THE IRISH STORYTELLER

The Irish Storyteller

Georges Denis Zimmermann

FOUR COURTS PRESS

Published by
FOUR COURTS PRESS
Fumbally Lane, Dublin 8, Ireland
email: info@four-courts-press.ie
http://www.four-courts-press.ie
and in North America by
FOUR COURTS PRESS
c/o ISBS, 5824 N.E. Hassalo Street, Portland, OR 97213.

ISBN 1-85182-622-X

A catalogue record for this title
is available from the British Library.

Printed in Great Britain
by MPG Books Ltd, Bodmin, Cornwall.

Contents

Abbreviations

ARV	Scandinavian Yearbook of Folklore
AT	International tale-type (Aarne-Thompson)
FFC	Folklore Fellows Communications
IFC	Irish Folklore Collection (UCD), main manuscripts
IFC S	Irish Folklore Collection (UCD), school manuscripts
OSL	Ordnance Survey Letters
RIA	Royal Irish Academy
RSAI	Royal Society of Antiquaries of Ireland
TCD	Trinity College Dublin
UCD	University College Dublin

Acknowledgments

I wish to thank the National Library of Ireland, the Department of Irish Folklore at University College, Dublin, and the Schweizerische Archiv für Volkskunde, for allowing me to consult their collections. Material from the manuscript collections of the Department of Irish Folklore was carefully checked by Dr Rionach uí Ógáin and is published by kind permission. I am also indebted to all those who have written on the subject and whose observations and interpretations are listed in the bibliography. My deep gratitude goes to Dr Paul Kirschner, who carefully read an earlier version of my text, improved style, and made useful suggestions. The team of Four Courts Press and their reader patiently helped me to lick a bulky typescript into shape.

Diarmuid Ó Giolláin's *Locating Irish Folklore*, which situates Irish folkloristic discourse within Irish history as well as in the development of theories around the world but without focusing on storytelling, appeared when my work was practically completed and is therefore referred to only in notes.

I

'Tell us a story ...'

The request is universal: we like to hear stories, known to be fictive or believed to be true, and the impulse to shape our experiences or desires in narrative form and thereby to control and share them is a fundamental human trait. Both teller and listener must have a command of the basic rules according to which narrative utterances can be generated and understood, and psychologists tell us that, from an early age, our minds gradually develop the competence for constructing or reconstructing ordered series of events. We use it as a way of finding connections between apparently disparate occurrences, drawing up plans, establishing and confirming our individual identity. Any sequence of statements which includes a temporal juncture may have some narrative quality, but we like a reported chain of events to involve some remarkable change from one situation to a different state of affairs; we call it a 'story' when the selected incidents form a concatenation which reverberates in our minds, conveys a sense of both progression and completion, and is worthy to be retold for display purpose, not just to communicate information. The code itself makes the development of stories partly predictable, but its multiple-choice possibilities allow surprises, which are appreciated because the tension between expectation and uncertainty is exciting.

We may derive aesthetic pleasure from identifying a shapely arrangement, heightened by the manner of telling. But oral narration involves more than an arresting set of events and a sense of formal achievement: although telling stories to oneself is possible, storytelling is essentially a social – co-operative – activity; to narrate is to act on listeners, and an audience's sense of sharing an experience and thus belonging together may be as valuable as individual imaginary release. The foundations of the art belong to a common heritage of mankind, but some formal details and performance patterns may be specific to a particular culture. People with a common stock of stories (and ways of telling them) form a community; conversely, different repertoires may divide audiences – but stories can cross ethnic barriers. Whether some societies collectively cultivate innate potentials better than others remains an open question, but it is obvious that some individuals are specially gifted: all of us resort to the narrative mode, but few can fully satisfy an audience. For this reason, mastery of this art confers prestige. The word 'storyteller' may also sometimes carry negative overtones, however, as in one of the *Oxford English Dictionary* definitions: 'Euphemistically, a liar'.

The focus of this book is on representations of 'Irish traditional storytellers', of different kinds and at different periods: I shall examine what has been said about them, and try to find out why. It seems necessary, at the outset, to weigh up some of the lexical and conceptual tools required to survey such a field, because they are susceptible of important shades of meaning which may reflect differences in approach and lead to conflicting interpretations. Beyond allowing that it may refer to several kinds of persons who, in diverse ways and circumstances, tell various kinds of stories, we do not have to dissect the term 'storyteller' here; but 'folklore' and 'tradition' may be more problematic, and we shall also be confronted with loaded terms like 'identity' and 'nationhood'.

Already with the notion of 'folklore' we risk entanglement in unsettled denotation and contradictory connotations. Today, when it does not dismissively refer to mere picturesque and perhaps fake obsolete stuff and retrograde attitudes, the term may refer to a distinctive cultural inheritance transmitted by practice or word of mouth, in an archaizing society. It may also denote any set of rituals and expressions in circulation long enough to have been made familiar, in any community whatsoever. 'Folk' is itself narrowly or broadly defined: as the unsophisticated part of a population retaining certain supposedly old manners and customs; or as the lower classes; or as any group of people forming a closely bound community. Folkloric items have been said to be relatively static – and this consistency may endow them with venerable qualities, or serve as an argument for rejecting them as outdated. But folklore is also said to be characterized by continual reworking and modulation, in which case a protean nature might be its most remarkable feature – unless it is perceived as mere degeneration. Folklore used to be seen as communally produced and anonymous; but now, though there seldom is reliable ascription to an 'inventor', greater emphasis may be placed on the role of individuality in the activation and continuing existence of folklore items, which are alive only if they can be reshaped. The folklore process may happen as long as certain modes of communication and human information storage are used. But debate continues about what should be called folklore, and whether the word itself is still useful.

For a long time, the traditionality of the material and of modes of performance has been an essential criterion for definitions of folklore; but 'tradition' is a term with various meanings and is subject to different valuations. When it is used broadly, both as the process of handing down cultural elements through generations and as the body of beliefs, values, patterns of behaviour and skills thus passed on, it is not contentious. Trouble begins when one has to decide if the process involves change, and whether what is said to be thus inherited is sacred. What is commonly called a 'traditional society' would tend to repeat what the ancients are said to have done, while 'modern societies' feel compelled always to innovate. Traditionality has often been associated with old people and antique customs whose origins are supposed to extend beyond recorded time.

Indeed, some continuity is involved in any definition of tradition, along with its social character: a group controls the canon. As an established way of thinking, feeling and doing, and as the force exerted by the past on the present, tradition may be denounced as social and cultural inertia. It is now admitted, however, that it is not as static and may not be as old as is supposed: it need not take long for repeated forms of expression or behaviour to be perceived as a collective heritage, and consequently ritualized. Tradition can be added to and modified. Aspects of the past are selected, interpreted, if necessary invented, and the adjective 'traditional' may be used manipulatively to imbue with authority certain socio-cultural interests and those who represent them. The dynamic and ideological dimensions should therefore not be ignored; in fact, traditions shift over time, more or less rapidly, in form or in function. Whenever the term is used in this book, it will emphasize one of these basic meanings: a mode of transmission controlling form and content, or a body of inherited cultural elements, or a way of symbolically designating something as ancient and venerable – or burdensome. I shall try in each case to make clear which of those senses applies.

'Folklore' consists, among other things, of ready-made plots, of codified ways of putting together basic narrative elements to produce partly new stories, and of manners of performing them in face-to-face communication. Such 'traditional narratives' are said to have a 'collective' dimension; but does it concern creation, or only temporary ownership? It is generally admitted that control belongs to those who share the same code and decide what can or should be repeated; innovations and effective developments are the result of individual talent, but what is produced is offered on probation and transmitted only if acceptable. Oral tradition is not always isolated from written communication: indeed, in Europe, oral arts and written literature have coexisted for a very long time and have exchanged elements and techniques. It has become clear that a written origin or the passage through a written form does not exclude the possible adaptation or return to oral expression.

Another cluster of words and notions is linked to the need to perceive oneself as fitting in a group set apart from others by some aspects of its culture, to which symbolic value is attached. A society would have an 'identity' when its members can distinguish it from others and feel that they belong together because they share some interests, a history, and a destiny. Although the persistence of distinctive traits is implied, identities may have to be repeatedly redefined. The concept of 'nationhood' is connected with that of collective identity, and invokes the idea of a community of people occupying a more or less defined territory, with a sentiment of unity, a shared culture and history and a shared attitude towards the outside world against which the nation defines itself. A nation is capable of constituting a state, to protect its integrity. It implies the positing of continuity and is supposed to be founded on a common heritage, the preservation of which would be a sacred duty. Folklore or traditions and nationalism have been closely interconnected: because a national consciousness is partly founded on shared memories, a common set of stories about the past may be of considerable significance.

The basic concepts examined in the preceding paragraphs will have to be scrutinized and qualified again, but I may now define more precisely the subject of the present investigation. Formerly, the main or only focus of attention for those who studied 'traditional oral narratives' was the narrated object: the story as a plot and its verbalization (perhaps also the beliefs it seemed to illustrate). But the importance of the individual who actualizes the narratives has gradually been recognized, as well as the peculiarities of his interaction with an audience. The telling may be more important than the tale. The storytelling event unites a community, clarifying or exorcizing its shared feelings and beliefs, its fears and aspirations. Meeting a good storyteller in performance can be a tremendous experience, and because of the power he seems to have, an individual practitioner can be depicted as a remarkable personage. A 'type' of the storyteller may be established, with generalized traits representing some qualities highly valued – or feared. This book will gather and analyse enduring or fluctuating and sometimes conflicting images of the so-called traditional storytellers of Ireland – keeping in mind the relative uncertainties of the concept of 'tradition' and the fact that we may be dealing with multilayered realities and changing perspectives.

Is it a subject worthy of exploration, and what can we hope to find? The Irish are often said to have great facility in verbal expression, to love eloquence, and to spin tales. In actual fact, verbal agility is unevenly distributed among them and there are good and bad storytellers everywhere, but it can hardly be denied that Ireland has enjoyed a highly verbal culture, that conversation and storytelling have been cultivated there as a game or a fine art, and that a good deal of the narrative exchange has been perceived as 'traditional'. Those who deplore the use or misuse of history as a misguiding model, or as a weapon, point to the mutually incompatible stories about the Irish past which opposed camps (now often referred to as distinct 'traditions') have obsessively cultivated. A common though generally undemonstrated explanation for certain excellences of written Irish literature in English – short-story writing for instance – is the impact on it of oral tradition. Books and brochures advertising national specialities to attract tourists used to recommend traditional story-telling – as if a hurried visitor could easily experience the real thing! Some non-Irish folklorists have singled out Ireland as particularly rich in tales, and its sorytellers as very skillful. Foreign travellers have sketched Irish raconteurs supposed to embody the qualities – good or bad, depending on the origin of the testimony – conventionally attributed to the Irish as a group.

It is tempting to define cultures as totally coherent, stable and autonomous sets of customs, beliefs and capabilities, but the notion of a pure Irishness preserved virtually unchanged must be treated cautiously. In recorded history, the population has never been monolithic, and the structure of society has been almost completely dislocated more than once. Until fairly recent times, insularity and a position on the western edge of the continent may have delayed and diluted the effects of some wider European movements; a predominantly rural life, unaffected by the Industrial Revolution except for the north-east corner of the island, was maintained longer than in many other western countries, and deep socio-cultural cleavages could make a large part of the population conservative. A separate language – largely replaced by another idiom in the last two centuries – may have isolated a community while somehow laying down lines along which habitual thought would follow. But how much continuity can be traced in Irish history is a matter of dispute. There was disruption through catastrophes, and accommodation due to contacts between different groups: successive waves of settlers (who may have arrived with their own stories and conceptions of story-telling) have left their marks, and in the dialectic process of adaptation certain 'original' features could be preserved unchanged while others evolved or disappeared. For centuries, different communities, each with a partly distinct heritage and ethos though all belonging to the broader European circle, have coexisted on a relatively small territory; they have interacted, while remaining attached to the identity markers which foregrounded distinct customs and beliefs. The image of the traditional storyteller could embody respectable Irishness for one part of the population, while some features of Irish storytelling might also be used by others to brand that part of the population as extravagant or menacing; on the other hand, positive views of the supposedly typical Irish storyteller could cross some socio-cultural frontiers when those striving to pacify a plural Irish society proposed to share in a larger patrimony. We may expect to find various strata of lore in Ireland, and to see the result of some cross-fertilization.

Frequenting Ireland yearly for half a century I soon paid attention to Irish singers and found it relatively easy to observe them. I also noticed how ordinary people animated conversation with narratives; but trying to learn something about the more formal storytelling as it had existed in the past was another matter. I had to turn to what others had written about it, which meant reading thousands of pages, often to find only brief relevant passages. Though I have had very little access to information available only in the Irish language, of which my knowledge is only rudimentary, there are translations, and I dare to hope that the mass of documents I have seen may validate some conclusions.

Examining particular or standardized written accounts of storytellers and storytelling in Ireland, I shall look for dominants and constants as well as for diversity and evolution: how images, once formed, persisted or changed, and how different representations of similar or dissimilar storytellers could coexist. It will be a study in reflected images, and in subjective evidence which expressed the biases and systems of values of the observers as much as the nature of what they were observing. The fact is that various Irish storytellers appeared, in different circumstances, to different people who could see them as representing ideals, oddities, or threats. They were described by Irish people and by foreigners, by persons who had an intimate knowledge of their world and art and by others who found them strange and responded with surprise, amusement or revulsion. When possible, we shall also examine the image Irish storytellers had of themselves and wanted to project, including in narrative accounts of acts of narration and in stories about storytellers. We shall meet not only the regular performers of grand tales, but also those who occasionally told shorter and less formalized narratives.

Studying representation means sifting secondhand information; in a way, we shall not see directly the storytellers themselves but rather what existed in the eyes of the beholders, rendered in the form of verbal constructs. Even when not accurate, those images may be significant, and if we are interested in what Irish storytellers really were like we should not despair of catching glimpses of observable realities. The relevant data were found in antiquarian publications, travel books, reminiscences, fiction with local-colour elements, folklore *collectanea* – an abundant but heterogeneous material, with variable degrees of detailing and reliability. Examining such a corpus of more or less factual, or idealized, or caricatural representations of Irish storytellers, I had to ask a series of questions: What do these images have in common, where do they differ, and how have they evolved in the course of time? What can be accepted as faithful description of actually observed facts, what seems to have been distorted or invented – and to what purpose? What may reveal the special qualities of an individual, and what has been based on generalization and stereotyping? To what extent did the presence of the observer in the field change what he was observing, and how did his interests or prejudices colour the representation? In brief, I have tried to establish who (from which position and with what bias?) proposed what image (concerning which kind of Irish storyteller?), to whom and why (to achieve what effect?). I also had to see storytelling in relation to a more general socio-cultural field, and to take into account environmental conditions and the changing historical context.

The first part of the book follows a historical course; but from the end of the eighteenth century, chapters follow parallel tracks corresponding to different kinds of sources. Chapter two summarily studies how storytellers and acts of storytelling were represented in a number of documents and literary texts originally written until approximately the twelfth century, and what modern scholars have to say about this early period. The third chapter covers information (and misinformation) from the thirteenth century to the eighteenth. The next one focuses on reports of antiquarians, from the beginning of the eighteenth century, and on the writings of those who, in the early decades of the nineteenth, carried out the first more or less systematic field researches (the purpose of which was not primarily to collect folklore), or began to explore ancient manuscripts. Chapter five is devoted to travellers' accounts of encounters with certain kinds of storytelling people in Ireland, mostly in the first half of the nineteenth century. Chapters six to eight explore other nineteenth-century perspectives: the first examines the testimony and opinions of early folklore collectors and the links between their publications, the situation of the Irish peasantry, and the influence of political movements in the first half of the century; the second deals with representations of Irish storytellers and traditional storytelling in written fiction, mostly of the same period; the third focuses on observations and collecting after the mid-nineteenth century, both from the point of view of 'folklore', as then understood, and as part of a growing national consciousness. Chapter nine examines the various representations or manipulations, by non-folklorists and for literary and/or political reasons, of Irish traditional storytellers in the twentieth century. The next two chapters deal with the store of information amassed by the folklorists in the same century. The last section of the book departs from the more or less diachronic framework: Chapter twelve examines fictional representations of story-telling in Irish folk stories; Chapter thirteen addresses itself to the complex and varying relationship between storytelling, truth and falsity, and the paradox of liars who may be telling the truth.

2

Colloquies of the ancients, and modern views or controversies

A distant past verging on the unknowable may pleasantly excite the imagination: the nature of Irish oral storytelling before the twelfth century remains obscure, but speculations have flourished on the strength of few documents. The first part of this chapter will consider representations of storytelling and storytellers in medieval Irish literature, in texts which belong more or less to what we would call fiction. Such material probably had roots in earlier periods, but is known to us through versions which may have been (re)composed and copied much later. The composite picture resulting from my compilation would therefore be deceptive if it were offered as that of a single historical moment; we may think, however, that at least part of what was considered important changed only slowly. At any rate, what was later believed to have been the functions and the status of poets and storytellers in protohistoric and early historic periods had an effect on definitions of supposedly permanent features of the typical Irish storyteller. The second part of the chapter relies upon the authority of modern specialists who have established facts or developed hypotheses about storytelling in early Ireland. It does not claim to be a contribution to advanced scholarship, but is rather a necessarily unassuming attempt at outlining some modern views and divergences of opinions, on a subject which is fraught with difficulty and abounds in pitfalls.

A. ANCIENT IMAGES

We start with an image which crystallized about 1200, when an anonymous writer hit upon the idea of combining into a vast literary compendium many episodes associated with Fionn (Finn) mac Cumhaill and his troop of warriors or adventurers. It is known to us as *Acallam na Senórach* ('Colloquy of the Ancients' or 'Conversation' or 'Dialogue with the Elders'), and versions of the text were copied until the nineteenth century. The author organized his text with a frame story including other narratives and poems, supposed to be communicated orally. The enframing structure is the meeting of St Patrick and his followers with survivors of the previous pagan world – live embodiments of a 'tradition' – and the journey they undertake together through Ireland. The representatives of the past, the most eloquent of them being Caoilte (Caílte) mac Rónáin, report the lore associated with hills, rivers, plains, or other notable features of the landscape, and a large number of tales, anecdotes and poems are thus inserted. Caoilte is not only one of the first Irish storytellers we hear about, but also the first Irish guide explaining his country to visitors – Patrick had come from Britain.

After a separation of a hundred and fifty years apparently spent in hiding, Caoilte and Fionn's son Oisín, each accompanied by a small band of warriors, are all that remains of a great fellowship. They meet again and exchange memories of bygone days; then, while Oisín goes to the fairy mound of Ucht Cleitech to visit his mother, Caoilte and his companions, with enormous wolfhounds, take their way over the plains of Meath. St Patrick and his monks watch their approach. This is how the passage was translated by Standish O'Grady at the end of the nineteenth century:

Patrick chanted the Lord's order of the canon, and lauded the Creator, and pronounced benediction on the rath in which Finn Mac Cumhall had been: the rath of Drumberg. The clerics saw Caeilte and his band draw near them; and fear fell upon them before the tall men with their huge wolf-dogs that accompanied them, for they were not people of one epoch or of one time with the clergy. Then Heaven's distinguished one, that pillar of dignity and angel on earth: Calpurn's son Patrick, apostle of the Gael, rose and took the aspergillum to sprinkle holy water on the great men, floating over whom until that day there had been a thousand legions of demons. Into the hills and 'skalps', into the outer borders of the region and of the country, the demons forthwith departed in all directions; after which the enormous men sat down. 'Good now,' Patrick said to Caeilte, 'What name hast thou?' 'I am Caeilte son of Crunnchu son of Ronan.' For a long while the clergy marvelled greatly as they gazed upon them; for the largest man of them reached but to the waist, or else to the shoulder of any given one of the others, and they sitting.[1]

After a meal, Caoilte evokes the greatness of Fionn, and Patrick praises his narrative skill for the first time: ' "Success and benediction attend thee, Caeilte," Patrick said; "this is to me a lightening of spirit and of mind; and now tell us another tale." "I will indeed; but say what story thou wouldst be pleased to have." '[2] And the performance goes on, as Caoilte recounts the legends relating to notable landmarks and to the origins of place names: 'Patrick said: "Good now, Caeilte, and wherefore was the name of *fionntalach* [white hill] given to this eminence on which we stand?" "I will tell you the truth of it," answered Caeilte.'[3]

Storytelling is the meeting of an old world and a new one, and our first Irish storyteller is a gigantic figure. Not only is he knowledgeable about the past: he is the past, still active in the present. He may claim to be an eye-witness to part of what he is narrating, which gives his account more authority. He is in

1 Tr. by Standish H. O'Grady *Silva Gadelica* 2.103, from the late-fifteenth-century Book of Lismore. (The spelling of proper names, in this and other quotations, cannot be consistent.)
2 Ibid. 2. 104. 3 Ibid. 2. 118.

touch with the supernatural, too, and is therefore, like the saint himself, a numinous figure. He reeks of paganism, but exorcism can make him acceptable: the saint baptizes him. Indeed, the first gesture of the 'big men' (*fir mhóra*) has been to show the way to a well of pure water, of which Caoilte sings the 'fame and quality'. (Traditions are adaptable: the pagan cult of wells was christianised, and in the twentieth century it has been calculated that there are 'some three thousand holy wells in Ireland, many of them still used'.)[4] As the representative of the older dispensation, Caoilte has much to offer: clear water which can be made holy, knowledge – and also entertainment, the latter element being absolved of the taint of profanity. Indeed, Patrick reacts first as the early monastic leader John Cassian (*c*.350-*c*.432) had done when he denounced fascinating pagan stories as frivolous or devilish fables which diverted him from prayer and contemplation;[5] but in Ireland a celestial intervention allays such scruples:

'All this is to us recreation of spirit and mind, were it not a destruction of devotion and a dereliction of prayer.' There they were until the morrow's morning came, when Patrick robed himself and emerged upon the green; together with his three score priests, three score psalmodists, and holy bishops three score as well, that with him disseminated faith and piety throughout Ireland. Patrick's two guardian angels came to him now: Aibelan and Solusbrethach, of whom he enquired whether in God's sight it were convenient for him to be listening to stories of the Fianna. With equal emphasis, and concordantly, the angels answered him: 'Holy cleric, no more than a third part of their stories do those ancient warriors tell, by reason of forgetfulness and lack of memory; but by thee be it, such as it is, written on tabular staffs of poets, and in ollave's words [*ollamh*: master-poet]; for to the companies and nobles of the latter time to give ear to these stories will be for a pastime.' Which said, the angels departed from him ...[6]

We note an awareness of the relative fragility of oral lore. Before being written down, however, memories and narratives were already inscribed on the landscape – and this was to remain true in Ireland.[7] In the rest of the *Acallam*, Patrick is a good listener and a diligent collector who repeatedly expresses his delight at what has been told and his desire to have it recorded: ' "Victory and blessing wait on thee, Caeilte!" said Patrick: "for the future thy stories and thyself are dear to us." ... "Success and benediction!" said Patrick: "a good story it is that thou hast told us there; and where is Brogan the scribe?" Brogan answered: "Here, holy cleric." "Be that tale written by thee"; and Brogan performed it on the spot.'[8]

As Caoilte and his troop are travelling on with the Christian missionaries,

4 E. Estyn Evans *Irish Heritage* 163 .   5 O. Chadwick *John Cassian* 9; and 148-9: 'The *Institutes* and *Conferences* dominated thought at Lérins ... There was probably a connexion between Lérins and the early Celtic monasteries of Ireland.' 6 O'Grady, op. cit. 2. 107-8. 7 Cf. L.T. Taylor *Occasions of Faith* 61: 'Those raised with the stories need only hear the name of a given place or else see it to rehear the story that is tied to the place – or at least know that there is a story that someone "has".' 8 O'Grady, op. cit. 2. 109, 115.

Oisín reappears and the recital continues. Recollections can induce nostalgia – a mood not typical of early Irish narratives as we know them, but which was to become dominant when similar stories were revived in English more than half-a-millennium later.

The *Acallam* shows that the storytellers mediate not only between present and past (and future, inasmuch as what they say will be preserved); but also between different levels of reality into which it is possible to travel – when it is not an otherworldly musician who comes to 'our' world in order to learn the human art of telling tales:

They saw draw near them a *scológ* or 'non-warrior' that wore a fair green mantle having in it a fibula of silver, a shirt of yellow silk next his skin, over and outside that again a tunic of soft satin, and with a timpan [a musical instrument] of the best slung on his back. 'Whence comest thou, *scológ* [scholar]? asked the king. 'Out of the *sídh* [fairy hill] of the Daghda's son Bodhb Derg, out of Ireland's southern part.' 'What moved thee out of the south, and who art thou thyself?' 'I am Cascorach, son of Cainchinn that is ollave to the *Tuatha Dé Danann*, and am myself the makings of an ollave [an aspirant to the highest grade]. What started me was the design to acquire knowledge, and information, and love for recital, and the Fianna's mighty deeds of valour, from Caeilte grandson of Ronan.' Then he took his timpan and made for them music and minstrelsy, so that he set them slumbering off to sleep. 'Good now, Caeilte, my soul,' said Cascorach, 'what answer returnst thou me?' 'That thou shalt have everything to seek which thou art come and, if thou have but so much art and intellect as shall suffice to learn all that the Fianna wrought of valorous deeds and exploits of arms, thou shalt hear the same. In this town once was an *óglaech* [warrior]: Finn mac Cumall, and great would have been thy wealth and stipend from him in lieu of thy minstrelsy, although to-day the place be empty!' And Caeilte uttered: – 'This night the Fianna's seat is void,/ To which Finn of the naked blade resorted ...'[9]

The tellers and their repertoire thus combine different levels of reality as well as different strata of time. Towards the end of the manuscript versions that have survived (leaving the frame story unfinished), the High King of Ireland reacts as Patrick did, showing that, like the spiritual authorities (including pagan ones represented by the 'people of the goddess Danu'), temporal authorities are well disposed towards storytellers:

'Success and benediction, Caeilte!' said Dermot grandson of Cerbhall: 'and where are Ireland's sages and antiquaries? In ollaves' diction be these matters written down upon the tabular staves of poets and in records of the learned; to the end that of all knowledge, the enlightenment, the hill-lore, and of all the doughty deeds of arms which Caeilte and Oisin have communicated to us, each and all make their way to their own country and to their land take back their stave.' Even so it was done.[10]

At the outset of our investigation, we are thus confronted with impressive

9 Ibid. 2. 187-8. 10 Ibid. 2. 167.

survivors, with a landscape interpreted as a repository of stories, as well as with
the glorification of a legendary past – and in a complex way at that, since a text
composed about 1200 (and known to us through fifteenth-century or later
copies, here filtered by a late nineteenth-century translation) sets in the fifth
century AD the telling of stories concerning the third century (according to the
chronology accepted at the time of composition);[11] much of the information on
which the present study is based will consist of what, from the start, was set *in
illo tempore*. Distance does not preclude authenticity – at least this particular
time-traveller's account is supposed to be reliable because Caoilte was a *féinní*,
and according to him the members of the fraternity were sustained through life
by 'the truth that was in their heart' and 'the fulfilment of what they promised'
as much as by the strength of their hands. He repeatedly introduces his stories
with the formula 'I will tell the truth of the matter'.[12]

What other accounts of narrative situations and of the effects produced on listeners do we find in the early fictional literature? The following survey may
indicate some constants. The sources in Irish are versions copied in different
centuries, from originals which were then more or less 'ancient'; but certain elements occur repeatedly – singly or in clusters. I leave out mere references to storytelling as part of a feast along with other forms of celebration.[13] The items I
have considered are classified in six basic categories according to the relative
importance to the plot of the character doing the storytelling, the more or less
decisive function of the narrative act in the development of the main story, and
whether the in-tale is reproduced, summed up, or just mentioned. Boundaries
are sometimes blurred – for instance, the narrator may be a minor character in
the whole text but the protagonist of the in-tale. The same criteria will be tentatively applied, in Chapter 12, to representations of storytelling in folktales collected between 1850 and 1950.

*1. A central character narrates and the narration – which we may 'hear' – is
decisive for the whole story.*
When age is associated with wisdom, it qualifies a character for good storytelling, and an extraordinary long survival will then make him really outstanding. Thus Fintan mac Bóchna, one of the first legendary settlers in Ireland and

---

11 J.F. Nagy developed an 'old saying' quoted in the text, '*gablánach in rét an scéluighecht*'
(storytelling is a complicated matter), to show that the intricate structure of this work is
founded on an organized tension between 'then' (the heroic past) and 'now' (the Christian
world), and between the cyclicality of ancient mythology with its repetitive stories and the
new linear eschatological sense of time. ('Compositional Concerns in the *Acallam na Senórach*',
in D. Ó Corráin, L. Breatnach, K. McCone eds. *Sages, Saints and Storytellers* 149-58.) 12
O'Grady, op. cit. 2.104, 105... 13 For example, when the heroes of Ulster are being entertained: 'Musicians came to play and sing and amuse. Poems and tales and encomia were
recited' – from *Mesca Ulad* ('The Intoxication of the Ulaid'), tr. Jeffrey Gantz *Early Irish
Myths and Sagas* 195.

'the true remembrancer', survived the Flood by turning himself into a salmon, then a bird of prey; according to some reckonings he lived for more than 5500 years, and he acquired additional knowledge from another long-lived creature, the old Hawk on Achill Island,[14] or from an angel of God. He appears in several texts as the memory of the island, and in a proud statement lists some of the favourite themes of ancient Irish storytelling: 'I am knowledgeable in [Ireland's] feasts, and in its cattle-raids, in its destructions and in its courtships, in all that has been done'.[15] In *Do Suidigud Tellaig Temra* ('The Foundation of Tara', a tenth- or eleventh-century text), he announces: 'I will establish for you the progression of the stories and chronicles of the hearth of Tara itself with the four quarters of Ireland round about; for I am the truly learned witness who explains to all everything unknown'.[16] He is not alone of his kind: in *Scél Tuain meic Chairill* ('The Story of Tuán mac Cairill', the oldest transcription of which is in the twelfth-century Book of the Dun Cow), another survivor is said to have arrived with the first settlers after the Flood and to have passed through a series of animal shapes until, in the fifth century, he was eaten as a salmon by a woman and became a man again. Having acquired wide knowledge of the Irish past, he could give an account of his successive lives and of what he had witnessed – 'the stories of Ireland'.[17] In both texts the imparting of knowledge in narrative form is a significant act. The main reason for imagining such cases of long life and total remembrance may have been that it allowed chroniclers to evoke an otherwise undocumented past, but we may also regard such quasi-immortal guardians of collective memory as representing the process of tradition itself: in Fintan's words, 'a continuity of existence still remains in me'. In the same manuscript as one of the versions of Tuán's story, we read of Lí Ban, who, when Lough Neagh burst forth and drowned her family, survived by being transformed into a mermaid; three hundred years later, many people came to see her and marvelled at her shape as well as at her narrative.[18] She became a saint – but in the Irish canon only.

Two stories involve acts of storytelling by Mongán mac Fiachna. Annals refer to him as a king who died in AD 625, but he was also said to be a reincarnation of Fionn, or the son of shape-shifting Manannán mac Lir, lord of the sea and of the Otherworld. During a night spent drinking in a strange house he recounted his own adventures, and the following day it appeared that the night had lasted a whole year – elastic time is a favourite motif of Irish folktales or legends involving transcendent experiences, but it may also be a way of point-

---

14 A poem in the Book of Fermoy details the exchange of stories between the man and the bird. See Eleanor Hull 'The Hawk of Achill, or the Legend of the Oldest Animal', in *Folk-Lore* 43 (1932). 15 Daithi Ó hÓgáin *Myth, Legend & Romance* 224-5. 16 'The Settling of the Manor of Tara', ed. and tr. by R.I. Best, in *Ériu* 4 (1910) 147. 17 Tr. Kuno Meyer *The Voyage of Bran Son of Febal* 2. 294-301. The text with another translation, by John Carey, is in *Ériu* 35 (1984) 93-111. 18 In S. O'Grady's *Silva Gadelica* 1. 234-7 and 2. 484-5. In the *Acallam*, we are told that Caoilte held a conversation with the same Lí Bán.

ing out that you forget time when listening to stories.[19] References to night-time
and timelessness as well as the motifs of intoxication and of expressive 'frenzy'
may emphasize the phantasmagorical dimension of storytelling, which remains
associated with heroic action. (For the other occasion when Mongán was associated with storytelling, see p. 29 below.)

Storytelling may have important consequences for the storyteller. The motif
of redress obtained by narrating predominates in *Airec Menman Uraird maic
Coise* ('The Stratagem – or Allegory – of Urard mac Coise'). The story concerns
a poet who died in 990. When his house was destroyed and his cattle seized, he
went to the king who had authority over the plunderers and was asked what
'news' or 'information' he was bringing; playing on the ambiguity of the word,
which also meant 'stories', he listed the chief narratives of Ireland, then offered
to tell one as yet unheard of. It included an in-tale according to which a fictitious poet (Mael Milscothach: 'Mael of the Sweet Words') demanded and
obtained compensation from a worthy king; Urard then revealed that it was his
own case, and obtained reparations plus a kingly recompense for his expertise.
Was this a true story, or a parable to assert the prestige of the profession and
show how narrative indirection may convey truth and influence reality?[20]

One of the many accounts of visits to and from the Otherworld, *Echtrae
Cormaic maic Airt*, dating from the twelfth century according to linguistic features though it survives in later manuscripts, combines the theme of the necessary link between a good king and truth with that of the peculiar relation of stories to truth. It tells how a mysterious youth, belonging to 'a land that has only
truth', took from Cormac mac Art his daughter, then his son, then his wife,
giving him in exchange a silver branch with three golden apples which, when
shaken, made delightful music and put people to sleep (a possible function of
art, particularly of music, according to ancient Irish texts). After the third
abduction, Cormac followed the young warrior into *Tír Táirngiri* ('the Land of
Promise'). He lost his way in a mist, witnessed various wonders, then came to a
magic palace where he was entertained and taught the power of truthfulness
(two other functions of art are to give pleasure and revelation). While a pig was
being cooked for the banquet, the owner of the palace said that true stories had
to be told – one for each quarter of the pig. The 'true' stories told are credible
only if wonders are believed; indeed, the last one – Cormac's contribution – is
even stranger than the others, yet accurately relates what has 'really happened'
thus far.[21] The host, who turns out to be the god Manannán, gives Cormac a
magic cup which breaks into three pieces when three lies are spoken over it, and
becomes whole again when three true statements are made. When Cormac
wakes, the following morning, he finds himself with his family on the hill of
Tara. The cup will henceforth serve him in his role of an Irish Solomon.

19 K. Meyer, op. cit.i. 57-8. 20 P. Mac Cana *The Learned Tales of Medieval Ireland* 33-5;
M. Dillon *The Cycles of the Kings* 115-17. 21 Book of Fermoy version, tr. Vernam Hull in
PMLA 64 (1949) 880-2. Another version is in Whitney Stokes (ed.) *Irische Texte*.

A later treatment of the motif of the hero forced by his host to tell stories is *Feis Tighe Chonáin Chinn-Shléibhe* ('The Festivities at the House of Conan of Ceann-Sleibhe'). It concerns the great Fionn mac Cumhaill and takes the form of a frame tale enclosing other stories, cruder and shorter than the *Acallam na Senórach* but perhaps inspired by it as a way of constituting a corpus of Fianna material. Although it may have been composed in the fourteenth or fifteenth century and the earliest complete version we have was copied in the last years of the seventeenth, it is said to have archaic features.[22] Fionn and his warriors are given hospitality in the residence (*bruiden*) of an Otherworld lord who compels the champion to narrate several of his adventures, and to supply various pieces of information in semi-narrative form.[23] And as in the *Acallam*, after each round of storytelling the host approves of the telling: ' "You are truly an intelligent and learned man, and it contributes much to my satisfaction and amusement to listen to you." ... "Win victory and blessings, O Fenian king," said Conan. "It is with clear memory and sweet words you relate these things".'[24]

The more general motif of storytelling in which a narrator-hero crosses some crucial boundary line between different times or levels of reality has been studied by J.F. Nagy, who regards it as the distinctive theme of a whole genre in medieval Irish literature: the dialogue involving narratives (the 'Colloquy of the Ancients' referred to at the beginning of this chapter would be the most famous and longest example).[25] K. McCone points to the presence of a Christian holy man in many of these stories, which would indicate that the aim often was to harmonize the pagan past with the Christian present[26] – indeed, to legitimate an exploration and exploitation of what was non-Christian.[27] In later texts, Fionn's son Oisín took over from Caoilte as the main narrator in shorter colloquies with Patrick, belonging to the special genre of verse tales known as 'lays' (Irish *laoithe*); more will be said about it in the next chapter.

In the probably earlier and not christianized *Echtrae Nerai* ('Adventures of Nera'), one Samhain night when elf-mounds are opened, Nera enters the

22 Maud Joynt (ed.) *Feis Tighe Chónain* vii: 'The substitution of Conan for St Patrick [as interlocutor] has made a difference in the tone of the story, which represents on the whole a more primitive and barbarous stage of society than that depicted in the *Acallam* and lacks the touches of chivalry frequent in the latter.' 23 Tr. Nicholas O'Kearney *Transactions of the Ossianic Society* 2 (1855) 127-9. In 'The Chase of Síd na mBan Finn', the same Fionn tells the story of how he got his drinking horn from another mysterious creature (K. Meyer *Fianaigecht* 56ff.). 24 Ibid. 133, 147. In other stories, Fionn has his own *file* (poet), Fearghus Fíonbhéil ('fair mouth'), who can interpret dreams, stop quarrels with his recitations, and fight when necessary. 25 'Close Encounters of the Traditional Kind in Medieval Irish Literature', in Patrick K. Ford (ed.) *Celtic Folklore and Christianity* 129-49; also by J.F. Nagy: *Conversing with Angels & Ancients* passim. 26 K. McCone *Pagan Past and Christian Present in Early Irish Literature* 199-201. 27 J.F. Nagy *Conversing with Angels & Ancients* viii: 'The *noíb* [saint] could rehabilitate and sponsor the recording of a pre-Christian "native past" discredited in the eyes of a Christian present, sanction the literary preservation of some of the elements of that past, and discover the past anew for a present that had lost touch with its roots.'

Otherworld through the cave of Cruachain near the residence of Ailill and Medb, and has a vision of future events threatening his people; after three days he returns to his companions and discovers that for them no time at all has passed.[28] He tells his people what he has seen and heard, so that they can take emergency measures, and the future is altered: the telling of a story can change history.

In *Síaburcharpat Con Culaind* ('The Phantom Chariot of Cú Chulainn', copied in three manuscripts including the eleventh-century Book of the Dun Cow), it is the chief hero of Ulster who is forced to narrate. He is brought up from the dead by St Patrick to prove the truth of the Christian doctrine to the High King of Ireland.[29]

Even divine beings may turn storytellers, like goddesses of war in *Cath Maige Tuired* ('The Battle of Moytura')[30] Supreme narrators control the future as well as the past, and what they say may be important even if it does not concern the main story in which they appear.

2. Storytelling by the protagonist is mentioned, not represented; we already know what is narrated and the narrative act is unlikely to advance the main story.
Less striking than the scenes in the preceding section, and in some cases no more than a conventional bridge or pause between more exciting episodes, the mere reference to narration may nevertheless be significant, but the precise degree of impact is difficult to assess. In the *Tóraigheacht Dhiarmada agus Ghráinne* ('Pursuit of Diarmuid and Gráinne': the earliest copy dates from the sevententh century, but there is evidence that the story was known quite early), the two male protagonists are just said to have turned narrators.[31]

In the second part of *Tochmarc Étaíne* ('The Wooing of Étaín', possibly ninth century but preserved in later manuscripts), the reincarnated Etaín listens to Midir who was her first husband more than a thousand years ago in the world of the Tuatha Dé Danann. He tells her how they were separated, and his description of the country they lived in is enticing; she is prepared to go with him if her second husband agrees – but he does not. Again, the act of narration can hardly be said to be decisive.

At the end of *Echtra Mac nEchach Muigmedóin* ('The Adventure of the Sons of Eochaid Mugmedón', eleventh century?), Niall of the Nine Hostages tells how he has been granted kingship by Flaithius (the Sovereignty goddess) – that is to say, he offers a brief summary of what was detailed before.[32]

A protagonist's narration may be a way of explaining at the end why the story can be told. In *Oidheadh Chloinne Lir* ('The Tragic Death of the Children

---

28 T.P. Cross and C.H. Slover *Ancient Irish Tales* 250-1. 29 Ibid. 347, 350. In *Aided Chon Culainn* ('Cú Chulainn's Death', from the 12th-century Book of Leinster), the dead hero appears to fifty women to prophesy the coming of Patrick and of of Christ (ibid. 340). 30 Whitley Stokes (ed. tr.) 'The Second Battle of Moytura', in *Revue Celtique* 12 (1891) 110-11. 31 Cross and Slover, op. cit., 404, 405. 32 Cross and Slover, op. cit. 512.

of Lir', earliest version known, *c.*1500), Fionnguala, after some nine hundred years of suffering with her brothers metamorphosed like herself into swans, relates their adventures to a young man on the shores of Erris, and we are told that this is how the story has survived. Towards the end of *Buile Suibhne* ('Frenzy of Sweeney', thought to date from the twelfth century), St Moling bids the mad king to return from his wanderings every evening, so that his story, as told by himself, may be written down before his death. A reference to narration by the protagonist may also be a way of launching the most pathetic final episode: in *Oidheadh Chloinne Tuireann* ('The Tragic Death of the Children of Tuireann', earliest surviving copy: sixteenth century) the unfortunate heroes tell their father and their sister what has befallen them while performing a series of apparently impossible tasks, only to discover that there are further quests to be undertaken, one of which will prove fatal to them.

As noted in the preceding section, an Irish hero may bring back stories from some incursion into the Otherworld. We may become acquainted with his adventures directly through his first-person narrative (see Section 1 above) or through an impersonal narrative, ending with a brief mention of his having related the experience afterwards. Bran mac Feabhail, the protagonist of one of the most famous 'wonder-voyage tales', *Immram Brain meic Febail* (a story said to date from the early eighth century), has been sumptuously entertained in *Tír inna mBan* (the Land of Women). Sailing towards Ireland again, he knows that he must not touch ground – it would lead to destruction. He speaks from his boat to the people who have assembled on the shore and tells what happened to him while conventional time, which did not affect him, was passing for them: 'Said Bran: "I am Bran the son of Febal," saith he. However, the other saith: "We do not know such a one, though the *Voyage of Bran* is in our ancient stories [*senchas* – in the sense of historical knowledge]" ... Thereupon, to the people of the gathering Bran told all his wanderings from the beginning until that time.'[33] Then he bids them farewell, 'and from that hour his wanderings are not known'. Here, to the motif of the hero as teller of his own story another is added, which was also to remain popular: the character, after a long absence, finds that he has become the stuff of legend. At the end of another voyage-tale, *Immram Curaig Maíle Dúin*, a christianized avatar of the story of Bran's navigations (possibly tenth century; earliest complete version in the late-fourteenth-century Yellow Book of Lecan), Máel Dúin returns from the Otherworld with his companions, one of whom has taken the precaution of bringing back a marvellous object to make their story more believable: 'They enter the house and are warmly received and clad in new garments, and they declared the marvels they had seen, and that God had revealed to them, according to the words of the sacred poet [Virgil] *Haec olim meminisse iuvabit*'[*Aeneid* 1.203: 'this will be pleasant to remember'].[34]

---

33 Tr. K. Meyer *The Voyage of Bran* 1. 32, 34   34 Eleanor Hull *A Text Book of Irish Literature* 1. 135. A late manuscript adds: 'And they related their adventures from beginning

Among other accounts of round-trips to the Otherworld which include acts of storytelling is *Echtrae Láegairi* ('Adventure of Laegaire', perhaps a ninth-century text). We are told that one day the people of Connacht were met in assembly when a supernatural stranger appeared. To Laegaire, the king's son, he told his story: Fiachna was his name, he had killed his wife's ravisher but now needed the help of human warriors to attack the fort where she was imprisoned – here, the narrative act is decisive: Laegaire and fifty men followed him into Loch Nen. In the Otherworld – now called the Plain of Delight or Plain of the Two Mists – they released Fiachna's wife. One year later they reappeared in Connacht to tell their story, carefully remaining on horseback to avoid touching the ground, then returned to the Otherworld for ever – the second narrative act has no consequence.[35]

In *Longes mac nDuil Dermait* ('The Exile of the Sons of Daol the Forgotten', a late medieval text), Cú Chulainn sails in a magical boat to a strange island where he must discover why the sons of the warrior Daol Dearmaid have disappeared (for the motif of the quest for an essential tale or explanation, see also Section 5 below). Cú Chulainn finally hears their story, then returns to Ireland, where he tells of his own adventures.[36] In the earlier *Tochmarc Emire* ('The Wooing of Emer', twelfth century), the same Cú Chulainn has travelled in space only, but wonders are not lacking; having learnt martial arts and magic in Scotland and returned to Ulster to win a wife, he 'came to Emain Macha and related all his adventures'.[37]

The hero of *Echtrae Airt meic Cuinn* ('Adventure of Art Son of Conn', in the fifteenth-century Book of Fermoy) has visited *Tir na nIonnadh* (the Land of Wonder) and, unlike his brother Connla who had followed a fairy woman and never reappeared, he returns to Tara: 'And the nobles of Ireland asked tidings of his adventures from Art; and he answered them, and made a lay.'[38] Then he banishes his wicked stepmother and restores fertility to Ireland, but it is not his narration that makes the difference.

A hero may be admired for telling a false story if he is motivated by good intentions. In *Táin Bó Fraich* ('Fraech's Cattle Raid', which may have been composed in written form in the eighth century) the protagonist, having won the heart of the daughter of Medb and Ailill, tells a noble lie when he must explain how a certain thumb-ring he had secretly received from her came to be found in a salmon; we already know what happened, but to reveal it to the fictional audience would have caused embarrassment; hence a feat of dramatic irony in

to end, and all the dangers and perils they found on sea and land. Now Aed Find, chief sage of Ireland, arranged this story as it stands here; and he did so for delighting the mind and for the people of Ireland after him' (H.P.A. Oskamp *The Voyage of Maél Dúin; A Study in Early Irish Voyage Literature* 179). 35 Ed. tr. K. Jackson in *Speculum* 17 (1942). Also in S.H. O'Grady *Silva Gadelica* 2.256-7. 36 D'Arbois de Jubainville, *Cours de littérature celtique* 5. 149 ff. Windisch *Irische Texte* 1. 164 ff. 37 Cross and Slover, op. cit. 169. 38 R.I. Best (ed. tr.) 'The Adventures of Art Son of Conn ...', in *Ériu* 3 (1907) 173.

which he deceives and pleases the fictional audience by inventing an explanation.[39]

3. A secondary character tells a story, which may be important.

In *Serglige Con Culainn* ('The Wasting Sickness of Cú Chulainn', copied in the early twelfth-century Book of the Dun Cow), the main hero turns listener. Loeg, the charioteer, has been sent to inspect Mag Mell ('Plain of Pleasures') before his master accepts an invitation to go there and, on his return, describes the marvellous country.[40]

In the most famous *Táin Bó Cuailnge* ('Cattle Raid of Cooley') as we know it from twelfth-century manuscripts, in-tales concerning Cú Chulainn's boyhood and youth are told to Queen Medb and her husband Ailill by exiles from Ulster. Nearly one-sixth of the *Táin* recensions that have survived is taken up by those narratives, which prepare us to understand the attitudes of the hero in the story of the cattle-raid. In various accounts of the recovery of the *Táin* after it had been lost, one of those who recounted the 'boyhood deeds of Cú Chulainn' in the main text, Fergus mac Róich, returns from the dead to recite the whole story; according to the Book of Leinster, it had been written down but the book was given away in exchange for a copy of Isidore's *Etymologiae*; in other manuscripts we are told that those who were responsible for oral tradition had become incompetent. The earliest known version of this story, *Faillsigud Tána Bó Cuailnge* ('How the *Táin Bó Cuailnge* was Found Again') may date back to the ninth century, and functions as one of the remscéla (prefatory tales) to the main story. The most recent version, which is also the most detailed, appears as *Tromdámh Guaire* (a fifteenth-century recension), known in English as 'The Great Visitation to Guaire', or 'The Proceedings of the Great – or Burdensome – Bardic Company'. Marbhán, a holy hermit, helps his brother the king of Connacht to get rid of an unruly rapacious band led by the chief poet Seanchán Torpéist. Storytelling is one of the skills of those leeches, but so is dangerous satirizing; they make a nuisance of themselves and must therefore be humiliated: let them find the lost story of the *Táin*.[41] A quest leads Seanchán and others to the burial mound of Fergus, and by fasting for three days and three nights they conjure him up from the dead. We meet again an image of the tradition-bearer who opens the doors of the past to the present: standing and surrounded by a mist, Fergus is so tall that he must sit down to enable the puny listeners to hear him – like Caoilte in the first text mentioned in this chapter, he dwarfs the men of the present; if they consider themselves more important than tradition and allow it to wither, they are mere parasites. Fergus relates the *Táin* from beginning to end.

A pathetic variant of the motif of the resurrected storyteller is found in *Cath*

---

39 Tr. A.O. Anderson, *Revue celtique* 24 (1903) 139. **40** Cross and Slover, op. cit. 188. **41** '*Imtheacht na Tromdhaimhe*', tr. Owen Connellan, *Transactions of the Ossianic Society* 5 (1860) 103.

Almaine ('The Battle of Allen'), a tenth-century account copied in a fourteenth-century manuscript, of events which would have taken place in the year 722. Fergal, son of Máel Dúin, had invaded Leinster to exact a tribute. On the eve of the decisive battle he asked Donn Bó, a widow's young son he had promised to protect, to entertain the camp: 'Said Donn-Bó: "I cannot have a single word on my lips to-night, so to-night let some one else amuse thee. Howbeit in whatever place thou mayst be tomorrow evening I will make minstrelsy for thee." '[42] On the following day the battle is a disaster: Donn Bó and his king are decapitated. The victors have the head of the dead king washed and dressed, and set up on a pillar. When the head of Donn Bó is brought too, he keeps his promise, and 'he raised his *cruinsech* [humming or chant] on high so that it was sweeter than any melody on the earth's sward; and all the host were weeping and sad at the piteousness and misery of the music that he sang.'[43] In reward for such art and faithfulness, the chanting head is fastened back to the body, and a revived Donn Bó can return to his mother and his people – now to tell the story of the battle. Other severed heads are heard speaking in ancient Irish literature, for instance in *Táin Bó Cuailnge*, *Togail Bruidne Dá Derga* and *Sanas Cormaic*.[44]

Certain objects may also have the power of speech, and turn narrators. In *Cath Maige Tuired* the sword of a dead king relates its feats: 'In that fight, then, Ogma the champion found Orna the sword of Tethra a king of the Fomorians. Ogma unsheathed the sword and cleansed it. Then the sword related whatsoever had been done by it; for it was the custom of swords at that time, when unsheathed, to set forth the deeds that had been done by them.'[45] But swords could also be an exacting audience: in *Serglige Con Chulainn*, we are told that when the heroes of Ulster related their combats their own swords would turn against them if what they declared was false.

From a secondary character (who may be divine ...), the protagonist can hear a particular kind of narrative in the future tense: a prophecy, as in *Baile In Scáil* ('The Phantom's Frenzy', eleventh century?) where the god Lug and the goddess of Sovereignty announce who will reign after Conn of the Hundred Battles; or advice and orders, as in *Echtrae Airt meic Cuinn* where Créide predicts the difficulties Art will come up against and tells him what to do. Secondary narrators may also contribute independent narratives which confirm the deeper meaning of the main one; thus the aged hermits who, at intervals, tell the stories of their lives to Máel Duín and his companions as the latter's boat drifts from island to island in *Immram Curaig Máile Dúin*.

42 Tr. Whitley Stokes, *Revue Celtique* 24 (1904) 45-7, 49-51. 43 Ibid. 61-3. 44 Cf. the talking head of Bran in the Welsh *Mabinogion*, the embalmed head of Midir which retained the power to tell Odin of things hidden from others, and the singing head of Orpheus. 45 Whitley Stokes (ed. tr.) 'The Second Battle of Moytura', in *Revue Celtique* 12 (1891) 107. In the *Mabinogion*, Peredur hears a talking spear.

4. The protagonist's opponent is a storyteller.

One can help or be helped, or entertained, by stories, but storytellers may occasionally be villains. The aforementioned story of *Tromdámh Guaire*, which led to the recovery of the *Táin*, also includes this motif – with a twist: the unpleasant storytellers cannot tell a certain story. Another illustration is found in an episode of the life of Mongán (cf. p. 21). He came into conflict with a proud and rapacious poet-storyteller, Forgoll, who was skilful enough since he could tell a different tale every night from the first of November to the first of May, but was not infallible and refused to admit it. Mongán dared contradict him concerning the place where a certain hero had been killed. The poet threatened to satirize him, which could amount to a death-sentence in the ancient Irish world, unless he received the queen herself in compensation. Happily, an unknown warrior came from the Otherworld to vindicate Mongán. He identified himself as Caoilte, who had killed the hero in question.[46] We are reminded that some storytellers are more arrogant than reliable, and therefore that not everything they say is valuable.

5. Storytelling, or a particular story, is considered valuable.

In *Altram Tige Dá Medar* ('Nurture of the Houses of the Two Milk-Vessels', copied in the mid-fifteenth-century Book of Fermoy), Eithne, a foster-child of the omnipresent Manannán, tells her story to a holy hermit before being baptized and dying. St Patrick is present and once again is said to be impressed by a voice from the pagan past; he orders that in future no one should sleep or talk during the telling of this story, and that it should be told only to a few good people. To those who listen properly, it will guarantee safety on a journey, good hunting, happiness and fertility in marriage, peace in drinking bouts, consolation if they are prisoners. The blessing has survived in oral tradition and 'is believed to be a prayer of great efficacy'.[47] It is not unique: a colophon to *Táin Bó Cuailnge*, in the twelfth-century Book of Leinster, blesses those who recite the epic without changing it. And parody – exaggerating the reality it plays with – only confirms the point: the comic *Aislinge meic Chon Glinne* ('Vision of Mac Con Glinne', composed in the eleventh or twelfth century), where recounting a vision of the Land of Cockaigne has the power to drive out the demon of gluttony stuck in the throat of a king, develops the formula of the blessings attached to the telling of a tale.[48] Here the accumulation of rewards may be laughable, but there is no doubt that stories and storytelling were prized in ancient Ireland.

That some stories could be more valuable than others is suggested by the motif of the quest for a particular tale, which plays an important role in the different versions of the recovery of the *Táin* (see p. 27) and in Cú Chulainn's investigation of the case of Daol Dearmaid's sons (see p. 26): he can neither sit

---

46 K. Meyer *The Voyage of Bran* I. 49-52: 'A Story from which it is inferred that Mongan was Finn Mac Cumaill, and the Cause of the Death of Fothad Airgdech'. **47** M. Dillon *Early Irish Literature* 72. **48** Cross and Slover, op. cit. 587.

nor lie down and sleep until he has found the truth, but succeeds in hearing the story of the young men and in freeing them . To be sent in search of the truth of a tale may mean risking one's neck, as in the case of Eisirt, the court poet in a lilliputian fairy land, who dared to proclaim that the men of Ulster were taller than his patrons, in the thirteenth-century version of *Echtra Fergusa maic Léite*.[49]

6. To become the hero of a story is the highest reward.

Storytelling was important not only for the pleasure and edification of listeners, but also for those who longed for wide renown. In *Echtrae Airt meic Cuinn* Bé Chuma claims 'that she was come from the Land of Promise in quest of Art whom she had loved from afar, because of the tales about him'.[50] We may doubt it, as she is of dubious character, but Étain, in *Tochmarc Étaíne* is honest when she tells her second husband 'it was for the noble tales about thee and for thy splendour that I have loved thee';[51] and everybody loves Baile mac Buain, the 'sweet-spoken' hero of a tragic love story, 'on account of the tales about him'.[52] In *Aided Derbforgaill* (in the Book of Leinster, twelfth century), Derbforgaill loves Cú Chulainn because she has heard stories of his prowesses; for the same reason Finnchaem loves him in *Longes mac nDuil Dermait*, and in *Táin Bó Fraích* Finnabair already loves Fraech before she has seen him. In *Togail Bruidne Da Derga* ('The Destruction of Da Derga's Hotel', perhaps composed in the eighth or ninth century), nine pipers come out of a fairy-mound to play for Conaire 'because of the noble tales about him'.[53] During the boasting contest of *Scéla Mucce meic Dathó* ('The Story of Mac Datho's Pig') one of the participants says: 'It shall be a famous tale even with the slave who drives the oxen, our meeting to-night.'[54]

Heroes are motivated by a longing for widespread renown, and the only immortality accessible to mortals depends on the stories that remain after them. Like Achilles, Cú Chulainn agrees to die young if his name lives on. In the earliest known version of the *Táin* (in the Book of the Dun Cow), he says: 'Provided I be famous, I am content to be only one day on earth';[55] in the Book of Leinster version it becomes: 'No matter that I be but a single day and a single night in the world, provided that my famous tales and my deeds [*m'airscéla 7 m'imthechta*] endure after me'.[56] In *Tochmarc Emire* he promises: 'Truly, I swear, O Maiden, that I shall make my deeds to be recounted among the glories of the strength of heroes'.[57] The Children of Tuireann (see p. 25) comfort themselves with the thought that their fame will live after them: 'We should prefer that our fame and our renown should be proclaimed aloud upon us, and that our cunning and our valour should be recounted after us, rather than folly and cow-

---

49 Ibid. 472ff. **50** Ibid. 493. **51** Ibid. 84. **52** 'Scél Baili Binnbérlaig', K. Meyer ed. tr. *Revue Celtique* 13 (1892) 224. **53** Cross and Slover, op. cit. 113. **54** Cross and Slover, op. cit. 205. **55** J.P. Mallory (ed.) *Aspects of the Táin* 73. **56** P.K. Ford 'The Idea of Everlasting Fame in the Táin', in J.P. Mallory and G. Stockman (eds) *Ulidia* 260. **57** Cross and Slover, op. cit. 158.

ardice should be charged aloud upon us.'[58] Therefore storytellers are important: heroes need celebrators and perpetuators of their actions, and ordinary people need stories to imagine themselves for a while living and shining in a heroic world.

Such a compilation foreshortens chronology, classifies themes or situations and roles by criteria which may not be airtight. The sources are works which were imaginatively elaborated, before being perhaps further distorted in transmission. Still, the authors could observe actual storytellers. We note that stories and storytellers are often represented as important, or that important people care for them; that repeated narration is said to bring glory; that travels through time and space make good stories – and that storytelling is a form of timetravel and spacetravel; that truth is valuable but that in certain circumstances a lie may be commendable. Narrating is depicted as an activity having sometimes a decisive influence: it may redress a wrong, or put the listeners in touch with another level of reality.

But in so far as what appears in these fragments may refer to reality, it does so selectively: it focuses on storytelling for, and often by, an elite, when the stories were first told they probably were already set in the past, and by the time the texts we have were transcribed it was easier to follow conventions than aim at ethnographic accuracy. To regard them as a complete picture would therefore be absurd, to take them as the products of *one* coherent tradition may be questionable, and to offer them – in all respects – as exclusively Irish would certainly be deceptive; but they do provide a few precious glimpses, and have influenced some later views of Irishness and Irish storytelling. Can we learn more from modern scholars' interpretations of documents?

B. MODERN RECONSTRUCTIONS AND DEBATES

What follows is a synthesis of information the validity of which I am not qualified to assess in detail, and of theories between which I am not competent to choose when they differ.

It may be true that, as Roland Barthes said, 'there nowhere is nor has been a people without narrative',[59] and we may therefore surmise that storytelling came to Ireland with the earliest settlers. We shall never know what stories instructed or entertained the growing population. Celtic culture had reached Ireland by the last centuries BC (but widely differing dates have been proposed); it must have involved more than linguistic elements, but exactly how much more is impossible to define, as there was no unified Celtic world. There seems to have been no mass migration towards Ireland, and some think that there was no

58 Ibid. 65. 59 R. Barthes 'Introduction to the Structural Analysis of Narratives', in *Selected Writings* 251.

fundamental discontinuity with the societies of the preceding age; but nobody knows the extent to which aspects of the culture of pre-Celtic people survived, nor can it be clearly demonstrated that new stories were brought at the time of the so-called 'arrival of the Celts'. There had been contacts before with what would become Britain and Spain, and with the Baltic region; some centuries later there was trade with Romanized Britain, and plunderage – but, again, whether stories were exchanged and any particular mode of oral art acquired then cannot be proven.

The coming of Christianity, which marked the end of protohistory around the fifth century, transformed Ireland; the transition may have been slow and some heathen beliefs and practices are said to have remained active for a considerable time. From the seventh century, networks of monasteries were established, and it was in this milieu that Irish written literature developed. To an existent and perhaps changing native oral base, Christian elements were added, along with, in learned circles, some knowledge of Greek – this is in dispute – and certainly familiarity with Latin texts. The result of that new cultural mix continued to evolve until the twelfth century, but historians recognize some constant features. The society was rigidly hierarchical, each member of it having a clearly defined rank. There was at first no centralization of power, but the political scene altered: powerful dynasties clashed with each other for supremacy.

On what sources of information can scholars rely to situate narrative activities in the early historic period? Unless they believe it is possible to extrapolate from what has been observed elsewhere, or in Ireland in more recent times, they must admit that the facts known about ancient oral narrating concern only the organization and the repertoire of a superior class of storytellers, and that they must rely for it on relatively scarce written evidence: dramatized and idealized images of storytellers such as the examples given above, or references to storytellers in semi-historical texts and legal prescriptions which perhaps described an ideal order rather than reality. Writing that preserved more than brief inscriptions came to Ireland with Christianity. For several centuries it remained generally confined to the scriptoria of monasteries, particularly of the more powerful ones controlled by the aristocracy. Although several epics or 'sagas' or tales now extant may have first been written down in the eighth or ninth centuries and embody older oral elements (how much, and how changed, is unknown), they may also have been considerably re-worked later. It must be borne in mind that 'early' documentary evidence was filtered by monks, likely to tone down or perhaps suppress what could not easily be brought into line with the principal tenets of Christianity as then understood in Ireland.

The copying of profane and pagan material along with sacred Christian books was not, as has often been said, a unique case of broad-mindedness: a passage of the seventh-century *Institutionum Disciplinae* written in Visigothic Spain by the Pseudo-Isidore and which may have reached Ireland as did some works by the real Isidore of Seville, recommends that the sons of the nobility (educated, in Ireland too, in monastery schools) should or could be exposed to the uplifting influence of poems about their heroic pagan ancestors; at about the same time Julian of Toled, in *Historia Wambae*, gave similar advice.[60] In the year 797, in a letter from the court of Charlemagne to the bishop of Lindisfarne, Alcuin rebuked the monks for listening to old stories about heathen – but meanwhile *Beowulf* was perhaps copied in Anglo-Saxon monasteries, and in his *Vita Karoli Magni Imperatoris* (*c.*826) Einhard says that the emperor had ordered the old barbaric poems to be collected and written down, so that they would not be forgotten.[61] It is also around the eighth century that vernacular literature is said to have begun to be written down in Ireland; but unlike what happened to most old pagan poems elsewhere, much seems to have survived for a longer time there.

What is found in Irish manuscript sources may have been variously edited, modified, mixed with topical allusions, edifying interpolations or imaginative flights. Using this material as historical source is tricky, but necessary caution should not be confused with excessive scepticism: what happened before the seventh century is bound to remain mysterious, but concerning the following four centuries, though the interpretation of a number of points are still disputed, reasonable assumptions seem to be possible about some codes and practices of storytelling in Ireland. Scholars agree that people with learning and skill (*aes dána*) enjoyed high status in a rank-conscious society, and that to reach and keep it the masters of verbal arts were subject to strict regulations.[62] The system must have undergone changes from proto-historic times to the eleventh century, yet part of it may have survived even beyond that time. The distinction between various employments is sometimes blurred: the preservation of learning, legal expertise, the interpretation of auguries, 'literature' and, until Christianity took over, religious rituals, may have been the prerogatives of the same class, sometimes perhaps of the same person acting in different capacities; but there were degrees of competence and standing, and specialization in certain branches. At the top of the scale of oral skills, in the periods for which written documents exist, was the *fili* (pl. *filid* – now *file*, pl. *filí*). Some think that he combined the most important aspects of three functions mentioned in classical descriptions of continental Celtic society: *druida*, *vatis* and *bardos* – in Old Irish *druí*, *fáith* and *bárd*. How distinct from bards and seers the druids actually were in earlier Ireland remains in dispute; in some manuscripts the terms *fili* and *druí* seem interchangeable.[63] A specifically druidic order is said to have died out after the fifth century – we

60 '*Solet virtutis esse praesidio triumphorum relata narratio animosque juvenum ad virtutis adtollere signum, quidquid gloriae de praeteris fuerit praedicatum*', quoted in Pierre Riché *Education et culture dans l'Occident barbare, VIᵉ-VIIIᵉ siècles* 211, 214, 504, 506. **61** '*Item barbara et antiquissima carmina, quibus veterum regum actus et bella canebantur, scripsit memoriaeque mandavit*', quoted in H. Munro Chadwick *The Heroic Age* 41, 62. **62** Eighth- or ninth-century legal texts detailed the grades, rights and obligations of poets and other 'privileged persons'. **63** Eleanor Knott *Irish Classical Poetry* 8. An example is in Leroux and Guyonvarc'h *Les Druides* 64. But for K. McCone 'it is hard to see how [the *filid*, after the seventh century] can use-

do not know how rapidly; by the seventh, the *filid* seem to have established a *modus vivendi* with the new ecclesiastical authorities.When information becomes available, bards appear as relatively inferior eulogists and reciters, and a poem on the duties of the poet or historian in the Book of Rights (*Lebor na Cert*, a late-eleventh-century compilation supposed to have very ancient sources) suggests that they were looked down upon by the *filid*.[64] The word *file* has remained in common use down to modern times in the sense of 'poet', but it does not do justice to the more complex role in the past: that of a master of wisdom and knowledge who could serve as an instructor of the young, and whose duty was to preserve important lore, perhaps to produce it at the royal banquet thus also acting in the capacity of storyteller (or employing subordinates for that task).

The *fili* was much more than a mere entertainer and storytelling was not his main function, but it was part of his *filedecht* (craft, competence) and was included among his official activities – as illustrated for instance in the anecdote concerning Urard mac Coise (see p. 22). A future *fili* had to undergo a long, rigorous course of training in the required skills: up to twelve years for the highest rank. Apart from becoming versed in *senchas* (Mod. Ir. *seanchas*: history, legal points, genealogical data), *dindsenchas* (explanation of place-names)[65] and principles of composition in various metres, he had to learn many tales; in the twelfth century, the conventional number was said to be seven times fifty, which may be a way of saying as many as there are nights in the year. According to the collection of legal pronouncements and commentaries known as *Senchas Már* ('Great Tradition') and to other documents, the seven grades of filid were distinguished by, among other criteria, the number and categories of stories they knew or were allowed to tell.

There were also different grades among the *báird*, whose main function was, or became later, the making of poems praising their patrons. The terms *scélaige* (storyteller) and *senchaid* ('receiver of lore', 'historian') appear in old texts, but it is not always clear that they were separate professions. The terms *cáinte* (satirist) and *glámh* (lampooner) might denote lesser classes of verbal artists – unless, again, they simply referred to occasional activities. In some texts 'harpers' are also called 'druids', and phrases like 'wherefore the *senchaid* sang this', alternating with 'whereof the *fili* said...', may refer to the same person.[66] In the story of Deirdre, although the father of the heroine is described as a storyteller and harper (*scélaige is chruittire*), his receiving a king in his house suggests that he was more than just an inferior entertainer. On a humbler level, the telling of cer-

fully be regarded as [the pagan druid's] more or less direct heirs' (*Pagan Past and Christian Present in Early Irish Literature* 86). **64** Here is the passage as translated by J. O'Donovan: 'This is the history of the King of Tara/ It is not known to every loud-mouthed bard/ It is not the right of a bard, but the right of a file/ To have a knowledge of each king and his law.' (*Leabhar na gCeart*, 183). **65** F.J. Byrne ' "Senchas": the Nature of Gaelic Historical Tradition', *Historical Studies* 9 (1974) 138. **66** 'Death of Crimthann son of Fidach ...', from the 14th- century Yellow Book of Lecan, *Revue Celtique* 24 (1903) 172ff., tr. Whitley Stokes.

tain stories was part of the activity of the *drúth* (fool, jester). There were roving troups, including a *crosáin* (buffoon), a *fuirseoir* (clown) and a *geocaigh* (mime), and the mere *bacaigh* (beggar) had to please those who had something to give; we know very little of such itinerants,[67] who may have had their own (lighter?) repertoire of tales (see Document A at the end of the following chapter for a view of their posterity in a later age), and even less of non-professional story-telling at home or in company.[68]

Apart from the narrative or non-narrative senchas already mentioned, the repertoire top performers had to master included *scéla* (tales): two documents, based on a lost model in existence by the tenth century, enumerates the *scéla* a fully qualified *fili* was capable of performing. One of the lists is part of Urard's story (see p.22); the other, in the Book of Leinster and in a sixteenth-century manuscript, is introduced as 'the qualification of poets in regard to stories and *coimcne* [complete traditional knowledge] to be narrated to kings and chieftains'.[69] The two versions partly differ in order of items and in detail of content, but both classify stories according to the types of events or deeds they deal with, as indicated by the first words of their titles: Destructions (murdering, ravaging), Cattle-raids, Courtships (with men as active suitors), Elopements (with women often taking the initiative), Battles, Caves, Sea-voyages (*immrama*: circumnavigation involving wonders), Death-tales (the manner and circumstances in which heroes died), Communal Feasts, Sieges, Expeditions and Adventures in the Otherworld (*echtrai*), Slaughters, Irruptions (the bursting forth of lakes or rivers), Loves, Military Expeditions, Invasions (the provenance and distribution of the tribes of Ireland), Conceptions and Births, Visions and Frenzies ... In a way, they look like an index of the different episodes which might be linked up as 'history', or as the archetypal pattern of a hero's career. Some of the titles correspond to lost stories, while a number of extant and supposedly early tales are not mentioned. Not mentioned either – obviously separated from semi-pagan or just profane *scéla* and *senchas* – were the lives of saints. Over a hundred Irish vitae written in Latin from the seventh century onwards and concerning sixty saints are still extant, and there are some fifty *beathí* in Irish about some forty saints. They could be used by monasteries to enhance their reputation and support their territorial claims. They were meant to be read (normally aloud), and could invoke oral sources: Muirchú introduced his life of Patrick (*c.*700) with a reference to what 'those who spread the word from the start have passed on',[70]

67 P.W. Joyce *A Social History of Ancient Ireland* 2. 484: 'Professional gleemen travelled from place to place earning a livelihood by amusing the people like the travelling showmen of the present day.' 68 G. Murphy *Saga and Myth in Ancient Ireland* 2: 'From the differences observable between different genres of storytelling, from references in literary texts to story-tellers of different ranks in society, and from analogy with the first steps of an ascending scale still to be noticed in Gaelic-speaking districts, it may be concluded that in ancient Ireland a whole hierarchy of storytellers existed.' 69 P. Mac Cana *The Learned Tales of Medieval Ireland* 41 (the book analyses those lists). 70 Quoted in J.F. Nagy *Conversing with Angels & Ancients* 41.

and the writing of Adamnán's *Vita Columbae* (before 700) was also preceded by a collection of all the evidence available, including oral lore 'from the account handed down by our elders' and 'from what I heard recounted without a trace of doubt by informed and reliable old men'.[71]

Whereas the medieval lists classified stories according to types of events, scholars since the end of the nineteenth century have preferred to divide them into four 'cycles': groups of stories centering on sets of heroes, who were supposed to have lived in distinct epochs and perhaps in different geographical settings.[72] They identify a 'Mythological Cycle' dealing with invasions of early Ireland by superhuman peoples and with more or less demoted pre-Christian deities. In the monasteries, this material was synchronized with the history-scheme provided by the Bible or the chronicles of Eusebius and Orosius. The 'Ulster Cycle' depicts a heroic world of cattle-raids, combat from two-horse chariots and head-hunting, with a peculiar honour-etiquette; scholars think that it may have constituted the literary tradition of greatest prestige until the eleventh century. The 'Fianna Cycle' (or 'Fionn Cycle', 'Fenian Cycle' or 'Ossianic Cycle'), which developed mostly in Leinster and Munster, evoking a later period, revolves around the less epic, more magical adventures of Fionn mac Cumhaill and the *fianna* he led, a band of hunters and professional warriors, or of young men who had not yet assumed adult status as full members of propertied society. Fionn's troupe is presented as defending Ireland against unwelcome human or superhuman invasions and living mostly in the natural wilderness beyond the borders of settled society. Whether, as has often been said, *fianaigecht* (Mod. Ir. *Fiannaíocht*: the exploits of the Fianna) actually began to be told long after the stories of the Ulster Cycle is not certain: before the *Acallam na Senórach*, the exploits of such outlaws may have been viewed unfavourably in the monasteries, and therefore not transcribed. They are said to have been originally preferred by *daoscarshluagh* (plebeians) and *criadhaireadha* (peasants)[73] – which would be hard to prove. What is clear is that the Fianna cycle becomes prominent in later manuscripts; new tales or lays, or new versions of old ones, continued to be composed at least until the late seventeenth century, and some lived on in oral Irish tradition – and in Gaelic Scotland – until the twentieth. The fourth group is more of a ragbag; when called 'The Cycle of the Kings' or 'Historical Cycle', it combines legend and history concerning rulers, with some Christian saints in secondary roles. Such stories accepted adventures and supernatural elements, but often the main point seems to be the definition of the *rí*'s power and responsibility, with his special *buada* (gifts, virtues) and his *gessa* (Mod. Ir *geasa*: prohibitions which were marks of heroic identity and des-

---

71 Adomnán of Iona *Life of Columba* (tr. Richard Sharpe) 105 (The Second Preface). The model for saints' lives throughout Europe, Athanasius' *Life of Anthony* (c.370), already referred to oral testimony. 72 An early example (1883) of such a classification is given in D'Arbois de Jubainville's *Cours de littérature celtique* 1. 357. 73 Gerard Murphy *The Ossianic Lore and Romantic Tales of Medieval Ireland* 5.

tiny). No system of classification is faultless, however, and characters and motifs from one cycle may turn up in another.

We have an idea of the repertoire of stories at the command of certain masters of verbal arts, and in *Airec Menman Uraird maic Coise*[74] it is made clear that they were intended for *oral* recitation. We would like to know what a storytelling performance was like and how the audience responded, but reports on this subject are very scant. It seems that storytelling had a role to play in assemblies held on regularly, like the great periodic festivals when people of high and low degrees and sometimes of different tuatha came together. There are also references to the telling of heroic tales on the eve of battles. And there were local occasions of joy or sorrow, or just leisure time;[75] in a late ninth- or early tenth-century text, among the instructions supposedly given by Cormac mac Airt to his son Cairbre concerning the proper behaviour of kings on such occasions, we read: 'What are the dues of a chief and of an alehouse [*cuirmthech*] ... Music in moderation, short story-telling. A joyous countenance. Welcome to companies. Silence during a recital.'[76]

But what were the performance modalities and manners of delivery? Here, again, we lack information. It appears that the normal medium of narrative was prose, but this defines written modes, not necessarily oral ones. Perhaps from the start some passages were rendered in a special rhythmical style without a fixed number of syllables, referred to by the scribes as 'rhetoric' (*retoiric*, *rosc* or *roscada*) because it was marked in some manuscripts by the letter r in the margin).[77] It featured series of short alliterative phrases multiplying unusual and often archaic words or lists of adjectives, without verbs; such passages were generally conventional descriptions interrupting the development of the narrative. Whether they were a specifically oral device and, as once asserted, of great antiquity, has been disputed.[78] Something of the form has survived in traditional Irish storytelling down to the twentieth century in the device known as 'runs' (see Chapter 11, Section 28). How recitation and music may have been combined, or alternated, is not clear.[79] In brief, there is very little certainty about what an audience actually heard – and saw; our knowledge is mediated by writing, which cannot fully recapture oral delivery.

---

74 P. Mac Cana *The Learned Tales* ... 50: Urard has 'heard' tales, 'remembers' them, and can 'tell' them to the king. **75** M. and L. de Paor *Early Christian Ireland* 106: 'Indoors, music and storytelling were probably the chief amusements'. **76** 'The Instructions of King Cormac mac Airt' (*Tecosca Chormaic*), ed. by Kuno Meyer, *Todd Lecture Series* 15 (1909) 3.13. **77** R. Thurneysen *Die irische Helden- und Königsage* 53ff; K. McCone 'Zur Frage der Register im frühen Irischen', in Tranter and Tristram (eds) *Early Irish Literature - Media and Communication* 80-4; J. Porthals 'Zur Frage des mündlichen oder schriftlichen Ursprung des Sage *roscada*', ibid. 201-20. **78** See for instance K. McCone and K. Simms (eds) *Progress in Medieval Irish Studies* 20, 21, 113, 126. **79** Alan Bruford explored the problem in 'Song and Recitation in Early Ireland', *Celtica* 21 (1990) – but known examples are of a much later date.

Some areas of disagreement between scholars must be mentioned here. They are interrelated in that they arise from the necessity of relying on the testimony of clerics who served a cause and could disregard less noble forms of storytelling and more shocking tales, and they all depend on the conception one has of the relationship of medieval manuscripts to what was actually heard in Ireland when they were written. Consequently, there are differences of opinion about the relative distance between the written and spoken modes; concerning the homogeneity or heterogeneity of oral narrative repertoire and techniques in the society we are trying to reconstruct through those documents; and on whether there was a close link between the texts as we know them and an oral 'tradition' reaching back to more ancient, pagan Ireland. In other words, to what extent were oral arts and older narratives the sources from which the written works we know drew their substance and perhaps their form?

It is difficult to decide how much a given work owes to preceding oral artists and how much to its literary redactors. Written texts are never mere, or complete, records of oral utterances – but how close to or how far from orality can they be? Is anything left of the oral storytellers' voices in written texts, and can we use them to try and know, not only the content, but also the form of ancient Irish storytelling? Even silent reading of some literary texts may induce auditory impressions, but both composition and reception are modified by the possibility of stopping to reflect or contemplate and of referring back to verify or compare; repetitions are no longer necessary and may be unwelcome; as ornamentation is less likely to be founded on rhythmic and sound effects, semantically-based figures of speech may become dominant. Telling a story or writing one involves partly different techniques – but tales composed in writing may be meant to be read aloud to an audience.

No serious scholar would assert that the texts in Irish medieval manuscripts are just scrupulous transcriptions of an oral corpus, which would have remained absolutely unchanged for centuries; nor, on the other hand, that they can show no trace whatsoever of oral devices. Between these extremes, however, some infighting has taken place. It has been suggested that in early Irish literature, along with the cosmeticizing of pagan beliefs, a particularly close interplay of oral and written expression may be observed. Even the supposedly basic distinction between variable oral tradition and relatively immutable written texts has sometimes been downplayed by those who believe that, like the ideal reciter blessed at the end of *Táin Bó Cuailnge* (see p. 29), the real Irish traditional storyteller would recite texts without any change; but the experience of modern collectors has shown that there is considerable verbal variation in most acts of oral storytelling. How the passage from orality to manuscript took place, and how much what was thus conveyed changed in the process, can only be guessed at: Patrick's repeated order to Brogan in the *Acallam* – 'Be that tale written by thee ...' – leaves us thirsting in vain for more information. Among the various possibilities, that of the *fili* telling his tale while a scribe recorded it on vellum does not seem very likely, and at any rate, implying a breaking down through dictation of rhythm and inspiration it would have been unnatural storytelling from the start. Alternatively, the scribe, having attended a genuine performance, might have tried to commit to writing as much of the story as he could remember, with inevitable omissions, summaries and perhaps misunderstanding. Finally, an author in the fullest sense of the word could compose a text, perhaps freely blending elements of oral tradition and written models to create something new.

It has been said that, although 'the manuscripts contain samples from interesting specimens of genuine storytelling', those were offered as out-of-date material 'arranged without much attention to artistic requirements';[80] not only was the original context lost and the function changed, but texts themselves could be abridged because the transcriber was either getting tired or could not follow the storyteller's delivery: 'Several of the best manuscript texts begin well, but tail off badly as the story proceeds'.[81] Miles Dillon suggested that the written texts were intended, not to be read aloud, but as mnemonic aids, mere outlines which the reciter would develop[82] – an idea already voiced by Douglas Hyde.[83] Poems had to be known word for word, but for prose stories only the general sense had to be remembered. Alan Bruford proposed a hypothesis, hard to substantiate, according to which the original epic Irish tradition consisted of improvised formulaic verse, of the sort collected in the Balkans and parts of Asia in the twentieth century; the Irish singers who knew this technique would have lost their audience after the fifth century, and when the protectors of monasteries asked for stories a couple of centuries later all that could be obtained were prose accounts of what had been orally extemporized, from which new texts were composed.[84] Other scholars have refused to see any significant link with orality; James Carney, for instance, thought that written tales and oral storytelling were far apart; the writers could borrow themes from a traditional background, but did not record oral narrative performances, nor try to imitate them, and it would be a fallacy to regard the medieval texts we have as in any way true reflections of oral art.[85]

Some scholars thought that, when written representations of orality were inadequate, they could be filled in by observing contemporary storytellers in the twentieth century, assuming that their 'tradition' had remained fundamentally unchanged.[86] In Proinsias Mac Cana's words, 'one may find it in some respects

80 G. Murphy *Saga and Myth in Ancient Ireland* 10. 81 Ibid. 7. 82 *The Cycles of the Kings* 2-3: 'We must suppose that these earliest texts are summaries of the matter of the story ...The form was given by the *fili* in actual performance and was his personal achievement.' 83 *A Literary History of Ireland* 297: 'the skeletons merely ... were in most instances all that was committed to the rare and expensive parchments'. 84 'Why an Ulster Cycle', in J.P. Mallory and G. Stockman (eds) *Ulidia* 24-5. 85 James Carney *Studies in Irish Literature and History* 321-2. 86 D. Ó hÓgáin *The Sacred Isle; Belief and Religion in Pre-Christian Ireland* 21: 'There is a time-honoured tendency in scholarship to attempt to decipher the culture of long-vanished societies from antiquated customs and ideas which survived into more modern times.'

useful, and certainly justifiable, to seek to bring the early Irish storyteller to life by pairing him with those of our own time ... since they belong to the same unbroken, if somewhat bruised, tradition'.[87] Gerard Murphy supported this idea, emphasizing the degradation that must have taken place in the passage from oral to written form.[88] But to utilize the present in order to reconstruct the past may be courting error.

The question of the distance between written and oral discourse, combined with that of the relative retentiveness of oral tradition, leads to another bone of contention: how far does the available medieval Irish literature reflect a 'tradition' going back to the pre-Christian past? Can we accept the texts we have as written traces of a more ancient culture, or did they sometimes deliberately invent that culture? Here too, extreme positions have been taken: either extant texts would have been recited generation after generation in the halls of kings before being written down, changing but little in the process, and thus providing us with 'a window on the Iron Age'[89] – or they would be essentially creations of the eighth and later centuries, with no great value as documents relating to earlier times. Again, there are intermediary positions. P. Mac Cana is not far from the extreme traditionalist view: 'The more closely one studies these early tales in their written form, the more one is persuaded that they are in substance, if not always in the accidents of style, a fair reflection of the oral narratives of pre-literate tradition.'[90] Others have insisted that whereas some older material might have survived, it had to be interpreted above all in the context of the medieval Christian culture which used and transformed it. In 1955, James Carney was criticizing scholars who, according to him, out of some 'nativist' nationalist convictions reconstructed the past through present folklore, exaggerated the importance of oral transmission and continuity with a pagan antiquity, saw in *filid* the heirs of the druids, and minimised the impact of Christianity and literacy upon the surviving early Irish texts. From approximately the mid-1970s, the attack developed against the tendency to see above all in those texts enduring features of an ancient Celtic past. The role of clerics would have been much more than scribal. This 'mandarin class ... sustained or at least endorsed by the church'[91] would have worked both as conscious literary redactors, and as propagandists. As members of monasteries they hated paganism and asserted the supe-

87 Mac Cana, op. cit. 11.   88 *Saga and Myth in Ancient Ireland* 8: 'When we think of the well-constructed narratives which even the unlearned peasant narrator to-day can produce, and when we judge of the greater power of Old Irish storytellers by consideration of certain passages scattered through the inartistic manuscript versions of their tales which have been preserved, we can be fairly certain that the tales, as really told to assembled kings and noblemen at an ancient *óenach*, were very different from the poorly-narrated manuscript versions noted down by monastic scribes as a contribution to learning rather than to literature.'   89 K.H. Jackson *The Oldest Irish Tradition: A Window on the Iron Age:* the Irish heroic sagas would reflect characteristic traits of Celtic culture prior to Christianization.   90 'Conservation and Innovation in Early Celtic Literature', *Etudes celtiques* 13 (1971) 97-8.   91 C. Etchingham, in K. McCone and K. Simms (eds) *Progress in Medieval Irish Studies* 125.

riority of the ecclesiastical scholar. Adopting an allegorical or typological mode of expression, they created analogues between a reconstructed early Irish history and the Old Testament, and manipulated the past to talk about the present – where there could be close links between the wealthiest monasteries and the secular aristocracy. The texts we have would thus be 'the literary and highly conventionalised products of specialised learned classes, retainers of the contemporary holders of power, who were at pains to legitimise all change by giving it the sanction of immemorial custom and who ruthlessly reshaped the past to justify the present';[92] they are 'first and foremost documents of their own time of composition, social and political propaganda that makes use of traditional materials in a kind of code'.[93] Inherited indigenous material is present, but the mark of foreign influence and more particularly classical learning can be felt too, as well as the pressure of what was topical at the time of writing. The 'Irish sagas' should therefore be treated essentially as 'literary compositions by men working in a literate monastic community'.[94] Others still think that a continuation of pre-Christian antecedents may be fruitfully studied in medieval Irish culture.

Yet another matter is argued about. What purportedly unified ancient Ireland was essentially the culture defended by an elite, and the standardized literary language used to convey and write it probably was anything but colloquial. If so, can we be sure that what we read reflects all of early Irish society – that there was not a different lore of the ordinary people (seldom seen in the texts we have)? Did all classes in this stratified world share the same narrative traditions, with or without significant nuances, or did each have its own lore? Was parchment too precious for recording what was not the literature of greatest social prestige? Some scholars invoke a 'relative universality or identity of taste'[95] – but they cannot prove it. It is not certain how far the commoners shared in the culture of the aristocracy, and the chances of ever being able to decide such matters are slight.

The debate continues about the close or distant relationship between the prose tales in Irish manuscripts and a then contemporary, archaic, or obsolete, oral tradition of storytelling.[96]

The preceding digest of what experts have found or discussed cannot size up all the problems they have been confronted with, nor do justice to their work; but it seems to permit us to make a few observations.

First, it induces us to be careful when using the catchy word 'Celtic': cer-

---

92 D. Ó Corráin, quoted in K. McCone *Pagan Past and Christian Present in Early Irish Literature* 244. 93 K. McCone, ibid. 244. 94 T. Ó Cathasaigh, in McCone and Simms (eds) op. cit. 61. 95 Mac Cana, op. cit. 7; also D. Ó hÓgáin *Myth, Legend & Romance* 391: 'It can safely be taken that the narrative genres current among the ordinary folk in medieval times were of the same general nature as those found in recent folklore'. 96 Different theses were presented in S. Ó Coileáin 'Oral or Literary? Some Strands of the Argument', *Studia Hibernica* 17/18 (1977-8) 7-35.

tainly not devoid of meaning and inapplicable to important aspects of Irish culture, it is easily overworked. In the content of the surviving Irish literature of the period surveyed in this chapter, it is hard to decide what would be specifically 'Celtic', what may be part of a wider Indo-European heritage, what came perhaps from more ancient strata, what was modelled on Christian sources, and what was the result of new creation; and there is little hope of our identifying an exclusively 'Celtic' way of narrating.

Secondly, we note that it is difficult to grasp exactly what oral narration was like up to the twelfth century. There have been various representations, and interpretations, but the most pregnant images may not be the most literally accurate. So far as we can judge, in the upper strata of the population storytelling was one of the varied duties of honoured professionals, who exhorted, glorified, informed and entertained the ruling classes; they were respected because they upheld order while justifying certain new interpretations of it, and because they built bridges between the present and the past, and between common sensory impressions and a normally invisible 'other' reality. Part of their repertoire of stories or set of motifs – through the intermediary of either written versions or a parallel oral transmission – may have survived and developed after the twelfth century, but how much of the older ways of telling those stories were retained seems impossible to know for certain. Impressive portrayals of performers as figures of authority may have already been those of legendary figures when the texts we have were written, and we may assume they were then further magnified. There must have been less exalted storytellers, who are virtually unknown. The storytellers of early Ireland thus remain mysterious figures – but the very vagueness of the portraits could be a valuable asset when they began again to catch a collective imagination centuries later.

Thirdly, we must beware of a view of ancient Ireland as static and perfectly homogeneous. In fact, there were enduring elements and transitions, with probably some variety. The advent of Christianity brought a new set of narratives, as well as a way of using them and of assessing and interpreting older ones. A political evolution resulted from struggles for hegemony. Then came the large-scale Scandinavian raids, beginning in the late eighth century. Irish historians used to emphasize the destructive role of the Vikings, but this view is now being tempered: by the mid-tenth century the Norsemen had established towns in Ireland, developed trade and increased communications with the outside world. To what extent did a mingling of cultures influence Irish oral storytelling? Competent scholars have analysed similarities between tales attested in Scandinavia and in Ireland, but cannot decide whether they were the result of direct borrowings or of a wider common inheritance.[97]

97 'Is there any direct connection between Scandinavian and Irish folktales? In this book I have endeavoured to answer this extremely difficult question, and the answer is in the main of a negative character' (Reidar Th. Christiansen *Studies in Irish and Scandinavian Folktales* 217). 'Only seldom, if at all, is it possible definitely to prove that similarities between the two

From the twelfth century, changes are better documented. They were due to continental influences, with the reform of the church along European lines and the development of Cistercian monastic houses which had little interest in Irish learning and no longer sponsored native literature. The *Acallam na Senórach*, examined at the beginning of this chapter, might have been a reaction to the new reformers' attitude: a timely reminder that Patrick would approve of efforts to rescue an Irish heritage.[98] The fact is that, just before the Anglo-Normans brought new continental ways of thought and literary modes, what seems to be an urge to safeguard what had been produced during the previous five centuries led to the compilation of ancient Irish texts, in the great manuscripts which provide much of our knowledge of earlier literature. Families of hereditary lay scribes and authors then took over, and texts composed or compiled later were intended for the houses of noblemen who, though they did have an interest in Irish stories, were also developing different tastes. By then, the ancient Irish stories first transcribed or composed around the eighth century might appear increasingly remote and strange, as already suggested perhaps by a comment – contrasting with Patrick's blessing in the *Acallam* – which was added in Latin by the scribe of the twelfth-century Book of Leinster after having copied out *Táin Bó Cuailnge*:

But I, who have written this story, or rather this fable, give no credence to the various incidents related in it. For some things in it are the deceptions of demons, others poetic figments; some are probable, others impossible, while still others are intended for the delectation of foolish men.[99]

areas [West-Nordic and Gaelic] are due to direct loans ... [yet there are] astonishing similarities between the two traditions' (Bo Almqvist *Viking Ales* xxvii). 98 D. Ó Corráin, in T. Dunne (ed.) *The Writer as Witness* 36-7. 99 *Táin Bó Cuailnge from the Book of Leinster* ed. Cecile O'Rahilly, 136, 272.

3

Powerful and dangerous or humble and innocent: storytellers as seen by Gaels and Galls

The period extending from the thirteenth century to the eighteenth is more obviously marked by reports of changes or fractures, of the disintegration of an old order and the ebbing of its culture, together with the incipient visibility of the peasantry which was later to provide collectors with folktales.

Ireland had been reached from outside before, but incursions now occurred repeatedly. Conquerors arrived in the last decades of the twelfth century; by 1350 some of their descendants were almost hibernicized, while others had segregated themselves in a separate territory. From the sixteenth century, new efforts to subjugate the whole of Ireland became systematic, and colonization led to more disruption; violent conflict alternated with silent mistrust, as two worlds were clashing or trying to ignore each other, but also to some extent acculturating. The 'first' inhabitants of the land, who called themselves *Goídil* (*Geil* in Modern Irish – *Gael* in the singular), had a word for 'foreigners': *Gaill* (sing. *Gall*). After the Reformation and the Tudor settlement, the Galls were subdivided into *Sean-Ghaill* ('old foreigners') also known as 'Old English', whose ancestors had come before the fifteenth century, who remained Catholic and seemed to be assimilated – and on the other hand *Nua-Ghaill* ('new foreigners'), the more recently arrived Protestant colonists who were seen by the others as intruders. A large Protestant community settled in the North-East in particular; much smaller groups of French and German refugees later appeared elsewhere. After a turbulent seventeenth century, the eighteenth was a period of relative peace – and separateness, with the now humble remnants of Irish culture under an eclipse from the viewpoint of the anglicized upper level of society. Over the centuries, alternation of violent clash and subdued hostility or indifference determined the views one community took of another, including of its storytellers or modes of storytelling. The Gaels could value their own traditions as essentially different, yet also borrowed models from the Galls; *Sean-Ghaill* might appreciate the verbal art of the Gaels; the *Nua-Ghaill* and English state servants temporarily stationed in Ireland were likely to have hostile or supercilious attitudes: in times of tension, they would denounce certain native poets or storytellers as barbarous and harmful; at other times, the Gaels and their oral artists could just be ignored, or inspire amusement, perhaps pity, even curiosity.

I shall distinguish four phases: first, the Norman settlement and the Gaelic resurgence, from the late twelfth century to the fifteenth; second, the Tudor conquest and resultant conflict with certain poets and storytellers in the sixteenth century; third, the collapse of the Gaelic order and the consolidation of the power of the new Protestant colonial classes in the seventeenth; fourth, the establishment and evolution of a new system of power in the eighteenth. We shall try to see what storytelling may have been like in each phase, and to form an idea of the types of storytellers that endured, changed, disappeared or emerged. The following questions will be considered: What was the impact on storytelling of the process of redistribution of land and power? What may the newcomers and their descendants have contributed to Irish storytelling? How were Irish storytellers seen, by themselves and by outsiders? The images we shall analyze are presented through partisan Gael or Gall eyes: the past and the heritage of stories and narrative modes supposed to come from it were represented by some native seventeenth-century scholars who resisted change; visitors and social semi-outsiders (members of the ruling minority) noticed some aspects of Irish storytelling which they abhorred when they seemed threatening, but began to find picturesque towards the end of the period under review.

The so-called Anglo-Norman Conquest which opened the first phase brought the institution of the manor, new ways of conducting war, new agricultural methods and a feudal system of land tenure and inheritance – for a long time the two populations would be distinguished according to which law they obeyed and were protected by. Two-thirds of the country were more or less under Anglo-Norman control by the middle of the thirteenth century, but the trend was then reversed: outside part of Leinster, Gaelic power reasserted itself and the frontier between English- and Irish-held areas was pushed back. Many colonists returned to England or died in the Black Death pandemic of 1348-9. Some Norman rulers had begun to adopt the ways of life of great Irish families with whom they intermarried. The authorities were alarmed by the weakening position of the settlement and by the tendency of a number of descendants of colonists to 'degenerate' into Irishness. The official policy was to segregate populations in the frontier society, by laws which preserved differences and prevented assimilation. In those passed in 1366 (in the Norman French which was still the legal language) and known as the Statutes of Kilkenny, along with prohibitions on intermarriage or alliances with the Irish and the use of their language, we find a teasingly brief reference to activities that included storytelling:

Item qe les minstrels Irroies venantz entre Engleis espient lez priuetz maners & Comyn des Englises dont graunz males sovent ad este venz, Accorde est & defende qe nulles ministres [minstrels] Irroies, cestascavoir Tympanors, fferdanes, skelaghes [*scéalaithe*: storytellers] Bablers, Rymors, clercz ne nullez autres minstrells Irrois veignent entre les Engleis et qe nul Engleis les resceiue ou don face a eux & qe le face & de ceo soit atteint soit pris et imp'son siton les Irroies ministreles come les Engleis qeles resceiuement ou

donent riens et puis soint reyntes a la volunte de Roy et les instrumentz de lor minis-
traeltees forfaitz a nre seignor le Roy.[1]

We should like to know more about those travelling storytellers and 'babblers':
what they told and how they told it. The explicit objection to them was that
they might collect sensitive information by entering the area directly controlled
by Dublin and its officials, or isolated Norman towers; but the general spirit of
those Statutes suggests that at least as much dreaded was an acculturation of the
colonists, to which Irish verbal arts might contribute. There had been earlier
legislative attempts to prevent the colonists from going native and there would
be others in the next two centuries, but it proved impossible to enforce the
decrees and to maintain a rigid separation between the two populations: a hybrid
society was developing along the line of contact.

The above quotation also illustrates the linguistic situation: several languages
were used in Ireland, and exchanges could extend to literary models. By the end
of the fourteenth century, however, French may have ceased to be spoken in
Ireland.

Ireland contributed to Britain and to the continent the matter of two of the
most popular religious stories in Latin of the late Middle Ages: *De Purgatorio
Sancti Patricii*, and more particularly *Navigatio Sancti Brendani* on the pattern
of the old *immrama*. A continental mode was imported: the *exempla* – Latin
outlines of narratives which preachers would fill in to interest their audience and
give point to sermons in the vernacular; they could be borrowed from oral tradition, and also supplied the latter with motifs and plots. Around 1275, an
English Franciscan friar who spent many years in Dublin and Cork compiled
such a collection, and the remarkable fact is that he situated some of his anecdotes in an Irish setting, for instance in the story of a bailiff who met the devil
on a lonely road at night and was protected by the power of confession, or those
of the woman of Balrothery who, 'in our times', tried to avoid paying tithes and
was punished, and of women in Drogheda and in Carrigtohill in County Cork;
there was also an account of the defeat of pestilent demons near Clonfert, which
the compiler had from the mouth of its protagonist, the bishop of Clonmacnois.[2]
Continental collections like *Gesta Romanorum* (compiled *c*.1300) may have
brought to Ireland some stories which were later found in Irish folklore.

---

1 H.F. Berry (ed.) *Statutes and Ordinances and Acts of the Parliament of Ireland, King John to
Henry V* 446-7; tr.: 'Also, whereas the Irish minstrels, coming upon the English, spy out the
secrets, customs and policies of the English,whereby great evils have often happened, it is
agreed and forbidden that any Irish minstrels, that is to say, tympanours, pipers, story tellers,
babblers, rhymers, harpers, or any other Irish minstrels, come amongst the English; and that
no English receive them or make gift to them. And that he who does so, and thereof be
attaint, be taken and imprisoned, as well the Irish minstrels as the English that receive them
or give them anything, and that afterwards they be fined at the King's will, and the instruments of their minstrelsy be forfeited to our Lord the King.' 2 A.G. Little (ed.) *Liber
Exemplorum ad Usum Praedicantium* items 95,105,180, 62,142.

Very little has survived of what may have been written in English during this period, but an Irish manuscript (British Library, Harley 913) shows that in the thirteenth and fourteenth centuries religious, satirical and other poems were composed. Evidence that native stories were known appears only later, for instance in the *Book of Howth* compiled in the early sixteenth century, some of the earliest accounts in English of Fianna adventures (see p. 36), including the representation of heroes as violent or melancholy storytellers.[3] But acquaintance with such stories did not lead the compiler to favour the natives from whom he got them: 'These men been variable and unstedfast, treacherous and guileful. Who that dealeth with them needeth more to beware of guile than of craft, of peace than of burning brands, of honey than of gall, of malice than of knighthood.'[4]

As for literature in Irish, although a sense of continuity with the pre-Norman past could be emphasized the milieu had changed. When Irish manuscripts multiplied again with the resurgence of Gaelic Ireland in the fourteenth and fifteenth centuries, professional families of *literati*, often working as chroniclers for the lay ruling houses, had taken over scribal activities. A new linguistic norm, Early Modern Irish, had emerged, and within it the professional poets set up a formalized literary language which remained the standard mode for literary composition until the seventeenth century.

Many noble families maintained house poets whose main function was to sing or recite in praise of the master and his lineage[5] – possibly Anglo-Norman despite the Kilkenny Statutes and similar edicts. It was fashionable to display Latin learning in poems in Irish, and love poetry was influenced by continental *amour courtois* themes.[6] The earlier distinction between *filidh* and *baird* became blurred, secular 'bardic schools' provided a rigorous training in style and

---

3 J.S. Brewer and W. Bullen *Calendar of the Carew Manuscripts* 5. 2, 7, 9. The story of how Garadh mac Morna was teased by women is in *Acallam na Senórach*, but the summary offered in the *Book of Howth* is closer to a fifteenth-century poem on the same subject: '*Toiteán tighe Finn*', *Eiriu* 1 (1904) 13-17. 4 Ibid. 5. 35. 5 M. Ó Riordan *The Gaelic Mind and the Collapse of the Gaelic World* 8, 9: 'The principal official function of the poet from the twelfth century was to provide support for the reignant or incumbent chief ... The functions of poet and chief were complementary.' P.A. Breatnach, 'The Chief's Poet' in *Proceedings of the Royal Irish Academy* 83c (1983) 37, 42: 'The [chief's poet], properly called *ollamh flatha*, is bound to his patron by ties that are often represented in the image of a marriage.' 6 J. Caerwyn Williams 'The Court Poet in Medieval Ireland' in *Proceedings of the British Academy* 57 (1971) 123: 'Not only were they authorities on all kinds of native learning, the legendary and historical as well as the poetic lore, but they also absorbed a great deal of the Latin culture of the period with the result that their poems are studded with apologues drawn from continental as well as from native literature.' James Carney *The Irish Bardic Poet* 10: 'they had to know so many stories that no situation could arise in their professional career but they would have a convenient analogy from the past to apply to the present.' The third Earl of Desmond, 'Gearóid Iarla' (1338-98), was credited with the introduction of courtly love conventions into Irish poetry; we shall meet him again as the hero of legends.

prosody, and the poets, still respected, had a high opinion of themselves; around 1260 one of them had written:

> Were poetry to be suppressed, my friends,
> With no history [*gan seanchais*], no ancient lays [*gan seanlaoidhe*],
> Save that each had a father
> Nothing of any man would be heard hereafter[7]

Mere storytelling may have been beneath the dignity of poets who had risen to the highest position, but it seems to have been pursued by others, and narrative prose is in plentiful supply in Early Modern Irish manuscripts. The older types of Irish narratives did not disappear[8] but earlier material was reworked to meet contemporary demands.[9] It seems that tastes were changing in the upper circles of the Gaelic or Gaelicized world: the truly heroic portion of the Ulster cycle ceased to develop, while stories of love and adventures were favoured. Chivalric romances of the French and Arthurian types were translated into Irish, and local *scéalta románsaíochta* (romantic tales) resembled them. A late document – a romance composed towards the end of the sixteenth century: *Eachtra Mhacaoimh-an-Iolair* ('Adventure of the Eagle-Boy') – shows how stories could pass from one language to another and from oral to written form or vice versa. In the introduction, the author states that he 'received the skeleton of this tale from a gentleman who said that he had heard it in French'.[10] Elements of the story – a king's son, who was snatched away as a baby by an eagle, must avenge the wrong done to his mother and reconquer his father's kingdom – are found in French and Irish romances, but no close parallel has been identified. Verse passages are spoken (or sung?) by the different characters at critical moments – a technique known both in French and in ancient Irish literature; there are 'runs' which sound more specifically Irish (see. p. 37). A. Bruford, who studied those romances, concluded that the best of them could probably be assigned to the late fifteenth and sixteenth centuries and are characterized by a loose episodic construction, the story-within-a-story technique and the use of 'runs'. He thinks they were meant to be read aloud, but versions transmitted orally have been collected.[11]

No doubt there existed oral narratives alongside written literature, but no

---

7 Giolla Bríghde Mac Con Midhe, tr. Eleanor Knott in *Irish Classical Poetry* 53.   8 James Carney, in *A New History of Ireland* 2. 700: 'The learned classes still read and copied the early sagas. But with every generation these were becoming less intelligible.'   9 C. Breatnach, 'Early Modern Irish Prose', in McCone and Simms (eds) *Progress in Medieval Irish Studies* 204: 'Recent research on primary sources strongly suggests that Early Modern prose compositions should be viewed as catering primarily for the needs of Early Modern patrons and dealing with issues of contemporary concern. It can no longer be maintained that the writers of this prose were motivated simply by a desire to preserve earlier traditions or to entertain an unspecified audience.'   10 J.F. Nagy *A New Introduction to Two Arthurian Romances* 3.   11 A. Bruford *Gaelic Folk-Tales and Medieval Romances*.

direct contemporary evidence shows how 'oral tradition' worked lower down the social scale, for instance among the native villeins the Anglo-Norman lords called 'betaghs' (from the Irish *biatach*: a food-provider); we must content ourselves with twentieth-century hypotheses.[12] Peasant storytellers begin to emerge from obscurity only in the second half of the eighteenth century.

A new phase opened when the Tudor power in England saw Ireland as a threat to its security: the Gall aristocracy had been a hatching-ground for plots, Gael chieftains were unreliable – by 1500 there were still more than sixty of them, and when division on religious lines widened the gap the island became a potential base for Catholic armies shipped from the continent. The English policy was to extend central authority, and political, legal and other cultural peculiarities were no longer acceptable; new measures were therefore taken to promote Englishness and to impose the system by which land was surrendered to the king, who then granted it back. Conciliation was tried, but by 1580 it was deemed that coercion, and if necessary terror, should be used. Those who resisted were termed subversives; efforts were made to quash all resistance by Gael chiefs ('wild Irish enemies') and their followers; to control or eliminate powerful Gall dynasties ('the King's rebels'); and to colonize stretches of Ireland with loyal new settlers from Britain, as the ordinary Gaelic Irish were considered hopeless: 'not thrifty and civil or human creatures, but heathen or rather savage and brute beasts'.[13]

In this context, the kind of storytelling that caught the limelight was the one suspected of fomenting rebellion and outlawry. Denunciations of the activities of 'bards' were revived, and specific charges were brought by colonial administrators and planters against people who sang or recited poems in Irish and could also practise storytelling. What was deemed criminal in their activity was at first the praise of those who were found unmanageable by the English power, but

12 Gerard Murphy 'Irish Storytelling after the Coming of the Normans', in Brian Ó Cuív (ed.) *Seven Centuries of Irish Learning* 72-3: 'The tales told by peasant firesides ... probably remained much as they had been before the Norman invasion violently changed the traditional life of the upper classes. But of the tales told by those peasants of past time we know nothing directly; we merely surmise that they must have been akin in matter and spirit to the folktales which their descendants continue to tell to-day in certain districts of Ireland. The only stories of past ages of which we have direct knowledge are those which belonged in a special way to the highest classes of society; for these alone were the stories which used to be recorded in manuscripts. Irish society in truly Gaelic times was undoubtedly less differentiated in intellectual interests than modern society: the lord knew and liked the tales told by the peasants; the peasants doubtless had heard the tales which more learned storytellers had designed mainly for reciting before a lordly company. But the distinction between the two types of tales is clear, and many traces of it were until lately to be found in Gaelic-speaking areas in Ireland and Scotland, where some storytellers, as well as folktales proper, knew also stories which are to be found in manuscripts, while other storytellers specialised in folktales proper and could not tell manuscript stories.' 13 Andrew Trollope in 1586, quoted in N. Canny and A. Pagden (eds) *Colonial Identity in the Atlantic World 1500-1800* 168.

they seemed to have a more diffuse evil aura.[14] A statute of 1549 forbade the composition of poems of praise 'to any one after God on earth except the king'.[15] The Drogheda custom officer, draughtsman John Derricke, who accompanied Sir Henry Sidney as war artist on campaigns again 'rebels' in Ulster in the 1570s, illustrated the customs of the Irish 'woodkernes' (outlaws); a plate in his book represents the chief of the MacSweeneys at dinner, entertained by his bard, his harper and other followers, and is commented upon in doggerel verse: the bard celebrated the past conquests of the listener or his ancestors and incited him to rebellion.[16]

From the English point of view there often was no clear distinction between the various kinds of poets or entertainers, as, for instance, in Edmund Spenser's tract written in the form of a dialogue between an advocate of extreme measures against the Irish and a relatively more moderate voice.[17] Behind the word 'bards' may be glimpsed the powerful 'men of skill' of the preceding age. Spenser might have deplored the fact that such people were not so highly estimated in England; the trouble with his Irish colleagues, however, was that they tended to celebrate what the English considered wrong.[18] Such themes were not suitable for poetry, and could be all the more dangerous as the Irish were inordinately addicted to narratives (*scéal*: news or story).[19]

For all those reasons he recommended that Irish poets and entertainers be severely controlled, tamed or perhaps exterminated, so that one could reduce 'that salvage nacion to better gouernment and cyvilitye'. Let them learn 'some honest trade', and stay put.[20]

Spenser was writing in 1596, during the ultimate phase of what was, by then, open war. Sir Henry Harrington, appointed as seneschal of the O Byrnes district in 1579, already had strict instructions concerning verbal subversion: 'He shall make proclamation that no idle person, vagabond or masterless man, bard, rymor, or other notorious malefactor, remain within the district on pain of whipping after eight days, and of death after twenty days.'[21] At about the same time, in Kildare, the mandate was 'to punish by death, or otherwise as directed, harpers, rhymers, bards, idlemen, vagabonds, and such horse-boys as have not their master's bill to show whose men they are'.[22] More detailed but equally biased information had been given in 1561 by Thomas Smyth, who listed the kinds of entertainers active then in the western Gaelic world, including those who must have practised narrative genres (see Document A at the end of this chapter). In his report the 'poet', or *file* (modern spelling, now) still had superior status and played a complex role, while the category 'bard' remained woolly, though by then English writers tended to lump together all 'poets in the Irish language'.

14 Quoted by B. Ó Cuív, in *A New History of Ireland* 3.521. 15 Ibid. 520-1. 16 *The Image of Ireland, with a Discourse of Woodcarne* Plate III. 17 *A View of the Present State of Ireland*, in *The Works of Edmund Spenser* 10. 124. 18 Ibid. 125-6. 19 Ibid. 128. 20 Ibid. 219. 21 Quoted by P. Walsh *Gleanings from Irish Manuscripts* 186. 22 Ibid. 186.

Such condemnation continued beyond the Tudor age. A particular case has been studied,[23] which throws light on deep motives for such attacks. It concerns a German who fled to Ireland in 1606 after having been declared bankrupt in London. He acquired an estate in King's County, studied spoken and written Irish, heard local storytellers, and could soon pose as an expert on Gaelic culture. But he was not driven by sympathy or intellectual interest: he used this knowledge to extend his estate at the expense of the local Gaelic lord and to acquire standing with the colonial administration by advocating the destruction of the cultural heritage he had acquainted himself with: a 'canker' had to be eliminated, namely 'the mere Irisch, called *Clan na Milegh* [*Clanna Míle*: the Milesians, referring here to the Gaelic rulers], and their bards and chroniclers which keepes their descents ... The maine point lyeth that we suppress their heads and their language that they maie not keepe any remembrance from whence they cam.'[24] Without history and genealogy the natives would have no right to the land, and having lost their identity they would become docile. In 1612, Sir John Davies, the attorney general for Ireland, in his list of dangerous customs dividing the country, still mentioned as a permanently obnoxious type the 'skelaghes' (*scéalaithe* meaning here both storytellers and rumour-mongers – Spenser's 'common carrier of news') who would 'by their false intelligence many times raise troubles and rebellions in this realm'.[25] In Fynes Moryson's memoirs, published in 1617, the bards are still denounced because 'in their songs [they] used to extoll the most bloudy licentious men, and no others, and to allure the hearers not to the love of religion and civill manners, but to outrages robberies living as outlawes, and contempt of the Magistrates and the Kings lawes'.[26] This battery of quotations (together with Document A), highlight one aspect of Irish storytelling, defined by such terms and concepts as 'abuses', 'disobedience' and 'dangerous', and threatened with repressive measures because it had infected the original colonists with Irish habits, it extolled an Irish savage 'disposition', and was now encouraging chieftains to resist English 'authority' and order. The notion of 'wildness', as opposed to the 'civility' which should distinguish men from animals, was important in this context: brutishness threatened civilized society. Those who refused to change should be treated harshly as 'recalcitrant subjects of the king'.[27]

The English thus tended to regard Irish poets and storytellers only as agents of disturbance. However, other odd but harmless uses of storytelling were occasionally mentioned. Edmund Campion, in his *History of Ireland* published in 1571, had noted an innocuous custom: 'One office in the house of great men is a taleteller, who bringeth his Lord on sleepe with tales vaine and frivolous,

---

23 Brian Mac Cuarta 'A Planter's Interaction with Gaelic Culture: Sir Matthew De Renzy (1577-1634)', *Irish Economic and Social History* 20 (1993) 1-17. **24** Ibid. 11-12. **25** John Davies *A Discovery of the True Cause Why Ireland Was Never Brought under Obedience of the Crown of England*, quoted in *Field Day Anthology of Irish Literature* 1. 219. **26** Quoted in J. Leerssen *Mere Irish & Fíor-Ghael* 52. **27** Ibid. 32.

whereunto the number give sooth and credence.'[28] And, trespassing on the next period, we may note here that Sir William Temple, who spent eight years in Ireland in the mid-seventeenth century and investigated the life of Irish chieftains in earlier times, confirmed Campion's observation:

The great men of their septs, among the many officers of their family, which continued always in the same race, had not only a physician, a huntsman, a smith, and such-like, but a *Poet* and a *Story-teller*: The first recorded the actions of their ancestors, and entertained the company at feasts; the latter amused them with tales when they were melancholy and could not sleep: and a very gallant gentleman of the North of Ireland has told me, of his own experience, that in his wolf-hunting therè, when he used to be in the mountains three or four days together, and lay very ill a-nights, as he could not well sleep, they would bring him one of these tale-tellers, that when he lay down, would begin a story of a king, or a giant, a dwarf and a damsel, and such rambling stuff, and continue it all night long in such an even tone, that you heard it going on whenever you awakened; and he believed nothing any physician give could have so good and so innocent effect, to make men sleep, in any pains or distempers of body or mind.[29]

Another witness had already attested, about 1580, that contemporary political issues were not the only source of inspiration, nor necessarily the most popular. The Irish had other stories: 'They think that the souls of the deceased are in communion with famous men of those places, of whom they retain still fables and sonnets, as of gyants, Fin-Mac-Huyle, Osshin Mac-Owim, and they say through illusion that they often see them.'[30] But nefariousness is the main theme again in an anonymous pamphlet published in London in 1689, though written half-a-century earlier.[31]

In short, when outsiders, did not depict the native Irish poets and story-tellers as dangerous (which was the main reason for mentioning them), they found them rather silly.

For Gaelic Ireland, the sixteenth century had been a troubled period but the policy of anglicization was still resisted; in this respect the seventeenth was disastrous. The end of native lordship, followed by 'plantation' (the allocation of the best land to new British owners on condition that they settled it with loyal tenants), then large-scale destruction and confiscation during and after Cromwell's military expedition, and finally the repressive measures against Catholics after the Williamites' victory, disrupted more and more what was left of the older world. At the beginning of the century, Catholics of Irish or Anglo-Irish stock may still have owned more than four fifths of the land; before the end of the same century, Protestants, who were not more than one quarter of

28 Quoted in James F. Kenney (ed.) *The Sources for the Early History of Ireland* 35. 29 W. Temple *Miscellanea*, quoted in J.C. Walker *Historical Memoirs of the Irish Bards* (1818) 1. 210-11. 30 *Camden's Britannia* (1586; tr. 1607) quoted in J. MacKillop *Fionn mac Cumhaill ...* 77. 31 *A New Irish Prognostication, or Popish Callender* quoted in D. O'Sullivan *Carolan* 1. 7.

the whole population, owned more than four fifths, and the proportion would further grow in their favour during the eighteenth. The last remnants of the Gaelic social order seemed to have been destroyed.

With the collapse of the earlier social system, the members of the 'bardic' caste who stayed in Ireland were marginalized and gradually slid down the social scale. Before the defeat, there had been a noticeable outburst of poetic activity; a poem by Tadhg Dall Ó hUiginn, describing a festive night spent in the house of the Donegal chieftain Maolmhuire Mac Suibhne, confirmed that a poet could function as a tale-teller – and that he worked for tangible reward of some sort: 'To the blossom of Tara and his three companions I relate a tale in return for reward; its dearness was a portent of fame for them, golden youth of the north. Four treasures endowed with virtue I take from them in payment for my story.'[32] The ruin of this aristocratic order swept away the privileges of the poets, who expressed their rage or despair. Those who had despised the peasants now could fear being reduced to manual labour or begging. According to some modern scholars they were essentially archaizing and conservative, and lamented the downfall of the Gaels 'not in terms of the "nation" or even the *patria*, but of the destruction of the class which had dominated the old order – the lords, clerics and poets'.[33] Others see in some of them an awareness of the contemporary crisis, an emergent national consciousness and innovative trends.[34] The debate continues.

Following the departure of the northern chiefs, a bard of the O'Neills wrote that, with 'the outlawry of all poets and the ruin of learning' it was no time for the telling of tales.[35] Another poet had lamented the same 'Flight of the Earls' as the end of his trade: 'No reciting of panegyrics: no telling of sleep-inducing story [*gan sgaoileadh sgeóil chodalta*]: no wish to examine a volume, nor hear a roll of genealogy.'[36]

An anonymous poem of the early seventeenth century, beginning with the question *Cáit ar ghabhadar Gaoidhil?* ('Where have the Gaels gone?'), blames the new foreign masters in similar terms: 'They find no sweetness in devotion to poetry, the sound of harps, and the music of the organ, nor the tales of the kings of Bregia [the plain around Tara] of the turreted walls, nor the numbering of the ancient generations of their forefathers.'[37] Dáibhí Ó Brudair, who lived from the second quarter to almost the end of the century, defined this

32 *The Bardic Poems of Tadhg Dall Ó hUiginn* ed. and tr. by Eleanor Hull, 2. 122. The blind poet received a dappled horse, a wolf-dog, a harp, and a manuscript containing great ancient Irish stories – which confirms the coexistence of oral transmission and written records. **33** T.I. Dunne 'The Gaelic Response to the Conquest and Colonisation: the Evidence of Poetry', in *Studia Hibernica* 20 (1980) 18. **34** See M. Caball *Poets and Politics: Reaction and Continuity in Irish Poetry 1558-1625*. **35** '*Táirnig éigse fhuinn Gaoidhil*' by Fearflatha Ó Gnimh, quoted in Leerssen *Mere Irish and Fíor-Ghael* 398. **36** Eoghan Rua Mac a' Bhaird, an *ollamh* of the O'Donnells, quoted and translated in M. Ó Riordan *The Gaelic Mind and the Collapse of the Gaelic World* 132.The same poem is ascribed to Ainnrias Mac Marcuis in another manuscript. **37** William Gillies 'A Poem on the Downfall of the Ghaoidhil', *Éigse* 13 (1969-70) 207.

period as that of *briseadh an tseanghnáthaimh* (the break up of the old custom).[38] A consequence for some Irish literati was that their verbal arts had to come nearer to the popular ones: though they could still feel superior and probably preferred a more distinguished audience when they found one, poets adopted simpler and often dialectal language and less intricate rules of syllable-counting.

We may suppose that the lower levels of society were less affected than the upper ones, and presumably they told and heard stories, but again they remain largely out of reach. If there were changes in their storytelling (and it remains a matter of conjecture), they may have been partly due to outside influences and to ethnic modifications with the arrival of new groups of colonists, whose influence could depend on the relative size of the different populations in a district. By 1641, more than twenty thousand planters from England had been settled in Munster and some thirty thousand Lowland Scots in Ulster; before leaving their homeland, some of them had known a way of life which materially may not have differed much from that of Irish peasants at the time – but religious and linguistic differences and conflicts of interest made them remain self-consciously a distinctive people. In the mid-century there were further confiscations of large tracts of land previously controlled by Catholic upper-class families: some twelve thousand Englishmen became new owners. With a new migration from Scotland in the last decade of the century, a predominantly protestant North-East was distinguished from the rest of the country and developed the mentality of a besieged garrison. Many Catholic peasants remained as small tenants or labourers; understandably, there were differences in loyalties, and no love lost between the earlier occupants and the new ones, but with time some cultural exchanges may have taken place. Smaller groups of foreigners also left a mark. Towards the end of the century there was an influx of French Huguenots: some ten thousand of them settled in Ireland, mainly in towns; there are proofs that those who moved to Germany brought tales there (their descendants were among the Grimms' main informants), but whether the same happened in Ireland is unknown. Also to escape persecution at home, more than eight hundred Protestant families from the German Palatinate of the Rhine, rendered homeless by wars, arrived in 1709 and settled in Counties Limerick, Kerry, Carlow and Wexford; some of their isolated communities continued their separate mode of life for almost a century; tales were collected from them[39] and a few traces of their traditions have survived into the twentieth century. It was also in the seventeenth century that English popular chapbooks (small pamplets sold by travelling pedlars) which could include tales, and broadsheets (leaflets with the texts of songs, or news), began to circulate in Ireland. At about the same time the close cultural links with Gaelic Scotland were loosening; the forms of what had

38 Dáibhí Ó Bruadair, quoted in S. Deane (ed.) *Field Day Anthology of Irish Literature* 1. 274.
39 See V. Hick, 'Images of Palatines from Folk Tradition, Novels and Travellers' Accounts,' in *Béaloideas* 64-6 (1996-7) 1-62. W.J. Thoms *Lays and Legends of Ireland* (1834) includes 'Tales of the Palatines'.

been a common language and a partly common narrative tradition now developed separately. Where disparate cultures came into contact with each other in Ireland, some new, mixed patterns may have emerged; just as classical mythology was accepted in Irish poetry, foreign popular models may have made an impact.[40]

The culture of Ireland was still largely oral-based, and contemporary accounts of Irish life confirm that narrative activities were enjoyed, from the simplest conversational level to more ritualized occasions. In a book published in 1674, the bookseller, hack and gambler Richard Head, who had been born in Ireland of English parents, noted that the natives were 'inquisitive after others' affairs and always babbling and telling tales', and that 'their greatest zeal [was] in keeping sacred some old sayings of their great grandsires, and preserving sacred relics of their grandmothers'.[41] In a description of County Leitrim a few years later, Tadhg Rody praised the sociability of its people: 'The natives or Irish inhabitants are civil, hospitable and ingenious, very fond of their ancient chronicles and pedigrees and as much abhorring theft, they are great lovers of music and fond of news.'[42] At the end of the century, the English publisher and bookseller John Dunton noted the pleasures of talk peppered with tales in Ireland, and caught glimpses of common beliefs. At an inn in Malahide he experienced the conviviality of people of different origins: English gentlemen like him mocked their own nation, a Catholic priest told a comic tale about confession, a Scottish lieutenant satirized his king, after which the Irish landlady sang 'an Irish Cronaan [*crónán*: singing in a low voice] which is so odd that I cannot express it, being mostly performed in the throat, only now and then some miserable sounds are sent through the nose'.[43] Travelling west, he became better acquainted with the exotic beliefs and pleasures of country people:

Old stories in this country [this letter was written from Mullingar] tell that where the Lough or lake now is a fair town once stood and people in a dry summer when cotting, that is rowing in a small sort of boat, have discovered the tops of many houses and steeples, but not having this from creditable eye-witnesses I do not impose upon your faith ...

[In County Galway] They told me when any of their family was near their end some spectre by them called a Banshee, or fetch, forewarned them of it, and that it had been heard several times of late using a lamentable cry about the house. I found they all believed stories of fairies, hobgoblins, or lemures, and to argue any thing against such beings was all in vain. So much were they prepossessed with the tales received from their forefathers, even the priest himself was of the same mind, though he had nothing more than tradition to confirm what he thought ...

40 Cf. N. Vance *Irish Literature; A Social History* 40: 'Seventeenth-century Irish letters reveal a pattern of cultural pluralism and tense cultural interaction coexisting with embattled cultural and political difference. Separate yet parallel and related traditions and identities begin to emerge.' **41** *The Western Wonder* quoted in E. MacLysaght *Irish Life in the Seventeenth Century* 40, 20. **42** Ibid. 22. **43** Ibid. 368-70. Dunton was in Ireland in 1691.

[In County Kildare] The Irish have another custom, to plant an ash or some other tree which will grow big in the middle of the village, though I never observed them to be planters of them anywhere else. In some towns these trees are old and very great, and hither all the people resort with a piper on Sundays or Holydays in the afternoon, where the young folks dance till the cows come home, (which by the by they'll do without anyone to drive them). I have seen a short truss[ed] young woman tire five lusty fellows, who hereby gets a husband: I am sure I should hardly venture myself with one who had been so able for so many. The elder people sit spectators telling stories of their own like feats in days of yore, and now and then divert themselves with a quill full of sneezing or a whiff of tobacco; for one short foul pipe of an inch long, the shorter and fouler the better, will serve a dozen of the men and women together, the first holding the smoke in his mouth until everyone has whiffed once or twice, and when the pipe returns to him he blows it out of his nose.[44]

We note that at this stage, at least for unconventional visitors like Dunton, the 'mere Irish' were not objects of fear or detestation but entertaining characters. Thomas Dineley, an English traveller who had visited Ireland around 1680, made similar observations but was less indulgent:

They have certain concomitant nastiness and laziness, wherefore having enough before hand to furnish them with potatoes milk & tobacco, which they toss from one another in a short pipe with this word, shaugh [*seach*: a smoke], sitting upon heir hams, like greyhounds in the sun, near their cabin, they'll work not one jot, but steal, which is an inseparable vice to them, that a gentleman in the county of Clare complain'd to me that they stole his box of pills because guilded ... Any news, report or rumour from towns is convey'd into the countries with dispatch above an Englishman's imagination, and they are so credulous that it is no sooner heard but believed. Irish wakes are an attendance upon the dead, which is perform'd with more solemnity and less noise in towns than in the country, where the coffin is placed under a table, or if the poverty of the defunct do not allow him that, then he is shrowded onely with flowers ribbons & sweet herbs, sewn'd to the shroud, about the corps, with a great many candles, lighted and set out upon the table. At these meetings the young fry, viz. Darby, Teige, Morogh, Leam, Rinett, Allsoon, Norah, Shevaune, More, Kathleene, Ishabeal, Nooula, Mayrgett, Timesheen, Shinnyed, &c, appear as gay as may be, with their holyday apparel, and with piper, harper, or fiddler, revel and dance the night throughout, make love and matches.[45]

A wake was also adversely described by Henry Piers, writing at the instance of the Protestant bishop of Meath:

At funerals they have their wakes, which as now they celebrate were more befitting heathen than christians; they sit commonly in a barn or large room, and are entertained with

---

44 Ibid. 324, 347 and 354. **45** *Observations in a Voyage through the Kingdom of Ireland ... in the Year 1681* (ed. J. Graves) 17-18, 21-2. For nineteenth-century accounts of an 'Irish way of sitting', see Chapters 5 and 6; for twentieth-century descriptions of the pipe ceremony, see Chapter 11.

beer and tobacco; the lights are set up on a table over the dead; they spend most of the night in obscene stories, and bawdy songs, until the hour comes for the exercise of their devotions; then the priest calls on them to fall to their prayers for the soul of the dead, which they perform by repetition of Aves and Paters on their beads, and close the whole with a *de profundis*, and then immediately to the story or song again, till another hour of prayer comes; thus is the whole night spent 'till day; when the time of the burial comes, all the women run out like mad, and now the scene is altered, nothing heard but wretched exclamations, howlings and clapping of hands, enough to destroy their own and others sense of hearing.[46]

'Nothing more than tradition', wrote Dunton, summing up what the Irish liked to repeat and talk about – 'the tales received from their forerunners'. It meant very little to outside observers, but for people in Ireland it was perhaps the only treasure left in a world that was breaking up before their eyes. And it was valued by those who compiled historical information to vindicate their people. Seathrún Céitinn (Geoffrey Keating, *c.*1580–*c.*1644), for instance, was of Anglo-Norman Catholic extraction and carefully distinguished *Sean-Ghaill* like himself from *Nua-Ghaill* (the new Protestant settlers), hoping to unite all Catholics – Gaelic and gaelicized Anglo-Norman – in the militant spirit of the Counter-Reformation. Between *c.*1620 and 1633 he travelled the country to collect material for his history of Ireland from the earliest times to the twelfth century: *Foras Feasa ar Éirinn* ('A Groundwork of Knowledge about Ireland'), written explicitly to counter the 'lies of the new foreigners' and the negative views of English writers. He thought that a country as worthy of honour as Ireland and people as noble as those who had inhabited it should not go down into oblivion till their story was told.[47] He had attended a bardic school before studying for the priesthood, and his sources may have included oral tradition; at any rate, he accepted as reliable, *because traditional*, much of the legendary account he found. Edmund Campion, the English author of a history of Ireland written in 1571, had dismissed Fianna tales as 'blinde legends'; Keating countered:

Whoever should say that Fionn and the Fian never existed would not be stating the truth. For, to prove that the Fian existed we have the three things that prove the truth of every history in the world except the Bible, namely, oral tradition of the ancients [*béaloideas na sean*], old documents, and antique remains called in Latin monumenta. For it has been delivered to us from mouth to mouth [*ó bhéal go béal*] that Fionn and the Finn existed ... And should anyone say that much of what has been written about the Fian is not to be believed, he would certainly state the truth; for there was no kingdom in the world in which there were not written tales called fabulae in Pagan times ... But there is no country in the world in which also true and credible histories have not been written. In the same manner, although many imaginative romances have been written

---

46 *A Chorographical Description of the County of Westmeath, Written A.D. 1682*, in C. Vallancey's *Collectanea de Rebus Hibernicis* 1. 124. 47 *The History of Ireland – Foras Feasa ar Eirinn* 1. 76 (tr. D. Comyn) – Keating's preface.

about Fionn and the Fian, such as *Cath Fionntragha* ['The Battle of Ventry'], *Bruighean Chaor Thainn* ['The Fairy Palace of the Quicken Trees'], and *Imtheacht an Ghiolla Dhecair* ['The Escape of the Difficult Servant' – three famous Fianna romances] and others of a similar kind, for the sake of amusement, still it is certain that true credible accounts of them were also written.[48]

In some cases, he admitted he was perhaps quoting fables: for instance, he concludes a story concerning Guaire with the words *más fíor*: if it is true. Manuscript copies of his book circulated widely and remained extremely popular; they were influential for two centuries as a source book for nationalistic historiography, and being read aloud in peasants' gatherings they certainly fed back oral tradition.

A similar desire to defend Ireland's reputation inspired Roderic O'Flaherty (1629-1718), who had studied both classical and bardic learning and whose family estate in County Galway had been confiscated after Cromwell's victory. In *Ogygia*, written originally in Latin in the early 1680s, he used source material critically:

Some are most certainly apocryphal and fabulous, written merely for entertainment; others are vitiated by the varieties of copies and ignorance of transcribers; and more, through motives of flattery and ambition, are fraught with hyperbolical accounts. However, the incontrovertible Truth shines through them with irresistible lustre, by the unanimous tradition and consent of antiquarians ... I totally reject and disbelieve all these monstrous and fabulous accounts that have been penned by poets such as that of Fintan [see pp. 20-1], the son of Borrat, one of Caesarea's [Cesair, queen of 'the first invasion of Ireland', according to the ancient 'Mythological Cycle'] triumvirs ... was resuscitated, after the deluge, and lived to the time of St Patrick, and also to the seventh year of Diermod, the first, king of Ireland; and that Tuan [see p. 21] ... the nephew of Partholon by his brother Starn, was alone preserved from the general fate of mankind, and metamorphosed into various kinds of animals for many ages; and that at last, from being a salmon, he became the son of Carill king of Ulster, and afterwards survived Fintan. The allegory of this fable may be unravelled, by considering that those fantastical notions of the Pythagorean and Platonic systems concerning metempsychosis, or transmigration of souls, pervaded our Druids in the times of ignorance and idolatry.[49]

He also recorded, cautiously, contemporary oral legends. In *A Chorographical Description* (1684), for instance, he collected an echo of the ancestral and universal theme of the Islands of the Blessed, perhaps from the mouth of the protagonist himself, Muircheartach Ó Laoi, who said he had been taken away by the fairies to a mysterious island in the Atlantic (Hy Brasil or O-Brasil) supposed to be visible every seven years.[50] O'Flaherty's phrase 'as he imagines' is a

---

48 Ibid. 2. 325-7, tr. P. Dinneen. 49 *Ogygia, or a Chronological Account of Irish Events* translated by James Hely in 1793, lxx and 5. 50 *A Chorographical Description of West or h-Iar Connaught* 70-2. At about the same time, in County Fermanagh, another 'modern' version of

polite way of making reservations. Collective fancy kept working on this story, and it was soon embellished with the important detail of O'Ley's receiving from the fairy inhabitants of Hy-Brasil a magic book which bestowed on him the gift of healing. The book survived – and turned out to be a man-made fifteenth-century medical manuscript. John O'Donovan heard the legend a century and a half later (see next chapter), and in 1902 Yeats wrote about a Drumcliff fisherman who saw, 'far on the horizon, renowned Hy Brazil, where he who touches shall find no more labour or care, or cynic laughter, but shall go walking about under the shadiest boscage, and enjoy the conversation of Cuchulain and his heroes'.[51]

If we know very little about the way stories were told towards the end of the seventeenth century and at the beginning of the eighteenth, we may have an idea of what kinds of stories there were. Beyond those mentioned in the preceding quotations, which are narrative justifications or illustrations of beliefs, we know that some of the medieval noble narratives and romances must have been kept alive by a combination of reading and memorization. We can suppose there already were 'wonder tales' (of the *Märchen* kind) and comic or cautionary tales, corresponding to types known elsewhere. Some of them could have developed independently by combining perennial themes while others were imported, perhaps with shifts of population and the seasonal migration of Irish labourers when they began working in Great Britain (from the eighteenth century), or through other channels.

There were also narrative songs, in two languages. The versified Irish texts known as *laoithe* constitute a special category. Attested in Ireland, Scotland and perhaps in the Isle of Man, they treat of the adventures or feelings of some heroes of the Ulster cycle and much more often, as *laoithe Fiannaiochta*, of heroes of the Fianna cycle. Whether they were meant to be sung, chanted or recited is not clear – indeed they seem to have been performed in different manners. The first known examples are in the twelfth-century *Book of Leinster*, and it remains a moot point whether the genre was a native development of the earlier verse passages marking climactic episodes in prose 'sagas', or an echo of the success of balladry on the Continent.[52] The bulk of the extant material, amounting to some 25,000 lines, is in manuscripts of the fifteenth century and later; lays were modified or newly composed until the eighteenth, by which time they had become a distinctive part of what would later be called folklore and were considered to have the highest status in it. The earlier ones were composed in

the island paradise legend appeared, concerning a Captain John Nisbet, who claimed to have landed on a lake island and met people who had been imprisoned there by a necromancer.; see T.J. Westropp 'Brasil and the Legendary Islands of the North Atlantic', *Proceedings of the Royal Irish Academy* 30c (1912) 223-60. 51 *Mythologies* 92. 52 Gerard Murphy thought they had been influenced, practically from the start, 'by the new genre of balladry' [*The Ossianic Lore and Romantic Tales of Medieval Ireland* 19); Hugh Shields says that they are not ballads: 'Ballads and lays are too different both in the matter they narrate and in their manner of using it' (*Narrative Singing in Ireland* 5).

'bardic' verse, with seven syllables in each of the four lines of a stanza; other songs in Irish were measured by stresses. The lays could be simply lyrical out-bursts connected with emotive situations, but some were more narrative. The set of themes included opposition to supernatural beings and mysterious visitors, adventures in distant lands, hunts – the usual Fianna lore. Narration often took the form of reminiscence by nostalgic survivors of the heroic age, but when the interlocutor was Patrick he could appear, in contrast to *Acallam na Senórach*, as a bigoted cleric pronouncing the damnation of the heroes of the past, while the main speaker – now Oisín more often than Caoilte – was the defiant pagan. (Some eighteenth- or nineteenth-century sketches of singers of such lays will be quoted in the following chapters.) As for ballads in English, there is no unitary definition embracing all their manifestations, beyond strophic form and a more or less narrative content. The terse elliptic type, with detached third-person dis-course or characters speaking in alternation, may have been introduced by sev-enteenth-century settlers;[53] a number of such 'early' (though generally post-medieval) 'English and Scottish ballads' were still collected from oral tradition in Ireland in the second half of the twentieth century. The more circumstantial 'journalistic' ballad kind, dealing with contemporary events, was also imported from Britain and developed first in towns on the east coast; significantly, 'The Boyne Water' in nineteen stanzas, one of the first notable historical ballads in English composed in Ireland perhaps in the 1690s, was a rallying cry of the Ulster Protestants.[54]

Cheap printed material diffused song texts and prose narratives. In 1769, a Dublin printer issued *The Companion for the Fire-Side, Being a Collection of Genuine and Instructive Adventures, Tales and Stories*, which opened with 'A Short Tractate on Story-Telling', said to be the art which people were most desirous of attaining:

> All love mutually to communicate and to hear a good story. Some are pleased with the grave, the solemn, the tragic tale; while others delight in the witty, merry and jocose. Now I have often observed that though all are desirous of excelling in this pleasing art, yet very few arrive at any manner of perfection; and the greater number become dull, tiresome and insipid; and far from gaining our applause, render themselves the objects of our ridicule ... Every person who wishes to attain to any degree of excellence in story-telling, so as to be capable of entertaining his auditors agreeably, should strictly scruti-nize the extent of his genius, that he may be the better able to make choice of such sto-ries as are adapted to his capacity.[55]

---

53 Hugh Shields, ibid. 40: '[These] ballads entered Ireland whole on the lips of immigrant singers of English and Scottish origin and neither altered nor, at first, were altered by the oral literature of the new environment.' 54 A. Hume 'The Two Ballads on the Battle of the Boyne', *Ulster Journal of Archaeology* 2 (1854) 9-21. 55 *The Companion for the Fire-Side* vi-vii.

Some fifty short narratives followed, most of them probably first published in Britain and some translated from the French.

Whereas the acclimatization of forms and of particular texts (and tunes) is obvious in the case of ballads, things are not so clear-cut in the oral prose repertoire. A hybridization of Irish and British cultural components may have developed in the period under discussion but, although borrowing or blending is conceivable, it may often be hard to prove beyond doubt. Story plots with similar narrative elements combined in similar ways may have a nomadic history across linguistic borders, develop new roots and be subject to reinterpretations; the date, channel and direction of dissemination – before the seventeenth century or later and towards or from Ireland, for instance – are difficult to ascertain. We can measure the complexity of such problems by looking at the resemblances between two stories, found in oral tradition in Ireland and elsewhere, which also appeared in written form within half a century as an in-tale in a *roman* in Paris, and a poem of some 200 quatrains in the west of Ireland.[56] The basic plot concerns a hero who enters the world of the immortals and may marry its queen, then is granted leave home provided he respects the prohibition of not dismounting from his horse; he disobeys and dies, or ages rapidly, on touching the ground.

Madame d'Aulnoy's *Histoire d'Hypolite, Comte de Douglas* (1690)	Micheál Coimín's *Laoi Oisín ar Thír na nÓg* (*c.*1750)
(The story is told to an abbess by a Scot, who is trying to remember '*un conte approchant de ceux des fées*' – rendered as 'after the manner of the fairies'.)	(The story is told by Oisín to Patrick.)
Prince Adolphe meets Eole's wife, and hears from her son Zephir about the Island of Felicity. He is transported there.	Oisín is enticed by Niamh, an Otherworld lady, to go with her to the Land of Youth. He is transported there.
There are extraordinary flowers, fruits, palaces built of gems, '*ils n'étaient jamais malades … leur jeunesse n'étaient point atteinte par le cours des ans.*'	There are extraordinary flowers and fruits, palaces built of gems, no sorrow, no decay or death.
After three hundred years – though he thinks he has been there only a short time – the prince wants to see his country again. He is told that once there he must not get off his horse.	After three hundred years – which seems to him a short time – Oisín wants to visit Ireland once again. He is told that once there he must not get off his horse.

56 An English translation of Madame d'Aulnoy's works was published in London in 1707. The *roman* that includes the tale was later published again in Ireland: *The History of Hypolitus, Earl of Douglas. Interspersed with Historical Anecdotes. Translated by a Gentleman* printed by William Flyn, Cork, 1768.

| | (In Ireland he is a giant among dwarfs who know him only as a legend.) |
| He does get off, to rescue an old man caught under an overturned cart – and he dies. (The old man was Time.) | He wants to rescue people caught under a block of marble; his saddle girths break; he falls and becomes extremely old. |

Madame d'Aulnoy's rendering of the tale is considered to have been the first notable 'literary' use of a *conte de fée* in seventeenth-century France (preceding Perrault). 'L'Ile de la Félicité' was an in-tale in a novel, but is known to have circulated separately in chapbook form in the eighteenth century, in several languages. The supposed author of the Irish text, Micheál Coimín (or Cuimín, or Comyn; 1688-1760) was a kind of cultural crossbred whose family, perhaps of Scottish descent, had been a victim of the Cromwellian confiscations but was compensated in 1665. He was a Protestant, reputed to have 'lived the wild, drinking, gaming life of the Anglo-Irish of his time',[57] but was bilingual, wrote in Irish and owned Irish manuscripts – which his embarrassed son destroyed after his death. He may have been acquainted with texts like Madame d'Aulnoy's – but he did not need to: the theme of the mortal who goes to some marvellous island peopled with immortal women, and of his potentially fatal return, had been treated in earlier Irish literature (see Chapter 2). The poem was copied in nineteenth-century manuscripts; prose versions of 'Oisín in Tír na nÓg' have been collected from oral tradition; on the one hand the eighteenth-century author of the poem may have used an earlier theme, and on the other the growing popularity of the poem in the nineteenth century may have affected oral tradition.[58]

Marie Catherine, baronne d'Aulnoy (*c*.1650-1705) was an unusual character too, twice involved in criminal cases, alleged to have been a secret agent in England and in Spain (but her biography mixes legends and facts) – and a talented writer. What were her sources? Here again it is impossible to be sure. It was claimed that she had heard a legend concerning Dónall Ó Donnchú (O'Donoghue of Killarney – more about him in Chapter 5) who was riding on Loch Léin whence Coimín's Oisín was transported to Tír na nÓg, or some legend concerning Gearóid Iarla Fitzgerald who had mysteriously disappeared but would return on Loch Gur – through an island which communicated with Tír na nÓg.[59] The Irish source may appear 'probable' to some and just possible

57 A. de Blacam *Gaelic Literature Surveyed* 324. **58** Ó Súilleabháin and Christiansen *The Types of the Irish Folktale* 96-7 lists some twenty versions from oral tradition. Máirtín Ó Briain, in 'Some Material on Oisín in the Land of Youth' (in D. Ó Corráin et al. eds. *Sages, Saints and Storytellers*) finds the attribution to Comyn 'somewhat unconvincing', thinks that the poem was founded on an older oral tradition, and notes that 'the widespread distribution of the folktale in Ireland and Scotland, in this century and the last, as well as the divergence between versions, proves that the tale has been in the oral tradition for some considerable time' (187). **59** Lady H.G.M. Chatterton *Rambles in Ireland during the Year 1838* 114-5: 'The tale respecting O'Donoghue's subaquaeous immortality was first printed in a French romance,

to others; but the longing for a lost paradise, the Otherworld journey and the perilous return are perennial and universal themes, and though the notion that time runs at different rates in different realms may be favoured by 'Celtic' storytellers it is not their exclusive property; enchanted islands as the abode of the blessed are at least as old as written literature itself – one of them appears in the story of Gilgamesh, and there are eastern and western parallels. In more modern literature there is the island where goddesses entertain Portuguese navigators in *Os Lusíadas*, or the Fortunate Isle where the magician Armida confines Rinaldo in *La Gerusalemme Liberata* – and Madame d'Aulnoy explicitly refers to the latter text in her own tale: *'tel etoit le brave Renault entre les bras de son Armide'*.[60] It concerns only part of the plot summarized above, but there is a twelfth-century Breton lay, 'Guingamor', which comes closer to it: after three hundred years in an otherworld castle of gold and *pierres de paradis* where he intended to spend only three days, the hero returns to his country and discovers that he has become a legend; though his *geis* (prohibition) is that he must not absorb food in the mortal world, he eats an apple and falls off his horse.[61] A famous Japanese story ('Urashima Taro'), and tales collected from oral tradition in Finland, Poland, Hungary, Corsica and France, follow more or less the same pattern combining motifs F116: Journey to the Land of the Immortals, F377: Supernatural Lapse of Time in Fairyland, C521: Tabu – dismounting from horse, D1896: Magic aging by contact with earth after otherworld journey, or C210: Tabu – Eating in Certain Place. In the French oral version, six hundred years are spent in the *île où l'on ne mourait point* and the hero gets off the horse to help a carter.[62] It is generally admitted that Madame d'Aulnoy must have heard folktales during her childhood in Normandy, and used them for the *Contes de Fées* she wrote later; but we cannot be certain that she heard a version of International Type 470*: The Hero Visits the Land of the Immortals and Marries its Queen. The lesson we may draw from this particular exploration is that, if resemblance may point to some common origin, it is often impossible to say how distant in space and time it was.

In eighteenth-century Ireland, a privileged minority of rulers seemed to be completely separated from a dispossessed majority, with language and religion clearly marking the social and ethnic divide. On the one hand some five thousand Protestant landowning families (who came to be known as 'the ascendancy')

---

entitled "Hyppolite, Comte de Douglas" which is known to have been the production of the Comtesse d'Aulnoy, who died in 1705. It appears probable that the Comtesse was told the fable, or the similar fables respecting the Earls of Kildare and Desmond [another Gerald Fitzgerald, and *Gearóid Iarla* himself], as a family tradition, by some of the officers of the Irish Brigade who had followed the fortunes of James II.' **60** *Histoire d'Hypolite, Comte de Douglas* 282. **61** This 'lai' can be found in P. M. O'Hara Tobin *Les lais anonymes des XIIᵉ et XIIIᵉ siècles; Edition critique de quelques lais bretons.* **62** A. Aarne and S. Thompson *The Types of the Folktales* 162; P. Delarue and M.L. Tenèze *Le conte populaire français* 2. 163–8.

adhered to the established Church of Ireland and were at the top, non-conformist Protestants being discriminated against. On the other hand, the large Catholic majority had practically no political existence, and land ownership among them had fallen to about five per cent by 1775. However, a more nuanced picture can be offered. The anti-Catholic legislation enacted between 1695 and 1727, to secure the political and social supremacy of Protestants and to weaken the majority, were more radical in theory than in practice and were gradually relaxed in the last third of the century. Not all Protestants were rich, and the Catholics were not all members of an oppressed peasantry: a stratum of Catholic merchants began to emerge. From the 1740s, with a demand for agricultural products for export and the development of linen manufactures, there was an economic expansion, though prosperity did not benefit all people and regions equally. There was some cultural interaction between the different social levels.[63] Middle-class Protestants who, at the beginning of the century, saw themselves as Englishmen born in Ireland, objected to the management of Irish affairs from London when their interests were perceived as differing from, or opposed to, those of the bigger island. But when they came to call themselves 'the Irish Nation' they did not want separation, and their 'patriotism' at first involved no veneration of an Irish past; they insisted on the differences between themselves and the 'native Irish', regarded as blinded by absurd papist/pagan superstitions.

If the life of the peasantry was not unmitigated despair, it could be very difficult: in 1739-41 a famine is said to have caused a quarter-of-a-million deaths; absentee landowners were becoming more numerous and the 'middlemen' to whom they let their estates divided them and sublet at a profit, the rising rural population and greater competition for farms pushing up rents. Regions in the West which had been barren and unpopulated were now occupied. Potatoes were becoming the staple food. There was a growing difference between prosperous tenant farmers and poor cottiers or labourers, the majority being reduced to a precarious status. Although animosity could be strong, there was no continuous general confrontation: the use of violence was episodic and in response to local problems and unwanted changes rather than against the established order. The material life of ordinary people in Ireland may not have been much worse than that of peasants in several other regions of Europe, but they had no rights whatsoever. Whatever culture of their own they had maintained was seldom noticed, and then mostly unfavourably; yet the masters of Irish verbal art and scholarship who now lived among them celebrated an idealized past – perhaps not exactly theirs. They were told that they were the descendants of glorious ancestors who had been wrongly dispossessed of their property; but one day, so they were given to hope, they would recover what had been stolen. (See

63 N. Vance, op. cit. 66: 'A recent study of popular culture in Ulster suggests that in the eighteenth and nineteenth centuries, Irish popular culture was the common possession of Catholic and Protestant to a considerable extent.'

Document B at the end of this chapter for a description of the poorer Irish peasants at the end of the century and the role of storytelling in their life.)

A few families belonging to the older aristocracy were able to keep estates, and while adjusting themselves to the changing world they still welcomed poets and harpists. But most poets were now patronless and survived as semi-clandestine schoolmasters, small farmers or labourers. In Munster, an attempt was made to keep the ancient bardic status alive with *cúirteanna eigse* (courts of poetry), meeting in public houses, barns or kitchens to recite new poems, try one's talent in extempore verse repartee, perhaps despise the lower classes, and exchange manuscripts[64] with texts from earlier centuries as well as new compositions, including narrative texts and lyrics.[65] In a way, these eighteenth-century poets represented the end of a literary line, but they transmitted some elements: the ancient view of the ruler as the symbolic spouse of the goddess of Sovereignty and of the land probably had something to do with the poetic genre of the aisling (vision), in which a personification of Ireland calls for help, and this form of poetry in Irish influenced more awkward popular songs in English; similarly, the Providential comparison of the Irish to the Hebrew slaves waiting for Moses, which had first appeared in bardic poems of the seventeenth century, flourished in street ballads in the first half of the nineteenth.

Poets could become legendary figures: many stories were told of them, and around 1900 Daniel Corkery, whose influential nationalistic book *The Hidden Ireland* in 1924 celebrated those Munster poets as the keepers of 'the soul of the Gael', witnessed the survival of their reputation.[66] If Irish poems of the eighteenth century are well known, conditions of their composition and performance comparatively well documented and the names of their authors celebrated, what was said of earlier periods concerning popular narrative activities still applies here: only a few scraps of information can be gleaned from contemporary sources. Oliver Goldsmith is one of them. Born in County Roscommon, he

---

64 D. Ó hÓgáin, 'Folklore and Literature: 1700-1850', in M. Daly and D. Dickson (eds) *The Origins of Popular Literature in Ireland* ... 3: 'Most of the literary men of the eighteenth-century Gaelic world stood as aloof as they could from the actual stories which circulated among the ordinary people, or at least from the form in which these stories circulated. To the literati, the "correct" versions of traditions were those in book or manuscript form.' 65 Brian Ó Cuív, in *A New History of Ireland* 4. 411: 'Manuscripts of the period [eighteenth century] contain a considerable number of tales which are not known from earlier sources, some belonging to the older Irish cycles, others showing the characteristic features of wizardry and magic, overseas adventures, romantic love and burlesque, which were already popular in preceeding centuries. Some of these have affinities with folk-tales, and of course storytelling was one of the most widespread forms of entertainment among a population of whom relatively few could read.' 66 *The Hidden Ireland* 234-6. For L.M. Cullen, in 'The Hidden Ireland: Re-Assessment of a Concept', Corkery's account of the socio-economic structure is simplistic: he reads 'into the poetry aspirations which it did not contain, and thus creates a continuity from aristocratic resentment to popular unrest more artificial than real' (47). D. Ó hÓgáin in *An File* explores the legends concerning those poets and their supposed powers; there is a shorter account in *The Hero in Irish Folk History*, Ch. 5: 'The Poet as Hero'.

spent part of his childhood in County Meath and heard the schoolmaster of Lissoy tell stories about ghosts, banshees, fairies and heroes like Hugh Balldearg Ó Domhnail, a messianic leader announced by prophecies and identified by his strawberry mark (*dearg*: red; *ball*: spot), who died in 1704. Goldsmith was an exception among the notable writers in English of that time in repeatedly referring to an Irish popular culture in two languages: he testified, for instance, that in the first half of the century British ballads were already acclimatized, while harpers and composers of songs in Irish, like Turlough Carolan, were appreciated by members of both communities. To people like Carolan he applied the term 'bard' in the loose sense it had acquired by then: 'their bards, in particular, are still held in great veneration among [the Irish]; those traditional heralds are invited to every funeral, in order to fill up the intervals of the howl with their songs and harps'.[67] An anonymous article, offered as a letter from an English gentleman visiting Ireland and of which Goldsmith was almost certainly the author, describes a meeting with a country storyteller, and a funeral wake:

My landlord [by which the author means his peasant host] offered to tell me the story of Kaul Kroodareg [Cathal Crobhdhearg – 'of the Red Hand' – O'Connor: a thirteenth-century king of Connacht who also became the hero of messianic legends announcing the liberation of Ireland] but continues he it will be nothing in English, but in Irish it is finer than fine itself. I declined his offer, pretending to have heard it before ... I was therefore obliged in spite of me to let the conversation take a general turn, and answer the news of the day, which was asked me by every one of the family. The questions I answered to the best of my power, but I found they looked upon my answers as no way satisfactory, they wanted something strange, and I had only news to tell them. [Again the double meaning of *scéalta – scéala*.] ... Before I left that part of the country, I went to see a wake or funeral, which is entirely peculiar to these people. As soon as a person dies he is immediately carried out into the best appartment, and the bed on which he died is burned at the door. The body is wrapped in linen all but the face, and thus laid upon the door of the house, which on this occasion is taken off the hinges, and claped under their large square table. Beer, pipes, and tobacco are immediately procured, and all the neighbours are invited to sit up the ensuing night, with the corpse, which they call waking it. Upon this occasion all the old men and women who are generally fond of beer and tobacco, and all the young ones of both sexes, who are equally fond of diversion, assemble at the house of the deceased, in order to howl, to romp, and to tell stories. If the deceased was of any substance there is always employed on this occasion a man whose only employment is story telling, and a woman whose only business is to bear a chorus in every howl. At nightfall the plays begin, the young folk, no way terrified at the scene of death before them, toy and play tricks and have twenty pastimes suited to the occasion, the old ones smoak, guzzle, and upon the appearance of every stranger, howl in the most dismal manner, to a particular tune which you may have seen set to music.[68]

---

67 'Carolan, the Last Irish Bard', *The British Magazine* July 1760. *Collected Works* 3. 118.   68 'A Description of the Manners and Customs of the Native Irish', *Weekly Magazine* 29 December 1759. *Collected Works* 3. 27-9.

Another essay confirms that he did know something of Irish narrative tradition, in ballad form and in prose, and that to him it did not seem monstrous or particularly damaging:

> Every country has its traditions, which, either too minute or not sufficiently authentic to receive historical sanction, are handed down among the vulgar, and serve at once to instruct and amuse them. Of this number, the adventures of Robin Hood, the hunting of Chevy Chace, and the bravery of Johnny Armstrong, among the English; of Kall Dereg, among the Irish; and Creigton ['the Admirable Crichton'], among the Scots, are instances.[69]

Other traces of popular 'oral traditions' in the eighteenth century appear in the 'county histories' written by an apothecary from Dungarvan, Charles Smith – particularly in his *Antient and Present State of the County of Kerry* (1756). Assuming the 'enlightened' attitude of contempt for superstition, Smith nevertheless listened to what local people said, though without taking pains to reproduce their exact words.[70] Those perpetuating such stories and beliefs did not seem worthy of respect: the 'common people' who lived among the ruins or geological oddities did not interest the antiquarian. One or two generations later, however, travellers would begin to find them entertaining and sometimes impressive. Already in 1767, James Parsons (1705-70), English-born but educated in Dublin before he became a renowned physician and an antiquary in London, praised Irish storytelling performances:

> In Ireland they have their bards to this day, among the inland inhabitants; and even among the poorest of the people; and so, I am informed, they have in Scotland and Wales; and it is a very common practice among them when they return home from the toil of the day, to sit down, with their people round them, in bad weather, in their houses, and without doors in fair, repeating the histories of ancient heroes and their transactions, in a stile that, for its beauty and fine sentiments, has often struck me with amazement; for I have many times been obliged, by some of these natural bards, with the repetition of as sublime poems upon love, heroism, hospitality, battles, &c. as can be produced in any language: and indeed, I have often regretted that so few gentlemen, of modern learning, understand that language enough to enjoy so fine an entertainment.[71]

In the last two decades of the century some members of the Protestant upper-middle class began to regard the Gaelic past more favourably and to collect or study what was sufficiently distant in time to look harmless and sufficiently mysterious to be fascinating. They now considered Ireland their country and found some comfort in the notion of an Irish cultural identity; coming from across the sea, there were also new tastes for 'savage nobility' and 'sublime environment', for what was essentially different or distant, for strong emotions or

69 'A Flemish Tradition', in *The Bee*, 1759. *Collected Works* 1. 420. 70 Op. cit. (1756), 83-4, 173, 196. 71 *Remains of Japhet: Being Historical Enquiries into the Affinity and Origin of European Languages* 148.

melancholy, and for picturesque regional peculiarities – I shall study these developments in the next chapter. The violent rebellion of 1798 checked the sympathy of the establishment for native culture; there was no reversion to the strident bardophobia of the Tudor age, but 'singing a ballad' (when it meant a political ditty) would remain a punishable offence throughout the nineteenth century.

As Irish society changed, sometimes gradually and sometimes catastrophically, much was lost – but not everything, and there could also be some cultural enrichment. The functions and modes of storytelling, which were always diverse, were evolving too: some native or long-naturalized genres and techniques slowly waned or adapted themselves to altered circumstances, while new genres, stories and perhaps techniques could enter Ireland and become acclimatized. Although different kinds of storytellers must have existed at any one time, the relatively few sources we have, mainly outsiders, tended to notice one kind only; but in the course of centuries they shifted their attention from the nobleman's familiar or rebel chieftain's firebrand to the wise or doting old peasant or brisk popular entertainer, and the attitude of such observers also changed, from fear to puzzlement or from condescension to amusement, and occasionally sympathy. Towards the end of the eighteenth century, a sentimental treatment became possible and wildness itself, formerly horrifying, came to connote freedom and moral purity.

Two views of the Gaelic world are offered as comparatively more extensive documents to round off the present chapter. They are mediated through the eyes of outsiders whose information and interpretations were limited and biased, and each of them addresses the English government to advocate a more effective policy. They illustrate two phases in the evolution just surveyed: the Tudor age and the very end of the eighteenth century.

The first illustrates the hostile attitude of settlers and English officials to an alien way of living, and contrasts its supposed barbarism with the order maintained in a beleaguered outpost of 'civility'. A denunciation coming from a party seeking clear directives and the means to root out a threat, it urges the authorities to take emergency measures against brigands and their entertainers. When it was written, in 1561, conciliation was no longer the order of the day: the Catholic majority was not likely to accept the Acts of Supremacy and Uniformity which a Parliament summoned in Dublin had extended to Ireland in 1556; 'plantation' in Leix and Offaly was being resisted; Shane O'Neill, in the North, had rejected all English titles in 1559 and was obviously going to be a dangerous opponent; on the west coast, Grace O'Malley, who would later be the heroine of many legends, was beginning to build her reputation as the 'nurse of all rebellions in the province for forty years';[72] eight years later, the first

72 According to Richard Bingham, governor of Connaught, 1593 (*State Papers of Ireland* –

Desmond Rebellion would break out in Munster. We do not know how near the informer ever went to those he is denouncing, but the letter contains a number of details which are corroborated by other texts: there were different kinds of verbal artists and entertainers in the Gaelic world; the poet's task, there, was to defend certain values that justified his own position and to exhort the chieftain to imitate examples of the past; genealogy was important; some classical erudition was respectable; the custom of cattle stealing (by then known as *crech* or *creach*: a raid or robbery) still played an important part in the prestige of Irish chieftains – something of the old less sedentary, more tribal Gaelic world survived at the end of the sixteenth century, but was marked down for suppression.

DOCUMENT A

Kept in the State Paper Office and dated 5 May 1561, it was published by Herbert F. Hore under the title 'Irish Bardism in 1561' in the 1858 issue of the Ulster Journal of Archaeology *(pp. 165-7, with a commentary on pp. 202-12). The author is presumably Thomas Smyth, a Dublin apothecary who became sheriff in 1576 and mayor in 1591.*

Their is in Ireland four shepts [septs] in maner all Rimers. The firste of them is calleid the Brehounde [*breitheamh*], which in English is calleid the Judge; and before they wille geave judgement, they will have paunes of both the parties, the which is callied in Irish *Ulieg* [*ualaigh*: burden], and then will they geave judgement according to their one discresions. Theis men be neuters, and the Irishmen will not paie them. They have great pleantie of cattel, and they harbour many vacabons and ydell persons; and if their be any reabell that moves any rebellione ageinste the Prince, of theis people they are chiflie mantayned; and if the English armye fortune to travell in that parte where they be, they will fle into montains and woods, by cause they wold not sucker [succour] them with vittals and other [means]; and further they will take uppon them to judge matters, and redresse causes, as well of inherytans as of other matters, althogh they are ignoraunt; the which is a greatte hinderans to the Queen's Majesties lawes, and hurtfull to the whole English Pale. The seconde sourte is the Shankee [*seanchaí*], which is to saye in English the Petigrer [genealogist]. They have also great plaintye of cattell, where withall they do sucker the rebells. They make the ignorant men of the country to belyve they be discendid of Alexander the Great, or of Darius, or of Caesar, or of some other notable prince; which makes the ignorant people to run madde, and cerieth not what they do; the which is hurtfull to the realme. The thirde sorte is called the Aeosdan [*aos dána*: poets], which is to saye in English, the bards, or the rimine sepctes; and these people be very hurtfull to the commonwhealle for they chifflie manyntayne the rebells; and, further, they do cause them that would be true, to be rebelious theves, extorcioners, murtherers, ravners, yea and worse if it were possible. Their furst practisse is, if they se anye younge man discended of the septs of *Ose* or *Max*, and have half a dowsen aboute him,

Microfilm 63/158.37 in the National Library of Ireland).

then will they make him a Rime, wherein they will commend his father and his aunche-
tours, nowmbrying howe many heades they have cut of, howe many townes they have
burned, and howe many virgins they have defloured, howe many notable murthers they
have done, and in the ende they will compare them to Aniball, or Scipio, or Hercules,
or some other famous person; wherewithall the pore foole runs madde, and thinkes
indede it is so.Then will he gather a sorte of rackells [rake-hells] to him, and other he
most geat him a Proficer [prophet], who shall tell him howe he shall spede (as he
thinkes). Then will he geat him lurking to a syde of a woode, and ther keepith him close
til morninge; and when it is daye light, then will they go to the poore villages, not
sparinge to distroye young infants, aged people; and if the woman be ever so great withe
childe, her they will kill; burninge the houses and corne, and ransackinge of the poore
cottes [cottages]. They will then drive all the kine and plowe horses, with all other cattell, and drive them awaye. Then muste they have a bagpipe bloinge afore them; and if
any of theis cattell fortune to waxe wearie or faynt, they will kill them, rather than it
sholde do the honeurs [owners] goode. If they go by anye house of fryiers [friars] or rely-
gious house, they will geave them 2 or 3 beifs, and they will take them, and praie for
them (yea) and prayes [praise] their doings, and saye his father was accustomed so to do;
wherein he will rejoise; and when he is in a safe place, they will fall to the devision of
the spoile, accordinge to the dyscresion of the captin. And the messinger that goithe of
their errants cleamith the gottes for their parcell; because it is an aunscient custome they
will not break it. Now comes the Rymer that made the Ryme, with his Rakry [*reacaire*].
The Rakry is he that shall utter the ryme; and the Rymer himself sitts by with the captain verie proudlye. He brings with him also his Harper, who please [plays] all the while
that the raker sings the ryme. Also he hath his Barde, which is a kinde of folise fellowe;
who also must have a horse geven him; the harper must have a new safern shurte, and a
mantell, and a hacnaye; and the rakery must have XX or XXX kine, and the Rymer
himself horse and harnes with a nag to ride on, a silver goblett, a pair of bedes of corall,
with buttons of silver; – and this, with more, they loke for to have, for reducinge distruxione of the Comenwealth,and to the blasfemye of God; and this is the best thinge
that ye Rymers causith them to do. The fourth sorte of Rymers is called Fillis which is
to say in English a Poete. Theis men have great store of cattell, and use all the trades of
the others with an adicion of prophecies. Theis are great mayntayners of whitches and
other vile matters; to the great blasfemye of God and to great impoverishinge of the
commonwealthe. And, as I have saied of the four secktes, ar devided in all places of the
fowre partes of Irland, as Ulster, Launster, Munster and Conet, and some in Methe; and
some in the Ilands beyond Irland, the land of Sainctes, the Ynce Bofine, Ynce Tirke,
Ynce Mayne, and Ynce Clire. Thes Ilands are under the rule of Homaile [the 'pirate
queen' Grace O'Malley, who was then approximately thirty, controlled Inishbofin,
Inishturk, Inishmaan, and Clare Island, among other places] and they are verie pleasaunt
and fertile, plentie of woode, water, and arabell ground and pastur and fishe, and a very
temperate ayer.

Their be many braunches belonging to the foure sortes, as the Gogathe [*geocach*:
rascal], which is to say in English, the glutayne, for one of them will eat 2 or 3 galons of
butter at a sittinge, halfe a mutton. And another, called the Carruage [*cearrbhach*: gam-
bler]; he is much like the habram's man [Abram-man or Tom o' Bedlam: a wandering
beggar who feigned insanity] and comenlye he goeth nakid, and carise dise and cardes

with him; and he will play the heare off his head, and his eares; and they be maintained by the Rymers.

Ther is a sort of women that be calleid the goyng women; they be great blasphemers of God; and they rune from contry to contry, soyinge sedicione amongst the people. They are comen to all men; and if any of them happen to be with childe, she will saye that it is the greatest Lord adjoining, whereof the Lordes ar glad, and doth appoincte them to be nurused.

Ther is one other sorte that is calleid the Mannigscoule [?]. Ther order is for to singe; and the chyfest of them most have but one eye, and he is called Lucas; they do much harme.Their is other towe sortes that goithe about with the Bachell [*bachall*: crozier] of Jesus, as they call it. Theis run from contry to contry; and if they come to any house wheir a woman is with child, they will putt the same about her, and wither she will or no, causithe her to geave them money. They will undertake that she shall have goode delivery of her childe; to the great distruxione of the people conserninge their soule's health. Other goith about with St Patricke's croysur, and playse the like partes or worse, and no doubte as longe as theis bene usyed, the worde of God can never be knowne amongst them, nor the prince fearyed, nor the contry prosper.

For the redresse theirof it might be esaly holpen if your honours will geave care ther unto; and if it may stand with your pleasures that I should make any further sertifycate how this nowghty people may be ponyste, and to cause them to leave their yle facions, I will, if it be your pleasurs, showe by what mayne they may be redressed. And as concerninge the fostering of the Irishe men's children [fosterage: the custom of entrusting one's child to foster parents] it needed as much redress as any other matter that can be movyed. The which I will showe your honours when it pleaseth you.

The text offered as Document B was written more than two centuries later. Its author takes a benevolent view of the Irish peasant, seen as a victim of landlordism but who can sometimes experience happiness and joy very intensely. The custom of seasonal migration to British farms is now established, but in Ireland itself itinerant herding, as still observed in the Tudor age, has been replaced by more settled farming. Professional storytellers have disappeared along with the chieftains; rural narration and other entertainments are placed in the relatively new socio-cultural context, and we find here one of the first fairly detailed accounts of what would later be described as 'Irish folklore'. The text was written after the rebellion of 1798 and its repression, yet makes no direct reference to it. Just as, in *Castle Rackrent* (see Chapter 7), Maria Edgeworth was looking back at the life of the landowners 'before the year 1782', this author is looking back at an earlier age; he uses the past tense because his observations were made some fifteen or twenty years before he writes them down, and also because he feels that things are changing, not necessarily for the better. The divine beings or heroes of the past seem to have shrunk to 'little people'; but for Bell as for Smyth the religion of the natives is founded on superstition and deception. Some elements of 'tradition' persist, like the reference to St Patrick's Crozier – or *Baculum Jesu* [*bachall Iosa*] – the staff of Christ which was said to have passed to Patrick and his successors and was burned publicly in Dublin during the time of the Reformation: both texts mention its legendary survival, and by the beginning of the twentieth century one could still swear *dar bachall Phadraig or dar iarann Phadraig* (by Patrick's crozier, or iron).

DOCUMENT B

A Description of the Condition and Manners as well as of the Moral and Political Character, Education, etc. of the Peasantry of Ireland, such as they were between the years 1780 & 1790, when Ireland was supposed to have arrived at its highest degree of prosperity and happiness, by Robert Bell LL.B.

Robert Bell thought that any legislator wishing to 'convert the native Irish into peacable, loyal, and industrious subjects' should first know the inhabitants, how they lived and what problems they faced. Speaking of himself in the third person, he states that he 'entertains no particular partiality towards those people whose manners he is describing: his chief object is to state, as accurately as possible, what he saw himself'. He has had 'an opportunity of becoming acquainted with their real situation, and habits of thinking [between 1780 and 1790, and] of knowing the truth of the facts which he now states, not only from his residence in several counties, and his personal knowledge of many families of peasants, but from the testimony of numbers of the gentry who came from these parts of the kingdom with which he was not acquainted [Munster in particular]'. He decided to share his knowledge, first in a series of articles in the *Weekly Dispatch*, then in a booklet published in 1804. According to him, three fourth of the Irish peasantry lived in extreme poverty; but descriptions of misery alternate with scenes of pastoral pleasures and fits of nostalgia for a vanishing state of innocence: 'Happy people! had not the strides of pretended civilization taught them the wants and the vices of polished society, without imparting to them any of its comforts!' Prudence and fairness were necessary to civilize Ireland – through London decrees, now that no parliament remained in Dublin (the Union had been proclaimed a few years before).

The following extracts, from pages 16 to 24 in the booklet, focus on Bell's interpretation of some customs and beliefs of the Irish peasants.

The manners of the ancient Irish have been very much done away with by the increase of English commercial civilization; such of them as survived the lapse of time, or escaped the restraints of law, have prevailed chiefly in places remote from towns, and seldom resorted to for the purpose of traffic. Here, if the people were not actually in want of the necessities of life, every man's door was open to a neighbour or a stranger, who might walk in without ceremony, even at meal time, and partake of whatever fare the house contained. Such a visit, so far from being deemed an intrusion, gave pleasure to every individual of the family, who were not only impelled by their natural feelings, but conceived themselves bound by a kind of sacred duty, to perform those acts of hospitality.

If the visitor was a stranger, he was received with the greatest attention; and if he could play on any instrument of music, or tell tales of old times calculated to excite the admiration of his hearers, the inhabitants of every neighbouring cottage vied with each other for the honour of entertaining him as a guest.

Living for the most part on vegetable food, and with scarcely any other beverage than water or milk, these people had a flow of animal spirits and a vivacity of temper unknown in countries whose inhabitants constantly feed on flesh and strong drink. After the labours of the day they never sat looking at each other in sulky silence; the aged would smoke one after another out of the same pipe, and entertain each other with stories; while the young would dance until near midnight either to the tune of some instrument or of their own voices: and although the rudest music was capable of rousing them into merriment, they had taste enough to distinguish and appreciate the performance of persons who played so well as to be sought after by people of a higher condition. Their national harp in later years fell into almost total disuse; their favourite and most frequent instrument was a bag-pipe on a different but superior construction to that of the Scotch-Highlanders. It is impossible to describe the joy that used to sparkle in the countenances of these rustics on the arrival of an itinerant performer of celebrity among them: they would flock to the house where he took up residence, and make it a scene of festivity as long as he remained there.

There was this strange peculiarity in the character of the native Irish; that on occasions of great joy and merriment they indulged themselves in grief and melancholy; and under circumstances of mourning and sorrow, they ran headlong into the most extravagant mirth. At a wedding feast they felt uncommon pleasure in singing and listening to the most plaintive ditties; and if they had drunk any quantity of whiskey, they would whine and weep at the relation of some woeful story. But on the death of a neighbour and a friend, although they went for the avowed purpose of weeping over the dead body: yet in the very room where it was laid out, they would spend the night in performing all kinds of sports and gambols that were calculated to excite laughter.

Those peasants who could afford the expence, used to give a feast to all their relations and neighbours when any female belonging to their family was married. The dinner, which was the only meal on this occasion, generally consisted of mutton, salt pork, bacon and poultry; with an abundance of potatoes and common garden vegetables. All these articles were supplied from the stock of the person who furnished the entertainment: but sometimes the relations of the parties would each contribute a share towards the wedding dinner. No part of the fare was purchased by money except the whiskey or beer: the latter was not always to be procured. The chief personage at this entertainment was the parish Priest or his deputy. The next in pre-eminence was the Squire: but it was not every country gentleman who could attain the honour of being present at a wedding feast: for if he had not resided long in the neighbourhood; if he had not by a gentle and familiar deportment, but above all, by conversing with the peasants in the Irish language, commanded their esteem, and conciliated their affections, he would not have been invited. The Squire, however, could have been easily dispensed with: but, next to the Priest, the Musician was the most necessary person to render the entertainment complete. He was generally a performer on the bagpipes; and the host was often obliged to send for one to the distance of near 20 or 30 miles. Doors taken off the hinges and laid on benches, constituted a dinner table, of which no part was covered with a cloth except the head: here the Priest sat as president or lord over all the guests, and had the most delicate of the viands placed before him. The others sat in order according to their rank; which was estimated by consideration of their property, their age, and their reputation. The meat was usually cut into pieces about the size of brickbats, and placed along the platters, out of which the guests helped themselves often without the aid of knives or forks: for the few instruments of this kind which could be procured, were appropriated to the service of the Priest and the select party whom he chose to honour with his conversation. The host and hostess, instead of sitting down to dinner, waited upon the company, and pressed them to eat with an earnestness and familiarity that would have been highly disgusting to persons of more refined manners. The marriage ceremony was generally performed before dinner; and on this occasion it was sometimes necessary to force the timorous bride from the place where she had concealed herself on the first approach of the company. The company afterwards amused themselves in dancing, singing and drinking. The Priest retired about eight or nine o'clock: and if great care was not taken after that hour, to prevent the distribution of liquor, the night would have ended in intoxication, riot, quarrelling and bloodshed. In the course of a week or fortnight, the bridegroom took his wife home to his own habitation; the portion he received with her, consisted chiefly in cattle. In places where English law and English manners were unknown, the married women were always called by their maiden names.

Of all the scenes of merriment enjoyed by those people, that which has been called an *Irish wake* appeared to afford them the highest degree of pleasure. An Irish wake was an assemblage of men and women round the corpse of a deceased neighbour. To accommodate as many persons as possible, the corpse was decently laid out in one corner of a barn or some other extensive place. The next of kin, together with some old men and old women sat near the dead body all night, and amused themselves the greater part of the time with smoking tobacco, and telling stories of ghosts, goblins and witches. The rest of the people began shortly after night-fall to arrange the plan of the sports and diversions, which hardly ever ceased until break of day. These sports consisted chiefly of rude buffonery, boisterous mirth, coarse jests, songs, &c. all of which were regulated by some one person, selected by the company to act as master of the ceremonies; and who was most noted for his drollery and vivacity. The mirth of the company was however interrupted once every hour, sometimes every half-hour, by the cries of those who sat next the deceased: the sports were then suspended, and every person present was supposed to join in the general lamentation, which lasted about five or six minutes. These cries have been described by the appellation of the Irish howl; and shocking as they would have been to a delicate English ear, they were not destitute of modulation. The tones were few but plaintive; and the voices of the women always predominated. While they were crying or howling they frequently repeated a set of unmeaning words, and would ask the deceased why he was so cruel as to leave them. Many women who had neither been related to, nor acquainted with the deceased, would join in the howl with every appearance of affliction, would beat their bosoms, dishevel their hair and bedew their faces with tears: the same women would perhaps, in ten minutes after, take a leading part in the mirth which succeeded. The corpse was accompanied to the grave by similar cries and howlings. It has often been said that persons were hired to cry at wakes and funerals; the author of these accounts cannot deny the existence of such a practice; but must say that he never knew an instance of the kind. He has also to add, that he never knew or heard of any liquor being drunk at wakes: the company was treated only with pipes, tobacco and snuff: and the whole experience of waking and burying an adult seldom amounted to a quarter of the sum which the interment of an infant three days old would cost in London.

The amusements of the native Irish chiefly took place on Sundays and holidays. On Sunday morning they regularly went to their popish chapel, which was sometimes not sufficient to contain one half of the people: those therefore who could not gain admittance prayed in the open air, near the doors of the chapel. As soon as the service was over, the greater part of the congregation went home and dined: after which during the summer season, they assembled in large bodies in some adjacent field; where the old sat in circles and entertained each other with stories, and the young danced to whatever music they could procure, and some of the young men exercized themselves in feats of bodily strength. Good humour and contentment always prevailed at those meetings as long as they drank no whiskey: but whenever that fiery spirit was introduced, intoxication and quarrels were the inevitable consequences.

In the winter season, they assembled on Sunday evenings at some house where whiskey was sold: but more commonly where some one belonging to the family played on an instrument of music. The people belonging to the later description of houses never demanded or expected any recompence for the accommodation thus afforded their neighbours, except the satisfaction arising from the consciousness of having contributed to the happiness of others. The love of society was, in short, so prominent a part of the character of those people that hardly any part of a peasant's family remained at home on a Sunday evening; and in winter they would often go a distance of three or four miles, through swamps and bogs, to any place where a considerable number of people were assembled. Even in their ordinary occupations both in the field and in the house, they shewed an uncommon fondness for social intercourse. Every evening in the week throughout the winter season, a party of young females went successively to the houses of their respective parents, with their spinning wheels, and dedicated a great part of the night to the double purpose of industry and innocent amusement. Hither they were generally followed by their lovers: the song and the tale went round, and labour ceased to be a toil. The happiness enjoyed by those simple rustics in places where oppression had not spread her iron hand, was such as those who live in polished societies might envy.

But of all the amusements of the native Irish, there were none so remarkable for variety, for the multitudes that partook of them, and for the interest they excited, as those which were called Patrons: nor were any of their meetings oftener concluded with drunkenness and broils than these. An Irish patron resembled, in some manner, the old English wake: probably they both sprung from the same origin. It was a large assemblage of people from all parts within a distance of ten or twenty miles, collected together round a sacred fountain dedicated to, and called after the name of the Saint, in honour of whom this festival was celebrated. In the morning or forenoon the priest of the parish performed mass on a large stone, which was called an altar. Several old men and women at the same time performed penance round the well. Here were all sorts of hawkers, mountebanks, conjurers and itinerant musicians: and tents and boots were erected chiefly for the sale of liquor. The day was not uncommonly concluded by a general battle. Outrages of this kind sometimes proceeded from family feuds; but more frequently from local animosities. If there were none others than the people of two parishes collected together; these, when elevated and maddened with liquor, would fight against each other, for what reason they knew not. If the assemblage of people had been collected from more distant places, the inhabitants belonging to one barony or county would contend with those of another. The battle was most commonly preceded by a challenge. Some fellow, whose bodily strength – whose boisterous and ferocious temper, gave him such an ascendancy over others as to be chosen their leader, would come forth, and flourishing his cudgel over his head bid defiance to all who did not belong to his clan, parish, barony, or county. A champion of the adverse side would instantly rush forward to meet him. Their followers soon joined them and the engagement became general.

The original inhabitants of Ireland were perhaps more credulous and superstitious than those of any other country. The system of Popery was no more like the Roman Catholic religion of Monarchical France, than the liberty of the modern French Republic resembles that of England. It was a compound of ancient paganism, together with all the absurdities into which Christianity had ever degenerated. To eat eggs during Passion Week was by them considered an unpardonable offence against Heaven: and on certain days of abstinence, it was more criminal to taste a drop of milk, than to get drunk with whiskey. Besides the Polytheistical worship prescribed by their Religion, they paid homage to several imaginary demons, to which, in their language, they gave names corresponding to those described in the old English mythology under the general denomination of fairies. But their veneration for these beings was entirely the result of fear, for they considered them capable of doing a great deal more mischief than good. The loss of cattle was often attributed to their malice: when a child died, it was frequently suspected that the fairies had carried it away while living, and that the corpse was nothing more than an artificial substance placed by them instead of the real body of the child. Similar suspicions arose if a child, from a good state of health, became sickly and consumptive. The poor little patient was no longer looked upon as the offspring of human parents, but the creation of demons. If the child survived the neglect occasioned by the idea of its unnatural origin, and recovered its former health, the fairies were thanked for their supposed interference.

In all whirlwinds and sudden tempests the fairies were thought to be the principal actors; especially if any damage was done to the houses or stacks or corn. They were also supposed to enter habitations at night after the family retired to rest, to indulge in sportive gambols, and particularly to wash themselves in clean water, but if there was no water in the house, it was understood they would play some mischievous tricks in revenge. Possessed with this belief, the people made a point not to go to bed, until they had deposited, in some large vessel, the libation which they conceived necessary to keep those whimsical divinities in good humour. The superstitious rustics would sometimes endeavour to find out a more respectful name for those beings than fairies [Note: They generally called them, instead of Fairies, the Good People]: and whenever they spoke of them, they made use of the expression – 'God bless them'.

The habitations usually assigned the fairies, were those small hills, or mounds, so frequently to be met with all over Ireland, called forts, because they were supposed to have been erected as places of defence, during the time of the Danish invasions of that country. Many of these hills might be seen, covered with wild shrubs, in the middle of arable fields: and the superstition of the cultivators would not suffer the sacred spots to be violated, either by the plough or the spade.

Many families were supposed to be followed by a female spright, who, on the death of any person belonging to the family, used to haunt the borders of some neighbouring lake or rivulet, whence her lamentable cries were said to be distinguished. This harmless mourner was called the banshee : and her existence was believed by several above the condition of peasants.

A general belief in ghosts and apparitions prevailed here as well as in other countries. The people had a variety of charms and nostrums to keep away and defeat the machinations of evil spirits. The most common were those of nailing an old horse-shoe on the threshold of the door of their dwelling house, and sprinkling the place once a week at least with holy water. Their superstitions, however, did not alone consist in fear of invisible agents: like most people in a state of barbarous ignorance, they always dreaded the effects of witchcraft. They believed there were many evil-minded persons, who had the power of destroying their cattle by a certain malevolent look, as well as by incantations: and that there were old women who, by a kind of charm, could take from the milk of their neighbour's cows all that part which constituted butter, and add it to their own: that they could raise storms, tempest &c. The people had their good, as well as their evil sorcerers and sorceresses; to whom, in case of theft or sickness, they applied much oftener than to magistrates or physicians.

Such was the credulity of the native Irish, that those among them who live in comfortable circumstances were always liable to be preyed upon by the vilest and shallowest impostors. Itinerant mendicants would frequently carry about them pieces of old wood, &c which they pretented to be sacred relics, possessing great virtue. The reputation which men of this description acquired for sanctity, caused them to be looked up to with reverence. They used to enter the houses of ignorant husbandmen without any ceremony: they were received, not only with hospitality, but with veneration: and, in return for the holy treasure which they left behind them, they were feasted with the best things the soil produced, and lodged in the best bed the house contained.

But there were no persons for whom the people entertained more respect and veneration than their priests. They considered them as the most virtuous, the most learned and religious of all men. In their private disputes they would often appeal to, and abide by, the decision of their priest; who, in many remote parts of Ireland, had all the authority, without any of the responsibilities of Civil Magistrates. From these men, the common people received all their religious, moral and political instruction; and placed implicit faith in every thing they said, however absurd or monstrous.

In taking an oath, these people consider the obligation as sacred, if the oath was sworn on a piece of iron. Of the bible, they knew little or nothing; because their priests prohibited those who had received instruction from reading it. There was a thing called St Patrick's Crosier, which was thought to possess such extraordinary power, that the persons swearing by it could not fail to obtain credit; for it was believed that, if they swore falsely, their faces would instantly become distorted and deformed. But as there were no more than two or three of those miraculous relics in Ireland, a cross made of iron, or some other metal, with mystic letters marked on it, was often provided as a substitute, and it was not uncommon to swear upon it in preference to the bible, even before persons authorised by law to administer oaths.

The moral character of the Irish peasants depended on the circumstances under which they lived. In some places they were not only simple and harmless, but extremely generous and benevolent: in others, they were selfish and depraved. They were all equally unacquainted with the principles of moral rectitude. Of those who laboured under hardships and oppression, the reaction was great and terrible: it was not a measure of equal retaliation regulated by the rules of reason; but a furious indiscriminate and unjust revenge, the exercise of which corrupted the heart and prepared the individual for the perpetration of every crime.

The sudden removal of men from habits of life nearly resembling a state of nature, to a state of civilized society, regulated by laws and upheld by commerce, has, but too frequently, a dangerous effect on the human mind. The individuals are not prepared to fill their new character: they are generally incapable of practicing the virtues required in this kind of society: the virtues which distinguished their former state, operating as vices, and producing private inconvenience and public evil, they at last become so mischievous, that if the persons on whom they act are sufficiently powerful, they must keep the government continually employed in resisting their violence, or counteracting their artifices. How much greater evils are to be apprehended if such men are treated so as to make them think they have been injured and oppressed.

4

Echoes of past virtues, heard or imagined by antiquaries, surveyors and philologists

In 1561, Smyth had nothing good to say about Irish customs. By 1800, Robert Bell thought that the loss of 'the manners of the ancient Irish' had been a 'perversion' because there had been too sudden a passage from 'a state of nature to a state of civilized society'. But others maintained that, though much had been subsequently destroyed, the ancient Irish had in fact reached an advanced stage of cultural development. This chapter will consider different revalorizations of the Irish past, in a conflictive ideological context, between the mid-eighteenth and mid-nineteenth centuries; Ancient storytelling was reconstructed, either by freewheeling imagination or from literary remains and encounters with those who seemed to be the last surviving practitioners of a venerable art. The first section examines influential cultural developments in Britain: a vogue for 'the dim mist of long ago', an increasing concern with the historical process and what was vanishing because of it, and a new fascination with wildness. The second takes us back to Ireland: in the last decades of the eighteenth century, both as an echo of and in reaction to what was published abroad, some members of the privileged minority became curious about crumbling monuments of the Irish past; but they often had fanciful notions and an inadequate grasp of the language. The third section focuses on official or semi-official attempts to gather information on Ireland's heritage, in the first half of the nineteenth century. The last section mentions the beginning of Irish philology. The unifying theme will be the retrieval of a culture and the images of real or supposed storytellers that developed then. We shall distinguish between an enthusiasm for the non-classical past of a country or region which led amateurs to collect relics for the sake of curious details, and perhaps to theorize about them ('antiquarianism'); systematic collection in the field, by a body of persons and ultimaterly for some state purpose, of data regarding a specific area (the 'survey'); and an approach to language consisting in the gathering and verifying of manuscripts and the critical treatment of the data therein ('philology'). There may not always have been a sharp divide between the relatively amateurish 'antiquarian', the contributor to a 'survey' and the more methodical and professional 'philologist'; but in a general evolution the third type tended to replace the first, and association with the academic world became its obvious if not infallible mark.

In his ode 'The Bard' written around 1755 and, according to a preface, 'founded on a tradition current in Wales', Thomas Gray established the image of an ancient poet with strange powers, striking an attitude in a wild landscape and embodying the values of a 'rude' but hale society. The hero of the poem was drawn partly from a living blind Welsh harper from whom Gray had heard tunes supposed to be 'of a thousand years old'. Transported into the thirteenth century with the help of historical texts (now partly discredited), and immensely magnified in the process, he was portrayed as a defiant old man, the sole survivor of an illustrious company – not for long: at the end of the poem, he plunges 'to endless night'. In a sensational scene on a Snowdon crag, he curses the English conquerors and foretells their doom. 'With haggard eyes ... loose his beard and hoary hair ...' and obviously carried away by 'prophet's fire', he is a very impressive figure. We witness here the construction of a new heroic type, at once 'Celtic' and pathetic, combining mastery of effective language, passion, visionary power and patriotism, surrounded by wild nature and darkness, and doomed to disappear.

A so-called first 'Celtic Revival'[1] enjoyed a vogue in Great Britain, but the adjective was imprecise. The term had reappeared during the Renaissance with the publication of Latin and Greek texts, and was applied indiscriminately: the Genevese scholar Paul-Henri Mallet, whose *Monuments de la mythologie et de la poésie des Celtes et particulièrement des anciens Scandinaves* (1756) was translated by Bishop Percy in 1770, confused Celts and ancient Germanic people – according to him the Old Norse *Edda* was the most authentic document of '*la religion celtique*'. The ancient world thus vaguely conceived was typified by the warrior, the druid and the bard. The warrior was brave and short-lived; views of the druids changed: at the beginning of the eighteenth century they were supposed to have built sites like Stonehenge for horrible human sacrifice and could represent any obscurantist tyrannical priestcraft, but later they became proto-Christian sages. 'Bard', as a loanword in English, first denoted the despised or feared rhymesters of northern or western enemies; then it acquired lustre and respectability – though little was positively known except that it had designated an order of singers of heroic exploits. In the eighteenth century its link with mysterious druidism could be stressed, and it had connotations of nobility as well as magic: the bard was thought to be an inspired poet, or the voice of a community. In fact, it often was a figment of the imagination and a projection of either fears or desires. In England, the mounting curiosity concerning 'bardism' freely applied the same label to minstrels and scalds, as did Bishop Percy in 1765.[2] In Wales, usage was more specific: the word *bardd* (poet) was part of the vernacular. By the mid-eighteenth century it was proposed to 'preserve and illustrate the ancient remains of Welsh literature', and in 1764 Evan Evans published *Some Specimens of the Poetry of the Ancient Welsh Bards*.

More must be said about what happened in Scotland, because it would have

---

1 See Edward D. Snyder *The Celtic Revival in English Literature: 1760-1800*. 2 'An Essay on the Ancient Minstrels in England', in *Reliques of Ancient English Poetry* 1. 346.

the strongest impact in Ireland. At first with local echo only, attention had been paid to what appeared to be a peculiar culture. In *A Description of the Western Isles of Scotland* published in 1703, Martin Martin had described the functions of the 'bards' attached to every chief. He had also observed that a gigantic hero known as 'Fin-Mac-Coul' was particularly celebrated – of whom more would soon be heard under the other name he had in Scotland since the early fourteenth century, Fingal (*Fionn gall*: 'fair foreigner' – others interpreted the name as *Fionn na Ghal*: Finn of valour). In the preface to *The Lives and Characters of the Most Eminent Writers of the Scots Nation* (1708), George Mackenzie combined his reading of Latin texts with recently observed reality: 'The Celtae had their Bards or Poets, who sang the Illustrious Achievements of their Ancestors; so have our Highlanders ... The Celtae had their Schaldres, who recited the Genealogies of their Great Men; and our Highlanders have their Senachies, who do the same.'[3]

Could a new literature in English tap this source? In 1749, in his 'Ode on the Popular Superstitions of the Highlands of Scotland Considered as the Subject of Poetry' William Collins exhorted the divine and playwright John Home to make full use of strange Scottish tales in remote settings:

> At ev'ry pause, before thy mind possest,
> Old Runic bards shall seem to rise around,
> With uncouth lyres, in many-coloured vest,
> Their matted hair with boughs fantastic crown'd. (St. 3)

A new interest in non-classical myths and in the pursuit of strong sensations could make such subjects fashionable. But this attitude also met with scepticism. In 1776 Samuel Johnson, touring the Highlands and the Hebrides, entered a poor cottage and saw the rather bleak indoor setting of storytelling among the common people – as could also be observed in Ireland at that time: 'No light is admitted but at the entrance, and through a hole in the thatch, which gives vent to smoke. This hole is not directly over the fire, lest the rain should extinguish it; and the smoke therefore naturally fills the place before it escapes.'[4] This was hardly the idealized 'bardic' décor. As must have been true in Ireland, however, narration was also practised in well-to-do society; Johnson experienced it at the house of the laird who put him up, on Skye, where he heard the story of a feud said to be the origin of a certain bagpipe tune, and commented: 'Narrations like this, however uncertain, deserve the notice of a traveller, because they are the only records of a nation that has no historians, and afford the most genuine representation of the life and character of the ancient highlanders.'[5] In Ireland too, the narrative background of a song or tune

3 Quoted in S.B. Hustvedt *Ballads Criticism in Scandinavia and Great Britain during the Eighteenth Century* 52. 4 *Journey to the Western Islands of Scotland* 54-5. 5 Ibid. 68.

can be given to inform the audience of the *brí*, or *míniú*, or *údar an amhráin*: the 'force', 'explanation', or 'justification of the song'.[6]

Did a Gaelic setting encourage wild thoughts? Johnson was interested in, and collected, oral reports of cases of 'second sight', which Martin Martin had defined as 'a singular faculty of seeing an otherwise invisible object'.[7] But he severely sifted information concerning the existence of a proper Gaelic literature in the past, for fear of being the victim of some imposture:

It seems to be universally supposed that much of the local history was preserved by the bards, of whom one is said to have been retained by every great family. After these bards were some of my first enquiries; and I received such answers as, for a while, made me please myself with my increase of knowledge; for I had not then learned how to estimate the narration of a highlander. They said that a great family had a bard and a *senachi*, who were the poet and historian of the house; and an old gentleman told me that he remembered one of each. Here was a dawn of intelligence. Of men that had lived within memory, some certain knowledge might be attained. Though the office had ceased [on Skye], its effects might continue; the poems might be found, though there was no poet.

Another conversation indeed informed me, that the same man was both bard and senachi. This variation discouraged me; but as the practice might be different in different times, or at the same time in different families, there was yet no reason for supposing that I must necessarily sit down in total ignorance. Soon after I was told by a gentleman, who is generally acknowledged the greatest master of Hebridean antiquities, that there had once been both bards and *senachies*; and that *senachi* signified 'the man of talk', or of conversation; but that neither bard nor *senachi* had existed for some centuries. I have no reason to suppose it exactly known at what time the custom ceased, nor did it probably cease in all houses at once. But whenever the practice of recitation was disused, the works, whether poetical or historical, perished with the authors; for in those times nothing had been written in Earse language. Whether the 'man of talk' was a historian, whose office was to tell the truth, or a story-teller, like those which were in the last century, and perhaps are now among the Irish, whose trade was only to amuse, it now would be vain to inquire.[8]

Had Johnson conducted the investigation farther, he might have learned that there still were reciters, and that manuscripts in Erse existed alongside a living oral tradition; but he remained sceptical and, still on Skye, when Boswell made an islander recite Fianna verse in Gaelic the Doctor was not convinced. His disbelief appears in another comment: 'if we know little of the ancient highlanders, let us not fill the vacuity with Ossian'.[9]

The latter name evoked a current topic of conversation and the subject of scholarly disputes which had ideological foundations. It was possible in Scotland to observe borderlines between cultures or between an old order and a new one, and the collapse of the clan-based society of the Highlands proved that history

---

6 H. Shields *Narrative Singing in Ireland* 63-6.   7 *A Description of the Western Islands of Scotland circa 1695* 321.   8 *Journey to the Western Islands of Scotland* 113-14.   9 Ibid. 119.

could extinguish a world, of which one might celebrate aspects while accepting inevitable change. There were ways of theorizing about it: the flowering of intellectual activity in the second half of the century, later known as the 'Scottish Enlightenment', was trying to promote a 'Science of Man', a tenet of which was that society could be analysed and general laws of its development uncovered, revealing an evolution through qualitatively different steps. Adam Ferguson's *Essay on the History of Civil Society* (1766), for instance, studied the emergence of 'civilized' society from prior stages characterized as savagery and barbarism. Three main stages had already been indentified in France, but in Scotland four phases were listed, depending on modes of subsistence, from hunting, then pasture, to agriculture and finally commerce. The evolution from 'rude' to 'refined' did not necessarily imply betterment. Upholders of the doctrine of progress would not look back to a golden age, because for them man's earliest stage was likely to have been that of a brute beast, but it was also fashionable to praise simplicity and contrast 'natural' and 'artificial' societies to the disadvantage of the latter. There was a growing esteem for sentiment and for simple virtues, and one could find something attractive in the supposed pastoral and heroic ages, the less 'advanced' stage of human development appearing more vigorous, spontaneous, uncorrupted, happier. Looking for contemporary traces of such a world could also satisfy a desire for self-definition: the observer asked how different he was, and whether he really enjoyed his own position.[10] If the earlier world, by being 'more natural', was better, then perhaps its pre-literary productions reflected its superior qualities. Ferguson thought that the 'traditionary fables' which were 'rehearsed by the vulgar' reflected the culture of their age of origin;[11] to examine them would therefore be a way of learning something about the remote past. Others, like William Duff, thought that more could be found in such traditions: 'in the early periods of society, original Poetic Genius will in general be exerted in its utmost vigour.'[12]

As the idea spread that the purest and greatest poetry might have been produced in the ancient stages of a society, James Macpherson was encouraged to translate surviving examples of such material and was sent to the Highlands to recover the great Scottish epic which *had* to exist. With his Ossianic texts in measured prose published in 1760, '62, '63 and collected in 1765, he offered what the public was beginning to ask for. It was a matter not just of satisfying a taste for the primitive but also of boosting national morale by asserting Scotland's past greatness.[13]

10 Fiona Stafford 'Primitivism and the "Primitive" Poet', in T. Brown (ed.) *Celticism* 82: 'What appears to be about primitive society very often turns out to be more concerned with the observer, who defines himself or his culture against a silent alternative'. 11 Quoted in Neil R. Grobman's 'Eighteenth-Century Scottish Philosophers on Oral Tradition', *Journal of the Folklore Institute* 10 (1973) 190-1. 12 *An Essay on Original Genius* (1767) quoted by J.V. Price, 'Ossian and the Canon in the Scottish Enlightenment', in H. Gaskill (ed.) *Ossian Revisited* 115. 13 A. Dundes 'Nationalistic Inferiority Complex and the Fabrication of Fakelore ...', *Journal of Folklore Research* 22 (1985).

The question of the authenticity of these texts and of their links with Gaelic originals is less vexed today than it used to be. We know that a great deal was invented, but that not everything was faked: Macpherson was a Highlander by birth and had grown up in a Gaelic-speaking area, where Fianna lore was 'part of the common cultural inheritance of Ireland and Gaelic Scotland'[14] – though the material available was probably not, as he claimed, literally a thousand and a half years old. On his collecting expedition in 1760, subsidized by John Home and others, he gathered some Gaelic manuscripts and took down a few fragments from oral recitation. He made use of some fourteen or fifteen 'Gaelic ballads' or lays, sometimes following the original fairly closely and sometimes offering little more than an allusion to it.[15] But in his commentaries he stressed the genuineness of the material he was using, as well as its antiquity:

> There can be no doubt that these poems are to be ascribed to the Bards ... By the succession of these Bards, such poems were handed down from race [generation] to race; some in manuscript, but more by oral tradition. And tradition, in a country so free of intermixture with foreigners, and among a people so strongly attached to the memory of their ancestors, has preserved many of them in a great measure incorrupted to this day.[16]

Actually, he does not seem to have trusted oral tradition and the manuscripts he collected: he saw them as corrupt texts and thought he could, indeed perhaps should, reconstruct ideal versions. Contrary to what he pretended, he was not a translator: he sometimes misunderstood the fragments he had collected or deliberately arranged them, combined them, and freely added episodes of his own fabrication enlarging upon atmospheric effects and pathos. He changed the tone and the themes to produce what his sponsors expected. And it worked: Hugh Blair, the professor of Rhetoric and Belles-Lettres at the University of Edinburgh, praised the combination of sublimity and tenderness and commented that 'throughout Ossian's poems, we plainly find ourselves in the first of these periods of society,' which were 'most favourable to the poetic spirit',[17] while the Edinburgh judge and philosopher Henry Home lumped together the Bible, Homer, the verbal arts of American Indians, Norse sagas, anonymous ballads, Shakespeare and Ossian as admirable examples of primitive poetry.[18]

The bards Macpherson depicted obviously had nothing to do with what he may have seen in the Highlands. His Ossian, the son of the *Scottish* king Fingal, has been a brave warrior and the 'king of many songs', but when we meet him he is old, blind and solitary. This, in itself, was a situation genuine Fianna lore had explored: in a distant past, the fictional speaker is a survivor looking back to even earlier times – a 'characteristic mood of retrospection'[19] defined the

14 D.E. Meek 'The Gaelic Ballads of Scotland: Creativity and Adaptation', in H. Gaskill (ed.) op. cit. 26. 15 D.S. Thomas *The Gaelic Sources of Macpherson's Ossian* 10. 16 Preface to *Fragments of Ancient Poetry* (1760). 17 Hugh Blair *A Critical Dissertation on the Poems of Ossian* (London 1763) 2. 18 N.R. Grobman, op. cit. 194. 19 J. MacKillop *Fionn mac Cumhaill: Celtic Myth in English Literature* 58.

Acallam na Senórach some six centuries before Macpherson, and more recent lays often were the retrospective dramatic monologues of an elderly *Oisín d'éis na Féine* (Oisín after the Fianna), occasionally of Fionn's leading rival Goll mac Morna who gave an account of his life as he was hungering to death on a promontory of the west coast, in one case of a speaking stone that revealed the story of the hero buried beneath it.[20] In Macpherson, secondary narrators tend to multiply, and tales within tales are rather awkwardly put together. But pastness and tradition are essentially embodied in Ossian and in his memories of what storytelling heroes of the preceding generation had been singing – the 'tales of the times of old' are repeatedly called 'songs', and harps are often referred to, though Macpherson stated in the preface to *Fragments of Ancient Poetry* that in his own experience they were 'not set to music, nor sung'. The obsessive repetition of some words and set phrases emphasizes certain themes and images. For instance, mood and inspiration are triggered off by remembrance of a lost world:

... Fingal sat at the beam of the oak. Morni sat by his side with all his grey waving locks. Their words were of other times, of the mighty deeds of their fathers.
... Fingal was next to the foes. He listened to the tales of his bards. His godlike race were in the songs, the chiefs of other times ... The wind whistled through his locks; his thoughts are on the days of other years.
... As flies the inconstant sun, over Larmon's grassy hill, so pass the tales of old along my soul, by night! When bards are removed to their places; when harps are hung in Selma's hall; then comes a voice of years that are gone! they roll before me, with their deeds!
... Did not Ossian hear a voice? or is it the sound of days that are no more? Often does the memory of former times come, like the evening sun, on my soul.[21]

It is a verbal kind of memory, and Ossian says he actually hears ancient bards:

... Ullin, Carril, and Ryno, voices of the days of old! Let me hear you, while yet it is dark, to please and awake my soul.
... then comes a voice to Ossian and awakes his soul. It is the voice of years that are gone: they roll before me, with all their deeds. I seize the tales, as they pass, and pour them forth in songs.[22]

Their poetry is sometimes associated with war; if the mode of the bards we hear is generally elegiac, the older voices they evoke could be martial, spurring heroes to battle:

... 'Go, Ullin, go, my aged bard,' began the King of Marven. 'Remind the mighty Gaul of war. Remind him of his fathers. Support the yielding fight with song; for song enlivens war.'[23]

---

20 *Duanaire Finn – The Book of the Lays of Fionn* 1. No.35, 2. No. 42. 21 *The Poems of Ossian* (Edinburgh 1805) 1. 498, 1. 108, 2. 341, 1. 297. 22 Ibid. 2. 221 and 'Oina-morul: A Poem' (1765). 23 Ibid. 1. 136, 2. 93.

And they also had an important role to play after the battle, for the glory of heroes:

... The bards pour their songs like dew on the returning war.
... 'We shall pass away like a dream. No sound will remain in our fields of war. Our tombs will be lost in the earth. The hunter shall not know the place of our rest. Our names may be heard in song.'
... 'Our renown would grow in songs.'
... 'But my name is renowned! My fame is in the song of bards.' [24]

More often than pride, however, we find moody contemplation of the transience of human works, in awesome settings. The voices of the dead bards are better heard at night:

... Night came rolling down. The light of an hundred oaks arose. Fingal sat beneath a tree. Old Athlan [formerly the chief bard of the king of Ireland] stood in the midst. He told the tale of fallen Cormac. [25]

Some relatively late Fianna literature had already evidenced an elegiac tendency, but Macpherson carried it to extremes. The stories themselves are generally sad ones:

... 'Mournful is thy tale, son of the car [of Cuthullin's chariot]', said Carril of other times [Cuthullin's bard]. 'It sends my soul back to the ages of old, to the days of other years'. [Here, Ossian remembers that Carrill was remembering ...]
... The tale of Althan was mournful. The tear was in his eye when he spoke. [26]

Yet such narrated sorrows give pleasure:

... Send thou the night away in song; and give the joy of grief.
... 'O bards of other times! Ye, on whose souls the blue hosts of our fathers rise! strike the harp in my hall; and let me hear the song. Pleasant is the joy of grief! it is like the shower of spring, when it softens the branch of the oak, and the young leaf rears its green head.' [27]

Such pleasant sadness, systematically associated with nature both in the evocation of setting and in the choice of similes, is in danger of vanishing, and the prospect of a loss of melancholy itself makes it even more valuable while it lasts:

[Ossian is dying] But age is now on my tongue; my soul has failed! I hear at times the ghosts of bards, and learn their pleasant song. But memory fails on my mind. I hear the call of years! They say, as they pass along, why does Ossian sing? Soon shall he lie in the narrow house, and no bard shall raise his fame! Roll on, ye dark-brown years, ye bring

24 Ibid. 2. 101, 1. 195, 1. 501, 2. 368. 25 Ibid. 2. 35. 26 Ibid. 1. 181, 2. 35. 27 Ibid. 1. 45, 1. 416.

no joy in your course! Let the tomb open to Ossian, for his strength has failed. The sons of songs are gone to rest. My voice remains, like a rock, after the winds are laid. The dark moss whistles there; the distant Mariner sees the waving trees![28]

Literary Europe responded with enthusiasm to moods which provided an escape from rationalism, and to images of a poet-hero associating bravery with solitude, or passion with melancholy, revealing himself as a voice travelling through time, on mist-clad mountains or wind-swept shores. For a couple of generations, the Scottish Ossian of Macpherson was the model of what a 'bard' should be. There were some ancient elements in the portrait, but it was mostly the projection of contemporary phantasms.

Macpherson's best-sellers were soon available in Ireland: the *Fragments* and *Fingal* were on sale in Dublin in 1762 and *Temora* in 1763. The effect of the Ossianic craze in Oisín's land was complex, and the reaction ambivalent: the now indigestible style, with its uniform lilt and hazy images, may have entranced some Irish readers as it did others at the time, and the dressing up of the past to appeal to new sensibilities might please; at the same time, as in Scotland the controversy over the authenticity of Macpherson's texts stimulated interest in real oral material and old manuscripts. Much more was involved, however: to whom did these 'traditions' belong? In London, in 1767, James Parsons (see p. 67), rashly vouched for the accuracy of the texts but said that they were Irish and still alive in Ireland:

I am acquainted with a gentleman of Ireland who has by heart several of the stories, in both *Fingall* and *Tamor*, taught him in his youth in that language; who expressed much surprize, when he found them exactly agreeing with some of those Mr M'Pherson has translated. This gentleman says, that many of the people in Ireland retain some of these very poems, which were handed down from time immemorial, in many families.[29]

Others, outraged that the Scots had appropriated Oisín and Fionn, reacted belligerently. Macpherson had tried to justify himself in 1761: 'Had the Senachies of Ireland been as well acquainted with the antiquities of their nation as they pretended, they might derive as much honour from Fingal's being a Caledonian, as if he had been an Irishman; for both nations were almost the same people in the days of that hero.'[30] So far he had a point, but the argument didn't satisfy those who wanted to prove the Irish origin of whatever material was genuine, and the offence became heinous when Macpherson argued, in his 'Dissertation Concerning the Poems of Ossian' (1773), that Ireland had been colonized by Scotland and that its culture was derivative; he further implied that Irish historians were fools and Irish bards mere pilferers. Fernando Warner, who had spent some time in Dublin gathering material for a *History of Ireland*, had

---

28 Ibid. 1. 468. **29** *Remains of Japhet* ... 158. **30** *The Poems of Ossian* 1. lxiv.

already asserted in London in 1762 that 'Fingal' was really Irish.[31] In the July 1763 issue of the French *Journal des Sçavans*, Terence Brady, a physician who lived in Brussels, insisted that the Fianna poems were '*l'ouvrage des anciens Bards d'Irlande*' and could still be heard there.[32] In five issues (261 pages) of the same Journal in 1764 and '65, John O'Brien, the bishop of Cloyne and Ross since 1747 and an active Gaelic scholar, gave his '*Mémoire de M. de C. à Messieurs les Auteurs du Journal des Sçavans au sujet des poëmes de M Macpherson* which was better informed and more acrimonious: Macpherson was guilty of robbery combined with lies and ignorance; Fionn was Irish and his son could not be a mere bard – that is to say a kind of servant; the real *Scotti* were the Irish who had colonized Scotland; the Fianna romances were Irish but not very ancient; there seemed to be a British conspiracy against the reputation of Ireland.[33] Protest was raised in Ireland too: in the second edition of his *Dissertations* (1766), Charles O'Conor denounced Macpherson as an impostor, as did Sylvester O'Halloran, first in an essay on 'The Poems of Ossine, the Son of Fionne Mac Comhal, reclaimed' and a 'Letter to Mr Macpherson occasioned by his Dissertation on the Poems of Tamora', both published in *The Dublin Magazine* for January and August 1763, then in his *Introduction to the Study of the History and Antiquity of Ireland* (1772). For several decades, Macpherson was blamed for having insulted Ireland, falsified tradition, and conflated stories belonging to different periods.

But despite all that censure, Ireland was impressed by the image of the poet-narrator constructed by Macpherson and by the shift from despicable to admirable in the connotations carried by the word 'bard'; henceforth it would be gratifying to find traces of this type of hero, and tempting to see whatever was extant through this distorting prism. The term 'bard', which John O'Brien had treated with disregard in 1764, now carried nobler associations,[34] and for a long time any evidence of the performance of an Irish 'Ossianic' item would be a most valuable catch for an antiquarian – so much so that one might be tempted to invent it (see Chapter 7).

The mixed reception of Macpherson took place in a context where any

---

31 *Remarks on the History of Fingal, and Other Poems of Ossian*, quoted in E.D. Snyder *The Celtic Revival in English Literature 1760-1800* 96. 32 'De simples villageois de mon pays, qui ne sçavent ni lire ni écrire, chantent jusqu'aujourd'hui des poëmes plus anciens de trois siè-cles que celui de Carthon' (the title of a Macpherson text translated in the same *Journal des Sçavans* in November 1762). 33 'On ne peut s'empêcher de plaindre le sort de la nation irlandaise, ainsi placée entre certains antiquaires écossais d'un côté, et quelques écrivains anglais de l'autre. Les uns lui enlèvent ses héros et ses grands hommes en tout genre, les autres s'attachent à avilir cette nation respectable; ils peignent tous les Irlandois comme des sauvages ou des bêtes, qui ne méritent pas de posséder la terre qu'ils habitent depuis si longtemps.' (Ibid. February 1765.) 34 Not always, though: 'The Bards of Ireland were always mere ballad singers [not a term of praise, then]', Charles Vallancey *A Vindication of the Ancient History of Ireland* (*Collectanea de Rebus Hibernicis* Vol. 4 in1786) 426; 'Bardic fictions and unfounded traditions are the oral records of every barbarous nation', Edward Ledwich *Antiquities of Ireland* (1790) 1.

treatment of native culture could give rise to heated arguments. In the latter part of the eighteenth century, the study of the local past could be a hobby in Ireland too, but had political overtones. One aspect of the ideology behind British anti-quarianism was most embarrassing: those who cared for the reputation of their country could not adopt the new fashionable use of terms like 'primitive' 'bar-barian' and 'savagery', which had been too often applied disparagingly to Ireland – by David Hume, for instance.[35] The notion that Ireland had no civilization before the Norman conquest had to be disproved. Those who wrote in Irish had not waited to vindicate the Irish past (see pp. 57-8), but to celebrate it in English was relatively new. Some native historians had begun to use this lan-guage earlier in the century: Hugh Mac Curtin (Aodh Buí Mac Cruitín) had written a *Brief Discourse in Vindication of the Antiquity of Ireland* in 1717, to prove 'that the Ancient Irish before the coming of the English were no way infe-rior to any people or nation in the known world for religion, literature, civility, riches, hospitality, liberality, war-like spirit &c.'[36] If Irish culture was respectable, one might also insist that it was distinct: Thomas O'Sullevane, who had been born *c.*1670 in County Tipperary but was now living in London, prefixed to the *Memoirs of the Marquis of Clanricarde* (1722) a dissertation which included the account of one of its peculiarities: the extraordinary modes of mental composi-tion in darkness taught in bardic schools before the middle of the seventeenth century.[37] How such information was gleaned is unknown, and, though it used to be considered accurate, some are less prepared to take it at face value today.

As Keating had done in the seventeenth century, Charles O'Conor and Sylvester O'Halloran, whose contributions to the Ossianic quarrel were men-tioned above, attacked those who had libelled their country; O'Halloran declared in 1778 that he had 'laboured to render that justice to our ancestors which had been so long denied them', adding that his information was 'extracted from pure native records'.[38] A defence of Ireland would be achieved by revealing true facts – but there were also shaky speculations: the same O'Halloran would assert for instance that 'from the birth of Phenius [said to be 'the inventor of letters' and the ancestor of the Milesians or true Irish] to the Incarnation comprehends a space of 2146 years. From this period the Irish chronology is accurate.'[39] The language itself was an object of lucubration. The Englishman Parsons, already quoted above, said he had 'spent several years of [his] life in Ireland, and there attained to a tolerable knowledge in the very ancient tongue of that country, which enabled [him] to consult some of their manuscripts',[40] and he dabbled in linguistics. According to the genealogies compiled from older sources in *Lebor*

35 David Hume *History of Britain* (1770) I. 454. He also wrote that 'The songs and traditions of the Senachies, the genuine poetry of the Irish, carry in their rudeness and absurdity the inseparable attendants of barbarism, a very different aspect from the correction of Ossian'. (Quoted in J. Leerssen *Mere Irish and Fíor-Ghael* 344.) **36** *A Brief Discourse* 286-7. **37** The relevant text is in *Field Day Anthology of Irish Literature* I. 972-3. **38** *A General History of Ireland* 'Dedication' I. v, vi. **39** Ibid. 'Preliminary Discourse' v. **40** Parsons *Remains of Japhet* vii.

Gabála, the Milesians were the descendants of Noah's son and grandson Japhet and Magog; it was the particularization to Ireland of an old idea, already mentioned by St Jerome and Isidore of Seville, about the origin of all Europeans, and Leibnitz himself believed in a 'Japhetic' family of languages. Parsons concluded that the purest 'Japhetian languages', close to the language shared by God and man before babelization, were Irish and Welsh.

Some members of the Protestant social elite in Ireland had also begun to feel that a unique character and history differentiated the country from Britain, and that the heritage somehow belonged to them too. Antiquarianism could be more than a hobby, for 'Patriots' with a sense of responsibility towards the society they belonged to. In 1782, they obtained the retrocession of parliamentary autonomy for the control of domestic affairs – until the Act of Union merged the two kingdoms in 1800. Anglo-Irish antiquarianism was not unanimous, though, and the 'Japhetian' school split into two branches: there were those who believed that the Irish descended from Japhet through the Scythians (hence their Latin name of *Scotti*), had crossed northern Europe and had therefore been primordially barbaric and in need of the English civilizing influence; others, preferring to think that the ancient Irish had a native culture of high civility which later invaders (the English) had tried to destroy, asserted that the descendants of Japhet had come through Phoenicia, Egypt and Spain. The clergyman Edward Ledwich belonged to the first school, and in the preface to his *Antiquities of Ireland* (1790) he contrasted native barbarism with imported civilization. A champion of the opposite theory was Charles Vallancey; posted to Ireland in 1765 as a military engineer he spent the following half-century there, took an interest in local antiquities and philology (without ever acquiring competence in Irish). His books written in the 1780s connected the ancient Irish with the Carthaginians; he also thought he had 'shown the perfect identity of the Irish language with ancient Persian'. He did not care much for literature, but could be interested in legends when they were associated with curious monuments. He was aware for instance of the vanishing-island motif (cf. pp. 58-9) and of the belief in submerged cities attested in different parts of Ireland.[41] One of his correspondents, E.W. Burton, had described in 1785 a megalithic monument on Slieve Callan, County Clare, which he thought was connected with such a legend, and perhaps also with the Fianna world:

A peasant who was acquainted in the dreary wild in which this monument was situated, told me he was well acquainted with Conane's tomb, and would show it to me; but it turned out to be a Druid's altar [dolmen], without any inscription... The common people of the mountain are well acquainted with the name of Conane, the hero supposed to be buried under the Ogham monument they cannot be convinced that the search was made for an inscription, but after an enchanted key that lies with the interred hero, which when found will restore an enchanted city, sunken on the neighbouring shore of the

41 C. Vallancey *A Vindication of the Ancient History of Ireland* 52

Atlantic sea, to its former splendor, and convert the hideous moory heights of Callan mountain into rich fruitful plains. Their imaginations are heated in this gloomy awful wild, expecting also great riches whenever this city is discovered.[42]

We still have here the generalized account of a legend, not the description of an oral performance: the stone monument was important, and inscriptions would be particularly valuable, whereas the oral tradition of 'the common people' was received as fanciful.

The Anglo-Irish antiquaries I have mentioned so far made only a few passing remarks about verbal arts, but in 1786 a different kind of book appeared, compiled by the wealthy dilettante Joseph Cooper Walker: *Historical Memoirs of the Irish Bards* (an enlarged posthumous edition was published in 1818). Edward Jones's *Musical and Poetical Relicks of the Welsh Bards* (1784) had served as model, and Walker paid attention mostly to poets and musicians. His book included the text of a Fianna *laoi*, but concerning prose storytelling he had little to say, beyond observing that at wakes 'the young sing and dance, and the old tell stories',[43] and briefly attempting to establish the native terminology: 'The Irish have several appellations for Tale-tellers, viz. Sgealaigh, Fin-Sgealaighe [teller of Fianna-tales or lays], Scelaigh, Sgealaiche, Scealaiche [other variants of *scéalaí*: storyteller], and Dresbheartach [perhaps from *dréachtach*: composer, poet – but Walker had another explanation: 'from *dres*, news, I suppose'].'[44]

The material in Walker's book most relevant to the present study was contributed by correspondents, including the already mentioned Charles O'Conor 'of Belanagare' (1710-91), whose ancestors had been High Kings before the Norman conquest and who had spent his childhood in a humble cottage until the family recovered possession of the house they had lost after the Williamite War. In his letters he had much to say about the harper and composer of praise-songs Turlough Carolan (see p. 66), whom he had known in County Roscommon. For Walker, this was 'our Bard', 'a genuine representative of the ancient Bard'. In fact, the wandering harper-composer-versifier had nothing to do with the old Irish bardic order, nor was there anything heroically 'ossianic' in his personality and career, but the term 'bard' now had a meliorative aura.[45] More specifically narrative art was treated rather dismissively by O'Conor: 'Of Irish story-tellers on the exploits of Finn, Oisin, Oscar, Goll, Conan, &c I have known many in my youth [in County Sligo]. They amuse the vulgar at wakes and weddings.'[46]

But an unusually precise piece of information appeared in the Appendix, with the first relatively detailed sketch and life-story of an itinerant singer and storyteller, contributed by Ralph Ouseley, of Limerick:

---

42 Ibid. 528-9. (Vallancey wrote an essay about the stone.) 43 Op. cit. (1818 ed.) 18. 44 Ibid. 210. 45 Donal O'Sullivan *Carolan: The Life, Times and Music of an Irish Harper* 1.161: 'It is to be regretted that so many writers have not been content to take him for what he was, but have persisted in attributing to him the imaginary qualities of a "bard".' 46 Ibid. 210.

Perhaps the subject of these memoirs is the last of that order of Minstrels, called tale-tellers, or *Fin-sgealaighte* ... [Footnote: 'Since writing the above, I have been informed that a few Fin-Sgealaighte or Dreis-bheartaighe still remain in Connaught.'] Cormac Common (or Cormac Dall, that is, Blind Cormac) was born in May 1703, at Woodstock, near Ballindangan, in the County of Mayo. His parents were poor and honest ... Before he had completed the first year of his life, the small-pox deprived him of his sight. Showing an early fondness for music, a neighbouring gentleman determined to have him taught to play the harp ... But his patron dying suddenly, the harp dropped from his hand, and was never after taken up. [He listened] eagerly to the Irish songs and metrical tales which he heard sung and recited around the 'crackling faggots' of his father and his neighbours. These, by frequent recitation, became strongly impressed on his memory. His mind being thus stored, and having no other avocation, he commenced a Man of Talk, or a Tale-teller ... He was now employed in relating legendary tales, and reciting genealogies at rural wakes, or in the hospitable halls of country squires. He has often been heard to recite some of those Irish tales which Mr Macpherson has so artfully interwoven with the texture of the epic poems which he does Oisin the honour to attribute to him. Endowed with a sweet voice and a good ear, his narrations were generally graced with the charms of melody ... He did not, like the tale-teller mentioned by Sir William Temple [see p. 52], chant his tales in an uninterrupted *even tone*: the monotony of his modulation was frequently broken by cadences introduced with taste at the close of each stanza. 'In rehearsing any of Oisin's poems, or any composition in verse', says Mr Ousley, 'he chants them pretty much in the manner of our cathedral service.' ... Cormac has twice married, but is now a widower. By both his wives he had several children. He now resides at Sorrell-town, near Dunmore, in the County of Galway, with one of his daughters, who is happily married. Though his utterance is materially injured by dental losses, and though his voice is impaired by age, yet he continues to practise his profession: so seldom are we sensible of our imperfections. It is probable that where he was once admired, he is now only endured. Mr Ousley informs me, that 'one of his grandsons leads him about to the houses of the neighbouring gentry, who give him money, diet, and sometimes clothes. His apparell is commonly decent and comfortable; but he is not rich, nor does he seem solicitous about wealth.' His moral character is unstained. His person is large and muscular.[47]

We note that the man is called a 'minstrel', not a 'bard' (Carolan being then generally considered the last representative of the second category), and that what could be really observed in the contemporary world was very far from the Ossianic construct.

Another contributor was Charlotte Brooke, who lived in County Kildare and whose father had an interest in antiquities. Walker was told that she had reacted to Macpherson's books like the gentleman mentioned by Parsons (see p. 87):

A young lady, on whose veracity I have the firmest reliance, informed me, that her father had a labourer, who was in possession of two volumes of Irish manuscript poems, which in her infancy she often heard him read to a rustic audience in her father's field ... The

47 Op. cit. 272-83. Corman Common must have died about 1786.

bold images and marvellous airs, of these poems, so captivated her youthful fancy, that they remained for some years strongly impressed on her memory. When Mr Macpherson's Ossian's Poems were put into her hands, she was surprised to find in them her favourite Irish tales, decked with meretricious ornaments; and her blustering heroes, Fin, Con, Cuchullin &c. so polished in their manners.[48]

Unlike Walker, she had a good command of the Irish language. Encouraged to present to the public a set of Irish poems with translations, and imitating the title of Percy's famous British collection, she published in 1789 *Reliques of Irish Poetry*, to which is subjoined an Irish Tale, with the motto '*A Oisín, as binn linn do sgéala*' (O Oisín, we are charmed by your stories). The tale announced in the title is the story of 'Maon' (Moen: 'speechless'), who was compelled to eat his father's heart and then became dumb; banished, he returned as an adult to take revenge. A 'bard' appears to the author in a dream and tells her the story – in fact, one of the sources of Charlotte Brooke's composition was Keating (see p. 58). The rest of the book gave authentic native material (including five 'Ossianic poems') with 'the originals in the Irish character' and translation in rather awkward English verse. The author explained her intentions in a preface which sums up the new patriotic programme of some late eighteenth-century Anglo-Irish antiquaries; Ireland was the 'elder sister' of Britain – a concise way of revealing one's position in the quarrel about cultural precedence; she used first person possessives to express her relation to Ireland, and thought that a 'cordial union' between the two islands should be possible, provided the value of Irish culture was acknowledged:

The productions of our Irish Bards exhibit a glow of cultivated genius, – a spirit of elevated heroism, – sentiments of pure honor, – instances of disinterested patriotism, – and manners of a degree of refinement, totally astonishing, at a period when the rest of Europe was nearly sunk in barbarism: And is not all this very honorable to our [Irish] countrymen? Will they not be benefited, – will they not be gratified, at the lustre reflected on them by ancestors so very different from what modern prejudice has been studious to represent them?[49]

Lyrical and narrative poetry, as well as information about authors and (less often) performers, had begun to be published; there remained to rescue the musical heritage. In 1792, a festival was organized in Belfast with this aim:

Some inhabitants of Belfast, feeling themselves interested in every thing which relates to the honour as well as the prosperity of their country, propose to open a subscription which they intend to apply in attempting to revive and perpetuate *the ancient music and poetry of Ireland*. They are solicitous to preserve from oblivion the few fragments which have been permitted to remain as monuments of the refined taste and genius of their ancestors. In order to carry this project into execution, it must appear obvious to those

48 Ibid. 57-8. 49 Charlotte Brooke *Reliques of Irish Poetry* (1789) vi.

acquainted with the situation of this country that it will be necessary to assemble the *harpers*, those descendants of our ancient bards, who are at present almost exclusively possessed of all that remains of the *music, poetry*, and *oral traditions of Ireland*.[50]

Ten Irish performers, most of them old and six of them blind, turned up. Edward Bunting, an organist, was appointed to transcribe their music, and soon started a more extensive collection. Patrick Lynch, a schoolmaster, accompanied him in Connacht in 1802 to note down the texts. The results were partly published in 1796, 1809 and 1840. The first volume expressed the opinion that the specimens which had survived were only 'the wreck of better times, the history of which is either lost, or incorrectly recognised in a confused series of traditions'. One should pay them due attention, not merely to 'gratify the national pride' but to trace 'the progress of the human mind'.[51] The last volume included some 'airs to which Ossianic and other very old poems are sung ... noted down from persons singing very old fragments of this class of poems, both in Scotland and in Ireland', as well as 'the Lamentation of Deirdre over the Sons of Usnach, [which] is still sung in various parts of the country, to words corresponding with those of the old national romance of the death of the Sons of Usnach, as preserved in Connaugt'.[52]

Bunting's persistence was rather exceptional. Nevertheless, the way was being paved for more rigorous scholarship by gathering material and formalizing the publication of results. In 1785 the Royal Irish Academy was founded to promote useful arts and sciences, and 'to awaken a spirit of literary ambition, by keeping alive the memory of [Ireland's] ancient reputation for learning'.[53] Vallancey and Walker were among the original members, and joined the 'Committee for Antiquities'. The academy soon began to collect manuscripts, and its published 'Transactions' would occasionally touch on oral traditions – but not in the first years. In the volume published in 1806, Walker dabbled in the question of how stories of 'magicians, knights, and damsels, with which Fairy-land is peopled' reached Ireland; they would have come from the East through Italy and France at the time of the Crusades, then to be diffused by monks along with 'holy legends', and 'thus obtained a footing in Ireland and furnished materials for the metrical tales of our early bards'.[54] A description of contemporary oral culture appeared only in the volume for 1825, in a report on the Aran Islands, which for the first time were elevated to the rank of 'Celtic' sanctuary (cf. Chapter 9):

50 E. Bunting *The Ancient Music of Ireland* (1840) Preface. On Belfast pioneers, including Robert S. Mac Adam who collected oral material in Irish, see D. Ó Giolláin *Locating Irish Folklore* 96-100. 51 *A General Collection of the Ancient Irish Music* (1796) Preface. 52 *The Ancient Music of Ireland* (1840) Preface. 53 Preface to the first volume of the Transactions of the R.I.A. in 1787, quoted in R.A. Breatnach, 'Two Eighteenth-Century Irish Scholars, J.C. Walker and Charlotte Brooke', *Studia Hibernica* 5 (1965) 89-90. 54 J.C. Walker 'On the Origin of Romantic Fabling in Ireland', *Transactions of the R.I.A.* 10 (1806) 3-6.,

The isles of Aran abound with the remains of Druidism – open temples, altars, stone pillars, sacred mounds of fire worship, miraculous fountains, and evident vestiges of oak groves ... The Aranites, in their simplicity, consider these remains of Druidism still sacred and inviolable; being, they imagine, the inchanted haunts and property of aerial beings, whose power of doing mischief they greatly dread and studiously propitiate. For entertaining this kind of religious respect, they have another powerful motive; they believe that the cairns, or circular mounds, are the sepulchres, as some of them really are, of native chiefs and warriors of antiquity, of whose military fame and wondrous achievements they have abundance of legendary stories. The well attended winter-evening tales of the scealuidhe, or story-tellers, are the only *historical* entertainments of this primitive, simple, and sequestered people. In this credulous and superstitious propensity, they exactly resemble their brethren, the Scots of the Highlands and Isles. Indeed, the solitude and romantic wildness of their 'seagirt' abode, and the venerable memorials of Christian piety and Celtic worship, so numerously scattered over the surface of the Aran Isles, fairly account for the enthusiasm, credulity, and second-sight of these islanders ... I have already glanced at the character of the people, and have stated that in language, habits, and customs, they retain, beyond comparison, more of the primitive Celtic character than any of the contemporary tribes of that stock, at least, in this kingdom. Sequestered and almost unmixed as the Aranites have been for a long succession of generations, history has always considered them as full of that ancient spirit, which has been elsewhere made to disappear by the force of revolutionary and colonial innovations. To delineate the character and peculiarities of the Aranites of the present day is, in fact, to call forth associations, mounting up not only to the times of Christian celebrity in this country, but even to the days of their sages and warriors of heathenism. Their immemorial traditions and practices may, without stretch of imagination, be viewed as the graphic annals of 'oldest' days. Here you have, on every lip, the exploits of Cuchullan, of Conal Cearnach, of Gol son of Morna, of Fionn son of Cumhal, of Oisin and of Oscar; here, they enthusiastically point out the very places which these invincibles had honoured with their presence; and here they tell us, their spirits rest, as in Elysian dales! ... The people of Aran, with characteristic enthusiasm, fancy, that at certain periods, they see Hy-Brasail, elevated far to the west in their watery horizon.[55]

Most antiquarian work in the last decades of the eighteenth century and the first decades of the nineteenth was done with more enthusiasm than method, though individuals could build up networks of correspondents. Later, amateurs would still gather and imaginatively interpret remains of the past, but they became more and more marginal to systematic and sometimes official investigations, and to professional scholarship.

The Royal Dublin Society, founded in 1731, aimed at 'improving husbandry, manufactures, and other arts and sciences'. At the beginning of the nineteenth century, it encouraged 'statistical surveys' – 'statistics' being then

55 John T. O'Flaherty 'A Sketch of the History and Antiquities of the Southern Islands of Aran, lying off the west Coast of Ireland; with observations on the Religion of the Celtic Nations, Pagan Monuments of the early Irish, Druidic Rites, &c.', *Transactions of the R.I.A.* 14 (1825) 97, 98-9, 137-8, 139.

understood as that branch of political science dealing with the assembly and analysis of data, not necessarily numerical, bearing on the condition of a community and potentially useful for the management of a state. To its 'suggestions of inquiry' limited to geographical circumstances, minerals, agriculture and cattle, habitations, roads and the use of the English language, Hely Dutton, in his *Statistical Survey of the County of Clare* (1808), added 'moral, manners and customs of the people'. He found that the 'labouring classes' believed 'in fairies, hobgoblins, witches, will o' the wisp, ghosts, and a multitude of legendary tales, which old women are fond of relating.'[56] He described a wake, and visited the 'celebrated tomb of Conaan on Mount Callan' mentioned by Vallencey (see p. 90): 'Many laughable anecdotes are told of the efficiency of Darby and Grana's bed, as it is called by the country people.'[57]

Another attempt at bringing together detailed information relevant to policy was launched in the second decade of the century and encouraged by Robert Peel, then Chief Secretary for Ireland: *A Statistical Account or Parochial Survey of Ireland*, under the direction of William Shaw Mason The Anglican rector of each parish was to answer a questionnaire, one section of which concerned 'the genius and disposition of the poorer classes; their language, manners, and customs'. Three volumes were published between 1814 and 1819. The choice of contributors limited the value of the reports: most of them had little to say about the 'poorer classes', which generally were of a different religion and could mistrust them, and which they tended to despise:

Of the genius of the common people little can be ascertained, for they are very shy in converse with their superiors, and confidentially communicative only to each other.[58] ... As to traditions, and legendary tales of darker times, together with marvellous stories of apparitions and witchcraft, we hear little or nothing of them in this part of the country: they may, perhaps, be preserved in some of the mountain townlands, which are inhabited by the aborigines alone.[59]

They could also be dismissed as not worthy of mention: 'The ridiculous notions of the existence of fairies and witches obtain implicit belief in the minds of the ignorant, who are extremely superstitious; and the number of absurd stories on this subject told among them, received with incredible avidity, repeated or believed, however inconsistent with reason and common sense, is hardly to be credited.'[60] A clergyman concluded that 'the common Irish are naturally shrewd, but very ignorant, and deficient in mental culture, from the barbarous tongue in which they converse, which operates as an effectual bar to any kind of literary attainment.'[61]

There was an exception, however: Alexander Ross, the rector of Dungiven

56 Op. cit. 363. **57** Ibid. 318. **58** Lismore, Co. Waterford. *A Statistical Account ...* 1.554. **59** Ibid. Maghera, Co. Derry. 1. 597. **60** Ibid. Athlone. 3. 72. **61** Ibid. Kilfergus, Co. Limerick. 2. 311.

in County Derry, was interested in the culture of the Catholics who constituted half the population of his parish. We are indebted to him for an important testimony on the persistence of Ulster and Fianna lore and on the ways in which 'tradition' (in the dual sense of transmission and preservation) functioned:

The poems attributed to Ossian, and other bardic remains, are still repeated here by the old seanachies (as they are called) with visible exultation. Eight of these have been written down, at my request, by a young mountaineer, named Bernard MacLoskie, from whose acquaintance with the native traditions, customs and language, the writer derived much assistance in this survey: he is himself a good Latin scholar, and possesses, by every account, a critical knowledge of the ancient Irish. These poetic records have been handed down, from time immemorial, by tradition alone, nor is it apparent whether they ever existed here in manuscript. A curious evidence of the accuracy of tradition, in preserving these remains, may be noticed: two of the poems transcribed, namely Deirdri (the Darthula of Macpherson) and Tailc, had been already published, from southern manuscripts, in a volume entitled Transactions of the Gaelic Society:[62] this book, which was accidentally in the writer's possession, afforded an opportunity of comparing the poems taken from viva voce recitation, with the printed copy; and strange as it may seem, they were found to agree together word for word, with the exception, however, of a few lines in Deirdri, and four entire stanzas in Tailc, which the written record has evidently lost, and tradition preserved. An old man, named Mulholland, who is now the most accurate depository of these poems to be met with, continues at an advanced age to sing them with enthusiasm and delight. As there is a separate air for each poem, in which the melody is suited to the subject, it is probable that the original music is also preserved. The manner of preserving the accuracy of tradition is singular, and worthy of notice. In the winter evenings, a number of Seanachies frequently meet together, and recite alternately their traditionary stories. If anyone repeats a passage, which appears to another to be incorrect, he is immediately stopped, when each gives a reason for his way of reciting the passage, the dispute is then referred to a vote of the meeting, and the decision of the majority becomes imperative on the subject for the future. This plan, aided by the measure of the poetry, and also that of the music, may account for the accurate preservation of these ancient poems.[63]

A much richer hoard of information was put together one generation later as a side-line of the Ordnance Survey of Ireland. In addition to mapping the land – a task accomplished by army engineers – it was hoped to fix the place-names, and to that end the way the locals pronounced them was listened to and compared with historical documentation. A description of localities was also planned, and the project became more ambitious still when an English officer, Thomas Larcom, expanded the toponymical programme: those who were engaged in this part of the Survey would also locate and describe ruined churches, holy wells, 'forts' and other prehistoric monuments such as standing

---

62 Theophilus O'Flanagan (ed. tr.) *Deirdri, or the Lamentable Fate of the Sons of Usnach ...* , in the first volume of the Gaelic Society Transactions, 1808. 63 1. 317-18.

stones and 'giants' graves', investigate the story behind each name, and describe the practices of people. The instructions which, in 1837, detailed the types of information to be collected read like an early questionnaire for ethnographers, with storytelling as one of the relevant objects:

Note the general style of cottage, as stone, mud, slated, glass windows, one story or two, number of rooms, comfort and cleanliness. Food; fuel; dress; longevity; usual number in a family; early marriages; any remarkable instance of either on these hands? What are their amusements and recreations? Patrons and patrons' days, and traditions respecting them? What local customs prevail, as Beal Tinne, or fire on St John's Eve? Driving the cattle through fire, and through water? Peculiar games? Any legendary tales or poems recited around the fireside? Any ancient music, as clan marches or funeral cries? They differ in different districts, collect them if you can. Any peculiarity of costume? Nothing more indicates the state of civilization and intercourse.[64]

The scrutiny of architectural remains, ancient names of places and 'traditions' were the special tasks of a department staffed by Irishmen. John O'Donovan served as Gaelic adviser from 1830; Eugene O'Curry joined in 1834. From 1835 they worked under George Petrie who supervised the Department of Topography, History and Antiquity. Part of its activity consisted in searching ancient manuscripts for information which one hoped to verify, county by county,[65] but when time came to collect local oral lore, discovering the right informants was not always an easy task. The field work was done first by John O'Donovan alone, then partly by his assistants; Eugene O'Curry occasionally shared in it, though his main function remained to supply those in the field with extracts from old texts. Petrie centralized the reports sent back by those who were exploring the country. These Ordnance Survey Letters written between 1834 and 1842[66] offer the fascinating cross-section of a society in which the oral heritage remained important – though in this matter the earlier reports are richer in details than later ones. It is such an unusual source of information for that time that extensive quotations seem justified. I shall sketch out the most fruitful campaigns, mainly in the North and West, and see what kind of oral information was obtained.

In his first expedition, in County Down in 1834, O'Donovan met people who, so far, had been almost invisible except to their immediate and often illiterate neighbours. It seemed quite an adventure:

64 Quoted in J.H. Andrews *A Paper Landscape: The Ordnance Survey* 148. 65 J.T. Gilbert *On the Life and Labours of John O'Donovan, LL.D.* 8-9: 'After the name of every important place in a county had been tabulated in the various forms in which it was found in old writings, O'Donovan and others of the staff, during the summer months, proceeded to the localities, inspected the existing remains of monuments, learned from the old Irish-speaking people the vernacular name of each townland, and carefully noted down all the local traditions and legends.' 66 The letters, kept in the Royal Irish Academy, were copied between 1924 and 1932, and I have used the typescripts.

[Newry, 10 April 1834] I travelled yesterday through the parish of Donaghmore, and discovered one of the aborigines, 100 years old, and on the point of death. He is blind, and though in the most feeble state, he retains his reasoning powers in a most surprizing manner. He is intimately acquainted with every field in the Parish of Donaghmore, where he was employed for half a century as a bailiff. He was able to give me the ancient name of every townland in the Parish in the most satisfactory manner. I travelled through fields and unfrequented ways until at last I discovered him in a little cabin lamenting his transgressions and preparing for death ... I certainly felt very shy in disturbing him, but as there was no substitute for him, I made bold to examine whether or not he had sufficient discernment to understand what he was about. He understood me immediately, and answered the questions I proposed him with great readiness. Several persons of whom I enquired the way to his house, told me that he was dead this 'many and many a year'. I had to return in the dark, and being far off the main road to Newry, it is with difficulty I made my way back. I tore my trousers across with the brambles. I suppose that I shall become wild before I return to Dublin.

Oral tradition did not survive on remote hills alone, but sometimes seemed out of reach:

[Downpatrick, 27 April] Yesterday I went through all the Gaol to see if I could find any of the aborigines in it, Mr Archbold having suggested that it was the most probable place to meet them; and tho' disappointed, I felt a kind of satisfaction in finding only one old man in the 89th year of his age from the Parish of Saul [Sawel] who could speak Irish. He is confined for debt, but so stupid, that he could not understand us, and his articulation so indistinct that I could not catch the pronunciation.

Such a setback could, however, be compensated by other encounters:

[Downpatrick, 29 April] It is surprizing to consider what intelligent people are to be met with in these sequestered places [the Mountains of Mourne], and it is a fact that the more *Irish* they are, the more civil, obliging and intelligent you will find them.

A few months later, when O'Donovan was in and around County Derry, his expectations were disappointed again: popular memory often failed to match what had been found in manuscripts, and the 'Ossianic' lore, the presence of which had been attested some twenty years before (see p. 97), seemed to have almost vanished:

[Londonderry, 30 July] I have travelled through the townlands of Stranagalwilly and Slaghtmanus in search of old Irish inhabitants; I have met many who can speak Irish, but they retain very few traditions of any kind excepting the exploits of Shane Crossagh O'Mullan, the celebrated Rapparee, many of whose leaps and retreats are pointed out.[67]

67 Raparees, from *ráipéir*: rapiers; the name was first given to irregular soldiers in the seventeenth century, then to outlaws like John Mullan 'the Pock-Marked', who was said to rob the rich and help the poor in Counties Derry and Tyrone.

[Dungiven, 1 August] I went on Thursday to see the ruin of the work of [?Bricriu mac Carbada] on the summit of a hill ... Is it possible that this can be the ruin of the celebrated palace of Aileach? [It was not.] ... I made every enquiry about it in its vicinity but could discover nothing; all the neighbours have lost their traditions and their old language – they could only tell me that the hill was called Grianan Gormley, and the ruin the *Ould Fourth*. I have been very much disappointed, but I do not give it up yet.

[Claudy, 11 August] I have also searched the glens [Glenullin and Glen- na-Benmada] for some of the old Tuireadhs [*tuireamh*: dirge, lament] or Elegies, sung at the wakes of the old families but I could not find one, except one fragment ... They can not recite any of Ossian's poems except odd lines here and there. These [they] have not from a succession of oral traditions, but from hearing old men (Irish scholars now dead) read them out of manuscripts now decayed or lost.

According to O'Donovan, and contrary to what the Reverend Ross thought, a 'tradition' (i.e. the material transmitted) was deteriorating when no manuscript served as guide:

[Londonderry, 12 August] I made every enquiry in the vicinity of Dungiven about Aileach but could discover no recollection of it; the people there know nothing about Irish monarchs or Irish kings, and it is curious that Fin MacCool and his followers are better remembered than Cormac mac Art or Niall of the Nine Hostages. This can be very easily accounted for: some time ago in these glens there were Irish scholars [people who could read Irish] whose principal amusement was to read over at their fire side on winter evenings tales and poems concerning the exploits of Fin and his Fians; such as the tale of the elopement of Grainne, the wife of Fin with Dermot, one of his warriors (their beds are pointed out in various places). The poem concerning 'the huge woman', daughter of the King of Greece. The chase by Fin on Slieve Gullion, the defeat of Manus, son of the King of Denmark, etc., etc. These poems have rendered Fin immortal (as the Iliad or Eneid have immortalized Achilles and Hector). A few lines of these are yet repeated in the parish, but I could not meet one able to recite the entire of any one poem, or to tell any one tale correctly. These tales and poems are yet preserved in manuscripts, but they are better recited in the mountains of Waterford and Kerry than in O'Kane's country.

Incredulity alternated with amazement:

[Maghera, 23 August] I have had great argumentations with the Shanachies of Glenullin and other places, about the meaning of *Aireagal* [oratory] (which O'Reilly translates refusal of a friend!). They can invent stories in an instant to account for the names of old churches.

[Draperstown-Cross, 17 September] I met a very interesting old man of the name of Murry in the townland of Moneyneany to-day, he is 88 years old, but perfectly sound in his mind. I asked him if he had ever heard why Moneyneany got that name? He answered that it signifies the 'hill of wonders' and then began to tell a string of stories about the wonders that are traditionally handed down as having happened in it.

The first season of field work ended in mid-Ulster, where O'Donovan heard more narratives – and missed an opportunity of collecting others:

[Belturbet, 12 November] I passed through the parish of Kinawley and met a very intelligent old man of the name Terence or Turlough Currain (Toirr McCurthain) who is deeply versed in traditionary and legendary lore. He requested that I would stop with him to night, but as I do not at present want to enter into any matters but the names, I got him to pronounce the townland names for me, and came on to Belturbet. He told me, however, a story about the patron saint of the parish that I wish to preserve.

[Enniskillen, 24 November] I met a very clever and enlightened Milesian in the Parish of Clones, Mr Con O'Neill, the Goban Saer of the district. [On Gobán Saor, see Chapter 12.] He is an architect, a goldsmith, watchmaker and a carpenter. It would be very difficult to convince Con that the round tower of Clones was older than the ruin of the monastery. He says that the country people always style it Sean-Chlaighteach a t-Seipel, or the Old Belfry of the chapel, and that there is a tradition current among the peasantry that there is a silver bell lying under ground in a place immediately under the tower, formerly a quagmire, but now converted to a meadow and garden. The peasantry also say that this tower was built by the daughter of Goban Saer, and that when she was finishing the cone a boy looked up under her clothes, which when she perceived she leaped down into the quagmire already referred to, where she was immediately swallowed and lost ... I can never forget the story of the two dogs [Fionn's greyhounds transformed into hills] nor the interesting individual who told it to me and Mr Taylor at Derrygonnelly ... I have been under considerable expense in entertaining old sheanchies for whom I sent to the mountains.

In the 1835 campaign after the winter break, Armagh, Monaghan and Donegal were explored. By then it was clear that Larcom's extensive project could not be realized with the means at disposal, but O'Donovan was still taking an interest in legends associated with toponyms:

[Monaghan, 4 May] I have got on famously to-day, there being a fair in the town, and many of the old aborigines having been sent to me to the office. I send you the name-books of the very large parish of Tedavnet ... The names were pronounced Hibernicé for me by an old man of the name Sheals (Hibernicé O'Sindhail), a very intelligent man who is well acquainted with the parish ... All the old inhabitants of the parish state that a Saint Damhnad, a virgin, was the first founder of the old church of Tedavnet, which they say is as much as to say as Toigh Damhnaide or the House of Davnet. They have no idea of the age in which she lived, but think it was a long time after the introduction of Christianity.

He met a man who was critical of the 'improved' toponymy established by surveyors:

[Ballybay, 11 May] The most intelligent old fellow I came across is named Mac Kahy, he was formerly a cess collector, but is now living in the most lamentable state of misery.

He is as naked as Adam before he clothed himself with the leaves of a fig tree! When I entered his cabin he had not a single article of dress upon him, nothing but an old blanket thrown across his shoulders. He sat upon a little stool and stooped with his face, hands, and knees over a small fire, which has actually roasted him. I never met such a spectacle of misery! And though living in this oyster-like condition, he retains his reasoning powers, and a very vivid memory. He says that gentlemen know nothing about Irish names of townlands, that they wish to harden, shorten, and make them look like English names, and as this work is going on since the reign of Oliver Cromwell, it is now most difficult to come at the *ould* name, for even through [thoroughbred] farmers are now forgetting the names which their grandmothers used to call these lands, and adopting the hard and shortened names, which they hear with their landlords. The old Druid illustrated these observations by shewing that the townland which his grandmother called Fionn Tulaigh, or the white hill, is now refined to Fintlie, though he thinks Fintally would do well enough.

But while certain items were vanishing, others were still remembered by some people:

[Carn[donagh], 21 August] Yesterday we travelled through the parish of Clonca, and got the names pronounced by John O'Dogherty of the townland of Bree, not far from Malin Well, a man full of years, traditions, and hospitality. He thus traces his pedigree [thirteen names] to Conor an Eny who, he says, was the first that got possession of Inishowen ... I got him to repeat this pedigree six times over to see if it were settled in his memory, and found that he can repeat all the names in succession with as much certainty as I could abcd to z.
    [Letterkenny, 21 September – concerning Scarrifhollis, a ford over the Swilly where a Royalist-Catholic army was destroyed in 1650] ... the old men only can tell that the name of the castle was Shar-Sollus, or Castle Sollus. In Kilmacrenan, however, Manus O'Donnell remembers and pronounces the name distinctly as Scairbh Sholais, and tells the story preserved by tradition, with great appearance of having retained a considerable deal of truth.
    [Ballybofey, 5 October] I marked as by far the most intelligent and skilled in ancient lore, an old man of the name Merly whose forehead and features spoke health, goodnature, and intelligence. He is intimately acquainted with the situations and meanings of the names of the townlands, and the repertory of the legends, stories and prophecies of Glen Finn.

In 1836, O'Donovan explored Louth, Cavan, Leitrim, Sligo and Meath:

[Castlebellingham, 21 January] A story prevails among the people relative to the building of this church [Kilsaran]. It is said that, when a site was choosing for its erection, a white horse laden with some burden was sent forth, to determine by his resting when fatigued (sárnighte) the spot whereon to build; it happened that becoming fatigued he rested where the church was afterwards built, unde nomen Cill Sárán.
[Castlebellingham, 22 January] ... there is a bridge ... which they call Droichet Atha na bhfianaibh, regarding which name there is a story told of Cuchullin having singly fought

against the Fians [the kind of conflation of 'cycles' for which Macpherson had been blamed is possible in oral repertoire] who were enchanted at that bridge, unde nomen. We could get no person to tell the story in full. Matthew Kennedy of Mansfieldstown Parish recollects from manuscript a few scattered scraps of it, which are not worth the telling, as no important names appear in them ... Matthew Kennedy has a few Irish manuscripts in his hands; he shewed us two, one of which was entitled Eachtra na g-curadh [a 'modern' romantic tale, in several eighteenth-century manuscripts], in which a good deal is said of Cuchullin, Feardhia MacDamon and others. Matthew had a manuscript in which was the story of Cuchullin's birth, the origin of his name, his life and death; he remembers a considerable part of the story, but not the names of the persons and places connected with it ... Cuchullin is well remembered even in this part of the county. We always hear that the entire story is to be had of some, but we have met none yet who could give it.

Clusters of legends could be associated with one place, or the same legend with different settings as appears in this report concerning Lios Ghearraid (Garret's Fort), two miles south-east of Ardee, where Gerald, earl of Desmond, or Gerald, earl of Kildare and his soldiers, would be asleep, waiting for a six-fingered man to enter and break the spell:

[Ardee, 27 January, a letter signed P. O'Keefe and T. O'Conor] In this fort is the habitation of the far-famed Gearraid Iarla and his forces who are said to be enchanted there waiting the time ... No one in the neighbourhood ever saw him except one Mathews, a very old man, who certainly 'ni eum oculi vani fefelissent' saw him. Some other old fellow, whose name we could not learn, is also said to have seen him. The people also tell a story in which there is not a word a lie, that a man named Ginnity, who lived in Paughanstown townland was going to the fair of Mullacrew to sell a colt; he was met by Garret on the road near his habitation, who having offered a price for the colt, desired Ginnity if he could get no more at the fair, that at his return the money was to be had in readiness: it happened that he could not exceed at the fair the price offered by Garret, he brought the colt back, and was met by Garret on the same spot, who brought him into his cave, where Ginnity delivered up the colt safe and sound and received payment in as good and as honest coin as he could get from any one. On another day it happened that there was a football near the place, by the shouts at which Garret roused out of his dwelling, asking in person was it the time, *An raibh and tam ann? A'd taine an uair?* ['Is it the moment? Has the hour come?'] but finding himself disappointed he retired to where he is still believed to remain. This is all we can learn about Garret.

This item illustrates the circulation of story elements between mainland Europe and Ireland, and within Ireland: the international theme (Thompson's Motif D1960.2 King asleep in mountain; Christiansen's Migratory Legend Type 8009) of the liberator asleep underground with his army, and awaiting the opportune time to return, appears in Irish legends concerning various leaders: Fionn mac Cumhaill, Donal O'Donoghue, Hugh and Red Hugh O'Neill, 'Balldearg' O'Donnell, and more particularly Gearóid Iarla Fitzgerald who, in a strong corpus, is said to wait under Lough Gur in County Limerick. It is also near Lough Gur that the story of the man who was going to the fair to sell his horse is often set.[68] In legends associated with various lakes, the question 'Is it time?' is asked by some *peist*, or *piast* (monster), doomed to stay there until Judgment Day.

Another passage in the same letter shows again how two stories could be fused into one, and how cycles of stories clearly separated by scholars could combine in the memory of simple people. The ancient territory of Muirthemne had been the scene of the four-day fight in which Cú Chullainn finally slew his friend Fear Diadh (cf. p. 103):

Ardee Town is called in Irish Baile Atha Fhir dhiadh [the town of Ferdia's ford] ... for which name the people account thus: Fionn Mac Cumhail, they say, kept his castle at Hacklim ... The Fear dhiadh hearing of Fin's fame came to challenge him to single combat ... [There follows the tale of Fionn pretending to be a baby in the cradle and terrifying a giant by biting him, 'one of the most popular tales in the folklore of Ireland'].[69] ... As he was drinking Fin's wife by preternatural means sent an enchanted poisoned dart (ga-builg) after him, which despatched him on the spot; from this circumstance the Ath (ford) was ever called Ath Fhir dhiadh, or the Ford of Fhir dhiadh. James Dolan a native of Ardee went with us to the Ford and pointed out where Fear dhiadh was killed, and also his grave ... Dolan told the story of his death thus: [now the 'correct' version, as told in *Táin Bó Cuailnge*] Cú Chulainn gave Fear dhiadh a mortal wound with the Ga builg of which he immediately died.

The first Fianna story told at Ardee was a version of the tale later made famous by William Carleton – the 'Legend of Knockmany', first published in *Chamber's Edinburgh Journal* in 1841 where the opponent is 'Cucullin'; an anonymous, different version had appeared in 1833 in the *Dublin Penny Journal*.[70]

The conflation of 'cycles' is also evidenced in these notes concerning Dún Dealgan, the prehistoric mound, west of Dundalk, which early Irish literature named as the home of Cú Chullainn:

[Dundalk, 15 February, signed O'K–O'C] The people here [at Castletown] do not retain by tradition that Cuchullen ever made this his *priomh-ánu*; they think that Finn Mac Conmhail had more to do with it. They ascribe the erection of the mount to the Danes;

---

68 David Fitzgerald, 'Popular Tales of Ireland', in *Revue Celtique* 4 (1879) 190-1, 198. For a detailed study of this tale or legend-type: Dáithí Ó hÓgáin ' "Has the Time Come" – The Barbarossa legend in Ireland and its traditional background', in *Béaloideas* 59 (1991) 197-207. 69 D. Ó hÓgáin *Fionn mac Cumhaill; Images of the Gaelic Hero* 305. The episode in which Finn hides in a cradle is an oikotype of international tale-type AT1149 Children Desires Ogre's Flesh. More than one hundred versions collected in Ireland are extant. Portraying Fionn as a trickster is much more common in oral tradition than in manuscripts, perhaps because cunning is an essential virtue for poor people like most storytellers. 70 J. MacKillop, op. cit. 128-33.

nor in all our enquiring through the County did we meet any person who knew that this was Cuchullen's habitation, except a few who read his story in manuscript.

In this campaign, as in those of the first two years, there were times when pickings seemed hopelessly slim: '[Cavan, 19 May] To our great disappointment, we found the ancient language and traditions quite extinct in that part of the county [between Belturbet and Ballyconnell]. The language is spoken by the old people only, and even these do not understand the meanings of the topographical names.' On the other hand the tactics of the collectors were improving; they knew when and where it might be possible to find informants: [Mohill, 10 June] 'We do more on Sunday than any other day because the old sages of the country are always idle on that day and willing to talk about Crom Cruach[71] or any other subject.'

It could be tempting to compare Irish stories and non-Irish mythologies:

[Kells, 29 July] I conversed for a long time on the banks of Lough Sheelin with an old man of the name Magheaghran [Magauran]... The legend about the original formation of Lough Sheelin is exactly similar to that about Lough Neagh and most other lakes in Ireland[72] ... The lake is enchanted even to this day: Magheaghran says that there are herrings and bream in it in great abundance, but the fishermen cannot take them! Magheaghran wore out my patience telling me how Sherridan lost the townland of Derrysherridan, but it is so like the story about Carthage and the Bull's hide that it is not worth preserving. [It was AT Type 2400 The Ground is measured with a Horse's Skin or Ox-hide – cut into thin strips.]

To be considered really worthwhile, the material collected orally still had to be confirmed by written material. In the 1830s, such adequacy was not easy to get:

[Sligo, 8 September, a letter from Thomas O 'Conor?] There is a tradition that this Ben Bolban took its name from Conall Bulbin. I requested a man, who neither understood nor could speak the English language but pure Machaireon Irish, to tell me the story, he said it would occupy too much time; he, however, related a great part of it, so that I understood it as a metamorphosis of a story about Conal Golban, which I heard Mr O'Donovan say was preserved in an Irish manuscript in the College. [According to the written tradition, the mid-fifth-century king Conall Gulban, got his nickname from the famous mountain: Benbulben or Beann Ghulban.]

A few days later, the problem was the name of a cave in Keshcorran Hill. A story about it was gradually pieced together:

71 A pagan god whose idol – a pillar stone inside a stone circle – is supposed to have been destroyed by St Patrick on the plain of Magh Sleacht, somewhere in County Cavan. 72 S. Ó Súilleabháin *A Handbook of Irish Folklore* 271: 'There are several lakes in Ireland whose origin is traditionally ascribed to some incident [like] forgetting to close a well ...'.

[Boyle, 12 Sept., from P. O'Keefe] The mother of Cormac mhac Airt, as she was passing in this neighbourhood was seized with her labour, and obliged to rest and give him [Cormac] birth, in the townland of Cloonagh at a well which is yet pointed out. She after parturition being weak and faint, a wolf snatched away the child and brought him to the cave called from his name Umhaigh Cormaic where she suckled him till he was about 7 years of age. He was then taken and adopted by a man in the neighbourhood after which I have not as yet been able to learn what became of him. [He became the famous king with the Cup of Truth] Some call him Cormac Carty; some also say that his mother was a king's daughter... The people told me they used to laugh at these stories looking on them as 'Fairy tales' ... Since I wrote the foregoing, I got a better version of the story of Cormac Mc Art, from Mr Conolly of Templeavanny...

The onomastics of other mountains in South Sligo caused some perplexity:

[Dublin, 21 Great Charles Street – the central office, in Petrie's house; a letter from O'Donovan to O'Conor dated 14 September] From Bellasadare you will have a view of the celebrated mountain Slieve Gamh [Ox Mountains]. Do you find any legend in the country accounting for its name? ... Is there any tradition now existing in the country about this wonderful well of Sliabh Gamh? ... You will, therefore, have to inquire for it in various parishes lying around the mountain.

The inquiry concerning the well illustrates the way field work was conducted, and what was finally uncovered by the Ordnance Survey employee offers a glimpse of the proliferation of legends. One started with four manuscript sources. There was a medieval poem which accounted for the name of Sliabh Gamh:

> Gam was the gillie of famous Eremon
> from whom bright Sliab Gam is called:
> from Gam indeed, without deceit or violence,
> comes the name of the mountain in the North.

> The gillie met with a strange death,
> Eremon's gillie, as I believe;
> he disputed violently with the [...]
> an offence against piety was the deed that was done there.

> On the edge of the spring on bright Sliab Gam
> his head was cut off in its beauty:
> the head was thrown a while into the well,
> that turned bitter for a time from that deed.

> One while in the day it was a salt stream grey and bitter
> another while it was pure water,
> so that it is a wonder in Erin,
> the tarnished spring of Sliam Gam.[73]

73 Edward Gwynn *The Metrical Dindshenchas* I. 12-13.

In some copies of the chronicle supposedly compiled by the Welsh monk Nennius in the early ninth century, a list of the 'Wonders of Ireland' follows a section on those of Britain and the Isle of Man. The seventh wonder of Ireland is 'A well of sweet water in the side of the Corann: the property of that well is that it fills and ebbs like the sea, though it is is far from the sea'.[74] In Giraldus Cambrensis' *Topographia Hiberniae* (twelfth century), it was still one of the Mirabilia Hiberniae: 'There is a well of sweet water in Connacht on the top of a high mountain and some distance from the sea, which in any one day ebbs and overflows three times, imitating the ebbing and flowing of the sea'.[75] The well is the fourth wonder in Roderic O'Flaherty's *Ogygia; or a Chronological Account of Irish Events*, written in Latin in 1685 and translated in 1793 by James Hely:

> In Sligo's district on Mount Gam's high side,
> A fountain lies, not washed by ocean's tide;
> Each circling day it different waters brings,
> The fresh, the salt, from it alternate springs.[76]

Another legend concerns St Patrick and explains why the well became a place of pilgrimage and 'pattern' (celebration of a patron saint's day). This version seems to have fared better in oral tradition, but there were hundreds or perhaps thousands of 'holy wells' in Ireland. Where was this one to be found? T. O'Conor, who tried to elucidate this point for the Ordnance Survey campaign, had trouble locating the right spot:

[Skreen, 23 September, O'Conor to O'Donovan] I am getting no information as to Sliabh Gamh, or even the locality of its enchanted wells, though my enquiry is incessant.

Finally he thought he had identified the 'wonder':

[Ballina, 4 October] I have not written one word respecting Sliabh Gham or its wonderful and miraculous well, till I see plainly after having traversed every part of the county on both sides and both ends of it, I have fully satisfied myself the people know no more about either ... There is no well on or near Sliabh Gamh, that I could hear of, which is changed as to its waters in the course of the day, excepting one which springing from between three large flags lies on the S.E. side of (near the summit) a little hill called Tullachan in the townland of the same name in the parish of Bellasodare. This Tullachan is a part of Sliabh Gham ... The well is generally called Tullachan well, Tobar a Tullachain. It has been dedicated to St Patrick and is frequented by persons performing stations at it. The tradition of it with the people is that St Patrick, when expelling the Daemons from the Rick (Cruach Padraic in the County of Mayo), he pursued one called Caorthanach (who according to some was the Devil's mother). This Daemon was polluting the waters all the ways to Tullachan, where St Patrick was seized with great

74 *Lebor Bretnach. The Irish Version of Historia Brittonum* ed. and tr. A.G. von Hamel (1932). **75** Op. cit. 62. **76** Op. cit. 2. 175.

thirst. He prayed to obtain a drink for himself and this fountain sprung up on the side of the little hill, which has been ever since frequented, and at which many were cured of several diseases. The saying is constantly afloat among the people that it comes and goes with the tide, it is never said that its waters become salt water, and though the saying is so prevalent yet every one denies it to have happened, it is said, no one ever saw it having either more or less water in it, than the quantity which is seen at every part of the day and night, whenever it be visited. [As for the alternating bitterness and sweetness mentioned in the old rhyme] it would take at least a whole day to ascertain whether the well of which I have spoken have any such property or not. It ought to be appointed in the moderate season for it is very cold to remain a day, or even an hour, on Tullachan hill.

O'Conor may not have been a stoic, but he had found the place. Half-a-century later, legends were still alive there, as a local archdaecon observed:

Pilgrimages or pious visits to the well have ceased, though traditions of the natural and supernatural prodigies that are said to have taken place in connection with it are still rife in the neighbourhood. The grown-up inhabitants of the district heard from their fathers that the well ebbs and fills with the tide, and that cures of all kinds were wrought on those who prayed around it; but, notwithstanding this, it is hard at present to meet anyone so credulous as to believe either in its tidal or healing properties. The qualities ascribed to the well do not, however, come altogether from imagination or invention; for there is something peculiar to it which gave occasion to the idea of its following the movements of the sea. There is no doubt that the water in it sometimes rises and subsides in a very remarkable manner ... Two trouts are said to have haunted the well, and, of course, to have been enchanted like the well itself. They are no longer visible, at least to ordinary eyes, but there are trustworthy persons who assure you that they themselves saw these 'odd fish' some time ago. How they came there it is not easy to say, though we are hardly bound to believe, with several simple-minded persons, that they have been in the well from the beginning of time. In proof of their enchantment a story is current to the effect, that though they were captured, killed, broiled, and eaten by some profane people of the neighbourhood, they were seen in their old *habitat* immediately after as lively as ever, and as 'wholesome as trout' proverbially are.[77]

In the late 1930s, pilgrims were still praying round the well at the festival of Lughnasa or 'Garland Sunday' (around the first of August), and children were still repeating legends concerning the place.[78] While searching for the wonderful well, O'Conor also found a story accounting for the name of the mountain chain:

[Ballina, 4 October, O'Conor to O'Donovan] The legend [of Sliabh Ghamh] among the

77 T. O'Rorke *History, Antiquities and Present State of the Parishes of Ballysodare and Kilvarnet in the County of Sligo.* 228-9. W.G. Wood-Martin also described the well in the 1880s: *History of Sligo, County and Town* I. 111-12. Marvellous trouts were said to haunt many other holy wells; see Eleanor Hull *Folklore of the British Isles* 112-13. **78** Máire Mac Neill *The Festival of Lughnasa* 117.

people runs thus: There was an ox of a monstrous size on Sliabh Ghamh, which lived to a great number of years. In a battle which took place on this mountain, and in which Flann fell by Fir-na-inse, this monstrous ox was killed by Cuaich, a hero in Tireragh ... It happened afterwards that Cuaich went to a country forge to get his sword whetted. The smith agreed to do the job on condition that Cuaich should tell him how Flann fell by the hand of Fir-na-hinse. Cuaich commenced the story and continued it as far as where he said that he concealed himself in the ox's horn from the violence of Rahan [Rohan, the owner of the ox], when he was interrupted by a man who was hidden behind the smith's bellows, saying if he was there at the time he would not call him Cuaich chonnacht but Cuaich na-adhairce (because he was concealed in the horn). The story ceased here, and it was never since ascertained how Flann and Fir-na-h-inse parted. From this ox in Irgh Damh it is thought Sliabh Gham – quasi Sliabh Dhamh i.e. *Mons bovis*, took its name.

This appears to be a rather confused account of a tale, an Irish oikotype of AT Type 1376A 'Storyteller Interrupted by Woman', involving Cú Chulainn or Fionn, of which more will be said in Chapter 12. Did O'Conor meet a bad storyteller, or did he fail to understand a good one?

In 1837, O'Donovan worked in Longford, Roscommon, Westmeath and Kildare – where he noted [3 December]: 'The people are entirely anglicized and have lost all their ancient traditions. I long to get to Connaught again as those of my own province [Leinster] are not only exceedingly ignorant on the subject of my inquiry, but also boorish and unobliging.' In 1838, the surveyors were in County Mayo and County Galway. Besides ascertaining names and locating famous sites they still occasionally had an ear for what might be vestiges of ancient myths:

[Westport, 29 June] I have heard all the versions of the story about Domhnall Dualbhuide and his wife Muinchinn or Munchaoin, the daughter of Maonghal, and think that Domhnall was no other than Damon the father of Ferdia the hero of Tain bo Cuailgne. All the Shanachies agree that Domhnall was slain by Fergus Mac Roigh King of Ulster. [Dónall Dualbhuí was Ailill Fionn, king of the Gamhanra sept in what is now County Mayo; he beheaded a smith who had refused him the loan of a boat. Muinchinn was 'soft-haired' Fliodhais, a goddess or fairy-lady who later became the wife of Fearghus mac Róich, bringing as dowry a herd whose most wondered beast was a cow called Maol – 'the hornless one'.][79]

Different layers of narrative tradition coexisted; it was possible to hear, successively, echoes of one of the supposedly ancient 'Three Sorrows of Storytelling', legends of saints, and fairy lore:

[Binghamstown, 5 June] A romance still repeated here [Inis Gluair] states that the chil-

79 D. Ó hÓgáin *Myth, Legend & Romance* 231-2: 'Because of its association with the area, versions of the story have been popular in the folklore of North-West Mayo in recent centuries.'

dren of Lir were transformed into the shapes of swans by the incantations of their stepmother ...

[Westport, 17 July] From a legend current among the aborigenes of this parish
[Burrishoole] it would appear that Saint Marcan was its original patron saint ... The
people still firmly believe in the fairies here.

Between Lough Mask and Lough Corrib, O'Donovan entered a region filled
with megalithic monuments and designated as the site of *Cath Maige Tuired
Cunga* (the first Battle of Moytura), where the Tuatha Dé Danann defeated the
Fir Bolg:

[Ballinrobe, 31 July] According to the present tradition in the country this battle was
fought at Nymph's field in the parish of Cong ... There is no one now living who could
describe the manner in which it was fought, nor name the monuments raised over the
fallen chiefs; but it is asserted that the grandfathers of the present generation were accustomed to recite the story of the battle of Moy-Turg at their fire sides, and to astonish
the rising generation by descriptions of the valour of Balor [in another battle...], and the
dreadful property of his eye, by which he metamophosed a line of warriors drawn up in
a circle into stones, where they remain to this day.

The informants seemed to take a greater interest in relatively more recent
events. Thus the 'minstrel' whose life-story had been published by Walker (see
p. 92) had become a kind of legend around Tuam – and a 'bard':

[Tuam, 13 August] We have no historical authority to prove when or by whom this
castle of Dunmore was erected, but the tradition is vivid, and I think true. It has been
preserved by Donnell Treacy who lives at the old castle from the lips of the poet Cormac
O'Comon ... who lived to the age of 110, and who was the living Fintan [see p. 20] of
the history of Connaught in his time.

[5 September] All the old people here assert that Cormac O'Comon was the last
Bard of Connaught, and that his likeness and poems have been published – I never heard
a word about him before. Has Mr Petrie ever heard of his poems? Old Donnell Treacy,
who lives at the Castle of Dunmore, says that he saw him about 50 years ago, and that
he was then more than one hundred years old. He was a blind man gifted with an extensive and tenacious memory.

More than a century and a half after Roderic O'Flaherty (see p. 58),
O'Donovan also heard what had become of the story of Murrough O'Ley's visit
to a fabulous island:

[Galway, 3 August 1839] ... This story is still told. Some few generations ago the crew
of a fishing boat passing an island which they did not know, landed thereon to refresh
themselves. They had no sooner landed than a man appeared and told them they had no
business there, as the island was enchanted. They therefore immediately returned to their
boat, but as they were going away the islander gave one of them a book with directions
not to look into it for seven years. He complied with this request, and when he opened

and read the book, he was able to practise surgery and physic with great success. This man's name was Lee, and the book got from the enchanted man in O'Brazil or New Aran, remained as an heirloom with his descendants until some 20 months since, when it was purchased by a bookseller in Dublin ... The truth seems to have been this, that Lee got his book from some of his relatives who were hereditary physicians, and turning it in his head to turn quack, forged the story.[80]

The reputation of Roderic O'Flaherty himself had been handed down by word of mouth: [Galway, 27 August] 'Tradition calls him Ruaidhri Mac Aodha, and states that he was a great shanaghie and scholar.' O'Donovan also heard the legend of *Bóthar na Mias* (the road of the dishes), which had appeared in Keating's book and according to which a great bowl of food was carried by an angel from King Guaire's dwelling to the hermitage of St Colmán, in the Burren:

[Gort, 10 November] The story told above is still vividly remembered in the country, and the road of the dishes shown in a mountain valley in the townland of Sliabh-carran, parish of Carran and barony of Burren in the Co. of Clare. The people imagine that they see the impressions of the hooves of horses in, and soup and wine spilt (congealed) on the stones! Tradition is positive in asserting that the castle of Dun Guaire near Kinvarra is the house in which King Guaire lived, when he followed the dishes.

Eugene O'Curry joined in to explore his native County Clare. From Ennistymon, on 21 October, he wrote that he had heard 'many wild legends in this district about the lake and family of Inchiquin ... Tradition has it here that Connor O'Quin [Earl] of Inchiquin had one day observed a beautiful lady on the southern brink of the lake ... ' The earl fell in love with her and she became his wife; but she was a fairy and imposed a condition of discretion, which he broke; she then vanished into the lake. The Inchiquin lake-lady story-type, which bears an affinity with tales from other lands (the Mélusine theme), has often been recorded from oral tradition and rendered in nineteenth-century literary and popular texts.[81] In the same letter can be found a version of the story of the one-legged smith Lon mac Liomhtha and his magic cow Glas Ghoibhneann (the 'grey-green' wonderful milker, whose hoofprints are preserved in the rocks of Teeskagh): ' [It was] very accurately taken down by Mr O'Donovan from the lips of the most illustrious seanchaidhe of the Kinel Owen now living, i.e. John Reagh O'Cahane, tailor of Corofin.'[82] Examples of Fianna lore were heard in

80 The story of 'An Dochtáir Ó Laoi agus Beag-Arainn' was still recorded in 1938 at Carna (*Éamon a Búrc Scéalta* 288-92). Though precisely localized in these versions, it is founded on an international motif F379.2.1 'Book (medical) brought back from otherworld'. 81 J. Kavanagh, 'The Melusine Legend in Irish Folk Tradition', *Sinsear* 8 (1995) 71-82 and B. Almqvist 'The Melusine Legend in the Context of Irish Folk Tradition', *Béaloideas* 67 (1999) 13-69. 82 According to T.J. Westropp's 'The Cow Legend of Corofin, Co. Clare' (*Journal of the Royal Society of Antiquaries of Ireland* 95 (1895) 227), it 'coincides with the shorter form of the legend still told at Tullyconane'.

County Clare during that campaign, including a version of *Feis Tighe Chonain* (see p. 23):

[Milton Malbay, 25 October] ... [we saw] a remarkable (conspicuous) mountain called Ceann-Sleibhe, i.e. the Head of the Mountain, and they have a tradition here that this head of the mountain was the scene of a romantic finian tale called Feis-tighe-Chonain-Chinn-tSleibhe.

But our circuit peters out here: though the Ordnance Survey continued for some time, there are fewer and fewer references to storytelling in the letters written after 1839. It had proved impossible to fulfil the programme set out in the original instructions; already in 1837 (Boyle, 27 July), O'Donovan had commented:

I have a letter from M. Petrie complaining that I am becoming a dry topographer. I agree with him but I do not understand how he conceives that I could do more than I am doing; all my time is consumed looking for townlands, lochans, and bits and noses of townlands to ascertain their correct names; this is what I conceive I am employed to do and nothing else. I don't look on the letters I write as any part of my business.

By then, the founding of the whole venture was becoming uncertain. The first of the 'memoirs' originally intended to complete the maps of the counties with various data had been published in 1835, concerning one parish only. As the authorities found it too costly, the project was drastically cut down and finally terminated in 1842.

We may now form an overview of the enterprise. In principle, the method combining the study of manuscript sources concerning the past with the search for present physical evidence and oral testimony in the field was faultless; but how was it applied and what does the material thus brought together contribute to our knowledge of 'Irish traditional storytelling' in the late 1830s? The quotations above illustrate the documentary value, as well as the limitations of, the Ordnance Survey Letters, regarding a subject central to this book but only marginal to the topographical project. We can prize information taken directly on the spot and not elaborated for publication: snapshots, at certain moments, of a complex and changing reality. The coexistence of oral transmission and manuscripts in popular hands is confirmed. We catch glimpses of inadequate informants, but also of people who were conscious of the importance of what they were remembering, be it particular genealogy or collective history seen from below. As in *Acallam na Senórach*, but without the fictitious frame, the land appears to be teeming with stories – but more in certain regions than in others.

As far as the study of oral narration is concerned, the incompleteness of the inquiry is obvious. It can be explained by the research design itself: since there was little time to cover wide areas,whatever did not directly concern the origin of place-names and legends associated with visible monuments remained on the periphery of the directing plan, and had to be sacrificed. The collectors had the impression that native knowledge about the past thrived more in some Irish-speaking districts, but as they were always on the move mere chance could put them in touch with the most eloquent keepers of tradition in one place and prevent their meeting such people in another. Nor did they build lasting and fruitful relations with informants.

Yet they might perceive the problems caused to local communities by a demographic explosion:

[Cavan, 21 May 1836 – concerning Glangevlin, which was another place associated with the marvellous 'Grey Cow of Goibhniu'] I find it chronicled by tradition that this immortal Glen derived its name from the famous Glas Gaibhlen... What caused her to forsake the Glen is no longer remembered by tradition, because the people being now too numerous, must be always at the loy, and cannot spare time to be rehearsing old stories, which, to a people now possessed of no ordinary quantity of cunning and sagacity, appear too silly and worthy only of the folly of their grandfathers, who having little or no rent to pay, spent a great part of their time idle, talking of the wonders of the golden age, when one cow afforded as much curds as would feed a triocha cheud [*triocha céad*: a barony], and when Saints were wont with astonishing success to revive bodies a long time mouldered, and to make stones swim.

No contemporary 'bard' was seen: none remained. No doubt there must have been masters of the complex wonder tales, but the surveyors do not refer to them either – it was not in their brief. The pertinent oral material would rather be 'legends' (for discussion of this concept, see Chapter 13), and the people to be consulted were regularly called (with protean spelling) 'the most illustrious seanchaidhe', 'old seanchies', 'old seanachies', 'some old Shanaghie', 'the best Seanachie or Historian', 'entertaining old shenachies' ... Walker had defined the term as used in the past: 'The Seanchaidhe were antiquaries, genealogists and historians. They recorded remarkable events, and preserved the genealogies of their patrons in a kind of unpoetical stanza. Each province, prince and chief, had a Seanacha'.[83] In the 1830s, *seanchaithe* were non-professional men particularly well informed about the local past. They were expected to be *old*; this in itself does not necessarily mean that storytelling was on the verge of death, as it is generally an activity associated with age, i.e. with greater, accumulated knowledge and a diminished capacity for other activities – but in the late 1830s our surveyors might have had the impression of walking through ruins: fragments of an older oral culture as well as of ancient stone monuments.

What they were trying to obtain from informants was 'tradition' (i.e. a certain kind of inherited knowledge) or the product of 'tradition' (i.e. the mode of

83 *Historical Remains of the Irish Bards* 1. 18.

transmission, or of storage). The term keeps appearing in the letters: 'the tradition among the old inhabitants', 'there is a tradition among the people', 'the story here preserved by tradition', 'still remembered traditionally by the people', 'according to present tradition', 'tradition is positive in asserting that ... ' Another formula reveals mixed feeling: 'if oral tradition can at all be depended upon ... ' The directors of the programme tended to assess the information received from the 'aborigines' according to whether it tallied with what had been found in old manuscripts. It soon appeared that only limited trust could be placed in popular oral sources:

[Granard, 9 May 1837)] These legends are in themselves of *no value*, but they illustrate, in a striking manner, the credulous simplicity of the people among whom they originated...

[Kells, 14 July 1836, O'Donovan] The legend connected with these crosses is laughable, but perhaps not altogether unworthy of notice as affording an example of the extreme simplicity of the minds of the people by whom it has been handed down.

According to the version referred to in the second quotation, Colum Cille had stolen crosses from St Ciarán of Cluain; more often, in the folklore of County Meath, it is Ciarán who took a cross from a church at Kells which belonged to Colum Cille and the latter tried to recover it, but it was broken on the way back:[84] legends were not only simplistic – they contradicted each other. Oral tradition did not seem to go very far back, and was being replaced by written sources:

[Boyle, 27 July 1838] I have made every inquiry for traditions connected with the monuments [Petrie] alludes to, and have found that there is not the faintest trace of a tradition in existence relative to a single fort, *rath*, *caisiol*, or *cathair* except that they were built by the Danes. Anything else the natives know about them had been acquired by reading. I could at once distinguish between a story preserved by pure oral tradition and one manufactured from 'an oulde histhory'. Several stories have been told me about St Patrick, Maeve of Croghan &c, but I have learned upon inquiry that they were not preserved by oral tradition, but read out of Keating, and Lynch's life of St Patrick. The only traditions connected with Cromlechs now, and perhaps for the last thousand years, is that they are giants' graves, or the Beds of Dermod and Grania. Not a word more!

Before he grew weary of travelling in difficult conditions, O'Donovan was already disillusioned about the possibility of approaching Cú Chulainn or Fionn through an informant's memory:

[Maghera, 3 September 1834] The more I look into the traditions preserved among the peasantry to account for names of places, the less I think of their title to historical credit ... I must lay it down as a kind of postulate, if not axiom, that respectable written

84 D. Ó hÓgáin *Myth, Legend & Romance* 89.

authority is preferable to any oral tradition ... The next argument against oral tradition [after the human mind's love for the wonderful] is that no two persons will tell the same story alike. Its parts are omitted, distorted, ornamented, and augmented according to the creative powers of the fancy of the narrator; and the fact is that he remembers a few prominent features in each story and fills up the vacancies according to his own ideas of things.

A fine account of the 'folk process' – but at this stage and given his assigned task it was something O'Donovan had no time for. Were written texts always more reliable, though? And was oral testimony quite worthless? He was led to try and evaluate the kind of truth to be extracted from either source:

[Loughrea, 25 October 1838] No memory is tenacious enough to retain all the details of any occurrence nor the human mind sufficiently clear to understand the motives of others in every instance. A distinction, however, should be made between a lie and a falsehood. A rogue tells a lie, knowing it to be such, but a candid man may, from the want of true knowledge, commit to writing what was really false, but which he believed to be true. The early Irish monastic writers were of a mixed character, for they some-times committed to writing floating traditional stories, which they believed to be true, but at other times, they fabricated prophecies some centuries after the incidents had occurred.

As often in fieldwork, the difference in codes of values between observer and informant could at first be disorientating. The collaborator who had the most awkward relation to his informants in the first months of his work may have been O'Conor:

[Sligo, 17 September 1836] I wish I had time to state something respecting the way people in this country get on, striving to impose (not intentionally, but out of too much officiousness, and a desire to find out whatever is asked, to gratify the inquirer) on a person, external objects, as bearing the names enquired after, whilst there is always a far different name prevalent among the people for each, which they endeavour to metamor-phose for one, into as near as possible the name asked; for instance, they would feign that the doon, called by them Dun Aibhinn is Dun Feich, making it Dun Ee, and then making all allowances for the difference in pronunciation; another would make Dun Iarach into it saying that Iarach was wrong, and first even concealing the pronunciation Iarach till extracted from them unawares. If one of them was asked, did he ever hear it called by the name Dun Feich, he would finally answer, saying 'not a one o' me ever *hard* that name on it'. These few remarks may give an idea to a person well acquainted with such a class, of their diffidence and want of strength of mind to tell at once, whether they know such a name, or such a place, or not.

Other travellers and inquirers would repeatedly comment on an Irish tendency to try and guess what 'Your Honour' wished to hear, then say it. They also noted that questions were received with suspicion, and it was difficult to explain the nature of the investigation. What were the outsiders up to? Why did strangers interfere with place-names? Why did they ask questions, the answers to which they would then deem unorthodox or ludicrous? It might be better to equivocate. O'Conor was learning his job:

[Tubercurry, 1 October 1836] I know three things are necessary for a serious inquirer; firstly, a method to elicit some information, which can be acquired only by knowing the manners of the people, secondly to happen on persons calculated to give him information, thirdly time and place (i.e. good dry lodgings, without the noise of drinking people and smoke) to digest, compare and write out what he collects.

As for O'Donovan, he could also be lenient, even respectful, towards what he considered naive information. Compare the common attitude of contributors to the earlier Parochial Survey (see p. 96) with these statements:

[Kilcar, 20 October 1835 – after witnessing a pilgrimage at Glencolumbkille] What their forefathers thought, believed, said, and did a thousand years ago, they think, believe, and say at present. They are primitive beings who have but a few points of contact with the civilized world. [But this does not allow a collector to look at it with a superior smile:] We must listen with patience and respect to the tale of the peasant in the 19th century who declares with gravity and sincerity that one of his own acquaintances not many years ago was carried off body and soul by the fairies or demons of this coast for his having been guilty of the crime of bigamy. I stated in a respectful manner that the phenomenon might be accounted for by supposing that he might have slipt off the cliff and become the prey of a shark, but this would not account for it so satisfactorily as that he was carried off by the devil.

The ethnographic part of the Ordnance Survey project was not completed, but archaelogy and work on Irish manuscripts progressed. More attention was paid to historical and textual accuracy, and research in those fields could be integrated in institutions of higher learning. This evolution will be briefly outlined in the remainder of the chapter.

Several of those who had been employed by the Ordnance Survey followed individual careers, which more and more discarded old-style antiquarianism as well as the still dilettantish mood of what was beginning to be called folklore for the exacting standards of true scholarship. By 1820, Dublin-born George Petrie (1789-1866) had developed a passion for ancient Irish architecture and for native music; he travelled the country, painting or sketching landscapes and ruins, and collecting tunes. Here is a striking account of an encounter with Gaelic rural culture in County Clare, in 1821:

During the two or three hours which we spent examining and sketching some of these antiquities, we were attended by a crowd of the peasantry, who, with that ardent curiosity for which the lower orders in Ireland are so remarkable, patiently watched our proceedings ... I confess that at first I felt their presence a considerable annoyance; but a little conversation with them made me ashamed of having indulged such an unmanly prejudice, and gave me another proof, in addition to many I had already met with, of the superiority in natural politeness, feeling, and sense of this class of society in many parts of Ireland, to that immediately above them ... The patience and cheerfulness, which the Irish peasantry display under the severest sufferings, resulting from poverty, have been too often remarked on to need illustration now. Of these qualities, however, an example came under my observation just previous to our departure from Kilfenora, so striking and, at the same time, so characteristic of the national amusements in the remote parts of Ireland, that I feel little hesitation in trespassing on the reader's patience with a notice of it. [In a Roman Catholic chapel] a crowd of forty or fifty persons were assembled, whose attitudes and occupations seemed scarcely appropriate to a temple of religious worship. On an elevation in the centre of this assemblage, stood a wild-looking, but well-formed, and rather youthful figure, his hair black and long, his neck bare, and his dress ragged; but his enthusiastic and impassioned gestures indicated the presence of a spirit not usual in one thus attired, and which seemed to have fixed the attention of the surrounding group as if they were spell-bound. An expression of intense interest marked the faces of the eager and delighted listeners, and – should I be ashamed to confess it? – as I got within the circle, I too became charmed and motionless. The cravings of hunger, the uncertainty of finding a resting-place, the friend I kept waiting for me, all were forgotten, and my only uneasiness for the time arose from the fear that the cause of this enchantment should be interrupted. The reader will, perhaps, scarcely expect to be told the effect thus produced by a pathetic Irish tale, sung with a sweetness and expression actually bewildering ... My presence, for a few minutes, caused no interruption to their enjoyment. The singer was unconscious of my intrusion, his back being turned to me; and those who observed me made no stir lest it might disturb their entertainer. But the direction of their gaze towards the door drew by degrees the eyes of others in the same way, and the singer at length, observing the movement, turned his head suddenly round. In an instant the place became as silent as if it were empty.[85]

Petrie did not always paralyse native artists, judging from the mass of musical material he later collected. He was an important member of the Royal Irish Academy, wrote serious essays on Irish architecture and published periodicals which included much antiquarian material and tales, from which I shall quote in the next two chapters.

Among the scholars were also Irish Catholics and Gaelic speakers. 'Folklore' does not seem to have been among the major interests of John O'Donovan (1809-61), though he wrote on the subject at least once and gave his assessment of the value of oral tradition – in nineteenth-century positivistic terms; reporting legends of his native parish in County Kilkenny, he commented:

I trust that no one will suppose, from the style of the above legend [concerning Loch Cuillin, which would have been created when a youth, pulling a tuft of rushes, produced a deluge and the coming of an oll-phiast or huge serpent, later to be killed by an

85 Quoted in William Stokes *The Life and Labours in Art and Archaeology of George Petrie* 44-6.

O'Donovan] that I think slightingly of our national traditional lore. Assuredly I do not, else why this paper? It has usurped too many of my nights and days, it has been the object and the solace of too great a portion of my by-gone years to meet with disrespect from me. But I respect it as a great influence that *has been*, and no longer is, or can be. It fed the poetical flame within the people's mind, and was the parent of true poetry in the more cultivated: it nourished the latent, instinctive aspirations of the Irish race, gave them aliment, and directed their movement, and rescued their ancestors from the dominion of brutish ignorance; stirred them up with insatiable thirst for true knowledge, which when established on a right basis, will raise this ancient and imaginative people to a truly noble standard among the civilized nations of modern Europe; but its office has been fulfilled; it is no longer necessary to the exigencies of modern society, with which the Irish race must either amalgamate or perish. The only interest it can have is a historical and a poetical one, and most men will acknowledge that nothing can be more interesting to us, in this point of view, than the progress of our ancestors, from rude primeval simplicity, to true civilization and positive science. I myself have lived long enough to experience the decay of the old traditions, and the introduction of something like true science among the natives of the County of Kilkenny ... Our *written* legends are sufficiently preserved, and they require only translation and illustration; but our oral legends are fast disappearing, and it has become our duty to preserve them as well as we can, while they still glimmer among the few old men who survive their contemporaries of the last century.[86]

By then, however, O'Donovan was devoting all his energies to the study of written material. In his edition of the *Annals* of the Four Masters, in 1856, he contrasted written sources, considered relatively more creditable, with an oral one he had collected on Tory Island, concerning the Fomorian Balor of the Evil Eye:

It is a curious specimen of the manner in which tradition accounts for the names of places, and remembers the names of historical characters. This story is evidently founded on facts; but from its having floated on the tide of tradition for, perhaps, three thousand years, names have been confounded, and facts much distorted.[87]

He co-founded the Irish Archaeological Society, and later became Professor of Celtic at Queen's College Belfast.

O'Donovan's brother-in-law Eugene O'Curry (1796-1862) may have been moved by deeper feelings towards oral tradition, having been more intimately linked with common people in his childhood:

It was not until my father's death [in 1825] that I fully awoke to the passion of getting these old fragments of history. I knew that he was a link between our day and a time when everything was broken, scattered and hidden; and when I called to mind all the knowledge I knew him to possess of every ruin, every old manuscript, every old legend

86 'On the Traditions of the County of Kilkenny', *Transactions of the Kilkenny Archaeological Society* 1 (1849-51) 368-9, 372. **87** *Annals of the Kingdom of Ireland* 1. 18-21.

and tradition of Thomond, I was suddenly filled with consternation to think it was all gone for ever, and no record of it.[88]

In his early years near Carrigaholt, in South West Clare, he had heard his own father and friends sing lays, and he referred to the experience in one of his later books:

I have heard my father sing these Ossianic poems, and remember distinctly the air and the manner of their singing; and I have heard that there was, about the time that I was born, and of course beyond my recollection, a man named Anthony O'Brien, a school-master, who spent much of his time in my father's house, and who was the best singer of Oisin's poems that his contemporaries had ever heard. He had a rich and powerful voice, and often on a calm summer day, he used to go with a party into a boat in the Lower Shannon, at my native place, where the river is eight miles wide, and having rowed to the middle of the river, they used to lie on their oars there to uncork their whiskey jar and make themselves happy, on which occasions Anthony O'Brien was always prepared to sing his choicest pieces, among which were no greater favourites than Oisin's poems. So powerful was the singer's voice that it often reached the shores on either side of the boat in Clare and Kerry, and often called the labouring men and women from the neighbouring fields at both sides to the water's edge to enjoy the strains of such music (and such performance of it) as I fear is not often in these days to be heard even on the favoured banks of the soft flowing queen of Irish rivers.

I do not remember having heard any other poem sung to the air of these Ossianic pieces but one, and that one is a beautiful ancient hymn to the Blessed Virgin, some seven hundred or more years old. My father sang this hymn, and well too, almost every night, so that the words and the air have been impressed on my memory from the ear-liest dawn of life. [It was '*Stiuradh me dod mholadh ...* ' – 'Direct me to praise thee'.] The air of this hymn is not popular; I never heard it sung but by my own father. I know it myself very well, and I know several old poems that will sing to it, such as the above poems ascribed to Oisin.[89]

O'Curry had even practised storytelling in his youth, according to O'Donovan.[90] But when his work for the Ordnance Survey of Ireland stopped, O'Curry like O'Donovan focused on manuscripts: he catalogued and analysed what was in the library of the Royal Irish Academy and in the British Museum. In 1855 he became Professor of Irish History and Archaeology at the newly founded Catholic University in Dublin; his pioneer lectures which began to be

88 Quoted in S. Ó Duilearga 'Notes on the Oral Tradition of Thomond', *Journal of the Royal Society of Antiquaries of Ireland* 95(1965) 135. 89 *On the Manners and Customs of the Ancient Irish* 3. 392. He was a member of the council of the Society for the Preservation and Publication of the Melodies of Ireland which issued George Petrie's *Ancient Music of Ireland* in 1855, including some tunes he had contributed. The air in question must be the 'ancient hymn, also the melody of Ossian's poem or tale' given as item 1205 in *The Complete Collection of Irish Music* edited by C.V. Stanford from Petrie's manuscripts. 90 Michael Herity, 'Eugene O'Curry's Early Life: Details from an Unpublished Letter', *North Munster Antiquarian Journal* 9 (1962-3) 144.

published in 1860, laid the foundation of much of modern knowledge concerning early Ireland. He was capable of patriotic enthusiasm – 'if we judge the value and proportions of the original literature of our Gaedhlic ancestors, as we may fairly do, by what remains of it, we may be justly excused the indulgence of no small feeling of national pride'[91] – but distinguished primary sources from imaginative additions, and criticized the earlier 'bold attempts of such ignorant, unscrupulous fabricators of facts, as Ledwich, and Vallancey, to impose their audacious forgeries on our presumed ignorance of the written and existing records of our national history'.[92]

A clearer view of ancient culture was emerging, and texts in Irish were made available to scholars and amateurs. There were ephemeral specialized associations: in 1806 Theophilus O'Flanagan, who had assisted Charlotte Brooke, had founded a Gaelic Society 'for the investigation and revival of Ancient Irish Literature', and in its transactions in 1808 he published texts in verse and prose including 'The Fate of the Sons of Usnach' with the Deirdre story (see p. 97). Edward O'Reilly had published an *Irish-English Dictionary* in 1817, and in 1820 his *Chronological Account of nearly 400 Irish Writers* from early times to the mid-eighteenth century. In 1829 Thaddeus Connollan edited *An Duanaire*, a selection of Irish poems, and James Hardiman's *Irish Minstrelsy or Bardic Remains of Ireland* appeared in 1831. In 1853 an Ossianic Society was founded to publish a series of Fianna romances. At about the same time, an individual attempt, rather belonging to the tail end of the Macphersonian craze, was John Hawkins Simpson's *Poems of Oisin, Bard of Erin*, in 1857, which included both translations from manuscripts and material taken from oral tradition – the latter being offered with some hesitation:

My first intention was to publish a volume consisting entirely of songs of Oisin which have been taken down for me, in the Irish language, from the lips of old people in Mayo. As it is, I have only given a selection from them [nine pieces], which will be found under the head 'Mayo Mythology'; thinking that I should best set forth the justice of Ireland's claim to the old bard, by first giving translations [by James O'Sullivan] of some old manuscripts relating to the Fenii of Erin (the Dialogue between Oisin and St Patrick being one) which were in existence long before Macpherson's time: prefacing them by short tusheries of Deardra and of Conloch, in order that the reader might judge for himself how much Macpherson has despised ethnological correctness. And secondly, by giving, in a separate form and for the sake of contrast, literal translations [by John MacFaden] of some of the legendary poems of Mayo extant, for the songs of Oisin or Ossian still delight the peasant in the west and south-west of Ireland: for him there is no greater treat than to listen to tales about the ancient warriors of his native land, Fionn MacCumhall, Goll or Gaul son of Morni, and Osgur 'of the dire deeds': at mention of their names his eye lights up with an expression of ingled pride, fondness and sadness.[93]

---

91 *Lectures on the Manuscript Materials of Ancient Irish History.* **92** *On the Manners ... 3. 321.*
93 Op. cit. 10-11.

The development of comparative philology in German universities gave a proper foundation for the study of Celtic languages, which were definitely accepted as a branch of the Indo-European family when Franz Bopp published *Über die celtischen Sprachen vom Gesichtspunkt der vergleichenden Sprachforschung* (1838). In 1853, J.K. Zeuss's *Grammatica Celtica* described the system of early Irish and Welsh. John O'Donovan produced a grammar of modern Irish in 1845.

Starting with fanciful speculations about the verbal efficacy of ancient bards and with the melancholy fascination of vanished glories, we have then focused on particular reactions to these trends in Ireland: a patriotic burst of enthusiasm – and of indignation, and a new awareness of the finality of change inspiring the desire to rescue some relics of the past. But the search for present-day bards could be disappointing, as reality looked dull and shabby compared with fashionable fabrications; the exploration of ruined monuments which remained mysterious, along with bold dabbling in ancient texts, was more satisfying. There were some concerted efforts to get usable oral information about the past from contemporary informants, but not much interest in what was alive and changing – though the word 'tradition' was now often used. The observers generally felt different from what they were observing. Irish studies were beginning to gain honourable status, and gradually became a specialized pursuit using rigorous methods; but the tendency was still to consider as worthy of serious scholarship only what was remote in time and represented by manuscripts or monuments.

Apart from antiquarians and some scholars who temporarily left their books, however, other people were in the field, listening to what the contemporary lower classes had to tell. They had different expectations, either as mere tourists in search of oddity, amusing incidents and picturesque characters; or as folklorists who had developed a taste for strange beliefs, or for the mysteries surrounding the origin of stories surviving on the lips of simple people; or as nationalists seeing evidence of Ireland's special values; or as fiction writers interested in oral fabulators and local colour. The next three chapters will examine those different perspectives, mostly during the first half of the nineteenth century.

5

Travellers and talkative guides

All representations are influenced by circumstances of observation, including the time devoted to it and the social, cultural or temporal distance, as well as by the fictionalizing power of imagination. It is certainly true of images of storytellers filtered through the minds and moods of travellers. Within those bounds, what information about storytelling in Ireland can be derived from the reports of foreign visitors, or from Anglo-Irish residents' accounts of sporting trips or lengthy stays in parts of Ireland other than those in which they normally lived? How do meetings with story-telling natives fit into the conventions of a mostly sub-literary genre and its prevailing theme: an encounter with otherness and the astonishment provoked by difference?

Travel to look at the country and its inhabitants without ulterior motive developed late in Ireland. In the Golden Age of monasteries people went there to study or on a pilgrimage; at other times, to conquer and colonize. Towards the end of the twelfth century, the Anglo-Norman prelate Giraldus Cambrensis wrote for the English king and his son the first extensive description by an outsider of Ireland and its *gens barbara*. He evoked strange facts, some of which he knew would seem incredible.[1] He had been told bizarre anecdotes about places where one could not die, floating islands, milk-stealing hares, werewolves ... He accepted them because he thought that on the fringe of the world, where Ireland was supposed to be, nature might tolerate abnormality. What he actually saw was less exciting: Irish musician were worthy of praise, but otherwise the country was 'barren of good things' and its inhabitants 'cruel and bloodthirsty'. The main purpose of his book was to justify the Norman subjugation of 'a filthy people wallowing in vice'. Four centuries later, when Tudor or Stuart colonists described Ireland, their main concern was to explain why it was worth exploiting and how the more or less devilish natives should be kept at bay. Travelling out of sheer curiosity may have begun at the end of the seventeenth century, though it seems that John Dunton, for instance (see pp. 55-6), was also trying to escape from creditors and his mother-in-law, and to sell books – those aborigines who could not read he denounced as 'a generation of vermin'. At least he could be amused, and decided that people in the West were not so bad after all: their customs were intriguing rather than revolting. At the beginning of the

1 *Topographia Hibernica – The History and Topography of Ireland* (tr. J.J. O'Meara) 56.

eighteenth century, most Englishmen still did not care much for Ireland and remained largely uninformed about its supposedly uncouth inhabitants; Swift caricatured this ignorance: 'As to Ireland, [the English] know little more than they do of Mexico; further than that it is a country subject to the King of England, full of Boggs inhabited by wild Irish Papists, who are kept in awe by mercenary troops sent from thence: and their general opinion is, that it were better for England if this whole island were sunk into the sea'.[2] He also noted that 'no strangers from other countries make this a part of their travels, where they can expect to see nothing but scenes of misery and desolation'.[3]

Many English people travelled abroad for recreation or instruction, but chose other parts of Europe where cities and monuments were considered worth visiting. From the middle of the century, however, some began to value the kind of experience that a trip to Ireland made possible. By then, pleasure travel in Britain itself was developing, as distinct from the Grand Tour of continental Europe and more adventurous explorations; travel in distant lands remained most prestigious, but wandering in Britain also became fashionable, and an account of it might be written. At least a hundred 'tours' of Scotland, the Lake District or Wales were published in the last three decades of the eighteenth century, and the trend was extended to Ireland as the country seemed less forbidding than it used to be and access became easier: by the middle of the eighteenth century, crossing the Irish sea was less hazardous and from the third decade of the nineteenth steamers would make it more rapid and regular; by 1800, the main roads of Ireland were considered as good as those of Britain, there were canals, and a regular stage coach service soon operated, to be supplanted by railways which launched large-scale tourism.

New tastes helped to make Ireland more attractive: rough nature, formerly thought repulsive, could be appreciated, and the kind of scenery the country offered began to be valued. The awe-inspiring 'sublime', as distinguished from the harmonious 'beautiful', was found in external nature and might be evoked in art and literature too: according to Edmund Burke (who may have begun to develop the idea in Ireland), if the body felt in safety when viewing mountains, oceans and 'druidic' obscurity, the mind was filled with a 'delightful horror' which suspended rational activity. If this experience seemed too strong, one could cultivate a sense of the 'picturesque', which still favoured contrasts and mysterious charm in natural settings but was only tastefully irregular – a middle ground between the grand 'sublime' and the serenely 'beautiful'; the presence of ruins would show nature's way of dealing with man's handiwork, yet at the same time some evidence of human intervention eased the scene. The theatre manager William Rufus Chetwood wrote in 1746 what may have been the first foreign praise of the Irish landscape since Spenser, associating legends with settings:

2 Swift *Drapier's Letters, Prose Works* 10. 103. **3** 'A Short View of the State of Ireland', *Prose Works* 12. 9.

'We stood to please our eyes with the gentle winding stream of the Barren, which washes the base of a beautiful hill ... This is a very solitary retirement, surrounded with awful towering trees, and much noted for stories of apparitions, which add to the gloomy face of this solemn old pile ... We left this delightful place with some regret'.[4] In 1806, another traveller wrote about Killarney : 'In this western Tempe, the artist will find everything he can possibly wish: the *beautiful* in the Lower and Mucross Lakes; the *Sublime* in the Upper Lake; *Variety* in the river that connects the lakes, and the *Savage* in the mountains that form the Pass of Dunloe'.[5]

Painters and drawers catered for those tastes and travel books were often illustrated, thus visual models helped to shape the travellers' expectations. Particular kinds of scenes were favoured: the positive image of Ireland now consisted of glens, rocks, cliffs, twisted trees, winding streams, lakes, waterfalls and ruins, perhaps with a few figures in the landscape but preferably not in the foreground. Yet a situation involving people could also play on sentiments – which points to another fashionable trend: 'sensibility' (i.e. sensitivity) or susceptibility to tender feelings and an emotional consciousness, a reliance on feelings as guides to truth and conduct, and a readiness to feel compassion for the sorrows of others. The sentimentally inclined could find gratification, when the view of victims aroused satisfying tenderness combined with sadness: 'Amidst the unspeakable miseries of those half-fed wretches, they enjoy in a very exalted degree poetry and song. It would seem that Providence, to cheer them in the vale of calamity – their only inheritance – had given them the talent of soothing woe.'[6] But something should also be said about another possible attitude, which was not so new: varieties of comic approaches stretching from sympathetic laughter or the smile of comprehension to buffoonery or contemptuous snigger. It was possible to go to Ireland in quest of the amusing, the incongruous or the grotesque (i.e. bizarre and rather frightening).

In addition to such contrasting aesthetic experiences, the country seemed to become quieter: the natives were more manageable, and for fairly long periods between local outbreaks of violence the sense of insecurity once associated with Ireland diminished. Travel there also came to appear morally safer than the kind of experience to be expected on the continent: 'Would not a tour round the islands of Great Britain and Ireland furnish a Briton with more useful, proper and entertaining knowledge, than what is called the grand tour of Europe, which for one person it hath improved, hath been the destruction of thousands!'[7] At any rate, the French Revolution and the Napoleonic wars practically closed off the continent for some time, and an alternative was to go westwards. Later, Ireland would be one of the regions where the vanishing pre-industrial landscape could still be found.

4 *A Tour through Ireland, in Several Entertaining Letters* (1746) 207, 211, 240. 5 Richard Colt Hoare *Journal of a Tour in Ireland, A.D. 1806* (1807) 81. 6 Charles Topham Bowden *A Tour through Ireland in 1790* (1791) 165. 7 James Robertson, *Monthly Review* 37 (1767) 282, quoted

Different kinds of travellers went there, with various motives: that of a systematic inquiry, or a mere holiday without making a point of acquainting oneself with the history and customs of the country. Some went to hunt, shoot or fish; others pursued interests like archaeology, or sought to cultivate their sensibility in awe-inspiring or delightful scenery. Their descriptions could omit squalor, or focus on it. Observers with a social conscience found problems writ large: poverty, the land question, confrontational religious and political relations. They could arrive with a relatively open mind or with some axe to grind (like anti-Catholicism: a number of travel books were written by Protestant proselytizers). Somehow the country seemed to adapt itself to the interests, tastes and moods of its visitors. In the eighteenth and nineteenth centuries, the majority came from Britain; some had Irish connections.

For all these reasons, accounts of travels in Ireland began to proliferate, and were particularly numerous in the first half of the nineteenth century.[8] Such books were meant to prepare people for the journey, to accompany them, to revive memories after the experience, or to help stay-at-home readers to imagine an alien environment. They ranged from impersonal guidebooks giving information on routes, transport facilities and inns, to impressionistic accounts of exciting or drab personal experience; and from didactic and normative representations of appalling conditions and the prescription of remedies to smug accounts of the odd manners of people who lacked the good fortune of being English. Comedy recorded the quaintness of natives for the amusement of readers at home – but tourists themselves might be held up for ridicule. Any kind of description would involve the selection of certain details, and thus acquired a certain meaning. There was a choice of writing strategies: one could work on the reader's feelings by evoking impressive landscapes and dramatic or pathetic situations, or try to enrich his mind with facts or wise meditations. The traveller could make himself/herself the central figure in a series of adventures. The book could take the form of a series of letters, of a personal diary perhaps 'originally not intended for publication' (to affect such self-effacement was a common trick); or of an informative summary interspersed with scenes and reflections. In brief, it was not a genre but a mixed bag of elements from different genres. What differed from the reader's everyday life was likely to add interest and was therefore emphasized; yet the form itself was conventional enough, because strong rules or habits largely determined what was likely to be shown: the traveller found in books confirmation of what he had experienced, but what he had read also directed his attention during his journey,[9] and what was known of readers' expectations influenced the writing after his return. Tourism may thus

in C.L. Batten *Pleasurable Instruction* 94. 8 J. McVeagh's *Irish Travel Writing: A Bibliography* lists some two thousand titles since the twelfth century. 9 A. Hadfield, J. McVeagh *Strangers to that Land; British Descriptions of Ireland from the Reformation to the Famine* 16: travellers' accounts establish 'a framework and a set of concepts for later travellers, helping to make sense of what they observe'. Sheer plagiarism was not unheard of.

imply more recognition than discovery: you must find what you have been told
to look for, and respond to it in the prescribed way. Still, description was always
by a particular person (reflecting his/her values), and the various sub-genres of
travel description claim validity by constant reference to personal experience.
More or less casual observation through chance encounters, and then selection
by the writer, meant that much was left out. Apparent eccentricities were more
likely to get attention than what might appear normal, since normal behaviour
remained the privilege of the visitor or was simply not interesting. To depart
from fact for the sake of effect was a constant temptation, and some visitors may
have fantasized a great deal.

Even when they had come for landscapes and sports, travellers would organize any experience of theirs through a certain set of attitudes; they were likely
to notice ways of life alien to their own, and they judged what they saw according to the norms of their own society, from which deviation might appear outrageous, or puzzling, or ludicrous. They arrived with certain assumptions, prepared to shudder, marvel or laugh at the cultural otherness of Ireland before
returning to the normality of their own world. One of the basic ingredients of a
travel book was the encounter with natives, who embodied the oddities associated with stereotypes which writers and readers had accepted concerning the
region they were visiting, actually or by proxy. A native could be perceived and
represented by the foreign observer as more extraordinary than he actually was,
while differences amongst a population might become invisible: the 'we–they'
dichotomy led to distortions and could reduce an entire society to a few traits.
At all times, brief contacts were likely to be a source of misunderstandings and
hasty judgements, with rigid role-playing on both sides. Thus visitors who came
to Ireland from England were likely to look for the supposed distinctive features
of the Irish character, and generally maintained a condescending attitude, forti-
fying their conscience with the conviction that their own society was intrinsically
superior. They seldom scrupled to generalize about 'Irishness' as a disposition,
without really trying to understand it – indeed, it was rather expected to be irrational, unpredictable and incomprehensible, and the experience of native elu-
siveness and incongruity was part of the 'fun'. Sir Jonah Barrington, who had
spent his childhood and early youth in County Laois in the 1760s and 70s and
wrote a comic history of his own Anglo-Irish class, warned would-be foreign
travellers against simplifications concerning the natives (while propagating them
himself):

In travelling through Ireland, a stranger is very frequently puzzled by the singular ways,
and especially by the idiomatic equivocation, characteristic of every Irish peasant. Some
years back, more particularly, these men were certainly originals – quite unlike any other
people whatever. Many an hour of curious entertainment has been afforded me by their
eccentricities; yet, though always fond of prying into the remote sources of these national
peculiarities, I must frankly confess that, with all my pains, I never was able to develop

half of them, except by one sweeping observation, namely, that the brains and tongues of the Irish are somehow differently formed or furnished from those of other people.[10]

The natives were no longer the dangerous savages in current clichés of the sixteenth and seventeenth centuries, but could be seen as comically bellicose or lazy boors, or as both friendly and unreliable creatures, servile yet unstable, with a propensity for abrupt transitions from grief to joy and from indolence to violence, superstitious, and – what especially concerns us here – wonderfully talkative: 'It is always a source of pleasure to listen to the conversation of the lower Irish'.[11] To some extent, with changing socio-political circumstances there was an evolution of the received images of Ireland and of the people to be met with there: Anglo-Irish settlers once presented as the pillars of civilization could become worthless duelling and squandering drunken louts; the natives as seen from Britain, tended to become buffooning figures or irresponsible children rather than malevolent enemies, and were sometimes shown as long-suffering victims of an unfair system;[12] but one way or another they remained inferior. The description of an amusing playground, in a good many books written before the middle of the nineteenth century, later tended to be replaced by the pathetic account of shameful conditions; portraits of amusing storytellers are thus much more numerous in books written before the Great Famine of the late 1840s. Indeed, storytelling itself may have been paralysed for a time by the disaster, or the more committed writers found it too frivolous a subject to be mentioned in serious books – except when the telling concerned some dreadful personal experience: 'The dismal tales of famine and distress I had heard among the people through whom I travelled occurred to my mind and weighed down my spirit'.[13]

The fact remains that Irish storytellers, drawn from life or invented, were portrayed by travellers, and that tourism, as we shall see, may have had a certain impact on the practice of storytelling. The variety of travel books written in different ways and for different purposes makes some attempt at classification both necessary and open to criticism. First, I shall consider three kinds of foreign professional writers who dealt with Ireland in different ways; I shall continue with accounts, thematically arranged, of meeting with storytellers or information about storytelling by various other travellers. Then I shall focus on a special occupation which appeared with tourism: that of storytelling guide. The last section will turn to Anglo-Irish residents who, though they were better informed, could still be thrilled or appalled when journeying through, or temporarily taking up residence in, what resembled aboriginal reserves in western or south-western Ireland.

10 *Personal Sketches of His Own Times* (1827-32), quoted in *The Cabinet of Irish Literature* 2. 3. 11 John Carr *The Stranger in Ireland* (1806) 157. 12 J.P. Harrington *The English Traveller in Ireland* 16-22. 13 *The Irish Peasant: A Sociological Study*, an anonymous book published in 1892 and quoted in Harrington, op. cit. 315.

Some foreign writers, who were not tourists, combined first-hand observation with extensive statistical data and political comments; their purpose was to explain a situation and to propose remedies. Arthur Young, for instance, was a propagandist for progressive farming and an observer of social conditions, and had already published a great deal on these subjects when he embarked for Ireland in 1776. He travelled about the country, then for about two years was a land agent in County Cork. He found that Irish agriculture lagged behind that of England, and recommended improvements; he concentrated on economy and social practices, and on temperaments in so far as they were connected with those two fields. He could occasionally praise a sublime landscape, but soon focused on ways of putting it to efficient use; of Killarney, for instance, he said it was 'the wildest and most romantic country [he] had anywhere seen ... There is something magnificently wild in this stupendous scenery, formed to impress the mind with a certain species of terror' – then he recommended that something should be done to make tourism more profitable.[14] Criticizing absentee or lazy landlords, he praised those who adopted the new methods of farming and were prepared to change the country 'from licentious barbarity into civilized order'.[15] He produced one of the many generalizing portraits of the natives which stressed their eloquence:

The circumstances which struck me most in the common Irish were, vivacity and a great and eloquent volubility of speech; one would think they could take snuff and talk without tiring till doomsday. They are infinitely more cheerful and lively than anything we commonly see in England, having nothing of that incivility of sullen silence, with which so many enlightened Englishmen seem to wrap themselves up, as if retiring within their own importance. Lazy to an extent at *work*, but so spiritedly active at *play*, that at *hurling*, which is the cricket of savages, they show the greatest feats of agility. Their love of society is as remarkable as their curiosity is insatiable; and their hospitality to all comers, be their own poverty ever so pinching, has too much merit to be forgotten. Pleased to enjoyment with a joke, or witty repartee, they will repeat it with such expression that the laugh will be universal. Warm friends and revengeful enemies, they are inviolable in their secrecy, and inevitable in their resentment; with such a notion of honour, that neither threat nor reward would induce them to betray a secret or a person of a man, though an oppressor whose property they would plunder without ceremony. Hard drinkers and quarrelsome; great liars, but civil, submissive, and obedient ... Many strokes in their character are evidently to be ascribed to the extreme oppression under which they live. If they are as great thieves and liars as they are reported, it is certainly owing to this cause.[16]

But he was not interested in the stories the people might have told. Other analysts of the socio-economic situation of Ireland could similarly cast off the convention of the 'tour' account. Gustave de Beaumont, for instance, a French lib-

---

14 *Tour in Ireland with General Observations on the Present State of that Kingdom ... in the Years 1776, 1777 and 1778* 1. 348ff. **15** Ibid. 1. 463 **16** Ibid. 2. 146-7.

eral monarchist and friend of Alexis deTocqueville, knew that he had to go to Ireland to understand it;[17] he went there in 1835 and again in 1837, but recorded his observations in a treatise (of more than 700 pages), not in the form of a travel book. He devoted a whole chapter to 'the character of the Irishman', but approached storytelling only to discourse upon 'a general aversion to truth', which complicated the researcher's task and could be explained by long suffering under tyranny.[18] Tocqueville had accompanied de Beaumont in July and August 1835 to study the land question, the problems of the Poor Law, and the administration of justice. He interviewed British officials and Catholic priests, and his notes have survived. The poor are described as very hospitable and generous, but (according to the secretary of the Poor Law Commission) 'there is no other country where it is more difficult to get the truth out of a man' (Tocqueville noted that 'this has always been the vice of the unfortunate or slaves'). The population had not the slightest confidence in justice: 'The poor believe themselves to be somehow outside the law'. Conversation could be 'impassioned, superficial, light, often interrupted by jokes and witty remarks. I might have been in France. Nothing resembled England.'[19] Young, de Beaumont and Tocqueville show that a good grasp of Irish social realities could be gained without giving undue importance to storytelling – a sobering thought.

W.M. Thackeray represents another professional approach: the literary figure who may occasionally use travel as his subject. Writing for a living and still comparatively unknown after the relative success of a *Paris Sketch Book*, he secured a contract from a London publisher to produce a book on Ireland which had to be informative but only up to a point: he assumed the role of 'a humble writer of light literature whose aim it only was to look at the manners and the scenery of the country, and who [did] not venture to meddle with questions of more serious import'.[20] His method was impressionistic and humorous. Part of the comedy consisted in mocking the clichés of travel writing; he foregrounded the role of the writing traveller, lamenting the number of books that had already been published on the subject when he undertook his journey (in 1842): 'What remains for me to discover?'[21] The people he met would tell him they had guided – and sometimes deliberately misguided – his predecessors, whose books he ridiculed because of their tendency to hyperbolize: 'Fond legends are to be found in Irish books regarding places where you may see a round tower and a little old chapel, twelve feet square, where famous universities are once said to have stood, and which have accommodated myriads of students.'[22] He presented

17 *L'Irlande sociale, politique et religieuse* 1.10: 'Il faut donc absolument, pour juger l'Irlande, se transporter dans le pays même'. 18 Ibid.: 'Celui qui, dans ce pays, cherche le vrai avec le plus de zèle et de bonne foi, a bien de la peine à le saisir; tout le lui dispute et travaille à l'égarer; tout est menteur en Irlande, depuis le riche qui cache son égoïsme jusqu'à l'indigent qui exalte sa misère. Toutes les passions de classe, de secte, de parti, qui y sont brûlantes, sèment sous les pas du voyageurs mille éléments d'erreur.' 19 *Journeys to England and Ireland* ed. by J.P. Mayer, 119, 133, 153. 20 *The Irish Sketch Book* (1843) 368. 21 Ibid. 250. 22 Ibid. 8.

his own method by antiphrasis: 'As that romantic and beautiful country has been described many times in familiar terms, our only chance is to speak thereof in romantic and beautiful language, such as no other writer can possibly have employed.'[23] In fact, he insisted more often on the discomforts of the journey and the dullness of the landscape; when he was confronted with a beautiful sight he declared that it would be vain to try and render it in words – or described it in mock-sublime style. He had to live up to his growing reputation as a wit, but if he was amused by some things he was indignant at others, like degradation and poverty: 'the traveller is haunted by the face of the popular starvation. It is not the exception, it is the condition of the people. In this fairest and richest of countries, men are suffering and starving by millions.'[24] He had something to say on Irish storytelling and on contradictory stories about Ireland; moderately interested in, or amused by, popular literature, he bought chapbooks and retold part of their content in his own words, marking a preference for genuine folktales: 'So great is the superiority of the old stories over the new, in fancy, dramatic interest, and humour, that one can't help fancying Hibernia must have been a very superior country to Ireland.'[25] When he heard the stories aimed at tourists, he generally judged their quality very poor compared with the kind of literature he wanted his name to be associated with: '[At Glendalough] there are numerous legends, too, concerning St Kevin, and Fin MacCoul and the devil, and the deuce knows what. But these stories are, I am bound to say, abominably stupid and stale; and some guide ought to be seized upon and choked, and flung into the lake, by way of warning to the others to stop their interminable prate.'[26] At the end of his tour he had the impression that what he had heard and seen was so full of contradictions that Ireland remained a mystery. The ways people spoke and wrote about Ireland were an obstacle in the path of would-be scholars: 'To "have an opinion about Ireland" one must begin by getting the truth; and where is it to be had in the country? ... In the midst of all these truths, attested with "I give ye my sacred honour and word," which is the stranger to select?'[27]

Our third kind of writer is represented by the German Johann Georg Kohl who was in Ireland the same year as Thackeray: he may be described as a professional traveller. His many books on European countries were addressed to German readers, that is to say, in contrast to Young and Thackeray's audience, to people with no immediate interest in, or sense of collective responsibility for, the Irish situation. Of repute as a geographer, he was a gifted observer interested in everything and relatively unprejudiced. More than the writers mentioned so far, he was disposed to listen to and value stories: 'I am convinced that a diligent collector could find matter enough in Ireland for more than a thousand-and-one nights.'[28] There was a problem of language, though; even those storytellers who spoke English were not always easy to understand: 'My Kerryman

---

23 Ibid. 253-4. 24 Ibid. 83. 25 Ibid 189. 26 Ibid. 266. 27 Ibid. 368. 28 *Travels in Ireland* 93. (First published as *Reisen in Irland* Dresden and Leipzig, 1843)

was the son of a peasant, he was about thirty years of age, talkative, animated, and really imaginative, like all the lower orders of the Irish. He narrated to me a multitude of stories and traditions [*Sagen und Geschichten*], all of which unfortunately I did not understand, on account of his peculiar dialect.'[29] Nevertheless, Kohl made interesting observations. He was put in touch with what was thought to be the oldest kind of Irish narrative art, through an entertainment organized for him by a Catholic priest in Drogheda:

The first person who came forward was an Irish declaimer, a man from among the people – I know not whether a gardener, a carpenter, a plough-man, or a 'broken farmer' (the broken farmers very often turn story-tellers in Ireland), but I was told he knew a countless number of old Irish poems and songs. He came in and thus addressed me: 'Out of friendship for him (meaning the priest) I am come: he told me that there was a foreigner here, who wished to hear some of our old Irish poems, and I will gladly recite to him what I know.' 'I am much obliged to you,' said the priest; 'but if you were to recite all you know, we would be obliged to listen to you all night, and perhaps many other nights besides'. 'It is true our forefathers have handed down to us a great number of poems from generation to generation; and very beautiful ones they are too, sir, if you could only understand them. How beautiful is not the song of *Tober a Jollish* [*Tobar a t-Solais*], that is, of the glittering spring, which is but three miles distant from our town; or that of *Cuchullin*, the Irish champion, who went to Scotland. Shall I begin with the song of Cuchullin, your reverence?' 'Do, my son, and God bless thee!' The man began to declaim, and recited for a quarter of an hour without once stopping. I, of course, did not understand a single word of all his recitation, but my host was kind enough to relate the story to me afterwards. To understand, however, was not so much my object as to convince myself, by my own ears, that this old Ossianic poetry is still living and extant here in Ireland among the people. [Here the original German text is more detailed: the text was a version of the fight between Cú Chulainn and his son.] The reciter was, as I have said, a simple man, and his recitation was as simple, unadorned and undeclamatory as himself. Sometimes, however, when carried away by the beauty of the poetry and the ideas, he became animated, and even appeared much affected: he would then look at his hearers, as if he expected their sympathy and admiration for himself and his poem ... After this he recited a 'Song of the Fairy Mounds' ... This reciter told me that most of what he knew was very ancient and was chiefly Ossianic poetry, of which there was a great deal here in Drogheda among the people. I had already heard this, and I afterwards heard it repeated at other places in the north. The county of Donegal in particular was described to me as full of living Ossianic poetry.[30]

Impressed by the value simple people placed on education, Kohl saw that manuscripts were preserved in families 'as precious heir-looms'.[31] He learned it while sailing down the Shannon, and could refute the assertion that there was quasi-total illiteracy in Ireland, as well as the notion that oral and written modes of transmission were incompatible:

29 Ibid. 61. **30** Ibid. 317-19. **31** In *A New History of Ireland* 4. 391, Brian Ó Cuív notes that 'in all, nearly 4,000 Irish manuscripts written in the eighteenth and nineteenth centuries are

In the bow of the boat sat a Kerryman, reading an old manuscript, which was written in the Irish language, and in the Celtic character. The manuscript consisted of several small and large sheets stitched together, which, to judge from the various colours and antiquity of the paper, must have been united to each other at different periods. It was all, however, neatly and regularly written. Some, the man told me, he had added himself; some he had inherited from his father and grandfather; and some had, in all probability, been in the family long before them. I asked him what were its contents. 'They are', answered he, 'the most beautiful old Irish poems, histories of wonderful events, and stories and treatises of antiquity; for instance, the translation of a treatise by Aristotle on some subject of natural history!' ... I inquired if there were any others on board who had manuscripts with them; a man from the county of Clare opened his travelling chest, striped with blue paint, and from beneath night-shirts and boots drew out an old manuscript. I asked why they carried these writings about with them? They replied that they did not like to part from them, and they were fond of reading portions of them on their journey. I afterwards saw several such manuscripts in the hands of the lower classes.[32]

For this kind of writer, a popular love for stories and learning was worth illustrating; not only because it provided picturesque or amusing exoticism but also because it seemed to reveal an important feature of the people he was trying to understand.[33]

Other professional authors of 'tours of Ireland' have similarities with Kohl, and differences. Anna Maria and Samuel Carter Hall, for instance, were also active writers, but unlike him they had Anglo-Irish connections, and were not globetrotters. In collaboration they produced several books, the most successful being *Ireland, its Scenery, Characters, etc.* (three volumes, 1842-3). They did not want just to offer practical advice, nor would they be satisfied with mere impressionistic accounts, but – essentially for English prospective visitors – proposed 'guidance' which included information on history, economics (without being as precise as Young), and ways of life, as well as descriptions of scenery. They gave numerous 'Irish stories', most of them in reported speech but some as told by natives (probably with some adjustments). I shall often quote from their books, and as Mrs Hall also wrote fiction she will appear again in Chapter 7.

The run-of-the-mill travel books were produced by amateur scribblers who had made a tour for recreation or professional reasons and, when back home, decided to write about it. The result varies considerably in quality and nature, therefore defies classification, and would perhaps not justify a detailed analysis; but there were standard themes, the constant recurrence of which must be significant. Practically all the travellers were struck by the poverty of the peasants, the number of beggars, the smoky cabins (they could seldom enter them); but they

extant'. **32** Kohl, op. cit. 71. **33** On those three writers, see Constantia Maxwell *The Stranger in Ireland* Ch. 14 'Arthur Young', Ch. 23 'William Makepeace Thackeray', Ch. 22 'Johann Georg Kohl'.

also tended to find country people of all classes relatively merry and very hospitable. If a journey through Ireland consisted in looking for the unusual, it was also marked by familiar beacons: places one had to visit, and situations one had to experience, for instance hearing incredible stories told in a certain way, and noticing the natives' willingness to listen to what others said.

There could be communication problems, however. The tourist was advised to volunteer entertainment as a way of triggering off native performances: 'If the visitor can relate a lively tale, or play upon any instrument, all the family is in smiles, and the young will begin a merry dance, whilst the old will smoke after one another out of the same pipe, and entertain each other with stories.'[34] But such entertainment was seldom witnessed close up, and honest travellers had to acknowledge the limits of their observations. First, despite the much publicized loquacity of the natives, those one met could be tongue-tied – as Thackeray had observed in Connemara: 'In the various cabins I have entered, I have found talking a vain matter; the people are suspicious of the stranger within their wretched gates, and are shy, sly, and silent';[35] but in many cases the main obstacle was the Irish tongue. And even when he/she understood, the traveller had to admit the impossibility of doing justice to Irish oral storytelling in giving it written form: 'one ought to have an Irishman beside one to tell an Irish story to good effect. Wit is marvellously strengthened by gesture and tone of voice.'[36] Apart from the language barrier and the difficulty of putting oral expression on paper, there was another problem: the normal conditions of traditional storytelling were hardly compatible with the traveller's timetable; tourists who quickly passed over the surface of Irish life could hear and perhaps appreciate music or see dances, but were unlikely to attend and understand performances of the longer tales in their natural setting. There were perhaps exceptions; this, for instance, may actually have been observed: 'In the evenings [at Churchtown, Co. Cork] some neighbouring lads come in and join the family at their kitchen fire-side; then they begin to relate stories of which all are passionately fond, and this they will prolong to a late hour.'[37] It was possible to gather second-hand information about storytelling:

From our entertaining gentleman [at Ballycastle, Co. Antrim] I learned that during the winter it is a general custom for the neighbouring cottiers to assemble alternately at each other's cabins about the blazing hearth of wood procured from the bog, and preserved for such occasions. The females bring their spinning-wheels and stools, while children and men complete the semi-circle on the floor; the oldest patriarch then takes the lead in narration, and is succeeded by his grey-headed juniors in turn. The 'tale twice told' loses no tittle of its force, or interest, but is listened to by all with delight.[38]

34 John Carr *The Stranger in Ireland* (1806) 252. 35 *The Irish Sketch Book* 225. 36 Margaret Scott Gatty *The Old Folks from Home, or A Holiday in Ireland in 1861* 117. 37 J.B. Trotter *Walk through Ireland in the Years 1812, 1814 and 1817* (1819) 157. 38 J.C. Curwen *Observations on the State of Ireland ...* (1818) 1. 166-7.

Another traveller succeeded in attending such a gathering in Ulster, but did not appreciate what he heard:

> A part of the evening I was an undiscovered eye-witness, and about the whole of it I was an ear-witness of their merriment. Had I appeared, I should in all likelihood have put an end to it; for whether or not it be true that forwardness makes a part of the genuine Irish character, the Northern character, as far at least as my observations go, is rather designated by bashfulness, or even sheepishness, The first effect of the whisky was to unloose their tongues in story-telling; but on these I can bestow no praise. They resembled the worst half of old Flamborough's [in Goldsmith's *Vicar of Wakefield*], for they were very long and very dull, not only not about themselves but not about any order of things or beings that ever existed. They seemed all of Eastern origin, combined with the vulgar mythology of fairies, and presented the magic and enchantments of Arabian tales transfigured by village narration and degraded by rustic language and homely circumstances. After story-telling, they proceeded to song-singing, and here they were more successful, for some of them had good voices, and sang good songs. Yet of these not one was Irish in its words, tune, or associations.[39]

Travellers from Scotland who knew Gaelic were more likely to understand what went on among the natives. Thus the Rev. Daniel Dewar, in 1812, claimed that he was able 'to enter more fully into the views and prejudices of the Irish nation than the mere English traveller could possibly have done' – but, probably prompted by missionary zeal, he could not be the ideal witness either. He confirmed what others had said about native curiosity and – unfortunately without giving concrete examples – the importance of the storyteller in Irish communities:

There is no mark by which the Irishman (always recollecting that by this I mean the original race of the country) is more distinguished than inquisitiveness. He will walk miles with you to discover where you come from, where you are going, and what is your business; he will appear merry to make you frank, and perfectly untutored and simple with a design constantly in view. This disposition has been cherished by the recitations of sceullachs, a species of legendary tales that have been transmitted from time immemorial. Every one is in possession of some of these; and the recital of them is one of the most favourite pastimes. As there is not one in a thousand of these people who can read, and as their priests do not often condescend to deliver sermons, this may be considered as the principal source of their instruction. And, however extravagant some of these stories may be, they are not altogether useless even in this point of view; they refer the mind from the present to the past, and the future, they sharpen the intellect and furnish it with ideas; and they tend to excite and gratify a powerful curiosity. A people possessed of this disposition, though sunk in ignorance and superstition, will nevertheless rise; and though circumstances for a time may repress its ardent impulses, yet their situation cannot be considered as hopeless while that impulse remains. The tales of the bards and senachies produce a powerful influence on individual character. They begin to make their

39 John Gamble *Views of Society and Manners in the North of Ireland* (1819) 289.

impression at that period of life, when almost any impressions may be made, and, when once made, can scarcely ever be completely effaced. Besides, the influence which the tale exerts is the more permanent, since the young listeners are generally allied, either by kindred, or tribe, or nation, to the hero, of whose marvellous exploits, or tragic death, it is the history: all the warm and sympathetic affections of the tender mind are thus awakened, and dwell with infinite delight on the fond image which an astonished imagination has formed.[40]

It was from overheard exchanges between Irish travel companions that a foreigner was most likely to discover the native art of conversation; but, as Thackeray noted, it could be difficult to follow:

... in the midst of this wild tract, a fellow met us who was trudging the road with a fish-basket over his shoulder, and who stopped the coach, hailing two of the gentlemen in it by name, both of whom seemed to be much amused by his humour. He was a handsome rogue, a poacher, or salmon-taker, by profession, and presently poured out such a flood of oaths, and made such a monstrous display of grinning wit and blackguardism, as I have never heard equalled by the best Billingsgate practitioner, and as it would be most useless to describe. Blessings, jokes, and curses trolled off the rascal's lips with a volubility which caused his Irish audience to shout with laughter, but which were quite beyond a cockney. It was a humour so purely national as to be understood by none but natives, I should think.[41]

Other standard themes in accounts of travels in Ireland were peculiar 'traditional' activities of the people, and their amazing beliefs. The prevalence of odd customs was regularly mentioned, as well as the fact that the rather strange Irish peasants seemed to believe in the existence of a yet stranger supernatural world. The amazing rural Irish funeral usages were a subject of constant comment, and some description of them was almost a must in the early nineteenth-century travel accounts – though how often really the result of personal observation is hard to say. Some travellers completed the usual description of keening and drinking with references to storytelling: '[At Charleville, Co. Cork] the old people amuse themselves in smoking tobacco, drinking whiskey, and telling stories in the room with the corpse.'[42] Or: 'The conversation was carried on in an undervoice, and turned on death and judgment, and ghosts and apparitions: more stories were told of these latter than I can remember: I was forcibly struck with the look and tone of terror and affright with which they were told and listened to.'[43]

By directly conversing with certain people who could adapt their discourse

40 D. Dewar *Observations on the Character, Customs, and Superstitions of the Irish* (1812) 26-7. According to him, unlike what happened in Scotland the ancient literature transmitted orally would have deteriorated in Ireland, partly under the influence of Catholicism which promoted a taste for the marvellous. **41** *The Irish Sketch Book* 45-6. **42** Th. Campbell *A Philosophical Survey of the South of Ireland ...* (1777) 210. **43** John Gamble *Sketches of History, Politics and Manners, Taken in Dublin and the North of Ireland in the Autumn of 1810* (1811) 340.

to his understanding, a traveller might become acquainted with narratives making natural features or monuments more significant, or illustrating beliefs. When visiting ruined churches, like those on Scattery Island in County Clare, one would perhaps hear about the local saint or some strange events that had taken place there:

Scattery, as may be supposed, has a thousand legends and stories connected with it. An old man who accompanied us said, as he looked on the time-stained ruins, – 'Ah! I couldn't repeat to you half the queer things I have heard tell of those ancient places. When I was a boy, my grandfather used to get us round his knees on a winter's evening by the blazing bog-wood, and tell us of what happened to himself often and often among them. He was fond of talking about them, and especially of a wonderful sight he once saw in one of the old churches ... [and the story follows].[44]

Of constant interest were stories concerning ghosts or fairies, like those illustrating 'the manners of the lower orders of the inhabitants' in a book which described a village near Cork as a remote and culturally backward area:

They are very superstitious; perhaps even more than the generality of people of their rank in other counties in Ireland. This appears, first, from an endless variety of glaringly fabulous stories current amongst them for undoubted truths; – stories of things said to be ominous; also, of ghosts and witchcraft; and of miraculous cures performed by charms, incantations, or superstitious ceremonies ... Any body who will hazard the open profession of a doubt, as to the truth of the [assertions] of the narrators; or, in their own phraseology, will not *'give in* to such matters' especially if he should happen to laugh, is immediately eyed with a look truly diabolical, and set down an *unbeliever*, and an enemy to *piety*! In sickness they have recourse to charms and superstitious ceremonies, warranted only by idle tradition. But these practices are chiefly resorted to when the patient is supposed either bewitched, or 'fairy-struck' as it is more usually termed ...

   I shall here, by way of specimen illustrative of my opinion, repeat a story told by a very decent woman of Brook Lodge, near Glanmire ... 'A certain man was buried in a churchyard, some miles distant from his family and friends. A few nights after the interment, he appeared to his wife in a dream, and often continued to do so, charging her to have his body removed forthwith; for, that the strange ghosts, at night, as he walked inoffensively about the place, used to pelt him with stones, as a cuggeriegh [*coigriochach*: foreigner] charging him to get amongst his own people; and, though he often climbed up into one tree or another to avoid them, they climbed up likewise into the other trees, as nimble as monkeys, and thence pelted him soundly. The poor widow, alarmed for the safety of her husband's ghost' – though it was not added that he was killed over again, nor even that he received any dangerous contusion from the stones – 'had the body removed to his family burying-ground; and then the poor ghost troubled her no more.' – A question from me, how the ghosts came by the stones, when up in the trees, was thought worthy of an infidel, and, as such it was severely reproved. The gravity with which the story was told to my wife, and the pains taken to impress it upon her mind,

44 M.F.D. 'Letters from the Coast of Clare' *Dublin University Magazine* 18 (1841) 547-8.

as an established and indubitable fact, appeared to me strongly indicative of heathenish principles, completely predominant over professed christianity.[45]

Indeed, legends of the supernatural were said to abound, among a particularly superstitious people: 'Marvellous, beyond the ordinary reach of romance, are many stories repeated by the side of the cabin fire, concerning the midnight revelry and wanton tricks of these malicious spirits, who, by the courtesy of fear, are termed the *good people*.'[46] Fairy lore, which had become more specially associated with Ireland, was much in demand but not always easy to get:

[Bridget, an old Killarney woman is speaking.] 'Sit down, sir; don't go, and I will tell you a story, which I remember very well ... ' [She tells the story of a man who ploughed a field too close to a 'fairy fort'; then she seems to be sorry for having touched on such a subject.] The whole night she would say nothing more about the fairies, and it was ever a matter of difficulty to draw from her her store of stories, which she seemed to keep to herself like a fearful secret.

[Another experience at Killarney.] I wanted to glean news, if I could, of the 'Good People' I might expect to find here. You would have laughed, had you been with me. There was a whole row of cottages, and I stood debating for a bit which I should enter ... [In one of them, the traveller meets the mother of a large family and the grandmother.] But from neither one nor the other could I get anything, at all at all, about the 'Good People'. 'She met with many more bad people than good', said the old woman; and the younger one had nothing to say. That girl however hinted that six miles off, lived a woman who could see the Good People, but it was not everybody that could; and she added, after we left the place, that 'the priest did not like them to talk about them'.[47]

The unusually detailed (but perhaps partly fictionalized) portrait of a native storyteller was drawn by an English journalist and man of letters paid by Dickens's *Household Words* and *All the Year Round* to travel and produce topographical sketches. We are on a jaunting-car 'between Ballyrobin and Ballynabrig':

Dennis is a Connaught man, pale and whiskerless, but with straight black hair and good features, with a serious, earnest manner, changing rapidly to rollicking fun and drollery, and with a fine swelling low-toned voice, capable of much rise and fall, much in and out, and endless subtle gradations of feeling. It is rather startling to a sober, cynical, sceptical Englishman, who believes what he sees and can handle, and little else, to hear, for the first time, an Irishman telling you a fairy story with a quiet, almost sad, air of intense conviction and feeling; it is startling to one accustomed to see sham ghosts brought up at police courts and sentenced to the tread-mill, one accustomed to hear aerial voices and winking statues accounted for by bespectacled men on scientific principles, to find a

45 James Alexander *An Amusing Summer-Companion to Glanmire, near Cork ...* (1814) 79, 81-2, 111-12. 46 J.N. Brewer *The Beauties of Ireland* (1825) clxxv. 47 Julius Rodenberg (an Austrian traveller) *A Pilgrimage through Ireland, or the Island of the Saints* (1860) 154, 156; Margaret Scott Gatty *The Old Folks from Home* (1862) 94.

person soberly and calmly relating, with a voice thrilling with emotion some narrative of
a dumbly prophesying banshee, or a child stolen by the fairies. At once a great mist rolls
away, and you see the centuries that roll between the Protestant and Catholic, the Saxon
and the Celt. You feel that you are in a twilight country, where faith is still unreasoning
and supreme; where miracles and relics, and ghosts, are still believed in; where ghost stories are matter of life and death to men; and where the beautiful monsters of our nurs-
eries still walk, even in daylight.

Dennis had heard the banshee in the blue cloak, with the grey dishevelled hair, wailing under the peat heap; he had seen the phooka, or demon horse, tear past at night,
with fiery mane and phosphorescent eyes; he had seen the fairies in green, garlanding the
mushroom; he had beheld O'Donohue on his white horse rise from the tranquil morning lake; he had stolen up and heard the cluricaun, or little dwarf in the cocked hat and
scarlet Hogarth coat, tapping at a shoe on the sunny side of a haystack; and here I am,
who love everything Irish, quite an outer barbarian, who has never been granted any of
these privileges![48]

Thornbury *did* go to Ireland, and may well have met talkative car-drivers
like Dennis O'Flanagan – but it is obvious that in this text he wanted above all
to offer a compendium of the Victorian view of Irish folklore, the main source
of erudition probably being T. Crofton Croker's *Fairy Legends and Traditions of
the South of Ireland* (see next chapter). Other travelling writers could be less
effusive, like this German prince who listened, near Headford in County
Galway, to an old man's account of his personal involvement in the mysteries of
Knockmaa, the seat of Finvarra, King of the Connacht otherworld community,
who lured young people away – as his consort Úna (or Nuala) also did:

To-day I took advantage of a leisure day to ride to Castle Hackett, a solitary hill in the
neighbourhood, believed by the people to be a favourite resort of the fairies, or 'good
people' as they call them. No nation is more poetical, or more richly endowed with
fancy. An old man who has the care of the woods of Castle Hackett, and has the reputation of knowing more than other men about the 'good people', told us the circumstances connected with the death of his son, in the style of a romance. 'I knew it', said
he, 'four days before – I knew he would die; for as I was going home that evening about
twilight, I saw them scouring in a wild chase over the plain: their red dresses fluttered
in the wind; and the lakes turned to ice as they came near, and walls and trees bowed
themselves to the earth before them; and they rode over the tops of the thicket as if it
were over the green grass. In front rode the queen, on a white stag-like horse; and by
her I saw, with a shudder, my son, whom she smiled upon and caressed; while he, with
a fevered eye, looked wistfully at her, till all were past Castle Hackett. Then I knew it
was over with him; – that same day he took to his bed; – on the third I carried him to
the grave. There was not a handsomer man in Connemara, and it was for that the queen
chose him.' The old man seemed so firmly and unaffectedly convinced of the truth of
his story that it would have offended him to express the least doubt about it.[49]

48 Walter Thornbury *Cross Country* (1861) 124-7.   49 H.L.H. von Pückler-Muskau *Tour in
England, Ireland and France* (1832) 1. 240-1.

Belief legends or personal experience stories, when obtained at all, could be reported by the traveller without comment, or with manifest amazement, or with more or less scornful remarks about credulity. In the following example, the traveller's perplexity is emphasized: 'The general tenor of their conversation is so interlarded with marvellous accounts of enchantments, and other supernatural concerns, that it is difficult to separate delusions from whatever solid information they may have gleaned by listening to the observations of the more intelligent of their number.'[50] The reaction could also be indignant, like that, earlier in the century, of an Anglo-Irish clergyman and antiquarian commenting on the Glendalough saint's legends: 'Let these impious and foolish tales of ignorant and superstitious ecclesiastics suffice, and let them warn us of that miserable degradation of the human mind, which alone could give them currency and credit.'[51] But most tourists found legends and odd beliefs just amusing. From the beginning of the nineteenth century, the vanishing of such picturesque beliefs was commented upon and sometimes deplored:

... the peasantry have grown 'mighty shy' of communications [concerning fairies]; they have become, for the most part, even sceptical concerning them; and deliver their anecdotes with an air of doubt, at the least, which indicates an abandonment of their cause approaching to contempt of their power. We venture to assert that a modern traveller, even in Donegal or Connaught, will not hear from veritable authorities a dozen stories of the 'good people'. A score of years ago he would have heard as many from a dozen persons, meet them when or where he would.[52]

Thanks to the National Schools in Ireland, there is scarcely a child of six years of age, from Skibbereen to Lough Foyle, who does not scout the whole fairy mythology, from the Pooka to the Banshee, and laugh at the credulity of his father and forefathers![53]

In fact, fairy-lore remained widespread and often believed in for several generations, but people might hesitate to open their hearts to foreigners: certain stories should not come to unprepared ears.

The idea that you would meet an innocent talker by mere chance when approaching a monument or some peculiar sight was unrealistic, or the rendering of such a scene could be a fiction: if someone was waiting for you there, he might be prepared to swap narratives for coins, and thus belonged to a new class of storytellers. His repertoire consisted of a selection of local lore, plus stories specially concocted for foreign visitors – which soon appeared in print. I shall now consider the general features of this peculiar trade, before focusing on a few famous or notorious representatives.

---

50 G.N. Smith *Killarney and the Surrounding Scenery* (1822) 15. **51** Edward Ledwich *Antiquities of Ireland* 2nd ed. (1804) 176. **52** A.M. and S.C. Hall *Ireland, Its Scenery, Character, &c* (1841) 3. 237. **53** James Johnson *A Tour of Ireland, with Meditations and Reflections* (1844) 312-13.

The guide was expected not only to point out places of interest but also to humour (and exploit) his client by telling stories supposed to be coming down from a distant past or from recent experience, in a tone likely to impress or amuse. He might deliberately 'play Paddy to the Saxon', thus cultivating his patrons' sense of superiority and giving them the means to expatiate later on 'Irishness'. As perceived by their more or less willing victims, the shabby guide became a type, which we shall reconstruct through a first series of quotations.

As soon as he had landed, a visitor would meet a car driver – 'carboy', or 'jarvey' – who took him to town; then many excursions would require the services of another coachman, who was expected to be inquisitive and talkative.[54] The typical Irish driver would be 'lightening the way with reminiscences and legends'.[55] Here are two late nineteenth-century sketches, the first in a nostalgic vein, the second exploiting an outworn convention as if it were still in its prime:

The old race of car-driver is nearly gone now. It went out with the whisky [because of Father Mathew's crusade against drunkenness, in the 1840s], and has not come back with its return. The drivers are now short in their answers, and seem as if they thought the person who seeks to stimulate conversation has some offensive motive for what he is doing. I doubt if a traveller who journeys from the Giants' Causeway to Cape Clear will pick up a dozen anecdotes from that source worth telling again; while half a century ago it would have been a barren harvest that did not yield a dozen in a day.[56]

The Irish carman – or 'the jarvey', as he is styled in his native isle – enjoys a wide celebrity as a comical fellow. Sometimes his humour is absolutely unconscious. He says the quaintest things imaginable without the slightest striving after effect or the least intention of being funny. But oftenest he is consciously droll.[57]

If the visitor was a sportsman, he could hear stories from the native 'gillie' (from Scots Gaelic *gille*: lad) who carried his gear and led him to good fishing grounds:

I universally found the companions of my fishing expeditions willing, obliging, and civil; ready and anxious to do what they could to promote my amusement and comfort; and extremely grateful for kindness received.[58]

One day, on a fishing excursion, being near the island, accompanied by old Shaun, the boatman, [the vacationer sees a mysterious inscription]. On inquiry of 'mine ancient brother of the angle' as to the cause of it, he replied, 'Ah, sir, that is a story indeed'. And casually remarking at the same time 'that story-telling was dry work, and that he would require another sup to keep up his spirits during the narrative', I handed him my flask and obtained the following account of him ...[59]

---

54 Charles Richard Weld *Vacations in Ireland* (1857) 6, 62-3. 55 Alexander Innes Shand *Letters from the West of Ireland 1884* 206. 56 S.C. Hall *Retrospect of a Long Life* (1883) 340. 57 Michael Mac Donagh *Irish Life and Character* (1898) 301. 58 [Belton] *The Angler in Ireland ... during the Summer of 1833* 1. 50. 59 *Leaves from My Notebook ...* (c.1877) 85-6.

Pre-eminently, however, the travellers' talkative Irishmen were those they met at celebrated beauty spots. Such people would help them through tricky rock passages or watery ground, point out interesting details – and, if they were at all gifted for the job, make themselves entertaining. Nineteenth-century travellers in Ireland found them particularly numerous, garrulous and often very intrusive, but they might supply the only real close contact one had with local people. The guide provided what seemed likely to bring a tip, adapting local legends or inventing them if nothing adequate was available. At first, it seemed any local person could fill this role – so thought the French traveller Jean-Gabriel Capo de Feuillide, in the 1830s: 'Le *paddy* est fort enthousiaste des beautés de sa terre natale, et, par esprit national, il ne veut pas qu'on la voie autrement que lui et ses ancêtres l'ont vue.' It was practically impossible for the traveller to contemplate a site alone and to form his own opinion. The guide would tell him what to look at and what story was associated with it – and Capo de Feuillide concluded that it was a rather pleasant experience after all.[60]

Non-professional guides might compete with star performers, as in this scene in the early 1840s:

Of the 'ould cave' [at Mitchelstown, County Tipperary] we heard the legend from the lips of one of our guides; and before we commence our descent into 'the bowels of the earth', we may give it as nearly as we can in the words in which we received it. 'Is it how the caves war discovered, ye'r asking, ma'am?' replied a "Tipperary boy" to our inquiry. 'Why, then, it was quare; though, to be sure, the sheep was not a right sheep, as any one might know that took a thought about it; for if she was right in herself – I mean nothing but a sheep to make mutton of – she could not have had the understanding of Christian language, as she surely had'. 'If ye'r going to tell the lady the story, tell it at once, and don't be riddling out your own ideas about what you don't understand, Reddy', interrupted another guide. 'And don't you be taking me up, or maybe it's too heavy for you I'd be', replied Reddy ... At last he was prevailed upon to commence his tale. 'A poor man lived hard by there, a poor man entirely; trusting to his quarter of potatoes for the bare food, and to God's marcy (like most of us) for everything else ... ' [the discovery of the more accessible set of caves by a quarryman, less than ten years before this scene, had already become a legend].[61]

The traveller sometimes failed to understand what he was told – particularly when it was a version of a strange ancient story like that of Cú Roí, who was first befriended and then slain by Cú Chulainn: 'On our return [from Inch, County Kerry], when we came again in sight of Cahir-con-righ, "the Rock of King Con", or the "Fortress of Con the King", our guide told us a wild and wondrous tale about it; but so confused and so crowded with hard Irish names, that I despaired of ever retaining it: which I regretted, as it was highly roman-

60 J.-G. C. de Feuillide *L'Irlande* (1839) 112-14. 61 A.M. and S.C. Hall *Ireland, Its Scenery, Character, &c* (1841) 2. 79-80. In the last decade of the twentieth century, the curator still had a short legend ready for every peculiar calcite formation in the cave system.

tic'.[62] Other travellers found their guides plainly ridiculous: 'One of the party asked our guide (who was an old inhabitant of the glen) what was supposed to be the use of that immense slab. "That, sir," replied he, "was the banquet table at which the giants regaled themselves in distant ages!" We all laughed heartily.'[63]

Meanwhile, a tourism industry was organizing itself around a few centres of attraction. Full-time guides, who knew best what tourists were prepared to hear and understand, occupied the unavoidable stopovers of fashionable itineraries. The visitor felt particularly duty bound to see Killarney, which soon became the most celebrated resort.[64] Texts praising it had already appeared in the middle of the eighteenth century. There was not a word about the natives and their stories in what may have been the first celebrations of 'the stupendous mountains hanging over the lake', the 'level and beautiful country on the opposite side of the lake' and 'an assemblage that charms the human mind, and raises admiration for the whole';[65] but according to another book first published in 1760, if the place 'awakes sentiments truly sublime ... the principal entertainment after supper was in hearing little pieces of history told over, very necessary to be known by adventurers going to embark upon this romantic piece of water'.[66] In 1764 there was another early allusion to storytelling for tourists at Killarney: 'On our return from the upper lake, through this most enchanting maze, we were most agreeably entertained by our pilot.'[67] At first, only the local landlords produced a minimum of amenities; but in 1812 there were three inns and the first specialized guidebook had already appeared: Isaac Weld's *Illustrations of the Scenery of Killarney and Surrounding Country*. In 1828 there were two hotels; by 1850 seven. A railway line reached Killarney in 1853. The poorer locals adapted themselves to the new source of income. They worked as boatmen, with whom tourists spent hours on excursions; one had to listen to them, and it was a pleasant experience. By 1828, each hotel had its own carmen and boatmen who knew that they were expected to tell local stories. Some could still seem more reluctant than others to touch on their own beliefs and had to be coaxed, but they might be play-acting:

One of our boat's crew – a man of about fifty, with long black hair, which the wind blew wildly about his temples, of an earnest and quiet but imaginative look, – was stealthily

62 (Lydia Fisher) *Letters from the Kingdom of Kerry in the Year 1845* 71. 63 *Notes from a Tourist's Journal, being a brief Sketch of a Visit to the Lakes on the Galtee Mountains* (1857) 18. 64 See Luke Gibbons, 'Topographies of Terror: Killarney and the Politics of the Sublime', *South Atlantic Quarterly* 95 (1996) 23-44. 65 Richard Barton *Some Remarks towards a Full Description of Upper and Lower Lough Lene, near Killarny, in the County of Kerry* (1751) 7. Another description, perhaps by the same author, had appeared the year before: *The Masterpiece of Nature, or the Beautiful Lake near Killarny*. 66 William Ockenden *Observations on Modern Gardening ... Letters describing the Lake of Killarney and Mucruss Gardens* 8. 67 John Bush *Hibernia Curiosa* (1769) 108. Exactly the same sentence appears in Philip Luckombe's *A Tour Through Ireland* (1780) 246.

pointed out to me by one of his companions, while they whispered in my ear that 'he had met him' [O'Donohue – see below]. You will believe that I quickly entered into connection with this boatman, and sought to gain his confidence, knowing that these people, whenever they anticipate unbelief and jesting, observe an obstinate silence. At first he was reserved; but at length he became warmed, and swore by St Patrick and the Virgin that what he was going to tell me was the naked truth.[68]

By the 1830s the composition of the Killarney boat-crew was fixed by usage: for a group of tourists it might include four or six oarsmen, with a gunner and a bugler to demonstrate the echo, and stories could be provided by any one of them:

The men are generally honest and sober, being well-informed about the localities, are useful and interesting guides, although they do sometimes take a pleasure in making John Bull swallow stories that are as veracious as the Adventures of Baron Münchausen, or the Travels of Sir John Mandeville.[69]

The sobriety marvelled at in the mid-nineteenth century must have been a result of the abstinence movement led by Father Mathew, but at the high-point of his crusade in 1841 the stipulated price per day for each of the boatsmen still included a bottle of whiskey.[70] One of the ritual jokes played on a naive tourist consisted in pretending to give his/her name to one of the thirty islands in Loch Lein – a ceremony accompanied by great libations.

As not everything could be admired from a boat, guides became available for more extensive tours. By 1822 they were already numerous: 'Early as was the hour, I was pestered with poor fellows offering themselves as guides, I accepted the service of one, and was attended by five others, each striving to do something for me that might entitle him to a trifle.'[71] Poverty promoted such vocations, much to the disgust of travellers like this one, writing some sixty years later: 'Go where you will, you cannot escape the nuisance of being beset by beggars, boatmen, and guides, by car-drivers hungry for fares now that the tourist supply is running short, and by wayside vendors of whisky and goat's milk and other beverages equally poisonous and detestable. It would be wise and benevolent if the local authorities, in their own interest and ours, would do something to abate an almost intolerable nuisance.'[72] But others thought that guides were necessary: 'The procuring of a guide who may have an intimate knowledge of all the paths and stations in the neighbourhood, and some perception of the beauties of nature, is of infinite advantage.'[73] The same piece of advice was still given a quarter of a century later, with the idea that a sense of the 'wild' and a taste

---

68 Pückler-Muskau, H. von *A Tour in England, Ireland and France* 1. 293. 69 Archibald G. Stark *The South of Ireland in 1850 ...* 203. 70 *Leigh's New Pocket Hand-Book of Ireland* 3rd ed. (1841) 362. 71 Thomas Reid *Travels in Ireland in the Year 1822* 274. 72 Alexander Innes Shand *Letters from the West of Ireland 1884* 201. (The first, violent phase of the Land War reduced the number of tourists in the early 1880s.) 73 G.N. Smith *Killarney and the Surrounding Scenery* (1822) 14.

for legends went together (sometimes expressed in a 'bardic' reference to the storyteller's hair as ruffled by the wind); but the guide might equally be described as funny:

In the various excursions we are about to describe, it is advisable, indeed we may say absolutely necessary, that the tourist should take a guide with him, not only to avoid the discomfort of being lost in the wild mountain glens and forest glades, but also for the sake of having an amusing companion, and one who is well-informed as to every object of interest in the district, and brimful of the wild legends and stories with which scenery so romantic is necessarily connected.[74]

A Killarney repertoire of stories for tourists seemed to be rapidly growing. There were narratives according to which Loch Leane had been formed when a girl forgot to replace the capstone on a well (the origin of several Irish lakes was similarly explained); and romantic tales in prose or verse about a hermit who had spent a number of years in the ruin of Muckross Abbey in the mid-eighteenth century. The guide could also tell of his own dealings with illustrious travellers – or with the supernatural:

The guide who rode round the lake with me mentioned a curious circumstance which occurred to him, and to the truth of which he said he could at any time take a solemn oath. He told me that he was one day driving a Kerry cow from Miltown into Killarney; that it was broad daylight, when he suddenly observed, at a short distance before him, a little boy who was attending a herd of cows. Presently the little boy (who had on a straw hat) drove his cattle through a gap into the field: the guide's cow followed them. He immediately jumped through the gap to regain his cow, when he found the boy and his herd had vanished. He was firmly persuaded of the fact; and escaping without harm, he set the urchin down for one of the 'good folk'.[75]

The tourist could be pleased by such contacts with Irish 'superstition'; but above all he wanted to hear more elaborate stories associated with the places he was visiting. In particular, he expected some variants of the corpus of tradition which elsewhere concerned Gearóid Iarla Fitzgerald and Lough Gur (see p. 103); at Killarney, they became attached to the twelfth-century local chieftain Dónall Ó Donnchú, whose story was already reported by Ockenden in 1760.[76] He was supposed to have been a magician, now asleep in a cavern under Loch Leane and forced to ride over the lake on May mornings until the silver shoes of his horse were worn out. He also protected local tenants from oppressive landlords. Many landmarks were associated with him, and through the eloquence of the guides 'the very rocks and stones of the countryside breathed to life to take part

74 R.M. Ballantyne *The Lakes of Killarney* (1859) 22.   75 John Barrow *A Tour Round Ireland, through the sea-coast counties, in the autumn of 1835* (1836) 312.   76 *Observations on Modern Gardening* 13ff.

in what was a constantly unfolding saga'.[77] Here are some references to this local hero in travel books, from 1776 to the second half of the nineteenth century:

The great O'Donahue [or O'Donoghue], the hero of this ancient race, still survives in the praises of his countrymen; who set off his virtues with all the colourings of enthusiasm. They represent him like the Demi-gods of old, a contemner of danger, a sworn foe to oppression, a passionate admirer of whatever is great and honourable.[78]

Still solicitous about the prosperity of his ancient dominions, it is believed, he quits at times the regions of immortal bliss, and appears in person among the descendants of his people. I have met men who related the tale with all the enthusiasm of religious faith, and who asserted most solemnly, they had themselves beheld the apparition: happily, however, for the cause of common sense, the numbers who give credit to it daily decrease.[79]

The guides and boatmen have all, of course, 'had a sight' of the chieftain, and will tell the tourist amusing stories – but those they have only heard – of their ancestors, who not only saw, but conversed with him and shared his hospitality in his palace below the waves.[80]

A more detailed account includes a sketch of the storyteller himself:

'I saw him once', whispered the old boatman to me, in a confidential tone. I started, and looked hard at the man, a strong figure of about fifty, with long black hair, which the least breeze scattered about his temples. I looked, because I did not at first believe him to be in earnest, but I was soon perfectly convinced that he was so. I have no doubt that the legend had taken full possession of his belief, and that he was firmly persuaded he had really met the chieftain; nor was he at all eager to tell me the particulars, seeming to regard it as a sort of profanation to throw away fresh details on a heretic. By dint of much questioning, however, I drew from him, that he had stayed out one night late fishing; it had rained hard all day, and but for his bottle of whiskey, he thought he must have perished. He was, and had been for a long time, the only living being on the waters, when all at once a boat, as if dropped from the clouds, came sailing towards him; it came rapidly on, but only one steersman was visible; a gigantic figure dressed in scarlet and gold, with a three-cocked hat trimmed with broad gold lace. Just as he passed him, Paddy saw two large black eyes glaring forth, which scorched him like coals. His wife called him drunken fellow, but 'it was not the whiskey done that', though he did not come to himself till the boat was ashore all right. He seemed rather sorry afterwards that he had told me so much; he repeated over and over that O'Donoghoe, though terrible, looked like a raal gentleman, 'a perfect gentleman', he added; 'He was, is now, and ever will remain.' The younger boatmen I found were much less credulous than this man; they were inclined to joke him, but his seriousness and anger soon silenced them.[81]

77 Donal Horgan *Echo after Echo; Killarney and Its History* 116. **78** (Dunn) *A Description of Killarney* (1776) 39. **79** Isaac Weld *Illustrations of the Scenery of Killarney and the Surrounding Country* (1807) 82. **80** A.M. and S.T. Hall *Ireland, Its Scenery, Character, &c* (1841) 1. 195. **81** Emily Taylor *The Irish Tourist ...* (1843) 138-9.

Some twenty years later, at a window from which the hero was said to have leaped, a guide's speech sounded more like a music-hall act:

'Well, you see, this O'Donohue was a mighty grate enchanter, and had dealings surely with the ould jintleman that bit a bit out of the mountain anent the Punch-bowll there. Now his wife got curious about those tricks of his, and one day tazed him till he would show her some of his power; "For," says she, "O'Donohue, I belave it's all sham, so I do." "Well," says he, "go up in the tower, and look out of the window, and you'll see what I can do, devil a doubt of it." So she goes and looks; and presently comes O'Donohue like an elephant, and roars till every stone of Ross Castle shakes again. But the wife wasn't a bit troubled; and so he turns into a leaping fire and a whale, and a red deer with a salmon head, and then into a lion in a cocked hat – and she wasn't troubled; – till at last he comes climbing up to this window like a big, rolling fiery serpent; and when the lady sees that, she out with a prayer, and O'Donohue leaps from the window and disappears for ever in the lake.'[82]

This past and future hero is still celebrated in Domnhall Ó Cathail (or Donal O'Cahill)'s compilation of texts, *Legends of Killarney*, a fifth edition of which was issued in 1964 to be sold to tourists in souvenir shops as well as by the only guides left at the time, the 'Killarney jarvies' (a group-photograph of twenty-nine of them adorns the booklet).

Less internationally famous but closer to Dublin, Glendalough, with the 'wild' beauty of its scenery, its monastic remains and the legends about St Kevin – how he banished a monster, allowed a bird to nest on his hand, was pursued by a young lady he pushed into the lake – became from the late eighteenth century another favourite stopping-place for tourists; and story-telling guides emerged there too. By 1817 there were still comparatively few of them:

When strangers appear in the valley, the local guide (there are two or three who assume that office) immediately attaches himself to the visitors, and gabbles over the fabulous and oral traditions which have been handed down for generations. We had, however, previously consulted Ledwiche's Antiquities, and listened to our guide more amused by his manner and his credulity than informed by his explanations, of which our learned antiquarian had rendered us independent.[83]

But before the middle of the century, the place swarmed with would-be escorts:

A peine avais-je mis le pied dans la vallée que je me vis assailli par une troupe dégue-nillée d'hommes, d'enfants et de femmes qui semblaient sortir du milieu des ruines, et qui, poussant mille clameurs bizarres, offraient de me servir de guides.[84]

---

82 W. Thornbury *Cross Country* (1861) 181. 83 *The Angling Excursions of Gregory Greendrake, Esq.* (1824) 57-8 (first published in *The Warder* in 1817). Rev. Edward Ledwich's *Antiquities of Ireland* had appeared in 1790. 84 J. Joseph Prévost *Un Tour en Irlande* (1846) 169.

[The place] is infested with harpies, who call themselves 'Guides'; and a more offi-cious set are not to be met between Killarney and the Giant's Causeway: at every point they swarm about, and cling like leeches.[85]

An American Quaker lady saw the same crowd and tried to shame the native who wanted to please her with his tales; it led to a typical distinction between lies and stories, and between transmitted stories and newly-minted ones:

The poor peasantry ... soon gathered in thick array around us when we arrived, to show us the wonders, or to ask a penny. Old men and maidens, young men and children were on the spot, each with the utmost servility ready to 'sarve' us in the best and 'chapest' manner. We were obliged to shake them all off except one, who was engaged, and handed over to me, as I was a stranger, and my party had visited it before. The sensible reader shall be troubled with only a little of the consummate nonsense with which my ears were stuffed during the long six hours we passed among the ruins ... [The guide] told me that the wonders he was about to relate had been told to him by his grandfather, and might be all believed ... When all was finished, I said, 'You do this for money, Sir.' 'I get my bread by it, lady, and yesterday I made eight shillings.' 'And do you believe one word of all the ridiculous stuff with which you have been cramming me?' 'I tell it, lady, as I heard it.' 'But do you believe it yourself?' He looked confounded, and answered, 'No: but I made only one story to fill up the time as we were passing along.'[86]

The Giant's Causeway, on the Antrim coast, was the third high point of a tour of Ireland. In 1693 the Royal Geographical Society had already decided that it was one of the great wonders of the world. At the beginning of the nineteenth century tourists were greeted by a vociferous throng: 'We had not yet come in sight of it, when we were assailed by a number of persons who called themselves Guides, and offered us their services. They had all strong claims to favour, which they urged with more violence than manners, and with such perseverance, that when we thought we had got rid of them, we only lost them at one side to see them start up at the other.'[87] Stories were not the only commodity; in the 1830s a whole industry had developed: 'Long before reaching the Causeway, we were met by one of the guides, who seemed to think that this rencontre gave him a legal right to take us under his charge. He kept up with the vehicle by running; and in the meanwhile, took care to describe the country as we passed, in order to show us that he had already entered upon his office.'[88] In the 1840s, Thackeray and the Halls also saw many guides there:

The traveller no sooner issues from the inn, by a back door, which he is informed will lead him straight to the Causeway, than the guides pounce upon him, with a dozen

85 Alfred M'Farland *Hours in Vacation* (1853) 15. **86** Asenath Nicholson *Ireland's Welcome to the Stranger; or Excursions through Ireland, in 1844 & 1845* (1847) 72-7. **87** John Gamble *Views of Society and Manners in the North of Ireland* (1819) 390-1. **88** Leith Ritchie *Ireland, Picturesque and Romantic* 124-5.

rough boatmen, who are likewise lying in wait; and a crew of shrill beggar-boys, with boxes of spars, ready to tear him and each other to pieces seemingly, yell and bawl incessantly round him. 'I'm the guide Miss Henry recommends', shouts one; 'I'm Mr Macdonald's guide', pushes in another.[89]

The guides at the Giant's Causeway are quite as numerous and almost as ragged as those at Killarney and Glendalough; but their character is altogether different. The Kerry and Wicklow guides delight in legends of fays and fairies, in snatches of songs, bits of ballads, and in 'impossibilities' of all kinds; there is nothing too wild and wonderful for them – nothing too airy or fantastic; their wit and their rags flutter together; they greet you with a jest, and bid you farewell with a tear. Not so the northern guides ... People of knowledge ... stiff and steady ... they are remarkable for the exactness and minutiae of their details ... Although very superstitious, their superstitions are of a marine kind, and of a gigantic and terrible nature.[90]

Some forty years later, the recital of the legends the tourist expected to hear had become perfunctory, contrasting with the telling of a personal experience story:

On the islands of Staffa and Iona the same formation reappears, giving rise to the legend that it was made by Fin McCoul, the Irish giants, out of politeness to a Scotch giant, whom he wished to come over and fight with him, 'without wetting the sole of his boot'. John King told us this, and many other stories, pointing out the Chimney-tops, the Giant's Organ, the Giant's Grandmother, &c. – Irish imagination gives a name to everything ... John King, though he conscientiously pointed out the spot and told the tale [of an Armada ship], seemed more interested in a modern shipwreck [he had been involved in as a rescuer] ... He spoke of it in a matter-of-fact way, as of an everyday occurrence.[91]

At about the same time, D.R. McAnally quoted or imagined a local fisherman who commented on the lore concerning a local hero, the 'Gray Man': 'all thim shtories bein' made be thim blaggard guides that set up av a night shtringin' out laigends for to enthertain the quo'lty'.[92] McAnally's book was probably in part a fabrication, as the style of even such a brief quotation suggests, but it is true that, from the late eighteenth century at least, Fionn mac Cumhaill (whose hair, according to a much older story, had turned grey or white after a dive into a magic lake on Slieve Gullion) was said to have built the road of basaltic shafts. Guides may have invented this 'tradition', or embellished it, for tourists impressed by Macpherson; it was still part of their repertoire in the mid-twentieth century:

... The local guides have a far better story to tell than all this dry geological stuff, and you can get it at first hand. 'Geology, me fut', they'll say. 'Sure doesn't all the world know Finn Mac Cool, the Irish giant, built the Causeway with his own hands, an' him itchin' to get at the Scottish giant that was boastin' about how he could knock the melt

89 Thackeray *Irish Sketch Book* 322. 90 A.M. and S.T. Hall *Ireland, Its Scenery* ... 3. 155. 91 Dinah Craik *An Unknown Country* (1887) 65-7. 92 *Irish Wonders* ... 153.

out of any Irishman in the world: and isn't the other end of the same Causeway over in Staffa, in Scotland itself, to prove it?' Believe what you like, but don't miss the grand stories these guides will tell you for that's more than half the fun.[93]

Practically everywhere, any 'traditional lore' the average tourist could learn was likely to be filtered through a guide, and one could expect some leg-pulling; the role he had to play included being an outrageous liar or being able to spin a new yarn. When he did so, one motive might also be the secret pleasure of fooling a foreigner who pretended he understood Ireland and was prepared to record absurdities in his note-book.

In the examples quoted so far, the guides were more or less interchangeable and often merged into a crowd. But in the second quarter of the nineteenth century, writers – particularly Anglo-Irish ones – selectively aggrandized some of them into legendary personages, for a time. To catch a glimpse of such living monuments became essential to a well-planned tour. The transition from mere walk-on parts to notoriety, as well as the mixture of observation and fabrication involved in such buildup, can be studied in Thomas Crofton Croker's curious fictional reportage *Legends of the Lakes, or Sayings and Doings at Killarney*, published in London in 1829. The author had won fame with his *Fairy Legends and Traditions of the South of Ireland* (to be taken up in the next chapter). R. Adolphus Lynch, a schoolfellow of his who had served at Waterloo and retired to Killarney on half-pay, sold him a collection he had assembled there. Croker decided to link the stories together with a fictional frame about *his* hearing them, and added a few other tales. As he had actually listened to traditional storytellers during his rambles in the south of Ireland, and visited Killarney, his descriptions are not worthless. A modified version issued in 1831, *Killarney Legends; Arranged as a Guide to the Lakes*, was shorter and 'pocket-size', so that the tourist could consult it *in situ*. When Croker meets Lynch in the fictional frame-story, the following conversation takes place – and we note the use of the adjective 'traditionary' (handed down orally from generation to generation) to refer to what might be particularly valuable:

'I have come to Killarney alone with the fancy of writing a Guide book'. 'Writing a guide book! Why, there's Weld, and Wright, and half a dozen others have written Guide books'. 'But I mean a traditionary one: have you forgotten all the *ould* stories you used to relate so well?' 'What, the foolish nursery tales of our childhood?' 'Any thing but foolish, if you please, Lynch; I cannot admit your assertion'. 'However, metaphysically speaking –' 'Oh, come, if you are about to enter into a metaphysical dissertation, like the bard of Highgate [?Coleridge], upon fairy tales –' 'Well, well,' said Lynch, smiling, 'many of them no doubt are curious ...'[94]

Although Croker used Lynch's written material, he preferred to offer it as

93 Richard Hayward *This Is Ireland: Ulster and the City of Belfast* 70. 94 Croker, op.cit. 1. 99.

coming straight from the mouths of natives, whom he named and personalized. His supposed collection starts on the box of the Killarney mail coach where he sits beside the driver:

'What castle is that, Crowley? 'The castle is it? Why then 'tis, it is the castle sure enough, without any kind of doubt! Did your honour never hear what Tool, the guard, said to a gentleman that axed him about that same Droumhoomper Castle – that's the rale name for it, though they calls it Coltsman's Castle ... [and the story of the castle is told].[95]

Then, like any visitor, Croker meets a guide:

The principal charm of a ramble through Killarney consists in being accompanied by an entertaining guide; one who can put you in possession of the mind of the place, who can tell a good story, and whose local anecdotes, though slight and sketchy, give you a more characteristic idea of the people than could possibly be gained from more laboured accounts. Such a one was Mahony, or as he was commonly called Mountain Mahony ... 'That's the very spot where Darby Minchan saw the fetch of O'Donoghue', said my guide. 'How was that?' said I. 'Ah, then, I'll tell you all about it', replied Mountain Mahony, 'for sure I ought to know ...' [and we are told about it].[96]

The 'real' Spillane, one of the established Killarney characters, puts in an appearance and sparks off a version of the widespread Irish legend about a monster banished to the bottom of a lake until Doomsday:

What a wild spot – this dark lake with its surrounding hills! – See, how its black waves roll against the shore, and break upon the rocks with an angry growl. It seems the very abode of melancholy; and I should not wonder if there was some wild story connected with the place.' 'By the by, sir', said Spillane, 'I believe there is a story, something about a great serpent, I think – do you know anything of it, Picket?' 'The serpent, is it?' said Picket in reply. Sure, every body has hard tell of the blessed Saint Patrick, and how he *druve* the *sarpints* and all manner of venemous things out of Ireland. How he "bothered" all the varmint', entirely. But for all that, there was one *ould sarpint* left ...' [the story follows]'[97]

The traveller also meets a storyteller – not a guide – who addresses believers only:

Barret had told his fairy tales so often, that constant repetition had all the efficacy of demonstration in impressing upon his mind a firm conviction of the truth of his stories. It was therefore necessary to use a little angling art, in order to hide all appearance of unbelief, which would infallibly have put a stop to his loquacity ... Satisfied that I was not an unbeliever, and ticked by the flattery, Barret commenced his story.[98]

95 Ibid. 1. 3.   96 Ibid. 1. 12 and 15.   97 Ibid. 1. 179–80.   98 Ibid. 1. 202

Perhaps most notable in Croker's book is the idea that storytelling was what characterized Ireland best, and that guides were the best storytellers a tourist could meet. As personae, they also were a useful literary convention, and the Advertisement to the second edition recognized it:

As three years had elapsed since the book was written, there naturally arose the question, whether the numerous individual portraits which were introduced should be retained or rejected? But since 'the lads of the Lakes' must naturally change, like the lights and colouring upon the majestic mountains which surround the lovely waters of Killarney – it was determined to preserve the sketches of the guides and boatmen, which it was the Editor's fortune to find, as faithful prototypes of their fellows, and as the best medium of communicating to the reader the tales of wonder which are the unquestionable inheritance of a scene of enchantment.[99]

Florid portraits of such 'prototypes' also appeared in the very popular travel descriptions and guidebooks published in the 1840s and 50s by Anna Maria Hall and her husband. In the second edition of *A Week at Killarney*, in 1864, the couple added nostalgic regrets: the great Killarney guides (the first generation of such professionals) were already figures of the past. The new breed was, on the whole, too refined to be fully 'Irish' – though it still included some remarkable cases:

Irish guides are the most amusing fellows in the world; always ready to do anything, explain any matter, go anywhere ... They enliven the dreariest road by their wit, and are, of course, rich in old stories; some they hear, some they coin, and, occasionally, make a strange hodge-podge of history – working a volume of wonders out of a solitary fact. Our pleasant memories of Killarney are associated with those of a guide – 'Sir' Richard Courtenay, who now sleeps in the mid-aisle of Mukcross. His picture, although that of a hero gone by, may be worth retaining, for it is a picture of a class in the old times; his successors being far less 'Irish', and much more refined. Note his peculiar hat – not quite a 'caubeen', although the mountain blasts have materially changed its shape since it was 'a bran-new beaver'; his small keen grey eyes; his loose good-natured mouth, that pours forth in abundance courteous, if not courtly phrases, and pronounces scraps of French with the true pronunciation of an actual native – of Kerry; for Sir Richard, having mixed in good society, 'parlez-voos' as well as bows with the grace of a travelled gentleman. His coat was certainly not made by a Stulz, nor his brogue by a Hoby; but the frieze suits well with his healthy and sunburnt countenance, and the shoes are a fitting match for limbs that have borne him a thousand times up the steep and high mountain of Mangerton. Alas! the Tourists who have experienced his courtesy will miss him now from his accustomed places; they will not fail to pay him a tribute of remembrance as they stand beside the graveside – as yet, we regret to say, unmarked by his name – that covers his remains, in holy Muckross, every spot of which knew his footstep well. Honour, then, to the memory of pleasant 'Sir Richard'; and if now enlisted in the troops

99 *Killarney Legends; Arranged as a Guide to the Lakes* 'Advertisement' dated 'Killarney, April 7, 1831'.

of O'Donoghue, the 'good people' themselves may listen with delight to the 'laagends' with which he was familiar, and follow him without dread, through every 'Glen and bosky dell' of their delicious dominions. We owe him much, and recall with gratitude the information he gave us, the stories he told us, and the wit and genuine humour that sparkled in so much he said and did.[100]

By the mid-century, some Killarney guides were advertised among the best local attractions. Verbal artists they may have been, but their reputation was established by being mentioned in books:

Those who go to Killarney go to stay for at least two days; and their 'best guide' is, when a survey and not a glimpse is contemplated, not a book, but one of the men who obtain their livings by hiring themselves out for a day as cicerones to the beautiful neighbourhood. These persons constitute a numerous class, all clever, ready, and intelligent, and some of them possessed of qualities which, through the books of literary tourists, have rendered them famous. Mrs Hall, in her book, acts as the Plutarch of successive generations of distinguished 'guides'. Two remain, and have always the preference with those who have heard anything of Killarney before visiting it. They are the Spillanes – father and son. The elder is a bugler (the bugle being indispensable to the guides for the purpose of awakening the echoes), of the highest order ... The old man's son, rejoicing in the bardic attribute of the inheritance of song, possesses not only the paternal dexterity of instrumentation ... but has won the merit of being an exquisite singer of the melodies of his country.[101]

I had been told, before leaving London, that when I reached Killarney, I ought on no account to lose the amusement which I would receive from employing Sir Richard Courtenay as my guide. Sir Richard is a very interesting personage. He is a man about forty-five or fifty years of age; below the middle height, and somewhat slightly made. But though there is no appearance of robustness about him, he rejoices in a very excellent constitution, and is capable of enduring very great fatigue. His countenance has much of that copperish hue which is one of the characteristics of the gipsy tribe, and which is most likely to be ascribed to his constant exposure to the sun. Sir Richard dresses too tidily and fashionably (though not exactly in the West End style either), to run any risk of being mistaken by the stranger for a member of the gipsy fraternity. His features are small and pleasing; his eye is black, quick, and full of intelligence. He is exceedingly polite, always obliging, and has an inexhaustible store of anecdotes, and of superstitious stories, wherewith to amuse his patrons. He never ceases speaking, – not from any self-vanity which he has to gratify, but from a desire to 'instruct, edify, amuse and delight' those friends who employ him. I could not have wished a more pleasant companion, had I been remaining a month at Killarney ... I have no reason to suppose that he was more talkative in my case than in that of others. Now, I had the honour of six hours of his society, beginning at six in the morning, and ending at twelve. During that time he could hardly be said to have ceased speaking. What he then said would have made a good quarter of a volume of the ordinary size ... The reader who has never heard of Sir Richard before, will be surprised at the seeming anomaly of a person of his title

100 Op. cit. 79-80. In the first edition, 1850, Sir Richard was said to be alive and ready to tell legends. **101** *The Irish Tourist's Illustrated Handbook* 2nd ed. (1852) 63.

employed in the humble capacity in which I have introduced him to the English public. A few words will explain all. Sir Richard is by birth a peasant, and has for the greater part of a quarter of a century supported a wife and a family in the humble but honest way I have mentioned. [But he once rescued the wife of the Lord-Lieutenant of Ireland and received the knighthood – so he said.][102]

There were legendary guides at Glendalough too, but they were more often treated as objects of fun. The first individualized portrait was drawn by John Carr in 1805, in a typically flourished composition:

I think it is but fair that the local historian of the place, who has never been known to fame by any other name than that of Joe, and who presents himself to every visitor in that studious undress so finely depicted in the statue of the great Dr Johnson, erected in St Paul's cathedral, namely, without shoes and stockings, and encumbered, if I rightly recollect, with only half a pair of breeches, should relate his story first, especially as the cunning, ingenuity, and drollery of the discourse, will serve to illustrate the character of the low Irish. The speech which succeeds I took down verbatim in my sketchbook under the pretence of sketching ... 'And plaze your honour, I will tell you the history of the place; *and true*', said he, 'as ever was made in Ireland. All that you see belonged to St Kevin, who lived one hundred and twenty years before he died. Long life to your honour; three generals have just given me only two ten-penny pieces, and that's little enough; for your honour may perceive' (pointing to his cabin upon the mountains, and smiling) 'that it is high living there. The fat little general told me to show him the Ivy Tower, as they wrongfully call it; but I said there are two jantlemen, meaning you, your honour, and the other jantleman, long life to you both, who are gone amongst the mountains there to see the loch, and I must not leave them.' [He keeps talking for a while.] 'And pray,' said I, 'Joe, how did you procure all this information?' 'Oh! your honour,' was the reply, 'I learned it all from my Great-Uncle, who lived 120 years before he died, he was the only man who knew anything about the place but me.'[103]

As in Killarney, such 'characters' (famous or notoriously odd persons) were sometimes more extensively described in travel books than the sights they were supposed to point out. One of them – perhaps the same – was well-known in the 1830s: 'that best of guides and most veracious of legendaries, our ingenious protege Joe Irwin'.[104] At about the same time George Winder (or Wynder) became even more famous: 'Yet who is this? – The Prince of the lot, old George Wynder, in his seal-skin cap and weather-beaten face'. Here are four vignettes of the 'prince':

From the moment he accosted me, I may almost say to the moment he left me, his tongue never ceased, but went on at such a clattering tremendous rate, rattling out his words, with a rapidity equalled only by the curate of a parish church in London when he publishes the banns of marriage ... 'It was I', said he, 'who accompanied Mr Tommy

102 J. Grant *Impressions of Ireland and the Irish* (1844) 1. 246-50. **103** *The Stranger in Ireland* ... (1806) 178-84. **104** *Guide to the County of Wicklow* (1835) 117-18.

[Moore] ... through all the scenes of his poems; it was I who told him all the various legends ... ' His head seemed overflowing with Irish legends, and I am sure if any one take the trouble to write down his stories, they would furnish materials for a second volume of Crofton Croker's "Fairy Tales" [see next chapter]. He never hesitated for a word, and altogether it had not been my fortune to meet such a character in any part of the world. He calls himself Winder.[105]

Once at Glendalough, when George Winder was relating to us a 'laagend', we said, 'Now, Winder, tell us truly, is that a veritable legend?' 'Well,' he replied, 'I'll tell truth to your honours: *it is not*, for ye see I make as many laagends over night as will do for the quality next day.'[106]

Among the crowd of guides, I soon recognized George Wynder, with his red beard, but not with bare feet, as drawn in the second volume of Mr and Mrs Hall's highly amusing work [*Ireland: Its Scenery* ...] ... 'George' had lost none of his volubility of tongue, whatever he might have done of the wit which Mr Hall has celebrated. I verily believe that he 'can coin laagends enough over night, to entertain the quality all the next day'. George has a smattering of Latin, in addition to a tolerable knowledge of the native Irish. He is, decidedly, one of the most amusing and intelligent guides I have ever met with on any part of this earth's surface.[107]

In 1874 a book was still illustrated with a portrait of 'George Winder, the Glendalough Guide'.[108] Joe Irwin and George Winder could also fuse into one composite character:

The old weather-beaten, but very intelligent historian and guide of Glendalough, George Irwin, as he escorts the visitors, points out to them the four openings at the top of the tower, and explains their use by stating that the priests of the Fire-worshippers used to mount to the top of the tower, and to the four quarters of the compass, cry 'BEAL! BEAL! BEAL!' by way of summoning the faithful to prayer, and announcing the arrival of the sun ... The old entertaining guide of Glendalough, George Irwin, confidently asserts that he escorted Sir Walter Scott, and his friend Miss Edgeworth, into St Kevin's Bed, and that they assured him there was no place in the world equal to Glendalough.[109]

Unreliability was part of the game. The Anglo-Irish traveller Caesar Otway (more about him presently) offered in 1829 one of the most detailed portraits (or caricatures) of Joe Irwin, caught in the act of cultivating his own legend:

Leaving my horse at a wretched inn near the bridge, I was accosted as I proceeded towards the churches, by a queer looking old fellow, attired in what once was a military frock coat, that might have been scarlet, but now by some dirty dye had assumed the hue of bog water; this hung in stripes about his heels, with an old shapeless felt on his head, such as country boys call a cobbeen – his countenance was not less uncommon than his attire – a leering cautious cunning in the wink of his eye, a hooked miserly formed nose,

105 John Barrow *A Tour round Ireland* (1835) 365-7. **106** A.M. and S.T. Hall *A Week at Killarney* (1850) 79. **107** James Johnson *A Tour in Ireland ...* (1844) 38-9. **108** Sir Cusack P. Roney *How to Spend a Month in Ireland* 37. **109** George O'Malley Irwin *The Illustrated Hand-Book to the County of Wicklow* (1844) 13-14.

a huge mouth, whose under lip hung loose and pendulous. The expression of the whole outward man denoted practised confidence, cunning, and meanness. Addressing me with the assurance that denoted his calling – 'Here I am, Joe Irwin, the best and only guide to the Churches – I'm the boy that can show your honour all, and tell you all; sure it's I that's in the book.' 'What book?' 'Why Doctor Wright's book [G.N. Wright *Tour to the Seven Churches* 1822], that tells the quality all about the County of Wicklow – sure I am down there, printed off in black and white – and sure it was nobody else but I, that showed the Duchess of R– all and every thing about the Churches – 'twas I, my own self, that handed her, all as one as if I was her Duke, into Kevin's bed – and there I brought also the great Sir Walter Scott, who though he be short of one leg, is an active and proper man sartainly, and very free and dacent and generous, as I may say, to a poor body. It was just at this hill where we now stand, that the Duchess ordered her coachman to draw up, and the darling lady looked out amongst us all, as we stood around, and a posy she was, with her cheeks as red as poppies among the corn; a proper woman too, as to size, as becomes a Duchess – So my dear life, out she drew her book, and then she axed "where is the guide that is down in this book, for no other, will my Grease have," says she; so says I to myself, "now's your time, Joe Irwin, to step forward, for you're the boy for her money"; so out I started from among the poor crathurs who were about the coach, for they all knew, sure enough, that I was the man in the book; so taking off my hat, and not forgetting to make a bow and a scrape of the heel, "I'm the boy you want, my *Grease*," says I; "I know the ins and outs of every thing here, and can tell yees all about St Kevin, and King M'Thoul, and Cathleen, and the dog, and the serpent, and the willow apple, and any thing else your Duchess pleases." "Come along then," says my Duchess, "you're the man for my money; and so let all the other spalpeens sneak off, about their business, for not a mother sowl shall be a follower or get a penny of mine, but the man that's down in the book, and that's yourself, honest Joe Irwin".' From this narrative of Mr Irwin, it was easy to see what a forward, self-sufficient, ignorant creature he was; greedy of gain, and jealous of the attentions of any other, who might share of the bounty of visitors. The man had none of the simplicity, and ready obligingness of my guide at Gougane Barra, nor any of the wild humour and fund of song and story that belonged to Alick M'Cock at the Causeway, but still he was a character, likely to serve my turn as well as another, and so I took him, and proceeded on foot towards the churches.[110]

An even more heavily charged send-up of 'that celebrated guide and *bore*, Joe Irwin' was drawn a few years later by another Anglo-Irish writer, Samuel Lover. Here we decidedly enter the world of fiction (on which we certainly began to encroach earlier). Lover's guide would warn the public that:

... 'there's a power of them spalpeens sthravaigin' about, sthrivin' to put their comether upon the quol'ty, and callin' themselves Irwin (knowin', the thieves o' the world, how his name had gone far and near as the rale guide), for to deceave dacent people; but never to b'lieve the likes – for it was only mulvatherin people they wor.' ... 'This, sir,'

---

110 'A Day at the Seven Churches at Glendalough', in *The Christian Examiner and Church of Ireland Magazine* 8 (1829) 51-3. The rendition of Irwin's gossip fills several pages.

said my guide, putting himself in an attitude, 'is the chapel of King O'Toole – av coorse y'iv often heerd o' King O'Toole, your honour?' 'Never,' said I. 'Musha, thin, do you tell me so?' said he. 'By gor, I thought all the world, far and near, heerd o' King O'Toole! Well, well! – but the darkness of mankind is ontellible. Well, sir, you must know, as you didn't hear it afore, that there was wanst a king, called King O'Toole, who was a fine ould king in the ould ancient times, long ago; and it was him that ownded the Churches in the airly days. [He tells the story of Kevin's goose; the gentleman smiles.] 'Oh, you may laugh if you like,' said he, half-affronted, 'but it's thruth I'm tellin' you ... [The story of the goose is continued:] Well, over the ind o' Luganure she flew, stout and studdy, and round the other ind av the *little* lake, by the Churches (that is, av coorse, where the Churches is *now*, but was not *thin*, by raison they wor not built, but aftherwards by Saint Kavin), and over the big hill here over your head, where you see the big clift – (and that clift in the mountain was made by *Fan MaCool*, where he cut it acrass with a big swoord, that he got made a purpose by a blacksmith out o' Ruthdrum, a cousin av his own, for to fight a joyant that darr'd him on the Curragh o' Kildare; and he thried the swoord first an the mountain, and cut it down ino a gap, as is plain to this day; and faith, sure enough, it's the same sauce he sarv'd the joyant, soon and suddent, and chopped him in two like a pratie, for the glory of his sowl and owld Ireland) – well, down she flew over the clift, and fluttherin' over the wood there at Poulanass (where I showed you the purty watherfall – and by the same token, last Thursday was a twelve month sence, a young lady, Miss Rafferty by name, fell into the same watherfall, and was nigh hand drowned – and indeed would be to this day, but for a young man that jumped in afther her ...)' ... 'Oh, you needn't laugh,' said old Joe, half offended at detecting the trace of a suppressed smile, 'you needn't laugh, for it's truth I'm telling you ... '[111]

We may complete this salvo of quotations with a relatively more sober recording of yet another avatar of the type: Miles Doyle, heard by an Austrian traveller in the 1850s:

'Have you ever heard of Dr Wilde and Dr Graves [noted scientists and antiquarians in the mid-nineteenth century]? Oh, all the Irish scholars know me; I found the old gravestones about here for them, and scratched away the earth that they might read the oghams. Show me that green book you have in your hand; oh, I see, it is Black's Picturesque Tour of Ireland. Mr Black knows me well [Adam and Charles Black published several guidebooks in the 1850s]; I told him all he wrote about Glendalough.' [When he tells a story about St Kevin and a perjurer, a tourist interrupts him:] 'You tell falsehood yourself,' Mr Macrie shouted, after looking long and cautiously through his Picturesque Tourist of Ireland. Mr Black doesn't say a word of it.' 'Look you, your honour', the guide replied; 'poor Miles knows many things which Mr Black doesn't tell'.[112]

Of course, in the preceding pages we have been confronted with stock characters, appearing only in one kind of scene. Why dwell upon such histrionic

111 'King O'Toole and Saint Kevin – A Legend of Glendalough', *Legends and Stories of Ireland* 2-4, 8-10. 112 Julius Rodenberg *A Pilgrimage through Ireland or the Island of the Saints* (1860) 62, 68.

role-playing? Partly because, as already said, it was the kind of storytelling most tourists encountered in the field, and in books they played a decisive role in the elaboration – after the dangerous firebrand and the inspired 'bard' – of a new image of the Irish storyteller; also because they show how an ethnic image may be projected for the outside world: such performers, consciously or not, intensified the visitors' prejudices. They may have fabricated special sets of legends, but were influenced by genuine tradition.[113] It had been the function of poets and *seanchaithe* to know the history of every notable place; what had served local people as a link with their past was diluted or fossilized to provide tourists with cheap souvenirs, or with material to pad out their books. To some extent it spread what only the natives had known, but it also encouraged some Anglo-Irish writers to cultivate a taste for buffoonery which could be curiously ambivalent: stigmatizing the natives or making them fascinating, and pleasing English audiences or ridiculing them.

After the middle of the nineteenth century, and particularly in its last decades, the authors of travel books tended to pay less attention to legends and those who told them – partly because Ireland had changed, or because what tourists expected was less flamboyant, in part also because such information now appeared separately as 'folklore', which had become marketable in its own right. A few references to talkative guides can still be found in the twentieth century,[114] but their golden age was by then long past. Today, speaking in the microphone of a whistle-stop coach-tour, he/she has little time for narratives, and may not be a local person. The tourist is invited to buy a video-cassette travelogue to play at home, and 'Heritage Centres' or theme-parks may offer condensed filmed versions of ancient stories.

Those who did not content themselves with clichés and who published their fresh impressions of what they had observed in remote parts of Ireland were not always foreign tourists: descendants of British settlers also sometimes left their urban dwellings, 'big-house' (country estates) or Anglican rectories, not to go to Dublin or London as was the fashion but to explore the island, or sojourn in out-of-the-way regions. Some of them recorded their experiences, writing for

---

113 Brian Earls 'Supernatural Legends in 19th-century Writing', *Béaloideas* 60-1 (1992-3) 105: 'Such figures should probably be thought of less as charlatans than as tradition-bearers whose art had coarsened to the degree that they had become aware of their own ethnographic picturesqueness.' 114 As in H.V. Morton's *In Search of Ireland* (1930) 135: 'The boatmen and the jarveys of Killarney are expert at feeling your pulse. They have a genius for telling you what you expect them to tell you! They sum you up in ten seconds ... 'Are there any leprechauns in Killarney?' I asked a jarvey. 'Leprechauns?' he said, taking a good look at me. 'Why, this is the most terrible place in all Ireland for them! You could not stir a foot in the old days for them'. As late as 1991 a booklet distributed by the Killarney Tourism Office recommended the by now old-fashioned 'Jaunting Car Trip': 'A unique experience and a must for the visitor, this is the traditional way to visit many of the well-known beauty spots, with a story-telling jarvey as one's guide'.

their Anglo-Irish countrymen or for English readers. They were themselves observed and commented upon by outsiders; for instance, the Scottish visitor Daniel Dewar (see p. 134) had met in Ireland at the beginning of the century 'two classes of people perfectly distinct in genius, manners, customs and dispositions': the 'original Hibernian' and the 'Anglo-Hibernian'. Of the latter, he thought that 'though he is proud of being an Irishman, he is full of prejudice against the aborigines of his country; he heartily hates their language, their customs, and their superstitions.'[115] However, we have seen in Chapter 4 that the last part of the statement was not true of all Anglo-Irish people. By briefly focusing now on half-a-dozen texts or groups of texts produced by members of the Protestant upper-middle class we may try and sample the views of this kind of witnesses who, though in some important respects socially and culturally separated from what they saw, were closer to it than foreign visitors.

Thomas Campbell, born in 1733 in County Tyrone, graduated from Trinity College Dublin and became a clergyman in his native county. In 1776 his *Philosophical Survey of the South of Ireland, in a series of letters to John Watkinson, M.D.* used the persona of an English traveller recording his tour, and pastiched the conventions of the genre when they were only beginning to crystallize. For instance, because Macpherson's versions of supposedly 'bardic' poetry were at the height of fame, Campbell's traveller gets acquainted with Ossianic remains in Ireland. It is difficult to decide if real knowledge is mixed with Campbell's own errors or with ironic parody of contemporary antiquarians' extravagant use of etymology:

The songs of Ossian are as familiar to the aboriginal natives of Ireland, as they are represented by Mr M'– to be in Scotland. Fin-mac Comhal (pronounced Fin macoal) i.e. Fin the son of Comhal is the great hero, to whom, as a Hercules, the common Irish assimilate all strong and gallant men ... [The visitor has seen dolmens, and heard the common legend attached to many of them.] A whimsical circumstance relative to these *Crom-liaghs* [*liag chrom*: bent stone] I cannot omit. They are called by the ignorant natives Granie's beds. This Granie is fabled to be the mother of Finmacoal, or Fingal; and of her, as well as of her son, they have wonderful traditions. I have heard songs in her praise, and was shown, in a stone, the mark of her foot, and have heard an huge rock called Finmacoal's finger-stone. The source however of the appellation Granie's bed, I conceive to be a corruption of the original Irish name of these altars. Grineus is, we know, a classical name for Apollo ... and Grian is a common name for the Sun in Irish.[116]

As in real foreigners' reports, 'absurd superstitions' are commented upon:

The Fairy Mythology is swallowed with the wide throat of credulity. Every parish has its green, and its thorn, where these *little people* are believed to hold their merry meetings, and dance their frolic rounds. Those forts and mounts I have described to you, are

115 *Observations on the Character, Customs, and Superstitions of the Irish* (1812) 21-2. **116** Campbell, op. cit. 83-4 and 229-30.

all regarded as fairy land, where the pigmy grandees keep their moon-shine courts, and star-light assemblies. It would be difficult to tempt any common labourer, and some could not be tempted, to apply their spade to these *sacred* remains; for they would be certain that some evil must befall either themselves, or their family, or their cattle, before the expiration of a year.[117]

We catch a glimpse of the anonymous crowd of helpful or curious talkative people with silly stories, from which 'guides' would emerge one or two generations later:

My short stay here [at Cashel, County Tipperary] has afforded me frequent opportunities of conversing with the common people; who, having observed me measuring one of the monasteries, would sometimes follow me at a distance, and sometimes throw themselves in my way, in order to get or give information. Their native humour was entertaining, and their remarks upon men and manners shrewd and sagacious; but nothing could be more ridiculous and absurd than their traditional tales. Asking them for the reason of the name of the Hore Abbey, they told me, that one of their queens, who in her youth had been a great whore, founded it for the salvation of her *poor* soul.[118]

Campbell may have deliberately associated the 'absurdity' of Irish traditional explanations with that of English or Anglo-Irish pseudo-scholarship, for instance in the 'Granie' episode – if he himself knew the real nature of Gráinne's relationship to Fionn.

Our next example comes from resident landowners rather than tourists: *Letters from the Irish Highlands of Connemara*, written in 1823 and 24 by three members of the Blake family of Renvyle House, relate a first journey to that remote region in 1811 and their experiences after they had decided to settle there. The texts, aimed at an English audience, tried to correct erroneous opinions about Ireland: 'The object has been to present to view the details of domestic life, to open the door of the lowly cabin, to portray the habits and manners of its neglected inmates, and preserve the memory of facts, which, although not worthy to become matters of history, are yet of intrinsic value in the delineation of national character.'[119] The letters described the life of Connemara people, sometimes deploring their 'gross superstitions', sometimes defending their character. 'That natural eloquence for which the Irish are so remarkable' is mentioned; yet the informants' prudent reticence is also noted:

I never cease to regret our ignorance of the Irish language. It completely shuts us out from that communication with the lower orders, so interesting in itself, and without which no judgment is to be formed of the character of a nation ... I feel this privation of intercourse more particularly when I am following our country guides over a bog or across a mountain: Naturally a communicative people, they would willingly beguile the way, but, checked by wants of words, they are reduced to answer our eager inquiries by

117 Ibid. 280-1. 118 Ibid. 134. 119 Op. cit. 'Introduction'.

tardy monosyllables. Perhaps, too, their uncertain comprehension of our meaning makes them suspicious of being the object of ridicule; and, aware that our religious opinions differ from their own, they carefully avoid bringing into notice those local superstitions, connected with anecdotes of traditional history, which to me have always an appropriate charm that adds to the beauty of picturesque scenery.[120]

It was possible, however, to listen to some bilingual and culturally amphibious persons:

> Your taste for anecdotes, which are characteristic of national peculiarities, might easily be gratified, if you could sometimes take my place by the fireside, and have near you the old lady who makes frequent use of the privilege which gives her the freedom of every room in the house, to call my attention from my book, or entertain me while I am at work, repeating some of her long stories. Her age, which carries her back more than half a century, and her profession as a nurse, which has gained her admittance, and a sort of prescriptive right to intimacy in every house in this part of Ireland, from the castle of the noblest lord, to the meanest and most neglected cabin, enables her to fur-nish tales and anecdotes in greater variety and abundance than any one I have ever met with. Add to this, that she herself belongs to a class altogether lost in England, but still to be met with here, where feudal feelings and affections, although, perhaps, no longer supported by the laws, yet find sufficient encouragement in the habits and manners of the people. Kind-hearted and charitable, she is always ready to listen to the complaints of the poor, enters into all their tales of distress, gives advice and assistance gratuitously, and acts as a sort of mediator between them and their richer neighbours ... It is when repeating the anecdotes connected with the history of families residing in the country that I like to listen to her: when seated by the fireside, close to the ground, resting on her heels, in the peculiar attitude which the peasantry of this country seems to prefer to the use either of chair or stool; her countenance lighted up by the recollection of scenes in which she formerly bore a distinguished part; her strong accent and native idiom giving force and energy to her language; while the addition of names and dates allows you to consider the narrative as somewhat better authenticated than the former; it is then that I listen with pleasure, as the repetition of one story calls up another.[121]

Other Anglo-Irish writers only sojourning in the west were less concerned with gaining sympathy for the natives; they wanted to amuse their peers and portrayed Ireland as a playground for gentlemen. William Hamilton Maxwell exemplifies them. Born at Newry in 1792, he travelled, enjoyed life, was for a time the dilletantish Anglican rector of a parish in County Mayo, and wrote a dozen books. His *Wild Sports of the West, with Legendary Tales* achieved great success in 1832. The first-person narrator is invited by his cousin to spend some time 'in the wilds of Erris', and the sports he goes in for are hunting, fishing, rambling and reading or listening to stories. The preface states that the tales and legends were actually heard; it may be true, but they have lost much of their real

120 Ibid. 168-70. 121 Ibid. 370-1.

oral style, and the reactions of the listening gentlemen steal the limelight. Antony, an old otter-hunter is the main oral sub-narrator. This is how he is introduced:

In his wanderings, he picked up tales and traditions among the wild people he consorted with: his memory is most tenacious, and he narrates strange legends which, in wildness and imagination, rival the romances of the east. In winter, when the snow falls and the fury of the storm is unloosed, Antony is settled in his rude but comfortable chair, formed of twisted bent. The women of my household listen to his love-stories with affected indifference, but there is always some apology for remaining near the otter-killer. At times, when the old man is summoned after dinner to receive his customary glass, I, if I be 'i' the humour', listen to his wild legends; and here, in this mountain hut, seated in this room, 'mine own great chamber', while I luxuriate over a bright bog-deal fire, an exquisite cigar, and an admixture of pure hollands with the crystal water that falls from the rock behind us, I listen in voluptuous tranquillity to Antony's monotonous romances, as he recites to his attentive auditory in the kitchen his narratives of former times.[122]

Such background noise is perceived by the gentlemen as part of the holiday atmosphere in a comfortable summer lodge. The local storyteller and the lower-class section of his audience are comic – though their 'wildness' might also be a bit frightening:

The credulity of these wild people is amazing, and their avidity for news, if possible, exceeded by the profound reliance they place in the truth of the intelligence. Hence the most absurd versions of passing events circulate over the district – and reports prevail, by turns, of a ridiculous or mischievous tendency, generally according to the mental temperament of the story-teller.[123]

Testimonies collected by an official commission at about the same time, mostly from Anglo-Irish residents, reflect the establishment's fear of 'mischievous' rumours:

[Parish of Headford, County Galway] I think it is highly prejudicial to the poor to give lodging to beggars; it causes dirt, and brings on fever. They often circulate false reports, and excite rebellious feelings.
    [Parish of Moore, County Roscommon] The trading beggars do injure by their dissolute habits, loose conversation, and the circulation of stories which it does not answer the people to hear, the moral state of the population.
    [Parish of Carlow] They are in many cases the means of spreading discontent, by repeating stories calculated to breed ill-will.
    [Parish of Naas, County Kildare] It was stated, also, that beggars often fabricate and spread mischievous stories.[124]

---

122 W.H. Maxwell *Wild Sports of the West* 79. **123** Ibid. 324-5. **124** *Selection of Parochial Examinations, relative to the Destitute Classes in Ireland* (1835) 283, 306, 320, 326.

Even a near-absentee Anglo-Irishman like Maxwell could glimpse a social tension which travellers from abroad might ignore.

Yet another type of Anglo-Irish traveller, the systematic explorer, may be represented by Caesar Otway, who was born in County Tipperary in 1780. Because he was a noted Evangelical preacher of the 'Second Reformation' movement and as such an obsessive anti-Catholic propagandist, this man has a bad name in Ireland; but when he toured the country and noted down his observations he did justice to the landscape and paid attention, though without much respect, to storytelling. (See his portrait of the Glendalough guide Joe Irwin, pp.154-5.) He asked local people for local legends: his books contain more than a hundred and fifty of them. *Sketches in Ireland* offers, for instance, an interview concerning a beast-in-the-lake legend associated with Lough Derg:

To beguile our mountain road, I asked the boy why the lake was called Lough Derg? – *derg* signifies red in Irish ... [Otway has proposed his own explanation.] 'Oh, indeed, Sir;' and mind here, reader, I pray you, that my memory does not serve me to give the following story exactly in the boy's words, 'that is not the reason I have heard the old people give: formerly, I hear say, it was called Lough Fin or Fin M'Coul's Lough, but afterwards it was called Lough Derg, or the Red Lough; and the reason for that, as I have heard, is, that once upon a time, long ago, there was an old wicked witch of a woman, who had a great big giant of a son ... [the story follows]'.[125]

The setting of the following extract is Gougane Barra in County Cork (with legends of the local saint, and another haunted lake):

There is no collection of cabins in Ireland that does not contain some idle, chatty, knowledgeable personage – a lounger about the smith's forge – a collector and dealer in news, stories old and recent – a man who knows how to live by his wits, just as well (though in a different way) as in Paris and London. Such a genius presented himself to my notice. The lazy gait, the lively eye, the quaint but intelligent features of the man announced just such a gossiping fellow as I wanted. 'If your honour wants to go to the blessed lake I'll show you the way and attend you, with a thousand welcomes ... '[126]

Another scene, in *A Tour in Connaught*, takes place by Lough Corrib; Otway is questioning people about Caisleán an Circa (or na Circe), a thirteenth-century island keep supposed to have taken its name from a magic hen which provided the besieged garrison with abundant food, until its leader, Donal-an-chogaidh ('of the war') O'Flaherty, grew tired of eggs and roasted the fowl:[127]

125 *Sketches in Ireland* 181. 126 Ibid. 303-4. 127 There were other versions of the story: 'The legends respecting its name, origin, and history, are as numerous as they are fabulous – how it was built in a night by a cock and a hen, how it was defended by the Lady O'Flaherty after O'Flaherty *an Coilean*, or the Cock, had been slain, whence the heroine derived the soubriquet of the Hen, or *an Chearc* – again, how it was built by a chieftain named Darka – and how the celebrated Gráine Uaille [see p. 68], after she had abducted the heir of Howth, car-

I was anxious to inquire about the castle, and therefore stopped at a range of cabins that stood in all their low dirty wretchedness on the roadside, and saluting the inmates, as I always do, with the usual Irish accost – 'God save all here,' out came a young woman with a child in her arms ... In answer to many questions, she with a sort of suppressed smile, said she did not know. The Irish never like to answer questions until they see what is the drift of the interrogator; but when I expressed admiration at the beauty of the country, and the fine position of the old fortress, and how sorry I was that I could not know any thing about it, she then said, Och, for that matter she'd tell me and welcome all she ever heard about it, but how could the likes of her know any thing for sartain? The place was called Castle Hen, and all the neighbours said that it was built by a witch ... [Later on Otway meets a 'bare-legged gossoon':] 'What old ruin is it, may I ask?' 'Och! then, I was just thinking as much – an' it isn't every body could tell you about that same. Sure, it's one of Grania's ould castles, an' a fine antiant place it is'. 'I dare say it is, but what may be the meaning of that long, outlandish name (Chrislane-a-Kirca)?' 'The manin', your honour! I'll tell you that – 'tis the Hen's Castle.' ... [Then an older man steps in:] 'Wait a minit, your honour, till I kindle the pipe, an' I'll tell ye all about it ... '[128]

William Robert Le Fanu's *Seventy Years of Irish Life; being Anecdotes and Reminiscences* (1893), takes a less humorous approach to the 'sports' Maxwell called 'wild'. He gives his account of an evening of storytelling in a thatched farmhouse where himself and his friends had taken refuge when lost in the Galtee Mountains, in July 1838. His brother, the ghost-story writer (see Chapter 7), disrupted the joyful atmosphere:

A huge turf fire was blazing on the hearth, at which we sat drying our nether garments which were thoroughly drenched; great mugs of hot goats' milk were supplied to warm our insides, our host informing us that he had upwards of eighty goats on the mountain. He and the boys (all unmarried men are boys in the south) and girls sat up with us by the cheery fire, talking, joking, and telling stories. After some time my brother happened to say to the man of the house, 'I suppose that was your horse that passed us on the mountain?' All were silent, and looked one at another half incredulous, half-frightened. One of them, after a pause, said, 'There is no horse on the mountain. What sort of a horse was it that ye thought ye seen?' 'A chestnut horse,' said we. 'Oh, begorra!' said our friend; 'they seen the yalla horse!' Then turning to us, 'It's a wonder ye all cum down alive and safe; it is few that sees the yalla horse that has luck after'. This was one of the superstitions of the dwellers on the Galtees.[129]

Le Fanu also acquaints us with yet another local belief concerning lake haunting:

The dreadful beast, the 'wurrum', half fish, half dragon, still survives in many a mountain lake – seldom seen indeed, but often heard. Near our fishing quarters in

ried him thither, etc., etc; some of which fables the guides and boatmen will no doubt relate to the tourist.' (W.R. Wilde *Loch Corrib, its Shores and Islands* 162.) **128** *A Tour in Connaught* (1839) 229, 233, 236. **129** Op. cit. 129-30.

Kerry, there are two such lakes; one, the beautiful little lake at the head of the Blackwater river, called Lough Brin, from Brin, or Bran, as he is now called, the direful wurrum which inhabits it. The man who minds the boat there, speaks with awe of Bran; he tells me he has never seen him, and hopes he never may, but has often heard him roaring on a stormy night. On being questioned as to what the noise was like, he said it was like the roaring of a young bull. To my suggestion that perhaps 'it might have been a young bull,' he made no reply, but the expression of his face showed what he thought of the levity, or perhaps even the irreverence, of the remark.[130]

Finally, one unlikely source on Irish storytelling is difficult to classify (except, perhaps, as ironic paternalism): John Pentland Mahaffy. The caustic provost of Trinity College and famous Dublin 'character' was a classical scholar hostile to Irish nationalism, who thought that no worthwhile culture or literature could exist in the Irish language; yet in his treatise on *The Principles of the Art of Conversation* he admitted that he was living 'in a country where the practice of [this art] is confessedly on a high level, and where the average man is able to talk well'.[131] He included Irish peasants among the masters – though from the point of view of a defender of the Anglo-Irish ascendancy they also had to be subordinates:

One chief cause of the talking and social ability of some peasantries over others is the fact that their proximate ancestors were a bilingual people ... constantly educated in intelligence by the problem of translating ideas from one language into another ... Conversation with these people [gentlemen like Mahaffy might know them only as 'gillies' – see p. 140], which is often prolonged through many hours, is not only very instructive – a secondary matter to us now – but exceedingly amusing, from the perfect frankness as well as tact with which they speak their mind to the sporting friend, whom they regard as their inferior or equal from a professional point of view. It is this perfect liberty, this spiritual equality, often designated as the free-masonry of sport, from which arises the charm of talking upon subjects of common interest to one confessedly inferior in many respects ... The most successful conversations with old men are, however, not those with the old raconteur, who is in the habit of narrating his experiences and expects to be asked to do so, but with some modest and apparently dull old person who is successfully probed by intelligent and sympathetic questions, till he is actually reminded of long-forgotten scenes which have perhaps not been suggested to him for years, and then he draws from his memory, with the help of further questions, some passage of life and adventure of the highest interest.[132]

---

130 Ibid. 115. **131** *The Principles of the Art of Conversation* vii. **132** Ibid. 133-5, 139-40. W.B. Stanford and R.B. McDowell *Mahaffy: A Biography of an Anglo-Irishman* 78: he had lived in his youth in County Monaghan, in 'a society in which conversation was one of the great sources of entertainment, family history providing a staple of talk, and stories about local heroes, reshaped in repetition, becoming legends ... In later life he liked to go to Donegal, his father's native county, for the trout fishing and grouse shooting in the autumn.'

At all times, in all countries, travellers have met storytellers, and guides may have been prepared to interest or entertain with a fund of anecdotes and legends wherever people flocked to admire celebrated landscapes or monuments. Travellers have also brought back tales of their own, often presumed to be lies. The reactions of people visiting foreign countries have generally oscillated between indignation, contempt, amusement, curiosity, compassion and admiration; many have looked for deviations from their norm, then shared their astonishment with their countrymen.

These general remarks also apply to the impressions of continental, British or Anglo-Irish people who visited Ireland, but there was room for differences: among those who could afford to travel, there were attentive observers commenting on living conditions and changes in Irish society, and tourists who cared merely for their comfort; some accounts seem truthful while others may be of doubtful authenticity; only occasionally was the traveller a writer of merit. But beneath such diversity we find obvious similarities: first, the confrontation with a more or less different way of life; secondly, a limited field of vision conditioned by time or chance and by preconceived notions – for instance, one had to visit certain places and to witness some 'typical' scenes, and many saw what they had been told to see. In fact, there wasn't a simple fixed reality, and some visitors were more aware of it than others; but the average English traveller was likely to accept the conventional definition of Irish people as an inextricable mixture of contradictory vices and minor virtues, including unreliability and native wit. On the whole, the travel books about Ireland produced between 1780 and 1850 tended to show sublime or picturesque settings (perhaps alternating with sordid ones), and friendly, eccentric or grotesque inhabitants.

From such sources we can hardly expect the very accurate presentation of an Irish storyteller addressing members of his own cultural group; the narrators we hear about are mostly those who deliberately acted a subservient role in front of 'your honour', and who were often considered as buffoons or sly liars but also as intriguing bizarre characters, too easily supposed to embody Irishness. In brief, to be worthy of 'touristic' interest the natives had to appear as curiosities while providing standardized experiences, and some adapted themselves to such expectations. With them, we have come a long way from the powerful, arrogant or dangerous *fili* represented in the distant past, and from the more recent construction of inspired 'bards'. In travel books we meet people engaged in more conversational narrative activities, and who were not listened to, as they were perhaps impatiently during the Ordnance Survey campaign, with the aim of obtaining 'true' topographical and historical information, but as part of the fun or as evidence of an irrational attitude. Meanwhile, much storytelling activity was taking place beyond the reach of mere travellers.

Other portraits of storytellers appeared in more specialized accounts of Irish traditions or in obviously fictional contexts, written by people who often had a much more intimate and extensive knowledge of Ireland than most travellers and who might take a more serious interest in cultural differences. The storyteller they preferred was the old 'peasant', sometimes endowed with bardic touches or with the same gift of the gab as the guides, but more likely to manifest ancient simple wisdom and a peculiar imagination, or to serve as the emblem of a common national identity. It is to such portraits that we shall turn in the next two chapters.

6

Protofolklorists and imitators, nationalists and peasants, in the first half of the nineteenth century

There is no hope of knowing *exactly* how stories were told in that period and how the audience they were naturally aimed at experienced them, but we may come nearer to the real facts by studying the evidence given by those who did not merely mention oral narration among other curiosities, but prized it because it had passed from teller to teller over a supposedly long time and would thus have acquired peculiar qualities. The first section of this chapter, after situating the reassessment of such material in a more general current of thought, examines publications which purported to document 'traditional' Irish storytelling. The second section will try to place this material and its aura in the context of growing nationalistic trends, and of the changing conditions of the Irish rural society. The detailed portrait of a storyteller, by a writer who had inside knowledge of that life, will conclude the chapter.

A. PUBLISHING IRISH TALES OR LEGENDS AND PORTRAYING STORYTELLERS

If the cultural situation of Ireland was in some respects special, it did not escape influence from British or more widely European ideologies. In England, one had started relatively early to collect odd local beliefs and customs. Such relics were known as 'fallacies', or 'antiquities' – the term *Antiquitates Vulgares* was introduced by Henry Bourne in 1725 to denote the 'ceremonies and opinions which are held by the common people'. Being a clergyman, he denounced such 'superstitions' as vestiges of paganism or of papistry. If some rejected them as contrary to religious truth, the upholders of the Enlightenment who believed in progress through the use of reason mistrusted the authority of tradition, and saw in the belief in marvels a mental aberration or a sign of obscurantism. Earlier in the century, in French aristocratic *salons*, literary *contes de fées* and later 'oriental' tales had been a source of amusement and a relief from the constraints of neoclassicism, but both genres were soon made fun of by parody or used for didactic purposes. Voltaire, for instance, said he had read the *Arabian Nights* fourteen times but rejected gratuitous fantasy, and invented the *contes philosophiques* which ironically explored a question for polemical use. In one of these texts, a sage wonders how people can like '*des contes qui sont sans raison et qui ne signifient rien*'; some women answer that '*c'est précisément pour cela que nous les aimons*',[1] but in another tale composed in 1773 the heroine protests against such fables, which are good only for the Irish and for some French theologians: '*Les contes qu'on pouvait faire à la quadrisaïeule de ma grand'mère ne sont plus bons pour moi.*'[2]

By the last quarter of the century, however, a movement in the opposite direction was gaining ground. In 1777, when John Brand reissued and completed Henry Bourne's collection it no longer seemed so necessary to save the populace from old habits and ideas, which had become interesting: 'New Lights have arisen since [Bourne's] time. The English Antique has become a general and fashionable study'.[3] To 'the Written Word', Brand opposed an 'Oral Tradition' transmitting 'vulgar rites and popular opinions'[4] which were not negligible. While the still dominant principles prompted generalizations about a universal human nature and fostered a cosmopolitan high culture founded on rational certainties, those who were prepared to respond to apparently sub-rational ways of thinking and to the peculiar modes of expression of lower-class people were becoming more numerous; what was uncorrupted by the artifices of sophisticated society could seem good. One began to try and rescue the popular heritage in the name of an organic collectivity. The supposedly unconscious and anonymous art of 'the people', which was said to preserve values formerly common to society as a whole, could be used to certify the specificity of a nation, and to justify the restoration of its rights if they seemed endangered by foreign political domination or cultural infiltration.

The bases of the new theory were formulated in Germany by Johann Gottfried Herder. From his reading of the Old Testament, of Macpherson's *Ossian* and Percy's *Reliques of Ancient English Poetry* as well as his experience of Lettish, Danish and German popular songs, he had conceived an 'enthusiasm for the uncultivated'. *Das Volk*, for him and his followers a kind of collective personality made up of people (peasants rather than the mob)[5] rooted in the same set of views and customs, would preserve values which a frenchified high culture had tried to suppress. Universal basic elements existed in human experience, but place, time, climate, mode of subsistence and history had developed in each of those distinct communities a certain consciousness and set of symbols – its 'spirit' or 'soul'. Every *Volk* had a mission to perform in the march of humanity towards a time when different cultures would flourish together in peace, but this duty could be carried out only if the unique creative potential of each remained pure. Unsophisticated strata of the community would best embody the distinctive qualities, and their oral traditions were thus the most

---

1 *Zadig*, in F. Deloffre (ed.) *Romans et Contes* 1. 84. 2 'Le Taureau Blanc', ibid. 2. 264-5. 3 Bourne and Brand quoted in R.M. Dorson *The British Folklorists: A History* 12,13. On the beginning and later development of partly similar attitudes in Germany and France, see H. Bausinger *Volkskunde* and N. Belmont *Paroles anciennes*. Also D. Ó Giolláin *Locating Irish Folklore* Ch. 2. 4 Quoted in R.M. Dorson (ed.) *Peasant Customs and Savage Myths* 1. 8,6. 5 *Stimmen der Völker in Liedern, Zweites Buch* 175: 'Volk heisst nicht der Pöbel auf den Gassen.'

authentic and highest expression of national characteristics. A plan of action to recover and use such powerful roots was outlined in an essay published in the November 1777 issue of *Deutsches Museum*. Herder generally favoured epic poems and songs, but in this text he cast his net wider:

Common legends, tales, and mythology also belong here. In a way, they derive from the beliefs of the people, from its way of seeing, its energies and instincts, when one dreams because one does not know, and believes because one does not see, and the whole uneducated soul is at work. This is also great material for the historian of mankind, the poet and the critic and the philosopher. Stories of a certain kind, diffused by Nordic people, have appeared in many countries and at different times, yet in each country and in each period they have taken particular forms. What are they like now in Germany? Where did the most common and most extraordinary stories first appear? how did they circulate? how far did they spread and to what extent have they become diversified?[6]

By collecting and studying such material, the *Volksgeist* of a nation, its ancestral energy, could be identified and preserved or revived.

Collections of German *Märchen* and *Sagen* began to appear in the 1780s, but the task recommended by Herder was really undertaken more than a quarter of a century later by the brothers Grimm, who, around 1807, started collecting 'the legends and folktales that still circulate among the peasants and that have been preserved for us in forgotten places'.[7] They insisted that it was a matter of urgency to record them ('*diese Märchen festzuhalten*') because those who kept them alive were ever fewer.[8] A vogue for folktales was launched in the second decade of the nineteenth century by their *Kinder- und Hausmärchen*. Elements of theory which developed gropingly in the successive editions were also influential: *Volksdichtung* (folk poetry) was not the conscious product of individuals but was communally created, perhaps from some divine source, in a mysterious process metaphorically conceived as the growth of a flower or the crystallization of a gem. The methods of the Grimms would later be criticized: while celebrating the supposed spontaneous utterances of natural artists, they thought *they* could decide what properly belonged to the *Volksgut*, and transformed documents they considered imperfect into texts that conformed to the ideal. They were sincere when they said that their concern was accuracy and truth ('*diese Märchen so rein als möglich war aufzufassen*'); yet they were not prepared to tour the country to collect stories and then publish them without reshaping. Their

6 '*Von Aehnlichkeit der mittlern englischen und deutschen Dichtkunst, nebst Verschiednem, das darauf folget*', in *Herders Werke* 3, Part 2. 262–3. 'Auch die gemeinen Volkssagen, Märchen und Mythologie gehören hieher. Sie sind gewissermassen Resultat des Volksglaubens, seiner sinnlichen Anschaung, Kräfte und Triebe, wo man träumt, weil man nicht weiss, glaubt, weil man nicht siehet, und mit der ganzen, unzerteilten und ungebildeten Seele wirket: also ein grosser Gegenstand für den Geschichtschreiber der Menscheit, den Poeten und Poetiker und Philosophen.' 7 Jacob Grimm, quoted in C. Kamenetsky *The Brothers Grimm and their Critics* 183. 8 Preface to the 1819 edition of *Kinder- und Hausmärchen*.

direct informants were very seldom from the *Volk* in the limited social sense; they received much material from educated town-dwellers, and also used written texts (some forty different contributors have been listed, and thirty other printed or manuscript sources). It seemed to them that the *Volk*, who had had a collective creative power in the past, now consisted merely of custodians of ancient treasures. The editors reshaped the material when they found it inadequate, decided what was to be considered the essence of the tales – the ideal plots as distinguished from individual ways of telling the stories – and tried to reconstitute the original by combining different versions. They admitted that the expression and execution (*Ausführung*) was theirs.

Be that as it may, the result was a literary masterpiece, which had a great influence. A less popular but notable feature was the commentary, offering parallels and analogues from other countries. It raised questions which were to inflame debates in the following generations. On one hand folktales supposedly provided evidence of national distinctiveness, and the Grimm brothers deleted from the second edition tales that were not 'German' enough. On the other hand the international dimension of the material became more and more obvious. The editors tried to account for this contradiction: the tales were fragments of old myths – some strictly Germanic, others part of a common Indo-European inheritance. When analogues were found on other continents, they offered another explanation: 'There are situations which are so simple and natural that they are found everywhere, just as there are thoughts which come by themselves anywhere (*die sich wie von selbst erfinden*); this is the reason why the same tales, or at least tales which are very similar, occur in very different countries.'[9]

In various parts of Europe, particularly in societies under foreign domination, there were similar attempts to revive a national culture by collecting and editing narratives. In some countries, the Grimms' *Deutsche Sagen*, a set of local and historical legends, was imitated first. In Great Britain, eighteenth-century ballad scholarship had prepared antiquarians and *literati* for the idea that certain anonymous verbal artefacts inherited from the past and having varied in temporal and geographical circulation were worth studying. The ballads were ennobled by the belief that 'minstrels' had originally composed them. Tales and legends were at first not deemed so worthy of attention, but the Grimms' publications directed attention to such prose narratives: a favourable review of *Kinder- und Hausmärchen* appeared in England in 1819[10] and a first translation in 1823. In 1834, William John Thoms, who had edited medieval romances and popular printed texts, began to publish 'Lays and Legends of Various Nations, Illustrative of their Traditions, Popular Literature, Manners, Customs, and Superstitions' – including an Irish volume (No. 3) along with those devoted to Germany, France, Spain and Tartary. He emphasized common features: 'The outlines of the traditions are, in fact, common to all countries; maintaining, in

9 '*Literatur*', in the 1856 edition of *Kinder-und Hausmärchen* 3. 405. 10 Kamenetsky, op. cit. 195-8.

despite of the varied colouring with which they have been tinged by the peculiarities resulting from climate, religion and moral and political causes, so strong
a family resemblance, as either to point to a common origin, or to stamp at once
the poverty of human invention.'[11] In 1846, launching in *The Athenaeum* an epistolary collect of British material explicitly modelled on the Grimm brothers'
method, Thoms wanted to avoid the restrictive or derogatory connotations of the
terms 'antiquities', 'vulgar errors', or 'old wives' tales', and coined a new word
to denote 'the manners, customs, observances, superstitions, ballads, proverbs,
&c, of the olden time': 'What we in England designate as Popular Antiquities ...
would be most aptly described by a good Saxon compound, Folk-Lore – the
Lore of the People.'[12] (Later developments in that field of study will be surveyed
in Chapter 8.)

Tales indigenous to or assimilated by Ireland were published through different
channels: some publications were aimed at common people who could use them
to perfect their reading skills or transmit them to illiterate members of their
community, after which they might be (re)adapted for oral performance; others
were meant to entertain a more polite public, as interest in living verbal lore
gradually merged with the already active antiquarian search for ancient mysteries or glories and with the travellers' thirst for picturesque native oddities. The
compilers used the material in different ways and to different ends, perhaps
transposing the tales into a posh language which created amusing contrasts and
affirmed the writer's superiority to his subject; some had scholarly ambitions,
which appeared mostly in comparative notes modelled on those of the Grimms.
While the first category – material printed for common people and more particularly for rural dwellers – is easily differentiated from what was published for
middle-class readers, the difference within the second group between entertaining and more or less informative aims may be blurred. It is possible to distinguish between what was printed in London mostly for a British audience and
what was published in Ireland; or between what appeared in book forms and
material published in periodicals – but here again there will be borderline cases.
Nothing came directly from the rural world, though a couple of writers had
grown up in it but had then moved up in the social scale.

The more popular material took the form of cheap prints produced in
Dublin, Belfast, Cork, Clonmel, Limerick, Monaghan, Newry and other places.
The early nineteenth century was in Ireland the period of widest diffusion of
'broadsides': loose sheets with more or less narrative songs dealing with love,
crimes and executions, politics, emigration and sport, some of them coming
from, or entering, oral tradition. Prose narratives of different kinds might appear
in 'chapbooks', small in format and sold at three- or sixpence each in grocery
shops or by peddlars who travelled the countryside. They included 'residues of

---

11 *No. 3. Lays and Legends of Ireland* v. 12 Quoted in R.M. Dorson (ed.) *Peasant Customs and
Savage Myths* 1. 53, 52.

oral tradition and were probably intended to be read aloud'.[13] In 1799, a collector of some of those booklets noted: 'They might be divided into the following classes: histories of robbers and pirates; books of chivalry; books of witchcraft and gross superstition; indecent books; these classes constituted about two third of the whole number [he had bought some eighty items], the remaining third consisting of useful or innocent books of voyages, travel, history or novels.'[14] The longer texts could be read or performed from memory in short sections. At least one Fianna romance, *The Battle of Ventry*, circulated thus in the 1820s and 30s[15], and what may have been the first Irish collection of folktales, *The Royal Hibernian Tales: Being a Collection of the Most Entertaining Stories now Extant*, was published as a chapbook in Dublin before 1825,[16] remained in print in that form at least until the middle of the century, and seems to have been widely diffused.[17] The anonymous compiler must have felt that he was performing a kind of patriotic work by doing in Ireland what had been done elsewhere; the models he quoted in an introduction seem to have been British chapbooks, some of which were reproduced in Ireland:

I have oftentimes seen, and with pleasure perused the English Nights' Entertainments, Arabian Nights' Entertainments, Winter Evening Tales, Persian and Chinese Tales; and in short, observed that there is no Country but what has given birth to some Native production of this kind. Finding nothing of this kind in Ireland, and knowing a great many curious Tales, handed down to posterity and held on record throughout the country, which I had an opportunity of hearing in many places, I thought I could not benefit my readers more than by committing them to print for their instruction and amusement ... All the stories will be found to be genuine, and never before offered to the public.[18]

Twelve of the thirteen stories in this collection have been frequently attested in Irish oral tradition at least until the middle of the twentieth century; ten of them fit in with the Aarne-Thompson catalogue of International Tale types, and four have cognates in the Grimm collection. The booklet has nothing to say about the narrators the editor had 'heard in many places'. Of another chapbook, published at Drogheda in 1829, the most impressive part is the title: *The Ancient Irish Tales, Being a Collection of the Stories Told by the Peasantry in the Winter Evenings*. It gave nine stories, some comic and others dealing with fairies, generally taken from 'respectable' books like Croker's *Fairy Legends* – of which more later.

Turning to representations of peasant narrative lore for urban middle class readers, we know that around 1800 some members of the Anglo-Irish world could

13 N. Ó Ciosáin *Print and Popular Culture in Ireland, 1750-1850* 11. 14 W. Stokes, quoted ibid. 14. 15 Ibid. 53. 16 It was reprinted in the tenth volume of *Béaloideas* (1940). 17 Thackeray bought a copy in 1842 and found in it 'the old tricks and some of the old plots that one has read in many popular legends of almost all countries, European and Eastern'. (*Irish Sketch Book* 156, 189ff.) 18 *Béaloideas* 10 (1940) 152.

be interested in a native past, but might be hard put to consider living members of the Catholic community as its noble inheritors and to follow the European trend associating the rural world with original purity; in the Irish context, intellectual curiosity and social benignancy soon conflicted with ethnic prejudices, and, whatever appeal distant stories and images might have, it was difficult to respect the culture of the contemporary peasantry. Moreover, when the brothers Grimm were at work and later when Thoms proposed a name for what their followers were studying, most collectors and editors of Irish oral material were confronted with more than just the general social obstacles their colleagues abroad would also meet: as soon as one went west or southwest, there was a language barrier and an important cultural divide had to be negotiated. Most of those who collected and published Irish material were limited to what they found in English, were apologetic about it, and – perhaps more than was the case elsewhere – tempted to select the more bizarre aspects, often resorting to the amused indulgence of humour or the more cutting superciliousness of wit.

It took time for mere folktales and legends to be taken seriously by educated people in Ireland, but they began to receive attention and be exploited in the second quarter of the century. In 1832 a mediocre anonymous poem obviously based on William Collins's 'Ode on the Popular Superstitions of the Highland of Scotland' (see p. 81) praised Irish popular legends and tales as potential literary themes:

> Such are the tales thy ancient legends tell,
> Land of renown, in times that are gone by –
> Such tales may bring before the poet's eye
> Shapes that but in the feverish fancy dwell ... [19]

The style aimed at by the anonymous poetaster shows what an abyss divided such material and what was supposed to have the dignity of print. But by then the breakthrough of Irish popular narratives into 'respectable' literature, and on the international scene, had already been achieved by Thomas Crofton Croker, who represented the transition from miscellaneous antiquarianism to an intensive exploitation of oral literature, and was at first generously treated as an equal by the Grimm brothers. His books were published in Great Britain. Born in Cork in a family that had come from England in the seventeenth century, Croker (1798-1854) made several excursions in the southern counties between 1811 and 1816, looking for physical antiquities but also observing the country people, 'sketching and studying the character and traditions of the country'[20] and

19 B.B.F. 'Ode on the Popular Superstitions of Ireland, Considered as the Subject of Poetry', *The Irish Monthly Magazine of Politics and Literature* 1 (1832-3) 506. 20 T.F. Dillon Croker 'Memoir of the Author', in *Fairy Legends and Traditions of the South of Ireland* (new ed. 1862) iv. Written by the author's son and first published in the *Gentleman's Magazine* in 1854. See also D. Ó Giolláin *Locating Irish Folklore* 100-2.

learning some Irish – how much is not clear. At eighteen he settled in London, but rambled again through the south and southwest of Ireland in 1821.

His *Researches in the South of Ireland, Illustrative of the Scenery, Architectural Remains, and the Manners and Superstitions of the Peasantry* was published in 1824, and the content justified what its long title announced: the book, for the first time to such an extent in Ireland, combines descriptions and antiquarian material with an interest in oral traditions irrespective of their possible links with ancient literature. The opening pages vindicated the collect of old vanishing expressive or behavioural items – from an 'enlightened' standpoint: 'The vulgar superstition – the traditionary tale – even the romantic legend – possess a relative value from the conclusions to which they lead; and every fragment that we glean, is important as preserving ancient and decaying peculiarities, from which alone a just estimation of former transactions can be derived.'[21] The argument was that one should study remains, but not necessarily admire them. A whole chapter devoted to 'Fairies and Supernatural Agency' contains comments like: 'There is an odd mixture of the ridiculous and the sublime in the prevalent notions respecting such beings'.[22] It was not new to perceive the 'sublime' in Irish landscapes, but one was less disposed to see it in popular beliefs. In this first book, what comes closest to our subject of research is a passage where Croker quotes, from a correspondent's letter, the account a woman of Castletown had given of her experience in fairyland: 'After considerable hesitation on her part, and persuasion on mine, she gave me the following history, which I will recount verbatim, as highly illustrative of fairy superstition and Irish manners ... ' (and she tells how she spent twenty years in fairyland while one thought her dead, then returned to find that her husband had married again).[23]

Here, the curious 'facts' are what matters, not the storyteller's way of presenting them. Croker also reports the story of the old woman changing herself into a hare in order to steal milk or 'dairy profit' from her neighbours, and observes that 'numberless variations [of it] are in circulation amongst the Irish peasantry';[24] but we do not 'hear' the traditional narrator. Like several travellers and antiquarians, Croker notes the existence of a written popular tradition with a partly different content, parallel to the oral one:

Modern manuscripts, in the Irish character, may be met with in almost every village, and they are usually the produce of the leisure hours of the schoolmaster: there is little variation in their contents, which consist of verses wherein Fingal, Oscar, Ossian and St. Patrick are important characters. A dialogue in particular between Ossian and St. Patrick, in which the latter endeavours to convert the bard to Christianity, and one of some length between Death and a Sick Man, are amongst the most common. In addition to

---

21 *Researches in the South of Ireland* ... 3. 22 Ibid. 78. 23 Ibid. 88–90. 24 Ibid. 94. Milk-stealing was mentioned by Giraldus Cambrensis, and the belief was also attested in Britain and on the Continent.

these are found translations from the classics, and frequently from some of Dean Swift's verses into the Irish, with a variety of receipts, prayers and charms. The possessor of such manuscript regards it with a degree of affection bordering on veneration, and only on particular occasions is it produced.[25]

He also saw chapbooks in English, including a highly popular celebration of noble robbers or bandit-heroes which had first appeared in the 1720s or 30s and was still going strong a century later: 'A "History of the Irish Rogues and Rapparees" is at present one of the most popular books amongst the peasantry, and has circulated to an extent that almost seems incredible; nor is it unusual to hear the adventures and escapes of highwaymen and outlaws recited by the lower orders with the greatest minuteness, and dwelt on with a surprising fondness.'[26]

But the book which made Croker famous, won praises from the Grimms and Walter Scott and practically revealed Irish folklore to Europe, was his *Fairy Legends and Traditions of the South of Ireland*. I shall quote from it at some length. The first part appeared anonymously in 1825 and was so successful that the publisher sent the author-editor on a field trip to collect material for a sequel, which came out in 1828; a third part gathered Welsh stories relating to fairies. (For Croker's Killarney books, see pp. 149-51.) In the preface to the first volume, he stated his aim as 'illustrating the superstitions of the Irish Peasantry, superstitions which the most casual observer cannot fail to remark powerfully influence their conduct and manner of thinking'; he also referred to 'the very extravagant imagination in which the Irish are so fond of indulging'.[27] Later, probably using information provided by the Grimm brothers, he compared elements of the stories he was editing with what had been collected in Denmark, Germany or Spain: 'It is curious to observe the similarity of legends, and of ideas concerning imaginary beings, among nations that for ages have had scarcely any communication.'[28] He promoted and romanticized his own image as a field collector – which to a certain extent he was. His account of the preparation for the second volume verges on the sensational:

On Friday, the first of April, 1825 – ominous day, and fool as I was – I started from London at four in the evening, for Bristol, with an intention of making a tour in the south of Ireland, for the purpose of gleaning, in the course of six weeks, the remainder of the fairy legends and traditions which Mr Murray, of Albermarle Street [his publisher] suspected were still to be found lurking among its glens ... I started from London, as I before said, with a firm determination of seeing the sun rise, and making a personal acquaintance with the shade of O'Donoghue, at Killarney, on May morning; and during the month that was before me, and till the day previous to that fixed on for our personal

25 Ibid. 331-2. **26** Ibid. 55. The complete title of the chapbook is *The Lives and Actions* [or *A History*] *of the Most Notorious Irish Tories, Highwaymen and Rapparees*. See Niall Ó Ciosáin 'The Irish Rogues', in J.S. Donnelly and K.A. Miller (eds) *Irish Popular Culture, 1650-1850* 78-96. **27** Op. cit. 1825, I. 18. **28** *Fairy Legends ...* (1862) 21.

introduction [Croker purports to be writing a letter to a friend] making the most of my time in hunting up and bagging all the old 'grey superstitions' I could fall in with. My sport was to have been 'shooting folly as it flies'; and pretty fair, though devilish wild sport I had, and rough enough it was into the bargain. After sundry adventures with Whiteboys [dangerous rural secret societies], in caves and out of caves, upon hill-tops, with bootmakers and broguemakers, with smugglers and coastguard-men, with magistrates and murderers, with pilgrims and pedlars, I returned to England within the prescribed time – bringing with me ... a budget of 'grey superstitions'.[29]

How much of the book is Croker's is uncertain; he is said to have lost his early notes and to have reconstructed them with the help of friends, who also gave him other stories and perhaps contributed some of the notes.[30]

On the one hand he wanted to astonish; on the other he thought his material was representative. In the preface to the second (1826) edition of the first volume, he defended as a positive quality the fact that the stories were widely known: he was not trying to be original, and the fact that the material was widespread was what made it significant.[31]

He referred to women as typical storytellers, which is interesting because others would tend to mention only male narrators in Ireland. Although he said he was giving the tales 'as he found them', it remains doubtful: indeed, they were filtered and 'arranged' – sometimes by different transcribers – and generally rendered in a written rather than colloquial style.[32]

In the preface to the second volume, Croker felt he had to distance himself more explicitly from ill-famed superstitions, while insisting on the necessity of knowing them: in 1826 a child thought to be a 'changeling' had been murdered by his mother, and to publish tales that revealed the beliefs involved in such behaviour was a way of exposing obstacles to the progress of civilization.[33] But the tone of the book is more often jolly: Croker contributed to the elaboration and diffusion of the image of the truculent Irish storyteller, well settled in a local community, which partly replaced the rather incredible solitary 'bard' and was definitely offered as contemporary. Let us stroll through this portrait gallery:

Tom Bourke lives in a low long farm-house, resembling in outward appearance a large barn, placed at the bottom of the hill, just where the new road strikes off from the old one, leading from the town of Kilworth to that of Lismore. He is of a class of persons who are a sort of black swans in Ireland: he is a wealthy farmer ... Tom Bourke is a little, stout, healthy, active man, about fifty-five years of age. His hair is perfectly white, short and bushy behind, but rising in front erect and thick above his forehead, like a new clothes-brush. His eyes are of the kind which I have often observed with persons of a quick, but limited intellect – they are small, gray, and lively. The large and projecting eye-brows under, or rather within, which they twinkle, give them an expression of

29 Quoted in *Fairy Legends* (1862) vi-vii. 30 *Dictionary of National Biography* 13 (1888) 133. 31 Ibid. xxi. 32 As shown by Neil C. Hultin, 'Anglo-Irish Folklore from Clonmel: T.C. Croker and British Library Add. 20099', *Fabula* 27 (1986) 288-307. 33 *Fairy Legends* xxvi.

shrewdness and intelligence, if not of cunning. And this is very much the character of the man ... It is not easy to prevail on Tom to speak of those good people [fairies], with whom he is said to hold frequent and intimate communications. To the faithful, who believe in their power, and their occasional delegation of it to him, he seldom refuses, if properly asked, to exercise his high prerogative when any unfortunate being is *struck* [he is a 'fairy doctor, who cures people from spells] in his neighbourhood. Still, he will not be won unsued: he is at first difficult of persuasion, and must be overcome by a little gentle violence. On these occasions he is unusually solemn and mysterious ... The character of Tom Bourke is accurately copied from nature, and it has been thought better to preserve the scene entire, rather than derive two or three tales from his confession. It affords an illustration of the difficulty with which an acknowledgment of supernatural skill is extorted from the gifted possessor, of the credulity of the peasantry, and of some national superstitions. [He tells how he acquired his power.][34]

Perhaps it *is* 'copied from nature' – though in this case not by Croker himself. The following portrait is interesting too, evoking the changing social setting in which the storyteller performed:

John Mulligan was as fine an old fellow as ever threw a Carlow spur into the side of a horse. He was, besides, as jolly a boon companion over a jug of punch, as you would meet from Carnsore Point to Bloody Farland ... John believed devoutly in fairies; and an angry man was he if you doubted them. He had more fairy stories than would make, if properly printed in a rivulet of print running down a meadow of margin, two thick quartos for Mr John Murray, of Albermarle-street; all of which he used to tell on all occasions that he could find listeners. Many believed his stories – many more did not believe them – but nobody, in process of time, used to contradict the old gentleman, for it was a pity to vex him. But he had a couple of young neighbours who were just come down from their first vacation in Trinity College to spend the summer months with an uncle of theirs ... and they were too full of logic to let the old man have his own way undisputed. Every story he told they laughed at, and said that it was impossible – that it was merely old woman's gabble, and other such things. When he would insist that all his stories were derived from the most credible sources – nay, that some of them had been told him by his own grandmother, a very respectable old lady, but slightly affected in her faculties, as things that came under her own knowledge – they cut the matter short by declaring that she was in her dotage, and at the best of times had a strong propensity to pulling a long bow.[35]

Here are two of the lively women narrators portrayed with their audiences:

Peggy Barrett was once tall, well-shaped, and comely ... But she is now upwards of sixty years old; and during the last ten years of her life she has never been able to stand upright ... Her powers of conversation are highly extolled, both for humour and narration; and anecdotes of droll or awkward incidents, connected with the posture in which she has been so long fixed, as well as the history of the occurrence to which she owes that misfortune, are favourite topics of her discourse ... Peggy, like all experienced story-

34 Ibid. 51, 52, 54, 65. 35 Ibid. 67-8.

tellers, suited her tales, both in length and subject, to the audience and the occasion. She
knew that, in broad daylight, when the sun shines brightly, and the trees are budding,
and the birds singing around us, when men and women like ourselves are moving and
speaking, employed variously in business or amusement ... we want that spirit of
credulity, without which tales of the deepest interest will lose their power. At such times
Peggy was brief, very particular as to facts, and never dealt with the marvellous. But
round the blazing hearth of a Christmas evening, when infidelity is banished from all
companies, at least in low and simple life, as a quality, to say the least, out of season;
when the winds of 'dark December' whistled bleakly round the walls, and almost through
the doors of the little mansion, reminding its inmates, that as the world is vexed by elements superior to human power, so it may be visited by beings of a superior nature: – at
such times would Peggy Barrett give full scope to her memory, or her imagination, or
both ... [She tells the personal story of the 'crookening of her back'.] There was a pause
when Peggy Barrett finished. Those who had heard the story before had listened with a
look of half-satisfied interest, blended, however, with an expression of that serious and
solemn feeling which always attends a tale of supernatural wonders, how often soever
told. They moved upon their seats out of the posture in which they had remained fixed
during the narrative, and sat in an attitude which denoted that their curiosity as to the
cause of the strange occurrence had been long since allayed. Those to whom it was
before unknown still retained their look and posture of strained attention, and anxious
but solemn expectation.[36]

    ... An old woman called Moirna Hogaune, with a long blue cloak about her, who
had been sitting in the chimney corner smoking her pipe without taking any share in the
conversation, took the pipe out of her mouth, threw the ashes out of it, spit in the fire,
and, turning round, looked Felix straight in the face. 'And so you don't believe there is
such things as Cluricaunes [*clutharacán*: a fairy pigmy or elf], don't you?' said she. Felix
looked rather daunted, but he said nothing. 'Why, then, upon my troth, and it will
become the like of you, that's nothing but a bit of *gossoon* [*garsún*: boy], to take upon you
to pretend not to believe what your father and your father's father, and his father before
him never made the least doubt of! But to make the matter short, seeing 's believing,
they say; and I that might be your grandmother tell you there are such things as
Cluricaunes, and I myself saw one – there's for you, now!' All the people in the room
looked quite surprised at this, and crowded up to the fireplace to listen to her. Felix
tried to laugh, but it wouldn't do; nobody minded him. 'I remember', said she, 'some
time after I married my honest man, who's now dead and gone, it was by the same token
just a little afore I lay in of my first child (and that's many a long day ago), I was sitting
out in our bit of garden with my knitting in my hand ... [A cluricaune appeared, and she
tried to get hold of his treasure – but failed as is usually the case in this type of stories,
because he made her look in another direction: 'there's your bees all swarming off with
themselves ...']'[37]

The introduction to 'The Lucky Guest' is particularly detailed:

The kitchen of some country houses in Ireland presents in no ways a bad modern translation of the ancient feudal hall. Traces of clanship still linger round its hearth in the

36 Ibid. 148-9, 152. 37 Ibid. 86-7.

numerous dependants on 'the master's' bounty. Nurses, foster-brothers, and other hang-
ers-on, are there as matter of right, while the strolling piper, full of mirth and music, the
benighted traveller, even the passing beggar, are received with a hearty welcome, and
each contributes planxty, song, or superstitious tale, towards the evening's amusement.
An assembly, such as has been described, had collected round the kitchen fire of
Ballyrahen-house, at the foot of the Galtee mountains, when, as is ever the case, one tale
of wonder called forth another; and with the advance of the evening each succeeding
story was received with deeper and deeper attention. The story of Cough na Looba's
dance with the black friar at Rahill, and the fearful tradition of *Coum an 'ir morriv* (the
dead man's hollow), were listened to in breathless silence. A pause followed the last relation, and all eyes rested on the narrator, an old nurse who occupied the post of honour,
that next the fireside. She was seated in that peculiar position which the Irish name
Currigguib [*ar do chorraghiob*: squatting, on one's hunkers][38], a position generally assumed
by a veteran and determined story-teller. Her haunches resting upon the ground, and her
feet bundled under the body; her arms folded across and supported by her knees, and
the outstretched chin of her hooded head pressing on the upper arm; which compact
arrangement nearly reduced the whole figure into a perfect triangle. Unmoved by the
general gaze, Bridget Doyle made no change of attitude, while she gravely asserted the
truth of the marvellous tale concerning the Dead Man's Hollow; her strongly marked
countenance at the time receiving what painters term a fine chiaroscuro effect from the
fire-light. 'I have told you,' she said, 'what happened to my own people, the Butlers and
the Doyles, in the old times … '[39]

A fine portrait, this; the catch – rather typical of the whole book – is that Croker
himself was not present when the tale he ascribed to Bridget Doyle was told: he
received it from a correspondent. Since he had really observed storytellers, we
may give some credit to such descriptions but there is little doubt that the
frames he provided for the legends or tales he had gathered were often free
reconstructions. As for the texts themselves, those he claims were taken down
'verbatim' do have some recognizable features of oral expression, but others are
obviously expanded and ornamented in the fashionable literary style of the time.
On the whole, however, he did not go as far in this direction as some of his successors did, and there is some comparative truth in the judgment passed by the
British Victorian folklorist Thomas Wright that he 'had the merit of giving the
stories as they are told simply by the Irish peasantry, and not, as is too generally the case, clothed in the artificial embellishments of the compiler'.[40]

    Wilhelm Grimm, who reviewed the first volume of the *Fairy Legends and
Traditions* in 1826, thought that the tradition had been represented with unusual
care: the stories would 'depict very truthfully the domestic existence, thought,
mode of life and customs of a country we still do not know well'.[41] Later the

---

38 Cf. the 'peculiar attitude' of a Connemara nurse quoted on p. 160. There could be a
simple practical reason for the crouched position: in smoke-filled chimneyless cabins, one tried
to remain below the smoke level – and anyway there was very little furniture.   **39** Ibid. 295-
6.   **40** Preface to his edition of Croker's book in 1862.   **41** *Göttingische Gelehrte Anzeigen*
January 1826: 'sie schildern nämlich mit vollkommener Wahrheit den häuslichen Zustand,

same year, part of the book appeared in German as *Irische Elfenmärchen, Uebersetzt von den Brüdern Grimm*. The preface stated again that all had been taken straight from the mouth of the people – and that the Irish might have preserved the best examples of the ancient belief in supernatural beings.[42] In 1828 Wilhelm was preparing another volume of translations, but it remained unpublished until 1986;[43] the work may have been interrupted by a nasty letter from one of Croker's ex-collaborators, the now dissatisfied Thomas Keightley, who denounced his successful rival as a charlatan.[44]

Croker may not have been a great scholar, his material was gathered in different ways, and often presented as funny: indeed, Wilhelm Grimm was embarrassed by the tone.[45] But his book placed the Irish living narrative tradition on the European map, and encouraged others to publish similar material: 'Till Mr Crofton Croker collected the legends of the South of Ireland, the value and interest of such stories were very little appreciated in this country, and our popular traditions were generally despised and very rapidly disappearing.'[46] His book supplies us with more portraits of Irish storytellers than anything previously published.

Some other Anglo-Irishmen who settled in London were active writers, for instance Thomas Keightley, born in County Kildare in 1789. Since his own reputation is not very good – 'he ludicrously overestimated all his performances'[47] – we do not have to take his negative comments on Croker at face value, but there is no reason to doubt that he had experienced storytelling in Ireland. In a late version of his *Fairy Mythology* (first published in 1828), and in the introductory chapter of another compilation where he wondered if similarities of tales in different European traditions resulted from borrowing or independent invention, he nostalgically evoked his early contacts with Irish oral narration.[48] In this volume, the Irish section only summed up information already published by Croker, but the elegiac-bucolic mood in the evocation of a lost paradise was different; and later folklorists often adopted it. It is also found in the other book, where Keightley remembers one narrator in particular and mentions a genre not represented in Croker's collection of 'legends', the international wonder tale:

Denkensart, Lebensweise und Sitten eines gerade nicht sehr bekanntes Land.' (Reprinted in W. Grimm *Kleinere Schriften* 2. 370.) **42** Op. cit. Preface: 'alles aus dem Munde des Volks und in dem Stil, in welchem es gewöhnlich vorgetragen werde ...' ' ... von einem Volke ... dessen Altertum und frühe Bildung die Geschichte bezeugt und das, wie es zum teil noch in der eigenen Sprache redet, auch lebendige Spuren seiner Vorzeit wird aufzuweisen haben, wovon der hier dargestellte Glaube an überirdische Wesen vielleicht eins der besten Beispiele abgibt.' A translation of the introductory essay '*Ueber die Elfen*' appeared in the third part of Croker's *Fairy Legends* (1828). **43** W. Moritz and C. Oberfeld (eds) *Irische Land- und Seemärchen*, with an essay on Croker by S. Heyer. **44** Ibid. 191-2. **45** 'Man muss bedauern dass die Darstellung zu dem ausgebildeten Geschmack der jetzigen Zeit sich etwas mehr zuneigt als zuträglich ist, zumal wenn sie jene Ironie anwendet, die uns zu verstehen gibt dass das Märchenhafte nur das Erzeugnis einer durch den Rausch erregter Phantasie sei, womit jede tiefere Bedeutung schwindet.' (*Kinder- und Hausmärchen* 3. 393-4.) **46** Thomas Wright, preface to the edition of 1862. **47** *Dictionary of National Biography* 30 (1892) 308. **48** *The*

It was my lot (no unenviable one) to be reared in the country, and near the mountains. In Ireland we are less aristocratic, and mingle more familiarly with the lower orders of the people, than seems to be the case here ... In consequence of this state of manners, a great companion of my younger days was Johnny Stykes ... Often, as memory looks back through the glade of life along which my course has lain, doth her eye rest on the figure of my humble companion, returning in the evening from the stubble with his feathered charge [turkeys] ... He had not his fellow in the whole country for what is called *shanahas* [*seanchas*], or old talk, that is, tales, legends, and traditions, handed down from age to age, and transmitted from mouth to mouth. And let me now fearlessly confess the truth. I have since seen some of Nature's finest scenery, I have conversed with the learned and the ingenious, and have read the master-works of the human mind; and yet I am convinced I have never, at most very rarely, felt a degree of pleasure at all comparable to what I enjoyed, when sitting with Johnny, of a summer's day, beneath a spreading tree, or on the bank of a purling stream, while the cows were feeding around, and the air was filled with the melody of birds, and listening to some wild tale of wonder and enchantment. Much would I give to be able to recollect his tale of The Fair Norah na Vodha and the White Bear of Worroway, a Beauty-and-Beast kind of story, in which the heroine is pursued by I know not who, and 'when he was on the hill she was in the hollow, and when she was on the hill he was in the hollow'; or another about a princess (for he had all kinds of high personages at command), who was confined in some dismal place all full of *sarpints* and toads and *vifers* ... Johnny, too, had a story answering to Robber-bride-groom in MM. Grimms' collection, in which the lady at the bridal banquet told, as if relating a dream, all that she had seen when she secretly entered the robber's den, and as she proceeded in her narrative, the disguised robber would get up and say, 'Dreams are but *feebles*, and *feebles* are but lies; By your leave, Gentlemen, pray let me by.' He also knew the Frog-king, and several others in the same collection; and he had tales of fairies without end.[49]

The second tale mentioned here – 'The White Bear of Norroway', a variant of International Type AT 425 'The Search for the Lost Husband' where the woman disenchants her spouse by burning his animal skin and must then suffer to regain him – appears as 'The Brown Bear of Norway' in Patrick Kennedy's *Legendary Fiction of the Irish Celts*; there are versions of this tale in Irish, as well as of the 'Robber Bride-groom' (AT 955) and of 'Frog Prince' (AT 440). The formula 'hill/hollow' was often used by Irish storytellers. In brief, Keightley here sounds reliable – but a few pages later in the same book he declares himself capable of inventing an Irish legend and the character of some old narrator, as well as his or her way of telling the legend.[50] As he was probably not the only one who had such a talent, we have better keep in mind this special conception of authenticity when reading the portraits of Irish storytellers drawn at that time.[51]

Fairy Mythology (1892 ed.) 362. **49** *Tales and Popular Fictions* (1834) 12-13. **50** Ibid. 16. **51** William Maginn (1793-1842), who was also one of Croker's occasional collaborators for the *Fairy Legends*, does not rank as a precursor of serious folklorists, but can be named here as a model of the writer who played the role of the good-humoured or bellicose, thriftless and

At first, the scholars who took Irish folklore seriously were more likely to be foreigners who had only second-hand knowledge of it, like the Brothers Grimm[52] or W. J. Thoms (see pp. 170-1); when the latter, in 1834, compiled a collection of *Lays and Legends of Ireland*, he found them 'wild and visionary', 'exquisitely national', 'exquisitely racy'. What had been revealed by Crofton Croker and the legends published in various periodicals should be completed by material in Irish, which would perish if not speedily collected:

Much as we admit what Mr Crofton Croker has achieved in his collection of the fairy tales of Ireland, and numerous and clever have been the imitations of his stories, and style of story-telling [a footnote adds: 'See series of "Legendary tales of the Irish peasantry" in the "Dublin and London Magazine", and in the "Dublin Penny Journal" a series of "Popular Legends of the South" by E.W. &c.'], it appears extraordinary to us, that by far the most extensive fields of Irish legendary tales should remain not only ungleaned, but that no attempt has been made to reap the rich crops which they present. Such, for instance, as the miraculous monkish tales and legends still current in 'the Isle of Saints'. The romantic narratives, recited by professional story-tellers, and those histories of enchantment, and series of wild adventures, which have been committed to writing in the Irish language; add to which many of the songs of the Irish bards and rhymers, orally preserved in the country, and that will perish if not speedily collected. [My] regret [of not knowing the Irish language] is heightened by the loss which literature has sustained in the death of Mr Edward O'Reilly[53] (the author of a valuable Irish Dictionary) and the dispersion of his manuscripts. Mr O'Reilly had long contemplated the translation and publication of a collection of Irish Tales of Enchantment – and we have seen several curious letters from him on this subject, written in the year 1816 and 1827. Indeed we have reasons for believing that at the time of his death, Mr O'Reilly had several of these tales prepared for the press. In speaking of them, he says. 'The stories are acknowledged to be fabulous, although the actors are sometimes real personages'; – and he particularized as complete the *Faghail Craoibhe Cormaic* or 'Finding of Cormac's Branch' – 'The Tale of Farvlay, daughter of Jameson of Turcall, King of Scotland, and Caroll, son of Donagh mor O'Daly' – 'The Story of Lomnotan of Slieve Riffe' – 'The Adventures of Torolb, son of Starn' – and 'The Adventures of Misadrice',

hard-drinking Irishman, and wrote humorous fiction in that line. Born in Cork, he was a learned schoolteacher, then schoolmaster, who wrote skits of local characters for *Blackwood's Magazine*. In the early 1820s he moved to London, where he contributed to several periodicals and founded *Fraser's Magazine*. Some of his comic pieces had a London setting, others an Irish one: 'Bob Burke's Duel with Ensign Brady' (as told by Burke) or 'The Legend of Knocksheogowna', 'The Legend of Knockgrafton', etc. – appeared in book form long after his death (*Miscellanies, Prose and Verse* ed. W. Montagu, 1885). He was one of those who realized that Irish material served with the proper sauce would sell. **52** *Kinder- und Hausmärchen* (1856) 3. 393-5. **53** Edward O'Reilly (1770-1829) compiled a *Dictionary of Irish Writers*, catalogued manuscripts in Dublin and worked for the Ordnance Survey. It is not certain that he collected from oral tradition: *Faghail Craoibhe Chormaic mhic Airt, Tormarc Fearblaide, Eachtra Lomnochtáin an tSléibhe Riffe*, and *Eachtra Thoirbealbargh mhicStáirn* are romances O'Reilly could read in the libraries of T.C.D. or of the Royal Irish Academy. His 'collection of Irish Tales of Enchantment' never came out (see also p. 120).

wherein the Gruagach, a domestic spirit which precisely accords with the Scotch Brownie, performs a conspicuous part. There is no work, we are convinced, which would be more gratefully hailed by the scholars of Europe than an Irish Mythology; and ample materials for the compilation, we believe, exist in the songs of the bards to which we have alluded.[54]

From the 1820s, there also was a market for printed 'folklore' (not yet so called) in Ireland itself. The vogue for such material may have followed British and continental models, and have something to do with the development of tourism (see Chapter 5). It was linked with a multiplication of magazines, most of them short-lived, in which some dilution of fashionable interests in elegant style or smartly jocular tone made of 'legends' (the term was often used)[55] good reading for gentlemen and middle-class families. Thus a partly new kind of sketches of 'traditional' Irish characters and customs appeared and became more or less standardized. In such texts, the dividing line between document and fiction enhanced with local colour may be hard to draw.

To offer a sampling of what can be found in that mass of publications, I start with a group of men who lived in Cork (as Croker and Maginn did for a while) and were published there. At the time, the city ranked second only to Dublin as a commercial centre. It had been prosperous until the early decades of the nineteenth century – though travellers saw many beggars, coming from the hinterland. Intellectual life was active, and one was closer to the Gaelic world than in Dublin. A circle of amateurs interested in popular customs had formed around the antiquarian John Windele (1801-65). Croker was a member; so was John Callanan (1795-1829), who taught in William Maginn's school. Stimulated by the relative success of Croker's *Researches in the South of Ireland*, he travelled in the south-west to collect ballads and legends.[56] In the summer of 1826 he composed a poem entitled 'Gougane Barra' about a place in the West-Cork mountains where could be 'glean'd the gray legend that long had been sleeping'. It was a favourite hunting-ground for Corkonian protofolklorists, because of the impressive scenery and a popular pilgrimage, described by Croker among others ('Patron at Gougaun' in *Researches in the South of Ireland*), which was so riotous that the Catholic Church for a while suppressed it. In January the following year, Callanan was writing to Windele: 'I have made a great harvest in the Irish way. If I'm not before Croker in one way, I think I shall be in another'.[57] Between 1826 and 1831 he contributed poems and an essay on 'Irish

---

54 *Lays and Legends of Ireland* vi, ix-x. The booklet includes a version of the 'Legend of O'Donoghue', various tales contributed by Thomas Steele, and a Fianna story, 'The Adventures of Fuin Mac Cual', with the following comment (ibid. 87): 'The variations of the traditions concerning the adventures of Fuin Mac Cumhall current in Ireland are so numerous and lengthy that it would require many large volumes to embody them.' **55** For a type list of 'migratory legends' in nineteenth- and early-twentieth-century Irish writing in English, see Brian Earls, in *Béaloideas* 60-1 (1992-3). **56** J. Windele *Historical and Descriptive Notices of the City of Cork and its Vicinity ...* 139. **57** Quoted in R. Welch *A History of Verse*

Druidism' to *Bolster's Quarterly Magazine*, edited by Windele. In the second volume, reissued in 1834 as *Tales and Legends of Ireland, Illustrative of Society, History, Antiquities, Manners and Literature, to which are added Translations from the Irish*, we find some accounts of storytelling sessions where genuine observation may hide behind verbiage. The following two detailed scenes involving travelling beggars as storytellers combine the older respect for bards, touches of breughelian grotesque, and the new curiosity for contemporary oral tradition. In the first, written by Windele under his pseudonym of Dr McSlatt, we are supposed to be in a kitchen near Gougane Barra, in 1827:

A few friendly neighbour-visitants, with a laudable curiosity to know all that could be known of the strangers, formed rather a crowded assemblage; at the upper end flamed a huge turf-fire, and over it hung a large black pot in preparation for our dinner, suspended on a black well sooted iron hook. The pig, below, grunted his vesper chime, sweet and euphonic, but an admonitory *cuch-ass* [*cuach*: whoop] from time to time would rouse up Hector from his *couchant* posture in the ash-pit, and give him warrant to exercise his tooth in the ear of the gentle minstrel. Here we found what pleased our city companion much to meet, a veritable sample of our genuine Irish boccaugh [*bacach*: beggar], a race for whom I entertain an ancient liking. I have always regarded them as reliques of our old Irish Society; the representatives of those numerous tribes of Carrouchs [*cearrbhaig*: gamblers] – Stocachs [*stócaigh*: youths] – tale-tellers and gillys, who once pursued their vagabond vocation, administering to the pleasure and entertainment of thanes and their retainers, in the old feudal halls and chambers, incurring by their attachment to their native chiefs, the displeasure of the poet Spen[s]er. Your sturdy boccaugh is still the repository and chronicle of all the legends and marvels of his own and of former times, a wandering rehearser of the tale and the lay – speaking the same language and still nearly clad in the ancient garb, with the slight drawback of a knee breeches, and some superabundant professional patches, and surely fearless may he be of comparison in the length of his beard or hair glibb [*glib*: lock of hair] or couleen [*cúilín*: forelock]. He of Rossalucha was no degenerate scion of his race, we found his motto to be, as with his confreres in Kerry, 'Ullin eyem nou arigid' [*ollainn, im, no airgead*]: wool, butter, or money; and his numerous and well fitted pouches and bags, set apart for each of these important and necessary articles, and many more besides, proved that his calling was not in disrepute ... The costume of our heavily laden vagrant was of a sufficiently antique and venerable fashion; what for instance could be more characteristic than his loosely hanging *Cota-mor*, or great coat of grey frize, fastened round the neck by a hook and eye. His inner garment was the indubitable *falleen* [*fallaing*: mantle], well enclosed within a stout leathern girdle, while his ample pockets, capacious in the superlative degree, and distorted to an enormous bulk, by the acquisition and spoils of his expedition, gave to him the truly antique appearance of my beau ideal stocach. His mighty brogues hobnailed and patched into a truly primitive form, gave the finish, and filled up the *tout ensemble* of his figure. Beside him lay his spiked staff, the trusty and well tried companion of many a weary mile, and the terror of every yelping cur and tooth-exhibiting mastiff; and under its shadow and protection rested his wallet, containing the *maxima*

Translation from the Irish: 1789-1897 61.

spolia of his recent campaign. A weather tanned face, illumined by a pair of sharp grey eyes, had a sinister expression of sly waggery and shrewdness, by no means repulsive to my humour, and, in a few moments, my friend and the ancient boccaugh seated together, were busily comparing notes of places and recollections, and contending, by anecdote and legend, telling of 'ladies, and knights, and arms'. He was just entering on a fine old Fenian romance, when our interview was suddenly broken up – '*Maw vee riav*', [*má bhí riamh*: if it ever was] said he, '*iss minnick a vee*', [*is minic a bhí*: it often was] – The great and renowned Fion mac Cuil, and his invincible band of heroes, being one day returning from the chase along the shore near Carrickfergus, beheld afar off a *fawhogh* [*fathach*] or giant, of monstrous dimensions. He was advancing from Scotland in the sea, through which he strided with as much indifference as if it were an insignificant brook [cf. p. 104]. 'Tut tut', cried the bard [one of the travellers, described as a mere versifier], who had just entered and caught me by the arm, 'this is all *ramesh* [*raiméis*: nonsensical talk] – come my good friend, I must find you other employment besides listening to such stuff.⁵⁸

The author must have observed real travelling beggars, who were indeed important agents in circulating and reactivating tales. The text is a curious 'assemblage' of mannered English and of Irish, also of fascination and repulsion ('venerable', 'primitive', 'marvels' – 'pig', 'sinister'). The portrait of another (?) story-telling *bacach* appears in the anonymous account of a gathering on a saint's festival day:

Amongst this tribe ... there was one superior fellow, a despot in his way, the terror and the admiration at once of all. He had a northern brogue, was tall and stout, and was such a voracious eater, that when invited to sit down, he made nothing of the family meal. He was said to be 'cracked', and from the superstitious veneration the lower orders entertain in common with the Turks for madmen, he was greatly respected – by women and children. At the same time, his appearance in a village spread consternation amongst many poor families, who hastily closed their doors before he approached too near, for whenever he made a lodgment, there was no possibility of dispossessing him of his hold. One evening, during the festival times I have described, in 1820, this famous 'poor cratur' made his way into the kitchen of a farmer's house, where I was regaling myself. After a benediction on the house, and the owner of it, a place was made for him within the large fire-place, where he seated himself. He asked innumerable questions about the 'childer', and answered as many more about those in neighbouring families, then entered on the genealogy of their parents and their connections; slowly displacing all the time he was speaking, a number of wallets, which he laid by his side, and over the whole, his large tin porringer which had hung by his waist. Being disincumbered, he pushed himself still farther into the chimney corner, and for my entertainment, he was now called upon to tell one of his 'owld stories'; he was very willing to comply with the request; but many were proposed and rejected. While I was complimented by being allowed to select one,

58 *Bolster's Quarterly Magazine* 2. 336-7: 'Gougaune Barra', a letter from 'Trismagistus MacSlatt' dated 'Macroom, June 1827'. The influx of beggars in the busy pattern season is also mentioned in Windele's *Historical and Descriptive Notes* ... 289.

it never occurring to the good-natured people that I could have no preference, not understanding Irish, but the Schoolmaster decided for me, by offering at the same time to give me the English, as Dhthermod went on slowly – Dhthermod himself fixed on the tale which I send, saying 'it would devart the gintleman, as may be he was a scholar'. The story began with an incoherent chant, consisting of verses which are omitted [from the text that follows this portrait]. After this prelude, he commenced a more monotonous but vehement strain, looking at times awful in the flickering gleams of light, which occasionally illuminated his large visage, old red cap, grey hair, which fell nearly to his shoulders, and beamed out of the darkness, whenever the fitful blaze of the fresh faggots or turf were put on the fire. Leaning his frosty chin sidewise on his folded hands which held his long upright staff, he appeared the Runic Bard a painter would have chosen for his model. Still there was something ludicrous in his ruling the monarch of the hearth, and his eyes were seldom for a moment remiss, during the whole recital, but were steadfastly fixed, watching the progress of a large pot of potatoes that swung over the fire, and he stopped at once in the middle of his declamation to announce the moment they were done. His tale being over, he found it necessary to cheer his depressed auditory with a roguish song, in a croaking senile voice, which had the effect of sending the country girls into the dark nooks and corners, blushing as hard as they could, while the men and married women laughed outright, Dhthermod's features remaining as unmoved as if he sang through a mask.[59]

The portrait introduces the translation of a tale in verse, 'Morna', and also comments on the distinctiveness of orality: 'If Irish poetry has an existence, it must be in tradition; an oral, not a written existence; and we may only hope to find it occasionally, in those secluded haunts to which it flies from the injurious "hand of the spoiler" – in spots yet unreclaimed by *improvements*.'[60]

We would probably look in vain for such a unified group in Dublin, but the following section will consist of different kinds of texts published there, ending with those of two contrasting writers: a city dweller who mimicked country brogue and an ex-peasant who tried to parade genteel style. Indeed, there was a choice of attitudes. Besides evokers of some lost paradise, entertainers who based their humour on incongruity between the realistic description of a setting and an extravagant enclosed narrative, and scholars trying to establish what had been the Irish contribution to world culture, there still were those who wrote to wage war on what remained of paganism – and ambivalent positions were possible. Thus Philip Dixon Hardy, a bookseller, printer and publisher, knew that books on Irish rural oddities might sell, but like Bourne a century before (see p. 167) he disapproved of at least some of them: his compilation on *The Holy Wells of Ireland*, in 1836, never misses a chance to denounce what he considered the folly and absurdity of Roman Catholic practices. In his *Legends, Tales, and Stories of Ireland* published the following year, he hoped that the beliefs expressed in the

---

59 Ibid. 406: 'An Irish Beggarman's Tale'. **60** Ibid. 405.

narratives would soon vanish, though he admitted that the narratives themselves could be collected as curious documents supporting some theories:

Now that 'the schoolmaster is abroad' [as a state-sponsored school system was established in the 1830s, the native 'hedge schools' were losing ground], there can be no question that the warm sun of education will, in the course of a very few years, dissipate those vapours of superstition, whose wild and shadowy forms have from time immemorial thrown a mysterious mantle around our mountain summits; shed a darker horror through our deeper glens; traced some legendary tale on each unchiselled column of stone that rests on our bleakest hills, and peopled the green border of the wizard stream and sainted well with beings of a spiritual world. While, however, the friends of Ireland cannot but be pleased in thinking that our peasantry should, from being better informed, renounce their belief in these idle tales of superstition, to which they, unfortunately, have for centuries been taught to listen with delight, to the exclusion of matters more rational and important, it is to be hoped that the two prominent features of our antiquity as a nation will not be altogether lost sight of, – namely, our vernacular language, and those extraordinary legends, which are esteemed by many as going a great length to prove, from their remarkable analogy with the tales of the eastern world, our oriental descent.[61]

Several periodicals published in Dublin focused on specifically Irish matters. In its first issue on January 5, 1833, the *Irish Penny Magazine* informed readers that among its main topics would be 'Antiquities, illustrating every memorial of former times in our country that can be considered historically or pictorially interesting ... and Ancient Literature ... with the Popular Traditions, the Legends and the Minstrelsy of the country'. But when the periodical ceased to appear in 1834 (it was reissued in 1842), relatively little had been done to illustrate the last-mentioned fields. Some texts which seem to be at the fictional end of the spectrum were introduced with factual portraits:

Patrick Mullaly was a fine old man, who had, for some *political* reason or another, emigrated from the County Tipperary in the days of his youth, and in the evening of his age was to be found working as a hedger in the neighbourhood of Leixlip. Patrick was a very clever hand at a story, and whenever a wake was going he was not only sure of being invited, but also certain of getting the hottest, and the strongest glass of punch that was handed round to the mourners. It was at the early hour of two in the morning, upon one of these melancholy and merry occasions, when the girls were tired of forfeits, and the boys of redeeming them with kisses, that ould Pat was called upon for a story, and a naggin of whiskey made into the sweetest of punch was promised him if he would tell the company something which not one amongst them had ever heard before. This was a request which puzzled Paddy for some time, but after taking off his old flax wig, rubbing his polished pate two or three times with a scarlet pocket handkerchief, he called for a sup by way of earnest, and then commenced his story in the following manner: – 'Boys and girls, I wish your very good health, entirely, entirely, – I wish you good health all round, from wall to wall, and an inch in the wall besides, for fear I'd leave any of you

61 Op. cit. 64-5.

out. I will now tell you a story which I never told you before, and the reason I did not mention it to you is, that it never occurred to myself, and I therefore could not answer for the truth of it; but it happened to an old grand-uncle of mine, one Denis Mullaly, who I heard tell it at a bone-fire, in Thurles ... '[62]

The opening of another anonymous tale in the same periodical is also typical; again drinking and storytelling go together, but this time dialect is emphasized:

On a dark and stormy winter evening in the beginning of the present century, a party of young people were congregated round an ample turf fire, in a little thatched cabin on the furthest coast of Donegal ... Old Ulick, who had numbered eighty winters, taking a long pull at the bottle, said: 'Ye talk of the gun, boys, but it's little ye know of it till ye're out before it, at say, on sich a night, as I was fifty years ago, which, God grant that none of yes ever may, is my worst wish;' and so saying, Ulick caused another glass of poteen to disappear very summarily. 'Arrah, Ulick, was that the night that ye saw the fairy ships?' demanded four voices at once. 'Troth, thin, an' maybe it was', he replied, looking very mysterious. 'Ah, then, can't ye tell us about it, Ulick; it's often we heard of Ulick Maguire an' the fairies, but nivir how it happened that ye saw thim.' 'Hand me that bottle, Jack Donnelly, an' ye shall hear it all.' Ulick's request was immediately complied with, and he commenced: 'Twas on a rough an' breezy evenin' in November, fifty years ago, that I was down upon the beach below ...'[63]

Apparently more authentic, another sketch may have been contributed by George Petrie himself (see p. 116) and confirms not only that accounts of fairy beliefs were well received but also that a storyteller in action was now a worthwhile subject:

During an excursion round the eastern shore of Lough Neagh, in July 1825, accompanied by a friend, I accidentally encountered a singular instance of belief in the existence of fairies. [On a rainy day, they took shelter in a ferry-house.] ... The landlady told us that one of the men now opposite to us knew the fairies better than any man in the country. He was a tall thin figure, and might be about sixty years of age. Flattered by the praise of our hostess, and encouraged by some enquiries from us, he narrated the following events, which I have written as nearly as possible in his own words. 'About twenty years ago, when I was stilling on Cunny Island [distilling *poteen*], I was lying awake one night, with Denis Conolly beside me. All at once I hears the sound of flutes and bagpipes ... [it was fairy music] ... The solemn manner in which he told his stories, the whiffs of smoke by which his face was occasionally obscured, the dim light of the appartment, and pattering of the rain against the window, formed a singular combination of accompaniments. The first spectacle he described was one of which he himself had been an eye-witness. 'In the year 94 or 95, in the time of the Wrackers ...' [he saw mysterious horsemen] ... Here he made a pause, and took the pipe from his mouth, – 'by the pipe in my fist, they vanished from my eyes.' The next tale proceeded thus: 'You have

62 *Irish Penny Magazine* 13 April 1833, 'The Unlucky Gift'. **63** Ibid., 5 February 1834, 'The Fisherman's Tale' – by 'B.'.

heard tell of Dr Leslie, the great man-midwife of Stewartstown? ... ' [he became midwife to the fairies – a very common legend type but the fact that the hero is a man makes this version more sensational] ... The conversation then turned on the manner of redeeming, on a Hallowe'en night, persons who had been taken away by fairies. I have no doubt that Ben really believed the tales, and relied on the power of the charms he repeated: – a surprising and singular instance of the power of imagination.[64]

Sober reporting was not the rule, however. With the next quotation we swing again towards the other extreme: exaggerated eccentricities to arouse amusement. In 1834, the Dublin *Salmagundi* published a legend supposedly heard at a wake; since it was an essentially comic periodical the dialect is laid on as thickly as possible:

I was once at a regular wake, where there was 'lashings and lavings', and grief and fun, all gloriously intermingled ... I retired to a quiet corner where an old man was sitting, 'calmly obsarvin' the 'divarshin', and from him I drained the veracious narrative which I give as nearly in his own words as possible. 'You must know thin sur', he began, 'that in the ould times ov all, that's beyant my recollecshun, or me father or me grandfather afore me, that thim two big mountains, there, wer'nt mountains at all, be reason ov their not bein rared up as they are now, an have been these many years, an will be plase God! But in the place ov thim, a big lake was swimmin about jist like thim boys there, not knowin what to do wid itself.' 'Wonderful!' ejaculated we, and 'wonderful' ejaculated a couple of others, who had left the dancers on seeing 'ould Paudheen beginnin to spake!'. 'In troth an gasons [boys, in the vocative case] yez may say that same, an idz no lie that's in id, seeing, as how a big lake becomin a pair ov mountains like them, and that too all in one night, is not a thing that a body 'ill meet with every day! bud howesomedever sur, as I was sayin, id was all one shinin lake full ov sportive fishes ... ' 'Psha!' I heard grunted beside me here just as I began to be interested, 'don't sit down, it's only the ould story ov the goint [giant], he's tellin! an shure wee've heerd that as often as wee've fingers and toes!' However, Paudeen, if he heard the remark was nothing disconcerted but continued ... [65]

Other accounts of storytelling and portraits of storytellers appear in the *Irish Penny Journal* (1840-41), launched by Petrie. The most interesting contribution is reproduced in extenso at the end of this chapter, but I give here a few excerpts from others. The first expresses the backward look at childlike innocence and lists some of the themes which, by then, were considered most typical of Irish folklore:

Well do I remember the thrill of fear, mingled with a degree of pleasurable awe, with which I listened some forty years since to the narratives of a venerable aunt, who was lingering out the evening of her existence at my father's fireside – her only occupation being, rocking the cradle and keeping the youngsters from mottling their shins. She

64 Ibid. 27 April 1833 'Fairy Superstitions of the North of Ireland' – by 'P.'. **65** *Salmagundi* 26 July 1834: 'Reminiscences of Jim O'Leary. No. 1. The Legend of the Holy Well'.

was an experienced dame, and withal pious, but would as soon doubt her own identity as that of witches and fairies, and her memory was well stored with instances of their interference. These I then believed most implicitly, particularly as in many of them 'the family' was concerned. She could relate how her grandfather one morning detected a hare in the act of milking one of his cows, which he fired at and wounded, and on tracking the blood, discovered it to flow from the thigh of an old crone who inhabited a neighbouring hovel [cf. p. 174]. She also could tell how an elder brother had surprised a leprachaun in the act of making shoes for the gentle people – could describe his dress minutely, and how he had escaped captivity by making a feint with his awl at my uncle's eye, and causing him to wink when in the very act of seizing him, and thereby marred his fortune [cf. p. 178].[66]

Next is an example of 'shortening the road' with stories (more about this in Chapter 12):

'I shall tell you the story as we go along, if your course lies in the direction of this pathway.' As we proceeded, he delivered the following legend. The old man's phraseology was copious and energetic, qualities which I have vainly striven to infuse into the translation; for an abler pen would fail in our colder English of doing justice to the very poetical language of the narrator.[67]

The introductory description required to provide a setting could focus on the audience:

While around the blazing turf fire, on a winter's evening, the story, the pipe, and the joke, take their rounds by turn, you will invariably discover that that tale always gains a double share of applause which may contain a relation of some clever successful scheme or trick, or the 'sayings and doings' of some remarkably clever fellow, albeit perhaps a great rogue; in fact, such stories as these are suited to the conceptions and tastes of a shrewd and ready-witted people. But without tiring my reader with any more 'shanachus', for so we term 'palaver' in Clare, let me endeavour to present him with one of these very stories ...[68]

Longer passages of atmosphere-building through adjectival description were possible, like this sketch by someone who came from a peasant family; it combines a bucolic mood, attempts at 'literary' formality or wit, and the conviction that the Irish peasantry had unique qualities:

One evening last winter – a holiday evening too – when the western wind was sweeping on wild pinions from the grey hills of Tipperary, athwart the rich and level plains of the Queen's County, when the blast roared in the chimney, and the huge rain-drops pattered saucily against the four tiny panes which constituted the little kitchen window, I was sit-

66 *Irish Penny Journal* 12 Sept. 1840: 'Orohoo, the Fairy Man, a Reminiscence of Connaught' – by 'A.'. 67 Ibid. 17 April 1841 'The Bald Barrys, or The Blessed Thorn of Kildinan' – by 'E.W.'. 68 Ibid. 27 March 1841: 'Rooshkulum, or the Wise Simpleton. A Legend of Clare' – by J.G. M'Teague.

ting in the cottage of a neighbouring peasant, amid a small but happy group of village rustics, and enjoying with them that enlivening mirth and sinless delight which I have never found anywhere but at the fireside of an Irish peasant ... Such a scene of fun and frolic and harmless waggery could not be found anywhere outside that ring which encircles the Emerald Isle, and even within that bright zone, nowhere but in the cabin of an Irish 'scullogue' [*scólog*: small farmer]. The songs of our sires, chanted with all that melancholy softness and pathetic sweetness for which the voices of our wild Irish girls are remarkable, the wild legend recited with that rich brogue and waggish humour peculiar alone to the Irish peasant, and the romantic and absurd fairy tale, told with all the reverential awe and caution which the solemnity of the subject required, long amused and excited the captivated auditors; but at length, more's the pity, the vocalist could sing no more, having 'a mighty great cold intirely'. The story-teller was 'as dry as a chip wid all he talked', and even the sides of most of the company 'war ready to split wid the rale dint of laughin'; whilst, as if to afford us another illustration of the truth of the old proverb, 'one trouble never comes alone', even the old crone who had astonished us with the richness and extent of her fairy lore was also knocked up, or rather knocked *down*, for the quantity of earthly *spirits* she had put *in*, entirely put *out* all memory of *un*-earthly *spirits*, and sent her disordered fancy, all confused as it was, wool-gathering to the classic regions of *Their-na-noge* (that imaginary region under ground, supposed by the peasantry to be the residence of spirits and fairies). Well, what was to be done? It was still young in the night, and, better than that, a good 'slug' [*slog*: a swig of liquid] still remained in the greybeard [jug], and as we all had contributed to procure the stock, so all declared that none should depart until the very last drop was drained. But how was the interval to be employed? The singer was hushed, the storyteller was exhausted, and vollies of wit and waggery had exploded until every one was tired; yet to remain silent was considered by all the highest degree of discomfort. ['An old sooty book', the English historian Sir Charles Coote's *Statistical Survey of the Queen's County* printed in 1801, is produced and the author of the essay, the 'peasant poet' John Keegan – more about him later – is asked to read a passage concerning Poor-Man's Bridge over the Nore.] 'Read that again, sir', said a fine grey-headed, patriarchal old man who was present; 'read that again', said he emphatically. I did so. 'He cannot learn the tradition of Poor-Man's Bridge, *inagh!*' [*an ea*: is it? indeed] said the old man with a sneer, 'faith, I believe not; I'd take his words for more nor that. But had he come to me when he was travelling the country making up his statisticks, I could open his eyes on that subject, and many others too.' Some of the present laughed outright at the old man's gravity of manner as he made this confident boast. 'You need not laugh – you may shut your potato-traps', said the old man indignantly. 'Grand as he was, with his gold and silver, his coach and horses, and servants with gold and scarlet livery, I could enlighten him more on the ancient history and traditions of our country than all the *boddaghs* [*bodach*: lout] of squireens ['gentlemen in a small way'] whom he visited on his tour through the Queen's County.' These assertions served to increase the storm of ridicule which was gathering around the old man's head; and to put a stop to any bad blood which the occasion might call forth, I requested of him to tell us the tradition of the 'Boccough Ruadh' [Red Beggar]. After some wheedling and flattery he complied, and told a curious story, of which the following is the substance ...[69]

69 Ibid. 23 January 1841 'The Boccough Ruadh. A Tradition of Poor-Man's Bridge' – by

Reported by the same observer is a preparation for the telling of a wonder tale, and an example of the association between a narrative and a tune (cf. pp. 81-2):

Garret [Dalton] was generous and hospitable; his house 'was known to all the vagrant train', and the way-worn pilgrim, the wandering minstrel, the itinerant 'bocough' [*bacach*: beggar] and the strolling vender of the news and gossips of the day, were always secure of a welcome reception at his comfortable fireside. Among the most constant of his guests was one Maurice O'Sullivan, a native of the County of Cork. Maurice was a most venerable-looking personage – tall, gaunt, athletic, and stone blind. He was about eighty years of age; his white hair flowed on his shoulders, and he played the Irish bagpipe delightfully. He was the lineal descendant of a family still famous in the annals of the 'green isle'; and although now compelled to wander through his native land in the garb and character of a blind piper, he had once seen better days, and was possessed of education and intelligence far superior to most of his caste. He was intimately acquainted with the sad history of his country, was devotedly attached to the dogmas of the fairy creed, could recite charms and interpret dreams, and was deeply conversant in all those witch legends and traditions for which the Munster peasantry are so peculiarly celebrated ... [He plays a tune.] 'And have you', he asked, 'never heard me play that tune before? and did I never tell you the strange story connected with it?' 'Never', was the reply. 'Well that is strange enough; that tune is an old favourite in Munster, and I thought the whole world had heard of it.' 'It never kem to Glen-Mac-Tir, any how', replied the farmer, 'or I'd surely have heard of it. How d'ye call the name of it?' '*Caith-na-brogueen* – that is in English, Puss in Brogues', said the piper. 'Well', said Garret, 'it's often I heard of Puss in Boots, but I never heard of Puss in Brogues afore [*bróg*: shoe, boot].' 'Well, I'll tell you and this good company all about it ... and a wild and strange tale it is,' said Maurice. 'However, it is a popular tradition in South Munster, and often when a boy have I listened to it, whilst my eyes, now dark for ever, would glisten with delight, and I would even fear to breathe lest one syllable of the legend might escape me.' Then emitting a deep-drawn sigh, and again wiping his polished brow, he thus began. 'At the foot of a hill in a lonely district of the county of Cork, about a dozen miles from my native village, there lived in old times a man named Larry Roche ... ' [His devilish black cat asks for two pairs of brogues and, when taken to be fitted with them, is destroyed by a dog, with the help of a 'wild huntsman'. The tune played by the piper was taught by 'the little people'.] Thus ended the strange tale of Maurice O'Sullivan, who in addition to the unanimous applause of the company present, was treated to another flowing tumbler of the barley bree, which he tossed off to the health of those who, to use his own words, were 'good people' in earnest – not fays or fairies, however, but the hospitable folks of Glen-Mac-Tir; adding at the same time that he was resolved to gratify the lovers of legendary lore with another of his wild Munster tales on the following night.[70]

The monthly periodical which best represents the Anglo-Irish spirit of the time,

John Keegan. 70 Ibid. 1 May 1841 'Puss in Brogues, A Legend' – by John Keegan. The story, classified as 2412C in Seán Ó Súilleabháin and R.T. Christiansen's *Types of the Irish Folktale*, is generally known as '*Cat ag lorg bróga*' or '*Bróga don Chat*'. The fairy-piper is generally not part of it, and it is not the usual International Type AT545B 'Puss in Boots' – also told in Ireland.

the *Dublin University Magazine*, was launched in 1833 and, unlike many others, had a long life. It combined Tory unionist principles with a policy of moderate cultural nationalism, the basic line being that the Protestant ascendancy understood and somehow owned the Irish past, and therefore was entitled to rule the country. From the start and until 1877 therefore the periodical had some space for Irish 'traditions'. They were sometimes treated seriously, but the humorous approach was often cultivated, and some fabrication was possible.

A case in point is Samuel Lover (1797-1868), who also wrote for other journals including the *Irish Penny Magazine* and collected his sketches as *Legends and Stories of Ireland* in 1832, a second series appearing in 1834 and a third, *Further Stories of Ireland*, thirty-one years after his death. He was also a painter, a songmaker, a novelist, and a one-man-show artist who toured Britain and North America with 'Irish Evenings' of his songs, monologues and stories, first tested on friends: 'It was as a teller of Irish stories Lover most delighted his audience. Few who heard him will forget the inimitable humour, the rich oily brogue, and the perfect ideal, he conveyed into the character.'[71] The notable point is that, whereas many writers were content to bring peasant storytellers to life in print, he actually impersonated them. This is how he introduced the first series of his *Legends*:

Though the sources whence these Stories are derived are open to every one, yet chances or choice may prevent thousands from making such sources available; and though the village crone and mountain guide have many hearers, still their circle is so circumscribed, that most of what I have ventured to lay before my reader is for the first time made tangible to the greater portion of those who do me the favour to become such. Many of them were originally intended merely for the diversion of a few friends round my own fireside; – there, recited in the manner of those from whom I heard them, they first made their *début*, and the flattering reception they met on so minor a stage, led to their appearance before larger audiences; – subsequently, I was induced to publish two of them in the *Dublin Literary Gazette*, and the favourable notice from contemporary prints, which they received, has led to the publication of the present volume. I should not have troubled the reader with this account of the 'birth and parentage, and education' of my literary bantlings, but to have it understood that some of them are essentially *oral* in their character, and, I fear, suffer materially when reduced to writing. This I mention *en passant* to the critics; and if I meet but half as good-natured *readers* as I have hitherto found *auditors*, I shall have cause to be thankful. But, previously to the perusal of the following pages, there are a few observations that I feel are necessary, and which I shall make as concise as possible. Most of the stories are given in the manner of the peasantry; and this has led to some peculiarities that might be objected to, were not the cause explained – namely, frequent digressions in the course of the narrative, occasional adjurations, and certain words unusually spelt. As regards the first, I beg to answer, that the stories would be deficient in national character without it; the Irish are so imaginative that they never tell a story straightforward, but constantly indulge in episode; for the second, it is only

71 S.C. Hall *Retrospect of a Long Life* 2. 134.

fair to say, that in most cases the Irish peasant's adjurations are not meant to be in the remotest degree irreverent, but arise merely from the impassioned manner of speaking which an excitable people are prone to; and I trust that such oaths as 'thunder-and-turf', or maledictions, as 'bad cess to you', will not be considered very offensive.[72]

There had been fake 'genuine Irish singers' before, and many an 'Irish fool' on stage, but by assuming the storyteller's role Lover seemed to be breaking new ground and vindicating the new image. One of his texts begins as follows: 'The only introduction I shall attempt to the following *extravaganza* is to request the reader to suppose it to be delivered by a frolicking Irish peasant in the richest brogue and most dramatic manner. "I'll tell you, Sir, a mighty quare story, and it's as thrue as I'm standin' here, and that's no lie".'[73] If we remember that at least some of his pieces were conceived as impersonations, with the exaggeration required by such form of entertainment, we understand the heavy load of Irishisms and the typifying of the narrators – including of the authentic Glendalough guide Joe Irwin in one of his first sketches (see pp. 155-6). In another text, Lover evokes an old woman on the banks of Lough Corrib:

'They say it's a fairy throut, yer honour, and tells mighty quare stories about it.' 'What are they?' I inquired. 'Troth, it's myself doesn't know the half o'them ... The people here has a mighty owld story about that throut.' 'Let me hear it, and you will oblige me.' 'Och! it's only laughin' at me you'd be, and call me an ould fool, as the misthiss beyant in the big house did afore, when she first kem among us – but she knows the differ now.' 'Indeed I shall not laugh at your story,' said I, 'but on the contrary, shall thank you very much for your tale.' 'Then sit down a minnit, sir,' said she, throwing her apron upon the rock, and pointing to the seat, 'and I'll tell you to the best of my knowledge'. And seating herself on an adjacent patch of verdure, she began her legend. 'There was wanst upon a time, long ago ... '[74]

We are also invited to meet 'Paddy the Sport', the perfect 'big house' jester:

He was a tall, loose-made, middle-aged man, rather on the elder side of middle age perhaps – fond of wearing an oil-skinned hat and a red waistcoat – much given to lying and tobacco, and an admirable hand at filling a game-bag or emptying a whisky-flask; and if game was scarce in the stubbles, Paddy was sure to create plenty of another sort for his master's party, by the marvellous stories he had ever at his command ... Paddy being a professed storyteller, and a notorious liar, it may be naturally inferred that he dealt largely in fairy-tales and ghost-stories. Talking of fairies one day, for the purpose of exciting him to say something of them, I inquired if there were many fairies in that part of the country? 'Ah! no, Sir!' said he, with the air of a sorrowing patriot – 'not now ...'[75]

There are many pieces of that ilk. In the Second Series we find the dialogue of

---

72 I quote from D.J. O'Donoghue's edition of *Legends and Stories of Ireland, First Series* (1899), ix-x. 73 Ibid. 148. 74 Ibid. 31-2. 75 Ibid. 176, 179-80.

a pair of Dublin street vendors, and we also learn the way of rewarding a story-teller:

The crone of every village has plenty of stories to make her hearers wonder how fortunes have been arrived at by extraordinary short cuts; and as it has been laid down as an axiom that there never was a fool who had not a greater fool to admire him, so there never was an old woman who told such stories without plenty of listeners. Now, Darby Kelleher was one of the latter class, and there was a certain collioch [*cailleach*: old woman] who was an extensive dealer in the marvellous, and could supply 'wholesale, retail, and for exportation', any customer such as Darby Kelleher, who not only was a devoted listener, but also made an occasional offering at the cave of the sibyl, in return for her oracular communications. This tribute generally was tobacco, as the collioch was partial to chewing the weed.[76]

The author's knowledge of rural Ireland may have been limited: he had spent part of his thirteenth year in a farm-house in County Wicklow,[77] according to D.J. O'Donoghue, but 'it was not until after several of the sketches had appeared in periodicals that Lover perfected his knowledge of the Irish peasantry by frequent visits into the remotest parts of the country – parts of which he had previously not visited at all, or only hurriedly for urgent artistic purposes, including the sketching of notable ruins for a Dublin magazine'.[78] It might seem questionable to mention him among some relatively better informed collectors, yet an accomplished impersonator must first be observant; at any rate we should bear in mind that by 'in the manner of the peasantry' he meant stage represen-tation to amuse an urban audience, and that the 'national character' he referred to might be the stereotype such an audience would accept.

The fact is that, before the end of this period, complaints began to be heard about the superficiality and patronizing attitude of such pastiches. John Keegan (two of whose articles were quoted on pp. 190-3) voiced the native's protest. Born in 1809 at Leix, he was of peasant stock and, having been educated in a hedge school in the Queen's County, became a teacher. A folklorist of the second half of the century vouched for his intimate knowledge of the subject: 'He was fond of attending the dances on the cross-roads – common at the time – sports, wakes, funerals and gatherings of the farmers and peasantry at their evening firesides. There he loved to hear old legends and traditions of men and times gone by, and relate in turn from his own stores of knowledge. Of ballads and stories he thus acquired a considerable assortment.'[79] One of his contribu-tions to the *Dublin University Magazine*, in 1839, denounced the assault on the dignity of Irish people and the distance between real lore and its representation

76 *Legends and Tales of Ireland* (1987) 230. **77** Bayle Bernard *The Life of Samuel Lover, R.H.A.* 1. 14: 'It was now he gained his first acquaintance with the peasantry of Ireland, and it was with the eyes that saw them now he ever continued to behold them.' **78** Introduction to the 1899 edition of *Legends and Stories* xxiii. **79** Canon O'Hanlon, quoted in D. O'Donoghue's 'Memoir', in J. Keegan *Legends and Poems* xiii-xiv.

in genteel periodicals. It may serve as a corrective to much of what we have
been quoting so far:

I venture to appear merely in the humble character of an Irish story-teller, and although
many have made their *entrée* on the same path before me, still I am bold to think that
there is still 'ample scope and verge enough' open to me – the more so, as I intend to
deviate a little from the route marked out by many of my more talented, but, at the same
time, more ignorant and prejudiced predecessors. It has been well observed that many of
those 'stories' and 'sketches' of 'Irish life' which have appeared of late years, were written more with a view to stigmatize and blacken the character of the lower order of the
Irish peasantry, than to exhibit a faithful delineation of the superstitions, habits, and
national prejudices of that remarkable people; and hence we find that the natives of
Great Britain, and even many of the higher orders in our own country, know less of our
customs, our peculiarities and predilections, than they do of the distinguishing traits in
the character of 'the shivering tenants of the frozen zone', or the painted and tattooed
natives of the South Sea Islands. And how can it be otherwise? when we see that most
of those who of late years have written of 'Ireland and the Irish' were either prejudiced
against us from habit or education, or were no further interested in what they said, than
as it merely regarded a pecuniary or money-making speculation? [Editor's protest in a
footnote: 'We believe the author to be mistaken, and we fear that in his secluded home
many of the splendid illustrations of the character and superstitions of our people, which
have appeared within the last dozen of years, may never have reached him.' Signed:
A.P.] Thus, their sketches were either mere dreams of fiction, in which we were held up
to the gaze of the contemptuous world, as a nation of demi-savages, or, at best, but caricatures in which the creations of the fancy were substituted for 'things as they are', and
the good-natured, generous, quick-witted and imaginative Irish peasant made to appear
as a mean, ignorant, cowardly barbarian. It was, therefore, gentle reader, the consideration of these facts which at first tempted me to add my humble name to the lengthened
catalogue of Irish 'story-tellers'; and perhaps I am as well qualified to undertake the task
as many of those who have gone before me. I am an Irish peasant – born and reared in
an Irish cabin, and educated in an Irish hedge-school. I have spent my years (and, as yet,
they are not many) among the lower classes of the insulted and despised Irish peasantry.
On Sundays I have knelt with them before the same rude altar; on the week days I have
wrought with them in the same fields, and in the same employments; on the summer
evenings I have joined them in the gaieties of the rustic dance, on the well-trodden vil-
lage-green; and during the long tempestuous winter evenings I have been with them at
the gaming table, or the wake, or formed a link with them in the laughing circle, around
the cheerful cottage fire, and there felt intense delight in listening to those numerous
romantic national songs, and wild legends, with which my native hamlet abounds. I,
therefore, fondly hope that the world will not reproach me with vanity or egotism when
I assert that, from the facts which I have mentioned, and the reasons I have just now
stated, I must necessarily be better acquainted with the affairs of the Irish peasant, and
with his life and habits, than those dandy caricaturists whose opportunities of observation were limited to a cursory survey of the scenery of the country, taken, perhaps, from
the top of a stage-coach, or, at most, to a few rambling excursions through the highways
or villages, made during some two or three weeks' sojourn at the villa of a noble friend,

or a few days' residence at some fashionable watering-place or country hotel; and to those still more dangerous and less honourable writers whose sole information is derived from the remarks of those more ignorant and malicious than themselves. Nor will I, I expect, be accused of arrogance or effrontery, when I announce to the public my intention of presenting them, henceforward, regularly, with a series of original [authentic] Irish stories, and that, under the title of 'Legends and Stories of the Queen's County Peasantry'. I intend to introduce my first series – not 'Sketches', however, professing to develop the personal character of the Irish peasant, or involving in their details an *exposé* of his faults, his foibles, or his virtues – but tales and narratives illustrative of the leading superstitions of the nation in general, and in particular of that part of the country in which I have been born and educated.[80]

Keegan deserves to be remembered as one of the first insiders among those who wrote about the rural folklore of Ireland; his production, however, was not equal to his literary ambitions, and he pales beside another writer from the same world: William Carleton (see the Document at the end of this chapter).

We may conclude that in the second quarter of the century the fashion for evocations of a perhaps long-established but now apparently vanishing body of popular lore had reached Ireland, and that some distinguishing characteristics of local 'folklore' were being identified. Interest was becoming less elitist than it had been with antiquarians; less obviously ancient stories and ways of telling them among the peasantry aroused more widespread curiosity. Of course, the tales said to have been picked up in the countryside varied in quality, and we cannot always trust the veracity of the portraits of rural Irish storytellers drawn by observers who, if they were not mere tourists (the demarcation line was not always clear, though ...), were nevertheless social outsiders, or by manipulators of popular material: high standards of accuracy were not the aim of those who wrote for effect and might accentuate the weirdness or drollery of characters and situations. Some could still play with the 'ossianic' ideal of the previous era, but others would present, sympathetically or not, simpler scenes of contemporary life; some only wanted to raise a laugh, while others had to see the natives as very different in order to reinforce their own sense of normality. It was also possible to combine those ingredients and attitudes. The usual format was that of the sketch: a relatively short arresting text in which a casual observer evoked a life-like situation, often in a conversational and perhaps witty manner, perhaps fusing fact and fiction. There could be a good deal of deliberate code-mixing: describing setting and characters, the writer used words that did not belong to the commonly spoken language, and he might carry elaborate prose to the point of affectation, treating the 'low' in grandiose language; such a style would clash with rude vernacular when the storyteller's voice was heard. Differences in social status were thus marked, and oddity further emphasised.

80 *Dublin University Magazine* 14 (1839) 366-7.

Most interesting for our purpose are the frames enclosing the narratives. The setting often was the kitchen of a comfortable farm; as we shall see presently, the Irish rural world could certainly not be reduced to that, but the field of observation remained limited. In terms of repertoire, though one occasionally finds traces of the older Fianna lore, the kind of material evoked by Robert Bell (Document B) is much more in evidence. Although Keightley and Keegan attested to the telling of long complex wonder tales, most adapters of Irish oral stories focused on relatively short legends of the supernatural – partly because they were easier to find (they could be told anywhere and at any time, by anyone), but also because, being less formalized in structure and expression than heroic or wonder tales, they were easily rendered in the style expected by readers, and not too long so that the experience did not become boring. With them it was possible to emphasize supposed typical Irish traits such as a propensity for flamboyant utterance, outrageous mendacity, or credulity.

The texts on which we have based this chapter do not reveal traditional storytellers in *all* their aspects and functions but at least show that they played a significant role, and confirm the shift from the repulsive or awesome to the picturesque and harmless in outsiders' perception. Even when the sketches can be suspected of only partly reflecting the reality of Irish traditional storytelling, they bear witness to certain common views, and even distortions show the writers' feelings about their subject. While pastiches should not be mistaken for the real thing, conscious imitation of the style or subject matter of a mode of expression becomes possible only when its peculiar conventions and relative originality have been identified.

In the 1840s, John Keegan – like William Carleton for a while – was associated with the nationalist periodical *The Nation*. He died of cholera in 1849, while the Irish peasantry was in the throes of the Great Famine. The often merry and generally harmless image one had formed of the Irish storyteller had helped conceal a conflictive and darkening background, of which we must now form an idea.

B. IRISH NATIONALISM AND THE RURAL WORLD

Why did a larger number of middle-class observers notice what was preserved orally by the ordinary people of rural Ireland? Were there political implications? And what was the socio–cultural context in which 'traditional storytellers' were active, in the first half of the nineteenth century?

They belonged to the demographically increasing majority of the population, in an age when the importance of 'statistics' (in the sense of the study of facts bearing on the condition of a state – see pp. 95-6) was also growing; they therefore attracted attention, stirring concern, but also hopes. The 'superstitions' illustrated in popular narratives were still considered objects of contempt by some members of the higher strata of society, or seen by them as mere cultural freaks which might be examined but were doomed to vanish. At the beginning of the nineteenth century, however, some found them fascinating because different from their own world, or admitted that what was popular had virtues of its own, particularly if they thought that stories transmitted by the 'people' might identify a 'nation'. But interpretations of the term 'people' varied, and 'nation', though it was developing as a central catchword, was used with various meanings. If the word 'people' denoted only the lower part of a population, any culture it might have was not likely to be taken seriously by most members of the upper one; but there were new ideas according to which the masses mattered and any power had to draw its authority from the 'people'; if the latter term referred to all those who shared the same language and history, it could become eminently respectable. Beyond the basic principle that mankind was naturally divided into competing communities, there were two basic views of the 'nation': the French Revolution had defined it as the freely constituted community of citizens and their collective supreme sovereignty; at about he same time, some German thinkers pointed to a particular cultural heritage as the basic bond. Both definitions might imply that one's nation was superior, and that it was entitled to have its own independent government; the second definition added that political boundaries should be coterminous with cultural ones. It was the middle-class intelligentsia of a country that tried to make of the whole population a nation, by appealing to the masses or claiming to speak for them.

The concept of what would soon be called 'folklore' could involve haughty or paternalistic attitudes towards the people (as *vulgus*), but in many European countries it was valued as a search for the roots distinguishing one collectivity from the others: the existence of 'traditions' of one's own would justify demands for political autonomy. Delving more or less selectively into the past, sometimes imagining what could not be proved, and looking for positive peculiarities – as opposed to the stereotypes formed by outsiders – one would then advocate ways of building a certain future. Herder (see p. 168) had already considered that each nation should develop in accord with its own innate abilities, and remain true to its 'spirit' or 'soul', which could if necessary be rediscovered in folk poetry.[81]

In Ireland, the concept of nation had to be adapted to the local reality. The notion that it consisted of equal citizens or of a common ethnicity, that each nationality should have a state of its own consisting of one national group, and that folklore provided insights into its character, could be difficult or dangerous to apply. The sense of belonging was far from being the same for all, and class differences coincided or intersected in intricate ways with religious and even linguistic ones. The ruling minority, which in the eighteenth century did call itself 'the Irish nation' and could have a 'patriotic' sense of civic duty, largely shared British upper-class culture; but it lost its parliament with the Act of Union of

---

81 William A. Wilson 'Herder, Folklore and Romantic Nationalism', *Journal of Popular Culture* 6 (1973).

1800, and some of its members resented what made them subjects of a distant government like their Catholic servants or tenants and other paupers who surrounded them. As for the Catholic majority, after fighting for full political enfranchisement and winning it in the late 1820s, it was becoming aware of its power. It was mobilised again in a campaign to repeal the Union, and was led in both fights by Daniel O'Connell, the hero of many folk stories, who invented the mass political movement and said that he was 'backed by the Irish people'. Although he repeatedly denied having sectarian aims, 'Catholic' and 'Irish' tended to be synonymous for him. He could refer to 'the Irish nation' but did not clarify the concept; in fact he was neither a revolutionary nor an advocate of total national independence. The emblems wielded by his supporters to rally the troops were a few simple symbols (shamrocks, harps, wolfhounds, round towers), not a complex narrative tradition, nor the Irish language. On the other hand, from the late 1820s, some members of the Anglo-Irish middle classes were paying allegiance to a Gaelic past and asserted their emotional attachment to a land of which they still considered their class to be the natural leader; the *Dublin University Magazine*, whose politics remained Unionist (see p. 193), advocated writing on Irish subjects and training the public to distinguish between their true and false representations.

A more radical and nationalistic movement, referred to as 'Young Ireland', became active in the 1840s with its weekly newspaper *The Nation*. Its followers were impatient of O'Connell's constitutional methods. The independence they advocated would be founded on a cross-class alliance reinforced by the re-establishment of an independent Irish Parliament, a refusal to introduce religious questions into public affairs, and a kind of comprehensive cultural renaissance. In the first issue of the journal, in October 1842, the motto was: 'To create and foster public opinion and make it racy of the soil'. The Irishness this movement invoked was a quality anybody could have acquired as the result of long residence in the land and sufficient assimilation; thus descendants of the ancient Gaels, of Normans or of seventeenth-century planters, could together be one people. 'Irish nationality' was thus to 'contain and represent the races of Ireland'; relations between them were 'about to become harmonious', because the Irish were now supposed to be 'rational', that is to say prepared to merge religious affiliations and classes in a new patriotic front – at least, so the 'Young Ireland' movement believed. In reality, there had been an increasing sectarianization of Irish politics since the 1820s, and to oppose those who defined Irish identity by a religious tag was to swim against the tide.

The main spokesman of this inclusive nationalism, Thomas Davis (1814-45), defined the aim as the creation of 'a race of men full of a more intensely Irish character and knowledge', with a revived self-respect he called 'a Nationality which will not only raise our people from their poverty, by securing to them the blessings of a Domestic Legislation, to inflame and purify them with a lofty and heroic love of country – a Nationality of the spirit as of the letter – a Nationality

which will come to be stamped upon our manners, our literature and our deeds
– a Nationality which may embrace Protestant, Catholic and Dissenter.'[82] A
nation of otherwise different citizens, but with some common cultural roots?
Davis thought that the study of selected chapters of Irish history would promote
the necessary spirit. The French romantic historian Augustin Thierry, one of his
inspirers, was quoted as having offered a version of the history of Ireland as a
long heroic resistance to British rule – a version that would flourish into the
twentieth century:

There are some peoples who have long memories, whom the thought of independence
never abandons in their slavery, and who, holding out against long habit, elsewhere so
potent, still detest and strive to shake off, after centuries, the yoke which superior power
has imposed upon them. Such is the Irish nation. This nation, reduced by conquest
beneath the English sway, refuses for these six centuries to consent to this government
and give it its sanction; it spurns it as it did the first day; it protests against it as the
Ancient Irish protested – by unsuccessful battles. Its revolts it does not regard as rebellion, but as just and legitimate war. Vainly has England spent her strength in efforts to
crush this undying spirit ... To maintain this chain of manners and traditions unbroken
against all the efforts of the conqueror, the Irish have made monuments which neither
fire nor sword can destroy – their music – that music in which they boast their skill, and
which, when they were independent, was their pride and pleasure. The Bards and
Minstrels became the chroniclers of the country. Wandering from village to village, they
brought to every fireside, memories of Old Ireland; ... he who knew best how to celebrate the freedom of days gone by, the glory of the patriot, and the grandeur of his
cause, was most welcome and the highest honoured.[83]

A problem was that the 'people', if by it was meant the Irish peasants, were
not naturally inclined to nationalistic politics: they identified with smaller local
units. But as they represented the bulk of the population they had to be invoked
as guarantors, and won over. Educated city-dwellers could reify *certain* aspects
of peasant culture as the *national* culture with which they desired to identify;
but, on the whole, members of the Young Ireland movement did not seem to
value highly the fantasy that pervaded tales or legends; this particular material
was not to be trusted, and could too easily be employed once again to discredit
the 'Irish People':

The practice of speaking and acting only the truth, more than military or commercial, or
intellectual eminence, makes a country great and happy ... The slave's vice of paltering
with the truth clings to our people like the rust of chains. They must unlearn the practice of boasting and exaggeration; they must learn – hard task to a demonstrative, imag-

82 Prospectus announcing *The Nation* Oct. 1842. On folklore and nationalism, see D. Ó
Giolláin *Locating Irish Folklore* Ch. 3. 83 'Sur l'esprit national des Irlandais, à propos des
Mélodies Irlandaises de Thomas Moore', *Le Censeur Européen* 22 February 1820 – translated
in *The Nation* 26 November 1842.

inative people – to be direct and literal. To be prompts in saying 'This is not true: I will not believe it.' 'This is not true: I will not say it' ...[84]

On the whole (though there might be exceptions), in the first half of the nineteenth century neither those who told Irish folktales nor those who collected them were likely to be staunch nationalists. But it seemed that something could be done with the popular genre that had been spreading through Ireland since the seventeenth century: ballads in English. The form could be used as a way of teaching Irish history and nationhood – and of course it would not be called propaganda: 'One of the essential qualities of a good historical ballad is truth'.[85] On the other hand, old beliefs which were not considered of a useful 'national' nature were not what one could hope to build upon; Davis, who agreed to a last harvest of documents, would not recommend keeping traditions at all costs:

We are in a transition state. The knowledge, the customs, the superstitions, the hopes of the People are entirely changing. There is neither use nor reason in lamenting what we must infallibly lose. Our course is open and is a great one, and will try us severely; but, be it well or ill, we cannot resemble our fathers. No conceivable effort will get the people, twenty years hence, to regard the fairies but as a beautiful fiction to be cherished, not believed in, and not a few real and human characters are perishing as fast as the Fairies. Let us be content to have the past chronicled wherever it cannot be preserved. Much may be saved – the Gaelic language and the music of the past may be handed uncorrupted to the future; but whatever may be the substitutes, the Fairies and the Banshees, the Poor Scholar and the Ribbonman, the Orange Lodge, the Illicit Still, and the Faction Fight are vanishing into history, and unless this generation paints them no other will know what they were.[86]

Davis wrote this in 1845. His list of what was doomed and what might endure proved partly inaccurate, but he was right when he anticipated great changes – only, they would first take the form of disaster rather than progress.

The 'traditions' one had begun to collect or imitate (selectively) were those of a rural population which was subject to dominion and adverse circumstances, formed particular social relationships, and may have had distinctive mental attitudes. We should not draw too static and unified a picture: although this rural world can be described as culturally conservative, by 1840 it was probably far from what it had been at the beginning of the eighteenth century and could differ in some respects from what Robert Bell had observed around 1780. It would be severely disrupted at the end of the 1840s, and partly transformed in the following decades. We must also acknowledge the relative heterogeneity of that population at any given time.

84 Quoted in C.G. Duffy *Young Ireland* 1. 60-1. 85 Th. Davis, 'A Ballad History of Ireland', *The Nation* 30 November 1844. 86 'Habits and Characters of the Peasantry', *The Nation* 12 October 1844.

Sociologists tell us that the concept of peasantry is an awkward one because it embraces very different kinds of social groups and modes of existence. The fact is that, while four-fifths of the population of Ireland in 1841 were rural residents (indeed, only 5% lived in cities of more than 50,000) and two-thirds directly depended on the land, there were various strata in that rural society. The structure of landholding determined conditions and ways of life, and the main stratifying feature was the relative degree of security or insecurity of access to sufficient land. The large majority lived on estates belonging to aristocrats or gentry. There were little more than eight thousand landed families, whose properties varied considerably in size. Between one-half and two-thirds of them lived on their estates; the others – often the richest – were 'absentees' who left the management of their land in the hands of agents (and perhaps through them to 'middlemen' who sublet to poor peasants, to make a profit); they lived more or less permanently abroad, but there was a growing tendency for landowners to take personal control. Some showed a paternalistic concern for their tenants, while others did not care for them at all and had only pecuniary interests. In the greater part of Ireland, landlords and tenants were further divided by religious barriers. Below the landlord class – and the generally detested agents who managed estates – were the tenant farmers with long leases and enough good land. Representing no more than a quarter of the agricultural society, they would not consider themselves mere 'peasants'; but there were grades among them, too, from the most prosperous large or 'strong' farmers, with extended tenure, to relatively small ones. The 'cottiers' (some 18% of the population in 1841) occupied a cabin and a very small plot let annually to the highest bidder and for which they could pay with labour; landless labourers, most numerous, might rent even smaller pieces for a period of less than a year, to grow a single crop for the subsistence of a family — this 'conacre' system had been expanding since the end of the eighteenth century. In parts of the west of Ireland the supposedly older 'rundale' form of agriculture was still applied: the joint holding of poor ground by a number of tenants, generally with family ties, who divided up the arable part into small portions every year so that each received different qualities of ground, the 'outfield' being shared as pasture land. In the 1840s, cottiers and landless labourers and their families may have been three million. Many labourers – the *spailpíní*, carrying their scythes or spades – hired themselves out for a season in the richer farms of other districts; the labourers of west Cork and Kerry would move to Tipperary or Limerick, and those of Galway and Mayo to the midlands, while others found temporary work in England and Scotland. There were mere vagabonds, too, and this mobile population was often regarded as dangerous. Strong divisions existed between landlords and farmers, and between small-holders and cottiers or landless labourers; oath-bound secret societies reacted violently to conflicts over enclosure, rent and evictions, but this agrarian protest rose and fell in accordance with economic fluctuations and was for the most part organized only locally. There were important regional differences: lowest density of population and better land in the eastern counties of Leinster and Munster for instance, and poorer conditions in the west, where holdings were getting smaller. Everywhere, relatively barren uplands and fertile lowlands had distinct conditions, and there was an evolution in time: in the south and east, depending on the demand for grain, shifts from cattle to tillage, then back to livestock production – to the detriment of labourers; spinning and weaving linen, which had been an important rural occupation and a boon to living standards in Armagh, Roscommon, Mayo, Sligo and Leitrim, collapsed by the 1820s when these activities were mechanized around Belfast.

Many foreign travellers in the late eighteenth century and the first half of the nineteenth were appalled at the material condition of life of the majority. Thousands had died from starvation and disease in 1727-9, 1740, 1800, 1816, 1822 ... In 1836, a commission was appointed to investigate the extent of poverty in Ireland and recommended that welfare schemes should be organized for some two-and-a-half million people. The Census of 1841 revealed that nearly half the families lived at poverty level in one-roomed mud cabins and that the number of wandering poors was increasing. Historians no longer believe that, as was often said then, national laziness was the cause of this situation: the land-tenure system had its share of responsibility, and there were demographic causes – the population almost quadrupled from the mid-eighteenth century to the 1840s, and the rate of growth was highest in the cottier or labourer classes, with increasing density as one travelled westwards and the most people being crowded onto the least fertile land. Except for the North-East, there was no significant industrial development as an outlet. In addition, the almost entire dependence of three million people on potatoes – by the 1840s the most extensively cultivated crop – made the situation of the poor particularly fragile. Plentiful and nourishing, potatoes were available from late August to May, but there regularly came a period of hardship ('the hungry months') before the new crop arrived; then one might be forced to eat nettles, or go begging. A longer interruption meant disaster.

While those at the bottom of the social pyramid led a precarious existence, there also seems to have been much energy and exuberance. Visitors often commented on what seemed to be paradoxical, as Walter Scott did, for instance: 'Their poverty is not exaggerated; it is on the verge of human misery ... Yet the men are stout and healthy; the women buxom and well-coloured ... Their natural disposition is turned to gaiety and happiness.'[87] There was a rumour, in England, that with only some four months needed to gather turf and produce potatoes, the Irish had eight months to drink, fight among themselves, dance and tell stories. Reality was of course not so idyllic; on a closer look, one noticed the negative effects of overpopulation (see p. 113), but it is true that life in local communities had its pleasant moments. Tobacco and drink – particularly the

87 Quoted in D.J. O'Donoghue *Sir Walter Scott's Tour of Ireland in 1825* 92.

latter – were not expensive, and there was plenty of music and dancing, sport, and other occasions on which people socialized, such as fairs, patterns (festivals celebrated at holy wells), weddings and wakes. Periods of little work could be spent by the men in going from house to house to discuss the news brought by beggars or by returning *spailpíní*. In brief, sociability was the main positive element. It was particularly strong where the communal 'rundale' mode prevailed; from ten to twenty huts would cluster in a *clachan* where there was constant interchange – for work, disputes, and entertainment. A Donegal 'improving landlord' of the 1840s noted that members of this type of society were 'great talkers; as firing is plentiful, they sit up half the night in winter, talking and telling stories; they therefore dislike living in detached houses.' When he tried to change the system, they resisted: 'The pleasure the people feel in assembling and chatting together made them consider the removal of the houses, from the clusters or hamlets in which they were generally built to the separate farms, a great grievance.'[88]

Were there particular ways of feeling and habits of thought? It is a delicate undertaking to analyse popular mentalities over a distance of almost two centuries, but no doubt some particular turns of mind, networks of beliefs and systems of representation must have been operating. One of the features most often commented upon by observers was the great role that seemed to be assigned to parallel worlds and magical practices. A Munster schoolteacher, Humphrey O'Sullivan (Amhlaoibh Ó Súilleabháin, 1780-1838), non-committally reported in his diary unelaborated reports of local news:

(24 Sept. 1827) There is an extraordinary story going around hereabouts just now. Eleanor Dorcey, daughter of James Dorcey of Ballyline was coming home from Kilboyne (Ballingarry) after hearing Mass, the 2nd day of this present month, Sunday, in the company of Nicholas Tobin and others, when she saw the fairy host around Machaire More. A dark person came out of the host and tried to wound her. She ran round Nicholas Tobin that she might not be hurt; but this was little help to her, for she would have been wounded and severely hurt, only that her mother (dead six years) came to save her. Her mother had a woeful expression. Then the fairy host left her and Nicholas Tobin and the other people took her home. She was speechless until cockcrow after midnight, when she recovered her speech; and then she lost the use of her leg which was as cold as ice. Thus she continued for thirteen days, that is till Saturday, the fifteenth day of this month weeping and wailing and sorrowing, till her mother came to her and asked did she wish to be cured. She said she did. 'I should have come to you sooner, but I could not as long as anyone was with you; but now as I find you in solitude, I will heal you. Come out to the roadside.' They both went out, though they did not take the same way. Her mother showed her a herb and told her to pluck it, for nobody else ought to pluck it. She plucked it, and it was without skin, leaf or flower. Her mother told her to boil it in water and to rub it to her leg six times, in the name of the Father and of the Son and of the Holy Ghost. Her mother then left her. She did as she had been told; and

88 George Hill *Facts from Gweedore* quoted in E.E. Evans *The Personality of Ireland* 100.

on her making the sign of the cross on the leg the first time it straightened out and it is whole and sound since. This is an extraordinary story, unless she became subject to hallucinations like a person in a fever, or unless it is a make-up of her own. But some of the neighbours say that her leg was as cold as ice. It is her own father who told me the story from beginning to end, and Denis O'Brien from Ballyline Bridge told it in the self same way. But in truth he is afraid that it is a bit of make-believe and that she merely pretended to be dumb and lame. He admits however that respectable people told him that her leg was cold as I have said already. Personally, I wash my hands of it![89]

The higher one moved in the social hierarchy, the more likely were such beliefs and practices to be derided as drivel, or denounced as popish nonsense by proselytizing Protestants; non-institutionalized forms of belief could also be condemned by the Catholic Church, as John O'Donovan observed in 1837: 'The priests, I am very sorry to see and say, inclining very much to Protestant notions, are putting an end to all those venerable customs.'[90] The Catholic Church, however, does not seem to have had as much control of the poorer classes then as it would later; there was on average one priest for a congregation of three thousand people and the disproportion was higher in the west where the so-called 'superstitions' and apparently 'pagan' practices were most strongly adhered to.

Is it possible to talk of a unified Irish popular culture?[91] Catholic, Anglican and Presbyterian traditions and attitudes would differ in important respects; we must distinguish between the popular culture of the countryside and that of towns, perhaps that of strong farmers and that of the rural poor, not to mention linguistic differences. Levels – or kinds – of education also varied. In 1835 it was estimated that one half of the population spoke Irish, but in many parts of the country English was also spoken: the two languages, and the oral traditions they conveyed, were not completely independent, and there were bridges between elite and popular cultures. Charles Smith had observed in the mid-eighteenth century, more particularly in Kerry, a surprising knowledge of Latin and even Greek.[92] It was picked up in the 'hedge-schools' which had developed for Catholics prevented by the Penal Laws from receiving a regular education; the local collectivity would guarantee the teacher's livelihood. In 1825, according to a government report, 9,000 of those schools served some 400,000 pupils. The teachers injected elements of ancient mythology and history into Irish peasant culture, and were also partly responsible for the copying of manuscripts. They gradually vanished after the establishment of the 'National schools' in the 1830s. Approximately half of the population, five years of age or older, was still illiterate in 1841, the proportion being higher in the western half of the country – in parts of Connaught it could reach 85 or 90 per cent. In 1822, in County Kildare,

89 *The Diary of Humphrey O'Sullivan* (tr. M. McCraith) 1. 135-6. **90** O.S. Letters, Roscommon, dated Castlereagh, 7 July 1837. **91** See S. J. Connolly 'Popular Culture in Pre-Famine Ireland', in C.J. Byrne and M. Harry (eds) *Talamh an Eisc: Canadian and Irish Essays* 12-28. **92** *History of Kerry* 67, 418.

the Quaker educationalist Mary Leadbetter, who wanted to awaken 'an interest in the concerns of a class of people whose faults are *much*, whose virtues are *little* known',[93] had shown how literacy and oral skill could go together:

Reading has stored [Elizabeth Brady's] mind with much entertainment for herself and others, her memory being very retentive, and the matter she has collected of great variety – truth and fiction, history and tradition, poetry and romance – but all of a blameless tendency, like her life, and with her modest, humble manners, she mingles a quiet, dry kind of humour, so diverting and withal so unoffending, that her hearers are surprised how her husband could desert so pleasant a companion.[94]

With important differences there were common elements, in a still predominantly oral culture.

Evidence presented in this chapter and the previous one confirms that stories could be told in different settings and in different ways, and were generally appreciated, as also noted by this English 'statistician' in 1812:

[The 'old native Irish'] delight in dancing, music, singing, and listening to old romantic stories, which some still continue to relate ... The women in the weaving districts are much accustomed to visiting each other, and these visits are called *Kealing*. A young female with her spinning-wheel on her head travels a considerable distance to the house of an aquaintance, where others are assembled, who spin, sing, and converse the whole evening ... In the neighbourhood of Nymphsfield, I met an old man who repeated a long history in Irish, which he called the *Poems of Osheen*, meaning, as I suppose, the Poems of Ossian. Having found a person to act as an interpreter, I spent two hours in writing down what he rehearsed. It seemed to have none of the requisites of a poem, but appeared to be a confused legend which the man had learnt by heart, for when I interrupted him he could not proceed without beginning again.[95]

There were various kinds of stories, long and short, local or widespread, fantastic and credible, relatively old or new. Fenian lays were still valued by older people. Travellers' reports and the protofolklorists' sketches reveal that long wonder tales inventing an ideal life were thriving, as well as shorter legends expressing beliefs. There were stories referring to true events which functioned as a collective memory; Charles Gavan Duffy, one of the 'Young Irelanders' who wanted to diffuse another view of the past, had a low opinion of such popular history: 'Beyond a vague sense of disaster and injustice the mass of the people knew little of the past. I can remember hearing when a boy from some of the *seanachies* to whom I was always ready to listen, a story of "the time of the troubles" in which the massacre in Rathlin (under Charles I) and the cruelties of the Ancient Britons (1798) made part of the same transaction.'[96] Most testimonies

93 *Cottage Biography: Being a Collection of Lives of the Irish Peasantry* Preface. **94** Ibid. 12. **95** Edward Wakefield *An Account of Ireland, Statistical and Political* 2. 738. **96** C.G. Duffy *Young Ireland* 1. 27.

agree that good narrators enjoyed social recognition, but some observers condemned a particular kind of storytelling: rumour-mongering. The commission
appointed in 1833 to investigate the condition of the Irish poor denounced the
bad influence of strollers and their stories on the moral condition of the labouring classes (see p. 161), but it also had this to say: 'The very poor are more
ready to feel for, and to help them according to their means, than any other
class, they are never sure but it will be their own case soon.'[97]

The economic bases of this society were unsound, however, and calamity
brought about dramatic changes between 1845 and 1850, with repeated failure
of the potato crop. Severe food shortages had happened before, but never on
such a scale and for so long. Perhaps a million people died from starvation and
famine-related diseases. More or less the same number emigrated during this
period; emigration had been a fact of Irish life since the eighteenth century but
it now increased dramatically, and remained a drain: in twenty years the population of Ireland was almost halved. The majority of the victims were the labourers and cottiers, and particularly the Irish-speaking population of the extreme
southern and western half of the island. Many landlords seized the opportunity
to clear their lands for more profitable use, or felt they had no other choice to
avoid bankruptcy, and in five years about a quarter of a million people may have
been evicted. The Great Famine disrupted communities and demoralized individuals. For a long time it left intense fear, and the Irish countryside in general
would never again see the liveliness it had once known. At first there seemed to
be no place left for storytelling, as William Robert Wilde wrote in 1849:

The great convulsion which society of all grades here has experienced, the failure of the
potato crop, pestilence, famine, and a most unparalleled extent of emigration, together
with bankrupt landlords, pauperizing poor-laws, grinding officials, and decimating work-
houses, have broken up the very foundations of social intercourse ... In some places, all
the domestic usages of life have been outraged; the tenderest bonds of kindred have been
severed, some of the noblest and holiest feelings of human nature have been blotted from
the heart, and many of the finest, yet firmest links which united the various classes in
the community have been rudely burst asunder ... The Shannaghie and the Callegh [*cailleach*: old woman] in the chimney corner, tell no more the tales and legends of other days
... In this state of things, with depopulation the most terrific which any country ever
experienced, on the one hand, and the spread of education, and the introduction of rail-
roads, colleges, industrial and other educational schools, on the other – together with the
rapid decay of the Irish vernacular, in which most of our legends, romantic tales, ballads,
and bardic annals, the vestige of Pagan rites, and the relics of fairy charms were preserved – can superstition, or if superstitious belief, can superstitious practices continue
to exist?[98]

97 *Selection of Parochial Examinations relative to the Destitute Classes in Ireland, from the
Evidence Received by his Majesty's Commissioners for Enquiring into the Condition of the Poorer
Classes in Ireland* 284. **98** *Irish Popular Superstitions* 9-11 'Discursive Introduction written in

Much of the older world disappeared, indeed, though something of it survived, as folklorists were to find out later in the century.

Before turning, in Chapter 8, to what they would observe then, we shall look again at the period we have already covered but from a partly different angle, in Chapter 7: if there is fiction in texts offered as factual accounts of Irish storytelling, isn't some factual information to be found in novels or literary tales? Meanwhile, as a kind of synthesis of the present chapter and also as a transition, I shall consider the longest portrait of an Irish storyteller written in the pre-Famine period, by a man who had intimate personal experience of rural life. This text assembles elements which had appeared piecemeal in sketches, and adds to them.

DOCUMENT C

During the winter of 1827-8, having just published his *Sketches of Ireland* after a tour in search of 'beastly rites' and strange stories (see p. 162), the Reverend Caesar Otway brought assistance to the man who was to contribute a distinctly new voice to Irish writings in English, by accepting some of his early short texts for a periodical he was editing. It was the time of the aggressively anti-Catholic 'Second Reformation', and a young convert who seemed prepared to attack his ex-religion was a useful recruit; but Otway may also have recognized that by this offspring of the peasant world something valuable might be chronicled. Indeed, from hack-propagandist, William Carleton (1794-1869) soon aspired to become the 'historian' of his people. He was for a time a fellow traveller of Young Ireland while maintaining links with Unionism, and was also prepared to attack all parties. He was too passionate and contradictory, and circumstances made him too opportunistic, to take the objective and sober view supposed to be that of a real historian, but when it was a matter of describing the peasant world in the first third of the century, and more particularly in Ulster, he could not be surpassed.

He defined his mission in the preface to his *Tales of Ireland* in 1834: 'I found them [the Irish peasants] a class unknown in literature, unknown by their own landlords, and unknown by those in whose hands much of their destiny was placed. If I became the historian of their habits and manners, their feelings, their prejudices, their superstitions and their crimes; if I have attempted to delineate their moral, religious and physical state, it was because I saw no other person willing to undertake a task which surely must be looked upon as an important one.'[99] In 1839, he stated his intention of offering 'a panoramic view of Irish life, characters and manners ... Old customs, superstitions and usages, that either have passed away or are fast disappearing, will be described with truth and accu-

1849 ... '. **99** *Tales of Ireland* 1.

racy; so that the work will be, in this point of view, valuable to the lover of Irish social antiquities as well as to the general reader.'[100] In the 'General Introduction' to the 1842 edition of his *Traits and Stories of the Irish Peasantry* he insisted again that he had given 'faithful delineations of Irish life': 'I come to a subject of such difficulty with unusual advantages on my side, and ... consequently, my exhibitions of Irish peasant life, in its most comprehensive sense, may be relied on as truthful and authentic ... I have endeavoured, with what success has been already determined by the voice of my own country, to give a panorama of Irish life among the people – comprising at one view all the strong points of their general character – their loves, sorrows, superstitions, piety, amusements, crimes and virtues.'[101] Thomas Davis, the advocate of non-sectarian nationalism in the 1840s (see pp. 200-1), was aware of the importance of the phenomenon:

Well may Carleton say that we are in a transition state. The knowledge, the customs, the superstitions, the hopes of the People are entirely changing ... It is chiefly in this way we value the work before us. In it Carleton is the historian of the peasantry rather than a dramatist. The fiddler and piper, the seanachie and seer, the match-maker and dancing-master, and a hundred characters beside are here brought before you, moving, acting, playing, plotting and gossiping ... Born and bred among the people – full of their animal vehemence – skilled in their sports – as credulous and headlong in boyhood, and as fitful and varied in manhood, as the wildest – he had felt with them, and must ever sympathise with them ... Here is a genuine Seanachie ...[102]

Carleton was born in County Tyrone, the fourteenth child of a small farmer just above the 'cottier' class; he first received the oral heritage from his mother, who was a singer, and from his father, a storyteller:

My native place is a spot rife with old legends, tales, traditions, customs, and superstitions; so that in my early youth, even beyond the walls of my own humble roof, they met me in every direction. It was at home, however, and from my father's lips in particular, that they were perpetually sounding in my ears. In fact his memory was a perfect storehouse, and a rich one, of all that the social antiquary, the man of letters, the poet or the musician would consider valuable. As a teller of old tales, legends, and historical anecdotes he was unrivalled, and his stock of them was inexhaustible. He spoke the Irish and English languages with equal fluency. With all kinds of charms, old ranns [*rann*: an epigram or quatrain], or poems, old prophecies, religious superstitions, tales of pilgrims, miracles, and pilgrimages, anecdotes of blessed priests and friars, revelations from ghosts and fairies, was he thoroughly acquainted. And so strongly were all these impressed upon my mind by frequent repetition on his part, that I have hardly ever since heard, during a tolerably enlarged intercourse with Irish society, both educated and uneducated – with the antiquary, the scholar or the humble *seanachie* – any single tradi-

---

100 A flyleaf in *Fardorougha the Miser* announcing another book, which perhaps did not materialise. 101 *Traits and Stories of the Irish Peasantry* 1. viii and xxiv. 102 *The Nation* 12 July, 1845: a review of *Tales and Sketches illustrating the Irish Peasantry*.

tion, usage or legend, that, so far as I can at present recollect, was perfectly new to me or unheard before in some similar or cognate dress. This is certainly saying much; but I believe I may assert with confidence, that I could produce, in attestation of its truth, the names of Petrie, Sir W. Betham, Ferguson, and O'Donovan [Carleton had met George Petrie, Samuel Ferguson and John O'Donovan while writing for the *Irish Penny Journal* and the *Dublin University Magazine*; he had exchanged a couple of letters with William Betham, Ulster King-of-Arms and archaeologist] the most distinguished antiquaries, both of social usages and otherwise, that ever Ireland produced. What rendered this besides of such peculiar advantage to me in later life, as a literary man, was that I heard them as often in the Irish language as in the English, if not oftener: a circumstance which enabled me in my writings to transfer the genius, the idiomatic peculiarity and conversational spirit of the one language into the other, precisely as the people themselves do in their dialogues, whenever the heart or imagination happens to be moved by the darker or better passions.[103]

His next source of narrative material was hedge-school education. One of the masters he later portrayed seems to have taught, among other things, verbal skills:

Every winter's day each brought two sods of turf for the fire, which was kept burning in the centre of the school: there was a hole in the roof that discharged the function of a chimney. Around this fire, especially during cold and severe weather, the boys were entitled to sit in a circle by turns. ... Sam was about eighteen years of age, a fine strapping young fellow, possessed of a great deal of dry humour. In consequence of his age and respectability he usually set at the fire beside the master, who used to indulge in a variety of anecdotes for Sam's entertainment. Sam, on the other hand, returned anecdote for anecdote, or in other words lie for lie.[104]

To the Irish fund of tales and anecdotes, the hedge schoolmaster added classical mythology. Later on, when the young Carleton, as a 'poor scholar' (wandering student), was walking through Ireland, he used this knowledge to pay for hospitality by telling stories, and realized that he could not only retell but also invent:

The neighbouring families began almost to quarrel as to which of them should receive me. The only equivalent I could bestow was the narrative of the old classical legends, which I transmogrified and changed into an incredible variety of shapes. I would have given them Irish legends, and sometimes did, but then the Irish legends did not show the 'larnin'. I made one discovery, while leading this extraordinary kind of life, and that was the power of my own invention. It did not indeed strike me very forcibly then, but since that time I have reflected on it with something like wonder. Finding that it would not do to go over the same ground so often, I took to inventing original narratives, and was surprised at the facility with which I succeeded. This new discovery was as great an

103 W. Carleton *Traits and Stories of the Irish Peasantry* 1. viii-ix.   **104** W. Carleton *Autobiography* 29.

212   *The Irish storyteller*

amusement to myself as it was to my audience. I used to compose these fictions in the course of the day, while walking about, and recite them at the fireside in the evening. I was beginning to enjoy a certain degree of local fame, which constituted me a treasure to whatever neighbourhood I stopped in. The number of people who came to hear me in the evening was surprising, as were the distances they came from. In fact I became a regular *improvisatore*, and was the subject of many a wondering conversation among the people.[105]

Another set of models was offered by chapbooks: as a youth, Carleton read and immensely admired Lesage's *Gil Blas*, which offered a model of adventurous life for a social misfit ('I did not then even know that it was fiction'),[106] as well as a formula for 'truthful' novels[107] consisting of disconnected and repetitive but lively scenes which reveal a society, and of adventitious stories told by the people the unheroic protagonist encounters.

If Carleton combined in himself the knowledge of different narrative repertoires and techniques, his life led to hesitation between priesthood and teaching and to shifting and confused allegiances; he was for some time a member of an agrarian secret society then condemned all such conspiracies and violence; he wrote for a while for a nationalist periodical but also courted the British government; he tried to 'show larnin' in his writings yet claimed, not without justification, the title of spokesman for the peasantry; and he repeatedly asserted that the culture he knew was that of a bygone era. The best part of his work explores memories of his childhood and youth, which he insisted he was exceptionally good at reconstructing: 'My memory, too, although generally good, was then in its greatest power; it was always a memory of association. For instance, in writing a description of Irish manners, or of anything else connected with my own past experience, if I were able to remember any one particular fact or place, everything connected with it or calculated to place it distinctly before me, rushed from a thousand sources upon my memory.'[108]

Carleton's contributions to George Petrie's *Irish Penny Journal* in 1840-41 may be his most 'documentary' work: he knew that the editor was a respected scholar. Nevertheless, the gallery of character studies he drew was filtered through creative memory, and the texts could straddle the frontier between fact and fiction. Amusement was striven for, but founded on sympathy rather than satire. The characters he portrays can be singled out for some special talent and function other than storytelling, but many of them can also narrate. Thus we meet a gossip or 'cosherer' (from the Irish *cóisir*: visiting a neighbour's house):

The cosherer in Ireland is a woman who goes from one relation's house to another, from friend to friend, from acquaintance to acquaintance – is always welcome, and uniformly well treated ... The whole business of her life is carrying about intelligence, making and

105 Ibid. 146-7. **106** Ibid. 110. **107** Cf. Lesage's introductory declaration: 'Je ne me suis proposé que de représenter la vie des hommes telle qu'elle est.' **108** *Autobiography* 128.

projecting matches, singing old songs and telling old stories, which she frequently does with a feeling and unction not often to be met with. She will sing you the different sets and variations of the old airs, repeat the history and traditions of old families, recite *ranns*, interpret dreams, give the origin of local customs, and tell a ghost story in a style that would make your hair stand on end.[109]

Another text concerns a fiddler who is never at a loss for words: 'All his anecdotes, songs, jokes, stories, and secrets, bring us back from the pressure and care of life to those happy days and nights when the heart was as light as the heel, and both beat to the exhilarating sound of his fiddle.'[110] In yet another, a midwife who had rescued an illegitimate child narrates this experience: 'Oh, many a thing happened me as well worth tellin', if you go to that; but I'll tell it to you, childre, for sure the curiosity's nathural to yez. Why, I was one night at home an' asleep, an' I hears a horse's foot gallopin' for the bare life up to the door ...'[111] The text focusing on a storyteller (who also has a variety of other talents) is reproduced here in full as it appeared in *The Irish Penny Journal* on 29 May 1841. It was reprinted in book form four years later with slight changes and a new title – 'Tom Gressiey, the Irish Senachie', in William Carleton's *Tales and Sketches Illustrating the Character, Usages, Sports and Pastimes of the Irish Peasantry*. 'Shanahus' is normally one of the possible renderings of the Irish word *seanchas* (important information or true stories), but in the first published version of this text it obviously refers to the *seanchaí* (a teller of such material).

THE IRISH SHANAHUS

The state of Irish society has changed so rapidly within the last thirty or forty years, that scarcely any one could believe it possible for the present generation to be looked upon in many things as the descendants of that which has immediately gone before them. The old armorial bearings of society which were empanelled upon the ancient manners of our country, now hang like tattered scutcheons over the tombs of customs and usages which sleep beneath them; and unless rescued from the obliterating hand of time, scarcely a vestige of them will be left even to tradition itself. That many gross absurdities have been superseded by a social condition more enlightened and healthy, is a fact which must gratify every one who wishes to see the general masses actuated by those principles which follow in the train of knowledge and civilization. But at the same time it is undeniable that the simplicity which accompanied those old vestiges of harmless ignorance has departed along with them; and in spite of education and science we miss the old familiar individuals who stood forth as the representatives of manners, whose very memory touches the heart and affections more strongly than the hard creations of sterner but more salutary truths. For our own part, we have always loved the rich and ruddy twilight of the rustic hearth, where the capricious tongues of blazing light shoot out from

109 *Irish Penny Journal* 'The Irish Match-Maker', 10 October 1840. **110** Ibid. 'Mickey M'Rorey, the Irish Fiddler', 15 August 1840. **111** Ibid. 'Rose Moan, the Irish Midwife', 26 December 1840.

between the kindling turf, and dance in vivid reflection in the well-scoured pewter and delft as they stand neatly arranged on the kitchen-dresser – loved, did we say? ay, and ever preferred it to philosophy, with all her lights and fashion, with all her heartlessness and hypocrisy. For this reason it is, that, whilst retracing as it were the steps of our early life, and bringing back to our memory the acquaintances of our youthful days, we feel our hearts touched with melancholy and sorrow, because we know that it is like taking our last farewell of old friends whom we shall never see again, from whom we never experienced any thing but kindness, and whose time-touched faces were never turned upon us but with pleasure, and amusement, and affection.

In this paper it is not with the Shanahus whose name and avocations are associated with high and historical dignity, that we have any thing to do. Our sketches do not go very far beyond the manners of our own times; by which we mean that we paint or record nothing that is not remembered and known by those who are now living. The Shanahus we speak of is the dim and diminished reflection of him who filled a distinct calling in a period that has long gone by. The regular Shanahus – the herald and historian of individual families, the faithful genealogist of his long-descended patron – has not been in existence for at least a century and a half, perhaps two. He with whom we have to do is the humble old man who, feeling himself gifted with a strong memory for genealogical history, old family anecdotes, and legendary lore in general, passes a happy life in going from family to family, comfortably dressed and much respected – dropping in of a Saturday night without any previous notice, bringing eager curiosity and delight to the youngsters of the house he visits, and filling the sedate ears of the old with tales and legends, in which, perhaps, individuals of their own name and blood have in former ages been known to take a remarkable and conspicuous part.

Indeed, there is no country in the world where, from the peculiar features of its social and political changes, the chronicles of the Shanahus would be more likely to produce such a powerful effect as in Ireland. When we consider that it was once a country of princes and chiefs, each of whom was followed and looked up to with such a spirit of feudal enthusiasm and devoted attachment as might naturally be expected from a people remarkable for the force of their affection and the power of imagination, it is not surprising that the man who, in a state of society which presented to the minds of so many nothing but the records of fallen greatness or the decay of powerful names, and the downfall of rude barbaric grandeur, together with the ruin of fanes and the prostration of religious institutions, each invested with some local or national interest – it is not surprising, we say, that such a man should be welcomed, and listened to, and honoured, with a feeling far surpassing that which was awakened by the idle jingle of a Provençal Troubadour, or the gorgeous dreams begotten by Arabian fiction. Neither the transition state of society, however, nor the scanty diffusion of knowledge among the Irish, allowed the Shanahus to produce any permanent impression upon the people; and the consequence was, that as the changes of society hurried on, he and his audience were carried along with them; his traditionary lore was lost in the ignorance which ever arises when a ban has been placed upon education; and from the recital of the high deeds and heroic feats of by-gone days, he sank down into the humble chronicler of hoary legends and dim traditions, for such only has he been within the memory of the oldest man living, and as such only do we intend to present him to our readers.

The most accomplished Shanahus of this kind that ever came within our observation, was a man called Tom Grassiey, or Tom the Shoemaker. He was a very stout well-built man, about fifty years of age, with a round head somewhat bald, and an expansive forehead that argued a considerable reach of natural intellect. His knowing-organs were large, and projected over a pair of deep-set lively eyes, that scintillated with strong twinklings of humour. His voice was loud, his enunciation rapid, but distinct; and such was the force and buoyancy of his spirits, added to the vehemence of his manner, that altogether it was impossible to resist him. His laughter was infectious, and so loud that it might be heard of a calm summer evening at an incredible distance. Indeed, Tom possessed many qualities that rendered him a most agreeable companion: he could sing a good song for instance, dance a hornpipe as well as any dancing-master, and we need not say that he could tell a good story. He could also imitate a Jew's harp or trump upon his lips with his mere fingers in such a manner that the deception was complete; and it was well known that flocks of the country people used to crowd about him for the purpose of hearing his performance upon the ivy leaf, which he played upon by putting it in his mouth, and uttering a most melodious whistle. Altogether, he was a man of great natural powers, and possessed such a memory as the writer of this never knew any human being to be gifted with. He not only remembered everything he saw or was concerned in, but everything he heard also. His language, when he spoke Irish, was fluent, clear, and sometimes eloquent, but when he had recourse to the English, although his fluency remained, it was the fluency of a man who made an indiscriminate use of a vocabulary which he did not understand. His pedantry on this account was highly ludicrous and amusing, and his wit and humour surprisingly original and pointed. He had never received any education, and was consequently completely illiterate, yet he could repeat every word of Gallagher's Irish Sermons, Donlevy's Catechism, Think Well On't, the Seven Champions of Christendom, and the substance of Pastorini's and Kolumb Kill's Prophecies, all by heart. Many a time I have seen him read, as he used to call it, one of Dr Gallagher's Sermons out of the skirt of his big-coat; a feat which was looked upon with twice the wonder it would have produced had he merely said that he repeated it. But to read it out of the skirt of his coat! Heavens, how we used to look on with awe and veneration, as Tom, in a loud rapid voice, 'rhymed it out of him,' for such was the term we gave to his recital of it! His learning, however, was not confined to mere English and Irish, for Tom was also classical in his way, and for want of a better substitute it was said could serve mass, which must always be done in Latin. Certain it was that he could repeat the Deprofundis, and the Seven Penitential Psalms, and the Dies Irae, in that language. We need scarcely add, that in these learned exhibitions he dealt largely in false quantities, and took a course for himself altogether independent of syntax and prosody; this, however, was no argument against his natural talents, or the surprising force of his memory.

Tom was also an easy and happy *Improviser* both in prose and poetry; his invention was indeed remarkably fertile, but his genius knew no medium between encomium and satire. He either lashed his friends, for the deuce an enemy he had, with rude and fearful attacks of the latter, or gave them, as Pope did to Berkley, every virtue under heaven, and indeed a good many more than ever were heard of beyond his own system of philosophy and morals.

Tom was a great person for attending wakes and funerals, where he was always a busy man, comforting the afflicted relatives with many learned quotations, repeating *ranns*, or spiritual songs, together with the Deprofundis or Dies Irae, over the corpse, directing even the domestic concerns, paying attention to strangers, looking after the pipes and tobacco, and in fact making himself not only generally useful, but essentially necessary to them, by his happiness of manner, the cordiality of his sympathy, and his unextinguishable humour.

At one time you might see him engaged in leading a Rosary for the repose of the soul of the departed, or singing the Hermit of Killarney, a religious song, to edify the company; and this duty being over, he would commence a series of comic tales and humorous anecdotes, which he narrated with an ease and spirit that the best of us all might envy. The Irish heart passes rapidly from the depths of pathos to the extremes of humour; and as a proof of this, we can assure our readers that we have seen the nearest and most afflicted relatives of the deceased carried away by uncontrollable laughter at the broad, grotesque, and ludicrous force of his narratives. It was here also that he shone in a character of which he was very proud, and for the possession of which he was looked up to with great respect by the people; we mean, that of a polemic, or, as it is termed, 'an arguer of Scripture,' for when a man in the country parts of Ireland wins local fame as a controversialist, he is seldom mentioned in any other way than as a great arguer of Scripture. To argue scripture well, therefore, means the power of subduing one's antagonist in a religious contest. Many challenges of this kind passed between Tom and his polemical opponents, in most or all of which he was successful. His memory was infallible, his wit prompt and dexterous, and his humour either broad or sarcastic, as he found it convenient to apply it. In these dialectic displays he spared neither logic nor learning: where an English quotation failed, he threw in one in Irish; and when that was understood, he posed them with a Latin one, closing his quotation by desiring them to give a translation of it; if this too were accomplished, he rattled out the five or six first verses of John in Greek, which some one had taught him; and as this was generally beyond their reading, it usually closed the discussion in his favour. Without doubt he possessed a mind of great natural versatility and power; and as these polemical exercitations were principally conducted in wake-houses, it is almost needless to say that the wake at which they expected him was uniformly a crowded one.

Tom was very punctual in attending fairs and markets, which he did for the purpose of bringing to the neighbouring farmers a correct account of the state of cattle and produce; for such was the honour in which his knowledge and talents were held, that it was expected he should know thoroughly every topic that might happen to be discussed. During the peninsular war he was a perfect oracle, but always maintained that Bonaparte never would prosper, in consequence of his having imprisoned the Pope. He said emphatically that he could not be shot unless by a consecrated bullet, and that the said bullet would be consecrated by an Irish friar. It was not Bonaparte, he insisted, who was destined to liberate Ireland: that could never be effected until the Mill of Louth should be turned three times with human blood, and that could not happen until a miller with two thumbs on each hand came to be owner of the mill. So it was prophesied by *Beal Deorg*, or the man with the red mouth, that Ireland would never be free until we first had the Black Militia in our own country, and that no rebellion ever was or could be of any use that did not commence in the Valley of the Black Pig, and move upwards from the tail to the the head. These were axioms which he laid down with great and grave authority; but on none of his authentic speculations into futurity did he rely with more implicit confidence than the prophecy he generously ascribed to St Bridget, that George the Fourth would never fill the throne of England.

Tom had a good flexible voice, and used to sing the old Irish songs of our country with singular pathos and effect. He sang Peggy Slevin, the Red-haired Man's Wife, and Shula Na Guira, with a feeling that early impressed itself upon my heart. Indeed we think that his sweet but artless voice still rings in our ears; and whilst we remember the tears which the enthusiasm of sorrow brought down his cheeks, and the quivering pause in the fine old melody which marked what he felt, we cannot help acknowledging that the memory of these things is mournful, and that the hearts of many, in spite of new systems of education and incarcerating poor-houses, will yearn after the homely but touching traits which marked the harmless Shanahus, and the times in which he lived. Many a tear has he beguiled us of in our youth when we knew not why we shed them. One of these sacred old airs, especially, we could never resist, 'the Trougha,' or 'the Green Woods of *Trough*'; and to this day we remember with a true and melancholy recollection that whenever Tom happened to be asked for it, we used to slink over to his side and whisper, 'Tom, don't sing *that*; it makes me sorrowful'; and Tom, who had great goodness of heart, had consideration for the feelings of the boy, and sang some other. But now all these innocent fireside enjoyments are gone, and we will never more have our hearts made glad by the sprightly mirth and rich good humour of the Shanahus, nor ever again pay the artless tribute of our tears to his old pathetic songs of sorrow, nor feel our hearts softened at the ideal miseries of tale or legend as they proceeded in mournful recitative from his lips. Alas! alas! knowledge may be power, but it is *not* happiness.

Such is, we fear, an imperfect outline of Tom's life. It was one of ease and comfort, without a care to disturb him, or a passion that was not calmed by the simple but virtuous integrity of his life. His wishes were few, and innocently and easily gratified. The great delight of his soul was not that he should experience kindness at the hands of others, but that he should communicate to them, in the simple vanity of his heart, that degree of amusement and instruction and knowledge which made them look upon him as a wonderful man, gifted with rare endowments; for in what light was not that man to be looked upon who could trace the old names up to times when they were great, who could climb a genealogical tree to the top branch, who could repeat the Seven Penitential Psalms in Latin, tell all the old Irish tales and legends of the country, and beat Paddy Crudden the methodist horse-jockey, who had the whole Bible by heart, at arguing Scripture? Harmless ambition! humble as it was, and limited in compass, to thee it was all in all; and yet thou wert happy in feeling that it was gratified. This little boon was all that thou didst ask of life, and it was kindly granted thee. The last night we ever had the pleasure of being amused by Tom was at a wake in the neighbourhood; for it somehow happened that there was seldom either a wake or a dance within two or three miles of us that we did not attend; and God forgive us, when old Poll Doolin was on her death-bed, the only care that troubled us was an apprehension that she might recover, and thus defraud us of a right merry wake! Upon the occasion we allude to, it being known that Tom Grassiey would be present, of course the house was crowded. And when he did come, heavens! how every young heart bounded with glee and delight!

The first thing he did on entering was to go where the corpse was laid out, and in a loud rapid voice repeat the Deprofundis for the repose of her soul, after which he sat down and smoked a pipe. Oh! well do I remember how the whole house was hushed, for all was expectation and interest as to what he would do or say. At length he spoke – 'Is Frank Magaveen there?'

'All that's left o' me's here, Tom.'

'An' if the sweep-chimly-general had his due, Frank, that wouldn't be much; and so the longer you can keep him out of that same, the betther for yourself.'

'Folly on Tom! you know there's none of us able to spake up to *you* , say what you will.'

'It's not so when you're beside a purty girl, Frank. But sure that's not surprisin'; you were born wid butther in your mouth, an' that's what makes your orations to the fair sect be so soft an' meltin', ha, ha, ha! Well, Frank, never mind; there's worse where you'll go to; keep your own counsel fast: let's salt your gums, an' you'll do yet. Whisht, boys; I'm goin' to sing a *rann,* and afther that Frank an' I will pick a couple o' dozen out o' yez "to box the Connaughtman".' Boxing the Connaughtman is a play or diversion peculiar to wakes; it is grotesquely athletic in its character, but full, besides, of comic sentiment and farcical humour.

He then commenced an Irish rann or song, the substance of which was as follows, according to his own translation: 'St Patrick, it seems, was one Sunday morning cross-ing a mountain on his way to a chapel to say mass, and as he was an humble man (coaches wern't then invented, at any rate) an' a great pedestrium (pedestrian), he took the shortest cut across the mountain. In one of the lonely glens he met a herd-caudy [Scots – cawdy: boy], who spent his time in eulogizin' his mashter's cattle, according to the precepts of them times, which was not by any means so larned an' primogenitive as now. The countenance of the dog was clear an' extremely sabbathical; everything was at rest barring the little river before him, an' indeed one would think that it flowed on with more decency an' betther behaviour than upon other sympathising occasions. The birds, to be sure, were singin', but it was aisy to see that they chirped out their best notes in honour of the day. "Good morrow on you", said St Patrick; "what's the raison you're not goin' to prayers, my fine little fellow?" "What's prayers?" axed the boy. St Patrick looked at him with a very pitiful and calamitous expression in his face. "Can you bless yourself?" says he. "No", said the boy, "I don't know what it means?" "Worse and worse", thought St Patrick.

"Poor bouchal [*buachaill*: boy], it isn' your fault. An' how do you pass your time here?"

"Why, my mate (food)'s brought to me, an' I do be makin' king's crowns out of my rushes, whin I'm not watching the cows an' sheep."

St Patrick sleeked down his head wid great dereliction, an' said, "Well, acushla [*a chuisle*: oh pulse (of my heart)], you do be operatin' king's crowns, but I tell you you're born to wear a greater one than a king's, an' that is the crown of glory. Come along wid me."

"I can't lave my cattle", said the other, "for fraid they might go astray."

"Right enough", replied St Patrick, "but I'll let you see that they won't." Now, any how St Patrick undherstood cattle irresistibly himself, havin' been a herd-caudy (boy) in his youth; so he clapped his thumb to his thrapple [Scots: the wind-pipe], an' gave the Soy-a-loa ['Loy-a-loa', in the text of 1845] to the sheep, an' behould you they came about him wid great relaxation an' respect. "Keep yourselves sober an' fictitious", says he, addressin' them, "till this boy comes back, an' don't go beyant your owner's property; or if you do, it'll be worse for yez. If you regard your health durin' the approximatin' season, mind an' attend to my words."

Now, you see, every sheep, while he was spakin', lifted the right fore leg, an' raised the head a little, an' behould when he finished, they kissed their foot, an' made him a low bow as a mark of their estimation an' superfluity. He thin clapped his finger an' thumb in his mouth, gave a loud whistle, an' in a periodical time he had all the other cattle on the hill about him, to which he addressed the same ondeniable oration, an' they bowed to him wid the same polite gentility. He then brought the lad along wid him, an' as they made progress in the journey, the little fellow says, "You seem frustrated by the walk, an' if you'll let me carry your bundle, I'll feel obliged to you."

"Do so", said the saint; "an' as it's rather long, throw the bag that the things are in over your shoulder; you'll find it the aisiest way to carry it."

Well, the boy adopted this insinivation, an' they went ambiguously along till they reached the chapel.

"Do you see that house?" said St Patrick.

"I do," said the other; "it has no chimley on it."

"No," said the saint; "it has not; but in that house, Christ, he that saved you, will be present to-day." An' the boy thin shed tears, when he thought of the goodness of Christ in saving one that was a stranger to him. So they entered the chapel, an' the first thing the lad was struck with was the beams of the sun that came in through the windy shinin' beside the altar. Now, he had never seen the like of it in a house before, an' thinkin' it was put there for some use or other in the intarior, he threw the wallet, which was like a saddle-bag, across the sunbeams, an' lo and behould you the sunbeams supported them, an' at the same time a loud sweet voice was heard, sayin', "This is my servant St Kieran, an' he's welcome to the house o' God!" St Patrick then tuck him an' instructed him in the various edifications of the larned languages until he became one of the greatest saints that ever Ireland saw, with the exception an' liquidation of St Patrick himself.'

Such is a faint outline of the style and manner peculiar to the narratives of Tom Grassiey. Indeed, it has frequently surprised not only us, but all who knew him to think how and where and when he got together such an incredible number of hard and difficult words. Be this as it may, one thing was perfectly clear, that they cost him little trouble and no study in their application. His pride was to speak as learnedly as possible, and of course he imagined that the most successful method of doing this was to use as many sesquipidalian expressions as he could crowd into his language, without any regard whatsoever as to their propriety. Immediately after the relation of this legend, he passed at once into a different spirit. He and Frank Magaveen marshalled their forces, and in a few minutes two or three dozen young fellows were hotly engaged in the humorous game of 'Boxing the Connaughtman'. Boxing the Connaughtman was followed by 'the Standing Brogue' and 'the Sitting Brogue', two other sports practised only at wakes. And here we may observe generally, that the amusements resorted to on such occasions are never to be found elsewhere, but are exclusively peculiar to the house of mourning, where they are benevolently introduced for the purpose of alleviating sorrow. Having gone through a few more such sports, Tom took a seat and addressed a neighbouring farmer, named Gordon, as follows: – 'Jack Gordon, do you know the history of your own name and its original fluency?'

'Indeed no, Tom, I cannot say I do.'

'Well, boys, if you derogate your noise a little, I'll tell you the origin of the name of Gordon; it's a story about ould Oliver Crummle, whose tongue is on the look-out for a drop of wather ever since he went to the lower story.' This legend, however, is too long and interesting to be related here: we are therefore forced to defer it until another opportunity.[112]

Tales and Sketches was dedicated to Charles Gavan Duffy, 'editor of the "Nation" Newspaper'– to which Carleton had contributed a few articles. The volume contains an illustration by Phiz, who at one time or another worked for Dickens, Ainsworth, Surtees and Charles Lever; it shows the 'senachie' looking at the skirt of his big-coat, surrounded by seventeen adults and children – and the pig which foreigners expected to see in an Irish cabin. In the preface dated 'Dublin, June 16, 1845', Carleton defines the book as 'delineations of several characters that are strictly national, and consequently not to be found in any other country, at least with the same traits of habit, thought, and feeling ... The author has reason to think that several of the originals who sat for their portraits here represented, were the last of their class which the country will ever again produce'. The whole is offered as 'a body of Irish Social Antiquities' – images of the past surviving mostly in the memory of the observer, but perhaps also in some out-of-the-way pockets of resistance to progress. In the text reproduced above, the author refers to 'our early life' and 'our youthful days': he had spent that period in County Tyrone, which he left in 1818. Different details confirm that the temporal setting is the beginning of the century: 'the peninsular war' (*c*.1810); 'coaches were not then invented' (Bianconi's coaching business started in 1815); 'new systems of education' (Irish education was reorganized in 1831); the 'poor-houses' (they appeared in Ireland in 1838). Gracey is a surname of Scottish origin found in Ulster, but whether the character existed as an individual is disputable: on the one hand, in his preface Carleton says that 'in every instance the characters have been drawn from actual life'; on the other he states that in those portraits 'the individual always represents not a person but a class'. Indeed, it may well be a composite creation, with elements borrowed from different people, including Carleton's parents.

   The variety of talents he attributes to the character is perhaps a result of this process of composition, but may also be true to fact: storytelling, which was no longer a profession, accompanied other activities. On the other hand, the fact that the man does not seem to touch long wonder tales and heroic material is also in accord with a division of vocations generally observed in Ireland. The feats of memory and ability to improvise are attested in other documents. If the man was really illiterate, he had nevertheless furnished his mind with the contents of some of the most popular chapbooks of the time: the *Irish Sermons* of

112 In the *Tales and Sketches* edition, the paragraph from 'Tom was punctual ... ' to ' ... fill the throne of England' has been deleted, and so has part of the following paragraph, from 'Many a tear ... ' to ' ... and sang some other', along with the very last sentence.

James Gallagher, bishop of Raphoe, went through many editions after 1735, as did the catechism written by a prefect of the Irish College in Paris, Andrew Donlevy, and first published in English and Irish in 1724. *The Seven Champions of Christendom*, following the medieval designation of the national patron saints of England, Scotland, Wales, Ireland, France, Spain and Italy, was first published in chapbook form in 1596 and for centuries had a wide distribution in Britain, then in Ireland. Prophetic poems ascribed to ColumCille circulated orally, appeared in chapbooks, and in book form in 1856.[113] Those of 'Pastorini' (Charles Walmesley, an English Catholic bishop) were part of a book published in 1771 and were frequently reissued as chapbooks in Ireland from the last years of the eighteenth century; they foretold the triumph of Catholicism in 1825. Predictions concerning Baldearg ('the red-spotted'), a messianic O'Donnell champion, had been mentioned by Goldsmith one century earlier (see p. 66). The Black Pig's Dyke, a series of earthworks dated to the Iron Age scattered between Donegal Bay and Newry, was said to have been ploughed up by a magician transformed into a ravaging boar; it was prophesied that one day the beast would return, and the 'Valley' of the Black Pig, sometimes located more precisely in the townland of Leaktha (Co. Sligo), was held in dread 'because it is in it that the battle at the end of the world, or, if not the final battle, at least a great battle between North and South, will take place'.[114] (The prophecy will be sounded again later in this book.) Several of the songs mentioned in the text are identifiable: the tune and an English adaptation of the text of 'the Trougha' appeared in 1809 as '*An Seann Triucha*' ('The Old Truigha') in Edward Bunting's *Collection of the Ancient Music of Ireland* (1809);[115] 'The Red-haired Man's Wife' or '*Bean an Fhir Ruaidh*' is in *The Complete Petrie Collection*, and 'Shula na Guira' in P.W. Joyce's *Old Irish Folk Music and Songs*. I cannot identify 'Peggy Slevin' – unless it is '*Peggi ni leavan*' in Bunting's *Ancient Music of Ireland* (1840), and have seen no ballad on 'The Hermit of Killarney' but the story was well-known (see p. 144). The 'wake-games' mentioned by Carleton are described in S. Ó Súilleabháin's *Irish Wake Amusements*.

A text written by Carleton at the beginning of his career and retouched by Caesar Otway for his Evangelical periodicals was a version of the 'Legend of St Kieran', signed 'James Clinton' (Carleton's usual pseudonym at the time).[116] An introductory paragraph, probably by Otway himself, contrasted the 'rational and scriptural education' provided by his magazine with 'such absurd matters on human credulity as the annexed', i.e. the legend itself; but the 'Clinton' version

113 N. O'Kearney *The Prophecies of SS Columbkille, Maeltamlacht, Ultan, Seadhna, Coireall, Bearcan, &c.* **114** Fionnuala Williams 'The Schoolmaster and the Black Pig's Dyke – An Irish Legend Associated with Linear Earthworks', in R. Kvideland and L. Solberg (eds) *The Eighth International Society for Folk Narrative Research Congress, Bergen 1984* 1. 421. See also R.S. Rogers 'The Folklore of the Black Pig's Dyke', *Ulster Folklife* 3 (1957) 29-36. **115** Text and translation in S. Ó Tuama and T. Kinsella *An Duanaire* 280-3. **116** *The Dublin Family Magazine, or Literary and Religious Miscellany* 1 (1829) 17-29.

was not more provocative than the one attributed to Grassiey twelve years later, which does not read today as anti-Catholic propaganda. The wording of the two versions is quite different. The legend told by Grassiey – obviously not a 'rann or song' (see p. 218) is related to International Tale-Type AT 759B: 'when holy man is upbraided for not coming to Mass, he hangs his coat on a sunbeam'. The basic motif of the sunbeam sustaining a hanging object appeared for the first time in writing in the fifth-century Pseudo-Matthew Evangelium, and the legend was told in Spain, France, Germany, Switzerland, etc. In Ireland it was associated with St Brigit (Cogitosus' *Vita Brigithe c.*650).[117] More than 160 versions in the manuscripts of the Irish Folklore Commission are listed in S. Ó Súilleabháin and R.T. Christiansen's *Types of the Irish Folktale* ('A sunbeam supports the coat of a holy man when he goes to church. It fails to do so later, because he has sinned in some way').[118]

Carleton accentuates the malapropisms, which he knows readers expect, but he also expresses his nostalgia for something good that was already on the wane – a dream of funny euphoria, idealizing the community he has chosen to leave and no longer quite recognizes: 'the shape of Irish society has changed' and 'a social condition more enlightened' means loss of 'simplicity' and the growth of 'heartlessness and hypocrisy'; to observe it induces 'melancholy'. There used to be 'dignity' in the 'humble', 'harmless old man', who was 'looked upon as a wonderful man gifted with rare endowments'.

The sketch in the *Irish Penny Journal* ended with the promise of another example from the same man's repertoire. Carleton kept his word: the following issue of the journal included 'The Castle of Aughentain, or a Legend of the Brown Goat, a tale of Tom Grassiey, the Shanahus', the first paragraphs of which again show the storyteller in action, but in a less striking way.[119]

---

117 Robert Wildhaber 'Zum Weiterleben zweier Apokrypher Legenden', in L. Carlen and F. Steinegger (eds) *Festschrift Nikolaus Grass* 2. 219-37. 118 Op. cit. 154-5. A version which must have been used as a popular *exemplum* to explain the concept of sin was collected in Mayo at the beginning of the twentieth century (L. M'Manus 'Folk-Tales from Western Ireland', *Folk-Lore* 25 (1914) 333-4). 119 *Irish Penny Journal* 5 June 1841.

7

Nineteenth-century Irish novelists
and traditional storytelling

Sharply to differentiate between antiquaries, travellers, folklorists – and now fiction writers – might lead to absurdities. Reference to some short fiction in a chapter focusing on novelists is probably acceptable, and one may even cope with the indefiniteness of the perhaps semifictional 'sketch'; more awkward is the presence of Thackeray as a 'traveller' rather than as a 'novelist', or of Carleton's detailed portrait of a traditional storyteller in the 'collectors' section though it may include some fiction, while the texts of the same writer to be quoted in the present chapter owe much to observation; and to see Lover, who first appeared as a 'traveller', then as a 'collector' or 'imitator', now pop up as a 'novelist', may give rise to mirth. 'Real' and 'imagined' elements may coexist in the same text, and an author and his reader may not have the same perceptions of what is and is not fictive. We expect a difference in kind between novels and documentary evidence, but it may be only a difference in degree, and there are cases which defy systematization. Novels are 'made up'; to a certain extent they can be treated as repositories of sociological data, but when we explore such material for its testimonial value we must remember that data are likely to have been tampered with to achieve certain effects.

The backcloth of actual life against which the fictional story is played may include so-called local 'traditions'. From the beginning of the nineteenth century there were readers who appreciated the representation of the distinctive modes of life of a particular region, and some novels evoked the rural world for an urban public; they would focus on what differed from the intended reader's world and might carry him pleasantly away from his usual surroundings. In that kind of literature, local colour was brushed in by quaint dialect and scenes illustrating odd customs, which might include storytelling. Apart from responding to readers' demands, a writer could be personally interested in oral communication, if he was curious about a form of narrative art that differed from the one he practised; then he would observe patterns appropriate to orality, note the special tricks of the teller or the peculiarities of his material, perhaps envy his direct exchange with an audience. He might look down on what seemed to him to be naive, and parody its subjects and devices – or pay homage to what his own mode of narration was perhaps superseding. In general, novelists are also likely to be interested in personalized narrators as instruments for organizing and animating their own creations.

As a distinctive kind of narrative, purporting to show life as it was in some specific time and place and combining the illusion of reality with emotional excitement or moral instruction and generally a measure of romance, the novel was imported into Ireland in the eighteenth century. In the nineteenth, a number of novelists chose rural Ireland as their setting and concentrated on its social scene. In addressing the problems of the Irish world, they could not help being conditioned by their own social status, cultural and religious allegiances, perhaps political options; nor could they ignore the expectations and prejudices of their readers. At first, most of these writers belonged to the Anglo-Irish world; their position as at once insiders and outsiders conditioned their vision, and they were likely to have ambivalent attitudes about at least some of the aspects of Irish life they dealt with: it was for instance difficult for them to understand fully the reasons why, at irregular intervals, the lowly social strata became dangerously violent. The Catholic novelists who began to write a couple of decades later were in some respects closer to certain subjects, but shared a problem with the Anglo-Irish writers: their publishers and main audience might be English, that is to say, a priori ignorant of, and perhaps biased against, Irish things. It affected the choice of topics and the way of presenting them.

It was perhaps the success of some travel books and picturesque essays on Irish cultural oddities which prompted publishers to offer novels set in Ireland, and conventions of the first two genres could influence the third. The focalizing characters in novels were often foreigners discovering Ireland. The more serious among the writers dealing with Irish subjects for the British market wanted to bring their readers' attention to facts they had previously ignored, while correcting misconceptions and negative representations; but they had to avoid certain subjects, or to treat them in acceptable ways. To pursue easy success, they could be tempted to use low comedy routines, but the label 'national tale', which seems to have appeared in the second decade of the century, pointed to more ambitious functions beyond the development of a melodramatic or amusing plot: to reveal the cultural specificity of Ireland and illustrate its religious and social polarities, perhaps to assert its rights.[1] One was often aware that the community to be portrayed was in a period of transition or crisis, and that part of what was being evoked was probably doomed.

A treatment of curious customs and beliefs, behind the main action, had the combined advantages of focusing on innocuous aspects of Irish reality, intensifying the sense of authenticity, and satisfying the taste for strangeness. One aspect of rural life worth rendering, because it might favourably impress or entertain readers and was considered a marker of nationality, was the weight of a traditional heritage, including native oral arts. It might be illustrated in a few pages or paragraphs of the novel only, and the traditional storyteller was most

1 Benedict Anderson *Imagined Communities: Reflections on the Origin and Spread of Nationalism* 25: the novel 'provided the technical means for "representing" the kind of imagined community that is the nation'.

often an incidental character conforming to a type – the main difference, after all, between the fiction treated here and the sketches previously referred to may be that in the latter form 'folklore' was not a sideshow but took the central stage. Some novelists had a more intimate knowledge of traditional storytelling than others, but even the Anglo-Irish could have heard, in their childhood for instance, folktales from members of the lower classes; some had a greater faculty of observation, or greater skill in stressing concrete details. They could have real models and try to portray them accurately. On occasions the telling of a tale, the personality of the storyteller and the participation of the audience created an important event in the book. The authors had of course different ways of writing, but the common techniques of the average novel at the time account for certain forms and devices; for instance, the generally loose episodic construction of most early novels lent itself to the old convention of dragging in extra tales supposedly told by characters to each other.

The present chapter will analyse representations of traditional Irish storytellers and scenes of storytelling abstracted from works generally offered as fiction. The relative literary merit of the works is not the essential point, and when I consider an aspect of the novel it does not imply I necessarily see it as the most important theme in the book.

A. THE FIRST HALF OF THE NINETEENTH CENTURY

Maria Edgeworth (1767-1849) saw Ireland for the first time when she was six, and from the age of fifteen spent the greater part of her life in County Longford. As a writer, she thought she was lacking in inventiveness, and compensated it by careful observation. Among the objects of her attention were her father's servants and tenants; she was socially and culturally distant from them, yet she shared her father's benevolent concern for the lower orders.[2] With him she studied their ways of using the English language, and the result was an *Essay on Irish Bulls* published in 1802, the main argument of which was that the common description of the Irish as clumsy and illogical in their speech was unjustified: logical blunders (bulls) were met with everywhere, but in Ireland they might be explained by the rapidity of thought of the natives and by a frequent use of rhetorical devices; actually, the Irish could sometimes be better speakers of English than the English themselves, and the book quotes anecdotes or pieces of dialogue to substantiate it – while also criticizing 'sentimental admirers of the Irish past' who only collected such oddities instead of doing something to improve the country.

Castle Rackrent: an Hibernian Tale – the first part may have been written in 1794-5, the second in 1796-8, and the book was published with additional mate-

2 Maria's father was an 'improving landlord' of the type praised by Arthur Young (see p. 128).

rials in 1800 – is generally considered the first major Irish novel (or novella), the first piece of 'regional' fiction in English, and the first 'big house' novel (showing the decline of the gentry). The general subtitle continues: ... *taken from Facts, and from the Manners of the Irish Squires before the Year 1782* – that is to say, before the temporary revival of the Irish Protestant parliament and before the arrival of the Edgeworths, thus implying that things were changing because 'the race of the Rackrents has long since been extinct in Ireland'.[3] As for ordinary peasants – 'a set of poor wretches'[4] – they seemed unable to progress honestly by their own means; the subject was the story of a landlord family, the predicament of the tenants being only implicit, and no profound social reform was advocated: an enlightened attitude of the ruling class would suffice. Yet the work may now also be read as prophetical of the revolution by which estates would later pass from the landlords to a new Irish class, represented in the novel by the narrator's son.

The book is filled with details about the mismanagement of an estate by members of the supposedly extinct species of irresponsible landlords. The ways of the common people are explained in footnotes and in a special glossary (prepared with the help of the author's father) to make things 'intelligible to the English reader'; a satirical intention has been seen here,[5] but there was a serious didactic purpose too: as 'Ireland [was losing] her identity by an union with Great Britain' (this statement is in the preface dated 1800, just before the centralization of government became effective)[6] the English had new responsibilities and should understand the Irish in order to help them. The book, therefore, was offered as 'a specimen of manners and characters, which are, perhaps, unknown in England. Indeed, the domestic habits of no nation in Europe were less known to the English than those of their sister country, till within these few years'.[7] Information was selective, however, because there were things potential readers would not like to hear: no reference was made to religious differences or to recent rebellions. On the other hand there is a good deal of factual information on traditional habits and attitudes; funeral customs are described, with the wake as an occasion for 'gossiping', and belief legends are commented upon: 'There are innumerable stories told of the friendly and unfriendly feats of these busy fairies; some of these tales are ludicrous, and some romantic enough for poetry.'[8] A special form of deception, the telling of long 'stories' to confuse a justice of the peace, is illustrated with an example offered as authentic: 'Their method is

---

3 *Castle Rackrent* 63. 4 Ibid. 69. 5 Gary Kelly, in *English Fiction of the Romantic Period* 78, sees 'mock-antiquarianism' in many of the notes, 'as if to suggest that antiquarians' loving, laborious, and bookish recording of particularities of folklore and folksay is beside the point in a world that needs reason, order, and "improvement", and not superstition, prejudice, and unexamined tradition, if modernization is to take place.' Marilyn Butler (*Maria Edgeworth: A Literary Biography* 364) also notes that, to the Edgeworths, 'Irish traditions meant ... the survival of irrational and inefficient habits: they thought that extensive education among all classes was the best remedy for tradition.' 6 *Castle Rackrent* 63. 7 Ibid. 121. 8 Ibid. 130.

to get a story completely by heart, and to tell it, as they call it, *out of the face*, that is, from the beginning to the end, without interruption.'[9] The abundance of such information is connected with the most remarkable decision made by the author: her choice as narrator of a native with typical verbal gifts, along with a play on the double meaning of the phrase 'to tell stories' (to report on what has happened – or to lie). We have the testimony of an 'illiterate old steward' who gives – in his own vernacular and 'out of the face'[10] – an account of the decadence of the family he has served for several generations. This choice is said by the supposed 'editor' to make the testimony more reliable, because such an unsophisticated and reluctant narrator would not try to mislead us. The context casts doubt on this statement: Thady would 'simply pour forth anecdotes and retail conversations, with all the minute prolixity of a gossip in a country town ... The authenticity of his story would have been more exposed to doubt if it were not told in his own characteristic manner. Several years ago he related to the editor the history of the Rackrent family, and it was with some difficulty that he was persuaded to have it committed to writing';[11] but some documents in the glossary seem to warn us that what is offered as 'a plain unvarnished tale'[12] may include fabrication, and that what Thady himself calls 'the whole truth of the story'[13] may be neither complete nor always truthful. His unpleasant son's statement that he is 'no fit witness, being so old and doting'[14] is yet another deliberately confusing indication.

Authors had claimed to be mere editors of documents long before Maria Edgeworth, and the pretence of having recorded a real, though perhaps not reliable person's spoken discourse was not new; there had already been narrators who belonged to the world of the story without being protagonists, yet without being objective witnesses either. The use of such a 'teller' was, however, preferably reserved for shorter stories inserted within a main narrative; the more original idea was to extend the technique to the whole text, and to give it a dialectal flavour. Maria Edgeworth said that her Thady Quirk was based on a real-life person, and admitted that parodic impersonation had something to do with her work, at least at an early stage:

The only character drawn from the life in *Castle Rackrent* is Thady himself, the teller of the story. He was an old steward (not very old, though at the time I added to his age to allow him time for the generations of the family). I heard him when I first came to Ireland, and his dialect struck me, and his character; and I became so acquainted with it, that I could think and speak in it without effort; so that, for mere amusement, without any idea of publishing, I began to write a family history as Thady would tell it, he seemed to stand beside me and dictate, and I wrote as fast as my pen could go, the characters all imagined ... [15]

9 Ibid. 133. 10 Ibid. 115: 'I told him the story out of the face, just as Judy had told it to me.' We learn eighteen pages later that it can be a way of evading truth. 11 Ibid. 62, 63. 12 Ibid. 62. 13 Ibid. 115. 14 Ibid. 110. 15 Letter to Mrs Stark, 6 Sept. 1834, in *A Memoir of Maria Edgeworth* ... (1867) 3. 152.

One of the rare physical details in the portrait of the storyteller is the 'long great coat' he wears winter and summer, the *cóta mór* which associates him with past traditions (see p.184, but it was already mentioned by Spenser). His fulfilling the duties of a *seanchaí* in the cultivation of a family legend is evoked, and may account for his unfailing, though not necessarily sincere, praises of the masters: as a child – and it is not indifferent to know that he was to go to the bad – Condy Rackrent 'would slip down to me in the kitchen, and love to sit on my knee, whilst I told him stories of the family, and the blood from which he was sprung.'[16]

Oral expression focusing on extraordinary scenes is better represented in the first part of the book, while a tone of controlled dictation is more perceptible in the longer second part which was later added to the original text; but in both sections we find early illustrations of a device favoured by many an Irish storyteller, re-identifying the speakers after every speech (in Irish, with the repetitive *a deir sé*: says he; *a deir sí*: says she) to remind us that a certain passage in the monovocal discourse represents dialogue:

'And what's all that black swamp out yonder, Sir Kit?' says she. 'My bog, my dear,' says he, and went on whistling. 'It's a very ugly prospect, my dear,' says she. 'You don't see it, my dear', says he, 'for we've planted it out, when the trees grow up, in summer time,' says he. 'Where are the trees,' said she 'my dear?' still looking through her glass. 'You are blind, my dear', says he; 'what are these under your eyes?' 'These shrubs?' said she. 'Trees,' said he.[17]

'She' is the wife Sir Kit brought from England, a Jewess he intends to strip of her fortune; being, like the author herself, as foreign as possible to the male Irish world of the novel, perhaps she sees the landscape as it really is – but Thady thinks she is a simpleton. We may remember this detail when reading the insistence on truth at the very end of his narrative: 'As for all I have here set down from memory and hearsay of the family, there's nothing but truth in it from beginning to end: that you may depend upon; for where's the use of telling lies about the things which every body knows as well as I do?'[18] While the fictional *male* editor affects to trust 'the plain round tale of faithful Thady', the *lady* author may caution us with the examples of Irish pleading that appear a few pages later in the 'Glossary': 'Please your honour, under favour, and saving your honour's presence, there's not a word of truth in all this man has been saying from beginning to end, upon my conscience, and I wouldn't, for the value of the horse itself, grazing and all, be after telling your honour a lie ... I'll tell you the whole truth about the horse that he swopped against my mare out of the face.'[19] (And another misstatement follows ...)

The reader is left to wonder how much irony is the author's and how much

---

16 *Castle Rackrent* 85. **17** Ibid. 77. The same technique is used on pp. 87-8 and 91-3. **18** Ibid. 121. **19** Ibid. 134.

Thady's – whether Thady is reliable though naive, or shrewd, or a blend of these traits, or not a consistent character. Perhaps the only thing that matters is that he has told a story worth the listening – a tale which is far from being 'plain' and 'unvarnished'; the editor repeats these adjectives at the beginning and at the end, but the reader is warned in the Preface that 'the truth of honest Thady's narrative' must be of a peculiar kind since his Memories will probably appear 'perfectly incredible'; he is also told at the end that Irish life mixes 'quickness, simplicity, cunning, carelessness, dissipation, disinterestedness, shrewdness and blunder'. Our first portrait extracted from a novel is thus one of the most complex: forms of storytelling may be elements of local colour, but here they seem above all to point to the theme of the impossibility of reaching absolute truth.

Rising to fame a few years after Maria Edgeworth, but with less subtlety, innovative technique and durable impact, Sidney Owenson (?1776-1859), who became known as Lady Morgan, had a different pedigree and was more self-consciously Irish. If Maria Edgeworth may be a late representative of the Enlightenment, Sidney Owenson was a romantic, and a professed patriot (of the sentimental brand) who repeatedly used the phrase 'national tale' as a subtitle to her books. The aim was not to promote order and efficiency but rather to restore the rights of an idealized native aristocracy, and in this programme storytelling would either represent the glory of the past in 'Ossianic' terms or be described as feeding hatred when justice was denied. Her usual mode of expression was melodrama and effusiveness, set in stormy landscapes and ruined castles. She may seem to have been a less reliable witness, but on the other hand she had acccess to some aspects of Irish life which her rival – no doubt a better writer – was less familiar with. Though she was educated in Dublin, Sidney Owenson had contacts with Gaelic Ireland: her father, an Irish-speaker born Robert MacOwen and the son of a Catholic peasant, made the conquest of a woman from the Protestant gentry, then became an actor and theatre-manager, sang Irish songs to his daughter's harp accompaniment, and told what she called 'shanaos' (*seanchas* – defined in a footnote as 'a kind of genealogical chit-chat, or talking over family antiquity, family anecdotes, descent, alliance, &c, &c, to which the lower as well as the higher order of Irish in the provincial parts are much addicted'):[20] 'In the course of my early life, and after years, it was a source of infinite delight to hear him narrate in broken episodes traits and incidents of his own story and of the times in which he lived, mingled with relations of habits, customs and manners still existing in Ireland down to the close of the last century.'[21] She toured the provinces of Ireland with her father, sometimes stayed in the houses of genteel cousins in the West, and became a governess. Far from being a scholar, she was in touch with some Anglo-Irish antiquaries who

20 *The Wild Irish Girl* 53. 21 *Lady Morgan's Memoirs* 1. 40.

informed – and misinformed – her; in her early years she fantasized about an Irish past coloured by Macphersonian inventions. In February 1806, during one of her stays in County Sligo, J.C. Walker, who still depended on correspondents for his research in literary antiquities (see pp. 91), told her what to look for: 'You are now in a part of the island where many of the Finian tales are familiarly known. You will, of course, collect some of them, and perhaps, interweave them with the work [*The Wild Irish Girl*] on which you are at present employed.'[22] One year later he insisted: 'As you visited a part of the country where society is, in some degree, in a primitive state, you will, of course, be minute with regard to customs and manners. You should also give all the traditions that prevail, particularly those relating to the heroes and heroines of the metrical tales of the Irish, some of whom, it is said, may be traced to medieval tales. It is not improbable but you may have heard stories similar to some of those which you have read in the *Arabian Nights Entertainments*.'[23] Consequently, when writing an account of her sojourn as a poor relation at Longford House near Beltra, she obliged by describing a meeting with a 'bardlike' young peasant in the Ox Mountains:

'This,' said Mr [Compton – her cousin], who accompanied us, 'is an *à propos* rencontre; for this is the young fellow I mentioned to you, who has obtained so much celebrity among his rustic friends for singing the songs of Ossian'; and in fact, after a few words of conversation with him, we discovered he was on his way to attend a wake [walking] seven miles for that purpose. Mr [Compton] asked him if he would come and sing the songs of Ossian for us at L [ongford] House; he replied, with a bow and a blush, that 'he did not think he could, not being used to sing before such a company;' adding that 'he was sure he could not make himself understood in English, as the songs were in such fine old *cramp* Irish, that few (save the old people) could understand them; and that though he *felt* all he sang, he could not himself well explain it, so as to *hit his fancy*.' In a word he gave us to understand, that the songs had descended orally in the pure ancient Irish ... At my particular instance, the young story-teller (for so he was named) repeated some stanzas from Ossian in a species of recitative, not unmusical: it was an account of Fingal's combat with the Danish monarch; and while he recited the combat with some degree of epic fire, he pointed to a mountain sacred to some of the feats of his heroes, and thus gave a superadded interest to his 'song of other times'.[24]

The book in which this appeared was not offered as fiction; but did she actually have the experience? With this writer, the problem is that it is not always easy to decide. The references to Ossian and the final quotation from Macpherson might arouse suspicion: could Sidney Owenson have invented the whole

---

22 Ibid. 1. 261 (a letter dated 4 Feb. 1806). **23** Ibid. 1. 314 (18 Feb. 1807). **24** *Patriotic Sketches of Ireland, written in Connaught* 2. 37-39. In *The Wild Irish Girl* (199-203), a 'venerable bard' – also called in Macphersonian terms a 'bard of other times' – is modelled on the real Dennis Hampton or Hempson of Magilligan who participated in the Belfast Harp Festival of 1792 (see pp. 93-4) and to whom a long footnote is devoted.

episode? On the other hand it is true that *Bruidhean Chaorthainn* ('The Hostel of the Rowan Tree'), a tale first written down in the sixteenth century which deals with the fight of the Fianna against the King of Norway's son and the King of the World, was in oral tradition in the early nineteenth century.

Owenson's first book, *St Clair, or The Heiress of Desmond* published in 1803, had already offered, in an avowedly fictional context, an account of the still fashionable craze for Ossianic literature. The protagonist of this epistolary narrative, writing from the Castle of L— (the link with the preceding quotation is obvious), repeatedly broaches the subject with her hosts:

In this part of Connaught you find the character, the manner, the language, and the music of the ancient Irish in all their primitive originality; and the names Ossian and Fingal are as well known among these old Milesians as in the Hebrides ... I expect to find many of those literary traditions which throw a light upon the history and character of every country which has preserved them from the wreck of time or the devastation of warfare ... [The local schoolmaster is not helpful:] I interrupted him to enquire into the possibility of procuring an old Irish poem I had heard my father repeat. He shook his head contemptuously, and replied that he never troubled himself with such barbarous productions ... [But the author or her persona is more successful in conversations with the owner of the castle – 'the only gentleman in these parts, who cultivates Irish literature, or appears anxious to rescue from total oblivion the poetry and music of his country':] We both displayed as much warmth in fixing the native place of Ossian as the commentators of Homer the spot which had the honour of giving him birth. Every mountain in the province was enriched by a feat of Fingal; not an old woman in the country, but could recite a poem of his inspired son; and he pointed to a promontory which distance almost reduced to a shadow, the extreme point of which is still called the Seat of Fingal (of whom the lower order report many improbable tales) ... The old gentleman (who is not wholly free from a superstition, which the liveliness of his imagination, even at threescore, is well adapted to nourish) repeats the various tales of [the castle] being still the haunt of 'witches and ghosts who rove at midnight hour', or digresses into the history of its former lords; generally concluding with an emphatic shake of the head, and a melancholy apostrophe from Ossian: 'Why doest thou build the hall, son of the winged days?'[25]

The book that made her famous, *The Wild Irish Girl* (1806), contains more documentary digressions and footnotes on Irish life and antiquities than action, but encounters with storytellers are part of the male protagonist-narrator's formative experience. The estranged son of an absentee landlord, he visits members of the Irish nobility who have been dispossessed by his own ancestors, and discovers the true nature of the natives during a forced stay in Connaught. He is in a world of ruins: old towers and abbeys, but also fragments of an ancient literature – all of it 'magnificent in decay'.[26] Remains of the Irish world are gradually revealed to him. First, he meets an old man who is 'a living chronicle'

25 *St Clair, or The Heiress of Desmond* 12, 16-17, 50, 89. 26 *The Wild Irish Girl* 35.

' "Och! it is a long story, but I have heard my grandfather tell it a thousand times ... " It would be vain, it would be impossible, to describe the emotion which the simple tale of this old man awakened.'[27] Then a nurse functions as tradition-bearer.[28] The host, a descendant of the ancient Irish rulers, values his cultural heritage:

[His] memory is rich in oral tradition, and most happily faithful to the history and antiq- uities of his country ... [He says:] 'Many a morning's sun has seen me climb that moun- tain in my boyish days, to contemplate these ruins, accompanied by an old follower of the family, who possessed many strange stories of the feats of my ancestors, with which I was greatly delighted.'[29]

The author was aware of the theory according to which poetry which first existed in manuscripts for the aristocracy could then survive orally. Her 'wild Irish girl' (an aristocrat) says. 'This was once the business of our Bards, Fileas, and Seanachies; but we are now obliged to have recourse to our own memories, in order to support our own dignity.'[30] The local Catholic priest upholds, against Macpherson, the thesis of the Irish origin of the so-called Ossianic tales.[31]

We may suppose that in these scenes imagination combines with second- hand information; yet the repetition of similar accounts may also point to some genuine observation which the author wanted to share. 'The great secret of the success of *The Wild Irish Girl*', she later wrote, 'was that it conveyed in a vivid and romantic story curious information about the social condition, the manners, customs, literature and antiquities of Ireland. There was in it a passionate plead- ing against the wrongs and injustice to which the people and the country were subjected.'[32]

Irish traditional storytelling plays some role in two of her later novels. In *Florence Macarthy: An Irish Tale* (1818), there is a critical view of post-Union Ireland – of the misery of Irish peasants deprived of their natural aristocratic leaders, and of the supposed destruction of native lore.[33] But in this novel tradi- tional storytelling is also shown to have dangerous aspects; a Kerryman who pre- serves the link with the past is portrayed as the embodiment of the power of oral history to foster hatred, and is

an epitome of that order once so numerous, and still far from extinct in Ireland, the hedge schoolmaster. O'Leary was learned in the antiquities and genealogies of the great Irish families, as an ancient Senachy, an order of which he believed himself to be the sole representative, credulous of [its] fables and jealous of [its] ancient glory; ardent in his feelings, fixed in his prejudices; hating the Bodei Sassoni [*bodaigh Sasanaigh*] or English churls, in proportion as he distrusted them; living only in the past, contemptuous of the present, and hopeless of the future; all his national learning, and national vanity, were employed on his history of the Macarthies More, to whom he deemed himself hereditary senachy.[34]

27 Ibid. 27, 32. 28 Ibid. 53, 102, 107. 29 Ibid. 54, 55. 30 Ibid. 111. 31 Ibid. 98. 32 *Lady Morgan's Memoirs* 1. 127. 33 *Florence Macarthy* 3. 117. 34 Ibid. 1. 283-5.

In her last and most complicated novel, *The O'Briens and the O'Flaherties: a National Tale* (1827), partly set in Connemara in the late eighteenth century, traditional storytelling is evoked through memories, and its emotional effects are carried to extremes. The hero's foster-brother, Shane, has assimilated traditions in the Aran Islands – which had begun to be described as a stronghold of Irish culture (see pp. 95; as far as we know, the author was not drawing here on her own observation):

[Shane's] powerful memory, and more powerful imagination (the one stored by his foster-mother, a celebrated *Scealuidhe*, or story-teller of Arran, and the other fed by the fantastic superstition of the Arranites) are proofs of his true Irish organization, which bad laws and institutions may have degraded, but have not destroyed ... From his cradle the auditor of his Irish foster-mother, the famous weird woman of the Isles of Arran, Mor ny Brien, his memory and imagination nourished these early associations; and recollections of family glory were the more fondly cherished, in proportion to the growing misfortunes and mortifications of his present struggling position.[35]

The story-telling foster-mother is evoked as a powerful woman, with an avalanche of Irish erudition which, this time, owes nothing to Macpherson:

'Mor ny Brien was greatly gifted; her memory was miraculous, and her voice most melodious.' '*Thah!*' [*tá*: indeed, yes] (exclaimed Shane, his stern features relaxing from their temporary compression) '*clarsagh na vallagh*, she was called far and near – ay, troth –' 'Which means the *harp of the village*, if I remember right?' '*Musha* [*A Mhuire*: Mary!] *thah!*' said Shane, much pleased; 'and [one] hears her voice in the mountains to this day, when the wind is asleep, keening th' ould moan!' The tears suddenly started to his eyes, and rolled down his haggard cheeks in big drops. 'With what delight,' said O'Brien, 'I used to listen to her stories of the tribe of Dalgais, and the feats of the heroes of our family – of Cas, son of Conal of the swift horses, and of Fionne Mac Cumhal –' '*Agus Ossin*', said Shane, suddenly brightening up, and shaking back his coolun [*cúilín*: forelock], and wiping his eyes in his hair. 'Yes,' said O'Brien, 'I remember the effect of her Irish cronan, that began "Corloch, haughty, bold and brave", and Cucullin's challenge to him. You remember that, Shane?' '*Thah!*' said Shane, swinging backwards and forwards his gigantic frame, and cheering gradually up. '*Agus an Moira Borb* [a mythic Munster woman, possibly a manifestation of a sun goddess]'. 'Yes,' said O'Brien, rather in soliloquy than in dialogue, and wholly borne away by the subject, which now called up, not only past, but present associations; – 'that tale of Moira Borb, the Irish enchantress ...' 'And there was a spirited controversial dialogue, too, between St Patrick and Ossian,' continued O'Brien, 'which she used to sing to a wild strain'. '*Ossin agus St Phaedrig*', repeated Shane, making the sign of the cross ... I suppose you have not one story-teller, one *sceadluidhe*, left in Arran?' '*Virgo Maria!* Ay, plinty,' replied Shane. '*Agus* ould Fergus, the *clashmanaigh*' [*cleasamhnacht*: a playful person, trickster, acrobat]. 'Indeed! those Arranites never die ...'[36]

---

35 *The O'Briens and the O'Flaherties* 1. 32; 2. 212-13. **36** Ibid. 2. 311-16.

There is less control in Sidney Owenson's books than in Maria Edgeworth's, much of the information was second-hand, and part may have been faked for sensational effects; but she was the first to adapt to the Irish novel what was left of the Ossianic craze, the new enthusiasm for Irish antiquities or oral traditions, the romantic taste for sublimity, and patriotic sentiments. Her heroes and heroines are members of the nobility, but they meet colourful 'common' people; and the storytellers among them are meant to be impressive, indeed, sometimes awe-inspiring, figures.

Not everybody in Dublin, however, was prepared to celebrate them. In 1808, Charles Robert Maturin (1780-1824), who was hoping – in vain – to share in the success of *The Wild Irish Girl*, published *The Wild Irish Boy* at his own expense. As in the model, in this novel which (according to the preface) 'purports to give some account of a country little known' there are footnotes explaining rural customs or dialect, and again an outsider must discover Ireland's landscapes and traces of Ossian; but very little is made of it. The emblematic scene with a beautiful 'wild' young woman playing a harp in romantic surroundings, launched by Sidney Owenson and soon to be reset in Scott's *Waverley*, is reduced by Maturin to a fancy dress ball. He made a more substantial attempt in 1812, with *The Milesian Chief*, stating in the preface: 'I have chosen my own country for scene, because I believe it the only country on earth, where, for the strange existing opposition of religion, politics, and manners, the extremes of refinement and barbarism are united, and the most wild and incredible situations of romantic story are hourly passing before modern eyes.'[37] He hated Catholicism, and for him 'Irish traditions' were on the side of barbarism, in a country where the very ruins and tombs relayed harmful voices from the past; one of his characters says: 'Here is a local genius: a spirit of eloquence and mortality seems to have taken up his residence between the living and the dead, and to interpret to one the language of the other. I feel who lies below: Every step I take awakes the memory of him on whose tomb I tread, and every hour seems weary till I lie down with them and am forgotten.' Morbid temptation is also exerted by the living voices of Irish storytellers: one of the protagonists is branded with fatal Irish patriotism because his grandfather had 'shut himself up in the old tower of his ancient demesne, and listened to the tales of his bards and the songs of his harpers',[38] thereby preparing his grandson to lead a vain uprising.

Maturin seems to have spent only a year far from Dublin (as a Protestant curate at Loughrea), and was less acquainted than Sidney Owenson with native Irish culture – or just had no respect for it. In his one great novel, *Melmoth the Wanderer* (1820) which begins and ends in Ireland and is a network of interlocking tales by many narrators, Irish potential storytellers play only an ancillary role and are rapidly silenced; in the prologue, an old servant tells part of the

37 *The Milesian Chief* 1. iv-v. 38 Ibid. 3. 49.

Melmoth family's history, but the main frame narrator does not care to quote her exact words: 'We spare the reader her endless circumlocutions, her Irishisms, and the frequent interruptions arising from her applications to her snuff-box, and to the glass of whiskey punch with which Melmoth took care to have her supplied.'[39] Another possible Thady-like contribution is completely erased a few chapters later: 'She began her narrative, the effect of which was to lull Melmoth into a profound repose before half of it was concluded; he felt the full benefit of the invalids mentioned by Spenser, who used to hire Irish story-tellers, and found those indefatigable persons still pursuing the tale when they awoke.'[40] We may conclude that this author did not have a high opinion of Irish traditional storytelling, whatever experience he may have had of it, and did not consider it useful material for his pursuit of Gothic sensation – though in *Melmoth* actual Irish violence in a recent rebellion does contribute to the gallery of horrors.[41]

An unexpected presence in a company of novelists is Thomas Moore (1779-1852), who made his reputation with song texts (sprinkled with 'minstrels' and 'bards') set to the traditional tunes. In one book fitting into the category of the novel in the loose sense of long prose fiction, and in the reply of an opponent, we see again how certain kinds of Irish storytelling could be connected with interpretations of the past and with contemporary violence. Having made a tour of south-west Ireland and observed misery and unrest due to falling agricultural prices and the fact that Catholics had to pay tithes for the Protestant church, the generally more circumspect writer published in 1824 – but anonymously – *Memoirs of Captain Rock, the Celebrated Irish Chieftain, with some Account of his Ancestors*, which more or less directly justified the reactions of the oppressed. The fictional 'editor', an Englishman who has been sent to Ireland as a Protestant missionary, receives a manuscript from a 'disguised gentleman in green spectacles' – the rebellious Captain Rock himself: it was one of the names used by peasant secret societies in Munster and South Leinster to sign their threatening messages, often promising the imminent doom of the Protestant ascendancy according to the prophecies of Pastorini (cf. p. 221). The *seanchaí* who keeps the rebel fire burning is Captain Rock's father, and his portrait is drawn, with comments on the supposed national character, by the more enlightened but still rebellious son who knows that there are different ways of wearing green spectacles, one of them being short-sighted partisanship encouraged by narrative traditions (cf. above, quotations from Owenson's *Florence McCarthy* and Maturin's *Milesian Chief*):

The pride which [my father] took in his ancestry, was the more grand and lofty, from being founded altogether on fancy – a well-authenticated pedigree, however noble, would

---

39 *Melmoth the Wanderer* 59. **40** Ibid. 115. (The source is William Temple of Campion, not Spenser.) **41** Ibid. 345: an episode of the Emmet rebellion of 1803.

have destroyed the illusion. He had a vague idea – in which the school-master used to help him out – of those happy days when Ireland was styled the Island of Saints, and when such of our ancestors as were *not* saints were, at least, kings and princes. Often would he hold forth, amidst the smoke of his wretched cabin, on the magnificence of the hall of Tara, and the wisdom of the great Ollam Fodhlah [*Ollamh Fódlach*: master-poet of Ireland] – much to the amusement, as I have heard, of the second Mrs Rock, who, proud of her own suspected descent from a Cromwellian drummer, used to laugh irreverently both at my father and at old Ollam Fodhlah. I was indeed indebted for my first glimmering knowledge of the history and antiquities of Ireland, to those evening conversaziones round our small turf fire, where, after a frugal repast upon that imaginative dish, 'Potatoes and Point' (when there is but a small portion of salt left, the potato, instead of being dipped in by the guests, is merely, as a sort of indulgence to the fancy, pointed at it), my father used to talk of the traditions of other times – of the first coming of the Saxon strangers among us – of the wars that have been ever since waged between them and the *real* Irish, who, by a blessed miracle, though exterminated under every succeeding Lord-Lieutenant, are still as good as new, and ready to be exterminated again – of the great deeds done by the Rocks in former days, and the prophecy which foretells to them a long race of glory to come – all which the grandams of our family would wind up with such frightful stories of the massacres committed by Black Tom (Lord Stafford) and old Oliver as have often sent me to bed with the dark faces of these terrible persons flitting before my eyes ... Of my father's happy talent for wit and humour, I could fill my page with innumerable specimens, – all seasoned with that indescribable sort of 'vernacular relish', which Cicero attributes to the old Roman pleasantry. But half the effect would be lost, unless I could 'print his face with his joke'; besides, the charm of that Irish tone would be wanting, which gives such rich effect to the enunciation of Irish humour, and which almost inclines us to think, while we listen to it, that a brogue is the only music to which wit should be set ... In the rapidity of his transitions from melancholy to mirth, my father resembled the rest of his countrymen ... He was a great believer in miracles, both old and new – but the newer the better; and, though sufficiently alive to the ridiculous on all other subjects, he would listen to any old woman's tale of a wonderful cure, with a gravity of belief which was by far the greater wonder of the two – nor was it altogether safe for a by-stander, on such occasions, to smile. This, however, I look upon as the natural consequence of his political position. They, whom all human means are employed to torment, may be allowed, at least, divine interposition to comfort them; and as a relief to pride, if nothing else, it is a sort of *set-off* for the slave against the insolence of his oppressor, to represent himself as worthy of the peculiar agency of Heaven.[42]

The invitation to compare some Irish storytelling with a 'potatoes-and-point' compensatory strategy is interesting.

Mortimer O'Sullivan (1791-1859), who had been born a Roman Catholic like the author of *Memoirs of Captain Rock* but later became a Protestant clergyman and an aggressive Tory, did not appreciate Thomas Moore's sympathetic humorous approach to 'disaffected' Ireland, and soon retorted, just as anony-

42 *Memoirs of Captain Rock* 242-8.

mously, with his grating *Captain Rock Detected: or, The Origin and Characters of the Recent Disturbances ... by a Munster Farmer* (1824). The emphasis is placed on the sinister connotations of Irish storytelling. We witness a meeting of Rockites, who smoke the communal pipe while telling 'superstitious' tales and plotting devilish crimes:

... the murderers had full dependence upon them, and are now in a hut, enjoying themselves with the utmost complacency. A plentiful but limited allowance of whiskey has been assigned to them, and they are sitting in perfect composure and indifference, smoking at intervals from a short black tobacco pipe, which passes from mouth to mouth, and speaking on subjects such as are frequently discussed amongst the lower Irish.

'Why then now, Denis,' said a soft-faced white hair'd young fellow, addressing himself to an elderly looking man, 'I wonder is hell such a cruel bad place as they say it is.' 'Devil a worse, can be, Larry, my jewel; I often heard all about it from Tim Condon, and sure enough, 'tis the Devil's own place ...' [The 'poor sowls' who suffer there cannot move.] 'How can that be,' said the third speaker, 'sure they sometimes appear on earth?' 'That's the sowls in limbo, that appear, for they never get out of hell.' 'If it was,' rejoined the other, 'how could I see young Cowley, on Wednesday night last, and he a heretic; and didn't he ride by me like a blast of wind, as I was carrying away a sheep that I stole from his father, and knock the sheep off of my back, and when I stoop'd to rise it again, Oh! Devil a one of me could stir it, no more than if it was Slieve-na-mon mountain; and there was he standing over me on his horse, and I reel'd into the ditch, and then when morning came, I took it up as aisy as ever I did in my life; and how could young Cowley be there if he was in one of the pans or the oven?'[43]

According to the Tory clergyman, those Catholics believe that to kill a heretic is no sin and that hell is for the other denomination; they are credulous and garrulous, and their tastes in stories reveal their most nefarious impulses.

But Irish storytelling could also connote old-fashioned innocence. Among the minor writers who tried to interpret Ireland for English readers was the journalist and novelist Eyre Evan Crowe (1799-1868), a benevolent Tory who contrasted contemporary violence with an idyllic world of rather childish old customs and beliefs – of which he foretold the death:

Certain it is, that the old superstitions of the people are fast fading into disrepute and oblivion. Their traditionary laws and history, although related casually, and handed down from parent to child, are no longer taught as a creed or a duty, but begin to be recounted with dubious credence, and with but half-seriousness, even by the lower orders. And universally as the knowledge of these tales is known and scattered through the peasantry, there exist few, or no longer any of those mysterious hags who used to consider themselves peculiar and living depositories of this dreadful lore. These do exist certainly; but they are few, and little either noticed or reverenced; and even they themselves seem affected by the incredulity of the age. It is in the eastern counties of Ireland, those most

43 *Captain Rock Detected* 94-6.

infected with incredulity and an unpoetic love of demonstration in those matters, that the decline we have mentioned is most evident.[44]

Yet the author, posing as a collector, finds (or imagines) a Glendalough story-teller who remembers the marvels of the past: 'After a gorgeous fairy-tale, related by one of these superannuated beings as having witnessed herself, it was asked, "And do you see no fairies now-a-days?" "Oh! not myself, nor anybody, – sure they are all gone to Scotland, the good people." '[45]

The idea that those aspects of Ireland were dying could arouse nostalgia. Anna Maria Hall (1800-81), quoted above as a traveller, was also the author of tales and novels; her first collection in that field combined fiction with memories of her Wexford childhood. This storytelling scene, written in the late 1820s, is clearly associated with rustic innocence:

How I did love to sit, during the long evenings – nurse's arms around me, to prevent the possibility of any irregular and restless movement terminating in an upset, and listen with delight to Frank's fairies, about whom the good old man so dearly loved to talk, only interrupting his narrative now and then by a necessary word of caution to his dogs. Whenever I urged him to tell me a story, he used to shake his head, and say, 'Och! Miss, honey, ye'll may-be think of old Frank and his fairies when ye'll be far from your native land, and my poor smashed bones at rest. But my blessing be about ye', he would add, patriotically, 'never deny your country'. My favourite story was 'The Stout and Strong of Heart'; and I believe it was Frank's favourite also, for many a time and oft has he repeated it to me, and always have I listened with attention, pleasing the old man while I was myself delighted. I will give it to my readers, although I fear it will lose much from the absence of my ancient friend, who with so much earnestness and native humour related it. [A man's wife and their child were abducted, but he rescued them as the fairies were riding along a path at midnight – a common legend plot.] 'They are still living in Dumraghodooly, and James is ever and always ready to tell his story over a glass of whiskey punch; but no inducement has yet prevailed on Ellen to give any account of her adventures in fairy-land.' 'Oh, Miss, don't laugh,' Old Frank would invariably add – 'it's as true as I'm a sinner, and it's bad to disbelieve the fairies. Sure I was an unbeliever once myself, and this was my punishment – one of their arrows right through the flat o' my hand; I shall carry the mark to my grave.' [It was believed that fairies threw 'blasting' projectiles at animals and people.][46]

Another storyteller begins his tale thus: ' "Asy, agra, till I tell ye a little story to divart ye a bit, and its all thrue, and I know ye'll find out my maning, for ye're cute enough." And Anty listened very attentively, pulling first one and then the other of Bang, the baste's ears, which [the dog] bore patiently, not even increasing her perplexity by moving his head from off her lap. "In the ancient

44 *To-Day in Ireland* 3. 261-2. **45** Ibid. 3. 267. **46** *Sketches of Irish Character* 350-4. The preface explains that the book was written to make the Irish character 'more justly appreciated, more rightly estimated, and more respected in England'.

times, when flowers, and trees, and fairies were on spaking terms, and friendly together ... ".'47

But Old Frank, the believer in fairies, also 'delighted in telling stories of the rebellion [of 1798]'. The coexistence of inocent storytelling and 'the poetry of Irish revolt' is stressed in a book Mrs Hall wrote some twenty years later, *The Whiteboy: A Story of Ireland in 1822* (1845), dealing again with agrarian unrest – the 'Whiteboys' had been the first widespread agrarian secret society in Munster in the early 1760s and the word remained in use in the first half of the nineteenth century. In the book, violence is frowned on but the author explains its historical causes. An idealistic young absentee landlord who has been educated in England crosses over – in a modern steamship – to take possession of an Irish estate: since *The Wild Irish Girl* it was the conventional way of initiating the British reader into the secrets of Ireland. Still on board, he receives his first special instruction from people who know the country:

'We are two nations on one soil; Celt and Saxon, Roman and Protestant, Irish Irish and English Irish; in England you do not understand this; but we do; perhaps you may – after a time.' ... 'The Irish peasant', continued [another mentor], 'lives amid the faded glories of his country, knows and feels it; his cabin is mud-walled and miserable, yet the ruined castle he passes by, to go to his ill-remunerated labour, bears his name. This yields him a gloomy satisfaction! He looks on the crumbling walls, and *knows* that the glories of his ancestors are not mere fables. His wife, while digging the potato garden, or whirring at her wheel, sings the cherished legends of his race; tells their triumphs and their oppressions to the children who tremble in rags at her knee; and dim prophecies of the future – when "Ireland shall be herself again" – when Ireland shall belong to the Irish – when Tara's kings shall dispense "justice to Ireland" – are repeated and listened to with avidity at every wake and fair; the story-teller vies with the piper in attracting listeners; and grateful as they feel for *individual* kindnesses of the Saxon race, they look upon them in a body, as not only intruders, but oppressors.'48

The same speaker later stresses the power of the past and of stories which keep it alive.49 The cruder members of the Whiteboy organization accept fantastic legends as well as the native version of history, and with some of them it would be difficult to sympathize: 'Murdogh of "the Strong Hand" was few removes, perhaps, from a savage. Keen, cunning, revengeful, cruel, but faithful, watchful, and undeviating in his few attachments – superstitious to positive weakness; his dark, deep, blood-shot eye, that never quailed at difficulty, would tremble amid tears of terror at the mention of a ghost or a tale of supernatural agency.'50 Yet others are depicted in more pleasant terms; when the protagonist has been captured by the rebels, his guard turns out to be an amusing storyteller, whose folklore is innocuous enough:

47 Ibid. 79-80. 48 *The Whiteboy* 2, 15. 49 Ibid. 212. 50 Ibid. 157.

'My grandfather's father had a power of lagends: and though he couldn't talk English, he'd the world and all of Latin in his head, and Ossian in the original on the top of his tongue; and as to the Druids' altar above there, and a fine sight it is–' 'I should like so much to see it,' interrupted Edward, 'I should like so very much to see it; do you know that in England we talk a great deal about your round towers, and your Druids' altars and Ogham stones.' 'I dare say you do – why not?' replied the mountaineer, not seeming to be at all astonished at the information, 'it's only natural that people that haven't such things should think a dale about them; they're so plenty with us, that we don't think any thing of them; and my grandfather's father –' 'But could I not see this Druids' altar?' 'Bedad, you could, Sir, if you wor there; it's so big every blind man in the country can see it – almost; but honour bright, Sir, you wouldn't get a poor boy like me into trouble; and until I'm tould, I dare not send yer honour out for a walk even that far.

But so little did my grandfather's father think about them Druid altars that once having wandered half the day until almost night-fall, about the hill-side, after an unruly young heifer, one of the rale Kerry breed that's first cousin to the goats, and that would win a steeple chase if any one would ride her; after spending his day that way, when he got under the shelter of the stone and the sun setting, he lay his gray head on his hand and fell to rest in two minutes, just as innocent and sleep-full as a new born baby. Well, he never could tell how long he slept, but at last he woke and wondered to see the beautiful colour of the setting sun all gone, faded away like a rose in hot July, and nothing above him but the moon and the dawshy stars sporting and sparkling through the heavens, and he wondered where the heifer could be, when he turned his eyes a little to the left, and there she stood as meek as a lamb, not a stir in her, and her wild wicked eyes fixed upon a bunch of blackberries, and her tail, that used to be stiff as a blast of the north wind, hanging down like a bunch of silk, and her ears quiet, and a sugaun [*súgán*: straw rope or collar] of fruit and fresh-made hay round her neck and one end of it in the hand of the most beautiful little creature the sight of his eyes ever looked upon, and she twisting and spinning about on the top of the heifer's little stumpy horn.

"Oh! murder, my lady," says my grandfather's father in Irish, "is it there you are, and is it my beautiful little *coween* yer going to whisk off to yer own country?" "Oh, fie!" she says; and saving yer presence, Sir, she says, "is it a Saxon you take me for, to be taking the good out of the country? I'm no such thing. I found yer little beast on the wild hill side, and I brought her to you; and there she is, as tame and as gentle as a new-born lamb".'[51]

Fairytale innocence and political convictions are thus curiously harmonized. The good leaders are not those who preach hatred, however, but paternalistic civilizing landlords.

Most of the writers mentioned so far wanted to explain, justify or condemn, but there were other modes which may be summarily labelled as 'comic' and 'antiquarian'.

In the 1830s and 40s, comic stereotypes inherited from the theatre like the boastful Irish soldier, the garrulous Irish sharper and the blundering or clever

51 Ibid. 215-16.

Irish servant still amused the English audience and were also found in prose fiction. I find less to harvest here, but may mention again Samuel Lover (see pp. 155 and 193-5). His novel *Handy Andy* (1842) includes a pseudo-folk story – 'The Marvellous Legend of Tom Connor's Cat' – and several funny storytelling scenes at different social levels, in an Ireland with no trace of misery and violence. The participation of the audience is repeatedly focused upon:

Larry puffed away silently for a few minutes, and when Oonah had placed a few sods of turf round the pot in an upright position, that the flame might curl upward round them, and so hasten the boiling, she drew a stool near the fire, and asked Larry to explain about the fright.'Why, I was coming up by the cross road there, when what should I see but a ghost' – 'A ghost!!!' exclaimed the widow and Oonah, with suppressed voices, and distended mouth and eyes ... With that eagernesss which always attends the relation of horrible stories, Larry and the old woman raked up every murder and robbery that had occurred within their recollection, while Oonah listened with mixed curiosity and fear ... 'I wish Larry did not tell us such horrid stories,' said she, as she laid rushlight on the table; 'I'll be dhramin' all night o' them.' ...
'A capital story, Randal,' cried Dick; 'but how much of it did you invent?' ' 'Pon my soul, it is as near the original as possible.' 'Besides, that is not a fair way of using a story,' said the Doctor. 'You should take the story as you get it, and not play the dissector upon it, mangling its poor body to discover the bit of embellishment upon it; and as long as a *raconteur* maintains *vraisemblance*, I contend you are bound to receive the whole as true.'[52]

Another novel, *Rory O'More* (1837) is set in the time of the 1798 rebellion but avoids representing it. Sentimental and comic scenes alternate, with plenty of dialogue, and an old schoolmaster is 'constantly recounting to [Rory] the glamorous deeds of his progenitors – or, as he called them, his 'owld anshint anshishters in the owld anshint times'.[53] It is worth noting that, while Lover wrote about Ireland in a comic vein, there were cruder forms of 'Irish' histrionics which he denounced as 'foreign, false and exaggerated' and 'without 'the true stamp of nationality'.[54]

The telling of anecdotes and playing with the notion of truthfulness are also part of the rollicking Irish student- or soldier-life evoked in Charles Lever's early picaresque narratives, which were very successful in England. But the author or his persona gives up trying to imitate rural storytelling – as in this excerpt from *Jack Hinton, the Guardsman* (1842): 'Could I have borrowed any portion of his narrative power, were I able to present in his strong but simple language any of the curious scenes [Father Tom] mentioned, I should perhaps venture relating to my readers one of his stories; but when I think how much of the interest depended on his quaint and homely but ever forcible manner, as, pointing with his whip to some ruined house with blackened walls and fallen

52 *Handy Andy* 75-8, 342. 53 *Rory O'More* 1. 8. 54 Preface to *The Lyrics of Ireland* (1858) ix-x.

chimneys, he told some narrative of rapine and of murder, I feel how much the force of reality added power to a story that in repetition might be weak and ineffective.'[55] The same reserve is noticeable in Lever's sombre later novels about the decline of the Protestant landlord class; in *Luttrell of Arran* (1865), for instance, we are just told that a little Donegal girl narrates with 'some of that assumed importance she had possibly seen adopted by story-tellers', or that an old man trying to remember could narrate too, in his own way: 'As if the strain on his memory to recall the precise words employed, and to bring back the whole scene, had been too much for him, or as though the emotions of the past had surged back to overwhelm him, the old peasant held his hand over his eyes, and sat several minutes without speaking.'[56] The author himself had a reputation as a skilful oral *raconteur* – but not of the traditional rural kind.

Another subgenus of fiction was the reconstruction of remote times, as in a set of texts by Samuel Ferguson (1810-86): *The Hibernian Nights' Entertainments*. It was part of the attempts (see p. 200) to make the Protestant accept their 'Irishness' by identifying with the Irish past, and thus prove their capacity for legitimate leadership: 'What we have to do ... is the recovery of the mislaid, but not lost, records of the acts, and opinions, and conditions of our ancestors – the disinterring and bringing back to the light of intellectual day of the already recorded *facts* by which the people of Ireland will be able to live back, in the land we live *in*, with as ample and as interesting a field of retrospective enjoyment as any of the nations around us.'[57] The effort to do it in prose narrative form had begun in *Blackwood's Edinburgh Magazine*, and continued in the *Dublin University Magazine* in the 1830s – to be collected in book form only in 1857. It was a framed set of stories, supposedly told by the old bard Turlogh O'Hogan in Dublin Castle in 1592, to captives like Red Hugh O'Donnell who needed encouragement before they could escape:

'When shall I sit again by the great hall fire, wandering in fancy with Finn and his old warriors, through enchanted castles and over magic seas? When shall I stand with the three sons of Usnach, holding the castle of the Red Branch against Conor MacNessa and his Ulster legions, with Deirdre by my side, still fearlessly bending over the chess-table on which she plays against her lover, lest he should catch alarm from her desertion of the game? Ho, Turlogh, do tell us this story of clan Usnach, without slip or blunder, and I will make thee bard of Tirconnell.' ... 'I would I had my harp here', said Turlogh, 'that I might sing the songs of Deirdre as they ought to sound from the string: but, alas! I had forgotten; the notes of a harp were dangerous to be heard from a prisoner's dungeon; so I shall chant the strains as best I may, and abstain from singing, lest we should be overheard.' So saying, Turlogh drew his seat nearer the cheerful blaze now flickering on the red hearth-stone, and with half-closed eyes began the tale of the Death of the Children of Usnach. 'The nobles of Ulster were feasting in the house of Felimy ...'[58]

---

55 Op. cit, 2. 33. 56 *Luttrell of Arran* 14-15, 80, 89. 57 *Dublin University Magazine* 4 (1840) 448. 58 *The Hibernian Nights' Entertainments* 15.

The bard has a wide repertoire: ' "I will tell your nobleness the names of some of my store ... and you shall choose which you like best among them." The young man gladly assented, and Turlogh proceeded to enumerate the titles of his tales. "Shall I tell your nobleness that ancient legend of the walls of Ross, or the story of Dame Kettle, or Coghlan na Cashleen, or Curby MacGillmore?" '[59] – he illustrates the unifying power of antiquarianism by alternating stories of Anglo-Norman and of Gaelic Ireland.

At first, most of those who published more or less documentary fiction about Ireland belonged to the Protestant communities (Thomas Moore was a Catholic – but a Dubliner). When addressing a British audience, they had the authority conferred by their relative proximity to the world they were evoking, but their attitudes towards the rural Catholic tenants combined, in varying proportion, curiosity and perhaps sympathy with a sense of unbridgeable difference, and sometimes fear. Novelists born in the provincial or rural Catholic world appeared in the second quarter of the century; they were of course better prepared to understand their coreligionists and, as the O'Connellite movement towards emancipation had given a new confidence to the part of society they belonged to, they were less likely to be on the defensive than the ascendancy and some members of the Protestant middle classes. It brought some changes in the content and form of Irish literary fiction: precise depictions of non-idyllic or non-farcical aspects of life, which so far one had to imagine or ignore, appeared in the books of the new writers. But these writers also had to please an audience of outsiders, and were therefore likely to combine pleading and attempts at realism with what still seemed to be expected of books about Ireland: in other words they were not likely to make local customs merely amusing, bizarre or shocking, and when they set their novels in the past their perception of history could differ from that of a Ferguson, but they were tempted to sensationalize or be laboriously didactic.

A model had been provided by Walter Scott: one hoped to do for Ireland what he had done for Scotland – whereas Scott himself said he had tried to do for Scotland what had already been achieved by Maria Edgeworth who, according to him, had been the first to make the characteristics of a country or region a subject for novels.[60] The difference was that the new Irish writers we shall now examine did not, like her, set the 'big houses' of landlords at the centre. In Scott, they saw that it was possible to treat seriously those characters from the lower-classes which so far had generally been clowns or pallid pastoral types, and they discovered a way of representing the experience of social and cultural change: the passing of an age and the coming of another, with gains and losses. He had created memorable figures of outcasts who were knowledgeable about the past, could foretell fatal events, and had grandeur; Edie Ochiltree, in Scott's

59 Ibid. 308. **60** 'Postscript' to *Waverley*, and 'General Preface to the Waverley Novels'.

Antiquary published in 1816, is akin to the beggars still portrayed in Irish periodicals some ten years later (see pp. 184-6) and, like them, is not just a grotesque; 'the news-carrier, the minstrel, and sometimes the historian of the district', he is the most convincing character in this particular novel. In Scott's books about eighteenth-century Scotland, Irish writers could also appreciate a use of the vernacular not designed to make its speakers 'low' and absurd.

Walter Scott was therefore the 'ideal of a National Novelist'[61] for the Banim brothers (John: 1798-1842; Michael: 1796-1874), the sons of a Kilkenny farmer and shopkeeper, who chose to be the spokesmen for those who had so far been portrayed only from afar. Their programme was summed up by John's first biographer: 'To raise the national character in the estimation of other lands, by a portrayal of the people as they really were; but at the same time to vindicate them from the charges of violence and bloodthirstiness, by showing, in the course of the fiction, the various causes which he supposed concurred to draw forth and foster these evil qualities.'[62]

With their experience of country life the two brothers were better equipped than Thomas Moore or Mrs Hall to illustrate and explain the darker sides of rural Ireland, including the peasant attitude to crime and to a foreign law; but they generally set their stories before their own time, perhaps to lessen unpleasantness. There is little humour or deliberate picturesqueness in the most impressive of their *Tales by the O'Hara Family* (1825), 'Crohoore of the Bill-Hook', written almost entirely by Michael, 'carefully copied from the life and the facts' but set in the eighteenth century. The mood rapidly shifts from the description of a warm Christmas Eve to that of a funeral wake, during which 'an aged retainer of the family' gives 'the circumstantial account of his master's death, here set down, to a circle of attentive and affrighted hearers',[63] then to a story of murder, Whiteboy conspiracy and revenge. We follow people who are approaching the supposed underground abode of supernatural creatures, and their beliefs are shown to be an integral part of their life; stories have swelled and multiplied in transmission, and the place where they are delivered is decidedly bleak – neither vaguely sublime as in Ossianic imitations nor jolly as in many sketches where legends were told.[64] Later on, when a changeling story is told, we may find it less sombre because the dialogue we hear, sprinkled with Irish words and phrases, evokes conviviality:

'I'm afeard the story 'ud be a long one.' 'Och, no, à-roon [*a rún*: my darling]; the night's young; an' better for us be here at this good fire, sayin' to the wind that's widout, blow your best, a-bouchal [*a bhuachaill*: boy], nor be perishin' alone by oursels in our could beds.' 'Well; hould your hands, now, Andy, an' I'll tell you about Biddy Grasse.' 'I will, a-cuishla [*a chuisle*: heart- pulse] ; I'll be a good boy.' They drew their stools – or stool – we disdain to say which – closer to the blaze, and prepared, one to speak, and the

61 P.J. Murray *The Life of John Banim* 92. 62 Ibid. 92-4. 63 *Tales by the O'Hara Family* 1. 39. 64 Ibid. 1. 160-1.

other to listen, with that peculiar pleasure story-telling imparts. 'Now, Andy, this is as thrue a story as ever you hard; I had id frum Biddy's own gossip, an' she had id frum Biddy's own mouth ... '[65]

Hallowe'en storytelling, and a Macbethian situation, are evoked in *The Ghost Hunter and his Family* (1833), also by Michael Banim and equally rich in 'folk-lore': we follow a character who 'was very particular in observing the customs, pranks, or rites, of each season of the year'.[66] He asks for a tale:

'Very willingly I'll tell you, Rendal' – and as the good woman had only been coquetting to have the question put, she now assumed the importance of the story-teller setting forward on her tale, with a peculiar smack of her lips, which told her relish of the occupation ... [Another member of the party has seen a ghost:] 'Do you know the place he was murthered at, in the bosheen [laneway]? 'tis asy to mark it to-night, there's such a fine moon shinin' out for 'em all. Well, 'twas along the bosheen I came to see ye, an' by course I passed the spot. No rain came since Joey was found sthretched there, to wash the marks from the ground; an' there's a red cross, made wid his blood, on a broad stone in the wall.' 'Well, Hester?' questioned Morris, fully absorbed. 'Well? for what do you cry your "well, well" at me? I met Joe Wilson's ghost on that spot; yes, there we met with one another; and he followed me when I passed him, givin' him my heavy curse; an' he crossed the thrashold o' this house, afther me! an' now he's between me and the fire, as I tould ye afore; I see him – I feel him.'[67]

In these texts, intensity of feeling and tragic circumstances tended to replace the extravagant or sentimentalized features of Irish peasants as they had often been portrayed hitherto. The author does not pretend to share his characters' beliefs, nor does he criticize or scoff at them: strange though they may seem to outsiders, they are shown to have coherence possibly, and certainly potency.

John Banim's most Scottian work was *The Boyne Water* (1826), an attempt to give a comprehensive vision of Ireland at a moment of crisis in its history and to suggest what it was like to those who lived through it. It follows the fortunes of two families fighting on opposite sides in the Jacobite-Williamite war of the late seventeenth century. As 'bards' and 'Ossianic remains' were still a must in evocations of the 'Celtic' past, a real character – Carolan, the 'last Irish bard' celebrated by Oliver Goldsmith (see p. 66) – puts in an appearance, and a singer of ancient lays in North Ulster contributes to the theme of monstrous civil war when he chants the story of Cú Chulainn's killing of his own son:

'Manus Oge! Come here, old Manus Oge!' The chronicler of the glen rose and advanced: his very tall figure was somewhat stooped from illness, his long limbs moved gracefully, his long arms swung or fidgeted about, and his shoulders often shrugged up and down, perhaps from an inward impatience or indisposition – 'Sit down here, near me, and sing us the *Laoidh* of Oisin that we all like best;' [Carolan] went on: 'Edmund, get your large

65 Ibid. 1.274. **66** *The Ghost Hunter and His Family* 7. **67** Ibid. 14, 21.

harp, and accompany him: you know the old chaunt; I will help you, now and then, with this little Clarseeech [*cláirseach*: harp]; tho' no man can play even my own airs worse than myself. I have often told you I only use the harp to assist me in composition; running over it with my fingers, in search of the melody that is in my brain and heart. Come, your harp, and sit down by Manus Oge.'

'Is it the *Laoidh* of Con-More mac-an Deirgh, you want, Carolan?' asked Manus – or the *Laoidh* of Cagavra, where Oscar was killed by Cairbre, the king? or of Conloach-Mac-Cuchullin'? and so he continued to run over the names of poems, others of which as well as those mentioned were on subjects which another chronicler has since given, in an adapted shape, to the world. 'It is Conloach-Mac-Cuchullin I want, Manus Oge,' replied Carolan; and the selection being thus made, and Edmund's harp ready, Manus began the recitation of a poem, which, in a different style of language and arrangement, may be found among the collection of Ossian's poems, before alluded to; but which, it is our impression, has not been improved in the hands of the Scotch editor, or in the hands of those from whom he received it; though even at this day, it may be obtained in Irish, very nearly word for word as it shall now be translated, from the lips of the descendant of Manus Oge, and on the very spot which is the present scene of our story. 'From Scotland came a haughty young hero, the valiant champion Conloach, unto the grand court of pleasure ... '.[68]

The scene is fabricated and looks conventional, but in a note by Michael to the 1865 edition of *The Boyne Water* it is said to have documentary value: 'As a fact bearing on a disputed question, which has to some extent occupied the literary world, I think I am called to state here, that the Ossianic remnant embodied in the tale is the literal translation of a poem recited in the Irish tongue for my brother, while he travelled the county Antrim. And the transcriber assured me that numerous relics of the same character could be obtained in the same locality.'[69] When the Banim brothers dealt with the contemporary rural world, they managed to convey the weight of its traditions and to make a more dramatic than comic use of peasant speech. Storytelling itself can be sinister when the life of the storytellers is bleak.

Another writer who tried to present the Catholic peasantry and middle-class in 'truthful' ways was Gerald Griffin (1803-40). The grandson of a County Clare 'strong farmer' and the son of a Limerick brewer, educated mostly in hedge schools, he went to London at the age of nineteen to try and make a career as a playwright. There he met John Banim and William Maginn (see pp. 181-2), and wrote some articles on Irish ruins, Irish rebels and the 'Irish Funeral Cry' – the latter being a subject that nineteenth-century English travellers and readers found particularly puzzling and impressive. The success of the Banims' *Tales by the O'Hara Family* – on which he had refused to collaborate – led him to try his hand at regionalist fiction. For his first attempts in the genre he adopted the international convention of the *Rahmenerzählung*, with a framing fiction enclosing stories told by several characters. It might be argued that the for-

68 Ibid. 62-3. 'Conloch' was translated in Charlotte Brooke's *Reliques*. 69 Ibid. 568

mula had long been known in Ireland; in written literature there had been the twelfth-century *Colloquy of the Ancients*, and in oral storytelling it was possible to combine several tales into one continuous performance: 'The most characteristic type of Irish folktale is the elaborate frame-story with a series of incidents more or less loosely strung together, often in surprising combinations.'[70] Alan Bruford, in his study of Irish romances, also noted that the technique of the story-within-a-story was highly developed – but that in practically every case the narrator of the 'in-tale' told of his own experience. (I shall return to the subject of interwoven oral tales in Chapter 12.) Thomas Moore's successful poem *Lalla Rookh* (1817) used the frame device, with an oriental prince in disguise telling tales to a princess; Griffin, who repeatedly exploited this technique, could also have been inspired by English (he mentions Chaucer) and continental models.[71] His first attempt, *Holland Tide* (1827), has a few peasants gathered on All Saints' Eve, 'at the house of a respectable farmer in the west of Munster'. Old women are gossiping and exchanging stories, and in the opening sequence folklore remains amusing:

As the noisier revellers grew comparatively silent, the voices of two or three old gossips who sat inside the hearth in the chimney-corner, imbibing the grateful warmth, and seeming to breathe as freely and contentedly amid the volumes of smoke which enveloped them as if it had been pure aroma – their knees gathered up to their chins [*ar do chorraghiob?* – see p. 179], and the tails of their cotton or stuff gowns drawn up over their heads, suffering the glazed blue or green petticoat to dazzle the eyes of the admiring spectators – the voices, as we said, of these old crones became more audible as the noisy mirth around them began to decrease, and at length attracted the attention of the other guests. 'What is it ye're doing there?' exclaimed the old master of the house, looking towards the corner with an expression of face in which much real curiosity and some assumed ridicule were blended. 'Oych thin nothing in the world', replied a smoke-dried, crow-footed, white-haired, yet sharp-eyed hag, whose three last teeth were employed in masticating a piece of 'that vile roguish tobacco'. 'Nothing; – only we to be talking among ourselves of ould times – and things – the quare doings that used to be there long ago –

> Onst on a time
> When pigs drank wine,
> And turkeys smoked tobaccy!

whin *themselves* [the fairies] used to be seen by the ould and the young, by day and night, roving the fields and places, and not to be scaming about as they do now (maning 'em no disparagement), in a whisk of a dusty road on a windy day, – whin goold was as plenty as bog-dust, and there used to be joyants there as long as the round towers; when

70 R.T. Christiansen *Studies in Irish and Scandinavian Folktales* 67. **71** The device had been revived in Germany: refugees, or travellers, or people joining together for amusement, exchange stories – from Goethe's *Unterhaltungen deutscher Ausgewanderten* (1795) through E.T.A Hoffmann's *Die Serapionsbrüder* (1813-21) to Wilhelm Hauff's *Im Wirtshaus im Spessart* (1827).

it was the fashion for the girls to come coorting the boys, instead of the boys going after the girls, and things that way, entirely.' 'Poh, what nonsense!' exclaimed the hero of the snap-apple, 'there's not a word ever to be had out o' the ould women, passing a chronicle of a fable about the fairies, and priests, and joyants, and things that we never seen, nor that nobody ever come back to tell us about – what kind they wor – or what truth was in 'em. Let somebody sit upright and tell us something that we'll know is it a lie that he's telling, or not.' 'Something about wakes and weddings, and them things', said (a note above her breath) the modest, small-mouthed Norry Foley. 'Or smugglers, or coiners, or fighting at fairs, or Moll Doyle, or rebellion, or murthering of one sort or another', roared he of the legs. 'Easy now – easy the whole of ye! – easy again!' said the host, waving his hand round the circle to enjoin silence, – 'there may be a way found to please ye all!' (this was said with an air of good-natured condescension, as if the speaker, in his benevolence, were about to tolerate rather than enjoy the silly amusement which the youngsters meditated). 'Gather round the fire, do ye, and let everybody tell his story after his own way; and let the rest hearken, whether they like it or not, until 'tis over, and then tell their own, if they think 'tis better.'

A clattering of chairs and stools, and a general bustle, announced the ready concurrence of the company in this polite arrangement. In a short time all were hushed into a most flattering silence, and the following tales passed round the circle, lulling some to sleep, keeping others awake, each finding its particular number of indulgent, gratified, and attentive auditors, though no single one, perhaps, succeeded in pleasing all.

Whether such may be the lot of the narratives among a more extensive and less considerate audience, remains to be seen. Avowing the source from which his materials were taken, the collector thinks himself entitled to tell the stories after his own liking.[72]

Griffin preferred not to imitate the oral narrator's style further. He also left the realm of fairytales aside; the book concludes that present rural life has sinister aspects which cannot be ignored:

Of late years, scenes like this have become rare in Ireland. Before the period of the year arrives when ancient and revived custom reminds the peasant of the domestic jollities of his father's and of his own childhood, the horn of the Whiteboy, or the yell of the more ferocious Rockite, has startled the keeper of the land, and warned the inhabitants to prepare for 'other than dancing measures'.[73]

Yet he had 'endeavoured in most instances, where pictures of Irish cottage life have been introduced, to furnish a softening corollary to the more exciting moral chronicles of our predecessors [he probably had the Banims in mind], to bring forward the sorrows and the affections more frequently than the violent and fearful passions of the people'.[74]

The book was successful enough in England, but Griffin, homesick, returned to Ireland where he produced, on a similar though looser pattern, *Tales of the Munster Festivals* (1827), announcing his intention to take an inventory of popular characters and customs with which politicians might be wise to get

72 *Holland Tide* 8-10.   73 Ibid. 373.   74 Introduction to *Holland Tide*.

acquainted. He defined the work as 'an attempt to illustrate the manners and other peculiarities of a particular district of Ireland (which, though presenting many highly interesting features to the eye of the novelist, has hitherto been altogether neglected), by a series of tales, each of which shall fix its main action on one of the popular festivals of the year, or days which are set apart for the observance of certain traditional rites and gala ceremonies.'[75] It seemed to be what publishers, and perhaps readers too, wanted at the time; but Griffin was not so confident that it was the right thing to do, and he brought forward in the book itself a criticism of the method he was following. In a fisherman's cottage near Kilrush, where he has just heard a story, the frame-narrator says that such material should be written down and published, but a 'sour old man' protests:

'Talking of tales,' I continued, wishing to analyse the old gentleman, as soon as we were left alone together, which happened shortly after – 'it is surprising that while so many able pens are employed in delineating the manners and scenery of all other parts of Ireland – this unique and interesting people, and the magnificent wonders of their coast should have altogether escaped attention.' This I said with a certain tone of authority and loudness, as if to compel a degree of deference from my morose companion. He replied, however, in a gruff tone, and without raising his eyes from the book – 'I'm very glad they have, I'm sure – I'd be very sorry it was otherwise.' 'I believe you are rather singular in that opinion,' said I, 'and it is fortunate for our novelists that you are so. Tales of this nature are, I believe, very popular at present.' 'I have something else to do besides reading them,' he replied. 'You are a fortunate man,' said I, 'if you can employ all your time more profitably and agreeably. For my part, I am of opinion that they might be made the vehicle of not only very agreeable, but very useful information. Besides, they throw a train of pleasing associations around the people whose manners they describe, which never fades nor is forgotten, and which is found to serve them among their neighbour-nations in a hundred ways.' ... 'I am one of those,' said the old gentleman, who appeared to be best pleased with rough usage, 'who think that a ruined people stand in need of a more potent restorative than an old wife's story ... We are in no wise indebted to those writers, however brilliant their acquisitions or endowments may be, who, professing to present faithful illustrations of the minds and hearts of our countrymen, greedily rake up the forgotten superstitions of our peasantry, and exhibit the result of their ungracious researches, the unhappy blemishes of our island, the weakness of the poor uninstructed peasantry, over which decency and good feeling would have thrown a veil, to the eyes of a world that, unfortunately for us, is but too eager to seize every occasion for mocking and upbraiding against our forlorn and neglected country.'[76]

The dispute over the advisability for Irish writers to treat such subjects, or how to treat them honestly and usefully, was to be revived again and again during the next century and a half. But though Griffin may have had his doubts – he later abandoned literature altogether to teach as a Christian Brother – his narrator-traveller kept listening to stories.

75 *Tales of the Munster Festivals* I.ii.   76 Ibid. I. xiv-xix.

In this book, the author was prepared to try and reproduce oral style, for instance in a boatman's transformation of *Táin Bó Cuailnge* into a folktale.[77] A servant contributes a religious legend.[78] Peasants at work exchange sensational news, or jokes and tall tales:

A number of peasants were occupied in *trenching* a field of potatoes, in a fine soft summer evening, in the earlier portion of the last century, on the borders of one of the south-western counties of Ireland. Their work proceeded merrily – all being engaged, as is customary in Ireland, in relieving the tediousness of their monotonous labour by wild tales, and light and jocular conversation, which we shall take up at random. 'An so you tell me Segur is off, Mick?' said one to a young peasant who worked beside him. 'He'll never see daylight again,' was the reply. 'An how coom that?' 'Simply enough – be killen of 'm.' 'Who kilt him?' 'O then that's more than I'll tell you this time – one o' the gang eastwards, they say.' 'An why did they kill him?' 'Sorrow one o' me knows – bekays he was alive, may be.' ... 'I'll tell ye a story then about that very thing, if ye like to hear it,' said the young fellow. After a few jibes on the propensity of the story-telling genius, his companions proceeded with their work in silence, while Jerry cleared his voice and commenced as follows (the English reader will at once perceive a striking similitude between this popular cottage legend and one of Chaucer's Canterbury tales) ...[79]

Griffin returned to the frame-narrative device, this time without the rural context, in *Talis Qualis; or Tales of the Jury Room*, published in 1842 after his death. An Englishman arrives in a town in the south of Ireland during the assizes, and strays into the room where the jury is locked for the night because its members cannot reach a unanimous decision. They while away the time telling stories, some of them traditional (including an early record of the famous Irish tale 'The Man Who Had No Story'; see Chapter 12 for different versions and interpretations of it).

His most ambitious and successful work was *The Collegians*, a full-length novel published in 1829. Based on a real murder case of 1819, it is set approximately half a century earlier and offers a broader view of Irish society than any previous fictional book, embracing all classes and conditions in Limerick, Clare and Kerry: the landless poor, peasants or mountaineers, servants, Catholic 'middlemen', 'squireens' or 'half-sirs', the gentry and the English 'Garrison'. It was customary in European literature to set novels in the not too distant past, but for Griffin and his Irish colleagues it seems to have been a way of reaching a 'more Irish' world; what Griffin had not seen he had heard about, and the word 'tradition' appears twice in the short first chapter. The melodramatic plot is interspersed with ceremonies like the 'Patrick Boys' procession or the 'May-day mummers', a race, a hunt, a duel, much ballad-singing, and a demonstration of the 'ingenuity of Irish witnesses' as a technique of survival: 'all the inimitable subtleties of evasion and of wile which an Irish peasant can display when he is

77 Ibid. 2. 26. 78 Ibid. 2. 94. 79 Ibid. 2. 170-2. The reference is to Chaucer's 'Friar's Tale'.

made to undergo a scene of judicial scrutiny'. A variant of the 'potato-with-point' technique of the poor (see Thomas Moore above, p. 236) is detailed: 'they'd peel a piate first, and then they'd point it up at the bacon, and they'd fancy within their own minds that it would have the taste o' the mait when they'd be aten it, after'. There is plenty of entertaining talk with rendition of regional speech, and scenes of storytelling. Events are commented upon by a chorus of secondary characters: 'The story, as usual, was circulated throughout the country in the course of the following day, with many imaginative embellishments'.[80] Repeatedly, an episode which has first been reported by the main anonymous narrative voice is re-enacted in much more lively terms by a local representative of Irish storytelling, standing aside from the action and speaking about it:

('Written narrative')	('Spoken narrative')
After sustaining a long and distressing altercation with her father and her mountain suitor, Eily O'Connor threw her blue cloak over her shoulders and walked into the air. She did not return to dinner, and her father felt angry at what he thought a token of resentful feeling. Night came, and she did not make her appearance. The poor old man in an agony of terror reproached himself for his vehemence, and spent the whole night in recalling with a feeling of remorse every intemperate word which he had used in the violence of dispute. In the morning, more like a ghost than a living being, he went from the house of one acquaintance to another to enquire after his child. No one however had seen her, except Foxy Dunat, the haircutter, and he had only caught a glimpse of her as she passed his door on the previous evening.[81]	'I was standing in my little place, above, shaving a boy o' the Downes's against the *benefit* at Batt Coonerty's, an' being delayed a good while, (for the Downes's have all very strong hair, – I'd as lieve be shaving a horse as one of 'em) I was sthrappen' my razhor, (for the twentieth turn) an' looken' out into the fair, when who should I see going by only Eily O'Connor, an' she dressed in a blue mantle, with the hood over her head, an' her hair curling down about her neck like strings of goold. (Oh, the beauty o' that girl!) Well, "It's a late walk you're taking, Eily," says I. She made no answer, only passed on, an' I thought no more about it till this morning, when her father walked in to me. I thought, at first, 'tis to be shaved he was coming, for, dear knows, he wanted it, when all at once he opened upon me in regard of his daughter. Poor girl, I'm sure sorrow call had I to [I didnt care for] her goen' or stayen' ...'[82]

The narrative comes to life when a commoner is speaking.

Variants of well-known tales and legends are told in this novel: punishing a butter-stealing witch; a child stolen by the fairies; trying to find a woman more foolish than one's own; successfully breaking a vow about never drinking in your house or out of it. There is a variant of the 'fearless boy' story, localized by the

---

80 The last three quotations: *The Collegians* 193-4, 253, 263. 81 Ibid. 9. 82 Ibid. 45.

naming of places and persons.[83] The cyclical nature of repeated traditional stories contrasts with the tragic linear movement of the 'real' plot; some storytelling scenes provide comic relief, while others may suggest homologies between traditional motifs and aspects of the novel – with an important difference: in the main narrator's Ireland evil is active, whereas in traditional stories it seems less harmful.

The Rivals (1829) is set at Glendalough, and an introduction links this novel with some travellers' sketches, as the main narrator is approached by a 'singular looking figure' who is no less a person than the 'celebrated guide' George Winder (cf. p. 153):

Touching his hat as he came near, he offered his services as cicerone during my ramble round the lake, enhancing their value at the same time by informing me that he had acted as guide to a number of celebrated literary characters; indeed, to all the well known people who had visited the lakes within the last ten years. As a farther inducement, he told me that some of those individuals, availing themselves of information which he had given them, 'bein' great ould historians themselves, and havin' recourse to other ould hishtories, at home, between 'em all had magnified that place to a very great pitch.' [The 'author' accepts the services of the guide.] Feeling an honest ambition to give value for his money, George immediately commenced operations with a volubility characteristic of his vocation. [Griffin turns into a poem his story of the woman who tried to tempt St Kevin, then he hears the story which will constitute the first half of the book.][84]

The prose fiction texts examined so far were composed by writers of different social origins, having observed 'traditional storytellers' from a distance which could vary but was never negligible. A pure unmediated insider's view of the role of the storyteller and of the functions of storytelling at the poorest levels of Irish rural society is impossible to find; we approach it, however, with a writer we have already met: William Carleton, the author of 'The Irish Shanahus' (see pp. 209ff). He knew the subject at first-hand – he *had been* an insider when living with his family in the Clogher valley of County Tyrone; but when he wrote, in Dublin, he was removed from the world he was evoking and, although he claimed his recollections were exact and always asserted that he was giving a faithful account of facts, he was more or less selecting, combining, heightening, and sometimes inventing to make a point or for sentimental or horrific effects. He is nevertheless a unique witness.

The factual ('traits', or 'sketches') and the fictional ('tales' or 'stories') were more clearly distinguished in the titles of his books than in the texts themselves, and they appear together in the title of the work where we can best assess how he drew on his experience of traditional storytelling: *Traits and Stories of the Irish Peasantry* (first series 1830, second series 1833, definitive edition 1843-4).

83 Ibid. 31-4. The Irish versions of International Type AT 326 concern a man who accepts to spend nights in a haunted house and is rewarded with the discovery of a hidden treasure.
84 *The Rivals and Tracy's Ambition* (introduction to the first edition).

In the 'General Introduction' which he wrote for the edition of 1842, he claimed special authority, in the terms he also later used in his autobiography: 'the subject is one which I ought well to understand'. As in the 'Shanahus' sketch, he also insisted on its vanishing nature:

The recreations of the Irish were very varied, and some of them of a highly intellectual cast. These latter, however, have altogether disappeared from the country, or at all events are fast disappearing. The old Harper is now hardly seen; the Senachie, where he exists, is but a dim and faded representative of that very old Chronicler in his palmy days; and the Prophecy-man unfortunately has survived the failure of his best and most cherished predictions ... The amusement derived from these persons was undoubtedly of a very imaginative character, and gives sufficient proof, that had the national intellect been duly cultivated, it is difficult to say in what position as a literary country Ireland might have stood at this day.[85]

Carleton felt he had a role to play in the transition. He had tried to correct the insulting portrait of the Irishman he found in English literature – 'a broad grotesque blunderer, every sentence he speaks involving a bull, and every act the result of headlong folly, or cool but unstudied effrontery';[86] his own contributions, on the other hand, would be 'faithful delineations of Irish life', and particularly of those aspects of it which were on the wane or already lost, yet were close enough in time to be remembered with accuracy.

Traits and Stories, which went through several revisions and additions,[87] was originally planned, like some of Griffin's books (see pp. 246-50) as a series of tales told around the fire – this time on successive winter nights at Ned M'Keown's *shebeen* in the Valley of the Black Pig where, according to one of the prophecies he placed in Tom Gressiey's repertoire (see p. 216) the liberation of Ireland would start with apocalyptic destruction. From general chat we move on to a ghost story, which soon seems to materialize in the unexpected arrival of a mysterious stranger. According to the Irish saying, one story leads to another (*tarraingíonn scéal scéal eile*): 'Sit down, gintlemen', said Ned; 'sit down, Father Ned, you and Father Pether – we'll have another tumbler; and, as it's my turn to tell a story, I'll give yez something to amuse yez, the best I can, and, you all know, who can do more?'[88] Ned tells the tale of 'The Three Tasks', in which we recognize International Type AT 313 'Girl as Helper in the Hero's Flight', with the motifs of the game of cards and the pledging of one's soul, things impossible to do, help received from the magician's daughter, and loss of memory through being 'kissed' by a dog.[89] For a while, the framing device is respected:

85 *Traits and Stories of the Irish Peasantry* 1. xxiii-xxiv. **86** Ibid. 1. 11. **87** Studied in B. Hayley *Carleton's Traits and Stories and the 19th Century Anglo-Irish Tradition*. **88** *Traits and Stories* ... 1.22. **89** Many Irish versions are listed in Ó Súilleabháin-Christiansen *The Types of the Irish Folk Tale* 68-71. Cf. G. Ó Háinle, 'The Gaelic Background of Carleton's Traits and Stories', *Éire-Ireland* 18-1 (1983) 16: 'Though we cannot establish how faithfully Carleton reproduced his original, his "version" has the ring of authenticity to it. There are untradi-

a more 'literary' presentation of the setting and speaker generally contrasts in style with the tale told in the vernacular, but the portraits of storytellers and accounts of storytelling sessions can also be presented as oral communication:

'Well, as I was telling you, there was great sport going on. In one corner, you might see a knot of ould men sitting together, talking over ould times – ghost stories, fairy tales, or the great rebellion of 41 [1641], and the strange story of Lamh Dearg, or the *bloody hand* – that, maybe, I'll tell you all some other night, plase God: there they'd sit smoking – their faces quite plased with the pleasure of the pipe – amusing themselves and a crowd of people that would be listening to them with open mouths. Or, it's odds but there would be some droll young fellow among them taking a *rise* out of [teasing] them; and, positively, he'd often find them able enough for him, particularly ould Ned Mangin, that wanted at the time only four years of a hundred. The Lord be good to him, and rest his sowl in glory, it's he that was the pleasant ould man, and could tell a story with any one that ever got up.'[90]

After the fourth story, however, Carleton drops the *Rahmenerzählung* device, with this comment:

It was the original intention of the author to have made every man in the humble group about Ned M'Keown's hearth narrate a story illustrating Irish life, feeling, and manners; but on looking into the matter more closely, he had reason to think that such a plan, however agreeable for a time, would ultimately narrow the sphere of his work, and perhaps fatigue the reader by a superfluity of Irish dialogue and its peculiarities of phraseology. He resolved therefore, at the close of the Battle of the Factions to abandon his original design, and leave himself more room for description and observation.[91]

The next story begins with an address to 'Our readers ...': the author's voice now tends to replace those of fictional characters in narrative parts, and authorial comments become more obtrusive. It is as if Carleton had decided that to have his Irish subject-matter accepted as literature he had to adopt a form that was then considered more serious. There is still plenty of dialogue, though, and some accounts of storytelling – or of the collective transformation of stories:

The next day the story spread through the whole neighbourhood, accumulating in interest and incidents as it went. Where it received the touches, embellishments, and emendations with which it was amplified, it would be difficult to say; every one told it, forsooth, *exactly* as he heard it from another; but indeed it is not improbable that those through whom it passed, were unconscious of the additions it had received at their

tional embellishments, it is true, but none basically alters the nature of his wonder-tale nor its component episodes. Carleton's courage failed him, however, towards the end of the piece, when the storyteller, Ned, informs his listeners and us, that Jack Magennis, the hero of the story, has dreamt all that had been narrated. This calls the very nature of the folk tale in question.' **90** Ibid. 1. 105. The 'bloody hand' may be the one the original O'Neill cut off and threw ashore when approaching Ulster to become the ruler of the province – unless it is yet another reference to 'Balldeaerg' O Domhnaill (see p. 216). **91** Ibid. 1. 144.

hands. It is not unreasonable to suppose that imagination in such cases often colours highly without a premeditated design of falsehood.[92]

Later retellings or pastiches of traditional tales need not be framed in represented acts of storytelling, but there still are details concerning this kind of activity. Here is a Sunday morning scene; while the more pious part of the population is already deep in religious thoughts, others

collect together in various knots through the chapel, and amuse themselves by auditing or narrating anecdotes, discussing policy, or detraction; and in case it be summer, and the day of a fine texture, they scatter themselves into little crowds on the chapel-green, or lie at their length upon the grass in listless groups, giving way to chat and laughter. In this mode, laired on the sunny side of the ditches and hedges, or collected in rings round that respectable character, the Academician of the village, or some other well-known *Senachie*, or story-teller, they amuse themselves till the priest's arrival.[93]

It is clear, however, that Carleton wanted to be known as a full-fledged novelist, not a mere picturesque sketcher: 'My friends began [about 1836] to hint to each other, behind my back, that indeed I was a very clever writer; that I knew Irish life remarkably well; but that they were of opinion there was more of memory than imagination in my writing. "He is a fine fellow in his way – that is, at a *short story* or so – but he wants invention, and has not strength of wing for a long-sustained flight. He will never be able to write a novel ..." Accordingly [I] sat down and wrote *The Miser*.'[94] To change his medium may not have been such a good idea: it is generally admitted that Carleton was best in the shorter form. In his novels, though dialogue sometimes still has the energy of the spoken word and there are impressive scenes, we often miss the intensity of shorter texts and may find the author's prolixity indigestible. There are comparatively fewer references to oral sorytelling, and a minimal use of it as a literary device.

We note, however, that one of the novels, *The Black Prophet, a Tale of Irish Famine* (1846-7), develops and individualizes a type Carleton had obviously been impressed by, because he repeatedly referred to it both in his 'documentary' texts and in his fiction:[95] the doomsayer who laid claim to some form of inspiration or knew by heart all that had been foretold by unquestionable authorities – for instance about the place where the last battle for Ireland would be fought, or how an empire, or the world, would end. Prognostication itself is a kind of narrative where the future is combined, in paradoxical ways, with past and present. Here are two evocations of this type of discourse, marked off by special rhetorical devices, which show how Carleton used the same material in the 'documentary' and 'fictional' modes: the first text, 'Barney M'Haighrey, the Irish

92 Ibid. 2. 85. 93 *Traits and Stories* ... 1.121-2. 94 Introduction to the new 1848 edition of *Fardorougha the Miser* , xv. 95 For instance in 'Tubber Derg, or the Red Well', in *Traits and Stories* ... 2. 386-8.

Prophecy Man', appeared in the *Irish Penny Journal*, June 18, 1841,[96] the second extract is from the novel *The Black Prophet*: [97]

I

'... Now, I have a little book (indeed I left my books with a friend down at Errigle) that contains a prophecy of the milk-white hind an' the bloody panther, an' a forebodin' of the slaughter there's to be in the Valley of the Black Pig, as foretold by Beal Derg, or the prophet wid the red mouth, who never was known to speak but when he prophesied, or to prophesy but when he spoke.'

'The Lord bless an' keep us! – an' why was he called the Man wid the Red Mouth, Barney?'

'I'll tell you that; first, bekase he always prophesied about the slaughter an' fighting that was to take place in the time to come; an' secondly, bekase, while he spoke, the red blood always trickled out of his mouth, as a proof that what he foretould was true.'

'Glory be to God! but that's wondherful all out. Well, well!'

'Ay, an' Beal Derg, or the Red Mouth, is still livin'.'

'Livin'! why, is he a man of our time?'

'Our own time! The Lord help you! It's more than a thousand years since he made the prophecy. The case you see is this: he an' the ten thousand witnesses are lyin' in an enchanted sleep in one of the Montherlony mountains.'

'An' how is that known, Barney?'

'It's known. Every night at a certain hour one of the witnesses – an' they're all sogers, by the way – must come out to look for the sign that's to come.'

'An' what is that, Barney?'

'It's the fiery cross; an' when he sees one on aich of the four mountains of the north, he's to know that the same sign's abroad in all the other parts of the kingdom. Beal Derg an' his men are then to waken up, an' by their aid the Valley of the Black Pig is to be set free for ever.'

'And what is the Black Pig, Barney?'

'The Prosbytarian church, that stretches from Enniskillen to Darry, an' back again from Darry to Enniskillen.'

'Well, well, Barney, but prophecy is a strange thing, to be sure! Only think of men livin' a thousand years!'

'Every night one of Beal Derg's men must go to the mouth of the cave, which opens of itself, an' then look out for the sign that's expected. He walks up to the top of the mountain, an' turns to the four corners of the heavens, to thry if he can see it; an' when he finds that he cannot, he goes back to Beal Derg, who, afther the other touches him, starts up, an' axes him, "Is the time come?" He replies, "No; the *man is*, but the *hour* is *not* !" an' that instant they're both asleep again. Now, you see, while the soger is on the mountain top, the mouth of the cave is open, an' any one may go in that might happen to see it. One man it appears did, an' wishin' to know from curiosity whether the sogers were dead or livin', he touched one of them wid his hand, who started up an' axed him the same question. "Is the time come?" Very fortunately he said *No*; an' that minute the soger was as sound in his trance as before.' [Cf. p. 103.]

96 Reproduced in *Tales and Sketches ...* (1845) 206ff. **97** Op. cit. 12-15.

'An', Barney, what did the soger mane when he said, "The man is, but the hour is not"?'

'What did he mane? I'll tell you that. The man is Bonyparty, which manes, when put into proper explanation, the *right side* ; that is, the true cause. Larned men have found *that* out.'

II

... a strongly built man, above the middle size, whose complexion and features were such as no one could look on with indifference, so strongly were they indicative of a two-fold character, or we should say, calculated to make a twofold impression. At one moment you might consider him handsome, and at another his countenance filled you with an impression of repugnance, if not of absolute aversion, so stern and inhuman were the characteristics which you read in it ... [He comments on the hard times – we are in 1817, at the beginning of a period of famine.] 'If that change has come on you, you know, it didn't come without warnin' to the counthry; there's a man livin' that foretould as much – that seen it comin' – ay, ever since the pope was made prisoner, for that was what brought Bonaparte's fate – that's now the cause of the downfall of everything upon him.'

'An' it was the hard fate for us, as well, as for himself,' replied Sullivan; 'little he thought, or little he cared, for what he made us suffer, an' for what he's makin' us suffer still, by the come-down that the prices have got.'

'Well, but he's sufferin' himself more than any of us,' replied Donnel; 'however, that was prophesied too; it's read of in the ould chronicles. "An eagle will be sick," says St Columbkill, "but the bed of the sick eagle is not a tree, but a rock; an' there he must suffer till the curse of the Father is removed from him; an' then he'll get well, an' fly over the world".'

'Is that in the prophecy, Donnel?'

'It's St Columbkill's words I'm spakin'.'

'Troth, at any rate,' replied Sullivan, 'I didn't care we had back the war prices again; aither that or that the rents wor let down to meet the poor prices we have now. This woful saison, along wid the low prices and the high rents, houlds out a black and terrible look for the counthry, God help us!'

'Ay,' returned the Black Prophet, for it was he, 'if you only knew it.'

'Why, was that, too, prophesied?' inquired Sullivan.

'Was it? No; but ax yourself *is* it. Isn't the Almighty, in his wrath, this moment proclaimin' it through the heavens and the airth? Look about you, and say what is it you see that doesn't foretell famine – famine – famine! Doesn't the dark wet day, an' the rain, rain, rain, foretell it? Doesn't the rottin' crops, the unhealthy air, an' the green damp foretell it? Doesn't the sky without a sun, the heavy clouds, an' the angry fire of the West foretell it? Isn't the airth a page of prophecy, an' the sky a page of prophecy, where every man may read of famine, pestilence, an' death? The airth is softened for the grave, an' in the black clouds of heaven you may see the death-hearse movin' slowly along – funeral afther funeral – funeral afther funeral – an' nothing to folly them but lamentation an' woe, by the widow an' orphan – the fatherless, the motherless, an' the childless – woe an' lamentation – lamentation an' woe.'

Donnel Dhu, like every prophecy-man of his kind – a character in Ireland, by the way, that has nearly, if not altogether, disappeared – was provided with a set of prophetic declamations suited to particular occasions and circumstances, and these he recited in a voice of high and monotonous recitative, that caused them to fall with a very impressive effect upon the minds and feelings of his audience. In addition to this, the very nature of his subject rendered a figurative style and suitable language necessary, a circumstance which, aided by a natural flow of words, and a felicitous illustration of imagery – for which, indeed, all prophecy men were remarkable – had something peculiarly fascinating and persuasive to the class of persons he was in the habit of addressing. The gifts of these men, besides, were exercised with such singular delight, that the constant repetition of their oracular exhibitions by degrees created an involuntary impression on themselves, that ultimately rose to a kind of wild and turbid enthusiasm, partaking at once of imposture and fanaticism. Many of them were, therefore, nearly as much the dupes of the delusions that proceeded from their own heated imaginations as the ignorant people who looked upon them as oracles; for we know that nothing so much generates impostures as credulity. [Later, Donnel Dhu tries to dupe the other man's family with fabricated prophecies, and is led to destruction because he has failed to interpret a dream which announces his own future ...]

This was only one peculiar type of 'storyteller'; other narrative usages and functions are illustrated in Carleton's novels. In *The Emigrants of Ahadarra; a Tale of Irish Life* (1847), for instance, we overhear informal conversation in a poteen still-house at midnight and witness the tantalizing *non*-telling of a story:

'I am right, I say: I remember it well, for although I wasn't there myself, my father was, an' I often h'ard him say – God rest his soul!' – here he reverently took off his hat and looked upwards – 'I often h'ard him say that Paddy Keenan gave Mullin the first knockdown blow, an' Pether – I mane no disrespect, but far from it – give us your hand, man alive you're goin' to be married upon my shister to-morrow, plaise God! – mashter, you'll come, remember? you'll be as welcome as the flowers o'May, mashter – so, Pether, as I was sayin' – I mane no offince nor disrespect to you or yours, for you are, an' ever was, a dacent family, an' well able to fight your corner when it came upon you – but still, Pether – an' for all that I say it – an' I'll stand to it – I'll stand to it – that's the chat! – that, man for man, there never was one o' your seed, breed, or generation, able to fight a Keenan – that's the chat! – here's luck!'[98]

In *The Tithe Proctor* (1849), seditious storytelling takes place between members of a peasant secret organization.[99]

Carleton's texts – particularly the shorter ones written in the 1830s and 40s – multiply details concerning material culture and popular entertainments: festivities and wakes, athletic competitions and ritual fights, drinking and socializing, games, singing, music and dancing – and narrative activities of all kinds. A number of traditional tales and legends are retold by him, including variants of international types and more specifically Irish ones: 'The Legend of Knockmany' about Finn disguised as a baby to defeat a giant (cf. p. 104), stories of benevo-

98 *The Emigrants of Ahadarra* 41. 99 *The Tithe Proctor* 134-5.

lent or malevolent fairies, of 'profit-stealing' witches, of treading on 'the hungry grass' ...). It does not make him a folklorist,[100] because he did not deliberately set out to collect such material, did not classify it, and freely adapted it to his own purposes. But his intimate knowledge of how country people had acted and talked in the first third of the century cannot be doubted; Maria Edgeworth generously wrote, in 1847: 'I have read all the works that Carleton has yet written, and I must confess that I never knew Irish life until I read them.'[101] His delight in language, his talent for rendering Irish dialogue and his skill in making people and situation live through speech, are obvious too. At the same time there are curious ambiguities in his attitudes partly due to uprootedness and frustration, and a mix of stylistic registers. He had chosen to become a semi-outsider, yet wanted to retain something of the old life and kept evoking the world of his childhood which his imagination never left ('I was happy then for the first and last time ... Nurchasy [where the Carleton family lived between about 1805 and 1809] to me was paradise')[102] – but he had separated himself from this cultural milieu to 'become a more important member of society',[103] earning with some the reputation of a renegade and with others that of a boorish upstart; he was torn between popular and high culture, somehow regretting the former but aspiring to the latter, and whereas critics have repeatedly tried to praise him by calling him a 'seanachie'[104] we may suppose that he would not be satisfied with such a title. He wanted to be a writer, though he was not always at ease in the mould his time seemed to impose on what was defined as 'literature'.

Differences between the early Irish novelists' ways of drawing verbal portraits of storytellers and of depicting traditional storytelling scenes may be due to the social angle from which they viewed the subject and to their degree of familiarity with it, to what they knew of their target readership – in London or at home, and of course to their individual perceptive power and creative talent. Similarities might be explained by the fact that the same objective reality was under scrutiny, but also by the established conventions of the genre in which those portraits and scenes had to function.

Storytelling scenes could make different contributions to a novel: they could have a decisive role to play in the main action, but more often they were relatively extraneous material contributing to the evocation of a social setting, provided comic relief, or generated an atmosphere, sometimes assuming a symbolic significance. The storytelling itself could be described as an arrested tableau of genre painting, or, essentially through dialogue, be recreated in a dynamic scene where the interrelationship between performers and audience was highlighted. Popular modes of narrative and of speech could offer contrasts to a more elabo-

---

100 André Boué *William Carleton, Romancier Irlandais* 208: 'Carleton n'est pas un folkloriste. Il n'en a ni les buts ni les méthodes'. 101 Quoted in *Illustrated Dublin Journal* 2 November 1861. 102 *Autobiography* 23, 40. 103 Ibid. 198. 104 Thomas Davis as quoted on p. 210, or Barry Sloan in *The Pioneers of Anglo-Irish Fiction* 173.

rate literary technique and style. An in-set narrative might be impregnated with thematic associations which planted some hints concerning what would later happen in the main plot. The 'traditional storyteller' could be marked with positive or negative values, but most often, as a secondary character or only part of the social setting, he/she tended to be a stock figure constructed around a limited set of traits. Even if reduced to a voice, an outward appearance and the focus of attention in a group, he/she might be endowed with some mysterious power. When the tale-spinner is shown in action and made real through speech, vivid details can be striking, particularly if the rest of the novel creaks with techniques which were accepted then but seem obsolete now.

When novelists of the first half of the nineteenth century referred to or represented aspects of Irish rural storytelling, their purpose may have been just to add picturesque touches to their books, but they could also make it significant — to emphasize social polarities, or point to an ambiguous relationship between truth and lies (Edgeworth); or romanticize a more or less mythical past and a relatively elementary conception of national specificity (Lady Morgan); or exaggerate supposed national characteristics so as to meet the demand for stage-Irish monologues and comic situations (Lover); or preach education and reconciliation while providing an element of local colour (Hall); or expose a symptom of Irish Catholic barbarity (O'Sullivan) ... The Banim brothers and Griffin showed that storytelling and rumours were a normal social activity associated with both pleasant and horrible aspects of Irish life. Carleton offered a view of diversified kinds of oral arts and of their essential roles in the life of a society which was vanishing like his own youth. Significantly, scenes of traditional storytelling were for the most part set neither in strictly contemporary Ireland nor in a distant past but one generation back, in a no-man's land between the present and the historical: a zone of more or less nostalgic recollection and testimony by old witnesses, when Ireland was supposedly not yet changing very much – for the better or the worse.

One aspect of the reality writers were trying to represent or to play with was language itself and the sociolects of a certain community, whether as a ridiculing mark of inferiority or as perhaps respectable evidence of originality. That there were peculiar Irish ways of using English was obvious, and those who lived in Ireland could notice that in fact several kinds of non-standard English were spoken: there was the English brought to Ireland by early planters and preserving features that were no longer common in England, while there was a strong influence of Scots and Scottish Gaelic in northern counties, and there were regional varieties spoken by people whose first or ancestral language was Irish and which preserved some of the latter's features, for instance using the sounds of Irish to pronounce English words, or imitating in English the Irish verbal system. Such details were hardly known abroad, however, and there were no clear linguistic concepts and methods to describe and analyse dialects. Most of the novelists who wrote about Ireland (as well as travellers and early 'folklorists') were confronted with the problem of rendering the peculiarities of spoken Hiberno-English in written form, and there was no perfect system to do it. A number of tricks had been used more or less intensively in comedies and were adapted to the prose essays or fiction of the first half of the nineteenth century. The easiest device to convey a flavour of the vernacular, at the lexical level, was the insertion of a few Irish words or idioms; the least knowledgeable writers contented themselves with ejaculations (*musha! wirra!*); others inserted words or even phrases which could be explained in notes or in a glossary, or left to produce an outlandish impression. As regards the English vocabulary, one could emphasize polysyllabic words: indeed, those whose native language was Irish had no particular reason to prefer Saxon words when a Latinized diction provided more congenial rhythm along with a touch of 'larnin'. For comic effects one could emphasize the resulting malapropisms (e.g. in Carleton's tales 'collusion' for 'allusion', 'embargo' for 'lumbago', 'metamurphied' for 'metamorphosed' ...). Another common device was the representation of non-standard pronunciation through peculiar spelling. Samuel Lover, who had reasons to be more concerned than others with phonology because he actually uttered the texts in his one-man-shows and knew that readers might want to memorize them for recitation, preceded his *Legends and Tales of Ireland* by 'some general observations ... on the pronunciation of certain sounds in the English language by the Irish peasantry'.[105] He mentioned the 'curtailing of words' (dropping the last consonant, usually replaced in writing by an apostrophe); 'sharpening' (marked by adding an 'h' to a 'd' or a 't'); and changes of vowels or diphthongs. His list of peculiarities is not exhaustive and he sees no system in it; but he cannot be blamed for living at a time when phonology and dialectology hardly existed, and when it was probably not uncommon to regard Hiberno-English as just another case of obscurantism and anarchy. Specific grammatical features were difficult to understand for those who did not know Irish, and were therefore at first not so often imitated. One settled for a few non-standard uses of demonstrative adjectives or pronouns, apparent breaches of concord, and non-orthodox past or participial forms of strong verbs. Other Irish turns of phrase and rhythmic effects would be systematically reproduced only from the end of the century. Relative linguistic imprecision did not embarrass the writers we have dealt with, but there were two problems they were likely to be aware of. First, deviant spelling and grammar tended to ridicule those who were thus placed outside the readers' norms: it was an advantage if one wanted to raise a smile or to stigmatize the Irish as inept, but a drawback for those writers who wanted to plead their cause. The other problem was that, in such attempts to capture Irish speech the accumulation of oddities in more than one sentence or paragraph made reading difficult. Would the reader accept a continual presence of such idiosyncrasies of speech? Maria Edgeworth used as few Irishisms as possible to maintain the

105 *Legends and Tales of Ireland* 16.

awareness of a distinctly Hiberno-English voice. Carleton, when he revised his texts for new editions, considerably reduced Irish or dialect features. But novels remained characterized by the presence of the voices of different societal groups, with an interplay of linguistic varieties.

B. IN THE SECOND HALF OF THE NINETEENTH CENTURY

In this period the number of novels written or set in Ireland may have increased threefold; I have read only a small proportion of them, but there seems comparatively less to glean for my research. Evocations of the Irish peasant society were less appealing, and renderings of 'traditional oral storytelling' less numerous in novels; perhaps in part because the rural world had lost much of its vitality or strangeness, or because many novel-readers now had expectations which did not favour such material. The changing taste of readers and writers may have reduced interest in ethnic peculiarities and serious native eloquence while a partly different national awareness, or reaction against it, could restrain for a time the exploitation of what had earlier seemed comic or picturesque. One characteristic of much writing about Ireland, however, remained: contrary to the convention abided by in the literature of several other countries, the poor were seldom represented as inarticulate. I shall focus on five (or six) writers, of unequal literary standing and belonging to different social environments, who did draw upon folklore, for varied purposes.

The first had started writing in the preceding period, but changed in the course of time. Born in Dublin of Huguenot stock and educated at TCD like C.R. Maturin, Joseph Sheridan Le Fanu (1814-73) is, like him, still read for his weird fiction; he seems to have had a better knowledge of Irish oral traditions, and certainly used them more extensively in part of his work. He was twenty-four when he began to publish stories in the *Dublin University Magazine*. They were offered as having been collected in the south of Ireland by a Catholic priest interested in 'the marvellous and whimsical' he found in local 'superstitions' – the first text, 'The Ghost of the Bonesetter' (January 1838), illustrated the belief that 'the corpse last buried is obliged, during his juniority of internment, to supply his brother tenants of the churchyard in which he lies, with fresh water to allay the burning thirst of purgatory', hence a furious race when two funeral parties were approaching the graveyard at the same time. The pseudo-collector reports the words of a supposed informant, with the current spelling tricks for the rendering of dialect:

I tell the following particulars, as nearly as I can recollect them, in the words of the narrator. It may be necessary to observe that he was what is termed a *well-spoken* man, having for a considerable time instructed the ingenious youth of his native parish in such of the liberal arts and sciences as he found it convenient to profess – a circumstance

which may account for the occurrence of several big words, in the course of this narrative, more distinguished for euphonious effect, than for correctness of application. I proceed then, without further preface, to lay before you the wonderful adventures of Terry
Neil.

'Why, thin, 'tis a quare story, an' as thrue as you're sittin' there; and I'd make bould
to say there isn't a boy in the seven parishes could tell it better nor crickther than
myself. For 'twas my father himself it happened to, an' many's the time I heerd it out
iv his own mouth; an' I can say, an' I'm proud av that same, my father's word was as
incredible as any squire's oath in the counthry; an' if a poor man got into any unlucky
throuble, he was the boy id go into the court an' prove; but that doesn't signify – he was
as honest and as sober a man, barrin' he was a little bit too partial to the glass, as you'd
find in a day's walk.'[106]

Formally typical of much of what was published in the first half of the century,
it is also a piece of macabre humour, which finally dismisses the supernatural
experience as a dream. The tone of Le Fanu's later writings would be different.

There is no doubt that he had heard storytellers, and there may be some
faithful report in his 'Ghost Stories of Chapelizod' ('these true tales', he calls
them), which appeared in the same periodical in 1851: he had spent twelve years
of his childhood (1814-26) near that place and situated the events he was reporting (not in the comic vein this time) 'about thirty years ago' or 'some thirty-five
years ago'. He had spent the next seven years on the Limerick-Clare border, and
heard there the 'Stories of Lough Guir' which were published much later (1870)
in *All the Year Round*. His informant, Anne Bailey or Baily (born *c.*1769), also
appears in Mary Carbery's *The Farm by Lough Gur*.[107] Here is her portrait by
Le Fanu:

When the present writer was a boy of twelve or thirteen, he first made the acquaintance
of Miss Anne Baily, of Lough Guir, in the county of Limerick. She and her sister were
the last representatives at that place, of an extremely good name in the county. They
were both what is termed 'old maids,' and at that time past sixty. But never were old
ladies more hospitable, lively, and kind, especially to young people. They were both
remarkably agreeable and clever. Like all old county ladies of their time, they were great
genealogists, and could recount the origin, generations, and intermarriages, of every
county family of note. These ladies were visited at their house at Lough Guir by Mr
Crofton Croker; and are, I think, mentioned, by name, in the second series of his fairy
legends ...

Miss Anne Baily's conversation ran oftener than her sister's upon the legendary and
supernatural; she told her stories with the sympathy, the colour, and the mysterious air
which contribute so powerfully to effect, and never wearied of answering questions about
the old castle, and amusing her young audience with fascinating little glimpses of old
adventure and bygone days. My memory retains the picture of my early friend very dis-

106 *Ghost Stories and Mysteries* 182. **107** Op. cit. 114: '[The Baily sisters] seemed to know
the genealogy and family history of half Ireland, and they liked to tell the legends and stories
of Lough Gur.'

tinctly. A slim straight figure, above the middle height; a general likeness to the full-length portrait of that delightful Countess d'Aulnois, to whom we all owe our earliest and most brilliant glimpses of fairy-land; something of her gravely-pleasant countenance, plain, but refined and ladylike, with that kindly mystery in her side-long glance and uplifted finger, which indicated the approaching climax of a tale of wonder.[108]

This portrait of a storyteller familiar with tradition but belonging to a class distinctly above the peasantry confirms that Le Fanu knew something of Irish folklore – from the distance which was normally that of the Anglo-Irish, though he also had brief but direct contact with the lower Catholic levels of the rural population when hiking through the country with his brother. The above quotation shows that he also had literary contacts with non-Irish tales of the supernatural – and not only Madame d'Aulnoy's fairytales. His 'Stories of Lough Guir', dealing with Geároid Iarla (see p. 103), with banshees and various apparitions, are not presented in the pseudo-oral mode of his early tales. Introducing a 'ghost story', he commented on the difficulty of rendering oral telling in print when not courting comic effects:

In my youth I heard a great many Irish family traditions, more or less of a supernatural character, some of them very peculiar, and all, to a child at least, highly interesting. One of these I will now relate, though the translation to cold type from oral narrative, with all the aids of animated human voice and countenance, and the appropriate *mise-en-scène* of the old fashioned parlour fireside and its listening circle of excited faces, and, outside, the wintry blast and moan of leafless boughs, with the occasional rattle of the clumsy old window-frame behind the shutter and curtain, as the blast swept by, is at best a trying one.[109]

The fact that, from 1861, one of Le Fanu's close friends was the folklorist Patrick Kennedy (whose work will be examined in the next chapter) may account for the return of folklore themes in some of his later stories; when he strayed from what had become a psychological terror of his own, he still preferred folktales of macabre humour to heroic fantasy, and his abiding concern with the occult was not attuned to 'Celtic' mysteries, as shown by a remark in a letter to his friend denouncing 'the Ossianic fables' as insupportable curiosities, and preferring a certain story of the 'wicked fellow in the coffin who pursued the girl looking for work'[110] – a version of 'The Man Who Had No Story'. The latter group of tales will be discussed in Chapter 12, but here we may note a possible link between its theme of telling or not telling and the fact that narrating, revealing or hiding, are almost obsessive motifs in a novel le Fanu was writing at about that time, and which would be one of James Joyce's favourites: *The*

108 Ibid. 144-5.   109 'Ultor de Lacy: A Legend of Cappercullen', first published in the *Dublin University Magazine* in 1861. *Best Ghost Stories* 444.   110 Quoted in W.J. McCormack *Sheridan Le Fanu and Victorian Ireland* 242.

House by the Churchyard. Published in book form in 1863, it had been serialized from 1861 in the *Dublin University Magazine* Le Fanu now owned and edited. The plot concerns the solving of two murder mysteries, but the book is also an evocation of life towards the end of the eighteenth century, at all social levels, in a small town or village near Dublin, and this 'little world of Chapelizod' (a microcosm of Ireland, though not set beyond the Bog of Allen as much 'national' literature would be) is characterized by constant chat and some ominous silences. The opening words of the loquacious narrator are 'We are going to talk, if you please ...'; then 'the gossip of the town' never ends[111] What is untrue is certain to be repeated:

> Next morning, you may be sure, the news was all over the town of Chapelizod. All sorts of cross rumours and wild canards, of course, were on the wind, and every new fact or fib borne to the doorstep with the fresh eggs, or the morning's milk and butter, was carried by the eager servant into the parlour, and swallowed down with their toast and tea by the staring company.[112]

While lies are accepted as truth, truth may be mistaken for fiction: the villain, who passes for an honest gentleman, has success with stories of crime and imprisonment he seems to be inventing but tells in a 'biting way'. The parson illustrates his sermons with moralizing *exempla* which are to the point – but also tells wild, obsolete or politically dangerous tales to his ailing daughter: 'He would relate stories of banshees, and robberies, and ghosts, and hair-breadth escapes, and "rapparees", and adventures in the wars of King James, which he heard told in his nonage by the old folk, long vanished, who remembered those troubles.'[113] His old servant is garrulous too ('She had all sorts of old-world tales of wonder and adventure')[114] and contributes an in-set narrative concerning the ghostly hand that is supposed to haunt one of the houses in the neighbourhood. On the clergyman's daughter, the eerie legend has the sedative effect the stories of ancient bards were supposed to bring: 'And so on, and on, and on flowed the stream of old Sally's narrative, while Lilias dropped into dreamless sleep.'[115] Meanwhile the real hand of the villain is active, and the Liffey seems to know that one should take him more seriously: 'The river at the foot of the walk seemed snorting some inarticulate story of horror.'[116] The criminal and his future victim are troubled by symbolic narratives: warning dreams. Not to say what one has experienced can have serious consequences; a doctor comments on this point: ' "I tell you what it is, Mrs Mack, you have something on your mind, my dear Madam, and till it's off, you'll never be better ... There's more paralysis, apoplexy, heart-diseases, and lunacy, caused in one year by that sort of silly secrecy and moping than by – ... Tell it you must to *some* one, or take the consequences." '[117] Those who know little, speak: '[The boy] could tell them but

111 *The House by the Churchyard* 95-6. 112 Ibid. 380. 113 Ibid. 262. 114 Ibid. 49. 115 Ibid. 52. 116 Ibid. 201. 117 Ibid. 128.

little – only the same story over and over.'[118] But the most crucial revelation is repeatedly postponed: ' "In Heaven's name, have you come to tell me all you know?" "Well, maybe – no", answered the clerk. "I don't know: I'll tell you something. I'm going, you see, and I came here on my way; and I'll tell you more than last time, but not all – not all yet." '[119] This, of course, is the technique of suspense which Le Fanu himself was practising. But there is probably more than that: for him, who was now haunted by recurrent inconclusive nightmares, the truth about the forces of evil around us and in us was difficult to reveal and to accept. Yet it was essential both to tell stories about it, and to know how to interpret and assess those one heard.

Le Fanu wrote for an Anglo-Irish and British audience, only part of which would appreciate his sophisticated interpretation of the nature of storytelling. For common people in Ireland and for the Irish abroad, the most popular novel was, for several generations, Charles Kickham's *Knocknagow; or, The Homes of Tipperary* (1873); it offered an elegiac celebration of ordinary rural life as well as strong condemnation of the land-tenure system, more particularly when benevolent paternalism was replaced by pecuniary self-interest. The novel opens with the arrival of the conventional stranger to a community: an English visitor will observe peculiarities of the Irish scene. 'I'd like to witness as many of the customs of the country as possible,' he conveniently announces.[120] He discovers religious practices, is initiated into customs like 'hunting the wren' and sporting events such as a hurling match, a sledge-hammer contest and bull-baiting. There is plenty of singing, instrumental music and dancing. He discovers 'the phraseology of the peasantry' – which the author sometimes finds difficult to render: 'We are not sure whether it is possible to convey by the means of the English alphabet the only name ever given to potatoes in Knocknagow ... The nearest approach we can make to the word we were about writing is "puetas" or "p'yehtes". "See if them puetas is goin' to bile," said Mat Donovan; " 'twould be time for 'em".'[121] But the foreign observer never attends a traditional storytelling session. As his limited perspective is gradually abandoned, we realize that there are – or have been – narrative traditions: '[Mat Donovan's] latch was often raised not only by neighbours who came in for a 'shanahus' of an evening, but travellers who were accustomed to pass the way made it a point to light their pipes at the bright turf fire.'[122] We hardly witness such sharing of *seanchas*, however.[123] Here and there, legends are alluded to: the discovery of a 'crock-of-gold'; what happened to the head of Father Sheehy, executed in 1766 for alleged involvement with the Whiteboys; a haunted house; the Black Dog waiting for victims at a well – but the stories are not told. We almost hear how Slievenamon

118 Ibid. 207. 119 Ibid. 271. 120 *Knocknagow* 3. 121 Ibid. 142-3. 122 Ibid. 146. 123 R.V. Comerford *Charles Kickham; a Study in Irish Nationalism and Literature* 46: 'Antiquarianism of any kind, if it lacked political significance for the Ireland of his day, held no interest for Kickham.'

('Mountain of Women') got its name when Fionn mac Cumhaill organized a running competition up the mountain in order to choose a wife – having already carried his favourite to the summit the night before: 'He was the great chief of the Fenians long ago. The top of Slievenamon is called Shee-Fen after him. My grandfather would keep telling you stories about him for a month ... '[124] – but the story is only summed up in drab terms.

Kickham (1826-82) came, like the Banim brothers and Griffin half-a-century before, from the rural Catholic middle class, and had acquired an intimate knowledge of the poorer members of his society: 'We have lived amongst the peasantry, joined in their sports, sat by their fireside, listened to song and story, proverb and prophecy – till every pulse of their hearts has become familiar to us.'[125] Someone who knew him remembered that he was 'an ardent gatherer of local tradition from the peasants';[126] but as his sight and hearing were severely impaired by an accident when he was thirteen, it must have been difficult for him to keep in touch with storytelling activities. Far more than the Banims and Griffin, he was politically committed; as a Fenian he had advocated armed rebellion against English rule and had been jailed for it. As a novelist, however, he was more sentimental and prone to idealize some rural ways, preparing the image of the noble peasant which would be an emblem of Irishness in the early twentieth century. Whereas the writers of the first half of the nineteenth century explained the Irish peasantry to outsiders, his audience consisted of members of this world, and of those across the seas who had left it.[127]

By the end of the century, contemporary observation of ancient customs from a liberal ascendancy point of view remained possible only in remote corners of Ireland. The Honorable Emily Lawless (1845-1913), in *Grania: The Story of an Island* (1892), lets us hear, as a secondary character, 'the professional story-teller and at that time the oldest inhabitants of Inishmaan':

'Murdough Blake, wisha!' She went on, emptying the small black pipe she was smoking with a sharp rap upon the stones. 'Truth, 'tis the poor lot those Blakes of Alleenageeragh are, and always have been, so they are! There was this one's grandfather – myself remembers him when he was no older than this one – no, nor so old by a year – a fine bouchaleen you'd say to look at him – broad and bulky, and a clean skin, and a toss to his head as if all the rest in the place were but dirt and he picking his steps about amongst them. Well, what was he? He was just nothing, that is what he was, and so I

---

124 Ibid. 314. **125** Kickham 'The Peasantry', in *The Celt* 10 October 1857. **126** Quoted in James Healy *Life and Times of Charles J. Kickham* 8 – but cf. note 123. **127** R.V. Comerford, op. cit. 210: '*Knocknagow* filled the role of a national epic. It depicted a past that possessed the aura of a golden age and was peopled with a goodly number of heroes and heroines. Here a society preoccupied with the ownership of the land could presume to see an explanation of its own origins in a struggle against the vicissitudes of insecurity of tenure. Most important of all, here painted in touching and memorable fashion, were the virtues that this society prized, the emotions that it felt, and the values that it exalted.'

tell you, women, not worth a thraneen [*tráithnín*: a straw], no, nor the half of a thraneen ... There is a story that I could tell you about that same Malachy Blake would make the very eyes of you start out of your head, so it would. But there – 'tis a poor case, God knows, to be telling stories to them that knows nothing; a poor case, a very poor case!' ... 'Did I ever tell you women both about Kathy O'Callaghan, that lived over near Aillyhaloo when I was a girl? ... She would laugh when you talked of the good people, and she would say that she would as soon go up at night to the Phooka's hole as not, which everyone knows is all but the same as death. As for the *cohullen druith* [*cochallín draíochta*: a little magic hood, to live in the ocean] with my own two ears I heard her say she did not believe that there was such a thing! though my grandfather, God save his soul! saw one once on the head of a merrow [*murúch*: mermaid] hard by the Glassen rock. But, faith! I haven't the time nor the strength to be telling you the half of her folly and nonsense, nor couldn't I if I took the night to do it! ... Well, one day' – here the narrator paused, looked first at one and then at the other of her listeners, coughed, spat, twitched the big cloak higher round her shoulders, and settled herself down again in her chair with an air of intense satisfaction. 'One day ... ' ... The two listeners remained silent a minute after the tale had ended. Peggy Dowd filled her pipe and puffed at it solemnly, with the air of one who has fulfilled a social duty and sustained a widely-known reputation.[128]

Emily Lawless was writing three quarters of a century after Lady Morgan (cf. p. 233), and her portrait of an Aran storyteller is not romantic; it rather embodies what the young and impetuous protagonist of the novel experiences as stifling in the close-knit community. Nationalists did not like the book.

To novelists looking for an epic subject, it now seemed that they should try and reconstruct the distant past. When Emily Lawless chose a *seanchaí* as the protagonist of one of her books set at the time of the Desmond Rebellion in 1583, she made him feel already outmoded then: 'All the tales are done and told, lady *girshas* [*girseacha*: young girls], all the good tales are done and told! There are no more left! All over! all over!'[129]

What could more popular prose fiction aimed at the Irish public do with the exploits or tragedies of ancient heroes? The material had been made available to a large audience by Patrick Weston Joyce in his *Old Celtic Romances* (1879): 'I have tried to tell the stories as I conceive the old shenachies themselves would have told them, if they had used English instead of Gaelic'.[130] Perhaps inspired – for the general frame but certainly not the tone – by Ferguson's *Hibernian Nights' Entertainments*, as well as by the publications of the defunct Ossianic Society and by P.W. Joyce's book, Patrick Joseph McCall first serialized in *The Shamrock* and then produced in book form his *Fenian Nights' Entertainments* (1897), to make 'the old legends of pre-Christian Erin known and attractive to the peasantry' and 'to illustrate the localisms of a district' (Forth and Bargy).[131]

128 *Grania* 88-9, 145-6, 150, 156. 129 *Maelcho* (1894). 130 Op. cit. vii. 131 *The Fenian Nights' Entertainments* 131. It was claimed that the dialect of English spoken in that part of Wexford was 'Elizabethan'.

McCall (1861-1919) was a patriot and a founder member, with Yeats and Hyde, of the Irish National Literary Society in 1892. He was also a ballad-maker and collector and therefore, though Dublin born, relatively familiar with oral traditions. But in this book he used conventions which by then seemed dated: the Samuel Lover brand of funny storytelling, and the early-nineteenth-century ways of rendering Hiberno-English in writing, which Emily Lawless for instance now generally avoided. For partisans of an Irish Literary Revival, he might be the epitome of what had to be replaced by a more sophisticated art, and for folklorists he might seem to have no respect for tradition – but this in particular he would have denied. The introduction is in the idyllic mode:

Reader, fair or brave, I am about to take you in spirit down to the rich, moory vales of Bargy, to a comfortable thatched farmhouse. There we will go each Sunday evening to listen to one of our country's most famous legends, told by the inimitable Mick Neill to an appreciative audience ... Lifting the latch we enter the house, and leaving the upper room and parlour to our left we turn into the kitchen. Ah, you are admiring the snow-white dresser ... But look now at the happy people assembled around the fire, some on forms, others, the more favoured visitors, seated in home made easy chairs with curved backs, while the cat and dog stretch in amiable ease at each side of the fire.[132]

Then the storyteller is introduced:

You would know Mick Neill at once, without any description. There he is, in the middle, pulling a lighted furze stalk from the blaze, and applying it, with grave danger to his nose, in an effort to ignite the hard tobacco in his pipe. Now he is puffing with the air of a philosopher. Well, we are just in time. They have discussed the news in *The People* paper, and gossiped a little over the talk of the country heard that morning at the chapel gate, and now being invisible, we can listen without 'disturbing the congregation', as Mick would say himself, for the sight of a stranger would put them on pins and needles. Hush, we are in luck! Mick Neill has been asked for one of his 'thousand and one' stories, with which he is accustomed to beguile the long Sunday evenings from Hollantide to Candlemas.[133]

After disciplining his audience (cf. Carleton's 'Shanahus', p. 218), he starts narrating:

'Long an' merry ago – are yous listenin', boys an' girls? – there lived a king over Forth an' Bargy, an' the name he went be was Creevan Skewball (Sciath-Bheil), it wasn't Skew-ball [a famous horse] all out, if yous *are* so particular; but it isn't a hunthered mile away from the name, an' the racehorse that ran with Miss Grizzle, the bonny grey mare, for five hundhered guineas on the plains of Kildare may have been called afther him for all we know. But anyway, talkin' ov king Creevan, for feerd yous 'ud be axin', I'm goin' to tell yous this much, that *I* didn't know him, an' I'm sure yous didn't know him, nor

132 Ibid. ix-x.   133 Ibid. x-xi.

did anyone else I ever heard tell ov know him, not even 'Jack the Road'; but sure, if he didn't live sometime or other we wouldn't be to hearin' about him, at all, at all! But live he did, an' that's as much as can be sed about the most of us when we're *planted* – God help us! Well, at the time I'm tellin' about – 'twas in the *old man'*s time, Mosey, if you want to know! – there was a gang ov English savages come over to gobble us all up, an' poor King Creevan was put to the pin ov his collar to know what to do with the bla'-guards ...[134]

The stories, as they are 'told', are crude pastiches of the art; but the story-teller's behaviour can be true to type, and perhaps to reality as well. On the fifth evening he is still interlarding his narrative with personal remarks to maintain contact while asserting his authority:

Well, long long ago, an' long beyant that even – musha, don't be lookin' so *groomach* [*gruama*: sad, sombre] Mosey! – shure, it's only a way I have –, as I was sayin', long, long ago, there lived a great prence in Ulster, be the name ov Cucullin. Be all accounts he was a great lepper in his day; it stood him upon (was useful), of'en and of'en, when he'd be circumvented be some vagabone or other, to be able to show his inimies a clane pair ov heels, be the fair dent ov soopleness. Well it so happened, that a purty little princess, be the name ov Emir, tuk his taste, an' as she didn't mislike him, up he goes to her father ...[135]

Ancient heroes and heroines are thus treated familiarly. The last night of story-telling comes at the end of the dark half of the year – an accurate notation:

An' now yous have h'ard me story; an' haith, it's the last I'll tell for another month of Sundas, till the nights get long agen; for we'll have somethin' else to think about besides storytellin'. There's me darlin' Mothy asleep, after all me trouble; an' the rest o' yous not much betther! So; I'm thinkin' yous have all got tired o' me stories Oh, was you ploughin' to-day, boys? Ho, ho! Then you was't in much humour for listenin', I can tell yous – faith, I wondher yous come down at all to-night; but plaze God, we'll have many a story together again, when we're not over busy![136]

With this particular book – hardly a novel, of course – we have moved from one extreme, the 'ossianic' bards or bardesses of a Lady Morgan at the beginning of the century, to another which was largely a fabrication too, though probably with some distillation of the qualities of real people. It was easy to build a case against McCall's attempt: his 'dialect' was over-obtrusive; the idea of using it to teach peasants their older traditions, taken from scholarly books but comically transformed, could seem ludicrous or pathetic when other urban patriots were brandishing the ancient repertoire as an object of veneration and as material for poetry or serious drama. Field collectors, however, would soon find out that the peasants themselves could treat Fionn and Cú Chulainn in a familiar way.

134 Ibid. 1-2. **135** Ibid. 41-2. **136** Ibid. 130.

For a comic treatment of contemporary conversational storytelling seen from the upper-class point of view, we may turn to the fictional *Experiences of an Irish R.M.* written by 'Somerville and Ross' (Edith Somerville, 1858-1949, and Violet Martin, 1862-1915), which began to appear in a periodical in 1898 and in book form the following year. The authors were in daily contact with the people of the west of Ireland, and were shrewd observers. In their best novels they recorded the decline of their own social world, and the lower classes remained in the background – there seemed to be no hope of improving them as some had been trying to do in Maria Edgeworth's day. The greatest success of the pair of writers was the series of comic sketches of Irish eccentricities mentioned above. They composed it together in conversation,[137] first looking for basic motifs and then carefully building plots where the 'master-servant' relationship was often reversed and imaginative anarchy triumphed. Ladies of quality, they felt no sympathy for Irish nationalism and did not idealize the peasantry, but they had an accurate sense of Irish dialogue. In two of their *R.M.* stories founded on farcically catastrophic series of events, a large part of the humour derives from the fact that outsiders take folklore more self-consciously than the natives do. In 'The Last Day of Shraft', the elderly stepbrother of the magistrate's English wife is – apparently without reason – an Irish language and folklore enthusiast; it already makes him odd, and at any rate he has only confused notions of what he is collecting. He is taken to an island said to be an 'unworked mine' of oral material; the natives make fun of him, and before the police arrive to find him in a place full of illicit *poteen* he collects only a fairly recent comic ballad (which another part of the story has enacted): ' "Sing up, Paddy boy, for the gentleman! Arrah, what ails ye, Paddy! Don't be ashamed at all! 'Tis a lovely song, your honour, sir!" (this to my brother-in-law). "Is it an ancient song?" I heard Maxwell inquire with serious eagerness. "It is, your honour: 'twas himself made it up lasht year".'[138] The atmosphere of the 'ceili' is well rendered and the contrast between the collector and the natives is interesting – (the R.M. is the one who reports the scene):

The door opened into the frieze-covered backs of several men, and an evenly blended smell of whisky, turf-smoke, and crowded humanity steamed forth. The company made way for me, awkwardly; I noticed a tendency amongst them to hold on each other, and there was a hilarious light in Mrs Brickley's eye as she hustled forward to meet me. My brother-in-law was sitting at a table by the window writing in a note-book by the last light of the waning day; he gave me a glance laden with affairs to which I was superfluous ...[139]

137 H. Robinson *Somerville & Ross: A Critical Appreciation* 42: 'The book in progress was talked into existence; the sentences were spoken, its phrases played with by both of them, and then the sentences written down by whoever happened to be holding the pen.'   138 *Experiences of an Irish R.M.* 270. The song – 'Nell Flaherty's Drake' – may have been composed in the first half of the nineteenth century.   139 Ibid. 268.

The element of caricature is obvious, but may be a useful corrective by insisting on the fact that popular verbal arts were intended primarily for entertainment as one of several activities inducing conviviality; and by the end of the nineteenth century it is perfectly fitting to have the collector as part of the picture. (A more subtle piece from the same book will be analysed in Chapter 13, along with the general theme of storytelling and truth.)

Though the Literary Revival, which will be examined in Chapter 9, was beginning to monopolize critical attention, the older local-colour school with its two basic tones – sentimental or comic – did not vanish overnight; indeed, it survived into the twentieth century, but more self-conscious literature now rejected it. As for renderings of Irish folktales and legends, they now tended to be treated as specialized material; I shall now resume the survey of such folkloristic activities as they developed, in a changing context, after the Great Famine.

8

Irish country life, folklore and nationalism in the second half of the nineteenth century

During this period, observers could get contradictory impressions of Ireland, because modern and archaic elements coexisted. Those who collected what was now more and more often called 'folklore' saw a fluid and conflictive situation, and some of them were influenced by the ways of approaching and publishing similar material abroad. This chapter opens with a rapid sketch of what was happening in rural Ireland, and more particularly of what might affect storytelling. It proceeds to an outline of theoretical issues and methods of folklore which dominated in this half-century, and of their relative impact in Ireland; then it examines what different kinds of collectors and editors had to say about storytellers there. Finally it evokes the crystallization, in the last decades of the century, of certain nationalist trends which assigned special functions to 'traditions' – a movement that would reach fruition after 1900.

We start in a devastated, demoralized rural world. Contemporary writers described the awful silence and apathy in the countryside during the Great Famine years (cf. p. 208), and half a century later an old person remembered the situation in Donegal: 'Sports and pastimes disappeared. Poetry, music and dancing stopped. They lost and forgot them all.'[1] After the 'Great Hunger', one had the impression that old patterns of behaviour had collapsed, that rural beliefs and values were discredited and the oral traditions of the Irish peasantry obliterated. William Wilde observed in 1851 that during the first three years of the calamity: 'the closest ties of kinship were dissolved; the most ancient and long-cherished usages of the people were disregarded; the once proverbial gaiety and lightheartedness of the peasant people seemed to have vanished completely, and village merriment or marriage festival was no longer heard of or seen throughout the regions desolated by the intensity and extent of the famine'.[2] The same year, in County Tipperary, John Dunne found collecting difficult:

Unfortunately, my researches cannot be now made with such facility as in by-gone days – and those not remote either – when the farmer and his group of labourers, from all parts of the country, sat down in the evening, their day of toil being over, with light hearts before a blazing turf fire and a *sciach* [*sciath*: a basket] of smiling potatoes, and

1 Quoted in Th. Gallagher *Paddy's Lament* 27 from a MS in the Irish Folklore Department at UCD. 2 Comment on the census of 1851, quoted in E. Estyn Evans *Irish Folkways* 295.

recounted in turn the tales of the olden time handed down to them from their fathers. Now, alas! the story-telling peasant is in the grave, the poor-house, or the wilds of America; and the farmer lies down at night with a heavy heart, brooding over his insurmountable difficulties and misfortunes.[3]

In the introduction to his *Ancient Music of Ireland*, in 1855, George Petrie also described a country where what used to be preserved – 'the songs and traditions' – had almost vanished.[4]

Historians may insist that the Famine did accelerate rather than initiate changes, but they have to admit that it was perceived as a great historical divide. The effects varied socially and geographically: some rich farmers whose sub-tenants no longer paid their rents had been the first to emigrate, but it was the lower classes who were decimated. The counties hardest hit were in the west and south-west, where the landless agricultural labourers and small cottiers were by far the most numerous victims. People could be filled with a sense of grievance, and some older traditions might pale in comparison with horrible episodes of this period – but it seems that what was fixed in the folk memory then was not willingly shared. When recollections of the ordeal were searched for a century later, after they had been transmitted through two or three generations of those who had stayed in the country,[5] many informants displayed a fatalistic attitude: it had been a punishment from God; the local community had not been directly involved, or at least the famine had been worse in other places; those who died in the parish were strangers ... The anguish of the time must have been remembered, but was too painful to be talked about or revealed outside the family circle; perhaps there was embarrassment or shame at a lack of solidarity (traditions of hospitality had been temporarily ignored), or just at having survived. On the other hand nationalist history gave the widest exposure to the catastrophe, and insisted on British responsibility.

Those who were interested in Irish folklore began to look back to rural life before the cataclysm, if not as a Golden Age for most people who had known it, at least as a much more festive, colourful world. Whatever apparently ancient custom or belief remained after the dislocation seemed precious – something to be collected before it was too late, as William Wilde stated: 'All the stories about the fairies and the pishogues [*piseoga*: charms, superstitions] are going fast, and will soon be lost to us and our heirs for ever. The old forms and customs, too, are becoming obliterated; the festivals are unobserved, and the rustic festivities

---

3 'The Fenian Traditions of Sliabh-na-m-Ban', *Trans. of the Kilkenny Archaeological Soc.* 1 (1849-51) 234. 4 Op. cit. xii. 5 Material concerning the Great Famine was collected by the Irish Folklore Commission through a questionnaire distributed in 1944-45. It was first examined by Roger McHugh, 'The Famine in Irish Tradition' in F.D. Edwards and T.D. Williams (ed.) *The Great Famine* (1956), then partly edited by Cathal Póirtéir in *Famine Echoes* (1995) and analysed by Carmel Quinlan, 'A Punishment from God: The Famine in the Centenary Folklore Questionnaire' in *Irish Review* 19 (1996). See also 'Famine Memory' in Cormac Ó Grada *Black '47 and Beyond* ... 194-225.

neglected or forgotten ... If, however, we cannot hope much for the future, let us for the present, at least, live in the memory of the past.'[6]

What actually had changed or was changing, in rural Ireland? First, demography: whereas the population had grown at unprecedented rates in the decades prior to the 1840s, afterwards it shrank continuously, as emigration removed a large part of each generation in rural areas. The social structure was affected. There were still landlords and tenants, but some landowners who were already in debt when the Famine began were bankrupt by the decline of rents and the increase of taxes; they were replaced by new entrepreneurs, often Irish and sometimes more brutal. About one seventh of the land changed hands in a few years, and by 1870 the majority of the landlords were new owners. As for the farmers, some were more prosperous than others; it had been possible to survive with a holding of eight hectares or more, which could now be increased by the plots of those who had died, emigrated or been evicted. The cottiers who existed at subsistence level on very small pieces of land sub-let on a yearly basis, and the other labourers, were a shrinking class: the proportion of 60% labourers and cottiers against 40% farmers in 1845 was reversed in 1881. Family patterns and modes of rural settlement also changed. At the beginning of the century, holdings tended to be subdivided into ever smaller pieces of land between all the sons, who married early (particularly in the poorer classes); now, to keep the farm viable, only one son would inherit while his siblings stayed on as unmarried and unpaid helpers or sought their fortunes elsewhere. Marriages were fewer and later, often arranged as a way of enlarging or securing property – but the birth-rate remained high. With the concentration into larger holdings, pasture farming became dominant: prices were rising for cattle and mutton. The rundale system and the *clachán* settlement in clusters of cabins where social life was intense (cf. p. 203) were replaced by scattered dwellings and individual leases, supposed to foster self-reliance. The poorest type of housing, the one-roomed mud cabins which according to the Census of 1841 housed some 85% of the population, was gradually vanishing – though some 150,000 such hovels were still occupied in 1881. Between those humble dwellings and substantial farmhouses, a new common type was the long house with two rooms and a kitchen in the middle. The face of the landscape changed as homesteads were dispersed, and the sense of communality may have diminished. At first, however, co-operation in work did not vanish, and fireside evenings could still bring neighbours together. There was also, from the 1870s, an expanding number of public houses for the social drinking of the male population, particularly of the large group of bachelors.

While magical beliefs and practices were declining, the Catholic Church increased its hold on people. It gave consolation in troubled times, and occupied the cultural space left vacant by a partial decay of 'traditional' life; a concerted

6 William Wilde *Irish Popular Superstitions* 14, 24.

campaign led by more assertive bishops bore fruit. Church building increased and the clergy became more numerous: there were some 5,000 priests, monks and nuns in 1850; in 1900 they were over 14,000 for a smaller Catholic population,[7] and exercised tighter moral control. The priests were more active and efficient in combating the older intermingling of the orthodox and 'pagan' in the countryside, and in suppressing the profane elements (drinking, dancing, fighting) associated with the celebration of local patrons or with funeral wakes.

The last quarter of the century saw further mutations. After a period of economic recovery there was a new depression: in 1877, disastrously wet weather and bad crops began an agricultural crisis, while prices were falling because of cheap grain arriving from America. The threat of a new famine and the landlords' policy of eviction of the tenants who could not pay the rent led again to rural agitation and violence. This time the tenants were organized in an effective mass movement. At first, it sought only modifications of the laws relating to land contracts: rent reductions and security in holdings, but then a fight developed for the transfer of land-ownership to the tenants: 'The land of Ireland belongs to the people of Ireland, to be held and cultivated for the sustenance of those whom God decreed to be the inhabitants thereof.'[8] A series of Land Acts improved the condition of tenants, then replaced landlordism with peasant proprietorship by a policy of annuities instead of rents after a massive land purchase by the state. In 1870, only 3% of those who worked the land owned their plot; from the mid 1880s and more particularly during the first decade of the twentieth century, Irish tenant farmers became small proprietors – by 1906, about 30% were owners, and some ten years later two thirds of Irish farmers would own their land. The values of those people now began to prevail, as well as those of shopkeepers who were the other rising group.

Some districts did not evolve as rapidly as others; in western areas, features of the earlier structure of rural life survived: people continued to marry young, farms were still subdivided, and one practiced seasonal migration to find work. Oral arts remained stronger in these areas, and the adjective 'remote' now regularly accompanied descriptions of the settings of impressive Irish storytelling, although with the development of the railway network even isolated areas were becoming more accessible. Elsewhere, mentalities – along with the choice and reception of stories – were not the same at all social levels. Some illustrations of the effects of changes and of the widening cultural gap may be found in the memories of Mary O'Brien, who was born in 1858, the daughter of a 'successful and progressive farmer'[9] in County Limerick. As a child in the 1860s she heard traditional stories, but from the servants:

The maids did not get into the other world in the way we did who knew more about it. Although they were thankful for holy days and went to Mass, they were really more

7 F.S.L. Lyons *Ireland since the Famine* 19. 8 Declaration of Principles of the Irish National Land League, 1879. 9 *The Farm by Lough Gur*, edited by Mary Carbury, 10.

interested in an old Irish world where fairies, witches and banshees took the place of our angels and saints. We children were forbidden to pry into that magic place which was, mother told us, imaginary and untrue, but we could not help knowing that the maids and most of the untaught people round Lough Gur believed that a third world, fraught with danger, was going on all round them.[10]

The culture of the farmer's family was different: 'At seven o'clock we sat down for a happy time round the table in the little room, a bright, shaded reading lamp in the middle, and while the rest sewed, one of us or our mother read aloud books suited to our years. ... We calculated that we read with mother in the evening at least five hundred hours a year.'[11] Mary O'Brien received a convent education and returned home (c. 1875) with firmer ideas about 'superstitions', while the older generation was more lenient towards them, like the old local priest: 'I bid you put away all fear. Dance the old dances, sing the old songs, remember, if you will, but with pity and tender laughter, the old heathen customs and charms of your forefathers, and be thankful all the time that Christianity has taught you to dread none of the heathen things.'[12]

The life of people was altering under the impact of these new conditions, and consequences of adopting new cultural traits and dropping old ones would be felt more strongly in the following decades, though part of the older ways could be observed for quite some time in certain regions.

In the second half of the nineteenth century, collecting folklore could still be a mere hobby satisfying sentimental attachment to a local heritage and requiring no complex theorizing; it was enough to think that the 'folk' in question consisted of rural social groups which were the backward part of a more modern world, and that their supposedly peculiar practices and beliefs were very ancient and fundamentally unchangeable (except that they might deteriorate and vanish and should therefore be documented and preserved before it was too late). But others treated folklore as a scholarly subject; what had been assembled had to be interpreted, according to hypotheses which some might soon treat as absolute laws. Theoretical principles could be borrowed from contemporary anthropology, philology or comparative mythology.

The nineteenth century was obsessed by questions of origins and relative place in an evolution. When British anthropologists investigated exotic cultures and folklorists the peasant lore in their own world, they made strong assumptions about degrees of civilization. The dominant model interpreted human history as the progress of all societies from the simple to the increasingly complex, following the same developmental pattern and order, but at different rates; the observer's society was taken to be at the most developed point, while others more or less lagged behind. French and Scots social and moral philosophers had

---

10 Ibid. 158. 11 Ibid. 23, 172. 12 Ibid. 165-6.

already proposed such schemes in the eighteenth century (see p. 83); now the archaeological notion of 'ages', the success of evolutionary doctrines in biology and their application by Herbert Spencer to society, gave a new impetus to the theme of unilinear cultural progress. The English anthropologist Edward B. Tylor proposed three stages: savagery, barbarism and civilization; he described them mostly in terms of the development of religion from animism through polytheism to monotheism, while Lewis Henry Morgan in America correlated each phase with economic, social and technological achievements. According to Tylor, the second stage could still be dimly seen on remote islands or in isolated valleys of Europe, where local cultures were cases of arrested development – vestiges of a level which the higher strata of the larger society had outgrown. Folklorists made the greatest use of this concept of 'survivals': according to them, as a society passed to the superior stage in the sequence of development, some traits of the earlier level remained, with a reduced, changed or virtually forgotten function, as 'folk traditions'. The object of their study would be anachronism, residual odd practices or apparently irrational ways of thinking, and stories used to illustrate or justify them. An earlier stage could be reconstructed by observing such cultural leftovers and by explaining them through analogies with practices and beliefs observed in contemporary 'primitive' cultures, which were 'living fossils'. An important corollary was that whatever did not fit the scheme might be explained away as corrupt or irrelevant.

The method of study used by many scholars was comparison: anthropologists would look for striking differences or similarities in the data provided by explorers, missionaries and colonial administrators – Tylor is said to have thus gathered information about 350 societies around the world. But a cross-societal (also trans-historical) comparison had its drawbacks: starting, as the cultural evolutionists did, from some a priori theory which needed confirmation, one might be tempted to exaggerate similarities between selected units and to ignore their varied contexts. At all events, there were puzzling results for folklorists: looking for evidence of the distinctive identity of their nation (because, apparently contrasting with the universalism of the dominant anthropological theory, the desire to promote a national identity based upon distinctive traditions still was a strong incentive in the second half of the century), they soon realized that their colleagues from other nations had made similar discoveries. There was a common stock of customs, beliefs, and tales; the publication of folklore material from different parts of Europe revealed many parallels, which in some cases could hardly be accounted for in strict evolutionary terms.

Other explanations were put forward. For instance, because all humankind shared the same essential mentality, different peoples could invent or re-invent the same cultural elements independently. But one could also decide that any complex invention, for example of a certain narrative plot found in different places, had occurred only once; then it might be an inheritance from common ancestors: developments in historical philology, plus the less easily demonstrable notion that generic relationship extended beyond linguistic kinship, suggested the idea that the folktales derived from a shared Indo-European foundation. But to account for ethnographic parallels, including the fact that folktales appeared in so many countries in similar forms, culture contacts and exchanges rather than common origin could be invoked: separate cultural items might migrate. Those who thus explained similarities as the result of diffusion did not necessarily invoke the prehistoric dispersion of Aryan tribes; Theodor Benfey, in Germany, who postulated that India had provided the originals of most European folktales, thought that much of the diffusion had followed trade routes in historical times, mostly since the tenth century. Other possible centres from which tales could have spread were 'identified', and diffusionism admitted that any society could give or borrow. It was possible to combine moderate cultural evolutionism with a dose of diffusionism to explain similarities: Tylor himself was not as doctrinaire as some of his disciples and could bridge the evolutionist and diffusionist theories of his time – both of which used the concept of 'survivals'.

Concerning the 'meaning' of the tales, a particular school of interpretation must be mentioned, evolving from the idea that some earlier mythology had splintered into various offshoots and become blurred. For the philologist and orientalist Max Müller, the original Aryans had expressed their observations of the sun in metaphorical language and through personifications, which were later taken literally. Some of Müller's followers carried this kind of explanation to extremes: the plots of folktales were degenerated forms of what had been composed, in a 'mythopeic age', to account for natural phenomena – sun, moon, stars, storms, etc. But while the 'comparative mythologists' were proposing and applying such ideas, the 'anthropological' evolutionist school remained powerful. Andrew Lang (1844-1912) challenged Müller and Benfey, defined folklore as 'the science of survivals', and applied Tylor's ideas and methods to the study of folktales. 'Primitive' people everywhere would have developed similar tales, corresponding to their minds at a stage where what now looked irrational appeared intelligible: 'we believe [fairy tales] to be derived from the savage state of man, from the savage conditions of life, and the savage way of regarding the world'.[13] Folklorists should collect and compare the 'immaterial relics of old races, the surviving superstitions and stories, the ideas which are in our own time but not of it ... The peculiarity of the method of folklore is that it will venture to compare ... the myths of the most widely severed races'.[14] Data from all cultures, not only Indo-European ones, were relevant to finding traces of a universal early stage of culture. Lang tabulated correspondences between European and African tales – but did not pretend that *all* parallels between tales could be accounted for *solely* by the evolutionary theory. He also paid some attention to structural principles which could generate tales:

13 Introduction to Margaret Hunt's translation of *Grimm's Household Tales* (1884) i. xli. **14** *Customs and Myth* 10-11, 23.

A tale will start with a certain opening, that, let us say, of the man with three daughters. Then it will glide either into one of the formulae in which an unkind Stepmother appears, or into a story of adventures to be achieved by each of the daughters, in which only the youngest usually succeeds, or into the narrative in which a giant or fiend claims one of the three. Any of these points having been reached, more crossroads branch off in every direction. There are dozens, if not hundreds, of other ways in which any popular tale, starting from whatever formula you please, may journey to any end, always by well known paths and through familiar adventures.[15]

In 1891, in the first chapter of *The Science of Fairy Tales*, E. Sidney Hartland tried to describe 'The Art of the Story-Teller'. Again, the comparative method and the evolutionist doctrine of survivals were applied, combined with the notion of possible distinctive ethnic or national qualities:

Some nations have developed the art of story-telling more highly than others, since some stages of civilization are more favourable to this development than others, and all nations are not in the same stage. The further question may, therefore, be put whether the various stages of development may not produce differences of manner in story-telling – differences which may indicate, if they do not cause, deep-seated differences in the value of the traditions themselves.[16]

But he concluded that 'national differences in the manner of story-telling are for the most part superficial'.[17] When he tried to identify a 'Celtic' art of story-telling, he found 'a social state in which the art of story-telling has received a high degree of attention'[18] – in fact, Hartland used mostly Scottish, Breton and Welsh sources, though he did mention collections made in Ireland.

Joseph Jacobs, a spokesman for diffusionism rather than evolutionism, included Irish material (which he had not collected himself, and which he rewrote) in his *Celtic Fairy Tales* (1891) and *More Celtic Fairy Tales* (1894); in the notes, he used the stories to support the theory he favoured: 'Celtic tales are of peculiar interest in this connection, as they afford one of the best fields for studying the problem of diffusion, the most pressing of the problems of the folktales, at present, at least in my opinion. The Celts are at the furthermost end of Europe. Tales that travelled to them could go no further and must therefore be the last links in the chain.'[19]

Another member of the Folklore Society of England, Alfred Nutt (1856–1910), preferred the evolutionist thesis, and as a specialist in pre-Christian religions and a Celticist he applied the doctrine of survivals in his work on ancient Irish texts: 'Of all the races of modern Europe the Irish have the most considerable and the most archaic mass of pre-Christian traditions'.[20] He compared the living folklore of Irish peasants with the manuscript versions of Irish sagas or romances, trying to identify still older creeds: 'What the Irish peasant of to-day

15 Ibid. 64-5. 16 Op. cit. 5. 17 Ibid. 20. 18 Ibid. 5. 19 *Celtic Fairy Tales* 241. 20 *Studies on the Legend of the Holy Grail* ... xii.

fables and believes of *the good people*, his ancestors of a thousand years ago fabled and believed of the Folk of the Goddess'.[21] He paid respect to the Indo-European theory, but saw in Ireland little evidence of diffusion: 'No other Aryan civilisation has developed itself so independently of the two great influences, Hellenic and Hebraic, which have moulded the modern world; nowhere else is the course of development less perplexed by cross currents; nowhere else can the great issues be kept more steadily in view.'[22]

Theoretical speculation may have been the more dignified activity in Victorian Britain, but recorded observations of people on the spot were necessary to substantiate it; to secure the relevant data, collectors were given for guidance ready-made questionnaires – which tended to impose certain concepts and categories. Such a checklist, contributed in 1874 by E.B. Tylor to a handbook for potential ethnographers, reflects the ideas of the time concerning narrative material. 'The collection of mythic stories' (he also uses terms like 'mythic legends' and 'fairy tales, etc.') is said to be important because 'they contain the ideas of the people, on religious subjects, names of gods, &c. often in more original and exact forms than those used in common conversation. ... It would thus be a serious mistake to suppose the mythology of the lower races of little scientific value. Few studies throw more light on the early history of the human race and the human mind'. Finding the equivalent of a European folktale among the 'primitives' of another continent might prove the doctrine of survivals, or that of borrowing – diffusionist premises are grafted on evolutionist bases:

Do any of the native stories contain episodes which seem as though they might have been learnt from modern Europeans? ... Are there any similar touches which betray contact with Mohammedans or Buddhists? Apart from these, are stories current which have a resemblance to well-known classical or folk-lore mythology, but may have a distinct or independent origin? ... The episodes, jests, &c. in mythic legends should be particularly noticed when they correspond to those known in the legends or folk-lore of other races, for such evidence throws light on the connexion or intercourse in former times between the two races.

Some questions also seem to accommodate the 'solar mythology' of Müller and his disciples:

What stories come under the heading of nature-myths, being told of the sun, moon, stars, rivers, &c as personal beings? Do any of the heroes and heroines bear names which suggest such origin? or do their feats seem to be suggested by natural phenomena? Are there, for example, myths relating to the sun, his birth, course, and death; day and night; eclipses; the changes of the moon?[23]

---

21 *The Celtic Doctrine of Re-birth*, vol. 2 of K. Meyer *The Voyage of Bran*, 159. 22 'Celtic Myth and Saga', *Archaeological Review* 2 (1889) 137. 23 'Mythology', in *Notes and Queries on Anthropology* 62-3.

A Folk-Lore Society, founded in London in 1878 and largely influenced by Tylor, produced its own guide for collectors in 1890: *The Handbook of Folklore*, edited by George Laurence Gomme. The activity of folklorists was defined as 'the comparison and identification of the survivals of archaic beliefs, customs, and traditions in modern ages', including 'superstitious belief and practice', 'traditional customs', 'traditional narratives' and 'folk-sayings'.[24] The section dealing with folktales, written by Hartland, summed up the prevalent views of the day:

All over the world and in all degrees of civilisation men have been addicted to telling tales. In the lower grades of civilisation, such as we know by the names of savagery and barbarism, these tales embody the ideas of the world, and the nature of things entertained by those who tell them. They contain very often a philosophy of the universe. As we ascend in the scale the same tales, or at least tales containing the same incidents, continue to be told, many of them as facts, others as mere romances. In our study of primitive thought stories are therefore of prime importance. They enshrine the beliefs of early ages, and they preserve relics of customs which have fallen, or are falling, into decay; and thus they are valuable evidence to the student of human nature as well as to the antiquary ... As we advance in the scale of civilisation the sagas told by savages are dropped or modified. They cluster round new names. Some of them are related of genuine historical characters. Some of them become attached to remarkable places. Or perhaps they may cease to obtain credit as facts: they may fall into the status of romances told simply for amusement, and particularly the amusement of children.[25]

The would-be collector is warned of difficulties, and advised to work with caution to oversome the informant's diffidence, then to avoid distorting the material: 'Care should be used in taking down the stories in the very words of the teller. Stories altered, or improved, into literary form are deteriorated in scientific value, and frequently too in real literary value, by every alteration. They ought to be given, imperfections, mistakes, and all, just as they are told, though mistakes may, and ought to be, pointed out in footnotes.'[26]

As it seemed necessary to bring order to a growing amount of collected material, a system of classification of tales established by Joseph Jacobs was proposed in the same *Handbook*, with seventy types divided into 'incidents' (later known as 'motifs'), but it was admitted that such a catalogue was far from exhaustive.

Whatever issues one chose to focus upon, it was not likely to be the personality of the individual storyteller or the conditions of performance. Tylor, in the guidelines of 1874, merely recommended 'to take [material] down verbatim from the lips of a skilled storyteller', and to note if there was 'any special class of priests, bards, &c. concerned especially in preserving [stories]';[27] beyond that, the storyteller and his art were ignored.

24 Op. cit. 5-6. 25 Ibid. 110-11. 26 Ibid. 115-16. 27 *Notes and Queries on Anthropology* 62.

In Ireland, the word 'survival' and the notion that some stories came from an earlier stage of culture were easy to accept, and might be charged with emotion: it was possible to believe at the same time in the relative general progress of the evolutionists and in some particular setback and loss. At any rate, it seemed that more had 'survived' there than in most of Britain until the beginning of the century. The diffusionist theory and the idea that elements from all cultures were comparable might be more difficult to reconcile with extreme forms of nationalism founded on a belief in uniqueness; on the other hand, the notion that ancestors had come to Ireland from somewhere in the east or south-east was well established, and there was no impassable barrier between the belief in a 'Japhetian' origin of the Irish language (see p. 90) and the new Indo-European explanation. In any case it was becoming clear that a number of stories collected in Ireland were in fact akin to what could be found elsewhere.

Some people interested in folklore knew about the activities and principles of British anthropologists or continental mythologists. The Folklore Society of England had members in Ireland, and a 'local secretary': George H. Kinahan, a geologist who contributed a dozen articles, mostly about County Donegal, to the society's *Folk-Lore Record* from 1879 onwards and its *Folk-Lore Journal* from 1883. The theories according to which folktales reflected the symbolism of solar, stellar or natural phenomena were criticized, parodied, and also defended at Trinity College in Dublin.[28] The boldest attempt to apply them to Irish material may have been an article concerning the content of ancient Irish manuscripts as well as living folktales, published in the French *Revue Celtique*. The author, David Fitzgerald, started with the axiom that divine and semi-devine mythic figures were always 'personifications of various powers or phenomena of nature'; Celtic myths, in particular, would systematize 'a few leading constants – the stars, especially Ursa Major and Orion; light and darkness; time; the year; winter and summer; the days; the shortest day'. Referring to 'inedited Irish tales' he had collected, Fitzgerald applied his theory to what was still found in oral tradition: the Black Pig referred to by Carleton and later by Yeats was connected with Circe and Ursa Major, and the cat in the 'Irish tale of the Cat and the Brogues' (cf. p. 192) was a 'twin-brother' of the Black Pig because shoes were associated with Ursa Major ...[29]

General propositions could thus provide principles of analysis or interpretation, but it was also possible to ignore foreign theories and work without caring for sophisticated deciphering systems: a number of collectors or editors had a more insular conception of preserving the Irish heritage. Folkloristic publications

---

28 See R.M. Dorson *The British Folklorists: A History* Ch. 5, and by the same author 'The Eclipse of Solar Mythology' in Alan Dundes *The Study of Folklore* 57-83. 29 'Early Celtic History and Mythology', *Revue Celtique* 6 (1883-5) 193-259. Fitzgerald also published in *La Revue des traditions populaires* (1890 and 1891), without such flights of interpretation, an Irish tale he had collected and an essay on St Martin's legend.

concerning Ireland in the second half of the nineteenth century may be sorted
roughly into five trends, which will be examined in the following pages. Some
still took the older antiquarian approach: a leisure activity for genteel persons
who would compare oral traditions and ancient written texts or monuments, perhaps knowing something of recent theories. Secondly, there was the sentimentalized – but also amusing – exploitation of Irish folklore, particularly for a new
audience consisting of people with Irish blood living abroad: here the distinction
between observation and fiction tends to be blurred. Thirdly, non-mercenary but
not particularly methodical amateur attempts were made at gathering contemporary local lore, which was then generally published in non-specialized periodicals or books and might not display much familiarity with the theories surveyed
above. I shall consider as my fourth subject two outstanding – but different –
collections inspired or at least encouraged by the evolution of folklore studies
abroad. Finally, other collections were connected with the new cultural nationalism that developed in the last decades of the century. Of course, there is nothing absolute about the divisions and individual cases may overlap these rough
categories.

The typical antiquary had been an amateur collector and student of different
kinds of relics, including what others now called folklore, as long as it could be
considered as remnants from the past; he might publish his findings in the
learned journal of some society of which he was a member.[30] Individual cases
varied, though. For instance, Nicholas O'Kearney (*c.*1802-*c.*1865), whose main
trade was copying manuscripts, worked for antiquarians and was not a dilettante
of gentlemanly rank; he published *The Prophecies of Columbkille*, edited and
translated an ancient text for the Ossianic Society, and contributed articles entitled 'Folk-Lore' and 'On Folk-Lore' to the *Transactions of the Kilkenny Archaeological Society*. In 1851, the same periodical published a paper read by John
Dunne (1815-92), a school-teacher and local historian – as well as an antiquarian in that he searched for links between contemporary oral traditions and old
manuscripts:

It appears to me that the curious old fairy legends of our country, much as their loss
should be deplored, were never half as valuable or as interesting as the traditions which
have long lingered amongst our peasantry concerning the primaeval inhabitants of
Ireland, the total obliteration of which is now, unfortunately, threatened from the same
causes. The pre-historic annals of this kingdom, which remain yet to be properly compiled, must be drawn not alone from the appearance of the existing primaeval monuments, but from the vivid traditions connected with them, long handed down from sire
to son in the localities in which they are placed, and which, though many of their features were marvellous, incongruous, or impossible of occurrence, are far from being

30 *The Journal of the Royal Society of Antiquaries of Ireland; ... of the Cork Historical and
Archaeological Society; ... of the Kildare Archaeological Society; The Ulster Journal of
Archaeology.*

worthless as aids to a proper investigation of that important subject. With such materials much may yet be done towards the elucidation of remote events in our national history; and though a very large proportion must, unquestionably, be thrown aside as profitless chaff, from amongst it many valuable grains of corn may be sifted. [He decides to focus on 'Fenian' – in the sense of ancient *Fianna* – tradition.][31]

The stories were what counted: Dunne had nothing to say concerning ways of telling them. When he portrayed individuals, a few years later, they were essentially native antiquarians – 'bards and scholars' who collected manuscripts; yet he did mention a performer:

A decent-looking and intelligent farmer, named Lahey, residing at Kyleatlea, at the foot of Sliabh-na-mBan, who surprised me by repeating from memory some of the longest of the dialogues between St Patrick and Ossian, stated that, in his opinion, several of the old people of Cloran still safely preserved some of the works of another local *seanchaidhe*, Walsh of Three Bridges, Carrick-on-Suir; and that he heard him recite the 'Chase of Gleann na Smóil' and other Irish poems, one Sunday morning, in a house at Cloneen, on which occasion he was handed thirty shillings by a few farmers who were present, towards defraying the expenses of publishing that and the other Fenian tales in Irish verse.[32]

Another antiquarian was Oscar Wilde's father, William Robert (1815-76). Born in Castlerea (County Roscommon), he is said to have spent much time in his boyhood exploring ruins and sharing in the entertainments of the peasantry. Later, with George Petrie as his mentor, he studied Irish prehistory and classified skulls found in old burials.[33] He wrote on various subjects: eye and ear surgery, medical history, the 1851 Census, ancient monuments, travels abroad and in Ireland. *The Beauties of the Boyne and Blackwater* published in 1849, and *Lough Corrib and Lough Mask* in 1867, combined landscape description, archaeology and legends. He was one of the first in Ireland to use in print a variant of the word folklore ('folks' lore', in 1852). Having collected 'particulars about the old customs and social antiquities of Ireland' from his boyhood on, he published them, in 1852, as *Irish Popular Superstitions* (parts of which had previously appeared in the *Dublin University Magazine*). He noted that the 'great amount of traditional, antiquarian, and topographical information' collected some twenty years before by the Ordnance Survey field-workers (see Ch. 4) might no longer be available after the Famine.[34] He was already aware of evolutionist theories and comparative methods which Tylor would formalize later:

---

31 'The Fenian Traditions of Sliabh-na-m-Ban', *Transactions of the Kilkenny Archaeological Society* 1 (1851) 333-4. 32 This article, published in 1854, is quoted in James Maher (ed.) *Romantic Slievenamon in History, Folklore and Song* 247-9. Dunne adds that the booklet was indeed printed, at Carrick-on-Suir, in 1816. 33 T.G. Wilson *Victorian Doctor; Being the Life of Sir William Wilde* 3, 7, 133, 137. 34 *Irish Popular Superstitions* 18.

There are certain types of superstition common to almost all countries in similar states of progress or civilization, and others which abound in nearly every condition of society. ... It would, no doubt, form a subject of great interest to trace back our traditional antiquities, and to compare them one with another – the German and Scandinavian with the Irish, Scotch, or English – those of the western and eastern continents generally, with the rites and ceremonies, or opinions, of which vestiges still exist among ourselves; when, indeed, strange affinities and similarities would be found to obtain among the North American Indians, and the Burmese and other Orientals, with those even yet practised in the Irish highlands and islands ...

It is scarcely necessary to inform the reader that a superstitious creed, and certain mystic rites derived from the remotest times, attach to almost every nation in a certain state of society, and are not peculiar to either race or creed; that some of these are of almost universal acceptation; that others belong to peculiar localities, and that their geographical distribution is a source of interesting investigation both to the historian and to the ethnologist.[35]

In the same book, informants are characterized by a flamboyance and a dialect close to the common mode of the first half of the century. One of Wilde's real or synthetic speakers had 'long been considered the knowingest man in the whole country, and could tell more stories about the ould times and the "good people" ... than "all the books that were ever shut and opened".'[36] We are invited to hear his voice:

'Troth, sir,' said Darby Doolin, an old Connaughtman of our acquaintance, when lately conversing upon the subject [the decay of traditions], 'what betune them national boords [the National Board of Education ran non-denominational schools for the lower classes], and godless colleges, and other sorts of larnin', and the loss of the pratey [potato], and the sickness, and all the people that's goin' to 'Merica, and the crathurs that's forced to go into the workhouse, or is dyin' off in the ditches, and the clargy settin' their faces agin them, and tellin' the people not to give *in* to the likes, sarra wan of the *Gintry* [fairies] (cross about us!) 'ill be found in the counthry, nor a word about them or their doin's in no time.'[37]

A more detailed account is given of 'Paudeen Brannagh (Anglice, Patrick Welsh)', a Roscommon fisherman who was 'thoroughly and peculiarly Irish':

Paddy was great at a wake ... He could tell them how to slap, and play forfeits, and shuffle the brogue, and rehearse 'the waits' [those were traditional games at funeral wakes]; or he could sing the 'Black Stripper,' and 'Nell Flaherty's Drake' [see p. 271] or repeat a rhan [*rann*: verse, quatrain] beyond compare. The young, and those unconcerned in the mournful spectacle, welcomed him with loud applause; even those in grief would smile through their tears, and the nearest relative of the deceased would exclaim: – 'Oh, thin, musha Paddy, you *summahawn* [*somachán*: an innocent child, or booby], bad cess to you, is it here you're coming with your tricks, and we in grief and sorrow this night?' 'Hould

35 Ibid. 30, 37.   36 Ibid. 23-4.   37 Ibid. 11.

your whist, shtore ma chree [*stór mo chroí*: my dear heart], sure it's for that I stept over, just to keep ye from thinking, and to anose the colleens.' ... It was said he had found a crock of gold in one of the towers of the old bawne [*bábhún*: a walled enclosure or a castle yard – here Toberbride Castle] of Ballintober which was not more than a mile and half distant from his cabin. ... We often endeavoured to worm the story out of the cunning angler; but, drunk or sober, he was always on his guard, and generally passed it off with a joke, or – 'Sure, Master Willie, you don't give into the likes – 'tis only ould women's talk. It's myself that would be glad to own to it if I got the goold, and not be slaving myself, summer and winter, by the river's brink, as I am.' 'Yes; but, Paddy, they say you made the attempt, at all events. Cannot you tell us what happened to you?' 'Oh, then, it's only all *gollymoschought* [*galamaisíocht* : in play]. But that's mighty fine parlimint [legal whiskey] your honour has in the little flask; 'tis a pity it doesn't hould more, and the devil a tail we are rising to keep up our spirits.' 'Come now, Paddy ... – just stick the rods and lie on your face in the grass there, and tell me all about the night when you went to look after the money in the old bawne. Do, and you'll see I'll squeeze another mouthful out of the cruiskeen [*crúiscín*: a jug].'

'Well, but you're mighty 'cute and disquisitive after old stories and pishogues. I suppose I may as well be after telling it to you while the breeze is getting up; but keep an eye to the river, awourneen, [*a mhúirnín*: my little darling] and try could you see e'er a rise ... But don't be tellin' on me, nor let on at the *big house* that I told you the likes at all. Sure the mistress 'ud never forgive me for putting such things in your head; and maybe it's Father Crump she'd be after repatin' it to the next Sunday he dines in Dundearmot; and if she did, troth I wouldn't face him for a month of Sundays. Maybe it's to St Ball or to St John's Well he'd send me for my night walkin'.' 'Oh, never fear, I'll keep your secret.'

'Well, then awourneen, to make a long story short, I dhramed one night that I was walking about in the *bawne*, when I looked into the old tower that's in the left hand corner, after you pass the gate, and there I saw, sure enough, a little crock, about the bigness of the bottom of a pitcher, and it full up of all kinds of money, goold, silver and brass. When I woke next morning, I said nothin' about it, but in a few nights after I had the same dhrame over agin, ony I thought I was lookin' down from the top of the tower, and that all the flures were taken away. Peggy knew be me that I had a dhrame, for I wasn't quite asey in myself; so I ups and tells her the whole of it, when the childer had gone out. "Well, Paddy," says she, "who knows but it would come thrue, and be the making of us yet; but you must wait till the dhrame comes afore you the third time, and then, sure, it can do no harm to try, anyways." It wasn't long till I had the third dhrame ... Oh, what's the use in tellin' you anything about it; sure, I know by your eye you don't believe a word I am sayin'.[38]

He kept collecting folklore data, and it is said – the man himself being a focus of legends in Dublin – that he accepted stories as payment from his poorer patients and kept the notes he had thus collected in a basket.[39] Towards the end of his life he was preparing a book on *Irish Fairy Lore*, which he never com-

---

38 Ibid. 84–97. Stories about such triple and therefore truthful dreams were common in Ireland. 39 W.B. Yeats 'Tales from the Twilight', *Scots Observer* 1 March 1890.

pleted. After his death, his widow (Jane Francesca, Lady Wilde, 1826-1896) used this material, and perhaps other sources as well, for two volumes which she compiled when living in London: *Ancient Legends, Mystic Charms, and Superstitions of Ireland* (1887) and *Ancient Cures, Charms, and Usages of Ireland* (1890). She claimed authenticity and accuracy, invoked a patriotic duty, and played the by then inevitable 'last-minute-rescue' theme.[40] The raw material to which Lady Wilde had access was obviously rich – but in editing it she gave no indication of sources, rewrote the legends, and commented on them with less authority than her husband. She had gathered a jumble of information and misinformation: the 'strange and mystical superstitions' had been 'brought thousands of years ago from their Aryan home. ... Here in our beautiful Ireland the last wave of the great Iranian migration finally settled [but she would also assert that there might be 'some truth' in the legend that Ireland was colonized by Egyptians]. ... It is, therefore, in Ireland, above all, that the nature and origin of the primitive races of Europe should be studied.'[41] She had nothing to say of the storytellers, with whom she may have had no direct contact.

Lady Wilde was an occasional editor of folklore material, not, as far as we know, a collector, and her place among antiquaries is questionable. Patrick Weston Joyce (1827-1914) may be more rightfully named here; apart from being professionally involved in the training of teachers, he wrote about life in ancient Ireland and the Hiberno-English dialect; collected traditional music and songs; and was for a time the president of the Royal Society of Antiquaries of Ireland. He also adapted Irish sagas and romances for a large audience (see p. 268), but unlike Standish James O'Grady (1846-1928) who wrote volumes of legendary history or historical fiction to reawaken enthusiasm for heroic Ireland, and his more scholarly cousin Standish Hayes O'Grady (1832-1915) who, having worked under the guidance of O'Curry, O'Donovan and Petrie, edited texts along with translations, Joyce occasionally had something to say about contemporary traditional narrative arts. He had observed storytellers since his childhood in County Limerick:

The ancient institution of professional story-telling held its ground both in Ireland and in Scotland down to a very recent period; and it is questionable if it be even yet extinguished. Within my own memory, this sort of amusement was quite usual among the farming classes of the south of Ireland. The family and workmen, and any neighbours that chose to drop in, would sit round the kitchen fire after the day's work – or perhaps gather in a barn on a summer or autumn evening – to listen to some local shanachie reciting one of his innumerable Gaelic tales. The storyteller never chose his own words – he always had the story by heart, and recited the words from memory, often gliding in a sort of recitative in poetical passages, or when he came to some favourite grandiose description abounding in high-sounding alliterative adjectives. And very interesting it was to mark the rapt attention of the audience, and to hear their excited exclamations when

40 *Ancient Legends* ... xii.   41 Ibid. xi, 3-4, 124.

the speaker came to relate some mighty combat, some great exploit of the hero, or some other striking incident. Three years ago [*c*.1875], I met a man in Kilkee, who had a great number of these stories by heart.[42]

But – and this may be an antiquarian's typical attitude – he did not take oral tradition on trust, for instance when looking for *The Origin and History of Irish Names of Places*:

Many of the legends with which the early history of our country abounds are no doubt purely fabulous, the inventions of the old shanachies or story-tellers. Great numbers, on the other hand, are obviously founded on historical events; but they have been so distorted and exaggerated by successive generations of romancers, so interwoven with strange or supernatural circumstances, or so far removed from their true date into the regions of antiquity, that they have in many cases quite lost the look of probability. It is impossible to draw an exact line of demarcation beween what is partly real and what is wholly fictitious.[43]

For others, collecting relics was not an end in itself. The nineteenth century saw, everywhere, the emergence of an exploitation of folklore for nonlocal consumption; the products were offered as authentic but not properly documented, and more or less doctored. My second category consists therefore of writers who produced books of Irish folklore which they knew would please a certain audience and perhaps prove lucrative, because they combined the picturesque and amusing with what might flatter patriotism. There were varieties and degrees, from mere forgery – an extreme I shall try to ignore – to genuine information modified to increase quaintness and jollity. Easy targets for this kind of publication were the Irish abroad: their number was rapidly increasing. Recent emigrants in a hostile environment were not the best customers for printed material, but in the second or third generation of Irish Americans approaching middle-class respectability, many were interested in their ethnic background and enjoyed the fantasized Irish identity of St Patrick's Day parades. A member of an Irish family recalled life at Bridgeport, Connecticut, about 1880: 'We used to sing and dance to all the old Irish songs and ballads and dance the Irish jig. We were always taught to be proud of being Irish and Catholic, and we knew all the history and legends of Ireland and followed the happenings in Ireland as much

---

42 *Old Celtic Romances* (1879) vii-ix. In this mixed group we may also place Thomas J. Westropp (1860-1922) who from his youth was interested both in archaeology and folklore; he contributed papers to the *Journal of the Royal Society of Antiquaries of Ireland*, and to *Folk-Lore*, the periodical of the British Folklore Society, comparing accounts of contemporary informants with manuscripts and occasionally with the Ordnance Survey letters of the 1830s. Colonel William Gregory Wood-Martin (1847-1917) was an enthusiastic antiquary and archaeologist, whose *History of Sligo County and Town* includes many legends associated with places, and who classified an enormous mass of information (unfortunately without giving sources) in *Traces of Elder Faiths in Ireland* – the title indicating that it was an inventory of 'survivals'.
43 Op. cit. 1.158-9.

as we did the local news.'[44] There also was a home market for such more or less synthetic and stereotyped folklorism. I shall confine quotations to three examples – not of the least creditable kind, though it would probably be unwise to vouch for the accuracy of the portraits they offer.

In 1888 the Irish-American David Rice McAnally compiled a book with a title calculated to appeal, *Irish Wonders; the Ghosts, Giants, Pookas, Demons, Leprechauns, Banshees, Fairies, Witches, Widows, Old Maids, and other Wonders of the Emerald Isle; Popular Tales as told by the People*:

> Go where you will in Ireland, the story-teller is there, and on slight provocation will repeat his narrative; amplifying, explaining, embellishing, till from a single fact a connected history is evolved, giving motives, particulars, action, and result, the whole surrounded by a rosy wealth of rustic imagery and told with dramatic force an actor might envy. The following chapters comprise an effort to present this phase of unwritten Celtic literature, the material having been collected during a recent lengthy visit, in the course of which every county in the island was traversed from end to end, and constant association had with the peasant tenantry. As, however, in perusing a drama each reader for himself supplies stage action, so, in the following pages, he is required to imagine the charms of gesticulation and intonation, for no pen can do justice to a story told by Irish lips amid Irish surroundings.[45]

The preface pleads authenticity, but the book emphasizes extravagance and, as Yeats noted, uses an incredibly unified 'dialect'. Narrators are introduced in a conventional way – though there is no reason to doubt that McAnally did travel through Ireland. He says for instance that he ran into 'a boatman on the Shannon, "a respectable man", who solemnly asseverated "Sure, that's no laigend, but the blessed truth as I'm livin' this minnit, for I'd sooner cut out the tongue be the root than desave yer Anner, when every man knows there's not a taste av a lie in it at all" '; or he heard a legend told 'by an old "wise woman" of the neighbourhood with a minuteness of detail that rendered the narrative more tedious than graphic. A devout believer in the truth of her own story, she told it with wonderful earnestness, combining fluency of speech with the intonations of oratory in such a way as to render the legend interesting as a dramatic recitation.'[46]

What may be a book of the same ilk, published in London, was John O'Neill's *Handerahan, the Irish Fairyman; and Legends of Carrick* (1854). Mrs S.C. Hall, the Irish travel-books expert and novelist, praised it in a rather mystifying introduction:

> These Fairy Tales have, to my mind, a decided advantage over all the fairy tales ever published – they are simply given as related by the people to each other ... I know that

---

44 Interview for the WPA Federal Writers' Project 1938, quoted in Marjorie R. Fallows *Irish Americans: Identity and Assimilation* 87.   45 Preface to the London edition, 1888 – not in the American reprint of 1993.   46 Op. cit. (American edition) 88, 172.

when I write a story, it is seldom written exactly as it was heard ... But John O'Neill's pen is *not* practised in story-telling, and the consequence is, that his *stories are truths*; this may read like a bull, but it is not so. He tells the tale, which to him is a truth, exactly as he heard it ... It is probably the last contribution of the kind that will be made to our literature: for the Irish Fairies are, even now, beings of a past tradition – of a gone-by generation. It is now-a-days impossible for the traveller in Ireland to obtain any stories concerning them; the old have departed and the young become sceptical.[47]

This book may be founded on genuine memories, but whether there is no fiction at all is doubtful. At any rate, we are referred to a remote past; the narrator says he witnessed, at the beginning of the century, the funeral of a Fairy Doctor (a man who could break enchantments) who would have been born about the year 1710, and he gathered information about him:

I remarked that it was almost beyond belief that any man could have the power they ascribed to the deceased. An old man who sat in the corner smoking a short pipe, which, from its black and smokey appearance, must have seen a long service, taking the dood-heen from his mouth, said – 'Ah! well, many a heart will ache for his loss; I have reason to remember and pray for him; I'll never forget how he brought me back my poor horse that was kidnapped from me, and I on his back, and never felt them changing him ... I will tell you of his history, and then give you living proofs of his power.' So saying, he gave the following recital, as nearly as I can recollect it, after a lapse of above half a century ...[48]

Less inclined to exaggeration or oddities which were too often associated with anti-Irish jokes, publications idealizing Ireland and its folklore were addressed to an Irish-American audience which sentimentalized memories of 'the Ould Sod'. The typical note is struck in this preface by Barry O'Connor:

In Ireland one need rarely trudge a mile without beholding some boreen, rath, lake, hill or mouldering stone to which is attached some humorous tale, or weird legend ... While trying to portray the Irish peasant, I endeavoured as much as possible to avoid caricature ... The American reader may rest assured that the so-called Irish peasant we sometimes see pictured as a compound of idiot and buffoon is simply a creature of imagination, to be found only in the stage farce or in the prejudiced pages of some anti-Irish magazine.[49]

Yet 'stage-Irish' style was not absent from the few vignettes of storytellers in O'Connor's book: 'Is it true? Troth it is, sir, just as true as that you're now saited forninst my fireside. 'Tis true I am an oulder man to-day than I was when the sportin' boys around used to be callin' me the goold-seeker. Yes, indeed, faix, that's the name they gave me. Danyeen, the Goold-Seeker. But

---

47 *Handerahan, the Fairyman* 6-7. **48** Ibid. 15, 21. **49** Barry O'Connor *Turf-Fire Stories & Fairy Tales of Ireland* (New York, 1890) vi

light your pipe and make yourself comfortable, and I'll try and make it all as
clear to you as I can ...'⁵⁰

In the third group I cut off from what others might prefer to see as a contin-
uum, we find Irish people who did not belong to learned societies and were
unaffected by new anthropological methods and theories; they continued the
older line of 'legend' publication, often (but not exclusively) read in Ireland
itself, perhaps including the display of some eccentric characters and a rendition
of conventional dialect but without the excess of some texts representative of the
second category. The only difference from what had been published half a century before might be a more pronounced sense of the passing of the customs
described, sometimes accompanied by a stronger touch of patriotic sentiment.
An anonymous text published in 1854 in *Duffy's Fireside Magazine* belongs to
this continuation of the proto-folkloric sketches of the first half of the century,
on the borderline of fiction. The setting is County Donegal, and the telling of
adventures among fairies is prepared by a conversation:

'There is a fine healthy nationality about the old traditions and imaginary tales that
delighted our fathers, roused their minds to deeds of daring and supplied fresh oil to the
lamp of patriotism that burned so brightly among them; no nation, in song or story, can
boast such a poetical creation of innocent, light-hearted, aerial beings as old Ireland.' ...
'There is one in our company at present, who is silent as the grave listening to everyone's opinion without a word of contradiction, while he could silence the whole of you
if he pleased.' This timely hint was received with general approbation, for the fact is, the
party had been invited to hear the latest news from fairy land from the lips of Diarmuid
O'Cathain, the poet, who had only returned a day or two before from that delighted
region. ... The bard O'Cathain rose slowly to his feet, and in the midst of the most profound silence, began in a clear, silvery voice, the following narration of his travels in fairy
land ... ⁵¹

The *Dublin University Magazine* kept publishing articles dealing with Irish folklore, like this 'Fire-Side Gossip about Ghosts and Fairies': 'Let but a social
party gather round the fire in country or town on a cold night, and anyone commence a weird tale connected with apparitions, and scarce a person in the company will fail to relate something beyond what ears and eyes are accustomed to,
which occurred if not to himself, at all events to some intimate acquaintance,
who would not utter a falsehood.'⁵²

Popular on both sides of the Atlantic were the books of John O'Hanlon
(1821-1905): *Irish Folk Lore – Traditions and Superstitions of the Country; with
Humorous Tales* (1870), *Legends Lays of Ireland* (also 1870), and *Irish Local
Legends* (1896). He had been ordained in the United States and, in 1853,

50 Ibid. 99-100. 51 'Diarmuid O'Cathain's Christmas Visit to Fairy Land', *Duffy's Fireside
Magazine* 4 (1854) 152-3. 52 *Dublin University Magazine* 62 (1863) 692 (an anonymous article).

returned to Ireland where he was later known as either Canon O'Hanlon or 'Lageniensis'. In trips he made later in life, he heard legends from local people who guided him (cf. Chapter 5):

The greatest enjoyment was experienced to ascend the higher hills and gaze with rapture over the level, diversified plains, or to track the windings of lovely glens and valleys, there to search for particular objects of exploration, while accompanied by some intelligent peasant. He had only the local legends to communicate, but he was invariably obliging, and anxious enough to report those fire-side narratives of his fathers that had been preserved to his time.[53]

Canon O'Hanlon occasionally used written sources, but also, having emigrated in 1842 at the age of twenty-one, his own memories of the pre-Famine times:

To visit the light-hearted peasant's cabin or to form one of its social circle during long winter evenings is popularly known as *courdgeaghing* [*cuardaíocht*: visit]. How agreeable to our youthful fancies, the harmless and pleasant jokes of young and old, at these humble cheerful *re-unions*. How many weird tales of goblin and fairy were told, and to auditors predisposed for receiving most wonderful descriptions and adventures with reverential assent! How many romantic and long-drawn narratives were spun out through the night by some professional story-teller, and which were only varied by the rustic ballad, containing an almost interminable quantity of verses! How often has not the Irish peasant child fallen asleep, through downright tension of eager desire to follow the story-teller to his denouement of a giant's mishap and a successful exit of adventure to the youngest son of some imaginary king or queen! The subject matter for such tales beguiled the hours of rest and often of field labour; among our humble classes.[54]

For all this effusive tone, however, he considered the beliefs of such people 'absurd and irreligious', and must have had only limited respect for the verbal art of traditional story-tellers because he did not hesitate to turn some of their tales into poor rhyming verse of his own.

Portraits – in the past tense – may be found in sketches by James Woods (born 1838), first published in the *Westmeath Examiner* and collected in book form in 1890:

Moodheen Chalke was an itinerant fiddler ... He was well versed in all the legendary lore of Lough Ree, traditional and otherwise, and he was acquainted with all the vicissitudes of all the famous old families in Roscommon, Westmeath and Longford, their duels, horse racing, cock fighting, and heiress hunting. He knew every haunted house in the country ... 'Musha, ye must be a stranger about here, and maybe ye niver hard the story about the ould lake and its islands.' I answered in the negative, and told him that I would feel obliged to know something about it, traditional and legendary. He cheerfully complied, and after applying to the flask for inspiration, he proceeded to relate the

53 *Irish Local Legends* vii.   **54** *Legend Lays of Ireland* (1870) xxvi–xxvii.

legend of Lough Ree. [The urine of a marvellous horse formed the lake.] ... [The writer
also listened to an old woman.] I expressed a wish as a stranger to hear some of the legends of the locality. Polly complied, and after the usual formalities were gone through by
her, viz., a short cough, resembling the peculiar chirrup of the grouse, and dredging the
nasal organ with Goodbody's high toast snuff, she asked me if I knew the little fort near
Mr Reddy's house on the roadside. I replied in the affirmative, when she proceeded to
relate the legend of St Enan after her own peculiar fashion: – 'Well, me dacent man, in
the ould ainshint times whin rich people wor plain an' humble, an' afore the ladies wore
improvers, an' whin pianyes wor as hard to be seen or got as a leprehaun, an' whin
gosoons [*garsúin*: boys] an' girshas [*girseacha*: young girls] spoke Irish wid the rale axsint
... ' ... Whilst Polly was narrating the legend she was frequently corrected and interrupted, as nearly all hearers had different versions of the story, all of which she treated
with the utmost contempt.[55]

More sober accounts of collecting made in Ulster by Letitia McClintock were
published in the 1870s and 80s in the *Dublin University Magazine, All the Year
'Round* and the *Cornhill Magazine*:

'Who are the fairies?' we asked an old man who had told several quaint fairy tales, full
of strange adventure, gravely vouching for their truth. The curious events described had
all, he declared, happened to neighbours and friends of his own, or had been handed
down from father to son in his family. 'The gentry [fairies] is allowed to be the fallen
angels,' he replied. 'When Satan and his angels were thrown over the battlements of
heaven, the greater part of them fell down to hell; but some fell into the sea – those is
the mermen an' mermaids; an' others fell on the earth – those is the fairies.' 'Why are
they now so rarely seen or heard?' we inquired. 'Weel, ma'am, there's them that says the
wee-folk is all awa' to Scotland; but others thinks there's as many o' them in Ireland as
ever, only they canna get making themselves visible, becas there's so much scripture
spread abroad over the country.' 'Is that your opinion?' 'It is not, ma'am. I think they
know that the judgment-day is drawing near; an' so they're keeping very quiet in the
hope that, if they do no more mischief, they may be saved.' We thanked our old friend
for his explanation, which was quite new to us. Our manifest interest in his conversation
led him to tell grotesque stories of circumstances which had, he said, taken place at the
beginning of the present century, when the elfin people had still the power of making
themselves visible.[56]

In the introduction to his *Fairy and Folk Tales of the Irish Peasantry* in 1888,
Yeats praised Letitia McClintock's controlled use of dialect.

Two books written by W. Hart (who signed 'Floredice') were devoted in
their entirety to encounters with storytellers and to what they had told. In
Memories of a Month among the Mere Irish, the author said he had heard them
as a boy, in the same County Donegal. Physical portraits are unusually detailed.
The same author's *Derrydeel. A Collection of Stories from North-West Donegal* was

55 *Ancient and Modern Sketches of the County Westmeath* 13-14, 31-4. The legend of St Enan,
patron of Drumrath, is also in Canon O'Hanlon's *Lives of Irish Saints* 8. 291-2. 56 *Cornhill
Magazine* 35 (1877) 172: 'Folk-lore of the County Donegal. The Fairies'.

said to have been compiled from similar notes. Here we encounter a storytelling woman:

On returning to Mrs Herraty's cabin, we found seated by the hearth, where the potato-pot seemed to have been in requisition, a cheerful little old woman, whom Mrs Herraty introduced as Nancy Mac Ilhenny, a personal friend of hers, informing us that 'she was, wanst on a time, Father McLoughlin's housekeeper,' and that she was 'full of divartin' stories'. On which I expressed an earnest desire to hear some of her reminiscences ... Another of Nancy's stories told in Mrs Herraty's chimney corner I thought an amusing one, and I shall here try to reproduce it, though with little hope of doing anything like justice to the old woman's histrionic mode of narration ... During the recital by Nancy Mac Ilhenny of her narrative of the Splay-Footed Princess, old Owen had evinced the interest he took in it by sudden ejaculations of wonder, pity, or applause at its various incidents, and, on its completion, thus announced his general approval: 'Troth, Nancy, that's a rael divartin' story ye've told us! Have ye another wan like it?' ' 'Deed have I,' replied she, 'but ye wouldn't want me to tire the gentleman out with me nonsense.' Old Nancy's scruples having been removed by a suitable assurance on my part, she commenced to tell, or rather to rehearse, the following story ... [57]

In the same mixed group of texts but at the most clearly documentary end of the spectrum, we find the portrait and biography, published in the *Irish Monthly* in 1886, of an old shanachie who was ending his life in County Clare; born around 1800, he was said to have learned his repertoire from an old hedge-schoolmaster who died in 1826:

I spent an hour to-day in Kildysart workhouse with the last of the Shanachies, blind Teague Mac Mahon. He must be as old as the century, if not older; but his broad, bent figure and his ruddy well-featured face are still full of vigour. The sightless eyes are closed, the white hair is long and thick and only the wrinkled hands, somewhat wasted from enforced illness, show how old the shanachie must be ... Teague only knows a limited amount of English. He speaks like a foreigner, with difficulty and deliberation, using the most dignified idioms and with a tantalizing slowness but with a wonderful good accent. He evidently picked it up late in life from educated people ... Blind Teague, partly himself in English, partly in Irish to his interpreter, told me of Peter Connell. Now, that schoolmaster in his youth not only crossed into Connaught to study 'all the old talk, and the old stories,' but visited every part of Ireland and even spent a long time in Scotland from whence he brought back much matter of song and story. [The paper then celebrates Connell's expertise in pedigrees.] ... Many a song, and many a story, and many a queer tradition blind Teague, then a stalwart young peasant, learned from the sage. I tested several of them as to dates and names by looking them up in authentic records, and allowing for exaggeration and certain elements of ghostly and diabolical nature, nearly all the people were living at the times stated, and performed the feats of bloodshed, love-making, or drinking, from which the legends spring. ... [Mac Mahon was a valuable informant for antiquaries like O'Curry, Petrie and Joyce in Dublin, before the

57 Op. cit. 14, 17, 41-2.

mid-nineteenth century.] Teague looks on the Royal Irish Academy as a sacred shrine, and it is his great boast that his was the only single knock that was ever answered at that learned door. Once a policeman ordered him off the steps as having no business there. The indignant shanachie responded. 'It is I that have business there with the gentlemen, and not the likes of you that would be let inside.'[58]

This portrait of a very old inmate of a poorhouse, the 'last' of his kind (but neither a 'bard' nor a 'minstrel'), speaking English 'like a foreigner', was offered as belonging to a lost world. Yet there still were storytellers in the 1880s. Could one collect from them more accurately and systematically, or more consistently use recollections of their art earlier in the century? That is what the folklorists we shall now deal with wanted to do.

The different kinds of portrayals (and perhaps sometimes pastiches) which the preceding sections have skimmed through were not innovative in their purposes and methods. In Britain and on the continent, some folklorists tried to develop new collecting and editorial techniques, but the Irish material quoted so far seems largely impervious to such efforts. However, a model of what could be done came from Scotland. In the 1850s, John Francis Campbell of Islay (1822-85) had undertaken the systematic exploration of Gaelic lore. Although narrative traditions were on the wane in large areas of the Highlands, he found them still in full vigour in the Outer Hebrides – which were close to Ireland in the types of tales most highly prized. He worked in the field himself and employed others as well, published the original Gaelic texts with their translation, and specified their provenance. He was interested in 'the nature of the people who knew the stories'[59] and portrayed several of them in action: 'I found them to be men with clear heads and wonderful memories, generally very poor and old, living in remote corners of remote islands, and speaking only Gaelic; in short, those who have lived most at home, furthest from the world, and who have no source of mental relaxation beyond themselves and their neighbours.'[60] The team of collectors he trained – another important innovation – had strict orders: 'I begged for the very words used by the people who told the stories, with nothing added, or omitted, or altered.'[61] He made a trip to Ireland, and there is a brief account of what he found in the fourth volume of his *Popular Tales of the West Highlands, Orally Collected*:

A lot of stories got from a carman in Waterford in 1861, included – 1. The water-cow and her progeny. 2. The Bansidhe, which the narrator 'had seen and heard'. 3. A version of the man who travelled to learn shivering. 4. A haunted tower. 5. Treasure finding. 6. A spirit haunting a road and asking for a ride. 7. A lake spirit. 8. The man and the dog in the subterranean passage, and many others were alluded. It was evident that the Irish peasantry had the very same legends as the Scotch, and these were told in a dif-

---

58 Mrs Morgan John O'Connell 'The Last of the Shanachies', reprinted in *Béaloideas* 30 (1962) 99-100. 59 *Popular Tales of the West Highlands* 1. xvii. Campbell also published in 1872 a collection of 'Ossianic ballads', *Leabhar na Féinne*. 60 Ibid. 1. xxiii. 61 Ibid. 1. xiv.

ferent, and very characteristic way. It is to be hoped that some Irishman will collect and publish the Irish popular tales. If it be honestly and faithfully done it will be the most amusing collection of all; but if any one polishes the language of Irish peasants, he will most certainly spoil it.[62]

At about the same time a more distant model became accessible, showing how the whole repertoire of a nation might be assembled and interpreted: romantic nationalism and the example of the Grimm Brothers had encouraged an interest in folklore in Nordic countries, and during the 1840s and 50s Jørgen Moe and P. Chr. Asbjørnsen collected and published Norwegian tales and legends. The methods of publication may have been less ethnographically sound than Campbell's – one of Asbørnsen's ideal examples was T.F. Croker, through Wilhelm Grimm's translation (see p. 180), and like him he fictionalized the descriptions of storytelling that framed the narratives,[63] but the books were rich in stories which proved valuable for comparative studies. The English scholar George Webbe Dasent, an authority in Scandinavian matters who encouraged Campbell, translated parts of them in 1859 with a long introductory essay on the 'Origin and Diffusion of Popular Tales', in which he developed the Grimms' hypothesis concerning an Aryan origin of folktales and urged collectors of different countries to gather like material. Read in Ireland, it could broaden perspectives.

In 1862, in a Dublin periodical, a detailed anonymous review of both Campbell's *Popular Tales of the West Highlands* and Dasent's *Popular Tales from the Norse* proved that in Ireland too there was sensitivity to the problem of accuracy, and awareness of comparative studies which now might be systematized not only to identify similar tales but perhaps also to distinguish national repertoires and modes of storytelling – including perhaps a 'Celtic' one – in the European concert:

All the great dialects of Europe – the German, the Scandinavian, the Celtic, the Greek, and the Latin – widely as, at first sight, they seem to differ from each other, are yet kindred tongues, children of the same parent, and referable to a common original. That original is to be sought in the East – in the old Sanscrit. If philology has led to the result which we have just stated, that result is powerfully confirmed by the various tales, which, for long ages, have been popular in different countries, and which are the foundations of those stories which, as children, we listen to with so much delight. When an old woman relates to us some fabulous tale, the matter seems insignificant and unworthy of much attention. If the tale is interesting, we listen to it, and then, perhaps, forget it; its value appears to be limited by the momentary pleasure which it gives. But if we are told that that very same story, or one at least which in its main incidents and its essential character, bears a very strong resemblance to it, is to be found in a book, written thousands of years ago, in a distant country, in a language which we cannot understand,

---

62 Ibid. 4. 401. 63 R. Kvideland and H.K. Sehmsdorf (ed.) *Scandinavian Folk Belief and Legends* 13, 24.

in letters even which are as strange as the words which they make up, our curiosity cannot fail to be awakened, and we must acknowledge that the fact is, at least, a striking one. If another step is taken, and we learn that, in addition to this, the story is one which, for an immense space of time, has been a favourite in a number of different countries, that in different forms it is to be found among the traditions alike of Hindoos and of Greeks, of Germans, and of Celts, our astonishment gives way to reflection. And then, when we are further told that this is the case, not with one story alone, but with an entire mass of stories, that several races which we have always been accustomed to look upon as total strangers to each other, have what is manifestly a common tradition, we cannot help feeling that, if there is a common tradition, there must be more, and we are borne on to the conclusion that those races have also a common origin.

There are scarcely any two branches of the human species which are generally thought to differ more widely from each other in manners, in character, and in their various modes of thought than the Celtic and the Scandinavian. Yet, when we read [the books under review], we are at once struck, as in the course of this article we shall show to our readers, at the vast number of instances in which the popular ideas of both races coincide, and in which both alike appear to draw from the same common fund of intellectual entertainment. But, while this is the case, we cannot help recognising at the same time the widely different manners in which each of the two races treats this common fund, and the great difference of style between the Norse tales and those of our Celtic brethren of Scotland. ... The Gaelic stories [wonder and hero tales in Campbell, as opposed to the generally simpler and more concise Norse pieces] are often long, full of wearisome, though strange detail, and crowded with episodes which branch off in a number of directions, and, of course, interfere with the progress of the main narrative.[64]

Campbell's scholarly method was assessed: the non-intrusiveness of the editor and the accuracy of transcription might complicate the reader's task, but were laudable:

Indeed, one of the most interesting portions of Mr Campbell's book is that in which he enumerates the sources from which he has taken his materials. Sailors, fishermen, gamekeepers, old women, travelling tinkers, discharged Highland soldiers, such are his authorities, and in every instance, he allows his informant to tell his story in his own way, and never permits the fastidiousness of the educated gentleman to introduce any refinements in the rude speech of the unlettered narrator. Another matter which, at least to a mere English reader, throws a good deal of strangeness into the style of these stories is this, that Mr Campbell gives these in almost a literal translation from the Gaelic, rendering word for word of his original, and carefully preserving even the most idiomatic Celtic expressions. All this, of course, often creates a good deal of harshness and obscurity, but for our own part, we must express approval of this mode adopted by Mr Campbell, for we thus, at least, get a true insight into the Gaelic mind, and are presented with a faithful picture of the mode of narration which has for centuries delighted the Celtic population of the Highlands.[65]

64 'Norse and Gaelic Popular Tales', *Duffy's Hibernian Magazine* 1 (1862) 319-21. 65 Ibid. 321-2.

The more 'scientific' mode of folklore studies would henceforth try to achieve such precision, while also testing general hypotheses.

Two folklorists who published Irish material more extensively and professionally than those mentioned earlier moved in this direction, each in his own way: Patrick Kennedy (who probably wrote the review of Campbell and Dasent quoted above), and Jeremiah Curtin. The first dealt with traditions in the English language and often worked from memory – which clearly distinguished him from Campbell. The other, coming from America, was familiar with new ethnographical methods and directly noted down from informants, in Irish-speaking districts. For both – and their immediate successors – folklore was still associated with rural culture only.

Born in County Wexford, Patrick Kennedy (1801-73) had lived among country people. In the early 1820s he moved to Dublin where he worked as a teacher and teacher-trainer for the 'Kildare Place Society' promoting the education of the poor, and later set up as a bookseller. He wrote books which included folklore items mingled with some fiction: *Legends of Mount Leinster* (1855), *The Banks of the Boro* (1867), *Evenings in the Duffrey* (1869), and three collections of traditional narratives: *Legendary Fictions of the Irish Celts* (1866), *The Fireside Stories of Ireland* (1870) and *The Bardic Stories of Ireland* (1871). He referred to oral sources, but was in fact dealing with what he had heard and observed in his rural childhood and youth, filtered through recollection and reconstructed in the style he thought his readers would accept. He had experienced oral traditions in a district where the English language was established; Douglas Hyde would describe part of the material as 'the detritus of genuine Gaelic folk-stories, filtered through an English idiom and much impaired and stunted in the process',[66] but had to admit that the collector himself had not falsified it.

A letter to the editor of the *Wexford Independent*, in August 1851, explained Kennedy's programme: 'Do not you and I and the others still retain many of the traditions and legends of our native place? In the present transition state of the country they are likely to be lost, and will it not be doing some service to preserve them, however imperfectly?'[67] Stories he remembered were published in this periodical, then in others. He commented on some of his informants, for instance in an article which testifies to the coexistence of different cultures in partly anglicized areas of Ireland:

The ensuing traditions, or legends, or whatever they may be called, have been altogether procured from oral authority in the county of Wexford ... The subjoined legend was heard from the lips of an intelligent woman [his godmother], who, despite the want of books in her neighbourhood, had amassed a considerable stock of information on the legendary history of Ireland, on sacred history, and even on the subject of Heathen mythol-

66 *Beside the Fire* xi. **67** Quoted by James Delany, 'Patrick Kennedy', in *The Past* 7 (1964) 58.

ogy. She had a retentive memory for poetry, and could recite many passages from the
Iliad and Paradise Lost, and the greater part of The Battle of Aughrim [a chapbook constantly reprinted between 1728 and 1850].[68]

Another article described a storytelling session and the way 'tradition' persisted:

When the circumstances attending the recital of fictions such as these are considered, the
tenacious hold they retain on the memory of uneducated people will cease to be a matter
of surprise. The scene is always the warm domestic hearth, the time the long cold night
of winter. The members of the family, and the neighbours who drop in, have nothing to
distract their attention. The hands of the women are mechanically occupied, the hands
of the men and boys are on their knees or in their pockets. The children, too, happy in
escaping banishment to an early bed, and ensconced among the legs of the seniors, fully
exist for the time in the wild tissue of the story. The grown-up folk may forget a tale
heard for the first time, but the children will not, and if only one in a dozen of the auditors turns out to be a good scealacht in his turn, the memory of what he has once or
twice heard is certain to endure.[69]

In his semi-fictional works, Kennedy regularly included scenes of storytelling. In what was probably the most factual of those books, *Legends of Mount
Leinster* (a miscellany of sketches), we first meet a storyteller of consequence,
Owen Jourdan, who would reappear in following volumes. *The Banks of the
Boro*, written in 1856 and published more than ten years later, had a fictional
protagonist, but the documentary part remained important; the preface acknowledged the distance between observation and the time of writing, while asserting
the authenticity of the report: 'The incidents of the following story occurred in
the years 1817 and 1818. ... The chief incidents, circumstances, and fireside conferences mentioned in this really occurred.'[70] The book multiplied accounts of
traditional customs and regularly gathered its characters around a fire to introduce tales, ballads, personal experience stories and rumours:

On passing through the kitchen, we found the large fireplace provided with its retinue
of labourers and servants, and a few of the half-witted strollers through the country. One
of this class called *Bet-na-Dheega* , was relating how she was annoyed last spring, coming
down Gurrawn road, from Mr Horneck's to the bridge, by a whole ditchful of frogs. ...
Neddy *Lannan* (Lennon), another of the fraternity, was reminded by this that he met
Murtheen Caum waumussing [feeling sick] down the same road this very day ... We had
formed a circle round the inmates of the kitchen fire, attracted by the conversation going
on, there being something in the demeanour and expressions of these poor children of
Providence, interesting to everyone that has a sympathy for his kind.[71]

---

68 'Fairy Lore and Pagan Relics in a County of the Pale', *Dublin University Magazine* 59
(February 1862) 241. 69 Ibid., April 1862, 455, 'Leinster Folk-lore'. 70 *The Banks of the
Boro* iii. 71 Ibid. 48-50.

Evenings in the Duffrey, a sequel to *The Bank of the Boro*, repeated the claim to authenticity: 'On all other points [apart from the love story of the protagonists] there is not a fictitious character, nor incident in the mere narrative, nor legend related, nor ballad sung, which was not current in the country half a century since. The fireside discussions were really held.'[72]

All fictional trappings were cast off in *Legendary Fictions of the Irish Celts* (dedicated to Joseph Sheridan Le Fanu, who 'was not without sympathy for story-tellers' – see p. 264) and in *The Fireside Stories of Ireland*. The second gathered fifty texts – often Irish versions of international tales: 'a more correct title for the present collection would be "The Fireside Stories of the Aryan peoples, as related in Ireland", for nearly every one of them is told in some shape at the social gatherings of Hindoos, Persians, Slavonians, or Teutons'.[73] A running commentary on the narratives shows that Kennedy was now prepared to think about the nature of traditional storytelling and had some ideas of what had been written about it outside Ireland. The preface conveyed the author's view of his role as rescuer of what was vanishing in a process of acculturation, or – in his opinion as a Dublin resident at the time of writing – had perhaps already disappeared:

Country folk of the small-farmer and peasant class resort to their neighbours' houses during the long winter evenings, urged by the same want which sends the shopkeepers and mechanics of a city to the reading or tap-room, or to the theatre. They soon exhaust the local topics, but are unwilling to withdraw to the comparative loneliness of their own homes; and if one of the company possesses the faculties of a good memory and a good utterance, and condescends to tell a story, he or she is a social benefactor for the time. In this way the great body of fireside lore has been preserved notwithstanding the small number of good story-tellers in any neighbourhood. Where the office devolves on an incompetent narrator, a change for the worse ensues. Having gone on correctly for a time, he finds his memory at fault, and is obliged to fall back on the sequel of a remembered tale. In this way stories, once popular in this or that locality, come to be remembered no more. Taking into account the fewness of story-tellers, and the odds against a regular succession of good ones in any given district, the preservation of so many household fictions is not easily accounted for, especially as they have lost the poetic form in which they could be easily retained in the memory. The easy access to cheap books, and the diffusion of the penny literature of our times, have given a death-blow to the oral literature of the fireside. Regret at the passing away of an institution from which my childhood and boyhood derived such pleasure, has set me on to preserve in print the naïve, and in many cases, excellent narratives which once delighted the unlettered folk of half the world.[74]

The preface to the *Legendary Fictions* situated Irish traditions in the European family tree, and repeated the refrain about the necessity of a last-minute rescue:

72 *Evenings in the Duffrey* Preface. **73** *The Fireside Stories of Ireland* vii. **74** Ibid. vii-viii.

From our early youth we have felt the deepest interest in the stories and legends which are peculiar to the Irish, or which they possess in common with all the Indo-European races, and our dearest wish is that their memory should not fade from the minds of the people. ... Taking into consideration the diminishing of our population by want and emigration, and the general diffusion of book learning, such as it is, and the growing taste for the rubbishy tales of the penny and halfpenny journals, we have in these latter times been haunted with the horrid thought that the memory of the tales heard in boyhood would be irrecoverably lost. ... The greater part of the stories and legends in this volume are given as they were received from the storytellers with whom our youth was familiar. A few of them thus heard we read at a later period, and in an improved form, in the Bardic historians and in manuscripts, kindly furnished by the late estimable archaeologist, John Windele, of Cork [see p. 183].[75]

The first part consisted of what Kennedy after the Grimms called 'household stories': 'those fictions which, with some variations, are told at the domestic gatherings of the Celts, Teutons, and Slavonians and are more distinguished by a succession of wild and wonderful adventures than a carefully-constructed framework'. He could move on from local details to a global view:

Presence in a crowd produces an uneasy state of expectation, which requires something startling or sensational to satisfy it. Thus it was with the hearth-audiences. It needed but few experiments to put the first story-tellers on the most effective way of amusing and interesting the group gathered round the blaze, who for the moment felt their mission to consist in being agreeably excited, not in applying canons of criticism. The number of good *Scealuidhes* dispersed through the country parts is but small compared to the mass of the people, and hundreds may be found who recollect the succession of events and the personages of a tale while utterly incapable of relating it. In remote neighbourhoods, where the people have scarcely any communication with towns or cities, or access to books, stories will be heard identical with those told in the Brothers Grimm's German collection, or among the Norse tales gathered by MM. Asbjornsen and Moe ... The ancestors both of Celt and Teuton brought the simple and wonderful narratives from the parent ancestral household in Central Asia ... Not only can a general resemblance be traced in all the fictions of the great Japhetian divisions of the human race [cf. p. 90], but an enthusiastic and diligent explorer would be able to find a relationship between these and the stories current among the Semitic races, and even the tribes scattered over the great continent of Africa, subject to the variations arising from climate, local features, and the social condition of the people.[76]

The book multiplies references to the folklore of other countries, and while the commentary reveals an awareness of the applicability to folktales of current publications abroad, the reference to the 'Japhetian' theory confirms that Kennedy had been in touch with older Irish antiquarianism; we also notice it when he gives a late example of the use of tale-telling as a sleep-inducer (cf. p. 52):

75 *Legendary Fictions of the Irish Celts* ix-xi. 76 Ibid. 3-4, 14-15.

The Rev. Matthew Horgan, the intimate friend and zealous fellow-labourer of the late John Windele in the fields of Celtic archeology, was during his later years obliged to have recourse to a similar auxiliary. This *scealuidhe* was Tim or Tighue O'Sullivan a man without education, but rich in the second stage of the Ossianic lore, in which all the original poetic form is lost, with the exception of some remarkable quatrains appearing here and there through the prose. He, taking his station near the good clergyman's bed, would commence, and conduct his mighty men of old through their trials; and by dint of the soft, guttural, gliding sounds of the Gaelic, uniform pitch of voice, and frequent repetitions, such as may be found even in Homer, would at last bring the thick folds of slumber down on the priest's eyes.[77]

In the section dealing with ghost stories and other legends of the supernatural, Kennedy insists on the sincerity of the informants. 'Ossianic stories' form another part, for which oral sources were scanty. One of them was Jemmy Reddy, who 'understood Irish, for his father and mother spoke it pretty fluently, but they would not suffer their children to speak it'.[78] According to Kennedy, such material had been degraded by 'descending ... to the care of uneducated peasants',[79] and he preferred to summarize from manuscripts.

He was interested in some technical features of storytelling, when trying to understand why a certain tale – 'The Corpse Watchers' – was heard more often than others in his Wexford childhood:

It probably owed its popularity to the bit of a rhyme, and the repetition of the adventures of the three sisters, nearly in the same words. It may seem strange that this circumstance, which would have brought *ennui* and discomfort on our readers, should have recommended it to the fireside audience. Let it be considered that they expected to sit up to a certain hour, and that listening to a story was the pleasantest occupation they could fancy for the time. Length, then, in a tale, was a recommendation, and these repetitions contributed to that desirable end.[80]

In the same book he named again his main informants, and gave his most detailed account of Owen Jourdan's art:

Poor Jourdan was a genuine story-telling genius. He was not the mere talented Scealuidhe; he not only had a sense of what pleased and interested, but he could invent, if needful – i.e. he could form a good narrative out of two or three independent ones. With all his native powers of deceiving his auditors while relating extraordinary things, as if they had happened to himself, he was suspected of believing in the existence of fairies. ... We have endeavoured to retain his style of narrative; but alas! it is more than thirty years since we sat near to his throne, viz. the big kitchen griddle in Tombrick.[81]

The last remark points again to one of the limitations of Kennedy's work as a folklorist: what he reported had not been directly transcribed, but was reached

77 Ibid. 177-8. **78** Ibid. 184. **79** Ibid. 158. **80** Ibid. 48 **81** Ibid. 247.

through memory. Another relative weakness was deliberate selection: if he did not censor beliefs (which others had denounced as 'superstitions'), as a true Victorian he eliminated situations and language which he considered as dirt not to be confused with pure folklore;[82] on the other hand he was not immune from the old temptation to overstress the picturesque. But he preserved a rich material and offered a fairly comprehensive panorama of the variety of narratives transmitted in a society.[83]

A decisive new step was taken fourteen years after Kennedy's death when a linguist and trained ethnographer, Jeremiah Curtin (1838-1906), came from abroad to take down, systematically and from the mouths of live storytellers, what was still traditionally narrated in Irish-speaking districts of the West. Opportunity to talk with German, Norwegian and Polish settlers near Milwaukee, where he lived with his Irish parents, had given him a start as a polyglot: by the end of his life he was said to know – not equally well – more than sixty languages. Though his father was probably bilingual, Curtin did not learn Irish as a child but began to pick it up by deciphering a New Testament in this language and by conversing with immigrants in Boston. He would later say that 'it's a waste of time to speak English if one knows Gaelic, a fine compact and flexible language, capable of expressing the most delicate shades of meaning'.[84] Having graduated from Harvard, he worked from 1864 as a secretary to the American legation in St Petersburg, resigning after a few years but remaining in Russia until 1877 as a businessman and traveller. Later he would translate Russian and Polish novels. From 1883 to the end of 1891 he was a member of the staff of the recently established Bureau of American Ethnology in the Smithsonian Institution, and made an intensive field study of Native Americans, collecting the oral traditions of half a dozen tribes. He also wrote about Mongol and Buriat cultures, and published Russian and Magyar myths and tales.

Having spent a six-months leave of absence in Ireland in 1887 (not his first visit), he went there again in 1891, and for more than a year (his longest stay)

82 *The Fireside Stories of Ireland* viii: 'I have endeavoured to present them in a form suitable for the perusal of both sexes and of all ages.' *Legendary Fictions of the Irish Celts* 20-1: 'Forty or fifty years since, several very vile tales – as vile as could be found in the *Fabliaux* or the *Decameron*, or any other dirty collection, had a limited circulation among farm-servants and labourers, even in the respectable County of Wexford.' 83 James G. Delaney 'Patrick Kennedy, Folklorist – A Preliminary Assessment', *The Past* 14 (1983) 55: 'Speaking as a folklorist of nearly thirty years experience of field work in many counties, especially those of the Midlands, and as one whose first task in the field it was to follow in the footsteps of Kennedy in the shadow of Mount Leinster and the White Mountain, I can say, after studying his writings ... that I have never discovered any inaccuracy of any kind. His touch is sure and his instinct unfailingly accurate. His folklore is always correct, even though there are sometimes many lacunae ... ' 84 Charles A. Curtin 'Jeremiah Curtin', *Journal of the American Irish Historical Society* 31 (1937) 56.

in 1892-3. When he began to gather Irish material in 1887, he knew what he was looking for:

For many years, I had been possessed with the idea that there was a great stock of myths current among the people of Ireland, as well as many of that class of facts which throw light on the history of the human mind. Facts of value to the scientific world. I hoped that there might still remain in the minds of the people of the remote districts of Ireland many idioms useful in explaining the language of the manuscripts preserved in the Irish Academy, and myths that would supplement and strengthen recorded mythology. I was going to Ireland to settle that question.[85]

In Kerry, he found men who knew 'of strange adventures, told their "beliefs" and their myths' – he obviously liked the latter word, referring by it to all orally transmitted material which seemed ancient and significant. But at Newcastle West he met a representative of a well-attested class of popular anti-quarians who believed that valid traditions were to be found only in manu-scripts:

O'Conner had asked an old man, an ex-schoolmaster, to meet me. He brought with him a manuscript a hundred and twenty years old. After patiently listening to a long story about the manuscript, I asked the old man if he could tell me a Gaelic myth. His answer was: 'I don't care to be telling lies that have been handed down from father to son. I care only for things that have been recorded and are authentic.' I told him that the manu-script contained myths which had been handed down for a thousand years or more, but I couldn't reason with him. 'What was written was true.' [86]

Most of the time he seems to have had no great difficulty in finding storytellers, though it often meant renouncing comfort: 'It is not in homes of ease and wealth that ancient lore is found.'[87] Field-work took him to Donegal:

At Teelin Point I found a man, Donald McBrearty, who knew a good number of fine myths, and later I spent many hours with him at his home. ... In a small house at the foot of the mountain [Slieve League], I found a man, James McLaughlin, who told me a good myth. I spent the following day at his house taking down what myths he knew. Work in a small room, where a peat fire is burning and hens roosting, is very wearisome for one accustomed to fresh air and light.[88]

He also worked in County Galway:

The second man I met [in the Claddagh] was a sailor. I asked if he knew an old man who could tell stories. He said that he did, and conducted me to one of the houses where I found an aged couple sitting by a turf fire, their morning meal on a chair in front of

85 *Memoirs of Jeremiah Curtin* (adapted by his widow from his notebooks and her own diary) 385. 86 Quoted by S. Ó Duilearga in his introduction to *Irish Folk Tales* xi. 87 *Memoirs ...* 457. 88 Quoted in *Irish Folk Tales* xii.

them. The meal consisted of a bowl of tea and some bread the woman had baked on the coals. They welcomed me pleasantly, and the old man told me a long myth.[89]

Two places produced 'no myths'; one was Killarney, where suspiciously new material was being tailored for the tourists, and the other (in the second field trip) was the Great Blasket, later to become known as a folklorist's mecca: 'I asked a man on crutches if he knew any Gaelic myths. His answer was: "I care more about getting the price of a bottle of whiskey than about old stories." Another man said: "If you'll give me the price of a bottle of whiskey, I'll talk about stories." I got no stories.'[90] But not far from there, at Ventry, he found more willing informants, like Maurice Lynch (who was born in 1810): 'He had kept in his mind the myths told him by his grandparents. He had repeated them to me with pleasure, realising that if not written down from his own lips they would perish, for even his children to whom he had told them a great many times could not repeat them entirely.'[91]

The result of the first expedition was Curtin's *Myths and Folk-Lore of Ireland*, published in 1890. In a long introduction he set forth his ideas on mythology, referring to Max Müller and to the Indo-European theory. He believed that the Celts had been the first of seven branches of 'Aryans' to move west, and therefore retained the most archaic features. He published what he had collected in 1891-93 in the New York newspaper *The Sun*, and in book form: *Hero-Tales of Ireland* in 1894, and *Tales of the Fairies and of the Ghost World Collected from Oral Tradition in South-West Munster* in 1895. In the introduction to *Hero-Tales*, he repeated the idea that characters in 'myths' were personifications of natural forces, and compared what he had heard from North American Indians and his Irish informants: 'We may affirm as a theory that primitive beliefs, in all places, are of the same system essentially as the American. ... A comparison of Gaelic tales with the Indian tales of America shows that the Gaelic contain materials some of which is as ancient as the Indian, while the tales themselves are less primitive.'[92] Influenced by the dominant evolutionist theories, he believed that earlier mental conditions were embedded in the 'myths' different peoples were still telling, and that Ireland was a good laboratory for comparative study of layers of tradition: 'The people of any purely Gaelic district in Ireland, where the language is spoken yet, preserve numerous remnants of pre-Christian belief. These remnants are in many cases very valuable, though they may seem grotesque, naive and baseless to most observers.'[93] By studying the heritages of different cultures and going back to the myth-making patterns of primitive peoples, one might reach, behind the already

89 Ibid. xiii. **90** *Memoirs* ... 455. **91** Quoted in Pádraig Ó Fiannachta (ed.) *Thaitin Sé Le Peig* 41. **92** *Hero-Tales of Ireland* xvi, xlv. **93** Quoted in *Thaitin Sé Le Peig* 34.

more differentiated 'Aryan' mythology, universals of human experience: 'All myths have the same origin, and all run parallel up to a certain point, which may be taken as the point to which the least developed people have risen.'[94]

Only in the book published in 1895, focusing on accounts of personal experiences of the supernatural, did he give accounts of the storytellers and circumstances of telling, which took place mostly in a house still to be seen near Ventry Strand:

I invited my host to come to me in the evening and bring two or three men to tell the strange adventures of our own time, true tales of the district ... After supper, the 'man of the house' came with two other persons, and we passed a very interesting evening. One of the two visitors was a blind man named Dyeermud Duvane, about forty years of age, and born in the neighbourhood, who had been in America, where he lost his eyesight. He related to me somewhat of his life in the United States. ... This blind man, though a sceptic by nature, knew some good cases of fairy action, and told the first story of the evening. The second man was seventy years old, white-haired, with a fair complexion and blue eyes which were wonderfully clear and serious. This was a genuine believer in fairies and a rare example of one type of old Irishmen. He lived near a fairy fort about a mile distant; his name was John Malone. His family and friends had suffered from fairies, and his daughter-in-law died from a fairy stroke ...

When the company came to my room on the following evening the host brought a fourth man, Maurice Lynch, a mason, who knew a good deal about ghosts and fairies. When he bade me good-bye the night before John Malone promised to open the present session with a tale which he knew to be true, for the chief actors in it were friends of his own, 'and himself was in it also' ...

My host brought a tinker who had 'walked the way' that day and was passing the night at the house. The tinker knew none of the old tales, but as the host said, 'He has two stories that will knock a laugh out of the company ...'

One day an old woman leaning on a staff and a blind man 'walked the way to me.' After some talk and delay they agreed to tell what they knew about fairies, ghosts, and buried treasures. I had heard of them before, and tried to secure their services. The old woman speaks English only when forced to it, and then very badly. The blind man has suffered peculiarly from the fairies. They have lamed the poor fellow, taken his eyesight, and have barely left the life in him ... I may say that the woman, whose name is Maggie Doyle, was unwilling to tell tales in the daytime. It was only after some persuasion and an extra reward that she was induced to begin ... This is all the old woman told. When going she promised to come on the following day, but I have not seen her since. The blind man informed me some evenings later that she was sick and in the 'ashpitl' (hospital). Her sickness was caused, as she said, by telling me tales in the daytime. Many of the old people will tell tales only in the evening; it is not right, not lucky, to do so during daylight.[95]

94 Introduction to *Myths and Folk-Lore of Ireland*. **95** *Tales of the Fairies* ... 4-5, 23, 43, 89, 132, 143. In 'Notes on some of Jeremiah Curtin's story-tellers', an appendix to *Tales of the Fairies*, other informants are identified by Pádraic Ó Siochfhradha who was ten years old when Curtin stayed at Ventry.

With Curtin, Irish folklore reappeared on the international scene and proved to be more diversified than the impression Crofton Croker's collection had made some sixty-five or seventy years before: there were fairy legends indeed, but also epic tales which were still being told and did not smack of pseudo bardic ossianism, as well as complex equivalents of international wonder-tale types. His investigations confirmed that, contrary to what had been foretold by Wilde and others, oral traditions had not vanished after the Great Famine, though they fared better in certain regions which retained the Irish language and where storytelling was still one of the major forms of conviviality; even there, audiences had thinned, along with the whole rural population, and, although old beliefs had not vanished, the proportion of those who trusted them was diminishing.

Curtin had devised his own phonetic system of rapidly recording in writing the sounds of spoken languages, even when he did not understand; whether he really mastered conversational Irish is questionable[96] – there is no doubt that, at least on occasions, he had local people assist him in deciphering the transcription, and was probably helped in the translation too. Sean O'Sullivan summed up the advantage of his books over Kennedy's in two ways: 'he had collected, not recollected, and in Irish not in English'.[97] But if his work represented a progress in having the stories transcribed on the spot and not through slow dictation, he did not publish the texts exactly as he had received them: they appeared in English, without the original version.

Curtin had taken advantage of his facility with languages to gather oral literature as a way of exploring the basic structures of the human mind. Others were beginning to gather such material essentially for linguistic studies. Thus in the autumn of 1895 the young Danish scholar Holger Pedersen, who was then adding Irish to his knowledge of living languages, visited Inishmore and noted down thirty-five stories from Máirtín Ó Conghaile (c.1826-1904), who may have been one of Curtin's informants in 1892 and who will reappear in the next chapter. Pedersen, however, was not impressed by the quality of the stories, nor by the art of the storyteller.[98]

Before focusing on yet another branch of folklore collecting, which was associated with the progress of cultural nationalism in the last two decades of the nineteenth century, it is necessary to glance again at the political situation and at the evolution of ideologies. For some time after the Famine, many were interested in local rather than national issues; then popular political consciousness grew. There were revolutionary movements, trusting in conspiracy and physical force: in the last third of the century, a secret organization whose members became known as 'Fenians' after the legendary warrior-band of Fionn mac Cumhaill drew support not only at home but also from Irish-Americans; it

96 See J.E. and G.W. Dunleavy 'Jeremiah Curtin's Working Methods: The Evidence from the Manuscripts', in *Eigse* 18 (1980). 97 *Folklore of Ireland* xi. 98 The stories were published in 1994 as *Scéalta Mháirtín Neile*.

achieved no direct result but was 'famed in songs and stories' and maintained a 'tradition' of plots to get an independent republic. Meanwhile, reformists believed in consitutional methods, and by 1880 their action was in the spotlight; the Home Rule agitation at Westminster for the restoration of a parliament in Dublin, with responsibility for domestic issues, was transformed by Parnell into a powerful machine with popular support, linked for a while with agrarian radicalism at the time of the 'Land War' (see p. 276) and even supported by some Fenians. After the third Reform Act had considerably increased the number of Irish voters, the 1885 elections revealed that this Parliamentary Party was the dominant political force, except in the north-eastern corner of the island where the Protestant 'loyalist' electorate was the majority. Those who refused the programmes of revolutionaries and reformists defended full political integration with Great Britain, and in the mid-1880, a Unionist organization cohered against the Home Rule movement; while opposing a nationalism, it fostered its own sense of a culturally defined community with its special history and set of heroes and villains.

At the same time, cultural nationalism would enhance the sense of a distinct Irish heritage and tried to revive a collective identity, without necessarily agitating for a separate state (but it was difficult to be utterly non-political). Groups and associations of various size and degree of organization emphasized roots that would bind a community together, and which they opposed to anglicization and/or modernism. Some of the ideas professed by the Young Irelanders in the 1840s (see p. 200), were pursued or hardened. The movement to regenerate Ireland was not monolithic: an interest in Irish cultures was not incompatible with Protestant Unionism when what was emphasized was a vision of ancient Ireland as a hierarchical society in which lord and peasant respected each other; but Irish distinctiveness could also serve to legitimize claims for political independence. On the whole, a need was felt for regeneration, and antiquarianism was being replaced by forms of revivalism.

A parallel trend was the international wave of 'Celticism' – which, as soon as it went beyond hard linguistics, ran the risk of freewheeling imaginings. In the second half of the century, it seemed possible to situate the peculiarities of Ireland within a larger Celtic cultural area, and in this respect Irish folklorists could follow the example of Campbell, who had compared his Scottish material with what could be found in Wales and Brittany. A degree of ethnic cohesion was thought to have survived over time, in spite of geographical dispersion; and more or less hazy notions of a special Celtic genius were elaborated, essentially in reaction to apparently more successful materialistic attitudes. In *La Poésie des races celtiques* (1854), Ernest Renan – who was born in Brittany, believed his ancestors had come from Ireland or Wales, and remembered his story-telling mother – ascribed to the marginalized Celt an essentially feminine sensitivity, a tendency to fatalism, and an infinite power of imagination which flourished in tales:

This race has an eternal spring of folly in its heart. The 'kingdom of faery', the most beautiful on earth, is its realm ... Invite those people to talk, and if they trust you they will tell you, half seriously and half jokingly, invaluable stories, of which comparative mythology and history will one day make the best use.[99]

Matthew Arnold met Renan and read his essay. He did not believe that the tales of the 'Populace' were part of the best that had been taught and said in the world, but learned about a nobler ancient Irish culture from O'Curry, O'Donovan and Petrie. In the four Oxford Lectures *On the Study of Celtic Literature* which he delivered in 1865-6, he used a marginalized 'race' as a stick with which to beat English 'Philistines': the Celtic genius had 'the power of quick and strong perception and emotion' as its main basis – which meant it was also 'undisciplinable, anarchic, turbulent by nature'. Arnold deplored the separatist movements of the Irish (their supposed excitability and ineffectuality would render them incapable of self-government), but hoped that the different 'bloods' of the United Kingdom would combine their complementary qualities. Lady Wilde, writing in London in the 1880s, seemed to follow Renan and Arnold when she listed the qualities to be found in the 'slender oval' head of Irish people:

The people are enthusiasts, religious, fanatical; with the instincts of poetry, music, oratory, and superstition far stronger in them than the logical and reasoning faculties. They are made for worshippers, poets, artists, musicians, orators; to move the world by passion, not by logic. Scepticism will never take root in Ireland; infidelity is impossible to the people. To believe fanatically, trust implicitly, hope infinitely, and perhaps to revenge implacably – these are the unchanging and ineradicable characteristics of Irish nature, of Celtic nature, we may say; for it has been the same throughout all history and all ages. And it is these passionate qualities that make the Celt the great motive force of the world, ever striving against limitations towards some vision of ideal splendour; the restless centrifugal force of life, as opposed to the centripetal, which is ever seeking a calm quiescent rest within its appointed sphere. The very tendency to superstition, so marked in Irish nature, arises from an instinctive dislike to the narrow limitations of common sense. It is characterized by a passionate yearning towards the vague, the mystic, the invisible, and the boundless infinite of the realms of imagination.[100]

But some details of the new stereotype, particularly the emphasis on a supposed melancholy and dreaminess or natural mysticism and visionary powers, had comparatively little echo in Ireland itself before the so-called 'Celtic Twilight' vogue at the turn of the century. Nevertheless, the Celtic element in an Irish national character was now emphasized much more than it used to be: in 1857-

99 *Souvenirs d'enfance et de jeunesse* 79-80: 'Cette race a au coeur une éternelle source de folie. Le 'royaume de féerie', le plus beau qui soit en terre, est son domaine. ... Faites parler les bonnes gens, et, s'ils ont confiance en vous, ils vous conteront, moitié sur un ton sérieux, moitié sur le ton de la plaisanterie, d'inappréciables récits, dont la mythologie comparée et l'histoire sauront tirer un jour le plus riche parti.' 100 *Ancient Legends of Ireland* ... 144-5.

8, a Celtic Union had already published a periodical called *The Celt* which rejected the idea of merging Irish identity into a British world.[101] Folklorists themselves had begun to use the adjective 'Celtic' as an ennobling term. A charged and confusing word that constantly appeared then was 'race'. By the late nineteenth century, the dominant belief in a common human nature was largely replaced by the conviction that different human groups had separate origins and unequal qualities; the term 'race' had rather vaguely denoted people of a common stock, but now tended, on supposed scientific grounds, to refer to biologically self-perpetuating characteristics carrying positive or negative traits, which could be used to discriminate against the so-called inferior. Many English people interpreted the Irish question in terms of innate hereditary weaknesses,[102] and Irish people subjected to racialization could hardly be blamed for trying to reverse the picture. The fact is that the phrase 'Irish race' was used more and more often by the Irish themselves, of course in a positive sense.

Ethnic identity offering a sense of continuity and dignity is perceived as more crucially important when it seems under threat; one is then encouraged to preserve from corruption supposedly irreplaceable cultural values. A Gaelic Athletic Association, founded in 1884, worked for 'the preservation and cultivation of our National Pastimes, and for providing amusements for the Irish people during their leisure hours':[103] 'ancient Irish sports' like Gaelic football and hurling prospered. Others thought that language was the foremost marker of ethnicity, and that it required the greatest efforts. While approximately a quarter of the population still spoke Irish as their first or only language in 1851, as against perhaps half of the population in 1841, in 1891 the proportion of bilingual people had shrunk to some 14%, with only 0.8% monoglots; the language was gradually retreating to discontinuous peripheral areas. Irish-speaking people were still emigrating in large numbers, elementary education was in English, and the Irish peasantry had come to consider the old language a handicap for those who wanted to gain social and economic advancement; it tended to be a shameful symbol of poverty – Matthew Arnold called it 'the badge of a beaten race'.[104] The first attempts to stem the decline had involved scholars only, with little effect; better results seemed to become possible when the Gaelic League (*Connradh na Gaeilge*) was established in 1893. It wanted to restore self-respect to Irish-speakers and advocated the preservation and promotion – where necessary the revival – of Irish as a spoken language. It would make real progress in the middle class at the beginning of the twentieth century, fostering an interest

101 *The Celt* 19 September 1857: 'Ireland has been inhabited from a very remote era, and her people are of Celtic origin ...'; 26 September 1857: 'The Celts have all the endowments fitting them for a truly great people ...' 102 T. Champion, in T. Brown (ed.) *Celticism* 71: 'Victorian concern for questions of race, and the hierarchical ordering of the races, produced a picture in which the Celts were near the bottom of the evolutionary scale of human societies.' 103 Circular issued on 27 October 1887 by Michael Cusack and Maurice Davin. 104 *Lectures and Essays in Criticism* 293.

in folktales both for their ethnic nature and their possible use to learn the native tongue. Consequences of the revaluation of the native culture, and its literary aspects, will be examined more closely in the next chapter; here we may consider the more specifically folkloristic activities of the League's spokesman and first chairman.

Douglas Hyde (1860-1949), the son of a Church of Ireland rector, was reared in County Roscommon and learned Irish among local people, first from a gamekeeper, Seamas Hart, who must have been at least sixty and was 'the best reciter [he] ever knew', with 'the greatest repertoire of stories of any shanachie [he] ever met'. Later, from John Cunningham (between seventy and eighty years of age), he collected long wonder tales and Fianna stories; from Martin Brennan, a mower, folktales including Irish variants of international tale-types; and from Mary Ellen Sarsfield – 'there was not a storyteller to compare with her in the county'.[105] They belonged to the last generations of Irish speakers in the region. He visited Mrs Sarsfield again in the 1930s, when she was eighty-six: 'Her daughter, Mrs O'Connell, has very good Irish, but this daughter has nine children and they do not understand Irish, and as far as I could make out, nobody in the locality had Irish'.[106] Hyde was convinced that language and 'tradition' were closely connected: 'where the language dies, these folk memories scarcely survive one generation'.[107] He retained from his boyhood a bright vision of 'traditional' life and a hatred of modernization which would govern his multiple activities, in a long career only partly devoted to folkloristic field work.

He published folktales in Irish – and folksongs or poems – in periodicals and in book form, starting in 1889 with *Leabhar Sgéuluigheachta* ('A Book of Storytelling'). Other volumes of folktales and legends followed until 1939. In 1890 he translated part of the first volume under the title *Beside the Fire*. A long preface began with the usual elegy: folk stories were, 'as a living form of literature, by this time pretty nearly a thing of the past', already swallowed up in England 'by the waves of materialism and civilization combined; but still surviving unengulfed on the western coasts of Ireland'.[108] Then he reviewed and assessed the work of earlier collectors: Croker's *Fairy Legends* were 'delightful' but with too much manipulation of the originals; Lover had published only 'some incidental and largely-manipulated' stories; Patrick Kennedy was more reliable but not precise enough concerning his sources, and his material coming from a non-Irish speaking region *had* to be, as Hyde saw it, of an inferior quality; Lady Wilde was completely ignorant of Irish and said nothing at all of the informants. Jeremiah Curtin, who had 'approached the fountain-head more

105 Information on these storytellers from Bairbre Ní Fhloinn, 'Folklore Collecting in Co. Roscommon – Douglas Hyde and his Legacy', in *Comhdáil an Chraoibhín: Conference Proceedings 1989* 24-46. 106 Ibid. 32 – quoting from *Béaloideas* 4 (1949) 425. 107 Quoted in Dominic Daly *The Young Douglas Hyde* 67. On Hyde as a collector, see also D. Ó Giolláin *Locating Irish Folklore* 107-9. 108 *Beside the Fire* ix, x.

nearly than any other',[109] did not present and credit his informants either (the reproach would not apply to Curtin's *Tales of the Fairies*, but this book appeared several years after Hyde's preface). Most collectors had given only plot-skeletons of the tales, 'padded round and clad' in a style that was far from that of the storytellers. Too many liberties had been taken with the oral legacy, and it was time to 'give the exact language' of the informants. Hyde pointed to the close relations between Irish and Scottish Gaelic tales and acknowledged the value of what had been done in Scotland: 'We have as yet no folk-lorist in Ireland who could compare for a moment with such a man as Iain Campbell, of Islay, [see pp. 296-7] in investigative powers, thoroughness of treatment, and acquaintance with the people, combined with a powerful national sentiment, and, above all, a knowledge of Gaelic.'[110]

He proposed a classification of the tales found in Ireland, distinguishing between native ones, like 'most of the *longer* tales about the Fenians, and all those stories which have long inflated passages full of alliterative words and poetic epithets',[111] and on the other hand tales that had become Irish by adoption. In accordance with diffusionist and evolutionist principles, the stories of the latter group were interesting too, inasmuch as they derived from the 'old Aryan heritage': 'Such myth stories as these ought to be preserved, since they are about the last visible link connecting civilized with pre-historic man'.[112] His presentation of informants was factual, but he lamented their diminishing number and even more the present lack of an audience:

The people who can recite [these stories] are, as far as my researches have gone, to be found only amongst the oldest, most neglected, and poorest of the Irish-speaking population. English-speaking people either do not know them at all, or else tell them in so bald and condensed a form as to be useless. Almost all the men from whom I used to hear stories in the County Roscommon are dead. Ten or fifteen years ago I used to hear a great many stories, but I did not understand their value. Now when I go back for them I cannot find them. They have died out, and will never again be heard on the hillsides, where they probably existed for a couple of thousand years; they will never be repeated there again, to use the Irish phrase, while grass grows or waters runs. Several of these stories I got from an old man, one Shawn Cunningham, on the border of the County Roscommon, where it joins Mayo. He never spoke more than a few words of English till he was fifteen years old. He was taught by a hedge schoolmaster from the South of Ireland out of Irish MSS. As far as I could make out from him the teaching seemed to consist in making him learn Irish poems by heart. ... His son and daughter now speak Irish, though not fluently, his grandchildren do not even understand it. He had at one time, as he expressed it, 'the full of a sack of stories,' but he had forgotten them. His grandchildren stood by his knee while he told me one or two, but it was evident they did not understand a word. His son and daughter laughed at them as nonsense. Even in Achill where, if anywhere, one ought to find folk-stories in their purity, a fine-looking dark man of about forty-five, who told me a number of them, and could repeat Ossian's

109 Ibid. xv. **110** Ibid. xvi. **111** Ibid. xxxv. **112** Ibid. xli.

poems, assured me that now-a-days when he went into a house in the evening and the old people got him to recite, the boys would go out; 'they wouldn't understand me,' said he, 'and when they wouldn't, they'd sooner be listening to *géimneach na mbó*' (the lowing of the cows).[113]

In the same preface, Hyde gave practical advice to collectors:

It is not as easy a thing as might be imagined to collect Irish stories. One hears that tales are to be had from such and such a man, generally, alas! a very old one. With difficulty one manages to find him out, only to discover, probably, that he has some work on hand. If it happens to be harvest time it is nearly useless going to him at all, unless one is pre-pared to sit up with him all night, for his mind is sure to be so distraught with harvest operations that he can tell you nothing. If it is winter time, however, and you fortunately find him unoccupied, nevertheless it requires some management to get him to tell his stories. Half a glass of *ishka-baha* [whiskey], a pipe of tobacco, and a story of one's own are the best things to begin with. If, however, you start to take down the story *verbatim* with pencil and paper, as an unwary collector might do, you destroy all, or your shanachie becomes irritable. He will not wait for you to write down your sentence, and if you call out, 'Stop, stop, wait till I get this down,' he will forget what he was going to tell you, and you will not get a third of his story, though you may think you have it all. What you must generally do is to sit quietly smoking your pipe, without the slightest interruption, not even when he comes to words and phrases which you do not under-stand. He must be allowed his own way to the end, and then after judiciously praising him and discussing the story, you remark, as if the thought had suddenly struck you, '*budh mhaith liom sin a bheith agam air pháipeur*' – I'd like to have that on paper.' Then you can get it from him easily enough, and when he leaves out whole incidents, as he is sure to do, you who have just heard the story can put him right, and so get it from him nearly in its entirety.[114]

An Sgéuluidhe Gaedhealach (first published in 1893) contained thirty-five tales, most of them from Próinsias Ó Conchúbhair (born in County Sligo but met by the collector in the Athlone workhouse), and from Máirtín Ruadh Ó Giollarnáth (a small farmer in County Galway). Hyde repeatedly vouched for the literal recording of his texts, with variants of the formula '*sgríobhta síos go díreach ó na bheul féin gan aon fhocal d'athrugadh* (written straight from his mouth without changing a word)'. In 1915 appeared *Legends of Saints & Sinners*, 'folk-stories and folk-poems which are either entirely founded upon Christian conceptions, or else are so far coloured by them, that they could never have been told – at least in their present shape – had not Christianity established itself in Ireland'.[115] Sources were still precisely designated: 'The following story I got from Proinsias O'Conchubhair when he was in Athlone about fifteen years ago, and he heard it from a woman who herself came from Ballintober, Co.

113 Ibid. xli-xliii. The whole paragraph, with a few variants, had already been part of a lec-ture on 'Irish Folklore' which Hyde had delivered in 1889; see *Language, Lore and Lyrics* 101. 114 Ibid. xlv-xlvii. Same precepts, more or less, in the 1889 lecture: *Language Lore and Lyrics* 102. 115 Op. cit. vii.

Mayo ... I got this story from Francis O'Connor [O Conchúbhair] ... The story was told by Joyce or Seoigtheach, of Poll na bracha, in Co. Galway, some years ago, for the Oireachtas [a Gaelic League festival with competitions for traditional performers] ... I wrote down the following story from the mouth of John Cunningham of Ballinphuill, Co. Roscommon, on the high road between Frenchpark and Ballaghaderreen, about twenty years ago ... I wrote down this story carefully from the mouth of Mártain Ruadh Ó Giollarnáth from near Monivea Co. Galway ... From the telling of Michael Mac Ruaidhre, of Ballycastle, Co. Mayo ...'[116]

Other tales collected from Próinsias Ó Conchúbhair in 1896 were published in 1909 as *Sgéaluidhe Fíor na Seachtmhaine* ('The True Storyteller of the Week'), a cycle of stories with a frame-tale according to which a man has to pay for hospitality by telling an incredible yet 'true' story every evening of the week – I shall look at it more closely in Chapter 12. His last publications gathered stories obtained from a Mayo man: *Ocht Sgéalta ó Choillte Mághach – Eight Stories from Kiltimagh* (1936) and *Sgéalta Thomáis Uí Chathasaigh – Mayo Stories Told by Thomas Casey* (1939). Casey had received his repertoire from his grandfather in the 1860s or 70s: 'He used to be telling his stories beside the fire at night, in his own house, and Thummaus used to be there, and he a young boy, listening to him, and he picked them up himself.'[117] The informant was said to be 'a very cute and clever man, and he used to have the full of the house every night listening to his stories'. Hyde added he did not think that he had ever heard a storyteller 'who was better at "putting a skin" on a story he made [*craiceann*: skin, *chuir sé craiceann ar an scéal*: he polished the story – he made the story sound plausible]'.[118]

Douglas Hyde was thus the first to explore in depth the repertoire of individual informants. He aimed at greater accuracy than his predecessors and published stories in the original Irish form. He represented his storytellers as normal human beings, not as 'picturesque characters'. As for his other activities besides folklore collecting and publications, I shall touch on them in the next chapter. William Larminie (1849-1900), who had begun to collect tales in Irish in 1884 under Hyde's influence, published in 1893 his *West Irish Folktales and Romances*. They had been taken from Irish speakers in Counties Donegal, Mayo and Galway, 'word for word from the dictation of the peasant narrators ... difficult and doubtful parts being gone over again and again. Sometimes the narrators can explain difficulties. Sometimes other natives of the place can help you.'[119] He tried to identify the repertoire of different 'races' in Ireland, and thought that it would account for the coexistence of different kinds of tales. As Hyde had done, he gave some biographical data about his informants, including their place – generally at a low level – in society:

---

116 Ibid. passim. 117 *Sgéalta Thomáis Uí Chathasaigh* ix. 118 Ibid. xiii, xi. 119 *West Irish Folktales and Romances* xxiii.

Terence Davis [of Renvyle] is a labourer pure and simple, a man of about forty-five years of age, and blind of one eye. Some of his tales he got from his mother. ... Pat M'Gale [Achill Island] is a man of middle age, a cottier with a small holding, and besides, a Jack-of-all-trades, something of a boatman and fisherman, 'a botch of a tailor,' to use his own words, and ready for any job. He can read Irish, but had very little literature on which to exercise his accomplishment. He knows some long poems by heart. ... John M'Ginty, a man of Donegal descent and name, has also some land; but his holding is so small that he is to a great extent a labourer for others ... He knows many Ossianic poems by heart, which, he told me, his father taught him, verse by verse.[120]

In addition to the distinctive manners of different individual tellers, he tried to identify styles associated with classes of stories. He also collected tales in English, perhaps in County Wicklow.[121]

This chapter and the previous ones concerning the same century have pointed to a few dominant features. First, whereas in other countries the personality of the informant from whom 'oral tradition' was collected often tended to be considered negligible, it seems that the Irish storyteller was likely to be treated as an interesting character, and the conditions in which stories were told were often evoked. But the descriptions tended to be brief and with recurrent traits; to a large extent the result may look like a *cliché* – though repetitiveness can also reflect constant aspects of performances. In general, the portraits we have read seem to have been less the representations of individuals than embodiments of a role and/or of an attitude, as perceived from a favourably or unfavourably prejudiced point of view. What went under the name of 'folklore' could not have the same significance for mere observers and for those who practised it, unselfconsciously, as part of their ordinary life; the point of view of the latter group is, by far, the most difficult to grasp.

Another general observation is that, while there always was the notion that efforts should be made to salvage swiftly dwindling remnants, in the period 1850-1890 one often preferred to reconstruct the social life of the first half of the century rather than describe contemporary rural reality; there also was a tendency to look for links with a much more distant and supposedly totally glorious past – a golden age that could be recovered only in the imagination. By the end of the century, the idea that decline and even death might give way to renewal was gaining strength.

Some Irish folklorists adopted the conjectural history of evolution and/or migrations which had become current abroad, but a sense of apartness was emphasized: one expected to find in Ireland what had not existed, or had long vanished, in other parts of Europe. Meanwhile, one began to realize overseas that Ireland was not just a bizarre place but that one could go there and collect stories which might be of universal interest.

120 Ibid. xxiii-xxiv. 121 Three of them appeared in *The Cabinet of Irish Literature* 4. 61-8.

There was much refashioning, for literary creation or commercial aims; the folk-lorists offered their texts as 'authentic', but even when they did not deliberately take liberties with actual facts they depended on fallible devices like memoriza-tion or dictation. In the first half of the century, publications gave the impres-sion that legends of the supernatural with their different kinds of fairies were, by far, the most numerous items; the way people reacted to the possibility of the supernatural remained fascinating, but later more and more attention was paid to the complex tales.

By the end of the century, the pressure of political and cultural nationalism was intensifying, and gave new motivations to some folklorists who would establish a partly new image of the traditional storyteller; the interest of Irish literary cir-cles in cultural roots took new forms and a different use began to be made of the resources of folk material as well as of ancient Irish texts. A few decades later, a large systematic collection of Irish folklore would be launched, and the traces left by 'traditional storytellers' seemed easier to follow – just as the models were vanishing. For a while, folklore would be used officially to reinforce the sense of ethnic identity and to try and inflect the course of history: to build a new Irish Ireland in which the traditional Gaelic storyteller would be somehow sacralized. The next two chapters will examine these developments.

9

Noble peasants and mythical islanders –
or 'tons of useless folklore'?

At the beginning of the twentieth century, broader and narrower views of 'Irishness' coexisted. Most relevant to my research are those which invoked immemorial 'traditions'. Later, when the greater part of the island achieved a political separation from Britain, nativist views seemed to dominate: for several decades, powerful voices advocated a return to roots in order to develop a distinctive way of life; but there were also attacks on the officially sanctioned ideals of the day. Three historical phases will be outlined in this chapter. The first section, starting with an apparently smooth continuation of trends observed in the last two decades of the preceding century, ends with the 1916-22 crisis; it considers the attitudes of 'Irish Revival' writers and their immediate successors towards oral narratives and their performers, and the question of whether Irish storytelling played any role in the preparation and form of a political revolution will have to be asked – without hope of offering a simple and final answer. Section B will trace those developments, from 1922 to the late 1950s, which had an impact on the image of the old-style Irish storyteller in official or semi-official manifestos, collective self-representation, and literature, reserving for Chapters 10 and 11 the examination of some results of the systematic campaign of folklore collection undertaken in the second third of the century and the evolution of theories and methods in that field. Section C will sketch out much more summarily the last third of the century; this phase is not completed. Older kinds and conceptions of Irish storytelling seem to be discarded, while the tracks that will be left by new forms are not yet discernible.

A. TRADITIONS AND MIRRORS

In the first decades of the century, old-style descriptions of Irish country life could still include account of storytelling events, tinted with nostalgic sentimentality or amusing picturesqueness. Renderings of raconteurs' performances in Daniel Deeney's *Peasant Lore from Gaelic Ireland* (1900), for instance, strike a familiar note: ' 'Tis often me father towld me the story, an' 'tis often me father's gran'father towld him the story. They're all dead, now, an' let not God allow that I'd put a lie on them – indade I widn't. Sorra fear o' me!'[1] A bilingual

1 Op. cit. 17.

schoolteacher at Spiddal, Co. Galway, Deeney knew his subject, but his rendering of dialect smacks of old-fashioned conventions. We may contrast such ostentatious Irishisms with the more neutral style of the literate farmer James Berry, born in 1842; at the age of seventy he evoked the raconteurs he had heard in his younger days in Mayo and later in Connemara, synthesizing experience into a unified impression:

Among all the vast assembly at 'the Cake' [a social gathering and dance competition] I noticed three old men who sat by themselves, and who in appearance and dress differed as much from those around them as the sun differs from the moon. These three noble-looking old men belonged to the eighteenth century and lived far into the nineteenth. They were the last of their generation ... When night set in, the company became hilarious and gradually the noise grew in volume until it was almost intolerable, so one of the grand old men of the West called for silence. 'Now', he said, 'we have had much dancing and singing, so why not have some stories for variety's sake?' This proposal was received with applause. The old gentleman called on the last of the packmen for a story ... 'Musha', said Hugh, a benevolent smile playing around the corners of his mouth, 'the sorra story I have, but I will give ye a piece of Shanachus, and as I proceed with it, if portions of it be dry and weansome, some of it may interest you, for you will hear things you have never heard before at any rate.'[2]

Séamus MacManus (1869-1960), one of the many who were awarded the title of 'last of the true Irish shanachies', was much more prolific and his books had a wide circulation until the mid-century. Most of them catered for Irish-Americans' wish to read about Old Ireland's sentiments and pleasant extravagance, but he had a real knowledge of folkways and some of his writings have documentary value. Born on a small farm in County Donegal, he worked with his father till the age of eighteen, then became a school-teacher and contributed short texts to local papers. He was active in the Gaelic League. At odds with the Department of Education for his nationalist activities, he went to America in 1899 and discovered that magazine publishers would pay well for his versions of the tales and legends he had heard in his native parish. He was in Ireland again in 1900-3, then settled in the USA where he had a ready market for the stories he published and often told to paying audiences. In his many books, including eighteen collections of tales (some of his own invention), he often thickened dialect and comic effects, or occasionally pathetic situations, giving the same tales several times in different versions, with details of contexts which could overdo local colour. The distance from genuine tradition seems to vary from one book to the other, and his descriptions of Irish ways may alternate true remembrance with playing to an audience. In his more restrained writings there are valuable comments on storytelling and portraits of storytellers; the introduction to *Donegal Fairy Stories* (1900 – already his ninth book), sketches various types:

2 *Tales of the West of Ireland* 16, 22, 93. (First published in the *Mayo News* between 1910 and 1913.)

The man who brings his shaggy pony to the forge 'reharses a rale oul' tale' for the boys whilst he lazily works the bellows for Dan. As she spins in the glow of the fir-blaze on the long winter nights, the old white-capped woman, with hair like a streak of lint, holds the fireside circle spellbound with such tales as these. When at Taig, the tailor's, on a Saturday night, an exasperated man clamours angrily for the long-promised coat, Taig says, 'Arrah, Conal, man, have sense, and be quate, and sit down till ye hear a wond-herful story of anshint happenin's.' And the magic of the tale restores Conal to a Christian frame of mind, and sends him home forgetful of a great procrastinator's deceit. When the beggarman, coming in at dayligone, drops his staff and sheds his bags in token that he deigns to honor the good people with his presence for that night, among young and old there is anticipative joy for the grand stories with which he will certainly enchant them till (too soon) *an bhean-an-tighe* [the woman of the house] shakes her beads and says it is rosary-time. The professional shanachy recites them to a charmed audience in the wake house, in the potato field, on the green hillside on summer Sundays, and at the cross-roads in blissful autumn gloamings [dusk], whilst the green marge rests his hear-ers' aching limbs.[3]

In *Yourself and the Neighbours* (1914), MacManus traced the changing func-tions of stories in the life of an individual and the growing recognition of his role as a storyteller. He would start as a mere listener, but with age and physi-cal work becoming too hard for him, the passive bearer of tradition could turn active teller; he first discovered his verbal skill entertaining children, then con-firmed it bewitching adults:

When they knew you would be story-telling, the neighbours, both young and old, gath-ered from far and near, crowding your house to listen once again to the astounding adventures of the brave King of Ireland's Son, or to the side-splitting tricks of tricksome Jack, the lucky, witty son of the poor widow woman, or to the magic romance (which it took three of the longest nights in winter to tell) of the wonderful wanderings of the King of Connacht's Thirteen Sons. The whole house held their breath as you came to your climax, till the wonder was that some of the more excited of them didn't burst entirely.[4]

MacManus could revive past experience in idyllic terms, or offer boisterous scenes: in the same book, after portraying the sedentary *seanchaí*, he sketched travelling storytellers in mock-epic style, with an account of a contest between two beggars for the possession of a territory.[5] In 1938, he portrayed his mother's way of bestowing on a story 'such perennial freshness that when she told it for the hundredth time (as musing persons will) it charmed the children even more than it did the first.'[6] In the same autobiography he remembered – or perhaps invented – an expert Fenian-lay reciter who was still praising his repertoire on his deathbed.[7] In one of his last books, the opening formula of a storyteller heard in childhood seems to convey the author's own sentiment: 'That was a long time

3 Op. cit. xi-xii. 4 *Yourself and the Neighbours* 86-7. 5 Ibid. 194-5. 6 *The Rocky Road to Dublin* 70. 7 Ibid. 164-5.

ago in Ireland, and a happy time too. And them that are here weren't there then, and them that were there then no toothache has tormented in the last ten thousand years ...'[8] For him, in some respects the course of time had stopped before the end of the nineteenth century; he could offer popular versions of the Macphersonian persona remembering heroes of yore, who themselves told in a heroic way what they remembered of a lost earlier age.

The antiquarian mode also continued, and may be represented by Stephen Gwynn (1864-1950) who served as MP for Galway between 1906 and 1918 and contributed to various scholarly periodicals. In *Irish Books and Irish People*, he later remembered how he had been looking for an illiterate man who would be able to recite 'the classic literature of Ireland, the epics or ballads of an older day'. He found him in a remote valley of the Cark Mountain, in County Donegal:

James had by heart not only the Fenian or Ossianic cycle, but also the older sagas of Cuchulain. He confused the cycles, it is true, taking the Red Branch heroes for contemporaries of the Fianna [cf. p. 104], which is much as if one should make Heracles meet Odysseus or Achilles in battle; but he had these early legends by heart, a rare acquirement among the Shanachies of to-day. Here then was a type of the Irish illiterate. A man somewhere between fifty and sixty, at a guess; of middle height, spare and well-knit, high-nosed, fine-featured, keen-eyed; standing there on his own ground, courteous and even respectful, yet consciously a scholar ... He chanted with a continuous vocalisation, and while he chanted, elbow and knee worked like a fiddler's or a piper's marking the time.[9]

Cultural nationalists, who wanted to build a new country by reviving selected ancient values, liked leaning on scholarly arguments but also made use of rhetorical effects. In a paper read to the National Literary Society in December 1892, Douglas Hyde had complained that Ireland, while claiming political autonomy and recovering possession of its land, was neglecting what guaranteed its distinctive qualities, 'hastening to adopt, pell-mell, and indiscriminately, everything that is English, simply because it *is* English'.[10] The trend should be reversed before it was too late. The necessary restitution of self-respect implied the cultivation of 'everything that is most racial, most smacking of the soil, most Gaelic, most Irish, because in spite of the little admixture of Saxon blood in the north-east corner, this island *is* and will *ever* remain Celtic at the core'.[11] Dress, Christian names and surnames, music, ideas – all had to be national again, but it was most important to restore Irish as a living language and to change the attitude of those who were ashamed of speaking it. In a footnote to the printed edition of his speech, Hyde illustrated this need with an anecdote which he was to use again when he acted the role of the platform-

8 *Heavy Hangs the Golden Grain* 23. 9 Op. cit. 48, 57. 10 'The Necessity for De-Anglicizing Ireland', in *Language, Lore and Lyrics* 153. See also D. Ó Giolláin *Locating Irish Folklore* 114-25. 11 Ibid. 169.

Irishman to collect funds; here side by side are the written summary account
and the oral histrionic performance in New York thirteen years later:

... I mention the case of a young man
I met on the road coming from the fair
of Tuam, some ten miles away. I
saluted him in Irish, and he answered
me in English. 'Don't you speak Irish',
said I. 'Well, I declare to God, sir', he
said, 'my father and mother hasn't a
word of English, but still, I don't speak
Irish.' This was absolutely true for him.[12]

... I was going from the fair of Tuam
I was selling cattle there (laughter and
applause). I am not ashamed of it; all
Irishmen sell cattle when they have
them to sell; and very glad to have
them (laughter), I overtook a young
man driving a cow before me and I
spoke to the young man in Irish, and
as I was speaking in Irish he was answering
in English (laughter), and at last I said to
him, 'Don't you speak Irish?' And what was
his answer? 'Well, I declare to God, sir, that
neither my father nor my mother has one
word of English and still I can't spake
and I won't spake Irish' (laughter). And I,
who had just left [three continental profes-
sors] living on buttermilk and potatoes on
the mountain sides in the houses of the
peasantry to learn to speak the language that
this reptile was discarding – to tell you the
honest truth I lost my temper (laughter and
applause). I lost my temper and I stood out
from him, and to tell the honest truth, I hit
him one kick. And mind you, it just shows
you what the loss of your native language
does for you, the poor, unfortunate devil, he
didn't have courage enough to turn around
and knock me down (laughter and
applause).[13]

The Gaelic League, which had fifty-eight branches in 1898, progressed to
some six hundred by 1908 with a total membership of a hundred thousand. It
was more active in towns than in rural areas but sent many people to the
Gaeltacht, where one of the cultic activities during linguistic stays consisted in
listening to tales. At the central *Oireachtas* and in county *Feiseanna* [*feis*: festi-
val], dancing, singing and storytelling competitions were held. The League's
periodicals, or those of similar organizations like the Gaelic Union with its magazine *Irisleabhar na Gaedhilge*, included transcriptions or simplified versions of
folktales. The first book-length new narrative in Irish, Canon Peter O'Leary (an
tAthair Peadar Ó Laoghaire)'s *Séadna* (first serialized in 1894), was important in
that it used *caint na daoine*, the contemporary everyday speech of the people,

12 Ibid. 160. 13 'The Gaelic Revival', in *Language, Lore and Lyrics* 185-6.

rather than antiquated literary forms. Founded on an Irish version of the international folktale-type in which a man manages to avoid fulfilling his part of a contract with the devil, it is supposed to be told by a girl to younger children. The in-tale (how Séadna struck a bargain with *An Fear Dubh* and was rescued by his own good works) remained formally rather close to a traditional narrative, while the frame (the telling) is not detailed as a remarkable occurrence.

The Gaelic League, according to its constitution, was supposed to be 'strictly non-political and non-sectarian'; but it was difficult to remain neutral, and problems became acute because social, religious and political affiliations did not necessarily coincide. Between an elitist Anglo-Irish revivalism and Catholic more or less sectarian and separatist movements, some tried to find a shared sense of Irish identity, not easy to define – some mysterious force in the land or in the 'Celtic' atmosphere would have assimilated and completely hibernicized the descendants of colonists, apart from a hopeless minority of perennially foreign occupants. For common inspiration, one looked back to a noble past contrasting with a mediocre present, and it was asserted that, though the heritage had been neglected by its legitimate claimants, it could be reaffirmed in all its glory against deleterious external influences. Late-nineteenth-century antiquarian publications remained influential; Standish James O'Grady (see p. 288) had praised such material: 'The legends represent the imagination of the country; they are that kind of history which a nation desires to possess. They betray the ambition and ideals of the people and, in this respect, have a value far beyond the tale of actual events and duly recorded facts.'[14] Younger writers like 'Æ' (G.W. Russell) remembered the power of fascination of his books: 'It was the memory of race which rose up within me, and I felt exalted as one who learns he is among the children of kings.'[15] New scholars also emphasized the importance of glorious memories to re-forge a national identity:

Patriotism does not rest to any large degree upon a national pride in the physical beauty of the country that gave us birth, nor yet on a legitimate satisfaction in its commercial or industrial prosperity; it rests upon what we may call the historic imagination. It connects itself with certain events in the past history of our country, or with occurrences, sometimes of a semi-legendary character, that have stamped themselves upon the mind of the nation in a series of vivid mental pictures, and have fostered a just pride in the deeds and epochs of their forefathers.[16]

In fact the whole spectrum of Irish nationalism cultivated – in different ways – a 'tradition' circulating both orally and in written form, which consisted of ancient and recent patriotic symbols, of the simplified narrative of centuries of continuous struggle for supposedly eternal principles, and of a Golden Legend of heroes and martyrs.

14 *History of Ireland: The Heroic Period* (1878) 1. 22. **15** Quoted in W.I. Thompson *The Imagination of an Insurrection* 22. **16** Eleanor Hull *The Cuchulain Saga in Irish Literature* (1898) xi.

There was now a marked tendency to portray the Irish storyteller as very respectable, and to produce a more demanding kind of texts. The so-called 'Irish Literary Revival' or 'Renaissance', which began around 1890, also ran parallel to the nationalist drive for independence, and to some extent exploited the same resources; but the members of that informal movement proposed what they considered more subtle values than those that had generally been defended so far, and took greater heed of form. The average Gaelic Leaguer had not included high arts in his view of revivalism, and D.P. Moran's 'philosophy of Irish-Ireland' – a fundamentalist scheme of 'de-Anglicizing' which defined Irishness as exclusively Gaelic and Catholic – did not care for literature. The writers of the new group, on the other hand, were not concerned with preservation only, nor prepared to restrict criteria of belonging: they would use ancient mythology and the contemporary set of oral traditions creatively, looking for universal as well as local significance. In 1892, in a letter to *United Ireland*, Yeats asked: 'Can we not keep the continuity of the nation's life ... by translating and retelling in English, which shall have an indefinable Irish quality of rhythm and style, all that is best of the ancient literature?'[17] Two other points were important: this unmistakably Irish literature should not be subordinated to politics, and should have a European impact. The past had always been extolled; what was new was that national pride was to be enhanced by showing that art of the highest aesthetic quality was again possible in Ireland, that heroes and noble deeds of long ago could still inspire artists, and that – with due stylization – the language and themes of the contemporary folk afforded more than picturesque idiom and quaint material. The phrase 'Celtic Twilight' might seem to connote the vanishing of vestigial elements, but was also intended to herald the coming of dawn; and in connection with 'twilight states' of paranormal daydreaming it connoted a longing for mysterious powers and the hope that, through them, some fundamental transformation might take place. The programme set forth by Yeats and Lady Gregory to attract subscriptions to a 'Celtic Theatre' summed up all that: 'We will show that Ireland is not the home of buffoonery and easy sentiment, as it has been represented, but the home of an ancient idealism.'[18]

Heroic inspiration was found mostly in translations of ancient Irish literature, but for unspoilt contemporary sources of energy one also turned to the peasantry. Folklorists could find there elements of continuity with what had been observed earlier; but as noted in the previous chapter, country life had been partly transformed since the 1850s and was still being profoundly modified by the transfer of ownership of land from the landlords to those who worked it. The new status of the rural population, more particularly the increasing power of the strong farmers and shopkeepers, changed mental attitudes. The Irish Parliamentary Party needed the support of the many rural voters; cultural nationalism wanted them to remain unaltered emblems of Irishness and to be

17 It was published on 17 December. 18 Lady Gregory *Our Irish Theatre* (1913) 20; from a letter written in 1897.

proud of a rediscovered cultural heritage – but, seen from Dublin, they might seem insufficiently aware of it: they needed to be told why they should be attached to a certain past. Now there were writers who did not portray them as comic, or picturesque, or bestial; embellished images emphasized their patriotism and/or stoic simplicity, their wisdom; the less glamorous realities of country life tended to be ignored. The 'peasant' could still be 'wild', but by now the adjective connoted impressive vitality rather than blind brutality. He could be seen as a noble and sometimes tragic figure, and (for some writers more important) he could appear as a spiritually superior creature shielded from the bad influences of modern mediocrity and the debilitating mercantile way of life associated with England. His Catholicism (which the fundamentalists considered essential) could be downplayed by Protestant writers in favour of a pagan sensitivity: he might be a seer and an expert in magic, and his belief in fairies might attest to his spirituality. The exploration and exploitation of his folklore was justified as a literary activity, not only as a patriotic one: folktales and legends, as well as the ancient mythology, constituted a resource with which Irish literature – in English – could be reborn.

The image of the rural storyteller was therefore exploited in new ways. We shall now see what the major writers of the movement, and some of their epigones and adversaries, had to say about Irish storytelling – granting that this perspective upsets the scale in which the importance of the various aspects of their works is usually measured.

The symbols W.B. Yeats adopted or invented intimated ideal solutions to his, or Ireland's, or the world's problems. For him, the 'peasant' could function as a primitive still close to a 'unified' life, and demonstrate how the personal and the collective might be harmonized; he could have a healthy energy which modern city people had lost – though the outcast (beggar, vagrant, fool ...) seemed better suited for this particular role; he had not lost touch with the concrete and the emotional: 'An impulse toward what is definite and sensuous, and an indifference toward the abstract and general, are the lineaments, as I understand the word, of all that comes not from the learned, but out of common antiquity, out of the "folk" as we say.'[19] He could also embody resistance to utilitarian materialism, be in touch with mysterious forces and thus give support to Yeats's own beliefs: country people would have kept something of the 'early phase of every civilisation' where myth and dreams gave access to wisdom. According to him, if Douglas Hyde and his League 'sought the peasant, ... we sought the peasant's imagination'.[20] Yet the peasant was also seen as an essentially passive and not individualized receiver of experience and tales: those Yeats said he had observed 'listening in Irish cabins to songs in Gaelic about "an old poet telling his sins", and about "the five young men who were drowned last year", and about "the lovers that were drowned going to America", or to some tale of Oisin and his

19 *Explorations* 43. 20 Ibid. 400-1.

three hundred years in Tir ná nOg' would be like the people Sophocles, Shakespeare and Calderon had written for.[21] At least some members of the peasantry were the custodians of an almost lost art; of course there were also narrow-minded people in the country, but they were 'not the true folk' – they represented 'the peasant as he is being transformed by the modern life'.[22]

Yeats's views of the Irish peasant and his traditions were partly founded on recollections of long holidays spent in Sligo. 'When I was a boy I used to wander about at Rosses Point and Ballisodare listening to old songs and stories. I wrote down what I heard and made poems out of the stories or put them into the little chapters of the first edition of *The Celtic Twilight*, and that is how I began to write in the Irish way.'[23] In *Reveries over Childhood and Youth*, he recollects his hope of being carried away by the fairies; what normally frightened the natives seemed to him highly desirable: 'I wandered about raths and faery hills and questioned old women and old men and, when I was tired or unhappy, began to long for some such end as True Thomas found [Thomas the Rhymer, the Scottish visionary poet who went to fairyland]. I did not believe with my intellect that you could be carried away body and soul, but I believed with my emotions and the belief of the country people made that easy.'[24] He had heard so many stories that the world seemed to him 'full of monsters and marvels'.[25] He also heard storytelling when living at Howth, in 1881-2: '[Yeats's mother] read no books, but she and the fisherman's wife would tell each other stories that Homer might have told, pleased with any moment of sudden intensity and laughing together over any point of satire. There is an essay called "Village Ghosts" in my *Celtic Twilight* which is but a record of one such afternoon, and many a fine tale has been lost because it had not occurred to me soon enough to keep notes.'[26]

The greater part of his knowledge of Irish folklore, however, was gathered in libraries, in the late 1880s and early 1890s, from nineteenth-century publications which he listed in an appendix to his *Irish Fairy Tales* as 'Authorities on Irish Folk-Lore'.[27] Like Hyde, he criticized mere dabblers in the field: 'When will Irishmen record their legends as faithfully and seriously as Campbell did those of the Western Highlands?'[28] But whether he himself did not inflect what came from tradition to make it tally with his own tastes and beliefs is questionable. Indeed, in the introduction to his anthology of *Fairy and Folk Tales of Ireland* he objected to a merely 'scientific' approach to folklore, defending literal

21 'The Theatre' (1900), in *Essays and Introductions* 167. 22 'Samhain: 1905', in *Explorations* 183. 23 *Where There Is Nothing* ... (1903), in *The Variorum Edition of the Plays* 232. 24 *Autobiographies* 78. 25 Ibid. 33. His sister said that in Sligo 'everyone talked of fairies' (R.F. Foster *W.B. Yeats: A Life* 1.21). 26 *Autobiographies* 61. 27 Nineteen names, from Crofton Croker to Carleton and from Kennedy to Curtin and Hyde, plus the titles of a dozen periodicals. For a study of his use of sources see M.H. Thuente's *W.B. Yeats and Irish Folklore* ; also S.D. Putzel 'Towards an Aesthetic of Folklore and Mythology: W.B. Yeats, 1888-1895', *Southern Folklore Quarterly* 44 (1980), 105-30. 28 *Providence Sunday Journal* 7 July 1889; in *Letters to the New Island: A New Edition* 91.

belief against rationalist methods: for him, fairies existed, or expressed something real, or at least offered a necessary refuge from the misery of life. He claimed at any rate that his information was not only bookish or recollective, and presented himself repeatedly as a field collector. For instance in 1887:

Have been making search for people to tell me fairy stories and found one or two ... I have been busy gathering fairy tales in the cabins. And have many new and curious ... I was going along the river a few days ago when a man stopped me and said 'I think I should know you Sir'. I found out he knew me well as a child. He asked me to go for a row with him saying 'Come we will tell old yarns' and with old yarns mainly fairy yarns collected round here I have filled two note books.[29]

In August 1891, staying in the family farm of Katharine Tynan near Clondalkin (Co. Dublin), he still had his 'note books' ready: 'I am back in Ireland for the time being, and writing out on the lawn of an old Irish farmhouse ... I am here looking for stories of the fairies and the phantoms.'[30] In the late 1890s, Lady Gregory took him round to some cottages to let him hear tradition-bearers. On Inishmore, he heard an old man who insisted on his truthfulness: 'Once, while he was telling this story, he thought I was not believing him, and he got greatly excited and stood up and said he was an old man and might die before he got to his house and he would not tell me a lie, before God he would not tell me a lie.'[31]

But if he had some direct contact with oral tradition, what he knew was more often mediated through non-traditional channels; and what came from both sources was shaped by his own preoccupations. His interest in the Irishness of that tradition was balanced by the conviction that it was also a link with a more universal mysterious knowledge: commenting on Renan's and Arnold's definitions of Celticism (see pp. 309-10), he observed that they had been given 'before the activity in the study of folk-lore and of folk-literature' had revealed that much of what they thought specifically Celtic was 'of the substance of the minds of the ancient farmers and herdsmen' – it was a European, perhaps a global, heritage of wisdom.[32]

Research into folklore and involvement with occultism and spiritualism often overlapped; Yeats was looking for remnants of ancient secret doctrines that might authenticate his own beliefs, for proofs of the existence of spirits or of communication with some transcendent reality ('My object [when collecting folklore with Lady Gregory] was to find actual experience of the supernatural ...'), and for contact with a primordial world ('When we passed the door of some

29 To Katharine Tynan 13 Aug. 1887; to H.H. Sparling 16 Sept. 1887; to Katherine Tynan 18 Nov. 1887 (*The Collected Letters of W.B.Yeats* 1. 33, 36, 41). 30 'The Celt in Ireland', *Boston Pilot* 12 Sept. 1891, in *Letters to the New Island* 53-4. 31 'The Prisoners of the Gods' (1898), in R. Welch (ed.) W.B.Yeats *Writings on Irish Folklore* 169. It was one of six essays published from 1897 to 1902, using material collected by Lady Gregory. 32 'The Celtic Element in Literature' (1898), in R. Welch ed. op. cit. 190.

peasant's cottage, we passed out of Europe as that word is understood').[33]
Folklore also opened a collective storehouse of pregnant symbols, like the Black
Pig of the prophecies mentioned by Carleton concerning an Irish Armageddon
which suited Yeats's own version of a necessary passage through chaos to regeneration: in 1896 it inspired a poem and in 1899 a long note in *The Wind Among
the Reeds* connected contemporary references to the prophecy with the mythog-
raphy produced by John Rhys, James Frazer and others. Yeats also valued examples of limitless fantasy or of unhampered behaviour in folktales: 'Here at last is
a universe where all is large and intense enough to almost satisfy the emotions
of man. Certainly such stories are not a criticism of life but rather an extension...'[34] Allusions in Yeats's prose writings to the context of traditional storytelling are often expressive of a wish: reading Hyde's *Beside the Fire* made him
'hear in imagination the very voice of the sennachie, and almost smell the smoke
of his turf fire'; and ten years later he thought of going 'at last down into
Connacht to sit by turf fires'.[35] In the same review he praised 'the charms of
folk- and fairy-tales', which rescued one from 'sooty and finite reality' and satisfied our 'imaginative impulse – the quintessence of life'.[36]

Folktales and legends thus had different valuable potentialities. But they still
had to be refined by a real artist: the tellers 'did not think sufficiently about the
shape of the poem and the story.'[37] To become superior art, oral tradition
needed writers who could control the 'wild anarchy of legends' and give it
'deliberate form'[38]; on the other hand the availability of a popular tradition was
good for the artist because it put him in touch with a community: 'I delighted
in every age where poet and artist confined themselves gladly to some inherited
subject-matter known to the whole people.'[39]

At the beginning of his career, Yeats was commissioned to compile two collections of Irish folktales[40] based on material published during the nineteenth
century; but he wanted to do more than borrow other people's images and plots.
He published his own material in *The Celtic Twilight, Men and Women, Dhouls
and Fairies* (1893; an expanded edition with a shorter title appeared in 1902),
which he offered as 'all real stories heard among the people or real incidents
with but a little disguise in names and places.'[41]

A couple of years later, however, his interest in peasants' beliefs and folktales seemed to have lessened and he was more concerned with elitist values; Cú
Chulainn and the other heroic figures that now inspired him offered better dramatic possibilities and belonged to an aristocratic world. The fairies may have
disappointed him because they did little more than perhaps exist. They had not

33 *Autobiographies* 400. 34 *Uncollected Prose* 1. 187. 35 'Irish Folk-Tales' (1891) *Uncollected
Prose* 1. 188, and 'Popular Poetry', *Essays & Introductions* 4. 36 *Uncollected Prose* 1. 186-9.
37 Yeats's preface to Lady Gregory's *Cuchulain of Muirthemne* 12-13. 38 'Bardic Ireland', in
the *Scots Observer* 4 January 1890. 39 *Autobiographies* 190. 40 *Fairy & Folk Tales of the Irish
Peasantry* in 1888 (instructed to edit a selection from Crofton Croker, he expanded the project), and *Irish Fairy Tales* in 1892 (aimed at a juvenile audience). 41 Quoted in M.H.
Thuente, op. cit. , 128.

consented to appear to him – or had they? The evidence is contradictory or ambiguous.[42]

It was in the nature of fairies, after all, to be evanescent. What about the human storyteller? When one of the *personae* of Yeats's imaginary world, he was defined in terms of his perennial function as keeper of a tradition: 'The influences that had moved Ireland deeply were the old influences that had come down from generation to generation, handed on by the story-tellers that collected in the evenings round the fire, creating for learned and unlearned a communion of heroes.'[43] And the ideal storyteller could, indeed should, be a strong personality like the wandering song-maker and fiddler Anthony Raftery, whose compositions and legend Yeats learned from Lady Gregory and Douglas Hyde: '[He would] not allow you for any long time to forget himself. Our Raftery will stop the tale to cry, "That is what I, Raftery, wrote down in the book of the people" … he knows how to keep himself interesting that his words may have weight – so many lines of narrative, and then a phrase about himself and his own emotions.'[44] But Yeats never met such a prodigious personage. His most detailed early portrait of a real but humble informant, first evoked in the introduction to *Fairy and Folk Tales of the Irish Peasantry*, is that of a man who lived at Ballysodare:

The most notable and typical story-teller of my acquaintance is one Paddy Flynn, a little, bright-eyed, old man, living in a leaky one-roomed cottage of the village of B— 'The most gentle – i.e. fairy – place in the whole of the County Sligo', he says, though others claim that honour for Drumahair or for Drumcliff. A very pious man, too! You may have some time to inspect his strange figure and ragged hair, if he happen to be in a devout humour, before he comes to the doings of the gentry [fairies]. A strange devotion! Old tales of Columkill, and what he said to his mother. 'How are you today, mother?' 'Worse!' 'May you be worse tomorrow'; and on the next day, 'How are you today, mother?' 'Better, thank God!' 'May you be better tomorrow.' In which undutiful manner he will tell you Columkill inculcated cheerfulness. Then most likely he will wander off into his favourite theme – how the Judge smiles alike in rewarding the good and condemning the lost to unceasing flames. Very consoling does it appear to Paddy Flynn, this melancholy and apocalyptic cheerfulness of the Judge. Nor seems his own cheerfulness quite earthly – though a very palpable cheerfulness. The first time I saw him he was cooking mushrooms for himself; the next time he was asleep under a hedge, smiling in his sleep. Assuredly some joy not quite of this steadfast earth lightens in those eyes – swift as the eyes of a rabbit – among so many wrinkles, for Paddy Flynn is very old. A melancholy there is in the midst of their cheerfulness – a melancholy of purely instinctive natures and of all animals. In the triple solitude of age and eccentricity and

42 Letter to Richard Le Gallienne, Oct. 1892. *Collected Letters* 1. 321. Cf. the interview in C. Weygandt in 1904, quoted in E.H. Mikhail *W.B. Yeats: Interviews and Recollections* 1. 14: 'Mr Yeats had never himself seen "The Other People" in the Woods of Coole, he said, but many of the neighbouring peasants had.' 43 George Moore's rendering of an after-dinner speech by Yeats in 1899, in *Hail and Farewell: Ave* 150. 44 'Literature and the Living Voice' (1906), *Explorations* 212.

partial deafness he goes about much pestered by children. As to the reality of his fairy
and spirit-seeing powers, not all are agreed. One day we were talking of the Banshee. 'I
have seen it', he said, 'down there by the water "batting" the river with its hands'. He
it was who said the fairies annoyed him.[45]

This mixture of 'apocalyptic cheerfulness' and sorrow was typical of Yeats's
imagined peasant at the time: 'that strange mystery, that sense of melancholy in
which there is no gloom, a sadness as of morning twilight which I find in the
legends of the west.'[46]

The introduction to *Irish Fairy Tales* portrays another storyteller:

It is not so long since I sat by the turf fire eating her griddle cake in [Biddy Hart's] cottage on the slope of Benbulben and asking after her friends, the fairies, who inhabit the
green thorn-covered hill up there behind her house. How firmly she believed in them!
how greatly she feared offending them! For a long time she would give me no answer
but 'I always mind my own affairs and they always mind theirs'. A little talk about my
great-grandfather who lived all his life in the valley below, and a few words to remind
her how I myself was often under her roof when but seven or eight years old loosened
her tongue, however. It would be less dangerous at any rate to talk to me of the fairies
than it would be to tell some 'Towrow' of them, as she contemptuously called English
tourists, for I had lived under the shadow of their own hillsides. She did not forget,
however, to remind me to say after we had finished, 'God bless them, Thursday' (that
being the day), and so ward off their displeasure, in case they were angry at our notice,
for they love to live and dance unknown of men. Once started, she talked freely enough,
her face glowing in the firelight as she bent over the griddle or stirred the turf, and told
how such a one was stolen away from near Coloney village and made to live seven years
among 'the gentry', as she calls the fairies for politeness' sake, and how when she came
home she had no toes, for she had danced them off; and how such another was taken
from the neighbouring village of Grange and compelled to nurse a child of the queen of
the fairies a few months before I came. Her news about the creatures are always quite
matter-of-fact and detailed, just as if she dealt with any common occurrence: the late fair,
or the dance at Rosses last year, when a bottle of whiskey was given to the best man and
a cake tied up in ribbons to the best woman dancer. They are, to her, people not so different from herself, only grander and finer in every way ... When she talks of the fairies
I have noticed a touch of tenderness in her voice. She loves them because they are
always young, always making festivals, always far off from the old age that is coming
upon her and filling her bones with aches, and because, too, they are so like little children.[47]

Whether or not the names were authentic, the models existed; but the texts
contain so much of his own aspirations that Yeats must have projected into these
portraits something of himself, perhaps what he considered a submerged part of

45 *Fairy & Folk Tales...* 5-6. A similar portrait appears in *Celtic Twilight.* 46 Letter to Nora
Hopper 27 January 1895, *The Collected Letters of W.B.Y.* I. 432. 47 *Fairy & Folk Tales ...*
301-3. See also *Reveries over Childhood and Youth.* (*Autobiographies* 70-1.)

his own personality. This tendency may be more marked in his overt creation of fictional folk artists, particularly in the stories collected in *The Secret Rose* (1897). Reckless Red Hanrahan is a poet more concerned with expressions of feelings than with narratives (and is thus more Yeats's man); but there is in the book at least one fictional storyteller who has a recognizable repertoire, not limited to fairy legends, including 'The Son of Apple', 'The Beauty of the World', 'The Feast of Bricriu', which in the 1908 version becomes 'The King of Ireland's Son', thus establishing a trilogy of three of the greatest Irish wonder folktales as distinguished from popular versions of ancients 'sagas'.[48]

Lady Augusta Gregory was much more important as a transcriber of Irish folklore.[49] According to Yeats, she 'was born to see the glory of the world in a peasant mirror'[50]; others might call her representative of the attitude of those members of the Anglo-Irish landed gentry who took an interest in some popular Irish peculiarities and attempted to revive the material by creating a new literary voice in English. Like several of them she had first come into contact with Irish stories as a child through a Catholic servant, but it was a reading of the first version of Yeats's *Celtic Twilight*, in 1893, that made her rediscover, at forty-one, the value of folklore. At about the same time she read Hyde's *Beside the Fire*, as well as – lighter stuff – a rather patronizing evocation of mostly comic aspects of life in Connemara by another Anglo-Irish writer: Jane Barlow's *Irish Idylls* (1882). Encouraged by Yeats, whom she first met in 1894, and by Douglas Hyde in 1897, she started learning Irish and collecting oral material, mostly in the Gort area of County Galway:

The Sligo legends in [*The Celtic Twilight*] made me jealous for Galway, and the gathering of legends among my own neighbours became a chief interest and a great part of my work for many years to come. The gathering was for the most part mine, but as it had begun so it was continued under Yeats's direction so to speak, so far as the lore of vision was concerned. The folk history and folk-tales and poems came later and made a foundation for many of my plays ... We searched for folk-lore. I gave him all I had collected, and took him about looking for more, and whoever came to the door, fisherwoman or beggar or farmer, I would talk to on the subject, and if I found the stories worth having would call him down that he might have them first hand.[51]

Even with Yeats along, *she* was the active collector. She admired the liveliness, abundance and variety of stories: 'This discovery, this disclosure of the folk learning, the folk poetry, the ancient tradition, was the small beginning of a weighty change. It was the upsetting of the table of values, an astonishing excitement.'[52] She was also fascinated by the way her informants spoke English while apparently thinking in Irish. Inspired by Douglas Hyde's translation of the *Love*

48 *The Secret Rose: A Variorum Edition* 73. 49 See Patricia Lysaght's 'Perspectives on Narrative Communication and Gender: Lady Gregory's *Visions and Beliefs in the West of Ireland*', *Fabula* 39 (1998) 256-76. 50 *Autobiographies* 457. 51 *Seventy Years; being the Autobiography of Lady Gregory* 308, 313. 52 *Kiltartan Books* 19.

Songs of Connaught (1893), she evolved her own literary idiom, intended to render dialectal peculiarities; she used it in plays and in her renderings of ancient epics or sagas. The first of those books, *Cuchulain of Muirthemne* (1902), was an attempt at unifying, in a continuous and occasionally bowdlerized narrative, the 'Ulster Cycle' material she found mostly in the publications of nineteenth-century scholars. Dedicating the result to the people of Kiltartan, she observed that those stories had almost completely vanished from their repertoire, and hoped that they might become current again. Like Maria Edgeworth a century before, but with a different intention, she had decided to impersonate an Irish storyteller : 'I have told the whole story in plain and simple words, in the same way my old nurse Mary Sheridan used to be telling stories from the Irish long ago, and I a child at Roxborough.'[53] A similar remark appears in the notes following *Gods & Fighting Men* (1904), her renderings of the arrival of the Tuatha De Danaan and of part of the Fianna Cycle: 'I have found it more natural to tell the stories in the manner of the thatched houses, where I have heard so many legends of Finn and his friends, Oisin and Patrick, and the Ever-Living Ones, and the Country of the Young, rather than in the manner of the slated houses, where I have not heard them.'[54]

Oral informants rather than books were the sources for parts of *Poets and Dreamers* (1903), the whole of *A Book of Saints and Wonders* (1907), *The Kiltartan History Book* (1909), *The Kiltartan Wonder Book* (1910), and – more particularly valuable as a collection of accounts of contacts with the Otherworld – *Visions and Beliefs in the West of Ireland* (1920). The material was collected shortly before or after 1900, concerning for instance the travelling poet Raftery (1779-1835) – 'legends are already growing up about his death'[55] – or Biddy Early (?1798-1874), the white witch of County Clare: 'I think as time goes on her fame will grow and some of the myths that always hang in the air will gather around her.'[56] In the first book, 'Workhouse Dreams' is the account of storytelling sessions among the inmates of a poorhouse:

I spent three happy afternoons in a workhouse in my own county, but not in my own parish; and after we had spoken of the Fianna for a while, the old men began to tell me these long, rambling stories I am about to repeat ... As I listened, I was moved by the strange contrast between the poverty of the tellers and the splendours of the tales. These men who had failed in life, and were old and withered, or sickly, or crippled, had not laid up dreams of good houses and fields and sheep and cattle; for they had never possessed enough to think of the possession of more as a possibility. It seemed as if their lives had been so poor and rigid in circumstance that they did not fire their minds, as more prosperous people might do, on thoughts of customary pleasure. The stories that they love are of quite visionary things; of swans that turn into king's daughters, and of castles with crowns over the doors, and lovers' flights on the backs of eagles, and music-

---

53 *Cuchulain of Muirthemne* 5. **54** *Gods & Fighting Men* 354; again, the sources were essentially books and manuscripts. **55** *Poets and Dreamers* 39. **56** *Visions and Beliefs ...* 32.

loving water-witches, and journeys to the other world, and sleeps that last for seven hundred years. I think it has always been to such poor people, with little of wealth or comfort to keep their thoughts bound to the things about them, that dreams and visions have been given. It is from a deep narrow well the stars can be seen at noonday ...[57]

Though impressed by Yeats's quest for the ideal and by her informants' fantasy, Lady Gregory had in fact a more realistic view of the traditional storyteller. But she drew no detailed individual portrait; we have to be content with passing notes such as: 'One of the old men told me a story in Irish – another translating it as he went on; for my ear was not practised enough to follow it well: "There was a farmer one time had one son only..." '; 'Another old man says: "There was a Protestant and a Catholic one time..." '; '... That's my story. Will you give me tobacco for that?" But this being the last day, they all had tobacco – story tellers and all.'[58] She was aware of the importance of talk and make-believe for such people, as shown by a character in her play *The Workhouse Ward* (1908): 'All that I am craving is the talk. There to be no one at all to say out to whatever thought might be rising in my innate mind! To be lying here and no conversible person in it would be the abomination of misery!'[59] In *Spreading the News* she illustrated (with comic exaggeration) another aspect of the Irish love of talk, the eagerness to multiply and inflate rumours: 'Telling lies the whole of the people of this town are; telling lies, telling lies as fast as the dog will trot.'[60] She introduced *The Kiltartan History Book* – a collection of legends or 'myths in the making' – with the brief comment: 'I have given this book its name because it is in this Barony of Kiltartan that I have heard the greater number of the stories, from beggars, pipers, travelling men, at my own door; or by the roadside or in a workhouse, though others I have been given to the north of Galway Bay, in Connemara, or on its southern shore.'[61] In *The Kiltartan Wonder Book*, including Irish versions of 'international tales' (for which she did not care much)[62], the narrative settings or the narrators are evoked in lively vignettes:

'Well, I will tell you the story of a Mule was in the world one time', says the old man who had promised me a codfish and had only brought a hake ... 'I will tell you the story of Beswarragal', said the old man of a hundred years old ... 'I'll tell you a story', says the old man who was bringing fish from the sea; 'and after that I'll be going on to Ballinrobe, to one that has a shop there and that was reared by my grandmother. It is likely he'll give me a tasty suit of clothes. Working all my life I am, working with the flail in the barn, working with a spade at the potato tilling and the potato digging, breaking stones on the road, and four years ago the wife died, and it's lonesome to be in the house keeping alone. There was a king long ago in Ireland ...' ... 'I'll tell you a story, now, and I'll not be with you again till Christmas; and I never saw a man that could read an open book, was able to tell a story out of the mouth ...' ... 'I have a new wife now,

57 *Poets and Dreamers* 128-30. **58** Ibid. 130, 133, 191. **59** *Seven Short Plays* 156. **60** Ibid. 25. **61** *The Kiltartan Books* 147. **62** Lysaght, op. cit. 266.

says the old man who had come back from Ballinrobe; to keep my victuals ready and the door open before me. She's a quiet woman at some times, but she has a queer way in her mind at the time of the full moon, but it will pass away after. And here is a story now, and I'll word it easy to you ...' ... 'And that's a nice story and a wonderful story, and a true thing that fell out. And Lofarey, the man that told it to me, said it was a true story, and that his own father told him he was speaking to the poor scholar who read the flag.' [63]

She concluded: 'I have not changed a word in these stories as they were told to me, but having heard some of them in different versions from different old people, I have sometimes taken a passage or a phrase from one and put it in another where it seemed to fit.'[64] Perhaps she needed an interpreter when the storyteller spoke Irish, and with hindsight her collecting and editorial practice might be criticized: she generally memorized the stories and wrote them down later, in a more or less synthetic style and with some conflation of sources. But such practice was still common in folklore publications at the beginning of the century, and she did not see it as an obstacle to what she aimed to do: to hold up 'a clean mirror to tradition'.[65]

Turning to John Millington Synge, we soon realize that the 'traditional' Irish world that attracted him was far from idyllic or merely picturesque; its denizens could be very tough characters, but capable of imaginative flights, and tramps or islanders living in 'primitive' conditions had a greater power of fascination over him than the average Irish peasant – unless the latter appeared in an extreme situation or mood. He was also born in the Anglo-Irish ascendancy, but unlike Lady Gregory he seems to have been ill at ease in his own class. In boyhood, he had spent his free time wandering in the Mountains of Dublin and Wicklow, and occasionally listening to the stories told by simple people. He learnt some Irish at Trinity College, but it was a lecture by the Breton folklorist Anatole Le Braz in 1897 and the reading of his books, while living in France, that made him realize the value of oral lore. A knowledge of continental collections and of medieval literature prepared him for a comparative approach to folktales, while the Celtomania of the late nineteenth century focused his attention on the vestiges of an old culture that might still exist in his own country. It seems that he was better able than Yeats to empathize with the feelings or thoughts and behaviour of the people he observed. He was not looking for occult significance and visionary outbursts, and as his usual attitude was taciturnity he had the makings of a good listener.

Between 1898 and 1902, he spent in all about four-and-a-half months in the Aran Islands. What immediately thrilled him was primitiveness: 'It gave me a moment of exquisite satisfaction to find myself moving away from civilisation ...'

63 Ibid. 153, 156, 180, 184, 186, 188. 64 Ibid. 210. 65 *Visions and Beliefs* ... 15. Yeats had applied the same phrase to his own folkloristic activities, in an article published in 1897 (see *Writings on Irish Folklore, Legend and Myth* ed. by R. Welch, 153).

– so he wrote as a curragh was bringing him to Inishmaan. Of his arrival for a second stay, he wrote: 'I was coming back to grow as strong and simple as they were among the islands of the west.'[66] He was impressed at least as much by the population as by the setting, the two being in fact inseparable in struggle and communion: a 'strange concord [existed] between the people and the impersonal limited but profound impulses of the nature that is round them'[67]. He praised the islanders' way of talking and telling stories 'lovingly'. As his linguistic competence improved, he acquired a better knowledge of 'the unlettered literature which was the real source of all the art of words'.[68] *The Aran Islands* (1907) contains a number of folktales ('all verifiable as belonging to genuine oral tradition'),[69] and several portraits of storytellers in action, including Máirtín Ó Conghaile (Mourteen Conneely), who had been an informant for George Petrie, Sir William Wilde, Jeremiah Curtin in 1892 and Holger Pedersen in 1895, on Inishmore:

As we talked he sat huddled together over the fire, shaking and blind, yet his face was indescribably pliant, lighting up with an ecstasy of humour when he told me of anything that had a point of wit or malice, and growing sombre and desolate again when he spoke of religion or the fairies. He had great confidence in his own powers and talent, and in the superiority of his stories over all other stories in the world. When we were speaking of Mr Curtin, he told me that this gentleman had brought out a volume of his Aran stories in America, and made five hundred pounds by the sale of them. 'And what do you think he did then?' he continued; 'he wrote a book of his own stories after making that lot of money with mine. And he brought them out, and the devil a halfpenny did he get for them. Would you believe that?' Afterwards he told me how one of his children had been taken by the fairies.[70]

On Inishmaan, Synge called his main informant Pat Dirane:

When I was going out this morning to walk round the island with Michael, the boy who is teaching me Irish, I met an old man making his way down to the cottage. He was dressed in miserable black clothes which seemed to have come from the mainland, and was so bent with rheumatism that, at a little distance, he looked more like a spider than a human being. Michael told me it was Pat Dirane, the story-teller old Mourteen had spoken of on the other island. I wished to turn back, as he appeared to be on his way to visit me, but Michael would not hear of it. 'He will be sitting by the fire when we come in', he said; 'let you not be afraid, there will be time enough to be talking to him by and by.' He was right. As I came down into the kitchen some hours later old Pat was still in the chimney-corner, blinking with the turf smoke ... While the old woman was cooking my dinner he asked me if I liked stories, and offered to tell one in English, though he

66 *Collected Works: Prose* 57, 142. 67 Ibid. 59. 68 Ibid. 75n. 69 S. Ó Súilleabháin 'Synge's Use of Irish Folklore', in M. Harmon (ed.) *J.M. Synge; Centenary Papers* 30. According to Nicholas Grene, the rewriting of tales from notes to published versions involved 'an attempt to use more definitely Irish idioms than in the original' (*Synge: A Critical Study of the Plays* 24–9). 70 *Collected Works: Prose* 50–1.

added, it would be much better if I could follow the Gaelic. Than he began: – There were two farmers in County Clare... [He tells a variant of International Type 882: 'The Wager on the Wife's Chastity' which inspired Boccaccio and Shakespeare.] He paused for a moment, and a deep sigh of relief rose from the men and women who had crowded in while the story was going on, till the kitchen was filled with people ... It gave me a strange feeling of wonder to hear this illiterate native of a wet rock in the Atlantic telling a story that is so full of European associations ... Pat told me a story of an unfaithful wife [the subject of *The Shadow of the Glen*] , which I will give further down, and then broke into a moral dispute with a visitor, which caused immense delight to some young men who had come down to listen to the story. Unfortunately it was carried on so rapidly in Gaelic that I lost most of the points. This old man talks usually in a mournful tone about his ill-health, and his death, which he feels to be approaching, yet he has occasional touches of humour that remind me of old Mourteen on the north island ...They say on the island that he can tell as many lies as four men: perhaps the stories he has learned have strengthened his imagination.[71]

In the first part of the book, this storyteller is little more than a voice, relatively fluent in English but preferring to narrate in Irish and mysteriously connected with distant archaic sources. When Synge returned to Aran after the death of Pat Dirane, the latter was the subject of other storytellers' narratives, in which he sometimes played the role of a trickster: 'I remember old Pat Dirane used to tell us... Pat was a great rogue.' [72]

Declan Kiberd notes that Synge discriminated between the two main types of Irish storytellers: the *scéalaí*, who told long wonder tale or stories of very olden times (*seanscéalta*) and the *seanchaí*, who narrated local lore, generally in the first person.[73] Some Aran people, like Pat Dirane, practised both genres: 'In stories of this kind [*seanchas* – supposedly true lore] he always speaks in the first person, with minute details to show that he was actually present at the scenes that are described.'[74] Old Mourteen was also at ease in both genres. Others could tell only the humbler kind of narrative: 'Another old man, the oldest on the island, is fond of telling me anecdotes – not folktales – of things that have happened in his lifetime.'[75]

The people Synge observed on Aran were seen by him alternatively as 'primitive' and as 'medieval', as 'wild animals' but 'with a touch of refinement', as poor but 'aristocratic', 'plaintive' and soon after 'passionate'. Yeats called him the 'rooted man', but he was in fact a man in search of roots, attracted by what was far from the world he had been raised in. When he discovered the Blasket Islands, he may have felt closer to his ideal: 'It is probably even more primitive than Aran and I am wild with joy at the prospect'.[76] But such spots were under a threat, and he felt that he was studying a dying culture, which induced morbid reflections: 'The thought that this island [Inishmaan] will gradually yield to the

71 Ibid. 60-3, 65, 70, 100. 72 Ibid. 154. 73 *Synge and the Irish Language* 157-8. 74 *Collected Works: Prose* 72. 75 Ibid. 95. 76 Letter to Lady Gregory, quoted in J.W. Foster *Fictions of the Irish Literary Revival* 99.

ruthlessness of "progress" is as the certainty that decaying age is moving always nearer the cheeks it is your ecstasy to kiss.'[77]

The closer he came to a community with which he would have liked to identify, the more he felt he was in fact an outsider:

> In some ways, these men and women seem strangely far away from me. They have the same emotions that I have, and the animals have, yet I cannot talk to them when there is so much to say, more than to the dog that whines beside me in a mountain fog. There is hardly an hour I am with them that I do not feel the shock of some inconceivable idea, and then again the shock of some vague emotion that is familiar to them and to me. On some days I feel this island as a perfect home and resting place; on other days I feel that I am a waif among the people. I can feel more with them than they can feel with me, and while I wander among them, they like me sometimes, and laugh at me sometimes, yet never know what I am doing.[78]

He admired their skill with words, the importance they attached to storytelling which made their life more interesting, and their 'delight in broad jests and deeds' – the more so as he was himself shy and relatively tongue-tied. He perceived 'an affinity between the moods of these people and the moods of varying rapture and dismay that are frequent in artists, and in certain forms of alienation'.[79] In fact, he noted what accorded with his own secret temperament, 'choosing what would express his own personality' and trying to see 'what lay hidden in himself'.[80]

The Playboy of the Western World admits many interpretations, but from the particuliar point of view I have adopted we may note that Christy Mahon, the protagonist, does not arrive, like the fugitive in a story Synge heard on Inishmaan[81], in a healthy community, but among a demoralized population whose narrative food is reduced to poor news items. Undergoing an identity crisis, he is confronted with mirrors: material ones like the glass in his father's house where he was a nonentity ('it was the divil's own mirror we had beyond, would twist a squint across an angel's brow') and the one in Mayo that seems to make him glamorous when girls admire him, or reflections provided by human beings like the false image of virility the Mayo people send back to him ('Is it me?')[82] before trying to destroy it. He must discover his true self and (like Synge?) become a master of verbal arts and an accomplished fictionist who goes 'romancing through a romping lifetime', or 'winning clean beds and the fill of my belly four times in the day, and I doing nothing but telling stories...'[83] The Irish audience did not like the image of Ireland they received from the stage;

---

77 *Collected Works: Prose* 103 (the passage was suppressed in the published version of the essay). 78 Ibid. 113. 79 Ibid. 74. 80 Yeats *Essays and Introductions* 299, 330. Cf. Padraic Colum: 'All his work was subjective, he once told me, it all came out of moods in his own life.' (*The Road Round Ireland* 365) 81 *Collected Works: Prose* 95. 82 Ibid. 121. 83 *Collected Works: Plays* 1. 173, 135. For more about Christy as a liar, see Chapter 13.

more precisely, city people who fostered the idealized image of the Irish peasant did not like what Synge made them see.[84]

'Æ' (George Russell) was the best loved person in the Literary Revival galaxy, but is the least read today. More than the others he could give in his writings and paintings the impression of embodying 'Celtic' dreaminess, yet he knew rural poverty and was more deeply involved than them in practical action to transform society. As 'A Visionary', he had made an anonymous appearance in Yeats's *Celtic Twilight*: 'His pleasure ... was to wander about upon the hills, talking to half-mad and visionary peasants.'[85] Bicycling through Ireland for the Irish Agricultural Organization Society, he sometimes felt relief when hearing legends of the supernatural rather than endless discussions concerning the price of eggs.[86] But his aim was not to publish such material and observe storytellers; his own spiritual adventures and visions were more important. The new Irish civilization whose emergence he announced was imbued with theosophy, pantheism or mysticism. He was interested in other people's dreams when they confirmed his, and he distilled from Irish traditions what vindicated his own prophetic message:

The gods have returned to Erin and have centred themselves in the sacred mountains and blow the fires through the country. They have been seen by several in vision, they will awaken the magical instinct everywhere, and the universal heart of the people will turn to the old druidic beliefs. I note through the country the increased faith in faery things. The bells are heard from the mounds and sounding in the hollows of the mountains. A purple sheen in the inner air, perceptible at times in the light of day, spreads itself over the mountains.[87]

Beyond Irish landscapes and mythology, he sought confirmations of ageless doctrines:

I think that the tales which have been preserved for a hundred generations in the heart of the people must have had such a power, because they had in them a core of eternal truth ... These dreams, antiquities, traditions, once actual, living, and historical, have passed from the world of sense into the world of memory and thought; and time, it seems to me, has not taken away from them their power nor made them more remote from sympathy, but has rather purified them by removing them from earth unto heaven.[88]

His conception of oral, literary and patriotic Irish traditions is illustrated in one of his later works, *The Interpreters* (1922): 'Michael', the eponymous hero of

84 Synge tried, in vain, to conciliate his patriotic adversaries by denying that he was holding the mirror up to Irish nature, in an interview for the *Dublin Evening Mail* quoted in J. Kilroy *The Playboy Riots* 23. 85 *Mythologies* 11. 86 He kept Yeats informed: see for instance *Letters from Æ* 25-7 (February 1898). 87 Ibid. 17: letter to W.B. Yeats, 2 June 1896. 88 From Russell's contribution to John Eglinton (ed.) *Literary Ideals in Ireland* (1899) 50-1.

a poem recited towards the end of a discussion, has lived in the west of Ireland and 'listened to old tales, or legends' which sent him on a visionary *immram* or voyage amidst heavenly islands; later, while vegetating in Dublin, he hears from a Donegal Gaelic speaker the story of Cú Chulainn and other 'warriors of Eternal Mind'. He dies in the Easter rebellion of 1916, and a crystal boat takes him back to 'the heavenly seas'.[89] The author's hopes for what he considered *the* sacred land were later crushed; by the early 1930s, he found the new Ireland intolerable and spent his last years in England.

If Yeats, Lady Gregory, Synge and Russell represent that part of the Anglo-Irish community that persistently – though with important nuances – believed in a Celtic revival, George Moore is a more complex and anomalous case. On the one hand he had been born an Irish Catholic – but in a family of landlords; later he turned against his family's religion. Unlike most of the Anglo-Irish writers he frequented, he was in no way a patriot and conducted a complicated series of quarrels and half-hearted reconciliations with things Irish. In his autobiographical novel *The Confessions of a Young Man* (1888), he had provocatively defined the dominant notes in his character as 'an original hatred of my native country and a brutal loathing of the religion I was brought up in. All the aspects of my native country are violently disagreeable to me, and I cannot think of the place I was born in without a sensation akin to nausea'.[90]

He had spent only the first nine years of his childhood, and one as an adolescent, at Moore Hall in County Mayo; he then returned only for a few brief stays. A comfortable life of artistic dilettantism in Paris was interrupted by the Irish Land War, when the tenants first stopped paying the rents he was living on, then succeeded in having them reduced. He settled in London, and declared: 'Ireland is a bog and the aborigenes are a degenerate race'.[91] In the 1890s, however, what was happening in Dublin began to intrigue him. He acquainted himself with the Gaelic League programme, and although he had earlier thought that 'nobody did anything in Irish except bring turf from the bog and say prayers', he was for a time won over, calling for 'a return to the language ... a mysterious inheritance in which resides the soul of the Irish'.[92] He sympathized with plans for an Irish theatre in which he hoped to play an important part, and believed in the promotion of culture in a country where so far, according to him, writers in English had 'written nothing of any worth – miserable stuff, no novel of any seriousness, only broad farce'.[93] The comedy of his ambivalences and expectations followed by disappointment between 1899 and 1911 is maliciously related in *Hail and Farewell*, with some brief comments on Irish storytelling. Before deciding to move to Dublin in 1901, he had tried to recollect the contacts he had had with folklore through a Mayo poacher turned gamekeeper: 'at

89 Op. cit. 157–68. The poem had been first published separately in 1919. **90** Op. cit. 84. **91** Introduction to *Parnell and His Island* (1887). **92** 'Literature and the Irish Language', in J. Eglinton (ed.) *Literary Ideals in Ireland* 47. **93** *Hail and Farewell: Ave* 4–5.

this distance of time it is difficult to recall the tales I heard of Carmody's life among the mountains'; but he considered making use of such material: 'I closed my eyes a little and licked my lips as I walked, thinking of the pleasure it would be to tell this story ... and to tell it in its place. [But] it would be necessary to live in Ireland, in a cabin in the West; only in that way could I learn the people, become intimate with them again ... The impulse in me to redeem Ireland from obscurity was not strong enough to propel me from London to Holyhead.'94 Still in London, he listened to Yeats telling stories, and found the performance rather comic: 'He continued to drone out his little tales in his own incomparable fashion, muttering after each one of them, like an oracle that has spent itself – "a beautiful story, a beautiful story!" '95

Having settled in Dublin, Moore went on a cycling tour round pre-Christian sacred places, including Slieve Gullion in County Armagh, with 'Æ' who wanted to 'drive Irish mythology and idealism on him';96 he described the expedition as a failure, because local people had forgotten the stories which he, as a neophyte, had read in books:

A local man by the roadside] had no Irish. But his father, he said, was a great Irish speaker ... He had never been to the top of Slievegullion himself [where, according to late medieval sources, Fionn mac Cumhaill met an otherworld lady and was transformed into an old man], but he had heard of the lake from those that had been up there, and he thought that he had heard of Finn from his father, but he disremembered if Finn had plunged into the lake after some beautiful queen. 'Things that have lived too long in the same place become melancholy, Æ. Let him emigrate. He is no use to us. He has forgotten his Irish and the old stories that carried the soul of the ancient Gael right down to the present generation.'97

Finally it was 'Æ' who had to revive 'tradition' by telling his own version of the whitening of Fionn's hair.98 Some time later, Moore was less enthusiastic than his fellow directors of the Irish Literary Theatre when they all attended a Gaelic League *Feis* in County Galway – one of those new occasions when folklore competitions were taking place before more or less open-minded adjudicators and comprehending audiences:

As soon as the jig was over the story-teller came in, and, taking a chair, he warmed his hands over an imaginary peat fire, and began his traditional narrative, which did not differ much from traditional singing. Now and then he seemed to wander, and I thought he must be telling of somebody lost in a field, who had to turn his coat inside out to rid himself of the fairy spell; and, glancing round the audience, I could see the eyes of the Irish speakers kindling (it was easy to pick them out), the wandering Celtic eye, pale as

94 Ibid. 34-8. 95 Ibid. 56. 96 Russell's letter to Yeats, late 1900, quoted in H. Summerfield *That Myriad-Minded Man: A Biography of George William Russell* 106. 97 *Hail and Farewell: Salve* 67. 98 This, like the following quotation, was written some ten years after the event; Moore's first reaction may have been different.

their own hills. How they listened! interested in the narrative, recognizing themselves and their forlorn lives in it. Creatures of marsh and jungle they seemed to me, sad as the primitive Nature in which they lived. I had known them from childhood, but was always afraid of them, and used to run into the woods when I saw the woman coming with the men's dinners from Derrinanny (the name is like them), and the marsh behind the village and the dim line of the Partry Mountains were always alien to me. 'Edward [Martyn], let's get away. We're losing the sunlight.' 'We're expecting a piper from Aran, the great piper of the middle island –' 'And a great number of story-tellers', Yeats added.[99]

George Moore did not find folklore inspiring after all, and the Celtic revival was not for him. Addressing Yeats, he made fun of his colleagues' activities: ' "I don't think that one can acquire the dialect by going out to walk with Lady Gregory. She goes into the cottage and listens to the story, takes it down while you wait outside, sitting on a bit of wall, Yeats, like an old jackdaw, and then filching her manuscript to put style upon it, just as you want to put style on me." Yeats laughed vaguely...'[100]

One of the short stories Moore produced in Ireland, 'The Curse of Julia Cahill' (a first version was completed in 1901), lets us hear an oral storyteller, in the common nineteenth-century situation: the frame narrator is a gentleman travelling through Ireland, and the sub-narrator a local jaunting-car driver who addresses him as 'Sir' or 'Your Honour'. The speech of the in-tale, which makes up the greater part of the text, is coloured with a few conventional markers for written renditions of Irish peasant dialect ('bedad', 'them that's in league with the fairies ...', 'agin', 'others do be saying ...'), while the frame narrator, not distinguishable from the author, writes Standard English. The story is that of a girl who had been 'with the fairies', and who laid an effective curse on the village when the priest banished her. The local man believes in the girl's magic, while the traveller is obviously skeptical.[101]

Having left Ireland in 1911, Moore published his autobiographical, satirical and perhaps partly fictionalized account of the revival movement, which Yeats and others resented: 'I am glad ... that George Moore's disfiguring glass will not be the only glass'.[102]

But Moore was not through with Ireland. In *A Story Teller's Holiday*, which he started writing by the end of 1916, he seems to have tried to do what he had contemplated in the late 1890s, with stories heard in childhood or youth. He now chose the device of an imaginary confrontation between himself, as an established writer, and several types of Irish storytellers. Arriving in Dublin

---

99 Ibid. 135-6. **100** *Hail and Farewell: Ave* 348-9. **101** The story was first published in 1902, then revised for *The Untilled Field* in 1903. In another story, 'A Play-House in the Waste', the man who hears a story is identified as an organizer of the I.A.O.S – like Æ – and his informant is again a car-driver: 'Faith! these jarveys can tell a story – none better' (ibid. 106). **102** Yeats, letter to Katharine Tynan, 12 Dec. 1913 (*The Letters of W.B. Yeats* 586).

shortly after the 1916 Rising (the inevitable ruins thus appear earlier than was usual in Irish travelogues, and are more recent ...) he listens to Oliver St John Gogarty, the arch wit of the day. Then, crossing Ireland by train, he hears a story from a fellow traveller. But it is in Mayo that he meets his main partner, Alec Trusselby, who lives in the woods in the summer-time, sleeping on a tree like the mad Suibhne of the medieval tale or like wood-kernes, those Irish outlaws of the sixteenth or seventeenth centuries. In the bad season he turns storyteller:

It was delightful to hear that in the winter he related stories about the firesides in the cottages, and that no one refused Alec bed and board if he could help it; Alec's company was sought for by everybody; and a suspicion was abroad that to treat him ill was to bring ill luck upon oneself. Gathering ferns in the summer and telling stories in the winter, I repeated, becoming possessed in a moment of an absorbing interest in Alec Trusselby. Is he an Irish speaker? I asked, and heard that he was one of the best in the county of Mayo. But, a girl cried across the table, 'mind, if he suspects you are laughing at him he will run away at once, and don't tell him you're a Protestant, he might refuse to go into the woods with you'.[103]

After repeated attempts on the part of the would-be collector, stories start pouring out:

It was often on my tongue to say: 'In the winter evenings I suppose you tell stories in the cottages', but I had restrained myself, and it is not unlikely that it was to break through my studied reserve that he began to speak, some days later, of Liadin and Curithir, saying that they used to meet by the druid stone under which we were now sitting, eating the food he had brought with us. 'And who may they be?' I asked. 'You don't read their names in the stories that are going round about old Ireland', he answered, 'but 'tis many and many's the time I've heard my father say that there wasn't the like of that pair for the making of poems'. The names seemed to kindle a new personality in him. The lantern is lighted, I said; we shall see whither it leads us. 'In the years back' he continued, 'it was a favourite story with the people, but they don't care much about it here. It is out of their minds now like the rest of the old shanachies, and all they have a taste for is the yarns they do be reading in the newspapers and the like; stuff without any diet in them. Well, since your honour is so pleasant, I'll tell it ...'[104]

Moore had found the ninth- or tenth-century story of the tragic love between a poet and a poetess, Cuirithir and Liadain, in Kuno Meyer's edition of the text (1902); in Trusselby's version it is enriched with elements of the tale of the 'man without a story', still popular in Ireland in the twentieth century (see Chapter 12).[105] By now it is clear that Moore's book, which first appeared in 1918 under the imprint of a totally fictitious Society for Irish Folklore, is poking fun at a fashion. In a possible dig at Yeats – or at himself – the author leads Trusselby

103 *A Story-Teller's Holiday* 1. 62-3. **104** Ibid. 1. 71-2. **105** Ibid. 1. 80-1.

to pass off as oral tradition what had been found in books, when it was not invented by the editor: 'Well, sir, I've told it the way I got it from the grandfather, just as he used to tell it when he was in the humour for dreaming over the old Ireland of long ago, and he had it from his father or from the old writings, for he was reading every evening in the National Library in Dublin.'[106] Moore appreciates the amphibious nature of this Irish 'shanachie' – whose name does not sound Irish, who despises the Gaelic League storytellers, and has a marked tendency to criticize the repression of sexuality by the Catholic Church:

His gift of story-telling amuses me because it is new to me, but it is as old as the hills themselves, flowing down the generations since yonder hills were piled up. Sheep paths worn among the hills. His grandfather or grand-uncle, whichever the Dublin scholar was, trimmed these paths a little. Sheep paths, nothing else. Alec is a creature of circumstance, and like myself can be accounted for. He tells stories against the priests and nuns of the twelfth century, for these are not far removed, in his knowledge and imagination, from druids and druidesses ... 'You've told me some wonderful stories, and without doubt are the great shanachie of Connaught.' 'Many's the one that has said the same to me, your honour, but if they were right itself, it isn't much of a brag to be above those going up for the competitions with no more than two and three and a half a story between the lot of them; and the fellows stuttering and stammering them out. But, compared with the shanachies that were in it in the old time, your honour, I'm not so much maybe.' [107]

When Trusselby invites Moore to tell stories in his turn, the writer, like a traditional storyteller, needs coaxing: ' "It would be a great honour to hear a story from yourself, your honour." ... "But you see, Alec, my stories are intended to be read; my stories are eye stories, yours are ear stories, and at an ear story you beat me easily".'[108] He finally complies, however; and a deliberately unorthodox question is raised: where, after all, is the difference between the supposedly distinct species of storytellers, traditional and sophisticated, since Moore now decides to tell a story he heard as a child from a Moore Hall labourer? His nature, too, is amphibious:

A great story-teller was Timothy, and many legends I heard from him in the stable-yard whither I was forbidden to go, and in the woods hiding from my governess – legends long passed out of my mind and out of the mind of the world. However closely I search my memory, I come on names only, a phrase, mayhap a broken outline, Of one story I have a beginning, a middle, and an end, a bare, meagre outline, it is true, but an outline, however, is enough for a story-teller.[109]

In this book, George Moore seems to have expressed his mixed feelings about Irish storytelling: there could be something fascinating about the ideal storytellers some of his contemporaries worshipped, but as far as he could judge

106 Ibid. 1. 143. **107** Ibid. 1. 173, 202. **108** Ibid. 1. 203. **109** Ibid. 2. 4.

only dim memories survived of their art, which after all was perhaps not so fundamentally different from that of writers. As for their descendants competing for medals in Gaelic League functions, he was unimpressed by them.

The new Irish writers could not be satisfied with the solutions adopted in the previous century to render the vernacular (see pp. 261-2). Non-standard language had been looked down upon as a ludicrous mark of ignorance, or at best as an entertaining difference; it now had to be made respectable, because those speaking it were often dignified and it had to function as a literary medium for noble artistic purposes. Consequently some markers were selected while others were excluded: for instance, the use of odd spelling to mimic a deviant pronunciation, which had been the favourite device during the nineteenth century, and the multiplication of verbal blunders from malapropisms to 'bulls', an even older literary convention for the rendering of Irish speech, were no longer acceptable. The solution lay in identifying certain turns of phrase (word-order, and cadence) proper to the Irish language, which would not appear grotesque and could be transposed into English. The Irishness of a discourse was now to be found in some syntactical structures, in rhythm, and in a certain kind of imagery. Douglas Hyde had shown the way – but more in the prose commentary on his *Love Songs of Connacht* (1893) than in his translations of folktales. Lady Gregory and Synge, in different ways, also stylized their selection of 'peasant' speech to suit their literary purposes. They used it more particularly in their plays.

As he did not trust his own ability to render Hiberno-English speech, Moore had asked James Stephens to season the dialogue of *A Story-Teller's Holiday* with peasant style: to 'heighten the colour ... sprinkle the idiom over the story'.[110] But the linguistic local colour in the book remained awkward. The literary talent of Stephens is not in question – he could skillfully play with Irish mythological and legendary characters – but although his origins and early years remain obscure we know that he was Dublin born and bred, had less experience of rural life than most writers of the Literary Renaissance, and resisted 'the present glorification of the peasant'.[111] His *Irish Fairy Tales* (published in 1920) were adaptations of mostly Fianna material he had found in translations; his storytellers – Tuan, Caoilte, Mongan and others – were the narrating heroes of medieval texts, and the same is true of Nera and Fergus who function as storytellers in *The Land of Youth* (1924). In *The Demi-Gods* (1914), however, where tinkers and angels exchange stories by the roadside, there is a good definition of the skilful narrator: 'He would tell you a thing you knew all your life, and you would think it was a new thing. There was no age in that man's mind, and that's the secret of storytelling.'[112]

James Stephens had been discovered and helped by 'Æ'. The same is true

---

110 Letters to Stephens quoted in J.W. Foster *Fictions of the Irish Literary Revival* 372. 111 Quoted in P. Craig (ed.) *The Oxford Book of Ireland* 308. 112 *The Demi-Gods* 185.

of Padraic Colum, with whom I end this overview of the Irish Literary Revival. His treatment of rural life sometimes came closer to that of a Séamus MacManus, but more restrained. In America, where like MacManus he had emigrated (in 1914), he was considered an authority on Irish folklore, though he did not try to play the role of a scholar: 'After all I'm not a folklorist, and am not a mythologist, and shouldn't be compared with a real folklorist in the field.'[113] He had had early experience of traditional Irish storytelling when he heard the poor in the Longford workhouse of which his father was the master, or when living with other members of his family:

I spent some years in my grandmother's house in County Cavan. It was not Irish-speaking, but at the time it was as close to the old life as any English-speaking locality could be. My grandmother often told traditional stories: she had a beautiful one that I never found in any collection, and that I made into a narrative poem. It had an imaginative phrase that I long remembered, 'As wise as the man who never told his dream'. But she did not tell the stories in any professional way. But there was an old man who came to the house, to the celidh [*céilí*: friendly visit or social evening], who was a shanachie, the story-teller and the local historian. I learned about local history by listening to exchanges between him and my grandmother. And in his very dilapidated house – he was afterwards evicted from it, and I now wonder why his neighbours allowed it to be done – by the light of the bog-deal on his fire, I heard him tell stories to the boys and girls who had come in. He remained seated on the bench by the fire as he told the story, a stick in his hand that he raised to emphasize the salient parts of the narrative, the runs and repetitions said rhythmically. It stayed in my mind as a performance. Afterwards when I came to write books that were based on legends, this method of oral delivery was in my mind.[114]

He revived similar memories in the introduction to his *Treasury of Irish Folklore*: 'I heard stories told in the professional way, with the timing, the gestures, the stresses that belong to an ancient popular art'.[115] And in one of his last books, he amplified his generalized portrait of the storyteller:

He told his stories in the evening; he told them by the light of a candle and a peat fire – often by the light of a peat fire only. There were shadows upon the walls around. Nothing that he told us had to be visualized in the glare of day or by the glare of electric light. He had a language that had not been written down; he had words that had not been made colorless by constant use in books and newspapers. He was free to make all sorts of rhymes and chimes in the language he used, and to use words that were meaningless except for the overtones of meaning that were in their sounds. He had various tags with which to end his stories. And he could make his hero start from a hilltop that was known to all his audience.[116]

113 'Ninety Years in Retrospect' (an interview conducted by Zack Bowen) in *Journal of Irish Literature* 2 (1973) No. 1. 26. 114 'Vagrant Voices, A Self-Portrait', in *Journal of Irish Literature* 2 (1973) 1. 65-6 115 *A Treasury of Irish Folklore* xx. 116 *Story Telling New and Old* (1968) 2-3.

He rewrote myths and legends, particularly for children; the education of the hero of *A Boy of Eirinn* (1915) consists mostly in listening to storytellers as he travels through Ireland.*The King of Ireland's Son* (1916) blends genuine folk material and invention. One of the motifs is the quest for a story – an element common enough in Irish tradition (see Chapter 12), and the whole is a complex composition of intertwined and framed tales.

In sum, the Literary Revival's treatment of Irish folktales and storytelling was both respectful (they were parts of a valuable inheritance) and free (they could be adapted to some specifically literary use, comic fantasy not excluded). The extent of direct knowledge of oral lore and actual experience of traditional storytelling varied from one writer to another, and books were an important source of information. Each writer was likely to find what he wished to see: Yeats expected the storyteller to be a visionary, or the embodiment of instinctive passion, or both; Lady Gregory and Synge looked for people who were materially poor but endowed with the power of inventing richness through words, but Synge, more fascinated by primitive settings, inclined to project onto those he portrayed something he wished to find in himself; for 'Æ', avatars of ancient gods were hiding among Irish peasants, and ancient stories pointed towards an Otherworld (the only real one); Stephens and Colum favoured the conventional device of the fictional hero turning narrator or listener. Moore played with the role of storyteller, and probably thought he saw the limits of the traditional forms of the art more lucidly than those who had been his temporary companions in an Irish cultural crusade.

James Joyce stood apart from the Literary Revival and, sometimes rudely, debunked its tenets. He reacted against its misty and mystical moods, and condemned folkish tendencies as yielding to the tastes of 'the most belated race in Europe'.[117] But in his own way he also used elements of ancient or popular Irish narratives, as well as oral techniques, and storytelling as a theme in itself. He was not a member or would-be member of the Anglo-Irish ascendancy who could select from native culture what suited him: in his youth, he wanted to shrug off a heritage he had received naturally and which he felt to be stifling. According to him, Ireland would revive by turning away from the past: 'Ancient Ireland is dead just as ancient Egypt is dead. Its death chant has been sung and on its grave stone has been set the seal ... If [Ireland] is truly capable of reviving, let her awake, or let her cover up her head and lie down decently in the grave for ever.'[118]

He resisted nationalism in its more extreme forms, and chose expatriation; rejected the notion that art should be subordinate to politics; dissociated himself from insularity and acquired a cosmopolitan culture. Yet through his family and

117 'The Day of the Rabblement' (1901), in *Critical Writings* 68-72. 118 In a lecture delivered in Trieste in April 1907 (*Critical Writings* 173-4).

his Dublin pub crawling he had received a fund of Irish verbal arts which he later exploited: anecdotes, songs and turns of phrase. He was typically a city man, and despised the rural world, whose inhabitants he saw as at best 'a hard, crafty and matter-of-fact lot'.[119] Critics warn us against taking his characters' utterances as authorial positions; it seems, however, that Stephen Dedalus is expressing Joyce's opinion when he says: 'I really don't think that the Irish peasant represents a very admirable type of culture.'[120] But was it just a way of distinguishing himself from his elders, or the fear of a constraining past, or the rejection of what did not appear to fit his criteria of high literature – or all that at the same time? When he reviewed Lady Gregory's *Poets and Dreamers* for the Dublin *Daily Express*, in 1903, he was ruthless and ironic: 'In fine, her book, wherever it treats of the "folk", sets forth in the fulness of its senility a class of mind which Mr Yeats has set forth with such delicate scepticism in his happiest book, "The Celtic Twilight" ';[121] in *Ulysses* she became 'that old hake Gregory',[122] and in *Finnegans Wake* her collections may be 'them bagses of trash'.[123]

In *A Portrait of the Artist as a Young Man*, the venerable rural storyteller evoked by Yeats, Lady Gregory and Synge has turned into a disturbing but perhaps also fascinating figure, in one entry of Stephen's diary:

April 14th. John Alphonsus Mulrennan has just returned from the west of Ireland. European and Asiatic papers please copy. He told us he met an old man there in a mountain cabin. Old man had red eyes and short pipe. Old man spoke Irish. Then old man and Mulrennan spoke English. Mulrennan spoke to him about universe and stars. Old man sat, listened, smoked, spat. Then said: – Ah, there must be terrible queer creatures at the latter end of the world.

I fear him. I fear his redrimmed horny eyes. It is with him I must struggle all through this night till day come, till he or I lie dead, gripping him by the sinewy throat till... Till what? Till he yield to me? No. I mean him no harm.[124]

Where is the 'latter end of the world' – in the Irish mountain cabin, or east of that questionable Eden? The second paragraph is also open to different interpretations. Is the old Irish man only a prejudiced senile peasant, or a Yeatsian visionary, or the angel who comes to reveal the brave fighter's true identity as in the biblical story of Jacob – in other words, isn't confrontation with this Irish tradition necessary after all, at least at a certain stage in the evolution of an Irish writer? Does he represent the burden of the past which an 'artist' will shake off, or the heritage it would be wrong to reject, or a mere nonentity that should be ignored? Is the struggle 'a literary combat, the clash of two literatures, two ways of perceiving and ordering the world'?[125] Is the old man also the father figure

119 Arthur Power *Conversations with James Joyce* 33. 120 *Stephen Hero* 59. 121 'The Soul of Ireland', *Critical Writings* 105. 122 Op. cit. 208. 123 Op. cit. 420. 124 *A Portrait of the Artist as a Young Man* 234. 125 J.W. Foster *Fictions of the Irish Literary Revival* 326.

who looked at baby Stephen through a glass in the opening lines of the book and impressed him with his first, incomprehensible fairytale? There is ambiguity again in *Ulysses*, when Stephen recalls 'the tramper Synge' – whom Joyce had met in Paris in 1903: 'In words of words for words, palabras. Oisin with Patrick. Faunman he met in Clamart woods, brandishing a winebottle. *C'est vendredi saint!* Murthering Irish. His image, wandering, he met. I mine. I met a fool i' the forest.'[126] In dreamlike confusion, Synge seems to be at the same time another Patrick listening to the voice of the ancients and that very voice heard by Stephen; it is not clear which of them, or what, will be murdered – remembering that 'murther' can be mere stage-Irish exaggeration (in Hiberno-English dialects 'to murder' or 'murther' may be 'to punish' or 'to distress'). Earlier in the text, Buck Mulligan announced that Synge was looking for Stephen to 'murder' him; but does Stephen feel threatened by Synge or by the same nationalist fanatics who attacked him? The 'fool i' the forest' is the court entertainer out of his milieu in *As You Like It*, but may also be a writer yielding to primitivism.

Whatever the deeper meanings of such perplexing passages there is a good deal of Irish storytelling in Joyce's books. It includes motif and forms from early Irish literature, and legends or songs from oral tradition, but often differs from what has been illustrated so far in this chapter: Joyce preferred to use Dublin oral arts, which folklorists took longer to discover. In 'Counterparts', for instance, Farrington tries to bolster his self-esteem with his rehearsed interpretation of the dressing-down by his boss.[127] In 'The Dead', Gabriel Conroy narrates and enacts an item of family lore: the story of Johnny, his grandfather's horse, who like Gabriel himself was hesitating between east and west. The teller (soon to be dispirited by his own image in a mirror) acts like a Dublin-pub raconteur:

Gabriel paced in a circle round the hall in his goloshes amid the laughter of the others.
– Round and round he went, said Gabriel, and the old gentleman, who was a very pompous old gentleman, was highly indignant. 'Go on, sir! What do you mean, sir? Johnny! Johnny! Most extraordinary conduct! Can't understand the horse!'
The peals of laughter which followed Gabriel's imitation of the incident were interrupted by a resounding knock at the hall door.[128]

In *A Portrait of the Artist*, Stephen's father plays, among other roles, that of 'a storyteller' and 'a praiser of his own past'.[129] Mr Casey, in the Christmas dinner episode, is his double:

[Mr Dedalus] took up his knife and fork again in good humour and set to eating, saying to Mr Casey:
– Let us have the story, John. It will help us to digest ...

126 *Ulysses* 192. 127 *Dubliners* 103. 128 Ibid. 237–8. 129 *A Portrait* ... 244.

– The story is very short and sweet, Mr Casey said. It was one day down in Arklow, a cold bitter day, not long before the chief died...[130]

The collective pressure which Irish tradition and patriotic storytelling can exert on the individual mind is epitomized in the case of Stephen's fellow-student, Davin:

The young peasant worshipped the sorrowful legend of Ireland ... His nurse had taught him Irish and shaped his rude imagination by the broken lights of Irish myth. He stood towards the myth upon which no individual mind had ever drawn out a line of beauty and to its unwieldy tales that divided themselves as they moved down the cycles in the same attitude as towards the Roman Catholic religion, the attitude of a dullwitted serf.[131]

The young man is paralysed by the directives of the Church, and is also described as an 'athlete' (no doubt a member of the Gaelic Athletic Association, itself linked with Fenianism) and a romantic nationalist. He is not really a 'peasant', if, like Lady Gregory but in a middle-class and Catholic family, he was initiated to Irish folklore by a servant. The narrative mode he thus acquired is 'unwieldy' – inefficient because shapeless. Yet it has enabled him to communicate his experience: when he has narrated his encounter with a young woman while crossing lonely hills at night, the story remains in Stephen's memory, and 'sings' there.[132]

In *Ulysses*, one reason why Stephen dislikes his roommate Haines is that he is an English compiler of quaint Celtic things – what is 'folk' and comes 'from west'. In the 'Scylla and Charybdis' chapter, revivalism is ridiculed along with occultism. The 'Cyclops' episode parodies the various rhetorics of nationalism and nineteenth-century renditions of ancient epics in Irishized English alternating with typical pub narration.

There is a peculiar picture of Joyce as a 'traditional Irish storyteller', and the story he told on this occasion is interesting. The witness was the French art historian Louis Gillet, who had joined the Joycean circle in Paris. He had read the English translation of Maurice O'Sullivan's account of life on the Blaskets, *Twenty Years a-Growing*, published in 1933, and when he praised its charm Joyce smiled and told a story he pretended to have from a friend – an ethnographer and naturalist – who had spent a fortnight on the islands. One day, a native crossed over with him to go shopping on the mainland. He bought a pocket glass, because when looking into it he thought he saw his father. Back home, he kept contemplating that face. His suspicious wife, thinking it was the portrait of some mistress, took a peep, and saw an ugly old woman. '*Pouah! une vieille! s'écria-t-elle et, de colère, elle jette le miroir qui se brise à terre sur un caillou.*'[133]

---

130 Ibid. 30. **131** Ibid. 167. **132** Ibid. 168-9. **133** *Stèle pour James Joyce* 170-7. (' "Ugh! An old woman", she exclaimed; and angrily she throws away the mirror, which breaks on a stone.')

The tale was not specifically attached to the Blaskets: by 1960, there were twenty-seven versions, collected in the four provinces, in the Irish Folklore Commission manuscripts.[134] Nor was it peculiar to Ireland: it is a form of International Tale-Type 1336A – 'A Man does not Recognize his own Reflection in the Water/Mirror'. It may be told as a mere joke, as a moral apologue, or even as part of an initiation to some transcendent perception of truth. The versions collected in Ireland tend to be jocular (but a joke may be an 'epiphany' – have revelatory power). Here are two of them, the first published in a popular periodical in 1907, the other collected from oral tradition in 1938:

Once upon a time a man was walking by the edge of the ocean and he picked up a looking-glass. Into the glass he looked and he saw there the face of himself. 'Oh,' said he, ' 'tis a picture of my father', and he took it to his cabin and hung it on the wall. And often he would go to look at it, and always he said, ' 'tis a picture of my father.' But one day he took to himself a wife, and when she went to the mirror and looked in she said: 'I thought you said this was a picture of your father. Sure, it is a picture of an ugly red-headed woman. Who is she?' 'What have you?' said the man. 'Step away and let me to it and he looked at it again. 'Ah', said he with a sigh (for his father was dead) 'tis a picture of my father.' 'Step away,' said she, 'and let me see if it's no eyes at all I have. What have you with pictures of women?' So he stepped away and let her to it, and she looked at again. 'An ugly, red-haired woman it is', said she. 'You had a lover before me', and she was very angry. 'Sure we'll leave it to the neighbour', said he. And when the neighbour passed by they called him and said: 'Tell us what it is that this picture is about ' I say it's my father, who is dead.' 'And I say it is a red-haired woman I never saw', said the woman. 'Step away', said the neighbour, with authority, 'and let me at it.' So they stepped away and let him to it, and he looked at it. 'Sure neither you nor the woman was right. What eyes have you? It is a picture of myself. I will take it.' And he took it away with him, to the

There was an old man and old woman there one time, and they lived in a very out-of-the way place entirely. They hardly ever went anywhere in their life before, except I suppose to go to Mass. They were never in a town in their life, and I suppose there was no trains or motorcars there then. Anyway, begor, this day they decided that they'd go to town and buy a few things. They had plenty money for they used never spend anything. So they yoked up the ass, and they started off into Ross. They were fooling about Ross for a while anyhow, and begob the old man went into a shop. The first thing he saw inside was a big mirror. When he looked into the mirror he saw his father inside in it he said, and he'd have to buy it. The man in the shop showed him several mirrors, and he saw his father in every one of them. He bought one nice handy one anyway, for a few shillings and he put it in here inside his coat. He said he wouldn't let the wife see it at all. They fooled about the town anyway and they come on home, after they had bought whatever things they wanted. Every now and again the old man would open his coat this way and he'd take a look at his father in the glass; and the wife was mad to find out what bedamned he had inside his coat, that he had all the looking at. Begob a couple of days after the old man was working at something and he went off out and left his coat after him inside. When he was gone out, the old woman went and searched the coat and found the

134 Ó Súilleabháin and Christiansen *The Types of the Irish Folktale* 237-8.

gladness of the wife, who hated the woman her husband had in the frame, and the grief of the man, who could see his father no more. But in the neighbour's house was the picture of himself.[136]

mirror. She held it up and she looked into it. 'Well,' says she 'if that's the old hag he is to running after he may carry on. There's no fear I'm going to try and stop him.[135]

Joyce probably invented the friend – a common authentifying device. The mix-ups on which the story depends can make us think of the double danger of an excessively traditional attitude: cultivating a false image of oneself and identifying with the past. Perhaps this is reading too much into a joke, but the fact is that problematic identification with, or difficult separation from, the father is a basic Joycean theme: in *Ulysses* Stephen 'proves by algebra that Hamlet's grandson is Shakespeare's grandfather and that he himself is the ghost of his own father', and he admires 'the subtle African heresiarch Sabellius who held that the Father was Himself His own Son'; towards the end of the book, when Bloom and Stephen seem to have reached a tacit union, they are said to be 'each contemplating the other in both mirrors of the reciprocal flesh of theirhisnothis fellowfaces'.[137] At any rate, Joyce's performance as described by Gillet, like that of Gabriel in 'The Dead' (see p. 348), resembles Dublin pub histrionics or music-hall acts rather than the usually static rural storytelling mode:

Joyce était à voir! Il mimait la scène de tout son corps, il rapprochait les mains en coupe de son visage, s'y souriait, comme s'il y tenait le miroir, s'écartait, puis vite se penchait avec un petit bruit de salive, comme s'il y humait une gorgée d'eau; il était le personnage lui-même, il imitait le ton, le geste avec une vie délicieuse. C'était une cascade de 'Papa! Papa!' répétés sur toutes les notes de la gamme, avec des petites mines, des petites moues, des petits cris, des expressions qui disaient la surprise, le reproche, l'amour, comme lorsqu'on revoit un être chéri que l'on n'espérait plus ... Tout cela répondait si bien aux pensées intimes du poète qu'il n'avait même pas la peine de faire semblant ... Mais ce qu'il fallait voir, c'était cette vie, ce style, cette mimique, ce diable au corps: quelle verve, quel humour, quel talent du récit! C'était le génie d'une race, la grace d'un peuple de conteurs, le don de la fabulation et du faiseur de mythes, le sortilège d'une île sauvage, d'une patrie de romanciers et de poètes, qui ont créé en foule les plus belles légendes qui aient enchanté le monde. Je venais de voir fonctionner pendant une heure, pour moi tout seul, l'exquise machine poétique. Par quel démon cruel et taquin cette cervelle de charmeur avait-elle fait le choix pervers de se changer en mécanique à logographes, le talent du conteur en la confection laborieuse d'un fatigant grimoire, d'un texte sybillin ...?[138]

Mirrors are used as symbols of various, sometimes contradictory notions: prudence, represented as a woman with two faces holding a looking glass

135 IFC 543:311-12, collected by T. Ó Ciardha from Seán Óh-Aodha, aged 70, County Wexford, July 1938. **136** 'Seen in the Glass: An Irish Legend', *Ireland's Own*, 11 December 1907. **137** *Ulysses* 18, 21 and 655. **138** *Stèle pour James Joyce* 174-5 and 177. Summary: Joyce was mimicking the scene, imitating the gestures and the voice of the old man, and at the same time expressing intimate thoughts (his own father had died in 1931).

(because, before acting you must consider good and bad possible consequences); divination; reversal; self-love or self-hatred... It is a way of knowing oneself, but when it reveals faults it is perhaps not believed ('Satire is a sort of glass, wherein beholders do generally discover everybody's face but their own')[139]. It frames, modifies what it shows, and may magnify it. It may represent truthful art – but the romantic conception rejects the notion of art as a mere reflector, and cubism or modernism fractured the representational planes. The 'broken lights of Irish myth' in the Davin passage of *A Portrait* (see p. 349) may be echoed in *Ulysses* by Stephen's definition of 'Irish art' as 'the cracked lookingglass of a servant'.[140] A 'cracked' mirror, like the one Buck Mulligan stole from a poor girl, can portend ill-fortune; what it reflects may be a false representation of Irish people or a true representation of the servitude they refused to admit: advertising *Dubliners*, Joyce wrote that Irish people should take 'one good look at themselves in my nicely polished looking-glass'.[141] Clairvoyant and deceptive mirrors, as well as lethal ones, appear in mythologies and folklore, and the stories of 'doubles' haunting nineteenth-century literature, generally to expose the hidden side of personality, often involve actual or metaphorical looking glasses.

Finnegans Wake blends linguistic, literary and mythological elements, including ancient Irish lore, contemporary demotic Irish speech and the Dublin landscape. At the beginning of the book, twelve drinkers are mourning the bricklayer Tim Finnegan, who fell from his ladder while building a tower with many storeys – and at an Irish wake there may be 'one thousand and one stories, all told'.[142] If the book is a dream, it has the condensing and shifting power of a dreaming mind and becomes a kind of 'tradition' where all stories can be fused. As a cyclical history of all mankind ('1001' suggests multiple stories before impending death, but in Joyce's numerology it also symbolizes a new start). The result, a 'new Irish stew',[143] babelizes language, has many layers (storeys) of meanings and is deliberately hard to decipher; it almost ends with the question: 'Is there one who understands me? One in a thousand of years of the night?'[144] Joyce's attitude towards storytelling seems to have been ambivalent: perhaps because while adding conviviality to Irish life, it could also be used as a paralysing ideological weapon.

The exploration of literary texts has taken us beyond the period covered in this section. Returning to the beginning of the century and casting a glance at the political background, we note that Irish nationalism still had the many facets and gradations observed in the last decades of the nineteenth. Some contented themselves with cultural action. It was not sufficient for those who wanted above all

---

139 Swift, preface to *The Battle of the Books*. **140** *Ulysses* 7, 16 – a phrase adapted from Oscar Wilde: in 'The Decay of Lying', to treat art as a mirror would 'reduce genius to the position of a cracked looking-glass', and in the preface to *The Picture of Dorian Gray*, Caliban is enraged both when he *sees* and when he does *not see* his face in the glass. **141** Letter to Grant Richards, 23 June 1906 (*Letters* 1. 64). **142** *Finnegans Wake* 5. **143** Ibid. 190. **144** Ibid. 627.

political sovereignty, but they themselves were divided into two currents: some stood for constitutional methods and would settle for a limited measure of self-government – and for a while the Home Rule they aspired to seemed within reach; others thought that an armed insurrection would lead to complete independence, and this minority included those who, by 1916, were convinced that a blood sacrifice was necessary to shake public opinion from its torpor. The dividing line between political activism and cultural programmes could fade; storytelling did play a role in the physical-force movement and in events – its relative importance depending on the tactics of particular leaders and the changing state of mind of the general public. First, the separatist ideology and the preparation for the rising involved the use of narrative weapons: a search for, and an idealization of, certain patterns of action to be found in the past, in other words, a partisan telling of Irish history in the light of the kind of future one proposed to achieve. Then, during the insurrection itself, misleading information was deliberately spread to mobilize the rank and file, and unconfirmed rumours seemed to multiply spontaneously. Later, a profusion of heroic or pathetic narratives, sung or spoken, glorified the events and their protagonists.

In popular biographies of rebel heroes, a required motif was the formative experience of patriotic narratives. Two examples may suffice: the first concerns George Clancy, the man who appeared in *A Portrait of the Artist as a Young Man* as 'Davin', nursed with 'the sorrowful legends of Ireland' (see p. 349). Here is the kind of information diffused some twenty years after his death, according to the by then well-established model of Republican hagiography:

Born in the village of Grange, Co. Limerick, Seoirse drank in the tenets of militant Irish Nationality with his mother's milk ... While yet a child he learned many things from his grandfather – also George Clancy – whose mind was stored with the history and legends of his native place, with the tales of Ireland's heroic age, and with the facts of Irish history at home and abroad ...To the knowledge acquired in the schools, he added a knowledge of the Irish language, laboriously learned from the old people in the neighbourhood, and an intimate acquaintance with the history, traditions and legends of Ireland ... He joined the Gaelic League; and his first Irish teacher was a shy, studious-looking, very earnest young man named Patrick H. Pearse. He knew and loved old Michael Cusack, founder of the Gaelic Athletic Association ...[145]

Then he taught Irish, was a founding member of the Irish Volunteers in Limerick, was arrested in 1916 and again in 1917, became mayor of Limerick, and was killed on March 7, 1921 – by the British Black-and-Tans in probably true Republican versions, though counter-propaganda blamed Irish Republican Army gunmen.

We find similar motifs in the life-story of one of the leaders of the 1916 Easter Rising: Patrick Pearse. They confirm that, if respect for traditional sto-

145 *Limerick's Fighting Story* 115-16.

rytelling may not have been the most important ingredient in an Irish heroic career, it was practically always there. One of the first detailed popular biographies begins in early childhood with his account of an initiation into Irish patriotism: '[A] kindly grey-haired *seanchaidhe*, a woman of my mother's people, telling tales by the kitchen fireplace ... spoke more wisely and nobly of ancient heroic things than anyone else I have ever known. Her only object was to amuse me, yet she was the truest of all my teachers.'[146] What the child heard, and the patriotic texts he read later on, offered mirrors of destiny: 'With every picture that I saw; with every story or song that I heard, I saw myself doing or suffering all the things that were dared or suffered in the book, or story, or song, or picture.'[147] As he developed an understanding of the mission for which he thought he was destined, the hero had to be an active defender of the native tradition which defined what he was to fight for; thus the young Pearse joined the Gaelic League in 1896 and explored the Gaeltacht, where 'he would spend long evenings in the people's homes, marvelling at their language and their stories, and finding in them all the virtues of his beloved Gaelic civilization'.[148] Here, Le Roux's biography was more colourful: '[He] wandered deep into Iar-Chonnacht, often for weeks disguised as a tramp, sleeping in the poorest of the poorest cabins, speaking Irish and collecting old songs and stories, always in search of his soul's Gaelic antecedents.'[149] The 'tramp' was also an Irish scholar who edited two Fenian romances and a folktale (Douglas Hyde praised his work). Padraic Colum likened him to a traditional performer: 'He sat in a chimney-corner, and in a deep voice, and with the heavy, occasional gestures of an old shanachie or professional storyteller, recited the same, long, vigorous and extravagant ballad.'[150] We are told that he used material he had collected in Connemara to create his own tales, like the story of *An Dearg-Daol* (the black chafer, or cockroach, which is the type of the informer because it was said to have revealed Christ's hiding place); its performer is imposing:

A walking-man, it was, come into my father's house out of the Joyce Country, that told us this story by the fireside one wild winter's night. The wind was wailing round the house, like women keening the dead, while he spoke, and he would make his voice rise or fall according as the wind's voice would rise or fall. A tall man he was, with wild eyes, and his share of clothes almost in tatters. There was a sort of fear on me of him when he came in, and his story didn't lessen my fear [151]

Pearse was not at first a political activist; his conversion from cultural nationalism to radical separatism came late, and for a while he had positive

---

146 Quoted in L. Le Roux *Patrick Pearse* 97. (The storyteller was Pearse's mother's octogenarian aunt.) 147 Autobiographical fragment quoted in R.D. Edwards *Patrick Pearse; The Triumph of Failure* 6-7. 148 Ibid. 51. 149 L. Le Roux *Patrick Pearse*, 43. 150 *The Road Round Ireland* 159. For other examples, see D. Ó Giolláin, 'Heroic Biographies in Folklore and Popular Culture', in G. Doherty and D. Keogh (eds) *Michael Collins and the Making of the Irish State*. 151 P. Pearse *Plays – Stories – Poems* (tr. by Joseph Campbell) 137.

things to say about folklore: 'Perhaps these tales are no more than poetical fancies. But poetical fancies are the most valuable part of history. History is often, as Napoleon said, no more than the lie on which the historians agree. In the fanciful tales of a people are told the true traditions of that people. Each one reveals something of the mind of its composer. In the fanciful tales of a people is understood the mind of that people.'[152] As might be expected, he valued above all the heroic legends and the ancient 'sagas' – particularly for their educational virtue: 'A heroic tale is more essentially a factor in education than a proposition in Euclid'.[153] St Enda's, the school he founded, had the Fianna motto: 'Courage in our hands, Truth in our tongues, And purity in our Hearts' (cf. p. 20). One of the pupils remembered: 'He believed strongly in story-telling as an essential part of education. *Sgéalaidheacht* [*scéalaíocht*: storytelling] had always a recognized place on the programme. He told his pupils the entire Cuchulainn and Fionn cycles and the main periods, movements, and men in Irish history during the hours devoted to *Sgéalaidheacht*.'[154] As he came to think that education should lead to specific political action, he voiced reservations about mere cultural revivalism: 'I protest that it was not philology, not folklore, not literature, we went into the Gaelic League to serve, but: Ireland a Nation.'[155] Literature had a role to play in the coming revolution, but as the aim was the creation of a *new* Ireland and folklore belonged to a former time, a different kind of writing was needed to cope with contemporary life and preoccupations.[156] But as late as April 1916 he described the free Ireland of the future in epic storytelling terms: 'Literature and art will flourish. The Tain and the Fionn-story will come again in mighty dramas. The voice of a people that has been dumb for many centuries will be heard anew.'[157]

During the Easter Rising, new legends seemed to be gestating, while startling events were taking place: 'Within an hour after the issuing of the proclamation, rumours were already rife throughout headquarters, wild rumours about German submarines, Turkish landings, and Volunteer victories throughout the country.'[158] Fantastic yarns spread around Dublin, and James Stephens experienced this narrative excitement:

Earlier in the day I met a wild individual who spat rumour as though his mouth were a machine gun or a linotype machine. He believed everything he heard; and everything he heard became as by magic favourable to his hopes, which were violently anti-English. One unfavourable rumour was instantly crushed by him with three stories which were favourable and triumphantly so. He said the Germans had landed in three places. One of these landings alone consisted of fifteen thousand men. The other landings probably

152 Quoted by Kevin Danaher in 'Folk Tradition and Literature', *The Journal of Irish Literature* 1. 2, 74. **153** 'The Murder Machine', in *Political Writings and Speeches* 38. **154** Desmond Ryan *The Man Called Pearse* 83. **155** 'Psychology of a Volunteer', in *Political Writings and Speeches* 107. **156** In *An Claidheamh Soluis*, 26 May 1906, 6. **157** Quoted in R.D. Edwards, op. cit. 338. **158** Ibid. 282.

beat that figure. The whole city of Cork was in the hands of the Volunteers, and, to that extent, might be said to be peaceful. German warships had defeated the English, and their transports were speeding from every side. The whole country was up, and the garrison was out-numbered by one hundred to one. These Dublin barracks which had not been taken were now besieged and on the point of surrender. I think this man created and winged every rumour that flew in Dublin, and he was the sole individual whom I heard definitely taking sides. He left me, and , looking back, I saw him pouring his news into the ear of a gaping stranger whom he had arrested for the purpose. I almost went back to hear would he tell the same tale or would he elaborate it into a new thing, for I am interested in the art of story-telling.[159]

When the rising was crushed and protracted repression followed, the tide of public opinion, which had been indifferent or hostile, turned in favour of the defeated insurgents. At once an effect and a cause of the change, flamboyant or elegiac accounts in poems and narrative songs multiplied. More 'rebel songs' and stories flourished during and after the guerilla war for independence of 1919-21. While 'on the run' in Roscommon, Donegal, and Clare or on the Aran Islands, Ernie O'Malley, as an officer of the Irish Republican Army, listened to older stories which inspired fresh actions and heard new stories created on similar patterns: 'Our people seized imaginatively on certain events, exalted them through their own folk quality of expression in song and story ... There was a tradition of armed resistance, dimly felt; it would flare up when we carried out some small successful raid or made a capture. Around the fire it would be discussed.'[160] He was one of those who had the rare experience of hearing how they themselves were becoming the stuff of legend, and he saw the danger:

Many of us could hardly see ourselves for the legends built up around us. The legends helped to give others an undue sense of our ability or experience, but they hid our real selves; when I saw myself as clearly as I could in terms of myself, I resented the legend. It made me other than myself and attuned to act to standards that were not my own.[161]

Post-revolutionary disillusionment made him end his book (in 1936) with the fairytale formula – but significantly changing the personal pronouns: 'Put on the kettle and make the tay; and if we weren't happy, that you may.'[162]

The 'old tradition of nationhood' and the voice of 'the dead generations' invoked in the 1916 Proclamation of the Irish Republic remained powerful, but there were people who thought that, for a bright future to rise from the ashes, many of the threads which tied Ireland to its past should be cut. This attitude appears in the novella 'The Weaver's Grave', the one great text written by the Sinn Feiner Seumas O'Kelly (1875-1918) at the end of his life. It seems allegorically to set the younger generation (the Ireland of the future) against the Irish past

159 *The Insurrection in Dublin* 28-30. 160 *On Another Man's Wound* 6, 114. 161 Ibid. 295-6. 162 Ibid. 320.

and its shroud of slowly woven traditions, which it was now time to tuck away. In a disused graveyard where only a few survivors of the old world retain the right to be buried, two old men are walking round and round and talking only of the dead, 'telling stories, reviewing all virtues, whispering at past vices'. The man whose hereditary plot they must locate had tried in vain 'to keep up the illusion of a perennial youth'; he was a *seanchaí* in the strict sense of the word: a person who made a specialty of local lore. His young widow seems totally passive, until we enter her mind; she has had to undergo the funeral wake as 'a grand review of family ghosts', a ritual similar to the present ceremony in the graveyard: 'There one hears all the stories, the little flattering touches, the little unflattering bitternesses. The traditions, the astonishing records, of the clan.' Bed-ridden, hidden beneath blankets and systematically referred to as the 'mummy', the 'skeleton', or 'that ghost of a man', the dead weaver's successor as the oldest bearer of tradition, is still capable of some miracles of energy, pulling himself up by means of a rope ('hoisting himself up from the dead') when he sees a chance to adopt his vatic role; but his discourse has become difficult or impossible to understand. For him, life is only a dream from which there is no awakening. At the end, however, the widow does awaken, when she sees her young future husband jump happily over the grave of the dead tradition-bearer to come and kiss her. The cyclic time of a closed world is broken, and an account of the liberation of the couple could in its turn become a tale worth telling, with a more modern narrative technique.[163] It is little wonder that James Joyce (cf. the statement quoted on p. 346), who had a poor opinion of O'Kelly's earlier folksy sketches, had 'a great admiration for this writer's remarkable short tale "The Weaver's Grave".'[164]

B. A GAELIC NATION ONCE AGAIN?

The new Ireland proved difficult to build, and divergences appeared between aspirations and reality. This section will focus on the ideology which, from the 1920s to the 1950s, clung to the conviction that 'the essential Irish reality was the uniquely desirable, unchanging life of small farm and country town in the Irish-speaking west',[165] and largely determined representations of 'Irish traditional storytelling' during this period. But it will also consider reactions against the officially promoted set of ideas and attitudes, which led to less romantic views of storytellers. The setting will be essentially the Free State, later the Republic of Ireland; not that folklore and folklorists did not exist on the other side of the Border, but the dominant ideology there was not founded on the

---

163 *The Golden Barque and the Weaver's Grave* (1919). O'Kelly was also the anonymous author of one of the many poems on the Easter Rising, 'The Shanachie tells Another Story', published in September 1917. 164 H. Gorman *James Joyce* 181, a footnote added at Joyce's request. 165 T. Brown *Ireland: A Social and Cultural History 1922-1979* 182.

same basis: those who ruled defended both their own Protestant distinctiveness
on the island and the union with Britain. Most of them did not care for 'Irish'
folklore, but they did not try to suppress it as long as it remained politically
innocuous.

The emerging state needed some slogans and symbols reinforcing cohesiveness
and legitimizing the power of the hegemonic group, and differentiation from 'the
other' seemed essential (more particularly from what was 'English' and
'modern'). Opinions differed on exactly what should be fostered, but among
those who now had the whip-hand the prevailing tendency was to consider that
the Catholics were more Irish and that the most Irish of all were Catholic Gaelic
speakers. The nativistic trend defined certain elements of culture as symbolic
markers of authentic Irishness. The golden age to which one should return was
no longer the ancient dream of heroism, but the idyllic image of a simple and
virtuous pastoral life. The Gaeltacht – the part of Ireland where Irish was
spoken and a supposedly immemorial way of life preserved – was the model.

The following text, describing a sojourn in Donegal and written during the
'War of Independence' by Aodh De Blácam, for the 'Catholic Truth Society of
Ireland', is typical (and not one of the most extreme, since this nationalist,
unlike some others, would admit that a Protestant writing in English might still
be an Irish author):

The musical racy Irish speech on every side of you brings to your mind a thrilling sense
of the reality of Irish nationality, such as the dweller in the cities amid English speech
and English papers, never feels. When you grow familiar with the language, and the lore
it bears with it, you get so absorbed in the vision of Irish-Ireland that you feel in your
very fibre the *wrongness* of anglicisation ... Until you have been there you cannot pretend
to know the secret Ireland, which is the real Ireland, the Ireland submerged by the Penal
Laws, but striving to-day to win back into its former place of sovereignty ...

Of the intellectual life of Donegal this is the highest and justest praise: that it is the
virile life of a complete community, which with all its seclusion has never manifested
degeneracy. From these humble children of simple life sprang, and still do spring, the
minds of distinguished ecclesiastics and laymen. These cottages around us are homes in
which the love of refinement, wit and imagination is kept glowing, and handed from generation to generation by a lively traditional culture. In the evenings the stools and
benches around the turf-fire will be crowded by the neighbours of three houses, who will
entertain one another with Gaelic songs of exquisite taste and melody, and tales in which
the ancient myths of Balor will now be told, and the doings of the Irish saints. To-night,
at our cottage fire, we shall see a student whose willingness to be absorbed in the
people's life distinguishes him from the superior person, whom they justly hate. Having
listened to their songs and tales, carefully studying the pure speech in which they are
delivered, he will possibly contribute an item himself.[166]

166 *From a Gaelic Outpost* (1921) xi-xii, 10-11.

The promised land was not really attained in 1922, but for several decades the new state maintained a Catholic-conservative social order and extolled an arcadian utopia. The revival of the Irish language was deemed an absolute necessity; as Daniel Corkery, one of the advocates of strict distinctions between truly Irish and embarrassingly Anglo-Irish, still put it in 1954: 'The tradition of the Irish people is to be understood and experienced with intimacy only in the Irish language ... To say tradition is to say language – and while this is true of every national tradition it is overwhelmingly true of ours.'[167] Collecting pure Irish material was praised as an essential service to the nation, and folklore was therefore highly valued. The way this task was conducted and the kind of material thus gathered will be examined in the next two chapters. But 'traditions' involved much more than a taste for folklore. Nationalist politicians and the Irish Catholic Church wanted to protect Ireland from the threat of modernity. What the Archbishop of Tuam reportedly said in 1926 typifies the association of non-Irish influence with vice: 'Company-keeping under the stars of night had succeeded in too many places to the good old Irish custom of visiting, chatting and story-telling from one house to another, with the Rosary to bring all home in due time.'[168] In short, the archaic rural way of life as now defined by the authorities was the good one. In the 1930s, de Valera's ideal was a self-sufficient country, satisfied with little material wealth and free from corrupting imports. In an overquoted radio-speech in 1943,[169] he could still celebrate its 'frugal comfort' and the firesides which would be 'the forum of the wisdom of serene old age', but by then he referred to it as the dream he had had at the beginning of the century rather than as present policy.[170]

What is idealized tends to be fixed in a state of perfection. In fact rural Ireland was changing, and conditions were hardly idyllic. Nor were 'traditions' eternal; inherited modes of storytelling, for instance, may survive socio-economic transformations, but provided certain basic conditions remain: the habit of gathering to swap news and to share entertainment; the coexistence of several generations to maintain transmission through time; accepted conventions controlling the permanence, and allowing the adaptability, of narrative techniques as well as of story plots and stylized expression. In these respects, what had survived the big mutations of the nineteenth century could still be observed to some extent in Ireland in the second quarter of the twentieth; but, as social life altered and new forms of entertainment developed, the perpetuation of this kind of storytelling and the continuity of transmission to younger generations were less and less assured.

The economy of Ireland was still predominantly agricultural: in 1926 more

167 *The Fortunes of the Irish Language* 13, 14. **168** Quoted in D. Keogh *Twentieth-Century Ireland: Nation and State* 28-9. **169** The text of the broadcast was published in *The Irish Press* on 18 March 1943. **170** Michele Dowling ' "The Ireland that I would have" – De Valera & the Creation of an Irish National Image', in *History Ireland* 5:2 (1997) 37-41.

than half of the active population were working on the land. Country people had accommodated their new situation as small owners-occupiers with some older customs, including forms of communal entertainment which could persist where cooperation between neighbours continued. In the early 1930s, a socio-anthropological study of small farmers in County Clare by the American Conrad M. Arensberg[171] described Irish rural life as that of an apparently highly integrated community. The year was still divided into two parts: a summer of work outside, which fostered cooperation, and a winter of intense sociability: according to a system of mutual obligation ('cooring', or *cómhar*), families could pair for the cutting and hauling of turf, the thatching of houses, harvest or haymaking, and in winter there was a round of parties and visiting, with talking, dancing and marriage-making – for the few who could marry in a society that no longer accepted the splitting up of property and where the heir had to postpone marriage until his parents retired or died. The strong emphasis on celibacy (due to the new type of family structure) and on chastity (promoted by the Church) segregated the sexes, with intensive male grouping. The father was the dominant figure: the sons remained 'boys' as long as they were not in power. Women tended to be excluded from public life, whatever influence they might have at home. The elders were in control. The younger generations – particularly the girls and young men with no future – had less reason to be satisfied with a system of which Arensberg may have exaggerated the stability.

The pastoral theme needed adjusting; yet for a while the countryman was still represented as pious, wise, dignified and conscious of his role as keeper of a flame. Any attempt to describe less pleasant or edifying aspects of rural reality was likely to be condemned; but one key element in the rosy picture might be worrying: the 'noble peasant' was invariably old. What would happen after the death of such patriarchs? They were still celebrated in a text written about 1930 (the setting is a Catholic part of Northern Ireland, in County Tyrone), but the younger generation is significantly absent: 'And now we old people drew our stools closer together round the fire, for the talk was of the Wee People – the 'Gentry' (Fairies) – of their malevolence, their tricks, their constant interference in the affairs of men and women. Old Cormic was speaking. "There was a man", he said ...'[172] How long would such stories still be admired? And if the world they were rooted in was receding, how much farther should amateurs go to hear them?

Those who needed a perfect incarnation of Irishness hoped to find it in the islands of the West. The hardshisps of life there could be described in the epic mode, and to go to those last outposts seemed to be a journey in time, back to the pure source. John Wilson Foster has shown how the old motif of imaginary

---

171 *The Irish Countryman*, published in 1937; with S.T. Kimball: *Family and Community in Ireland*, in 1940. 172 Rose Shaw *Carleton's Country* 57.

islands as meeting-points for mortal men and immortal beings combined with memories of the medieval reality of islands as Irish monks' or hermits' refuges against pagan darkness and temptations, and with the modern philological reputation of the same islands as places where undefiled Irish was spoken: 'The western island came to represent Ireland's mythic unity before the chaos of conquest: there at once were the vestige and the symbolic entirety of an undivided nation.'[173] Listening to storytellers at least once in such inspiring settings was a must for anyone who wanted to really get in touch with archetypal Ireland. Accounts of pilgrimages to such revered places multiplied, and texts written or dictated by those who lived there became best sellers.

The Aran Islands were at first the most famous of those ethnic shrines. Synge had made a comparatively early contribution to this kind of literature, though the place and its inhabitants had already been celebrated in the first half of the nineteenth century, and more in the second: 'The extreme politeness of the islanders, and their desire to impart any knowledge they possess of antiquarian lore or of the legends or fairy tales with which the islands abound, must strike with force the mind of the observing tourist.'[174] It became customary to write down one's impressions after even a brief visit, as did Arthur Symons, who visited Inishmore in 1896 with Yeats and Edward Martyn; he portrayed a storyteller – probably Máirtín Ó Conghaile, who worked with Synge and others (see p. 335):

Coming back from Dun Aengus, one of our party insisted on walking; and we had not been long indoors when he came in with a singular person whom he had picked up on the way, a professional story-teller, who had for three weeks been teaching Irish to the German philologist who had preceded us on the island [Franz Finck, whose *Die Araner Mundart* was published in 1899]. He was half blind and of wild appearance; a small and hairy man, all gesture, and as if set on springs, who spoke somewhat broken English in a roar. He lamented that we could understand no Irish, but even in English, he had many things to tell, most of which he gave as but 'talk', making it very clear that we were not to suppose him to vouch for them. His own family, he told us, was said to be descended from the roons, or seals [at the same place, I was told the same thing by a member of the Conneely family in the 1950s], but that certainly was 'talk'; and a witch had, only nine months back, been driven out of the island by the priest; and there were many who said they had seen fairies, but for his part he had never seen them. But with this he began to swear on the name of God and the saints, rising from his chair and lifting up his hands, that what he was going to tell us was the truth; and then he told how a man had once come into his house and admired his young child, who was lying there in his bed, and had not said 'God bless you!' (without which to admire is to envy and to bring under the power of the fairies), and that night, and for many following nights, he had wakened and heard a sound of fighting, and one night had lit a candle, but to no avail, and another night had gathered up the blanket and tried to fling it over the head

173 'Certain Set Apart: The Western Island in the Irish Renaissance', *Studies* 66 (1977) 265.
174 O.J. Burke *The South Isles of Aran* (1887) 61.

of whoever might be there, but he had caught no one; only in the morning, going to a box in which fish were kept, he had found blood in the box; and at this he rose again, and again swore on the name of God and the saints that he was telling us only the truth, and true it was that the child had died and as for the man who had ill-wished him, 'I could point him out any day', he said fiercely. And then, with many other stories of the doings of the fairies and priests (for he was very religious), and of the 'Dane' [Pedersen – see p. 308] who had come to the island to learn Irish ('and he knew all the languages, the Proosy, and the Roosy, and the Span, and the Grig'), he told us how Satan, being led by pride to equal himself with God, looked into the glass in which God only should look, and when Satan looked into the glass, 'Hell was made in a minute'.[175]

A generation later, some Aranmen had begun to write about their islands. In the 1930s, Pat Mullen gave some accounts of storytelling there, but mostly as memories of his younger days because living conditions were already different: 'The men of Aran in those days read little fiction. They lived in their stories, and their eyes flashed with fire or grew dim with emotion as a tale reached great heights of courage or sank down to sadness.'[176] In other books, Mullen evoked the warm-up act when a storyteller was asked to perform: 'He bent his head and covered his face with his hands and seemed to be lost in profound thought. They all waited expectantly, some with serious faces and some with sly winks at one another that said: "He has the story in his mind all the time, he just wants to get us all worked up so we will take more interest in it." After a couple of minutes, with a couple of coughs and clearing of his throat, the Cobbler began his story';[177] or he described storytelling as an activity for which those not cut out for manual work could be valued: 'I stood one day by the door brooding on the ups and downs of life, when I saw Pat Lee, a story-teller, coming down the road. Pat had never been physically strong, having been through much illness in his youth, in consequence of which his parents did not expect him to do much work. So he had spent the ealier years of his life in listening to old men's tales, sitting by the fires, in the village cottages, where the story-tellers and the young men of the village used to gather.'[178] Mullen also noted that one took pride in having a supposedly exceptional repertoire: 'I found the story-tellers much inclined to hold back some specially good tale till last, and each one claimed that he himself had at least one story that nobody else had. Michael Dirrane (Mikeleen Pipe) said very earnestly that "Cos mac Orshen's Visits to Tir-Na-N-Oge" [cf. pp. 61ff.], which he told, had been handed down in his own family for centuries – nobody had ever written it before in any language.'[179]

By the 1930s, Aran was drawing foreign visitors who might still cast themselves in the role of bold explorers, and give accounts of storytelling sessions.[180]

175 *Cities and Sea-Coasts and Islands* (1897), quoted in B. and R. Ó hEithir (eds) *An Aran Reader* 88. For Yeats's account of that meeting, see p. 327 above; he also mentioned the mirror story. 176 *Man of Aran* 15-16. 177 *Hero Breed* 221. 178 *Irish Tales* 8 179 Ibid. 10. 180 See for instance Ian Dall *Here are Stones: An Account of a Journey to the Aran Islands* 134-5, 152-4; and C.C. Vyvyan *On Timeless Shores: Journey in Ireland* 123-5, 149-50.

But the international reputation of this place notwithstanding, Celtic scholars and people in pursuit of values which the modern world had lost gradually turned to the Blasket Islands. Nineteenth-century travellers to the extreme south-west tip of Kerry had merely caught glimpses of those rocks and were told that their inhabitants led a miserable life. In 1905 Synge was in the area, still associating narration with wild settings: 'The scene last night of story-telling had an old-fashioned dignity and this outside pageant of curiously moving magnificence made me shudder to think of the seedy town life most of us are condemned to.'[181] He decided to delve deeper into that 'old-fashioned dignity' by spending a few weeks on the Great Blasket, and was deeply impressed: 'What mystery of attraction is in that simple life.'[182] After the experience, he knew he had been only an 'interloper' there, 'a refugee in a garden between four seas', and the idea that another stranger had already replaced him in the cottage of the 'king' of the island made him unhappy.[183] By then, people had indeed started sojourning on the island to learn Irish or improve their fluency. Among them were Irish patriots, and also foreign philologists; the latter had no nationalistic motivation but were interested in what they saw as a culture on the verge of extinction – a society which, though not illiterate,[184] was still in an essentially oral stage and seemed to have retained impressive elements of a proto-historic European culture. The mere presence in it of outside observers may have contributed to its transformation. (The work of specialized folklorists with Blasket people will be mentioned in Chapter 10.)

One of the first 'discoverers' was Robin Flower, who belonged to the staff of the British Museum Library. He went to the Blaskets for the first time in 1910, bidding farewell, as he stepped into the curragh at Dunquin, 'not only to Ireland, but to England and Europe and all the tangled world of today'. After the crossing, he discovered a 'vanishing mode of life'[185], which he loved and described. Others followed. A curious comparison of the island culture and archaic Greece was launched by a British Marxian hellenist, George Thomson, who stayed on the Great Blasket for the first time in 1923: 'The conversation of those ragged peasants, as soon as I learnt to follow it, electrified me. It was as though Homer had come alive. Its vitality was inexhaustible, yet it was rhythmical, alliterative, formal, artificial, on the point of bursting into poetry ... Returning to Homer, I read him in a new light.'[186] A Trinity College professor developed the analogy 'between the social and cultural situation of the Blasket islanders and the early Ionians', and between the oral arts of two populations separated in time and space: 'The Blasket Island culture ... had impressed well-qualified observers with its archaic and heroic qualities. I want to suggest that it deserves the even more explicit epithet "Homeric", in the sense that it exhibits

---

181 *Collected Works: Prose* 263-4. 182 Ibid. 258. 183 Ibid. 259. 184 Muiris Mac Conghal *The Blaskets: An Island Library* 40. See also D. Ó Giolláin *Locating Irish Folklore* 125-8. 185 *The Western Island* 6, and preface to O'Crohan *The Islandman* vii. 186 *Studies in Ancient Greek Society: The Prehistoric Aegeans*, quoted in MacConghal, op. cit. 154.

some features which were also characteristic, as far as we can tell, of the communities in which Homeric poetry flourished.'[187] He pointed to resemblances in style and narrative modes, as well as to 'a similarity of ethos which is pervasive ... a simple and virile humanism, unpolished yet dignified'.[188] We do not have to discuss this theory – which may seem to revive the eighteenth-century homerization of northern and ossianic texts; the point is that the viewpoints of visitors determined and dignified what they wanted to see, be it a primitivist dream, some supposedly pure example of Irishness, or resemblance with another valued culture.

On the Blaskets too, the eighteenth-century 'Lay of Oisín in the Land of Youth' (see pp. 61ff. and 362) was still recited, and poems were improvised on the main island in the nineteenth century. Above all, there were storytellers who knew some old Irish stories and international folktales, and who livened up conversation with accounts of local or distant events. They had a gift for personal-experience narratives: 'In these autobiographical tales the narrator recalls events of his own life, which he relates just as they occurred, except that he has reshaped them to some extent in his imagination in order to make a good story out of them; and he does this with all the skill he has acquired, as practitioner or as listener, in the storyteller's art.'[189] It was put to use when the narrators were encouraged to write about their experiences: thus in 1917 Tomás Ó Criomhthain – anglicized as O'Crohan (1856-1937) – was incited by one of the visitors to write his autobiography, and other islanders followed his example.

Detailed individual portraits of storytellers were drawn by visitors. Robin Flower met an old man who had tales of the Fianna:

At times the voice would alter and quicken, the eyes would brighten, as with a speed which you would have thought beyond the compass of human breath he delivered those highly artificial passages describing a fight or a putting to sea, full of strange words and alliterating rhetorical phrases which, from the traditional hurried manner of narration, are known as 'runs'. At the end of one of these he would check a moment with triumph in his eye, draw a deep breath, and embark once more on the level course of his recitation.[190]

Flower also described the different, more homely, mode of a woman telling the story of 'The Square Dog'.[191] After her performance, a man who had the heroic repertoire and technique declared that his own kind of narratives could no longer be told:

'Well, well, well', broke in Seán [Seán Fada – Long John O'Dunleavy], 'it's a good tale enough, but we wouldn't have called that a tale at all in the old times. Devil take my

187 J.V. Luce 'Homeric Qualities in the Life and Literature of the Great Blasket Island', in *Greece and Rome* 16 (1969), 153. 188 Ibid. 164. 189 George Thomson *Island Home: The Blasket Heritage* 27-8. 190 *The Irish Tradition* 105. 191 *The Western Island* 62.

soul, it's long before I'd put a tale like that in comparison with the long Fenian stories we used to tell. It was only the other day that I had all the old tales in my mind, and I could have spent the night telling them to you without a word out of its place in any tale. But now I couldn't tell a tale of them. And do you know what has driven them out of my head?' 'Well, I suppose you're losing your memory', I said. 'No, it isn't that, for my memory is as good as it ever was for other things. But it's Tomás [Ó Criomthain] has done it, for he has books and newspapers and he reads them to me, and the little tales one after the other, day after day, in the books and the newspapers, have driven the old stories out of my head. But maybe I'm little the worse for losing them.'[192]

This drew elegiac comments from Robin Flower: what he had been lucky enough to observe would soon vanish.

The Blasket storyteller most often portrayed and recorded was born on the mainland: Peig Sayers (1873-1958), whose father had been one of Jeremiah Curtin's informants. The earliest portrait was also by Robin Flower:

Big Peg – Peig Mór – is one of the finest speakers on the Island; she has so clean and finished a style of speech that you can follow all the nicest articulations of the language on her lips without any effort; she is a natural orator, with so keen a sense of the turn of phrase and the lifting rhythm appropriate to Irish that her words could be written down as they leave her lips, and they would have the effect of literature with no savour of the artificiality of composition. She is wont to illustrate her talk with tales, long and short, which come in naturally along the flow of conversation, and lighten up all our discourse of the present with the wit and wisdom and folly and vivid incident of the past ... As Peig was telling this tale I watched her, in admiration of her fine, clean-cut face, with the dark expressive eyes that change with the changing humours of her talk, all framed in her shawl that kept falling back from her head as she moved her arms in sweeping gestures, only to be caught and replaced above her brow with a twitch of the hand.[193]

Towards the end of her life she held little hope for the art she had learned from her father:

That was the chief pastime then, story-telling and talking about old times. But that's not the way now. They no longer care for stories, and the stories would have died out altogether, for the young people weren't ready to pick them up. But now, thank God, there's a gadget for taking them down, if there were any story-tellers left, but there aren't. For the old Gaels are dead and the new generation rising up don't know Irish well.[194]

Flower had brought the first recording machine to her; this is how her son remembered the scene:

192 Ibid. 70. **193** Ibid. 49, 56. **194** W.R. Rodgers, Introduction to *An Old Woman's Reflections* ix-x.

'Now, Peig', said he at last, rising and opening it', I suppose you never before saw the likes of this talking machine. When I was here last, you used to be telling me grand stories beside the fire. It ran into my head then that if I had this machine, I could take all those stories away with me, so if I lived to come to the Blaskets again, I would bring it. Would you mind at all putting one of the fine stories you have into it?' 'Blahín', said my mother, 'all that's in me is a poor tormented woman, but I wouldn't mind if I thought the boys and girls of my own country would profit from my labours.' 'My hand and word to you', said he, 'that's the way it will be.' Then my mother started with her stories, and well able she was to tell them, even though I say it myself. But, by my palms, Doctor Blahín never let her go thirsty, for he always gave her a drop of whiskey.[195]

By then, she was widely known in Ireland as 'the Queen of Storytellers'; but the high point of 'Blaskets culture' seems to have been reached at the turn of the nineteenth century; after the First World War gradual decay set in, with the emigration of most young people. When the number of visitors multiplied, the community was already on the wane. The twenty survivors were relocated on the mainland in 1953.

There was still Tory Island, off the north-west coast of Donegal, which had preserved a peculiar life-style. The British anthropologist Robin Fox went there in the 1960s to explore the local conceptions of kinship, land tenure and marriage arrangements. Narrative folklore was not his object but he listened to the *seanchaithe*, whose social functions he emphasized:

When a 'storyteller' launches into his tale, it is law, tradition, pedigrees, and gossip that are always involved. Even the highest of the high tales sound at times like gossip about the doings of the gods and heroes – including the interminable discussions of their ancestries. There is no such thing as *idle* gossip; it always works overtime. For it is but one name for that endless fascination with each other, with relationship one to another, and with the traditions and laws that govern this, that consume all little communities like Tory more than the rest; for knowledge-for-its-own-sake – the highest expression of man's humanity – is often more treasured in the lowliest of settings.[196]

Later an American visitor sill collected tales on the island,[197] but even on distant Tory it could not last: 'The advent on the island of twenty-four hour electricity in 1981 – and therefore television – had meant the death of the old-fashioned custom of storytelling.'[198]

The number of inhabited islands around Ireland has decreased by approximately two thirds in a century and a half, and it is probably not there that twentieth-century folklorists have gained the richest ore.

Some could deplore the vanishing of what they saw as a reserve of Irishness or

195 Micheál Ó Guiheen (or Gaoithin – Peig's son, who wrote from dictation her two volumes of memories) *A Pity Youth Does Not Last* 79-80. 196 *The Tory Islanders: A People of the Celtic Fringe* 64-5. 197 D.H. Therman *Stories from Tory Island* 27. 198 Ibid. 12.

an escape to timelessness. By the middle of the century, however, the image of a pious Eden seemed less and less to tally with reality: between 1922 and 1939 the number of native speakers of Irish halved; ownership of a piece of land did not guarantee an adequate income; emigration was endemic. Many of those who experienced rural life were complaining of its deprivation. The emphasis was more and more on what was paralysed or paralysing; an official commission, which had worked between 1948 and 1954, noted in its report: 'We were impressed by the unanimity of the views presented to us in the evidence on the relative loneliness, dullness and general unattractive nature of life in many parts of rural Ireland at present.'[199] The sociologist Hugh Brody, who researched in the west of Ireland between 1966 and 1971, gave a bleak picture contrasting with what Arensberg had described some thirty-five years before (see p. 360) – but perhaps he was exaggerating the sense of demoralization where his predecessor may have overestimated integrative forces. The fact is, in 'traditional' regions there was less mutual aid and social interaction, a decline of interest and faith in the older ways, and a generally atrophied atmosphere: 'Today almost a majority of country people of the remotest districts find their way of life a burden to be avoided if possible.'[200] This may not have been true in all of rural Ireland, nor for everybody in any region, but Brody was not the only severe judge – while others were sensitive about any questioning and still denounced what looked like the introduction of novelty.

Although they had difficulty making themselves heard and were apparently still a minority some twenty years after the creation of the Free State, the number of those disenchanted with the practical results of independence was growing: they tried to shake complacencies and to criticize an Ireland which was at the same time stultified by stagnant economic conditions and afflicted by a hardening conservatism. Behind conformity or flag-waving discourse, frustration made itself heard and officially praised 'traditions' were challenged. I shall give only two examples.

Sean O'Faolain (1900-91), exploring the Gaeltacht as a young patriot before 1920, had also idealized rural life: 'Then we foresaw the new Ireland as a rich flowering of the old Ireland, with all its old simple ways, pieties, values, traditions' he recalled in the 1960s; now impatient with this regressive mentality, he added: 'Only the old men went on thinking like that ... Let me drag my life free of that dream-world, that drunk-world, that heavenworld to try to look at it lucidly, now that it has left me and left all of us.'[201] Already in the late 1930s, when he visited the Blaskets, it seemed to him that the place was 'not altogether magic'. 'The island's famous shanachie, Tomas Ó Criomhthain', was not impressive: 'I thought he was a pompous old man.'[202] In the 1940s, O'Faolain in his influential magazine *The Bell* was criticizing Gaelic romanticization:

199 *The Commission on Emigration and Other Popular Problems* (1956) quoted in T. Brown *Ireland: A Social and Cultural History* ... 185. 200 *Inishkillane: Change and Decline in the West of Ireland* 72. 201 *Vive Moi!* 141. 202 *An Irish Journey* 142-3.

It is a mystique ... an impossible bundling together of disparate facts ...The mystique has tried to discover in the old Gaelic world a model, or master-type ... to which we must all conform. [About 1900] there were still places where men and women told ancient folktales by the fireside, believed in the *sidhe*, held in their rude hands the thin thread of Ariadne back to the forgotten labyrinth. All one needed to get back to that wonder world was to be able to speak Irish ... [But that programme] produces nothing positive. On the contrary its effect is wholly negative and inhibitory.[203]

Patrick Kavanagh (1911-66), who had lived on a small farm in County Monaghan, and known the desolation of rural life, was another critical voice, more strident. He attacked the Irish language movement, deflated all revivalist postures including the 'Celtic' trappings of the Literary Revival (which he termed an 'English-bred lie', his sharpest attacks being aimed at Synge), and rejected what he considered false representations of country nonlife by writers who had not suffered from it. In 1939 he even denounced the activities of the Irish Folklore Commission as gathering dust to blot out real present problems: 'Folklore collecting, like its modern sister, mass observation, is an attempt by sentimental science to do without the poets, who are now starving to death.' The tons of manuscripts gathered by folklore collectors would just 'blind the eyes of the coming historians': with good reason, the *seanchaí* in his native parish kept a pitchfork ready to chase 'the folklore fellas' away. 'Not only is this stuff culturally useless, it is definitely harmful. Let Dr Delargy [the director of the Folklore Commission] say what he may, this weighty collection is a rubbish heap that sooner or later will have to be destroyed.' It was wrong to try and 'build up a synthetic culture from the dust of sages and the spittle of fools'.[204] Such provocative opinions were then seldom publicized, and Kavanagh was known to be particularly embittered, iconoclastic and disposed to attack any institution; but in his sharp tone he may have voiced what less outspoken persons felt – namely, that the pastoral dream was now utterly obsolete.

Not that all Irish folklore was dead or generally considered useless, towards the end of the period now under consideration! If Irish references to 'traditions' could by then be toned down and sometimes ambivalent, foreign amateurs of Celtic twilight or would-be time-travellers still marvelled at the archaic features they observed. The German A.E. Johann, travelling through the country in the early 1950s, multiplied accounts of legends and visited the storyteller Anna Nic an Luain in the Blue Stack Mountains of Donegal; he noted that local people still regularly came to listen to her lively storytelling, which she kept improving by observing the reactions of her audience.[205] On the other hand, Scottish-born David Thomson, looking for variants of the seal legends he had heard in the Hebrides, noticed that audiences were becoming hard to please and that storytellers were shying away from publicity:

203 'The Gaelic Cult', an editorial in *The Bell*, December 1944. 204 'Twenty-Three Tons of Accumulated Folk Lore: Is It of Any Use?', *The Irish Times*, 18 April 1939. 205 *Heimat der Regenbogen: Irland* 193-202.

Many people asked me not to mention them by name in print and often they were reluctant to tell a story until I promised to disguise the names of families mentioned in it, and even the names of some places. I believe that the very request meant more than a normal misgiving about betraying family secrets, that it was a sign of changing attitudes, for many of the older story-tellers gave their names freely. It was their younger friends who held them back – those who were beginning to feel self-conscious about the old tradition.[206]

The first part of this chapter has shown that most writers of the 'Revival' used oral traditions, to various ends. Later, such elements became less common in sophisticated literature, and when scenes of storytelling were evoked they could be treated in new ways, because the ideals, and social reality too, were different. I shall now examine some of these new treatments, related to the evolution sketched in the preceding pages.

In the autobiographical novel *The Green Fool* (1938), which in 1947 he still claimed to be 'one of the truest books ever written' but in 1964 dismissed as 'stage-Irish lie'[207] – too folksy –, Patrick Kavanagh described the growing detachment of the younger generation from traditional storytelling: old George, the only adult in the Monaghan community who still believes in fairies, knows many stories but cannot tell them because his daughter regards them as rubbish: 'Don't be makin' a cod of yerself'.[208]

In a short story written in Irish by Máirtín Ó Cadhain and published in 1939, an old man who masters songs, tales and legends has been silenced by the indifference of his community: 'He knew he was no longer wanted'. When he wins the All-Ireland Award at the Gaelic League Oireachtas in Dublin, his neighbours are impressed and prepare a reception; but he ignores them, and dies soon after.[209] In Bryan Mac Mahon's 'The Good Dead in the Green Hill', written in the 1940s, an old storyteller is deprived of his audience by the newly installed radio.[210]

In *An Béal Bocht* (1941), which 'Flann O'Brien' (Brian O'Nolan) published in Irish under the compound pseudonym of 'Myles na gCopaleen', Gaelic revival excesses were ridiculed, including the false vision of rural life, the stereotyped lament about its demise, inadequate interpretations and overexploitation of the Blasket autobiographies, and conventional features of other 'good Gaelic books' like *Séadna* (see pp. 322-3). Above all, it was the fakeness the author detected in too many language-enthusiasts that he subjected to parody and savage satire. The peasant protagonist is not noble and serene, but dirty and

---

206 *The People of the Sea: A Journey in Search of the Seal Legend* (Introduction to the New Ed.) 12. 207 A. Quinn *Patrick Kavanagh: a Critical Study* 60. 208 Op. cit. 169. 209 '*Fóide Cnapanacha Carracha Uachtair a' Bhaile*' in *Idir Shúgradh agus Dáiríre agus Scéalta Eile* 177-87 – translated as 'The Gnarled and Strong Clods of Townland's Tip' in *The Road to Bright City*. D. Ó Giolláin, in *Locating Irish Folklore* 149-53, discusses Ó Cadhain's critique of a necrophiliac tendency in Irish folkloristics in lectures given in 1949 and 50. 210 *The Lion-Tamer and Other Stories* 138.

starving in a dismal place. There are storytellers, but without the earlier aura of
glamour and prestige: 'In each cabin there was ... a worn, old man who spent
the time in the chimney-corner bed and who arose at the time of night-visiting
to shove his two hooves into the ashes, clear his throat, redden his pipe and tell
stories about the bad times.'[211] This man might have something to say, but outsiders would not understand it anyway: the *Gaeilgeoirí* – literally Irish speakers
or learners of Irish, but here fake revivalists – are ignorant of the language they
praise, and so dense that a 'scholar' records the gruntings of a pig as an authentic example of native verbal arts. The violence of the caricature can be explained
by the rigidness of the ideology it was reacting against. At least the book was in
Irish, and probably for that reason not censored. The English translation of *An
Béal Bocht – The Poor Mouth* – appeared only in 1964. What was in English,
and therefore much more accessible to the large majority of Irish people, easily
offended those in power: briefly leaving fiction aside we may note that at about
the same time, when Eric Cross published *The Taylor and Ansty* collecting the
anecdotes and actual fireside talk of Tim Buckley (1863-1945) from Inchigeela
near Gougane Barra, the relative unholiness of his chat as reconstructed by the
author could not be accepted as the truth about Irish peasant life; consequently,
the book was banned until the 1960s, and local clergymen terrorized the old
raconteur into burning a copy in his own fireplace.[212]

In two short stories written in the 1940s, Sean O'Faolain portrayed the
break with older oral arts. In the significantly titled 'The End of the Record', a
folk collector brings his machine to a poorhouse, in quest of 'any story at all
only it has to be an old story and a good story'. Most of the inmates have forgotten what they used to know, but the widow of a famous storyteller is there.
The microphone is brought to her bed and she starts narrating, but soon passes
out, and only the cry of some lonely bird outside is recorded – a tradition is
waning or becoming unintelligible. In 'The Silence of the Valley', modern
people holidaying in a remote Gaelic area learn that the last renowned storyteller
of the region has just died; they attend his wake as an interesting oddity. The
following day, the last sound they perceive is the noise of the coffin going down
into the grave, after which the valley is definitively voiceless. This story somehow contrasts with Seamus O'Kelly's 'The Weaver's Grave' (see pp. 356-7): the
weaver was not quite the last of his kind, whereas O'Faolain's cobbler is; in the
story composed in revolutionary times there seemed to be a promising future for
the younger generation, but the more recent story ends with the phrase 'like a
curtain falling'.[213]

In 1937, Frank O'Connor had also treated the theme of the dying old sto-

---

211 *The Poor Mouth* (tr. Patrick Power) 65. 212 Cross was not a professional folklorist. He
also produced a collection of short stories – *Silence Is Golden* (1978) – with some scenes of
storytelling.   213 'End of the Record' first appeared in *New Statesman and Nation* (1949);
'The Silence of the Valley' in *The Bell* (1946). The two stories follow each other in *The Finest
Stories of Sean O'Faolain* (1957), in an order chosen by the author.

ryteller and of the changing attitudes of members of the new generation; in 'The Story Teller', children are puzzled:

'Mom said', continued Nance in the tone of one reciting a lesson, 'that 'twould be better for grandfather now if he hadn't so much old stories and paid heed to his prayers when he had the chance.'
    'Grandfather always said his prayers. Grandfather knew more prayers than mom.'
    'Mom said he told barbarous stories.'
    'But if they were true?'
    'Mom says they weren't true, that they were all lies and that God punishes people for telling lies and that's why grandfather is afraid to die. He's afraid of what God will do to him for telling lies.'[214]

But when he has passed away, they hear other adults who remember that storytelling used to be of value:

'There was nothing he cared about only the stories.'
    'No, then. And he was a wonder with them.'
    'He was. You wouldn't miss a day in a bog or a night in a boat with him. Often he'd keep you that way you wouldn't know you were hungry.' Afric's father spat. It was not often he made such admissions. 'And there were times we were hungry.'
    'You never took after him, Con.'
    'No, then. 'Twasn't in me, I suppose. But 'twasn't in our generation. I'd get great pleasure listening to him, but I could never tell a story myself.'[215]

Benedict Kiely, well versed in folklore, repeatedly used storytelling and traditional stories as subsidiary or central elements in his writings. In his first novel, *Land without Stars* (1946), young men from Northern Ireland who have joined an Irish-language summer school in the Rosses of County Donegal hear a local storyteller. He is proud of having fooled a folklorist, but his stories and scraps of partisan history have a powerful impact on members of the audience:

Mandy spat, slapped his knees, inserted his own naive inventions into stories that burned with the passions of men dead for centuries. Fionn and Oisin and Conan the Bald, Diarmuid and red Grainne, Goll who wrestled with God on the Fenian meadows, jostled with clever third sons, slightly obscene giants, maidens from royal Spain, evicting soldiers, lads from Burtonport, potato-pickers in Ayrshire or Roxburghshire. Teachers from Belfast and civil servants from Dublin, holiday-makers and earnest students sat round in circles and listened. It was part of the national resurgence. Without a language, without a nationhood Pearse had said 'Ireland Gaelic and Ireland free.' The King of Spain's daughter. The flag of Tone's republic above the burning post office in Dublin in 1916. Connolly the internationalist dying like a prince for the freedom of one small nation. What under God did it all mean? Had any people on earth put forward so many complicated claims to what the world called nationalism?[216]

The listener on whose mind the narrative is focused here may have mixed feel-

214 *The Cornet Player Who Betrayed Ireland* 66. 215 Ibid. 71. 216 Op. cit. 149.

ings; another – his brother – will die an IRA man, killed by circumstances, history and stories.

Storytelling is a central structuring principle in *The Cards of the Gambler* (1953), by the same author. Segments of a traditional tale – an Irish version of International Type 330C (the Devil is defeated; Heaven is entered with a magic pack of cards) combined with Type 332 (a poor man chooses Death as godfather for his son, who receives the power of predicting the course of an illness; Death is tricked, and avenges itself) – alternate with chapters transposing the story into a modern setting and form. The opening pages, the description of a traditional storytelling event, are a deliberately stylized, archaizing construct:

The stage is set for the telling of a story ... The old man is ninety years of age. He isn't tall, but he is heavily built, and when he was young he was strong and active. His face is still a healthy red from wind and sun and good circulation. His eyes are as grey as the grey lakes, but, unlike the lakes, they are deep with happiness. He is not bearded, but he has a bristling moustache. He wears a good tweed suit and a sailor's cap with a glossy peak. His fingers knitted around the crook of a stick, he is preparing carefully to tell a story.

This story he has heard from his father, who heard it from his father, who heard it from his mother, who heard it from her uncle, who heard it from his father, who sometime in the eighteenth century heard it from a travelling man whose ears had been cut off for threatening the life of a squireen. It is quite possible that the travelling man heard it from his father or his uncle or his mother or another travelling man. It has been added to, subtracted from, divided, and multiplied. It has borrowed something from this place, from that period, from that individual twist of mind or tongue. As for me, I heard it from the man you're watching, and you, if you wait, will hear it from me. When I come to tell it, I will also add, subtract, divide, and multiply.[217]

The modern, 'written' treatment of the theme is much longer than the traditional tale and displays the more varied techniques of novels; but the interlacing of the two mutually reflecting narratives, and the recurring symbol of the circle, suggest that traditional stories, like myths, embody fundamental truths or mysteries and enact series of events which can be told and experienced again and again, in different forms and in a changed world.

C. BLURRED OUTLINES

It is a commonplace that, after the frustration and bitterness of the 1950s, Ireland has been undergoing rapid transformations and now seems to have altered radically. I cannot possibly analyse the detail of an evolution which is still in progress but I must mention some of the profound changes in daily life and in the overall patterns of society which could have repercussions on the main

217 *The Cards of the Gambler* 1-3.

object of my study: the storyteller as an icon that suggests emotional significance and communicates values, and as a mirror revealing the desires or fears of the person who looks at it.

Today, the majority of the population is urbanized: the proportion of those of working age employed in agriculture declined from almost 44% in the early 1950s to less than 15% in the 90s; the total number of farms has more than halved since the mid-20s, and the small ones, which half a century ago were still seen as the foundation of genuine Irishness, are no longer considered viable and may even be denounced as obstacles to progress. Agricultural production now accounts for a smaller part of the national output. Industries, often foreign-owned, have been promoted, and a new prosperity has generated a mood of self-confidence in certain circles – while other sectors of the population remain poor. Society is growing more secular; values which used to be transmitted as common standards seem less clear, or more questionable; in an age of globalized economy and new communication systems, Ireland is more open to the influence of imported mass culture – which may be combined with newly interpreted native elements. Parts of the Gaeltacht are turning into a tourist resort, and what is left of the arcadian dream is marketed for foreigners. Practically every home has a TV set, and one regularly complains that 'the TV killed the conversation' in the family.

Violence erupted again in Northern Ireland and the issue was often called one of 'identities' and 'traditions' founded on 'history' and the existence of 'two nations' : terms we have often come across are thus still loaded, but at the turn of the century one hoped to be moving towards a peaceful pluralist society.

In the Republic, some older themes seem to be slipping out of fashion, as the formerly dominant ideology slowly becomes residual: active revivalists are now a minority. The weight of the past may be resented. In 1983, while refusing to be called a 'British poet', Seamus Heaney rejected images that emblematized subservience and encouraged division or violence:

> It's time to break the cracked mirror
> Of this conceit
> It leads nowhere so why bother
> To work it out?[218]

Some historians propose to 'reinterpret the past', by which they mean exploding nationalist 'myths' and emphasizing the mixed nature of Irish identity. Young people in urban areas, influenced by the mainstream of American popular culture, may be tired of what one used to force-feed them with: a slogan (or mock-slogan) for a rock festival in the summer of 1995 was 'Peig Sayers is dead, but Elvis lives' – Peig's autobiography in Irish had been for decades an unavoidable subject at school while the world and the attitudes it illustrated were

---

218 'An Open Letter', in *A Field Day Pamphlet Number 2* (Derry, 1983) 11.

becoming increasingly remote to the students. But can history be simply erased and the whole inheritance denied? Others are trying to find out what aspects of an Irish cultural heritage still make sense and can live on, in renewed form and spirit. It fares well with 'traditional music', for instance, where respect for what is considered 'old style' and some fusions with other 'traditions' or new fashions may coexist.

What about 'traditional storytelling', in this profoundly altered context? The kinds of stories which had long been considered typically Irish are less generative today and seem less adaptable to new circumstances. Some may regret this evolution: the American Lawrence Millman, who visited the west of Ireland in 1975 to find out what was left of the celebrated masters of the art of storytelling, entitled his book *Our Like Will Not Be There Again* (using one of the last phrases in Ó Criomthain's *An tOileánach*: '*Mar ná beidh ár leithéidí arís ann* – which had been ruthlessly parodied in *An Béal Bocht*). The dominant tone of his report was sad because he found that people who 'had the old tales' were indeed getting fewer and fewer. In interviews, they could begin by pleading incapacity: ' "Stories? In truth, stories? I have them all forgot", he protests.' [219] Others thought they would still be able to perform, if only they had an audience. But Millman also found Irish people who resented the systematic association between Irishness and storytelling: ' "I hate stories, and I wouldn't listen to one if you paid me. Stories didn't do this country one bit of good", says the proprietor of the Irish crafts shop [where tourists buy 'traditional' souvenirs].'[220]

Evocations of rural life are still being published as images of a world that is long gone, but the younger writers are less likely to exploit folklore than their predecessors; dialogue including narration and verbal flourishes remains abundant, but the pastoral orientation is generally replaced by depictions of urban culture – or suburban void. There is, however, one relatively new theme: the complex relationships between the folklorist or ordinary listener, the teller, the 'tradition', and present issues. Novelists and short-story writers may thus focus on the observer's experience (O'Faolain's stories already did so). In a more recent text by Bryan MacMahon, 'The French Cradle', an American woman gathering material for her Ph.D. dissertation is overpowered by emotions and perhaps reborn after listening to a 'wild-eyed' storyteller at Ballyferriter.[221] In 'The Mermaid's Legend', by trained folklorist Eilís Ní Dhuibhne, the tale of the captive sea-maiden who returns to sea when she has recovered her magic cloak gives a woman the impulse and energy to win back her own freedom.[222] In *The Inland Ice and Other Stories* (1997) by the same author, a version of 'The Search for the Lost Husband' (AT 425), broken into fourteen tellings, ironically alternates with thematically linked modern episodes.

Drama has its own ways of representing, heightening or criticizing Irish storytelling, or of using it emblematically. The question whether stories from the

219 *Our Like Will Not Be There Again* 18. **220** Ibid. 12. **221** In *The Sound of Hooves* (1985). **222** In *Eating Women Is Not Recommended* (1991).

past can help the individual or the group is one of the themes in Thomas Murphy's pair of plays first performed in 1985, the full titles of which already point to one of the main types of Irish traditional narratives: *Bailegangaire; The Story of Bailegangaire and how it came by its appellation*, and *A Thief of a Christmas; The Actuality of how Bailagangaire came by its appellation*. The second play enacts a laughing match, the loudest laughs being in response to the evocation of misfortunes and the last laugh that of a dying man. The other play evokes the contest in a prolonged and confused act of storytelling some fifty years later. The setting is 'a country kitchen in the old style'[223], but the people of the township depend for a livelihood on a Japanese-owned computer plant about to close down. Mommo, an 'old woman in the bed' – and it is difficult not to think of the 'traditional' representation of Ireland as *seanbhean bhocht* – is a repetitive and tyrannical storyteller: 'Let ye be settling now, my fondlings, and I'll be giving ye a nice story tonight when I finish this. For isn't it a good one? An' ye'll be goin' to sleep ... And no one will stop me! Tellin' my nice story.'[224] It is not, though, the kind of 'nice' (naive and pretty) fairytale which used to be dear to literary people, but the obsessive evocation of harsh rural life, with death and grief. The storyteller prevents the listeners – her daughters – from living, and when it is at long last completed, her tale turns the past into a nightmare. Finishing the senile narrative will perhaps make life possible again. Connor McPherson's play *The Weir* (1998) consists of a set of eerie stories told in a small rural bar: three legends of the older type (the house built on a fairy road; a ghost story; the dead man supervising the digging of his grave) make a lesser impact than a modern urban legend (the phone call from a dead child).

Considering current social and cultural changes, how much of what we have been studying can survive? What may a radically reshaped culture do to oral storytelling? As we have seen, the passing of old ways in Ireland has often been lamented – the elegiac refrain itself providing an element of continuity. The fact is that certain kinds of storytelling, still in full force a century ago, may now be vanishing from Irish life: those who can tell 'the old stories' are hard to find and no longer have the audiences their predecessors had, with the inclination and competence to listen to long tales: rural gatherings just to listen to a local storyteller are no longer natural and common, though one may still pander to the tourist's dream of an enchanted land: I have before me the advertisement for a storytelling and *sean nos*-singing workshop on Inishmore in August-September 1999; no Irish is required, but '*un bon niveau d'anglais est nécessaire pour comprendre les récits.*' In part of the urban Irish population, however, there is – as in the rest of the western world – an interest in revived 'traditional' storytelling.

Narrative activities have always adapted to the environment. The *seanchai* has not completely disappeared as a part of Ireland's self-definition, even if in real life he no longer is the important figure he used to be: many Irish people

---

223 Tom Murphy *Plays: Two* 91.   224 Ibid. 91-2.

still have a knack of telling about the local past, or their own experience. People still like to meet, and feats of verbal skill remain a welcome part of collective entertainments – what is now fashionably called 'crack' (Irishized as *craic*: having a good time, with drink and talk). Perhaps the concept of folklore will remain in use, but it may have to be at least partly redefined, and applied to material conveyed through different media. My diachronic survey ends in a time of transience or mutation.

Whatever the future has in store, the enormous fund of 'traditional' material collected by folklorists during the century is – *pace* Patrick Kavanagh – a treasure worth exploring. The next two chapters will dip into this ocean of tales and tellers, single out some notable traits, and try to see them in a European or wider context.

Folklorists meet storytellers or those
who remember them

In the early years of the twentieth century, 'folklore' was said to combine continuity (durability and diffusion) with variation (the interchangeability of its elements and some degree of improvisation in performance), in expressive forms, beliefs and customs. It had to be transmitted in face to face contact and controlled by the community. It would be found in highly cohesive groups relatively unaffected by modern ways, though living alongside the urban and industrialized world. The idea that a particular set of folkloric items distinguished the culture of a region or nation was still potent, though it was more and more obvious that a vast proportion of what was found in any given cultural unit was not unique to it.

The discipline that studied such material had to define its subject, methods and concepts. There were boundary problems between the social sciences which had developed since the nineteenth century, and what was later called folkloristics may have had more difficulty than others carving out a field of its own. It could appear relatively independent from anthropology/ethnology only as long as the latter was looking at distant non-Western societies while folklorists were working in the rural hinterland of their own country. They tended to have more conservative views, both in valuing archaism for itself and in clinging to obsolescent tenets: thus the principles of evolutionism (with folktales and customs seen as survivals from earlier stages in one ascending scale) were invoked in writings about folklore long after anthropologists decided that the distribution of cultural differences in space could not be so simply interpreted as the result of more advanced or delayed development. In the 1920s, when functionalist principles emerging in anthropology tended to insist on the stability and homogeneity of a culture at a certain moment in time and to discard what had lost its utilitarian value, folklore remained obsessed with the idea of salvaging what no longer served immediate sociological purposes. But folklore studies could learn from the anthropological approach how to produce a monograph about a single society after long-term participant observation, first trying to empathize with the insider's perspective and then moving back to write a partly detached report. In folkloristics as well as in anthropology, the scholar who worked in archives instead of carrying out field research and collecting his own data could be downgraded. In some countries, ethnology has absorbed folklore; in others, where it

is institutionalized in university departments or some state-sponsored organizations, folklore remains more autonomous. But, everywhere, theories and research
practices have been borrowed from other fields: sociology explained how people
interact and how to scrutinize the interrelations within confined locations; from
psychology came the idea of studying folklore items as the expression of cognitive systems, or of interpreting them as responses to specific stimuli; linguistics
made it possible to analyze systems of differences in signs, or the structure of
discourse, or how people organize communication; philological and literary studies, which had already provided ways of establishing texts, also propounded
models of narrative forms. The various approaches were perhaps more often
complementary than contradictory.

It will be the object of this chapter to outline the work of collectors in
Ireland during the twentieth century, and what they learned about storytellers –
but only after briefly characterizing some theoretical positions, each of which
might bring attention to certain features of storytelling and overlook others.

Diffusionism asserted that a complex tale, variants of which were collected
in different countries, must have been created once only at a certain place and
then spread out to other areas, either through migration of peoples or through a
borrowing process. Could the earliest version be reconstructed and the paths of
dissemination mapped? Those who addressed such questions made use of techniques of inductive language reconstruction and textual criticism developed by
comparative philologists and literary scholars: from the 1870s they had been
applied to the Finnish epics, and were later extended to folktales. The assumptions were that every tale had its own history and that it was possible to reconstruct the archetypal plot, determine its place of origin and establish its migration routes. The partisans of this 'historic-geographic' method would accumulate
a large number of variants of 'the same basic story', then take an inventory of
the constituent elements that were ever-present and therefore considered essential; the country where the variants most resembled the reconstructed *Urform*
would be the tale's homeland. 'Vertical' transmission from generation to generation within one cultural area was not supposed to introduce major changes,
whereas 'horizontal' transmission to new cultural areas could result in considerable modifications – but general laws were supposed to delimit them. Variations
tended to be seen as deviations, stylistic peculiarities of the versions gathered
were not taken into account, and the storytellers themselves did not attract interest. Monographs on specific tales were produced with great care, and there is no
doubt that this way of working was an improvement on some nineteenth-century wild speculations; but the 'Finnish method' was criticized because it was
based upon library research rather than fieldwork and its conclusions were contingent on the nature of a corpus of written texts that was not very adequate; it
tended to ignore the context of narration; the quest for the *Urform* was dismissed as a wild-goose chase; roads of diffusion remained guesswork; and the

definition of the 'mechanical laws of thought and imagination that prevail in the rich variation of oral tradition'[1] was questionable.

Scholars applying this method were confronted with problems of classification: a uniform system of reference was needed to facilitate the comparative analysis of versions of the 'same story' told in various languages and in different parts of the world. For the kinds of 'international' tales which were of particular interest since the days of the Grimms, folklorists proposed a taxonomy based on 'types': recognizable plot patterns which can manifest themselves in many versions and variants. The general – in fact mostly European – catalogue (*The Types of the Folktale* established by A. Aarne and S. Thompson) was supplemented with indexes that applied the same system to particular regions or ethnic groups, including their 'oikotypes' – distinct subtypes of international tales tied to a particular cultural setting. The value of the tale-type concept has been questioned: first because plot abstracts may not be what is most important, a story being more than a set of identifiable plot kernels or 'motifs' (figures, objects, situations and actions sufficiently unusual to impress themselves on the listener as salient features, and which reappear in a variety of tales); secondly, there was disagreement as to the identification of the constituent units. Also, sequences of 'motifs' can float in and out of tales; a particular narrative can be only a segment of a recognized 'type' or combine episodes belonging to different such categories. But, as indexing tools more than as instruments of analysis, 'types' and 'motifs' catalogues remain useful; it is still argued that 'phenomena are identifiable as folklore only when and because they can be configured with like phenomena into set types'.[2]

The historic-geographic method and its classificatory extensions seemed to neglect much of what determined the shape and the power of stories. Other theories focused on the formal properties of so-called traditional narratives. Was it possible to identify the general principles by which they were governed? There were early attempts to establish rules of universal application, or the compositional scheme corresponding to a specific narrative genre. The so-called 'epic laws' or 'rules of composition' formulated in 1908 by Axel Olrik focused on modes of opening and closing tales, the use of repetitions, and patterns like polarization and concentration. Later, the 'oral-formulaic' theory of (re)composition in performance by drawing from a stock of building blocks, first applied to Homer and to Slavonic epics, was extended to other genres. More recent schools of narratology have tried to identify, in the light of Russian formalism, of structuralism or of semiotics, the ways in which all narratives would function: certain principles would govern the combination of a finite number of minimal constituants – roles, relations, and actions decisive for the progress of the narrative, and a plot structure was thus defined; or, on a deeper level, analogies and oppositions of significant elements, independently of their sequential relation-

1 K.K. Krohn *Folklore Methodology* 98.   2 R.A. Georges and M.O. Jones *Folkloristics: An Introduction* (1995) 119.

ship, would establish a semantic structure. From such basic schemata, the wide
variety of stories would be generated. When an overall 'model' was discovered,
it was formalized in a kind of algebra, and some thought that it expressed an
inbuilt universal logic at work in the human mind. Such methods of analysis
were often applied to folktales by non-folklorists, who chose, and sometimes
conflated, texts which folklorists would find doubtful as examples of oral productions. Another approach focuses on folk narratives in less abstract terms,
looking for the emotional load they carry, and what is intended to be signified
or may be unwittingly implied in their fantasy and symbolic representations.
The 'meaning' is produced by a combination of effects, and is highly subjective:
it varies for different persons – those who created the earliest versions of the tale
or those who transmitted it; this storyteller on a particular occasion, his customary audience, or the collector, or the outsider who is trying to put some construction on the collected item. A story makes sense in a certain context, and for
someone: the significance (now both in terms of fundamental meaning and of
important effect) of an oral tale does not reside in the text itself but depends on
the listeners, taken individually and as a group.

The formalist or structuralist approaches mentioned above owed something
to the linguistics that aimed at abstraction in representing a system of elements
and rules for combining them, and with Roman Jakobson and Piotr Bogatyrev
the Saussurian distinction between the general code of communication within a
speech community and the utterances of individuals was applied to folklore.
According to them, the storyteller would use as a code the system of representation and models of action accepted by his/her group. The group exerted a corrective influence: only what was ratified by the community would enter the
chain of transmission, and survive. But a certain freedom of choice and innovation being possible within the code, there were individual acts of creative
artistry.[3] Later, linguistics had other concepts to offer, when it studied the situations in which people communicated and the social functions of language.
Specific developments in folkloristics have grown out of the models thus provided. From the 1970s in the United States, for instance, much research on oral
narration shifted 'from the static view of artificially constructed and isolated oral
narrative sequences to the dynamics of telling and transmitting stories from
person to person and from people to people through means of direct contact'.[4]
Social interactions within a given context were emphasized and the act of telling
was considered as 'artistic communication in small groups [where] folklore is not
an aggregate of things but a process. [...] The telling is the tale'[5] – the latter
phrase became a motto. Each 'performance' would involve a shift from ordinary
speaking to a heightened mode of communication put on display; the audience
evaluates the relative effectiveness of the performer, who assumes a special role
and adopts a certain conventional behaviour for a limited time. Often prepared

3 'Die Folklore als eine besondere Form des Schaffens', in *Donum Natalicium* 3. Mei 1929. 4
L. Dégh *Narratives in Society* 47. 5 Ibid. 12, 10.

for and programmed with a clear scenario, marked as a special event, the performance is thus the product of a complex interplay of individual competence and community rules; among interacting variables are the physical setting, a social and psychological ambiance, the expectations of the listeners and their role as participants in a creative process – the spoken utterance being only a part of a larger whole which includes non-verbal features. This doctrine seemed to threaten much of what had been piled up in folklore archives, now devalued as 'collections of dead artifacts, arbitrarily limited texts'.[6] New systems of transcription would be required to keep a record of the distribution of pauses, shifts in volume or speed and tone of voice, the attitudes of different people – an exhaustive micro-analysis of all the parameters might be endless, and collecting all the data would probably disturb the performance. But it is undoubtedly important to study storytelling as an act of communication, with people interacting in a particular place at a particular time, and to find out how it is patterned in specific cultures. With the shift from 'texts' to performative aspects, the audience was recognized as an active shaper and the central performer became much more than a source of information.

Some literary critics have been accused of dwelling too much on the biography of authors; folklorists, on the contrary, tended in the past to dwell on the narratives, and paid little attention to the actors in oral arts, both as persons and as members of a community: how they had assimilated the material they were using, how they behaved when narrating, and with what constraint and freedom they adapted tales to their own tastes and preoccupations as well as to their audience. There had been exceptions, though: while many folklorists considered their sources as mere transmitters, some tellers in the nineteenth century had been granted a personality, and in the twentieth there was a growing awareness of the role of individual creativity. Carl von Sydow, who criticized some schematic aspects of the 'historic-geographic' ('Finnish') approach like the assumption that tales spread more or less automatically, thought that they were preserved, shaped and transmitted only by a select minority: a few 'active bearers of tradition ... equipped with a good memory, vivid imagination and narrative powers', who were regularly called upon to narrate and therefore were very influential; it is with them that tales could migrate. 'Passive bearers', aware of the content and conventions of the 'tradition', played no creative role but provided a competent audience and made sure that the active bearers performed correctly.[7] It was important, therefore, to study the lives and particular skills of storytellers; to see whether, consciously or not, they wove personal elements into the narratives; to examine variations in the way they told the 'same story' on several occasions; to find out how they differed from each other in age, gender, temperament, verbal proficiency, inventiveness. There were early examples of

6 Lauri Honko 'Methods in Folk-Narrative Research', in *Ethnologia Europaea* II (1979-80) 18.
7 'On the Spread of Tradition' (originally published in 1932), in *Selected Papers on Folklore* 11-15.

such an approach: a famous study established correlations between the facts of a Siberian taleteller's life, the tales she chose to tell, and her mode of telling.[8] In Germany and in Scandinavia, exhaustive monographs were produced on single tradition bearers, their whole repertoires and the communities where they were active. In Hungary the importance of the storyteller and the social conditions of production of the tales was stressed: 'the forms the Hungarians folktales assume cannot be separated from the person telling them;'[9] in 1962, an epoch-making study of storytellers and their community concluded: 'The narrator weaves his own person into the tale, he imparts his own point of view when he tells the tale. His own fate is involved in all the situations of the tale; he identifies himself with the tale action; and he interprets all the life expressions of his people. Every narrator does this, but the means depend on his personality.'[10] In Finland too, in order to understand the significance of a tale it was deemed necessary to know the social position of the person telling it: 'When the communication of oral tradition is analysed as social behaviour, one should examine tradition bearers not only as individual transmitters of tradition but also as the possessors of certain social roles, who again are expected by the community to fulfill those roles.'[11] Indeed, the storyteller functions in a social context, and it is important to know how the tales are received by regular listeners: 'In folk culture the essence and process of the "public poetry" are provided by the tension that naturally arises from the relations between individual talent and the tradition of the community.'[12] The tendency to choose the narrator and his natural audience as objects of research, either concentrating on the most proficient artists or considering all the members of the community, became widespread in the second half of the century.[13]

New formulations of old issues have determined some of the questions scholars are asking. The problem of origins is no longer considered essential, and there is less preoccupation with the 'extremely old': it may seem more important to study living communication, and folklore is seen less as a set of survivals representing the past than as ongoing cultural processes. A 'folk' could be any group that shows at least one factor in common, not just the illiterate peasants in a literate society. New 'lore', perhaps thriving in urban contexts, is valued. The social units where folklorists find their materials may now be not just rural groups in remote places but any persistent combination of people, at any level of society, who maintain contact and share special practices and memories; instead of dealing with 'national' customs, folklorists may focus on the lore of such discrete groups. Although many still think that continuity of oral trans-

8 M.K. Asadowskij *Eine sibirische Märchenerzählerin* (1926). 9 G. Ortutay *Hungarian Folklore* 226. 10 Linda Dégh *Folklore and Society; Story-telling in a Hungarian Peasant Community* 182. 11 J. Pentikäinen *Oral Repertoire and World View* 16. 12 G. Ortutay op. cit. 268. 13 Bibliographies in B. Biebuyck 'A la recherche du conteur', *Cahiers de Littérature Orale* 11 (1982) 195-214; R. Wehse 'Past and Present Folkloristic Narrator Research', in R.T. Bettingheimer (ed.) *Fairy Tales and Society* (1989); R. Schenda *Von Mund zu Ohr; Bausteine zu einer Kulturgeschichte volkstümlichen Erzählens in Europa* (1993).

mission establishes the 'authenticity' of folklore items, the concept of orality can be assigned a less central role: what is studied is not as free of literary intervention as was formerly assumed, and there are new channels. More attention has been paid to the complex nature of the fieldworker's relationship with informants, the effect of his/her presence in the group, and the subjectivity of the reports. Anthropologists/ethnologists have grown suspicious of the word 'tradition', and the concept has been reassessed by historians who have shown that it can be the mere construction of a link between aspects of the present and an advantageous interpretation of the past: a society selects, interprets and modifies what it needs to legitimize as ancient, or an elite defines the permanent identity of a society according to the current situation, and new features may quickly win recognition as 'traditional'. Around 1970 a new definition of folklore was proposed in America, according to which 'it is not the life history of the text that determines its folkloristic quality but its present mode of existence', and the concept of tradition would be of secondary importance: 'The traditional character of folklore is an accidental quality, associated with it in some cases, rather than an intrinsic feature of it ... Tradition should not be a criterion for the definition of folklore in its context.'[14] But older views of 'tradition' have remained, and the word is still in constant use. At any rate, without the notion of something being transmitted the very concept of folklore might dissolve.

Preceding chapters have shown that in Ireland one did not wait for the recent developments mentioned above to pay attention to storytellers and to the circumstances in which tales were told; but the nineteenth-century observers, when the notion of 'folklore' meant something to them, very seldom specialized in that field, often favoured the extremely picturesque, or cultivated stereotypes. The main changes illustrated in this chapter will be the drawing of more realistic portraits (though still with a tendency to typify); the advent of professional Irish folklorists engaged in a more systematic and sustained campaign than individual enthusiasm or occasional pastime had made possible; and the fact that major collectors, particularly from the 1930s on, could be less distant from informants than many of their predecessors, and consequently not likely to perceive what they heard or observed as strange or grotesque. If they were seldom full-time members of the smaller communities they were studying, they often lived in the neighbourhood, spoke the language, and understood local perceptions. They would not buttress their work with jargon-packed theories, but could be affected by some concepts and principles developed abroad, as they certainly were by ideological trends in Ireland itself. The following pages will show how intermittent and isolated action was replaced by wider and permanent efforts; how and according to what principles the new collectors carried out the task; then how they saw storytellers.

14 Dan Ben-Amos 'Toward a Definition of Folklore in Context', in A. Paredes and R. Bauman (eds) *Toward New Perspectives in Folklore* 14, 13.

The need for concerted action was felt, as shown in two articles written by the scholar Eleanor Hull in 1911. The first of them detailed a plan of campaign: it was the last opportunity to 'preserve from complete extinction what still remains of the folk-lore of Ireland', and a group of some forty collectors in different parts of the country had agreed to make a simultaneous effort during the next three or four years and to pool the results. Stories should be handed to Douglas Hyde and Joseph Lloyd. Advice was given: 'The best material is that which is communicated in the course of ordinary conversation; any attempts to go about officially as a collector will probably result in the invention of incidents by the obliging narrator, or in putting an end to his communications ... Tact and experience are needed to sift the information given, and to discriminate truth from invention.'[15] The other article gave the philosophy of the enterprise, quoting Tylor: folk custom: 'is the lingering remains and testimony to an earlier stage of thought; folk-tales are all we have to remind us of an ancient philosophy of life'.[16] The proposed venture was essentially an anthropological search for the 'primitive' level of culture, still in evolutionist terms. The oral tales one hoped to collect were not the respectable 'mythology' of Celtophiles – Eleanor Hull herself had founded the Irish Texts Society for the publication of early manuscripts, and in 1928 she would consider folklore as 'the essential handmaid of studies more ancient and dignified, in the general estimation, than itself ... [i.e.] of ethnology, or history, or religion and literature'.[17] Patriotic motives were not mentioned, and the second article of 1911 stood aloof from some conceptions of folklore held by the Literary Revival:

There is a disposition in the library man to be a little jealous and uneasy in view of the folklorist; he looks upon him as a profane person spoiling in an unscrupulous manner a rich field from which we can draw picturesque materials. 'Heaven only knows,' suggests Mr Yeats, 'what the folk-lorist is on the gad after!' What we are on the gad after is a knowledge of ourselves, a knowledge which can only be true when it is brought into connection with the older knowledge and beliefs of our ancestors. We want to build up a true history of thought, just as the historian seeks to build up a true history of the outward aspects of life. From this point of view even the wildest folktale has a double interest; it is not merely a fanciful creation of the imagination, it is an expression of what, in the old days, or in primitive conditions to-day, the folk thought about life.[18]

The last pages of this article restate the programme; but nothing seems to have

15 'Folk-lore Collecting in Ireland', *Journal of the Royal Society of Antiquaries of Ireland* 41 (1911) 188-90. Joseph H. Lloyd (1865-1939) edited the *Gaelic Journal* from 1899 on, collected and edited tales under the name of Seosamh Laoide between 1901 and 1915; T.J. Westropp (see note 42 on p. 289) was to serve as secretary of the proposed society. A British manual was recommended: G.L. Gomme's *Handbook of Folk-Lore* (1890), by then in the process of being revised by E.S. Hartland, then by Charlotte Sophia Burne. 16 *Journal of the Cork Historical & Archaeological Society* 17 (1911). 17 *Folklore of the British Isles* 1, 2. 18 *Journal of the Cork HAS* 17 (1911) 28-9.

come of the project because Ireland entered a period of turmoil: revived Home-Rule agitation, Ulster Protestant reaction, the growth of rival paramilitary formations ... For some time, it would not be easy, indeed at a certain stage it might become dangerous, to ramble and ask questions in out-of-the-way places.

The plan for a concerted action was revived some fifteen years later, when things had relatively settled down in the Free State. Two Scandinavian folktale scholars, R. Christiansen of Oslo and C.W. von Sydow from Lund, had visited Ireland and insisted that something should be done with the rich material they glimpsed there. By then, however, the aim from the Irish point of view was no longer to reconstruct a mental history of mankind: a Folklore of Ireland Society (*An Cumann le Béaloideas Éireann*) was founded in 1927 to collect what was left of the national folk legacy lest it perish, as its motto said: *Colligite quae superaverunt fragmenta, ne pereant.* Indeed, much seemed in danger of disappearing with the oldest living generation born about the middle of the nineteenth century, and the general idea was that Ireland might thus lose part of its now much-praised separate identity. Among the founders of the society were members of the pioneer period of the Gaelic Revival movement such as Douglas Hyde or Pádraig Ó Siochfhradha; they clearly distinguished genuine *béaloideas* (Irish for 'oral tradition' – *béal*: mouth, and *oideas*: instruction) from the 'leprechaun' or '*begorra*' stuff that had been exploited for a century. Their journal opened with a mission statement: 'The aim of our Society is a humble one – to collect what still remains of the folklore of our country. We are certain that the nonsensical rubbish which passes for Irish folklore, both in Ireland and outside, is not representative of the folklore of our Irish people.'[19] It was an independent venture, but an Irish Folklore Institute (*Institiúid Bhéaloideas Éireann*), established in 1930, was funded by the government to do what a mere voluntary body could not undertake; the better endowed Irish Folklore Commission (*Coimisiún Béaloideasa Eireann*) was set up in 1935. Ways of documenting folk culture were learned in Scandinavia and an indexing system for what was gathered, based on the Uppsala model, was adapted to Ireland. The tasks of the Commission were defined as: '(a) the collection, collation and cataloguing of oral and written folklore materials, and (b) the editing and publication of such materials where thought desirable'.[20] What was in the Irish language, considered most valuable and threatened, received special emphasis.[21] Long wonder tales and hero tales were at first more eagerly sought than other genres, but shorter narratives found their way into the collections, as did much non-narrative lore. In 1971 the Department of Irish Folklore of University College Dublin incorporated the

19 Séamus Ó Duilearga (James Delargy) *Béaloideas* I (1928) 5. 20 Quoted by Michael Tierney, 'Foreword' to B. Almqvist and others (eds) *Hereditas* xi. On institutionalized Irish folklore studies, see D. Ó Giolláin *Locating Irish Folklore* 128-36. 21 'At first [full-time collectors] concentrated on the Irish-speaking districts along the southern and western sea-coasts. Traditional lore of all kinds was richest in those areas and, with the passing of time, was in greatest danger of being lost.' S. Ó Súilleabháin 'Research Opportunities in the Irish Folklore Commission', *Journal of the Folklore Institute* 7 (1970) 117.

Commission, and teaching programmes were developed. By then, more than one-and-a half million pages of informants' contributions had been gathered. A team of 'full-time' paid collectors had been employed (their number varied between three and nine).[22] The Commission also had some 'special' collectors, and unpaid 'part-time' ones, who worked in their own neighbourhood: 'These collectors knew their respective areas and the people intimately, and, what was of equal importance, they were known to the people of the areas in which they worked. They would not be mistaken for tax collectors, gunmen on the run, or whatever else a stranger in an area can be mistaken for. People had confidence in them and willingly shared what they knew with them.'[23] There were many correspondents – often schoolteachers; approximately a hundred and fifty questionnaires on specific topics were circulated. Even primary school-children were mobilized: in 1937 and 1938, following specially prepared guidelines, they filled exercise books with what they heard from their grandparents and elderly neighbours. Their main service was to provide data from parts of Ireland where little 'professional' collecting was done, or to call attention to potential informants with whom trained collectors could later work methodically. According to the card indexes in the Department of Folklore, the corpus assembled in different ways involved some two thousand collectors and some forty thousand informants; many of the latter, in the 1930s, were elderly people whose own sources could have learned their 'traditions' before the Famine. Later there were adaptations to the changing realities in Ireland (with the collection of material in English for instance, and of songs, gaining in importance), perhaps also to shifts of interest in international folkloristics: more attention was paid to 'legends', and in 1980 full-time workers were occupied in an 'Urban Folklore Project' in Dublin City which found examples of 'modern legends' (the latter term will be discussed in Chapter 13).[24] Nevertheless, the accent remained as long as possible on out-of-the way rural places.

Collectors mandated to conduct a rescue operation that had direct relevance to national concerns were not likely to be bickering about terminological fads, but their activity had theoretical implications; the organizers of the campaign were in touch with ideas aired in the international congresses they attended, or debated in international periodicals, and the Scandinavian connection remained important. Definitions of the subject could be conservative in Ireland, like this one which was given in 1967: 'Folklore is one of the oldest and most international inheritances of the human race. It brings us into close touch with a men-

22 Bríd Mahon, who acted as secretary of the Commission, noted: 'I can safely say that without exception the collectors disliked visiting Dublin and were always anxious to get back to their bases.' (*When Green Grass Grows: Memoirs of a Folklorist* 87.) 23 Bo Almqvist 'The Irish Folklore Commission: Achievement and Legacy', *Béaloideas* 45-7 (1977-9) 12. 24 Since the 1980s, another study of popular life as remembered by Dubliners has been conducted by Kevin C. Kearns, of the University of Northern Colorado: *Stoneybatter: Dublin's Inner-Urban Village; Dublin Street Life and Lore: An Oral History; Dublin Tenement Life ...* ; *Dublin Pub Life ...*

tality that embraces all countries and all times. It must not be regarded as the debris of any system of religion or theology, but as a continuation and survival of a very ancient way of thinking. Underlying its patchwork and seemingly disordered pattern is a deep, silent substratum of folk thought, which serves to maintain an unbroken link with primitive mentality.'[25] But the government that subsidized the Commission, the national-nativistic ideology summed up in the preceding chapter (see p. 358) – and the organizers' sincere devotion, also promoted conceptions of *Irish* folklore as a very special heritage which could be regarded as sacred. Continuities were posited with an earlier but by no means 'primitive' Gaelic world, and one of the particularities of Irish folklore was said to be the coexistence in it of two kinds of constituents – survivals of an age-old fund, which after all might not be so specifically Irish, and the oral persistence of supremely Irish material, formerly the written literature of a higher stratum of society: 'To this ancient, orally preserved stock of West European tradition was grafted in the course of time a portion of the literature of the upper classes and of the written tradition of the schools of native learning, common to the cultivated Gael of both Ireland and western Scotland. For a thousand years this native literary manuscript tradition had run its course side by side with, although not entirely independent of, the oral tradition of the peasant; now, by force of circumstances, the two streams of tradition were joined.'[26] The notion that at least part of what was found in folklore had first evolved among the educated class, then filtered downward, had been defended by continental folklorists – and was the subject of disputes;[27] in Ireland it did not connote debasement, but heroic preservation.

Primitivistic moods might also be expressed, as in the following remarks during the Second World War (by the Professor of Early and Medieval Irish at UCD):

Folklore, the study of the folk-mind and the investigation of the world and ways of ordinary people, is ... a reaction against the intolerant primacy of letters and the exclusive rights of the intellectual. Folklore is the charter of the liberties and rights of the lowly. In the last century the rationalists, champions of the supremacy of the 'intellect,' reigned supreme. Now it is different. The bankruptcy of the intellectuals is too apparent to be disguised ... When truth and beauty and goodness cannot be found in modern civilisation, we are forced to seek for those values in other places. The world has obviously taken a wrong turning; and men in many lands are coming to realize that, if it is to be put right, we must retrace our steps to where we strayed from the road.[28]

To have competent investigators, proper techniques of collecting had to be

25 Seán Ó Súilleabháin *Irish Folk Custom and Belief* 8. 26 J.H. Delargy *The Gaelic Storyteller* 3-4. 27 At the beginning of the twentieth century,the German Hans Naumann coined the term *gesunkenes Kulturgut* to refer to much of what was collected as folklore: it would have originated among the elite, and then 'descended' (being thus debased) when the lower stratum copied it. 28 Francis Shaw S.J. 'The Irish Folklore Commission', *Studies* 33 (1944) 36.

taught. Sean O'Sullivan or Ó Súilleabháin (1903-96), the Commission's archivist from 1935, set guidelines, listing relevant questions in *Lámhleabhar Béaloideasa* in 1937. The following extracts from the much extended English version of 1942, *A Handbook of Irish Folklore*, show that, as regarded storytelling, the aim went far beyond the mere accumulation of texts:

Write down the name, age, and full address of the person from whom the storyteller learned the tale. How long ago and under what circumstances did this happen? Try to find out, if possible, how long that particular tale has been told in the parish, and how or by whom it was introduced ... Write down an account of his (her) life from each storyteller. Give the storyteller's genealogy, if possible. Give an account of the setting in which the story was told ... How were storytellers usually induced to tell a tale? What conditions were necessary on the part of the storyteller and his audience? ... Did storytellers tell only tales of their own choice, or did they comply with requests for particular tales? Did they use gestures? Describe. Were interruptions or interjections during the telling of a story resented or welcomed by the storyteller and the audience? What was the usual type of comment or interjection by a member of the audience during the course of a tale? ... Were certain houses particularly recognised as storytelling centres? ... What types of persons usually told tales? men or women? Age of storytellers? Profession or occupation? Did men or women act as professional storytellers? ... Were storytelling competitions held locally?[29]

Among other recommendations, collectors were told to make sure that a tale had not been learned from a written source but from 'genuine popular tradition'. One should not hesitate to multiply transcriptions of the same tale: 'the more variants recorded the better'. No changes or emendations should be made 'to suit convention'. In an interview, or even a series of interviews, the collector could of course not cover all the points mentioned in the handbook, and in any case he was urged not to produce a standardized questionnaire leading in one direction: the exploration had to appear spontaneous, in a free-ranging conversation. Beside the transcription of the *béaloideas*, collectors had to keep 'diaries' in which they described the occasions of collecting, identified each informant, and if possible detailed the type of house he/she lived in, his/her general occupation, and particular ways of narrating.

The gathering of folktales met with special difficulties. All occasional contributors until the middle of this century had to write down from dictation (which decontextualized the telling and ruined the flow of live delivery), or to reconstruct from memory after the interview (which led inevitably to imprecision and possible distortion). But recording equipment appeared; in the 1930s, some full-time collectors began to travel with cumbersome Ediphone clockwork dictation machines, whose wax-cylinders had to be changed after some eight minutes. By 1937 the normal procedure was as follows:

29 Op. cit. 555-7.

The collector finds out who the most noted storytellers and custodians of tradition are in each district, visits them, draws them into talk, makes lists of stories, songs, anecdotes, etc., which they possess, and, then arranges to record from them. This is usually done round the turf-fire at night when the day's work is over. The storyteller speaks into the mouthpiece of the recording-machine the stories and songs which he has heard from his forebears. This continues until it is time for the collector to gather together his apparatus and make his way home. At his own home he transcribes from the records made by the storytellers into notebooks supplied by the Commission. These, when filled, are sent into the Commission's headquarters, where the notebooks are bound into stout volumes, catalogued, and preserved for the future researches of scholars.[30]

Padraig Mac Gréine remembered how he worked, in the same decade:

I would tell the narrator to hold the voice box close to his mouth ... then when the bell rang at the end of the cylinder, I would write down the last sentence and put on a new cylinder and remind the narrator what he had finished saying. At night, after I had taken my tea, I'd transcribe the cylinders. It might take two or three hours to transcribe a story. I wrote exactly as the narrator spoke, that was to present English as it was spoken in the Midlands, as it was spoken then ... When I finished the box of cylinders, I'd take them to the bus station and send them back to Dublin to be shaved.[31]

Indeed, the cylinders were normally pared and recycled after transcription; few have survived, so that it is no longer possible to experience the vocal artistry of most speakers. The recording itself created unnatural conditions of performance, but many old Irish storytellers soon became expert in speaking to the machine, and delighted in hearing their own voices played back to them afterwards. From 1947, disc-cutting machines began to be used, but were still heavy. The wire recorder appeared in Ireland around 1955, and portable tape recorders later simplified the collectors' task. Non-verbal aspects of the narrator's performance and the listeners' responses still could not be captured; video-recording came too late for the most celebrated masters of the spoken word, but some of the 'last remaining Gaelic storytellers' began to be recorded thus in the 1980s.[32]

The Irish collectors who worked for many years in the field often spent a long time with the same persons or returned regularly, and developed personal relations with them; their attitude towards the storytellers and other informants they worked with could mix intimacy and reverence. The materials they gathered now constitute the enormous holdings of the Department of Irish Folklore at University College Dublin. The following pages sift through statements made by persons in charge of the Commission; the rest of the chapter, and much of the next one, is essentially a selection of what is said about so-called traditional

30 S. O'Delargy 'The Irish Folklore Commision and its Work', *Travaux du Congrès International de Folklore, Paris 1937* 38-9. 31 Interviewed in 1977 by George Gmelch, *To Shorten the Road* 13. 32 'The Dying Art of the Storyteller is Preserved for Posterity', in *Ireland of the Welcome* 35 (1986) no. 2.

Irish storytellers in the relatively small but perhaps representative part of the archives I have explored.[33]

It is only natural to begin with the remarkable evidence given by James H. Delargy – or Séamus Ó Duilearga (1899-1980) – who was the driving force from the start. A graduate in Celtic studies at UCD, he worked as Douglas Hyde's assistant. In 1928 he studied in Sweden under the direction of von Sydow and Åke Campbell. His interest in folklore had been awakened by storytellers he heard while holidaying in his native County Antrim. He was one of the founding members of the Folklore of Ireland Society in 1927, by which time he had already been collecting in County Kerry. He later gave his views on the importance of the task and described his encounters with storytellers, in various lectures and articles often harking back to the same subjects.

In a speech delivered in 1937, he outlined the field to be covered: 'In Ireland we have an immense body of oral literature and folklore, in extent and variety incomparable in Western Europe.' But 'although Irish popular tradition is still a living force it is receding swiftly before the new international culture of the towns. It is richest where the Irish language is strongest, and its custodians are among the older generation'.[34] He did favour narratives, and particularly when they were in Irish, but in an article published in 1942 he insisted that one should collect much more than tales, and not only in the Gaelic part of Ireland: 'I am not content to know something of the fireside tales of Kerry or the folksongs of Connemara. I am interested in the folklore of Ireland, in the speech of Ireland, in the geography of Ireland. Ulster planter and Leinster palesman, Norman and Saxon, they are all Irish, and in their traditions or what has been preserved of them I am equally interested.' He found in Ireland 'more of medieval literary remains than anywhere else in western Europe. There is in the Gaeltacht a wealth of oral traditions which has preserved the memory of custom and belief and the Gaelic *Weltanschauung* at one time common to most of Ireland and Scotland – indeed common all over the Atlantic culture-district when the world was young'. But the work of the Commission should 'spread over the Gaelic border into the rest of Ireland whose tongue is English but whose heart is Irish. In every townland throughout the length and breadth of Ireland are still living men and women who have preserved in English much that the present Gaeltacht never knew or has forgotten. And all this too we are taking down. We know no linguistic or political borders.' Indeed, the Commission also collected in Northern Ireland. (As a remedy for any lack of humility, I must swallow another passage from the same text: 'No one can understand Irish folklore if he does not know English, nor can he understand it if he has a polite smattering of Irish only. Still more difficult to understand than

---

33 Only one quarter of the holdings are in English, and I am far from having read all of that.
34 *Travaux du Congrès International de Folklore, Paris 1937* 37-8. On Delargy's 'Vision of Irish Folklore', see D. Ó Giolláin *Locating Irish Folklore* 136-40.

either English or Irish are the Irish people who speak these languages.')[35] In his introduction to Sean O'Sullivan's *Handbook* (1942), Delargy voiced his patriotism:

We have suffered great cultural losses as a nation, and can ill afford to let pass unrecorded and unappreciated the spirit of Ireland, the traditions of the historic Irish nation. It was for the old ways of life – for the *petite patrie* – that our forefathers fought and died, more than for kings, principalities and powers. The traditions of Ireland are the background of our history; they have helped in large measure to mould the Ireland of the past; they are part and parcel of the Irish nation of to-day. We desire to see them known and honoured, for the Ireland of to-morrow will have need of them, finding in them a source of inspiration and pride.[36]

Elsewhere, he summed up what, according to him, should be the folklorists' guiding principle, namely, respect for their informants: 'The only real authorities on Irish tradition are the storytellers; they belong to a different world from the commentators. And even the best-equipped collector, no matter how much he knows of the material he is recording, feels at times, or should feel, like a child in an infant school under the tutelage of a benevolent but omniscient master. One must cultivate an academic humility and a feeling of respect when working with these exponents of ancient lore.'[37] In a later text, he generalized about the informants he was relying upon:

All the story-tellers whom I and my colleagues have known are country people, of the small farmer-fisherman type, or farm labourers. I have never got a story from anyone else. The custodians of the oral archive of memory have been a gifted élite of the illiterate poor of the centuries, a tiny fraction of the population, be it noted, for it is not given to all to be a story-teller or a singer. What the necessary conditions are to belong to this chosen – or, rather, self-chosen – few are not so easy to determine: First of all, a good memory; secondly, the blessed gift of intelligent illiteracy which is the mainstay of memory, and, above all, a rude but nevertheless genuine artistic feeling, added to a desire to save something of value which might easily be lost. A story-teller must also have something of the actor in him, for he is the sole interpreter on the stage by the footlight of the turf-fire of the events of the tale, the delineator of the character of the various actors who pass to and fro across the stage of the narrative.[38]

A lecture he delivered in 1945, *The Gaelic Story-Teller*,[39] remains the most authoritative account of the subject; I shall repeatedly refer to it later in this chapter and in the next one.

Delargy's various publications contain successive sketches of the same indi-

---

35 'The Study of Irish Folklore', *The Dublin Magazine* 17 (1942) 20-4.) **36** Op. cit. v-vi. **37** From a lecture at Kilkee, 19 May 1969, quoted in *Dal gCais* 6 (1982), 119. **38** 'Irish Tales and Story-tellers', in H. Kuhn and K. Schier (eds) *Märchen, Mythos, Dichtung* 68. **39** 'The Sir John Rhys Memorial Lecture, 1945', *Proceedings of the British Academy* 31(1946). Reissued

vidual storytellers. The first one he worked with, from 1923, was Seán Ó Conaill (1835-1931), a farmer and fisherman at Cillrialaigh near Ballinskelligs, County Kerry, in 'the last of all inhabited places on the edge of the known world. Here I met the man in whose tales and traditions I found the inspiration to collect or have collected, in so far as in me lay, the unwritten oral literature and tradition of the people of Ireland.'[40] His family had lived in the same place for at least five generations and he himself had never left his native district: 'He had never been to school and could neither speak nor understand English. He was a man of old-time nobility with great respect for the oral tradition ... The people of the place thought Seán was sometimes rather odd. He had never been in the least irrational, but he had a certain strange way that some of his neighbours found incomprehensible. Seán had always the greatest respect for his tales and anecdotes, and he would have preferred to lose his worldly goods than to forget them.'[41] Delargy repeatedly evoked the evenings he spent in Ó Conaill's two-roomed thatched cottage, writing down from his dictation some two hundred pieces of prose narrative: 'From the doorway one gazed right down into the sea, and the distant roar of the waves crept into the kitchen and was the ever-present background of the folk-tale. While I wrote from Seán's dictation, the neighbours would drop in, one by one, or in small groups, and they would listen in patience until the last word of the tale was written. Then the old story-teller would take a burning ember from the fire, light his pipe, lean back in his chair, and listen to the congratulations of the listeners, who, although they had probably often heard the tale before, found pleasure in hearing it again.'[42] In the diary he kept, Delargy gave an account of what must have been one of the last encounters (so far, the work had been done without a recording machine):

Saturday, 12 April 1930. Seán Ó Súilleabháin, Seán Óg, his son, and I went west to Cillrialaig. We had a horse and cart, and we put the Ediphone carefully in the middle of the cart, with a big lot of straw under it and about it for fear of its being damaged on the miserable uneven road. The whole hamlet gathered into Seán Ó Conaill's house to hear the wonderful instrument which had come to us from America to collect the old-time lore. The horse was unyoked, the machine was taken inside, and put on the kitchen-table. I lifted the cover, and put it (the machine) in order. The little house was full to the beams; you would find it hard to walk between them, the people were so packed together. 'The greater the novelty in a house, the more attention it gets!' Then I asked Seán to tell an *eachtra* [Irish tale]. '*Airiú* [ah!], dear man, you have me picked as bare as a shorn goose!' said he. 'My stories have been told in the other part of my life!' But to please us all, he took the speaking tube, and told a short little *eachtra* of the Cailleach Bhéarra [the Hag of Beara']. As soon as he had said his say, I asked him to put

by the University of Chicago in 1969. **40** 'Once Upon a Time', in G. Jenkins (ed.) *Studies in Folk Life* 50. **41** Foreword to *Sean Ó Conaill's Book. Stories and Traditions from Iveragh* (tr. M. MacNeill) vi, x; first published in Irish as *Leabhar Sheáin i Chonaill*, it includes the informant's own account of his life. **42** 'Irish Tales and Story-Tellers', in *Märchen, Mythos, Dichtung* 73.

the tube to his ear. The talk came out to him in a flow, every word and every turn as clear and direct as he had said. His eyes dilated, and one can say he was amazed, and so was the whole company.[43]

A witness described one of J.H. Delargy's earlier working sessions with Ó Conaill:

I had heard from Séamas that they were midway in one of the major tales which took two nights to tell at dictation speed: 'The Guileful Blanait' (*Blánait na Ceilge*). Séamas had told me how far the tale had gone at the previous session and had shown me, with the light of the bicycle lamp, the last sentence he had written in the notebook. 'Seán will begin with those very words tonight, to link up the story, and will carry on in the same words and sequences that were used the first time he heard them, fifty years ago.' I knew already how immutable were the form and substance of the ancient tales, but I noted the sentence Séamas showed me ... , just to make sure. And sure enough, when Seán saw that we were all seated and that Séamas was waiting, pen in hand to begin, he took off his cap, lowered his eyes, though the massive head was still high against the wall and tuned his voice to the oracular tones of the shanachies ...

For me that was a memorable experience. Even for those who had heard the tale again and again and could recite it themselves without dropping a word, the recital was a display of the ancient art of the shanachie at its rarest and best. It proved too much for Séamas to listen to the engrossing story and, at the same time, write it down in cold script. Long before Seán had reached the inevitable end, the scribe had closed his book and delivered himself to the free and delectable enjoyment of the tale and the telling. Tomorrow was another day. He would come again.[44]

Some twenty years after this scene, Delargy was applying von Sydow's distinction between two kinds of potential informants (cf. p. 381): 'Really outstanding storytellers such as Seán Ó Conaill are now rarely to be met with in Ireland. Most of those from whom folk-tales have been recorded in recent years have been passive bearers of tradition; that is to say, they have remembered many tales, but through lack of opportunity, natural shyness or unfavourable circumstances, have neither practised telling their tales, nor given others the chance of learning them.'[45]

By 1929, he had started collecting in North Clare, where he thought he would be the first to search for folktales. He referred to this experience in various publications, quoting from the diary he had kept. One of the first houses he visited turned out to be that of a storyteller, Seán Carún (Johnny Carey): 'When I called he was not to be found anywhere for a long time, but at length he returned, and we spent the evening together. Some months later, I learned from

43 Quoted in *Seán Ó Conaill's Book* 423. 44 Joseph O'Connor 'The Last of the Shanachies', *The Capuchin Annual 1958* 371-2. The story of Cú Chulainn's slaying of Cú Roi with the help of the latter's treacherous wife Bláthnat is found in medieval manuscripts and in Keating's history. 45 'The Gaelic Story-teller – No Living Counterpart in Western Christendom', *Ireland of the Welcome* May-June 1952, 4.

his wife that on the second occasion, when he was not to be found, he had gone into a cave in the mountain above his house to wrestle with his memory, striving to recall tales which he had heard from a native of the Aran Islands some forty years before, and which he had forgotten: he had returned in triumph with three of these tales restored to their home in his memory, and I wrote them down.'[46] The presence of a collector could provoke a change from a passive attitude to an active performing role, and perhaps also increase the audience's estimation of the performers. The fact is that people flocked to the place where Delargy was working:

In the evening John Carey, junr., and I went to Paitsín Ó Flannagáin, and then all three of us walked down the hill to Anthony Maloney's house, which was ablaze with light. A huge fire was lighting in the room reserved for us, and a large crowd of people had gathered. Anthony had selected some eight singers and storytellers and these were brought into what must be the doctor's room when he has his dispensary. It was a small room, and the rest of those assembled had to wait in a larger room outside, but the door to the small room was open and the others could hear what was going on. Anthony kept order, but the people themselves were so interested that they listened with great attention and in complete silence to the songs and stories which lasted for five hours![47]

Later, the Ediphone seemed to revive a perhaps languishing taste for storytelling:

[Tómas Ó Húir] was born in 1845. He was an archive of tradition himself, a fine old man of stately manners, and unaffected courtesy ... We pushed against a wall of wind, with our heads down, and at length arrived at a neat thatched house, with a pillared gateway surmounted by two huge white stones. The house crouches for shelter among the sand-dunes, and the roar of the sea and of the wind which drums at one's ears outside is stilled when one gets inside and the doors are made fast. A huge fire on the hearth; an old man of patriarchal appearance with a well-cared white beard in a súgán chair beside the fire, wearing a frock-coat and billy-cock hat – there was old Tomás Ó Húir, waiting eagerly together with his son John, and John's wife and son, and some neighbours, for the arrival of the 'Ireeshian' [a person interested in the Irish language] with the wonderful machine which was to take down all the stories ... Well, we set to work. The first thing to do is to get the speaker to sing a verse of a song or the like, to ask him to put the tube of the Ediphone to his ear, and then to sit back and see what happens! This is a time-honoured ritual, and the effect is always the same. In this case I asked Tomás to start with *sean-phaidreacha* [old prayers] which he says morning and evening. He did so. I asked him then to put the mouthpiece to his ear. He took the tube up slowly, put it to his ear and listened. He was amazed and a bit startled, for this was the first time he had ever heard his own voice. He called out across the kitchen, and the others came eagerly but slowly forward and listened. From that on there was no difficulty. Tomás could not be kept back ... I went to Tomás early next day to continue my

46 *The Gaelic Story-Teller* 14.   **47** Quoted in Dáithí Ó hÓgáin's introduction to *Leabhar Stiofáin Uí Ealaoire* xviii.

work of recording. The old man had slept little last night, but spent the time trying to remember stories, with the result that I have now the names of about fifty tales which he has to give. But I should have come years ago to record his tales ...

[Another session:] It was 7.30 p.m. before I was able to walk through the storm to Ó Húir's and the old man was restless and worried wondering why I hadn't come. I questioned Tomás about many tales, and he had obviously been thinking deeply and probing into the corners of his memory for he had many more to add to the ever-growing list. He must have had a vast number of tales ten years ago, but he cannot remember more than 50 to 70 now.[48]

Still in North Clare, Delargy counted Stiofán Ó hEalaoire (1862-1944) among the best storytellers he had ever heard: 'On 15th August Stiofán came to see me and told me the finest tale I have heard before or since – and I write these lines twenty-five years later. This was *Conall Gulban* [the hero of a sixteenth-century romance very popular in manuscripts, from which it entered oral tradition to become 'possibly the most popular of all the hero tales'].[49] It was not only an excellent version but Stiofán showed himself as a really first-rate artist – a magnificent story in inimitable style. It took nearly two hours to tell, and he spoke very fast'.[50]

Delargy also portrayed storytellers from other regions. In West Cork, in 1935, he visited one of the last storytellers in his district:

Ó Murachú was a tall, well-built handsome man. He had been blind since childhood and had lived quite alone in this backward spot for many years, his sole companion a huge and very intelligent sheep-dog. Well, of course, following Irish and oriental custom, we first talked of many things which had no bearing on the purpose of my visit – the weather, the price of cattle, the wet harvest, politics, but eventually we came down to business. Yes, he knew a few tales – but he hadn't told them for years – the 'young people nowadays did not want to hear them any more' – he was out of practice. But there are many things in an old man's head if there be someone to question him. First of all, I had to show the old man that I knew many tales myself, and, finally, I told one tale (which I guessed he knew) wrongly so that he would interrupt me! This little trick always works with a real story-teller. So the old man told me that the version I had was wrong, but that *he* knew the right way to tell it, and then he began. I knew the tale by heart, but it was a real pleasure to hear it told by a master as the light of a flickering turf-fire flitted over his blind face, and the hills themselves seemed to listen, so profound was the stillness in which this age-old tale was told. His Irish was a delight to listen to, for this corner of Ireland was once a land of poetry, where verse came as easily as prose to the lips of southern peasants. As the night wore on, under careful questioning the list of tales grew – it ran to 26 numbers when I rose to go.[51]

---

48 'Notes on the Oral Tradition of Thomond', *Journal of the R.S.A.I.* 95 (1965) 140-1. 49 Seán Ó Suilleabháin *Storytelling in Irish Tradition* 37. 50 *Leabhar Stiofáin Uí Ealaoire* xix-xx. 51 'Irish Tales and Story-Tellers', in H. Kuhn and K. Schier (eds) *Märchen, Mythos, Dichtung* 76.

A similar scene took place in Connemara:

I shall never forget, as long as I live, the tale I now heard. It was AaTh 313,[52] and although I have often heard it I never met anyone who told it so well. Ó Briain was the finest story-teller I have ever met – or ever shall meet. He would have been regarded as a good storyteller 500 years ago. A few months afterwards, I brought a dictaphone to the house, and now when I wish to recapture the magic of that amazing version I listen again to the tale and hear the voice of the dead story-teller. On that occasion thirty years ago I wrote the following in my diary:

'At 4 p.m. to Seán Ó Briain where I recorded AaTh 313, the finest story I ever heard, and also wrote from dictation 21 large quarto pages of the hero tale, Sir Slanders.[53] It was somewhat difficult to write as there were five of the old man's grandchildren playing on the floor of the tiny house, and these ran in and out chasing hens and chickens, dogs and geese which persisted in coming in through the open door. The house is situated within a few yards of the sea, and in a high tide, the water seeps in under the door and comes up the floor "but", said the old fellow, "it never yet put out the fire, thanks be to God!" The old man had his eyes on the grazing cattle which he could see through the little window beside him, and now and again he would stumble to the door, giving orders in unmistakable language to the children to keep out the cattle from the patch of cultivated ground among the boulders which he called the "garden".'[54]

It is now admitted that even ethnographic accounts may aim at rhetorical effects. In the corpus of portraits of storytellers by Delargy, certain devices heighten atmosphere and attitudes. That the general tone should be celebratory is natural: who would systematically forgo comfort if it were to meet despicable people and collect worthless things? The portraits combine epithets ('old', 'patriarchal', 'strange') or abstract nouns ('natural shyness', 'deep perception', 'nobility', 'courtesy') and indirect presentation by actions (the simple but perhaps ritual motions in and around the house) or appearance ('a white beard' ...) with the suggested links or analogies between the storyteller and his surroundings ('on all sides stretched a wilderness', 'it was getting dark but there was still a glimmer of light', 'the roar of the sea and of the wind', 'the hills themselves seemed to listen' ...). These old people were not supermen, and were shown amid simple 'realistic' details of everyday life – yet they appeared in faraway places and seemed in touch with some cosmic natural forces. There was a sense of 'tableau': freezing in place and outside time what was about to vanish, or already survived only in memory.

What had been collected for the Irish Folklore Commission had to be catalogued, and if possible, published;[55] when the Department of Irish Folklore at

---

52 'The Girl as Helper in the Hero's Flight', in Aarne and Thompson's *The Types of the Folktale*. 53 Caol (slender) Glas, who married the daughter of the King of Greece – or Caol an Iarainn, the champion runner who helped the Fianna. 54 'Irish Tales and Story-Tellers' 77–8. 55 In *Béaloideas: The Journal of the Folklore of Ireland Society* and in a series of books under the auspices of *Comhairle Bhéaloideas Eireann* (The Folklore of Ireland Council).

UCD took over, there were also teaching duties. All this required a staff based in Dublin. Sean O'Sullivan, one of the schoolteachers roped in by Delargy in 1935, analysed and filed the material received from collectors and published parts of it;[56] but he also had direct contact with some informants and scrutinized what had been garnered from others – 'each like Oisín after the Fianna, the almost last of a centuries-long line of accomplished narrators of tales'.[57] With R.T. Christiansen he compiled *The Types of the Irish Folktale*: oikotypes of the international repertoire catalogued by Aarne and Thompson (see p. 379) – the number of versions dealt with, in 1956, amounted to 43,000. For more specifically Irish narratives, a type-index is outlined in O'Sullivan's *Handbook of Irish Folklore*. He also wrote a short account of *Storytelling in Irish Tradition*, but it concerns the different genres represented in the common repertoire rather than narrators' techniques. Kevin Danaher (Caoimhín Ó Danachair), who had taught Irish at Uppsala, was for a while the specialist of sound recordings and later became the 'ethnologist' of the Commission, which means he was responsible more particularly for the study of customs and material culture (house types, agricultural implements); he also collected and published tales, especially from his native County Limerick. On J.H. Delargy's retirement the direction was entrusted to Professor Bo Almqvist, who had studied at Uppsala, worked in Iceland and collected in Ireland (particularly around Dunquin); through him, contacts between Nordic and Irish folklore studies were maintained. His successor as head of the department, Professor Séamas Ó Catháin, has collected in Donegal and North Mayo and edited material from the manuscripts.

Those who did essentially fieldwork and were constantly in touch with informants often portrayed storytellers or described their performances. Without claiming to call the roll of honour of outstanding Irish storytellers in the twentieth century, the present section will offer a few excerpts from the rich documentation thus amassed.

One of the most famous informants in West Cork was Amhlaoibh Ó Luínse (1872-1947), a farmer who lived near Ballyvourney: an entire number (35-6) of *Béaloideas* is devoted to his versions of international tales, and other issues contain a number of his hero-tales; a volume of his miscellaneous lore, *Seanachas Amhlaoibh Í Luínse*, was edited in 1980. Seán Ó Cróinín, who worked for the Commission from 1938 to 1944, had collected this material, and also filled 1500 pages with stories from Seán Ó hAo, in Carbery on the south-west coast.[58] We have two different views of Tadhg Ó Buachalla (Tim Buckley), a *seanchaí* and raconteur rather than a master of the higher repertoire. As 'the Tailor' he was

56 *Scéalta Cráibhteacha*; *Folktales of Ireland*; *The Folklore of Ireland*; *Legends from Ireland*. More information can be found in P. Lysaght 'Ó Súilleabháin, Seán', in *Enzyklopädie des Märchens* 10. 442-6. **57** 'Irish Oral Tradition', in B. Ó Cuív ed. *A View of the Irish Language* 55. **58** Part of this material was published as *Seanachas ó Chairbre* in 1985, edited, like the other volume, by the collector's brother Donncha.

the subject of Eric Cross' book (see p. 370), which was not composed according to modern folkloristic requirements:[59] the writer had frequented his model but never written down anything during their conversations, which took place in English, and he recreated from memory his impressions of an extremely witty survivor. In 1942, Seán Ó Cróinín recorded and then transcribed what Buckley actually said, in Irish. Cross's book has lifelike qualities, whereas what was collected with an Ediphone recorder is less evocative but more accurate; the two sources may be complementary. Ó Cróinín's material was published, then translated,[60] and the editor's introduction sums up what was remembered of the by then long-dead informant:

The Tailor was a remarkable folk raconteur with an unconventional narrative flair. By way of introduction, for example, he might initially treat his audience to some jesting witticism, or to what would seem to be an inconsequential triviality, but from which he would proceed to some substantial yarn or traditional tale, or to tell of things wondrous or adventurous – all subtly related to his introductory levity. He might, too, deftly interpolate, between tales or anecdotes, a proverb or speech expression prompted by what he had just related, but he never would be put off his track – proving the excellence of his narratory craft ... The Tailor too, in congenial company, was a great conversationalist. On everything he would have his own particular comprehension or solution, often quite out of the top of his head, but displaying an intelligence and an imagination which enabled him to unravel everything, rightly or wrongly, to his own satisfaction. His facility in that regard was really extraordinary, especially for one who, as he himself has informed us, was nearing nine years of age before he ever went to school and was only thirteen when apprenticed to tailoring. Good though he was as a storyteller and conversationalist he knew hardly any of the great romantic or valour tales, though he held in the highest regard those who had these.[61]

County Kerry was rich ground for collectors. One of the first to work there for the Commission, Tadhg Ó Murchú, was very close to his informants. Born in 1896 on a farm near Waterville, he heard folktales told by members of his family. From 1925 he was an itinerant teacher of Irish in adult night classes. He contributed to the Irish Folklore Society journal *Béaloideas* as early as 1927, and from 1935 to 1958 was a full-time collector working in his native county. The American Richard M. Dorson, who accompanied him in 1951, saw how well accepted he was by those he interviewed and recorded: 'The observer notices curiously how the rural families now take for granted the visits of the field collector. He has become an institution, like the priest and the postman, and receives a friendly welcome and often a high tea when he arrives. The old men respond eagerly to his coming, both from social pleasure and from a vague

59 See James M. Cahalan 'Tailor Tim Buckley: Folklore, Literature and *Seanchas an Táilliúra*', *Éire-Ireland* 14 (1979) No. 2, and B. Almqvist 'The Tailor and the Critics', *Béaloideas* 48-9 (1980-1). 60 Aindrias Ó Muimhneacháin (ed.) *Seanchas an Táilliúra* (1978), tr. as *Stories from the Tailor* (1989). 61 *Stories from the Tailor* 7-8.

appreciation of the significance of his work.'[62] As said earlier, the collectors for the Irish Foklore Commission had to hand in, along with the texts they had gathered, notebooks (diaries) containing precise information on their work and their informants. This portrait by Tadhg Ó Murchú is quoted in Delargy's *The Gaelic Storyteller*:

His piercing eyes are on my face, his limbs are trembling, as, immersed in his story, and forgetful of all else, he puts his very soul into the telling. Obviously much affected by his narrative, he uses a great deal of gesticulation, and by the movement of his body, hands, and head, tries to convey hate and anger, fear and humour, like an actor in a play. He raises his voice at certain passages, at other times it becomes almost a whisper. He speaks fairly fast, but his enunciation is at all times clear. I have never met anyone who told his tales with more artistry and effect than this very fine old storyteller. He says that his storytelling has been spoiled by being forced, through love of the tales, to tell them in English to young people who did not know Irish. In that way, through lack of practice and an appreciative Irish-speaking audience, he had lost command over his vast store of tales, and in the end had forgotten almost all of them. He does not like to tell his tales on the Ediphone recording machine, as it hampers the movements he considers essential to heighten the effect of the story. Once he became so exhausted that he gave up in the middle of a tale, but I coaxed him to continue.[63]

On the Great Blasket island it was possible to study a close-knit community (see pp. 363ff). At the beginning of the twentieth century, among approximately a hundred and fifty persons living in one cluster of houses there were five or six noted storytellers (four of them women), but everybody seems to have known tales and legends: 'While members of the audience might not be capable of such sustained performance themselves, they were nevertheless familiar with the plot of many tales and might interject during the performance in order to point out any omissions or errors.'[64] The common repertoire included lays of the Fianna, international tales, and relations of events from the storyteller's own life which could adopt the ancient style. The older generation was illiterate. The islanders lost their meager livelihood – fishing – and most young people emigrated; the diffusion of printed material changed the attitudes of the others: 'From the outbreak of the first world war, and particularly as a result of the changing political scene, people's attention was focusing more sharply on outside events. Newspapers fed discussion and debate which began to displace islanders' interest in storytelling.'[65]

We saw in the preceding chapter that Blasket visitors, in the first three decades of the century, often were scholars interested in Celtic philology and

---

62 *Folklore and Fakelore* 187. In an article, *Scéalaithe dob aithnid dom'* ('Storytellers I know'), Ó Murchú sketched two dozen of them, from his grandmother to those he heard when working for the Commission. *Béaloideas* 18 (1949) 3-44. **63** *The Gaelic Story-Teller* 16. **64** *The Blaskets: A Heritage Report* 8 (by a research team directed by Patrick Ó Flannagáin). **65** Ibid. 89-90.

impressed by the noble archaism of the life to be observed there; they would not have called themselves folklorists. Things changed in the 1930s. Kenneth Jackson was a Celtic scholar, but he published a collection of Peig Sayers' tales in *Béaloideas* in 1938.[66] In 1940 Seosamh Ó Dálaigh (Joe Daly), a full-time collector between 1936 and 1951, began to work with the same informant when she was still on the island, then more assiduously in 1942-43 when she had returned to the mainland, and again in 1950-1:

I wish I had the ability to describe the scene in Peig Sayers' home in Dunquin on a winter night when the stage was set for the *seanchaí*. The evening meal was over, the day's work done, the family rosary finished. On the hearth glowed a small peat-fire and on the side-wall an oil-lamp gave a dim light. Peig dominated the scene, seated on a lower chair right in front of the fire (this was most unusual in the locality; *bean a' tí* , the woman of the house, usually seated herself at the side) and smoked her pipe. Mícheál her brother-in-law sat with his vamps (stockinged feet) to the fire at one side of her and Mike her son at the other. When the visitors arrived (for all gathered to the Sayers house when Peig was there, to listen to her from supper-time till midnight) the chairs were moved back and the circle increased. News was swapped, and the news often gave lead for the night's subject, death, fairies, weather, crops.[67]

Much material was collected from and by her son, Mícheál Ó Gaoithín (1904-74): thousands of pages written by him are in the archives of the Department of Irish Folklore at UCD. Bo Almqvist has compared mother and son:

On the level of style and performance, we ... note a stark contrast between Peig's all but classical, smooth and even-flowing way of telling and Mícheál's *Sturm-und-Drang*-like, nervous, dramatic and staccato delivery. Symptomatic of this is the use of interjections – such as *mhuise, dhera, is ea, am baiste* – which occur remarkably more often in Mícheál's renderings than in Peig's. Something similar holds true about oaths, insults and other strong expressions. Mícheál seems to take a pleasure in having his characters address each other as devils, fools (*diabhal, amadán*) and the like – often in instances where Boccaccio [whose *Decameron* he adapted in Irish and partly included in his 'traditional' repertoire] has nothing corresponding – while Peig only sparingly resorts to this kind of language. Another way in which Mícheál is more eloquent, or – if you would – verbose than Peig is in the use of strings of synonymous expressions and alliterating word pairs, e.g. *fiach is fianscoraíocht, searc agus síorghrá*. The reasons for this preference of Mícheál's are likely to be twofold: his familiarity with written Irish romances where such phrases are legion (as we have seen, Mícheál, unlike Peig, read Irish and was well read) and the fact that he to a much greater extent than Peig told the long and elaborate Fenian tales – considered to be the prerogative of men – where such expressions also abound.[68]

66 Reissued in book form as *Scéalta ón mBlascaod* in 1998. 67 S. Ó Dálaigh, quoted in the introduction to Peig Sayers *An Old Woman's Reflections* xii-xiii. He collected about two hundred tales from her. Another large collection was made by the Swiss linguist Heinrich Wagner and partly published in *Oral Literature from Dunquin* (Belfast, 1983). 68 'The Mysterious Mícheál Ó Gaoithín', *Béaloideas* 58 (1990) 122-3.

In the Dingle peninsula, Seosamh Ó Dálaigh collected from Muiris Sheáin Connor and from Pats Dhónaill Ó Ciobháin, whose tales are said to have filled 500 Ediphones cylinders.

As noted above, J. Delargy made the main collection of tales in North Clare. Kevin Danaher and others collected in West Limerick. Findings were plentiful in County Galway, and the parish of Carna was celebrated as particularly rich in storytellers. One of them, Éamon a Búrc (1864-1942), who had emigrated to America and returned lame at seventeen, became a tailor and was 'possibly the most accomplished narrator of folktales who has lived in our own time'.[69] He excelled at the long hero-tale and also told fairy legends. Liam Costello (Liam Mac Coisdeala, 1908-96) collected his stories from 1928: 'During the years I visited Éamon he would never boast about the extent or variety of his knowledge; his attitude was quite the opposite, always making little account of himself. He would say he had never made a practice of storytelling as had those who came before him, and I believe sure enough that he told me some stories – especially some of the long heroic tales – which he had never told a second time.'[70] The same collector also said:

He was usually quiet, shy, retiring. But when he took on himself the role of storyteller he handled the business like no other. He had an attractive speaking manner although he was over-rapid at times; the narration was duly suited, calm and quiet, or lively and vigorous, to the occasion, without undue recourse to exaggerated gesture or the like. He was a true artist ... He expresses himself with extraordinary clarity and directness. Often the thought continues to evolve when it is already partly dressed in words, so that the storyteller adds qualifying phrases and afterthoughts, and at times interrupts himself, fired by the very process of his thought, or perhaps by his vision.[71]

According to Delargy, only part of his repertoire could be recorded:

Perhaps the memory I cherish most of all is the last message of an old Galway storyteller from whom we had recorded 158 tales. One of these ran to 34,000 words. He died before we could get the rest – and we had drawn up a list of 150 more. Well, poor Éamonn Burke died, and that was the end of the tales, for they went with him, with a wealth of imagery, of thrust and parry, and with all the other traditional graces associated with the lost art of medieval story-telling. A short time before his death he told a friend of mine to send me this message: 'When I am dead, bury me in the old graveyard of Muigh-inis, beside the sea, where I can hear the waves on the beach, and the cry of the sea-birds, and let you and Liam Costello come to my grave and raise the three keens of sorrow over me'.[72]

In Mayo, one also met people who told long wonder tales, as well as entertain-

69 Sean O'Sullivan *The Folktales of Ireland* 262. 70 *Béaloideas* xvi (1946) quoted and translated by Kevin O'Nolan in his edition of a Búrc's long tale *Eochair Mac Rí in Éirinn* 19. 71 *Eochair* 29, 177. Another volume, *Éamon a Búrc: Scéalta*, gives a sampling of his repertoire. 72 'Irish Tales and Storytellers' 74.

ers who specialized in short jokes and witty remarks. Others conveyed only local legends and personal memories, like this woman from Ballinrobe portrayed in the 1940s:

Mrs Flannery, from whom I have collected most of the information in this manuscript, is well over eighty years of age. She is a lively alert little woman with an intelligent face and a friendly word for everyone who happens to come in contact with her ... Every night when the work is finished and the lamp is lighted, she sits on her favourite chair, a big comfortable-looking bed-chair, beside the fire, and she entertains the family and any callers who may have dropped in for the evening to a varied selection of tales about ghosts and fairies and seanchas of every kind. There is no need for any person to talk once Mrs Flannery has started, and nothing delights her more than to see everybody around her listening attentively ... Instead of tiring as the night goes on Mrs Flannery becomes more and more talkative. One story reminds her of another ... She is, however, at her best when describing some incident in her past life – for instance the death of her mother-in-law. She can recall the scene so vividly that for the moment one can almost hear the jingle of gold sovereigns as the old woman on her deathbed counted them from a stocking, one by one on to a plate, and left instructions as to how they were to be divided. This story becomes all the more realistic as the 'cailleach' [in traditional houses of the north-west, a small outshot in which a bed is fitted] in which the old woman died is just to the back of Mrs Flannery's chair. As she carries on with the story describing the priest's visit, and his answer (she is dying a nice natural death) to her query of what he thought of the patient, and the last few days of the old woman's life 'when she became very quiet and wasn't doing any talking at all' (the old woman during her life was as great a talker as Mrs Flannery herself is), one cannot help looking in the direction of the 'cailleach' just to make sure that there is nobody in it. Mrs Flannery is a firm believer in fairies and ghosts and does not at all approve of people who are inclined to be sceptical about them. She knows of many people who have been 'away with' or had contacts with the fairies, so she sees no reason why anyone should doubt their existence.[73]

Donegal was a major repository of oral lore. Mícheál Ó hIghne (or Ó Híne), of Atharach near Teelin, was one of the storytellers from whom Seán Ó hEochaidh, a native of the region who had started in life as a fisherman, collected between 1935 and 1983.[74] In *The Gaelic Storyteller*, J.H. Delargy summed up and particularly praised the data this collector had gathered:

Ó hEochaidh points out that the old story-tellers seemed to be loath to tell folk-tales in their own homes, and would rather go to a *toigh áirneáil* [*teach airneáin*: a house frequented by night-visitors – there was one in every townland] than tell their tales in the presence of their own families. In the congenial atmosphere of the house of story-telling, undisturbed by the noise and prattle of children, their sensitive artistry was appreciated by the grown-up audience, mainly men, for whom these tales were intended ... The teller

---

73 IFC 1015: 121-3. Written by Bridie Molloy (also known as Brigid Ní Maolmhnaidh or Bríd Ní Ghamhnáin). **74** *Síscéalta ó Thír Chonaill: Fairy Legends from Donegal* published in 1977.

of Finn- and hero-tales was held in highest esteem, and his tales were more popular than the shorter and more realistic stories ...

An old Teilionn [Teelin] story-teller named Dónal Eoin MacBriarty was dying. A friend went to see him. The dying man had his face turned to the wall, and had apparently said good-bye to this world; but on hearing the voice of his old friend, he turned around slowly in the bed, and, fixing his eyes upon his visitor, he said: 'Is that you, Hughie Hegarty?' 'Yes,' said Hughie. 'Give me your hand,' said the old story-teller. 'You are welcome. Sit down there until I tell you the last story I shall tell in this world.' He began the story then, and took over an hour to tell it. It was a tale his friend had never heard before. As he came towards the end, he faltered, but continued, although with difficulty, until the last word was said. He then pressed his friend's hand, turned his face to the wall, and said not another word until God closed his eyes.[75]

Other fruitful regions of Donegal where Ó hEochaidh collected were the Blue Stack mountain range (among its notable tradition-bearers were Anna Nic an Luain, and Pádraig Eoghain Phádraig Mac an Luain, also recorded by Séamas Ó Catháin),[76] Arranmore and Gweedore; at Rannafast was a nest of tradition-bearers, with Micí Sheáin Néill Ó Baoill (material collected from him ran to almost 1,400 pages) and members of the Ó Grianna family.[77]

In Leinster, stories were gathered in Wicklow and Wexford, and James G. Delaney, ranging from his Athlone base, worked in most of the central counties between 1954 and 1986. Pádraig Mac Gréine, who had collected in Longford already before the Folklore Commission was established, wrote this obituary for a local storyteller – a small farmer and egg-seller who died in 1932, aged sixty-seven:

Hughie [Gilnagh] was a small stout man with a cheery, happy face, cleanshaven save for a small wispy moustache. His rosy face and humorous blue eyes gave him the appearance of limitless good humour, and good-humoured he was. His flow of conversation was endless and when he talked, everyone listened. His house was always full of *céilí*-ers (visitors) at night and from October until the long days came again, was the principal card school of the district ... As a storyteller, Hughie was good; very good. He made no compliment of telling his stories. The words flowed from his lips without halt or stay – never had he to pause and think. He entered into the spirit of the characters and by word and gesture carried you along with him. He was, I should say, the last of the storytellers in County Longford. Beside stories, his mind was a storehouse of ancient lore, *pisreoga* [?*piseogacht*: supersitious practices], and beliefs and customs. It is rather unfortunate that I had not the time to drain his fountain dry.[78]

More recently, Patricia Lysaght described the personality and repertoire of

75 Op. cit. 19-21. 76 *Uair an Chloig Cois Teallaigh – An Hour by the Hearth*, texts and cassette, issued in 1985. 77 G.W. MacLennan *Seanchas Annie Bhán – The Lore of Annie Bhán*. Seán Ó Grianna and Seosamh Mac Grianna, Annie's brothers, had written in Irish about the life and folklore of their native region. 78 IFC 82: 246-8 – quoted in Séamas Ó Catháin *The Bedside Book of Irish Folklore* 64.

a tradition-bearer in changing midland life: Mrs Jenny McGlynn of Mountmellick, Co. Laois. Born in 1939, she began to be recorded (seventeen hours of audio-tapes, plus video-tapes) in 1976. She had learned some narratives from her grandparents and parents; the family house was a 'rambling house' or *céilí*-house: the local meeting-place for what in Irish was also known as *cuairt* (visiting). She had forgotten the Irish she had studied at school. Her husband's family also lived in a 'rambling house', and her father-in-law encouraged her to tell short narratives.

This was an important social and psychological achievement for Jenny. Her emergence as an active tradition bearer gave her confidence and a sense of belonging in her new surroundings after her marriage and helped her to integrate into the Bay Road community. In a family situation in which the extended family-in-law control network maintained a high level of conformity in behavioural pattern, Jenny gained, and maintained, a special position and identity, by virtue of her abilities as an active bearer of tradition.
[Storytelling sessions in her new home continued until the seventies.][79]

A more extensive selection from one collector's particularly elaborated reports may compensate for deficiencies of the foregoing skim. Michael J. Murphy (1913-96), whose diaries I have examined more closely, left school aged fourteen, worked as a farm labourer in South Armagh, and in 1940 began to write, broadcast and publish what he had heard from the old people of the region: 'When they tell one "some o' thim oul' tales" they are not aware that they are doing a service to the nation and an honour to the listener. One veritably hears a breath from down the centuries, and an important breath. One hears something that has been handed down from family to family, and is yet sweetly alive for all its age. And there it reposes in the mind of an old person sitting on a low form, hugging his or her knees before the fire. It is a unique experience in an age of spurious values, of artifice and snobbish sophistication.'[80] He started working for the Irish Folklore Commission in the early 1940s and collected materials in English in several counties of Ulster, more extensively in Armagh, Tyrone, Louth and on Rathlin Island. The diaries he kept in 1949-50 (IFC 1215 and 1216) during a prolonged period of 'participant observation' in the Sperring valley of Glenhull and the surrounding areas were published as *Tyrone Folk Quest*. One of his informants was Francis McAleer, portrayed here in action when he was sixty-two:

Abruptly he got up, whispered to one of his daughters, then went to the room and after a while returned, not to the former chair, but to a long red-painted stool along the 'Cooltyee' [*cúl an tí* : 'back of the house'] from which the curtains had been drawn back to expose the bed itself. He still wore his cap. With his hands behind his head and lean-

79 'A Tradition Bearer in Contemporary Ireland', in L. Röhrich and S. Wienker-Piepho (eds) *Storytelling in Contemporary Societies* 199-214. 80 *At Slieve Gullion's Foot* 10 (his first book, published in 1941).

ing his elbows on the bed behind him he said he would try one of Netchy's 'old rehearsals' [tales]. Again he warned me that it was thirty years since he had told the tale; told how he had heard it; how Netchy [McRory] used to tell it in Gaelic, then in English translation; and how he told sections of the tale only, one on each night. 'If me and Annie McCrae's son weren't fit to tell him where and how he had left off the night before he wouldn't tell us. He'd tell the same piece again.'

He slipped his pipe into his waistcoat pocket and waited: his wife returned from the room as quietly as a shadow and sat on her usual seat. Only the clicking of the girls' knitting needles broke the silence under the lamp-light and the glow from the embers of the turf fire. He began to tell a tale called 'Old Lord Erin's Son'. Throughout the tale he smiled or frowned at appropriate junctures, made comments like: 'Wasn't that smart of him?' and so on, while his family interpolated comments of their own: 'See that now' and 'Mark you'. I wrote from his [rendition]. His power of vivid characterisation was astounding; his swift descents to whisper or hoarse croak just incredible. Unlike some traditional storytellers who religiously repeat and tediously recapitulate details of events occurring to a character, McAleer had an artistic sense of narrative talent which condensed with skill in proper portion to the tale. Like McCullagh he kept pulling at his cap until the peak lay over one ear. He gave a quick smile as interlude each time he erected himself from his leaning stance on the bed but it vanished as soon as he leaned back and went on with the tale. Above all he unashamedly believed in the tale while he was telling it, as any good storyteller in any medium must believe, and was totally without halt, hesitation or inhibition in earthy detail or language when and where it was required: all, of course, within the purely rural norm when no 'outsiders' are present. When he finished the tale he swung up from the bed, fished out his pipe and not until it was lit did he ask me what I thought of the story.[81]

McAleer's version of 'Old Lord Erin's Son' – the son of a blacksmith goes to England in search of a wife; the father of a rich girl sends a servant to Ireland to investigate the status of the suitor's family, and receives a report that disguises poverty as wealth – was published with the following comments: 'The tale has minor defects: there is some omission and a touch of confusion. These were inevitable since the storyteller hadn't told a tale for over thirty years until I came along: I've watched him in a kind of frustrated agony trying to remember dozens of others. So conscientious was he about his art that he wouldn't even try to tell one until he felt he had remembered it as he had learned it.'[82]

Murphy's sketches of storytellers (he called all his informants 'storytellers' or 'narrators', whatever kind of lore they contributed) tend to follow the same pattern: they generally describe the face and its expressions, often the eyes; the voice; the temperament; the manner of telling. The belief of the storyteller in what he/she is telling is often emphasized. Above all, Murphy expresses his own feeling of sympathy or admiration, sometimes puzzlement. Among the numerous portraits in his unpublished 'diaries' are his 'Notes on some Clonduff storytellers, Co. Down':

81 *Tyrone Folk Quest* 36-7. 82 *Ulster Folk of Field and Fireside* 146.

Anne Savage, aged 96 when writing (April 1945) is the loveliest character I've met in the Mournes, or indeed anywhere else. Here you meet again with delighted glee a breath of the old Irish world which one thought had gone for ever. She is clad like the old women of the countryside of about twenty years ago. The handkerchief still on the head, the apron. For a woman of her age, her face is remarkably full, and fresh although not coloured. Her eyes are clear and reposed. Her voice is a joy to listen to, with its beautiful inflection, that touch of natural country pathos; that fling of joy, especially in welcome – like the antics of cloud shadows on an April day ... Her voice is still strong. She talks with just the slightest suggestion of weariness, and her inflection just noticeably – though naturally – adjusts itself to the mood or crises of her tale. A lovely old soul. A privilege to meet, and an inspiration to know. Her expressive face, marked with much care and a world of trouble and much sorrow, is simply beautiful. It is the kind of face I have seen before a few times, the times one can never forget.

Patrick Carroll (known as Carville) Leitrim, Clonduff. About 5 feet ten in height and very heavily built. The hair is white, and stands upright like a hedge. The face is large and deeply sunken. He tells his stories and lore with that fluency which comes from a clear knowledge of the facts. There is, nevertheless, a shyness about the man. He is fond of a good crack, and impulsively enthusiastic ...

Felix O'Hanlon (aged 75) Carcullion, Clonduff ... He talks with verve and determination, throwing himself agreeably into the spirit of his talking. His eyes dance and fix on you. His voice is high, but not loud in volume ...

Lizzie McCarville, Carcullion, Clonduff. She is a small woman, of very slight build ... Her face is a study of massed wrinkles, the complexion coloured like wet brown paper. She has a pair of vivid eyes, very large ... Her voice is amazingly strong, clear, with ample volume. She talks with a pronounced vigour, and drifts into awe when the crisis or part of her telling demands such expression; and at this juncture, she always rolls her eyes on one. There is no conscious artfulness in this art. With an obvious belief in what she is telling, the inflections and expressions of awe are the natural effects of an unquestioning sincerity ...

Willie McComiskey, Mullaghmore ... This man is a natural artist at storytelling, and easily the best and most interesting in his manner whom I've met in Clonduff ... An aristocratic air hovers about his countenance and evokes instantly a respect for the man. He gestures very little when talking, and keeps his hands underneath the bib of his overalls. He stares almost continually into the fire. He rarely smiles – if at all – and seldom laughs. In temperament grave and sincere, and solid – almost to the point of being introspective one would think – and as if aware of the dignity of his speaking, and the respect due to the people he talks of, or the tales they told him. When telling a tale, he is like an old monk telling gravely of the works of God. He interests and grips. There is a classical restraint about his speech, never being overloaded. A natural artist of the sincere and respectful kind. He talks as if awed, the voice dropping to huskiness. Then he may lean back in his [chair], and resume with a touch of gusto for a moment. A staunch believer in active Christian ethics. Voice firm and speech fluent. Inflection is used very sparingly ...

Stephen the Catholic (Stephen Fitzpatrick), Stang. Next to Willie McComiskey, this man is the best storyteller in Clonduff, and in some respects is indeed a better narrator. Stephen is small, compactly built, and must have been a wiry little man in his day. He was much crippled with pains when I saw him, sitting on a rope chair at the fire, or in the porch of the door. His face is as merry as a schoolboy's, eyes dancing to anticipate glee. Imagine a benign lauchraman [*lochram*: leprechaun] and you have the jovial Stephen ... He sat always at the right hand of the fire, and kept his hand always on the head of one of his sticks, even when lying back. He gestures none at all. When talking, he looks across the hearth out through the window, and maybe piling his dancing glance on you at the end of a story. He is ready to laugh at a comic turn in his story, and will laugh heartily into the roof at a funny story of one's own. And when Stephen tells a tale, you think of a brook bubbling along under early summer bracken. He tells his stories faithfully with few if any imaginative additions of his own ...

Mary Anne the Catholic (Fitzpatrick), Stang. She is taller than Stephen, with a sallow face and slightly haunched shoulders ... She has a very kindly disposition, and likes to hear Stephen tell stories ... She, too, speaks quickly, and tells her stories almost with indifference.[83]

The same year (1945) M.J. Murphy portrayed storytellers he met at Kilkeel, also in County Down:

John Donnan, 79 years, Harbour Cottage, Kilkeel. A man of about six feet, and of powerful build. Although 79 years, he is still agile, and still possesses amazing strength ... He tells his fairy tales quite happily, fluently – when he told the ones in present collection he was mending a box in which herrings are usually seen in 'cadgers' carts'. But he tells lore somewhat grudgingly. He interjects now and then that he doesn't believe it; even tells a story to prove superstitions aren't true; and he tells it so, with reticence, lest one thinks he is superstitious ...

Jimmy Donnan (The Lucky Fellow). He has iron grey beetling brows, and the eyes study you long and determinedly from the focus of long experience before he speaks. He smiles very very slowly, and it fades as quickly as it comes. He has a phenomenal memory, not only for dates, but for the actual day, sometimes even the weather of a particular day [for] some event heard from his father. 'The Lucky Fellow', say Kilkeel folk, 'has good stories, and better than all, he can give you day an' date for what he says'. He has composed many songs, and claims to remember about four hundred. His enunciation is clear, and reflective.[84]

In his 'Notes on Crossmaglen storytellers' (South Armagh), Murphy drew this portrait of a gossip and genealogist aged 73:

As Mary Daly says herself: 'I'm an old thrug-gwullian' a word I give in my own phonetics, and which means, huge, awkward and not too supple on the feet [the *Concise Ulster Dictionary* defines 'thrumgullion' as 'big-boned, loose-jointed, untidy woman']. I collected most of the lore from her sitting by her own fireside, sometimes in morning, even afternoon – in fact at all times – and at night. I feel I've drained her recollections dry. She is literate, but she was careful always to tell me when she was telling something which had 'come out of a book she had read'. For she loved talk. She took a detailed interest in the tittle-tattle and gossip of the countryside. She had that phenomenal memory which can follow up the intricate pattern of relationships, gathering other rela-

83 IFC 976: 79-91.   84 IFC 976: 353 and 525.

tionships on the way, until I was able to thread my way among the maze ... She told her material with an interested zest, as if happy to recall all the items and episodes. And while she talked, she kept her eyes closed, or the lids fluttering, while with hands joined, her two thumbs kept twirling on her lap ... I have never met anyone who knew so much lore.[85]

The death of old informants was regularly recorded in Murphy's diaries with a last portrait, like that of Tom Dunne, of Dromintee, South Armagh, who died at 74 in 1947:

He was perhaps the raciest of Dromintee storytellers, illustrating his talk with images of his own. He was forever lamenting that he knew 'loads of stories' if he could remember them. He dramatised everything, even a walk to the town; out of a traditional instinct or a natural one I can't say ... He could make an account of the lighting of his pipe in a wind an interesting story. He was fairly literate, but seldom read or wrote.[86]

... or of Pat Reid, who died in 1953:

Pat was one quiet and kindly soul ... He lived alone in a thatched house which adjoined another, 'under the one roof' as we say in South Armagh ... He always sat at the left-hand side of the fire, smoked a pipe, and each time I went wanted to treat me to a bottle of stout which I would not take, as I told him I could get it more easily than he ... He was no artist in narration, and the manner of telling had a jerkiness of voice which, as I now know and suspected, was due to some illness. What depth of lore he possessed only Heaven knows: I was getting on to that plane of comradeship and confidence, which I always cultivate first, which would have unsealed the memory. Nevertheless, he was not a poor narrator: he had neat turns of description and phrase and an equally neat leavening of detail. He always said to me: 'Next time you come back I'll have thought of more. I try to think of things to tell you.'[87]

Another obituary praised a woman who knew that stories arousing 'party' or sectarian feelings should be treated with caution:

Mary Nugent died on the 5th December 1948, aged 94 or 95 (R.I.P.) ... I do not know how to describe Mary Nugent; because her grand soul and charitable personality occupied a special place in my gallery of Slieve Gullion story-tellers ... In the end I saw her as a living symbol of an age and a people: an age built and centred around community spirit, and a people whose underlining characteristic was a great, great charity of soul and heart and mind that easily overshadowed any of the other frailties and humane defects of character. Mary Nugent could make me feel, actually, that I was in another age. Because, of course, she felt so herself. For instance, the perils of supporting the Jacobite cause ... were still impending: it was some time before she would mention, except without a cautious inflection of voice, 'The White Cockade' [a Jacobite emblem]. She would

85 IFC 1112: 385 (December 1945). 86 IFC 1113: 303-4. *Béaloideas* has regularly published obituaries of major informants. 87 IFC 1360: 77-9.

never fully explain to me what this meant, no doubt fearing it might get around the country. It was the same with the Famine memories, which is a familiar trait perhaps: she was reluctant to tell me who were 'Soupers' [those who had become Protestant to get food]. Even then she would say: 'That's what they said, but they're always saying something'.[88]

Other narrators had doubts about the social acceptability of their repertoire: 'When he has what some might regard as risque short tales and anecdotes to tell, that is brief folk-tales – not community accounts only – he is very hesitant: his idea is that it wouldn't do to "have the people in Dublin hearing that". Yet much of the material he tells I have heard in this valley and elsewhere over all my years. In the end he does consent to record.'[89] In 1969 he sketched an informant who, shy at first, turned out particularly talkative:

[James] Mitchell [of Corglancy, Dromahair], who is 78, and a farmer, is one of the freest-speaking narrators I've met, one tale leading to another from his own memory [a common saying in Irish – *tarraingíonn scéal scéal eile*: one story leads to another], so that to question and query one had to memorize much (and forget some) and do this off-tape ... Mitchell is a well-built man, maybe five feet ten, clean shaven, a face far from florid, but very agreeable and welcoming and easy. It appears he had some qualms about meeting me, so much so that Jim Reynolds thought it was advisable that he be present when I met the man for serious talk. A smooth, level voice, not too affected by emotion arising from tale or account.[90]

But storytellers grow old, their strength and faculties diminish, and stories can fade away. In the same year Michael Murphy paid one of his last visits to Frank Campbell, of Forkhill, County Armagh, once a valuable informant:

Poor Frank Campbell (he was 75 on Saturday last he says) visibly wizening. He is a genial old fellow, loves the crack, loves to 'get stuck into an argument' and drinks bottles of stout. He wanted to tell me about donkeys, a tradition he had remembered. From this he went on to other items I'd heard him mention; and in addition got some anecdotal tales, earthy as cow-dung, (and all rural life had a damn good streak of healthy vulgarity anyway, though the pious-platitudinising townees don't know this fact for reasons often stated) and he told a few folk stories: which surprised me. Folk stories that are now much reduced to the anecdotal form, confused, a mingling maybe of another: but hasn't such happened with all or many tales?[91]

M.J. Murphy found everything 'traditional' relevant, and he constantly expressed the respect his informants inspired, as well as his sense of being, through them, in contact with the past. He had already done so in 1940 before he became a professional collector: 'The old people remain the same to-day as they have been for years, despite the changes which have come over the coun-

---

88 IFC 1215: 2. 89 IFC 1788: 29. 90 IFC 1749: 159. 91 IFC 1749: 112-13.

tryside. The quaint, frank and even graphic phrasing of their idiomatic speech, the simple but deep faith which marks their activities and contacts, and the old sayings and traditions remain also ... Although they are not Gaelic speakers here, the influence of the native tongue and tradition is yet strong enough to give their speech an air and a feeling of old worth and dignity.'[92] More than thirty years later, his sense of wonder had not faded: 'Sometimes with Frank talking folklore I find a sense of the unreal gathering about me: wondering who is talking and where this memory comes from. I seem to realise that, when in a short while he has gone and no one can talk lore as he can, there will be that strange sense of a living void: that awareness that as time goes by and someone reads his stuff in conjunction with his own speech off the tape that whatever the technological marvels in and around the place this lost world will be a greater marvel still.'[93] And he would repeatedly express the same feelings: 'The thought occurred to me as I wrote this morning: we who collect take so much for granted the talents and abilities and personalities of our storytellers and informants: it can be a stunning thing to realise just what they are in this day and age ... Does one good to realise the point sometimes. They are now unique truly.'[94]

The admirable work of the Irish Folklore Commission should not obscure other efforts. Individual and institutional collecting was also initiated in Northern Ireland, for instance: T.G.F. Paterson had been active in County Armagh from the 1920s or 30s. In 1956, the writer and broadcaster Sam Hanna Bell published some of the Ulster folklore he had collected, including 'industrial folklore' of the Belfast shipyard and country lore gathered for the BBC: 'Did our story-tellers believe in fairies? They were mostly seventy years of age and upward; but they were not as old as the whitethorn bush their grandfather feared as a child [a solitary hawthorn, or *sceach*, is often said to belong to the fairies]. Doubt the story and they showed you the thorn; doubt the thorn's age whence came the story? The question of *belief* then did not enter the matter. A great number of the tales were family history and therefore, so far as they were concerned, incontrovertible.'[95] From 1928, E.E. Evans (1905-89), head of the Geography Department of Queen's University Belfast, had stressed the interaction between culture and environment; a survey of megaliths in the North led him to gather ethnographic data as well, which he used in his *Irish Heritage* (1941) and more extensively in *Irish Folkways* (1957). He became the first director of the Institute of Irish Studies in his university. A Committee on Ulster Folklife and Traditions had been set up, and since 1955 an annual journal was published; in 1961 an Ulster Folklife Society was established and in 1964 a Folk Museum was opened at Cultra near Belfast. The orientation towards material culture remained domi-

---

92 *At Slieve Gullion's Foot* 9. 93 IFC 1788: 117. 94 IFC 1801: 65. 95 *Erin's Orange Lily* 68-9. With M.J. Murphy, Bell produced a series of broadcasts entitled 'Fairy Faith'.

nant, because 'the links that [had] been forged [were] with geography and archeology rather than with the departments of language or history';[96] but just as the
Dublin Commission, for all the attention it paid to oral arts, did not neglect
material culture, so contents of the periodical *Ulster Folklife* proves that oral arts
are not ignored in the North. Folklore is also taught at University College, Cork,
where an important fieldwork project is in progress.

Foreign scholars visited Ireland;[97] some did fieldwork there. In the 1930s,
the British Celticist Kenneth H. Jackson (1909-91) collected in Kerry (see p.
400), and in 1936 he synthesized a portrait of the Irish storyteller from the performers he had observed:

Let us look at the *seanchaidhe* of the twentieth century. He is a man of from sixty to
ninety years of age or more, living in a small cabin in some tiny hamlet near the western coast. Maybe he has never travelled further than the nearest town, and probably he
can neither read nor write, nor speak much, if any, English. The village people will
gather at his house of an evening to be entertained by his professional stock and by the
wit and point of his talk, by the social amusement, *'cuideacht' is caithamh aimsire'* [to be
in company is a pastime], which the Irish folk love so much; and it will be the grown up
people, quite as much or more than the children, who will listen with keen appreciation
to his tales. He may have upwards of two hundreds of these in his repertoire, in addition to scores of songs and proverbs and other folk material which he has learned entirely
orally; and he will tell them with an extraordinary dramatic delivery, half acting them as
he sits in his chair by the fire, living the tale, never hesitating, and all in a fine simple
prose which any modern Irish literary movement should be proud of.[98]

A later generalization was still based on Jackson's experience in Kerry:

What kind of people are those story-tellers? They represent the intelligentsia of the old
rural Gaelic tradition; men of high intelligence, with keen minds and memories sharp-
ened by practice, devoted to stories and legends, the enthusiastic guardians of their
inherited oral Gaelic literature, and true artists in their craft. They are men widely educated in the old oral learning of their people though generally illiterate in their own language and not infrequently in English as well, at any rate until recent times. They play,
or used to play, a highly important part in the life of their community because they were
the focus of its intellectual activity; they held a sort of unofficial position as if unpaid
professional men, which gave them a standing in the neighbourhood.[99]

A German professor, Ludwig Mühlhausen, was in Teelin (Donegal) in
September-October 1937 to collect tales in Irish from James Cassidy (Seámus Ó

96 E.E. Evans 'Folklife Studies in Northern Ireland', *Journal of the Folklore Institute* 2 (1965)
361. 97 Stith Thompson, in 1937: 'Ireland has preserved this custom of telling and listening
to folktales better than most countries of western Europe, and it probably gives us a chance
to observe the process in the same kind of social setting that was very common a thousand
years ago and before' (*The Folktale* 455). 98 'The International Folktale in Ireland', *Folk-Lore*
47 (1936) 269-70. 99 *The International Popular Tale and Early Welsh Tradition* (1961) 51-2.

Casaide), aged 82. Cassidy had emigrated to America in 1888 to work there as a pedlar and had returned to Ireland in 1897. When Mühlhausen went to him, he obviously enjoyed having an audience again; like a number of old people met by Irish collectors, however, he had to make efforts to revive what remained latent in his memory:

He often told me at the end of our sessions, when I asked for more stories: 'Let me think first'. The result of a more or less sleepless night was a new tale the following morning – one which he had perhaps not performed for decades but which was now present again to his mind and could be repeated several times word for word. The collecting took place in the following way: I had every story told in whole without taking notes. Only then would I write it down from his dictation. It was not always easy: I often had to re-read long stretches of what had already been transcribed, when he was losing the thread. Yet the work was not too severely hampered. As soon as a session (which often lasted several hours) was over, I ran to my own lodging with my manuscripts, to decipher a text full of abbreviations and to make a fair copy as long as I remembered the sound and content of the telling. The following day, I read this second version to the storyteller, asked questions, had him tell some passages again. For Seámus, contrary to my fears it was quite enjoyable: he kept insisting that it was exactly what he had told, and that he could not tell the story better ... With some bitterness he sometimes told me, as we parted, that I was the last person to whom he would tell the stories. He was thinking of the younger generation, which had little taste for them and preferred other forms of entertainment.[100]

Another German, Heinrich Becker, was in the Aran Islands and in Connemara from 1937, and collected memories of personal experience from fishermen and seaweed harvesters, which were published in 1997.[101] American anthropologists John and Betty Messenger worked on Inisheer (Aran Islands) between 1958 and 1962.[102] Joe O'Donnell (1889-1963) gave them some information on formal storytelling sessions in the past and on the qualities that marked a good storyteller, but old-style performing could no longer be observed.[103] John Messenger's original mode of 'participant observation' included composing a narrative song on some local events and noting how it had changed after being performed for some years. He also experienced the adverse criticism a foreigner might expect from Irish people when he intruded into their field.[104] In the late 1960s, Artelia Court recorded material from Irish 'tinkers' (now officially known as travellers – more about them in the next chapter). One of her informants, John Cassidy, said:

'I'll tell you the stories and I'll tell you the history now: the story is in me generation [family]. The stories is in the Cassidy generation, in the seven generations and they was

---

100 *Zehn irische Volkserzählungen aus Süd-Donegal* 7-8 (my translation).   101 *I mBéal na Farraige.*   102 J.C. Messenger *Inis Beag: Isle of Ireland.*   103 'Joe O'Donnell, Seanchai of Aran', *Journal of the Folklore Institute* 1 (1964) 197-213.   104 J.C. Messenger *An Anthropologist at Play.*

true one time. I don't be like me father, now, going from house to house, stopping months in this house, months and months in the next one, but I do have the stories yet, or I have some of them. And those stories is worth me remembrance. It was where me life lain. I was only a year and eight months when me mother died, and me father he reared five of us, two brothers and three sisters, without a mother. I was the youngest one of them all and he carried me from house to house, carried me in his arms. And that's how I used to be listening to the stories more. You know, I'd have to listen to 'em 'cause I wasn't able to go any farther on me own. We'd go in the nighttime to the house and he'd tell those stories over the big fire. We used to be sitting down alongside of him, and maybe I'd be sitting down on the hearth between his legs. Every night. And it come so that any of the family could tell the stories – me sisters could tell 'em ... Me father was constantly telling stories, like, every night, from house to house where he'd go. And those neighboring men, from other farms around, they'd come to the house we was lodging in to hear him telling the stories, and they'd tell more of 'em. Well, he'd be learning the stories off of them and they'd be learning 'em off of him. That's the way it was.'[105]

A major contribution, applying recent developments in American folklore theory and practice (performance analysis and a holistic approach), was Henry Glassie's *Passing the Time: Folklore and History of an Ulster Community*. Glassie worked in the 1970s at Ballymenone in County Fermanagh, observing a set of 129 people divided into 33 Catholic households and 9 Protestant ones: 'It is my goal in this book to study not the total repertory of an individual, but the total repertory of all the individuals who compose a living community of artists.'[106] He is concerned with the geography of the place, the whole pattern of social connections, and material culture: how houses are built and used, how work is done in the fields, how turf is cut ... And he offers detailed descriptions of different situations in which discourse may lead to narration, stressing the importance of speech acts, the skill with which they are conducted and the 'mental associations woven around texts during performance to shape and complete them, to give them meaning'.[107] The function of stories in conversation is emphasized: we are shown how 'ceilis' develop – are not planned but 'happen' – and how, 'at the peak of an evening, at the nexus of force, the story emerges'.[108] The personal narrative, or 'experience' (relating events of one's own life), is accepted but is not called a story by the community; 'exploits', celebrating feats of strength or courage by respected people of the past, and tales of 'wit' (examples of intelligence) are more important. Most valued, however, are 'stories of history' concerning the local past and considered deepest in truth. They give cohesion to the community, with their clear spatial location and their situation within well-defined sequences of history marked out by crucial events; in a part of Ireland where the population is divided on religious-political lines, views of history of course differ and conflict. Henry Glassie closely analyses some narrative texts which start with a brief informational prologue then group

105 *Puck of the Droms: The Lives & Literature of the Irish Tinkers* 181-2. **106** Op. cit. 723. **107** Ibid. 33. **108** Ibid. 469.

the following sentences in clear-cut units (often triads), with systems of repetition and ways of emphasizing important words, and come to a brief conclusion perhaps raising the issue of the story's veracity and leading back to conversation: 'The folklorist's practice of isolating tales out of conversations, rather than letting them follow from happening to happening, topic to topic, has prevented understanding the nature of the experience story and its role in investigating reality's shape.'[109] This collector's practice, like that of several of his predecessors in Ireland, was to listen before recording: 'I wanted to hear live stories, stories enjoyed by their tellers and audiences, and I returned to record them so I could avoid the difficulties that have undermined attempts to analyse narrative content.'[110] Transcribing spoken words posed problems: to represent live performance, Glassie wanted texts to 'look like they sound',[111] and adopted a technique devised by American 'ethnopoetics' which consisted in arranging units in lines, like verse, to render rhythm and segmentation: such 'narrative sentences' are not separated on syntactic grounds (there may be no overt verb, or two verbs ...), but are generally delimitable by pauses and the initial occurrence of markers, like 'And then ...', 'But ...'. Words emphasized in speaking are typographically stressed and blank spaces indicate pauses.

Glassie called the people of Ballymenone his 'teachers', and portrayed them in this and other books; for instance Hugh Nolan, who was born in 1896: 'They name him the "historian". His memory is vast, the past is impeccably ordered within it, and he settles disputes among his neighbours over boundaries and rights of way across fields. His pleasure in youth, he says, came from listening to the old people talking, and his delight in old age, he says, is keeping the truth and telling the whole tale.'[112]

Another American anthropologist, Lawrence J. Taylor, who worked in County Donegal in the late 1980s, could still observe the power of storytelling there: 'It is clear to any ethnographer or historian working in Ireland that narrative discourse has had a generally important role in expressing and thus defining the way the surrounding world had been perceived ... I saw what was left of formal storytelling, but it was the general attention awarded narrative in whatever form and situation that I found most striking. An anecdote, when told well, riveted the audience in house or pub.'[113] Taylor arrived in 1975, studied the interaction between 'folk discourse' and that of 'established' (Catholic) religion,[114] and became Professor of Anthropology at Maynooth.

Clodagh Margaret Brennan Harvey's field work in 1983-4, focusing on storytelling in English within the framework of modernization and social change, led to a doctoral dissertation at the University of California, Los Angeles.[115] It

---

109 Ibid. 743. **110** Ibid. 731. **111** Ibid. 40. **112** *Irish Folktales* 6. **113** Lawrence J. Taylor 'The Language of Belief', in M. Silverman and P.H. Gulliver (eds) *Approaching the Past: Historical Anthropology through Irish Case Studies* 162, 149. **114** The results were published in 1995: *Occasions of Faith; An Anthropology of Irish Catholics*. **115** Partly published as *Contemporary Irish Traditional Narrative; The English Language Tradition* (1992).

was based on interviews with forty-three individuals, including fifteen story-tellers, most of them in County Clare but also in Roscommon, Galway, Mayo, Kerry and Armagh. The question of who can rightly be called a 'storyteller' was tentatively answered with a set of criteria such as: being so considered in the community, perceiving oneself as one, having being recorded by some official collector. The informant's background, the audience for the tales in the past and at present, perceived changes in the storytelling tradition, the nature of the rela-tionship between folklore collectors and storytellers – such topics were investi-gated with each of the fifteen main informants. Narrators appeared to be of dif-ferent kinds, not only as regards repertoire and skill. Some had long been passive bearers of tradition: they could report stories (relate the outline) rather than perform them with embellishments. Some would speak loud and quickly, others tended to whisper; some moved around the room and gesticulated while performing, others were very restrained. Many had been born into large, poor families, and had received only basic formal education; they all felt that changes had taken place in communal life which had considerably reduced the impor-tance of their kind of storytelling. Folklorists tended to be the only informed and receptive audience left; some people began to think of themselves as story-tellers only when contacted by collectors, and some thereby gained a local rep-utation.

Ethnographic documentation is acquired by a researcher cooperating with his informants, and it is now recognized that the investigator has an effect on what he observes and therefore should be an integral part of the investigation. Some folklorists were foreigners, many were 'strangers' in the local communities where they worked; with their particuliar knowledge, tastes and aims, all could differ somehow from those they were studying,[116] and thus orient the event and per-haps alter the result – concerning folklore, it has been said that 'the only truly natural context, of course, is one in which no collector is known to be pre-sent'.[117] The informant's perceptions of the collector's interests and intention may condition his answers. Being scrutinized may be inhibiting; Séamus Ó Catháin described the attitude of an informant when he first met an official folk-lore collector: 'He was both shy and wary on the one hand and terribly anxious to please on the other – a delicate and dangerous combination of attitudes famil-iar to all collectors engaged in "opening up" new informants.'[118] The presence of a person known to have official status can also convince the tradition-bearer of the importance of a role his own community no longer recognizes; the field-worker may replace the original audience and stimulate his informant to recol-lect long-forgotten tales – but they are conveyed in conditions differing from those in which storytelling naturally occurred earlier.

116 R. Finnegan *Oral Traditions and the Verbal Arts* 72: 'What you collect and record is affected by a whole series of prior decisions: theoretical preconceptions, aims, equipment, set-tings, and decisions about who or what is to be recorded.' **117** K.S. Goldstein *A Guide for Field Workers in Folklore* 82. **118** *Béaloideas* 48-9 (1980-1) 138.

How did informants see the folklorists? Anecdotes about city scholars duped by wily *seanchaithe* had only the truth value of jokes, and Patrick Kavanagh's view of the old *seanchaí* receiving the 'folklore fellas' with a fork (see p. 368) was certainly not the rule. It could happen that the collector came at the wrong time, and he might occasionally be laughed at, as M.J. Murphy noted in his diary in May 1970: 'I sometimes run into the minds which must satirize, out of inferiority complex essentially, sometimes out of sheer ignorance. I am known, of course: "Here's a fellow after old history, Martin. Can you give him an old history" ... "It's the history of the future we want to be thinking of".'[119] But James G. Delaney noted that the ethnographer and his informant generally got on well together: 'The fact [that the folklorist] is recording an old person's memories for an institution in Dublin, which will preserve them for future generations, is a cause of delight, and a source of pride for the informant, who is pleased to realize that his material is much sought after by scholars of folklore and folk life. The visit of the collector then becomes an eagerly awaited event. The informant feels a sense of purpose, which he previously lacked, and takes a new interest in life. The collector and his informant become united in a bond of sympathy and friendship.'[120]

The folklorist himself could be changed by the experience, and he determined how it was reported: he was likely to select the data according to his own leading concepts and perhaps emotions. But the account he gave also followed certain conventions. There were inevitable topoi: we have seen that practically from the start the theme of iminent loss was inherent in the impulse to collect, and as long as folklore was thought to consist of survivals of the past collecting was regularly presented as last-minute attempts to preserve a culture on the verge of dying out, or to reconstruct what it might have been like before modern corruption. Throughout the twentieth century, folklorists in Ireland had the conviction that something remarkable was rapidly vanishing. In 1932, Tadhg Ó Murchú complained: 'Each month which passes brings to us the news of the death of storytellers and informants who were living repositories of tradition. We cannot replace these old people; their knowledge is *not* passed on to a younger generation, as a rule, but goes with them into the grave.'[121] Seven years later, T.G.F. Paterson noted: 'Most of [the storytellers heard in South Armagh between 1927 and 1930] have since passed on, amongst them old and valued friends who remembered such far-off events as the famine days of 1846-1847 as if they were events of yesterday ... The tragedy is that the old stories are dying out with these old people. The younger country people now seek their pleasure in the towns. The cinema and the dance-hall are more to the liking of the boys and girls of today than the simple entertainment of the countryside. The recital of these tales is fast becoming a thing of the past.'[122] And in 1945 J.H. Delargy

119 IFC 1788: 72. 120 'Three Midland Storytellers', *Béaloideas* 50 (1982) 44, 52-3. 121 *Béaloideas* 3 (1932) 517. 122 *County Cracks: Old Tales from the County of Armagh* 15.

agreed: 'Although there are still many hundreds of Irish people who can tell these tales from an older world, it is but rarely now that they are told. The days of the folktale are numbered even in Ireland.'[123] In 1957, a lament was raised for Glencar, in County Donegal, once a repository of 'traditions': 'The young people have much broader horizons than ever their parents had and look outside the Glen for their entertainment, to Kerrykeel, Milford and Rathmullen. As a result the old musical parties and ceilidhes which used to be important events have now died out, even the old people preferring to remain at their own fire-side and listen to the wireless. The visiting of neighbours has declined as well, and this, combined with the general broadening of outlook which accompanies the advent of radio and newspapers, has meant that opportunities for storytelling are now rare.'[124] In 1970, Kevin Danaher focused on the storyteller's own sense of loss: 'With the passing of the interested and critical audience, the storyteller has lost the incentive to display his art and skill. He knows, too, that he is the last of his race and that nobody will learn how to tell his tales and pass them on to the future generations.'[125] Audiences and opportunities for 'traditional' tale-telling disappeared before the potential performers did themselves. Various explanations have been put forward: depopulation in the districts where story-telling had been active; a decline in the custom of neighbourly night-visiting; the growing number of bicycles with which young people left the immediate neigh-bourhood when looking for entertainment; the modern stove replacing the old fireplace which had been the traditional gathering place; the advent of radio (slowly from the late 1920s) and, apparently more lethal, of television (which spread rapidly from the early 1960s).

We find another kind of portraits in folklorists' reports: they received informa-tion concerning storytelling and storytellers they did not meet and who belonged to the past. The sources were members of the community concerned, but what they said was filtered through recall and perceptions of changes in the social environment and the style of life. The dominant impression was that things no longer were as lively as they used to be, and reminiscences were often punctu-ated by the refrain that the giants of yore 'are all gone now'.

Greatness might be defined in different terms: where dedicated folklorists saw 'nobility', the storytellers' natural audience could admire the ability to make time fly, a performer's tricks, and sometimes even unpleasant qualities that made of him a remarkable 'character'. The following pages give a selection of such informants' recollections of storytellers and old-style storytelling, again from the manuscripts in English in the archives of the Department of Irish Folklore. The first two were collected in the Dingle peninsula by Seosamh Ó Dálaigh:

In my grandmother's house there would be three or four people rambling every night in

---

123 *The Gaelic Storyteller* 13. **124** *Ulster Folk Life* 3 (1957) 40. **125** 'Stories and Storytelling', in *Automobile Association Handbook of Ireland* 27.

the year and they'd nearly stay up until morning and they used tell stories and discuss everything and I wouldn't know there was a revolution in France but for them. Then there was 'The Dane' down here in Lyre, his name was James Costello and when we grew up we used go rambling there. The house would be full. He'd bring his chair to one side of the fire and in front of it and he'd be pivoted there on the chair with his heels on the hob. He lived to be ninety-six years and he had stories for ever. He used tell us the story of the Black Thief of Sloe and those long stories. He had a story for every night of the year. You'd have the first one forgotten when he'd tell the second one. He was a small little man. He's dead now fifteen years. He was a powerfull storyteller. He had English and Irish. He was better at the Irish songs than at the English songs. He used tell the stories in his own house and at wakes. Anyone wouldn't play any tricks on him and if any two lads started talking between themselves while he'd be telling a story he'd stop up and wouldn't continue till everything was quiet again. The lads would be lying around the hearth listening to him. We'd have no women there for there were few women and girls around the place at the time. He had long long long tales and he was great to tell a story about landlords and he wouldn't miss a thing in the story. He'd tell it again and again and it would be always the same.

There was another man down there then, Jack Dillane or Jack Dillon. The Dillons and the Dillanes were so mixed up that some people called them Dillanes and more called them Dillons. But Jack Dillane was a great storyteller. He was living in this *clachán* [a cluster of houses] over here, *clachán na gCléireach* ... Dillane was able to read and write. He was a native of Abbeyfeale. He's dead with years now ... Jack Dillane the great storyteller when he married, he was married to a great aunt of mine in Ballagh. He had twelve cows when he married there and he went and he took Pallas and he had a great place there. If you came in to the house in the middle of the day he'd sit down and he'd hold telling stories till you'd have to go home from him.[126]

Seán [Munnic or Molyneaux] was a great storyteller here. He'd be telling stories all the winter-nights and he'd always keep the best story till home-time. He's dead now fourteen or fifteen years. He was about seventy-four years when he died. He was a delicate poor man. He was married to a niece of my mother's.[127]

Also in the Dingle peninsula, P.J. O'Sullivan received more elaborate information concerning Johnny Sayers and his 'school of storytelling' near Annascaul, towards the end of the nineteenth century – 'school' in the sense of a group gathered for any purpose rather than a place for instruction, though those who regularly met, the youth of the district, thus acquired a repertoire of stories:

About two miles from the village of Annascaul at Maum-Inch lived a certain Johnny Sayers and his wife. He was a labourer, who probably gave a hard day's work for 7d. – a munificient wage at that time I believe. We can picture him rising at a very early hour, descending the steep Maum road, putting in a hard day's work, and afterwards returning to his home in the evening. His favourite time for storytelling was during the winter months. Night would fall early, and the fire would be kindled. Every now and again the latch would be lifted to admit between 15 to 20 boys and girls, whose ages ranged from

126 IFC 1169: 201-4 and 230-1, from Éamon Mac Síthig (Sheehy), aged 74, at Duagh in 1950. 127 IFC 1177: 9, from Jack Kelleher, aged *c.*75 in 1950.

14 to 21 years, to hear a new story or perhaps just an often repeated one. Johnny Sayers, by the way, was a small man with a quiet serious face, small eyes and a pointed chin. He had a hump. He wore invariably corduroy knee breeches, a swallow-tail coat and a tall hat. Each evening he adjusted his hat to a particular angle on his head, sat by the side of the fire whilst his wife occupied the seat opposite. Here and there on upturned old wooden tubs, buckets and sods of turf were balanced his audience, who were mainly from Maum and the nearby villages. Johnny then produced his short clay pipe (a *dúidín* it was called) which had its cover attached to it by a chain. Then began the ceremony of setting tobacco alright, and what with a spittle into the fire and an odd malediction on it, which was generally the introduction to the night's entertainment. By the light of the turf fire Johnny Sayers was opening up in his own unique way of storytelling in a tone that was quiet and tense and earnest that compelled your belief. He paused a moment to see what effect his story was having, and being satisfied on this score he went on with tales of dragons, saints, ghosts, monsters and the 'good people'. Thus passed the night 'till 11 o'clock when all took leave of the old man and his wife. They went out into the biting night air, and to their own respective homes. In return for storytelling, Johnny was treated to an odd oz of tobacco which in those days could be had at 1d per oz; also they provided the potato seed and planted his potatoes on Sundays before and after Mass (Sundays being their free days). In the same way they saw to his fuel for the winter's fires, and incidentally for their storytelling. This turf they cut in Breckin Bogs, while Johnny stood over them supervising their work as it were ... Today, I am in touch with only [one] living member of that school, Bill Garvey, aged 65, who can give an almost verbatim account of each story told by poor old Johnny.[128]

In County Limerick, someone remembered a 'champion storyteller':

According to Mr W. Hanley, Mr Michael (Mike) Dawson was the 'king of them all', a real champion. The others like Dan Egan might 'know tales' but 'Mike was the one to tell them'. Mr Hanley had a great chance of hearing Dawson in 'action' as it were. About fifteen years or so ago when the National Insurances Act came into operation [c.1911], a number of people, among them Dawson, had to travel to Kilmallock to meet the official who looked into their cases and administered the Act ... As they generally turned up much earlier than the official, some one, one day, called on Mike Dawson for a story. So it began, and the party enjoyed themselves, till the inspector came. Even he as well as Mr Hanley fell under the charm of the seanchaí, and often after the insurance business was done Dawson would be asked to tell another one or perhaps add to, or finish, the tale in progress before the interruption. Mike had a wealth of tales, long and short and could add sequels to the short ones and curtail the long ones at will. He didn't like to repeat any of the tales, 'too soon anyway', except after great 'begging' or persuasion, but was 'never short' and could time his tale so nicely, or finish it off so well at a moment's notice, that the idea grew among his listeners, that he had 'foreknowledge' of the coming of the inspector.[129]

128 IFC 744: 467-9, from Bill Garvey, in 1941. 129 IFC 1380:14-16. Contributed by P. O'Connell, Kilfinane district, Co. Limerick.

From Mayo, and with the usual backward skipping of approximately half a century, comes this sketch of a 'great' Belmullet storyteller:

About fifty years ago there died a famous storyteller who was known as the name of Martin McNulty. This man lived in West Mayo in a place known as Gladree. Martin McNulty was a native of Crossmolina, and he came to Gladree herding cattle at the age of twelve years. He lived in Gladree at a man known as Heally. He worked at this man for six years, and he bought a place in Gladree. This man was a great storyteller. He used always speak Irish and never used to talk any English. He can understand English but he cannot speak it. Crowds used to come listening to him telling stories in Irish. He can tell stories of all the history of Ireland and other countries. He used to tell stories and rimes of all sorts. He got sick with a flu when he was about sixty years and he was sent to Belmullet hospital for treatment. During his stay in hospital crowds gathered from around Belmullet town and Ballina and one night he got fifteen pounds for telling stories and rhymes. Fifteen pounds at that time was a big amount of money. Before he would tell a story he would always start a rhyme first and then the story. If he lived up till now he would be a millinore.[130]

This one is from Achill Island:

My father God rest him was a great man for stories, and it's often times there'd be about twenty or thirty old people sitting around telling story after story, and they'd be competing with one another, but my father would always be able to get one better on them even if he had to invent it ...

'Now' said [Micheal Carr, aged 57] 'isn't it wonderful that they [the Folklore Commission] 'd take so much interest in an old story like that. Sure dang it' he continued 'if I could only remember all the yarns that ould Thomas Lavelle used to be telling they'd fill a book. He used to be down in the old house there night after night and I was only a lad of ten years or so at the time, and I used to be listening to him telling them himself, and my father and a few other old men. Thomas is dead witt about forty years now, and I never heard anyone since that could hold a candle to him for old yarns.'[131]

Other counties can be represented in this selection. County Longford, for instance:

When I was a boy, there lived an old man named Michael Cuinin in a small thatched house, right on the edge of Kinard bog. Kinard bog is in the parish of Legan, South Longford ... Micky, as we used to call him, was born before 'the Big Wind' [1839], and when I first remember him, was old, small, and crabbed ... He died about 1910 or 11. A few years ago, a neighbour of mine Thomas Moran (56) of Corraboola, parish of Legan, told me that Coinin was a great storyteller, and that he and other young fellows of his time used to listen to him telling stories in a house where he used to céilí every winter. Micky was hard to humour, and would brook no noise, comment, or interruption while he was telling a story. If anyone annoyed him, he usually got up and left the house.[132]

130 IFC 1417: 427-9, from Michael Howard, aged 72 in 1955. Collected by Miceal Ó Carolan. 131 IFC 1015: 31 and 201a-2a. Collected by B. Molloy. 132 IFC 1117: 138-9.

Or County Cavan (involving the collector's own family):

Sixty years ago, when I was a lump of a lad, I used to go to kailey [*céilí*: visit] houses around the Loughinlay Mountain, and it was as good as any concert to listen to the old people telling sories. They would sit round the fire on a winter's night, and it was a case of which of them would tell the best story. You could hear a pin falling while a story was being told, and well dare anybody interrupt or make the slightest noise. Even the woman of the house would not put a fresh sod of turf on the fire till the story was finished. My father (the late John Argue who was a shoemaker by trade) and your father (the late James Gaynor) would be among the bunch, and they could tell stories that would make the hair stand on your head.[133]

Or County Wexford:

An old woman that lived in a little house out there (the house is down now) was telling me that. I heard her telling it often and often. She is dead about twenty years now. Mrs Blake was her name. She was the best hand you ever hear to tell stories. I often stayed up half the night listening to her telling stories about the fairies, and about ghosts and everything. All the old people that were able to tell these things are all dead and gone now. And the young people rising up are different altogether. There is too much amusement now. Long ago when we were young we usen't be going here and going there. We'd be inside at home in our own house. Well, that's how we'd pass the night telling yarns and stories. I heard all these ould stories but I'm no good to think of anything like that.[134]

Particularly admired was skill in making the impossible sound credible:

Ah, if L. was alive now! He's the man could tell you the stories and the yarns. He'd make them up and invent them for you as fast as he'd walk. I often heard him at a wake and he telling them. And one story would hold for the whole night; and you'd swear that he was telling the truth, he'd finish them off so well. He would sit down there, and he'd start off telling the story to one fellow – some real serious old fellow that would pay attention, and maybe believe it too. You'd swear there was only the two of them in the house. I heard him hundreds of times but I'm no good to think of any thing like that at all. I usen't pay any attention that time to them things.[135]

The same year, also in County Wexford, an informant gave Seán de Buitléir several portraits of raconteurs who specialized in anecdotes and 'lies' (more about the latter genre in Chapter 13). They could use sharp language, and claim victims:

Contributed in 1943 by Pádraig Mac Gréine of Ballinalee. **133** IFC 791: 201-2, from James Argue, aged 75 in 1941. Collected by P.J. Gaynor. **134** IFC 543: 383-4, from Mrs Pat Mullins, aged 75 in 1938, collected by Tomás Ó Ciardha in Co. Wexford. **135** IFC 544: 60, from Tomás Mac Gearailt, collected by T. Ó Ciardha in 1938.

I'll tell you what it is, I was never very good for telling stories myself but I used to take a great delight in listening to an old man in Barmoney telling old tales when I was a young fellow. This man's name was C. and he's dead now this long time, God be good to him. He never had what you could call a good long story but he had bits of almost every old story that any one ever heard. The only time that he would start at the stories would be when he'd be at a wake and there would be a crowd of people listening to him. Some one would know that the lad was there and they would start some story that would remind him of one and then he would be away with it and there would be right fun with him. He told one story anyhow and I can't think now what it was and some one asked him was it long ago since that happened and he said that it was in the time when the streets were paved with two-penny loaves and the houses thatched with pancakes and the pigs were going round with a knife and fork stuck in their sides and saying 'who'll eat who'll eat!' Oh muise it is an awful pity that he is not alive for he had some very good ones and I was never any good to think of stories at all. I remember well though that there used to be an awful take on him at the wakes or at the threshing dance or any place where they would be a crowd of people gathered together.

There was another famous old storyteller and D. was his name and he had some choice ones and no mistake. Well when these two would get together there would certainly be some fun as one of them would be trying to best the other one you see and they used to draw right ones out of each other. Old D. was a devil all-out and he would never laugh at a yarn that C. would tell but when C. would be telling it the lad you know would be trying to think of another one to tell, and sure if he couldn't think of one he had a hell of a head for making them up. They would tell the damnest things that any one ever heard in all their lives and they would nearly get vexed with each other sometimes. An argument would arise as to which of them was the best and begor then the fun would be and no mistake. They were two devils for old riddles and old sayings and I don't know in the hell how the dickens they used to think of half the things that they used to say at all, and they used to be always across each other and would always be giving each other short answers and such like and it used to be a [?] to listen to them and no mistake. One night the two of them were in a public house and begor C. was after getting twenty pounds from America and the story got round that he had it and this night anyhow in the pub D. said to himself that he would give the lad a 'dig' about it. They were drinking away for some time anyway and then D. said to C., 'What are you going to do with that twenty pounds that you get from America?' C. was slightly taken by surprise, but he didn't show it very much and said 'Oh I'm thinking of buying a public-house where nobody but decent people will be let in.' There was a great laugh then all over the place and D. was waiting for them all to be done until he would start to say somehing. The laugh died down anyhow and then says D.: 'That would be alright but how would you get in yourself?' The laugh that followed that was twice as loud as the other one and then the two of them started and begor it was as good as ever you listened to. But as I said before I was never any good for remembering things at all. I'd forget them as quick as ever they'd be told to me however the dickens it is I do not know. I know fellows but they are all nearly dead now and they could sit down by the fire for the whole length of a night and spin out these yarns and could remember things that happened and give day and date for them but I'm not one of them. I think that it is marvellous about these fellows for they must take trouble and worry very easy and put aside all the cares of the world, for if anything was troubling them they surely wouldn't be able to tell all these stories as well as they do and remember all these things in detail.[136]

It was also remembered how, already in the past, some storytellers would complain about an unreceptive audience, as in this item from County Cork:

There was an ould man lived around here long ago. He was a very droll old man, and used to tell very funny stories about all that used to happen to himself when he used to be travelling by night drawing loads to and from Cork City. The old men of his own time used to listen to him, although they knew that more than half of what Thade was telling were lies, but when the young lads of the time would be listening they'd all start laughing at poor Thade. He would get mad over it. ' 'Tis no use to be telling stories to these young fellows, man-in-age, they're too clever' he used to say. 'Every generation is getting smaller an' hardier, man-in-age. When me, and Jem, here, were like them young fellows we would do twice their work, and we done it too, didn't we Jem?', and he used to turn to the old man of the house. 'That's true for you, Thade, and every word you're saying is true. And 'tis the old prophecy Thade that every generation would be getting smaller and hardier'. With such words of encouragement, Thade would begin to tell what himself was able to do when he was young.[137]

Oral information could also be twice removed: here is the account, collected in County Galway, of what had been heard in the past concerning narration in Kerry:

I heard a story once from an old man that was travelling around from place to place gathering rags and old clothes. He stayed one night at my house but sure I was only a kid that time about eight years of age, but young and all as I was I remember him telling his tale. My father and mother the Lord have mercy on them gave him his supper of potatoes and milk, and you never heard a shanachie better than him from that out ... I'm a native of Kerry myself said the traveller, and as you know, it is many a fairy tale the old people of Kerry used to tell on a winter's night, before the turf fire, after the day's work and it isn't out walking on the roads they were then, but the neighbours gathered into one house this winter and in the next house the following winter and so on. First of all they would spend half or a quarter of an hour chatting about the day's work, or about a fair or market that was in the locality asking did this man sell his or what price did he get, or who bought from him. Had any person in the company been at the fair? Did he sell? Or when would he put them out? Some of them would be fishermen, and they would describe the day's boating, and often exaggerating and boasting about how they succeeded in capturing a big pike or trout or maybe a mackerel. Then when all was told and said they would enter into details about the weather and if a storm came the night before telling about the damage it did, and maybe some of the roof, or thatch, blown off such and such a person's house, and from that, maybe it would remind them of the big storm of 1839 and comparing it with the storm of today. Some saying it wasn't

---

136 IFC 545: 633-9, from Mícheál Ó Murchada, aged 67, Glynn Co. Wexford. **137** IFC 1011: 360-1, from Sean McCarthy, aged 76, in 1946. Collected by D. Ó Cruadhlaoich.

half as bad as its account, and that the houses long ago were not half as well looked after as the present day.[138]

Similar social evenings in County Galway itself, at the beginning of the twentieth century, were remembered after the same interval of approximately fifty years:

When you went to visit at night when I was young, seventeen or eighteen or nineteen or twenty years of age, some nights we would be card-playing. Other nights they would be telling stories and everyone had to tell a story. One fellow would begin telling a story and then everyone had to tell a story when it came to his turn. I had a lot of stories in my head one time but they are all gone from me now – I have lost the memory – I'm gone eighty since last May, and when a man is that age he's losing his memory.[139]

I conclude this particular selection of echoes of storytelling and reflected images of storytellers with some items heard in Ulster by Michael J. Murphy:

Frank Mulligan of Drummalane – it's a pity he's dead, and he's only dead a year ago. He could have told cracks till morning about fairies and everything. And times ago, I mind here a big long man they called John Stringers. He was a schoolmaster at times of his life he told me. He could have told cracks better nor anyone. One after the other. He used to go about on crutches. He'd do a day's thrashing with the flail for you and things like that. He's dead a long time. A big long man he was. Then there was John Lathan. He used to work in Ballymacart Mill down the road. He could have told you that he seen the fairies tumbling over the bags in the mill and knocking them on them ...

My grandfather was great at telling all these old cracks, and they used to have great cracks at wakes. That's where they'd all be told. I never heard or knew of any beggarman or beggarwoman comin' in an' tellin' cracks like that. They'd talk and joke, but they'd never tell cracks. And my grandfather would say to me at night – see, he'd only tell you a passage every night, an' you be to remember the last word or he wouldn't tell you any more the next night: 'Remember the last word now, or you'll hear no more'.[140]

Did you ever hear tell of a James McGovern of Stranamount? – I did. A very famous man for telling stories; he told me a lot of stories. He was a great man – he's not that long dead: he died in 1962, James Thomas – Tommy's father. Many's a night I put in with him céili-ing. Many's a night I put in rambling, céili-ing with him. Long ago. And he had ghost stories and everything. He had a great memory. He was a man. He was the greatest gifted man ever I seen.[141]

The informants who celebrated storytellers of the past were not always passive tradition bearers; acknowledged storytellers could draw portraits of those who had taught them their trade. Here is the kind of information Michael Murphy collected from storytellers Michael Rooney and Francis McAleer (cf. pp. 404-5):

---

138 IFC 844: 376-80, from Donncha Ó Cinnéide, aged 55. Collected in 1942 at Cill Mac Duach Co. Galway by Máirtín Ó Mainnín. 139 IFC 1227: 727. Collected by Ciarán Bairéad, Claregalway, 1952. 140 IFC 975: 616; IFC 976: 412 and 465. County Down 1945. 141 IFC 1809: 70-1. County Cavan 1973.

I do remember well when [Michael McLaughlin] told that tale.He'd be sixty-five or sixty-six when I'd go to ceilidhe to them; sitting round the fire, and he'd take off his shoes, and' he'd put on a creel of turf you know. A married man with a big family, seven sons, no daughters. The wife died when they were very small, and he kept them all together ... I'd be forty-six or forty-seven when I heard him tell that story. He was a second cousin of my mother's. A great céili-ing house; sure they'd all come to it. And Michael would be like this and his shoes off and a great big pair of grey socks, home spun socks, after his day's work, and he'd light his pipe and he'd start to tell these yarns. And there'd be a creel of turf; the bog was at the back of the house, turf to no end. Ah, it was America at home! ... It would be a pity, as I said before, for them stories to die away. Oh yes, I enjoyed them when I was young. And I have them word for word and I just learned it in one night; got them, heard them and can repeat them as they told the story to me, Michael McLaughlin. He'd start a story, it was a céili-ing house. He never asked me: 'Would you like to hear a story?' This was a thing that used to go round, telling stories, and he'd start just off, just to amuse people, and of course you'd have to laugh at them; you'd take such an interest in them that you'd swallow them; you'd just take them in the same as a drink of milk.[142]

I can tell you where I heard these stories. I heard the old people tell them and I learned off from them. I heard a man in the next house here the name of John Bradley tell them – Oh, he had bags of them; and I heard James McRory in the next townland to this tell them. James McRory could fill a fodder bag with stories. He could tell as far as sixty in a night. He was great ... It was a man named McRory (or McCrory) that I learned most of my stories from. He was then a native of this part – but not here. He lived in the next townland ... He lived in a wee thatched house there, and the house would be full at night. But not all of them would listen to the stories. Some of them wouldn't bother their heads to listen; they'd be playing cards. But I always took a great interest in him. Me and a fellow named Dan McCrea. That was old Annie McCrea's son that lives beside you in Teebane (Glenhull). If he was alive he could tell you some of McRory's stories as well as me. But he couldn't tell them much better. For many's the time I went back to McRory and he'd say: 'Well, have you it off now?' And I wouldn't be far out. 'You're wrong in a word or two,' he'd say. 'You haven't that bit right.' I kept at it till I got them off by heart. We used to go nearly every night, and we'd say: 'Tell us another story, James.' 'Well,' he'd say, 'what stories did I tell last night. Ah, sure I told that one,' he'd say. 'No matter; let us hear it again.' That's how I got my stories. If only I had ever known someone like you would be coming round for them I could have them better, for it's years since I told them. Lord God, we never thought they were of any value at all, or I'd have them all. He had as many as would fill a fodder bag. James McRory heard all his stories from the old people. He told us he did. He heard some from Oiney McGurk, too, and he had them all from his own people.They lived to a terrible age. James McRory died about seventeen and half years ago. He was aged 78 at that time ... McRory was a big lump of a man. I helped to shave him when he was dead, and it took three of us to lift him.[143]

142 IFC 1803: 113-14; IFC 1786: 202-3, from Michael Rooney, Co. Cavan, in 1972 and 1971.
143 IFC 1215: 266, 290-1, 392 and IFC 1216: 36, from Francis McAleer, County Tyrone, 1950.

The adjective 'terrible' was applied to some storytellers; it might carry ambivalence, connoting either 'great' or 'fearful' and unattractive – or somehow blending those qualities.

Even when they were not considered active traditional storytellers themselves, informants talking about the storytellers of the past could adopt narrative modes and verbally recreate figures by showing them in action. They might emphasize the oddity of what they were evoking. While the preservation of remnants of the past before they sank into oblivion was a matter of national or scientific urgency for folklorists, those they were interviewing were personally involved: most of them would probably agree that at least some standards of living had gone up, but they could also regret a vanished condition of social wholeness, or simply the time of their childhood and youth. The people they talked about were often associated with circumstances now irrecoverable, and were becoming 'legendary'. Where some folklorists might idealize, insiders could sensationalize; in both cases, distortion revealed the symbolic power of the object.

The documentation quoted in the last few pages carries weight because it comes from people who were or had been in the so-called traditional world; professional folklorists, on the other hand, were trained to be precise and factual. The two sources could emphasize different traits as the characteristics of a type – or set of types: personal dignity was one of the defining features recognized by collectors, but was far from being as conspicuous in portraits drawn by their informants. As for occasional contributors to the building up of a general mass of documents relating to folklore, they ranged from the painstaking to the more desultory and sometimes glib, but serious work could be done by them.[144] And a word may be said here about approaches to folklore that had little to do with the strict garnering of information, and even less with scholarly analysis; at the lowest level, only the picturesque was exploited. More respectable perhaps were the generalized celebrations inspired by the idea that what was evoked represented the collective soul of the nation; it found outlets in popular publications, often local ones but sometimes widely distributed like the periodical *Ireland's Own* which, from the beginning of the century, was diffused in rural areas, including those where oral arts had been particularly rich and had not yet vanished. The material was often cheap and vague, but could include usable information, like this portrait of a Donegal storyteller, probably based on genuine memories:

144 Seán Mac Giollarnáth published material collected in County Galway: *Peadar Chois Fhairrge* (1934), and *Loinnir Mac Leabheair agus Sgéalta Gaiscídh Eile* (1936); Tomás de Bhaldraithe published material from another Galway informant: *Seanchas Thomáis Laighléis* (1977); Edmund Lenihan, who tells his versions of older stories in public or on cassettes, published material collected from Jimmy Armstrong, born in 1914 in County Clare: *Long Ago by Shannon Side* (1962). The list is not exhaustive.

I found him seated on the right-hand side of an open turf fire – the place of honour in an Irish homestead. As the performance (if I may be permitted to use that term) had not yet commenced, I had an opportunity of studying him closer than I otherwise could have done. The most remarkable feature about him was his eye. His keen, penetrating glance made you feel somewhat uncomfortable. You felt as though you were under the 'subdue' waves of a hypnotist ... He knew perfectly well how to utilize his voice to the best advantage. He made use of the rhetorical pause just as he was coming to some hair-raising adventure ... His vocabulary was full and accurate. In technical terms, relating to battles, he employed phrases far more picturesque than any to be found in the living speech of to-day. He seemed to have the story in set words, for once or twice I noticed that he used a modern phrase quite correctly but instantly substituted an archaic form therefore ... In a few isolated instances I am afraid that his language was slightly beyond the grasp of his listeners. And now a word about his audience; standing there in perfect silence for four long hours, were rude fishermen. An atmosphere of awe and reverence filled the house. To be present was an education of itself, of no mean order. The sheanachie, undoubtedly, was held in high esteem.[145]

145 J. O'Hare 'The Passing of the Irish Story-Teller', *Ireland's Own* 23 March 1921.

Irish traditional storytelling in the twentieth century: how much do we know?

In the mass of evidence collected mostly during the second third of the twentieth century, is it possible to identify essential constituents of storytelling, and to see how they worked together? Without making it my ambition to come to a final synthesis, in the first part of this chapter I propose to examine the distribution of storytellers according to special functions, gender, age, sedentariness or mobility; then their training: from whom, and how, skills and individual stories were learned and repertoires built, preserved or modified; how far one was aware of a code, and whether it could be circumvented. I shall try and define the place of the storyteller in the community, then the situations in which narrative performances most often occurred, and conventions of storytelling as a social transaction. The relationship of the performers to their listeners will be looked into, as well as the criteria by which the latter recognized talent and assessed storytelling acts. What the narrative power did for the participants and what the stories meant for them will be tentatively explored. The more or less stable or malleable parts of repertoire and craft will be identified. Finally we shall examine special devices and techniques, verbal or otherwise, by which storytellers achieved certain ends.

A few words of caution. First, concerning each of the topics listed above, my data base cannot be complete. Secondly, although they will be treated separately, the elements of storytelling are interdependent and much criss-crossing will therefore be involved. Thirdly, we must remember that it is dangerous to generalize without regard to individual propensities, the different sorts of tales and telling occasions, as well as regional styles and customs. And fourthly, data should be carefully weighed, because in some cases those who produced them may have been tempted to highlight unusual features rather than ordinary ones; I have tried to lessen the risk by accepting, as a rule, only what had been reported by several observers. Though part of what follows may be specific to Ireland, much else has been documented – perhaps with different emphases – from other European countries and even from farther away. What was distinctively Irish, then, and what can we regard as common to a larger area? A limited choice of possible expressive processes and basic narrative techniques may be universal, and we know that tales have often ignored frontiers – as even very patriotic Irish folklorists admitted: 'Irish folk-tale and romance is perhaps the most international feature of our culture'.[1] On the other hand comparisons are risky if elements are isolated from their context and called identical when in fact they function in different ways. I shall mention a few parallels or analogies in notes, essentially as a reminder that what is observed somewhere may be related to a wider context; I make no pretence of thus mapping the distribution of traits. The working hypothesis is that, perhaps, no single detail is unparalleled, though the whole configuration may well be unique. The second part of this chapter will dwell on a particular case: that of one Irish storyteller in English who was considered good and 'traditional' by experts. What is known of his personality, repertoire and means of expression will be discussed, in the light of what is established in the analytic first part.

A. THE COMPONENTS OF STORYTELLING

The first three sections will concentrate on ways of distinguishing storytellers. (How their talents were evaluated will be examined in Section 21).

1. Identifying and differentiating storytellers

Anyone may use narrative forms to organize and relate personal experiences or has heard stories considered worth retelling, but not everyone repeats them with enough persistence and talent to be specially valued for narrative proficiency. In Ireland too, many people were familiar with stories but were not active in their transmission, while a few others performed them in public – the borderline between active and passive tradition bearers perhaps being crossed one way or the other during a lifetime. To the division proposed by von Sydow (see p. 381) between informants who remembered stories they had heard but did not tell them (unless a collector tactfully extracted them – in the form of a 'summary' rather than an actual 'performance'), and regular practitioners, a third category might be added: occasional tellers, who knew a very limited number of stories and recited their pieces, always in the same manner, when some special opportunity occurred.[2] Few persons were known as 'storytellers' in most local communities, and really outstanding personalities practising the more complex narrative art were scarce: 'The number of such gifted story-tellers even in the richest districts of folk-tale is, as a general rule, very small – often only half a dozen in a community of many thousands'.[3] But some regions were reputed to

1 J. Delargy 'Irish Stories and Storytellers', *Studies* 31 (March 1942) 31. 2 The threefold division was proposed by L. Uffer in *Rätoromanische Märchen und ihre Erzähler* 10-14. 3 J. Delargy *The Gaelic Story-Teller* 34. Michael J. Murphy concurred: 'Though everyone has a story just a few people can be called storytellers' (*My Man Jack* 15). Cf. G. Henssen (Germany) *Volkstümliche Erzählkunst* 10: 'Nicht jeder, der in seiner Jugend Gelegenheit hatte, den Ueberlieferungen der Vorfahren zu lauschen, wird dadurch nun später zum Erzähler; immer sind nur einige Menschen von bestimmter Sinnesart und besonderer Begabung die

have more storytellers and stories than others, which led to extreme claims like 'it is generally conceded that the parish of Carna, in West Galway, had more unrecorded folktales in 1935 than did all the rest of western Europe'.[4]

Contrary to what had been observed at the upper level of society in the past, the Irish 'folk culture' we are now analysing had no professional storyteller; but there was a degree of specialization among performers. It was the kind of repertoire they used and their way of presenting it, consequently the function they had in the community they belonged to, that first defined them. The nomenclature in Irish tended to distinguish between *scéal* (story): preferably a stylized and often relatively long, complex narrative;[5] and *seanchas*: accounts, not necessarily narrative, of customs, encounters with the supernatural, local history or genealogies, all valued more as inherited information than as material for entertainment and aesthetically marked performances. A third category, loosely defined, would consist of anecdotes or jokes, and – out of the narrative field – of witty exchanges: *ciútaí* (clever remarks) and *nathaíocht* (wisecracking, use of aphorisms and proverbial sayings). The *scéalaí* performed the first type of material, which functioned as art; the *seanchaí* told the second type, mainly valued for informative truthfulness even when it included wonderful occurrences; there seems to have been no equally charged Irish term for the teller of jokes. (For more concerning the different genres see Section 11 below.) Narrators tended to specialize in one kind of repertoire, though some had a wider range of tastes and competence. In conservative circles there seemed to be a hierarchy, with the *scéalaí* considered – or at least considering himself – superior: 'A storyteller, whose reputation has been made on his skill in telling the old time Fenian tales or other *Märchen*, is, as a rule, somewhat scornful of these short trifles [*seanchas*] and must be pressed to recite them'.[6] There were probably always fewer *scéalaithe* than *seanchaithe*, and the former group was the first to wane. The distinction, however, is not always clearly made: there is nowadays a tendency to call 'shanachie' any Irish storyteller satisfying certain criteria of 'traditionality'. On the other hand some collectors have felt the need to subdivide the native categories. Michael Corduff identified five classes of storytellers in North Mayo:

1. Those who specialized in mythological or heroic tales, such as wonder-voyages, tales of magic and wonder and the like. 2. Those who favoured apocryphal and Biblical narratives, religious legends and stories of the supernatural world ... 3. Persons who preferred to tell local tales, such as stories of adventures by sea and land of named characters (usually natives of the locality) ... 4. Others who specialized in humorous stories or

künftigen Träger der Überlieferung' (few of those who have heard the tales in their youth become active tradition bearers). 4 S. O'Sullivan *Folktales of Ireland* xxxviii. 5 The word *scéal* may have other meanings: historical account, piece of news, state of affairs, matter for reproach, etc.; I use it to refer to complex fictional narratives. 6 Máirtín Ó Cadhain in *Béaloideas* 4 (1934) 87. Also Bo Almqvist in *Béaloideas* 39–41 (1971–3) 19: 'first-rate storytellers combine pride in the long hero tales and *Märchen* with a certain ... contempt for shorter anecdotes and jokes.'

anecdotes for the amusement of their audience. 5 ... those whose tales were of a more modern trend, ... evictions, resistance to baillifs, faction fights ...[7]

The two basic native categories can be recognized in Corduff's number 1 (*scéalaithe*) and in numbers 2 and 3 (*seanchaithe*, perhaps also including 5 unless the material was too recent and rather belonged to the category of personal experience report). Number 4 covers the skilful raconteurs who enlivened informal social occasions. Those who did not narrate 'in public' – for instance a mother addressing her children – could be talented but were generally not counted as 'storytellers' in the same sense of the word.

Acknowledged storytellers, in Ireland like elsewhere in Europe, were often said to belong to the humblest social classes. There is no convincing evidence that the most indigent members always were the most imaginative and articulate, but the fact is storytelling as an art requires no costly equipment.

2. Gender

In the preceding chapters, masculine pronouns and possessives have often been used to refer to traditional storytellers. Was it fair? In Northern-, Central- or East-European countries, some collectors either explicitly associated the telling of complex stories and even the possession of narrative talent with men[8] – or simply counted a large majority of males among their informants;[9] but others in the same regions, and more so in Mediterranean areas, defined storytelling as predominantly a female activity.[10] There might be gender-specific repertoires, favouring male or female protagonists or reserving certain kinds of narratives,[11] and occasions for narrating could differ (men performing particularly for adults, perhaps of both sexes; women for children or for other women).

Patriarchal Ireland is supposed to have been one of the parts of Europe where the traditional distribution of roles defined 'important' storytelling as a male activity. Whether this is objective truth or an assessment made from a dis-

7 'Notes on Storytellers and Storytelling in Iorrus, North Mayo', *Béaloideas* 19 (1949) 178. 8 To give but one blunt example: '... Weiterhin lässt sich feststellen, dass der Mann der bessere Erzähler zu sein scheint als die Frau. Vielleicht hat er mehr Fantasie.' ('One may state that man is a better storyteller than woman. Perhaps he has more fantasy.') L. Uffer *Rätoromanische Märchen und ihre Erzähler* 17. 9 In Germany, in the 1930s, Matthias Zender counted 88% men; in Rumania, in the 1960s, Ovidiu Bîrlea counted 86%. (Quoted in R. Schenda *Von Mund zu Ohr* 153 and 155.) 10 Paul Sébillot 'Les femmes et les traditions populaires', in *Revue des Traditions Populaires* 7 (1892) 449, agreed with great collectors like the Grimm brothers and Luzel who had observed that women provided them with the best versions of tales: 'une expérience déjà longue des conteurs de la Haute-Bretagne me permet de confirmer pleinement ces appréciations.' Yordanka Koceva, in D. Roth and W. Kahn (eds) *Märchen und Märchenforschung in Europa* 29, finds more women, with larger repertoires, in Bulgaria today: 11 A. Van Gennep *La formation des légendes* 268: 'En règle générale, les vieillards et hommes faits récitent plutôt des fragments épiques, les vieilles femmes et sages-femmes content des récits merveilleux à personnages démoniaques et les jeunes femmes des contes ordinaires.'

torting male perspective is now a disputed point.[12] The fact is that Jeremiah Curtin stated, more than a century ago, that great storytelling in Ireland was specifically masculine: 'It is supposed by many persons that women are the chief depositaries of tales touching fairies and other extra-human characters, but they are not. It is a rare thing to find a woman in possession of wonderful tales of the best quality ... In Ireland I have found few women who can tell tales at all, and none who can compare with the best men'.[13] It was often said that although women could produce *seanchas* (indeed, several observers insisted that it was a genre in which they might excel), they were not expected to tell *seanscéalta* (old tales) or tales of the Fianna, which would be the preserve of some men: for women to tell them was 'like hens crowing before the cock'. Nevertheless, they might be passive tradition bearers of that material, remembering the complex narratives they had heard:

Seanchas, genealogical lore, music, folk-prayers, were, as a rule, associated with women; at any rate they excelled the men in these branches of tradition. While women do not take part in the story-telling, not a word of the tales escapes them, and if their relatives or close friends make any slip or hesitate in their recital, it is no uncommon experience of mine to hear the listening woman interrupt and correct the speaker.[14]

Even as mere listeners, however, women were handicapped: they might still be busy with domestic tasks when the men relaxed, and they had less opportunity to assert themselves outside the home (men did the 'night visiting', 'courting' or 'rambling', to be described in Section 14 below). It was not impossible for women to go out, and they might meet to discuss the news, perhaps even exchange tales; but those who ran after stories or gossip and hawked them had a bad reputation, not only as silly rumourmongers but also as women who did not fulfil their real duties; in Ballymoe, Co. Galway, there was a word for it:

She's a 'rambler'. She's a 'cabin hunter' conveys, when passed on a woman or young girl, a very slighting meaning and a severe remark. A bad housekeeper who goes around from one neighbour's or friend's house to the house of another neighbour or friend carrying stories and spends much of her time which should be passed in her house engaged at her own household duties, mending and sewing for her husband and children instead of 'cabin hunting' and idle gossip about people's business.[15]

Still, there were women who addressed audiences, and some exceptions were recorded to the general rule against the telling of important heroic tales by women: the most famous was Peig Sayers, from whom some tales of the Fianna were collected; but the fact that she knew them and told them to a collector does

12 See C. Brennan Harvey 'Some Irish Women Storytellers and Reflections on the Role of Women in the Storytelling Tradition', *Western Folklore* 47 (1989) 109ff, and P. Lysaght 'Perspectives on Narrative Communication and Gender ...', *Fabula* 39 (1998) 256ff. 13 *Tales of the Fairies and of the Ghost World* 144. 14 S. Delargy *The Gaelic Story-Teller* 7. 15 IFC 925: 14. Contributed by Kathleen Hurley.

not prove that, a few years earlier, she would have told them in public to an all-Blasketian assembly.[16] To sum up, kinds of narratives, time and location of performance, and style, may have been gender-specific in Ireland; but information about women's lore and oral skills is relatively scarce, perhaps simply because most collectors were men who did not record what happened in gatherings, known to have existed, in which only women participated. It is obvious, however, that within the family the women played an essential role in the transmission of part of the cultural heritage to children. They could be particularly active as singers. Whether they had a different way of narrating and actually preferred stories with female protagonists is not clear, at least to me.

3. Age

In pre-modern societies, elders generally served as a reservoir of wisdom for the community, and age could be a requirement for an authoritative storyteller. The fact is that recognized storytellers tended to be old, in Ireland as elsewhere: '[In the 1950s and 60s] the ages of most of my storytellers ranged from about sixty to over ninety years'.[17] In 1945, J.H. Delargy noted that storytellers in their twenties were not rare but extremely few of them could tell the 'hero tales' in the 'traditional' manner,[18] mostly because the younger generation was turning away from some older customs and tastes but perhaps also because it took time to master the special craft. In the nineteenth century and probably earlier, those who told stories in public generally did so when they were relatively advanced in years (see Seamas MacManus's account of storytelling as a part of successful aging, p. 320). Younger people had their own kinds of group entertainment; those who wanted to become storytellers had first to be polite listeners and wait until their elders asked them to perform – and thus expose themselves to criticism:[19]

Most storytellers were men passed the age of sixty years, but some were between forty and sixty and a few even younger. An old narrator of reputation often called on a young man to recite in order to give him practice, if he felt that the neophyte had the makings of a *scéalaí* or *seanchaí*. When the young storyteller performed publicly, he had to be cer-

16 F. Alvarez-Pereyre mentions women in Rumania who transgress rules and thus '*postulent symboliquement leur pouvoir sur le village*' – symbolically claim for power (' Règles du contage et stratégie de la parole', *Ethnologie française* 5 (1975) 81-90). 17 M.J. Murphy *Now You're Talking* ... viii. Cf. L. Dégh *Folklore and Society* 169: '[In Hungary] only older men and women tell tales. These storytellers are usually between 60 and 80 years old, and rarely under 40.' Matthias Zender, who interviewed four hundred storytellers in the German Rhineland between 1924 and 1934, found that only 4% were under twenty, 4.5% between twenty and forty, 32% between forty and sixty, 51% between sixty and eighty, and 9% over eighty. (Quoted in R. Schenda *Von Mund zu Ohr* 149.) 18 *The Gaelic Story-Teller* 23. 19 Cf. L. Dégh, op. cit. 378: 'The narrators would come forward only in a favourable situation or after the passing of other outstanding storytellers. Only then did they recite the *Märchen* they had heard since early childhood; from passive carriers of tradition they became active narrators.'

tain of himself, for if he paused too often or too long or left out portions of the tale, he was ridiculed by the islanders and not called on again.[20]

Did the rules deciding who had the right to perform reveal an urge to keep the young, and women, under control?

4. Resident or itinerant storytellers

Walter Benjamin distinguished between two kinds of storytellers: the long-time member of a community, who knew its history and stories, and the traveller who brought news or new tales.[21] In Ireland as in other European countries there were storytellers who did not leave their native place; Seán Ó Conaill is a good example: 'I was born in this village seventy-seven years ago. I have never left this place and I am sure that I shall not leave it until I die'.[22] But there were also people on the roads, and the same informant remembered: 'I used to watch out for anyone with a story, and when the travellers (beggars) would come and one of them would stop in the village, we used to go to the house they stayed listening to them telling stories, and trying to pick them up from them'.[23]

There had always been itinerants in Ireland. In ancient society they had included 'men of skill' with relatively prestigious positions, and well into the eighteenth century vagrants could be respected by the native population – while Tudor colonists had diabolized them. In the first half of the nineteenth century, large sections of the so-called 'settled' population were often on the move (labourers, cattle drovers, tailors, pedlars ...), and there were many homeless beggars. The numbers of such people dwindled in the second half of the nineteenth century but some remained or were remembered in the first half of the twentieth. Settled people had generally welcomed them, not only because the rules of hospitality commanded it but also because wayfarers carried oral messages from one household to another and were a source of news as well as of entertainment:

I heard my father say that one time a travelling man named Gillen, I think it was Paddy Gillen his full name was, came to some house in Carnanrancy one winter; and that he was a great story-teller. I never heard him say where he came from; only he said that the house used to be full, everyone would gather in at night to hear him tell stories ... The people generally welcomed the arrival of travelling people in earlier times, because of the news they had to tell gleaned from their travels, of the songs and stories, and because it was told to be unlucky to turn a travelling person away, especially if they asked for help or shelter in the Name of God.[24]

Each poor traveller had a certain house to face and stop in every night, and when they came at night they were welcomed almost as a member of the family whom they

20 John Messenger 'Joe O'Donnell, Seanchai of Aran', *Journal of the Folklore Institute* 1 (1964) 203. 21 'The Storyteller', in *Illuminations* 85. 22 'Seán Ó Conaill's Own Story', recorded in 1930 (*Sean Ó Conaill's Book* xvii). 23 Ibid. xviii. 24 IFC 1218: 188, 192, from Michael Morris, Co. Tyrone. Collected by M.J. Murphy in 1959.

had not seen for some time, for the people liked to hear the news the poor travellers had brought from outside districts, and listen to the long fireside stories.[25]

'Twas an old tramp I heard telling this story years and years ago, when tramps were plentiful in the county an it seems this tramp in his wandering happened to spend a few nights in a townland called Tullyhough in the North of the county, for it was there he told me that he heard the following yarn ...[26]

Some of those newsmongers and narrators belonged to a special social group known as 'tinkers' (the neutral term is now 'travellers', or – most politically correct – 'our indigenous ethnic minority' as in the *Irish Times* of 10 June 1995). The origins of this population are obscure: quite distinct from Gypsies and Romanies, they are sometimes said to be the descendants of ancient nomadic craftsmen, or of people dispossessed in the Cromwellian era or at the time of the Great Famine. They used to cover regular circuits, and provided marginal service to the settled community as tinsmiths, chimney sweeps, hawkers, horse or donkey dealers, while the women begged. Until the late nineteenth or early twentieth century, it seems they often sought accommodation from the country folk, with whom they had much contact; later, they would camp on the outskirts of villages and towns, in tents or barrel-top wagons. In the evening they would sit around the campfire – not in a semi-circle facing the fireplace as settled people did – and could take turns telling stories. Occasionally a local man would join them, as one informant remembered in 1972:

In the country [in the 1930s and 40s] in poor cottages the labourin' man was very poor. The pay wasn't much good. Well they'd come up and sit down by the fire with the Travellin' People. And the Travellin' People would go down to their house for a ramble at night. There was no television at that time, and there wasn't much radios either. So they used to sit around the fire and tell stories and sing a song. That's what the Travellin' People were very fond of. Fairy stories and all this carry on, and without any drink. They used to be far happier and have a better laugh.[27]

A special category of occasional entertainers with their own sub-culture thus lived outside the settled community and were considered socially inferior, but had some special skills. Their folktales did not seem to differ fundamentally from those of the settled people, but their language sometimes did. They were not often recorded by the collectors of the Irish Folklore Commission, probably because they generally told their stories in English and also because it was difficult to keep in touch with people who were always on the move. Traveller-settler relations have deteriorated; some may still idealize 'free' nomadism, and others consider the lifestyle of those who practised it a cultural curiosity; more

25 IFC 107: 46, from Patrick Martin, aged 65, of Ballymitty Co. Wexford. Collected by T. Ó Ciardha in 1935. **26** IFC 485: 151, from S. P. Ó Breathnach, 72, of Cloghoge Co. Sligo. Collected by B. Molloy in 1938. **27** G. Gmelch and B. Kroup *To Shorten the Road; Traveller Folktales from Ireland* 33.

despise them as social misfits, and discriminate against them. In the second half of the twentieth century, as their crafts and services were no longer needed in the country, many moved to urban ghettos.[28] The whole group was estimated at 20,000 in the early 1990s.

The next four sections examine how and from whom storytellers acquired narratives and modes or strategies of narration, and how tales or elements of tales could be stored in the mind.

5. *Learning from oral tradition*

In modern times, there was no organized training for the kinds of storytelling we are concerned with. How, then, were tales and skills learned? Innate aptitudes (a good memory, a talent for speaking) and inclinations were necessary; but beyond gift and taste, experience was essential: you discovered the craft by listening to older performers, learned it by trying to imitate them, then took every opportunity to improve a command of narrative construction, voice control and tricks of the trade to catch and hold an audience's attention. You also had to acquire a fund of stories, which was likely to be perceived as a link with the past: storytellers generally remembered from whom this or that story had been obtained. The sources were often relatives: 'At night in the house one of us would get on every side of him at the fire and lean an elbow on every knee. "Tell us a story, grandda." And he'd tell us stories: that's how I know so many of the old pieces.'[29] Performance styles were also observed within the kinship group in childhood and youth.[30] It may have been a kind of osmosis rather than conscious learning: 'Anything I'm telling you I got from the old people; and how the hell it comes through my head I don't know'.[31] Peig Sayers' model was her father. So was Johnny Cassidy's:

He learned it from his father, and I learned it from me father. But I forgot the best part of the stories me father had. Just, they're only in history yet. But if I was going, like him now, through the houses again, I'd be telling 'em constantlier. The same as I'm telling 'em for you now, I'd be telling 'em constantlier, and they'd come back in me memories again, all complete, you see. But he was more used to the job, and he followed it up more. In them days, some years ago, that was the whole go: storytelling through the houses. But now it's all over.[32]

He had ambivalent feelings when his sons tried to emulate him:

28 See Jim Mac Laughlin *Travellers and Ireland: Whose Country, Whose History?* 29 IFC 1693: 235, from Johnny McAteer, Kileen, South Armagh. Collected by P.J. Murphy in 1965. 30 G. Henssen *Volkstümliche Erzählkunst* 6: 'Erkündigt man sich bei den Erzählern nach ihren Gewährsleuten, so nennen sie in der Mehrzahl der Fälle den häuslichen Kreis oder auch den der Nachbarschaft' (... the sources were in the family circle or in neighbouring houses). 31 IFC 1801: 113, from Frank Campbell. Collected by M.J. Murphy in 1972. 32 Artelia Court *Puck of the Droms* 182.

Johnny, a masterly storyteller, routinely disparaged his sons when they had the temerity to retell his stories in his presence or to try to help when he stumbled over a phrase or passage. The excellence of a son's rendering did nothing to lessen Johnny's ferocity, for it was his family leadership – most fully realized in occupational mastery – that he defended. But when his sons were not around to hear him and misconstrue his remarks as an invitation to rebellion, Johnny could speak proudly of their storytelling abilities.[33]

The father-son (or -daughter) line was often stressed: 'I heard that story from my father may the Lord have mercy on his soul about forty years ago. About fifty. I often heard him telling it';[34] or: 'And here's another story I heard my father telling: something that happened during the life of his grandfather from whom he heard the story.'[35] But the source could also be the mother, or could skip a generation; and it was possible to go beyond that circle:

As the word passed around the village that old Billy [in Connemara] was telling stories, the neighbours began to drift in and soon the walls were lined with interested listeners. One of the most eager of these was a young boy of twelve, who was himself learning to be a shannnecha. Hardly a phrase of the old man's tale escaped him. Little by little he is working up a repertoire.[36]

In the beginning of my life, when I was growing up, I was very interested in learning the Finn-tales if I heard of anyone who could tell them, and I often heard about them at home and what fine entertainment they were on a long night, that you would not feel the time passing. Whenever I heard a tale I would take it up so that I got a strong wish for them. There was no one very near to me who could tell them, but there was a man in the village called Micheál Ó Conaill, and he used to spend his time after Michaelmas going around the countryside making baskets – there were few people at that time able to make them – and he used to be away until Christmas. When he came home after his rounds he had a collection of tales to tell, and I would be well to the fore in the crowd listening to him, and whatever he said I took it from him! So as I was growing up and taking things in, if I went out at night with anyone else and heard a story, I would want to return again and again if someone would come with me, but those of my own age were not interested in stories; they preferred other kinds of amusement. I used to go off by myself at night.[37]

For singing, an old master might choose a younger disciple who would inherit his art and repertoire;[38] the same may have happened with storytelling (I have no conclusive Irish evidence of it, but see Francis McAleer's statement p.

33 Ibid. 47. 34 IFC 628: 253, from Jim McMahon, aged 60, Newcastle-West. Collected by S. Ó Dálaigh in 1939. 35 Conchúr Ó Siocháin *Seanchas Chléire* (tr. R.P. Breathnach) 5-6. 36 Stith Tompson 'Folktale Collecting in Ireland', *Southern Folklore Quarterly* 2 (1938) 56. 37 *Seán Ó Conaill's Book* (tr. Máire MacNeill) xx. 38 Daniel Fabre 'Pierre Pous, conteur du Pays de Sault', *Cahiers de Littérature Orale* 11 (1982) 146-7: 'Les bons narrateurs se forment ainsi, entre sept et dix ans, en ajoutant à l'audition publique des contes au cours des veillées cette communication plus intime, cette transmission volontaire, appliquée, du vieux conteur vers l'héritier qu'il a élu' (the period between the ages of seven and ten is crucial, and an old storyteller can choose an heir and train him).

425). Mature storytellers could still learn new tales from neighbours or travellers. Some could 'pick up stories' very easily: 'I knew people and if they heard a story told tonight they'd be able to tell every word of it to you after'.[39]

As we shall see later, it was probably the internal organization of the story – a certain combination of situations and events – that was stored in the memory, along with verbal formulae adaptable to any tale. But just to memorize tale schemata and phrases was not enough; the would-be storyteller also had to assimilate the techniques with which he could flesh them out again, amplify or reduce them at will, and find the best tone his own personality and voice made possible. Expressive competence would develop slowly, through practice and perhaps failure.[40] It seems reasonable to conclude that the bulk of the repertoire was established early[41] but could keep increasing, and that the perfecting of the techniques took time. There must have been differences between the training of a great *scéalaí* and that of an occasional transmitter of *seanchas*.

6. Learning from written sources

For old-style folklorists, this was abominable: 'traditional' tales were supposed to be passed on exclusively by the mouth to ear process. In actual fact, written and oral channels may interfere with each other in countries like Ireland where literate and non-literate lines have coexisted for centuries. Those who wanted informants who had absolutely no direct contact with written material might find such people; nevertheless, written material often had an influence, which was not necessarily disruptive if what was borrowed was assimilated and used according to the principles of oral arts: 'The teller can take a tale from a book, and if he invests it with culturally derived power, it will ascend to folklore'.[42] Such 'folklorization' of read narratives has been documented in Ireland:

These three stories were told by a woman of sixty, named Una Canavan. Her grandfather had a big book full of stories written in Irish ... Una had heard the stories from her aunt, who had heard her grandfather read them out of the book.[43]

While a few of the narrators [interviewed in the early 1980s] emphatically stated that they would not tell tales that they had learned from books or other printed media because they were 'not folklore', a surprising number know, have told, or tell tales that they originally read or heard recited from printed sources. Sean Ó Duinnín, for example, an accomplished narrator in Irish, frequently performs tales he learns from printed collections, but only after he has 'put his own Irish' on them.[44]

39 IFC 1169: 320, from Donncha O'Flaherty, 70, Mountcoal, Kerry. Collected by S. Ó Dalaigh in 1950.   40 Cf. L. Dégh *Folktales and Society* 169: 'Generally they heard the *Märchen* during their youth, and only much later attained the rank of storytellers.'   41 Cf. B. Holbek's observation in Denmark: 'It appears that tales were learned in childhood and adolescence, but mastery in storytelling was only achieved later' (*Interpretation of Fairy Tales* 173).   42 H. Glassie *Passing the Time* 147.   43 L. M'Manus 'Folk Tales from Co. Mayo, Ireland', *Folk-Lore* 26 (1915) 182.   44 C. B. Harvey *Contemporary Irish Traditional Narrative* ... 13. Cf. L. Uffer *Rätoromanische Märchen und ihre Erzähler* 71: '[Spinas Plasch] hat in

The influence of written forms seems to have been particularly important for lays and romances of the Fianna – 'indeed the tales which the unlettered storytellers themselves respected most'[45] – through the reading aloud of manuscripts, or consultating them when the accuracy of an oral performance was challenged, until the middle of the nineteenth century. But even there, oral transmission could bring improvements when medieval romances which, as A.J. Bruford noted, were 'often long and rambling and sometimes dull', were tightened up.[46]

For the *Märchen* kind, there was the spread and reading aloud of chapbooks like the *Royal Hibernian Tales* (see p. 172). From the late nineteenth century, some popular periodicals gave tales taken from or aping oral tradition, which could be memorized by a reader, and (re)adapted to oral telling. The widely diffused *Ireland's Own* (see p. 426) played such a role:

Its popularity down the years in the homes of Ireland has created a situation where, frequently, only the greatest skill and patience on the part of the collector will save him or her from laboriously noting a story, legend or proverb which forms part of the oral tradition but which has its ultimate origin in the columns of *Ireland's Own* rather than in the ordinary corpus of local folk tradition ... [Yet] the process of transmission from the printed words in say, *Ireland's Own*, through the medium of the storyteller and back to the notebook page of the collector ... is very frequently not simply a case of garbled regurgitation, for a gifted storyteller may add or subtract, censor or embellish at will, drawing on a store of traditional motifs and narrative techniques which may often serve to leave the finished product a cut above the original printed version.[47]

7. Owning, stealing or sharing tales

Just as the importance of illiteracy as a condition of folklore may have been exaggerated, so may the notion that there are no rights of personal ownership attached to 'folk' compositions. Important pieces of a repertoire could be considered to belong to a certain individual in the community, as long as he performed them efficiently. It was common courtesy not to tell or sing a valuable item in the presence of the master from whom you had heard it. Learning a certain tale from a reputed storyteller could be difficult if he regarded it as personal property to be protected from rivals: 'A good story was much valued, and the reciter of a good one might refuse to part with it or teach it to another, in order

---

seinem Leben gern und viel gelesen. Auch Geschichten hat er gelesen und etwa nacherzählt [he told stories he had read]. Aber wie Zahn erklärte: "Chellas tg' ins ò santia rachintar, ah chegl è ensatge tot oter" [... the stories one has heard told, ah, that's quite different]'. In Hungary, Linda Dégh found '40 percent of the total body directly or indirectly related to book tales. Narrators were actively seeking to expand their repertoires by listening to the reading of stories, which they then kept retelling and gradually shaping.' (In J. McGlathery, ed. *The Brothers Grimm and Folktales* 69.) **45** Máire Mac Neill 'Irish Folklore as a Source for Research', *Journal of the Folklore Institute* 2 (1965) 344. **46** *Gaelic Folktales and Medieval Romances* 168. **47** Séamas Ó Catháin *The Bedside Book of Irish Folklore* 11.

that he might not lose the glory attaching to its recitation'.[48] I have witnessed the refusal by an Irish ballad-singer to produce one particular item in his repertoire because another singer was present and obviously eager to have it. A tale could also be given, or symbolically 'sold': a Dunquin storyteller said that he was told a certain story by an old man on condition that he fetched him a few pailfuls of water on a rainy night.[49]

We are perhaps crossing the borderline between observation and sensational stories about storytelling (a subject developed in the next chapter) with narratives of how a tale had been 'stolen'. In a detailed version given by David Thomson, the thief is a tailor who has tried for years to get an old man's best story, which 'took more than an hour in the telling'; but the old man would never tell it in his presence. One evening, the tailor hid in the old man's loft; the story was told at last. ' "I have it," [the tailor] shouts, and his voice is high like a little pipe. "I have it now!" and he's down from the ladder with that and out the door'.[50] A shorter account of the subterfuge is in Delargy's *The Gaelic Story-Teller*: ' "I have the tale now in spite of you!" cried Lynch to the poor beggar-man'.[51]

In real life, the rule may be that a story belongs to whoever tells it well, but a storyteller is someone who is willing to share what he knows. A tale lives on provided that it is transmitted, and the principle of reciprocity applies to the exchange of tales.

8. Memorization

'I have it now' – but exactly what did one 'have' when a tale had been learned, and how did one 'keep' it? How was a story processed in comprehension, then committed to memory, and subsequently recalled and reproduced? Psychologists and anthropologists tell us that what people record is what they think is important, which is influenced by their culture, and that its reconstruction later involves transformations. We know that long-term memory can either store chronologically sequenced units or reorganize the information according to other patterns; that it is not static but dynamic and generative; that it is not infallible but labile; that the act of recalling is conditioned by the present context.

What can documents on Irish storytelling tell us about this? First, we note that researchers or their informants have often marvelled at some individuals' memorizing capacity, and several storytellers asserted that a long item of folklore could be perfectly preserved after one hearing:[52]

48 J.G. McKay 'Scottish Gaelic Parallels', *Béaloideas* 3 (1932) 145. 49 IFC 256: 240. 50 David Thomson *The People of the Sea* 60-2. 51 Op. cit. 26. 52 Cf. Gottfried Henssen, concerning a German storyteller, in *Überlieferung und Persönlichkeit: Die Erzählungen des Egbert Gerrits* 236: 'Das einmalige Hören einer Geschichte genügt ihm, um sie festzustellen und noch nach Jahresfrist in allen Einzelheiten widerzugeben' – several years after hearing a story only once, he could tell it exactly.

I wouldn't be any more than fourteen when I heard that story and I'm seventy-three now. He told it to me the once now; he didn't tell it a second time and I have it word for word as I was telling you, everything the same as the man told me, and I was only fourteen or fifteen at the time. I was interested in it. You know ... Oh yes, I enjoyed them when I was young. And I have them word for word and I just learned it in one night; got them, heard them and can repeat them as they told the story to me.[53]

For prose narratives, 'evidence for exact repetition of long pieces does exist', but by and large, and beyond special forms like proverbs and charms, 'exact repetition of standardized verbal forms, whether narrative or not, whether short or long, is rare'.[54] 'Exact' may, paradoxically, be used in a loose sense, or selectively, if one retains only some guiding scheme and ways of filling it: 'Recall in folk narratives is not mere reproduction ... [It] is essentially constructive'.[55] The process by which a narrator stores the relevant information in his memory may consist in ways of organizing the 'macro-structures' of a plot (relations between events or characters, and major turning-points), along with genre-specific stylistic devices; in that case, even if a certain tale is heard only once, having heard many similar ones would help: 'From experiencing hundreds of [folktales] over their lifetime people acquire this abstract framework about simple stories. They then apply this tacit framework to sort out and understand any new story they hear: they instantiate concepts such as setting, protagonist, goals, and problem-solving actions in terms of the concrete particulars of the given story. They also use this framework to reconstruct a story they have heard.'[56]

Perhaps some tellers succeed in grasping abstract relationships contained in the deep structure of a plot, but most of them need props to encode and retrieve a story. The process of recall may be based on the system of memorization known to ancient Greeks and Romans: the *ars mnemonica* of visualizing clues while progressing through some imaginary building, 'so that the order of the places will preserve the order of the things, and the images of the things will denote the things themselves'.[57] Some traditional narrators would essentially remember the hero's itinerary, or some striking images (the choice of which is partly subjective) would function as markers: 'It seems likely that the average story-teller, who does not memorize a whole story word for word, remembers much of it in the form of a series of tableaux, possibly actually visualized, which he then describes in his own words; it may even be the normal way of learning stories for all story-tellers.'[58] The method was said to have been used in Ireland

53 IFC 1838: 132-3 and IFC 1786: 202, from Michael Rooney, recorded by M.J. Murphy in 1974 and 1971. **54** Jack Goody *The Interface between the Written and the Oral* 176-7. **55** M. Hoppál 'Folk Narrative ...', in N. Baralakoff and C. Lindhal (eds) *Folklore on Two Continents* 297. **56** G.H. Bower 'Experiments on Story Understanding and Recall', in A.K. Pugh (ed.) *Language and Language Use* 387. **57** Quintilian, quoted in Frances Yates *The Art of Memory* 2. On the memorization of folktales, see N. Belmont and G. Calame-Griaule (eds) *Les Voies de la mémoire*. **58** Alan Bruford *Gaelic Folk Tales and Medieval Romances* 217. See also D.A. Macdonald 'A Visual Memory', in *Scottish Studies* 22 (1978) 1-26, and 'Some Aspects of

as well: 'The storyteller's chief gift is a sort of visionary power which enables him to see the persons and events he describes'.[59] S. Ó Cahan heard this comment from a Mayo storyteller: 'I would believe the man from Scotland, Séamas, about seeing the thing in front of him on the wall. The way I am too when I'm telling a story, especially old stories of old warriors long ago, ... it seems to me when I'm telling the story that I should see them standing on the floor and that I should be able to describe their real height and breadth and strength, so much does it run through my mind.'[60] Another technique is known to have been used in Brittany: between 1919 and 1925, a storyteller born in 1904 learned more than a hundred pieces, some of them one hour long, from an old man who refused to tell his tales more than once, perhaps to make sure his successor really qualified. The apprentice was advised to reduce the story he heard to a limited number of brief statements, like 'the hero did this, then he went there, then he did this', and to memorize the synopsis; thirteen such elements woud be sufficient to individualize a tale.[61]

It was possible to memorize the set verbalization of some key-passages, and to fill in the rest extemporaneously. Informants often claimed word-for-word reproduction, and collectors could sometimes confirm it (except for very minor variations), but we may assume that some improvisation or accident during performance was possible. No doubt individual talents and methods varied in this respect,[62] and the degree of recomposing also depended on the kind of narrative: a singer hardly changed the ballads he/she knew well – after having shaped *his/her* versions of them; stories recognized as particularly venerable required more precision and the 'correct' wording had to be learned, through many repetitions, sometimes checking a passage in a manuscript (see p. 100): 'My own father ... had the old *scéalta Fiannaíochta* [stories of the Fianna] and he told me that when he was learning them 'twas verse by verse he picked them up'.[63] Delivering standard texts by rote was supposed to be the rule for 'Ossianic' lays, and perhaps also for some prose versions of Fianna stories; J. Delargy vouched for such a feat achieved by Seán Ó Conaill:

Visual and Verbal Memory in Gaelic Storytelling', in *ARV* 37 (1981) 117-24; or A. Bruford 'Memory, Performance and Structure in Traditional Tales', ibid. 103-9: a storyteller of South Uist, interviewed in 1973, said he remembered the tales because he saw them as a moving picture on a wall. John Stewart, in *Tocher* 31 (1979) 48: 'I jist lie an picture them, think them. Picture them in ma own head and then put them – put it intae words, ye know.' Stanley Robertson, in *Tocher* 40 (1986) 177: 'I see [the story I am telling] as though I was watchin a film or a play.' 59 Kevin O'Nolan 'The Use of Formula in Storytelling', *Béaloideas* 39-41 (1971-3) 245. 60 *Béaloideas* 48-9, 254. 61 Donatien Laurent 'The Mnemonic Process of a Breton Storyteller', in ARV 1981, 111-15 and 'Un conteur breton de Haute Cornouaille et son système de mémorisation des contes merveilleux', in J.B. Martin (ed.) *Le Conte; Tradition orale et identité culturelle* 267-73. 62 Cf. Max Lüthi *Once Upon a Time* 71: 'Some changed the story each time they told it, and others kept the same wording intact, as if the words were sacred and inviolable – and both versions were acclaimed.' 63 IFC 354: 284, from S. Ó Flannagáin, of Kiltartan, Co. Galway.

As for his memory, it was a marvel. 'I never heard a Finn-tale,' he said to me once, 'from the time I was a twelve-year-old boy, that I did not have in my head as soon as it was told.' That was true. I remember that at Christmastime 1923 I heard him tell the story of Diarmuid and Gráinne almost word for word as it is in Standish Hayes O'Grady's edition[64] ... He told me he had heard the story read twice by someone who had the book, but the reader did not go further than that point of the story ... ; it was about fifty-five to sixty years since he had heard it, but the wording in the book had remained in his memory. I knew I might not be believed if I said I had met a man with such a memory, and so I wrote down what Seán had heard of the story, and I have kept the written document as proof.[65]

But for 'ordinary' prose narratives, and particularly for *seanchas*, it was different; we may suppose that most of those who said they could learn such stories from hearing them only once, and repeat them 'word for word' after a lapse of half-a-century or more, were probably deceiving themselves as far as verbal accuracy was concerned. In reality they remembered kernels of plot and key phrases, and used the common phraseology stored in their minds to revive the whole. The kind of memory this involved was 'constructive recollection', partly a new 'composition'.[66] Still, a gifted Irish storyteller was often said to repeat exactly what he had heard, and could sincerely believe that he did.

Different storytellers could memorize differently[67] and memorizing, whatever form it took, was not sufficient to make a good storyteller:

Tom is feeble and finds it very hard to express himself. He is not and never was a storyteller and any peculiar idioms which he uses are ones that slip from him unconsciously having been picked from his grandmother by continuous repetition. He is easily confused and has not himself a very clear picture of the things of which he speaks – he is rather a dictaphone record of his grandmother's stories.[68]

What sense of 'tradition' (both as cultural continuity and as a valuable heritage) was there in the so-called 'traditional' community? How adaptable were received narratives supposed to be? How large and varied could an individual's

---

64 *Toruigheacht Dhiarmuda agus Ghrainne*, first published in 'Ossianic Society Transaction 3', 1855. **65** *Seán Ó Conaill's Book* xi. **66** Cf. I. Sándor 'Dramaturgy of Tale-telling', in *Acta Ethnographica Academiae Scientarum Hungariae 16*: '[The storyteller is not] reproducing mechanically a precisely memorized text. Tale-telling is a far more complicated psychological process: the narrator must call to mind the skeleton of the tale as a dynamic scheme, then, moving from one passage to the other, he has to embellish this scheme in his fantasy and add an emotional excitation to the story while entering fully into its spirit, and finally, he must make the stylistic elaboration of the subject and pronounce the text.' **67** Gyula Ortutay distinguished two types of storytellers in Hungary: 'One sticking faithfully, and as far as possible without changes, to the traditional material, the other characterized by a freer presentation and a gift for making alterations, exchanging motifs or even introducing new ones. Outstanding talents, skilful storytellers as well as hesitant beginners can be found in both types.' (*Hungarian Folklore: Essays* 230). **68** IFC 265: 3, collector Patrick O'Toole, 1935.

repertoire be? How were stories classified – by the narrators themselves, and by scholars?

9. Respect for 'tradition', invention and creativity

In the first half of the twentieth century the word 'tradition', familiar to folk-lorists and irishized as *traidisiún*, does not seem to have been in common usage among their informants: the concept of cultural heritage existed, however, and the term in Irish that came near to express it was probably *sean* (old), in words like *seanfhocal* (a proverb), *sean-nós* ('old style' – a supposedly old manner of unaccompanied singing), *an seanreacht* (the old order or law), *seanscéal* (a story of olden times). In all those cases, ancientness, which is of course a relative notion, connoted worth, and what had been transmitted from generation to generation was treated with respect. Two favourite phrases were 'It was always said that ...' and 'The old people used to tell us long ago that ...', or variants of those formulae in Irish and in English.[69] It is in the nature of 'tradition' to stress links with the past and a communion with the dead: meetings of 'traditional' musicians in Ireland often include praises of local pipers, fiddlers or singers who have passed away. Storytellers also felt that they were links in a chain, and no one wanted to be the last. According to J. Delargy, 'many of the best of the old storytellers were conscious that they had many ancestors'.[70] Perhaps the awareness of acting as transmitter was increased by the coming of collectors, but irrespective of that and despite, or because of, a series of socio-cultural ruptures in Irish history, the perpetuation of something could be seen as particularly important.[71]

It was generally thought that to play the role of guardian of a cultural heritage and of a bridge between the past and the future meant avoiding to alter even the mere form of the message.[72] Hence the insistence, already mentioned, on 'word for word' accuracy as a guarantee of genuineness: 'So that's my story, and I didn't take from it or put to it. It just stands this minute the way the tramp told it to me forty-five years ago'.[73] As noted in the preceding section, however, some qualifications are necessary: for merely informative narratives, accuracy concerned facts rather than the words used to report them; for some elaborate and respectable pieces, on the other hand, blatant formal variation would be perceived as betrayal; but for many stories told to entertain, provided he/she respected community standards defining appropriate forms the skilful storyteller could choose better words, omit certain details or develop certain parts or add interpolated episodes, and combine elements in different ways: 'A

69 Seán Ó hEochaid *Siscéalta Ó Thír Chonaill* ... 126, 252. 70 *The Gaelic Story-Teller* 21. 71 R.S. Allison, in T.A. Green (ed.) *Folklore: an Encyclopedia* 800: 'For the bearers of a particular tradition or set of traditions, the performance establishes a connection between the present group and their predecessors.' 72 L. Dégh *Folktales and Society* 166: '[A certain woman in Hungary] felt herself responsible for the text which she had inherited from her parents; she did not consciously change one single word, because she would have considered any variation a falsification.' 73 IFC 485: 153, S.P. Ó Breathnach, Cloghogue, to Bríd Molloy, in 1938.

competent tradition bearer not only reproduces formerly learned material, but also, according to mastered rules, transforms familiar elements into new wholes.'[74] If the individual could shape the material to his own taste, the community decided what was acceptable and worth reproducing; but then it was again an individual who chose what he wanted to learn and how he would treat it, according to his own inclinations – without ignoring the general habits or the particular mood of the audience in front of which he might test out new bits.[75] And something could become 'traditional' rapidly enough: 'In Ireland, north and south, what was a sentimental innovation yesterday can, by a bit of astute and unanimous support from the right quarters, become an ancient and unquestionable tradition by tomorrow.'[76] Conservative and apparently rigid though it may appear to be, tradition was thus relatively flexible and allowed some scope to the individual.

Was it possible to produce something entirely new? While many singers and musicians are said to have composed songs or tunes in the 'traditional' manner, the possibility of making up new tales which become integrated into the common corpus is hardly acknowledged – except for personal experience stories, but even those tend to follow received patterns. Were good storytellers really unable, or unwilling, to invent stories, then? Some, to the embarrassment of folklorists, are known to have adapted stories from non-Irish books and offered them orally in Irish;[77] it is not unthinkable that they might also have invented plots (though I have no certain proof that twentieth-century collectors' informants did so). Of course, any complex tale must have originated with someone, and it is always possible to create 'new' tales according to a certain code, but the usual definition of the folktale tends to rule out the present informant as originator.

This does not exclude the possibility of deliberate variation or unplanned improvisation in the course of narration. It often affected verbalization and circumstantial details, but might also effect a new combination of larger elements to produce a new, composite tale. Each 'traditional' craftsman endowed with personality could modulate his observance of rules and norms, playing with the audience's expectations and deciding which of the structural or verbal devices he knew should be used on a particular occasion; selectivity in itself is already a form of creation. Performance is generally not the mere reproduction of rehearsed material; although there are limits to the amount of change acceptable as still 'traditional', a performer can use his creative power – perhaps with increasing freedom as he gains confidence in his skill.[78]

74 Juha Pentikäinen *Oral Repertoire and World View; An Anthropological Study of Marina Takalo's Life History* 19. 75 Cf. G. Ortutay, *Hungarian Folklore; Essays* 227: 'It is the special tension prevailing between the personality and the tradition preserved by the community that gives us the clue to an understanding of the essence of popular culture, and a one-sided emphasis on any of the factors may well lead us astray.' 76 S.H. Bell *Erin's Orange Lily* 105. 77 See James Stewart *Boccaccio in the Blaskets*. 78 A. Kaivola-Bregenhøj *Narrative and Narrating: Variation in Juho Oksanen's Storytelling* 20-1: 'The teller is active at each of these

10. Losing tales and building a repertoire

One of the components of the memorizing process is screening, which entails oblivion; indeed, the capacity to forget, though often bemoaned, is necessary. As a kind of collective memory, oral tradition selects, reshapes what it keeps – and laments the fact that so much seems to disappear irretrievably. At the individual level, certain tales are simply not registered, and some of those that are latent in the memory may never be transmitted while others are performed and retain relevance.[79] Thus parts of the fund of narratives undergo extinction, and awareness of it is quite common; collectors seem always to have been told that if only they had come a bit earlier they would have met storytellers, now dead, who had marvellous tales; or that the informant himself used to know much more than he can impart now: 'I heard most of the stories from Michael McLoughlin of Guberveeny ... Had I known that one day someone like yourself would come recording them I could have heard three times as many.'[80] The mass of 'lost tales' was a constant theme in interviews: 'Many though the tales be which I have told to you, I have forgotten as much again';[81] 'He told me, too, that if I had come to him five years earlier he could have told me an heroic tale for every day in the year but he had now forgotten most of them';[82] 'Sure God bless you I heard hundreds on tops of hundreds and I forget most of them, You have only a small part of what I heard here in my time with the old fellows'.[83]

Remembering may not be effortless, and is not infallible. Storytellers have been seen to struggle with their memory. They might require solitary rehearsal to make sure they could still tell a certain story in public after a long interval, and it was not rare for the storyteller simply to dry up; thus Michael J. Murphy, in County Down, heard the phrase ' "I can't get a-hold of it", when a speaker gave up his attempt to remember and tell the gist of the story'.[84]

What was left, and could be added to, constituted the individual's repertoire: the stock of tales he was prepared to perform. It might be homogeneous or varied in terms of genres (see the next section). At any given time there were favourite pieces, while others – which then might be revived only with some effort – could later become regular pieces in their turn.[85] The reputation of a

three stages [learning the story, storing it in his memory, and telling it], in other words he can influence what he learns or does not wish to learn, how much of what he learns constitutes his active repertoire and how much belongs to the latent store of folklore with which he is familiar, the way he varies the tale and the way he adds to and renews his repertoire.' **79** L. Dégh *Folktales and Society* 175: 'He adds certain tales to his repertoire, while he leaves out others without even considering them. Then, at storytelling occasions, he selects from his repertoire only the kind of tale which fits the occasion in question.' **80** Michael Rooney, born 1900, in M.J. Murphy *Now You're Talking* 154. **81** Seán Ó Conaill, quoted by S. Delargy *The Gaelic Story-Teller* 12. **82** Collector T. Ó Murchadha, quoted by Kevin Danaher 'Stories and Storytelling in Ireland', in E.S. Norton (ed.) *Folk Literature of the British Isles* 109. **83** M.J. Murphy *Now You're Talking ...* 152. **84** IFC 1620: 141 (in 1962). **85** Cf. J. Pentikäinen *Oral Repertoire and World View* 331: 'Marina Takalo's repertoire of folklore did not seem to be any stable, unchangeable whole; rather it appeared to change in accordance with the development of the individual personality and the epochs of her life story.'

storyteller could be partly based on the number of pieces he was said to know: 'As regards [Éamon a Búrc], it is not now possible to make even a guess at the number of stories he could tell: perhaps a thousand, perhaps five hundred. Certainly about one hundred and fifty tales were recorded from him, some of them very long.'[86] Indeed, given the very different lengths of narratives and the incompleteness of most collections, it is impossible to put forward useful figures. A way of praising a storyteller for his large repertoire consisted in saying that he could tell a different tale every night the whole winter through – from *Samhain* to *Bealtaine*. A moderate variant was, nightly for at least a month; hyperbolically, throughout the year.[87] But collectors soon learned the relative insignificance of the mere number of items one informant could produce; better criteria may be the rarity of certain tales and, above all, the manner of telling.[88] Nevertheless, we may assume that a storyteller who knew many tales was more likely to have assimilated the basic principles of the art and the formal peculiarities of specific genres.[89]

11. Categorizing narratives

How far were the storytellers aware of differences between kinds of narratives, and did they specialize in one 'genre'? Do the nice distinctions upon which scholars have more or less agreed also operate in 'traditional' communities?

In fact, 'the whole idea of "genre" is relative and ambiguous, dependent on culturally-accepted canons of differentiation rather than universal criteria'.[90] The discrete categories supposed to apply transculturally are abstractions scholars and archivists have found useful; the people who use the material may have their own systems of classification, which they do seldom bother to define. The main criterion according to which the material is divided may be a certain subject matter (themes, types of protagonists); or the tone (serious, comic); or the relative truth-value; or distinctive formal characteristics; or some performance conventions (on what occasion, more or less ritualized, and before which audience); or the main purpose normally served; or the supposed ancientness and origin. It is difficult to combine and balance the requirements, and they may blur. Lauri

---

86 Liam Costello, Introduction to *Eochair, A King's Son in Ireland* 17. 87 In Finland, the blind storyteller Berndt Leonard Strömberg (1822-1909) claimed that he knew 366 stories, one for each day of the year (R. Schenda *Von Mund zu Ohr* 137). 88 I. Sándor 'Dramaturgy of Tale-Telling', *Acta Ethnographica* ... 306: 'At an earlier stage of research, the prominence of the narrator was primarily represented by the richness of his repertory ... Subsequently the center of interest was shifted on the analysis of qualitative elements: the way the narrator handles, performs and revives the traditional text.' 89 M.-L. Tenèze 'Du conte merveilleux comme genre', in *Arts et Traditions Populaires* 18 (1970) 57: 'S'il apparaît que la qualité va de pair avec la quantité, c'est que la communauté de structure entre contes apparentés, alors même qu'elle favorise les "contaminations", facilite très probablement l'apprentissage, l'imprégnation dans l'esprit et la mémoire du conteur. Sous les différents "vocabulaires", le conteur semble bien enregistrer l'existence d'une même "syntaxe" ' (knowing many tales, one knows narrative syntax). 90 Ruth Finnegan *Oral Poetry* 15.

Honko notes that a theme may be treated in several genres (though some messages are preferably associated with one class of texts); he also says that each genre may establish itself in opposition to another one in the particular system of communication. He proposes to tabulate sets of stories as more or less factual (close to everyday reality) or fabulated (imaginary, ideal) and, on another axis, as more or less sacred or profane (referring or not to numinous beings and events). But he admits that 'the average user of folklore is more interested in the messages that genres convey than in the genres themselves'.[91]

After many others, Ludwig Mühlhausen at Teelin in 1937 observed the basic division between *seanchas* and *scéalta* (mentioned in Section 1 above):

If I had to describe briefly the attitudes of old people to the stories, I would distinguish between two groups; first the stories which have local features ..., secondly those which are set in some indefinite past and deal with kings, princesses, warriors, giants, magicians, and so on. Those of the first group will often start with '*bhí 'na chomhnuidhe ar an bhaile seo*' – 'There lived at this place ...'; the others with something like '*bhí ... uair amháin*' –' There was once a ...', and often one will add '*fad ó shin*' – 'a long time ago'. The first group is accepted as 'true', somehow as would an article in the newspaper dealing with an earthquake, a flood, or some extraordinary accomplishment.[92]

The broad category of oral narratives in twentieth-century Ireland – ranging from fictional to factual, or from sung or recited verse to more or less conversational prose, for instance – may be subdivided further. As the most distinctly native part of the general repertoire, folklorists in the first half of the twentieth century still found narratives, in Gaelic-speaking Scotland as well as in Ireland, which required considerable expertise. They included a few remnants of the Ulster cycle of stories, a much larger body of *scéalta fiannaíochta* connected with the 'literary' Fianna cycle (see p. 36)[93] and other relatively ancient 'romantic tales' (see p. 48) featuring adventures and encounters with the marvellous. Somehow connected with them, the 'hero tales' (*scéalta gaisce*) were a less tidily unified group of stories telling the adventures of distinctively Irish warriors, kings or kings' sons who journey to foreign lands, fight giants or ogres (*gruagaigh*) and hags (*cailleacha*), bring back abducted women and perform other valiant deeds; these tales can mix international and native motifs, and require

---

91 'Folkloristic Theory of Genre', in A.L. Siikala (ed.) *Studies in Oral Narrative* 13-28. 92 *Zehn Irische Volkserzählungen* 16-17 (my translation). Cf. G. Henssen *Volkstümliche Erzählkunst* 17: 'Das Volk ist sich des Unterschiedes von Sage und Märchen wohl bewusst' – German storytellers are aware of the difference between 'legends and tales'. 93 J. Delargy *The Gaelic Story-Teller* 37: 'The Finn-tales, so far as I know them in oral tradition, appear to belong to two types: 1. tales of undoubted manuscript origin which have been partly remoulded and refurbished with the tricks and trappings of Irish *märchen*, and 2. tales which do not occur in manuscripts but use characters and incidents from the Finn-cycle as part of the intricate framework, together with stock motifs from wonder-tales of the international type.'

feats of verbal skill in Irish (see Sections 27-8 below). In the first half of this century, *fiannaíocht* (telling stories about the Fianna) and the telling of *scéalta gaisce* tended to be the preserve of a small number of storytellers, and the audience knew that it was something special. If *laoithe fiannaíochta* (Ossianic lays) were no longer sung in Ireland after the middle of the century, ballads in English – which can be more or less narrative – are still alive today. The same story may exist in parallel prose and song modes, and a song may be combined in performance with a prose introduction. Narratives in English, known as 'recitations' and distinguished by a fixed form which is often verse, circulate orally as well as in print.[94] Still on the *scéalta* side of the narrative spectrum are tales which have cognates (related versions) in several countries and may have taken on local characteristics (oikotypes). They include 'magic' or 'wonder tales': multiepisodic stories with no particular temporal or geographic location, often following the progress of a protagonist through strange encounters, transformation and potentially tragic obstacles and reaching a happy end which emphasizes cosmic justice – the triumph of the weaker but kinder party. There are also stories of incredible luck and coincidences rather than magic, which emphasize qualities like cleverness or patience. Of the thousand-and-a-half 'international plot types' listed by Aarne and Thompson, S. Ó Súilleabháin and R.T. Christiansen identified some seven hundred in Ireland.[95] Other tales may have originated in Ireland, but the limits are blurred between local versions of international stories and stories composed locally by combining motifs which exist elsewhere and may have been imported or independently reinvented.

On the *seanchas* side of the spectrum, 'legends' are commonly said to be stories told as truth; in fact, they accept various degrees of belief or non-belief. They are set in the historical past and in recognizable settings, with precisions concerning supposedly identifiable people. Unlike the wonder tales, they do not have to end with the return to some positive equilibrium. In theory, any member of the community can perform them. They may be used more often as abbreviated allusions in informal conversation than in fully developed story form. Among other conversational narrative genres are repeated accounts of personal experience, and brief anecdotes which reinforce the stereotyped picture of an individual or group, and jokes which mock what troubles people or deal with some inadequacy in character, situation or reaction, usually with a surprise resolution. There is no entry for obscene jokes in S. Ó Súilleabháin's *Handbook of Irish Folklore*, the list of what the Irish Folklore Commission was looking for; but such material existed, and M.J. Murphy gathered and published what he found in Ulster.[96] Rumours, and mere gossip (conversation about absent people) would also have to be placed somewhere on the spectrum. Each kind of narra-

94 The 'monologue' was defined by K.S. Goldstein, *Southern Folklore Quarterly* 40.1 (1976) 8, as 'a solo, stylized, theatrically-mannered oral performance from memory of a self-contained dramatic narrative in either poetic or prose form'. 95 *The Types of the Irish Folktale.* 96 *My Man Jack: Bawdy Tales from Irish Folklore* (198).

tive may have its own form and mode of enunciation. Certain subgenres declined in usage while others became prominent.[97]

Most examples of traditional stories quoted in this chapter are taken from the *scéalta* or 'tale' group; I propose to look more closely at *seanchas* or 'legends' in Chapter 13, in connection with the problem of truth. The categories defined above should not be viewed as watertight, however: they can blend, and elements of stories may float from one class to another. Some Irish storytellers ranged freely over a large variety of stories while perhaps respecting a hierarchy among them; Stith Thompson seemed to believe that variety was the rule: 'Irish *shanachies* [he was using the term in its modern, loose sense of 'storyteller'] will shift without notice from the fairytale to a pious story, a saint's legend, or an account of the warlike deeds of the O'Flahertys. But they seem to feel that explanatory or local legends belong to a different order of story-telling. They will tell them if called in, but as an artistic medium such tales are not to be taken very seriously.'[98] Irish collectors met people who practised only one genre.[99]

What was the importance of the storyteller in his society?

12. The storyteller's social position and self-image
Every member of a community has a place determined by special qualities and functions, and the behaviour expected of whoever occupies that place is his or her 'role'. Even a part-time role may confer 'status': some prestige. Thus the storyteller, permanently or for the duration of the storytelling act only, had duties, some power, a reputation, and a certain sense of his/her worth. The term 'role' suggests a distinction between the individual when not performing and specific rights and obligations contingent on the performance. The same person can be a narrator in certain circumstances and have other functions in

---

97 Lauri Honko 'Methods in Folk-Narrative Research', *Ethnologia Europaea* 10 (1997-8) 13-14:' The degeneration and decline of a genre is normally a symptom of cultural and social change, which has many manifestations within and outside folklore. In our time, demographic changes in rural populations and the mechanization of agriculture, along with the expansion of mass-media, have bereft many a traditional genre of the social condition for its existence. Folktales and some forms of legends are on the verge of dying out in many places in Europe, recent reports tell us. An upsurge of "short, personal narratives" (memorates, chronicates, joculates, etc.) is discernible and folklore archives are flooded with ethnological memoirs and other materials previously regarded as non-traditional.' **98** *The Folktale* 451. **99** See p. 443, and cf. L. Dégh 'What kind of people tell legends?', in Kvideland (ed.) *Folklore Processed* 106: 'Recognized traditional Märchen-tellers conscious of their craft are careful to distinguish legends from tales. The legends they tell appear to be marginal in their repertoire, as first-hand learned true events that may be part of their life history. They know that their audience appreciates high-flying fantasy in the formulation of tales but at the same time would not tolerate artistic embroidery of the truth they believe in. It is one thing to tell a Märchen, to enjoy the liberty of creating a fictitious story, and another thing to tell a legend and reproduce reality. None of the village storytellers I personally knew [in Hungary] included their legends in their repertoires.'

everyday life; so it was with the Irish 'traditional' storytellers in the nineteenth and twentieth centuries. The role of narrator could be more significant than others, when it was considered an essential activity fulfilled to general satisfaction. It might compensate for physical limitations: a number of good storytellers were lame.[100] A reputation was attained on the basis of skills, but the kind of stories told might also be determinant. Storytellers of course ranged from those who were famous, sometimes beyond local limits, to those who were practically unknown outside the family circle; but as long as there was an audience, a performer could expect recognition.

To the examples of the appraisal of storytellers by members of their community and of mutual recognition among peers given in the preceding chapter can be added what an American observed in the West of Ireland in the 1930s: 'Such artistic performances by these men are not a casual thing either to them or to their audiences. When the rumour goes about a village that one of them is in action a crowd of interested listeners will always gather and give absorbed attention. They have doubtless heard the tale he is telling, but they love to hear it repeated, and especially with such elaboration as the skilled raconteur is sure to give the story.'[101] The following two excerpts from the material collected in 1937-8 in County Galway by the school of Barnaderg give the point of view (and spelling) of children who knew simply that the local storyteller was both important and entertaining:

Death of Tom Coen. Tom Coen was a great story-teller, and I have all his stories written in a foke-lore book. I am very sorry for him and all the winter I sat by the fire listing to all the storys as I would not be tird listing he was so good he would spend hours telling them and if I stayed he would stay all night telling them I think he had the best in this district but when he was getting sick I could not get any story from him.

[From another pupil:] Tom Coen is dead. He died on Thursday last. I am very lonesome now. He was a great storyteller. All the winter I used to sit by the fire listening to the stories he was never tired of telling. He would spend hours telling the stories and would stay up all hours of the night if I could stay. The sleep used to get the better.[102]

How did the Irish storytellers (*scéalaithe* or *seanchaithe*) see themselves and their art? They may not have claimed to be 'the voice of the community', but, as noted in Section 9, they generally revered what they had received, and considered it their duty to keep it alive. Most of them would probably not analyse the mental processes involved in the storytelling act, and their knowledge of rules and devices could be implicit rather than explicit; but J.H. Delargy described a good informant as 'a conscious literary artist' or 'a creative artist with a sensitive temperament'.[103] The storyteller was not indifferent to praise,[104]

---

100 A. Bourke *The Burning of Bridget Cleary* 54. **101** Stith Thompson *The Folktale* 454. **102** IFC S26: 164. **103** *The Gaelic Story-Teller* 10, 17. **104** L. Dégh *Folktales and Society* 170: 'Each good storyteller or folk artist seeks special recognition of his talents ... The storytellers

and pride could make him jealous of his reputation.[105] An Aran Islands master
was said to have wielded his authority despotically: 'The late *scéalaí* carried a
short sally rod with which he used to prod listeners who appeared to be weary.
It is alleged that he once tried to gouge the eyes of a nodding youth with his
forked fingers, an incident which often is alluded to when his past performances
are recollected.'[106] Such tyranny was unusual; the storytellers' attitude was generally more subdued – though perhaps not when defending the art itself against
bunglers: 'Good storytellers, proud of their art, were intolerant of badly told
tales, and sometimes stopped the unskilful narrator in the middle of his story,
saying such nonsense should not be allowed to represent the real traditional narrative!'[107] Many informants were described by collectors as modest, even bash-
ful: 'Some story-tellers are shy and sensitive to the possible banter of their
neighbours. Seósamh Ó Dálaigh tells in his diaries of an old Kerry woman who
insisted on having the door of her house bolted lest any neighbours should enter
while she was telling stories.'[108] With others, their 'everyday' personality contrasted with the authority they showed when narrating. The ideal or archetypal
Irish storyteller enjoyed prestige as an exceptional character, but actual performers were also ordinary members of the community. They became the focus
of attention when the need was felt for their special functions as unifying agents
of a group and as its links with the past. Between performances, they resumed
less remarkable activities, but the special role they could play was not forgotten
– until, with a change in the lifestyle or the disintegration of their community,
they lost that importance. Aware of the value of their stories and often also of
the fact that their craft was threatened, at least in what they considered its genuine forms, they often were willing, sometimes even anxious, to have their treasure collected. Deprived of an audience, a storyteller was unhappy:

In Seán Ó Conaill's youth [that is to say, in the 1870s] storytellers were quite common
in the district, but as he grew older the old tales were not so much heard as formerly.
Finally, there came a time when it was but rarely that he had an opportunity himself of
practising his art in public. So, lest he should lose command over the tales he loved, he
used to repeat them aloud when he thought no one was near, using the gesticulations and
the emphasis, and all the other tricks of narration, as if he were once again the centre of
a fireside storytelling. His son, Pats, told me that he had seen his father thus engaged,
telling his tales to an unresponsive stone wall, while herding the grazing cattle. On
returning from market, as he walked slowly up the hills behind his old grey mare, he
could be heard declaiming his tales to the back of the cart! In this way he kept a firm
grip on stories which he had not told to an audience for over twenty years; and when I

---

let it be known that they are well aware of their own capabilities.' **105** Cf. G. Ortutay
Hungarian Folklore 255: 'Fedics was at once proud and jealous of his ability to relate tales.
When, trying to spur his ambition on, I told him there were storytellers elsewhere, too, whose
tales I was going to listen to, he pooh-poohed them without even knowing who they were and
made every effort to dissuade me from listening to anyone else. He said no one knew as many
stories as he did and no one could match the way he told them'. **106** John C. Messenger *Inis
Beag: Isle of Ireland* 116. **107** J. Delargy *The Gaelic Story-Teller* 24. **108** Ibid. 17.

began to visit him for the dual purpose of learning Irish and writing down his stories, I found that he could repeat these tales without hesitation.[109]

Storytelling takes place under certain physical conditions and with the participation and reaction of an audience, as 'the interplay between communicative resources, individual competence, and the goals of the participants, within the context of particular situations'.[110] A 'performance' (see pp. 380-1), offering 'a heightened intensity of communicative interaction',[111] may be marked off from casual public interchange by some signals warning the audience that what is produced must be received in a special way. Unlike the ordinary conversational exchange (see Section 18), the special verbal-art event gives one individual the power of retaining the right to speak provided he displays adequate skill, and even when a story is embedded in a stretch of non-narrative discourse the listeners have the right to judge the speaker's effectiveness. A receptive competence is therefore needed to decide if an offering was good, just acceptable, or inadequate; shared conventions define different opportunities for various kinds of storytelling, the degree of formalization of the transaction and how participants should interact. In the following six sections, I shall focus on storytelling as an event in time, space and social context – bearing in mind that the normal mode was not interview by a collector (but the collector could also attend normal performances). Each act of storytelling is determined by a physical setting (where and when the performance takes place), an opportunity (a gathering, for entertainment or for some ritual, or a less formal insert in conversation); the selection of participants (differentiated or not by gender, age, profession); and a specific code. The greatest changes in Irish storytelling were probably determined by modifications of such frames.[112]

13. Storytelling away from home

Narration might take place out of doors; for instance to 'shorten the road' while walking in group, as the *seanchaí* Conchúr Ó Siocháin, dictating his memories, recalled in 1935-6: 'We set off on the road, but because we had no experience of a long walk we thought that we would never get the journey over. The officer was gossiping and telling us stories, and that shortened the road greatly for us ... "Let us shorten the road again" (*Bí mis ag ciorrú an bhóthair arís*) he said.'[113] Opportunities for tale-telling in the open were also offered by communal work, and more particularly by intervals such as waiting for the tide and for

109 J. Delargy *The Gaelic Story-Teller* 12. **110** R. Bauman *Verbal Art as Performance* 38. **111** Ibid. 43. **112** G. MacLennan *Seanchas Annie Bhán* 35-6: '[since the late 1920s or 30s] instead of the oral tradition being a community function it is becoming a performance for outsiders [for instance in Irish-language summer schools]. The new function gradually ousted the older one as the community discovered modern amusements to replace the old, and as the growing interest of outsiders in folklore and language reinforced the demand for a non-community performance.' **113** *Seanchas Chléire* (tr. by R.P. Breathnach as *The Man from Cape Clear*) 45, 65. A common saying goes: *Ciorraíonn beit bóthar* – 'two people shorten the road'.

better fishing conditions, or resting when a group of neighbours gathered: 'Working on the bog cutting turf or in the meadow saving hay were great occasions for storytelling: one man would tell a story and then another would follow, and the tales and yarns would continue while the *meitheal* [a band of farmers helping each other for a day or two] worked together.'[114] Someone might narrate while the others did work, like these men making a road: 'My father was time-keeper for the Relief Works and the good storyteller wouldn't have anything to do but to tell stories and my father had a big store of them. The rest of the workers would pick up for the storyteller.'[115] In parts of Ireland, there was a form of transhumance, 'booleying' (*buailteachas*): driving cattle to distant pastures and spending the summer season or half the year together; it was a time of much merriment for young folk, and storytelling could be part of it.[116] Other people met and chatted at crossroads and at fairs. News was exchanged at the creamery. The well was a meeting place for women, who often sat down and talked for a while. The forge was a rallying-point for men – a place where they had to wait, or gathered on wet days simply because it was pleasantly warm and there would be chatter, short narratives, maybe some longer stories:

In my young days I mind as far [as many] as thirty and more men in the forge at night out at our place. They'd gather in at night; every nights they'd be here there and everywhere in the forge, in your way or sitting up on the hearth behind the fire if they could. That's what they called the fun of the forge. Any fellow them times would be glad of an excuse to get to the forge.[117]

The forge remains one of the important places, with the pubs and the square in front of the church after a Sunday mass, where the inhabitants of the parish meet to exchange news.[118]

Storytelling was also expected where cobblers were at work: 'He was a shoe-maker; and they'd gather in there every evening in the time of the year and sit there till eleven and twelve cracking and spinning yarns, and talk of all kinds.'[119] The public house was suitable for tricks and jokes, not for the more respectable kinds of tales – which were perhaps also excluded from the other occurrences mentioned in this section.

14. At the fireside: family gatherings and 'courting'
Given the vagaries of the Irish climate, storytelling was primarily an indoor activity. Most tales were told in family houses, where it was possible to narrate at a comfortable pace: 'The storyteller ... is happier and more at ease when

---

114 M.J. Murphy *My Man Jack* 22. 115 IFC 659: 243. The informant was a Kerryman, aged 75 in 1939. 116 Seán Ó hEochaidh, 'Buailteachas i dTir Chonaill' *Béaloideas* 13 (1943) 130-58. 117 IFC 1215: 33, from Mickey Gormley, Eskragh, Co. Tyrone. Collected by M.J. Murphy in 1949. 118 Translated from Robert Cresswell *Une communauté rurale de l'Irlande* 425. 119 IFC 976: 305. Collected by M.J. Murphy at Kilkeel, County Down, in 1945.

seated by his own or a neighbour's fireside.'[120] The open hearth was naturally the focus of family and social life, and the domestic fire was felt to be associated with the prosperity of the household. It had first been kept burning in the middle of Irish huts, but in the period covered by this chapter it was either at a gable or against a wall that transversely divided the rectangular building. It was important not only for the preparation of food and the provision of heat and light, but also as the place for guests to converge: 'The turf fire burning continuously day and night, throughout the year, is the symbol both of family continuity and of hospitality towards the stranger ... It is to the fireside seat that the visitor is invited, for this is the place of honour, and it is around the fire that tales of old time are told.'[121] The right corner when looking at the fire might belong to the householder (*fear tí* or *fear an tí*) while the woman-of the-house (*bean tí*) would rather sit on the left-hand side to have her right hand free for cooking duties – but M.J. Murphy may have seen the opposite allocation: 'He sits at the left hand side of the fire on a low chair ... He always sat at the left-hand side of the fire ...'[122] The important point was to be close to the hearth (*cois na tine*). 'It was the height of discourtesy for anyone else to sit in one of these [corners] without being bidden to do so';[123] the honour could be conferred on a respected guest storyteller.

The evening gathering of the family could generate storytelling, but to visit other houses at night, in the winter months, was the main semi-formal social entertainment: the *céilí* (in the sense of friendly call and informal party). Certain '*céilí* houses' had a special reputation:

There were certain houses at which the same few neighbours met every night [note in the margin – 'From the year 1880 to 1900']: houses whose owner was a bright-minded talkative man and whose wife was a motherly woman, one who got on well with her neighbours and never had a hard word for anybody. Her work was finished before a certain fixed hour, a time before the 'ramblers' were expected to arrive, a good fire threw a glow around the kitchen; the fire hearth was clean, there may be a chair or perhaps two, but there was always to be found a few three-legged stools and perhaps a long wooden form; the woman of the house sat in the corner under the lamp knitting or darning, her seat was of plaited straw stuffed with fine straw. She listened to the conversation of the men whilst her fingers were busy with the knitting needles and her husband's or son's sock grew under her touch. At 10 p.m. the ramblers got to their feet and after a friendly good night to the man of the house and his wife they made for their own houses to meet

120 M.J. Murphy *Now You're Talking* ... viii. **121** E. Estyn Evans *Irish Folk Ways* 59, 71. Cf. Alessandro Falassi (Italy) *Folklore by the Fireside: Text and Context of the Tuscan Veglia* 25: 'The fireplace and the fire provide that place where ultimate if inconstant illumination takes place, where experience and the symbolic rendering of life come together perfectly. The real and the symbolic reflect each other as long as the flame endures. While the flame of the candle or of the little light was an operator of eminently individualistic images, the flame of the fireplace, social light, was an operator of an imagery appropriate to the group and shared by its members.' **122** IFC 1113: 525 and IFC 1360: 78. **123** K. Danaher *The Hearth and Stool and All! Irish Rural Households* 42.

again the following night on the same house and so passed the long winter nights. When they reached home a supper of hot porridge awaited them.[124]

The institution of night-visiting had many other names, with regional variations: *scoraíocht* (a social evening), also called *bothántaíocht*; *cuairt* or *cuaird* or *cuartaíocht* (visiting); *ránaíocht* (roving); *ragairne* (late-night carousing) or *airneán* (keeping late hours, chatting beside the fire late at night); in English 'courting' and 'visiting' – or 'rambling' and 'cabin hunting' when perhaps done to excess. Men were more likely than women to participate in these activities: 'the women do not go out on *cuaird* like the men';[125] or they might go visiting separately.

Age groups could keep apart. In some cases the meeting point might be some common premises rather than a private house, as observed in County Down:

The Bunk: this is the term used locally to designate the house, or céilí-house, in which the foregoing material was recorded. It is situated some hundred yards from Milltown village, Clonduff Parish ... Its clientele is old men and 'settled' men, and settled bachelors. Few or no young men go to it. They go to the Irish National Forestors' St Patrick's Club in Milltown village for recreation at night of card-playing, billiards, and debating. But in the 'bunk' the men sit around a fire on long stools or forms and smoke and chat. It is regarded as a céilí-house for old men; and young men incur some satire of a hopeless kind ... if they are known to be going to 'the bunk' ... The people of the parish, the young people and middle-aged, are still clannish in a microscopic sense. There are céilí-houses throughout the parish. These are frequented by a regular clientèle; and the intrusion of a 'newcomer' is more or less resented.[126]

Michael Corduff evoked night-visiting in North Mayo: 'Frequently, the house was crowded, and seating accommodation had sometimes to be improvised by people sitting on one another's knees; on inverted turf creels, on sheaves of straw; or by sitting on the floor near the hearth, while the kitchen bed was usually congested with the younger patrons.'[127] Arensberg and Kimball described a houseparty in North Clare in the 1930s:

The hob by the fire belongs to the old couple by right. The younger people, the sons and daughters, sit behind them round the room on other chairs or on the window seats of the rectangular kitchen, which makes up the principal room of the usual small farmer's house. This arrangement shows itself best in the *cuaird* or visit, where the old

---

124 IFC 1925: 124-5, from Kathleen Hurley, Ballymoe, Co. Galway. Cf. Joe Neil MacNeil, in John Shaw (ed.) *Tales until Dawn; The World of a Cape Breton Gaelic Story-Teller*: 'there were special houses for story-telling. Most of the visiting houses were good enough. Any of a number of nice houses could be visited, but people were more willing and eager to go to some houses in particular because there were more people frequenting these. There were also houses where people went expressly to hear tales.' 125 C.M. Arensberg and S. T. Kimball *Family and Community in Ireland* 203. 126 IFC 975: 22-4. Noted by M.J. Murphy in 1945. 127 'Notes on Storytellers and Storytelling in Iorrus, North Mayo', *Béaloideas* 19 (1949) 178.

men of the district drop in on neighbours and 'friends' to sit around the hearth together passing the evenings of winter in conversation, singing, discussing the news, and telling the old stories of legend and folklore. At the *cuaird* younger men and women, if they attend, sit behind, usually leaving the centre of the stage to the old men, and the children stand up in silent admiration. The younger men have their own pursuits, of course, though at present the divergence may be more marked than formerly.[128]

The same observers elsewhere described in detail the proceedings in the house where the 'old fellows' would regularly convene: 'Soon after supper they begin to gather. Perhaps this or that *habitué* may not come, but it is always the same group of men who stride across the threshold with a 'God bless all here' and take their accustomed places. O'Donoghue [the man-of-the-house] has the place of honour. He sits in the chair to the right of the fire ... In the nightly discussions which take place round his hearth he has a judicial role. He is regarded as a wise man.'[129]

A *céilí* could be essentially talk; and storytelling, which was not the only feature, was not necessarily of the most artistic kind. For instance the *cuaird* studied by Arensberg at the North-West Clare place he called Rynamona does not seem to have included the noblest kinds of narrative performance; *seanchas* was practised, and the speciality was traditional jurisprudence, with a particular pattern of fixed roles: the man he called the 'judge' could tell anecdotes as well as anyone but usually contented himself with a word of affirmation now and then during the nightly discussion and some measured authoritative opinions to which all deferred; the 'drawer down' would bring up topics and questions interesting enough to start a new set of exchanges; the 'public prosecutor' would raise objections and help to sift the truth from the lies or the right from the wrong; the 'senator' would draw from his powerful memory anecdotes that would confirm or infirm general statements. With time, and change of social position (getting married and acquiring householder status), one could graduate from youthful card-playing to the *cuaird*, which was (or considered itself) more respectable: 'Seven men make up the old men's *cuaird* . One can see how closely knit a clique they are. They have a code and values of their own, strong enough to enforce specific personalities on each of the members, in accordance with the role of each in the group ... The old men's house includes all the farm fathers of complete families. It is made up of those who are married and "have a responsibility on them".'[130]

The practice of the more complex verbal arts required a quiet intimate context, an expert narrator, and an attentive sympathetic audience. Everywhere in western Europe, the most important and most natural institution for such storytelling was an evening gathering of family and neighbours (*veillée*, *veglia*,

---

128 Arensberg and Kimball, op. cit.131. **129** Ibid. 135, 137. **130** C.M. Arensberg *The Irish Countryman: An Anthropological Study* 130-7. Some fifty years after Arensberg, L.J. Taylor observed a 'Parliament' at Teelin (*Occasions of Faith* 21).

458 The Irish storyteller

Abendversammlung, Meien ...) governed by special conventions. Ireland was not essentially different in this respect.[131]

15. The right time for storytelling
As a rule, folktales in Ireland were told only at night, but the telling of jokes and of legends which did not touch on the supernatural was less regulated; time restrictions were said to be particularly strict for Fianna material, the telling of which in daytime would have been dangerous: *Feadaíl san oíche nó Fiannaíocht sa ló, sin dhá n'nach bhfuil buan* ('Whistling at night or telling stories of the Fianna by day, these are two things which are unlucky'),[132] and the rule might extend to the telling of other genres as Jeremiah Curtin observed in Kerry (see p. 307). The idea that there are 'night words' as distinguished from 'day words' and that tales *must* be told at night is widely spread around the world.[133] Explanations for it may be pragmatic: daytime storytelling would be a distraction from more important activities, whereas in the evening there is nothing else to do; also, darkness heightens the more dramatic aspects of the tales. But other arguments are put forward: to tell of magic by daylight might provoke some supernatural powers.

The appropriate season was from the end of October until April: the Irish year was divided in two, and a common formula was *ó Shamhain go Bealtaine is ó Bhealtaine go Samhain* – from Hallowe'en to May Day and from May Day to Hallowe'en. In the dark half of the year, it was good to 'shorten the night' (*an oíche a ghearradh*) with stories.[134]

16. Special occasions and the wake for the dead
Some forms of storytelling could be part of ceremonial customs at certain times of the year like Midsummer or 'harvest home' (*clabhsúr*) festivities, Christmas, christenings, 'stations' (religious services conducted in private houses), pilgrimages or 'patterns' (patron saints' days).[135] More particularly, it was an integral part of funeral wakes (*tórraimh* or *fairí*), which combined sympathy with the bereaved, homage paid to the departed, a celebration of life, and the reestablishment of social order: the group manifested its continuity, while the deceased was incorporated into the afterlife.[136] Using entertainment in order to cope with

131 Cf. Angelika Merkelbach-Pinck *Lothringer erzählen* 10-11: ' "Meien gehen", das heisst, den andern zu einer gemütlichen Unterhaltung, zu einem verbunten und zwanglosen Gedankenaustausch aufsuchen, bei ihm geruhsam verweilen.' See also Daniel Fabre and Jacques Lacroix *La tradition orale du conte occitan* 1.110-42: 'Les institutions de transfert', and R. Schenda *Von Mund zu Ohr* 114-24. 132 Quoted by P. Mac Cana in *The Learned Tales of Medieval Ireland* 4. 133 Most often observed in Africa. 134 Same seasonal division in Belgium, for instance: 'les veillées commençaient dès que les jours raccourcissaient. Elles débutaient selon les contrées à des époques différentes, souvent après la récolte des pommes de terre ou à la Toussaint et se terminaient le premier dimanche de carème' (G.Laport *Les contes populaires wallons* 4). 135 Cf. Kevin Danaher *The Year in Ireland* 131, 140, 156, 182, 236, 241. 136 G. Ó Crualaoich 'The Merry Wake', in J.S. Donnelly and K.A. Miller (eds)

the disruption caused by death of a member of the group was not an exclusively Irish trait, but since the seventeenth century writers have insisted on it to amaze their 'civilized' readers (see pp. 56, 74-5, 91, etc.). Along with drinking, what they considered most sensational were wailing and the 'keen' (*caoineadh*): a dirge in which the 'keener' named the deceased, then praised him or her in extempore verse, and finally started the 'cry' of the whole company cantillating on interjections like *ochón* (alas). At other stages of the night, there were games and farcical interludes – and storytelling. The degree of entertainment or licence up to the removal of corpse to church varied; it could reach its heights in the case of the 'timely death' of an elderly person: 'The young people of every district looked forward with keen anticipation to the death of an old man or woman, which would offer them "a night of turf-throwing and frivolity".'[137] On the other hand, 'storytelling did not usually occur at wakes held for young people or children, as these would be occasions of great sorrow'.[138]

Having fun was not perceived as disrespect for the deceased: 'We went to a wake, not to increase the sorrow of the bereaved family by our tears, but to help them to forget their trouble in a flood of good stories.'[139] People needed to be kept awake because to fall asleep might be considered an insult when social intercourse had to be activated. But outsiders did not understand it; in 1833, a philanthropic Co. Wexford clergyman quoted, or imagined, a local peasant's description of a wake and a foreigner's reaction:

MURPHY First and foremost some of us sat down to play five and forty, and more of us to hunt the slipper, and more of us to smoke, and more of us to tell stories, and more of us (this is the truth of it) were coortin.

MACDUNCAN [a Scots steward]. What! in the very hoose and room with the dead man!

MURPHY Oh, by no manner of manes ... , the corpse was inside the other house [i.e. room], and the dead [i.e. complete] wall between us and it.

MACDUNCAN And no respect for the widow and the family in grief!

MURPHY And who hindered them from crying their fill? and crying they were, poor things, and a good right they had to cry.[140]

In poorer houses, there was no separate room for the corpse. Local practices varied; generally it seems that stories were told when smaller groups remained after the departure of the crowd, or could isolate themselves – and then there might be several storytellers, each with an audience. Here is one of the many nineteenth-century descriptions: 'The company, in Sunday attire, sat round the fire, smoking, drinking tea or whisky, and telling stories to beguile the long

Irish Popular Culture 1650-1850 173-200. **137** Seán Ó Súilleabháin *Irish Wake Amusements* 26. To throw turf at the door of a house where older people had assembled was common practice for riotous youth. **138** C. B. Harvey *Contemporary Irish Traditional Narrative* ... 11. **139** Maura Laverty *Never No More* 155. **140** 'Martin Doyle' *Irish Cottagers* 42.

hours of the vigil, and to divert the sad thoughts of the daughter of the deceased.'[141] The following description (the first version of which, in Irish, was published in 1961) is retrospective:

The start of the night at a wake was usually spent in the kitchen, if there was room for all. Affairs of the day were discussed: local gossip went on, and any big news in the world of politics or such was the subject for comment. In addition, humorous anecdotes were told about local people and happenings, causing a titter of laughter among various groups ... Most of the visitors to a wake went home about midnight, leaving behind only a dozen or score of people. After the Rosary had been recited, storytelling began. This was usual even in districts where the more lively type of wake was unknown. The storytelling was carried on everywhere in Ireland, and followed an informal pattern; in one corner of the kitchen, a storyteller, usually an elderly man, sat surrounded by a group of interested listeners, while another recited his tale to a different group elsewhere. It was not difficult to get some good narrators of tales in most districts in former times, especially when the Irish language was the normal means of expression. They were welcome at wakes, as the stories helped to while away the long night hours and kept the listeners from becoming drowsy or falling asleep towards dawn.[142]

From other twentieth-century recollections or observations, I extract the following representative statements:

On the first night of the wake they'd be all crammed together in the room with the person that died and two candles. Afterwards they'd talk about ghosts. People would say funny things, for example that they'd seen lights before people died, all the signs of the banshee ... They'd play cards at wake. There was conversation with old stories and different sorts of chat ... pipes, tobacco, snuff, drink of all kinds, criers, singers, stories, ridiculing neighbours, planning tricks, matchmaking for marriages ...[143]

[In County Galway] It is the custom for some piece of clothing belonging to each individual at a wake to be collected into a shawl and brought to the centre of the room. Each item is held up in turn and its owner identified. Unless the owner can perform with either a story or a song, the item of clothing is first threatened with a lighted candle and is finally burned with the candle flame so that a hole is left in it, should its owner absolutely refuse to perform.[144]

Already in the sixteenth century, and more particularly from the nineteenth, the Church condemned the manner in which wakes were conducted. What was objected to above all was drinking and horseplay – Seán Ó Súilleabháin noted that storytelling was generally tolerated, though in 1676 a bishop had written that prayers should be recited rather than *ineptae fabulae* (in fact, there were prayers too). By the middle of the twentieth century it could be said that 'tales

141 Letitia McClintock 'Folk Lore of Ulster' *Dublin University Magazine* 89 (1877) 751. 142 Ó Súilleabháin *Irish Wake Amusements* 26-7. 143 B. Sherry and R. McHughs (eds) *Along the Black Pig's Dyke, Folklore from Monaghan and South Armagh* 73, 74, 72. 144 G. Ó Crualaoich 'The Merry Wake ...', 186.

are still occasionally told at wakes in the Gaeltacht, but the custom has died out over the greater part of Ireland'.[145]

17. The etiquette of the storytelling house-party

Returning to the kinds of reunion described in Section 14, we note that they ranged from an impromptu which seemed to 'happen' rather than to be 'organized' – the narrative parts being informal elements embedded in other activities, to special meetings where storytelling artistry was the main or sole object, with a degree of formality and special norms. Whereas in casual public interchange anybody could join in, and voice overlap was expected, in more specialized sessions centred on verbal art performance some rules were recognized, even when not overtly expressed. There was for instance the principle summed up in the saying *ar fhear an tí a théann an chéad scéal*, which 'gave the man-of-the-house the right and duty to tell the first story, ... followed by one or more other narrators'.[146] Only talented participants were expected to hold the stage. Depending on circumstances, there was alternation among several voices or one-way discourse if a preeminent teller was present; he would probably need some coaxing, and his great tale of wonder might not come at the beginning of a session. During and after his performance, the audience was expected to express approval, then gratitude. Here is the whole agenda as observed in North Mayo by Michael Corduff:

The big turf fire was kept well stoked by the man of the house, who acted as master of ceremonies; and before the introduction of paraffin oil in remote parts of the country ... domestic lighting was provided by thrusting blocks of bogwood (*crompán*) head foremost into the turf fire. This shed a fitful light on the scene and enhanced the setting for the telling of wonder-tales ... After the news and topics of the day had been discussed and debated by the community present, someone would call on the *seanchaí*, if one was present, to 'shorten the night' by telling a story. The request was supported by a chorus of

145 *Irish Wake Amusements* 27. On funeral storytelling elsewhere, cf. for instance A. Merkelbach-Pinck *Lothringer erzählen* 34: 'Die Geister- und Armenseelengeschichten werden besonders gerne erzählt bei den allgemeine verplichtenden Totenwachen'; A. van Gennep *Manuel de folklore français contemporain* I.1. 703-4: 'très souvent [the funeral wake] ne présente rien de triste, ou n'est triste qu'au début ... On conte des anecdotes propres à dérider l'assistance.' O. Bîrlea 'La Fonction de raconter dans le folklore roumain', *Laographia* 22 (1965): 'dans certains endroits plus archaïques l'on raconte pendant les veillées funèbres des contes fantastiques mais plus souvent des "contes à rire". Les risées provoquées par de tels contes sont si bruyantes qu'il n'y a plus aucun trait funèbre dans la veillée, excepté la présence physique du mort.' R. Schenda, in *Von Mund zu Ohr* 125-30, mentions German, Hungarian and Swiss examples. **146** S. Ó Súilleabháin *Storytelling in Irish Tradition* 11. Cf. J.T. Campbell *Popular Tales of the West Highlands* 1.vi-vii: 'It was a common saying, "The first tale by the goodman, and tales to daylight by the *aoidh*," or guests.' Calum Maclean 'Hebridean Storytellers', in *ARV* 8 (1952) 129: 'There are strict rules of etiquette regarding the telling of tales. When a stranger visits a house, the good man tells the first tale. The stranger has then to continue for the rest of the night. No son tells a tale to a company in the presence of his father, and no younger brother in the presence of an elder brother.'

acclamations from the audience, and the story-teller would make some conventional excuse by saying he was not in form owing to a cold or toothache or some ailment, and declaring his urgent need for a couple of glasses of *poitín*, this remark evoking sympathetic and approving exclamations from the company. However, under the mild pressure and encouragement of the more veteran members of the assembly, he would acquiesce, saying 'Well! maybe it's as well! Yes, I will tell a short piece'. Of course, 'the short piece' would turn out to be a very lengthy story. Then the difficulty of selection had to be overcome. Some wanted this and others that, and as it was impossible to satisfy individual preferences, the man of the house would suggest that the selection of the narrative be left to the *seanchaí* himself. The proposal was carried by an overwhelming majority, and then all eyes were turned on the storyteller, the high priest of the ceremony. There were numerous laudatory and encouraging remarks, such as: 'Long life to yourself!', 'God bless you!', while at the same time those of the audience in possession of chairs or forms would pull up their seats nearer and huddle closer to the speaker for more advantageous positions. Occupying pride of place near the corner of the fireside, the *seanchaí* began with the customary preamble of all stories. ... The conclusion of the tale had its usual epilogue or conventional formula of phrases like the prefatory opening of the story. Then followed a chorus of praises and benedictions on the *seanchaí*. From the beginning to the end of the narrative, including interruptions, the time occupied would be approximately two hours in many cases. If time permitted, there might be another story told, perhaps a shorter one. If the hour was considered too late for further dissertation, the company broke up quietly and went out into the night, bidding one another 'Good night' and 'God speed' on their respective journeys homewards. This social function of storytelling was always observed with much decorum and reverence on the part of the assembly.[147]

In relatively formalized sessions with several potential tellers, a master of ceremony (normally the *fear tí*) could decide who should perform, and perhaps in what genre. It could turn into a contest. Or one star 'raconteur' was surrounded by people who encouraged him to shine. Tim Buckley, 'the Tailor', described both trends, involving one of his colleagues:

When [he] had come to a house the neighbours would congregate in there every night. It would be a great get-together with a house full of them seated around. Each would have a story to tell – one trying to outdo the other. Heroic tales would be told and, hold your tongue, you have never heard stories such as they would have, however it was they could have remembered them. They couldn't be excelled. You would have thought the night too short had you been listening to them. It wasn't heroic tales at all the tailor would have to tell but of his own affairs and adventures here and there, and I doubt if it was the truth he always had to relate. No one believes a word from anyone who is known to be a liar, and that is the reputation which some tailors had. Still people visited the house at night, to which he had come just to hear what he might have to relate, and they thoroughly enjoyed it all.[148]

147 M. Corduff 'Notes on Storytellers and Storytelling in Iorrus', *Béaloideas* (19) 1949, 178-80. **148** Aindrias Ó Muimhneacháin (ed. tr.) *Stories from The Tailor* 64-5.

A customary practice, particularly important at wakes but observed in other circumstances as early as the seventeenth century, was the passing round of a pipe among the men and perhaps older women as well. It was still mentioned in the twentieth:

And the pipe would go round them all; a clay pipe. The pipe would be filled and lit in that corner and passed from one to the other till it was empty at this corner of the hearth, and it was filled again and went back round again. The one pipe, with a chain on the lid.[149]

The host furnished pipe and tobacco, and the pipe was passed back to him by each person in turn after being puffed on for several minutes. Only if the story was a long one was the pipe proferred by the host to the narrator from time to time.[150]

When the house was full to the door, the man of the house would fill his pipe with tobacco, and give it to the most respected guest. The person thus favoured smoked it for a while, then handed it back to its owner; after that it went round the company from one to another. By the time the last man had had his smoke, all the current topics of interest had been discussed, and the storytelling could now begin.[151]

The type of performance designated by the performer himself as a special moment outside the rules of ordinary communication could consist of *scéalta* rather than *seanchais* – but one should not be dogmatic on this subject.

18. The place of narration in general discourse

Some storytelling can be embedded at any time in the ordinary conversation whose function is to confirm the existence of a social fabric. Previously mentioned rituals do not then apply if both the occasional speaker and the interlocutor are participating on the same plane, but there still are general norms of verbal exchanges, for instance turn-taking mechanisms. The skills of a storyteller involved in such a semi-informal gathering include ways of inducing the shift from open conversation to a relatively extended narrative; first, he has to signal that he is about to perform a particular act of expression and to hold the floor for some time; then he must prove, by the authority of his voice and the quality of his contribution, that the initiative was worthwhile; finally he can indicate the return to open exchange. Transitions can be marked by such devices as variations in volume and pitch of voice, or by verbal means: a story inserted into conversation may be introduced, in English, by an utterance like 'This reminds me of ...', 'Did you ever hear tell of ...' or 'They say that ...'; the return to normal turn-taking routine may be signalled by a formula like 'That was a true story', or some other conclusion.

A good storyteller breaking into the conversation is able to adjust to the situation and select the appropriate item in his repertoire; he might try to connect

149 IFC 1113: 525, from Paddy O'Hare, of Dromintee South Armagh. Collected by M.J. Murphy in 1948. **150** J.C. Messenger *Inis Beag: Isle of Ireland* 115. **151** J.H. Delargy *The Gaelic Story-Teller* 19.

it with previously raised topics. He also has to know how to move from one narrative to another: self-contained narratives can be linked (*tarraingíonn scéal scéal eile*: one story leads to another). In the more formal storytelling sessions dealt with previously, a storyteller could intertwine tales in a continuous performance: 'By combining several tales their compositions might swell into a tale of many chapters, each taking an evening for the telling ... The most characteristic type of Irish folktale is the elaborate frame-story with a series of incidents more or less loosely strung together, often in surprising combinations.'[152] In more conversational sessions there were chains of narratives on the same topic, which different speakers could tell in turn: 'Many of the tales about [Daniel] O'Connell were collected in clusters, of perhaps around six stories, where one O'Connell tale appears to lead into another, and once a storyteller had told one anecdote about O'Connell, it frequently brought another to mind.'[153]

19. Competition

Reciprocity is central to the organization of social life. If stealing a tale is questionable (see Section 7), refusing to share it is not very commendable either. Storytelling is a give-and-take process: the person who tells a story may expect to receive something in exchange – perhaps another story, and such swapping of tales keeps them circulating. A non-narrative countergift may be the acknowledging of a superior status by the one who cannot surpass or even equal the teller.

Competition is another natural tendency: organized tests of comparative skill can be conducted in fun, though even then some prestige is at stake. The limited number of very good *scéalaithe* on the one hand, as well as the usually ordered turn-taking in ordinary conversation, would in most cases moderate aggressiveness, but when there was more than one storyteller in the assembly a contest could be adjudicated by general acclaim, or by the older people who were accepted as experts:

I mind when I was a young lad the old people would gather in, and they'd sit round the fire, trying to best one another at telling stories, and maybe it would be up to four o'clock in the morning before they'd leave, and they'd be arguing with one other going out the door even at that time as to who spun the best one during the night, and we'd all have to give our opinions on it to try and settle the argument.[154]

The sense of rivalry could be exploited by a collector; to refer to an absent contender for the title of supreme storyteller might get the best out of an informant: 'The best way to get [an Irish storyteller] started with telling a particular tale is to remark that a certain rival has told it well. He will then insist that you

152 R.T. Christiansen *Studies in Irish and Scandinavian Folktales* 10, 67. **153** R. uí Ógáin *Immortal Dan* 122. **154** IFC 485: 55-6, from John Gallivan, aged 90, County Sligo. Same collector.

have never heard the story really told as it should be, and he then proceeds to demonstrate.'[155] More often than long stories, short comic anecdotes or preposterous lies were exchanged in open contests:

It was the usual thing that used to happen by the fireside, the ceilis that used to be longgo. One man would tell somethin, then another man would tell somethin forenent [opposite to] that, and it would go on around, and that's what they'd spend their night at. And then there'd be a discussion on whose pant [a lark, or an amusing incident] was the best one. Well, the people used to come along for to get a number of these stories, for to judge which of them would be the best to tell if they were in some company. They used to analyse it from beginning to end and judge for themselves which story was the best, do ye see. Someone would propose this round of storytellin. Then if there happened to come strangers along, the natives would be watchin to see what stories that these men would give.[156]

For an oral storytelling event to take place, a storyteller is needed (who will prove his or her competence), a story must be told (old or new, but in either case following certain schemata which can be recognized and used to interpret the message), and it must take place in an adequate setting. There must also be a receiving end offering adequate feedback: a sympathetic audience – narration can be a solitary mental exercise, but storytelling is a social transaction. Performer and audience must collaborate, and the success of tales as well as their survival through transmission depend on how well they accord with the tastes and views of the community. Those to whom the tale is delivered influence the performance, which in turn does something for them. The interaction is examined in the next three sections.

20. The audience, and how to control it

A storyteller's audience is never the whole community he/she belongs to: not everybody is willing or able to hear tales at the same time. And contrary to the dream of some folklorists of the past, the 'traditional' community is always composite: even the fraction represented by a given audience is likely to be diversified. Yet the storyteller must try to unify it and collaborate with it. The narrative act must be negotiated, and each particular performance is partly conditioned by the composition of the audience (who is accepted and who excluded, by reason of age, gender or status), and by its relative competence. Real connoisseurs, even when not in the majority, would exert a stronger influence than novices or mere bystanders; but even experts may project their individual preoccupations onto what they hear, which leads to different reactions. Nevertheless, all the willing members of a 'traditional' audience are prepared to behave in conventionalized ways.[157] The acceptable degree and form of partici-

---

155 S. Thompson *The Folktale* 454. **156** Henry Glassie *Passing the Time* 71, from Hugh Nolan, Ballymenone, Co. Fermanagh, *c*.1970. **157** J. Pentikäinen 'Oral Transmission of Knowledge', in R.M. Dorson (ed.) *Folklore in the Modern World* 241-2: 'The participants do

pation may vary from one culture to another and the same group may be more or less receptive according to circumstances, but it is generally true that 'audience members expect, and are expected, to be stimulated by the behavior of narrators and to respond in ways that in turn stimulate narrators'.[158] They may even correct a teller who diverges from what they want.[159]

If Irish storytellers have been commended, so have Irish audiences. An American woman who was trying to revive the telling of tales in her urban world and who visited Ireland around 1900 praised the receptivity of listeners there: 'I had once promised to tell stories to an audience of Irish peasants, and I should like to state here that, though my travels have brought me in touch with almost every kind of audience, I have never found one where the atmosphere is so "self-prepared" as in that of a group of Irish peasants. To speak to them, especially on the subject of fairy-tales, is like playing on a delicate harp: the response is so quick and the sympathy so keen.'[160] It is a fact that the process of listening to a tale can in itself be a creative act.

Most of the participants in a session where some reputed storyteller was performing were probably male adults; the women present were likely to be those living in the house, and their children could listen but were tolerated only if relatively unnoticed (tales specifically directed at them were told in more intimate contexts). The number of persons might vary from less than a dozen to twenty or more. They generally knew each other, and shared enough experience to develop collective attitudes. As noted above, there was a code of behaviour for listeners: what position to take in the room, how to humour a storyteller, when to be silent and when to make oneself heard, how to thank the performer ... Although they were expected to be quiet if some mesmerizing storyteller was in action, they should at least show that they were paying attention. It is possible to commune and give support in silence, but a certain amount of oral expression was accepted, provided it did not disrupt the rhythm: stimulus would be provided with 'yes', 'ah', 'well done', and Irish equivalents like '*Maith thu*' (good on you), '*Is fíor dhuit*' (true for you) – or with longer ejaculations like '*Go mba slán an seanchaí*' (may the storyteller prosper), which proved the effectiveness of the more dramatic scenes:

When recounting deeds of prowess by the hero, there would be cries from the listeners of 'My love!', 'The best!', 'It is good!' etc. and when the hero subdued the witch or some evil female there were ejaculations (in Irish of course) of 'The devil mend her!', 'That

not function simply as individuals but, rather, control each other and adopt certain role behaviour ... '. **158** R. Georges 'Communication Role and Social Identity in Storytelling', *Fabula* 13 (1990), 55. **159** Cf. G. Henssen *Volkstümliche Erzählkunst* 12: 'Jede gut erzählte Geschichte [ist] ohne Unterbrechung vorgetragen; nur dann, wenn der einzelne nicht den Stoff beherrscht, erfolgt eine Auflösung der Geschichte in Form eines allgemeinen Wechselgespräches, bei dem der eine sich dieser, der andere jener Einzelheit erinnert und darauf aufmerksam macht' [helping a storyteller's failing memory). **160** M.L. Shedlock *The Art of the Story Teller* 8-9.

was the fix of her!'. During the progress of the tale there might be an occasional question from an individual for the clarification of a certain matter. Sometimes, other members of the audience would resent such interruptions, and tell the inquirer to keep his ears open, pay attention, and not be distracting the storyteller.[161]

How the listeners participated in the course of events, although they had already heard the story quite often! They accompanied the telling with sighs and moans or with smiles and laughter, with a slap on the thigh, or an interjection, and at the end they were breathing more freely.[162]

Responses helped the narrator to decide how to continue: 'The tale becomes more beautiful and colourful when the narrator feels that his listeners are with him, living each moment along with him; the more complete the audience cooperation, the more perfect becomes the tale.'[163]

What has been described so far in this section applies to the performance of *scéalta*. Legend-telling could take a more polyphonic form, with turn-taking and collective comments. Even in a *scéal* session, someone in the audience could step in to fill a gap if no master was present or active: 'It often happened when the regular storytellers were absent, or when they were tired or indisposed, or perhaps when a long folktale came to an end, some ordinary man came in with a tale. These were generally of a humorous nature, and were generally short.'[164]

If a knowledgeable audience somehow influenced the storyteller, the competent performer, for his part, would of course know how to get a grip on his public and remain in control. It implied taking into consideration the reactions of the audience: not only would he adapt the performance to time constraints, making it longer or shorter, and do his best to arouse and satisfy curiosity, but he would quickly respond to the listeners' changes of attitude. A time came, however, when the storyteller's natural local audience stopped giving support: 'Storytelling is now almost a dead art because in many places the storytellers are laughed at and only tolerated when listeners are weatherbound or otherwise compelled to listen.'[165] As previously noted, when the community began to default collectors might occasionally mobilize some listeners, or become the only remaining audience. They restored self-confidence to the storyteller (if he had lost it), as well as a kind of renewed quality label in the community when it was known that people came from afar to listen to him; but, as also noted, collectors changed the conditions of storytelling and may have had some effect on the performances.

21. How the audience assessed a storyteller

The storyteller and his audience have a kind of contract, according to which one party is entitled to receive full attention and the other can expect that a story

---

161 M. Corduff 'Notes on Storytellers and Storytelling in Iorrus', *Béaloideas* 19 (1949) 179-80. **162** Ludwig Mühlhausen *Diarmuid mit dem Roten Bart: Irische Zaubermärchen* 9 (my translation). **163** Linda Dégh *Folktale and Society* 119. **164** IFC 1380: 24 – P. O'Connell, County Limerick, 1954. **165** IFC 630: 27 – John O'Donoghoe's comment when collecting in County Kerry, in 1939.

will be well presented. A narrator must demonstrate his skill, his story must be interesting, and the audience may rate the performance. But we must keep in mind the difference between 'natural' (or 'traditional') audiences and 'modern' ones, and in the former beween the potential judges' degree of competence or authority. The 'traditional' listeners could pass judgement on a teller's command of repertoire if they were themselves familiar with a wide range of tales; they might evaluate the handling of certain motifs, and the teller's verbal dexterity compared with what they had already heard. The necessary competence could be learned without conscious analysis through cultural conditioning, and personal tastes made divergent appreciations possible within the same set of conventions.

Some storytellers are generally better than others but may not always be in good form, and aesthetic criteria are not the only principles on which a judgment is based: a mediocre storyteller could occasionally give satisfaction just by being available at the right time at a gathering which felt the need to increase or express its cohesiveness, or to recall some fact or event. At other times the audience would not tolerate inadequate renditions: 'A poor storyteller soon lost his audience and, moreover, earned scorn and contempt as one who had set himself above his station as expert in an art beyond his talent.'[166] Sometimes, only the more competent listeners would react; embarrassment or anger could be voiced by a better performer who happened to be present:

I have seen expression ... given to outraged feelings by two really good Irish storytellers when I was being told a tale in a country kitchen by a countryman who had not inherited the gift for storytelling of his father; the story was being mangled and so badly told that the two old men, who had up to a certain point contented themselves with despairing gestures, at last could not restrain their feelings any longer, jumped up, and told the storyteller to stop, that he did not know the tale at all and that he should not attempt to recite a story which he could not tell properly.[167]

A Barra man, quoted by Alexander Carmichael, reacted differently in the Hebrides:

I went one night to a *céilidh* in the house of John. He was telling that story to the people who were in before I arrived. I listened to him as long and as patiently as I could, and, Mary Mother, it was not easy for me to listen to my own brother spoiling the good story! There was vexation upon me for the bad treatment of the good tale, but I was keeping check on myself, but at last I could keep check on myself no longer, and I rose softly and dumbly, and I left the house and returned home.[168]

This comment was quoted by J.H. Delargy from his County Clare notebook:

166 K. Danaher 'Stories and Storytelling in Ireland', in *Automobile Association Handbook of Ireland* 27. 167 S. Delargy 'Irish Stories and Storytellers', *Studies* 31 (March 1942) 38. 168 *Deirdire* 5.

'30 December, 1929. This is the worst told tale I have ever heard, and to one familiar with it the omissions, hesitations and inconsistencies were exasperating. The audience was quite disgusted. Now and then I would catch the eye of Johnny Carey and Stiofán Ó hEalaoire, who were sitting beside the fire smoking, and they would shake their heads sadly. To them it was a sacrilege to mishandle a story so. The unfortunate reciter, who was really doing his best, used to cough at times – he had a cold, but it suited him to cloak his deficiencies with a loud cough now and then, and the resting place in the narration thus created allowed him time to think. Very often story-tellers cough when they are not sure what they are going to say! Finally, old Carey stood the strain no longer being outraged beyond endurance, and he shouted at the story-teller telling him what he had omitted and admonishing him.' [Delargy later commented:] They had their standards, these old people. These standards were applied only to the more intricate forms of narrative, the long hero-tale, in particular, with its wealth of incident, its large number of characters.[169]

It is not easy to say exactly what would give rise to approval: aesthetic canons of storytelling may have existed but were not articulated. This anonymous passage in a school-book tries to list some of them:

The following were the qualities of a good *seanchaí* [in the loose modern sense of 'storyteller']: he told stories often and he loved to tell them; he had an outstanding memory and was able to master a huge body of narratives and recite them perfectly; he had a musical voice when speaking Gaelic and English; he used few bodily movements and spoke slowly; he knew when to pause for effect (especially after an important event in the story, to allow each listener to picture the event in his imagination and savour it), and these pauses were never more than ten seconds or so; he looked at each member of the audience, then down for a time, then into the fire for a time; and he smiled but did not laugh after telling something amusing that aroused great merriment among his listeners.[170]

Clear enunciation and a sense of varying tempo certainly counted, and – more difficult to define – the storyteller's 'presence' or personal magnetism must have been an important element. Other criteria were proposed: 'Not only were long and complex tales considered a necessary attainment, but the audience expected him to show ability in disputation and adroitness in repartee.'[171]

Precise norms are said to exist for the assessment of storytelling in Irish; they are applied, for instance, in adjudicating competitions organized by the Gaelic League (and here we may be leaving the 'natural, traditional' audience), where an estimation of general narrative skills may decide if the candidate is 'talented', but at least as much stress is laid on richness of diction and ability to introduce well-known fixed pieces. In fact, the display of linguistic skill seems

---

169 'Notes on the Oral Tradition of Thomond', *Journal of the R.S.A.I.* 95 (1965) 146. **170** *Island Stories: Tales & Legends from the West* 238. **171** T. Ó Broin 'Scéalaí Tíre' (Co. Galway), *Béaloideas* 24 (1955) 131.

to count most: 'For the native Irish narrators used to the formulaic and archaic diction of the storytelling tradition, the challenge in telling such stories lies in the opportunity they provide for them to exhibit their command of this special language ... Participants [in the yearly *Oireachtas* competition] are judged on the basis of their linguistic virtuosity; they are expected to be able to narrate the long, multi-episodic tales (*scéalaíocht*) and to incorporate the rhetorical descriptive passages associated with Irish heroic narrative ('runs').'[172] On the other hand, the same observer notes that for storytelling in English the performers themselves may be unable to define clear evaluative standards[173] – which of course does not mean that their own performance is artless and that they have no opinions about the value of other storytellers.

22. The functions of storytelling and the significance of the tales

What does storytelling contribute to the life of individuals and of the group? It may perform several actions at once, and one of them may be manifest to the participants while others, perhaps not less important, pass unnoticed. Different kinds of narratives can meet different kinds of needs; and one story may have different purposes and effects, depending on who tells it, to whom, and in what circumstances. In Ireland as elsewhere entertainment was expected: a way of passing time, of escaping for a while from the hardness or drudgery of daily life, also of relieving tension and of seeing dreams of justice fulfilled. But if storytelling could be a substitute for unsatisfactory reality, it could also be a means of ordering and making sense of actual experience through the awareness of analogies and the magnifying, or systematizing, of what was so far only half-perceived: in other words, although stories may put people to sleep, they can also awaken them to new insights into reality. Socially, storytelling sessions were also important in bringing people together, cementing communal bonds and reinforcing a sense of group continuity. Beyond making them feel comfortable together, they implicated all listeners in a value-system or set of beliefs and, in more or less didactic modes, they could lay down important norms. As simple expedients, stories might terrify children into obedience, and deter naive persons from getting into trouble: 'When I was a youth, I used to be afraid to go outside the door in the dark. The storytelling by the old people sitting at the fire would make you afraid.'[174] They could overtly be vehicles of cultural instruction, setting examples of what to do and what to avoid, but might also suggest that certain ends are achieved through defiance of rules, or fantasize about a reversal of normal conduct, or bring relief by evoking what is difficult to talk about openly. The relation could be with inner, rather than social, experience: for the individual certain stories would objectify conflicting feelings and wishes by fictionalizing them, and thus provide an outlet for frustration. A story can also

172 C.B. Harvey *Contemporary Irish Traditional Narrative* 56-8. **173** Ibid. 58ff. **174** *Béaloideas* 3 (1932) 181, from Michael Gaynor, aged 87, Co. Roscommon.

soothe or uplift when it is perceived as not merely pleasing or useful but, for some reason, beautiful – but in the 'traditional' world little was made explicit in terms of aesthetic evaluation.

The ways of thinking that inform tales and the mental processes used in telling or receiving them are not easy to grasp, and the problem of their 'meaning' is therefore complex. Can stories which seem to be irrational make coherent sense? A storyteller would probably choose a story because it struck some sort of responsive chord; but exactly what would it signify to him or her? What can a tale reveal about the world listeners live in or an imaginary world that somehow concerns them? It may, in certain circumstances, communicate meaning symbolically, suggesting feelings, fears and hopes in indirect ways. But what 'sense' emerged for a given audience at a given time is a matter of debate: any interpretation is likely to select some tales and consider only some of their aspects, reading them as the expression of the resentment or hopes of the powerless, or as shamanistic initiatory experiences, or practical guides in the maturation process, or ready-made sexual fantasies, etc. A full investigation is beyond the scope of this study,[175] but we may reasonably assume that a meaning emerges from the interaction of the listener with the teller, the group, and some objective features of what is being told; the listener is the final arbiter of the tale's meaning, and one tale may thus lead to different responses. More precise information would be necessary to decide if, in this respect, there was anything peculiar to Ireland.

Of the various functions mentioned above, the one most appreciated by the individual might well be entertainment. For the community as a whole, what was most important could be the conveying of a value-system and the validating of collective beliefs, or just the strengthening of relationships within the group.

After focusing on the tellers, then on audiences, we may look at what is told. The following sections will touch on some formal aspects of stories, starting with their length and the arrangement of their narrative line. Unwritten laws tended to determine – according to genres and with some latitude in practice – the size of a narrative, the shape of its plot, what tended to remain immutable in it, and where changes might be tolerated or desirable.

23. The length of the tale
There were stories which filled several 'nights': J.H. Delargy heard of a beggarman who took seven of them for one tale.[176] The longest heroic tale actually

175 E.B. Gose *The World of the Irish Wonder Tale* 180: 'the best wonder tales not only possess a close-knit texture of plot and character but also connect those elements with a theme of psychic and spiritual depth'. He tried to apply freudian, jungian and structuralist approaches to some Irish tales. **176** J. Delargy *The Gaelic Story-Teller* 21. Cf. N. Philip *The Penguin Book of Scottish Folktales* xxiii: 'The *Sgeulachd Cois' O'Cein*, the longest and most testing of all Gaelic tales, was intended for narration over twenty-four consecutive evenings.'

recorded for the Irish Folklore Commission, in October 1938, filled twenty-two Ediphone cylinders (30,000 words, taking perhaps two hours and a half, or more), and in the course of the telling the narrator said that he was omitting certain parts which would have made it longer. But it was told in three sessions, spread over three nights;[177] dividing a story into several tellings might be a way of managing suspense or just of saving one's strength, but this particular story-teller said he needed time to ponder the course of the following section.[178] More often told at a stretch, some stories could be fairly long. In 1936, an informant from County Waterford remembered: 'The people around here used to tell a lot of Irish stories about thirty years ago. There were Billy O'Sullivan from Toor and he'd keep the whole house going with a story called *Scéal an Ghamhna Bhuí* from ten o'clock in the night till three o'clock in the morning.'[179] A number of tales recorded in the twentieth century took about an hour and several were longer, but many more came closer to a half-hour or twenty minutes.

A storyteller could be proud of his ability to tell very long and perhaps com-posite tales,[180] but their length did not necessarily make them good. In any case a master would control the length of any story, deciding what might be devel-oped or added, shortened or deleted, depending on the time available, the response of the audience, and his own mood. Some narrative acts gain by being lengthy, others by being brief: a proverb says that *an seanchas gearr an seanchas is fearr* (a short *seanchas* is the best *seanchas*).[181] What will be said in the follow-ing section concerns *scéalta*.

24. Plot elements and organizational principles

There was perhaps a time when oral narratives were thought to be formless and to develop randomly, but it is now admitted that in all of them, and particularly in those that deserve to be called 'tales', the action develops in accordance with a logic of its own. A complex story consists of several sequences of narrative propositions; each sequence may be defined as the transition from one state to another (but there may also be delatory elements, or semi-independent sequences within the main story); and each (except perhaps the last) is likely to end with a situation which can develop in a number of different ways, the actu-alization of one of those possibilities opening the next episode. Apart from kernel events, there are secondary ones which just fill in the outline. The overall move-

177 E. a Búrc *Eochair, Mac Rí in Eirinn* 23, 35-6. 178 Ibid. 97, 117, 159, 171 (about dele-tions); 23 (about division into 'nights'). 179 IFC 259: 524, from Johnny Power, of Toor. Collected by Nioclás Breathnach. Cf. C. Maclean 'Hebridean Storytellers', *ARV* 8 (1952) 127: 'Some of his [i.e. Angus MacMillan, on the Island of Benvecula] longer romantic tales took from seven to nine hours to narrate.' 180 G. Henssen *Volkstümliche Erzählkunst* 23: 'In kühner Weise verbindet er häufig Geschichten, die nur lose miteinander in Zusammenhang stehen; entscheidend ist für ihn hier die Möglichkeit, den Faden recht lang ausspinnen zu können. Gerade auf ihre langen Geschichten sind die Erzähler besonders stolz' (a storyteller may loosely combine tales, and is proud of the length of his performance). 181 A. Partridge *A Hundred Irish Proverbs and Sayings* 5.

ment may be from imbalance to peace or from problem to resolution; or – most common in wonder tales – from happiness to degradation with a return to the starting point and final improvement (for the protagonist). Tension is created by the interaction of 'good' and 'evil' forces, including helpers and opponents. Characters which no longer contribute to the development of the plot simply disappear. Action is emphasized rather than description, and characterization is subordinated to incidents: it is by what happens to the protagonists and the decisions they make that their value is revealed. The story is told most often in the third person but from the point of view of the hero, with whom both the teller and the listener identify. The chronological order of events is generally respected: there may be ellipses, and warnings or commands may be anticipations, but a return to events of an earlier period is more likely to correct an accidental omission (' I forgot to tell you that ...') than to be a deliberate flashback. Plot patterns may be regulated by numbers (pairs of scenes, with oppositions or symmetries; triads, with some progression: the third son is better, and his third attempt is a success ...); or by chains (e.g. of tasks or transformations). The structural schemes underlying the narratives are simple enough to be easily applied by skilled storytellers to reconstruct a tale and to adapt it to the kind or degree of attention of which his audience is capable: the point is to make the listeners want him to keep speaking.

In addition to these general principles – which of course I have not discovered! – different genres may have their own special organization. In the wonder tale or *Märchen*, the essential point generally lies in reaching, with magic help and through some transformation, a conclusion we would like to achieve in real life but know we probably can't; the initial crisis may determine the goal of the action but it is also possible to say that the particular ending to be reached determines what happens before. The Irish 'hero-tale' may have a more complicated plot trajectory, with many characters, and descriptive (stereotyped) passages; but other principles of the wonder tale tend to apply. As will be shown later, the most distinctive features of the 'hero-tale' may belong to the texture rather than the plot, with the use of verbal devices that make of the telling a stylistic challenge.

25. What is variable and what is stable in a plot
There are variable and invariable elements in folklore, transformation and persistence – at the same time inertia and dynamism.[182] The listener likes to hear the same wonder tale several times (less so the same joke), but he also appreciates surprises. The performer must respect a certain style and a recognizable material, yet is given some licence with them. If the nucleus of a story remains the same, some incidents may vary; but if a detail is altered, others may have to

182 B. Toelken *The Dynamics of Folklore* 38: 'We can probably say, then, that those artifact productions that remain traditional do so because they have retained their variability.'

change to maintain a sense of consistency – which is not of the same kind when a story is heard and when it is read.

In an apparent paradox, on the one hand it was admitted that *bíonn dhá insint* (or *seacht n-insint*) *ar gach scéal* – 'there are two (or seven) ways of telling every story', but on the other the very idea of variation could be condemned as *claonadh seanchasa* – 'a deviation, or perversion, of tradition'. The overwhelming majority of the narrators interviewed by C.B. Harvey in the early 1980s certified that they were trying to tell their stories exactly as they had first heard them, but the same collector also met a teller of stories in Irish who said that she 'never told a tale the same way twice', adding that 'her mood or the circumstances affected her narratives and even, at times, her capacity to tell a story at all'.[183] As we have seen (in Section 8), Irish storytellers often asserted, and believed, that they were not changing what they had received;[184] in practice, certain genres were more stable than others on the textual surface, and texts in verse are relatively more fixed than texts in prose. In most cases, absolute verbal accuracy was unnecessary, and hardly possible.

But what about the plot pattern itself? Would certain elements be more flexible than others? Could the general development be modified by a storyteller? Folklorists tended to doubt it: Douglas Hyde said that 'the incidents and not the language were the things to be remembered', and J. Delargy confirmed that 'the tale must be passed on as it has been received, unaltered, not in regard to language, but in form and plot'.[185] Nevertheless, some structural changes can be made, by the permutation of parts, the choice of this rather than that stereotyped sequence from a common stock, the omission or drastic reduction of some elements or the addition of episodes borrowed from other tales; a whole story could be grafted on another; and it was possible to string different tales together to produce a longer and more complex piece. But what is subject to variation is not likely to be the basic set of hinge points that identifies a particular story-type. The degree of familiarity of the local audience with a narrative could play a role in defining the limits of flexibility, as an account from the Aran Islands confirms:

Myths, legends, and tales were never embellished but told as accurately as possible. If a narrator attempted to alter such a story, his audience interrupted and corrected him. Stories newly acquired or otherwise unknown to the islanders were embellished by the narrators who introduced them and by subsequent storytellers until they were well

---

183 C. B. Harvey *Contemporary Irish Traditional Narrative* 14. 184 Cf. L. Dégh *Folktales and Society* 166-8: 'the majority of the narrators themselves [in Hungary] affirmed that nothing must be changed in a tale ... [But] the inviolability of the tales learned from the older generation is pure fiction.' 185 *Beside the Fire* xxiv. and *The Gaelic Story-Teller* 20. Cf. L. Dégh ibid. 172: 'Since the narrator has at his disposal the ready-made traditional raw material, he does not have much choice concerning the plot – the inventory of motifs, incidents, stylistic formulae – and what he himself can add. He can move only in a very restricted space; his innovations are controlled by tradition and audience and can be seemingly very slight.'

known. Gradually they became standardized and the point reached where no one telling them could effect further alterations.[186]

26. 'Same story', same performer – different tellings

Larger differences might be expected between performances of the 'same tale' by two tellers than between two tellings by the same person who had established and tested his/her basic version.[187] Yet the interpretation could vary with the narrator's state of mind or with a new context, and if the storyteller noticed the special interest taken by the audience in some part of his performance, he might dwell on it longer in the next telling.[188] But the storyteller's particular mode of presentation remained recognizable: a stable manner might function as a kind of trademark, showing that the tale 'belonged' to him.[189]

The permanence and relative flexibility of a story in repeated performances by the same individual, as far as narrative content and structure are concerned, may be illustrated with an unadorned example in the Irish Folklore Archives, collected by M.J. Murphy: two tellings within two years, by the same informant (Michael Rooney, of Blacklion, Co. Cavan), of 'The Well at the World's End' – a story which also exemplifies the implantation in Ireland of an 'international tale type'. The motif of the 'water of life' to be brought from some far-off place is part of numerous tales around the world; the water restores youth or health, or confers immortality. It is often secured with the help of an animal or some supernatural being, and may be replaced by life-giving fruit or plants.[190] In the romance of Alexander (Greek 'original' *c*.200 AD, followed by Latin versions, and by vernacular versions since the eleventh century) the hero fails to locate the Fountain of Life or Fountain of Youth. The earliest known version of what would later be classified as AT 550 and 551 (The Quest for the Golden Bird, and The Sons on a Quest for a Wonderful Remedy for their Father – '*Das Wasser des Lebens*' in the Grimm collection) is in *Scela Caeli* (*c*.1300), a compilation of *exempla* by the Provençal Dominican Jean Gobi.[191] The well of healing is also a motif in ancient Irish narratives[192] and a constant in beliefs and customs.

186 John Messenger, 'Joe O'Donnell, Seanchai of Aran' 203.   187 A . Kaivola-Bregenhøj *Narrative and Narrating* (Finland) 199: 'Some of the narrator's decisions may become established and defy variation from one performance to the next.' B. Holbek *Interpretation of Fairy Tales* 181: 'A narrator could work considerable changes in a tale when adapting it for his or her own use. Once a tale had been adapted its form tended to stabilize.'   188 Ibid. 28: 'Narrative variation never takes place on the narrator's terms alone: it is always the outcome of interaction between the narrator and the audience.'   189 Cf. Flori Aloisi Zarn (1859-1943), Switzerland, in L. Uffer *Rätoromanische Märchen und ihre Erzähler* (67, 66) he wanted to tell the stories always in the same way '*per ch'ins satgi ca quellas ein las historias dil Zarn*' ('so that one would know those are Zarn's stories'). It was also to give them truth value: '*Que san ins beca ruschanar quella ga aschia e l'aultra ga autruisa, schiglioc vess la glieut getg: quel ei in manzaser*' ('You cannot tell this time one way and the next time another way, or else people will say: he is a liar').   190 Claude Lecouteux 'Lebenswasser', in *Enzyklopädie des Märchens* 8. 838-41.   191 Bolte-Polivka *Anmerkungen zu den Kinder- und Haus Märchen* 1. 512-13.   192 T.P. Cross *Motif-Index of Early Irish Literature* 134, 351.

Numerous versions of AT 550 and 551 have been collected in Ireland, along with versions of AT 513A (' Six Go through the World'), and include the race with a hag.[193] The tale quoted below may be seen as a combination of international motifs, including Q45 Hospitality rewarded, H1321.2 Quest for healing water, R231 Obstacle flight – objects are thrown back, which stop the pursuer. In each column, narrative units are numbered in the order they took in the second performance – not only to show that some permutation is possible but also that a unit can absorb or duplicate another. When three dots appear, they mark the teller's hesitation.

October 1971 (IFC 1786: 161-2)

October 1973 (IFC 1811: 35-40)

1. The king had a daughter and she got very ill. And nothing in the wide world would cure her only a bottle of water from the Well at the World's End.

1. Well, there was a king and he had the one, only the one daughter, and she got terrible ill and she took to her bed. And the king was very annoyed about this girl, the only one daughter he had. And eh – somebody told the king if there was any young man would get a bottle of water from the Well at the World's End, it would cure your daughter. Three or four months in bed she was in a coma, she couldn't speak or she could do nothing, and the king was very annoyed about her.

2. So every man that ... tried his hand to cure the king's daughter; if she was cured, well, he could have her in marriage, no matter where he came from or who she was, because she got very ill and she was there and she couldn't talk and she was in a coma.

2. So several men tried to go to the Well at the World's End to get a bottle of water to cure the king's daughter. Everybody failed, because it was impossible to get to the Well at the World's End. Because the first thing they met was a wall of spears, projecting out straight, they couldn't get through, they had to turn back.

3 A. So this man was sitting at the fire one night, a young man, and there came a rap to the door; this old woman appeared at the door and she says: 'Can I come in?' 'O, definitely,' he says. 'Can I sit down at the fire?' ' O, yes, definitely; why wouldn't you.' He had a big turf fire. 'Well, now,' she says to him, 'there's a king's daughter

3 A. Well, this young fellow was sitting at the fire one night and he was after a day's work, and he was sitting at the turf fire, and he had his shoes off, and he was sitting there after a cup of tea. And there came a knock to the door. 'I wonder who is this?' he says. And this old woman appeared at the door. She says: 'Would you let me have a shink

---

193 Ó Suilleabháin and Christiansen's *The Types of the Irish Folktale* lists eighty-seven versions of AT 550 ('The Sons on a Quest for the Wonderful Remedy for their Father') collected in the four provinces of Ireland.

very ill. Would you take a chance and go to the Well at the World's End for a bottle of water to cure the king's daughter?' 'Ah,' he says, 'how many have tried that and failed?' She says: ' You can do it'. 'Well,' he says, 'how would I go?' She says: 'There's a wee wand; a wand: and no matter what you meet wave your wand like that and you'll have a clean passage.'

heat at your good turf fire?' 'Aw – and why wouldn't I? And you look very cold. Will you take a cup of tea?' 'I will'. And he gave it to her. He made the cup of tea, he had the teapot there at the fire, put a drop of water on it, a great turf fire. And she sat over on a chair. She says to him: 'Now, for your kindness to me would you like to be married to the king's daughter? For the king'll give her to any man that could take a bottle of water from the Well at the World's End to cure his daughter.' 'Aw – 'twould be an impossibility. I couldn't do it.' 'Well,' she says, 'you can. Now for your kindness to me,' she says, 'and you're a very nice young man, and I'll tell you what you'll do, and take my advice. You'll encounter a lot of trouble on your way, but,' she says – and she took out a wee wand: 'Now,' she says, 'take that wand,' – a wee stick – 'and there's three apples' – three apples

3 B. – and 'there's an old witch watching that well in case the king's daughter would be cured, an old witch. And be careful of that old witch, because she's a desperate character' – this old woman said to the young man. And he says – she says to him: 'There's the wand and there's the three apples, and you'll be married to the king's daughter,' she says, 'for your kindness to me.' 'Well, begod ... Nearly an impossibility.' 'Not at all,' she says, 'not at all, for the king said that anybody that'd get a bottle from the Well at the World's End to cure his daughter would have her in marriage.' The only one that he has. 'Now there's three apples and there's the wee stick, and you start in the morning.' 'I'll start in the morning.' 'Will you start in the morning?' 'I will,' he says, 'I'll start in the morning.' So she went out and absconded.

4 A. The first place he went to was a wall of steel points; nothing could go through it, not even a bird. He wove his wand like this, they fell down, and he passed through it. The next place

4 A. He came to this – when he went about a mile, he came to this wood of spears, all projecting out straight in front of him; and no man that ever wore a coat could go through that. And he waved his

he encountered was a big, big fire
straight across, that he had to pass,
he couldn't go any way. He waved his
wand like this and the fire went to that
side and he passed through. The next
thing was a big wall fifteen foot and it
all spiked with glass; he waved his
wand like this and the wall opened,
and he passed on.

wand three times, and the swords
moved over and made a pass for him
to get through. 'That's alright,' he says.
He went on again then a bit further and
he met a wall about seventeen foot
high. 'I couldn't get across that,' he
says. He waved his wand three times
and the stones parted in two and he
went on through. And he came to a
shocking fire. 'I'm finished now,' he says,
'anyway; I'll be burned into a cinder.' And
he waved the wand and the fire parted like
that and let him pass.

3 B. 'Now,' she says to him, 'be careful;
there's an old witch guarding that well
and be careful now, and here's four
apples; and be careful when you're
lifting that bottle of water out of the
Well at the World's End that she won't
push you in – she'll drown you if she
gets a chance. Now this is the position
you'll stand in: you'll stand in like this
and keep your head like this [*erect,
eyes forward*] and get stooped down
this way [*bending the knees only*] and
when you think your bottle is full lift it
up. And she'll make a honch to fire you
into the well, and fire an apple – she's a
queer [fast] runner – and you'll have to
run back to the king's house, for she's a
queer runner,' she says, 'but you'll beat
her. But you'll have to beat her with tact.
 When she's getting tight [close] on
you drop an apple and she'll wait to eat
that apple, and you'll be a fair distance
gone by the time she has the apple
eaten.' And she says: 'If she's in front
of you at the king's castle you're a lost
cat. And be careful now, my young
man; that's a warning.'

4 B. She told him, you see, that when he'd
go through all that there'd be a bush, a
lone bush, and a well in about a
hundred yards from that, a lonely bush.
'There's where the Well is. And be
careful,' she says, 'for there's an old
witch watching that. Don't attempt now,'
she says, 'to lift a bottle of water from
the Well. Here's an apple. Cast that
apple as far as you can, fire it as far as
you can.'

5. So he took her advice and this old
witch appeared – Oh, a desperate looking
character, when he had the bottle going to
go down the steps, and he fired this apple.
She ran after it: 'She's very fond of fruit,'
says the old woman.
   She ran a good few yards, and by

the time she – he had the bottle of
water lifted out of the well and the cork in
it. He took a bee-line back again, as quick as
lightning, the way he came. 'Now she could
be catching you, and fire the second apple,
and by the time she's coming near you fire
it again and she'll run to get this apple;
she's very fond of fruit.'

6. Well, coming to the king's castle
she was coming in tight and he had
his last apple like this and he dropped
it within about a hundred and fifty yards
of the king's castle and she knew she
was lost, she ate the apple and she
could come no further.

6. He done what she – what he was told.
She was coming very tight on him,
nearly put – he fired one back again
and she lifted another apple. He went
as quick as ever he could and he made
– almost made the castle gate. Begod
she was coming tight on him and she was
putting her hand on him when he fired this
other apple back, and she ran back and he
got in on the king's gate.

Well, she let a scream that – it could
be heard in Belcoo.

7. And he went in with the bottle of
water from the Well at the World's End:
and as soon as the girl took the first
cup she opened her eyes and she
smiled and looked around. 'My daughter
is cured,' says the king; 'you'll marry my
daughter.'

7. And he went in with his bottle of water.

In this pair of tellings, we may observe the combination of stability and variability typical of 'oral tradition'. The basic organization of events into sequences,
and of sequences into a recognizable wonder tale, is preserved: 1. A king has one
daughter who gets ill, and only water from a certain well can cure her; the man
who brings some of that water will get the daughter. 2. The well is hard to
reach, and several attempts seem to have proved that it is impossible to return
from it. 3. A young man gains a helper by being kind, and receives magic help
which will enable him to reach the well. 4. He goes to the well. 5. On the way
back, with more magic help, he wins a race against a supernatural pursuer. 6. He
reaches the king's castle. 7. The princess is cured, and marriage follows. A tripartite structure is easy to identify: exposition and start of the action (1-3); com-
plication (4-5, with the series of obstacles leading to a climax: the race); denouement (6-7, with a final situation – only implicit in he second telling – linked
with the initial one); but it is not necessary to be conscious of the architecture
to enjoy the tale. Events and sequences follow one another both temporally and
causally (with possible anticipation as in unit 3B); but the order of the units may
change a bit from one performance to the next. Some of the sequences, or sets

of narrative propositions within one sequence, may be rearranged, expanded or eclipsed (in unit 5, for instance), while others do not change fundamentally and are always present: the elements which determine and advance the series of moves cannot be left out (the 'coma' of the princess, the king's promise, the old woman's visit ...), while details which are there to give a sense of familiar concreteness (the cup of tea) or to prolong scenes (the conventional description of some of the obstacles) can be replaced by others, or simply omitted. Events narrated as a forecast (twice in the second version: 3B and 4B) may also appear as actual action (5 in the second version, not in the first). The set of characters or 'roles' follows the typical pattern of this kind of tale: there is the young 'hero' (his only distinctive trait here is that he is at first apathetic and must be given the will to act, knowledge how to behave, and magic devices to achieve the impossible); a 'sender' who initiates the action (here a role first played by the king, who is also the 'receiver' of what the young man must fetch, then by the old woman who is also the 'helper'); an 'object' to be gained (the water of life, and the princess); and an 'opponent' (the hag).

The way the plot is put in concrete form may change, but the basic model cannot be fundamentally modified without producing 'another story'. Certain steps in the narrative can be repeated or not (for instance, the overcoming of successive obstacles may or may not be re-verbalized in detail and in similar terms). The first performance seems to have been more 'dramatized' in some respects, with a greater part played by gestural language in unit 3B, which may also have had a stronger impact by its position closer to the climax than in the second version. Dialogue could be extended or shortened at will; the redundancy in unit 3A of the second version would be considered awkward in a written text but might be perceived more favourably in oral storytelling.

Michael Rooney's tellings are minimalist: he obviously did not try to give the tale its fullest possible extension, as he might have done if invited to do so by a responsive audience: here, he was addressing only a folklorist and his tape recorder. Another storyteller could have modified certain points: the protagonist might be a king's son; the quest could be for a golden bird; the person to heal could be the father of the hero. The addition of other episodes could make the tale more complex: the protagonist might meet, in a series of scenes, a set of extraordinary characters who would later help him; he might find a princess asleep beside the object of the quest and beget a son, who would later search for him; the protagonist may have brothers, whose failure in the same quest can be related, and who might steal the object he is bringing back ... On the other hand the quest for the miraculous fountain may also be just one episode, perhaps dispensable, in a long hero-tale. Having selected the basic narrative material for his own 'permanent' version, Michael Rooney could then modify its verbal rendition. He varied the importance of the proleptic narration by the old woman in relation to his own direct narrative of the expedition. He could be more concise or more verbose, and might practically stop the action while multiplying repetitions (see unit 3A, in version B). Relatively few phrases remain unchanged; on the whole the narrator verbalizes freely, within the limits of the diction and phraseology familiar to him (e.g., introducing new steps in the development of his story with 'so' or 'well'). The manuscripts in the Irish Folklore Archives include many other examples of the re-telling of tales by one storyteller.

I shall now look more closely at the linguistic substance: the languages of Irish storytellers, their distinctive use of rhetorical ploys, and some of the stylistic devices and modes of delivery they used to achieve certain effects.

27. Language – Irish or English

Some think that languages, having the same genetically programmed bases ('linguistic universals'), are not semantically impermeable. Others believe that the special structure of a given language affects the way its speakers think and that experiences encoded by it are not easily rendered by a different system of verbal expression. I shall not try to decide the question, but I note that in Ireland, ever since nationalism became associated with the exaltation of Irish, the question of which language storytellers use proved a sensitive issue. There was a tendency to associate genuine 'Irish tradition' with only one language. Leading members of the Irish Folklore Commission reacted against such simplification (see Delargy's statement, p. 390); but here is an example, dated 1969, of what was often said or written: 'Had Irish remained the normal everyday language of our people, it is probable that storytelling in that language would have survived fairly normally even up to this age of mass-communications. But the coming in of English almost put an end to storytelling, as the tales never passed over, in any but a very small degree, to the new language.'[194]

Some storytellers could tell the same tales in both Irish and English: 'He told them in English and Irish. They used to translate it then you know after';[195] or: 'He heard it [a Fianna tale] from his father ... who could, so I was informed, have told the story either in Irish or English'.[196] Others, probably more numerous, used, or were at ease in, only one language:

Well now, and I a young lad, I went to a house one night, and there was an old woman there – Clancy's house. It was not in this village – very near it – here over – about a mile away from us – right outside the village – Clancy's – Pat Clancy's. His wife, an old woman, seated in the corner, started this story for me – she was feeble and old – and I hadn't it by heart the first night. So I went over to her again the following night and she told the story back again in Irish, but I am not able to tell it in Irish. And I'll tell it as well as I can in English, according to how she told it.[197]

194 S. Ó Súilleabháin, 'Irish Oral Tradition' in B. Ó Cuív (ed.) *A View of the Irish Language* 55. **195** IFC 1177: 411-12, from Tade Keane, aged 82 in 1950. Collected by S. Ó Dálaigh in County Kerry. **196** IFC 1257: 38-46, dictated by Matthew Early, in County Leitrim in 1895. **197** IFC 961: 135-6, from Mihíl Brannagh, aged 77 in 1943. Collected by Tadhg Ó Murchú in County Clare.

Stith Thompson, accompanying Irish collectors in County Galway, heard a story-teller asserting that it was impossible for him to convey his Irish repertoire in English: '[We] met one of the best of the local shannechas. He spoke some English to us, but told Seamus [Delargy] that he would not undertake to tell any tale in English. He had learned them in Irish and could not transfer their style to another language.'[198] And Tadhg Ó Murchú met a Kerry storyteller who thought it harmful to narrate in English what should have remained in Irish: 'He says that his story-telling has been spoiled by being forced, through love of the tales, to tell them in English to young people who did not know Irish. In that way, through lack of practice and an Irish-speaking audience, he had lost command over his vast store of tales, and in the end had forgotten almost all of them.'[199]

Were the tales really better in one language than in the other? From the early days of the Gaelic League movement, many Irish collectors had firm views: narration in English was inferior in style, in organizing skill and effect, in wealth and quality of repertoire. According to Douglas Hyde for instance, only the oldest, preferably monolingual, members of the Irish-speaking population could narrate properly; those who spoke the other language ignored the best tales, or made a mess of them: 'English-speaking people either do not know them at all, or else tell them in so bald and condensed a form as to be useless'.[200]

It seems to be primarily a question of genre. When applied to some specifically Irish tales, Hyde's statement can hardly be questioned if those were characterized by a special variety of language with archaic qualities ('hard Irish'), and by stylistic devices for which it might be difficult to find equivalents in English, particularly if the latter was less well mastered: 'Because of the style, no doubt, *fiannaíocht* seldom passed into English, and when it did, it did not last long; this is quite different from international tales, which, according to the generally accepted theory, have no difficulty in crossing linguistic frontiers.'[201] Also, inasmuch as storytelling was a more formal activity where Irish remained the vernacular, it was tempting to generalize that *all* tale-telling in English was *always* inferior – J.H. Delargy almost agreed:

Both the international as well as the native *Märchen* are more generally to be found in Irish than in English, and although many folktales of this kind have been recorded in English, the Anglo-Irish wondertale of the international type compares very unfavourably both as to style and content with similar tales in Irish. I have known storytellers in Clare who could tell folktales (*Märchen*) in both Irish and English, but it was quite evident that they told them much better in the Irish language in which they had heard them.[202]

I have myself seen what happens when a tale is bandied back and forth between

---

198 'Folktale Collecting in Ireland', *Southern Folklore Quarterly* 2 (1938) 55. 199 Quoted in J. Delargy *The Gaelic Story-teller* 16. 200 *Beside the Fire* xli. 201 A. Bruford *Gaelic Folk-Tales and Medieval Romances* 61. 202 J. Delargy *The Gaelic Story-Teller* 6-7.

Irish and English, and I have taken down the same tale in Clare in English as well as in Irish, from different narrators, just to observe what process – if any – was at work. Certain types of peculiarly Irish tales succumbed irremediably, being stifled when translated into a different linguistic milieu ... The Irish hero-tale lives and dies a monoglot – it belongs entirely to the old Irish world and can never speak any language but Irish. Some *Märchen* of the international type passed readily enough from English to Irish; the change, however, from Irish to English is not so easily effected.[203]

And R.T. Christiansen went further: 'The characteristics of Irish-Gaelic storytelling ... were intimately associated with the Irish (Gaelic) language and they do not seem to survive in English translation, even when plot and incidents are faithfully preserved. The vigour and style of the original has evaporated, and where English had become the daily language, the stories were sooner or later forgotten.'[204] In 1983-4, C. Brennan Harvey met some storytellers who could use both languages but expressed a preference for Irish: 'There's more talent in it', one of them would say.[205] Such opinions voiced by knowledgeable people cannot be dismissed as mere patriotic enthusiasm; but what lies behind them, rather than the inbuilt superiority of one language, may be the conjunction of Irish-speaking and a kind of society where storytelling had especially thrived. Well-deserved or not, the relative disregard for storytelling in English was accentuated by the Gaelic Revival: to narrate in Irish meant addressing an audience of linguistic *connaisseurs* – and skill in language is, indeed, what adjudicators in the storytelling competitions organized by the Gaelic League have looked for and rewarded. As one contestant put it: 'I try to give out as much of the fluent Irish that's in the story. I tell it for the sake of the vocabulary'.[206] That a change of language entailed losing contact with some textual qualities of a repertoire and craft is easy to concede, but the barrier was not absolutely impassable; in the late 1920s, J.H. Delargy found at least one storyteller, Paddy Sherlock, who did not speak Irish but told stories in a style not incomparable with that of Gaelic speakers (see the second part of this chapter).

A non-Irish observer might be less inclined to admit that the kind of language used absolutely determines the quality of the telling, and that English is an inadequate medium; J.C. Messenger, in the 1960s, noted: 'Contrary to the opinions of nativists, storytellers of the past [i.e. earlier in the century] in Inish Beag [Inisheer] were as proficient in English as in Irish, and tales were told in both tongues with equal ease and audience appreciation.'[207] This view, however, remains an exception. Another American observer voiced a more balanced opinion in the 1980s: traditional performers in Irish and in English could tell the same stories, but when English was used, although there might be an attempt to imitate some aspects of the diction in Irish, the language more clearly

---

203 'Notes on the Oral Tradition of Thomond', *Journal of the RSAI* 95 (1965) 147. 204 *Studies in Irish and Scandinavian Folktales* 10-11. 205 *Contemporary Irish Traditional Narrative* 56. 206 Ibid. 56. 207 *Inis Beag: Isle of Ireland* 116.

approached that of everyday communication, and expression was likely to be less stylized.[208]

In sum, what was considered most 'traditional' in the sense of most representative of the national or ethnic heritage was associated with Irish. If it was true it was because of the socio–cultural set-up of the world where the language was used, rather than for specific virtues of the language itself. Something might be transferred from one world to the other, probably with a loss; in some cases, however, storytelling in English shared with storytelling in Irish certain formulaic devices, one of which I shall now examine.

28. The 'runs', and formulaic composition

Perhaps the most distinctive stylistic feature of an elevated kind of storytelling in Irish (and Scottish Gaelic)[209] is a system of recurrent phrases for which there are various terms in Irish: *ruthag* (run) or *rithlearg* (alliterative run of speech); *culaith ghaisce* (literally martial equipment – a metaphor for high-flown speech); or *cóiriú catha* (battle array). It has often been said to perpetuate, while simplifying it, the *retoiric* of some Irish manuscripts which itself might be a 'survival' of ancient epic oral style (see p. 37) – but the link with an earlier oral form has been questioned and the 'similarity' between medieval manuscripts and later oral techniques qualified.[210]

When certain situations occurred, the informed audience expected the storyteller to resort to set passages. He would change his mode of speech and recite as fast as he could, perhaps with a nasal twang. The language could be partly incomprehensible even to Irish speakers; alliterations particularly marked nouns and adjectives, and the rhythm was emphasized. While a narrator tended to use the same words every time he repeated a particular 'run', another storyteller could favour a different rendition. The device could be considerably stretched: Pádraig Mac Donncha, a Carna storyteller heard by J. Delargy, 'was able to put a *culaidh ghaisce* – a rhetorical run – on a story to last for ten minutes'.[211]

Such prefabricated segments of discourse fell into well-defined classes according to the story-situations they adorned. Alan Bruford, who made a detailed and authoritative study of this phenomenon in late manuscripts and in their oral analogues, described the 'battle run' as the most celebrated kind of verbal acrobatics, which could include a description of weapons and armour, the challenge, the comparison of the combatants to noble fighting beasts, the praise of the fight itself as a spectacle (it was worth coming from far off to see), the

208 C. Brennan Harvey *Contemporary Irish Traditional Narrative* 54ff. 209 'The brief descriptions of most European *Märchen* may be replaced by strings of alliterating adjectives, or whole stereotyped accounts of recurrent happenings such as fights, journeys or hunts, known in English as "runs", derived from similar set-pieces in manuscript stories.' (A. Bruford, Introduction to *Scottish Traditional Tales* 17.) 210 A. Bruford *Gaelic Folk-Tales and Medieval Romances* 36: 'the runs are not, as I have often heard suggested, descendants of the old Irish *retoric … retorics* are speeches uttered by a character, usually in a prophetic mood; runs are descriptions by the narrator'. 211 *The Gaelic Story-Teller* 17.

description of its effects on the landscape, of the wounds inflicted and of the final state of the loser. There were also 'travelling runs', particularly for sea-journeys (preparing the ship, starting the journey, enduring a storm, sighting wonderful sea-creatures, approaching land, drawing the ship ashore); runs for 'descriptions of people' (types of beautiful women or of ugly giants and hags); and 'festive runs' (seating arrangements, the division of the feast into three parts – one of which was often devoted to storytelling). 'Dialogue runs' often involved the imposition of some obligation quasi-impossible to fulfil, or a prohibition impossible to respect (*geis*).[212] If the technique actually passed from manuscripts to oral tradition, there were some modifications: 'With oral transmission the archaic alliterative words may degenerate into nonsense, but often a verse-like rhythm develops in compensation, which may make them sound even more impressive.'[213]

The problems of comprehension which 'runs' may create are obvious in William Larminie's attempt to render a sea-journey formula in English:

When Bioultach went on board the ship they raised their great sails, speckled, spotted, red-white, to the top of the mast; and he left not a rope unsevered, nor a helm without * * * * * in the place where there were seals, whales, crawling, creeping things, little beasts of the sea with red mouth, rising on the sole and the palm of the oar, making fairy music and melody for themselves, till the sea arose in strong waves, hushed with magic, hushed with wondrous voices; with greatness and beauty was the ship sailing, till to haven she came ...[214]

He noted that there were several words, marked in asterisks, which he was unable to translate, and added that the narrator himself did not know the meaning of part of what he was saying.[215] Eileen O'Faolain rendered 'battle runs' in her translation of tales from various storytellers: 'They rushed at each other then like two bulls of the wilderness, or two wild echoes of the cliff; they made soft ground of the hard, and hard ground of the soft; they made low ground of the high, and high ground of the low. They made whirling circles of the earth, and millwheels of the sky; and if anyone were to come from the lower to the upper world, it was to see those two that he should come.' Another version was: 'They went for each other then, as would two whirlpools in an eddy, two calves to the suckling or two warriors to a fight. They kept fighting each other till they made hard places soft, and soft places hard, and until they were drawing wells of spring water up through the gray stones.' A simple 'travelling run' was rendered thus: 'They went so quickly that they could keep up with the March wind in front of them, and the March wind behind them could not keep up with them'. It also took this form: 'I will give you my slender brown steed that can overtake

212 A. Bruford *Gaelic Folk-Tales and Medieval Romances* 37-9, 182-209. 213 Bruford, Introduction to *Scottish Traditional Tales* 17. 214 *West Irish Folk-Tales and Romances* 50. 215 Ibid. 253.

the March wind in front of him and who cannot be overtaken by the March wind that's behind him'. And here are two versions, by the same translator, of a 'welcoming run': 'His wife welcomed him with great joy, and he thought she would smother him with kisses and drown him with tears until she dried him with towels of silk and satin'; 'His wife then ran to the king's son, and it was small wonder that she nearly smothered him with kisses, and drowned him with tears, and that she dried him with mantles of silk and satin.'[216] Simplified runs in tales told in English (with balanced rhythm but fewer alliterations than in Irish) already adorned Patrick Kennedy's rendering of what he had heard in the early nineteenth century.[217]

J. Delargy found that although runs were generally confined to hero-tales, they occasionally appeared in tellings of international *Märchen* which had been fitted into a more specifically Irish pattern. He noted that both the storyteller (who welcomed this chance to show his skill) and the competent audience 'held in low esteem the tale which did not include the traditional and often semi-obscure runs without which they held no hero-tale was complete'.[218] The technique would not be used in 'legend' telling.

That this device is typical of a certain kind of Irish storytelling is undeniable, and it was used to show off virtuosity. Whatever particular forms they took in Ireland, however, such standardized and rhythmed expressions tending to recur and to fill certain slots in the story have also been observed in 'oral literature' elsewhere. A fund of verbal formulae, from single phrases to longer passages, would even enable the performer to improvise.[219] Strictly speaking, this mode of 'oral-formulaic composition-in-performance', when the artist knows combinative plot elements and recurrent scenes along with a stock of phrases that fit half-lines, lines, or series of lines,[220] is harder to apply to texts not in regular verse form. As the Irish narrative material consists essentially of prose, the building-block principle works more at the level of plot construction than in verbalization. Nevertheless, after describing the formula as 'a device which arises from the nature of oral narrative, whether that narrative has a metrical pattern or the more fluid sequences of prose', Kevin O'Nolan analysed Éamon a Búrc's technique as a formulaic system of 'runs', often combined in sequences.[221] In another essay he distinguished between fixed collocations – doublets like *cath agus comhrac* (battle and combat) or noun-epithet pairs like *fiacla geala* (bright-teeth) – and the longer 'runs' which separates moments and/or suggest duration.[222]

216 *Children of the Salmon and Other Irish Folktales* 101, 142, 119, 291, 200, 273. 217 *The Fireside Stories of Ireland* 4, 50. 218 *The Gaelic Story-Teller* 34-5. 219 See Bengt Holbek 'Formelhaftigkeit, Formeltheorie', *Enzyklopädie des Märchens* 4. 1416-40. 220 As analysed in A.B. Lord *The Singer of Tales*. 221 'The Use of Formula in Storytelling', *Béaloideas* 39-41 (1971-3). 222 'Formula in Oral Tradition', in R. Thelwall (ed.) *Approaches to Oral Tradition* 32: 'Formula arises in the heroic tale, for the most part, and the language itself is formulaic, especially in the twin devices of the noun-epithet and the doublet. Recurring occasions generate longer formulae, and these formulae are the means by which a great continuity is both

29. Opening gambits, closure tags, links and breaks

Other set phrases may open a tale and get it under way, punctuate it, or round it out. Those functions may be fulfilled either by deliberately blank statements or by stunning ones. Irish storytelling shares with many other 'traditions' the use of opening and closing formulae to catch and then release the audience's attention, or to transport listeners in and out of a fictitious world and indicate the attitude to be assumed.

Openings serve to make contact with the audience, and perhaps sometimes to test the speaker's voice. They also announce what kind of experience is in store, for instance by setting off the story from the everyday world or on the contrary asserting its factuality. Conversely, bewildering statements or conversational tags at the end of a story can mark the recrossing of the fictional frontier back to everyday reality, or reassert the veracity of a report. Such formulae may be genre-specific.[223] Individual-experience stories generally open with some convincing facts concerning place and names of characters, or a formal guarantee of authenticity. The introduction to an Irish 'legend' may be 'There was a (man, or woman, or boy) *in this place* ...', 'There was a man *by the name of Walsh living to the east of the lake* long ago ...', 'There is a townland *called Cashel* here ...'; or 'Here's a story that I'm going to tell you now, and I promise you that there's no lie in it ...'; and such a narrative may conclude: 'That's a true story, I'm certain of it', or 'That story is as true as any you heard'. The last sentence may repeat the key initial element: 'I heard the banshee, myself, and it happened in this way. 'Twas of a Saturday night. ... 'Twas only the banshee!'[224] Not specific to Ireland, the ritual announcement of a joke may be: 'Did you ever hear what happened to ...?', or 'Do you know the one about ...'

The various opening formulae for overtly fictional tales often emphasize their extra-temporal nature: the past referred to is *not* historical. A common gambit in Irish is:

Bhí ann fadó agus fadó a bhí, dá mbeinnse an uair sin ann ní bheinn anois ann, dá mbeinn anois agus an uair sin ann bheadh scéal úr nó seanscéal agam, nó bheinn gan aon scéal; mar bhí sin rí agus bantiarna fadó in Éirinn agus phós siad. (A long, long time ago – if I were there then, I wouldn't be there now; if I were there now and at that time, I would have a new story or an old story, or I might have no story at all – there was a king and queen in Ireland, and they were married ...)[225]

For storytelling in English, it becomes: 'There was wance, an' wance, an' a very

broken and maintained.' **223** Examples from many countries, several of them close to some of the Irish ones quoted below, can be found in Kurt Ranke 'Eingangsformel(n)' in *Enzyklopädie des Märchens* 3. 1228-44, J. Bolte and G. Polívka *Anmerkungen zu den Kinder- und Hausmärchen der Brüder Grimm* 4. 13-19, and F.M. Luzel 'Formules initiales et finales des conteurs en Basse-Bretagne' in *Revue celtique* 3 (1876-8) 336-41. **224** IFC 575: 62-3 (from Mrs Manaher, Tarbert, in 1938). **225** *Éamon a Búrc: Scéalta* 44; tr. S. O'Sullivan *Folktales of Ireland* 38 .

good time it was. 'Twas neither my time nor your time, but 'twas somebody's
time. There was an old woman, a widda woman, an' she had wan son ...'[226]
Another version by the same narrator goes: 'Once, an' once an' very good times;
an' 'twas neither my time nor your time, but 'twas somebody's time; when
turkeys chewed tobacco and swallows built their nests in old men's beards, an'
that's neither my time nor your time, there was a very rich man an' he had
three sons ...'[227] A shorter and often less committing phrase is, in both languages: '*Bhí fear ann fad ó shin, agus ...*' (There was a man long ago and ...);[228]
or 'There was a man one time and he had a big grey cat ...';[229] or 'There was a
black thief there long ago – often was and will again ...'[230]

Apart from signalling, often by more patterned language, the passage to 'art
communication', recognizable stereotyped phrases stress that what one is about
to hear is a *story*, not to be taken as factual truth. This can be confirmed by
foregrounding more nonsense at the very end, or simply re-introducing everyday reality in a striking contrast. Here are some informants' recollections: 'He
used begin his stories with: "Once upon a time and a very good time it was
when the swallows built their nests in old men's beards ... " '; or 'Mary Daly,
Faughart, who told me much material, recalls now (1946) that storytellers began
their stories with expressions; thus: "Once upon a time when pigs were swine
and monkeys chewed tobacco ...".'[231] In a conversation recorded by M.J.
Murphy, different formulae were compared:

Sheridan: 'Once upon a time when ...' *Carrigan*: 'When men were bold ...' *Sheridan*:
'Once upon a time when men were bold / And turkeys chewed tobacco ...' You said
'monkeys': he said 'turkeys' and that was just the difference. And then when he'd be finished he'd say: 'And they lived happy ever after, and that if they didn't that we may /
Put on the kettle and make tay.' *Frank Maguire*: That's the very way the woman finished
the other day: 'Put on the kettle and we'll make a sup of tay'. *Sheridan*: That's the way
that my father used to tell the story, and when he would be just finished, that ending
had to be. Aye.[232]

The return to reality at the end of the tale could also be signalled by the following formula (offered here as translated from Éamon a Búrc's Irish), where
slapstick is followed by piety:

They returned home and held a feast which lasted for seven nights and seven days. I was
there with them but, if I was, the devil a taste of the feast did they give me. All that I
got from them was paper shoes and stockings of thick milk. I threw them back at them.
They were drowned, and I came safe. Not a word of news have I got from them for the

226 Oney Power, in G.Gmelch and B. Kroup *To Shorten the Road* 62. 227 Ibid. 79. 228 S.
Ó hEochaidh *Síscéalta ó Thír Chonaill* 60-1. 229 IFC 791: 137, collected by P.J. Gaynor in
Co. Cavan, 1941. 230 IFC 1608: 3, collected by P.A. de Brún in Co. Kerry, 1961. 231 IFC
1169: 401,collected by S. Ó Dálaigh in Kerry, 1950, and IFC 1113: 277, collected by M.J.
Murphy. 232 IFC 1811: 53, collected in Co. Fermanagh in 1973.

past year and a day. May this company and the storyteller be seven thousand times better off a year from today. And the dear blessing of God and of the Church on the souls of the dead.[233]

A neutral conclusion, very common in Irish, is *Sin é mo scéal*, the English equivalent being 'that's my story'.

Leaving aside such openings and endings, examples of which could easily be multiplied and are not peculiar to Ireland, we turn to spacers and links, which work as signposts between one part of the story and the next: within a tale, there are transitions and also breaks which may be signalled or enhanced by formulae. Spoken language being characterized both by fragmentation and by apparently endless drift, there may be numerous pauses, false starts and backtracks; in long utterances, it may therefore be difficult to identify sentence boundaries, and some lexical punctuation marks and connectives are therefore indispensable. Brief words may suffice as signals, and fillers (' you know ...') maintain contact with the listener and allow the speaker time to think. To tie together stretches of discourse, simple connectives like 'and' and 'so' are often emphasized; breaks or relationships may also be suggested by tones of voice or by gestures.[234] Language forms indicating relations between narrative segments and binding them into larger units with explicit cohesive ties or marks of development may also be minimal: in the two tellings of 'The Well at the World's End' (Section 26) one finds 'eh', 'aw', 'and', 'so', 'well' ... In spontaneous conversational narration, which tends to develop by fits, there may be hesitation noises ('er', 'um' ...). More formal storytelling is made to sound better organized with obvious rhythmic patterns, echoes, and verbally explicit ways of expressing pauses or linkage. To punctuate the narrative there are formulae or tags like: *Bhí go maith* (that was all right), or *Bhí go maith agus ní raibh go holc* (that was good and it wasn't bad).[235]

Connective formulae mark the transitions between different phases of the story. A common English tag is used when a storyteller decides not to repeat certain sequences, and thus not to expand his narrative: 'To make a long story short', or 'Well, it would take me too long to tell yez all the fine things he said to her ... But the long and the short of it was ...', or 'So we'll make a long story short and a short one merry'.[236] Irish equivalents may be: *le scéal gairid a dhéanamh de* or *le scéal fada a dhéanamh gairid* (to make a long story short), or *níl trácht air sin anois* (there is no talk of that now).

If the use of 'runs' could be the touchstone of a good storyteller, mere tags

---

233 *Éamon a Búrc: Scéalta* 61; tr. Sean O'Sullivan *Folktales of Ireland* 56. (In France, the shoes could be made of sugar or lard, and the menu of which the storyteller was prevented from partaking may be detailed: F. Sautman 'Variabilité et formules d'ouverture et de clôture dans le conte populaire français', in V. Görög-Karady (ed.) *D'un conte à l'autre* 133-43.) **234** See D. Tannen 'Oral and Literate Strategies in Spoken and Written Narratives' *Language* 58 (1982). **235** Éamon a Búrc *Eochair* 79, 95. **236** P. Kennedy *Legendary Fictions* 17; G. Gmelch and B. Kroup *To Shorten the Road* 66.

were easy to handle, and some might try to avoid stereotyped phrases, as did
one of Jeremiah Curtin's informants: 'His command of language was extraordinary. He was one of those who rely hardly at all on clichés or set phrases to
express themselves, but compose new phrases to illustrate their original thought
in speech-moulds of their own making.'[237]

30. Levels of style, rhetorical devices and voice control

Some oral storytelling has the general characteristics of much spoken discourse,
with a few peculiar turns of phrases: in English, the preference for deictic mod-
ifiers ('This man' rather than 'The man'); in Irish as well as in English, a preference for the present tense ('The storyteller may suddenly switch over to the
historic present')[238]. Such features, obvious in conversational recollections, may
also be observed in formal storytelling, but here the poetic function of language
can be heightened by the foregrounding of some selected modes of utterance. It
seems that the language more approximated that of ordinary speech for storytelling in English, though even there the diction occasionally departed from that
of everyday speech (as in 'absconded' at the end of unit 3 in the B-telling of
'The Well at the World's End' above). There might be regional idioms, and of
course individual artists had their own idiolects. In formalized narration, the
shift from ordinary conversation was signalled with the use of formulae and
other devices, and expression was more obviously patterned. A range of deviance
from the common usage was accepted, and as noted above a certain kind of storytelling in Irish could even turn into a display of linguistic virtuosity. There
were degrees of *recherché* expression, as noted by collectors: 'The language of a
good *seanchaí* is not quite that of everyday speech. It is often slightly more
archaic, more grammatical, and less slipshod; and it is only in certain circumstances in certain types of tales that it is at all bombastic'; or, confirming the
existence of the special style of *fiannaíocht* which others observed (see p. 482),
'One old story-teller friend of mine, speaking of old men whom he had known
in his youth, was full of admiration for their "hard Irish" *(crua-Ghaelainn)*,
remarking that "they had such fine hard Irish you would not understand a word
from them!"[239]

There were also what might be called rhetorical tricks to achieve effects on
the audience: interjections, strong comparisons, and more particularly some
forms of repetition or parallelism. The recurrence of elements is a basic part of
communication and a preponderant strategy for emphasis or clarity in speaking;
it is a fundamental characteristic of oral literature where it is exploited systematically to relieve the work of memory or composition but also to please the ear,
establish a rhythm, and make the whole utterance sound structured. Repetition

---

237 P. Ó Siochfhradha 'Notes on some of Jeremiah Curtin's Storytellers', in J. Curtin *Irish
Folk-Tales* 169. 238 J. Delargy 'Irish Tales and Story-tellers', in *Märchen, Mythos, Dichtung*
68. 239 Kenneth Jackson 'The International Folktale in Ireland', *Folk-lore* 47 (1936) 270fn.;
J. Delargy *The Gaelic Story-Teller* 33.

at all levels (sounds, words, phrases and longer units – it can also control the organization of the plot) is as common in Irish folktales as in those of other countries, for similar reasons: to give importance or for climactic effects; as a way of extending the narrative, or of allowing the narrator and the audience to relax for a short while; to establish a mesmerizing beat; to provide a sense of coherence, and a feeling of security with the return of the familiar. The trinary pattern (as a series of actions, rendered in the same words, often with a modification in the third step) is observed in Ireland as elsewhere in Europe; in other cases of parallelism, an element can also be conspicuously changed to emphasize a reversal.

Oral narratives get much of their power from voice inflections and from significant silence, shifts in pitch, volume, stress and speech rate, a particular cadence at the end of a sentence, pausing to point up a word or phrase – all of which largely escapes written notation. The storyteller's delivery may remain identical to that of speech, or can be more monotonous or more varied, with a regular or changing pace and greater or lesser importance given to pause. Gaps and hesitations, a feature of natural speech, may be feigned to achieve certain effects. M.J. Murphy often commented on the voice qualities of his informants. Henry Glassie (see p. 414) analysed rhythmic peculiarities of his Fermanagh narrators and distinguished between two modes: one, neutral prose, is used to orient the listener or to digress; the other, to impress the listener while also manifesting the teller's own involvement, may be almost chanted and is broken into 'lines' of various lengths, often delimited by recurrent words at the beginning and strong verbs at the end.[240] Of one of his raconteurs, Glassie says: 'In conversation he uses two voices artistically. One is low, slow, measured; it is appropriate to serious reminiscence and stories of the weird caprice of fairies and ghosts. The other soars in melodic runs, in looping long sentences that descend to short, punctuating statements.'[241]

31. *Making characters speak*

Dialogue may give life to a story. It can be reproduced, or – less efficiently – reported, as briefly or as fully as the narrator likes; spells and essential statements *must* be in direct speech. Irish storytellers and their audiences certainly liked direct speech: 'A good story-teller rarely departs from *oratio recta* ... He appreciates how much well-constructed dialogue can add to the effect of his tale on a critical audience, familiar themselves by everyday practice with witty epigrammatic talk and telling riposte.'[242] A.J. Bruford confirmed this tendency: 'Folk-tellers often put into dialogue passages which, in [manuscript] romances, are expressed in *oratio obliqua* or as the thought of a character: this gives a more direct and dramatic picture'.[243] But the teller had to make it clear whether he

240 *Passing the Time* 40. **241** *All Silver and No Brass* 27. **242** J. Delargy *The Gaelic Story-Teller* 27. **243** *Gaelic Folk-Tales and Medieval Romances* 172.

was speaking in his own voice or for a character. Hence the repetition, of forms
of the verb *abair* (say), as in *deir sé* or *deir sí* – or the English equivalents 'says
he' and 'says she' – as a constant reminder that what the audience is hearing is
supposed to be the voice of a character in the story. Whether the frequent punctuation of a narrative by 'says he' or 'he said' is specifically Irish remains
unproved. It has been observed elsewhere, but sometimes with a possible Irish
influence, as in the United States:

One characteristic of the southeastern tradition that can be pinpointed ... is the frequent
use of 'says', 'say', or 'said', functioning not just to introduce dialogue but also, apparently, as a rhythmic device and reminder that this is a story heard rather than experienced directly by the narrator. The origins of this feature – especially prevalent among
upland whites but also found with blacks, though usually omitted from published texts
in the past – are uncertain, but one possibility is the Scotch-Irish strain in the upland
population.[244]

To command attention and lead the audience to perceive the cohesion of
different elements of a story or to infer what was not said, the storyteller also
used paralinguistic features of communication. With its verbal and non-verbal
aspects, a telling can, to a varying degree, display theatrical qualities.

32. Posture, gestures or facial expression, and 'dramatizing' the tale
Ways of sitting or standing, movements of hand, head nods to reinforce words,
facial expression, eye contact to involve a listener into the story – these are
important components of storytelling, capable of acting as signs and producing
effects which overlap with, or counterpoint, verbal communication.[245]
    An Irish pub raconteur may stand, and gesticulate, but the *scéalaí* or *sean-
chaí* narrating from a seated position by the fireside was in semi-darkness; the

---

244 J.A. Burrison *Storytellers. Folktales and Legends from the South* 19. Max Lüthi found eighteen '*i dit*' (he says) or '*a dit*' (she says) in a short French-Canadian tale (*The Fairytale as Art
Form* 45). **245** Cf. I. Sándor 'Dramaturgy of Tale-Telling', *Acta Ethnographica* 16 (1967) 308-
10: 'the whole man is narrating, not only with the modulation of his voice, but with the variable compass of his glance, his expression, his movements and his behaviour ... Speech is
nothing more than the leading part, while the total effect is produced not only by the communicative function of speech but by every means establishing contact between the reciter and
his audience ... The uttering of words and sentences results by itself in a permanent movement of the facial muscles, but the face of the narrator shows also the emotional agitation
surging in the texts. In this respect, the eyes and the mouth play the most important role.
Narrowing or enlarging the pupils, fixing the glance in a certain direction, lifting or closing
the eye-lids, lifting or frowning the eye-brows – all this can suggest a number of emotional
conditions and characteristics. Pursing or curling up the lips, opening the mouth, chewing,
sticking out the tongue, gnashing the teeth, etc. are equally forceful expressive means.
Bending the head forwards, backwards or sideways, up and down or to the right or left, may
also be meaningful ... Usually the narrator is sitting while telling the tale, but it may occur
that he gets up, goes up and down, jumps, dances during certain passages of the tale.'

main visual effect he could achieve tended to hieratic immobility, with perhaps just a few perceptible movements thereby rendered all the more striking. Different behaviours were observed, however, ranging from absolute stillness to selective miming:

Feet fixed to the floor and hands to his knees, Johnny delivered his stories with an intensity that made him seem to levitate as his voice grew high with excitement.[246]

He used begin his stories with 'once upon a time and a very good time it was when the swallows built their nests in old men's beards'. And when he used say the word 'beard' he used stroke his fingers through his long faded brown beard and we used think that he'd expect to find a swallow's nest in it and then he'd start his story, 'There was a king in Ireland ... '.[247]

He makes few gestures; he raises the staff he holds in his hand at some impressive moments; he beats his hands together when he comes to a 'run'.[248]

The faces of the audience are ever before the storyteller, for he looks at them and to them seeking for their silent and at times their openly expressed approval. Not so the singer – often he sings, his face half-hidden by a hand, his head turned aside from his neighbours.[249]

[He] never gestured except once or twice when he lifted his stick to indicate distance.[250]

The tale itself may be 'dramatic' in that it is constructed as a sequence of scenes building up tension, with a great deal of direct speech. But in another sense of the word 'dramatic', the storyteller may 'enact' his tale by impersonating the various characters, imitating their voices, and using gestures. The above quotations suggest that in Ireland strictly vocal means tended to predominate. But effects can still be produced without much bodily action: 'So far as it is possible for a man sitting in a chair, the storyteller acts his story.'[251] Some storytellers were more 'physical' than others. The following set of quotations is ranged here from one extreme to the other:

[John McLoughlin, North Mayo, in the 1980s] brought a degree of intensity to his performance that I did not encounter in other storytellers: speaking quickly, moving around the room, gesticulating a great deal.[252]

Willie [Rourke, in South Roscommon] was a born actor and he brought his stories to life as he acted the part of each character during the progress of the tale. Sometimes, he would suddenly raise his voice to a shout, only to lower it dramatically to almost a whisper and repeat what he first said so loudly once or twice for added emphasis. As he

246 Artelia Court *Puck of the Drums* ... xiii. **247** IFC 1169: 401, from Ned Sheehy, in County Kerry. Collected by S. Ó Dálaigh in 1950. **248** P. Colum 'Story-Telling in Ireland', *Horn Book Magazine* 10 (May 1934) 194. **249** J. Delargy 'Irish Tales and Story-tellers', in *Märchen, Mythos, Dichtung* 66. **250** IFC 1112: 386 – a storyteller observed by M.J. Murphy at Crossmaglen, County Armagh, in 1945. **251** Kenneth Jackson *The International Popular Tale and Early Welsh Tradition* 54-5. **252** C.M. Harvey *Contemporary Irish Traditional Narrative* ... 292.

believed all the events, no matter how fantastic, that occurred in his tales, it was easy for him to put all the power of his – by no means small – histrionic ability into the telling.[253]

On a sunny afternoon we recorded a very fine version of Aa. Th. 890 [the international tale-type of 'The Pound of Flesh'], lasting one hour fifteen minutes, from a Kerry storyteller who, leaning at his ease on a grassy bank in a meadow beside the sea, told the story in quiet, measured tones. On the evening of the same day, in a farmhouse a few miles inland, another storyteller was so carried away by his telling of the hero-tale 'The Well at the World's End' that he suddenly changed in the narrative from the third to the first person and described the hero's adventures as happening to himself, meanwhile striding about the kitchen, waving his arms, while the local collector pursued him with the microphone, and the operator steadied the recording gear on a rickety table and prayed for patience. In the first recording, the level tones of the speaker are heard against a faint background of the beat of the waves on the shore, and the whole impression is one of quiet intensity. In the second, there is an air of bustle and excitement, with sounds of movement and, frequently, the delighted comment of one or other of the audience – which the storyteller expected, and for which he paused at appropriate moments.[254]

[Seán Ó Briáin, in Connemara] had a sensitivity as keen as that of any prima donna – he insisted on silence during the recital of his long hero-tales, but was not averse to the usual encouraging remarks which your folktale audience often makes during the course of the narrative. He used a great deal of gesture and had some of the tricks of the orator – the dramatic pause, the changing of the tone of voice to suit the characters and incidents, and so on. He was a real storyteller.[255]

[Micí na gCloch] had also a fine voice of great tonal range, and had an instinct to coordinate sense, sound, voice, and gesture to produce the most effective and musical speech, which he always delivered slowly and impressively, but without artificial or oratorical flourishes.[256]

The *seanchaí* never rose from the corner of the fireplace, and if he gestured too much in attempting to act out the story he was laughed at.[257]

Most of these quotations stress gesticulation, but the collectors probably noticed it because it contrasted with more usual impassiveness.[258] More often, the words alone conjured up the events.

253 J.G. Delaney 'Three Midland Storytellers', *Béaloideas* 50 (1982) 45. 254 C. Ó Danachair 'Irish Folk Narrative on Sound Records', *Laos* 1 (1951). 255 J. Delargy 'Irish Stories and Storytellers', *Studies* 31 (March 1942) 43. 256 P. Ó Siochfhradha 'Notes on some of Jeremiah Curtin's story-tellers', in J. Curtin *Irish Folk-Tales* 169. 257 *Irish Stories: Tales & Legends of the West* 238. 258 Cf. Joe Neil MacNeil, in J. Shaw (ed.) *Tales until Dawn; The World of a Cape Breton Gaelic Story-teller* 37: '... there was not much gesturing or anything to be seen with his hands. I wouldn't have seen; I wasn't looking anyway. The room was dark except for a light shining through the doorway. So I don't believe that they did much of that at all. Nonetheless I was told of an accomplished story-teller whom people went to hear recite and when he came to an awesome tale – the terrible feats that a hero performed which surpassed the valour of many – he would have to stand up and raise his hands and introduce some of his own embellishments; he might add some words of English to the tale. But it was not at all usual in company for the people that I often saw telling tales to do much of this, and if

What emerges from the evidence is that the 'traditional Irish storytellers' directly observed in the first two thirds of the twentieth century tended to have a number of features in common but also differed in some respects, according to the kinds of stories they might specialize in, and of course also to individual talent and personality. Their activity was an interplay between constraints, opportunities afforded by the social context, and originality. They varied in their ways of treating the material: some of them concentrated on scrupulously reproducing what they had inherited, while others to some extent could play with it; but creativity pertained to interpretation rather than to new composition. The plot elements a storyteller had at his disposal were generally not his invention, but could be developed within certain limits. At the level of verbal realization too, there were ready-made formulae, but it was possible to improvise. The principles controlling plot and texture were comfortable for hearers, who were used to them; they were not absolutely constraining. Some storytellers offered stylized, self-conscious and even ceremonial performances, while others narrated only in the course of informal conversational exchange. The telling could be fairly regular or exceptional, public or strictly domestic, done reluctantly or with eagerness. There were degrees between all those extremes, and perhaps shifts in the course of an individual life. Respect for what came from the past, individual creative impulse, and selection by a community whose tastes might not have been as uniform and immutable as was sometimes thought – all this determined the particular blending of continuity and variation.

Awareness of the existence of some particular repertoire and code would nourish the notion of a tradition, which functioned as evidence of a collective identity. A storyteller was respected for his skill as a communicator, but perhaps also for the perceived 'Irishness' of the stories he told and of his way of telling them. Yet a number of basic plots, in different genres, were not specifically Irish; some rules governing the behaviour of storytellers and audiences were not peculiar to one ethnic group or country; nor were the basic storytelling techniques. That much of what has been found in Ireland must be considered as part of a general European complex now seems fairly obvious. But along with narratives and modes of narration not exclusive to Ireland, there are native stories and a specific use of some formal devices: for instance, verbal flourish contrasting with a restrained use of other expressive modes.

B. AN IRISH STORYTELLER'S ART

To try and see how the ingredients and methods detailed in the first part of this chapter may work together, I shall now consider what is known of the life-story, repertoire, style and techniques of a single Irish storyteller of the same period.

you find one of the old people who can still recite a tale you will see that they stay very still; they don't make much of a commotion at all about it.'

Like the rest of the book, this section is based on other people's views of a man who is no longer here to be interviewed, on transcriptions of his tales by one collector, and on a couple of recordings. What can we know of his 'art'? – by which I mean the ability to play on listeners' emotions through a series of pregnant images and to offer the pleasure of perceiving formal qualities in a particular use of language and of narrative devices. It is generally admitted that a 'good story' (a potentially interesting plot) may be ruined in the telling, and that an unpromising one may lead to an excellent performance if the narrator is talented and inspired; indeed, what really matters is not so much the 'story' (plot) but the manner (art) of its telling. In the case we shall now examine, much of the *draíocht* (charm, spell) is likely to remain elusive.

I have chosen as my example a man of low social rank who led the life of an itinerant in a limited area and told his tales in English: Paddy Sherlock. The main reason is that I could not seriously cope with a mass of material in Irish, and better qualified persons have portrayed great exponents of the art in this language (see Chapter 10). Also, there may be some advantage in examining the legacy of a man who lived on the margin of two cultures, and whose talent was recognized by experts on the Gaelic mode. Other storytellers might differ, not only in their spoken language and position in society but also in their repertoire and ways of dealing with it, but we may assume that they were not *entirely* different. The relative paucity of information about the storyteller I have chosen is in itself representative of the major problems in exploring oral arts of the past.

Paddy was born in 1892, at Ennistymon. For at least three generations, his male ancestors had been itinerant chimney-sweeps and thatchers in County Clare, and enjoyed a reputation as good storytellers. He must have learned most or all of his tales in his youth, from his father Thomas. Neither father nor son spoke Irish, but the grandfather (born *c.*1800) did, and his storytelling was still praised around 1930 by a connoisseur who had heard him *c.*1870. Paddy followed in his father's and grandfather's footsteps, his only heritage consisting in practical skills which provided bread, and qualifications for storytelling which made him welcome. Service in the British Army between 1913 and 1922 did not make him forget the tales; when he returned to North Clare he resumed the family trade of chimney-sweeping, travelling with donkey and cart from farm to farm. In the 1980s, at Ballyvaughan, C.B. Harvey interviewed a man who remembered him: 'Paddy was a regular visitor to the area, he and his family ... If he was camping here for a week, I would visit him about, maybe four or five times. And I would sit around the open turf fire, together with other people in the area. Mainly old people. We would sit around the fire, and we would listen to Paddy relate these stories.'[259] Several collectors mentioned him, and agreed that, though he did not narrate in Irish, he represented 'a part of the native tradition ... in a style of English which could be a literal translation of tales in Irish

259 *Contemporary Irish Traditional Narrative* 10–11.

in the same area'.[260] More generally they noted that in North Clare 'the story-telling tradition spilled over into English with much of the verve and vitality of tales in Irish'.[261] J.H. Delargy, the only one who collected from him with some persistence (thirty tales, twenty-eight of which were recorded with the Ediphone), did not meet him often and gave only very brief indications concerning his personality, describing him as 'a fine, sturdy fellow, pleasant in his manner, and as honest as the sun ... [who] was an honest man, a loyal friend, and Nature's gentleman'.[262] Delargy was in the region of Doolin in August 1929 to continue the collection of long tales in Irish he had started in Kerry, and he returned several times for brief periods. During the Christmas holidays of December 1929, he heard about Paddy Sherlock who was then in the neighbourhood. At his request, Sherlock came three times to the kitchen of Seán Carún's house (and once more a year later) to tell his stories. In May 1950, at Lisdoonvarna, four of Sherlock's tales were recorded again by David Thompson, for the BBC Third Programme; these recordings have survived. Paddy died in 1956.

I shall consider first what we know of Paddy Sherlock's repertoire of stories and motifs and what seems to have been his preferences in those matters; the study of some stylistic features will follow; then I shall turn to properties of plot structure and to his particular treatment of them in some tales.

In four sessions, his repertoire was most probably not exhausted, and there is no way of knowing how much larger and more diversified it may have been. Nor do we know how far what was chosen for recording, and what was later selected for publication,[263] represented the storyteller's own preferences or the collector's particular interest. Nevertheless, some conclusions may be drawn from the corpus available. The repertoire and range of skills of a storyteller consists of a number of stories he can interpret (i.e. partly recreate) again and again, as well as a set of shorter narrative units and of patterns to combine them; there is also a stock of verbal formulae which may function as beginnings and endings, descriptive elements and fillers, or punctuation marks; finally, he has his own peculiar turns of phrases.

The majority of Sherlock's published texts were assigned by the collector-editor to Aarne-Thompson 'international types'; in other words, each of them was seen as a particular realization of some basic plot structure found in various countries and belonging to a special group within folktales in general. There are obvious versions of, or only partial similarities with, AT 300 (The Dragon Slayer – a rather loose category into which many Irish tales would fit); AT 325

---

260 Kevin O'Nolan, in Éamon a Búrc *Eochair* 176. **261** Máire MacNeill, 'Seamus Delargy and North Clare', *Dal gCais* 6 (1982) 112. **262** S. Delargy in *Béaloideas* 15 (1945) 263 and 30 (1962) 2. **263** One of the tales collected by J. Delargy was published in *Béaloideas* 3, two in Volume 5, one in Volume 15, and fourteen in Volume 30.

(The Magician and his Pupil); AT 326 A* (Soul Released from Torment – more precisely the story of the man who spends nights in a haunted room and learns where to find a treasure, as in Griffin's *The Collegians* – cf. p. 251); AT 330 (a trickster defeats the devil and sneaks into Heaven); AT 400 (The Man on a Quest for his Lost Wife); AT 506 (a grateful dead man helps the hero rescue and disenchant a princess); AT 550 (Search for the Golden Bird) and AT 551 (The Son on a Quest for a Wonderful Remedy for their Father); AT 567 (The Magic Bird-Heart); AT 613 (The Two Travellers, or the question of whether truth or falsehood is better); AT 750A (three wishes are foolishly made); AT 882 (The Wager on the Wife's Chastity); AT 1536A (the corpse of an old woman is made to pop up in various places to extort money and restore justice); AT 1641 (dishonest servants are led to confess their guilt). There is also what may be a more specifically Irish tale ('The Black Dog', see below) and a version of part of an *Arabian Nights* story, 'The Second Kalandar's Tale'. As already noted, however, the concept of type should not be reified: the latitude for variation in such pigeon-holing before another type is identified may be hard to define. A text can be a fragment of a type, or combine episodes that fit several of them: in Sherlock's repertoire there are tales that seem to result from the interbreeding of several types, or floating elements that reappear in different texts. But the same can be observed in other 'national' realizations of a common 'European' repertoire, and if the link with the platonic international idea may sometimes be loose, Sherlock's tales have counterparts in Ó Súilleabháin and Christiansen's *Types of the Irish Folktale*.[264] Whether Sherlock ever told 'legends' (*seanchas*) is not mentioned; as far as we know he favoured wonder tales, though he was not averse to comic pieces.

The compositional core of the plot tends to be always the same, which may reflect both his taste and the principles of a 'tradition' he was attuned to. In most of the tales collected from him, we find a basic movement towards fulfilment: the protagonist departs (is banished or given a mission, or goes out on an adventure), is tested, encounters helpers and opponents, undergoes temporary setbacks, and is finally successful. The components of episodes are often arranged in antithetical pairs whose conflict advances the action: obstacles and their overcoming, a lack and its remedy, the setting of a task and its fulfilment, kidnapping and rescue, an enigma and its solution, enchantment and disenchantment, disguise and unmasking, separation and reunion, death and resurrection. Triads are also common: interdiction, violation, consequence – or the breaking of a prohibition, suffering, then proof that the transgression was fortunate. Characters are built on polarities: rich/poor, beautiful/ugly, kind/unkind ...; opposed traits are given to a couple of characters, or one character suddenly shifts from one extreme to the other. If contrast is a major device, repetition is

---

264 Sherlock's versions tend to be shorter and in less ornate style than those collected in Irish, half-a-century earlier or more, by Curtin, Hyde or Larminie.

also a hallmark. Sherlock seems to have liked stories ending with a positive mood, and he favoured certain plot kernels: encountering and defeating three giants; being forced to undertake apparently imposible tasks after losing the third in a series of card-games; finding supernatural or animal helpers like the recurring 'dirty, scabby, mangy-looking pony' that gives good counsel when well fed (some helpful animals may ask to be killed, thereby becoming helpful in another way or regaining a human form); receiving magic objects; being cured by the content of an ubiquitous 'little bottle'; winning a game which consists in hiding oneself or finding a hidden adversary. Among other typical international motifs common in Ireland and adopted by Paddy Sherlock, is D610 (Chain of transformations), or D671 (Transformation flight): 'He turned himself into a pigeon and flew into the cloud. Instead of they being seven ferrets they turned themselves into seven hawks and went after him till he came to a large building, perched upon the chimney and flew down to a cross-stick. There was young ladies sitting by the fire. He turned himself into a gold ring and dropped unto the young lady's finger.' Other recurrent propositions include H901.1 (Heads placed on stakes for failure to perform a task): ' "Well, on this seven gates that you're after coming through, there are fourteen spears; there is thirteen heads on thirteen of them. There is one vacant, and I'll have your head on it – that is," says he, "if you can't gain the Golden Bird" '; Q502.2 (Punishment: Wandering till iron shoes are worn out, when a husband or wife has broken some prohibition): 'She wrote upon the label for Jack again never to find her out for what he had done upon her, until he had the pair of metal boots wore up to his knees and his knees along with the metal boots'; H1321.2 (Quest for healing water; it may be the core of a tale – Sherlock's version is much more elaborate than Michael Rooney's above pp. 475ff – or only one episode in a complex tale): 'If I bring you back a bottle of water from the Land of Youth, the one that take three drinks o' this water at the age of ninety years he'll become as young as he was at the age of twenty-one'; D2004.2.1 (Licking by a dog induces forgetfulness): 'So when he was leaving, she told him to take care for his life and peril would he let any lips touch his lips, or, if he did, he'd forget all about her and lose his memory. So when he came home, everyone was welcoming him, and shook hands, and also they were trying to kiss him, but, at the same time, he let no one kiss him. He sat down in his chair in the room, and a little dog came in and went in between his legs and travelled up along his clothes till he never felt him till the dog left his lips against his lips, and he lost his memory and forgot all about what happened.'[265] The Lord of Animals – a staple character of tales around the world – appears in Sherlock's stories in the role he often plays in European folktales: he (or she) controls birds, the animals of the forest, or the creatures of the sea, calls them with a horn or whistle and orders them to help the hero or forces the one that comes last to carry him: 'She went outside, and

265 *Béaloideas* 30 (1962) 15, 23, 34, 39, 74.

she sounded her whistle three times till she thought she had all the fish o' the
sea around her. She sounded her whistle the fourth time when the whale made
his appearance. She demanded the whale for to bring this man across the ocean
to the Land of Youth'; or: 'While Jack was eating his breakfast the following
morning, the old man went outside the door, and he sounded his whistle three
times till he thought he had all the birds of the world around him ... So the
fourth time he sounded his whistle this bird landed in at his feet, and she was
called the Roc.'[266]

All the elements listed so far, and assembled by Paddy Sherlock in his own
way, were 'international' stock material. Some more typically Irish motifs occasionally appear, like the traditional *geis* (prohibition or binding injunction – it has
become a means of developing the plot, rather than the mark of a special destiny as in ancient Irish stories): 'At the same time I'm going to cross and command you never to eat the second bit off e'er a table, never sleep the second
night in e'er corner!'[267] As E.B. Gose noted, whereas breaking a *geis* had fatal
consequences in 'ancient' Irish stories, in folktales it may be a roundabout way
to greater gains.[268] There are also references to contemporary Irish customs:
'"Oh, well," says Jack, "it's generally always the case that the man of the house
would always tell the first story." "You're perfectly right! says the woman" '(cf.
p. 461); or: 'They drew into a village, an' it was of a Saturday night. They were
ashamed to go on the road on Sunday; they were just as much ashamed to
remain inside of the house without goin' out to the Mass.'[269]

More idiosyncratic, though not unique, is the comic (but not parodic) treatment of some motifs: 'For it must be you that killed my brother yesterday [says
a monster]. 'Twas easily known you got him young and innocent; he was only
one hundred years of age, and 'tis ere yesterday he left the cradle.'[270] Sherlock's
'fee-fi-fo-fum' blood-sniffing giant seems about to tell an ethnic joke – which
turns instead into gruesome images: ' "What is he?" says the giant. "Is he an
Irishman, an Englishman or a Scotchman?" "He's an Englishman," says Jack. "If
that's the way," says the giant, "if I catch him near me tonight I'll have his liver
and lights [eyes] for my supper, an' his blood for my mornin' draught." '[271] The
stock evocation of a marvellous happening or sequence may end with a lifelike
detail, as in this rendering of motif D615 (Transformation conflict): 'Instead of
their being seven men they turned theirselves into seven turkeys ... He turned
himself into a fox, knocked their seven heads right and clear off o' their bodies,
left them jumping around the floor.'[272] The passage from the ordinary to the

266 Ibid. 41, 37. Cf. Lutz Röhrich 'Herr der Tiere', in *Enzyklopädie des Märchens* 6. 866–79,
and V. Voigt 'Elemente des Vorstellungskreises vom Herrn der Tiere in ungarischen
Volksmärchen', in *Acta Ethnographica* 11 (1962) 391-430. The fabulous bird in the second
quotation is, of course, an *Arabian Nights* element, often found in European tales. 267 Ibid.
18. 268 *The World of the Irish Wonder Tale* 85. 269 *Béaloideas* 30 (1962) 35, and 15 (1945)
264. 270 *Béaloideas* 30 (1962) 16. 271 *Béaloideas* 15 (1945) 268. 272 *Béaloideas* 30 (1962) 16.

fantastic is also possible: 'The cat got up from the fire, and he shook his back. He shook seven acres and a half of yellow ashes off o' the top of it'.[273]

The hardships the storyteller must have suffered in his life may give particular force to evocations of misery: 'He'd only got a sup of water and bit of hard bread for his supper ...'; or 'His bed he'd get to lie to sleep upon was a bed of furze, and the supper he'd get was a drink of cold water ...'; or 'It was in very bad times, and they were starving with the hunger ...'[274] A common fairytale motif could then be a compensative dream: 'They sat down on the road, and the man put his hand in his pocket, and he pulled up a towel, and he spread it on the ground, and all sorts of eating and drinking came upon it.'[275] And humble wisdom was voiced: 'If I married fine young ladies, I couldn't ask them to bring my mother a bucket of water for fear they'd only spit in my face'.[276]

Certain narrative devices repeatedly appear in Sherlock's tales, for instance the summary of the action by the protagonist towards the end of the tale, as a way of proving his identity. We find it in two tales which, without being identical in plot, have more in common than their titles: both are connected with AT 550, and in both a crucial earlier episode is briefly retold:

'The Golden Bird of Ivyland'	'The Golden Bird'
Béaloideas 30. 27	*Béaloideas* 30 .46
'Well, if you're the man,' says she,	'Well, if you're the man that took
'what did you first see when you entered,'	the Golden Bird from my palace in the
says she, 'my father's place?'	Land of Youth, tell me what did you
'The first thing I seen when I entered	first see?'
your father's place was seven gates. Myself	'The first thing I seen when I entered,
and my pony, we leaped those seven gates.	says he, 'to the Land of Youth,
The way your father put the game on me was	I seen the well. I took three bottles of
this that we had to play hides. I went to hide	water,' says he, 'from it. I also,' says he
three days in succession for two hours each	'took three apples from the tree that
day, still he could not find me, so I had you	was growing o'erhead it. I went along
gained. He told me then that I had not you	till I met the iron gate. Inside that iron
gained, that he'd have to go on hide for two	gate there was wolves, lions, and kang-
hours every day for three days. So the first	aroos, and they all asleep. I passed
day he went on a hide he was in a poker	them in till I went into your kitchen. The
underneath the fire, the second day he went	first thing I seen there was a cat as big as
on a hide he was in a currant loaf on the table	a bull. At the same time, he didn't interfere
you were sitting alongside him on a chair	with me. So I said before I'd lay the tea,
knitting a stocking. The first day of his hide	I'd walk through it to see if it was as nice
he was in a ring on your finger. I took your	a palace as my father's palace.
finger to leave it on the table to cut your finger	I walked into different rooms and seen
off when he he leaped out'. 'You're the	different sights until I came into the room
man,' says she, 'that best gained me and	where I seen a beautiful lady sleeping in

273 Ibid. 7. Cf. J. Curtin *Hero-Tales of Ireland* 366: 'He rose up, and shook seven tons of ashes from himself, with seven barrels of rust'. 274 *Béaloideas* 30 (1962) 4, 14, 69. 275 Ibid. 65. 276 Ibid. 17.

not those two men, so therefore,' says she, 'we'd better get those two men executed!'

bed. I lay down by the side of her. I took the gold garter from her knees, I took the the golden ring from her finger, I took the currant loaf, and I took her bottle of wine and her knife, and if I don't make a mis-take you're the same lady!' 'I'm the lady,' says she, and you're the man'.

'A currant loaf' ... Some props in Sherlock's tales add a 'modern' touch to ageless events: the weapon used by the hero or his antagonist may be a revolver, and there is the photograph of a giant on the wall in his version of an *Arabian Nights* tale. Details reflecting the social reality of the narrator and his audience appear in other stories: 'He called upon his tenants this day for to pay the rent at 12 o'clock ...'; 'She is sitting on a chair reading a paper ...'; 'There was a big heap of dung outside the door ...'; 'So they were this day in a garden digging out potatoes ...'; 'So this day he was sitting in the window reading a book. His mother was at the fireside knitting a stocking'.[277] Magical events may be more striking – or amusing? – when they take place among details belonging to the familiar world. (The same has been observed in other countries).[278]

Characters in folktales act and do not ponder; so do those in Sherlock's sto-ries. We note that his protagonists are always men; when Cinderella puts a brief appearance it is as a dull secondary figure: 'She was an *óinseach* [fool, idiot], always sitting in the corner ... full of ashes'[279] – she is soon forgotten, and the tale concerns her brothers. When a hero (or his helper) is named, he is often called Jack. The name typifies the common man in narrative tradition in English, and more particularly the unpromising hero with more luck than virtue who overcomes powerful adversaries by cunning or deceit – and sometimes out-smarts himself, as tricksters do. It has been noted that although Jack appeared as a tale-hero in England as early as the fifteenth century[280], he is 'not necessar-ily English in character; Irish collectors have pointed out with some surprise that "Jack" figures largely in the Irish tradition, even among Gaelic-speaking story-tellers'.[281] In Scotland, Duncan Williamson, like Sherlock an itinerant, stated in 1979 that Jack was the special hero of 'travelling people':

Jack was the great man. They looked up tae him. And naturally that's why if they wanted tae tell a story, even if the chap in the story's name wasnae Jack, then it became Jack tae the travellers, because it was their man, their hero ... They visualized themsels

277 Ibid. 22,25, 33, 55, 3. 278 Cf. M. Simonsen 'Folktales and Reality ...', in M. Chesnut (ed.) *Telling Reality* 124: The purpose is to 'help the storyteller to build up the mental pic-ture of a universe which resembles our own world, in order to ensure an illusion of "realism" and maintain the voluntary suspension of disbelief which is the basic covenant between an author and his audience. In short, references to real life are selected not according to the facts of reality, but according to the needs of fiction.' 279 Ibid. 46, 48. 280 Carl Lindahl 'Jack Tales', in *Enzyklopädie des Märchens* 7. 379-83. 281 H. Halpert, appendix to R. Chase *The Jack Tales* 186.

as Jack ... The only way they could compete and be superior tae the settled community, tae the landowners and farmers, wis be somebody. So in their beliefs like, I mean they were all children at hert, you may say, they were Jack. They could deceive the Devil, anyone. Take 'Jack and the Laird', 'Jack and the Poacher', 'Jack and the Water Bailies'. He was it. He deceived 'em. He tricked 'em. So they believed that was them. They were gettin their own back at the other sides. That's why there're so many Jack stories around today.[282]

Paddy Sherlock applied the name to different kinds of characters, but they are generally endowed with more than a touch of cleverness.

As concerns linguistic surface structure, we may also expect to observe the relative inertia of a received medium (the style of a genre) and distinctive marks of individual preferences. Sherlock used commonplace expressions, but was also capable of choosing among lexical and syntactic variables, and could produce striking turns of phrase which stimulated the listeners' imagination: 'So where the cattle stopped grazing you could shake pins and needles in it and find everyone of them in less than five minutes, it was that bare in grass!'; or, 'I seen his children running around the road, and if you left the top of a pin to their face and they'd bleed, they were that red in the face from eating meat and drinking soup!'[283] Comparison (conventional or original) is more frequent than metaphor, as is often the case in oral narration: 'They told him to go back home, or, if not, they'd cut him up as small as tobacco ...'; or, 'She thought more of the dirty water which was running through the streets than she thought of the king's son'.[284] When a woman must choose between two lovers and prefers the one she thought she had lost, she develops an allegory based on an erotic symbol: '"Well, ladies and gentlemen" says she, "some time ago I had an old key, and I was very fond of this old key, and I lost it. And when I lost this old key, I left a new one making. And as luck happened now, I'm after finding the old key; and which would you advise me for to keep the old key, or to get the new one?"' [285]

Humour, often an important ingredient, is probably another mark of the storyteller's personality. For instance, when the protagonist has created a commotion by appearing in a girl's room, the following dialogue ensues: 'I'm just as good a king's son as what you are a king's daughter'. 'Why didn't you say that long ago to-night and there'd be no shouting?'[286]

Paddy Sherlock also made use of stock devices; for instance, his way of rendering dialogues does not differ from that of other Irish storytellers in English (cf. p. 492):

'I don't know,' says he, 'who's speaking to me,' says he, 'or who isn't, but at any rate,' says he, 'I'll do your bidding' ...

282 Quoted by Barbara Mc Dermitt, 'Duncan Williamson', *Tocher* 33 (1980) 144. 283 *Béaloideas* 30 (1962) 4, 67. 284 Ibid. 22 (both quotations) 285 Ibid. 39. 286 Ibid. 15. 287 Ibid. 30, 45

She asked the witch to know did any man pass the way. 'Yes, there did,' says the witch, 'for he remained here,' says she, 'one night, and he left,' says she, 'that currant loaf on this table'.[287]

His connectives and ways of marking successive steps in the story, or mere fillers, tend to be simply 'and', 'so' and 'well': 'After a short time what came down the stairs but a bull, an' this bull had two big horns, an' a coffin laid on the top of them, came down to the fireside, stooped down on her knees, an' left the coffin down by the soldier's side ...'; or, 'So [the bird Roc] asked for a bit to eat. So he was cutting a piece off of each bullock to keep him balanced upon her back till she'd the two bullocks eaten into the bone; and there was no sight of land. So, anyway, she asked for another bit to eat ...'; or, ' "Well, I couldn't work" says he, "for I was never brought up to labouring work." "Well, couldn't you feed cattle and clean out stables?" '[288] But he also uses an adverbial phrase more idiosyncratically: 'Still and all, she wouldn't be satisfied'; 'Still and all, he couldn't see the young lady that done it ...'[289] The phrase 'but well and good' occasionally performs the same function.

Paddy Sherlock's most common opening formula includes an English rendering – 'in it' – of the Irish adverb predicating mere existence (*ann*): 'There was a woman one time in it, and she had a son o' the name Jack ...'; 'There was a king one time in it, and being in it, he got married ...'; 'There was a captain one time in it; and he came ashore ...'[290]

Closing formulae do not seem to have been used systematically, and when they appear in transcriptions they may be short: '... That's all is in it'; ... So that's the finishin' of my story'; '... And that's all the story.'[291] But he could also develop a longer formula: '... So Jack and The Golden Rose got married. And when Jack and The Golden Rose got married the wedding held for seven days and seven nights. I was there myself for the seven days and seven nights. The donkey got a feed of oats, myself got a bowl of stout; and if they don't live happy that we may!'; or, '... The king's son and the Sleepin' Beauty they got married. They lived in their own country ever after, and if they don't live happy that we may!'[292]

Some of Paddy Sherlock's wonder tales would take some twenty to thirty minutes in the telling or a bit more; there are shorter ones – some of them only a few minutes, like his version of 'The Three Wishes' (AT 750A). In the recordings, the storyteller's delivery tends to be rapid, and the tone is never emphatic: it always sounds like a narrative, not a dramatization, but the fact that there was the cumbersome Ediphone or another machine between the audience

---

288 *Béaloideas* 5 (1935) 26; 30 (1962) 38, 55. **289** *Béaloideas* 30 (1962) 8, 31 *et passim*. This equivalent to 'nevertheless' was of course not Sherlock's invention, as shown in B. Share *Slanguage: a Dictionary of Irish Slang* 275; but he favoured it. **290** *Béaloideas* 30 (1962) 16, 21, 53, *et passim*. **291** *Béaloideas* 30 (1962) 56; 5 (1935) 27; 3 (1931-2) 434. **292** *Béaloideas* 30 (1962) 39, 46.

and him may have had an influence. Segments of discourse between pauses, with or without a clear sentence construction, are short. There are very few adjectives; in 'The Seven-Year-Old Child', for instance (see below), they represent less than 0.7% of the whole text and are always very simple: the pedlar, the King of England and the giants' parents are 'old'; the wicked animal is a 'big red' cat; the king's cattle are led into a 'big large' demesne and must be brought back 'safe and sound'; the giants have 'big ugly' heads; the wizard touches 'green' stones with a 'little' rod; and when his enemy is killed the king is 'proud and glad'. There are few adverbs. Concrete images and verbs are what is essential.

All the stories of Paddy Sherlock, with the 'logic' of their action and characters, the narrative techniques (how to start, how to create suspense, how to end ...), and also the phraseology he used, must have been received by word of mouth from earlier generations. Individuality could appear in the selection of genre or motifs and of verbal formulae.

To learn more about Paddy Sherlock's ways of laying out the elements of complete stories, we can focus on three of his tales.

'The Beauty of the World' uses the international motif of the 'Grateful Dead Man', known throughout Europe and in part of Asia: having met creditors who refuse to permit a burial until the dead man's debts have been paid, the hero gives all he has to ransom the corpse and have it decently buried; later, he is helped by the dead person. This motif or set of motifs functions in several tale types, particularly AT 506 (The Rescued Princess) and 507A (The Monster's Bride), both widespread in northern and western Europe. The general pattern of the variants collected in Ireland[293] is as follows: at the start of a quest for a girl he loves without having seen her, the hero ransoms a corpse; later, he is joined by a stranger who magically helps him in a series of tasks, after being promised half of any gain. The girl, enslaved to a monster, is rescued – but must still be freed from the monster's evil spell. The helper identifies himself as the dead man, and the problem of the sharing of gains is solved. This basic scheme can work in different ways; for instance, in a version collected by Jeremiah Curtin around 1890[294] the girl's beauty is announced by a floating hair, and the tasks consist in answering hard questions. Paddy Sherlock's version comes closer to the one collected, soon after Curtin's, by William Larminie.[295] A comparison of their synopses, splitting the story into narrative moments, may give an idea of how the Clare itinerant treated a tale-type, and to what extent he

293 More than a hundred are listed in Ó Súilleabháin and Christiansen's *The Types of the Irish Folktale*; they are generally combined with elements to be found in other international types. 294 'Baranoir, Son of a King in Erin, and the Daughter of King Under the Wave', in *Irish Folk-Tales* 55ff. 'Jack the Master and Jack the Servant', in P. Kennedy's *Legendary Fictions of the Irish Celts* 18ff., is closer to Sherlock's version. 295 *West Irish Folk-Tales and Romances* 155-67.

cared, or did not care, for concatenation of plot. (Numbers in the right-hand column correspond to the units in the left-hand one.)

Paddy Sherlock (1929 or 30)
Luogh, Co. Clare
Coll. S. Delargy
Béaloideas 15

1. 'There was a young prince one time in it.' He goes hunting, sees a drop of blood on the snow and is told that only the lady Beauty of the World is more beautiful. He decides he will 'never sleep a second night in e'er a house or eat the second bit off o' any table' till he has found her. He starts his quest.

2. A dead man can be buried at last when the prince pays his debt (a hundred pounds).

3. The boy who is accompanying him refuses to go farther with such a fool. The prince meets an old man , Raggedy Jack, who decides to travel with him.

4.A. Raggedy Jack finds accommodation for them in the 'brass castle' of a giant – his brother. The following morning the giant gives him 'the Coat of Darkness'.

4B. Second castle; second giant (with two heads). The travellers receive the 'Sword of Strength'.

4C. In the third castle, the prince sees the Beauty of the World – and tells her: 'the hen-woman that my mother has at home is a better-looking woman than what you are ...' (to avoid irritating her jealous master, the third giant). *[The storyteller does not say here that the third giant had three heads.]*

5. Raggedy Jack follows Beauty of the World, who is crossing the sea to the Castle of Greenland'. *[The storyteller*

Pat. Minahan (*c.*1890)
Malinmore, Co. Donegal
Coll. William Larminie
West Irish Folk-Tales and Romances

2. A dead man can be buried at last when a prince pays his debt (five pounds).

1.The prince goes hunting, and, having killed a raven, decides to find the girl who combines certain colours: 'he would not marry a woman whose head was not as black as the bird's wing, and her skin as white as the snow, and her cheeks as red as the blood on the snow'. He starts his quest.

3. He meet a 'red-haired young man', who decides to travel with him.

4A. The red-haired young man frightens his uncle, a giant, by announcing that the prince is coming to kill him. The giant hides in an iron room and is locked in. The following morning the giant is killed and the travellers leave with his 'Dark Coat'.

4B. Second castle; second giant. The travellers leave with the 'Slippery Shoes'.

4C. Third castle; third giant. They leave with the 'Sword of Light, and plenty of gold and silver'.

5. They reach the house of a king and sees Beauty of the World: 'her head was as black as the bird's wing, her skin

forgets to say that Jack is invisible, and he is anticipating a later episode.]

6A. Beauty of the World gives the prince 'a scissors', which he must still have the following morning, on pain of death. She steals it back and gives it to the three-headed giant (on the island?) but, Jack, invisible, takes it back and brings it to the prince, who is saved.

6B. She orders the prince to cut the 'middle head' of the giant. Jack cuts it with the Sword of Strength. 'Now Beauty knew that she was all right.'

7. On the way back, Jack 'fired the sword' into the second castle. He makes the first castle disappear with the magic coat.

8. Jack reveals that he is the dead man of sequence 2. He is entitled to receive Beauty of the World, but proves generous. Then 'he shook hands to the prince and also to the Beauty o' the World, turned himself into a pigeon, and flew upon the young prince's shoulder, from that to the Beauty o' the World's shoulder, from that to the horse's neck – right into the clouds.'

9. Marriage. 'They were makin' children in basketfuls, they were flingin' them out the door in shovelfuls, an' if they don't live happy that we may.'

as white as the snow, and her cheeks as red as blood'.

6A. She gives the prince a comb, which he must still have the following morning, on pain of death. The object vanishes. The red-haired young man, invisible, follows the princess to an island where she gives the comb to the giant, her master. He steals it and brings it back to the prince, who is saved.

6B. She gives him a pair of scissors, etc. The red-haired young man brings it back, so that the prince can produce it the following morning.

6C. For a third test, the prince has to produce the 'last lips' the girl will kiss that night. She kisses the giant on the island. The young man cuts the giant's head and brings it to the prince .

7. The princess still has to be exorcised, by a beating. Three devils come out of her.

8. The young helper reveals that he is the dead man of sequence 1. He is entitled to the new couple's child, but proves generous.

Sherlock's version of the narrative follows the usual pattern of his preferred genre, the quest-tale. After the brief evocation of a state of equilibrium, something disrupts it and the main character has a goal to achieve; a preliminary test reveals qualities that will enable him to win – here, spontaneous generosity (whereas the first two giants are *forced* to be generous); a series of obstacles complicate the action, and the hero receives useful – or dangerous – objects; in the final resolution, with an act of spontaneous generosity echoing the first one, the goal of the protagonist is attained and a new stable state ushers in. Touches of humour in Sherlock's version (4C, 9) may be his individual contribution.

With cold analysis it might seem that clarity of plot was not his strong point, if we compare sequences 4-7 in the two versions and note the rather obscure development concerning the third castle as distinguished from the 'Castle of Greenland', due to the 'confusion' of the third giant with the one who owned the princess; and the episodes of the vanishing castle or castles in the return journey are left unexplained. This, however, is obvious only when we analyse a transcription; in an aurally received narrative the drive may be of another nature, produced through means the transcription does not account for: a listener might accept the alternance of high predictability with complete surprises, and though explicit connections are sometimes weak, the overall pattern remains satisfactory. What looks awkward on paper may thus be accepted in oral communication where each episode is self-contained and there is no time (or desire) to scrutinize. We should not be too easily tempted to condemn a variant as 'incomplete' and 'imperfect' by applying to it the demands of written narration.

As usual in European folktales, abstraction is avoided, and there is hardly any descriptive detail; characters are simply what they do and are reduced to basic qualities: steadfastness, resourcefulness, generosity, hostility; the only 'portrait' of the princess is the phrase 'Beauty of the World' – which has equivalents in Arabic, Greek, Italian, or Spanish folktales.[296] To identify 'beauty', like Larminie's informant, Sherlock uses Motif Z 65.1.1: 'red as blood, white as snow, and black as a raven', with the three symbolic colours of ancient 'Celtic' literature and of the European Middle Ages.[297]

The relative unimportance of certain gaps when a narrative is received aurally and one concentrates on the immediate scene is confirmed by the few recordings I have heard of Paddy Sherlock. As they concern tales which were collected twice within some twenty years, it is also possible to see how items of his repertoire were modified or remained unchanged. Both tales, 'The Seven-Year-Old Child' and 'The Black Dog of the Wild Forest',[298] deal with a young man's successful fight with monsters.

'The Seven-Year-Old Child' is distantly related to International Type AT 300 (The Dragon Slayer), with the peculiarity that in the very many versions of the Irish oikotype the hero, a cowherd, does not kill a dragon (*piast*) but a giant (*fathach*) – or three giants, along with their mother; and having been launched

---

296 Sherlock used it in another folktale: 'So it happened that the first woman's child was the nicest an' the beauty of the world' (*Béaloideas* 30, 83). In Irish, to be the 'beauty of the universe' (*ar ailleacht na cruinne*) is to be 'most excellent' (P.S. Dinneen *An Irish-English Dictionary*).   **297** See Pierre Gallais 'Le sang sur la neige – le conte et le rêve', in *Cahiers de civilisation médiévale* 21 (1978) 37-42, and Madeleine Jeay 'Sanguine Inscriptions...', in F.C. Sautman et al. (eds) *Telling Tales* 137-54. Ancient Irish examples are listed in T.P. Cross *Motif-Index of Early Irish Literature* 529. It is also found in the Welsh 'Peredur fab Efrawg'.   **298** Ibid. 2-10, 56-65, and BBC recordings of 1950. There are references to hundreds of versions in *The Types of the Irish Folktale*.

upon a dangerous quest he does not necessarily marry the princess he has rescued[299] – indeed, not in Paddy Sherlock's version, the narrative line of which may be summarized as follows:

1A. A farmer has a daughter. 1B. Every seven years a pedlar visits him.

2. The daughter is made pregnant by the king of Ireland's son, but for seven years, through magic devices, the queen prevents the girl from giving birth.

3. The seventh year, the pedlar returns and breaks the charm: the Seven-Year-Old Child is born.

4. Seven years later the boy, enormously strong, decides to marry the king's daughter. The king says that the boy must first succeed in making the King of England laugh three times; if he fails, he will be beheaded.

5. The boy goes to England, and is set the job of herding the king's cattle.

6. A giant comes to steal a cow. The boy defeats him, receives from him a magic present, beheads him, then prevents the head from jumping back onto the monster's neck (a motif which may be peculiar to Irish tales). The King of England laughs when he hears what has happened, and his cows give more milk than usual.[300]

7. The following day a giant with two heads comes to steal two cows and is killed after giving a magic object. The king laughs, and there is more milk.

8. The following day, a giant with three heads comes to steal three cows, and is killed after giving the keys to his 'brass castle'. The king laughs, etc.

9. The boy enters the castle, is confronted by the giants' father and mother and by a talking cat. He kills the parents, but is killed by the cat.

10. The King of England's daughter brings the boy back to life with the content of a magic bottle.

11. The cat attacks again, but this time is killed by the boy.

12. The King of England tells the boy that his two sons and his daughter's suitor have been kidnapped by a deer, seven years before. Every time there is a visitor, the deer comes and shames the king, by dirtying (pissing into?) his mouth.

13. When the deer appears, the boy follows it and wounds it before it vanishes into a cave.

14. In the cave, the boy finds a wounded butcher (the deer), who has transformed his three victims into green stones. The boy passes a test of strength, and rescues the three young men. The butcher is pursued for seven days and seven nights, and killed.

15. The boy returns home and marries the King of Ireland's daughter, 'and

---

299 R.T. Christiansen 'Giants and Dragons', *Studies in Irish and Scandinavian Folktales* 33-80. 300 Motif B597. Cf. J. Curtin *Myths and Folk Tales of Ireland* 103-4: 'The cows never gave so much milk as that night. They gave as much as in a whole week before ... The king said: "I have the luck since you came to me. My cows give three times as much milk to-day as they did yesterday." ... That evening the king's cows had more milk than ever before.'

if they don't live happy that we may, and when they're drinking bog-water that
we may be drinking tea!'

The central section (sequences 5-8), built on the triplicating principle, may
look more tightly knit than in Paddy Sherlock's 'Beauty of the World'. Here is
part of sequence 6:

He went up in the apple tree and he fell eating the apples. He wasn't very long there
when a big giant came through the forest. He was walking away with one of those cows
when the Seven-Year-Old Child spoke to him and asked him where was he going with
that cow. 'For I was sent here in charge of those cows. Those cows I'll have to carry
home safe and sound to my master.'

'Well,' says the giant, 'if I had you off o' that tree I'd put you from talk!'

'It would be better for you,' said the lad, 'to leave me where I am!'

'Out of that he vexed the giant. The giant caught a hold of the cow, he furred h[er]
up in the tree; [the boy] caught a hold of the cow with his one hand, left her to the
ground without a bit of injury. At the same time he came down out of the tree he caught
a hold of the giant. The giant caught a hold of him. So the first wheel he took out of the
giant he put him to his knees, the second to his middle, and the third to his neck.

'Spare me my life!' says the giant. 'If it's a thing you'd do, you're one of the best
men I ever knocked across in my life in this forest. Another thing,' says the giant, 'what
I'll do with you. I'll make [a present] of that lamp there. That lamp'll show you light all
over the world the darkest night in winter.'

'I'll have that lamp,' said the lad, 'and I'll also have your big ugly head off your
body!'

Along with that, he up with his sword. He cut the giant's head quite and clear off
his body. The giant's head started to leap backwards and forwards along the grass till the
lad got the top of his boot underneath it. He struck the head three kicks in succession
without ever letting the head stand upon the ground. The body of the giant spoke to
him and said: 'It's a good job for your soul what you're after getting done to my head,
for that head to get on my body, you or the wealth of men would never get it off!'[301]

The next two sequences in the tale (the encounters with the other giants)
are verbalized similarly. The repetition of numbers seven and three, as well as
the rapid tempo and constant action, contribute to unify a story which combines
well-known motifs while at the same time giving an impression of free-wheeling
fantasy. In fact, wonders crowd in, become relatively familiar through repetition,
then surprise us again with a change, and practically prevent us from realizing
that at the end the hero seems to marry his own aunt. We no longer hear about
the queen when she has been replaced by another opponent, and the pedlar vanishes when he has completed his role as helper: both are there to round off a
first episode and provide the protagonist with a distinctive feature, an extraordinary birth – delayed like that of Heracles and other heroes around the world.
The synopsis above follows the first of the versions collected from Paddy

301 *Béaloideas* 30 (1962) 5-6.

Sherlock. In the second, unit 1B comes after 2, and 9 to 11 are missing; no doubt the tale could also be told without sequences 12-14, or made longer by adding another triadic episode, but the later telling leaves out part of the numerical game. Some elements are interchangeable as long as their functions remain the same; thus among the gifts with which the giants try to cheat the boy but which in fact reinforce him, the Sword of Strength may become the Sword of Lightness and a lamp may be replaced by a magic coat (many folk tales and hero tales in Irish use these motifs).

The other narrative of which two tellings may be compared is 'The Black Dog of the Wild Forest', a version in English of a tale which has more often been collected in Irish. Its relatively uncertain status is shown by the fact that it is listed in Ó Súilleabháin's *Handbook of Irish Folklore* as a native 'hero-tale',[302] whereas in *The Types of the Irish Folktale* it appears as a distant oikotype of AT 934B (The Youth to Die on his Wedding Day) – a type attested from Finland to Greece and from India to Spain.[303] Paddy Sherlock's grandfather is known to have told the story in Irish, and was heard by Stiofán Ó hEalaoire, whose own telling of it in the same language some fifty years later was recorded by S. Delargy.[304]

The synopsis of Paddy Sherlock's version follows:

1. When Prince John (Seán, in Ó hEalaoire's version) was born, a travelling 'poor scholar' placed a 'gospel' (charm) under his head.

2. Nineteen years later, Prince John reads the 'gospel': it prophesies that he will be killed by the Black Dog of the Wild Forest (Ó hEalaoire: The Black Dog with Eight Feet).

3. He sails away, accompanied by a faithful boy, and reaches a seaport.

4. He is told that this is the country where he will encounter the Black Dog. He sends home the boy, who is sorry to leave (contrasting with the unfaithful boy in 'The Beauty of the World' 3).

5. He travels through the forest and spends the night in a remote hut; from an old man he receives a dog which helps him defeat the black monster's attack.

6. Riding on his dog, Prince John travels on and spends the second night in

---

302 'A stepmother places her stepson under *geasa* to procure Madadh na Seacht gCos (Seven-footed Dog) for her. By aid and directions given him on the way he reaches a castle where a girl helps him to obtain An Cú Glas (Grey Hound) from her father. The Hound kills all other dogs in a chase, and the father asks the girl to release the Madadh which is hidden under a stone. Hound pursues Madadh which changes into a daisy. The hairs of the Hound become sheep which eat all daisies including Madadh. Hero is then sent by the girl's father to the Eastern World in quest of a sword. cloak, and wand. These he secures and, having married the girl, returns home to win a hurling match for Ireland against Scotland' (op. cit. 605-6). 303 'A prince hears a prophecy that on his wedding day he is to fall victim of a frightful wolf. He tries through various magic means to avoid the enemy. He succeeds in killing the wolf but one of the wolf's claws pierces his breast. By means of life-giving water he is resuscitated' (Aarne-Thompson *The Types of the Folktale* 329). 304 'Madara Dubh na nOcht gCos', *Béaloideas* 14 (1944) 113-29; *Leabhar Stiofáin Uí Ealaoire* 143-58.

another hut, where he receives from another old man a second dog which helps him defeat the black monster again.

7. Riding on the two dogs, he travels on and spends the third night in another hut, where he receives a third dog which helps him defeat the black monster.

8. The prince and his dogs stay overnight in a 'brass' palace (cf. 'The Beauty of the World' unit 4A, and 'The Seven-Year-Old Child' unit 8); he has been warned to beware of the lord's daughter.

9. Indeed she is in love with the Black Dog, who will regain human shape if he kills the prince; she is ordered to lock up Prince John's three dogs during the next fight, and should he defeat the Black Dog she must then drive one of its poisoned nails into the young man's heart – or just leave the nail in his bed.

10. When the Black Dog attacks the prince, the three faithful dogs break the three locks of their prison and kill the monster.

11. Prince John returns to the castle, where the lord's daughter drives the nail into his heart; but the faithful dogs rescue him with a magic leaf found 'at the other end of the world'. The lord's daughter is punished.

12. The first dog asks the prince to chop off its head; he reluctantly grants the request.

13. The second dog asks to be beheaded; the prince reluctantly complies.

14. The third dog asks to be beheaded; the prince reluctantly complies.

15. Prince John meets two gentlemen and a lady; they take him to a 'gentleman farmer's house'.

16. It is revealed that the three noble persons are the three 'dogs', returned to their normal human form. The prince marries the lady (who was the third dog).

17. He returns home with his wife. (Meanwhile, the boy of units 3 and 4 has been working for him.)

Whereas the protagonist in 'The Seven-Year-Old Child' is relatively active, making independent decisions, this protagonist seldom acts on his own initiative, and helpers keep rescuing him. But again, and this applies to the whole genre, character delineation is practically non-existent. Wonders are not less tremendous in this tale than in 'The Seven-Year-Old Child', and the structure allows shortening or lengthening of episodes: thus the boy's story (3, 4 and 17), which is merely sketched out in the two recorded versions, might disappear altogether without damage, but could just as easily have been developed to make a longer tale with two sets of adventures. Threefold repetition of incidents and triplication of actors are conspicuous again.

In performance, the verbalization of some parts may vary considerably; for instance in this section of the third unit of 'The Seven-Year-Old Child' (in my transcription of the 1950 text, stressed words are in bold type, oblique lines mark slight pauses and line-changes correspond to longer pauses. A detailed score with varied coding symbols could be more accurate – and less readable;

this one may suffice to show how reductive most written versions of oral tales can be):

(1929-30)

So when he came back again he didn't know a bit of the farmer's house, it got so wrecked looking and withered and worn. He asked the farmer to know what happened him that he got so poorly since he was there last.

(1950)

The **pedlar** come along / after it's **seven** long
                                                                years
And he **called in** to this / gentleman farmer's
                                                                house
Now / it got **so worn down** that he **wouldn't**
That he could **hardly** know it .
He **couldn't believe** in his **own mind** / that it
                                could be the **same** house
And the same people that lived there.
So he **went in**
And he **asked** this farmer
'**Could I** stay here' says he / 'for tonight?'
'Oh **certainly**' says the farmer says he '**Why not?**'
'Why you are that good' says he 'There's
welcome here for you now.'
So the pedlar said nothing till he had his tea taken
Then he **turned back** and he **asked** the farmer
'**Could** you tell me' / he says
'**Which**' he says' I'm **ashamed** to ask you
And to be **so inquisitive** in this
Has anything happened to **you** / since I stopped
                                here / seven years ago?
Your **house** and your **place** looks **very miserable** to
                                                my eyes
    Not as it was seven years ago.'

'Well, I'll tell you that,' said the farmer, 'as you asked me the question. All over a good girl of a daughter I have within in that room. I'm robbed from paying doctors and priests, and each one of them is telling me that my daughter is going to have a youngster.'

'**I know**' says the farmer
'That / what **happened** to me'
'Is **one** thing.
That's **all over**' says he '**one** girl of a daughter
That **I** have' says he 'within' says he 'in my ... /
                                                her bedroom
I'm all out' says he, 'and I'm **robbed** of
All my cattle' says he and the **price of them**
And the price of my **horses and land**
All gone' he says 'from paying **doctors** and **priests**'
                                says he' / to **cure** her
And still and on
None of them says he can do anything for her
They **all tell you**' says he / 'that she's in the family
                                                way
But **how** could I **believe** this
That **my daughter**
Would be in the family way?'

Other parts are more stable and, unsurprisingly, they are the more formulaic ones, like these passages from sequences 5, 6 and 7 in 'The Black Dog', including the simplified and anglicized version of 'runs' (cf. Section 28 above), quoted here from the first telling, and italicized:

... a big dog leaped out there as big as a year-old calf. Prince John pulled his sword from his side for to cut the head off him, when an old grey-headed man hopped upon the door, and he called Prince John by his name.

'Prince John, don't you cut the head of that dog, for if that dog doesn't do you any good tonight, he'll do you no harm!'

He brought Prince John in, gave him plenty to eat and drink, washed his feet up to his knees, gave him sleeping drops, and hopped him into bed at once. The old man called the dog by his name:

'Hearwell, if you haven't this man safe and sound for me in the morning, if it's what he dies tonight a prisoner in bed, I'll burn you into ashes, I'll distribute you all over the world the way a bit of you can never be put together again!'

Out o' that they did hear the Black Dog coming from the other end of the world, *with the oul' trees breaking and the young trees shaking, till they made the hard ground soft and the soft ground hard, till they drew spring-water through the green flags,* until the cock crew in the morning, until the Black Dog of the Wild Forest had to retire back again!

The old man went in and he woke Prince John.

'Well, Prince John, you're safe after last night!'

'Yes,' says Prince John, 'thank God and you!'

'Well, now, Prince John, I'll make you a present of a good dog, and if you forget this dog, this dog will forget you'.

Prince John thanked the old man for the dog, and travelled forward that day. Every bit that Prince John would eat he'd give two bits to the dog.[305]

The same text is delivered twice more, with minimal adaptation. In this tale, another 'run' goes:

'Prince John, do you ride?'

'Yes, I do,' say Prince John.

'If that's the way, throw your legs across me, and get a hold of my two ears'.

Prince John did.

The wind that was in front of her [the dog] *couldn't come in rear of her, and the wind that was in rear of her couldn't come in front of her, till she arrived to the second hut that was in the wood.*

Later, it becomes: '*The wind that was in front of them couldn't come in rear of them, and the wind that was in rear of them couldn't come in front of them, till they arrived to the third hut that was in the wood'.*[306]

Paddy Sherlock's opening formulae for these tales are fairly stable, though extensible. Compare:

305 *Béaloideas* 30 (1962) 59-60. **306** Ibid. 61

('Seven-Year-Old-Child' I)
There was a farmer one time in it,
and being in it, he buried his wife; and
he had one girl of a daughter ...

('Seven -Year-Old-Child' II)
Well, at one time there was a very
wealthy farmer, and being in it,
at this time, he had plenty horses,
plenty cattle, and land, and all he
had was one girl of a daughter.

When closing formulae are used, they seem more prone to vary:

('Seven-Y.-O.-Child' I)
... The lad himself came home, and he
got married to the King of Ireland's
daughter, and if they don't live happy
that we may! When they're drinking bog-
water that we may drink tea!

('Seven -Y.-O.-Child' II)
And he come home and he got married
to the King of Ireland's daughter. And
they lived happy from that day on, and
so may all people who are in this
kitchen.

Repetitions occur on several levels: words, word groups, longer formulae, plot sequences, in the same tale – and repetition of the same kinds of events and of the same narrative structure from tale to tale. The telling sounds efficient and conveys an illusion of coherence in spite of ellipses and shifting scenes, fantastic surprises and the sudden vanishing of secondary characters.

How did Sherlock's listeners respond – what kind of satisfaction did they experience, and what was the significance of the tales for them? From an unimaginative point of view, much in his stories is highly improbable: if events follow laws, they do not seem to be those of everyday causality. But it is difficult to believe that, when listening to him, the audience found only the pleasure of being mystified, or some vague dreamlike quality: if everything were inconsistent, how could such tales have been faithfully transmitted for so long? Of course we are in an imaginary world, but there are controlling patterns; first, some plotting principles – the sequence of events is made necessary by the structural rules of the genre, recognition of which could bring contentment. Do the tales also *mean* anything? A scheme of contrastive cognitive and emotional elements is established: powerlessness/potency, poverty/wealth, fear/courage, age/youth, awkwardness/grace ... Symbols (characters, settings, actions or situations connoting ideas, values or problems) may have special meanings within a cultural context, and stimulate emotions and ideas – or remain dead clichés. Hyperbole and stylization, displacement, interpolation or contraction may transform, hide or intensify what is expressed, and, while the whole audience shares the experience, each of its members has a creative role in constructing what the story means to him or her. Scholars who try to interpret such tales refer to the basic experiences of growing up, gaining power, proving oneself and being accepted in adult society; or to the celebration of moral principles like kindness and persistence – or of luck as a form of grace; or to the manifestation of latent fears, hopes, or resentment ... Whatever meanings Sherlock's audience perceived, it is certain that they found something valuable in his performances. What has survived of a humble master's activity illustrates one way of treating one kind of story, but we may accept it as representative of what a 'traditional' audience appreciated when this genre was performed. We may assume that it was charged with feelings and values, and gave consolation and hope; beyond this, it would be presumptuous to try and decide exactly what went on in the minds of his listeners.

The opposition between a sophisticated artist perfectly in command of his craftsmanship and (in 'traditional' modes) a mere echo unaware of what he is doing is not a tenable proposition. 'There does, of course, exist an "art" of the storyteller, which is the ability to generate narratives (messages) from the structure (code)', and the artist in this field is 'not the person who invents the finest stories but the person who best masters the code',[307] realizing the virtualities of a narrative mode and of a repertoire. What he produces must have a discernible, coherent and satisfactory form. The audience's pleasure and approval depend on the combination of a high level of predictability with uncertainty as to how a foreseeable end will be attained. The effect is culture-bound: those with whom the product is normally shared respond to it according to norms and values which may differ from those of an outsider. The art of a storyteller combines personal choices and skills with what he has in common with the other narrators in his society and a knowledgeable audience; at a deeper level, it may be founded on some universal principles.

The example of Paddy Sherlock also reveals how incomplete our information is bound to be when we try to reconstruct an oral phenomenon that belongs to the past: we have a few sentences, by one collector, concerning the career of a man – for whom storytelling was only a part of his life but in which he probably found personal fulfilment; a few adjectives are not sufficient to establish his real character. The transcriptions of a number of texts probably do not represent his full repertoire; very few recordings have survived, and even they cannot give a full picture of what happened when he told the stories: we may form an idea of Paddy Sherlock's ways of manipulating narrative patterns and language, but we know nothing of the non-verbal dimension which must have contributed to the live experience – unless we admit that what was observed in other Irish acts of storytelling, at about the same time, also applies to this case.

307 R. Barthes *A Barthes Reader* 253, 286.

12

Stories about storytelling: storytellers in stories

Different Irish storytellers have been observed in various situations, from several points of views. We must now consider one more set of representations: those which nineteenth- or twentieth-century storytellers themselves offered in the stories they told, when an act of narration by one of their characters was a significant event, or when the main story or a secondary one was framed within a scene of narration. Is storytelling shown to be good or bad? Is the presence of a teller within the tale a way for the actual storyteller to define his own role and draw the audience's attention to the act of telling?

Describing acts of narration and giving characters the role of storytellers in written narratives is as old as literature itself. In the Egyptian story of 'The Shipwrecked Sailor', preserved on a Twelfth-Dynasty papyrus, the returned protagonist recounts what a huge serpent-god made him say on a vanishing island in the Red Sea, then what the divine reptile told of its own life and revealed concerning the future: personal and received narratives combine retrospective and predictive elements. In the latest version of the epic of Gilgamesh, the hero hears the story of the Flood from the man who survived it. In the *Odyssey*, the protagonist himself tells his most amazing adventures – and we cannot exclude the possibility that he is making them up; there are other storytellers in this text, including professionals and noble amateurs. Do the various storytellers mirror the author himself – if such an individual existed, or contrast with him, or represent the multiple voices that shaped and kept the set of stories alive and from whose 'traditional' repertoire the unified poem later recited by rhapsodes may have been composed? The problem of the reliability of oral transmission from one country, generation and individual to another seems to be raised in Plato's *Timaeus* when Critias tells the story of Atlantis as his grandfather heard it from Solon, who had it from an Egyptian priest. Inserted tales are common in Hellenistic romances, and there are stories within stories in the *Aeneid*, the *Metamorphoses*, *Satyricon* and *The Golden Ass*. More than twenty narrative parables are told in the Gospels, and the attitude of the audience can be significant when part of the message is that some understand the lesson while others don't (Matt. 13.1-23). Medieval European romances include stories told by the characters. When the taste for novels grew, the concept of a pseudo-oral narrative voice developed, and the situation in which someone narrated how the main story had been discovered was an enduring device. Mimicking a storytelling situation and holding up the main narrative while a character interpolates his tale can be a mere trick to lengthen the work or vary the entertainment, without establishing a significant relationship between the two story levels; but inserting a narrative within a longer story may also provide explanations necessary to understand the main text, for instance what led to the present situation and how newly revealed information concerning the past may change the way characters interact; or an inset story may work thematically by pointing (through similarity or contrast) to some basic issue which the main narrative is meant to illustrate. The illusion of a 'voice', by suggesting a living presence, can be a compensation for the reader's separation from the writer, and a plurality of narrating voices when a group of individuals swap stories may express collective consciousness. Separate accounts of the same event may be a way of making the reader aware of contradictory conceptions of 'truth', or direct the reader's attention to the artefactual nature of the text. Twentieth-century narratologists have devised theories and coined terms, including 'metanarration', for such foregrounding of narrative procedures.[1]

Long before those developments, however, attention had been paid to the *Rahmenerzählung* structure, or cycle of tales supposedly communicated orally within a frame situation whose outcome may be determined by the embedded elements. It is possible for an inner narrative to include yet another act of storytelling, in Chinese-box construction. The stories may remain independent, or each is a commentary on another. The device may be the homage of written literature to oral narration, or just a facile way of lending a semblance of unity to a heterogeneous collection. Used systematically in ancient Indian literature, it spread to Persia, and then farther west. The *Book of Sindibad*, for instance, translated into Arabic, Byzantine Greek and Hebrew, finally reached Europe where, in various languages, it was in vogue from the twelfth century as *Roman des Sept Sages de Rome*, *Il Libro dei Sette Savi*, *Libro de Los Engannos* or *The Seven Wise Masters*; the earliest English version dates from the beginning of the fourteenth century: a prince has been falsely accused by his stepmother and cannot defend himself because he must keep silent for a week; each morning, a wise helper tells a tale to persuade the emperor of the evils of ill-considered judgement or of the perfidy of women, and the emperor decides to relent, but at night the wicked accuser persuades him with other tales that the death sentence must be carried out. On the eighth day, the boy can tell his father what actually happened, and the accuser is sentenced to death. The *Rahmenerzählung*

---

1 The concept was adapted to folktales by B. Babcock-Abrahams: 'Metacommunication in narrative performance may be described as any element of communication which calls attention to the speech event as a performance and to the relationship which obtains between the narrator and his audience vis-à-vis the narrative message ... The frame tale, the embedding narrative is the essence of metanarration for it is the narration of a narration that calls attention to the act of narrating itself ... Even more explicitly, the embedded story itself may be a story about someone telling a story...' ('The Story in the Story: Metanarration in Folk Narrative', in R. Bauman (ed.) *Verbal Art as Performance* 66, 71-2).

method was often used in the late Middle Ages and Renaissance periods, in Italy, in England where Chaucer had the tales characterize their tellers, and in sixteenth-century France. The combination of texts framed by a storytelling situation had been carried to near-obsessive extremes in the *Arabian Nights* where Scheherazade prolongs her life by telling stories of which the characters may turn narrators too, or hear other storytellers. When the collection was translated at the beginning of the eighteenth century, into French and soon other European languages, it was widely imitated. From the late eighteenth century, several German writers used a fictional framework within which contemporary Germans were telling tales or legends. The fortune of the device in nineteenth-century Anglo-Irish literature was mentioned in Chapter 7.

The simpler forms of secondary narration may have developed naturally in oral storytelling, but the intricate polyphony which is played with in some written texts may remain beyond reach here. I shall examine some examples of oral narrative discourse about narrative discourse, first in a couple of oral *Rahmenerzählungen* known in Ireland, then as more or less instrumental elements in separate tales, according to the simple classification that was used for the analysis of more ancient texts (in Chapter 2). The second part of the chapter will focus on a tale-pattern, or pair of tale-types, based on the predicament of a person who is unable to tell a story and must acquire material for one through extraordinary experiences.

A. STORYTELLING WITHIN STORIES

There is in Ireland plenty of evidence for a high valuing of eloquence or a fear of curses, as well as for an awareness of the value and danger of both outspokenness and silence, as shown in proverbs like 'it is a bad thing not to have some story on the tip of your tongue', 'the silent mouth is sweet to hear' or 'a closed mouth – a wise head'.[2] References to, or representations of, the power of speech as it manifests itself in the narrative mode of discourse are also common in the oral repertoire. Not all of them are very significant – they may just represent moments of relaxation and sociability for the characters, or play an explanatory role – but in some interesting examples special effects are achieved, pointing to the nature of narrativity itself.

The structural device of the frame narrative containing within itself a series of tales was known in medieval Ireland, as attested most notably by the *Acallamh na Senórach* and, more crudely and probably later, *Feis Tighe Chonáin Chinn-Shleibhe* (see Chapter 2). *Scéalta rómánsaíochta* (romances) composed between the fifteenth and the seventeenth centuries and combining imported with native material and style also include scenes of storytelling; thus in *Eachtra an Mhadra*

---

2 S. Gaffney and S. Cashman *Proverbs & Sayings of Ireland* 39 and 82.

Mhaoil ('Story of the Crop-Eared Dog'), the ugly beast, a transformed prince, forces an Arthurian knight to tell news or stories: ' "Not to tell a story have I come here," said [the knight], "for I think it more fitting that I should give gold and silver for stories to be told to me, than for myself to be telling them" '3 – but he does say why he has come to the 'Dangerous Forest', and later the Crop-Eared Dog tells him his own story as well as that of their common enemy.

It has been said that one of the characteristic features of more recent Irish storytelling was the fact that 'by combining several tales [the storytellers'] compositions might swell into a tale of many chapters, each taking an evening for the telling' ... 'Fenian tales ..., having the same group of heroes, may be strung up together by folk-tellers as they were by literary ones'.4 This did not necessarily imply dramatized tellers. If the device of the story set in a frame that bounds it at beginning and end needed foreign models, they could be found in chapbooks: *The Seven Wise Masters* was already circulating in that form before the end of the seventeenth century.5 A version offered in Dublin as the thirty-eighth edition in 1814 has the complete set of tales told to influence the emperor, and is followed by another set on the same pattern with women replacing men.6 In a chapbook printed in Dublin in 1734, *Winter Evening Tales, being a Collection of Entertaining Stories related in an Assembly of the Most Polite Persons of the French Nation*, a game is played which was later practised in Irish rural wakes (see p. 460): objects belonging to the 'polite persons' are collected, and whenever one of them is drawn the owner is 'obliged either to relate some of [his/her] own adventures, or at least some story in which [he/she] has had some share'.7 Along with *The Seven Wise Masters and Mistresses of Rome* and many other texts, Carleton listed *The Arabian Nights Entertainment* as a chapbook used in his hedge school.8 That it was very popular was also noted by an English visitor:

In October 1808, I met in the neighbourhood of Adare, a boy who had travelled from Carrick, a distance of forty miles, for the purpose of begging. I gave him some money, and, meeting him again a few hours after, observed a remarkable change in his looks. His whole demeanour announced a comparative degree of happiness. He had got his pockets filled with bread; and, after thanking me for my bounty, he told me that he had purchased the *Arabian Knight's* [sic]*Entertainment*. In the morning he seemed famished, and almost naked; but his misery was now forgotten in the enjoyment of his book, which he considered as a great treasure.9

---

3 R.A.S. Macalister ed. and tr. *Two Irish Arthurian Romances* 12-15. 4 R.T. Christiansen *Studies in Irish and Scandinavian Folktales* 10; A. Bruford *Gaelic Folk-Tales and Medieval Romances* 312. 5 Niall Ó Ciosáin *Print and Popular Culture in Ireland, 1750-1850* 74. 6 *The History of the Seven Wise Masters and Mistresses of Rome*, printed by A. Fox. 7 Op. cit., 'reprinted and sold by George Faulkner', 2. The stories are not folktales. 8 *Traits and Stories of the Irish Peasantry* 1. 313. 9 Edward Wakefield *An Account of Ireland, Statistical and Political* 2. 726. According to P.J. Dowling (*The Hedge-Schools of Ireland* 69), among chapbooks used in these unofficial native schools before the 1820s was 'Alibaba' or 'The Forty

But such chapbooks did not necessarily include the Scheherazade frame story,[10] and the idea of binding a series of tales together in a narrative frame may have been re-invented several times.

A complete Irish cycle of tales was collected from oral tradition in 1896 by Douglas Hyde, in the Athlone poorhouse, from Próinsias Ó Conchúbhair who said he had it from a Sligo man. It was first published in 1909 as *Sgéuluidhe Fíor na Seachtmhaine* ('The True Storyteller of the Week'), with some editing: Hyde replaced one original 'night' he deemed improper by a version of the Gobán Saor story (about which I shall say more later). According to the frame story, an inscription on the house of a never-aging noblewoman says that anyone will enjoy good hospitality there, provided he can narrate every night. A young man has regularly listened to what old people said, but dares not enter the house before he has acquired a story which will sound new and true. One night, having accepted to 'pick the teeth' of a mysterious big man in a graveyard, he is shown Hell, Purgatory and the road to Heaven. He now has something to tell. After hearing the beginning of his tale, the lady interrupts him, calls a dozen male guests and their women, and makes the young storyteller start again from the beginning. His performance is praised. The following night, as he is telling the second story, he is interrupted by one of the women – who are all punished by being transformed into white greyhounds and regain human form only when the tale is ended. The third night, the storyteller, now uninterrupted, tells the tale of 'The King's Son and the Knight of the Sword' which sounds like an Irish hero tale, including 'runs'. And so on until the seventh night; by then, the audience has increased, because each lady is now breastfeeding a baby. When the young man has finished, members of the audience stand up one by one to testify that it was all true, since they are the heroes and heroines of the various stories. The last three men to speak are Oisín, his son Oscar, and Fionn Mac Cumhail himself who rewards the storyteller with an ever-full purse. The storyteller falls asleep; when he wakes up, the house is empty. He returns to his family, lives comfortably, has many sons and daughters, and after death goes to Fionn's fairy castle on the Hill of Allen.[11] We are invited to ask what heroes would become if storytellers were not celebrating them, and to wonder whether good storytellers themselves should not be treated like heroes.

The storyteller was probably conscious of commenting on his own art. The process of learning tales through assimilating and practising is reduced here to

Thieves'. Cf. also this statement collected by Seósamh Ó Dálaigh in Kerry in 1950: 'They used be telling stories in a house here and the house used be crowded and some of them couldn't get in. They got the stories out of a book called "The Arabian Nights". ' (IFC 1169: 320). 10 *Arabian Tales*, printed in 1810 by Edwards & Savage in Cork, did not – but it had the 'Second Kalandar's Tale', a version of which was told more than a century later by Paddy Sherlock (see p. 498). 11 A version with two nights only was collected in Munster by S. Ó Dálaigh in 1937 (IFC 316: 98-124). It includes the episodes of pulling a tooth from a dead man, seeing Hell, Purgatory and Heaven, and the interruption by women who are transformed into hounds. The setting is still County Galway.

memorization, but with a formula often applied to real storytellers: 'He would go from house to house every night to listen to the stories of old people. He just had to hear a tale once to keep it for ever.'[12] The way of using 'tradition' to compose 'new' stories is accurately described: 'Now, my worthies, here is a story nobody else knows in Ireland; I did not get it from one, two, or three persons, but found the elements everywhere and assembled them in such a way that it is absolutely true.'[13] A possible link between oral and written transmission is acknowledged: 'Just before he died, he told his story to a man who could write, and it was written exactly as it was coming from his lips. I have told it to you as I heard it from my grandfather's lips.'[14] The frame narrative and the stories related within it echo each other: several tales in the cycle include details such as the protagonist benefiting from overheard stories, or telling someone what has happened to him – or being warned not to do so; one character is punished for telling lies which he has offered as truth, and another is accused of lying when he is telling the truth. The notion of 'truth' in storytelling works as a refrain: 'It's a fine story and a true story'; 'All the stories I told you are true, though I cannot prove it'; 'Every word of the story is true'.[15] Some rules of behaviour for storytellers and audiences, including the principles of non-interruption and reward (both to be mentioned again later in this chapter), are stressed.

I know no other oral Irish example of so complex a chain of tales, but there are simpler items. For instance, Seán Ó Súilleabháin and R.T. Christiansen, in *The Types of the Irish Folktale*, add a category to the Aarne-Thomson classification, 2412A: 'Who Has Seen the Greatest Wonder? Two men vie in telling of the greatest wonder each has seen; or else a very old hag tells of strange things she has seen or experienced.'[16] The Irish Folklore Archives have versions of this group of tales collected in Kerry, Galway, Mayo and Sligo, and the marvels may be wild hunts at sea, transformations into animals, or combats with the devil. The teller of strange 'true' stories in oral narratives may be an ancient mythological figure, the Cailleach Bhéarra (Hag of Beare), sometimes supposed to be an avatar of some nature goddess beautiful and hag-like by turns, or the incarnation of sovereignty over a territory. With her extreme longevity, she has witnessed many things and may be invited to recount them:

'Though I don't know your age,' said the friar to the hag, 'I know that you haven't lived up to this time without seeing marvellous things in the course of your life, and the greatest marvel that you ever saw – tell it to me, if you please.' 'I saw one marvel which made me wonder greatly,' said the hag. 'Recount it to me,' said the friar, 'if you please' ...'[17]

A narrative act in a folktale or hero tale may function as mere transition or pause

12 *Sgéuluidhe Fíor na Seachtmhaine* 2-3 (tr.).   13 Ibid. 42.   14 Ibid. 98.   15 Ibid. 69, 98, 99.
16 *The Types of the Irish Folktales* 343.   17 D. Hyde *The Stone of Truth* 69. Also in *An Sgéaluidhe Gaedhéalach* 2.287. On the Cailleach Bhéarra, see G. Ó Crualaoich, in *Béaloideas* 56 (1988) 153-78.

between decisive events, or be a more or less important step in the development of the story. It may just represent passing time in company – to quote but one example: 'Daniel Crowley was asked to sit down and commence to shorten the night; that is, to tell stories, amuse himself and others'.[18] The circulation of stories in a community may be emphasized: 'The story spread in the country, so that all men, women and children of County Galway heard it, and there have been many versions of it before this evening', or 'shortly after, the story went from mouth to mouth through the country, as I have told it to you..[19] The following pages will focus on references to storytelling which tend to advance the plot, reinforce a theme or show that a good tale well told can solve a problem. The examples may be considered 'context-free units that have an independent existence and therefore have the capacity to enter into innumerable narrative relations'[20] – in other words 'motifs'; indeed, Stith Thompson's *Motif-Index of Folk-Literature* includes some references to acts of storytelling, but scatters them under different headings.[21] In an attempt to coordinate the examples found in Irish tales I shall apply the criteria already used in Chapter 2.

1. A central character narrates, and his narration is decisive for the whole story
Narrating in order to achieve some good or delay some evil is not peculiar to Irish folktales, but fairly common in them. Important too, the episode in which a protagonist reveals himself/herself or unmasks the enemy, may take the form of telling one's life story or some particular event; what has already been narrated may thus be repeated, or only summed up, with happy results for the teller and bad ones for the persecutor:

There was drinking and music and storytelling; there was no shortage of storytellers there. At last the stranger was asked to tell a story. He began, and what did he start telling but what had happened to himself from the day he was born up to that time. The stepmother, who was guilty of all that, was sitting listening to him, and as he told his story, she quickly guessed who he was. When he had finished his story, 'Now, people,'

18 Jeremiah Curtin *Tales of the Fairies and of the Ghost World* 47. 19 D. Hyde *An Sgéaluidhe Gaedhéalach* 2.218, 487-8. 20 D. Ben-Amos 'The Concept of Motif in Folklore', in V.J. Newall (ed.) *Folklore Studies in the Twentieth Century* 18. 21 MANIFESTATION OF MAGIC POWER: D1962.4.1 'lulling to sleep by sleepy story', MARVELS: F954.2.1 'dumb princess is brought to speech by tale ending with question to be solved', TESTS: H11 'telling of story known to both persons brings about recognition', H252.0.1 'telling true story', H1382.2 'quest for unknown story' (marked as more specifically Irish), WISE AND UNWISE CONDUCT: J571.5 'king restrained from hasty judgment by being told story', CLEVERNESS: J1177.1 'story told to discover thief', J1177.0.1 'leaving during story reveals guilt', J1185 'execution escaped by story-telling', DECEPTIONS: K555.2.1 'formula tale saves girl from devil', K835 'dragon deceived into listening to tale – hero cuts off his head, BARGINS AND PROMISES: M231 'free keep in inn exchanged for good story', ROYALTY AND NOBILITY: P14.14 'king requires everyone who comes before him to tell a story' (more specifically Irish), REWARDS AND PUNISHMENTS: Q482.4 'cast-forth wife must sit at horse-block of palace and tell story to each newcomer' ...

said he to the company, 'I'll leave the decision to ye as to what punishment the woman who did that should get.'[22]

Here is another example: ' "Don't stop him," said his mother, "till he tells the story to his grandfather." The child told him all the rest, and when he heard the story he hung the woman for what she did; and he brought the son of the herd into the house, and gave his daughter to him in marriage.'[23] The decisive revelation may also take the form of a non-verbal allegorical narrative, as in the last move of the story of the bride who was forgotten when a dog kissed her lover:

The king's son was very lonely, and he heard there was a woman in the village [the forgotten bride] who was a good storyteller, and he sent for her to tell him some stories to cheer him. She came and said she had no story to tell, and she took out a little box, and there was a little cock and hen within it ... [she puts on a play without words, enacting what happened between the prince and herself, so that his memory is revived].[24]

To have a character relate his/her experience (already known to the actual audience) can be more than a way of filling time or satisfying a taste for repetition; even when it does not change the course of the events it may contrast with the present state of affairs; towards the end of a story, retrospection distances the situations with which the actual audience previously empathized and thus prepares for the return to everyday reality: 'Nóinín told her whole story; told all, told everything in the way it had happened; how she had seen Sgiathán Dearg, and followed and caught him, then lost him, and followed a second time ...'[25] Or: 'He told her his story from beginning to end, how the sea had come on him when he was filling the pail under the flow of the stream and how he had been taken into a boat in which the little red-haired man was sitting in the stern ...'[26] A heroine's story ends with her telling her adventures to her husband:

'I have a long story to tell about [our three children] and about many other things, but I will tell it to you some other time.' 'I will not stir a foot until you tell me,' said he. 'You must tell me everything now.' She began on her story then, and she told to him from beginning to end ... Moireen and the nobleman lived happily from that out, without any trouble or anxiety of any kind. He never grew tired of listening to Moireen's story of how she and her sons lived in the sea.[27]

The motif of narrating in order to delay or prevent death is found in many countries; in Ireland, the most popular tale based on it is 'The Black Thief' (*An Gadaí Dubh*), an oikotype of International Type 953: The Old Robber Relates

22 Sean O'Sullivan *Folktales of Ireland* 129. 23 'The Nameless Story', collected by William Larminie, *The Cabinet of Irish Literature* 4. 168. 24 L. McManus 'Folk Tales from Co. Mayo, Ireland', *Folk-Lore* 25 (1914) 194. 25 Jeremiah Curtin *Irish Folk-Tales* 105. 26 S. Ó hEochaidh *Síscéalta Ó Thír Chonaill* 291. 27 Eileen O'Faolain (tr.) *Children of the Salmon* 218-9 (from *Imtheachtaí an Oireachtais* 1890).

Three Adventures to Free his Sons. In the Irish versions, three brothers have been forced by a wicked stepmother to try and steal the Steed of Bells from a knight or king; they are captured, together with an older man. The old robber secures their freedom by telling how he had already been near to death three times, and his last story reveals that, long ago, he saved the life of the knight or king. The earliest written rendering in Ireland is in the early-nineteenth-century *Royal Hibernian Tales*.[28] Curtin noted that 'there are many variants of this tale, both in the north and south of Ireland. It seems to have been a great favorite, and is mentioned often, though few know it well'.[29] Here is a passage transcribed from a shorter twentieth-century oral telling:

... When he was taking off the bells they rattled and when the king's army heard him he was arrested. He was carried before the king and the king said to put him to death and the death he gave him was to get three barrels of tar and to light the tar and to hang him over them till he'd burned to death. Before he was to be burned, the king came to him and asked him 'were you ever before as near death?' and he said he was and the king asked him how. He described to him then. 'I'll tell you. I was crossing a house and I heard a woman crying inside.' And he told him what he had done. How he made the pie and put the child's finger into it. 'More than that' says he 'I had to lie between the dead bodies and the giant came and cut one of my hips off. Then he was throwing a magic ring after me and where did it go but on my big toe. So I had nothing to do but cut off my toe with two stones. And here I am now with only one big toe.' The king was listening to him. 'Right you are, my man,' says the king, 'you're telling all the truth. I'm the baby, and here I am now,' says he. 'I've only four fingers in one hand. I'll give you your freedom and whatever you'd like to take and I'll keep you for the rest of your life if you'll stay.' But the black thief would not stay – he'd sooner go to the road.[30]

This story implies that an incredible tale may convey a most valuable truth. Blatant lying, however, may be useful too: also very popular in Ireland was International Type 852, where a king (or some other powerful figure) promises his daughter to the man who forces him or her to say 'that's a lie'; a poor boy takes up the challenge and succeeds by making outrageous statements:

There was once a grand gentleman who lived in a great, big castle. He had a lovely daughter, and he said he would give her to any man that would make him say 'You are a liar'. A great many of the nobility visited the castle and told the most outlandish stories but the old fellow listened to them all and never said 'You are a liar'. Now, at that time there was a young fellow called Jack – a jolly, jovial sort of fellow, and when he heard of the offer made by the gentleman he made up his mind to have a try at winning the daughter. So he went to the castle and introduced himself. The gentleman showed him 'round the place and said: 'Isn't that a great castle?' 'It isn't half as big as my father's. My father's castle would make two like that one.' The gentleman said nothing

28 *The Royal Hibernian Tales*, in *Béaloideas* 10 (1940) 156, 157,158, 160. 29 *Hero-Tales of Ireland* 551. 30 IFC 1608: 5-6. Collected in 1961 from Hannah Delaney (aged 78) at Ballyduff, Co. Kerry, by P. de Brún.

but took him to the rear of the castle and showed him a big garden of cabbages. 'Isn't that a great garden of cabbages?' asked the gentleman. 'It isn't half as good as my father's,' said Jack. 'How do you make that out?' asked the gentleman. 'Well,' said Jack, 'there was a regiment of soldiers in the garden one day, and there came a shower of rain, and the whole regiment went under one of the heads of cabbage and it gave them shelter from the rain.' The gentleman made no answer to this, but he took Jack some distance from the castle and showed him a new castle that was being built. 'What do you think of that?' asked the gentleman. 'It is not half as good as a new castle that my father is after building,' said Jack. 'Why do you say that?' asked the gentleman. 'Well,' said Jack, 'when they were finishing the roof one of the men shouted for a box of matches and it was stones that were sent up. He was so far from the ground that they couldn't understand what he was saying. And when they were finishing the tower one of the men dropped a trowel, and it was rusty before it came to the ground. The man leaped down after it, and his drop was so great that he sank in a solid rock and all of him that could be seen above the ground were his head and two shoulders. A fox came along and whipped the head off him. But he jumped up and followed the fox and took his head back off him.' 'You're a liar,' said the gentleman; 'that couldn't happen.' So Jack succeeded in making the gentleman call him a liar; the old fellow had to give him his daughter, and they were as happy as the day is long.[31]

In many versions, the father or the daughter is brought to say the required words when the youth makes up shameful lies about their family. In another tale, lying saves a life:

There was a king one time, and he made a law that every man in the country would be put to death when he was seventy years of age. He put them to death by burning them. He had a lot of workmen, and there was a fellow among them that had his father concealed. The old man was over seventy. And the king didn't know that he was still alive. He was a very wise old man – he had great wisdom and he was great at answering questions that were hard to answer. One day the king called all his workmen together and said: 'Any man that is able to tell which is the butt or the top of the trunk of a tree after it has been plained and painted, I will give him £5.' This workman came home and told his father about the king's offer. 'Oh,' says the old man, 'he knows that I'm still to be had yet, but all the same let you earn the £5. Bring the stick to the river and throw it in, and the top will sink and the butt will fall behind, with the rim above the water.' Next day the king had the workmen all gathered together, and he asked if any of them could tell between the butt and the top of the tree. The young fellow did what the old man told him, and he got the £5. The king then said to the men: 'Any man that is able to tell me what best loves man, what man loves best, and what is his greatest enemy, will get £5 from me.' The young fellow came home and told his father. 'Ha! ha!' says the old man; 'he knows I'm to be had yet, but let you earn the £5. Get your horse, and put your son before you, and your wife behind you, and bring your dog with you. Your dog is what loves you best; your son is what you love best; and your wife is your greatest enemy.' The young man did as he was told. He rode to the king's palace and says he,

31 IFC 791: 588–91. Collected in 1941 from Eugene O'Brien (aged 55), Kingscourt Co. Cavan, by P.J. Gaynor.

pointing to his dog: 'There is what loves me best.' And says he as he held up his little son: 'There is what I love best.' And turning round to his wife, he said: 'There is my greatest enemy.' She got vexed at what he said, and says she: 'If I were your greatest enemy I'd have told where you have your father hid in a cave behind the house.' The words were no sooner out of her mouth than the soldiers were sent out, and the old man was arrested and brought to the palace. There was a day appointed to burn him, and great crowds of people gathered on that day at the place where he was to be burned. Every man was supposed to tell a story before the burning would take place. The old man's son went to the king, and says he: 'Will you give me leave to tell a story?' 'I will,' says the king. 'Well,' says the young fellow, 'I want one condition in it – any man that interrupts me while I'm telling the story, will be burned instead of my father.' The king agreed, and the young fellow started to tell his story. 'Well,' says he, 'I ploughed all Erin over in one day. I sowed it on the second day, and on the third day I reaped it. I put my grandfather to the North, and my grandmother to the South, and my great-grandfather to the West, and my great-grandmother to the East. My grandfather ris [roused] a hare, and he fixed a hook at her and the hook stuck in her, and he hunted her over to my great-grandfather. The hook was cutting the corn as she ran along. And when she came to my great-grandfather, he hunted her to my great-grandmother, and my great-grand-mother hunted her to my grandmother, so in that way I cut all Erin in the one day. I drew it home in another day. I brought it on horse-back across a river, and when cross-ing the river the horse fell with the weight of it, and broke his back. I skinned a sheep, and put the skin round the horse's back and I bound it with briars. And every year I took nine pecks of blackberries and a ton of wool off the horse's back. When I took the horse out of the river I had nine salmons caught on the nail of every shoe.' There was an old fisherman in the crowd, and says he at the top of his voice: 'You are a liar and a damned liar, and you told nothing but lies since you went up here.' 'Burn that man instead of my father,' says the young fellow: 'He's after interrupting me.' The king ordered his men to seize the fisherman, and so they did and burned him at the stake instead of the old man. The old man was set free, and the son had him home with him.[32]

This story combines the 'Prince of Liars' theme (more will be said about actual contests for this title in the next chapter) with the 'Interrupted Storyteller' theme. Forced interruption is the decisive moment in stories belonging to 'the Endless Tale' group (International Types 2300ff), of which there are Irish oiko-types: a certain incident is repeated so often that the listener loses patience – and here the principle of repetition is carried to an absurd extreme:

There was a big lord some time ago there. He couldn't sleep, day or night. Any doctor couldn't give him any drugs to make him sleep. Well he'd give a thousand pounds to any man that would give him sleep. They were trying and he couldn't sleep. There was a poor scholar going around and he heard of it and faith he said he'd go. Oh yes. If they didn't make him sleep the head would be cut of him. There 'tis for you, for the thou-sand pounds. So this poor scholar whatever said he'd attack him, for the thousand pounds, and he'd sit down outside the bed and his meals would be only brought to him,

32 IFC 815: 157-63. Collected in 1942 from Michael Coyle (aged 60), Blackhills Co. Cavan, by P.J. Gaynor.

leave him there and begin at the story. He would tell the story until he'd fall asleep, do you see, a long story. Very well this poor scholar went to him and he came and he sat down outside the bed, he in bed always, couldn't sleep. Well he begins at the story and the story was:

'There was a large barn of corn alongside a man's house. A locust came in, he took away a grain. Another locust came in, took away a grain. Another locust came in, took away a grain. Another locust came in, took away a grain. Another locust came in, took away a grain.' Well, to make my story short, the king was tired of listening to him. He was that way for a whole day and a night. 'Is that the story you have? says he. 'It is,' says the poor scholar, he says. 'Listen on,' he says, 'an' youl'll fall asleep.' He was there for a whole week. 'Another locust came in, carried away a grain. A locust came in an' carried away a grain.' That was his story. At length and at last the old king said: 'God blast it for a story,' says he, 'yourself and your locusts,' says he, 'to put me asleep.' He had to give him a thousand pounds and [he] walked out the door.[33]

When they are telling 'serious' tales, however, storytellers resent interruptions, as appears in International Motif J1177.0.1: None should interrupt or leave the Room while Story is told: Treachery revealed. It is developed in Irish as a story generally concerning Cú Chulainn and his other nickname, *Cú na hAdhairce* (the hound of the horn). To have his sword fixed, he agrees to tell a smith about one of his rare defeats – provided no woman is listening. When the smith's wife, who has been hiding, comments on the hero's humiliation (a giant had flung him into a cow's horn), the hero-storyteller stops and kills the interrupter, or just refuses to complete the narrative. Here is the milder ending:

'May the devil take you!' roared Cú Chulainn rising from his seat and making for the sheaf [in which the woman was hiding]. 'Didn't I tell you,' said he to the smith, 'that no woman was to hear my story?' He would have killed the woman, only for the boy protecting her. 'If you had kept silent, you would have heard the finest story that was ever told!' said Cú Chulainn. 'Now I have done with you. That's the end.'[34]

Thomas O'Conor, one of the Ordnance Survey collectors in the 1836, may have heard a variant of this story (see p. 109). In another version the interrupted storyteller is Finn.[35]

The king who demands stories at night because he cannot sleep may be a fearsome tyrant, and the storyteller who defeats or unmasks him must be particularly skilful, as in the oral tale concerning wicked Lugaid mac Con (who was half-human, half-amphibian animal) and the son of a king he had killed:

... the old man told him how bad a king Conn was. Someone had to sit up with him every night telling him stories, and anyone whom he disliked or didn't satisfy him was

---

33 IFC 659: 505-6. Collected in 1939 from Mrs Lane (aged 90) at Finuge Co. Kerry, by S. Ó Dálaigh. 34 Sean O'Sullivan *Folktales of Ireland* 79, the translation of a tale collected in Donegal by S. Ó hEochaidh, IFC 142: 1334. 35 D. Hyde *Irisleabhar na Gaedhilge* 5. 10-13.

shot or hanged next morning ... 'Start off now,' said [the king] to the youth, 'and tell me the best stories you have'. The king turned his own face toward the wall with the bed-clothes drawn up over his head. When dawn was breaking next morning, he turned to face the youth. 'You are the best man at *fiannaíocht* and storytelling that has ever entered my palace or my city,' said he. 'I don't believe you heard the half of what I told you,' said the youth. 'I heard every word you said since you sat down there last night,' said the king. 'You couldn't have,' said the youth. 'You were asleep half of the time.' 'I wasn't asleep,' replied the king. 'I haven't closed my eyes in sleep for seven years, or maybe for seven more along with that.' 'Then,' said the youth, 'you must be half like an otter.' [He kills the sleepless villain.][36]

Everybody should have at least one story to tell: his own life-experience; and as already shown in 'The Black Thief' it can be particularly useful: 'Then Shaking-head said to the king's son: "You are no good, you have never told me a story since the first day I saw you." "I have but one story to tell you, except what happened since we met." ' The hero tells how he secured a decent burial for a corpse; the interlocutor reveals that he was the corpse, and rewards him: here we find again Motif E341.1, 'the Grateful Dead'.[37]

2. Storytelling by the protagonist is mentioned, not represented; we already know what is narrated, and the narrative act is unlikely to advance the main story
What distinguishes such acts of storytelling from those in the preceding section is that, instead of representing crucial turning points in the development of the main narrative or signalling its completion, they function as minor links or as periods of rest for the hero – and perhaps the teller and his audience; however, they may still play a role. We do not get a detailed account of what was said but a brief reference to narration may tell us how a potential helper or opponent learns of the protagonist's situation. The different impacts of such narrations are illustrated, for instance, in a tale where a young woman who has escaped from the fairies is still not saved because, when she returns home and tells her people – '*Agus d'inis sí óna thús go dtina dheireadh dóibh ansin an scéal*' (and she told them her story from beginning to end) – they ignore an essential detail; but later an old beggar-woman hears the same account – '*ag inseacht di mar a d'insigh mé dibhse*' (and what I told you was told to her) – spots the key detail, and is able to cure the young woman:[38] telling is ineffective the first time, then becomes effective.

That briefly mentioned acts of storytelling could function as mere enter-tainment is shown in a triadic pattern already attested in ancient Irish culture and later used as a 'run': a company is often said to 'make three thirds of the night', and though the occupation for each third may vary (drinking, eating, music, dozing, deep sleep), storytelling is generally one of them: 'The Greek

---

36 Translated by S. O'Sullivan in *Folktales of Ireland* 31-5. **37** Jeremiah Curtin *Myth and Folktales of Ireland* 133. **38** *Éamon a Búrc: Scéalta* 271.

magician's daughter smothered him with kisses, drowned him with tears, and dried him with fine silken cloths and her own hair. They divided the night into three parts: a third at storytelling [*trian le scéalaíocht*], a third at *fiannáiocht* [telling stories of the Fianna], and a third in deep and restful sleep until morning.' Other examples: 'They passed the night, one-third at storytelling, one-third at romancing, and one-third sleeping soundly until next morning'; or 'So he and she spent the night together – a third in talking, a third in story-telling, and a third in soft rest and deep slumber'; or 'They spent that night merrily – a third of it with Fenian tales, a third of it with telling stories, and a third of it with the mild enjoyment of slumber and of true sleep'; or ' "I never was at a place like this but one man sang a song, a second told a story, and a third played a trick." '[39]

3. A secondary character tells a story, which may be important

In his journey, the hero meets someone who tells him something strange and/or useful: ' "There's a man in that house who knows what fear is. If you go up to him, he'll tell you the whole story ... " '. The protagonist goes to the man – a knight. ' "Tell me now what fear is," said he. "Put away the sword and sit down. Then I'll tell you," said the knight. The boy laid down the sword once more and sat near the knight to hear his story. "I was living here with my three sons," said the knight ... [and the story incites the boy to perform an exploit]'.[40] Another example: 'While the table was being got ready for the others, Conall asked the warrior to tell his story. " 'Tis I that will tell it," said he ... [the warrior is then hired as guide, and Conall finds and defeats their common enemy].'[41]

A special kind of important narration by a secondary character is the commanding or predicting of actions which are then performed, and related again, as in these two examples from Curtin's version of 'The Bird of the Golden Land', (the hero is being instructed how to win a game of hide-and-seek):

'Walk into the garden', said the mare. 'You will find it full of beautiful maidens, each one will praise you, show you beautiful flowers, ask you to look at her, walk with her. Give no heed to the maidens, look not at one of them; go straight to the end of the garden where there is a tree and on it a single red apple. Pluck that apple, make two of it. The king will come out.'

The King's son did all as the mare had commanded. Every maiden in the garden was teasing the young man to go with her, was showing beautiful flowers, but he never lifted his eyes to look at the flowers or the maidens. He hurried forward to the tree and picked the apple ...

'Go straightway from this to the castle kitchen. A great many maidens will be there

39 Sean O'Sullivan *Folktales of Ireland* 40-1 and *The Folklore of Ireland* 55 or 58 or 59 (thrice the same formula – translated); William Larminie *West Irish Folk-Tales and Romances* 69; Douglas Hyde *Beside the Fire* 34-5, Jeremiah Curtin *Myth and Folk Tales of Ireland* 13. 40 Sean O'Sullivan *Folktales of Ireland* (tr.) 65-6. 41 Ibid. 92.

before you. They will laugh at you, tease you, push you, and slap you with towels, but never look at them or mind them. Walk up to the fire. The cook will give you a bowl of warm broth with no spoon in it. You will say, "I must find a spoon". Walk then to the cupboard. There you will see a three-headed pin. Take the pin, cut it open with your knife. You will find the King.'

The King's son of Erin did as the mare had commanded; went to the kitchen, avoided the maidens, took the bowl of broth, and saying, 'I must have a spoon for my soup', went to the cupboard, found a three-headed pin, and took it up.[42]

In the 'vision' (*aisling*), a form of political poetry widely practised in Irish in the eighteenth century, and in nineteenth-century ballads in English, a 'sky-woman (*spéirbhean*) personifying Ireland appears to the poet and announces a millenarian triumph of the Irish Catholics; her prophecy may include a modicum of narrativity.

As in ancient Irish literature (and in some continental tales), the occasional narrator may be a talking object: in Anthony Raftery's early nineteenth-century poem '*Seanchas na Sceiche*', an old bush under which the wandering poet has sought shelter from the rain narrates the history of Ireland. One of the strangest cases is that of the speaking loaves of bread, in another tale:

The King put [the King of Erin's son] in the cell, and said: 'I have heard that every man from Erin knows how to tell tales. I will bring you up to my chamber this evening. You must tell me some tales.' The King brought him up to the chamber. The youngest daughter had a bed made at each side of the chamber; one for her father and one for the King's son. She made the light burn very low, so that the chamber was almost in darkness. She took then three loaves of bread which she had made, put one in the couch of the King's son, one in the middle of the chamber, and one at the door. Then she and the King's son of Erin started off together and fled in great haste.

The King said: 'Now, King's son, begin your tale.' The loaf in the couch began a tale, and the tale was so long that it kept the king listening a good part of the night. When the first tale was ended the King said: 'That is a good tale, and it pleases me; tell me another tale now.' The loaf in the middle of the floor began to tell a tale, and was so long telling that when it was finished the time was near morning. 'That tale is very good also,' said the King; 'tell me a third one'. The loaf at the door began and said: 'It is I that will tell you a tale now to rouse your attention. King of the Green Island, your daughter fled last evening with the King's son of Erin. They are far from you now, and you are the man that ought to be following them.'[43]

4. *The protagonist's opponent is a storyteller*
The inner storyteller may function as the protagonist's adversary. In ancient Ireland, the main characters in heroic stories were usually kings or warriors, but professional storytellers were powerful persons with whom they might clash. In the tales of nineteenth- or early-twentieth-century rural Ireland, the occasional

---

42 J. Curtin *Irish Folk-Tales* 20-21. **43** Ibid. 33-4.

storyteller, when he is not the protagonist himself (Section 1 above) is more likely to appear as his helper or neutral informant (Section 3); but the encounter may lead to a contest. It provides the framing device for a series of amazing anecdotes, for instance in the exchange between a farmer and a sea-captain, each boasting of the wonders he has seen, the sea-captain finally admitting that the farmer's tale is more wonderful than his own;[44] or a competition in riddle-posing and -solving (with numerous Irish versions of International Type 851 'The Princess Who Cannot Solve the Riddle'); or a lying contest. The opponent may also be a dangerous liar who misleads the hero.

5. *Storytelling, or a particular story, is considered valuable*
The next category no longer centres on the part the narrator plays in the plot, but is determined by the value attributed to storytelling and its practitioners — a criterion which may cut across those I have used so far: for instance, the tales referred to earlier where storytelling saves lives show it to be eminently useful, and others make lesser claims but at least defend it as a source of pleasure.

To make a long journey seem shorter is a simple functions already mentioned by Chaucer: ' ... That ech of yow, to shorte with your weye,/ In this viage, shal telle tales tweye.' In Irish tales, it may unfold into a full episode, as in one of the adventures of the Gobán Saor (*saor* : craftsman), the fabulous master builder. The origins of this Irish Daedalus have been traced to a member of the Dé Danaan divine tribe, Goibhniu, associated with smithcraft (*gabha*: smith). The episode of the 'shortening of the road' (*an bealach a ghiorrú*) connected with him involves his clever daughter-in-law (or real daughter, according to some versions) and his not-too-bright son (or pseudo-son after a substitution of babies). As usual, the story is impossible to date but was already considered 'ancient' at the beginning of the nineteenth century; one of the first printed transcriptions was published in 1833.[45] Printed texts multiplied from the 1890s, and there are many oral renditions in the Irish Folklore Archives, like these, collected from two generations of Kerry storytellers:

I ... She was about two months in the house when the father said to his daughter-in-law to make two loaves of bread that they were going on a journey, himself and the son for to make a spire far away. The bread was made and she tied it up. There was no trains, no nothing going at that time, they had to tramp it. He had to carry the bread. Well they were about a mile of the road when the father said to the son: 'Shorten the road for me', says the father to the son. 'Twas far away. 'I can't shorten it,' says he, 'shorter than it was made.' Allright, they turned back again in to her, didn't go farther. This day they went on again and they were about a mile away when he asked him to shorten the road. 'I can't shorten it shorter than what it was made,' says this old half-fool. He turned back home again. Very well. Faith the daughter-in-law thought of herself and she said to her-

44 S. Ó Suilleabháin 'Scéalta Cráibtheacha', in *Beáloideas* 21 (1951) 321-2. 45 E.W. 'The Goban Saer', *Dublin Penny Journal* 6 July 1833.

self: 'Well,' says she, 'there must be something in this, to be turning back everyday.' She said to herself that it was something against herself. When they went to bed that night: 'Tell me,' she says to her husband, 'why are ye turnin' back,' she says, 'everyday and coming back home again?' 'I'll tell you', he says. 'We don't be a mile of the road when my father says to me to shorten the road an' sure I couldn't shorten it,' he says, 'shorter than it was made.' 'Is that the way?' she says. ' 'Tis'. 'Well now,' she says, 'when he'll ask you,' she says, 'to shorten the road begin to tell him a nice story, and I'll engage you,' she says, 'he'll carry you on.' Faith 'twas the same story. He told him to shorten the road and he began to tell him some little story and the father said to him after the story being finished: 'Who told you,' he says, 'to tell me the story?' 'My wife,' he says. 'Oh,' says the father, he says, 'she'll do'.[46]

II ... So they were married and some time after the Gobán got a letter from a gentleman in England to go to him building a castle. So away they went. They travelling along the road the father said to the son: 'Why don't you shorten the road for me?' 'Faith,' says the son , 'I couldn't shorten it.' 'Go home from me,' says he, 'I don't want you.' 'What brought you?' says the wife. 'He told me to shorten the road for me,' says he. 'Sure I couldn't shorten any road.' 'Be off now,' says she, 'as hard as ever you can and commence telling stories to him,' says she, 'the lie and the truth,' says she, 'as well as you possibly can because,' says she, 'it is telling stories the road is shortened.'[47]

The anecdote can also be told as a separate apologue, with unnamed characters. *What* story is told is generally not specified, but in a version from County Mayo[48] it is the endless tale of the bird taking grain after grain of corn out of a barn (see p. 528).

The value of a story entitles the teller to some reward but, in a society where it was not a professional activity, just showing one's gratitude might suffice. A short tale, sometimes classified as a religious one and known as 'Pay Me For My Story', of which some two dozen versions are attested, teaches the proper response. It tells how a man, or child, learns to appreciate the gift of a story. Because he does not know how to react, he is successively transformed into various animals, each time for a period of a year, at the end of which he is again asked to give payment and still does not know how to do it. Finally, in bird form and having perched on a chimney, he overhears through it a scene of storytelling, at the end of which someone in the audience blesses the speaker. The next time the instructor demands payment, he gets satisfaction. In some versions of this tale, God's favour may be called upon the souls of the dead, but more often it is on the storyteller himself. Here is a version contributed by a

46 IFC 659: 557-9. Collected in 1939 from Mrs Lane (aged 90) at Finuge, Co. Kerry, by S. Ó Dálaigh. 47 IFC 1169: 80-1. Collected in 1950 from Muiris Seoigh (aged 82) in Co. Kerry, by S. Ó Dálaigh. 48 IFC 1169: 349-51. Collected in 1950 from Doncha Flaherty (aged 70) in Co. Kerry, by S. Ó Dálaigh. The collector asked: 'Whom did you hear that story from?' 'He's a man that was over a hundred years. The man I heard that story from had a book called "The Arabian Knights".' (I failed to find exactly the same sequence in the *Arabian*

child in the Irish School-Collection of 1938, which shows that the lesson was taught early:

Once upon a time there lived a little boy who was very inquisitive. One day, he met an old man, and he asked him if he had heard strange news. 'Well,' said the man, 'if you will come along the road with me, I have a very strange story to tell you.' Of course the boy went immediately. When the man had finished the story, he said, 'now give me the price of my story'. The boy did not know what to give, so the man changed him into a hawk for a year and a day. When the time was up, the man came and asked him for the price of his story. The boy did not know what to give him, so he was changed into a hawk for another year and a day. The same thing happened at the end of the second year. The last year was nearly over. The last day was raining and there was a great gale blowing. So the poor hawk was very miserable. He took refuge in a chimney. There was a great many people gathered around the fire telling stories. A man was just finishing a story when the hawk came. When he finished, he asked for the price of his story. Immediately, all the people said, 'God be merciful to your seven generations.' So the next day when the man asked for the price of his story, the boy said, 'God be merciful to your seven generations.' 'Well,' said the man, 'If you did not know it today, you would be a hawk forever.' So he changed the hawk back into his human form.[49]

Other versions are more elaborate. With Paddy Sherlock, for instance, a man has asked for three stories, has undergone several transformations, when he is at the top of a chimney, as a pigeon, this is what he overhears:

There were two or three girls sittin' by the fire. One says to the other: 'Tell us a story.' The girl told the story. 'Pay me now for my story!' said the girl. 'Tell another an' you'll be paid for the two.' She told the second story. 'Pay me now for my two stories!' 'Tell the third an' you'll be paid for the three!' So she told the third story. 'Pay me now for my three stories!' The one sittin' at the fire said: 'The Lord have mercy on the souls that left you!' The pigeon was listenin' to that. In the end o' the year the man sounded his whistle an' the little pigeon approached towards him. He tipped the pigeon wi' the rod an' turned him back into the fine young man. 'Pay me now,' says he, 'for my three stories!' The man said: 'The Lord have mercy on the souls that left you!' 'Why didn't you tell me that before,' says he,'an' you'd be all right.'[50]

A Galway storyteller introduced the tale with the question 'Do you know the proper way to bless a story?'; in Kerry, another commented on the blessing formula 'that should be said whenever someone tells a story'.[51] To try and educate a particularly uncouth audience, the storyteller could turn to this shorter anecdote:

Nights.) **49** IFC S 650: 376-7. Written down by Eibhlís Ní hAodha, Kilmeadan school, Co. Waterford, and reproduced, with a study of this tale-type, in Barbara Hillers and Críostóir Mac Cárthaigh 'Pay Me For My Story: The Etiquette of Storytelling', *Sinsear* 6 (1990) 50. **50** *Béaloideas* 5 (1935) 24-5. **51** Quoted by B. Hillers and C. Mac Cárthaigh in *Sinsear* 6. 51

There used to be an ould man here in Bóthar na Trá and he used to be telling stories long ago and he was at a wake one night and he was telling a story and there was nobody listening to him and nobody thanked him when the story was said but they heard a voice to say in the chimney, *Faid saoil chugat a Fhiannaí* [Long life to the storyteller!]. All the people wondered who spoke when they heard the voice say it three times.[52]

Another evidence of the possibility of associating storytelling and the numinous appears in the belief that the devil would avoid houses where storytelling was going on – a notion also attested in Rumania.[53]

In tales, telling stories may bring material rewards. In very free Irish oiko-types of AT1525: The Master Thief, Aristotle's brother has three sons. Each of them must learn one more thing from the great scholar, in order to excel in a profitable profession. One has chosen to become a storyteller, and in a version collected by Douglas Hyde at Kilmacduagh, Co. Galway, he introduces himself to 'Harraidh' (Aristotle) as 'a teller of tales and historical stories in the evening' (*fear-innseacht-sgeulta, fear seanchais ann san oidche mé*), still looking for the answer to the question who should be the first to narrate in an evening session (cf. p. 461). The scholar's answer is: 'When entering a house, if you see that the master is weak, dark and bending his head, it is for you, the stranger, to start ... But when entering a house, if you see that the master feels like talking, don't cut him short – let him speak.'[54] By the end of the story, the young man's skill and good manners have made him gain a kingdom.

If certain stories or modes of telling and receiving them can chase evil away, others, or perhaps the same, can be denounced as sinful: a corollary of the power of storytelling is the risk one may incur. The danger for the listener is illustrated in the tale of the king to whom it has been prophesied that he will not die as long as no son of his tells him a story; he has all his wives killed before they get pregnant, until the eighteenth secretly bears him a son. Not knowing who the boy is, the king sends him in search of a story. When the boy returns and gives an account of his journey through the Otherworld, the king falls dead, or is crushed by a falling tree.[55]

Talebearers who spread gossip, and informers, are detested; and indiscreet prattle may turn against the speaker himself, as in gruesome Irish versions of 'The King of the Cats': when a man who has killed a monstrous cat goes home and boasts of this exploit in the presence of his own cat, the animal leaps at his throat.[56] In other tales, a fairy-wife or supernatural gifts are lost by telling how

and 55. **52** IFC 259: 635. Collected in 1936 from Sean Moylan (aged 35) in Dungarvan Co. Waterford, by Nioclás Breathnach. **53** O. Bîrlea 'La fonction de raconter dans le folklore roumain', *Laographia* 22 (1965), 25: 'On recommendait dans les habitations isolées – surtout dans les cabanes de bergers – de raconter chaque soir trois contes qui se donnent la main et entourent la bergerie que tu habites et le diable ne peut s'approcher, l'on peut dormir sans être troublé.' **54** *An Sgéaluidhe Gaedhéalach* 490-1, 492-5. **55** S. Ó Súilleabháin *A Handbook of Irish Folklore* 564. **56** Many versions of AT113A are listed in O'Sullivan-Christiansen *The Types of the Irish Folktale* 45-6. See also E.R. Ó Néill 'The King of the Cats. ML 6070B', in

they were acquired: 'Do not let anyone know that you have such a one as me in your house', said the wife to her human husband. But 'he told his brother how she had come and everything about her' He thus lost her for a time, then definitively when he told the story again.[57] A storyteller must know what or what not to tell in given circumstances.

If storytelling is necessary in social life, indeed sometimes a way of saving one's head, and if storytellers are important people (whose task is difficult and even risky), tales themselves are valuable when their hidden meaning is revealed. This is suggested by a peculiar motif in ancient Irish texts and more recent tales: there exists a 'Unique Story', which the hero must find (perhaps along with other marvels, like the 'Sword of Light'). It would solve a mystery, and is called in Irish *fios fátha an doimhin scéil* (knowledge of the cause of the profound tale), or *fios fátha an aoin scéil* (knowledge of the cause of the unique tale). The search for it may be a binding obligation (*geis*): 'They played with the gruagach [enchanter]'s dice, and Art lost. "Give your sentence", said he to the gruagach. "You will hear it too soon for your comfort. You are to bring me the sword of light, and the story of the man who has it" '; or, 'The magician had placed a judgment on Art not to sleep two nights in the same bed or eat two meals at the same table until he would bring him the Truth of the One Story and the Sword of Light. [Art finds the man, or god, who knows it:] When the feast was over, Balor said to Art, "Now I'll tell you the Truth of the One Story ... " '; or, ' "I put you under *geasa* of heavy magic not to sleep for two nights in the same bed nor to eat two meals at the same table until you bring me the knowledge of the Only Story and the Dúdán's sword!" "Very well," said the King of Ireland's Son.' When he has found the sword, he uses it to force a wizard to reveal the secret: ' "I will cut off your head at once unless you tell me the knowledge of the Only Story!" "Well," said the wizard, "I will tell you the knowledge of the Only Story to the end ... " '[58] In the perplexing Grail legend, the quest is not just for an object but also for some explanation of its origin and power; when the explanation is found in the Irish stories referred to here, it tends to be the account of magic transformations.

6. To become the hero of a story is the highest reward
Unlike the others, this possibility attested in ancient Irish narratives is not exploited in the tales collected in the last two centuries. A simple explanation would be that it belongs to the reality or ideal of an heroic age, where honour and fame are considered the greatest goods. But although it vanished from popular fantasy, this theme, partly because it had been rediscovered in ancient literature towards the end of the nineteenth century and partly because it ties in naturally with definitions of heroism, became one of the basic precepts of Irish

Béaloideas 59 (1991) 167-87. **57** *Siscéalta Ó Thír Chonaill* 293-9. **58** Jeremiah Curtin *Hero-Tales of Ireland* 325; Sean O'Sullivan *Folktales of Ireland* 109, 114; Myles Dillon *There was a King in Ireland* 82-90.

Republicanism: to die for the cause will make you join the long line of heroes celebrated in ballads.

No doubt the references to storytelling I have quoted vary in significance; very few of those motifs – none, perhaps – exist only in Ireland, and there are no statistics proving without doubt that Irish storytellers used them much more often than their colleagues in other countries. But at least it is possible to conclude that, beyond what we expect to find anywhere as a convenience for organizing narration, certain tales or themes emphasizing the importance of storytelling transactions were quite popular in Ireland. The group of stories I shall analyse in the remainder of this chapter should suffice to confirm the tendency to foreground narrating acts.

B. ON NOT BEING ABLE TO TELL A STORY

Everyone is likely to have experienced the predicament of drying up when expected to speak. The opinion that a person who is unable to tell stories is not an estimable member of the community can be expressed crudely: *is cuma nó muc fear gan sceal* (a man without a story is of no more account than a pig). But if an artist's inspiration flags, he can use dejection over the failure of his powers as his theme; or he can feign incapacity to enhance the value of his contribution when it is finally coaxed out of him.

In a very popular set of Irish tales, the protagonist does not know any story, or enough stories, and acquires one through some strange experiences. It appears as number 2412B in Ó Súilleabháin's and Christiansen's *Types of the Irish Folktale* ('The Man Who Had No Story'); Bo Almqvist prefers to call it a common 'frame' or a structural device,[59] but it seems possible to combine the classifying terms. There is a plot, with two constituents: (A) having no story to tell, and (B) learning one the hard way. The nature of the first element, more particularly the status of its protagonist, determines two basic types or groups of stories. In both, the initial situation reappears, but reversed, at the end (A'). (A) and (A') frame (B), and the fantastic moment embedded between two 'realistic' ones offers the possibility of narrating sensational events.[60] The first part (A – 'having no story') may appear independently and is not necessarily exploited as being decisive: it may remain a kind of unopened door, while the story develops in another direction; but one may suffer consequences because of the non-act; it may also lead to the non-verbal message towards the end of many variants of The Girl as Helper in the Hero's Flight (AT 313), with motif D2006.1.3 Forgotten fiancée reawakens husband's memory (see p. 524).

---

59 Notes to a Donegal version of *An fear nach rabh sceal ar bith aige*, in *Béaloideas* 37-8 (1969-70) 60. 60 Such series of 'fantastic experiences or dream sequences' are also the central part of what Ó Súilleabháin and Christiansen define as Type 2412A. 'Who Has Seen the Greatest Wonder?' (see above, p. 522).

What distinguishes the two groups of tales founded on the full three-part plot scheme (A - B - A') is that one of them concerns a professional storyteller who has too limited a repertoire and is therefore in danger of losing status – perhaps his head too (I shall call it Group 1), while the other set (Group 2), much more widely represented in twentieth-century collections, and often in Irish,[61] concerns an ordinary person, sometimes a child, who has never been able to tell stories and must acquire at least one, generally during a journey (a way of gathering interesting experience and also of having to pay for hospitality). The central section of both types or groups of tales consists of wonderful or gruesome scenes. More than a hundred versions of this pair have been collected in Ireland, and they have occasionally appeared in Scotland.[62] The argument may be analyzed as follows:

1. The professional storyteller's failure	*2. A naive person must become a storyteller*
1.A.1. The king's (or some rich man's) storyteller must produce a new story every night.	2.A.1. A man (boy) or woman (girl) is walking at night, gets lost, and arrives at an isolated house.
1.A.2. One morning, he realizes that he is unable to find a new one for the next performance.	2.A.2. He/she is offered hospitality, and asked to repay it with a story, which he/she is unable to do.
1.A.3. He sets off for a walk (with his wife).	2.A.3.1. He/she is or 2.A.3.2. He/she is expelled. allowed to stay, and falls asleep.
1.B.1. He meets an old man, who proposes a card game and wins everything, including the wife and the storyteller himself, who is transformed into a hare and subjected to strange experiences.	2.B.1. He/she has extraordinary experiences.
1.B.2. Then he is restored to human shape.	2.B.2. He/she returns to the house and reports what has happened.
1.A'. He now has a new story – and it is so good that the king will never ask for another.	2.A'.1. He/she is told that from now on he/she will always have something to narrate.
	2.A'.2. When he/she wakes up the next morning, the house has vanished.

61 The story is then known as *An fear gan scéal*, or *An fear ná raibh scéal aige*, and *Bean gan scéal* when the protagonist is a woman. **62** What was defined above as part A of the plot appears in J.F. Campbell *Popular Tales of the West Highlands* 2.33. The A-B-A' plot is given in Angus MacLellan's *Stories from South Uist*, and there are manuscript versions in the collections of the School of Scottish Studies, Edinburgh: see the version including a sex-change in N. Philip *The Penguin Book of Scottish Folktales* 55-9. A version has been collected among descendants of Irish emigrants in Newfoundland: see C.J. Byrne and M. Harry (eds) *Talamh an Eisc: Canadian and Irish Essays* 223-4.

What happens in the (B) section of both groups of tales is a set of wild motifs, including international elements: for Group 1: D117.2 Man transformed into hare, and D1852 Climbing into air on a magic rope, etc.; for Group 2: E422 The living corpse, E491.1 Phantom funeral procession, F990 Inanimate objects act as if living, H1400 Fear test, N762 Person accidentally met unexpectedly knows the other's name, S112.6 Roasting man alive, X422 The corpse with his feet cut off or G313 Shortening the legs of a live person, etc. The bawdy motif of the guest tricked into entering the bed of the host's wife is sometimes used.

As is the case with many folktales, there is little hope of solving the problem of convergence or filiation – in other words the question whether similar stories developed independently or derived from one base. A storyteller's real or pretended incapacity to perform, as in Group 1, is a situation that may arise everywhere. The *Povre Clerc* of a thirteenth-century French fabliau is invited by his host to tell a story, pretends that *il ne sait de fables*, but tells of the real fear he has just experienced – a way of denouncing the infidelity of the host's wife.[63] The starting point of Group 1 may also evoke Scheherazade's predicament; but a more obvious affinity is with one of the transitions to an inner tale in the *Arabian Nights*: a king has heard all the tales of Araby, Persia and India, and his storyteller, whose repertoire has been stretched to the limit, must find a new story on pain of death; he sends his servants in search of the most beautiful story, and one of them brings it back.[64] As far as I know, the story did not appear in chapbooks and is therefore not likely to have entered Irish oral tradition in this way. Anthony Hamilton (1646-1720), who was probably born at Roscrea County Tipperary and was made governor of Limerick by James II, whom he then followed to France, is said to have used various tale motifs he may have 'heard in his youth in Ireland'.[65] In his posthumously published mock addition to the *Arabian Nights*: *Histoire de Fleur d'Epine*, by the thousandth night, Scheherazade's energy and repertoire are exhausted and she is on the point of becoming a storyteller without a story or without an audience – and soon without a head. Her sister Dinarzade does not mince her words before successfully replacing her (using the trick of forced interruption illustrated above on p. 527):

'Je vous vois à la fin de votre Recueil, et par conséquent, bientôt à la fin de vos jours. L'histoire que vous venez de lui conter est si misérable qu'il n'a fait que bailler, et moi

63 W. Noomen and N. Van Den Boogaard *Nouveau Recueil Complet des Fabliaux* 7. 263. The story has survived as a French folktale connected with AT 1358C: A trickster surprises an adulteress and her lover, and, while saying he is unable to tell tales, informs on them. 64 This particular tale is not in Galland, but appears in later translations of the Bulaq and Calcutta versions: 'How King Mohammed Ibn Sabaïk forced the merchant Hasan to get the story of Prince Saif el-Muluk and the Princess Badi' Al-Jamal'. See R. Burton's *Book of the Thousand Nights and a Night* (Vol. 6, pp. 95ff in the edition of 1894). 65 P. Delarue *Le conte populaire français* 1. 341 (but this Irish link is only hypothetical).

aussi, pendant ce long récit. Ma patience à vous tenir compagnie depuis si longtemps est une preuve suffisante de ma tendresse; mais je n'en puis plus, & vous trouverez bien, s'il vous plaît, que je m'absente cette nuit ... [But she has a plan for the following night – which will be the last one.] Dès que le Sultan se sera mis au lit, avant que de vous y mettre, jettez-vous à deux genoux ; feignez quelque subite indisposition, & conjurez bien humblement ce vilain bourreau de trouver bon que je l'entretienne pour la dernière fois au lieu de vous; dites-lui bien que c'est pour la dernière fois, puisque vous ne demandez grace qu'à la condition que si l'Histoire que je lui conterai n'est plus extraordinaire que toutes celles que vous lui avez faites; il n'aura qu'à vous étrangler dès le lendemain, mais aussi, qu'il vous donnera la vie en cas qu'il m'interrompe avant la fin de mon récit ... '[66]

As for the starting point of Group 2 (never having been able to narrate), it may be seen just as a particular case of the slow-witted or tongue-tied person who miraculously becomes eloquent, like Moses (Ex 4.10), Jeremiah (Jer 1.6-9), Caedmon, etc. Another ingredient, the idea that hospitality should be repaid with stories, is not exclusive to Ireland either: in Italy an informant remembered that travelling people were received on this condition: 'If you can tell us a story you may stay; if not, off with you'.[67] In an Eskimo story collected in North Alaska, a young man must always leave the *karigi* (the place where the community meets) because he cannot take his turn at telling stories; his uncle gives him a piece of wood with which he sees narratable things, and from then on he is a great success in the *karigi*.[68] The second story pattern may well have been independently and orally devised in Ireland; perhaps the first one was, too, but it seems less probable.

As far as I know, the pattern concerning a professional storyteller appeared for the first time in Anglo-Irish writing in 1842, in Gerald Griffin's *Tales of the Jury Room* (see p. 250).[69] Relatively few versions of this story-pattern have been collected from oral tradition in the twentieth century. Here is a short one from County Clare:

There was a gentleman in Ireland one time and he had one only daughter and she was a very beautiful girl. He'd give the daughter in marriage to no one except to someone who could tell him a fresh story every night in the year for twelve months. Anyone who failed even for one night his head went on the spire, and there were series of heads on the spires. One young man ventured, and had a fresh story every night in the year except

---

66 *Oeuvres du Comte d'Hamilton* Utrecht 1731, 2. 2-3: Dinarzade tells a tale that forces the Sultan to interrupt her, and then, as promised, he pardons his wife. I shall not try to list all occurrences of the 'storyteller at fault' theme in literature, but Salman Rushdie's *Haroun and the Sea of Stories* is worth mentioning as one of the most recent, with Eastern connections. 67 Marino Anesa and Mario Rondi *Fiabe bergamasche* 33. 68 E.S. Hall *The Eskimo Storyteller: Folktales from Noatak, Alaska* 254ff. 69 *Talis Qualis; or Tales of the Jury Room* 74-6, 97-8. The text, partly rewritten from Griffith's version and combined with elements borrowed from a Scottish tale, appeared with the title 'The Story-teller at Fault' in Joseph Jacobs *Celtic Fairy Tales* (1892).

the last night. The day before that he was abroad in the yard and he looking up at the spire, and he very gloomy looking. That day he did not come into his dinner at all. The gentleman's daughter went out. 'Come in to your dinner' says she. 'I won't' says he. 'I can eat nothing. It is short until my head be on yonder spire!' 'What is on you?' says she. 'I had a fresh story for your father every night in the year' says he, 'but I have no fresh story to-night, and my head is to go on the spire!' 'Never mind' says she. 'Take courage, and we'll have a fresh story before night. We'll tackle the horses' says she 'and we'll go out, and we'll see something that will make a fresh story about.' They tackled the horses and off they went, and they having two hounds for a bit of a hunt. They went off out on a wild mountain, and they thought they saw a bulk on the top of a rock. They pulled up, and there they saw a little grey man sitting on the top of a rock, and he shuffling a deck of cards. 'Muise welcome Jack' says the little grey man, 'and 'tis many a day I am waiting for you to come the way! Will you play a game of cards Jack?' 'I have no money,' says Jack. 'I'll stake one hundred pounds for you' says the young lady. So they played and the little grey man won. 'Play again Jack' says he. 'I have no money' says Jack. The young lady laid down another hundred pounds and the little grey man won. 'Play again Jack' says he. 'I have no money' says Jack. The young lady had no more money to lay down. 'I'll put two hundred pounds against your horse, hounds, and carriage' says the little grey man. 'But how could I go home then?' says Jack. 'Chance it' says the young lady,' and maybe you might win.' He did. The little grey man won. 'Play again' says the little grey man. 'I have nothing at all now' says Jack. 'I'll put all the money, horses, hounds and all against your wife,' said the little grey man. 'I'd be killed if I went home without her' says Jack. 'You chance it' says she. He did. The little grey man won her, and she went and stood by his side. 'Play again' says the little grey man. 'I have nothing at all, at all, now' says Jack. 'Put yourself against all' says the little grey man. ' 'Tis all a case now' says Jack, 'and I might as well chance it.' He did. The little grey man won Jack.

'Now' says the little grey man 'I can turn you into anything I like – a fox, a hare, or a deer? 'Well if he turns you into a fox' says the young lady, 'you will be always roguing and stealing geese, and if you're a deer your horns will get caught in the wood. Be a hare!' The little grey man pulled out his handkerchief, and shook it, and turned Jack into a hare. The two hounds were there. The little grey man let him off and the two hounds at his heels. Off he goes and the hounds after him, and when they had him nearly killed he faced the young lady until she'd save him. She gave him a kick and off he goes again, and the hounds at his heels, and this time when the hunt was too tight on his heels he faced the little grey man, and the little grey man took him up in his arms and saved him. The very minute he did, he turned him into his own shape and form and he became Jack again. The little grey man then gave him the money, lady, horses, grey hounds and all. 'Go home now' says he 'and you'll have a fresh story for the king.'

He went home, himself and the young lady, and he told the king the best story he ever heard in his life. So they got married, and they had two sons and a daughter and that is my story.[70]

The earliest comment on Group 2 (a tongue-tied innocent is socialized the

70 IFC 707: 10-16. Collected in 1939 by Seán O Flannagáin, from Jamesy Brody (aged *c*.80) at Feakle.

hard way) appeared in 1828 in the second part of T. Crofton Croker's *Fairy Legends and Traditions of the South of Ireland*, after the tale 'Ned Sheehy's Excuse':

Several versions of this whimsical adventure are current in Ireland: one, which was noted down many years since, from the writer's nurse, is given as a proof how faithfully the main incidents in these tales are orally circulated and preserved. The heroine is Joan Coleman of Kinsale, who, after being driven out from an enchanted house, for having no story to tell, when called upon by an invisible speaker to do so, finds herself in a dark wood. Here she discovers a very old man, with a long beard, roasting another man as old as himself on a spit before a great fire. When the old man, who was turning the spit, saw Joan, he welcomed her, and expressed his joy at seeing his gossip's daughter, Joan Coleman of Kinsale. Joan was much frightened; but he welcomed her so kindly, and told her to sit down to the fire in so friendly a manner, that she was somewhat assured, and complied with the invitation. He then handed her the spit to turn, and gave her the strictest charge not to allow a brown or a burned spot on the old man who was roasting until he came back; and with these directions left her. It happened to be rather a windy night, and Joan had not turned the spit long before a spark flew into the beard of the roasting old man, and the wind blowing that way it was speedily on fire. Joan, when she saw what had happened, was much troubled, and ran away as fast as possible. When the old fellow felt his beard on fire, he called out to Joan, in a great passion, to come back, and not to allow him to be burned up to a cinder. Joan only ran the faster; and he, without ever getting off the spit, raced after her, with his beard all in flames, to know why, after the orders she had received, he was treated in that manner.

Joan rushed into a house, which happened to be the very same that she had been turned out of for want of a story to tell. When she went in, Joan Coleman was welcomed by the same voice which had directed her to be turned out. She was desired to come to the fire, and pitied much, and a bed was ordered to be made for her. After she had lain down for some time the voice asked her if she had now a story to tell? Joan answered that she had; having 'a fright in her heart,' from what had happened to her since she left, and without more words related her own adventure. 'Very well,' said the voice, 'if you had told the same story when you were asked before, you would have had your comfortable lodging and your good night's rest by this time. I am sorry, Joan, that I was obliged to turn you out, that you might have something to tell me, for Father Red Cap never gives a bed without being paid for it by a story.' When Joan awoke next day at the crowing of the cock, she found herself lying on a little bank of rushes and green moss, with her bundle under her head for a pillow.[71]

This early summary includes the basic ingredients: the obligation to entertain when offered hospitality, the macabre element – the turning of the spit is only one of the possible ordeals in this set of stories – and the return to waking activities. Before his comment, Crofton Croker gave his own version of the tale

---

71 *Fairy Legends and Traditions* 292-3. *Far Darrig* or *Fir Dhearga* (the Red man) is a red-clad fairy who specializes in practical jokes. He appears in L. McClintock's version mentioned later in this chapter.

(using material collected by R. Adolphus Lynch of Killarney): a servant, scolded for having been out all night, alleges that a dead man gave him night's lodging; a voice coming from a cupboard asked: 'Have you any news [*scéal*: news or story ...] for me, Ned Sheehy?' As he had none, he was expelled, forced to turn a man on a spit, and pursued back to the mysterious house where he had something to say at last, and heard this comment: ' "If you had told me this before, you would not have been turned out in the cold," said the voice'.[72]

A rambling anonymous version, said to have been heard in Munster, appeared in 1833 in the *Irish Penny Magazine* and was reissued in 1841 and 1866. It is introduced as voiced by a travelling man who, unlike his character, has stories to offer in exchange for hospitality.[73] Another wordy nineteenth-century magazine version appeared one year later. It also starts with the description of a storytelling scene and continues with the 'no story' adventure. Here, the imitation of the vernacular smacks of caricature, perhaps aimed at country 'culchies' — the text appeared in a Dublin comic paper – but also parodying the new 'literary' taste for pseudo folk-speech.[74] These lengthy written compositions confirm that already in the first half of the nineteenth century the tale in question was associated with 'typical' Irish storytelling. In the version from County Wexford published by Patrick Kennedy in 1866, the link with oral tradition is already closer. As in the *Salmagundi* version, the teller is supposed to be the protagonist:

The narrator of the following travelling sketch was a half-witted woman, who, although she had heard it from someone else, was under the impression that she had undergone part of the adventures in some form or other. She was a very honest, inoffensive creature, and would do any work assigned to her carefully enough; but she had a certain district of the country under her supervision, and it was essential to her well-being that she should perambulate (*serenade* was her term) this portion about once in the year. She went by the name of Cauth (Catherine) Morrisy, and this is the style in which she related her juvenile experience:

'Well, neighbours, when I was a *thuckeen* (young girl) about fifteen years of age, and it was time to be doing something for myself, I set off one fine day of spring along the yella high-road; and if anybody axed me where I was goin' I'd make a joke about it, and say I was goin' out of Ireland to live in the Roer [a district in Kilkenny]. ... [While looking for a lodging, she was chased out of a first house after setting fire to the thatch, ran from the second place where a sheepstealer wanted to kill her, and reached a third house where she was given food and shelter by an old man, who asked for a story.] ... "Musha, an the dickens a story meself has," says I. ... [As in the *Salmagundi* version, she must help carry a coffin; the corpse makes her open the lid and offers to play cards with her; she escapes, and returns to the old man.] ... "Ah, is that you, my little colleen? I thought you were asleep. Maybe you have a story for me now." "Indeed an' I have, sir," says I, an' I told him all that happen me since I saw him last. "You suffered a good deal," says

72 Op. cit. 290. 73 'The Beggarman's Tale', in *Dublin Penny Journal* 15 June 1833, 406ff. 74 'A Fairy Legend', *The True & Original Salmagundi* 27 Sept. 1834.

he. "If you told me that story before, all your trouble 'd be spared to you." "But how could I tell it, sir," says I, "before it happened?" "That's true," says he, and he began to scratch his wig. I was getting drowsy, and I didn't remember anything more till I woke next morning in the dry gripe of the ditch with a *bochyeen* (dried cow-dung) under my head. So –

There was a tree at the end of the house and it was bending, bending,
And my story is ending, ending.' [75]

A Donegal version, published in 1877 by Letitia McClintock, combines the spit and coffin elements. A tinker, in Inishowen, cannot find a night's lodging: 'none but them that can tell a story will get in here'. Hiding in a barn, he witnesses the roasting act, in which he is forced to participate; then he must help carry the coffin[76] and dig a grave, but is rescued by the cock's crow.[77] Printed versions multiplied in the twentieth century: Seumas MacManus produced the story, with minor variants, in several of his books, and other versions often appeared in the very popular periodical *Ireland's Own*.[78]

Twentieth-century direct transcriptions from oral performances abound. In the Irish Folklore Archives, versions in Irish of the second group of stories are four times more numerous than those collected in English. A survey of these texts[79] tried to identify regional traits, placing the 'man-roasting' episode in the South and the 'coffin-carrying' motif in the West, while the protagonist's involvement in a wake and the shortening of a corpse's leg would be associated with Donegal. Supernatural elements may be stronger in the North. The author of the survey prefers to call the piece a 'folk legend' rather than a 'folktale' because of the precise (though varying) localization of the framing part, the naming of the central character (who has as many identities as there are versions), and other 'realistic' details. This argument is relativized by the fact that, like early Irish narratives which were characterized by their high rate of personal names and place names, later wonder tales in Ireland, including some international types, may introduce such particulars. The fact, noted by Bo Almqvist,[80] that motifs associated with migratory legends are numerous in the central fantastic sequence would carry more weight; on the other hand it seems to me that the question of credibility, or the possibility of debate which according to some legend scholars would define the genre, is less important here than the presence

75 *Legendary Fiction of the Irish Celts* 141-5. 76 To meddle with a 'fairy funeral' was to court disaster: you might be forced to carry the shrouded corpse or the coffin on your back. 77 'Folk Lore of the County Donegal', in *The Dublin University Magazine* 89 (1877) 244-5. Yeats, who reproduced this text in *Fairies and Folk Tales of the Irish Peasantry*, gave another version heard at Rosses Point in *The Celtic Twilight* (*Mythologies* 90-2) with the corpse-roasting motif. 78 S. Mac Manus: *Bold Blades of Donegal*, *Heavy Hangs the Golden Grain*, and *The Bold Horses of Hungry Hill*. In *Ireland's Own*: 'Brian Roe, the Cow Doctor' by Richard Mahoney, 22 April 1908; 'Going to the Fair, An Old Meath Tale' by Miss M. Hanrahan, 3 Aug. 1935, etc. 79 Criostóir Mac Cárthaigh 'The Man Who Had No Story', *Sinsear* 2 (1980) 115-21. 80 *Béaloideas* 37-8 (1969-70) 60.

of an organized plot with a web of causation, the management of suspense and surprise, the sense of an ending – and the theme of storytelling.

A fine version in Irish was collected by Séamas Ó Catháin from Michael James Timoney at Fintown (Donegal) in 1965, published, translated and analysed in *Béaloideas* in 1969, with comments which tend to confirm the 'tale' quality: 'The story-teller himself considered The Man Who Had No Story to be one of the best tales he had ever heard. He told it with great gusto and with every appearance of enjoying himself. He had good reason to be proud, too, because although a great many versions of this tale have been collected, I think I can vouch for the fact that none is so perfectly balanced, and none conveys the sophisticated mixture of humour and horror, as well as his.'[81] In this version, a basket maker gets lost at night and finds a house where he must confess he is unable to tell a tale. Sent out to fetch a bucket of water, he is swept off by a big blast of wind, and reaches another house where a wake is in progress. He is forced to play the fiddle, say mass, shorten the legs of the corpse – things he has never done before, like storytelling. Then he must help carry the coffin to the graveyard. Another blast of wind sends him back to the first house, where he can say: 'I am the man who has got a story to tell (*Is mise an fear a bhfuil an scéal agam le hinnse*)'. The next morning, he awakes near home.

Here is a version from oral tradition in English collected in County Limerick. It exemplifies the strong local colouring and factual precision leading to, and contrasting with, the fantastic sequence:

There was a horse trainer there long ago by the name of Micín Murphy. He used to be training horses for a gentleman near Kilmeedy. He was sent to the Munster Fair of Limerick, and the night before he stopped at Fortetna near Patrickswell, in another gentleman's place. Two of the boys at Fortetna took Micín with them for a drink. By all accounts the three of them drank their enough. They then went torching birds to Greenmount (near Patrickswell). The night was very dark, stormy and wild. The light they had got quenched in the wood, so the other two boys wanted to play a trick on Micín and they left him in the wood. So he was trying to make his way through the wood; he saw a light, and he thought it was on the Railway line, where a stream used to cross the road. To his surprise, he saw a little house near the stream so he went in. He saw an old man sitting in the corner beside a nice cosy fire. The old man asked Micín if he came far. So Micín told him where he was from, and how he went astray. Then the little man persuaded Micín to stay with himself that night. 'Now my good man' said the little man, maybe Mr White would shoot you if he sees you around this place this hour of night.' Glad Micín was to get an invitation to stay with the old man. After a little

---

81 Bo Almqvist's note to 'An Fear Nach Rabh Scéal Ar Bith Aige', *Béaloideas* 37-8 (1969-70) 59-60. The translation is also available in S. Ó Catháin's *Bedside Book of Irish Folklore*. Other notable printed versions from oral tradition: Sean O'Sullivan *Folktales of Ireland* 182-4 (roasting motif: collected in Irish in County Cork); Kevin Danaher *Folktales of the Irish Countryside* 13- 15 (coffin motif: collected in English in County Limerick); *Béaloideas* 2 (1929-30) 52-3 (roasting motif: collected in Irish in County Kerry).

while the little man asked him if he had any story to tell. Micín said 'No the devil a one'. 'Muise 'tis time for us to go to bed so,' said the old man. 'Go out there to the stack Micín' said he 'and bring in a sop of straw for your bed.' So out with him, he caught the straw, and the stack made a jump away from him. So he tried it again, and this time he caught the straw so firm, that when the stack jumped, he was thrown in the yard. The next thing Micín did was to make for the old man's house. He couldn't find a door or a window to get in. He was trembling with fear.

Poor Micín ran away until he came to a big tree in the lawn. So he climbed up on the branches to stay there until morning. Micín wasn't too long there, when three men came the way and made down a fire underneath the tree. There they commenced to roast some meat. One of them said that he should go for bread. He went. The other said he should go for salt, he went. The third one looked upon the tree; he saw Micín above. He told him to come down. Micín got afraid of him. The second time he told Micín to come at once or he'd make him. The third time that he called him, Micín started to come. When Micín came down from the tree and was landed in the ground, he gave him a little rod to stir a piece of meat that was on the fire. 'Mind that Micín' said he, 'or if it will burn you'll replace it.' Micín began to twist and turn the meat. When he looked around him, suddenly didn't the fire disappear. Away Micín ran as fast as he could. So the light appeared to him again, and he made towards it. He went in again – to the house, and he saw he old man inside before him. The old man asked Micín where he was and he told him all that happened to him. 'Well now Micín my good man' said he 'wherever you'll go again you'll have a story to tell. Now you can go to bed.' In Micín went, he was so tired and worn out that he fell asleep before long.

When poor Micín woke the following morning, he found himself lying outside in the corner of Mr White's lawn, and a few stones under his head.[82]

In an unusual version, still from County Limerick, the fantastic middle section is eclipsed as the protagonist enters a state of non-life, but a lengthened final section introduces the ancient and still popular theme of temporal distortion: it seems that only a few minutes or hours have been spent in the otherworld, but in 'reality' years have elapsed.[83] When the man returns home, he is believed to be dead:

... Daniel when he recovered as it were off of the trance or dream he was in, when he saw where he was he did not know where it was and he made for home.

He was walking up for a long time till he come to some place he knew. 'Well,' said he, 'I'm on the road for home now.' So he came on and when he came in to his own farm it was a Sunday morning and he saw the people going to Mass as usual. He made for his own house and yard and they were all gone to Mass, the door was bolted. So he went off then and went for Mass and when he got into the chapel-yard there were some

82 IFC 279: 74-7. Collected *c*.1935 from Concubhair Ó Cadhla, at Kilmeedy, Co. Limerick, by Máire Ní Chadhla. 83 A contrary distortion takes place in the Hebridean versions: a boat without oars or sails takes the man to Donegal; he gets married and spends four years there; when taken back to Mull, he finds that no time has elapsed and the party is still waiting for his story.

as usual kneeling outside the door at each side and when they see Daniel coming on, the report was of course that he was dead for a year. They got up and they ran wit' fright ... So there and then the priest told him what was after occurring that he had prayed for him as being dead a year or up to it ago. So Daniel told him all the story as it was ... Daniel went home along with the family and if they don't live happy that we may and if they don't be drinking coffee that we may be drinking tea and that's my story. I heard that story from my father may the Lord have mercy on his soul about forty years ago. About fifty. I often heard him telling it.[84]

Long-winded or concise, skilfully told or awkwardly put across, independent or incorporated into composite stories, framing one or several prodigies which can be more or less awful or grotesque, this tale, pair of tale-types, or convenient formula is intriguing. Whereas many of the motifs it combines are known separately elsewhere, their fusion and relative prevalence in one country calls for some explanation. What made such stories successful, and why was the second pattern in particular so popular? A simple answer would be that what is said to happen on the literal level entertained audiences and that occasional storytellers found it easy to handle; but is that all? The fact that it was generally treated as comic[85] should not preclude a search for something serious below the surface. On the other hand, attempts to find deeper significances may run wild. In any case one story may mean little or much, and different things, depending on the circumstances in which it is told (an ordinary joke session or a funeral wake for instance) and the personality and state of mind of each listener. No doubt it exploited the common fear of having to speak in public, and played on the embarrassment of those in an audience who might secretly be afraid of being asked to perform ('More than once, when I have asked for stories in Ireland, I have received the answer: "I don't know any, unless it would be The Man Who Had No Story"').[86] At a primary level of signification, the reference to the laws of hospitality and reciprocity is obvious: a society functions properly as long as its members give and repay. The receiver of hospitality, for instance, should respond by some gesture, and a narrative can be the adequate countergift;[87] violations of such a custom can be condemned, and our tale illustrates this principle. Of course the value of storytelling is stressed, along with the idea that some talent enhancing conviviality offers rescue from social death. If we want to probe into some more profound significance – of which tellers and listeners were not necessarily aware – we should focus on what is constant in all the variants. We find that the permanent thematic nexus concerns an individual with some failing who undergoes a painful but enriching experience in some kind of nightly

84 IFC 628: 252-3, told by J. McMahon (aged 60) of Newcastle-West, Co. Limerick, in 1939. Coll. by Seosamh Ó Dálaigh. 85 Sean O'Sullivan *Folktales of Ireland* 274: 'generally told as a humorous tale'. 86 Bo Almqvist *Béaloideas* 37-8 (1969-70) 64. 87 O. Bîrlea 'La fonction de raconter dans le folklore roumain', *Laographia* 22 (19) 24: 'Il y a chez nous la coutume de récompenser l'hospitalité en débitant un conte avant de se coucher.'

otherworld or dreamworld and usually in the presence of death,[88] and who returns to normal life with some new power. We may be tempted to recognize, in the pair of opposed states separated by experiences out of the ordinary world, the common tripartite sequential structure of rituals marking the passage from one stage of life into another, with their three phases of separation, then transition (a liminal phase of chaos, timelessness, ordeals, role reversals and symbolic death and rebirth), and finally reincorporation into society with heightened powers. Many wonder tales have been traced, not always very convincingly, to 'rites of passage' in which the protagonists' transformations would also be potential initiatory experiences for the listeners;[89] it really seems to be the case with the stories quoted in the preceding pages. Some may also perceive in them the notions that the path from birth to death (or vice-versa!) constitutes a story, and that time can stand still for a good storyteller.

So far, attempts at interpretation have concerned the second of the two story-patterns. Taking both together, we note that they posit two different kinds of storytellers: on the one hand the man who already has the title and status and must live up to it, and on the other the person who has no such position but may have to narrate, now and then, to enter a social network and remain there. The first has received a repertoire and the skills that go with it, but should be able to add to what he has inherited; the other has no such foundations on which to build – Bo Almqvist observes that in a version recorded in Donegal (see p. 545) the protagonist specified he could not tell Fenian stories or wonder tales, two of the most elaborate and highly-prized kinds of Irish narratives.[90] But the message may be that an occasional storyteller's own life-experience sometimes compensates for lack of skills; thus when circumstances require, everybody should be able to narrate.

This chapter has shown that storytellers as living presences, and acts of narration as what linguists would call 'performatives' (because they 'do' something), appear in the world of Irish tales in a variety of ways but with some constants. On the one hand, the stories or fragments we have examined may refer to kinds of characters and activities with which the natural audience was familiar; but through a fantasizing process the images could also be detached from everyday experience. Indeed, fictional representations of storytellers in oral tradition seldom seem to have been self-portraits; indeed, they might sometimes clearly be what the actual teller was not – very important, or utterly unskilled. Picturesque details, or sentimentalism, or nobility are hardly emphasized, con-

---

88 Particularly strong when the protagonist is threatened with burial, as in a version collected by Kevin Danaher in County Limerick: 'The coffin was empty, although it was a frightful weight to carry. "Who will go in the coffin?" says the first man. "Who will go in but Paddy Ahern [the man who had no story]?" says they.' (*Folktales of the Irish Countryside* 13.) 89 Geneviève Calame-Griaule 'Pour une lecture initiatique des contes populaires', *Bulletin du Centre Thomas More* 21 (1978) 11-29. 90 *Béaloideas* 37-8 (1969-70) 63.

trary to what often happens in literary portraits, but the functions of storytelling may be reflected upon. The real audience could be confronted with a factual or reversed image of itself in those who, in the tales, can ask for stories; at the same time it was reminded of the fact that a storyteller is a person who has some power and to whom strange things may happen.

For a good many situations involving storytelling within stories, analogues may be found elsewhere, but their relative abundance in Ireland suggests that storytelling received much attention there. A fictional storyteller could be cunning or silly, brave or cowardly, lucky or victimized; but his function was essential. Like other sources of information, the stories themselves show that storytelling was valued as a recreational occupation, an occasion for tightening social links, a way of sharing experience and of instigating some action. It was also a means of revealing or deceiving, and perhaps of revealing through a deception, thereby raising the question of the kinds of truth and lies to be expected from storytellers. It will be examined in the next chapter.

13

'That was all true enough ...'

The Irish have often been represented as particularly offended when their truthfulness is questioned: 'Not speaking the truth, is it?' explodes Pegeen Mike in *The Playboy of the Western World*. 'Would you have me knock the head of you with the butt of the broom?'; but the same character approves of 'poet's talking' which beguiles listeners and transmutes reality through verbal exuberance. Eloquence seems 'always' to have been valued in Ireland, and it depends on means of persuasion which may have little to do with plain truthfulness. In popular lore, stories are occasionally dismissed as sinful lies, as in this saying ascribed to a 'poor scholar' (i.e. a young adult travelling in search of great hedge-schoolmasters and living on the charity of the population):

> He that tells stories is lost
> For stories are but fable and fables are but lies
> And he who tells lies shall go down in the Pit.[1]

But if some of those young men despised activities they considered futile or morally doubtful, there is no doubt that most of those who gave them hospitality enjoyed 'lies' such as those William Carleton as a 'poor scholar' (see pp. 211-12) obligingly produced. The most common claim Irish storytellers made about their stories was: 'it is true', but a good storyteller could be known as 'the best liar' in the parish. The storytellers themselves might wear this badge proudly if the word 'liar' was used in a special sense: Ireland is one of the countries where 'let's lie' could be an invitation to exchange tales[2] – though not for all kinds of stories. 'Truth', 'lies', 'fiction' and 'belief', sometimes inextricably mingled, were important in Ireland. Their relevance to different kinds of storytelling is the subject of this chapter.

Wihout raising a philosophical debate, we must size up the complexity of those concepts. Truth has been defined as a faithful account of 'reality' (though the nature of that reality is itself in dispute if our knowledge of it is only a mental construct); as the quality of propositions which do not contradict the laws of

1 IFC 462: 309. From P. Mac Domhnaill, Co. Carlow. 2 Linda Dégh 'Folk Narrative', in R.M. Dorson (ed.) *Folklore and Folklife, an Introduction* 60: 'a Russian storyteller boasted that he was a renowned liar who could fill three sacks with lies.' She gives similar examples con-

valid reasoning; or as what is part of a system characterized by inner coherence (but a wild fairytale might be self-consistent too); as conformability to a particular purpose: what is a good basis for action and produces satisfactory results, would be true (but mere propaganda may fit this definition). Different truth-finding procedures have been recommended: obtaining intuitive glimpses, or apprehending the truth in flashes of mystical insight; receiving a communication from a higher world (which must still be correctly interpreted); accepting the authority of tradition; deducing from established premises according to logical techniques, in a purely intellectual process; trusting sense perceptions when they are verified by experience ... But we are also told that we should be wary of what is registered emotionally; that authorities can disagree or may be questioned; that 'reason' can err; and that our senses are subject to delusion. Many think that we can only reach to a limited degree of truth, and extreme sceptics deny that knowledge of any kind can be certain: 'truth' would be another name for opinions, conditioned by historical, social and individual factors. Hierarchies of truths have been established. At the beginning of the seventh century, Isidore of Seville distinguished between the certainties of faith (*veritas*) and knowledge of mundane things, subordinating the second to the first: *maior est veritas quam verus*; other medieval theologians agreed that *veritas* about salvation was indeed 'more true' than earthly factual accuracy. Preachers could not always ignore that on the latter level some of their narrative *exempla* were inventions, but they considered the truths of religion thereby implanted into the minds of ordinary people more important: the outward fable, oftened likened to a husk, contained a kernel of essential reality. Thus *veritas* was aimed at in the two 'Irish' stories which were among the most popular European texts of the later Middle Ages (see p. 46) in Latin and in vernacular languages: the *Navigatio Sancti Brendani* could be read for edification as an allegory of the soul's quest for salvation – though many took it literally; the story of Knight Owein's experience in St Patrick's Purgatory (the earliest version, *Tractatus de Purgatorio Sancti Patricii*, is generally credited to a twelfth-century Cistercian monk) may have been written to give valid answers to those who wanted to know what happened after death. Omitting to tell the whole truth about worldly things was also justifiable: the collection of *exempla* compiled by a Franciscan preacher in Ireland in the thirteenth century (see p. 46) includes the story of a monk who led a disgrace-

cerning Hungarian storytellers in *Märchen, Erzähler und Erzählgemeinschaft* 92. G. Henssen *Volkstümliche Erzählerkunst* 21: in Germany, it was said of a good storyteller '*He kann am besten leigen* (but the folklorist notes that the dialect form *leigen* did not have the derogatory connotation of *lügen*: to lie) – *die Leute verstehen darunter die Kunst des dichterischen Gestaltens* (by it, people mean creative art).' Ada Martinkus, 'Trois conteurs lithuaniens qui croient un peu, beaucoup ou pas du tout à leurs récits', in *Cahiers de littérature orale* 11 (1982) 160: 'lorsque les villageois voulaient que le grand-père de Ilgevicius se lance dans des récits, ils lui disaient: 'Tu es un bon menteur, tu sais bien conter; mens-nous quelque chose [you are a good liar, you narrate well, lie for us] ... pour un conteur, savoir mentir constitue une qualité [for a storyteller, to know how to lie is a good thing].'

ful life, until he had a vision of Hell and saw the place prepared for him there; the compiler recommends not to say that the protagonist is a monk when telling the story outside the clerical world, the essential message being in no way compromised by presenting him as a lay drunkard.[3]

Wrong interpretations may be honestly voiced and phantasms sincerely expressed, but lies involve deliberate falsification. Just as there may be different kinds, degrees or levels of truth, there are different ways of consciously deviating from it. Lying may be an acquired social skill, used in self-defence or to smooth out problems; yet it is condemned on social grounds because the group cannot interact fruitfully without a fair amount of trust. One of the basic tenets of what H.P. Grice called the 'cooperative principle', implicitly governing ordinary discourse behaviour, is that in effective conversational partnership we are *normally* not expected to state what we know to be false, nor to say things for which we have no evidence. Neglect of this maxim is anti-social behaviour because it imperils mutual confidence; but there are times when the rules can be relaxed or even ignored, provided the real intention of the speaker is perceived.[4] Some philosophers, theologians and moralists of the past unreservedly condemned asserting something while knowing it to be false.[5] Others conceded that lies were not all equally bad: for Aquinas, for instance, the 'officious' or helpful lie and the 'jocose' one told in jest, though sinful, were less damnable than deliberately harmful deceptive statements (*mendacium perniciosum*); Plato had already allowed rulers to practise a 'noble lie' which kept the citizenry contented with their station in life and thus protected social harmony. Common wisdom resigns itself to the existence of lying as an unfortunate defensive necessity and admits that codes of honour, politeness or solidarity may recommend false assertions. Deceit to evade persecution may be legitimized. The skill of a trickster may amuse, if we do not sympathize with his victim; and there may even be connivance between the deceiver and his half-deceived or consenting prey when the trick is played for the fun of it. A certain kind of 'lying', the use of imagination, is one of life's pleasures: Oscar Wilde went to provocative extremes in celebrating 'the telling of beautiful untrue things' as the graceful remedy for 'a morbid and unhealthy faculty of truth-telling', and as 'the proper aim of Art'.[6] Should the question of truth arise with regard to art, and what is the relationship of fiction to truth? In its most common usage, 'fiction' is opposed to 'fact' and equated with 'untruth'; but – leaving aside the possibility that all knowledge might be fiction insofar as it is fashioned by our mind, and the certainty that all texts are verbal artefacts and not life itself – if we restrict the term to texts that openly invent, we find that imaginative elements may also be at work in essentially 'non-fictional' stories, and conversely that no 'fictional' work would make

3 A.G. Little (ed.) *Liber Exemplorum ad Usum Praedicantium* 115 (exemplum 95: 'De Gula'). 4 'Logic and Conversation', in P. Cole and J.L. Morgan (eds) *Syntax and Semantics 3: Speech Acts*. 5 'Lying lips are abomination to the Lord; but they that deal truly are his delight' (*Prov.* 12. 22). 6 'The Decay of Lying', first published in *Nineteenth Century*, January 1889.

sense without some plausibility and reference to the world of experience known to the receiver.[7] Tales have been condemned because they deal in illusion, but have also been defended as the vehicles of enduring general truths, or because they make us share an experience more intense than everyday perception. It has also been argued that fictive utterances are not subject to the criteria of truth and falsity, or not in the ordinary way; they should be distinguished both from a message which purports to be strictly informative and from acts of deceit. They would constitute a special kind of communicative act, to which the audience is expected to respond by consciously accepting a game of 'make believe' and doing *as if* the content of the story were true. Mutual agreement is necessary, however, and certain rules must be implicitly obeyed: the statement should be identifiable as a 'nondeceptive pseudo-performance',[8] for which a certain kind of interpretation is required. We may retain that we have fiction when we are invited to *imagine* that something has happened and to experience it vicariously; that a fictional discourse has its own mode of coherence; that it may convey, symbolically or metaphorically, general and fundamental truths rather than literal accuracy; and that the fiction/nonfiction distinction may be blurred.

One more concept requires preliminary comments: the notion of belief, and with it the problem of the interaction between individual views and those held by a community. The crux of the matter is the relation of truth to knowledge: for some, knowledge is belief backed by facts (but faith, as a strong belief in undemonstrable truth, might be considered eminently reliable); for others, knowledge and belief are quite distinct, the latter being only a mental attitude of assent combining values and feelings and involving more emotion than reason. It tends to be stronger than mere opinion, but admits of varying degrees of certainty from mere surmise to absolute conviction. Apart from characterizing a state of mind or an attitude, 'belief' also refers to what is believed; and whatever its truth-value, a belief can be an operative force manifested in action or verbally and possibly in a narrative. Stories illustrating beliefs can strengthen them, or leave them open to debate, or play with them. A set of beliefs can be shared by a group, and the process of enculturation includes acquiring such a collective mentality. In a tradition-oriented culture, what has been told by the living elders and supposedly by more distant ancestors should, on principle, not be questioned; even there, however, beliefs can change over time. The world view held by a group includes widely accepted values and convictions, but whether those always make up a perfectly coherent system is doubtful: apparently incompatible beliefs can coexist or alternate in the same society, and in the same individual; a person may repeat without full personal commitment what the collectivity says, or change his mind as circumstances vary and emotions wax and wane. The extent to which the listeners' beliefs (and doubts) coincide with or diverge

7 John Searle *Expression and Meaning; Studies in the Theory of Speech Acts* 74: 'A work of fiction need not consist entirely of, and in general will not consist entirely of, fictional discourse.'
8 J.A. Searle, op. cit. 65.

from those explicitely or implicitely put forward in a story determines its interpretation and evaluation; but what people really believe is not easily accessible to the observer. With those reservations, we may still speak of shared beliefs signifying membership of a collectivity. A cultural group will naturally tend to respect its own heritage of beliefs, and to deprecate those of another culture by branding them as 'superstitions'. Just as there may be links as well as oppositions between lies and fiction, there are special connections and differences between truth and belief: to believe a statement or a fact is to consider it to be true; but, to some extent, what is true for me is what concords with my beliefs, and crediting may sometimes be an emotional attitude.

I do not see why issues of truthfulness and lying, fiction and falsehood, or belief and certitude, should appear in completely different terms in Ireland; but there may be particular inflections, and I shall look for them in comments on supposedly typical attitudes and in the way stories were told and received.

The Irish have formulae to vouch for the truth of what they say; in Gaelic *Dar m'fhíor!* or *Ar m'fhíor!* (by my troth!), *B' fhíor é* (it was true, it really happened), *Níl focal bréige ann* (literally translated in Anglo-Irish as 'no word of a lie'), *Níl aon bhréag ansin* (there's no lie here). Such protestations are a universal rhetorical ploy, but may be more or less insistent, and may be toned down to 'that was all true enough'.

In ancient Ireland, truth concerned much more than discourse: it was the basis of honour and justice, and had a magical power. The 'Act of Truth' was the confirmation or refutation of a statement by an extraordinary event[9] and involved cosmic consonance, social order and individual balance. The warriors' code of honour prescribed *fír fer* (manly truth) or *fír ngaiseid* (truth of weapons), both meaning fair fight.[10] *Fír* was the wisdom possessed by an able poet or judge. For a king, there was *fír flathemon* (truth of the ruler, or being the rightful ruler). During the kingship of Eochaid mac Eirc, as 'falsehood was banned from Ireland ... and he it was who first established the rule of justice there', the weather was good and harvest plentiful, according to *Lebor Gabála*; in the eighth-century *Audacht Morainn* (Testament of Morann), a young prince is taught the importance of *fír flathemon* for general peace and fertility. The 'truth' in question combined the right to rule, the giving of good judgement, and integrity of action, but seems also to have implied that a king could not lie and should protect those who told the truth.[11] A ruler's falsehood (*gáu flathemon*) led to natural and social disaster. The power of ascertaining the truth of a statement could be objectified in literature: Morann, the legendary wise judge mentioned

9 Motif H252: Person asserts a thing as true declaring 'If my words are true, may this or that happen'. 10 P. O'Leary '*Fír Fer*: an Internalized Concept in Early Irish Literature', *Éigse* 22 (1987) 1–14. 11 Myles Dillon 'The Hindu Act of Truth in Celtic Tradition', *Modern Philology* 44 (1947) 137–40. Heinrich Wagner 'Old Irish *fír*: "truth", "oath" ', *Zeitschrift für Celtische Philologie* 31 (1970) 1–45, 57–8 and 146.

above, had a *sín* or *iodh* (magic collar – in fact the remnant of his caul) which would tighten around his neck if he was about to pronounce an unjust verdict, or could be placed on an accused person to 'separate truth from lie'. Cormac mac Art's cup broke if a lie was told over it and became whole again with truth (see p. 22); we note, however, that such infallible ways of distinguishing truth from falsehood did not remain in our world: the collar and the cup vanished with their legitimate owners. Absolute truth might belong to the Otherworld, which Loeg in *Serglige Con Chulainn* describes as 'a bright free land where no falsehood is spoken nor deceit'; in *Togail Bruidne Dá Derga* King Conaire meets creatures who have been expelled from it for having lied. Important stories were probably considered true, though there came a time when they were no longer credited: 'some things in it are devilish lies or some poetical figments', wrote one of the Christian copyists of *Táin Bó Cuailnge* (see p. 43). At all times there must also have been stories deliberately offered as untruth, and a twentieth-century Irish writer argued that 'a satisfactory novel should be a self-evident sham to which the reader could regulate at will the degree of his credulity'.[12]

While the Irish asserted their conception of truthfulness, outsiders might call them dangerous or childishly ridiculous liars. Edmund Spenser found the 'base Irish people' deceitful. In 1623, Sir Henry Bourchier noted that 'perjury is so usual in the realm, especially among the common sort of peasants, as against any great man of the natives no right can prevail on a stranger's side'.[13] For Richard Head, half-a-century later, the Irish were 'always babbling [talking childishly] and telling tales [falsehood]'.[14] Sir Henry Piers, who described Westmeath in 1682 at the instance of the Protestant bishop, found the lower class untrustworthy: 'As to the inferior rank of husbandmen called Sculloges [*scolóige*], which may be Englished farmer or husbandman, or yet more properly, boors, they are generally very crafty and subtile in all manners of bargaining, full of equivocations and mental reservations, especially in their dealings in fairs and markets; where, as if lying and cheating were no sin, they make it their work to over reach any they deal with.'[15] In English slang, from the late seventeenth century to the mid-nineteenth, the phrase 'Irish evidence' meant 'false witness, false evidence'.[16] For Arthur Young, the poorer classes in Ireland were 'great liars'.[17] According to a secretary of the Poor Law Commission interviewed by Tocqueville in 1835, 'there is no other country where it is more difficult to get the truth out of a man'.[18]

In fact, malevolent lies were considered offences in Ireland as elsewhere. A deceptive assertion was seen as a breach of faith and an attack on the social contract, therefore as something harmful to the community; of course lying was also

---

12 Flann O'Brien *At Swim-Two-Birds* 25. 13 Quoted by E. MacLysaght *Irish Life in the Seventeenth Century* 74. 14 Ibid. 41. 15 *A Chorographical Description of the County of Westmeath*, publ. by C. Vallancey in *Collectanea de Rebus Hibernicis* 1. 115. 16 E. Partridge *A Dictionary of Historical Slang*. 17 *Arthur Young's Tour of Ireland* 2.147. 18 *Journey in England and Ireland* 119.

known to be a sin and one of the attributes of the Devil. On both social and religious grounds, therefore, it would entail punishment; but there might be nuances in the interpretation of the basic principle, and even reversals: one Irish proverb says that 'God does not like the lying tongue', but according to another 'The lie often goes further than the truth',[19] or, less cynically, 'Truth is better, but a lie is savoury at times'.[20] Speech could be used as a way of hiding one's true thought from a superior, or of ingratiating oneself with him – William Robert Le Fanu, like many others, noted that an Irishman of the lower class might invent information in order to please the interlocutor: 'In giving answers the Irish peasantry, as a rule, have no great regard for truth, but like to give the answer which they think will be most agreeable to the questioner.'[21] In other circumstances, it seemed normal to meet with deceit what was considered deceitful, and lying to an official could pass for an excusable or even laudable act: for many an Irish peasant in the nineteenth century it was justifiable when confronting an alien justice. In 1833, Carleton commented on the Irish ability to lie under oath:

Put him forward to prove an alibi for his fourteenth or fifteenth cousin, and you will be gratified by the pomp, pride, and circumstance of true swearing. Every oath with him is an epic – pure poetry, abounding with humour, pathos, and the highest order of invention and talent. He is not at ease, it is true, under facts; there is something too commonplace in dealing with them, which his genius scorns. But his flights – his flights are beautiful; and his episodes admirable and happy. In fact, he is an *improvisatore* at oath-taking; with this difference, that his *extempore* oaths possess all the ease and correctness of labour and design. He is not, however, altogether averse to facts; but, like your true poet, he veils, changes, and modifies them with such skill, that they possess all the merit and graces of fiction. If he happen to make an assertion incompatible with the plan of the piece, his genius acquires fresh energy, enables him to widen the design, and to create new machinery, with such happiness of adaptation, that what appeared out of proportion or character is made, in his hands, to contribute to the general strength and beauty of the oath ...

Some persons, who display their own egregious ignorance of morality, may be disposed to think that it tends to lessen the obligation of an oath, by inducing a habit among the people of swearing to what is not true. We look upon such persons as very dangerous to Ireland and to the repeal of the Union; and we request them not to push their principles too far in the disturbed parts of the country. Could society hold together a single day, if nothing but truth were spoken? Would not law and lawyers soon become obsolete, if nothing but truth were sworn? What would become of parliament if truth alone were uttered there? Its annual proceedings might be dispatched in a month. Fiction is the basis of society, the bond of commercial prosperity, the channel of communication between nation and nation, and not unfrequently the interpreter between a man and his own conscience. For these, and many other reasons which we could adduce, we say with

19 S. Gaffney and S. Cashman *Proverbs and Sayings of Ireland* 65. 20 R. MacAdam 'Six Hundred Gaelic Proverbs Collected in Ulster', *Ulster Journal of Archaelogy* 6 (1858) 257; L. Flanagan *Irish Proverbs* 85. 21 *Seventy Years of Irish Life* 194.

Paddy, 'Long life to fiction!' When associated with swearing, it shines in its brightest colours. What, for instance, is calculated to produce the best and purest of the moral virtues so beautifully, as the swearing an alibi? Here are fortitude and a love of freedom resisting oppression; for it is well known that all law is oppression in Ireland.[22]

Carleton himself was tampering with the truth in this hyperbolic humorous text, but he was pointing to serious issues which were observed by others, for instance by Isaac Butt in 1866: 'The Irish peasant regards the Law and the Government as his natural enemies.'[23] In his short story 'In the Train' (1935), Frank O'Connor offered a twentieth-century rendering of the same attitude on the part of an isolated community where truth is for insiders only.

There may be necessary or excusable lies. There are also enjoyable ones: an intensification of truth, or invention, brings salutary escape from dull reality, provided the group and its conventions control the game. This special relationship between storytelling and truth intrigued some Anglo-Irish fiction writers who observed the rural population at the end of the nineteenth century or at the beginning of the twentieth. The Irish may be caricatured in 'Lisheen Races, Second Hand'[24] by Somerville and Ross, but the real target of the satire is the outsider: the Honourable Basil Leigh Kelway, a thick-headed Briton who has come to Ireland to collect statistics for a book that should at last clarify the Irish drinking problem. His more acclimatized Anglo-Irish guides know that he is unlikely to understand the subject; nevertheless, they try to initiate him into the Irish way of life by taking him to the local races. Arriving too late for the sporting events, he hears in a public house a colourful report on them by 'Slipper', one of the natives. While carefully gauging the responses of his audience, this storyteller multiplies protests like 'faith', 'sure', 'I declare on my sowl', 'I declare to ye, on the value of me oath' – but meanwhile transforms drab reality into a mock-epic, ending with the supposed death of a rival, who afterwards turns up alive and kicking. The author of the canard is not blamed by members of the local audience, who obviously have not been deceived: having seen the races, they enjoy narrative fantasy as a normal addition to the day's merrymaking. The liar and the local subject of his lie are soon reconciled, but Kelway is so bewildered that he resolves 'to abandon Ireland to her fate'. The book he intended to write would probably have been an inaccurate picture anyway, and less amusing than Slipper's yarn.

At first sight, Synge's Christy Mahon behaves in a Mayo *shebeen* as 'Slipper' did in West Cork; but, this time, when the putative corpse appears, the audience turns against the fictioner: 'You're a liar!' Why this opposite reaction? One possible explanation is that, unlike the other fabrication, Christy's lie could not be seen through by his audience from the start; also, it was a long-winded affair

22 'The Geography of an Irish Oath', in *Traits and Stories of the Irish Peasantry* 2. 2-3. 23 'Land Tenure in Ireland; A Plea for the Celtic Race', in S. Deane (ed.) *The Field Day Anthology of Irish Writing* 2. 225. 24 In *Some Experiences of an Irish R.M.* (1899).

and repeated too often, not always when his audience wanted to be humoured ('You've told me that story six times since the dawn of day'); worse still, Christy could be seen as a 'schemer', 'making up a story' to gain material advantage through a deception. When the illusion is punctured, Pegeen dismisses him as 'an ugly liar [who] was playing off the hero'. There is another explanation, however: the audience may be deficient. They are no longer the community of connoisseurs who used to admire a storyteller like Marcus Quin, 'and he a great warrant to tell stories of holy Ireland till he'd have the old women shedding down tears about their feet'. Great old men have given way to drunkards, and the only younger man left after the talent-drain of emigration, Shawn Keogh, is no entertainer: 'I'm a poor scholar with middling faculties to coin a lie, so I'll tell the truth.' The Widow Quin, herself a liar who can interpret narratives and would like to have again 'the wisest old men' telling tales in her cottage, is less gullible and remains Christy's last defender. Christy, on the other hand, seems to be learning something: not only 'the power of a lie', but also the rules of acceptable fabulation. From now on he may know how, to which audience, and in what circumstances he can offer lies as acceptable fiction, so that he can 'go romancing through a romping lifetime' and make life less boring for those who deserve it.[25]

Outside clearly marked situations, there are strong group injunctions against lying: Henry Glassie, who studied a County Fermanagh parish in the 1970s, found it hard at first to understand why people classed lying, theft and murder as almost equally serious crimes; then he recognized that 'a lie is an act of contempt and withdrawal, a theft of honor from individuals and order from society'.[26] He also learned from one of his informants that the condemnation did not always apply:

There was someone at one time and he asked a clergyman was it a sin to tell *lies*. And the clergyman replied, it depended on the source of the lie that you told. If you told a lie that would injure your *neighbour*, that would be a sin. Or that would spread any kind of scandal or anything like that. But he said, the lie that no one would believe there was no harm to telling that lie. Aye. A thing that no one would believe.[27]

Can one establish what people actually believe? The stereotyped Irish person used to be characterized by a propensity to swallow what others would find incredible; but the better observers knew that what they did not give credence to was not by that very fact despicable. During the Ordnance Survey campaign of the 1830s, John O'Donovan noted that the beliefs of a group, and possible vagaries of collective memory, should not be called lies by an outsider: 'No memory is tenacious enough to retain all the details of any occurrence nor [is] the human mind sufficiently clear to understand the motives of others in every instance. A distinction, however, should be made between a lie and a falsehood'[28] – without giving offence.

It has often been assumed that, until not so long ago, most active bearers of Irish traditions accepted the stories they valued as literally true; elsewhere, some collectors found that those who believed in the reality of their tales were exceptions but might have been more numerous in the past; others noted that, according to their informants, what happened in the tales might have been possible long ago but of course no longer was.[29] Indeed, a variety of attitudes have been observed in Ireland itself, often enough with strong emphasis on credence but with some changes over time. In 1902 a collector in County Mayo observed:

[Tales] were told simply and with belief, as if the speakers were asssured of the existence of a hidden world lying within the one visible to the senses. In several instances they were told as the adventures and seeings of the speakers. In what were clearly folk-tales ... the incidents were spoken of as if they had happened quite recently, and the locality and the names of the actors were given with what seemed certainty of knowledge, as of intimate acquaintance with place and persons. The story nearly always took for its time the present or the very recent past. It began with the well-known and familiar, but swiftly reached the marvellous and the mysterious.[30]

J.H. Delargy noted:

Many of the old story-tellers believed in all the marvels and magic of the typical wonder-tale and if some forward youth were to inquire if these things could possibly be true, the answer of most would be like that of an old friend of mine: *Bhíodh druíocht ann sa tseana-shaol!* 'There was magic in old times.' I remember vividly the horrified dismay of an old Kerry story-teller when one of his audience cast doubts on the return of the hero Oisín from the Land of Youth, questioning if Oisín had ever existed![31]

But the past tense used in this statement may be a sign that attitudes were changing when it was made, in 1945. Another collector remembered: 'My mother, from whom I heard the first folktales, told me once that the people from whom she heard them, when she was a child in her native district of Ballymitty in South Wexford, believed firmly in them and so did she at the time.'[32] In the 1980s, an American anthropologist still observed in Donegal that narratives had a special power of conviction:

28 O.S.L. Loughrea, Oct. 25, 1838. 29 Cf. G. Ortutay *Hungarian Folklore* 233: 'The position taken with regard to beliefs and tales is one of the safest barometers of change in the peasants' mind and rise of their cultural standards. In the peasant culture of bygone times one people's attitude to those was one of involuntary identification and a spontaneous creative fallacy, whereas today the position they take is either one critical and contemptuous, or embarrassed concealment and repugnance. Of course there are still many transitional forms.' 30 L. M'Manus 'Folk-Tales from Western Ireland', *Folk-Lore* 25 (1914) 324. 31 *The Gaelic Story-Teller* 8. 32 J.G. Delaney 'Three Midland Storytellers', *Béaloideas* 50 (1982) 45.

If we consider discourse to mean a way of talking about and hence seeing the world (or some section of it) that depends on a range of critical words, oppositions, and so on, then narratives, or stories, are perhaps the most affective, and hence effective, expression of any discourse. Belief and knowledge are often, and certainly most strongly, embodied in the form of stories. Aside from whatever deep structures or unconscious repressions they might express (or secrete), narratives about human or anthropomorphic subjects command attention through their ability to make abstractions concrete and to provide opportunities for identification.[33]

The members of an audience may react differently to what seems to be asserted. An individual may pretend belief, or half-believe in a made-up story while it is told, yet remain aware, or half-aware, of its being invented. John Messenger, conducting an ethnographic research on Inisheer in the early 1960s, observed generational gaps: 'Most of the storytellers believed the narratives they related, and this fact added to the joy of hearing them, for the narrators became deeply involved emotionally in the events they were describing. The youngsters also believed the stories, but the young men did not, or at least they said they did not.'[34] Indeed there may have been age-group attitudes, with young men asserting themselves against their elders: comments on a sceptical attitude of young adults multiplied from the early eighteen hundreds. But storytelling being practised more efficiently later in life, with the possibility of gaining authority, some young sceptics might come to believe at least in a certain truth-value of the tales. It is a commonplace that a good storyteller must 'believe' in what he says; but there are different ways of believing or seeming to believe, and for one individual it may vary with circumstances.

Performance context is likely to suggest the kind of message to be expected and to determine whether the audience will receive it as literally true or not. A verbal frame may also provide guidance – the difference between the imparting of true information ('facts') and the spinning of an imaginary tale ('story') was sometimes stated explicitly: 'I'll give you, not a story, but an account of what happened to a man named Tom Connors, who lived beyond Dingle, and there's a ghost in it. Connors told me all himself, and it's only a year since he died.'[35] A simpler example goes: 'Now, this is no crack or story; this really happened.'[36] Often, however, the words 'story' and 'true' seem to be compatible, because the former does not necessarily connote fictional status: 'This is a true story, as true as ever was told and it's a local one too ...'; or, 'This is as true a story as ever happened, that I'm going to tell you. Sure me father knew the man well that it happened to, and I knew him myself too ...'; or, 'I suppose you often heard tell, that there was a treasure at Heapstown, well it's true, and there's many a story

33 L.J. Taylor 'The Language of Belief: Nineteenth-Century Religious Discourse in Southwest Donegal', in M. Silverman and P.H. Gulliver (eds) *Approaching the Past* 146. 34 'Joe O'Donnell, Seanchai of Aran', in *Journal of the Folklore Institute* 1 (1964) 203. 35 J. Curtin *Tales of the Fairies and of the Ghost World* 58. 36 IFC 1215: 34.

told about attempts that was made to dig it up. It's as long as I mind of now to hear poor old Micky Walsh telling this story about it, and as sure as I'm here it's a true one too, for Micky was never a man to invent anything.'[37] Naming some respectable source lent a greater air of veracity: 'This one was true, true, true, I heard. My mother was telling me about it ...', or 'That's from the old people; the old people used to tell me that. And that was true ...', or *'Deireadh na seanúdair* (the reliable old people used to say) ...'[38] Other conventional phrases could conclude stories by vouching for their veracity: 'When he'd finish a story one of our crowd would say: "I don't believe that". "Well then, as sure as you're sitting there, that happened", he'd say ...'; or, 'Brian was telling me that for a fact truth. And he wasn't a fellow for telling lies ...'; or, 'I don't know for certain, now, whether 'twas to my grandfather or my great-grandfather this happened, but whichever of them 'twas, every word of it is true, and no lie in it ...'; or, 'This happened long 'go. An' 'tis as true as I'm telling it to you here this minute ...'; or, 'And this happened, for a fact, for 'tis the man it happened to told me.'[39] In Irish, claims of truth include *ba shin scéal fíor* (that was a true story); *dar m'anam* (upon my soul); *gan dabht* (without a doubt).

On the other hand *sin é mo scéal* (that is my tale) is non-committal and may conclude any narrative. The storyteller may also explicitly reserve his opinion on the authenticity of what he has reported, and signal that he is passing information without making any personal claim to it. He may even suggest in conclusion that it should not be taken as gospel, as in these examples: 'This is another crack I heard with old men in this town, whether lies or truth I don't know, but they told it anyway ...'; or, 'But the stories may not be true. The old people told them anyhow ...'; or, ' 'Twas Sally Fity (Old Tom Fity's wife, she was) who told me this yarn – though I won't say that 'twasn't true, or didn't happen just as she said ...'; or, 'Many queer things happened in the olden days, and the likes of them is often hard to believe.'[40] One formula to end wonder tales in Irish was *'Sin é mo scéal-sa, agus má tá bréag ann, bíodh. Ní mise do chum ná do cheap é'* (that is my story, and if there be a lie in it, be it so. It was not I who composed or made it).[41]

Linda-May Ballard, having collected in Ulster in the 1970s, described more recent and sometimes more embarrassed positions:

Increased enlightenment may lead to scorn for, or perhaps doubt about traditional beliefs. Some people hold a curiously ambivalent attitude, as is illustrated by a remark made by

---

37 IFC 485: 44, 103, 130, from three different informants in County Sligo, 1938. 38 D.H. Therman *Stories from Tory Island* 54, 132 and *Béaloideas* 59 (1991) 225. Cf. Anatole Le Braz *La légende de la mort chez les Bretons armoricains* 'Je le tiens de ma mère qui avait seize ans à l'époque et qui n'a jamais menti' (32), 'Ceci est la pure vérité: je le tiens de mon grand-père' (475). 39 IFC 1169: 402; 543: 34; 575: 33-4, 241, 247. 40 IFC 1218: 266; T.G.F. Paterson *County Cracks* 87; IFC 575: 48, 51. 41 Kevin Danaher *That's How It Was* 5. Cf. P.J. Hélias *Le Cheval d'Orgueil* 90: 'Et croyez-moi si vous voulez: il n'y a pas un poil de mensonge dans cette histoire, du moins de ma part à moi.'

a narrator, on concluding a tale: 'It's only fables; it happened though.' Desire to believe is matched by a natural reticence if scornful reaction may be incurred ... Sometimes, narrators accompany their tales with a vehement assertion of their validity ... Why so much stress is laid on [the tale's] authenticity remains to be investigated. A possible reason may be encapsulated in the remark of one story-teller: 'These stories are true insofar, now I'm telling you they're true, but they're true insofar as we believe; like I tell you that an aunt of mine seen a fairy. Now she believed that, and I believe it, because I knew her, and she wouldn't tell a lie.' Respect for the previous holders of a belief may, in itself, be a sufficient reason for sharing that belief.[42]

Another informant hinted at some truth above mere factual accuracy: 'There's something that, there's a ... I'd say a mystery you can't ... it can be truth you can't comprehend, do you know what I mean?'[43] There are distinctions which a 'traditional' audience may perceive without putting forward abstract arguments.

Different kinds and degrees of belief may be commanded by different genres of narratives. We may start with the native Irish taxonomy (see pp. 430 and 448-9) establishing two basic repertoires, depending on whether an item was thought to have verifiable referents (the informational value defining *seanchas* – which was not always a narrative), or was offered as an aesthetic presentation (to be enjoyed and admired as a *scéal* – but this term could also be used in a looser sense). You could prefer one of these basic modes, as did 'Paddy the Cope' when he was a youth in the 1890s:

[After hearing fairy-music] we then went to Peggy and asked her what did she know about the fairies [*seanchas*]. She gave each of us two turfs and told us to sit on them and she would tell us what to do whenever we met them. Then she told us the story of the old ruins on top of the spinks [steep hillside] and the misfortune that followed the farmer and his family who failed on Hallow Eve night to leave a pot of praties and a can of milk full to overflowing for the good people to eat and drink their fill ... [my companion] was crying more than I was because Peggy's story was very sad ... [The following night they went to another house.] When we went in my father was telling a story [*scéal*]. Its name was 'Speed Heavy and Light Foot'. It was a very good story ... When we were going home, I said to Charlie, ' ... I am sorry I did not go into Peggy's. I would rather her story than my father's. Peggy's are true ones but that story my father told could not be true. The man called Speed could not have left Donegal in the morning for the Indies and be back before night, that was not true.'[44]

When Douglas Hyde was consulted about the existence of fairyland by the American W.Y. Evans Wentz,[45] he referred to the same typology, with

42 'Ulster Oral Narrative: the Stress on Authenticity', in *Ulster Folk Life* 26 (1980) 37-8. 43 Ibid. 39. 44 Patrick Gallagher *My Story* 53-4. 45 Evans Wentz (1878-1965) published in 1911 the results of his field and library research, *The Fairy-Faith in Celtic Countries*; the thesis was that 'Celtic' beliefs in fairyland retained elements of a pre-Christian religion, that fairyland existed, and that some human beings could occasionally perceive it.

scéalaíocht (the telling of long, complex tales accepted as respectable verbal art) calling for a suspension of disbelief, and a kind of *seanchas* (including short accounts of encounters with the supernatural accepted as factual) which he translated by 'belief':

The *sgéal* or story is something much more intricate, complicated, and thought-out than the belief. One can quite easily distinguish between the two. One (the belief) is short, conversational, chiefly relating to real people, and contains no great sequence of incidents, while the other (the folk-tale) is long, complicated, more or less conventional, and above all has its interest grouped around a single central figure, that of the hero or heroine. I may make this plainer by an example. Let us go into a cottage on the mountain-side ... and ask the old man of the house if he ever heard of such things as fairies, and he will tell you that 'there is fairies in it surely. Didn't his own father see the "forth" beyond full of them, and he passing by of a moonlight night and a little piper among them, and he playing music that mortal man never heard the like?' or he'll tell you that 'he himself wouldn't say agin fairies for it's often he heard their music at the old bush behind the house' ... Again, ask the old man if he knows e'er a *sean-sgéal* ... and he will ask you at once, 'Did you ever hear the Speckled Bull; did you ever hear the Well at the End of the World; did you ever hear the Tailor and the Three Beasts; did you ever hear the Hornless Cow?'[46]

We may object that, if credence is to be the criterion, more than two categories are needed. There are factual accounts which are accepted as truthful because they reflect the everyday life of the narrator's natural audience, and others which are accepted because they depend on shared beliefs; but there are also 'ancient stories', elaborated, told with 'gravity and solemnity', and not treated as inventions – they may be considered 'true' in another sense than those dealing with recent events. On the other hand, some stories that are made to sound like real experience may be perceived as deceptive. And all members of a community do not react in the same way: some may believe unreservedly, while doubters find the same narrative disquieting, or just entertaining. If a story founded on a belief may thus receive limited credence, or none at all, a wonder tale can be made to appear factual by being localized, and occasionally offered as the true experience of a named individual, perhaps of the storyteller himself.

The *scéal/seanchas* dichotomy resembles (without exactly matching) the folklorists' distinction between two basic forms of narrative: *Märchen*, accepted as artful and entertaining fiction, and *Sage* ('legend'), a simpler story not entirely verifiable but popularly regarded as true, whose function is to impart information; Jacob Grimm, who introduced this classification, opposed 'more poetical' to 'more historical'. But the degrees of belief which are supposed to help define those genres may fluctuate.[47] The 'legend' side will be examined later in the pre-

46 Ibid. 23-4. 47 L. Röhrich *Märchen und Wirklichkeit* 10: 'Die Glaubensgrenze, nach der man immer wieder Sage und Märchen auseinandergehalten hat, ist jedoch zweifellos keine geschichtliche Konstante und gewährt deshalb keine objektive Scheidelinie.' (The limit based

sent chapter. Concerning the word 'tale', when it is applied to all short prose narratives offered as fiction it is not exactly synonymous with *Märchen* if the latter term is restricted to stories filled with marvels (more precisely *Zaubermärchen*). For Lutz Röhrich, the characteristic feature of the latter is a mixture of 'realism' (plausibility) and fantasy, and there are limits to the wonders that are accepted in it.[48] The universe of tales 'must be made *credible* if not *believable*'.[49] It has been said – but it is questionable – that Irish *Märchen* tend to be more realistic than others;[50] also that no division appears between *Märchen* and *Sage* in Ireland[51] – but this doubtful statement may be due to the fact that the Grimms translated Croker's Irish *Fairy Legends* as *Elfenmärchen*.

The teller of 'tales' can be in a peculiar position. Linda-May Ballard observed in 1980 that, in Ulster, the traditional storytellers were still occasionally called 'liars' and resented it when they were narrating seriously; but earlier evidence suggests that the same label could also be a term of praise in the same province. In the following reminiscences, it connotes something pleasant:

It's sixty-three or four years ago that I heard most of these stories. You could hardly say where you heard a lot of them, but I heard a lot of them in Isaac Cousin's house in Mullycartan. He was a man of seventy then, and as far as I know had always lived about here. The people would have gathered in in the evening – just to hear him telling lies. No matter what he would come off with, the wife would always say when he'd finished, 'And that's true, Isaac, for many's a time I've heard you telling it'.[52]

This interesting conception of truth points to the power of traditional narration: what is repeated may sound increasingly valid, or, as said in *The Hunting of the Snark*, 'what I tell you three times is true'.

At any rate, a tale of wonder, heroism or adventure may denounce the practice of lying, and, when norms are violated, show what sanctions should be expected. Thus we find Irish folktales in which lying is punishable by death: 'When the king saw that the other two sons told him lies he shot them and he went to live with his youngest son [who had been truthful].'[53] But there are also tales that seem to celebrate such breaches of standards; a hero may use disguise and deception to do good – for instance to discover the truth or defeat evil, and

on belief is neither historically constant nor objectively definable.) **48** Ibid. 3: 'Jedes Volksmärchen ist noch irgendwie mit der Wirklichkeit verbunden. Zwar stehen real-mögliche und real-unmögliche Geschehnisse unbekümmert neben- und durcheinander, und das Kausalgesetz scheint oft genug aufgehoben zu sein, aber dennoch bestehen gewisse Kausalitäten weiter. So ist das Volksmärchen phantastisch und realistisch zugleich, und diese Mischung macht einen wichtigen Teil seines Wesens aus.' (The possible and the impossible are mingled; tales combine fantasy and realism.) **49** B. Holbek *Interpretation of Fairy Tales* 198. **50** L. Röhrich, op. cit. 168: 'die nüchterne Bestimmtheit und der Realismus des irischen Märchens ...' **51** Ibid. 169: 'Im irischen Erzählgut scheint weitgehend noch keine Trennung von Sage und Märchen eingetreten zu sein ...' **52** IFC 925: 235. Collected in 1943 from Mrs Taggart, aged 76, in Antrim. **53** IFC 1417: 457. Collected by Mícheál Ó Carolan in Belmullet in 1955.

as shown in the preceding chapter there are stories whose protagonists ingratiate themselves with the audience by their tricks or preposterous lies. (For stories *about* lying, particularly those connected with International Type 1920F — He who says 'That's a lie' must pay a fine – see pp. 525ff.)

The relation to reality, which is not simple in *Zaubermärchen*,[54] may be clearer (in opposition) in comic narratives exploiting ludicrous situations and absurdities. Blatant falsehood is at the root of 'tales of lying', uttering incongruities in the frame of a 'realistic' narrative. The basic devices are exaggeration, reversal of established relations and values, and impossible occurrences. First, the teller must make the story sound realistic, often giving it the form of a personal experience narrative; then he proceeds to utter preposterous inventions, testing the limits of his listener's credulity. Straight-faced control is appreciated by those in the know. The 'licensed liar' does not expect to be believed by the members of the community who have been socialized into seeing a joke and identifying deliberate assaults on credibility, but the presence in the audience of some naive outsider or credulous fool who is taken in may enhance the fun. Indeed, this kind of verbal practical joke may serve as an initiatory rite. There may also be lying contests between yarn-spinning experts. The resulting 'tall stories' belong to the common stock of western European (and American) folktales, and form a section in the Aarne-Thompson classification of tale-types.[55] It has been said that they were particularly developed in Ireland;[56] in fact their quantity and quality may not have been so extraordinary there, but such stories (and songs)[57] can be found. An Ulster informant told M.J. Murphy: 'They used to gather in here you know. My father God be good to him and old Jemmy Maguire, och you wouldn't know him, but you be to hear tell of him; and Phelim McManus ... It was for who could tell the biggest lie.'[58] A generation earlier, a 'liars' club' in Ulster had been described, in a mild 'stage-Irish' mode:

When we would all be gathered about the oul' Sergeant's fire of a long winter evenin', and the stories would be goin' round, the Sergeant, for he was a jokey fella, would say:

---

54 M. Simonsen, in M. Chesnut (ed.) *Telling Reality* 139: 'We must conclude that folktales get their starting point and their basic dynamics from reality, the real situation of storytellers and their audience, and that their very *raison d'être* is to help people to come to terms with reality. In order to do so, they make use of textual references to the reality outside the tale, but submit reality to a number of distortions.'   55 See Gerald Thomas 'Lüge, Lügengeschichte' and Erich Wimmer 'Lügenwette' in *Enzyklopädie des Märchens* 8. 1265-70 and 1274-81. 56 Fr. von der Leihen *Die Welt der Märchen* 2. 238: 'Das Lügenmärchen, das die Iren zur Vollendung brachten ...' 57 Rather than narratives progressing from the factual to the impossible, songs tend to accumulate impossibilities. See '*Amhrán na mBréag*' (the song of lies) in Donal O'Sullivan *Songs of the Irish* 173-4: (tr.) 'This is a comical sight that I have seen on the roads,/ An eel with bagpipes playing music for us all the time,/ The sportive trout in the pool – oh! what fine shoes she has!/ And did you see the sheep in the winter cutting turf?'... Some nineteenth-century broadside ballads in English are of the same kind. 58 IFC 1113: 338. Collected from Jack Rafferty, Dromintee (Armagh) by M.J. Murphy (1948).

'There's not a crowd of better or bigger liars from one end of Tyrone to the other, an' I've listened to some good ones before the Binch of Magishtrates in my time. Sure it's "The Liars' Club" we should style ourselves' ... Most of them was oul' hands and had seen a good many sides of life in their time, and that made their stories worth listenin' till. In tellin' stories they didn't always keep to the rael truth, but I must be fair to them now that they're all dead an' gone and say that it wasn't done with the intention of hurtin' anybody's feelin's, but just to polish off the story, and give it a humorous turn ... Well, sure, things went that far in the story-tellin' line at the club that the Oul' Sergeant sayed he would give a prize of a half-hundred bag of Indian mail to the member that could tell the best and biggest lie, and so a night was fixed for the competition. [The winner is the one who dares to pretend that he is 'no good at the lies'.][59]

'Artistic' and competitive lying was cultivated elsewhere in Ireland. In County Wexford, Tomás Ó Ciardha (Carey) gathered in 1938 a number of testimonies illustrating the Irish custom of having a local 'king of the liars' (*Rí na mBréag*). A reader may not find the stories hilarious, but must realize that it was the teller's skill that counted. Here are two retrospective portraits of 'magnificent liars' in full swing:

I. Do you know B. down there on the Green Road? Well B. could tell the most awful lies you ever heard and he'd persuade you 'twas the truth; and there'd be no face at all to the things he'd tell. He was telling us one day that he saved turnips in the field below the road. 'There was one corner in the field' says B., 'and there was three or four loads of dung and road stuff on it. Begob' says he, 'I sowed the turnips anyway, and a few seeds happened to fall in this corner. They grew up, and I thinned them and left one. Begob it grew and grew till it got to a terrible size altogether. The turnip grew so big that the whole corner of the field was covered with it. That one turnip done us half the winter. One of the workmen would come out and draw away a load of it today and then another in a few days time. It held that way for half the winter, and we taking two or three loads out of it every week.' Well, wasn't that a barefaced lie?[60]

II. Ah if L. was alive now! He's the man could tell you the stories and the yarns. He'd make them up and invent them for you as fast as he'd walk. I often heard him at a wake and he telling them. And one story would hold for the whole night; and you'd swear that he was telling the truth, he'd finish them off so well. He would sit down there, and he'd start off telling the story to one fellow – some real serious old fellow that would pay attention, and maybe believe it too. You'd swear there was only the two of them in the house. I heard him hundreds of times but I'm no good to think of any thing like that at all. I usen't pay any attention that time to them things. He was down in Fenacre one time, he said, himself and a chum of his. They were at the races. There was a great crowd of people there, and games and singing and every devil of a thing you could mention. He got drunk, he said, and he lost his chum in the crowd, and he had to come home by himself. When he was coming home he got in on the mountain. (He was telling this at a wake. I was listening to him.) 'And by the Houlya' says L., that was a great

59 Robert Bratton *Round the Turf Fire: Humorous Sketches of Ulster Country Life* 103-4. **60** IFC 543: 556. From Séamus de Faoite, aged 53, at Newbawn, Co. Wexford.

word of his, when he'd stop to think of something. He went up on the mountain, and up and up, and after a while he kind [of] knew where he was. The next place he came to was a big opening and a gate in it. He fooled about for a while, and begor, he went in; and where did he find himself but in a robber's den. [Here three pages in the manuscript develop a classic folktale sequence describing how robbers were fooled, which L. told as if he were the protagonist: a folktale can be transformed into a lie by being told in the first person singular.] ... Well then he come on to where he got the robbers all caught and he read of a bit of paper, by the way, the sentence they all got. Some got ten years and more of them twenty years and so on. Well if you had to hear him, you'd swear 'twas the truth he was telling; and that story would hold for the whole night. And five or six real serious old fellows around him and not a stir out of them listening to that, and they paying the greatest attention to every word of it. He was an awful man. A right quare fellow that's what L. was.[61]

B.'s lies about prodigious harvests might comfort people still traumatized by the nightmare of famine. In other performances, L. seems to have been more mischievous, but, from his community's point of view, if the victims had been too quarrelsome or credulous or cowardly they deserved to be punished, and thus perhaps improved. Clever people, on the other hand, had the pleasure of not being fooled because they knew the man, and what to expect in this kind of story-telling session.

Carrying a certain kind of fictionalization to extremes, 'tales of lying' may explode it. If we now turn to the other end of the spectrum, we find stories told to explain or question, which deny fictional status – but may reveal the extraordinary in the midst of life. The vague collective term for such narratives is 'legend'.

Legends have been collected more abundantly than tales; their telling probably was the more common activity. Many of them were published in the nineteenth century with the adjunction of a literary form, but for a long period folklorists tended to be less interested in them than in the artful multiepisodic tale of wonder. They have become more fashionable lately because, having outlived the once more respected wonder tale as a productive genre, they can still be studied *in situ* and *in vivo*; also, less often dissected than *Märchen*, they may offer scope for new theories. In so far as the concept can be acceptably defined, the distinctive features would be the topics treated and/or or the attitudes of speakers and listeners: a legend would depict undocumented but supposedly real and localised occurrences, and might be taken on trust. The nature of the communicative act, and some ensuing formal features, are specific: the telling often – today, mostly – takes place in conversation, with the interaction of various persons offering comment, support or contradiction, and a legend may be assembled from bits and pieces by several individuals. The tellers may adopt rhetori-

61 IFC 544: 60-5. From Tomás Mac Gearailt, aged 70.

cal devices, but generally do not seek to embellish what they are transmitting. The structure of the narrative seems loose in comparison with that of a *Märchen*: the plot may not be so clearly developed, the sense of completion brought about by the resolution of conflicts at the end of tales is seldom achieved, and a legend can be just alluded to or talked about rather than told. But what we know of the *seanchaithe* of the past shows that the same material could also be the object of extended utterance by a respected performer: 'though usually short, it may, on the lips of an expert narrator, especially when he is telling of a personal experience, reach the length of even a folktale and comprise more than one episode.'[62] Imagination might be at work here, too, with the selection and amplification of details, condensation (several elements are fused), and displacement (a new item is substituted for another).

The criterion of belief, in the older definition of legend, has been taken issue with. As noted above, even *Märchen* have sometimes been taken literally, though the magic that functions in them is generally not expected in ordinary life.[63] The legend, on the other hand, accepts controversy,[64] and may be communicated deliberately to provoke dispute and negotiation about what is being asserted: 'The topic of the legend is raised as an unuttered question that is being discussed at the legend-telling session by supporters and non-supporters ... [The legend] takes a stand and calls for the expression of opinions in the question of truth and belief.'[65] Although a legend is not likely to be told as overt fiction, it can be offered tongue-in-cheek, or at least, as David Buchan said, 'told within a frame of only partial belief or disbelief ("Well, that is what the old folks said, anyway ...") though the teller feels some compulsion to repeat it'.[66] Bill Ellis emphasized the polemical aspect: 'a legend is a narrative that challenges accepted definitions of the real world and leaves itself suspended, relying for closure on each individual's response.'[67]

What has been observed in Ireland confirms the view that legends were often told in conversation and in a loose form – but not always; and recent attempts at downplaying the link with belief may have gone too far, according to an expert:

---

62 S. O'Sullivan *Legends from Ireland* 12. 63 L. Röhrich, op. cit. 63: 'Nur weniges von dem, was uns im Märchen an Wunderbarem begegnet, scheint sich zunächst mit einer lebendigen Volksglaubenswirklichkeit in Verbindung bringen zu lassen.' 64 Linda Dégh 'Legend', in T.A. Green (ed.) *Folklore: An Encyclopedia* 489: 'As a conversation about the truth of the presented case, the legend is a discussion between believers, doubters, skeptics, and nonbelievers. It is this discussion of the feasibility of the narrated legend that is essential, not its resolution or the settling of the dispute. It is also inconsequential whether the tellers are believers or nonbelievers; what counts is that they are attracted to the universal questions of the world and human life entertained by the legend and that they like to express their attitudes towards it.' 65 L. Dégh and A. Váznonyi 'Legend and Belief', in D. Ben-Amos (ed.) *Folklore Genres* 113, 119. 66 D. Buchan *Scottish Tradition* 18. 67 'When is a legend? An Essay on Legend Mythology', in G. Bennett and P. Smith (eds) *The Questing Beast* 34.

The Irish [collectors'] texts are – I dare say – more often than those of other countries accompanied by statements from the collectors to the effect that the tellers believed in them (and in most cases such statements are not based on flimsy impressions obtained perhaps through a single recital by a teller met only once, but rather on long and intimate acquaintance with the respective tradition bearers). In the case of material that has been taken down on tapes, the voices will also with a fair degree of certainty provide a give-away as to whether the informants' own statements, to the effect that they believe what they tell to be true, is only a narrative device to create illusion or whether it is to be taken at face value. In situations where we also have access to videotapes or films we have further opportunity to assess the degree to which legends have actually been the objects of belief. Though it is an obvious and oft-stated fact that the amount of belief that tellers place in migratory legends would be less than that with which they embrace personal experience legends or *memorates*, experience from my own field-collecting has taught me that a surprising number of tellers of migratory legends of the supernatural are firmly convinced that what they tell actually happened and that the final tag in many of these recitals *scéal fíor é sin*, 'that is a true story', means to them exactly what the words convey.[68]

This quotation uses the term 'migratory legend', which was introduced around 1930 to refer to 'a narrative of a certain length, usually shorter than a fairy tale, in prose, existing in a limited number of variants, some, if not all, of which may become localized in quite different places'.[69] R.T. Christiansen distinguished the 'migratory legend' from the 'memorate' (a repeatedly told episode in the life of the teller, often but not always involving an encounter with a supernatural being), in that the former 'no longer has the direct personal touch and instead follows a definite pattern' and 'will pass from one country to another'.[70] An international ordering system was suggested, and intensive work continues in this field. A number of Irish legends have affiliations with the international corpus.[71]

I shall look more closely at two categories of Irish legends and their modes of telling. My first set of examples come from the subgroup of so-called 'supernatural legends', treating of the manifestations of mysterious powers in the world of the tellers and their audience, the numinous quality of the events being a distinctive issue – unlike the *Märchen*, where the marvellous is generally taken for granted and is not particularly awe-inspiring. We must of course remember that the term 'supernatural' refers to phenomena which, though considered incompatible with known physical laws, may nevertheless be accepted by some (or many) as part of reality. I shall then turn to the 'historical legends': traditionally received but unverified 'truth' concerning attested personages and events.

68 Bo Almqvist 'Irish Migratory Legends on the Supernatural', *Béaloideas* 59 (1991) 41. 69 A.H. Krappe, *The Science of Folk-Lore* 101. 70 *The Migratory Legends: A Proposed List of Types with a Systematic Catalogue of the Norwegian Variants* 5. The catalogue is an extension of the system adopted for *The Types of the Folktale*. 71 D. Ó hÓgain *Myth, Legend & Romance* 228. A whole issue of *Béaloideas* (volume 59) and several articles in other issues have studied such international material.

Ideas about what is a 'supernatural' occurrence, and the credence given to it, may vary from one culture to another, and also within a society in the course of time and at any given time. As this is no place to embark upon a detailed inventory of the beliefs which observers have associated with rural Ireland, I shall focus on the telling of stories concerning only three kinds of awe-inspiring beings: 'witches', 'fairies', and 'ghosts'.

Special powers, not necessarily evil, were attributed to certain humans, often women: the *bean feasa* was wise and useful, while a *cailleach* (a very old woman or hag) might be a witch who could casts spells (*piseoga*), was perhaps able to shape-shift or to make herself invisible, to fly, raise storms and sink ships; she could use her powers for ill and was often feared – but Gaelic Ireland was generally free from the prosecution of witches as devil-worshippers. The following experience, reported from the Aran Islands at the end of the nineteenth century, illustrates the attitudes of a collector, his informant and members of the latter's community; it confirms that a belief may not be shared by all, and shows that the teller's purpose is more to inform and explain than to shape a story:

In May 1892, I was on hands and knees one morning, poring over a promising stretch of sandy pasture near the sea at Killeany, Aranmore, in search of the rare Milk Vetch (Astrologus hypoglottis), a species peculiar in Ireland to these islands, when I was startled by this remark, which came from one of the knot of puzzled Killeany-men who had gathered round me to watch my doings with embarrassing patience: 'That's a very dangerous thing you are about; I've known a man killed that way.' At first I thought the speaker, a grave, middle-aged man, meant to warn me against injury from some poisonous plant, but on close cross-questioning, it became evident that he was a firm believer in disease-transference by witchcraft.

His story was shortly this. Some years ago a friend of his, a man named Flanagan, living in the neighbourhood of Oghill, in Aranmore, lay sick of an incurable disease. He had been 'given over' by the doctors, and face to face with death, his fears, after a long struggle, got the better of his religion, and he made up his mind to call in the services of a *cailleach*, who lived in Onaght, at the other end of the island. This hag was well known to have the power of transferring mortal sickness from the patient, wicked enough to employ her, to some healthy subject, who would sicken and die, as an unconscious substitute. This was her method, evidently a combination of a plant-spell with the *gettatura*, or evil eye. When fully empowered by her patient, whose honest intention to profit by the unholy remedy was indispensable to its successful working, the *cailleach* would go out into some field close by a public road, and setting herself on her knees, just as I was kneeling then, she would pluck an herb from the ground, looking out on the road as she did so. The first passer-by she might happen to cast her eye on, while in the act of plucking the herb, no matter who it was, even her own father or mother, would take the sick man's disease, and die of it in twenty-four hours, the patient mending as the victim sickened and died. My informant had known the *cailleach* well, but had only heard for certain of one case, the case of his friend Flanagan, where she had worked a cure in this way. The name of the man she had killed to save Flanagan's life was O'Flaherty, and he had known him, too. This, in substance, is the story drawn from the

Killeany-man by a laborious cross-examination, under which he remained perfectly serious, and perfectly consistant in his answers. Three or four younger men who were in the group, Killeany-men, too, openly scoffed at his credulity, yet he clung tenaciously to every point in his story, and gave all the signs of an honest belief in it.[72]

While witches and enchanters act as powerful opponents or helpers in complex Irish tales, more 'ordinary' *cailleacha* appear in shorter and supposedly factual stories. Particularly widespread examples concern the old woman who, by magically appropriating the 'profit' of the milk, prevented the making of butter (cf. p. 77). In another common type of legend (cf. p. 174), the old woman transformed herself into a hare to suck milk from other people's cows: 'As any folklore collector worth his salt will tell you, individuals of this ilk are still widely talked about in many parts of the country. It may not even be too much of an exaggeration to say that these women and their doings not only constitute a continuing subject of conversation in a good many parts of this island, but that actually a lot of people still go in fear and dread of warranting their attention.'[73]

But from the end of the eighteenth century to the first decades of the twentieth, the beliefs that, according to outsiders, most markedly characterized the Irish were a particularly strong and complex set of notions associated with otherworld entities, usually invisible to the human race but living alongside with it, single or in groups, not human but in some respects resembling mankind though differing from it in 'powers, properties and attributes'.[74] They are grouped in English under the term 'fairies'. Such beliefs have been reported from every part of the world but there may be local peculiarities and, according to the specialist just quoted, 'the Irish fairy beliefs are the most explicit and generally held'.[75] For T. Crofton Croker, at the beginning of the nineteenth century, there was no questioning that many Irish actually believed in fairies: 'It would be in the power of every one conversant with the manners of the country to produce instances of the undoubting belief in these superstitions.'[76] At that stage it was impossible to be sure how old such 'traditions' were, and what exactly was the link with more sophisticated ancient Irish literature.[77] It was generally believed

---

72 Nathaniel Colgan 'Witchcraft in the Aran Islands', in *Journal of the Royal Society of Antiquaries of Ireland* 25 (1895) 84-5. 73 Séamas Ó Catháin 'Hags and Hares', in *Irish Life and Lore* (1982) 22. Ten years later, in an article listing more than sixty versions with recurrent elements, and showing that the belief was found in various parts of Europe since the Middle Ages, Eilís Ní Dhuibhne noted that this story was no longer widely told: ' "The Old Woman as Hare": Structure and Meaning in an Irish Legend', in *Folklore* 104 (1993) 77-85. 74 K.M. Briggs *The Vanishing People: A Study of Traditional Fairy Beliefs* 26. 75 K.M. Briggs *The Fairies in Tradition and Literature* 87. 76 *Fairy Legends and Traditions* xxvii (preface to the second volume). 77 According to D. Ó hÓgáin, *Béaloideas* 60-1 (1992-3) 72, 'There can be little doubt but that some lore of Celtic deities intermingled with notions concerning the living dead and was thus an important fountainhead of the tradition of the *Sí* people or fairies in Ireland.'

that fairies should not be named but referred to by some euphemistic circumlocutions like *daoine sídhe* (the people of the mounds, shortened to *sídhe*, now spelt
sí), or *daoine maithe* (the good people), or *daoine uaisle* (the noble people, the
gentry), or *daoine beaga* (the little people – 'wee folk' in Ulster), or *an dream so
lasmuigh dhínn* (the tribe apart from us), or *slua beatha* (host of life), or *bunadh
na gcnoc* (hill-folk).[78] Different accounts of their origin were given: they were the
dead, or guardians of the dead,[79] or (according to a medieval theory imported
from the continent)[80] half-fallen angels who had not decided between God and
Lucifer. Some antiquarians favoured the idea that they had been earlier inhabitants or ancient gods of Ireland (the *Tuatha Dé Danann*). They were said to live
in the ' fairy forts' (earthworks or ring-forts), in hollow hills or old tumuli, and
in other 'noble' or 'gentle' places (*áiteanna uaisle*). Their realm impinged on the
mortal world at in-between times and places: they would change their haunts at
the basic junctures of the Irish year and were therefore most likely to be
encountered at the beginning of November and of May. They should be pla-
cated or, better, avoided, because any contact with them was risky: they could
be benign or mischievous or just resentful of human intrusion, and their reactions were unpredictable. They had a habit of abducting pretty young women,
occasionally young men, and children which they replaced by sickly creatures
(*iarlaisí* or *síofraí*: changelings); why they did so remained in dispute.[81]
Sometimes those who were 'taken' or had received a 'fairy stroke' (*poc sídhe*)
remained present among humans, as specially gifted people or as half-wits. But
attempts to survey this Otherworld may be vain:

Fairy belief is in fact a very vague, ill-defined area, embracing subtleties no classificatory
system can hope to encompass ... [The folklorist compares two versions collected in the
1970s of 'The Departure of the Fairies': how, when and why fairies left Ireland.] One
man holds mutually contradictory beliefs, but has somehow reconciled the contradictions.
He can reconcile contradictions both in his own system in itself, and as it conflicts with
the system of another story-teller as is evidenced by the contradictory departure tales. It
seems that, to the believer, these contradictions are unimportant, so long as the tales
concur in the fact that the fairies actually exist. This general vagueness makes it possible for contradictory tales to be told, without any sense that they do conflict. Clearly, the
word 'fairy' must communicate something, but fairy beliefs allow for a vast range of elaboration and interpretation, depending on by whom they are handled.[82]

From the Middle Ages onwards, it was said in Europe that the fairies were van-

---

78 Other Irish names are listed in S. Ó hEochaidh *Síscéalta Ó Thír Chonaill* 26-7.   79 D. Ó
hÓgáin *Myth, Legend & Romance* 185: 'lore of the dead still tends to become confused with
that of the fairies in living oral narrative.'   80 Attested in the late-thirteenth-century *South
English Legendary*.   81 Críostóir MacCarthaigh 'Midwife to the Fairies', *Béaloideas* 59 (1991)
133-43; Séamus MacPhilib 'The Changeling', ibid. 121-31.   82 Linda-May Ballard 'Aspects
of Contemporary Ulster Fairy Tradition', in V.J. Newall (ed.) *Folklore Studies in the Twentieth
Century* 401-2.

ishing, or had already departed. In Ireland, throughout the nineteenth century some writers claimed that actual belief in fairies was dying, while others attested that it was still very much alive. Angela Bourke thinks that 'The question of whether ... storytellers "really believed" in the fairies they told stories about is less important than the use they made of them as scaffolding for the construction and maintenance of a whole world-view'.[83] She carefully documents the notorious case of the burning, in rural Tipperary in 1895, of a young woman thought to be a fairy-changeling, and interprets it as a way of 'reasserting the authority of an older way of life'.[84]

At the beginning of the twentieth century, Lady Gregory found it difficult to distinguish between genuine experience, received belief, and creative imagination: 'It is hard to tell sometimes what has been a real vision and what is tradition, a legend hanging in the air, a "vanity" as our people call it, made use of by a story-teller here and there, or impressing itself as a real experience on some sensitive and imaginative mind.'[85] At about the same time, Douglas Hyde held the view that 'beliefs in the *sidhe* folk, and in other denizens of the invisible world [was], in many places, rapidly dying'.[86] In the 1930s, informants might conclude their accounts of fairy doings with remarks like: 'That's a story I heard. I don't know is it true or not, but if it is a lie, 'twasn't I who made it up! The blessing of God on the souls of the dead!'[87] S. Ó hEochaidh, who collected in South-West Donegal from the mid-1930s, noted that belief in the fairies had been gradually declining, and that references to them were generally set in the past, as in this statement by Conall Ó Beirn: 'When I was a child I used to hear my grandfather talk about the hill-folk. No man in the countryside had more tales of the fairies than he had. He himself was a firm believer in them, and he never went to the bog for a creel of turf without expecting to see them.'[88] A study of Ulster folklore published in 1951 still stated that 'it is surprising how many people claim to have seen fairies';[89] in 1959, at Toorglas, County Mayo, the course of a projected road had to be altered because it would have cut through fairy territory and the local farmers explained that, although they did not believe in the Little People, it was better to change the project[90] – illustrating the oft-quoted Irish paradox: 'of course I don't believe in them, but does it prevent them from being there just the same?' In 1959, D.A. MacManus published a number of first-hand stories of 'seeings' and other mysterious manifestations ascribed to fairies, which he offered as 'authenticated' because a reliable

83 *The Burning of Bridget Cleary* 60. 84 Ibid. 135. 85 *Visions and Beliefs in the West of Ireland* 15. 86 W.I. Evans Wentz *The Fairy-Faith in Celtic Countries* 26-7. 87 IFC 529: 51 (collected in Co. Galway in 1938), tr. S. O'Sullivan *Legends of Ireland* 72. 88 *Síscéalta Ó Thír Chonaill* 34-5. 89 J.C. Cooper *Ulster Folklore* 66. 90 Quoted from the *Daily Mail* of 23 April 1959, in R.T. Christiansen 'Some Notes on the Fairies and Fairy Faith', *Béaloideas* 39-41 (1971-73) 102. Stories or legends concerning people who went on strike because they believed in fairies appear in Merwyn Wall's *Leaves for Burning* (1952) and in Patrick Byrne's *Irish Ghost Stories* (1965).

central character in each incident was still alive and was prepared to swear to it.[91] In 1967, Sean O'Sullivan could write that the belief in fairies was 'still strong in our own day in rural areas'.[92] Still later, T. Robinson noted that on Inishmore 'most islanders, if asked about the truth of such stories, would reply, "You wouldn't know".'[93] But many, today, would probably find such an inquiry insulting.

If the telling of fairy lore has diminished (except for tourists perhaps) and is given less credence, ghost stories still have audiences prepared to share a narrator's conviction, at least temporarily: 'The fairy gives way more and more to the ghost in rural Ireland today', Arensberg noted in the 1930s;[94] almost half-a-century later, another American observed that in Ireland 'more people credit ghosts than fairies, more credit tokens [signs heralding death] than ghosts.'[95] When something which can be interpreted as the manifestation of a dead person occurs, culture-determined models of interpretation give it a certain meaning; established narrative patterns condition the way it is conveyed, and repeated communication gradually shapes the message according to some basic types. Of course the resulting ghost stories may be told for the odd thrill of being afraid in company, but they generally strike a responsive chord. The belief is abundantly attested in Ireland, as in this introduction to a set of stories published anonymously in 1863:

> Were we assured that narrators were always as accurate as they are frequently honest, we should conclude that ghostly visitations are as common in these counties, at this day, as they were in the darkest ages that have slowly swept over the earth. Let but a social party gather round the fire in country or town on a cold night, and anyone commence a weird tale connected with apparitions, and scarce a person in the company will fail to relate something beyond what ears and eyes are accustomed to, which occurred, if not to himself, at all events to some intimate acquaintance, who would not utter a falsehood for any 'Earthly crown' ... Of [the stories] we are about to relate, we are as sure of the good faith of the tellers as of any ordinary truth or fact that has occurred to us, but are yet of opinion that, could all circumstances connected with the occurrences be ascertained, everything related might probably be referred to natural causes.[96]

In the twentieth century, it could still be said that 'innumerable stories are told in Ireland of people who were said to have returned to earth after death for some reason.'[97] 'There are an infinite number of ghost traditions current in Ulster' says a contemporary folklorist, who adds that ghost-beliefs are not confined to the Catholic section of the community.[98]

91 *The Middle Kingdom: The Faerie World of Ireland* 11. 92 *Irish Folk Custom and Belief* 82. 93 *Stones of Aran: Labyrinth* 81. 94 *The Irish Countryman* 214. 95 H. Glassie *Passing the Time...* 66. 96 'A Fire-Side Gossip about Ghosts and Fairies', in *Dublin University Magazine* 62 (1863) 692. 97 S. O'Sullivan *A Handbook of Irish Folklore* 244. 98 L.M. Ballard 'Before Death & Beyond – A Preliminary Survey of Death & Ghost Traditions with Particular Reference to Ulster', in H.R. Davidson and W.M.S. Russell (eds) *The Folklore of Ghosts* 37, 13.

As far as we know, ancient Ireland does not seem to have been all that rich in revenants that frightened, warned or attacked the living; it may be that they belonged to a popular level of lore not represented in the texts we have. There was undoubtedly a belief in parallel and sometimes communicating worlds, but whether death meant passing from one to the other with the possibility of returning is not clear. Christian views of Purgatory and the other places may have changed the picture: 'the mediaeval church not only tolerated a belief in ghosts, but was active in disseminating the belief, and the ghost story had an important role in the church's system of instruction — especially instruction of the populace.'[99] In nineteenth-century Ireland, dead people who had committed heinous sins were thought to become evil spirits who harmed the living (but such *sprideanna* were not always dead humans); one risked meeting them at intermediary places such as bridges or crossroads. 'Ordinary' apparitions (*taisi*) were not so formidable: they could be well-meaning dead people who tried to assist relatives and to whom the family house was open at certain times of the year; some were suffering temporary punishment and needed assistance; others returned to pay a debt, look after someone, or restore justice. In reports of personal ghostly experiences and in repetitions of such accounts by the neighbours, even in openly fictitious wonder tales, the returning dead (the 'Grateful Dead', for instance — see p. 505) were not disembodied spirits.

In 1939, Henry Traynor, a contributor to the Irish Folklore Archive, tried to classify the stories he had heard in County Wexford. There were stories in which the ghosts had been seen by the storytellers themselves, who might perhaps recognise them as people they had known: 'I am genuinely convinced that in certain cases the storyteller really believed he had seen a ghost and was not telling an idle tale to amuse his hearers.' Then there were ghosts the storytellers had heard about but had not seen: 'In such stories it was hard to discover at times whether the storyteller really believed the story or not. According to some of these stories there were black dogs, rattling chains on every road. This kind of story I would say was carried sometimes to ridiculous length.' There were also stories concerning ghostly noises and mysterious lights.[100]

Oral ghost stories tend to be short and simple, unlike the literary ones written in the second half of the nineteenth century. They may range from factual reports of genuine experience to inventions, with ambiguous cases in between: there may be no clear borderline between the sincere report and a narrative organized for effect.

A delicate question is whether all such accounts should be called legends. The ticklish point is not their narrative form: it can be short or long, rudimentary or elaborate, and they can be told by groups or by individuals, untrained or experts. The area of dispute rather concerns the more or less extended trans-

99 R.A. Bowyer 'The Role of the Ghost-Story in Medieval Christianity', in Davidson and Russell, 190. 100 IFC 1059: 115-21.

mission of the items – their 'traditionality' in that sense of the word. Loosely organized accounts of personal experience ('memorates') may not be so widely transmitted; but in them the experience is formulated and interpreted on the basis of collective, 'traditional' models,[101] and the account of a personal supernatural experience might in time develop into a legend.

What follows represents such a borderline case, as well as the 'polyphonic' form of telling when varied individual contributions complete each other. I have chosen three complementary accounts of a local apparition, collected by M.J. Murphy in the parish of Clonduff, County Down, in February-March 1945. They illustrates the resilience of a belief (Motif E415.4: Dead cannot rest until money debts are paid) as well as a collective reconstruction of facts, which are uncanny enough to be arresting and sufficiently harmonized with a common mental attitude to be acceptable when shaped into a story – in this case more implied than told:

Barney O'Hagan's contribution

Do you believe the dead can return and speak? Well, I'll tell this, and you can verify it on others if you like. It's quite true. It happened about – Oh, it might be thirty years ago. Why man, it used to be a common expression at the time: 'Is F. failed?' It was F. used to be seen. I believe it was on a pad [path] it happened. F. was killed off a car coming out of Castlewellan. And this man – a great chum of F.'s – I believe he was comin' now from a card playing. But he met him. And he was visible from the waist up only. Met him and knew him. The man who met him was the name of G. He went to the priest about it, too. It's a fact.

James Gribben's contribution (same session)

Oh, begod, there's no lie in that. Barney Hogan wasn't telling a word of lie. I never heard about F. being visible from the waist up; but many's the time I heard my father tell it as well. Sure Ghosty G.'s alive yet. He's the fellow seen F.. He lives in Foffally. F. was killed off a sidecar comin' from Castlewellan. And him and Ghosty was always great mates. They used to be at a céilí-house in Jemmy Ducks. Like, there was a near cut to it – a sort of pad [path]. And Ghosty was coming home the night he seen him. Oh, he knew him well. So he went to the priest the next morning about it, and told him. And the priest put him down on his knees at the altar, and read over him. And whatever he read he says: 'You seen F. alright!' So he says then: 'Go the same pad to-night, and you'll meet him again. And come to me in the morning.' And he done what the

---

101 L. Bødker *International Dictionary of Regional European Ethnology and Folklore* 2. 195-6: 'A memorate has not the nature of fiction, and is not tradition. It may, however, be strongly influenced by *sagen* [legends] about similar events. For a memorate to become tradition it is a condition that other people think it interesting enough to retell it, by which it is likely to become subject to stylistic alterations, what with elimination of details which seem less interesting to the new narrator, and adaptation of the content to conform with prevalent conceptions.' See also L. Honko, 'Memorates and the Study of Folk Belief', *Journal of the Folklore Institute* 1 (1964).

priest told him, an' he seen F. again. So the priest says to him: 'Well, go again to-night an' you'll see him again, and speak to him,' says he. 'Speak,' says he, 'and ask him his troubles. And ask him in the name o' God.' That was in Kilcoo. G. wasn't a bit afeard at all. He spoke to him the same as if he was coming in reality. But you'd feel the worst of it – though it didn't do G. much harm. He's alive and well yet. But they say if you meet anything like that and speak to it in the name of God, it can answer you. I heard that at it. But they say you'll not live only a short time after it. But, of course, G. went to the priest.

Ketty Courtney's contribution (a couple of weeks later)
There's a man out there in Foffally the name of Ghosty G. that seen a man. Oh, that's true enough. I mind it well at the time. He got odd looking since, but sure who would wonder at that. But he went to the priest. It was a man was killed off a car. He was out this night with a party, coming off their céilí, and he stopped behind to tie his boot, and this man was standing over him. He told him who he owed money to. I mind there was a tailor was still to get money. And others I can't mind. Oh, he told him all after he spoke to him. That was after he seen the priest. And he told too the way the carts was annoying him passing over him. That was all true enough.[102]

Our first impression might be of a disorganized series of attempts at clarifying an episode in the local past, involving comparatively little narrative skill. We recognize a common foundation of memories, but details of the events may be unequally distributed among members of the community. There seems to be a shared field of beliefs and of simple narrative schemata by which the material of experience is shaped and coloured, to meet the expectations of those who know what the account of a ghostly experience should be like. The facts of the case, which had been puzzling and perhaps significant a generation before, are gradually pieced together,[103] and the particularity of this set of testimonies is that it takes the contribution of someone not present in the first session to approach a more 'complete' version – but we cannot exclude the possibility that, had the collector met other cooperative informants, the whole pattern might be different.

The collective account is not as erratic or amorphous as individual tellings may seem to be. We may recognize the essentials of the paradigm established by William Labov in his study of 'natural narrative' embedded in ordinary conversation[104] – at least if we consider the full model approached by degrees through

102 IFC 975: 512, 534-5, 546. 103 Linda Dégh 'The "Belief Legend" in Modern Society', in W.D. Hand (ed.) *American Folk Legend; A Symposium* 63: 'The fragmentary character of the modern legend is closely related to its collective nature. Current legends seem to be generated by certain groups at specific occasions through communal cooperation. The participants of legend-sessions put together their pieces of knowledge.' The same author, writes: 'The proponent who starts a story will be joined by coproponents who add their information to the telling as the story unfolds. Those present contribute to a communal version, adding their information, making corrections, and expressing their opinions concerning the veracity of the event.' ('Legend', in T.A. Green (ed.) *Folklore: An Encyclopedia* 488.) 104 W. Labov and J.

the conflation of three fragments of conversational narration. In the synthetic version we have in mind after the third telling, we find the introductory signal that one of the conversationalists wants to turn storyteller because he feels he has something to relate, which can make a 'point' about some important theme: 'Do you believe the dead can return and speak? Well, I'll tell this ... ' It also functions as what in Labov's terminology is called the 'abstract': an opening routine giving the subject of the story before the actual telling. In the first fragment, the alliterative question 'Is F. failed' could be another possible introduction, but would normally be followed by the story of this man's faults or misadventures, whereas what we have is rather the story of G. What Labov calls 'orientation', necessary background information such as the place and time of the encounter and the identity of the actors, is at first kept to a minimum, probably because the local audience is familiar with it; but, an outsider (the collector) being present, it is developed piecemeal. In the 'complicating action', events should lead to a climax – hardly exploited at first; but the story is arresting enough from the first version, and is gradually clarified. When the third version has been told, a sequence with causal and other links is more or less established. By then, the relative complexity of the subject is revealed: what seemed at first to be just the story of the ghost ('It was F. used to be seen ...') turns out to be the story of the man who met the ghost ('He's the fellow seen F.'), and the role of yet another character, the priest, is gradually sketched out. The successive reports establish four facts which the community would find significant: F.'s sudden death after a reckless life; G.'s ghostly experience and the danger it may have involved; the priest's competence; and finally the precise cause of the haunting, some unpaid debt – which indeed was commonly believed to be a possible reason for a dead man's return. The 'coda' (Labov's term for a rounding-off statement), 'that was all true enough', signals to the audience that the story is complete and confirms that a basic issue has been raised about life and life-after-death. The story has a 'point' because it is 'evaluated' as both extraordinary and more or less plausible – or intriguing. These narrators seem to believe in ghosts (though the first one begins in a non-committal way) and in the events they are reconstructing after some thirty years: 'It's quite true', 'It's a fact', 'There's no lie in that', 'That's true enough'. They know G., who is still alive. But they have his story only by hearsay: 'I heard ...', 'They say ...'.

If G. himself told about his experience – and, after all, how else would we know about it? – it probably started as a brief account in the first person, conveyed as mere information. Nevertheless, the first telling may already have had some shape, imposed upon it by earlier experiences as a listener. Such 'traditional' fashioning would not imply an intention to deceive: 'The kind of readjusting and rearranging that goes on as people recount their experiences is not the sort of purposeful misconstrual we normally call lying',[105] but narration

Waletzky 'Narrative Analysis: Oral Versions of Personal Experience', in J. Helms (ed.) *Essays on the Verbal and Visual Arts* 12-44; W. Labov *Language in the Inner City* Ch. 9. **105** B.

introduces some order and sense. Because it was dealing with odd facts on the verge of what the community was prepared to believe, the experience was 'tellable' – worthy of being told again and again. To be considered 'story-worthy', however, it could hardly be strictly personal: it had to fit the interests and accepted beliefs, or perhaps worrying doubts, of the group, as well as its conception of how satisfactory narrative discourse should be organized. Did G. become too 'odd' to be a very effective storyteller? Anyway, being repeated by different neighbours who had not experienced the events personally, the story could be further altered to become increasingly consonant with the group's convictions and its standards concerning such 'true-narrative' stereotypes. Whatever undocumented career G. may have had as a memorate-teller, his experience became part of a collective local repertoire: 'I heard my father tell it as well ...'; it became an example used when its 'point' was the topic of conversation. After some thirty years, factual details were no longer easily verifiable, but the story was accepted as in some sense 'true enough', which may be paraphrased as: significant and therefore worth telling. It had somewhat crystallized as a close-knit common story in which a core of beliefs or questions now decidedly mattered more than some unique individual experience; but it may have vanished with the generation of informants met by the collector, perhaps to be replaced by other 'true' stories on a similar pattern, or on a partly different frame of reference imposed by changing values.

Still on the outskirts of the 'legend' nebula, folklorists and sociologists in the second half of the twentieth century paid attention to brief sensational stories subject to variation, circulating by word of mouth but also through the modern channels of mass communication, with a wide international distribution. They have been called 'modern legends', 'contemporary legends', 'urban legends' or 'urban belief tales'. Some of their narrative motifs may be ancient, but the events are said to have actually happened recently, are relevant to present preoccupations, and may express normally censured opinions. The subjects can be horrible or bizarre encounters, and are made plausible by the fact that the victim or the witness is often said to be a friend of one of the teller's friends. Adaptable geographical references strengthen the impression of veracity. Such stories are therefore often believed to be true, but may also be told tongue in cheek. They are said to combine characteristics of several genres: 'Modern legends seem to be like fables in their ability to focus fears, warnings, threats and promises, and to be like tall tales in the way the just-barely-possible occurrence is exaggerated to the point of wild improbability.'[106] When communicated orally, they are conversational, informal, and potentially controversial. There are problems of denomination: to call them 'modern' is questionable when they are avatars of old stories, and they are not exclusively 'urban'. Whereas the tellers of the earlier

Johnstone *Stories, Community, and Place* 9.   **106** W.F.H. Nicolaisen 'Perspective on Contemporary Legends', *Fabula* 26 (1985) 223.

kinds of legends often were the elders who embodied the 'tradition' of the community, these 'new' stories rather belong to the repertoire of the younger generation. Such material has been collected in Ireland too.[107] One item in the Irish Folklore Archives adapts to the setting of the 'Troubles' in Northern Ireland the most famous of those international floating story-types, that of 'The Vanishing Hitchhiker', first noticed by folklorists in the 1940s but based on Motifs E332: Non-malevolent road ghost, and E581: Dead person rides, which have been used by storytellers for several centuries (see p. 296); the most obvious 'modern' element is the replacement of some old-style mode of transport by a motorcar. A driver picks up someone on the road, usually at night; then the mysterious passenger, having perhaps offered some prophetic message, disappears and is later revealed to have been dead for a long time. Ghost stories developed in Northern Ireland after the bombing near Warrenpoint on 27 August 1979 in which eighteen British soldiers died: the place was said to be so haunted that it had to be exorcized. To the accounts of sightings of British ghosts were added stories of live soldiers pretending to be dead to terrify local people.[108] In this context, the international 'contemporary legend', which had circulated orally and through the media on both sides of the Atlantic, found a peculiar Irish expression, of which the following is a digest rather than a verbatim transcript:

A soldier in the North is driving along one night. It is near the border. He is flashed down by somebody on the road, who turns out to be a Scottish soldier. He picks him up, of course, and the soldier sits in the back-seat. He is driving, and hears no sound. So he turns back to have a look, and finds the seat empty! The soldier is gone. He goes home and of course the story spreads around the neighbourhood very quickly. The following night, somebody else is driving along the same stretch of road, and he is flashed at by two soldiers. He decides not to stop, but puts the boot down and flies on – a courageous thing to do in the North, where you could be shot if you didn't stop for a soldier. After a while he hears some noise in the back of the car. He turns around, and sees the two soldiers sitting there. The first man learned that the Scottish soldier had been killed on that patch of road.[109]

A cruder kind of communication involving belief is 'rumour': news, mostly unpleasant, of doubtful accuracy and from unidentified sources, widely disseminated by hearsay and perhaps gaining in detail as it spreads. It consists of one item of information rather than of a narrative and tends to be short-lived, yet a 'new' rumour may be the adaptation of an old pattern to new circumstances. It

107 See Eilís Ní Dhuibhne 'Dublin Modern Legends: an Intermediate Type List and Examples', *Béaloideas* (51) 55-70. 108 L.M. Ballard 'Tales of the Troubles', in P. Smith (ed.) *Perspectives on Contemporary Legend* 11. 109 IFC 2022 ('Urban Folklore Project' 1980): 94 (contributed, in Dublin, by a student of 23 who had heard it in County Derry). Cf. J.H. Brunvand *The Vanishing Hitchhiker: Urban Legends and their Meanings* 30-45; G. Bennett 'The Phantom Hitchhiker: neither modern, urban, nor legend?' in P. Smith (ed.) *Perspectives on Contemporary Legend* 45-67.

arises in situations of uncertainty, to propose an interpretation of unexplained or supposed facts when authoritative information is lacking, or when news spread by official channels is not trusted. It sets off a chain reaction: people listen to it because they need 'reliable' information, and transmit it partly because it may enhance their status as knowledgeable persons, but also because it contains what they are afraid of. Some legends may have originated as rumours, and a rumour may give new life to a half-dormant legend.[110] As with the formation of legends, a distorting/constructing process is at work in the evolution of rumours: reduction – irrelevant details are eliminated; sharpening – those that have been retained are stressed; and adjustment – alterations and additions produce more congenial utterance to the state of mind of the transmitter and of his interlocutors.

The combination of a ghost motif with political events provides the transition to another Irish repertoire: 'historical' narratives. An essential difference is the fact that, if individual experiences involving the supernatural may be questioned and uncertainties about them played with up to a point, such latitude hardly ever applies to the way one represents and interprets the collective past. One of the various senses of the word 'myth' may be relevant here: an imaginative construction of peculiar seriousness and emotional power, held to be true but without factual basis, and serving as explanation or justification of the present state of affairs. It may be valued as a manifestation of truth and a necessary support for common identity, or denounced as a dangerous illusion or wicked deception.

History itself is a vast and problematic field – perhaps particularly in the Irish context. On the basis of purpose and target audience, methods, medium, and consequently also content and form, I shall distinguish between four modes of treatment of past events: academic, popular, propagandistic, and oral-traditional history – admitting that in practice boundaries can be blurred.

Trained academic scholars have rigorous methods for sifting documentary evidence and establishing facts. They must make no assertion without referring to a verifiable source. Although they are supposed to know that absolute objectivity is impossible and that they have access to limited truths only, they must try to be impartial. They may admit that, in a sense, there is some fictionality in all historical discourse since it involves the selection of data, imaginative reconstruction, and the shaping of an argument. To represent development in time, historiography often adopts a narrative form, which means carving segments out of continuous reality and organizing series of scenes – creating a plot, with a starting point and transformations through causally related episodes, leading to a new situation. And the serious historian cannot ignore that he himself operates in a society which determines what is of interest, and conditions its

---

110 P.B. Mullen 'Modern Legend and Rumor Theory', *Journal of the Folklore Institute* 8 (1971) 95-109.

treatment. It would be rash, however, to conclude that there are only subjective interpretations: even if no observer is omniscient and capable of complete disinterestedness, it is possible to confront versions and, being aware of their potential bias, to draw some new conclusions – themselves provisional but already better informed.

The second kind of representation is simplified for the general public, less methodical and with little or no critical apparatus: statements are just offered as authoritative. This history may be sensational or sentimental and is produced to satisfy the curiosity of lay readers or to educate the young. Without intending to deceive, the writers of such texts are prone to generalization, and they 'fictionalize' much more than the historians of the first group. Legends, as distinct from verifiable facts, may be exploited. Some have argued that what is offered thus may be a necessary illusion, since groups and nations depend on collectively shared images. Popular histories of Ireland multiplied from the last decades of the nineteenth century, and could be closer to imaginative literature than to scholarship. The opening of one of them, in 1881, frankly admitted it: 'Let me tell you the story of Ireland. It is not a history ... '.[111] Standish James O'Grady's romanticized histories of 'the heroic period' of Ireland belong to this group, and Douglas Hyde, reviewing one of them in 1886, voiced his opinion: 'History is, we believe, the same word as story, and certainly the most universally interesting historical works are those of the story-telling sort.'[112] We move imperceptibly from popular and didactic patriotic evocations to the manipulation of the past used as an ideological weapon, which defines my third category.

Ireland, with its antagonistic factions, was bound to produce irreconcilable accounts of past events, subordinated to political aims. Such 'history', invoked to bolster a cause, promote certain attitudes and validate programmes – and denounced as dangerous ruminations, a burden, a plague, a nightmare – is of course not an exclusively Irish phenomenon: everywhere, propaganda combines truth, half-truths or selective amnesia and lies, asserts dogmas for which no verification is required or allowed, and stirs emotions; but the fact is that in Ireland it may have been carried to extremes. History, conceived thus, raises ghosts from the past as a way of nourishing a conflict. A claim to veracity can be made by any party preaching to its converts: the nineteenth century nationalist John Mitchell announced that his *History of Ireland* would exhibit 'the naked truth concerning English domination since the Treaty of Limerick, as our fathers saw it, felt it',[113] then produced a biased account; prefacing Dorothy Macardle's partisan *The Irish Republic* in 1937, de Valera praised her both for writing 'as a Republican' and for having 'the supreme merit of being sincerely devoted to the truth'.[114] Ulster loyalism has its own version of history that legitimizes resistance

111 Dion Boucicault *The Fireside Story of Ireland*, quoted in J. Leerssen *Remembrances and Imagination: Patterns in the Historical and Literary Representation of Ireland in the Nineteenth Century* 153. 112 Quoted in D. Daly *The Young Douglas Hyde* 74. 113 *The History of Ireland* (1868) Introduction. 114 *The Irish Republic* 20-1.

to 'papism'; in 1939 the Grand Master of the Orange Lodge of Ireland introduced a two-volume work as an effort to perpetuate 'truths, acknowledged to be at once fundamental and eternal'[115] – and all those writers were probably sincere. The same emblem can serve opposite causes: Cú Chulainn is a nationalist icon on some Belfast walls and a loyalist defender of Ulster on others.[116] The use of history to stir up feelings and advocate a cause can be the subject of ferocious controversy; in the second half of the twentieth century and more particularly in the last quarter, some professional historians condemned what they saw as an obsession with past wrongs in nationalist historiography, and what they called the 'myth' (the term being used pejoratively) of a seven-centuries-old struggle against oppression; this trend was, in turn, denounced by its opponents as not as neutral as it pretended.[117]

A fourth kind of historical narrative, groups' perceptions of their past elaborated and transmitted wholly or partly in oral form, is the one that most directly concerns the present study, but it is connected with the second and third kinds. What is referred to vaguely as a 'collective memory' (which generally manifests itself in individual representations ...) retains basic attitudes, as well as details which may be accurate, distorted, or perhaps invented to make a point. Parts of this historical lore do not survive for more than a couple of generations, but others are much more persistent and as with all 'traditions', continuity is combined with adaptation and innovation. What is preserved in the memory of a group was shaped at the start, both by a certain view of events and by narrative conventions, then modified by the conditions of transmission and circumstances of telling. It evolved only slowly, as the group and the world around it changed. The fallibility of memory may be partly compensated by some fixed forms and by a force of inertia in mentalities: after a certain time the eyewitness's account is replaced by a stylized and stereotyped version. How trustworthy is the information received from such sources? Academic historiography used to distance itself from accounts of the past transmitted orally, which indeed were hard to verify, short-sighted (ignoring the larger movements), and ranging from the truly factual to the fabulous. But 'oral history' may preserve information concerning events that are not documented in other ways, or offer a corrective to other sources; it may have captured ordinary people's reactions to historical processes and social conditions, what was felt then – and what is felt now – about what happened. When some specific details are obviously false, something can still be learned by trying to understand how such 'legends' came into being, how they functioned and changed. The line of transmission may have been solely oral, or relayed by school teaching, or by the reading of popular or partisan texts. The convergence of versions may be a mark of truth – or

115 R.M. Sibbett *Orangeism in Ireland* 1. vii. 116 A.D. Buckley (ed.) *Symbols in Northern Ireland* 57, 95. 117 See C. Brady (ed.) *Interpreting Irish History: The Debate on Historical Revisionism*, and G. Boyce and A. O'Day (eds) *The Making of Modern Irish History: Revisionism and the Revisionist Controversy.*

of a collective obsession. Folk history may have to be interpreted more as symbolic messages than factual information.[118]

Oral testimonies transmitted from generation to generation abound in Ireland. Seán Ó Súilleabháin's *Handbook of Irish Folklore* lists many questions to be asked by collectors concerning 'Individual Personages', 'Important Historical Events', 'Local Happenings'. It seems possible to distinguish between two fields: on the one hand stories, likely to remain strictly oral, concerning local events and characters, or local repercussions of wider disruptions; on the other hand stories which have been diffused through Ireland, partly in popular printed form, and which are more likely to be politically committed. In the first, *local* heritage, general history is mentioned mainly to provide points of reference in time: this or that happened before or after a certain outstanding event – which may be a natural phenomenon like the 'Big Wind' of 1836 or a political one like the 'Year of the French' (1798). Genealogy may be the 'historical' kind of information which requires most precision and feats of memory; but ethnographers have shown how, in 'traditional societies', pedigrees can also change, or be dismissed as false when they are not adaptable. Hugh Glassie, who made a detailed study of the 'historical' part of oral tradition in Fermanagh in the 1970's, noted that 'stories of history' are more than tales, and that 'the teller of historical story has more than words. He has the facts, rich and right',[119] and his contribution is essential for the community:

The most important of the ceili's tales are those deepest in truth, unimpeacheably true, the stories called 'history'. They are owned by the whole community, so – unlike pants [news, or adventures] – they lack authors. They were not learned as entities from individuals; they were 'gathered up' from every reliable source by certain old men called 'historians' ... Such information about past people and events floats free, unorganized in vast quantity, waiting to be selected and attached to something about which people do 'have the history'. When you have the history, you can cluster facts into an account that may be informational, even sequential and causative, but is less than a 'story'. The 'story of history' corresponds roughly to the folklorist's 'historical legend', but unlike folklorists, the people of Ballymenone are not combative about their definitions. As a story, it is entertaining, a full and artful narrative. As history, it is important and true.[120]

118 'The "truth" of historical legends is not identical with the "truth" of legal documents and history books, and official documents themselves are not necessarily "objective" reports. In many instances we should consider them the representation of one view of an event. Legend tradition constitutes another view. In epic form, historical legends reveal the reactions and reflections of the common folk, their impressions, experiences, and their explanation and evaluation of events that are important to them.' (B. Alver 'Historical Legends and Historical Truth', in R. Kvideland and H.K. Sehmsdorf *Nordic Folklore* 149.) 119 *Passing the Time* 128. 120 Ibid. 69-70. and 112. Glassie also notes (44-5) that 'Ballymenone's "historian" fills the role of "seanchaí" ... These older men know the "old history", the neighbours' genealogies, and the community's folk law. They tell the tales of their locality, and settle its small disputes.'

He confirmed that when local stories were set in a larger context of Irish history, the latter was reduced to a few select focal points, 'particularly powerful in their meanings for modern people'.[121] He obtained this insider's comment:

Hugh Nolan, the community's revered historian, told me that narrators must, at once, hold to the truth and use words of their own ... To hold the truth, Hugh Nolan said, one must tell the whole tale ... When accounts differ, as they generally do in the legends that he considered most important, the teller's task is ... to gather up and rehearse, synthesizing the truest version. Then cleaving to that version, a creation of the responsible self, the teller is obliged, owing to the limitations of memory and the peculiar needs of every audience, to use words of his own ... Hugh Nolan discriminated between what was essential and what was expendable in the tales he had heard. He reduced the past to features worthy of preservation – events in sequence, key quotations – then held them ready at hand to be shuffled, combined, and strung together when he invented a story to fit the flickering moment.[122]

The same informant affirmed: 'The job of the historian [i.e. the one who tells stories about the past of a collectivity – which may have biases] is keepin the truth'.[123] Only a few members of the community tell such stories, and it is 'men's work'.[124]

The widely spread 'folklore' of Irish nationalism was diffused and constantly renewed or confirmed in newspapers, cheap booklets and broadsheets. It enlisted individuals and groups in a cause, vilified the opposing side and brandished emblems. A typological principle tends to be at work in those texts: former events or persons provide models to be realized again, and the story of a martyr whose death was a moral victory may invite listeners to fight and die for the same ideal. In additions to stories or shorter anecdotes and non-narrative pieces, songs (or 'ballads') may convey emotions more effectively than prose. There are strictly local and oral songs, but I am referring now to printed material sung and sold in the street and achieving wide circulation; much of it was ephemeral, but some songs were constantly reissued and could become part of the oral tradition; indeed, a few of them originally came from it. The 'street ballad' form in English was appropriated by Irish political movements by the end of the eighteenth century and remained potent until the twentieth. Partisan history, 'ballad' testimony and the power of memories transmitted orally can be illustrated, and compared, by juxtaposing accounts, from conflicting standpoints, of an event which academic history would probably not focus upon. It took place in County Wicklow just before the rising of 1798. The Militia, set up in 1793 with members of both religions, was purged by some of its Protestant officers; soldiers suspected of being sympathetic to the non-sectarian radical movement of United Irishmen were eliminated one way or the other, sometimes summarily executed.

---

121 Ibid. 661. 122 H. Glassie 'Tradition', in *Journal of American Folklore* 108 (1995) 407.
123 *Passing the Time* 651. 124 Ibid. 62.

For the fiercely anti-Catholic Richard Musgrave, who produced in 1802 the first detailed defence of governmental repression, this was perfectly legitimate. A ballad, which seems to have been produced locally at about the same time and was later disseminated by broadsheet sellers, gives the opposing point of view.

The loyalist historian's version

Captain Saunders, of the Saunders-grove corps, having received a hint that some of its members were seduced by United Irishmen, called a full parade of them on the twentieth of May, and exhorted them, if any of them had been unfortunately tempted to swerve from their allegiance, to acknowledge it to him either publicly or privately; but his address to them did not produce any effect. Such of them as were disaffected, had resolved that evening to disclose their guilt to their captain, but that James Dunn, the corporal, who had seduced them, persuaded them to adhere to the united cause, and not to violate the oath of secrecy which they had taken. Full information having been received of the guilt of Dunn, he was taken up on the twenty-first of May, by the Wicklow militia, and on being arrested, he impeached some of the members of his own corps. This discovery induced Captain Saunders to call a full parade, the twenty-second of May, when he announced it to his men, in presence of a party of the Wicklow militia, and the Dunlavin cavalry: and having desired three or four of the most guilty to come forward, no less than twenty of them, touched with the stings of compunction, advanced, and confessed that they had been sworn. They were immediately conveyed as prisoners to Dunlavin, where many of them were shot on the morning of the twenty-fourth of May, when the general rising took place ... It may be said, in excuse for this act of severe and summary justice, that they would have joined the numerous bodies of rebels who were moving round, and at that time threatened the town.[125]

The anonymous ballad

In the year one thousand seven hundred and ninety eight,
A sorrowful ditty to you I'm going to relate,
Concerning those heroes both clever and rare to be seen,
By false information were shot upon Dunlavin Green.

Woe to you, Saunders; disgrace me you never shall,
That the tears of the widows may melt you like snow before the sun;
Those fatherless orphans! their cries nor moans can't be screened,
For the loss of their fathers, who were shot upon Dunlavin Green.

Some of our heroes are 'listed and gone far away,
There are some of them dead, and some of them crossing the sea;
As for poor Andy Ryan, his mother distracted has been
For the loss of her son, who was shot upon Dunlavin Green.

As for Andy Farrell, I'm sure he has cause to complain,

125 Richard Musgrave *Memoirs of the Different Rebellions in Ireland* 1. 383, 299. Preface to the first edition (1802): 'The author has made truth his polar star in the course of his work.'

And likewise the two Duffys, I'm sure they may well do the same;
Dwyer on the mountain to the Orange he owes a great spleen,
For the loss of his comrades, who were shot upon Dunlavin Green.

They were marched from the guard-house up to the end of the town,
And when they came there the poor fellows were forced to kneel down;
Like lambs for the slaughter that day, it was plain to be seen,
Their blood ran in streams on the dykes of Dunlavin Green.

That we may live happy the joyful tidings to hear,
When we will have satisfaction for the murders they did in that year;
There were thirty-six heroes, both clever and rare to be seen,
Both loyal and united, shot one day on Dunlavin Green.

Now to conclude and finish my mournful tale,
I hope all good Christians to pray for their souls will not fail.
Their souls in white pigeons a-flying to heaven were seen,
On the very same day they were shot upon Dunlavin Green.[126]

There are other versions, which can be sung to different tunes, and the song was still in oral tradition in the twentieth century. Typical of Irish ballads is the fact that there is comparatively little consecutive narration, with more space devoted to lyrical expressions of feelings: in this song, past-tense third-person narrative is not dominant. We note the use of the first person – singular for the singer, but often plural to involve his audience – while the second person alternately refers to the audience (a way of buttonholing people), and to the enemy. Repetitions make the song impressive to hear (not to read); names make it sound factual, but there are also simple and potentially emblematic images (green, snow, orange, blood) and references to 'traditional' beliefs (the power of a widow's curse, the souls a-flying), as well as clichés. One of the common ballad formulae appears in the second line of another version: 'the truth unto you I'll relate';[127] despite the fact that we hardly expect objectivity in such songs, we hear statements like: 'For to tell you the truth I like always to tell ...', or 'You true Irish heroes to me lend an ear/ For soon in a moment the truth you'll ear ... ', or 'Now listen awhile, the truth I will state ...', or '... the truth unto you I'll declare.'[128] Around 1860, the Rev. John F. Shearman, who was curate at Dunlavin and an antiquary, collected 'oral history' from 'some few persons still

126 A broadsheet printed in Cork by James Haly, who was active from the 1820s to the 1850s. Michael Dwyer, mentioned as still active in the fourth stanza, led a guerrilla band in the Wicklow mountains until 1803; it may be a way of dating the composition of the song. 127 In Colm O Lochlainn *Irish Street Ballads* 106, 'from a manuscript collection of ballads made about 1820'. 128 G.D. Zimmermann *Irish Political Street Ballads and Rebel Songs* 211, 242, 287, 103. A study in local history published in 1998, Chris Lawlor's *The Massacre at Dunlavin Green*, quotes documents of 1798 and refers to twentieth-century interpretations: 'Tradition has it that the Catholic priest of Dunlavin was the author of the ballad'. (96)

surviving [who had] a vivid recollection of the cruel and savage scenes'. They remembered that 'All fell – dead and dying – amid the shrieks and groans of the bystanders, among whom were their widows and relatives.' The number of victims (thirty-six, as the ballad said) was confirmed and explained: men from another corps, also thought by their officer to be potiential rebels, were killed with those arrested by Saunders. In the list of the slain as given more than half-a-century after the event, we find all the names mentioned in the ballad, along with that of John Dwyer (uncle to Michael). The collector could give every guarantee 'for the truth and correctness' of those from whom he had elicited information.[129]

Lies can be harmful but so can, in some circumstances, the conviction of being in possession of the absolute truth. We perceive reality through grids which shape our perception of it: we see what we are prepared to see, and our beliefs may colour facts. We also adjust the past to our present perceptions and preoccupations, and history can be a construction conditioned by present circumstances; but what is deemed historical without being authenticated should not be dismissed as insignificant, because it can deeply affect people's life and reveal their attitudes. With *truth* and *lies*, we may consider *fiction* as the third angle of a triangle, linked with the other two and often closer to one of them, but relatively independent; here, the referents may be an illusion accepted by the recipient of the story, or 'reality' itself – often a mixture of both. What matters is inner cohesion, clarity, opportuneness and interest. Narratives always tend towards fiction inasmuch as they impose a shape of their own, even when dealing with real events: the account of a personal experience, for instance, follows accepted norms, and increasingly so, because 'after several repetitions the creator's formative inclination and aptitude or certain psychological factors will greatly alter the account of whatever has happened'; taken up by others, those stories 'move more and more away from reality, are known in a wider circle of people, and are more polished',[130] acquiring turns which clarify them and make them *sound* convincing, while perhaps growing away from the original events. There are narratives which purport to be factually true and are told to share information, or interrogations; they must be distinguished from others which depend on the hearer's willingness to enter an illusion and are honestly feigned to stir emotions, be admired and provide entertainment – perhaps a certain kind of knowledge too.

I do not think that such issues are much more, or less, riddled with problems in Ireland than elsewhere. Yet some Irish people have admitted a tendency to hyperbolic distortion: 'We in Ireland are rather prone to exaggeration, perhaps more so than the average run of peoples.'[131] Some have prided themselves

129 W.J. Fitzpatrick *'The Sham Squire'; and the Informers of 1798* (Appendix) 308-11. **130** H. Dobos 'True Stories', in Linda Dégh (ed.) *Studies in East European Folk Narrative* 173-4. **131** P.W. Joyce *English as We Speak It in Ireland* 120.

on their expertise in lying, as did for instance Brendan Behan: 'What I told was ninety per cent lies, and that's being more than fair to myself for I was an able liar, but my stories were often funny.'[132] It is not necessary, however, to think with Matthew Arnold that the 'Celts' are in permanent revolt against 'the despotism of fact' (nor, of course, that all Irish people are 'Celts'). Carleton's observation (see p. 556) is more subtle: '[The Irishman] is not at ease, it is true, under facts', yet not 'altogether averse to facts.' But why should the dividing line between fantasy and reality be more blurred in the Irish climate than elsewhere?[133] One explanation might be the importance of talk in popular Irish activities, a taste for high-coloured narratives: the more one speaks to please or convince, the easier it is to depart from strict factualism. The role played by storytelling in consolidating a group, and separating it from outsiders perceived as possibly hostile and certainly alien, must also be taken into account. It may modify the rules of communication, if requirements of truthfulness are adapted to the basic principle of special obligations towards the group you belong to: you may lie to outsiders, or about them. In certain circumstances, you are licensed to lie playfully within the group too, provided you do it according to a recognizable code. Stories may then develop on an imaginary level where almost anything goes, the utterances being inventions marked off from other verbal acts and thus easily identifiable: some signals of fictiveness must announce a special mode of speech,[134] and the audience is invited to suspend judgment and to enjoy pretending that it is true while knowing it is feigned.

In a narrative, an act of lying can be presented as wicked, insignificant or amusing; tales may expose lying as devilish or ridiculous, or blur an oversimple distinction between truth and lie, or exorcize the dull and unsatisfactory truth of actual life. Storytelling involves a degree of manipulation; facts may be expanded, embellished and embroidered: 'Never spoil a good story for the sake of the truth.'[135] The problem is to decide what is acceptable to a given audience, under certain conditions, but storytellers and listeners everywhere are likely to think that a story worth telling and hearing is 'true enough'.

---

132 *Borstal Boy* 314. **133** As Larry Doyle asserts in Shaw's *John Bull's Other Island* Act 1. **134** Cf. B.H. Smith 'Afterthoughts on Narrative', in *Critical Inquiry* 7 (1980) 235: ' Different situations and structures of motivation elicit and reward different kinds and degrees of truth claims. Under some conditions, as when we exchange narrative jokes or present certain other kinds of fictive tellings ... the interest and value of an account-of-something-that-happened may be altogether independent of the extent to which veridicality might be claimed for or attributed to it.' P. Lamarque and S.H. Olsen *Truth, Fiction and Literature* 37: 'Any attempt to explain how fictive stories are told and enjoyed in a community, without deceit, without mistaken inference, and without inappropriate response, seems inevitably to require reference to co-operative, mutually recognized, conventions.' **135** A statement Benedict Kiely attributes to his father, in *God's Own Country* ix.

14

'Now to conclude and finish ...'

This half-line formula, which often launches the last stanza of nineteenth-century Irish street ballads, can be completed with a choice of other half-lines: ' ... and make an end unto my song', or ' ... no more I have to say', or (perhaps unwittingly subtle) ' ... I'll end as I began'. Some rounding-off of certain pieces of discourse is expected, with a final emphasis, a last bird's-eye view of the field, the brief outline of a larger frame of reference, or some other gesture. For these final pages, I choose as guidelines a few questions which, I feel, naturally arise at this stage.

Springing from the preceding chapter which suggested that 'truth' may often be made rather than found, one of the relevant questions is: how much truth can a book like this hope to attain? I must admit that my information has generally been obtained at several remotes, and remains fragmentary. The farther back we try to go, the more conjectural is what we can say – there is a shortage of documentary sources concerning oral storytelling before the nineteenth century. Even for later periods, when we know what kinds of stories prevailed, not much is said about the way they were told and how they were listened to. On the other hand I have not used all the information available for the twentieth century: no doubt much more can be extracted from the collectors' manuscripts in the Irish Folklore Archives. I have taken a risk in combining scraps of information gleaned from documents of unequal value, which may show or hide, faithfully express or deform, and sometimes invent. But I think the method would be really odious only if such dangers were not recognized, and if unauthenticated quotations were marshalled to fit a theory while pretending to present a totally accurate picture. At least I have shown that different kinds of Irish storytellers have been looked at, for different reasons and in different ways, by different observers; also that part of the knowledge to be drawn from these images concerns the opinions and feelings of the observers themselves. Even a tangled web of fact and fiction can evidence a response to something real.

What do those who have provided images of Irish storytellers reveal, and how can we use what they say? This book has brought together diverse accounts of meetings with storytellers, and noted that the ways of speaking or writing about them aimed to generate certain responses. Attention had to be paid to who was drawing the portrait, from what distance in time or social status and turn of mind, and with what conscious or unconscious purposes. A first step in the classification of testimonies may separate on the one hand members of the storytelling community they observed, and non-members on the other; but it soon appears that it oversimplifies the issue, because there are gradations between being a complete alien and fully an insider. Furthemore, changes of attitude take place: with different circumstances or moods, what is far from brilliant may be idealized, what is innocent diabolized, what is common presented as exceptional or vice-versa.

Some of the 'outsiders' who tried to make sense of socio-cultural otherness expressed their disapproval of what they saw or heard in Ireland, and thought that at least part of it, including some forms of storytelling, should be suppressed. As they naturally believed that the values of their own group were superior, what contradicted them was shocking and could be perceived as impending danger. Their representation of the other tended to be the opposite of what they thought of themselves: he/she was an incomprehensible barbarian, haunting a still untamed territory. Until the seventeenth century, therefore, when British observers (rulers, settlers, or visitors) were confronted with Gaelic verbal arts, they tended to despise them or to find them puzzling, and in both cases to regard them as potentially subversive or openly menacing; storytelling was not at the centre of their preoccupations, however, and opinions or anecdotal statements concerning it appeared marginally in their writings, not always as direct eyewitness reports. When the 'Irish bards' were no longer in a position to be threatening, more positive (though not always more accurate) views became possible: wildness, irrationality and strange powers now had a certain charm, and the picturesque and the unfamiliar could be attractive; inverted ethnocentrism even led some to romanticize differences and to admire what they thought were unspoiled virtues. The image of the monstrous native gave way to that of the inspired natural poet, or of the odd but somehow predictable and therefore controllable childlike rustic. It was pleasant to look down (perhaps benevolently) on inferiors, and to discover that those who had been considered 'voiceless people' actually told each other curious stories. When portrayed by visitors, and for people who had not seen Ireland, the Irish storytellers tended to be quaint superstitious actors in a backward society – singers of political ballads were still considered dangerous. At the same time, descendants of settlers who somehow identified with the country in spite of what set them apart socially and culturally from the common folk, noticed the passing of certain customs and found them interesting. Antiquarians began to collect vestiges of a now apparently harmless past. Writers of fiction also drew upon this material; some of them merely exploited what seemed to be Irish peculiarities, including storytelling, for the sake of local colour with amused or sentimental overtones, while others were genuinely interested in a kind of verbal art different from theirs, and used it for calculated literary effects.

Distinctions must also be made among the viewpoints of 'insiders', because there was more than one way of being in Ireland: that of members of the old-stock gentry; that of descendants of assimilated settlers (and here the definition of the categories 'insider'/ 'outsider' is part of an ongoing debate), or that of the common people who, still with some diversity, formed the majority of the population. The culture of the first group, the Gaelic elite, probably differed from that of the lower orders of society, but exactly to what extent remains unknown. Until the seventeenth century, the poets whose main function was to celebrate their patrons in verse could also tell prose tales (but how they did it is far from clear); then, with the defeat of their sponsors, they lost their status and, if they stayed in Ireland, reluctantly adapted themselves to less exalted audiences. Full-time specialization in Irish verbal arts vanished with them, but it is generally admitted that part of their techniques and repertoire survived. We also have the point of view of members of the middle class. Their perspective could be directly or indirectly influenced by nationalism, which had spurred folklore collections and studies in continental Europe and later did the same in Ireland: reciprocally, the revelation (and perhaps in some respects invention) of folklore strengthened the idea that some unique cultural heritage defined the national singularity and justified political claims. By the end of the nineteenth century and at the beginning of the twentieth, when the idea was in the air that one should remain or once more become Irish, going back (selectively) to cultural roots meant, for some, favouring distant 'Celtic' sources and perhaps entering an Otherworld and approaching a sacred well from which they might drink the Water of Life, while others (but sometimes also the same) conferred an aura of nobility to contemporary peasants. The rural storyteller, as then defined, was preferably an old Irish-speaking westerner, who lived a hard healthy life and was a model of native virtues. The peculiarities of a sub-group were thus offered as an ideal for the whole society, and particular aspects of storytelling in prose or in verse were made to serve different political programmes: for some factions, there were stories for which one was prepared to kill or die. But if a certain folklore could become a form of flag-waving, one could also undertake serious research: devoted collectors recorded vanishing items of oral culture and respectfully observed those who were still keeping them alive, noting how the teller would appropriate a story, how the kind of story might determine a mode of enunciation, how storytelling functioned in the local community, and what an essential role was played by a trained audience. Those who were fully insiders were the 'traditional storytellers' themselves and their natural audience. We know extremely little of their perception of storytelling before the nineteenth century, and in the following generations relatively few comments by those who produced and consumed this kind of storytelling were collected, except, at a later stage, through a retrospective and magnifying glass. But the popularity of some tales highlighting narration and narrators may be a sign of the value placed on storytelling.

Different storytellers, approached from various angles, were portrayed by selecting and accentuating certain features. There were Irish-produced stereotypes and others imposed from outside, and some images could be constructed against those proffered by others. Several dominant views crystallized and prevailed in turn, but elements of an earlier account could survive in a new one; indeed, supposedly or truly archaic traits were often stressed, and when 'traditional storytelling' was considered valuable the acme of the art was generally projected into the past; but at all times the experienced present, with its preoccupations and ideological biases, influenced views of a past as a nobler or darker world. At every stage, each layer or segment of society could have its own stories and storytellers, and transformations came about in the course of time. In brief, variety is certainly one of the facts this study has established: the impression one had of meeting avatars of the same figure was largely an illusion.

But is it impossible to identify some constants in the mass of portraits, beyond the universal basics of narration and the mere geographical setting of their application? Can Irish storytellers be thought of as forming a relatively coherent group? A first prudent generalization may consist in saying that there seems to have been an enduring interest attached to them – and therefore a good deal of fiction about them too, including slanderous or idealizing distortions. In the accounts given by many observers, the Irish, generally male, storyteller tended to appear in a limited set of roles: as a clown, a crafty old codger, a firebrand, a madman, a dreamer, a cultural hero or a person with charismatic authority acting as intermediary between the supernatural world and the community and exercising his powers in a state of self-induced trance – always remarkable. He could be said to possess highly valued qualities or abhorred vices, to embody some noble ideal or to be utterly ridiculous. Historical developments and sociocultural divisions account for such contrasts. Each of the basic images tends to depend on the stressing of some particular selection of characteristic details. If we single out adjectives and adjectival phrases used to characterize Irish storytellers, we note the tendency of certain terms to appear together and the changing valuation of recognizable qualities. For instance, and without getting caught in too rigid a binary logic, we find the following pairs of predicates:

with negative connotations	*with positive connotations*
wild: brutish	wild: energetic
old: weak, in his dotage	old: powerful, wise
superstitious	visionary
incoherent	inspired
clownish and servile	unassuming and independent
shameless	proud
rebellious: a trouble-maker	rebellious: a freedom fighter
garrulous	eloquent
deceptive	truthful

different: deviant
repetitive and boring
predictable
unpredictable
dangerous

different: original
respected as a keeper of customs
'traditional'
free
fascinating.

But the above schema is deceptively neat. In actual fact, certain traits (wild, old, rebellious, different) can be treated as either meliorative or pejorative. No single 'portrait' is likely to include all the possible constituents listed in one of the columns above; indeed, some of them might appear incompatible (proud and unassuming, predictable and unpredictable, original and traditional ...), but categories of non-contradiction are not as tight as sometimes supposed, and even the collocation of terms listed in different columns is possible (weak and inspired, unpredictable and visionary, incoherent and fascinating ...). No single set of characteristics inherent in storytelling would at once characterize all the Irish practitioners of the art and separate them from non-Irish ones, but certain persistent factors can be discerned, forming more than two possible clusters of properties. To the possibility of choosing between different combinations of epithets might be added, as an invariant, the very belief in some underlying continuity. At any rate, the idea persisted that, because the storyteller was rehearsing a heritage in ways which were themselves considered age-old, he was the heir to, and an essential link with, the past. He could embody the essence of plain Irishness – but was also likely to be considered peculiar, in the sense of special (unique) or/and bizarre (odd and perhaps awesome). There is also a lasting tendency to think that since a hero's immortality depends on the enduring fame of his deeds, those who sing them play an essential role. Perhaps we may add to all that a disposition to regard literal truth as somewhat adaptable, but 'Irish traditional storytelling' is or was aware of the distinction between two kinds of narrative speech acts: one, essentially the medium through which the speaker keeps alive what supposedly actually happened and should not be forgotten, and gives it a renewed power; the other, the creation of an alternative and aesthetically satisfying 'reality' which seems to be an end in itself. For individuals, the limits could vary to a certain extent. Both modes of storytelling can be vehicles of wisdom.

The survey suggests that a few focal points are stable. But reality is more varied than stylized pictures: there were individual attitudes, skills and tastes, in both models and painters. Also, the evolution of sets of expectations was interwoven with larger historical changes, and depended on the strata of society the acts of storytelling were taking place in: for instance, in some periods, the importance of a certain caste of storytellers was evidenced in their being richly rewarded and associated with the great; at other times and from the point of view of certain observers, poverty was a proof of independence and healthy asceticism and another mark of real value. The change of language must have had drastic effects, but without necessarily causing total interruption.

Perhaps most significant and permanent is the tension between different sets of attributes supposed to characterize the Irish storyteller. It resulted from the incompatibility between some of the perspectives from which they could be viewed: for instance, the heritage that storytellers kept alive was often considered sacred and glorious, but could also be perceived as nightmarish and crippling by those who aspired to a different mode of life, while others would invoke the dark barbarism of the Irish past to justify the coming of new civilizing masters. When a storyteller was seen as the epitome of some supposed collective features, he could be admired for them or seen as an obvious case of hopeless Irish irrationality. On the whole, the Irish storyteller was more likely to be aggrandized or belittled than presented life-size, and also more often emblematized than individualized.

Within a complex and developing field of forces, certain selections of qualities and attitudes seem to recur. But what could set off Irish storytellers from those of other countries, and what common properties did they share with them? Does the research now being concluded attest to the persistence of a specific Irishness, and did certain images of storytellers contribute to the elaboration of a sense of collective identity? Generalizations based on nationality are suspect, the notion of ethnic purity is a dangerous figment, and to try and define 'Irishness' has always been a hazardous enterprise. Confronted for long periods with detraction, conflicts and pains, many Irish people have been sensitive to hostile or laudatory definitions, and concerned with what might be essentially and exclusively theirs. It has been said that a distinctive Irish culture in the last few centuries was characterized by the primacy of speech over other modes of communication; people would have been inclined to try and cope with predicaments through verbal means – and perhaps sometimes have been taken in by their own words. An attachment to the past might be another marked trait. Rather than founded on objective criteria, communal identity has an affective dimension and is partly defined by the feeling of being in touch with forebears. The storyteller, whose words skilfully (re)created the past, could thus embody some aspects of a 'national character'. Other aspects of Irish culture could be invested with at least as powerful a symbolic significance, but narratives concerning a shared past and suffering at the hands of others, also affirming some link with the Pre-Conquest world, have contributed to a certain cohesiveness. Some analysts say that, individually, we *are* the stories we tell ourselves about ourselves, and it may apply to groups as well. A people's sense of identity is neither fixed nor without contradictions, however. Memories and symbols can work in different ways for separate sections of society, and Irishness may therefore have been different things for different people, at different times or simultaneously, because the society was not only changing but also plural. An individual may draw his self-image in agreement with, or in opposition to, what he sees in the mirror offered by the ideology of his society; thus the image of the Irishman as a storyteller may be what he expects to be, or what he unfortunately is not, or what he does not like to be, or what he no longer recognizes as an important part of his nature.

As for the notion of an unalloyed heritage, we must remember that, from the beginning, Ireland was populated by successive waves of immigrants, perhaps never numerous enough to supplant totally those who had arrived before them; each wave must have brought its customs, and layers of culture could accumulate, to some extent fuse. Relations between Ireland and the outside world have never ceased, and the intrusion of external forces repeatedly produced important effects. It is reasonable to assume both importation and indigenous creation or re-invention of stories as well as of storytelling modes; what satisfied a need could take root. Human cognitive and expressive potentialities seem to be everywhere similar, and there is much evidence for the relative unity of a western European cultural area. But if basic techniques, motifs and principles of plotting are transcultural constants, their combination, the elaboration of details and the meanings they convey can be locally modified. In point of fact, many techniques and conventions of storytelling observed in Ireland are instanced by 'traditional cultures' in other parts of Europe or elsewhere, and a significant part of the repertoire may be shared, but as the elements were synthesized again they could acquire a particular Irish inflection. What is unique may be the combination. There was also some grace in the formation of paradoxical keys to the mysteries of human experience, matrices for beliefs or symbols of collective tendencies – of jewels for the poor.

It is now time for a last look at one of the contentious terms that often appeared in this study: 'traditional'. What have we learned about it? 'Tradition' used to be the central object of folkloristics, both as a force maintaining beliefs, behaviours and expertise over a long time span, within a given society, and as what was thus transmitted. Anthropologists are less concerned with traces of the past than folklorists, and today they tend not to give much importance to this concept when they see sociocultural systems as essentially dynamic. Some historians have shown that, rather than being quasi-immutable ancient elements still active in the present, 'traditions' may be variable interpretations, always from the point of view of the present, of selected aspects of the past. It has also been proved that recently developed practices and notions may be artificially given a patina of age to establish a spurious link with hallowed origins, and to support current institutions and interests. But such possibilities of fabrication and exploitation should not prevent our seeing that there may be some kind of permanence in the midst of change, that something does persist (though not without being transformed), and that, if cultures are dynamic, they also depend on some enduring fund. We have found examples of survivals, and lines of continuity are not all inventions: although their functions and valuations may have varied, some cultural traits have ancient roots and remain active. Our study also confirms that different traditions may coexist. In any case, the importance the loaded concepts of tradition and continuation have had in Ireland can hardly be denied.

How much of that complex and perhaps sometimes overworked heritage can survive? For the kinds of storytelling most often described in this book, the vanishing process seems to have gone on for a long time, but it accelerated sharply and perhaps decisively in the second half of the twentieth century. One thing is obvious, however: oral storytelling may have changed, but has never ceased. Many Irish people still have a knack for telling about the local past, or their own experience. Some are still attached to 'the old ways'; others may disown them but still feel that feats of verbal skill are a required part of collective entertainment. Only time – *is maith an scéalaí an aimsir* (time is a good storyteller ...) – will tell how much of its relative distinctiveness Ireland may lose and how local and global factors will articulate with each other. Whatever mutations may yet occur, it takes no visionary gift to predict that, needing to comprehend and share experience and equipped with memory, imagination and language, human beings who are able to describe, relate, joke, lie, play games of pretence and conjure up what has never existed will keep narrating. They will certainly need new tales, but may not have finished with the old ones. In all likelihood, 'tell us a story' is a request that will continue to be heard.

Bibliography

A. BOOKS AND ARTICLES INCLUDING PORTRAITS OF, QUOTATIONS FROM,
INFORMATION OR OPINIONS ON, IRISH STORYTELLERS AND STORYTELLING

Unpublished material
IFC: Main Manuscripts Collection; Department of Irish Folklore, University College,
Dublin.
IFC S: Schools' Manuscripts Collection; Department of Irish Folklore, University
College, Dublin.
OSL: Ordnance Survey Letters; Royal Irish Academy, Dublin. Copies in the National
Library of Ireland.

Published material:
(Anonymous) (A.) 'Orehoo, The Fairy Man, a Reminiscence of Connaught.' *Irish Penny
Journal*, Sept. 12, 1840.
— *Aftermath of Easter Week*. Dublin, 1917.
— *The Ancient Irish Tales, being a Collection of the Stories Told by the Peasantry, in the
Winter Evenings*. Drogheda, 1829.
— (B.) 'The Fisherman's Tale.' *Irish Penny Magazine*, 5 Febr. 1842.
— (B.B.F.) 'Ode on the Popular Superstitions of Ireland, Considered as the Subject of
Poetry.' *The Irish Monthly Magazine*, 1 (1832-3), 503-6.
— 'The Beggarman's Tale.' *Dublin Penny Journal*, 15 June 1833.
— *The Companion for the Fire-Side: being a Collection of Genuine and Instructive
Adventures, Tales and Stories. Selected from the best writers in several languages, many
of which were never before published*. Dublin, printed by William Sleater, 1769.
— (Celt) 'Diarmuid O'Cathain's Christmas Visit to Fairy Land.' *Duffy's Fireside
Magazine*, March and April 1854.
— (E.W.) 'The Goban Saer.' *Dublin Penny Journal*, 6 July 1833.
— (E.W.) 'The Bald Barrys, or The Blessed Thorn of Kildinan.' *Irish Penny Journal*,
April 17, 1841.
— 'Fairy Legend.' *The True and Original Salmagundi*, Sept. 27, 1834.
— 'A Fire-Side Gossip about Ghosts and Fairies.' *Dublin University Magazine*, 62
(1863), 691-700.
— *Guide to the County of Wicklow* (1834). Dublin, 1835.
— *Killarney – Heaven's Reflex*. Killarney, n.d. (*c*.1980).
— *Island Stories: Tales & Legends from the West*. Dublin, 1977.
— *Leigh's New Pocket Hand-Book of Ireland*. (3rd ed.) London, 1841.

— (M.F.D.) 'Letters from the Coast of Clare. Letter No. 12.' *Dublin University Magazine*, 18 (1841), 547-8.

— 'Norse and Gaelic Popular Tales.' *Duffy's Hibernian Magazine*, March 1862.

— *Notes from a Tourist's Journal, being a Brief Sketch of a Visit to the Lakes on the Galtee Mountains.* Limerick, 1857.

— (P.) 'Fairy Superstitions of the North of Ireland.' *Irish Penny Magazine*, 27 April 1833.

— *Popular Tales and Legends of the Irish Peasantry.* Dublin, 1834.

— 'Reminiscences of Jim O'Leary. No.1: The Legend of the Holy Well.' *Salmagundi*, 26 July 1834.

— *The Royal Hibernian Tales; being a collection of the most entertaining stories now extant* (c.1820). In *Béaloideas*, 10 (1940), 148-203.

— *Selections of Parochial Examinations Relative to the Destitute Classes in Ireland from the Evidence Received by His Majesty's Commissioners for Enquiring into the Conditions of the Poorer Classes in Ireland.* Dublin, 1835.

— 'Seen in the Glass. An Irish Legend.' *Ireland's Own*, 11 December 1907.

— 'The Shanachie.' *Ireland's Own*, 62 (1933), 841.

— *Tales and Legends of Ireland, Illustrative of Society, History, Antiquities Manners and Literature* (= *Bolster's Quarterly Magazine* 1-2 1826-7). London, 1834.

— 'The Unlucky Gift.' *Irish Penny Magazine*, 13 April 1833.

a Búrc: *see* Bourke, Éamon.

Adamnán. *Life of St Columba* (ed. tr. R. Sharpe). London, 1995.

AE (G. Russell). *The Interpreters* (1922). New York, 1923.

— *Letters from AE* (ed. A. Denson). London, 1961.

(Alexander, James) *An Amusing Summer-Companion to Glanmire, near Cork; being a Picturesque Delineation of that Beautiful Village, together with certain Prospects of the Surrounding Country; to which are added Strong Sketches of the Manners of the Inhabitants.* Cork, 1814.

Almqvist, Bo. *Viking Ale; Studies on Folklore Contacts between the Northern and the Western Worlds.* Aberystwyth, 1991.

Anderson, A.O. 'Táin Bó Fraich.' *Revue Celtique*, (24) 1903), 127-154.

Andrews, J.M. *A Paper Landscape: The Ordnance Survey in Nineteenth-century Ireland.* Oxford, 1975.

Arbois de Jubainville, H. d'. *Cours de littérature celtique.* Paris, 1883-1902.

Arensberg, C.M. *The Irish Countryman.* London, 1937.

Arensberg, C.M. and S.T. Kimball. *Family and Community in Ireland.* Cambridge, Mass., 1940.

Ballantyne, R.M. *The Lakes of Killarney.* London, 1859.

Ballard, Linda-May. 'Tales of the Troubles.' In P. Smith (ed.) *Perspectives on Contemporary Legends.* Sheffield, 1984, 1-17.

— 'Three Local Storytellers: a Perspective on the Question of Cultural Heritage.' In Gillian Bennett and P. Smith (eds) *Monsters with Iron Teeth; Perspectives on Contemporary Legend* III. Sheffield, 1988, 161-82.

— 'Ulster Oral Narrative: the Stress on Authenticity.' *Ulster Folklife*, 26 (1980), 35-40.

— (Smith, Linda-May) 'Aspects of Contemporary Ulster Fairy Tradition.' In V.J. Newall (ed.) *Folklore Studies in the Twentieth Century.* Woodbridge, 1980, 398-403.

Banim, John. *The Boyne Water* (1826). Dublin, 1865.

Banim, John and Michael. *The Ghost Hunter and his Family.* (1831) New York, 1896.

— *Tales by the O'Hara Family.* London, 1825, 1826.

Barrow, John. *A Tour Round Ireland, through the Sea-Coast Counties, in the Autumn of 1835.* London, 1836.

Barton, Richard. *Some Remarks towards a Full Description of Upper and Lower Lough Lene, near Killarney, in the County of Kerry.* Dublin, 1751.

Bernard, Bayle. *The Life of Samuel Lover, R.H.A.* London, 1874.

Béaloideas: The Journal of the Folklore of Ireland Society. Dublin, 1927–. [The articles quoted from this periodical are not detailed in the bibliography.]

Beaumont, G. de. *L'Irlande sociale, politique et religieuse.* Paris, 1839.

Becker, Heinrich. *I mBeal na Farraige: Scéalta agus seanchas faoi chúrsaí feamainne ó bheal na ndaoine.* Galway, 1997.

Behan, Brendan. *Brendan Behan's Island.* New York, 1962.

Bell, Robert. *A Description of the Conditions and Manners as well as of the Moral and Political Character of the Peasantry of Ireland, such as they were between the Years 1780 and 1790.* London, 1804.

Bell, Sam Hanna. *Erin's Orange Lily.* London, 1956.

(Belton, William) *The Angler in Ireland, or an Englishman's Ramble through Connaught and Munster during the Summer of 1833.* London, 1834.

Berry, H.F. (ed.) *Statutes and Ordinances and Acts of the Parliament of Ireland, King John to Henry V.* Dublin, 1907.

Berry, James. *Tales from the West of Ireland* (1966). London, 1984.

Best, R.I. (ed .tr.) 'The Settling of the Manor of Tara.' *Ériu* 4 (1910), 121–72.

Binns, Jonathan. *The Miseries and Beauties of Ireland.* London, 1837.

(Blake, Henry et al.). *Letters from the Irish Highlands of Connemara.* London, 1825.

Boué, André. *William Carleton, romancier irlandais.* Paris, 1978.

Bourke, Angela. *The Burning of Bridget Cleary: A True Story.* London, 1999.

Bourke [a Búrc], Éamon. *Éamon a Búrc: Scéalta* (ed. P. Ó Ceannabháin). Dublin, 1983.

— *Eochair Mac Rí in Eirinn A King's Son in Ireland* (ed. tr. Kevin O'Nolan). Dublin, 1982.

Bowden, Charles T. *A Tour through Ireland in 1790.* Dublin, 1791.

Boyce, George and Allan O'Day (eds) *The Making of Modern Irish History; Revisionism and the Revisionist Controversy.* London, 1996.

Bradshaw, B. and A. Hadfield (eds) *Representing Ireland; Literature and the Origins of Conflict, 1534–1660.* Cambridge, 1993.

Brady, Ciaran (ed.) *Interpreting Irish History: The Debate on Historical Revisionism.* Dublin, 1994.

Brady, Terence. 'Lettre aux Auteurs du *Journal des Sçavans.*' In *Journal des Sçavans*, July 1763.

Breatnach, P.A. 'The Chief's Poet.' *Proceedings of the Royal Irish Academy*, 83c (1983) 37–79.

Breatnach, R.A. 'Two Eighteenth-Century Scholars: J.C. Walker and Charlotte Brooke.' *Studia Hibernica*, 5 (1965), 88–97.

Brett, David. *The Construction of Heritage.* Cork, 1996.

Bratton, Robert. *Round the Turf Fire: Humorous Sketches of Ulster Country Life.* Belfast, 1931.

Bray, Dorothy Ann. *A List of Motifs in the Lives of Early Irish Saints.* FFC 252. Helsinki, 1992.

Brewer, James N. *The Beauties of Ireland (Leinster)*. London, 1825.

Brewer, J.S. and W. Bullen (eds) 'The Book of Howth', in *Calendar of the Carew Manuscripts* V. London, 1871.

Britten, James. 'Irish Folktales.' *Folk-Lore Journal* 1 (1883), 52-5, 184-7, 316-24.

Brody, Hugh. *Inishkillane, Change and Decline in the West of Ireland* (1973). London, 1986.

Brooke, Charlotte. *Reliques of Irish Poetry*. Dublin, 1789.

Brown, Terence. *Ireland, a Social and Cultural History: 1922-1979*. London, 1981.

— (ed.) *Celticism*. Amsterdam, 1996.

Bruford, Alan. *Gaelic Folk-Tales and Medieval Romances*. Dublin, 1969.

— 'Song and Recitation in Early Ireland.' *Celtica*, 21 (1990), 61-74.

Buckley, Anthony (ed.) *Symbols in Northern Ireland*. Belfast, 1998.

Bunting, E. *The Ancient Music of Ireland* (1796, 1802, 1840). Dublin, 1969.

Burke, Oliver J. *The South Isles of Aran*. London, 1887.

Bush, John. *Hibernia Curiosa: A Letter from a Gentleman in Dublin to his Friend at Dover in Kent*. London, 1769.

Butler, Marilyn. *Maria Edgeworth: A Literary Biography*. Oxford, 1972.

Byrne, C.J. and M. Harry (eds) *Talamh an Eisce: Canadian and Irish Essays*. Halifax, 1986.

Byrne, Fr. J. ' "Senchas": the Nature of Gaelic Historical Tradition.' *Historical Studies* 9 (1974), 137-59.

Caball, Marc. *Poetry and Politics: Reaction and Continuity in Irish Poetry 1558-1625*. Cork, 1998.

Caerwyn Williams, J.E. 'The Court Poet in Mediaeval Ireland.' *Proceedings of the British Academy*, 57 (1971), 85-135.

Cahalan, James M. *The Irish Novel*. Dublin, 1988.

— 'Tailor Tim Buckley; Folklore, Literature and *Seanchas an Táillióra*.' *Éire-Ireland*, 14 (1979) No.2, 110-18.

Campbell, T. *A Philosophical Survey of the South of Ireland, in a Series of Letters to John Watkinson, M.D.* London, 1777.

Carbery, Mary. *The Farm by Lough Gur* (1937). Cork, 1973.

Carleton, William. *The Black Prophet* (1847). London, 1899.

— *The Emigrants of Ahadarra*. London, 1847.

— *Fardorougha the Miser*. Dublin, 1839.

— 'The Irish Shanahus.' *Irish Penny Journal*, 29 May 1841, 378-80.

— 'Legend of St. Kieran.' *Dublin Family Magazine, or Literary and Religious Miscellany*, April 1829, 17-29.

— *Tales and Sketches Illustrating the Character, Usages, Sports and Pastimes of the Irish Peasantry*. Dublin, 1845.

— *Tales of Ireland*. Dublin, 1834.

— *The Tithe Proctor*. London,1849.

— *Traits and Stories of the Irish Peasantry* (1830 and 1833). Dublin, 1843.

— *Valentine M'Clutchy*. Dublin, 1845.

—*The Life of William Carleton; Being his Autobiography and Letters* (ed. D.J. O'Donohue). London, 1896.

Carney, James. *Studies in Irish Literature and History*. Dublin, 1955.

Carr, John. *The Stranger in Ireland, or a Tour in the Southern and Western Parts of the Country in the Year 1805.* London, 1806.

Casey, Daniel and R. Rhodes (eds) *Views of the Irish Peasantry 1800-1916.* Hamden, 1977.

Chatterton, Henrietta G.M. *Rambles in the South of Ireland during the Year 1838.* London, 1839.

Chetwood, W.R. *A Tour Through Ireland, in Several Entertaining Letters.* Dublin, 1746.

Christiansen, R.T. *Studies in Irish and Scandinavian Folktales.* Copenhagen, 1959.

Clark, Samuel and J.S. Donnelly (eds) *Irish Peasants: Violence and Political Unrest 1780-1914.* Manchester, 1983.

Coffey, Diarmuid. *Douglas Hyde: President of Ireland.* Dublin, 1938.

Coimín, Micheál. *Laoidh Oisín ar Thír na n-Óg* (ed. tr. David Comyn). Dublin 1880.

Colgan, Nathaniel. 'Witchcraft in the Aran islands.' *Journal of the Royal Society of Antiquaries of Ireland*, 25 (1895), 84-5.

Colum, Patrick. *The King of Ireland's Son* (1916). Edinburgh, 1986.

— *The Road round Ireland.* New York, 1927.

— 'Story-telling in Ireland.' *Horn Book Magazine*, 10 (May 1934).

— *Story Telling New and Old.* New York, 1968.

— *A Treasury of Irish Folklore.* New York, 1954.

— 'Vagrant Voices, a Self-Portrait.' *Journal of Irish Literature*, 2 (1973), 63-75.

Comerford, R.V. *Charles Kickham; A Study in Irish Nationalism and Literature.* Portmarnock, 1979.

Connellan, O. (ed.) *Imtheacht na Tromdhaimhe, or The Proceedings of the Great Bardic Institution.* Transactions of the Ossianic Society 5. Dublin,1860.

Corduff, Michael. 'Notes on Storytellers and Storytelling in Iorrus, North Mayo.' *Béaloideas*, 19 (1949), 177-80.

Corkery, Daniel.*The Fortunes of the Irish Language.* Cork, 1956.

— *The Hidden Ireland: A Study of Gaelic Munster in the Eighteenth Century.* Dublin, 1924.

Court, Artelia. *Puck of the Droms; the Lives & Literature of the Irish Tinkers.* Berkeley, 1985.

Craig, Patricia (ed.) *The Oxford Book of Ireland.* Oxford, 1998.

Craik, Dinah. *An Unknown Country.* London, 1887.

Cresswell, Robert. *Une communauté rurale de l'Irlande.* Paris, 1969.

Croker, T. Crofton. *Fairy Legends and Traditions of the South of Ireland* (1825, 1828). London, 1862.

— *Killarney Legends, arranged as a Guide to the Lakes.* London, 1831.

— *Legends of the Lakes, or Sayings and Doings at Killarney.* London, 1829.

— *Researches in the South of Ireland, illustrative of the Scenery, Architectural Remains, and the Manners and Superstitions of the Peasantry.* London, 1824.

Cronin, Michael. *Translating Ireland; Translations, Languages, Cultures.* Cork, 1996.

Cross, Eric. *The Tailor and Ansty* (1942). Cork, 1970.

Cross, Tom Pete. *Motif-Index of Early Irish Literature.* Bloomington, 1952.

Cross, Tom Pete and C.H. Slover. *Ancient Irish Tales.* London, 1936.

Crowe, Eyre E. *To-Day in Ireland.* London, 1825.

Crozier, M. (ed.) *Cultural Traditions in Northern Ireland.* Belfast, 1989.

Cullen, L.M. 'The Hidden Ireland: Re-Assessment of a Concept.' *Studia Hibernica*, 9 (1969), 7-47.

Curtin, Charles A. 'Jeremiah Curtin.' *Journal of the American Irish Historical Society*, 31 (1937), 55-71.

Curtin, Jeremiah. *Hero-Tales of Ireland* (1894). Boston, 1911.

— *Irish Folk-Tales* (ed. by J.H. Delargy). Dublin, 1943.

— *Myth and Folk-Lore of Ireland*. London, 1890.

— *Tales of the Fairies and of the Ghost World Collected from Oral Tradition in South-West Munster* (1895). Dublin, 1974.

Curwen, J.C. *Observations on the State of Ireland, principally directed to its Agriculture and Rural Populations*. London, 1818.

Dall, Ian. *Here are Stones: an Account of a Journey to the Aran Islands*. London, 1931.

Daly, Dominic. *The Young Douglas Hyde*. Dublin, 1974.

Daly, Mary and D. Dickson (eds) *The Origins of Popular Literacy in Ireland: Language Change and Educational Development 1700-1920*. Dublin, 1990.

Danaher, Kevin. *A Bibliography of Irish Ethnology and Folk Tradition*. Dublin, Cork, 1979.

— *Folktales of the Irish Countryside*. Cork, 1967.

— 'Folk Tradition and Literature.' *Journal of Irish Literature*, 1 (1972), 63-76.

— 'Oral Tradition and the Printed Word.' *Irish University Review*, 9 (1979), 31-41.

— 'The Progress of Irish Ethnology, 1783-1982.' *Ulster Folklife*, 29 (1983), 3-17.

— 'Sound Recording of Folk Narrative in Ireland in the Late Nineteen Forties.' *Fabula*, 22 (1981), 312-15.

— 'Stories and Storytelling in Ireland.' In *Automobile Association Handbook of Ireland*, 1970, 26-7.

— *That's How it Was*. Cork, 1984.

— *The Hearth and Stool and All; Irish Rural Households*. Cork, 1985.

— *The Year in Ireland*. Cork, 1972.

Danaher, Liam. 'Memoirs from my Youth.' *Béaloideas*, 17 (1947), 58-72.

Davis, Thomas. *Selection from the Prose and Poetry*. London (1914).

Deane, S. (ed.) *The Field Day Anthology of Irish Writing*. Derry, 1991.

De Blacam, Aodh. *From a Gaelic Outpost*. Dublin, 1921.

— *Gaelic Literature Surveyed*. Dublin, 1929.

Deeney, Daniel. *Peasant Lore from Gaelic Ireland* (1900). London, 1973.

Delaney, James D. 'Patrick Kennedy.' *The Past*, 7 (1964), 9-88.

— 'Patrick Kennedy, Folklorist – A Preliminary Assessment.' *The Past*, 14 (1983), 49-66.

Delargy, James H. *The Gaelic Story-Teller. With Some Notes on Gaelic Folk-Tales*. Rhys Memorial Lecture. London, 1945.

— 'The Gaelic Story-teller – No Living Counterpart in Western Christendom.' *Ireland of the Welcome* , 1, No. 1 (1952), 2-4.

— 'Irish Folklore.' In *Saorstát Éireann: Irish Free State Official Handbook*, Dublin, 1932, 264-6.

— 'Irish Stories and Storytellers.' *Studies*, 31 (1942), 31-46.

— 'Irish Tales and Story-Tellers.' In H. Kuhn and K. Schiers (eds) *Märchen, Mythos, Dichtung*. München, 1963, 63-82.

— *Leabhar Stiofáin Uí Ealaoire* (D. Ó hOgáin ed.). Dublin, 1981.

— 'Notes on the Oral Tradition of Thomond.' *Journal of the Royal Society of Antiquaries of Ireland*, 95 (1965), 133-47.

— 'Once Upon a Time.' In G. Jenkins (ed.) *Studies in Folk-Life: Essays in honour of Iorwerth C. Peate*. London, 1969, 48-58.

— *Sean Ó Conaill's Book. Stories and Traditions from Iveragh*. Tr. by M. MacNeill of Delargy's ed. of *Leabhar Sheán I Chonaill* (1948). Dublin, 1981.

— 'The Study of Irish Folklore.' *Dublin Magazine*, 17 (1942), 19-26.

de Paor, Liam and Máire. *Early Christian Ireland*. London, 1958.

Derricke, John. *The Image of Irelande, with a Disclosure of Woodkarne* (1581, ed. J. Small). Edinburgh, 1883.

Dewar, Daniel. *Observations on the Character, Customs, and Superstitions of the Irish*. London, 1812.

Dillon, Myles. *The Archaism of Irish Tradition* (1947). Chicago, 1969.

— *The Cycles of the Kings* (1946). Dublin, 1994.

— *Irish Sagas*. Dublin, 1959.

— 'The Hindu Act of Truth in Celtic Tradition.' *Modern Philology*, 44 (1947), 137-40.

— *There Was a King in Ireland: Five Tales from Oral Tradition*. Austin, 1971.

Dineley, Thomas. *Observations on a Voyage through the Kingdom of Ireland ... in the Year 1681*. (Ed. J. Graves) Dublin, 1870.

Dinneen, Patrick S. *Foclóir Gaedhilge agus Béarla – An Irish-English Dictionary*. Dublin, 1927.

Dobbs, Margaret E. (ed. tr.) *'Altromh Tighi dá Medar.'* *Zeitschrift für Celtische Philologie*, 18 (1929) 189-230.

Doherty, G. and D. Keogh (eds) *Michael Collins and the Making of the Irish State*. Cork, 1998.

Donnelly, J.S. and K.A. Miller (eds) *Irish Popular Culture 1650-1850*. Dublin, 1998.

Dorson, Richard M. 'Collecting in County Kerry' (1953). In his *Folklore and Fakelore*. Cambridge Mass., 1976, 183-211.

Dowling, P.J. *The Hedge-Schools of Ireland* (1935). Cork, 1968.

'Doyle, Martin' (W. Hickey). *Irish Cottagers*. Dublin, 1833.

Duffy, Ch. Gavan. *Young Ireland*. Dublin, 1884.

Dunleavy, J.E. and G.W. 'Jeremiah Curtin's Working Methods: The Evidence from the Manuscripts.' *Éigse*, 18 (1980), 67-86.

(Dunn) *A Description of Killarney*. Dublin, 1776.

Dunne, John. 'The Fenian Traditions of Sliabh-na-m-Ban.' *Transactions of the Kilkenny Archaeological Society*, 1 (1849-51), 333-62.

Dunne, Tom (ed.) *The Writer as Witness: Literature as Historical Evidence*. Historical Studies 16. Cork, 1987.

Dunne, T.I. 'The Gaelic Response to the Conquest and Colonisation: the Evidence of Poetry', in *Studia Hibernica* 20 (1980) 7-30.

Dutton, Hely. *Statistical Survey of the County of Clare*. Dublin, 1808.

Edgeworth, F. (ed.) *Memoirs of Maria Edgeworth, with a Selection from her Letters*. London, 1867.

Edgeworth, Maria. *Castle Rackrent* (1800). London, 1992.

Edgeworth, R.L. and Maria. *Essay on Irish Bulls*. London,1802.

Edwards, Ruth D. *Patrick Pearse: The Triumph of Failure* (1977). Swords, 1990.

Egan, John. 'The Dying Art of the Storyteller is Preserved for Posterity.' *Ireland of the Welcome*, 1, No. 1 (1986), 30-2.

Eglinton, John (et al.) *Literary Ideals in Ireland*. London, 1899.

Evans, E. Estyn. 'Folklife Studies in Northern Ireland.' *Journal of the Folklore Institute*, 2 (1965) 355-63.

— *Irish Folk Ways*. London, 1957.

— *Irish Heritage: The Landscape, the People, and their Work*. Dundalk, 1942.

— *The Personality of Ireland* (1981). Dublin, 1992.

Ferguson, Samuel. *The Hibernian Nights' Entertainments* (1834-6). New York, 1857.

Feuillide, Jean-G. Capo de. *L'Irlande*. Paris, 1839.

(Fisher, Lydia) *Letters from the Kingdom of Kerry in the Year 1845*. Dublin, 1847.

Fitzgerald, David. 'Early Celtic History and Mythology.' *Revue Celtique*, 6 (1883-5),193-259.

— 'Popular Tales of Ireland.' *Revue Celtique*, 4 (1879), 171-200.

Fitzgerald, William J. *'The Sham Squire' and the Informers of 1798*. Dublin, 1866.

Flanagan, L. *Irish Proverbs*. Dublin, 1995.

Flanagan, Thomas. *The Irish Novelists, 1800-1850*. New York, 1958.

'Flann O'Brien'. *At Swim-Two-Birds* (1939). London, 1967.

— *The Poor Mouth* (tr. by Patrick C. Power from Myles na gCopaleen *An Béal Bocht* 1941). London, 1988.

'Floredice' (W. Hart). *Memories of a Month among the Mere Irish*. London, 1881.

— *Derryreel: A Collection of Stories from North-West Donegal*. London, 1889.

Flower, Robin. *The Irish Tradition*. Oxford, 1947.

— *The Western Island*. Oxford, 1944.

Foley, T. and S. Ryder (eds) *Ideology and Ireland in the Nineteenth Century*. Dublin, 1998.

Ford, P.K. (ed.) *Celtic Folklore and Christianity*. Santa Barbara, 1983.

Foster, John W. 'Certain Set Apart: The Western Island in the Irish Renaissance.' *Studies*, 66 (1977), 261-70.

— *Colonial Consequences: Essays in Irish Literature and Culture*. Dublin, 1991.

— *Fiction of the Irish Literary Revival: A Changeling Art*. Syracuse, 1987.

Foster, R.F. *W.B. Yeats: A Life: The Apprentice Master*. Oxford, 1997.

Fox, Robin. *The Tory Islanders: A People of the Celtic Fringe* (1978). Notre Dame, 1995.

Gaffney, S. and Cashman, S. *Proverbs & Sayings of Ireland*. Dublin, 1974.

Gallagher, Patrick. *My Story. By Paddy the Cope*. London, 1939.

Gallagher, Th. *Paddy's Lament: Ireland 1846-1847 – Prelude to Hatred* (1982). Swords, 1988.

(Gamble, John) *Sketches of History, Politics and Manners, Taken in Dublin and the North of Ireland, in the Autumn of 1810* (1811). London, 1826.

— *Views of Society and Manners in the North of Ireland*. London, 1819.

Gantz, Jeffrey (ed. tr.) *Early Irish Myths and Sagas*. London, 1976.

Gatty, Margaret S. *The Old Folks from Home, or A Holiday in Ireland in 1861*. London, 1862.

'Gerald of Wales'. *The History and Topography of Ireland* (tr. John O'Meara). London, 1982.

Gibbings, Robert. *Lovely is the Lee*. London, 1945.

Gibbons, Luke. 'Topographies of Terror: Killarney and the Politics of the Sublime.' *South Atlantic Quarterly*, 95 (1996), 23-44.

— *Transformations in Irish Culture*. Cork, 1996.

Gillet, Louis. *Stèle pour James Joyce*. Marseille, 1941.

Gillies, William. 'A Poem on the Downfall of the Gaoidhil.' *Éigse*, 13 (1969-70), 203-10.

Glassie, Henry. *Irish Folk History: Texts from the North*. Dublin, 1982.

— *Irish Folktales*. New York, 1985.

— *Passing the Time; Folklore and History of an Ulster Community*. Philadelphia, 1982.

— 'Tradition.' *Journal of American Folklore*, 108 (1995), 395-412.

Goldsmith, Oliver. *Collected Works of Oliver Goldsmith* (ed. Arthur Friedman). Oxford, 1966.

Gorman, Herbert. *James Joyce: A Definitive Biography*. London, 1941.

Graham, Brian (ed.) *In Search of Ireland: a Cultural Geography*. London, 1997.

Grant, James. *Impressions of Ireland and the Irish*. London, 1844.

'Greendrake, G.' (?Coad, J.).*The Angling Excursions of Gregory Greendrake Esq*. Dublin, 1824.

Gregory, Augusta. *Cuchulain of Muirthemne* (1902). Gerrards Cross, 1970.

— *Gods & Fighting Men* (1904). Gerrards Cross, 1970.

— *The Kiltartan Books* (1909, 1910). Gerrards Cross, 1972.

— *Our Irish Theatre* (1913). Gerrards Cross, 1972.

— *Poets and Dreamers* (1903). Port Washington, 1967.

— *Seven Short Plays*. Dublin, 1909.

— *Seventy Years; being the Autobiography of Lady Gregory*. New York, 1976.

Grene, Gerald. *Synge: A Critical Study of the Plays*. London, 1975.

— *Visions and Beliefs in the West of Ireland* (1920). Gerrards Cross, 1970.

Griffin, Gerald. *The Collegians* (1829). Belfast, 1992.

— *Holland Tide*. Dublin, 1827.

— *The Rivals, and Tracy's Ambition* (1829). Villeneuve d'Ascq, 1978.

— *Tales of the Munster Festivals*. London, 1827.

— *Talis Qualis; or Tales of the Jury Room*. Dublin, 1842.

Grimm, Wilhelm. *Irische Land- und Seemärchen* (W. Moritz, C. Oberfeld, S. Heyer eds). Marburg, 1986.

Grimm, Wilhelm and Jacob. *Irische Elfenmärchen* (1826). Frankfurt, 1987.

Gwynn, Edward. *The Metrical Dindshenchas*. Dublin, 1913.

Gwynn, Stephen. *Irish Books and Irish People*. Dublin, 1920.

Hadfield, Andrew and McVeagh, J. *Strangers to that Land, British Perceptions of Ireland from the Reformation to the Famine*. Gerrards Cross, 1994.

Hall, Anna Maria.*The Irish Tourist's Illustrated Handbook*. London, n.d.

— *Sketches of Irish Character* (1829). London, n.d.

— *The Whiteboy. A Story of Ireland* (1845). London, 1867.

— *Tales of Irish Life and Character*. London, 1910.

Hall, Anna Maria and Samuel C. *Ireland, Its Scenery, Character, &c*. London, 1841-3.

— *A Week at Killarney* (1843). London, 1865.

Hall, James. *A Tour through Ireland, particularly the Interior and Least Known Parts*. London, 1813.

Hall, Samuel C. *Retrospect of a Long Life*. London, 1883.

Hanrahan, M. 'Going to the Fair, an Old Meath Tale.' *Ireland's Own*, 3 Aug. 1935.

Hardy, Ph. Dixon.*The Holy Wells of Ireland*. Dublin, 1836.

— *Legends, Tales, and Stories of Ireland*. Dublin, 1837.

Harmon, M. (ed.). *J.M. Synge; Centenary Papers*. Dublin, 1972.

Harrington, J.P. *The English Traveller in Ireland*. Dublin, 1991.

Harvey, C. Brennan. *Contemporary Irish Traditional Narrative; The English Language Tradition*. Berkeley, 1992.

— 'Some Irish Women Storytellers and Reflections on the Role of Women in the Storytelling Tradition.' *Western Folklore*, 48 (1989), 109-28.

Hayward, Richard. *This is Ireland 2: Ulster and the City of Belfast*. London, 1950.

Healy, James J. *Lifes and Times of Charles Kickham*. Dublin, 1915.

Heaney, Seamus. 'An Open Letter.' (*A Field Day Pamphlet Number 2*). Derry, 1983.

Hennig, J. 'The Brothers Grimm and T.C. Croker.' *Modern Language Review*, 41 (1946), 44-54.

— 'Contes Irlandais.' *Modern Language Review*, 42 (1947), 237-42.

Henry, John. *Scéalta Chais Cladaigh – Stories of Sea and Shore, told by John Henry, Kilgalligan, Co. Mayo* (ed. Séamus Ó Catháin). Dublin, 1983.

Herity, Michael. 'Eugene O'Curry's Early Life: Details from an Unpublished Letter.' *North Munster Antiquarian Journal* 9 (1962-3) No. 1-2, 143-7.

Hillers, B. and Mac Cárthaigh, C. 'Pay Me For My Story: The Etiquette of Storytelling.' *Sinsear. Folklore Journal*, 6 (1990), 50-60.

Hoare, R. Colt. *Journal of a Tour in Ireland, A.D. 1806*. London, 1807.

Hore, Herbert F. 'Irish Bardism in 1561.' *Ulster Journal of Archaeology*, 6 (1858), 165-7, 202-12.

Horgan, Donal. *Echo after Echo; Killarney and Its History*. Cork, 1988.

Hull, Eleanor (ed.) *The Cuchullin Saga in Irish Literature*. London, 1898.

— 'Folk-Lore Collecting in Ireland.' *Journal of the Cork Historical and Archaeological Society*, 17 (1911), 27-33.

— 'Folk-Lore Collecting in Ireland.' *Journal of the Royal Society of Antiquaries of Ireland*, 41 (1911), 188-90.

— *Folklore of the British Isles*. London, 1928.

— 'The Hawk of Achill, or the Legend of the Oldest Animal.' *Folk-Lore* 43 (1932), 376-409.

— *A Text Book of Irish Literature*. Dublin, 1906.

Hull, V. (ed. tr.) 'Echtra Cormaic Maic Airt.' *PMLA* , 64 (1949), 871-83.

Hultin, Neil C. 'Anglo-Irish Folklore from Clonmel: T.C. Croker and British Library Add. 20099.' *Fabula*, 27 (1986), 288-307.

Hunt, B. *Folk Tales of Breffny*. London, 1912.

Hyde, Douglas. *Beside the Fire; A Collection of Irish Gaelic Folk Stories* (1890). Dublin, 1978.

— *Contes Irlandais: Leabhar Sgeulaigheachta, An Sgéuluidhe Gaodhalach* (1893, 1901.) Paris-Genève, 1980.

— *Language, Lore and Lyrics; Essays and Lectures* (ed B.O Conaire). Dublin, 1986.

— *Legends of Saints & Sinners*. London, Dublin, 1915.

— *A Literary History of Ireland from Earliest Time to the Present Day* (1899). London, 1967.

— *Love Songs of Connacht*. Dublin, 1893.

— *Sgéalta ó Thomáis O Chathasaigh – Mayo Stories Told by Thomas Casey*. Dublin, 1939.

— *Sgéaluidhe Fíor na Seachtmaine*. Dublin, 1909.

— *The Stone of Truth and Other Irish Folk Tales*. Dublin, 1979.

Irwin, George O'Malley. *The Illustrated Hand-Book to the County of Wicklow.* London, 1844.

Jackson, Kenneth. 'The International Folktale in Ireland.' *Folk-lore*, 47 (1936), 263-93.

— *The Oldest Irish Tradition: A Window on the Iron Age.* Cambridge, 1964.

— 'Scéalta ón mBlascaod.' *Béaloideas*, 8 (1938), 3-96.

Jacobs, Joseph. *Celtic Fairy Tales.* London, 1891.

— *More Celtic Fairy Tales.* London, 1894.

Johann, A.E. *Heimat der Regenbogen: Irland* (1953). Gütersloh, 1958.

Johnson, James. *A Tour in Ireland, with Meditations and Reflections.* London, 1844.

Joyce, James. *Critical Writings.* New York, 1959.

— *Dubliners* (1914). London, 1959.

— *Finnegans Wake.* London, 1939.

— *A Portrait of the Artist as a Young Man* (1916). The Modern Novel Series, London, 1964.

— *Selected Letters* (ed. R. Ellmann). New York, 1975.

— *Stephen Hero* (1944). London, 1969.

— *Ulysses* (1922). World's Classics, Oxford, 1993.

Joyce, Patrick W. *English as We Speak It in Ireland.* London, 1910.

— *Old Celtic Romances.* London, 1879.

— *Old Irish Folk Music and Songs.* Dublin, 1888 and 1909.

— *A Social History of Ancient Ireland.* London, 1903.

Joynt, Maud (ed.) *Feis Tighe Chonáin.* Dublin, 1936.

Kavanagh, Jean. 'The Melusine Legend in Irish Folk Tradition.' *Sinsear*, 8 (1995) 71-82.

Kavanagh, Patrick. *The Green Fool* (1938). London, 1975.

— 'Twenty-Three Tons of Accumulated Folk-Lore.' *Irish Times*, 18 April 1939.

Kearns, Kevin C. *Dublin Pub Life and Lore: an Oral History.* Dublin, 1996.

— *Dublin Street Life and Lore: an Oral History.* Dun Laoghaire, 1991.

— *Dublin Tenement Life: an Oral History.* Dublin, 1994.

Keating, Geoffrey. *Foras Feasa ár Éirinn – The History of Ireland.* Ed. tr. David Comyn (vol. 1) and P. Dinneen (vols 2-4). Irish Texts Society 4, 8, 9, 15. London, 1902-13.

Keegan, John. *Legends and Poems.* Dublin, 1907.

— 'Legends and Tales of the Queens County Peasantry.' *Dublin University Magazine*, 14 (1839), 366-74, 487-94, 580-86.

— 'Puss in Brogues, A Legend.' *Irish Penny Journal*, 1 May 1841.

— 'Tales of My Childhood. No.1 – The Boccough Ruadh.' *Irish Penny Journal*, 23 January 1841.

Keightley, Thomas. *The Fairy Mythology* (1828). London, 1892.

— *Tales and Popular Fictions; their Resemblance and Transmission from Country to Country.* London, 1834.

Kennedy, Patrick. *The Banks of the Boro.* Dublin, 1867.

— *The Fireside Stories of Ireland.* Dublin, 1870. *Legends of Mount Leinster.* Dublin, 1855.

— 'Leinster Folk-lore.' *Dublin University Magazine*, 59 (1862), 453-65 and 61 (1863), 81-93.

— *Legendary Fictions of the Irish Celts* (1866). London, 1891.

Kenney, James F. (ed.) *The Sources of the Early History of Ireland.* New York, 1929.

Keogh, Dermot. *Twentieth-Century Ireland: Nation and State.* Dublin, 1994.

Kiberd, Declan. *Synge and the Irish language* (1979). Dublin, 1993.

Kickham, Charles. *Knocknagow, or The Homes of Tipperary* (1879).

Kiely, Benedict. *The Cards of the Gambler* (1953). Dublin, 1973.

— *God's Own Country*. London, 1993.

— *Land Without Stars*. London, 1946.

Kilroy, James. *The 'Playboy' Riots*. Dublin, 1971.

Knott, E. (ed.) *The Bardic Poems of Tadhg Dall Ó hUiginn*. Irish Texts Society 22-23. London, 1922, 1926.

— *Irish Classical Poetry, Commonly Called Bardic Poetry*. Dublin, 1960.

Kohl, J.G. *Travels in Ireland*. London, 1844.

Lacey, Brian. *Colum Cille and the Columban Tradition*. Dublin, 1997.

Larminie, William. *West Irish Folktales and Romances* (1893). Totowa, N.J., 1973.

Laverty, Maura. *Never No More* (1942). London, 1985.

Lawless, Emily. *Grania; The Story of an Island*. London, 1892.

— *Maelcho*. London, 1894.

Lawlor, Chris. *The Massacre at Dunlavin Green*. n.p., 1998.

Leadbetter, Mary. *Cottage Biography: Being a Collection of Lives of the Irish Peasantry*. Dublin, 1822.

Ledwich, Edward. *Antiquities of Ireland* (1790). Dublin, 1804.

Leerssen, Joseph. *Mere Irish & Fíor Ghael; Studies in the Idea of Irish Nationality, its Development and Literary Expression prior to the Nineteenth Century*. Amsterdam, 1986.

— *Remembrance and Imagination*. Cork, 1996.

— 'Wildness, Wilderness, and Ireland: Medieval and Early-Modern Patterns in the Demarcation of Civility.' *Journal of the History of Ideas*, 56 (1955), 25-39.

Le Fanu, Joseph Sheridan. *Best Ghost Stories*. New York, 1964.

— *Ghost Stories and Mysteries*. New York 1975.

— *The House by the Churchyard* (1863). Belfast, 1992.

Le Fanu, W.R. *Seventy Years of Irish Life* (1893). London, 1928.

Lenihan, Edmund. *Long Ago by Shannon Side*. Cork, 1982.

Le Roux, Louis. *Patrick Pearse*. Dublin, 1932.

Lever, Charles. *Jack Hinton, the Guardian* (1842). London, 1901.

— *Luttrell of Arran*, London, 1865.

Little, A.G. (ed.) *Liber Exemplorum ad Usum Praedicantium*. Aberdeen, 1908.

Little, George A. *Malachi Horan Remembers* (1943). Cork, 1976.

Lover, Samuel. *Handy Andy* (1842). London, 1907.

— *Legends and Stories of Ireland* (First Series – 1832). Westminster, 1899.

— *The Lyrics of Ireland*. London, 1858.

Luce, J.V. 'Homeric Qualities in the Life and Literature of the Great Blasket Island.' *Greece and Rome*, 16 (1969), 151-68.

Luckombe, Philip. *A Tour Through Ireland*. London, 1780.

Lynd, Robert. *Home Life in Ireland*. London, 1909.

Lysaght, Patricia. 'Perspectives on Narrative Communication and Gender: Lady Augusta Gregory's *Visions and Beliefs in the West of Ireland*.' *Fabula*, 39 (1998) 256-75.

— 'A Tradition Bearer in Contemporary Ireland.' In L. Röhrich and S. Wienker-Piepho (eds) *Storytelling in Contemporary Societies* . Tübingen, 1990. 129-214.

Mac Adam, Robert. 'Six Hundred Gaelic Proverbs Collected in Ulster.' *Ulster Journal of Archaeology*, 6 (1858), 172-83, 202-12, 250-67.

Macafee, C.I. (ed.) *A Concise Ulster Dictionary*. Oxford, 1996.

Macalister, R. (ed.) *Two Irish Arthurian Romances*. Irish Text Society 10. London, 1908.

MacAnally, D.R. *Irish Wonders; the Ghosts, Giants, Pookas, Demons, Leprechauns, Banshees, Fairies, Witches, Widows, Old Maids, and other Wonders of the Emerald Isle. Popular Tales as Told by the People*. Boston, 1888.

Mac an Luain, P. *Uair an Chloig Teallaigh – An Hour by the Hearth*. Ed. tr. Séamas Ó Catháin. Dublin, 1985.

Macardle, D. *The Irish Republic* (1937). Dublin, 1951.

McAuliffe, James. 'The Connaught Shanachie.' *Ireland's Own*, 24 Oct. 1917.

McCall, P. J. *Fenian Nights Entertainments; being a Series of Ossianic Legends Told at a Wexford Fireside*. Dublin, 1897.

McCana, Proinsias. *The Learned Tales of Medieval Ireland*. Dublin, 1980.

Mac Cárthaigh, Criostóir. 'The Man Who Had No Story.' *Sinsear, The Folklore Journal*, 2 (1980) 115-21.

(MacCarthy, J.M.) *Limerick's Fighting Story*. Tralee, 1948.

McClintock, Letitia. 'Folk-lore of County Donegal. The Fairies.' *Cornhill Magazine*, 35 (1877), 177-81.

— 'Folk Lore of the County Donegal'. *Dublin University Magazine*, 88 (1876), 697-14.

— 'Folk-Lore of Ulster.' *Dublin University Magazine*, 89 (1877), 747-54.

McCone, Kim. *Pagan Past and Christian Present in Early Irish Literature*. Maynooth, 1990.

McCone, K. and K. Simms (eds) *Progress in Medieval Irish Studies*. Maynooth, 1996.

Mac Conghail, M. *The Blaskets: A Kerry Island Library*. Dublin, 1987.

Mac Cuarta, Brian. 'A Planter's Interaction with Gaelic Culture: Sir Matthew De Renzy (1577-1634).' *Irish Economic and Social History*, 20 (1993), 1-17.

MacCurtin, Hugh. *A Brief Discourse in Vindication of the Antiquity of Ireland*. Dublin, 1717.

McCormack, W.J. *Sheridan le Fanu and Victorian Ireland*. Oxford, 1980.

M'Farland, Alfred. *Hours in Vacation*. Dublin, 1853.

Mac Giollarnath, S. *Peadar Chois Fhairrge: Scéalta Nua agus Seanscéalta d'innis Peader Mac Thathaláin*. Dublin, 1934.

McHugh, Roger J. 'The Famine in Irish Oral Tradition.' In R. Dudley Edwards and T. Desmond Williams (eds) *The Great Famine, Studies in Irish History 1845-52*. Dublin, 1956, 391-436.

MacKillop, James. *Fionn mac Cumhaill: Celtic Myth in English Literature*. Syracuse, 1986.

Mac Laughlin, Jim. *Travellers and Ireland: Whose Country, Whose History?* Cork, 1995.

MacLennon, G.W. *Seanchas Annie Bhán: The Lore of Annie Bhán*. Dublin, 1997.

MacLysaght, E. *Irish Life in the Seventeenth Century* (1939). Cork, 1950.

MacMahon, Bryan. 'Peig Sayers and the Vernacular of the Storyteller.' In Alison Feder and Bernice Shranks (eds) *Literature and Folk Culture; Ireland and Newfoundland*. St John's, 1977, 83-109.

— *The Sound of Hooves*. London, 1985.

MacManus, D.A. *The Middle Kingdom; The Faerie World of Ireland*. London, 1959.

M'Manus, Henry. *Sketches of the Irish Highlands; Descriptive, Social, and Religious*. London, 1863.

M'Manus, L. 'Folk-Tales from Western Ireland.' *Folk-Lore*, 25 (1914) 324-41.

— 'Folk Tales from County Mayo, Ireland.' *Folk-Lore*, 26 (1915) 182-95.

MacManus, Seamas. *Donegal Fairy Stories* (1902). New York, 1968.
— *Heavy Hangs the Golden Grain*. Dublin, 1951.
— *Hibernian Nights*. New York, 1963.
— *The Rocky Road to Dublin* (1938). Dublin, 1988.
— *Yourself and the Neighbours* (1914). New York, 1932.
MacNeill, Eoin (ed. tr.) *Duanaire Finn. The Book of the Lays of Fionn* 1. Irish Texts Society 7. London, 1908.
— *Early Irish Laws and Institutions*. Dublin, 1935.
MacNeill, Máire. *The Festival of Lughnasa*. Oxford, 1962.
— 'Irish Folklore as a Source for Research.' *Journal of the Folklore Institute*, 2 (1965) 340-54.
— 'Seamus Delargy and North Clare.' *Dal gCais*, 6 (1982), 110-12.
M'Teague, J.G. 'Rooshkulum, or the Wise Simpleton.' *Irish Penny Journal*, 27 March 1841.
McVeagh, John. *Irish Travel Writing; a Bibliography*. Dublin, 1996.
Maginn, William. *Miscellanies, Prose and Verse*. London, 1885.
Maguire, Conor. 'Western Folk-Tales.' *New Ireland Review*, May 1906 to April 1907.
Mahaffy, J.P. *The Principles of the Art of Conversation*. London, 1887.
Maher, James. *Romantic Slievenamon*. Mullinahone, 1964.
Mahon, Bríd. *While Green Grass Grows: Memoirs of a Folklorist*. Cork, 1998.
Mahoney, Richard. 'Brian Roe, the Cow Doctor.' *Ireland's Own*, 22 April 1908.
Mallory, J.P. (ed). *Aspects of the Táin*. Belfast, 1992.
— and G. Stockma (eds) *Ulidia; Proceedings of the First International Conference on the Ulster Cycle of Tales*. Belfast, 1994.
Martin, Augustine. 'The Past and the Peasant in the Stories of Seumas O'Kelly.' In J. Genet (ed.) *Rural Ireland, Real Ireland?* Gerrards Cross, 1996, 185-200.
Mason, W. Shaw. *A Statistical Account or Parochial Survey of Ireland*. Dublin, 1814, 1816, 1819.
Maturin, Ch. R. *Melmoth the Wanderer* (1820). London, 1977.
— *The Milesian Chief*. London, 1812.
Maxwell, C.E. *The Stranger in Ireland from the Reign of Elizabeth to the Great Famine*. London, 1954.
Maxwell, W.H. *Wild Sports of the West* (1832). London, 1838.
Mehan, Helen. 'The McManus Brothers.' *Donegal Annual 1994*, 5-18.
Messenger, J.C. *An Anthropologist at Play: Balladmongering in Ireland and its Consequences for Research*. Boston, 1983.
— *Inish Beag – Isle of Ireland*. New York, 1969.
— 'Joe O'Donnell, Seanchai of Aran.' *Journal of the Folklore Institute*, 1(1964), 197-213
Meyer, Kuno. *Fiannaigecht: Being a Collection of Hitherto Inedited Irish Poems and Tales Relating to Finn and his Fianna*. Dublin, 1910.
— 'Scél Baili Binnbérlaig.' *Revue Celtique*, 13 (1892), 220-5.
— 'The Instructions of King Cormac mac Airt.' *Tood Lecture Series* 15. Dublin, 1909.
— *The Voyage of Bran, Son of Febal, to the land of the Living, with an Essay upon the Irish Vision of the Happy Other World and the Celtic Doctrine of Rebirth, by Alfred Nutt*. London, 1895-7.
Mikhail, E.H. (ed.) *W.B. Yeats: Interviews and Recollections*. London, 1977.

Millman, Lawrence. *Our Like Will Not Be There Again; Notes from the West of Ireland.* Boston, 1977.

Mitchell, John. *The History of Ireland.* Glasgow, 1868.

Moody, T.W. (et al. eds.) *A New History of Ireland.* Oxford, 1976-.

Moore, George. *Confessions of a Young Man* (1888). London, 1933.

— *Hail and Farewell.* London, 1911, 1912, 1914.

— *Parnell and His Island.* London, 1887.

— *A Story-teller's Holiday.* London, 1928.

— *The Untilled Field* (1903). Dublin, 1990.

Moore, Thomas. *Memoirs of Captain Rock.* London, 1824.

Morgan, Lady. *Florence Macarthy: An Irish Tale.* London, 1818.

— *The O'Brien and the O'Flaherties: A National Tale* (1827). London, 1838.

— *Patriotic Sketches of Ireland Written in Connaught.* London, 1807.

— *St. Clair; or The Heiress of Desmond* (1803). Philadelphia, 1807.

— *The Wild Irish Girl* (1806). London, 1986.

— *Lady Morgan's Memoirs, Diaries and Correspondence* (ed. W.H. Dixon). London, 1862.

Morton, H.V. *In Search of Ireland.* London, 1930.

Mühlhausen, L. *Zehn irische Volkserzählungen aus Süd-Donegal.* Halle Saale, 1939.

— *Diarmuid mit dem Roten Bart: Irische Zaubermärchen.* Kassel, 1956.

Mullen, Pat. *Hero Breed.* London, 1936.

— *Irish Tales.* London, 1938.

— *Man of Aran.* London, 1934.

Murphy, G. *Duanaire Finn – The Book of the Lays of Fionn.* 2-3. Irish Texts Society 28 and 43. London, 1933, 1953.

— *Glimpses of Gaelic Ireland.* Dublin, 1948.

— *The Ossianic Lore and Romantic Tales of Medieval Ireland.* Dublin, 1955.

— *Saga and Myth in Ancient Ireland.* Dublin, 1955.

Murphy, Michael J. *At Slieve Gullion's Foot.* Dundalk, 1941.

— 'The Folk Stories of Dan Rooney of Lurgancanty.' *Ulster Folklife*, 11 (1965), 80–6.

— *My Man Jack; Bawdy Tales from Irish Folklore.* Dingle, 1989.

— *Now You're Talking ... : Folk Tales from the North of Ireland.* Belfast, 1975.

— *Rathlin: Island of Blood and Enchantment.* Dundalk, 1987.

— *Tyrone Folk Quest.* Belfast, 1973.

— *Ulster Folk of Field and Fireside.* Dundalk, 1983.

Murphy, Tom. *Plays: Two.* London, 1993.

Murray, P.J. *The Life of John Banim, the Irish Writer.* London, 1857.

Musgrave, Richard. *Memoirs of the Different Rebellions in Ireland.* Dublin, 1802.

Nagy, Joseph F. 'Close Encounters of the Traditional Kind in Medieval Irish Literature.' In P.K. Ford (ed.) *Celtic Folklore and Christianity*, Santa Barbara,1983, 129–49.

— *Conversations with Angels & Ancients: Literary Myths of Medieval Ireland.* Dublin, 1997.

— *A New Introduction to Two Arthurian Romances.* Dublin, 1998.

— *The Wisdom of the Outlaw, The Boyhood Deeds of Finn in Gaelic Narrative Tradition.* Berkeley, 1985.

Nicholson, A. *The Bible in Ireland, or Excursions through Ireland in 1844 and 1845* (1847: *Ireland's Welcome to the Stranger*). London, 1946.

Ní Dhuibhne, Eilís. *Blood and Water.* Dublin, 1988.

— *The Bray House*. Dublin, 1990.

— *Eating Women Is Not Recommended*. Dublin, 1991.

— *The Inland Ice and Other Stories*. Belfast, 1997.

— 'The Old Woman as Hare: Structure and Meaning in an Irish Legend.' *Folklore*, 104 (1993), 77-85.

Ní Fhloinn, B. 'Folklore Collecting in Co. Roscommon – Douglas Hyde and his Legacy.' *Comdháil an Chraoibhín: Conference Proceedings 1989*. Boyle, 1993. 24-46.

Norton, E.S. (ed.) *Folk Literature of the British Isles*. Metuchen, N.J., 1978.

Ó Cadhain, Máirtín. *The Road to Bright City* (tr. of *Idir Shúgradh agus Dáiríre agus Scéalta Eile*. 1939) Dublin, 1981.

O'Cahill, Donal. *Legends of Killarney*. Killarney, n.d. (*c*.1950).

Ó Casaide, S. 'Crofton Croker's Irish Fairy Legends'. *Béaloideas*, 10 (1940), 289-91

Ó Catháin, S. *The Bedside Book of Irish Folklore*. Cork, 1980.

— *Irish Life and Lore*. Cork, 1982.

Ockenden, William.*Observations on Modern Gardening, Illustrated by Descriptions, to which is added an Essay on Design in Gardening; Letters describing the Lake of Killarney and Mucruss Gardens*. Dublin, 1770.

Ó Ciosáin, Niall. *Print and Popular Culture in Ireland, 1750-1850*. London, 1997.

Ó Coileáin, Seán. 'Oral or Literary? Some Strands of the Argument.' *Studia Hibernica*, 17-18 (1977-8), 7-35.

O'Connell, Mrs. Morgan John. 'The Last of the Shanachies.' *Béaloideas*, 30 (1962), 99-104. (From the *Irish Monthly*, 1886).

O'Connor B. and M. Cronin (eds) *Tourism in Ireland; a Critical Analysis*. Cork, 1993.

O'Connor, Barry. *Turf-Fire Stories & Fairy Tales of Ireland*. New York, 1890.

O'Connor, Frank. *The Cornet Player Who Betrayed Ireland*. Sword, 1981.

O'Connor, Joseph. 'The Last of the Shanachies.' *Capuchin Annual* 1958, 368-72.

Ó Corráin, D., L. Breatnach and K. McCone (eds) *Sages, Saints and Storytellers: Celtic Studies in Honour of Professor James Carney*. Maynooth, 1989.

Ó Cróinín, Donncha. *Seanachas Amhlaoibh Í Luínse*. Dublin, 1980.

— *Seanachas Ó Chairbre*. Dublin, 1985.

— *Seanachas Phádraig Í Chrualaí*. Dublin, 1982.

Ó Cróinín, Daibhí. *Early Medieval Ireland 400-1200*. London, 1995.

Ó Cuív, Brian (ed.) *Seven Centuries of Irish Learning*. Dublin, 1961.

O'Curry, Eugene. *Lectures on the Manuscript Materials of Ancient Irish History*. Dublin, 1861.

— *On the Manners and Customs of the Ancient Irish* (ed. W.K. Sullivan). London, 1873.

Ó Danachair, Caómhín: see Danaher, Kevin.

O'Dea, Séamus. 'A Première for Stiofán.' *Dal gCais*, 6 (1892), 119-22.

Ó Dónaill, Niall. *Foclóir Gaeilge-Béarla*. Dublin, 1977.

O'Donovan, John. *Annals of the Kingdom of Ireland, by the Four Masters* (ed.). Dublin, 1856.

— *Leabhar na gCeart, or The Book of Rights* (ed.). Dublin, 1847.

— 'On the Traditions of the County of Kilkenny.' *Transactions of the Kilkenny Archaeological Society*, 1 (1849-51), 362-72.

Ó Duilearga, Séamus: see Delargy, James S.

O'Faolain, Eileen. *Children of the Salmon and Other Irish Folktales* (1965). Swords, 1984.

O'Faolain, Sean. *Collected Short Stories*. London, 1983.

— *An Irish Journey*. London, 1940.

— *Vive Moi!* London, 1964.

Ó Fiannachta, P. (ed.) *Thaitin Sé Le Peig*. Ballyferriter, 1989.

O'Flaherty, John.T. 'A Sketch of the History and Antiquities of the Southern Islands of Aran, Lying off the West Coast of Ireland; with Observations on the Religion of the Celtic Nations, Pagan Monuments of the Early Irish, Druids & Rites, etc.'. *Transactions of the Royal Irish Academy* 14 (1825), 79-139. .

O'Flaherty, Roderic. *A Chorographical Description of West or H-Iar Connaugh*. Dublin, 1846.

— *Ogygia, or, a Chronological Account of Irish Events*. (Tr. J. Hely.) Dublin, 1793.

O'Flanagan, Theophilus. *Deirdri, or the Lamentable Fate of the Sons of Usnach*. Dublin, 1808.

Ó Flannagain, P. (dir.) *The Blaskets: a Heritage Report*. n.p., 1990.

Ó Giolláin, Diarmuid. *Locating Irish Folklore: Tradition, Modernity, Identity*. Cork, 2000.

Ó Gráda, Cormac. *An Drochshaol, Béaloideas agus Ahráin*. Dublin, 1994.

— *Black '47 and Beyond: The Great Irish Famine in History, Economy and Memory*. Princeton, 1999.

O'Grady, Standish Hayes. *Silva Gadelica, a Collection of Tales in Irish*. London, 1892.

O'Grady, Standish James. *History of Ireland. I. The Heroic Period. II. Cuculain and his Contemporaries*. London, 1878, 1880.

Ó Guiheen, M. *A Pity Youth Does Not Last* (tr. T. Enright from *Is trua na fanann an óige* 1953). Oxford, 1982.

O'Halloran, S. *An Introduction to an History of Ireland* (1772). Dublin, 1803.

— *A Vindication of the Ancient History of Ireland*. Dublin, 1786.

Ó Háinle, C.G. 'The Gaelic Background of Carleton's *Traits and Stories*.' *Éire-Ireland*, 18.1 (1983), 6-19.

O'Hanlon, John. *Irish Local Legends*. Dublin, 1896.

— *Legend and Lays of Ireland*. Dublin, 1870.

— *Lives of the Irish Saints*. Dublin, 1875ff.

O'Hare, J. 'The Passing of the Irish Story-Teller.' *Ireland's Own*, 23 March 1921.

Ó hEithir, Breandán and Ruairí. *An Aran Reader*. Dublin, 1991.

Ó hEalaoire, St. *Leabhar Stiofáin Uí Ealaoire* (ed. J.H. Delargy). Dublin, 1981.

Ó hEochaidh, S. *Síscéalta Ó Thir Chonaill – Fairy Legends from Donegal* (tr. M. MacNeill, ed. S. Ó Catháin). Dublin, 1977.

Ó hÓgáin, Dáithi. *An File: Staidéar ar Osnádúrthacht na Filíochta sa Traidisiún Gaelach*. Dublin, 1982.

— *Fionn mac Cumhaill: Images of the Gaelic Hero*. Dublin, 1988.

— *The Hero in Irish Folk History*. Dublin, 1985.

— *Myth, Legend & Romance: An Encyclopaedia of Irish Folk Tradition*. London, 1990.

O'Kearney, N. (ed.) *Feis Tighe Chonáin Chinn-Shleibhe – The Festivities of the House of Conan of Ceann Sleibhe*. Transactions of the Ossianic Society 2. Dublin, 1854.

— 'On Folk Lore.' *Transactions of the Kilkenny Archaeological Society*, 1 (1849-51) 144-8.

O'Kelly, Seumas. *The Golden Barque and The Weaver's Grave*. Dublin, 1919.

O'Leary, P. '*Fir Fer*: an Internalized Ethical Concept in Early Irish Literature'. *Éigse* 22 (1987) 1-14.

O Lochlainn, Colm. *Irish Street Ballads*. Dublin, 1939.

O'Malley, Ernie. *On Another Man's Wound* (1936). London, 1961.

Ó Muimhneacháin, Aindrías (ed.) *Stories from the Tailor* (Irish ed. 1978). Cork, 1989.

Ó Muirithe, D. *A Dictionary of Anglo-Irish*. Dublin, 1996.

Ó Murchadha, T. 'Scéalaithe dob aithnid dom.' *Béaloideas*, 18 (1948), 3-44.

Ó Néill, Eoghan R. 'A Preliminary Study of "The King of the Cats is Dead" in Irish Tradition.' *Sinsear. The Folklore Journal*, 4 (1982-3), 117-26.

O'Neill, John. 'Mémoire de M. de C. à Messieurs les Auteurs du Journal des Sçavans au sujet des Poèmes de M. Macpherson.' In *Journal des Sçavans*, June 1764-February 1765.

O'Neill, John. *Handerahan, the Irish Fairyman; and Legends of Carrick*. London, 1854.

O'Nolan, Kevin. 'Formula in Oral Tradition.' In R. Thelwall (ed.) *Approaches to Oral Tradition*. Coleraine, 1978, 24-34.

— 'Homer and the Irish Hero Tale.' *Studia Hibernica* 8 (1968) 7-20.

— 'The Use of Formula in Storytelling.' *Béaloideas*, 39-41 (1971-3), 233-50.

O'Rahilly, Cecile (ed.) *The Stowe Version of Táin Bó Cuailnge*. Dublin, 1961.

— *Táin Bó Cuailnge from the Book of Leinster*. Dublin, 1967.

O'Rahilly, T.F. *Early Irish History and Mythology*. Dublin, 1957.

Ó Raifeartaigh, T. (ed.) *The Royal Irish Academy; a Bicentennial History*. Dublin, 1985.

O' Riordan, M. *The Gaelic Mind and the Collapse of the Gaelic World*. Cork, 1990.

O'Rorke, T. *History, Antiquities, and Present State of the Parishes of Ballysadare and Kilvarnet in the County of Sligo*. Dublin, n.d.

Ó Síocháin, C. *The Man from Cape Clear* (tr. R.P. Breathnach from *Seanchas Chléire* 1940). Cork, 1975.

Ó Siochfhradha, P. ('An Seabhac') *Laoithe na Féinne*. Dublin, 1941.

Oskamp, H.P.A. *The Voyage of Máel Dúin: A Study in Early Irish Voyage Literature*. Groningen, 1970.

Ó Súilleabháin, Seán: see O'Sullivan, Sean.

O'Sullivan, Donal. *Carolan: The Life, Times and Music of an Irish Harper*. London, 1958-59.

— *Songs of the Irish*. Dublin, 1960.

O'Sullivan, H. *Cinn-Lae Amhlaoibh Uí Shúileabháin –The Diary of Humphrey O'Sullivan*. Irish Texts Society 30. Tr. M. McCraith. London, 1928.

O'Sullivan, M. *Captain Rock Detected*. London, 1824.

O'Sullivan, Sean. *The Folklore of Ireland*. London, 1974.

— *Folktales of Ireland*. Chicago, 1966.

— *A Handbook of Irish Folklore*. Dublin, 1942.

— *Irish Folk Custom and Belief*. Dublin, 1973.

— *Irish Wake Amusement* (Irish. ed. 1961). Cork, 1967.

— *Legends from Ireland*. London, 1977.

— 'Peig Sayers.' *Éigse-Ireland*, 5 (1970), pp.86-91.

— *Storytelling in Irish Tradition*. Dublin, 1973.

— 'Synge's Use of Irish Folklore.' In M. Harmon (ed.) *John Millington Synge: Centenary Papers*. Dublin, 1972, 18-34.

— and R.T. Christiansen. *The Types of the Irish Folktale*. FFC 188. Helsinki, 1967.

Ó Tuama, S. (ed.) *The Gaelic League Idea* (1972). Cork, 1993.

Otway, Caesar. 'A Day at the Seven Churches at Glendalough.' *Christian Examiner and Church of Ireland Magazine*, 8 (1829) 45-53, and 9 (1829) 113-19.

— *Sketches in Erris and Tyrawley* (1841). Dublin, 1850.

— *Sketches in Ireland, Descriptive of Interesting and Hitherto Unnoticed Districts in the North and South*. Dublin, 1827.

— *A Tour in Connaught, Comprising Sketches of Clonmacnoise, Joyce Country, and Achill*. Dublin, 1839.

Owenson, Sidney: *see* Morgan.

Parsons, James. *Remains of Japhet: being Historical Enquiries into the Affinity and Origin of European Languages*. London, 1767.

Partridge, A. *A Hundred Irish Proverbs and Sayings*. Dublin, 1978.

Paterson, T.G.F. *Country Cracks, Old Tales from the County of Armagh*. Dundalk, 1939.

Pearse, Patrick. *Plays – Stories – Poems*. Dublin, n.d.

— *Political Writings and Speeches*. Dublin, n.d.

Pedersen, Holger. *Scéalta Mháirtín Neile* (ed. Ole Munch-Pedersen). Dublin, 1994.

Petrie, George. *The Ancient Music of Ireland*. Dublin, 1855.

— *The Complete Collection of Irish Music, as Noted by George Petrie* (ed. C.V. Stanford). London, 1902-5.

Power, Arthur. *Conversations with James Joyce*. London, 1974.

Prévost, J. Joseph. *Un Tour en Irlande*. Paris, 1846.

Pückler-Muskau, H.L.H. (Fürst von).*Tour in England, Ireland and France in the Years 1826, 1827, 1828 and 1829, by a German Prinz*. London, 1832.

Putzel, Steven D. 'Towards an Aesthetic of Folklore and Mythology: W.B. Yeats, 1888-1895.' *Southern Folklore Quarterly*, 44 (1980), 105-30.

Quinlan, Carmel. ' "A Punishment from God": The Famine in the Centenary Folklore Questionnaire.' *Irish Review*, 19 (1996), 68-86.

Raftery, Barry. *Pagan Celtic Ireland; The Enigma of the Irish Iron Age*. London, 1994.

Read, C.A. and K. Tynan (eds) *The Cabinet of Irish Literature*. London, 1903.

Rees, A. and B. *Celtic Heritage; Ancient Tradition in Ireland and Wales*. London, 1961.

Reid, Thomas. *Travels in Ireland in the Year 1822*. London, 1823.

Ritchie, Leitch. *Ireland, Picturesque and Romantic*. London, 1838.

Robinson, Hilary. *Somerville & Ross: A Critical Appreciation*. Dublin, 1980.

Robinson, Tim. *Stones of Aran: Labyrinth* (1995). London, 1997.

Rodenberg, J. *A Pilgrimage Through Ireland, or the Island of the Saints*. London, 1860.

Rogers, R.S. 'The Folklore of the Black Pig's Dyke.' *Ulster Folklife*, 3 (1957) 29-36.

Roney, Sir C.P. *How to spend a Month in Ireland, and what it will cost*. Dublin, (1867).

Ryan, Desmond. *The Man Called Pearse*. Dublin, 1919.

Sayers, Peig. *An Old Woman's Reflections* (tr. Séamus Ennis from *Machtnamh Seanamhná* 1939). Oxford, 1962.

— *Peig: the Autobiography of Peig Sayers* (tr. B. MacMahon from *Peig* 1936). Dublin, 1974.

Shand, Alex. Innes. *Letters from the West of Ireland*. Edinburgh, 1885.

Shaw, Francis. 'The Irish Folklore Commission.' *Studies*, 33 (1944), 30-6.

Shaw, Rose. *Carleton's Country*. Dublin, 1930.

Sherry, Brian and McHugh, R. (eds) *Along the Black Pig's Dyke; Folklore from Monaghan and South Armagh*. Castleblaney, 1993.

Shields, Hugh. *Narrative Singing in Ireland.* Dublin, 1993.

Sibbett, R.M. *Orangeism in Ireland.* London, 1939.

Silverman, M. and P.H. Gulliver (eds) *Approaching the Past: Historical Anthropology through Irish Case Studies.* New York, 1992.

Simpson, J. H. *Poems of Oisin, Bard of Erin, 'The Battle of Ventry Harbour,' &c.* London-Dublin, 1857.

Sloan, Barry. *The Pioneers of Anglo-Irish Fiction 1800-1850.* Gerrards Cross, 1986.

Smith, Charles.*The Antient and Present State of the County of Kerry.* Dublin, 1756.

Smith, George N. *Killarney and the Surrounding Scenery.* London, 1822.

Somerville and Ross. *Some Experiences of an Irish R.M.* London, 1899.

Spenser, Edmund. *A View of the Present State of Ireland. The Works of Spenser. A Variorum Edition.* Vol. 10 (ed. E. Greenlaw et al.) Baltimore, 1949.

Stark, A. G. *The South of Ireland in 1850; being the Journal of a Tour in Leinster and Munster.* Dublin, 1850.

Stephens, James.*The Demi-Gods.* London, 1914.

— *The Insurrection in Dublin.* Dublin, 1916.

— *Irish Fairy Tales.* London, 1920.

Stewart, James. *Boccaccio in the Blaskets.* Galway, 1988.

Stokes, Whitley. 'Cath Almaine (ed. tr.).' *Revue Celtique*, 24 (1903), 41-70.

— 'The Death of Crimthann son of Fidach, and the Adventures of the Sons of Eochaid Muigmedón.' *Revue Celtique*, 24 (1903), 172-207.

— 'The Second Battle of Moytura.' *Revue Celtique*, 12 (1891), 52-130.

Stokes, William. *The Life and Labours in Art and Archaeology of George Petrie.* Dublin, 1868.

Swift, J. *The Drapier's Letters.* Oxford, 1966.

Synge, John M. *Collected Letters.* Oxford, 1983.

— *Collected Works.* London, 1962-8.

Szövérffy, Josef. *Irisches Erzählgut im Abendland; Studien zur vergleichenden Volkskunde und Mittelalterforschung.* Berlin, 1957.

Taylor, Emily. *The Irish Tourist, or Tales of the People and the Provinces of Ireland.* London, 1843.

Taylor, Lawrence J. *Occasions of Faith: An Anthropology of Irish Catholics.* Dublin, 1997.

Thackeray, W.M. *The Irish Sketchbook* (1843). Dublin, 1990.

Thelwall, R. (ed.) *Approaches to Oral Tradition.* Coleraine, 1978.

Therman, D.H. *Stories from Tory Island.* Dublin, 1989.

Thompson, Stith. 'Folktale Collecting in Ireland.' *Southern Folklore Quarterly*, 2 (1938), 53-8.

Thompson, W.I. *The Imagination of an Insurrection.* New York, 1967.

Thoms, William J. *Lays and Legends of Ireland.* Lays and Legends of Various Countries, Illustrative of their Traditions, Popular Literature, Manners, Customs and Superstitions, No. 3. London,1834.

Thomson, David. *The People of the Sea; a Journey in Search of the Seal Legend* (1954). London, 1980.

Thomson, George. *Island Home: The Blasket Heritage.* Dingle, 1988.

Thornbury, Walter. *Cross Country.* London, 1861.

Thuente, Mary H. *W.B Yeats and Irish Folklore.* Dublin, 1980.

Thurneysen, R. *Die irische Helden- und Königsage bis zum Siebzehnten Jahrhundert*. Halle, 1921.

Tocqueville, Alexis de. *Journey to England and Ireland* (ed. J.P. Mayer). London, 1958.

Tracy, Robert. *The Unappeasable Host: Studies in Irish Identities*. Dublin, 1998.

Trotter, J.B. *Walks Through Ireland, in the Years 1812-1814 and 1817*. London, 1819.

Tynan Hinkson, K. (new ed.) *The Cabinet of Irish Literature*. London, 1903.

Uí Ógáin, R. *Immortal Dan: Daniel O'Connell in Irish Folk Tradition*. Dublin, 1995.

Vallancey, Charles. *Collectanea de Rebus Hibernica*. Dublin, 1770-1804.

— *A Vindication of the Ancient History of Ireland*. Dublin, 1786.

Vyvyan, C.C. *On Timeless Shores: Journeys in Ireland*. London, 1957.

Wagner, F. *Remarks on the History of Fingal, and Other Poems of Ossian*. London, 1762.

Wagner, Heinrich. 'Old Irish *fir*: "truth, oath".' *Zeitschrift für Celtische Philologie*, 31 (1970), 1-45.

Wakefield, Edward. *An Account of Ireland, Statistical and Political*. London, 1812.

Walker, J.C. *Historical Memoirs of the Irish Bards* (1786). Dublin, 1818.

Walsh, P. *Gleanings from Irish Manuscripts*. Dublin, 1937.

Welch, R. *A History of Verse Translation from the Irish 1789-1897*. Gerrards Cross, 1988.

— (ed.) *The Oxford Companion to Irish Literature*. Oxford, 1996.

Weld, Ch. Richard. *Vacations in Ireland*. London, 1857.

Weld, Isaac. *Illustrations of the Scenery of Killarney and the Surrounding Country*. London, 1807.

Wentz, W.Y. Evans. *The Fairy-Faith in Celtic Countries*. London, 1911.

Westropp, T.J. 'Brasil and the Legendary Islands of the North Atlantic.' *Proceedings of the Royal Irish Academy*, 30c (1912), 223-63.

— 'County Clare Folk-Tales and Myths.' *Folk-Lore*, 24 (1913), 96-106, 201-2, 365-81; 29 (1914), 377-8; 26 (1915), 189-95.

— 'The Cow Legend of Corofin, Co. Clare.' *Journal of the Royal Society of Antiquaries of Ireland*, 95 (1895), 227-9.

Whitaker, T.K. 'James Hamilton Delargy, 1899-1980.' *Folk-Life*, 20 (1981-2), 101-6.

Wilde, Lady Jane Francesca. *Ancient Legends, Mystic Charms, and Superstitions of Ireland*. London, 1888.

Wilde, William R.*The Beauties of the Boyne, and its Tributary the Blackwater*. Dublin (1849), 1850.

— *Irish Popular Superstitions*. Dublin, 1853.

— *Loch Corrib, its Shores and Islands* (1867). Dublin, 1955.

Williams, F. 'The Schoolmaster and the Black Pig's Dyke.' In R. Kvideland and Solberg (eds) *8th International Society for Folk Narrative Research Congress*. Bergen, 1984 , 4. 417-22.

Wilson, T.G. *Victorian Doctor, Being the Life of Sir William Wilde*. New York, 1946.

Windele, J. *Historical and Descriptive Notices of the City of Cork and its Vicinity, Gougaun-Barra, Glengariff, and Killarney* (1839). Cork, 1848.

Windisch, Ernst. *Irische Texte* 1. Leipzig, 1880.

Wood-Martin, W.G. *History of Sligo, County and Town*. Dublin, 1882.

— *Traces of the Elder Faiths of Ireland: A Folklore Sketch*. London, 1902.

Woods, James. *Ancient and Modern Sketches of the County Westmeath*. Dublin, 1890.

Yeats, W.B. *Autobiographies*. London, 1955.

— *The Collected Letters of W.B. Yeats* (ed. J. Kelly, E. Domville). Oxford, 1985-.
— *Essays and Introductions*. London, 1961.
— *Explorations*. London, 1962.
— *Fairy & Folk Tales of Ireland* (includes *Fairy & Folk Tales of the Irish Peasantry* 1888, and *Irish Fairy Tales* 1892). London, 1979.
— *The Letters of W.B. Yeats* (ed. A. Wade). London, 1954.
— *Letters to the New Island. A New Edition*. London, 1989.
— *Mythologies*. London, 1959.
— *The Secret Rose; a Variorum Edition*. Ithaca, 1981.
— *Uncollected Prose* (ed. J. Frayne and Colton Jones). London, 1970, 1975.
— *Where There Is Nothing*. London, 1903.
— *Writings on Irish Folklore, Legend and Myth* (ed. R.Welch). London, 1993.
Young, Arthur. *Arthur Young's Tour in Ireland in the Years 1776, 1777 and 1778* (1780). London, 1892.
Zimmermann, Georges Denis. *Irish Political Street Ballads and Rebel Songs*. Geneva, 1966. (Also published as *Songs of Irish Rebellion*. Dublin, 1967.)

B. BOOKS AND ARTICLES ON MORE GENERAL SUBJECTS

(Anonymous) *Arabian Tales, translated from the French*. Cork, 1810.
— *The History of the Seven Wise Masters and Mistresses of Rome* (38th ed.). Dublin, 1814.
— *Winter Evening Tales, being a Collection of Entertaining Stories*. Dublin, 1733.
Aarne, Antti and Stith Thompson. *The Types of the Folktale* (1961). FFC 184. Helsinki, 1973.
Alvarez-Pereyre, F. 'Règles du contage et stratégie de la parole.' *Ethnologie Française*, 5 (1975), 81-90.
Anesa, Marino and M. Rondi. *Fiabe bergamasche*. Milano, 1981.
Anderson, B. *Imagined Communities: Reflections on the Origin and Spread of Nationalism*. London, 1983.
Arnold, Matthew. 'Lectures on Celtic Literature' (1867). In R.H. Super (ed.) *The Complete Works of Matthew Arnold* 3. Ann Arbor, 1962.
Asadowskij, Mark. *Eine sibirische Märchenerzählerin*. FFC 68. Helsinki, 1926.
Babcock-Abrahams, B. 'The Story in the Story: Metanarration in Folk Narrative.' *Studia Fennica*, 20 (1976), 177-84. (New version in R. Bauman ed. *Verbal Art as Performance*.)
Barthes, Roland. *Selected Writings*. London, 1983.
Bascom, William R. (ed.) *Frontiers of Folklore*. Boulder, Col., 1977.
Batten, C.L. *Pleasurable Instruction; Form and Convention in Eighteenth-Century Travel Literature*. Berkeley, 1978.
Baughman, E.W. *Type and Motif-Index of the Folktales of England and North America*. The Hague, 1966.
Bauman, R. *Story, Performance, and Event: Contextual Studies of Oral Narrative*. Cambridge, 1986.
— *Verbal Art as Performance* (1977). Prospect Heights, 1984.
— (ed.) *Folklore, Cultural Performances, and Popular Entertainments*. New York, 1992.

Bausinger, H. *Volkskunde.* Darmstadt, 1971.

Belmont, Nicole. *Paroles anciennes: mythe et folklore.* Paris, 1986.

Belmont, N. and G. Calame-Griaule (eds) *Les Voies de la mémoire.* Cahiers de Littérature Orale, 43 (1998).

Ben-Amos, D. (ed.) *Folklore Genres.* Austin, 1976.

— and K. Goldstein (eds) *Folklore, Performance and Communication.* The Hague, 1975.

Biebuyck, Br. 'A la recherche du conteur.' *Cahiers de littérature orale,* 11 (1982), 195-214.

Bîrlea, Ovidiu. 'La fonction de raconter dans le folklore roumain.' *Laographia,* 22 (1965), 22-6.

Blair, Hugh. *A Critical Dissertation on the Poems of Ossian.* London, 1763.

Bødker, L. *International Dictionary of European Ethnology and Folklore.* 2. Copenhagen, 1965.

Bolte, Johannes and Georg Polivka. *Anmerkungen zu den Kinder- und Hausmärchen der Brüder Grimm.* Leipzig, 1913-32.

Boskovic-Stulli, M. (ed.) *Folklore and Oral Communication.* Zagreb, 1981.

Briggs, Ch. and A. Shuman (eds) *Theorizing Folklore. Towards New Perspectives on the Politics of Culture. Western Folklore,* 52 (1993).

Briggs, K.M. *A Dictionary of British Folk Tales in the English Language.* London, 1970-1.

— *The Fairies in Tradition and Literature.* London, 1967.

— *The Vanishing People: A Study of Traditional Fairy Beliefs.* London, 1978.

Brinkmann, Otto. *Das Erzählen in einer Dorfgemeinschaft.* Münster, 1933.

Bruford, A.J. 'Memory, Performance and Structure in Traditional Tales.' *ARV* 37 (1981), 101-9.

— 'Recitation or Re-Creation? Examples from South Uist Storytelling.' *Scottish Studies,* 22 (1978), 27-44.

— and MacDonald, D. (eds) *Scottish Traditional Tales.* Edinburgh, 1994.

Bruner, Jerome. 'The Narrative Construction of Reality.' *Critical Inquiry,* 18 (1991), 1-21.

Brunvand, J.H. *The Vanishing Hitchhiker* (1981). London, 1983.

Buchan, David. *Scottish Tradition.* London, 1984.

Burlakoff, N. and C. Lindahl (eds) *Folklore on Two Continents; Essays in honor of Linda Dégh.* Bloomington, 1980.

Burrison, John A. *Storytellers: Folktales and Legends from the South.* Athens, Ga., 1989.

Burton, Richard. *The Book of the Thousand Nights and a Night.* London, 1885-6.

Calame-Griaule, Geneviève. 'Pour une lecture initiatique des contes populaires.' *Bulletin du Centre Thomas More,* 21 (1978), 11-29.

Campbell, J.F. *Popular Tales of the West Highlands, Orally Collected* (1860-62). London, 1890-93.

Chadwick, H.M. *The Heroic Age.* Cambridge, 1926.

— and N.K. Chadwick. *The Growth of Literature.* Cambridge 1932.

Chadwick, N.K. *The Druids.* Cardiff, 1997.

Chadwick, Owen. *John Cassian.* Cambridge, 1950.

Chase, Richard. *The Jack Tales.* New York, 1943.

Chesnut, Michael (ed.) *Telling Reality: Folklore Studies in memory of Bengt Holbek.* Copenhagen and Turku, 1993.

Christiansen, R.T. *The Migratory Legends.* FFC 175. Helsinki, 1958.

Cocchiara, G. *The History of Folklore in Europe*. Philadelphia, 1980.

Cole, P. and J.L. Morgan (eds) *Syntax and Semantics 3: Speech Acts*. New York, 1975.

Currie, Gregory. *The Nature of Fiction*. Cambridge, 1990.

d' Aulnoy, M.C. *Histoire d'Hypolite, Comte de Duglas* (1690). Bruxelles, 1704.

— *The History of Hypolitus, Earl of Douglas*. Cork, 1768.

Davidson, H.R. and W.S. Russell (eds)*The Folklore of Ghosts*. Cambridge, 1981.

Degh, Linda. *Folktales and Society; Story-telling in a Hungarian Peasant Community*. Bloomington, 1969.

— (ed.) *Folklore Today; A Festschrift for R.M. Dorson*. Bloomington, 1976.

— *Narratives in Society: A Performer-centered Study of Narration*. FFC 255. Helsinki, 1995.

— (ed.) *Studies in East European Narrative*. Bloomington, 1978.

Delarue, P. and M.L. Tenèze. *Le conte populaire français*. Paris, 1976-85.

Dorson, R. M. *The British Folklorists: a History*. Chicago, 1968.

— (ed.) *Folklore and Folklife, an Introduction*. Chicago, 1972.

— (ed.) *Folklore in the Modern World*. The Hague, 1978.

— 'Nationalistic Inferiority Complexes and the Fabrication of Fakelore: A Reconsideration of Ossian, the *Kinder- und Hausmärchen*, the *Kalevala* and Paul Bunyan.' *Journal of Folklore Research*, 22 (1985), 5-18.

— *Peasant Customs and Savage Myths*. Chicago, 1968.

Dundes, Alan. (ed.) *The Study of Folklore*. Englewood Cliffs, 1965.

Fabre, Daniel and J. Lacroix. *La tradition orale du conte occitan*. Paris, 1974.

Falassi, A. *Folklore by the Fireside: Text and Context of the Tuscan Veglia*. London, 1980.

Finnegan, Ruth. *Oral Traditions and the Verbal Arts*. London, 1992.

Gallais, Pierre. 'Le sang sur la neige – le conte et le rêve.' *Cahiers de civilisation médiévale*, 21 (1978), 37-42.

Gaskill, H. (ed.) *Ossian Revisited*. Edinburgh, 1991.

Georges, R.A. 'Communication Role and Social Identity in Storytelling.' *Fabula*, 31 (1990) 49-57.

— 'From Folktale Research to the Study of Narrating.' *Studia Fennica*, 20 (1976), 159-68.

— and Jones, M.O. *Folkloristics: An Introduction*. Bloomington, 1995.

Goldstein, K.S. *A Guide for Field Workers in Folklore*. Hatboro, Penn., 1964.

Gomme, G.L. *The Handbook of Folklore*. London, 1890.

Goody, Jack. *The Interface between the Written and the Oral*. Cambridge, 1987.

Görög-Karady, V. (ed.) *D'un conte ... à l'autre: La variabilité dans la littérature orale*. Paris, 1990.

— and Griaule. C. (eds) *Le conte. Pourquoi? Comment?* Paris, 1982.

Green, Th. E. (ed.) *Folklore: An Encyclopedia of Beliefs, Customs, Tales, Music, and Art*. Santa Barbara, 1997.

Greenway, John. *Literature Among the Primitives*. Hatboro Penn., 1964.

Grimm, J. and W. *Kinder- und Hausmärchen* (ed. H. Rölleke). Stuttgart, 1980.

Grimm, Wilhelm. *Kleinere Schriften*. Gütersloh, 1882.

Grobman, Neil R. 'Eighteenth-Century Scottish Philosophers on Oral Tradition.' *Journal of the Folklore Institute*, 10 (1973) 187-95.

Hall, Edwin S. *The Eskimo Storyteller; Folktales from Noatak, Alaska*. Knoxville, 1975.

Hamilton, Antony. *Oeuvres du Comte d'Hamilton*. Utrecht, 1731.

Hand, W.D. (ed.) *American Folk Legend: A Symposium*. Berkeley, 1971.

Hartland, E.S. *The Science of Fairy Tales: An Inquiry into Fairy Mythology*. London, 1891.

Hélias, P.-J. *Le Cheval d'orgueil*. Paris, 1975.

Herder, J.G. *Stimmen der Völker in Liedern* (1778-9). Stuttgart, 1975.

— *Herders Werke III.2* (ed. H. Lambel). Stuttgart, 1893.

Hobsbawm, E. and T. Ranger (eds). *The Invention of Tradition*. Cambridge, 1983.

Hofer, Tamás. 'The Perception of Tradition in European Ethnology.' *Journal of Folklore Research*, 21 (1984) 133-47.

Holbek, Bengt. *Interpretation of Fairy Tales*. FFC 239. Helsinki, 1987.

Honko, Lauri. 'Memorates and the Study of Folk Belief.' *Journal of the Folklore Institute*, 1 (1964), 5-19.

— 'Methods in Folk-Narrative Research.' *Ethnologia Europaea*, 11 (1979-80), 6-27.

Hustvedt, S.B. *Ballad Criticism in Scandinavia and Great Britain during the Eighteenth Century*. New York, 1916.

Jakobson, R. and P. Bogatyrev. 'Die Folklore als eine besondere Form des Schaffens.' *Donum Natalicium Schrijnen*. Nijmegen/Utrecht, 1929. 900-913.

Jackson, Kenneth. 'The Folktale in Gaelic Scotland.' *The Proceedings of the Scottish Anthropological and Folklore Society*, 4 (1952), 123-40.

— *The International Popular Tale and Early Welsh Tradition*. Cardiff, 1961.

Johnson, Samuel. *A Journey to the Western Islands of Scotland*. Harmondsworth, 1984.

Johnstone, B. *Stories, Community, and Place*. Bloomington, 1990.

Jones, J.R. and J.E. Keller (eds) *Disciplina Clericalis –The Scholar's Guide*. Toronto, 1969.

Kaivola-Bregenhøj, Annikki. 'The Context of Narrating.' In R.Kvideland (ed.) *Folklore Processed in honour of Lauri Honko. Studia Fennica Folkloristica 1*. Helsinki, 1992, 153-66.

— *Narrative and Narrating; Variation in Juho Oksanen's Storytelling*. FFC 261. Helsinki, 1996.

Kamenetsky, C. *The Brothers Grimm and their Critics*. Athens, Ohio, 1992.

Kelly, Gary. *English Fiction of the Romantic Period*. London, 1989.

Köhler-Zülch, Ines. 'Who Are the Tellers?' *Fabula*, 38 (1997), 199-209.

Krappe, A.H. *The Science of Folklore* (1930). London, 1974.

Krohn, K.K. *Folklore Methodology* (1926). Austin, 1971.

Kvideland, R. (ed.) *Folklore Processed; In honour of Lauri Honko*. Helsinki, 1992.

— and H.K. Sehmsdorf (eds) *Nordic Folklore: Recent Studies*. Bloomington, 1989.

— *Scandinavian Folk Belief and Legend*. Oslo, 1988.

Labov, William. *Language in the Inner City*. Philadelphia, 1972.

Labov, William and J. Waletzky. 'Narrative Analysis: Oral Versions of Personal Experience.' In J. Helms (ed.) *Essays on the Verbal and Visual Arts*. Seattle, 1967, 12-44.

Lamarque, P. and S.M. Olsen. *Truth, Fiction, and Literature: A Philosophical Perspective*. Oxford, 1994.

Lang, Andrew. *Custom and Myth*. London, 1884.

Laport, G. *Les contes populaires wallons*. FFC 101. Helsinki, 1932.

Laurent, D. 'The Mnemonic Process of a Breton Storyteller.' *ARV*, 37 (1981), 111-15.

— 'Un conteur breton de Haute Cornouaille et son système de mémorisation de contes merveilleux.' In J.B. Martin (ed.) *Le Conte: Tradition orale et identité culturelle*. Saint-Fons, 1988.

Leach, Maria (ed.) *Funk & Wagnalls Standard Dictionary of Folklore Mythology, and Legend* (1949). New York, 1984.

Le Braz, Anatole. *La légende de la mort chez les Bretons armoricains* (1902). Paris, 1966.

Le Roux, F. and C.J. Guyonwarc'h. *Les Druides*. Rennes, 1986.

Leyen, Fr. von der. *Die Welt der Märchen*. Köln-Düsseldorf, 1954.

Lord, A.B. *The Singer of Tales*. Cambridge Mass., 1960.

Lüthi, Max. *The Fairytale as Art Form and Portrait of Man* (1975). Bloomington, 1984.

— *Once Upon a Time ... On the Nature of Fairy Tales* (1962). New York, 1970.

McDermitt, B. 'Duncan Williamson.' *Tocher*, 33 (1980), 141-8.

MacDonald, D.A. 'A Visual Memory'. *Scottish Studies*, 22 (1978), 1-26.

— 'Some Aspects of Visual and Verbal Memory in Gaelic Storytelling.' *ARV*, 37 (1981), 117-24. McGlathery, J. (ed.) *The Brothers Grimm and the Folktale*. Chicago, 1988.

McKay, J.G. (ed.) *More West Highland Tales*. Edinburgh, 1940.

— 'Scottish Gaelic Parallels.' *Béaloideas*, 3 (1932), 144-5.

Maclean, C.I. 'Hebridean Storytellers.' *ARV*, 8 (1952), 120-9.

Macpherson, J. *The Poems of Ossian*. Edinburgh, 1805.

Mariotti, Martine. *Marie Nicolas, conteuse en Champsaur*. Aix-en-Provence, 1990.

Martin, Martin. *A Description of the Western Islands of Scotland circa 1695* (1703). Stirling, 1934.

Martinkus, Ada. 'Trois conteurs de Haute-Lituanie – Qui croient un peu, beaucoup ou pas du tout à leurs récits.' *Cahiers de littérature orale*, 11 (1982), 158-63.

Mullen, Patrick B. 'Modern Legend and Rumor Theory'. *Journal of the Folklore Institute*, 9 (1972), 95-109.

Nicolaisen, W.F.H. 'Perspective on Contemporary Legends.' *Fabula*, 26 (1985), 213-18.

Noomen, W. and N. Van Den Boogaard (eds) *Nouveau Recueil Complet des Fabliaux*. Assen, 1983-93.

O'Hara Tobin, P.M. *Les lais anonymes des XIIᵉ et XIIIᵉ siècles; édition critique de quelques lais bretons*. Geneva, 1976.

Ortutay, Gyula. *Hungarian Folklore: Essays*. Budapest, 1972.

Paredes, A., and R. Bauman (eds) *Toward New Perspectives in Folklore*. Austin, Tex., 1972.

Pentikäinen, Juha. *Oral Repertoire and World View; An Anthropological Study of Marina Takalo's Life History*. FFC 219. Helsinki, 1978.

Percy, Thomas. *Reliques of Ancient English Poetry* (1765). London, 1886.

Philip, N. (ed.) *The Penguin Book of Scottish Folktales*. London, 1995.

Pugh, A.R., V.J. Lee, and J. Swann (eds) *Language and Language Use*. London, 1980.

Ranke, Kurt et al. (eds) *Enzyklopädie des Märchens*. Berlin, 1975-.

Renan, Ernest. *Essai sur la poésie des races celtiques*. Paris, 1854.

— *Souvenirs d'enfance et de jeunesse* (1883). Lausanne, 1961.

Riché, Pierre. *Education et culture dans l'occident barbare, VIᵉ-VIIᵉ siècles*. Paris, 1962.

Röhrich, Lutz. *Märchen und Wirklichkeit*. Wiesbaden, 1956.

— and S. Wienker-Piepho (eds) *Storytelling in Contemporary Societies*. Tübingen, 1990.

Röth, D. and W. Kahn (eds) *Märchen und Märchenforschung in Europa*. Frankfurt a. M., 1993.

Sándor, István. 'Dramaturgy of Tale-telling.' *Acta Ethnographica Academiae Scientarum Hungariae*, 16 (1967), 305-35.

Sautman, F.C, D. Conchado, G.C. Di Scipio (eds) *Telling Tales: Medieval Narratives and the Folk Tradition*. London, 1998.

Searle, J.A. *Expression and Meaning: Studies in the Theory of Speech Acts*. Cambridge, 1979.

Schenda, Rudolf. *Von Mund zu Ohr: Bausteine zu einer Kulturgeschichte volkstümlichen Erzählens in Europa*. Göttingen, 1993.

Sébillot, Paul. 'Instructions et questionnaires.' *Annales de la Societé des Traditions Populaires*, 2 (1887), 97-166.

— 'Les femmes et les traditions populaires.' *Revue des Traditions Populaires*, 7 (1892), 449-456.

— *Traditions et superstitions de la Haute-Bretagne*. Paris, 1881.

Searle, J.A. *Expression and Meaning: Studies in the Theory of Speech Acts*. Cambridge, 1979.

Shaw, John (ed.) *Tales until Dawn; The World of a Cape Breton Gaelic Story-teller: Joe Neil MacNeil*. Edinburgh, 1987.

Shedlock, M.L. *The Art of the Storyteller*. New York, 1915.

Siikala, A.-L. *Interpreting Oral Narrative*. FFC 245. Helsinki, 1990.

— (ed.) *Studies in Oral Narrative*. Studia Fennica 33. Helsinki, 1989.

Smith, B.H. 'Afterthoughts on Narrative: Narrative Versions, Narrative Theories.' *Critical Inquiry*, 7 (1980), 213-36.

Smith, P. (ed.) *Perspectives on Contemporary Legend*. Sheffield, 1984.

Snyder, Edward D. *The Celtic Revival in English Literature: 1760-1800*. Cambridge Mass., 1923.

Sydow, C.W. von. *Selected Papers on Folklore*. Copenhagen, 1948.

Tannen, D. 'Oral and Literate Strategies in Spoken and Written Narratives.' *Language*, 58 (1992), 1-21.

Tenèze, M.-L. 'Du conte merveilleux comme genre.' *Arts et Traditions Populaires*, 18 (1970), 11-65.

Thompson, Stith. *The Folktale*. New York, 1946.

— *Motif-Index of Folk-Literature*. Copenhagen, 1955-8.

Thomson, D.S. *The Gaelic Sources of Macpherson's 'Ossian'*. Edinburgh, 1952.

— 'Macpherson's Ossian: Ballad to Epic.' *Béaloideas*, 54-5 (1986), 243-64.

Toelken, J.B. *The Dynamics of Folklore*. Boston, 1979.

Tonkin, Elizabeth. *Narrating Our Pasts; The Social Construction of Oral History*. Cambridge, 1992.

Uffer, Leza. *Rätoromanische Märchen und ihre Erzähler*. Basel, 1945.

Van Gennep, A. *La formation des légendes*. Paris, 1910.

— *Manuel de folklore français contemporain*. Paris, 1943-58.

Voltaire. *Romans et contes I-II* (ed. F. Deloffre). Paris, 1992.

Wehse, Rainer. 'Past and Present Folkloristic Narrator Research.' In R.B. Bottigheimer (ed.) *Fairy Tales and Society*. Philadelphia, 1989, 245-58.

White, Hayden. 'The Value of Narrativity in the Representation of Reality.' *Critical Inquiry*, 7 (1980-1), 5-27.

Wildhaber, Robert. 'Zum Weiterleben zweier Apokrypher Legenden.' In L. Carlen and F. Steinegger (eds) *Festschrift Nikolaus Grass*. Innsbruck, 1975, 2. 219-37.

Wilson, W.A. 'Herder, Folklore and Romantic Nationalism.' *Journal of Popular Culture*, 6 (1973), 818-35.

Index

*(This is an index of subjects. A few names of persons appear in the entries
'antiquarians', 'Celtic scholars', 'fiction writers or playwrights and oral traditions',
'folklorists of the 19th century', 'Irish Folklore Commission', and 'Literary Revival'.)*